John Salony

W9-ATC-135

20's

(1) List the reasons the
author gives for
saying business is:
① the ~~finest game~~
② the fullest education
③ the fairest opportunity

② WRITE REBUTTAL TO
ANE ARVCLE AGINEST

Oscar Bedolla

Computer

THE
UNITED STATES

A HISTORY OF THE REPUBLIC

Historian Reviewers

Robert H. Ferrell, Indiana University, Bloomington, Indiana
Aubrey C. Land, University of Georgia, Athens, Georgia
Edmund S. Morgan, Yale University, New Haven, Connecticut
Anne Firor Scott, Duke University, Durham, North Carolina
Kenneth M. Stampp, University of California, Berkeley, California

---

High School Reviewers

Sarah Lawrence Davis, Briarcliff High School, Atlanta, Georgia
William J. Fetsko, Liverpool Central School District, Liverpool, New York
Ronald W. Kruse, Ygnacio Valley High School, Concord, California
D. Margaret Lubberts, Olathe High School, Olathe, Kansas
William J. McCusker, Cardinal O'Hara High School, Springfield, Pennsylvania
Kay Norman, Denton High School, Denton, Texas
Thomas A. Payne, Broad Ripple High School, Indianapolis, Indiana
Evelyn Rodak, Detroit Public Schools, Detroit, Michigan
Robert Taylor, Hoke County High School, Raeford, North Carolina
Ernest G. Woizeschke, Coon Rapids Senior High School, Coon Rapids, Minnesota

---

Curriculum Consultants

Ricardo L. Garcia, Coordinator of Multicultural Education,
University of Utah, Salt Lake City, Utah

Ruth Polk Patterson, Supervisor of Minority Studies,
Little Rock Public Schools, Little Rock, Arkansas

Winona Elliott Sample, Consultant to the Office of Child Development,
State Department of Education, Sacramento, California

Beverly Sanders, Consultant on Women's Studies,
New York, New York

Susan Chong Wong, Asian American Legal Defense and Education Fund,
New York, New York

THE UNITED STATES

A HISTORY OF THE REPUBLIC

 James West Davidson   Mark H. Lytle

PRENTICE HALL, Englewood Cliffs, New Jersey

FOURTH EDITION

SUPPLEMENTARY MATERIALS
Annotated Teacher's Edition
Teacher's Resource Book
Computer Test Bank

© 1988, 1986, 1984, 1981 by Prentice-Hall, Inc., Englewood Cliffs, New Jersey 07632. All rights reserved. No part of this book may be reproduced in any form or by any means without permission in writing from the publisher. Printed in the United States of America.

ISBN 0-13-937400-0   10 9 8 7 6 5 4 3

PRENTICE-HALL OF AUSTRALIA, PTY. LTD., Sydney
PRENTICE-HALL CANADA INC., Toronto
PRENTICE-HALL HISPANOAMERICANA, S.A., Mexico
PRENTICE-HALL OF INDIA PRIVATE LTD., New Delhi
PRENTICE-HALL INTERNATIONAL (U.K.) LIMITED, London
PRENTICE-HALL OF JAPAN, INC., Tokyo
PRENTICE-HALL OF SOUTHEAST ASIA PTE. LTD., Singapore
EDITORA PRENTICE-HALL DO BRASIL LTDA., Rio de Janeiro

Prentice Hall
A Division of Simon & Schuster
Englewood Cliffs, New Jersey

Cover

The cover illustration is a display of historical American flags. From left to right on the bottom are the Taunton flag raised in Taunton, Massachusetts, in 1774; the Liberty Tree flag flown by American ships in northeastern waters in 1775; the Gadsden flag, the personal emblem of the First Commander of the Navy; the Continental Colors, the first national flag (1775–1777); the flag of 1777. From left to right on the top are the flag of 1818, known as the Great Star Flag; the 48-star national flag (1912–1959); the 50-star national flag.

Photo Coordinator: Michal Heron
Photo Researcher: Roberta Guerette/Omni-Photo Communications
Text Maps, Graphs, and Charts: Lee Ames & Zak, Ltd.
Reference Maps: R.R. Donnelley & Sons Company

Illustration Credits

Frequently cited sources are abbreviated as follows: AMNH, American Museum of Natural History; LC, Library of Congress; MCNY, Museum of the City of New York; MFA, Museum of Fine Arts, Boston; MMA, Metropolitan Museum of Art, New York; NA, National Archives; NASA, National Aeronautics and Space Administration; NG, National Gallery of Art, Washington, D.C.; NYHS, courtesy of the New York Historical Society, New York; NYPL, New York Public Library; NYSHA, New York State Historical Association, Cooperstown; SI, Smithsonian Institution; UPI, United Press International; WW, World Wide; Yale, Yale University Art Gallery.

key to position of illustrations
b, bottom; *l*, left; *r*, right; *t*, top.

(continued on p. 889)

CONTENTS

UNIT TWO
Creating a Republic   90

UNIT FOUR
An Era of Expansion
230

UNIT FIVE
A Nation Torn Apart   310

UNIT SIX
Transforming a Nation 372

UNIT SEVEN
Entering a Modern Age 474

I THINK WE'VE GOT ANOTHER WASHINGTON AND WILSON IS HIS NAME

UNIT NINE
A Time of Trial

Special Features

Spirit of America

American Profiles

Voices of Freedom

America's Heritage

American Enterprise

Arts in America

Skill Lessons

Writer's Handbook

xix

Maps

Atlas

Charts and Graphs

A Letter From the Authors

"History is more or less the bunk," auto maker Henry Ford once remarked. "We want to live in the present." The two of us are often surprised by how many students and even friends seem to agree with Ford. Yet whatever you do today becomes history the day after.

All of us, whether we realize it or not, have to draw on the past in everything we do. Decisions that were made years ago, often by other people, continue to affect us in major ways. That's one reason why science fiction stories about time machines are popular. They give their heroes a chance to go back and change the events that have shaped their lives.

Although we can't physically go back in time—at least, not in a machine—studying history offers a way. It is not as easy as pulling a lever and being instantly transported to long ago. But it can be a good deal of fun, because studying history is often like doing detective work. On the page after next, we tell the story of a farmer who became a good historian just by examining the rings of a tree. But he

had to know what sort of questions to ask about the rings to make them interesting.

Try an experiment. Take whatever objects are in your pocket or purse, and ask a few questions about the history behind them. We tried it and brought out of one of our pockets a couple of train tickets, a watch, keys, and some spare change. Nothing particularly unusual. But we began looking at each item, asking questions, and thinking about its history.

Take the ticket stubs, for instance. Today anyone can pick up a phone, dial an 800 number, and make train reservations from one city to another. But what sort of history lies behind those simple actions? A traveler of the 1860s would have had a much harder time purchasing tickets. There was no national booking system that sold one ticket for a journey that stretched over several rail lines. There was no telephone system that made it possible to call in reservations. Before a national railway network could be put into place, the United States had to build a highly complex industrial system.

The frontier had a tremendous impact on the course of American history. As a result, whether your ancestors were born in Europe, Asia, Africa, Oceania, or the Americas, the frontier experience is part of your history.

Even the contents of someone's pocket can be historical evidence.

Or think about the pocket watch. Time is something we all take for granted. Clocks and watches sell for only a few dollars. Yet ordinary people could not afford to buy accurate clocks before the mid-1800s. Even when they did, each town set its own official time by taking measurements on the position of the sun. Travelers had to constantly reset their watches. (New York and Boston, for example, were 11 minutes and 45 seconds apart.) No national system of time existed.

By 1882 there were about 50 systems of time—all different. To help passengers, train stations often had several clocks showing the time on different lines. Only in 1883 did the railroads set up four stan-dard time zones across the United States. These time zones correspond to the ones we have today. Time zones are one example of how decisions of the past affect our lives today.

For each object in our everyday lives, it would be possible to find similar histories. Taken together, these histories would provide a fairly good picture of how your own life got to be the way it is. But it is the responsibility of a textbook to go further. Along with the stories of Presidents and politicians are the stories of ordinary people—nurses and soldiers, sports heroes and ministers, teachers and farmers. A textbook must synthesize their stories into a bigger picture to show the important themes that have characterized American history.

Running through this textbook are many themes that have made our history special —religion, ingenuity, mobility, self-improvement, and volunteerism are all there. By understanding how they affected the past, we can better understand our present.

Despite time machine fantasies, we can never go back and change the past. But by understanding it, we can do something better: profit from its lessons and use them to shape our future.

James West Davidson
Mark H. Lytle

About the Authors

James West Davidson has written books and papers on a wide range of American history topics. He and Mark H. Lytle are the authors of *A History of the Republic: The United States From 1865* and *After the Fact: The Art of Historical Detection*. Dr. Davidson also wrote *The American Nation* and *A History of the Republic: The United States to 1877* with John E. Batchelor. With teaching experience at both college and high school levels, Dr. Davidson consults on curriculum design for American history courses.

In his spare time, Dr. Davidson is an enthusiastic hiker and canoeist. *One River Down* is his own documentary film of a canoe trip in Labrador. *The Complete Wilderness Paddler*, written with John Rugge, is a how-to book for the wilderness canoeist. *Great Heart* is the true story of a 1903 canoe trip in Labrador.

Mark H. Lytle is chairperson of American Studies at Bard College, where he also serves on the Women's Studies faculty. Author of numerous articles on the United

States and Iran and *Origins of the Iranian-American Alliance, 1941-1953*, Dr. Lytle has taught high school social studies, including black history in the Buffalo public schools. Dr. Lytle wrote *A History of the Republic: The United States From 1865* and *After the Fact: The Art of Historical Detection* with James West Davidson.

Dr. Lytle is an avid sportsman and tennis player. He is co-author of *Shang*, a book about the traditional art of carving duck decoys. Dr. Lytle lives with his wife and two children in Rhinebeck, New York, not far from where Robert Fulton docked the *Clermont*.

Mark H. Lytle (left) and James West Davidson

The Art of Historical Detection

*T*he following anecdote is from After the Fact, *a book of historical detection by James West Davidson and Mark Lytle. It describes an incident that focused the authors' attention on how historians work.*

One day while working on another project, we went outside to watch a neighboring farmer cut down a large old hemlock that had become diseased. As his saw cut deeper into the tree, we joked that it had now bit into history as far back as the Depression. "Depression?" grunted our friend. "I thought you fellows were historians. I'm deep enough now so's Hoover wasn't even born yet."

With the tree down, the three of us examined the stump. Our woodcutter surprised us with what he saw.

"Here's when my folks moved into this place," he said, pointing to a ring. "1922."

"How do you know without counting the rings?" we asked.

"Oh, *well*," he said, as if the answer were obvious. "Look at the core, here. The rings are all bunched up tight. I bet there's sixty or seventy—and all within a couple of inches. Those came when the place was still forest. Then, you notice, the rings start

getting fatter all of a sudden. That's when my dad cleared behind the house—in '22—and the tree started getting a lot more light. And look further out, here—see how the rings set together again for a couple years? That's from loopers."

"Loopers?" we asked cautiously.

"Sure—loopers. You know. The ones with only front legs and back." His hand imitated a looping, hopping crawl across the log. "Inchworms. They nearly killed the tree. That was sometime after the war—'49 or '50." As his fingers traced back and forth among the concentric circles, he spoke of other events from years gone by. Before we returned home, we had learned a good deal about past doings in the area.

Now, it occurs to us that our neighbor had a pretty good knack for putting together history. The evidence of the past, like the tree rings, comes easily enough to hand. But we still need to be taught how to see it, read it, and explain it before it can be turned into a story. Even more to the point, the explanations and interpretations *behind* the story often turn out to be as interesting as the story itself. After all, the fascination in our neighbor's account came from the way he traced his tale out of those silent tree rings.

About This Book

This book is organized into 10 units and 41 chapters. The Table of Contents (pages v–xx) lists the titles of the units and chapters. It also lists special features, skill lessons, writing lessons, and maps, charts, and graphs in the text. At the back of the book is a reference section with useful maps, charts, and documents.

Many features have been included in this book to assist you during your course of study:

1. **Unit Opener.** Each unit begins with an illustrated time line that correlates major events in politics and government, society and culture, economics and technology, and world history.

2. **Chapter Outline.** Each chapter begins with an outline of the contents to give you an overview of the chapter.

3. **Introduction.** The introduction provides a setting for the material in the chapter.

4. **Time Lines.** A time line appears after each chapter introduction. By highlighting major events and developments, it will help you understand how events discussed in the chapter are related in time.

5. **Important Terms.** Historical terms and vocabulary words are italicized and clearly defined the first time they appear in the text. You will be asked to define each term in a section review question. Important historical terms also appear in a glossary at the end of the book.

6. **Maps, Graphs, Charts.** Numerous maps, graphs, and charts appear throughout the book to help you understand major historical developments and events. Their clarity makes them useful additions to the narrative. Captions provide background information and relate the maps, graphs, and charts to what you are reading.

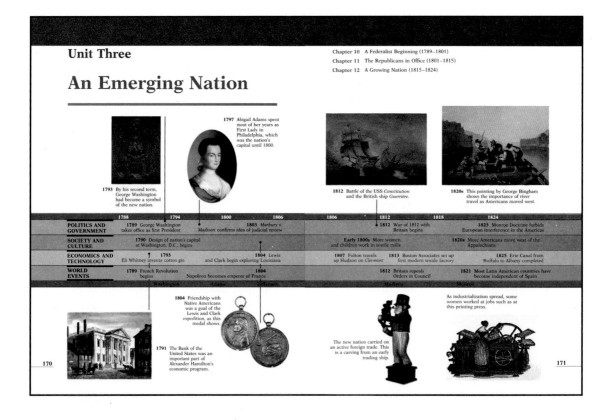

Unit Three

An Emerging Nation

Chapter 10 A Federalist Beginning (1789–1801)
Chapter 11 The Republicans in Office (1801–1815)
Chapter 12 A Growing Nation (1815–1824)

1797 Abigail Adams spent most of her years as First Lady in Philadelphia, which was the nation's capital until 1800.

1793 By his second term, George Washington had become a symbol of the new nation.

1812 Battle of the USS *Constitution* and the British ship *Guerrière*.

1820s This painting by George Bingham shows the importance of river travel as Americans moved west.

	1788	1794	1800	1806	1806	1812	1818	1824
POLITICS AND GOVERNMENT	**1789** George Washington takes office as first President		**1803** *Marbury v. Madison* confirms idea of judicial review			**1812** War of 1812 with Britain begins		**1823** Monroe Doctrine forbids European interference in the Americas
SOCIETY AND CULTURE	**1790** Design of nation's capital at Washington, D.C., begins				**Early 1800s** More women and children work in textile mills			**1820s** More Americans move west of the Appalachians
ECONOMICS AND TECHNOLOGY	**1793** Eli Whitney invents cotton gin		**1804** Lewis and Clark begin exploring Louisiana		**1807** Fulton travels up Hudson on *Clermont*	**1813** Boston Associates set up first modern textile factory		**1825** Erie Canal from Buffalo to Albany completed
WORLD EVENTS	**1789** French Revolution begins		**1804** Napoleon becomes emperor of France			**1812** Britain repeals Orders in Council		**1821** Most Latin American countries have become independent of Spain
	Washington		Adams	Jefferson		Madison		Monroe

1804 Friendship with Native Americans was a goal of the Lewis and Clark expedition, as this medal shows.

1791 The Bank of the United States was an important part of Alexander Hamilton's economic program.

The new nation carried on an active foreign trade. This is a carving from an early trading ship.

As industrialization spread, some women worked at jobs such as at this printing press.

7. **Illustrations.** The text contains many historic paintings, photographs, cartoons, and posters to enliven the study of each historical period. The captions contain useful information about the illustration and the people or events pictured.

8. **Special Features.** Boxed features give you a close look at people and events in American history. They include vignettes, biographies, and selections from diaries and other contemporary sources.

9. **Skill Lessons.** Special boxed lessons help you understand and practice important skills, such as reading maps and graphs, using visual evidence and statistics, recognizing propaganda, and analyzing conflicting sources.

10. **Section Reviews.** Each section ends with a set of review questions including identifications, vocabulary definitions, and a critical thinking question to test your understanding of what you have read.

11. **Major Events.** Near the end of each chapter you will find a chronological list of major events. This will help you review what you have learned and place historical events in proper sequence.

12. **In Perspective.** The chapter summary, called "In Perspective," reviews the developments you read about in the chapter and puts them in perspective.

13. **Chapter Review.** Four sets of questions end each chapter.
    - "Vocabulary" questions help you review the definitions of important terms.
    - "Chapter Checkup" questions help you review the basic content of the chapter.
    - "Critical Thinking Questions" ask you to analyze historical issues.
    - "Developing Basic Skills" calls for you to practice such basic skills as classifying, comparing, map and graph reading, interpreting source

material, and relating past to present.

14. **Writer's Handbook.** At the end of each chapter, there is a lesson to help you develop the writing and research skills associated with the study of history. The subject matter of each lesson is integrated with the chapter content. The lessons cover the skills necessary to organize effective paragraphs and write a research paper.

15. **Spirit of America.** Each unit contains a four-page feature that focuses on an important theme in American history. The Spirit of America feature contains an essay that discusses the historical development of a particular theme, the biography of a person who exemplifies it, and a document related to it.

16. **Reference Section.** The Reference Section can be found on pages 803–889. It includes:
    - Atlas with seven maps of the United States and one of the world.
    - A Chronology of American History with major events and developments in American history.
    - Glossary with definitions for all vocabulary words and other key terms.
    - Suggested Readings for additional reading for each chapter.
    - The Fifty States includes the capital, date of entry into the Union, area in square miles, recent population figures, and number of Representatives in the House for each state.
    - Presidents and Vice-Presidents of the United States includes the terms served and party affiliation of each President and Vice-President.
    - The Declaration of Independence.
    - The Constitution of the United States of America is annotated to help you understand its historical roots and its enduring significance in American life.
    - Index that tells you where to find a subject in the book. The Index is alphabetical and includes the names of people, events, and ideas in American history.

Unit One

The Americas

Pre 1450 This early American bowl shows the skill of Indian potters in the Southwest.

1590 View of Roanoke Island where the first English colony was established

	1450	1500	1550	1600
POLITICS AND GOVERNMENT		**1492** Columbus reaches the Americas	**1500s** Iroquois League formed to end warfare among Indian nations	
SOCIETY AND CULTURE	**1300s–1400s** Aztecs develop precise calendar and system of mathematics		**1500s** Plains peoples become nomadic	
ECONOMICS AND TECHNOLOGY	**1400s** Invention of caravel at Sagres spurs exploration		**1573** Laws of the Indies outline economy of New Spain	
WORLD EVENTS		**1517** Protestant Reformation begins in Europe	**1588** English defeat Spanish Armada	

1400s The caravel allowed sailors to explore regions far from Europe.

1500s Fishing provided abundant food for Native Americans on the Atlantic coast.

1609 The landing of a relief ship at Jamestown shown in a painting by John Gadsby Chapman

1700s Colonial cities were bustling centers of economic activity.

1600	1650	1700	1750

1607 Jamestown founded as first successful English colony

1673 Joliet and Marquette explore Mississippi River

1754 French and Indian War breaks out in North America

1647 First public school law passed in Massachusetts

1734 John Peter Zenger found innocent of libel

1660 Navigation Act regulates trade of the American colonies

1740s Eliza Pinckney raises indigo as a cash crop

1660 Charles II restored to throne of England

1756 War spreads to Europe where it is called the Seven Years' War

1600s Selling oysters was one way settlers in the American colonies made their way in the New World.

1745 New Englanders carried this flag in an early battle between the English and the French in North America.

1

1

Two Worlds

(Prehistory–1492)

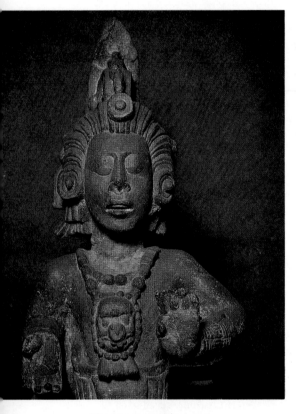

Mayan corn god

Chapter Outline

1 *The First Americans*

2 *Many Cultures Among the First Americans*

3 *Great Empires*

4 *Europe Awakens*

In the late 1400s two worlds met, and the destinies of both were changed forever. For most of human history the continents now known as North and South America were isolated from the rest of the world. There was probably some contact between the original Americans and individuals from other parts of the world. But generally Europeans, Asians, and Africans did not know of the existence of the American continents until the late fifteenth century.

In this chapter you will read about the original Americans and learn about some of the hundreds of cultures existing in North and South America by the 1400s. You will also read about developments in Europe that led explorers farther and farther into the open sea. By the late 1400s the two worlds were on the verge of an encounter that would alter the course of human history.

	Mayan civilization			Crusades in Europe		
500	700	900	1100	1300		1500

500 Middle Ages begin in Europe	**1000** Leif Ericson reaches America	**1200** Aztecs conquer Toltecs	**1400s** Incas dominate Andes region	**1418** Sailing school at Sagres opens

1 The First Americans

Fifty thousand years ago huge herds of animals roamed across what is now known as North and South America. Wild horses, bison, and camels grazed in vast fields. Jaguars stalked their prey. Woolly mammoths—large, shaggy-haired elephants with long, sweeping tusks—wandered from present-day Alaska to Texas.

Just when and how people came to be a part of this landscape is uncertain. Although scientists have attempted to answer these questions, no one theory has been conclusively proven. Moreover, discoveries made during the 1970s have served to intensify the controversy rather than to settle it. Therefore, questions still remain: How long have men and women inhabited the Americas? Did these people come from another continent? How did these first Americans live?

Studying Early People

The first Americans belong to the *prehistoric period*, the time before recorded history. Cultural groups in the prehistoric period had not developed a system of writing so they could not keep records. The lack of records makes the study of early cultures difficult.

Scientists who study the life and culture of ancient peoples are called *archaeologists*. In making educated guesses about the lives of early groups of people, archaeologists examine skeletons and *artifacts*, objects the people made. Skeletons provide information about the age and appearance of early people, while artifacts reveal the kinds of tools and weapons they used.

Whenever archaeologists discover an area where prehistoric people might have lived, they seal it off. Then they divide the ground into squares and carefully reproduce each square on a map. Next the digging begins. Using hand tools and screens, the diggers sift away the soil. Whenever they locate a significant object, workers use smaller tools such as dental picks and brushes. They mark on the map the location of each stone tool, bone chip, or skeletal piece that is found. In this way archaeologists get a clear picture of the site.

After artifacts and skeletons have been gathered, scientists test them for age. With the results of this analysis they can develop theories about the prehistoric people who lived on a given site. Using such procedures, archaeologists have drawn some conclusions about the first Americans.

Archaeological Theories

For decades many archaeologists have held that people first arrived in this hemisphere from 12,000 to 20,000 years ago. During this period the earth underwent one of its periodic ice ages. Vast amounts of water froze into glaciers, and as a result the depth of oceans dropped as much as 200 to 300 feet (about 60 to 90 meters). Underwater ridges were exposed and formed land bridges, linking some continents and islands. As the glaciers advanced southward, ice covered large areas of North America, Europe, and Asia. People and animals were then forced to migrate in search of food and warmer climates.

Experts who adhere to this theory believe that a land bridge perhaps 1,000 miles (about 1,600 kilometers) wide connected Asia and North America during this period. According to these experts, herds of animals moved eastward across the bridge and Asian hunters followed, tracking them throughout North and South America. When

Some early Americans drew sand paintings as part of religious ceremonies or to heal the sick. The paintings were then brushed away. This copy of a Navajo sand painting shows Father Sky and Mother Earth. Symbols of corn, squash, beans, and tobacco are pictured on Mother Earth's body.

the climate warmed again, the glaciers melted and the oceans rose. Water that today forms the Bering Strait then covered the land bridge, ending the migration. To prove this theory, scientists have traditionally used the *carbon-14 test*, a method for determining the age of plant and animal remains.

In the 1970s, however, a small group of scientists challenged the earlier theories. They asserted that the carbon-14 test had a limited use in studying prehistory. First, the test can date only those remains that are less than 40,000 years old; second, it works only on large objects as much as a pound (454 grams) in weight. Few archaeologists find bone fragments that large, and those who do are usually unwilling to destroy them, as is necessary to run the procedure. Therefore, the challengers of the theory argue, the carbon-14 test provides only an incomplete view of the first Americans.

To solve these problems a young California chemist developed a new method of testing, *amino acid racemization* (ras eh mih ZAY shuhn). With this method archaeologists can determine the age of remains up to a million years old, and they can test objects weighing less than an ounce (28 grams).

In the late 1970s racemization tests on pieces of bone found in a California dig indicated that people might have lived on the site over 48,000 years ago. Some scientists suggest that humans may have come to the Americas as long as 70,000 years ago, when another ice age had exposed the land bridge across the Bering Strait. Over thousands of years, these hunting peoples would have migrated southward until they reached recently examined sites in California.

Although racemization has led to some important discoveries, the controversy remains. Most archaeologists are reluctant to accept the new theories without further investigation. However, in spite of disagreements over these theories, archaeologists can agree on certain features of prehistoric cultures. As a result of studies done to date, a partial picture of the earliest Americans has begun to emerge.

Climate and Culture Change

Although scientists do not agree on the origins of the earliest Americans, most agree that about 10,000 years ago certain environmental changes took place in the Americas. The glaciers retreated, temperatures warmed, lakes dried up, lush vegetation died, and many large animal species became extinct.

These changes forced prehistoric peoples living in the Americas to alter their way of life. As the climate became more diverse, people living in different parts of the Americas developed the skills needed to survive in their new environments. When the huge game animals disappeared, people turned to hunting smaller game. Groups who lived close to the sea usually depended on fishing for a livelihood. Many organized their daily lives, their holidays, even their religions around fishing.

Other people followed similar patterns. For example, groups living in the present-day San Francisco Bay area found vast supplies of acorns. Although they fished to supplement their diet, they spent much time collecting and storing acorns. The acorn was the main ingredient of their meals.

During this period, people not only adapted their lives to their surroundings, they also changed their natural environment to meet their needs. Instead of following herds of animals or gathering wild foods, some groups learned how to grow such plants as beans, squash, and maize, or corn. With the emergence of agriculture, people no longer had to move from place to place in search of food. They were able to settle in permanent communities.

Over the centuries a wide variety of cultures developed in North and South America. Some people lived in small hunting and gathering bands, while others lived in larger, more permanent communities. Each had its own forms of government, religion, and art, reflecting and expressing its culture.

SECTION REVIEW

1. Define: prehistoric period, archaeologist, artifact, carbon-14 test, amino acid racemization.
2. What do archaeologists study to learn about prehistoric cultures?
3. (a) What is the land bridge theory of how people came to the Americas? (b) Where would the land bridge have been located?
4. **Critical Thinking** How might people today adapt to a warming climate?

2 Many Cultures Among the First Americans

Most early American peoples did not have names that you would recognize. They referred to themselves as "the people," "the ancient ones," or "the genuine people." Such names illustrated the pride they had in themselves and in their long-felt association with the land on which they lived. The map on this page and the discussion in this section and the next give some idea of the rich and diverse cultures that existed in the Americas by the fifteenth century.

Life in the West

Many of the early Americans who lived in the western region extending from the Arctic Circle to the warm Pacific coast of California lived by hunting, fishing, or gathering plants. Within the region, diverse cultures developed. Among them were the Eskimo, the Northwest Coast, and the Great Basin cultures.

The Eskimos inhabited the plains and seacoasts of the Arctic region. For most of the year they faced bitter cold and heavy snows. Because few plants grew in the frigid climate, the lives of the Eskimos revolved around hunting and fishing. Animals such as the seal, walrus, whale, and caribou were a source not only of food, but also of clothing, tools, weapons, boats, household implements, and other necessities. The crucial

■ *This map shows American cultures in the 1500s. Color indicates groups with similar styles of living.*

Major North American Cultures in the 1500s

Plentiful food, especially salmon, along the northwest Pacific coast allowed early Americans leisure time to develop the arts. The carved and painted canoe in this painting is typical of the designs they used. Cedar trees provided wood for building and bark for weaving.

importance of these animals to the Eskimos is shown by the prominent part they played in Arctic folklore, religion, and art.

The first Americans who settled along the northwest Pacific coast, with its mild climate and abundant food, had a much easier life. Salmon and other fishes thrived in the many streams and rivers. Offshore the seas teemed with seals, whales, and otters, while on land herds of deer, moose, and elk roamed the thick forests. The food supply of these people was plentiful.

These favorable conditions left the people of the northwest Pacific free to engage in other, more diversified activities. They built huge, elaborately decorated houses, fashioned handsome copper shields, carved great totem poles and canoes, and made beautiful wooden masks, furniture, and utensils of all kinds.

Gradually, they developed a complex society based on wealth. Each person's status depended on the possessions he or she owned. To demonstrate their prosperity people held feasts called *potlatches* (PAHT latch ehz). At these ceremonies, which lasted several days, the host family entertained guests lavishly and gave away valuable possessions. Those who received gifts held their own potlatches in return. Anyone who could not do this lost status in the social hierarchy of the community.

The groups living in the Great Basin had a more difficult life. The Great Basin is a dry, bleak region between the Sierra Nevadas and the Rocky Mountains. It supports few animals or edible plants. Peoples such as the Ute and Shoshone had difficulty finding food, so they were forced to move about in small bands often no larger than a single family. Family members spent most of their time searching for scarce food. The adult men dominated the bands, and women and children held low status.

The Desert Tradition

The environment of much of the region that now comprises part of Arizona, New Mexico, southern Utah, and northern Mexico was also harsh for people who lived there. In the north, rapidly flowing rivers had carved steep-walled canyons into the land or washed away the soil to form huge mesas* thousands of feet high. In the south, foothills and mountains gave way to flat stretches of desert. There, summer temperatures reached over 100° Fahrenheit (38° Celsius) and winter temperatures dropped well below 0° Fahrenheit (-18° Celsius).

Despite these extreme conditions, several imposing civilizations emerged in the area. One of the earliest groups was the Anasazi (ah nah SAH zee). An ingenious people, they turned the desert into productive farming land with a system of dams and irrigation canals. Within the remote canyons of much of today's Southwest, they built cliff dwellings resembling modern high-rise apartments. On the rock walls of the canyons they drew *pictograms*, pictures conveying their ideas about life. The Anasazi were also skilled weavers, basketmakers, and potters.

The Anasazi disappeared mysteriously; however, several later groups traced their origins to the Anasazi. One group, the Pueblo†, lived in the area of present-day Arizona and New Mexico. The Pueblo were a farming people who grew beans, cotton, tobacco, squash, and gourds—a difficult task in a region that received so little rain.

Like the Anasazi, the Pueblo often built their dwellings on the summits of mesas or along the sides of steep cliffs. With stone and *adobe*, sun-dried clay brick, they constructed oval, square, or rectangular structures several stories high. They grouped the buildings around a broad, open space, forming a kind of town with a main square.

At the center of each town lay a room called the *kiva*. Within the kiva, Pueblo men met to conduct religious ceremonies. The purpose of the rites varied. The Pueblo held some to bring rain, others to cure the sick, and still others to please the gods or to ask for a blessing. The kiva societies controlled Pueblo life. They emphasized conformity and the importance of society over the individual. A warrior class enforced the rules of conduct.

The Pueblo were a matrilineal society. In other words, they traced descent within a family through the mother's line. Women headed the families and held all property rights. A wife who wanted to divorce her husband just put his belongings outside her door—a signal that the husband had to go back to his mother's house. Pueblo women were also exceptionally skilled potters and basketweavers—crafts the Pueblo probably learned from the Anasazi.

During the sixteenth century, another important southwestern group, the Navajo (NAV uh HOH), migrated into what is now northern New Mexico. There, the Navajo came under the influence of their Pueblo neighbors, from whom they learned farming and weaving.

The early Navajo lived in settlements consisting of "forked stick" homes, made by piling logs against three poles joined together at their tops, then covering the outside with mud. Later, they fashioned *hogans*, earthen domes with log frames.

Navajo religion, which was influenced heavily by that of the Pueblo, centered on the idea that a person's life should be in harmony with the universe. Immortal beings called Holy People, who had to be pleased through strict rituals, could affect the lives of mortals, called Earth Surface People. To the Navajo illness indicated disharmony. Harmony and health returned when the Holy People were satisfied.

On the Great Plains

Between the Rocky Mountains and the Mississippi River lies a large area of relatively flat grasslands known today as the Great Plains. For thousands of years, most inhabitants of the Great Plains lived near rivers so they could be sure of a water supply for farming. Women were responsible for the farming and plowed their garden plots with digging sticks and hoes made from large animal bones. Maize, squash, beans, and sunflowers were the principal crops.

For most of the year, the Plains people lived in fairly permanent villages. There they built lodges by covering log frames with brush and sod. But during the summer, the

---

*mesa: a high, flat plateau or tableland with steep sides.

†The name "pueblo" (PWEHB loh), which means "town" in Spanish, was given to these people by Spanish explorers in the 1500s. These explorers thought the settlements looked like European towns.

men often left the villages for weeks at a time to hunt buffalo.

Sometime in the mid-sixteenth century most of the Plains people became more *nomadic.* Instead of living in permanent villages all year long, they moved from place to place, building temporary settlements near water and food supplies. Migrations were carried out on foot. Dogs dragged travois* carrying the owners' possessions. The change may have been caused by drought or by enemy attacks.

The nomadic settlements still relied on farming for much of their food, but the men engaged in many more hunting expeditions. On the hunt they lived in portable teepees made from buffalo hides. Farther to the west, Americans who were completely nomadic lived in teepees year-round.

The semiagricultural, seminomadic groups of the Plains included the Osage, Missouri, Omaha, Kansas, Iowa, Wichita, and Mandan, as well as the Pawnee. The Blackfeet achieved the greatest power in the western part of the Great Plains. The Crows hunted the land between the Missouri and Yellowstone rivers, and the Comanche, Kiowa, and Apache dominated the southern plains.

Each of the Plains groups had a well-developed religion. In most of them visions played an important role because people believed that visions revealed their destinies. To intensify their visions and thus to get a clearer picture of their destinies, young men and women would go out into the wilderness and fast.

Supreme status in the Plains communities belonged to the chief. He achieved this honor by demonstrating bravery, good judgment, skill in public speaking, or some other outstanding quality. A council made up of the most prominent men ruled each group. The council's decisions usually had to be unanimous.

In the Eastern Woodlands

Three major groups of people lived in the woodlands east of the Mississippi River: the Algonquin (al GAHN kwihn), the Iroquois (IHR uh kwoi), and the Muskogean (muhs KOH gee ehn).

The Algonquins inhabited the forests that covered the Northeast from present-day Labrador and Quebec as far south as Maryland and Virginia. They lived in small bands, hunting deer and caribou or gathering wild nuts and berries. The Algonquins also used the resources of the forest to build efficient transportation: snowshoes and toboggans in the winter, canoes in the summer.

Algonquin society was relatively simple. Each band shared the major food resources of the territory. Although families within the band hunted primarily in one area they regarded as theirs, they willingly shared their catch with others. Food was often scarce during the harsh winters, and every family knew that one day it might have to depend on another's support.

The Iroquois were several related tribes that originally lived in southeastern North America. Around 1300 they migrated north to the area of present-day New York State and drove out the Algonquins. However, not long after the departure of the Algonquins, the Iroquois began to feud among themselves. During the sixteenth century, the warfare became especially bitter. The waste of tribal energies on fruitless conflict threatened to undermine the Iroquois people.

According to legend, two reformers, Dekanawidah, a Huron religious leader, and his disciple Hiawatha, a Mohawk chief, responded to the situation by preaching the idea of a political confederation, or alliance, of the Iroquois tribes. They believed that such a union would not only end the bloodshed among the tribes but would also provide a strong defense against the Iroquois' enemies.

The goal of the two reformers was finally achieved during the 1500s. Five tribes—the Mohawk, the Seneca (SEHN ih kuh), the Cayuga (kay YOO gah), the Oneida (oh NĪ duh), and the Onondaga (ahn uhn DAH guh)—gradually joined together to form a confederation known as the Iroquois League.

The league, whose values were based on those of traditional Iroquois culture, proved successful. A representative council, consisting of the chiefs of each tribe and 50 specially chosen leaders called *sachems* (SAY chehms), governed the league. The sachems were responsible for all matters involving relations among the tribes.

Iroquois society, like that of the Pueblo, was matrilineal. All property passed

---

*travois (trah VOI): two poles with an animal skin mounted between them. After the Spanish reintroduced horses to the Americas, the Plains people used horses rather than dogs during their migrations.

from generation to generation on the female side of the family. Thus, women owned the gardens of the settlements and the spacious longhouses in which several related families lived. Although they did not serve on the league council, women who headed the clans appointed the male sachems.

Other eastern woodlands groups also had complex social and political systems—the Muskogeans, for example. These farming people had a highly structured class system based on worship of the sun. At the top of the system was the chief, called the Great Sun. Just below him in status were the nobles, known as Suns. Below them were the Honored People, and lowest of all was the class known as the Stinkards.

The reigning Great Sun had the power of life and death over the Muskogeans, who worshiped him as a god. The group's complicated marriage rules insured that membership in each class changed over time, however, so that no one family could hold the position of Great Sun indefinitely. In the space of several generations, a Great Sun's descendants would become Stinkards.

SECTION REVIEW

1. Identify: Hiawatha, Iroquois League.
2. Define: potlatch, pictogram, adobe, kiva, hogan, nomadic, sachem.
3. Which people had the most abundant food supply: Eskimos, people of the northwest Pacific coast, people of the Great Plains?
4. (a) Name one thing the Pueblo probably learned from the Anasazi. (b) Name one thing the Navajo probably learned from the Pueblo.
5. How did the travois and the teepee contribute to the lives of the Plains peoples?
6. **Critical Thinking** Why did Indians in the better climates develop more complex social and political systems?

3 Great Empires

Many scientists believe that the Muskogeans and other southeastern peoples were influenced by cultures that had developed to the southwest of them, in present-day Mexico. There the Mayas and later the Aztecs built great empires, sophisticated civilizations that influenced many early American societies. In South America the Incas also established a powerful empire.

The Mayas

Mayan civilization flourished on the Yucatan peninsula of Mexico and in present-day Guatemala from about 300 to 900 A.D. The Mayans built great cities, where as many as 40,000 people lived. While these cities were centers of trade, their most important purpose was religious. Towering over all other buildings in the city were huge temple-pyramids covered with carved pictures. It was there that the religious ceremonies took place. The pyramids show the Mayas' great engineering skills.

The Mayas were skilled in many sciences. Mayan priests were excellent astronomers. They could predict eclipses of the sun and moon and could chart the movements of the planet Venus. Their knowledge enabled them to work out exact calendars, an important part of their religion. The Mayas also developed a complex system of writing that is still not completely understood.

Rise of the Aztecs

Farther to the north, in the Valley of Mexico, a people known as the Toltecs rose to power around 900 A.D. Unlike the peaceful Mayas, the warlike Toltecs extended their influence through conquests. They conquered tribes around them with well-organized armies and new weapons such as the atl-atl, a hand-held catapult that increased the force of a thrown spear. The Toltecs in turn were conquered sometime after 1200 A.D. by the even more warlike Aztecs, who adopted many Toltec customs.

Aztecs called themselves the People of the Sun. As their power grew, they forced their neighbors to pay tributes of food and labor. They erected a spectacular capital city, Tenochtitlán (tay NOHCH tee TLAHN), in the middle of a large saltwater lake. An

Mayan Ideograms

The Mayas had a system of writing that used pictures, or ideograms, to represent sounds and ideas. For example, if a Mayan scribe wanted to show the idea of travel, he or she would draw two parallel lines, the symbol for road. Then the outline of a human footprint would be added between them to show travel.

The Mayas carved ideograms onto large stone shafts known as stelae and onto altars, doorways, and wall panels. The Mayas also had books consisting of large sheets of bark paper enclosed between boards. Their books concerned religion and science, especially astronomy. Some also recorded important events.

enormous pyramid now called the Pyramid of the Sun dominated the other structures in the city. Here Aztec priests sacrificed humans to Huitzilopochtli (WEE tsee loh POHCH tlee), the chief god.

Floating artificial islands, made by piling dirt on log rafts, surrounded Tenochtitlán. Some formed the foundations for homes; others were cultivated as vegetable gardens. Fresh water flowed into the city through aqueducts. Several long causeways connected the island-city to the mainland. Inside the city, paved streets led to the elaborate homes of the wealthy, to beautiful temples, and to zoos, orchards, and public gathering places.

The construction of Tenochtitlán, as well as the Aztec irrigation systems, bridges, causeways, and amphitheaters, indicates an advanced technology. The Aztec calendar reflects a knowledge of star formations precise enough to predict certain stellar locations on a 52-year cycle. The Aztec system of mathematics probably was better than European systems of the time.

The Incas

Other imposing civilizations developed along the western coast of South America and in the highlands of the Andes Mountains. By 1400 A.D. one group, the Incas, dominated settlements along a band 1,500 miles (about 2,400 kilometers) long, from what is today southern Ecuador to Chile.

Incan engineering achievements surpassed even those of the Aztecs. Sometimes the Incas constructed cities on the tops of mountains or along the faces of steep cliffs. Although no one can be sure how they accomplished it, the Incas moved massive stones from remote quarries, then cut them so precisely that they fit together like pieces of a puzzle. No cementing was required. Even today Incan structures survive earthquakes that demolish modern buildings; the stones move apart under stress, then slide back together.

The Sapa Inca, or supreme ruler, possessed absolute power over his subjects. He ruled a highly efficient economy based on diversified agriculture, with goods transported over an impressive system of roads, footpaths, and floating bridges. The Incas, like the Aztecs, worshiped the sun, and religious leaders performed various rituals to prepare the way for life after death.

The Mayas, the Aztecs, and the Incas were among the first Americans who would feel the impact of European exploration in the late fifteenth century. One by one their complex civilizations would fall to the invading newcomers. In the process, many valuable traces of their cultures would be destroyed—sometimes deliberately, sometimes out of carelessness. What is known of them today comes largely from the remains of their huge stone temples and public buildings. Through these, all three groups have left an indelible imprint on the imagination of the world.

SECTION REVIEW

1. Identify: People of the Sun, Tenochtitlán, Huitzilopochtli, Sapa Inca.
2. List two scientific accomplishments of the (a) Mayas, (b) Aztecs, (c) Incas.
3. **Critical Thinking** How were the Incas able to control their empire?

4 Europe Awakens

Until the late fifteenth century, people in the Americas remained largely isolated from the rest of the world. In Europe, however, an age of discovery was beginning that would soon end that isolation. The new spirit of discovery had its roots in developments that had been under way for many years.

Europe in the Middle Ages

During the Middle Ages (500–1500 A.D.) people in Europe focused largely on local affairs. Since the fall of the Roman Empire in the fifth century, the continent of Europe had been split into hundreds of small, independent states, each ruled by a lord.

Most of the people, peasants called *serfs*, were bound by custom to the lord's land. They gave the lord part of their crop in return for protection against bandits or invaders. Serfs could not leave the land to take up another kind of work, nor could they travel even short distances without the lord's permission.

Theoretically, the lord also owed allegiance and services to a superior: a king, an emperor, or a higher lord. He was the king's *vassal*, or tenant. According to the law of the time, a lord received lands from his superior in return for loyalty. For the most part, however, lords ruled their territories absolutely and independently of one another. This political and social system is known as *feudalism.*

Most medieval states were divided economically into *manors*, or large estates owned by lords. Peasants grew food for everyone on the manor and produced most of life's other necessities. A manor would have, for example, a cobbler who made shoes, a blacksmith who forged tools, a brewer who made beverages, and a miller who ground grain into flour. As a result, few goods had to be traded between manors.

The religious ideas of the Middle Ages further contributed to a lack of interest in the wider world. Christians learned that their life on earth was merely a preparation for life after death. They saw this world as a place of suffering and sadness, or of riches and corruption, but they believed that their station in life was God's will and did not question it.

A New Age Dawns

Around 1100 A.D. life in Europe began to change. People's horizons gradually widened, and they became more curious about the world beyond their own localities.

The Crusades were a major cause of the new atmosphere in Europe. Beginning in 1099, European Christians conducted a series of holy wars, or crusades, with the aim of recapturing the city of Jerusalem and the Holy Land from the Muslims.*

The Holy Land had fallen into the hands of the Muslims in the seventh century. Until around 1000 A.D., however, Muslim rulers allowed Christians to come and go as they wished. At that time, the Seljuk (sehl JOOK) Turks, Muslims not as tolerant of Christianity as their predecessors, conquered the Holy Land. Pilgrims returning to Europe from the Holy Land claimed that the Turks were killing and torturing Christians and turning Christian churches into Muslim temples.

---

*Muslim: a believer in the Muslim religion, in which the supreme deity is Allah and the chief prophet and founder is Mohammed. The Muslim religion is also known as Islam and the Muslims are sometimes known as Moslems.

Europeans quickly acquired a taste for the spices Crusaders brought back from Asia. At first only the rich could afford the scarce cinnamon, pepper, and cloves sold by merchants such as the man at right. The search for a less costly route to Asia helped spur sea exploration.

The Crusades against the Turks lasted for about 150 years. At first the Christian armies were successful, but by the end of the thirteenth century all the territory they had won was again under Muslim control.

Although the Crusaders did not achieve their goal, they did affect life in Europe. For example, they brought back books written by Arabic scholars. The new ideas and knowledge the books contained sparked curiosity about the world beyond local borders.

The spices, perfumes, fabrics, and other items the returning Crusaders introduced to Europe also gave people new tastes in foods, new fashions in clothing, and new ideas of comfort in their homes. Soon, a profitable trade arose between the countries of Europe and Asia.

Expanding Horizons Eastward

At first, Europeans traded only with the countries of the Middle East; however, merchants eventually became curious about what lay beyond that area. In 1271 Venetian merchants Maffeo and Niccolo Polo and Niccolo's 17-year-old son Marco set off from Venice. Their destination was Cathay, as China was called, a land celebrated for its fabulous wealth.

The Polos traveled over sea and land for three years, reaching the court of Kublai Khan (koo blī KAHN), China's emperor, around 1275. They remained in China as guests of the Khan for 17 years. During that time, Marco Polo traveled far and wide throughout the vast empire of China. Little escaped his notice, and in 1295, three years after the Polos had returned to Venice, he dictated the story of his travels to a scribe.* Marco Polo's account of the wonders he had seen revealed to Europeans a civilization beyond anything they had dreamed of.

In addition to describing the wonders of China, Polo provided some very practical information. He told readers that Asian goods were much cheaper in China than they were in Europe. Furthermore, he noted that China was bordered by oceans, not by huge, impassable swamps as had been thought. Therefore, a sea route to Asia would be possible if one could be found.

Over the next 200 years, interest in trade with China and with India, China's neighbor to the southwest, grew. Fine silks, gold, and jewels attracted mainly the wealthy, but nearly all Europeans wanted to buy Asian spices.

In the years since the Crusades, Europeans had discovered that cloves, ginger,

---

*In the Middle Ages, few men and women could write, so they hired professional writers called scribes.

cinnamon, and pepper did wonders for food. Without these spices, food had a bland, flat taste. Furthermore, many foods were extremely perishable and could be preserved only by heavy, often unpalatable, salting. It was not unusual for a medieval cook to have to pick worms out of meat before cooking it. Sauces made with Asian spices covered up the taste of rotten meat and other spoiled foods.

Because of the growing demand for products from Asia, merchants and adventurers began to search for faster and cheaper routes to Asia. They hoped to avoid paying extremely high taxes charged by rulers along the land routes, so they looked to the sea.

Exploration and Politics

A changing political scene in Europe further contributed to a growing interest in exploration. During the Middle Ages kings and queens for the most part had ruled in name only. Real power lay in the hands of the feudal lords.

As a new middle class grew and prospered, merchants, bankers, and other well-to-do commoners began to wish for the kind of power and status that the nobility had. Kings and queens discovered that they could increase their own power by taking advantage of the merchants' aspirations. Over a period of a hundred years or so, they allied themselves with the merchants and bankers, using their wealth to help create strong monarchies and powerful nations.

Merchants and bankers also profited from the alliance. With the backing of a strong nation, merchants could compete with the city-states* of Italy, which had a virtual monopoly on the Asian trade. Such a monopoly could not be broken by one merchant, or a group of merchants, no matter how powerful. But it could be broken by the combined power of a country's merchants and its government. A city-state like Venice, no matter how wealthy, was no match for the might of a united nation.

Changes in Outlook

Politics and economics were not the only areas in which significant changes took place. During the period of intellectual revi-

*city-state: a governmental unit made up of an independent city and the surrounding territory it controlled.

val known as the Renaissance (REHN uh sahns), which began in the 1300s, attitudes toward life, learning, and religion also changed profoundly.

The work of Arabic scholars brought back by the Crusaders made a deep impression on European learning. Arabic translations reintroduced European scholars to the writings of many classical Greek and Roman thinkers whose works had been lost to Europe since the fall of Rome. Europeans also studied Arabic science, especially advances made by Arab mathematicians.

Interest in one branch of knowledge stimulated curiosity about others. Increasingly, people wanted to learn more about the world in which they lived. They began to investigate their surroundings and to question what they found.

This new inquisitive attitude toward the world sparked advances in science and technology, including new inventions in sea travel. For example, a ship's captain could

At age 17 Marco Polo left home with his father and uncle to journey beyond the limits of the known world. His destination was the splendid court of Kublai Khan in China. This illustration from a manuscript of the 1300s shows the wedding of Ghazan Khan, son of Kublai Khan, to Princess Cocachin. Polo's tales of the Khan's court increased European interest in trade with Asia.

use a *compass* to tell direction, even when neither land nor the sun was visible. With the *astrolabe* (AS truh layb), the captain was able to fix the ship's location by sighting the stars. With the *quadrant* the captain could take bearings from the sun or the stars in order to plot the ship's position on a map.

By making more precise measurements of distance and location possible, new inventions also advanced the art of map making. Another invention, the printing press, made the improved maps more widely available. All these developments contributed to a growing interest in travel and exploration.

Prince Henry the Navigator

Of course, mariners had to be taught to use new instruments. One person more than any other was responsible for doing this—Prince Henry of Portugal, known as the Navigator.

Portugal was the first European nation to begin systematic exploration of the world beyond Europe and the Mediterranean Sea. Prince Henry played the leading part in this effort. In 1418 Henry established a school of navigation in his castle at Sagres (SAH grehs) on the southwestern tip of Portugal. From there he sent expeditions to Africa.

★ America's Heritage ★

Realms of Wealth and Culture

The Portuguese were first attracted to West Africa by reports of great wealth. The wealth they sought had grown over many centuries as great African empires rose and fell. The ancient West African empire of Ghana began to develop in size and importance around 700 A.D. Most people of Ghana were farmers. But it was Ghana's commerce that made it rich. Because it was located midway between the salt mines in the Sahara and the gold mines in the tropics, Ghana controlled the trade in gold and salt.

At its peak around 1100 A.D., Ghana's capital, Kumbi (KOOM bee), consisted of two connected cities. Kumbi had a magnificent palace, a merchants' trading center, and a prison. Scholars and priests met in its mosques.

The kingdom of Mali became important in the 1200s and 1300s. Like Ghana, Mali had a well-run government. It, too, drew much of its wealth from the gold and salt trade. Flourishing cities attracted many scholars as well as merchants. The city of Timbuktu (tihm buhk TOO) became a major center of learning for the Islamic world.

Stories about the fabulous riches of West Africa began to thrill Europeans around the 1500s. In one spectacular hajj (haj), or pilgrimage to Mecca, Mansa Musa (MAN suh MOO sah), the ruler of Mali from about 1312 to 1332, traveled with 12,000 slaves. Five hundred slaves carried six-pound staffs of gold. Each of 80 camels bore a 300-pound load of gold dust.

Having reached the height of its power under Mansa Musa, Mali became part of the empire of Songhai in the 1600s. The rulers of this third empire continued the tradition of stable and effective government. They created a civil service, a system of courts, a standing army, and even a navy.

The West African kingdoms of Ashanti, Dahomey, Benin, and Oyo also developed sophisticated cultures expressed in their beautifully woven fabrics, ornate jewelry, carvings in wood and ivory, and bronze sculpture. It was little wonder that Europeans who learned of these civilizations were eager to make contact with them.

Prince Henry had several reasons for sending explorers to investigate the western shores of Africa. Like other European princes, Henry felt that his nation had the duty to convert people to Christianity. He had heard the popular tale of Prester John, who was said to rule a Christian empire in the heart of Africa, and he hoped to be the first to find this legendary kingdom.

A concern for the commercial well-being of his country further heightened Henry's interest. Legends of rich kingdoms in western Africa had been circulating in Europe for years. In fact, gold from these kingdoms had reached Europe as early as the tenth century. However, it had come to Mediterranean ports by a long and costly route across the Sahara. Prince Henry hoped to find a quicker, cheaper route to the source of this gold by sea. Finally, Prince Henry, like other Europeans of his time, dreamed of finding a sea route to India, a place that symbolized riches.

For many years Henry could not convince his sailors to dare a trip beyond Cape Bojador (boh huh DOHR) on the African coast. At that time ships had difficulty sailing into the wind. Since the prevailing winds blew from the north, the sailors wondered how a ship could turn around once it headed due south. The sailors worried that if they passed Cape Bojador, they would not be able to sail back to Portugal. In addition, many sailors had heard that the water of the southern oceans was so hot it boiled.

At Sagres Henry encouraged his shipbuilders to experiment with new model ships. Eventually, they developed a vessel called the *caravel* (KAR uh vehl), which could sail into the wind. It had sleeker lines than the older *carracks* (KAR ukz), which looked like squat wooden tubs, and it used triangular rather than square sails. Henry also showed his captains how to use the quadrant so that they could sail out of sight of land and still be confident of getting back. In 1434 one of Henry's ships finally sailed beyond Cape Bojador. The crew found that it was able to turn around and sail back home. And the sailors discovered that the southern seas really did not boil.

Prince Henry died in 1460, but Portuguese explorers continued to push farther and farther down the African coast, building stone pillars on the shore to mark their progress. Gradually, they established a profitable trade with West African kingdoms. The bulk of their trade was in gold, but they also bought some African slaves. The explorers took the slaves back to Portugal to work as domestic servants. Some were eventually freed, took Portuguese names, and within generations became assimilated into the population.

In 1487 Bartolomeu Dias sailed around the Cape of Good Hope, the southernmost tip of Africa. He had planned to go on to India, but his crew mutinied and forced him to return to Portugal. Ten years later, in 1497, Vasco da Gama made the complete trip to India. Europeans had finally reached Asia by water, and Portugal was well on its way to becoming a powerful trading empire.

Early Contacts

By 1490 Europeans were on the verge of discovering the Americas. Yet this would not be the first contact between American cultures and people from other parts of the world. The first European visitors to the Americas were the Vikings. Sometime around 1000 A.D., Scandinavian sailors led by Leif Ericson reached the northern tip of North America.

Major Events	
300–900	Mayan civilization flourishes
1000	Leif Ericson lands in North America
1099	Crusades begin
1100	Height of Ghana's empire in West Africa
1200	Aztecs conquer Toltecs
1275	Polos reach China
1312–1332	Rule of Mansa Musa in Mali
1400	Incas establish dominance on west coast of South America
1418	Prince Henry founds navigation school at Sagres
1487	Dias sails around Cape of Good Hope
1497	Vasco da Gama reaches India

Throughout the winter of their arrival, they roamed up and down the rough Atlantic coast exploring present-day Labrador and Newfoundland. Then they went home.

Twenty years later, another group of Scandinavians arrived. Their settlement, built in a sheltered Newfoundland bay, lasted little more than two years and was abandoned. The only trace of these early visitors are the half-buried foundations of their houses and a few stone objects.

According to legend, a few Irish fishermen crossed the Atlantic to North America. But if they did, they left no evidence of it. Some maintain that a group of Chinese sailors reached Mexico around 450 A.D., and others claim that Africans explored parts of the Americas several hundred years before Columbus. Present-day Norwegian explorer Thor Heyerdahl believes that ancient Egyptians and Polynesians may have piloted large reed boats to the Americas long before European exploration.

None of these Europeans, Africans, or Asians left lasting traces of their presence in the Americas, nor did they develop any lasting relationships with the first Americans. America continued to go its own way until the late fifteenth century, when the new spirit of discovery that was infecting Europe ended its isolation.

SECTION REVIEW

1. Identify: Marco Polo, Henry the Navigator, Bartolomeu Dias, Vasco da Gama.
2. Define: serf, vassal, feudalism, manor, compass, astrolabe, quadrant, caravel, carrack.
3. (a) What were the Crusades? (b) List two ways the Crusades increased people's interest in the world beyond local borders.
4. How did each of the following contribute to an age of discovery: (a) Marco Polo's explorations; (b) desire for spices; (c) alliance between monarchs and merchants?
5. What new technology made sea travel safer and easier?
6. Why did Prince Henry of Portugal want to explore the west coast of Africa?
7. **Critical Thinking** Why have the Crusades been called a "successful failure"?

★★★ Chapter 1 Review ★★★

In Perspective

Although scientists debate the origins of America's first people, most agree that humans lived in the Americas as many as 20,000 years ago. Over thousands of years, people learned to use the resources available to them to survive. They built diverse cultures. Some groups hunted and fished or gathered plants. Others planted crops, even in harsh desert climates.

Each culture had its own religious traditions, art forms, and ways of life. The first Americans developed a variety of government and social systems.

While hundreds of cultures were developing in the Americas, many other cultures were growing up in Africa, Asia, and Europe. Changes in Europe, especially, would in time bring together the Americas and the rest of the world. During the 1300s and 1400s, alliances of monarchs, merchants, and bankers encouraged the unification of nations. These nations would sponsor explorations to other parts of the world. The meeting of the two worlds seemed to be only a matter of time.

Vocabulary

On a separate sheet of paper, write the word or words that best complete each of the following sentences.

1. Archaeologists study ___, or objects made by ancient peoples.
2. In the Northwest, people demonstrated their wealth by holding a ___.
3. ___ is sun-dried clay brick.
4. The ___ was the site of Pueblo religious ceremonies.
5. The ___ was a vessel that could sail into the wind.

Chapter Checkup

1. What methods do archaeologists use to study a site where early peoples may have lived?
2. (a) How were the lives of the Eskimos and the people of the Great Plains different? (b) How do you explain the differences?
3. How did the Anasazi, the Pueblo, and the Navajo cope with the harsh conditions in the desert?
4. Describe the building achievements of the Mayas, the Aztecs, and the Incas.
5. How did the changes caused by the Renaissance climate in Europe contribute to the age of discovery?

Critical Thinking

1. **Recognizing Relationships** Explain how differing environments and natural resources may have contributed to the diversity of early American cultures.
2. **Comparing** Describe how the Pueblo, the Plains people, and the Iroquois governed themselves. What factors do you think accounted for the similarities and differences among their systems of government?

Developing Basic Skills

1. **Classifying** Make a chart with two columns. In column 1 list the factors that inhibited European exploration before 1500. In column 2 list the factors or developments that encouraged exploration. Do you think that the factors that encouraged exploration made the European discovery of the Americas inevitable? Explain.
2. **Map Reading** Locate the following on the world map (pp. 806–807): Mediterranean Sea, Atlantic Ocean, Europe, Africa, Asia, Portugal, India, and China. (a) Why do you think Portugal led in the exploration of the West African coast? (b) What advantages did an all-water route to the East have for European traders?

See page 827 for suggested readings.

Writer's Handbook

Answering Essay Questions

In order to answer an essay question, you must understand what the instruction word is telling you to do. Some of the most common instruction words and the type of answer each calls for are listed below.

Discuss: tell the significance of a person or event

Describe: write a full account of *what* happened

Explain: tell *how* or *why* an action or event affects something else

Identify: give a person's or event's place in time and its relation to other persons or events

Compare: give similarities and differences or only differences

Sometimes an essay question will have a question word. Some of the most common question words and the type of answer each calls for are listed below.

Why: give reasons

How: tell in what way or by what means something was done

What: give specific examples or illustrations

Practice: Analyze each of the Critical Thinking questions in this Chapter Review. Tell which type of response the question calls for.

2

Europe's Age of Discovery

(1492–1608)

Christopher Columbus *by Sebastiano del Piombo*

Chapter Outline

1 *A New World for Europeans*

2 *Exploration and Conquest*

3 *Spanish Settlement of the Americas*

4 *The French and English Look North*

European sailors and adventurers were not looking for a new world in the 1400s. They were searching for the fastest route to Asia. The governments that financed their voyages planned to set up trading posts where European goods could be exchanged for the fabled riches of Asia. However, things did not turn out as planned.

Instead of finding a new route to Asia, Christopher Columbus and the explorers who followed him found two continents whose existence no one had predicted. Instead of meeting the Asians Marco Polo had described, they met people who were not mentioned in any of the books they had read.

In this chapter you will read about the meeting of the Old World and the New World as Europeans discovered the wealth of great American empires and the attraction of establishing colonies in the Americas.

Spanish establish empire in New World

1490	1510	1530	1550	1570	1590	1610

1492
Columbus reaches America

1513
Balboa discovers Pacific Ocean

1534
Cartier explores St. Lawrence River

1573
Laws of the Indies proclaimed

1585
Roanoke founded

1608
Champlain founds Quebec

1 A New World for Europeans

As Portuguese sailors were sailing along the African coast, other adventurers sought still faster routes to the wealth of Asia. Among them was Christopher Columbus, a tall, stubborn, and well-seasoned sailor from the Italian port of Genoa.

Columbus: A Determined Explorer

Columbus had sailed much of the then-known world in the service of the Portuguese. An insatiably curious man, he had studied geography and had read and reread Marco Polo's account of his travels.

Scholars had believed for hundreds of years that the world was round, and Columbus accepted their conclusions. He was also convinced, on the basis of his own calculations, that the earth was much smaller than people thought it was. Thus, he maintained, the distance between Europe and China, sailing west, could be navigated in "a very few days" if winds were favorable.

Armed with these convictions, Columbus tried to persuade King John II of Portugal to support a westward voyage to Asia. Portugal was a logical choice, but King John remained unconvinced. He preferred to concentrate his energies on an eastern route around Africa. Columbus spent the next ten years pleading his case at the courts of Europe. He approached the French, then the English. Rebuffed by both, he turned to Spain as a last resort.

The Spanish were not a seafaring people by tradition. However, they were a venturesome, ambitious nation, eager to spread the power of Spain and the influence of Christianity. Against the advice of cautious counselors, Queen Isabella agreed to back Columbus's venture. She outfitted him with three ships, the *Niña*, the *Pinta*, and the *Santa María*, and a crew of 90 sailors.

Columbus paid for part of the voyage himself. However, he demanded and received important concessions from the Spanish crown. Queen Isabella agreed to make him an admiral, to name him ruler of all the "islands and the mainlands" he discovered, and to give him one tenth of all the riches he "bought, bartered, discovered, acquired, or obtained."

Arriving in the Americas

Admiral Columbus set sail from Palos, Spain, on August 3, 1492. Two months later, on October 7, sailors spotted great flocks of birds flying southwest. Suspecting that the birds were heading for land, Columbus altered his course to follow them. Four days later the crew saw tree branches and flowers floating in the water.

Finally at two o'clock in the morning on October 12, the *Pinta*'s lookout spotted white cliffs on the horizon and raised a shout. Columbus and his crew had discovered a world unknown to Europeans, though no one on board the ships knew it yet.

Columbus, convinced that he had reached India, called the friendly people who greeted him Indians. "They invite you to share anything that they possess," he reported, "and show as much love as if their hearts went with it."

The Europeans saw no evidence of the fine silks or large buildings Marco Polo had described. The inhabitants of the island, the Arawaks (AR uh WAHKS), seemed to lead a simple life. The Arawaks did produce enough gold ornaments, however, to convince Columbus that he was not far from the Asian mainland.

Three months later, after exploring neighboring islands, including present-day Haiti and Cuba, the expedition sailed home to Spain. Columbus's success gained him immediate popularity in Spain. Queen Isabella and her husband Ferdinand were impressed by the "Indians" whom Columbus brought back to the Spanish court as evidence that he had found a western route to Asia. Consequently, the queen financed a more extensive expedition by Columbus in 1493. Columbus made two further voyages for the Spanish crown, one in 1498 and another in 1502.

Thirty women went along on the third expedition. By that time the Spanish had decided to establish settlements in the West Indies, as the Caribbean islands came to be called. The island of Hispaniola, or Little Spain, was chosen for the first settlement and a colony was organized. Eventually, the settlers established outposts on other islands.

Rivals for the New World

Word of Columbus's discoveries spread rapidly. Portugal's King John refused to believe the news that Columbus had reached India or China, nor would he recognize Spain's claim to the Caribbean islands. He argued that they were actually part of the Azores, islands in the Atlantic already owned by Portugal, and he claimed them for himself.

The two neighboring kingdoms were suddenly embroiled in a bitter dispute. Worried that the rivalry would lead to war and weaken European Christianity, the Pope offered to mediate. After months of negotiation papal ambassadors convinced Spain and Portugal to agree to the Treaty of Tordesillas (taw day SEE yahs). The treaty, signed in 1494, established the Line of Demarcation. Drawn on a map of the world about 1,100 miles (1,770 kilometers) west of the Azores, the line divided all undiscovered lands between Spain and Portugal.

The treaty granted Spain the right to the territory west of the line and Portugal the territory east of it. What neither Spain nor Portugal knew in 1494 was that the eastern part of South America extended across the line. When a storm blew Portugal's Pedro Álvares Cabral (AHL vah rehz kuh BRAHL) off his course in 1500, he landed in this part of the Americas and promptly claimed it for King John. The territory is now part of Brazil.

A Western Route to Asia

Although Spain and Portugal showed some interest in settling what came to be known as the New World, discovery of a fast route to Asia remained the top priority for most explorers. After Columbus's voyages, many believed that Asia lay just beyond the western coast of North America. To reach it a person only had to find a water passage through the continent.

In the early 1500s hundreds of people joined expeditions sailing from the ports of Spain and Portugal in search of this passage. These included sailors from many European nations as well as a number of Africans, who had been brought to Europe originally by Portuguese and Spanish traders.

Vasco Nuñez de Balboa (NOO nyehht day bal BOH uh), a Spanish explorer, discov-

ered the shortest route across the New World. In 1513, Balboa made a grueling journey across what is now called the Isthmus of Panama, the narrow strip of land connecting North and South America. His route cut through rain forest so thick that an explorer who followed the same trail 350 years later could not see the sky for 11 days.

Balboa's courage and stamina were rewarded at the end of the trek. Emerging from the rain forest onto the top of a mountain, the explorer gazed down on the vast ocean now known as the Pacific. He named it the South Sea, assuming that it was south of Asia.

Balboa was the first European to see the Pacific Ocean, but he had no idea of its great size. It remained for Ferdinand Magellan (muh JEHL uhn) to discover its immensity by sailing across it.

Magellan's expedition sailed from Spain in 1519, made its way around the stormy southern tip of South America, and then crossed the Pacific to the Philippine Islands. There Magellan died in a battle with the island's inhabitants.

What was left of Magellan's fleet continued the eastward journey. In 1522 the one remaining ship limped back to Spain. Of the 237 men who had set sail three years earlier, only 18 survived. Those 18 sailors were the first to have *circumnavigated*, or sailed around, the globe.

The discoveries of Balboa and Magellan added to Europe's store of knowledge about the world and to Spain's position as a world power. Spain now possessed the key both to the largest ocean on earth and to the lands on the western side of the vast American continent.

The Fate of Columbus

And what became of Columbus, the original discoverer? After three voyages he still believed he had found India, although in fact, he succeeded only in exploring the eastern coast of Central America.

Eventually, Columbus was hauled home in chains by Spanish authorities. Some Spaniards who had come to the Americas had begun to enslave and kill the original Americans. Authorities in Spain held Columbus responsible for the atrocities. Furthermore, when the promised gold and riches

Voyages of Discovery

NORTH AMERICA

EUROPE

ASIA

PACIFIC OCEAN

AFRICA

PACIFIC OCEAN

SOUTH AMERICA

Line of Demarcation

INDIAN OCEAN

3000 Miles
5000 Kilometers

ATLANTIC OCEAN

AUSTRALIA

Spain | Portugal

Portugal | Spain

Line of Demarcation

EXPLORER FOR ENGLAND
Drake 1579-1580 ⟶

EXPLORERS FOR PORTUGAL
Dias 1487 ⟶
Da Gama 1497-1498 ⟶
Cabral 1500 ⟶

EXPLORERS FOR SPAIN
Columbus **(1)** 1492, **(2)** 1493, **(3)** 1498, **(4)** 1502 ⟶
Balboa 1513 ⟶
Magellan 1519-1522 ⟶

■ *The hope of discovering a fast route to Asia led European explorers all over the world, as this map shows.*

did not appear, complainers at the Spanish court began calling him "Admiral of the Mosquitoes."

Even more insulting to Columbus, the new continent was not even named after him. Instead it was called America after Amerigo Vespucci (ah may REE goh veh SPOO chee), a merchant from Florence, Italy, who realized that the coast he had scouted on a voyage in 1501 was "a very great continent, until hitherto unknown."

Although Columbus did not get the fame or riches he had dreamed of, his skill as a sailor and his grand visions earned him a lasting place in history.

SECTION REVIEW

1. Identify: King John II, Queen Isabella, "Indians," Arawaks, Hispaniola, Pedro Álvares Cabral, Amerigo Vespucci.

2. Define: circumnavigate.

3. Why did Portugal refuse to support Columbus's plan for a westward voyage?

4. (a) What roles did Balboa and Magellan play in the exploration of the world? (b) How did their discoveries benefit Spain?

5. **Critical Thinking** Why was the Line of Demarcation to Spain's advantage?

2 Exploration and Conquest

Even though Columbus had not discovered a western route to Asia, his voyages led the way to further exploration of two vast continents. Spanish adventurers were soon exploring North and South America.

The Conquistadores

To gain a strong foothold in the Americas, Spain originally relied on *conquistadores* (kohn KEES tah DOH rehs), or conquerors.

21

Well-known for their boldness, ruthlessness, and daring, these professional soldiers had various motives for venturing to the New World. The lure of fabled riches was powerful, and the appeal of adventure in an untamed wilderness was strong.

Many, however, were also drawn to the Americas by a missionary zeal to convert the continents' inhabitants to Christianity. Bernal Díaz (DEE ahs), one of the conquistadores, aptly described their motives: "We came here to serve God, and also to get rich."

Each conquistador received permission from the Spanish crown to establish outposts and settlements in America. In return for a license to colonize the New World, the conquistadores agreed to send one fifth of any gold or silver they mined back to the royal treasury.

The adventure, as the conquistadores knew, was a calculated risk. They had to equip and finance their expeditions, taking the risk of huge losses or even complete ruin. If they succeeded, they stood to gain a fortune. If they were shipwrecked or suffered other accidents, they stood to lose everything—including their lives.

For many years the Spanish government was content to leave colonization to these military adventurers. Under this system Spain extended its power and authority with little expense. In fact, gold and silver from the New World eventually made Spain one of the wealthiest countries in Europe.

Great Empires Fall

Spain gradually gained control of most of South and Central America and parts of North America. Until 1519, however, colonization was limited to small settlements in the West Indies. In that year Hernando Cortés (kawr TEHZ) gathered a small army and prepared to look for the gold and riches rumored to exist in present-day Mexico.

An unusually intelligent leader, Cortés understood the value of psychological warfare as well as physical combat. When he discovered the skill of Aztec warriors, he decided to ally himself with other tribes who resented paying tribute to the Aztecs.

Cortés also acquired the services of a translator, speechmaker, and negotiator, a Native American woman whom the Spanish named Doña Marina (DOH nyah mah REEN ah). Doña Marina "possessed such manly valor," reported one soldier, "that . . . [she] never allowed us to see any sign of fear in her."

Cortés then made one of the most daring—some might say the most foolhardy—moves in military history. He marched 400 heavily armored soldiers into Tenochtitlán, the Aztec capital city of 250,000 people, and confronted the Aztec ruler, Montezuma (MAHN tee ZOO muh).

Tenochtitlán, as you will remember, was located on an island. At any time the Aztecs might have trapped Cortés and his army simply by raising their bridges. But, as Cortés knew, Montezuma believed that the Spanish had come to fulfill an ancient Aztec prophecy. According to the prophecy, the Aztec god, Quetzalcoatl (keht SAHL koh AH tuhl), would return to Mexico from the east, the direction of the rising sun. So Montezuma allowed Cortés and his army to enter the city unharmed.

In a tense game of diplomacy lasting over six months, Cortés held Montezuma a virtual captive in his own city. Then the Spanish fought their way out, losing half their number in the process. With their Native American allies, they surrounded Tenochtitlán. Through battle and starvation they destroyed the city, and with it the Aztec empire.

22

An Aztec artist–historian recorded this meeting between the emperor Montezuma (seated at left) and Cortés at Tenochtitlán. Doña Marina, a Native American, translated for them.

Tenochtitlan.

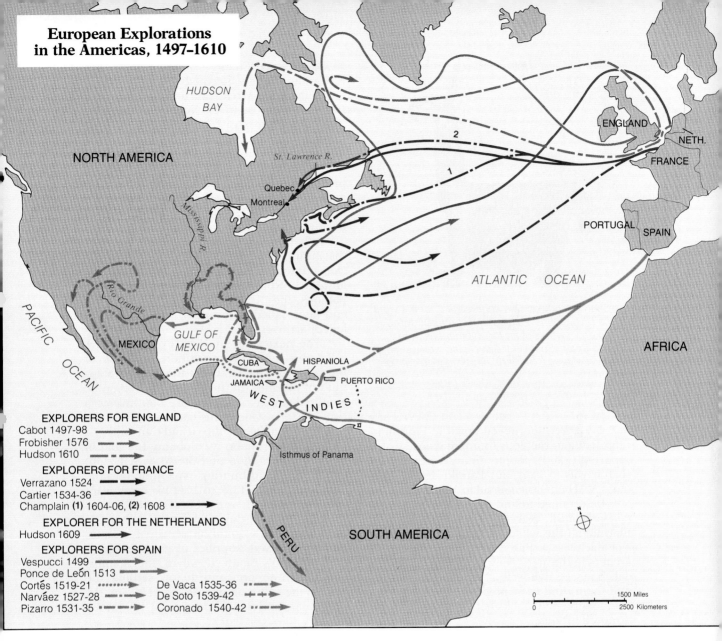

European Explorations in the Americas, 1497–1610

HUDSON BAY

NORTH AMERICA

ENGLAND

NETH.

FRANCE

St. Lawrence R.

Quebec
Montreal

Mississippi R.

PORTUGAL SPAIN

2

1

PACIFIC OCEAN

Rio Grande

ATLANTIC OCEAN

MEXICO

GULF OF MEXICO

CUBA

HISPANIOLA

JAMAICA

PUERTO RICO

WEST INDIES

AFRICA

Isthmus of Panama

PERU

SOUTH AMERICA

N

EXPLORERS FOR ENGLAND
Cabot 1497-98
Frobisher 1576
Hudson 1610

EXPLORERS FOR FRANCE
Verrazano 1524
Cartier 1534-36
Champlain **(1)** 1604-06, **(2)** 1608

EXPLORER FOR THE NETHERLANDS
Hudson 1609

EXPLORERS FOR SPAIN
Vespucci 1499
Ponce de León 1513
Cortés 1519-21   De Vaca 1535-36
Narváez 1527-28   De Soto 1539-42
Pizarro 1531-35   Coronado 1540-42

0   1500 Miles
0   2500 Kilometers

■ *After the first voyage of discovery, English, French, and Dutch adventurers raced to explore and claim sections of the New World. (See page 28.) The more numerous Spanish explorers claimed most of Central and South America as well as large areas of North America.*

Ten years later, in 1530, Francisco Pizarro (pee ZAHR oh), another conquistador, received permission to conquer the Inca empire of present-day Peru. With 180 metal-clad soldiers—less than half of Cortés' force—Pizarro marched into the Andean kingdom. Luck was with him. When he arrived, the Incas were embroiled in a civil war.

Pizarro launched a surprise attack, imprisoned the Inca leader, Atahualpa (AH tah WAHL pah), and killed most of his attend-ants. The attack stunned the Incas, weakening their resistance to the Spanish. By 1535 Pizarro had captured Cuzco, the Inca capital, and crushed nearly all opposition.

Exploration to the North

Legends of great wealth drew Spanish adventurers to the northern regions of the Americas as well as to the south. However, these expeditions were much less profitable to Spain than those of Cortés and Pizarro.

23

The Spanish showed little appreciation for the work of Inca silversmiths. Instead, the conquistadores melted down works of art for shipment as pure metal to Spain. Some of the surviving work, such as this silver alpaca from Peru, hints at the talents of Inca artists.

In 1513 Juan Ponce de León (PAWN say day lay AWN) journeyed north to Florida in search of a miraculous fountain whose water reportedly kept people young forever. His search was in vain, but Pánfilo de Narváez (nahr VAH ehz) tried again in 1527.

Determined to find the legendary "fountain of youth," Narváez marched deep into Florida, all the while under attack from the Appalachees (a pah LAH chees), the best archers in the area. They strung their six-foot oak bows so tightly that no Spaniard could pull them. And their precisely aimed arrows could pierce the cracks between the soldiers' armored fittings.

Unable to withstand the Appalachees' attack, the Spanish retreated to the coast. There they rigged makeshift boats—their ships had been destroyed by a hurricane—and sailed across the Gulf of Mexico to present-day Texas.

Only four of the original expedition of 260 soldiers survived. The rest perished at sea. The two most famous survivors were Cabeza de Vaca (kah BAY sah day VAH kah), a Spanish conquistador, and Estevanico (ehs tay vahn EE koh), an African.

For six years the four lived as the slaves of Native Americans, gradually gaining reputations as medicine men. After they were freed, Cabeza de Vaca, Estevanico, and the other two explorers made their way on foot across the hot, dry plains of present-day

western Texas. Finally after two years they met another Spanish expedition.

Cabeza de Vaca returned to Spain, but Estevanico stayed in the New World to join a new expedition organized by Francisco Coronado (KOH roh NAH doh). Coronado hoped to find the legendary "seven cities of gold" reportedly nestled in the hills of present-day New Mexico. Because of Estevanico's experience with the Native Americans of the Southwest, Coronado chose him to head the scouting party.

When the expedition reached the first of the Zuñi pueblos, the villages named in the exaggerated tales, the inhabitants launched an attack. Refusing to retreat with his companions, the "Black Mexican," as Zuñi legend later called Estevanico, was killed by a hail of arrows.

The next year, in 1540, Coronado himself led a full-scale expedition in search of the seven cities. He found the Zuñi pueblos but not the gold. In the process, however, he explored much of the future southwestern United States. One of his lieutenants was the first European to see the Grand Canyon.

While Coronado was looking for gold in the west, Hernando de Soto (day SOH toh) led another gold-hunting expedition into the Southeast. From 1539 to 1542 his army wandered as far north as the Carolinas and as far west as present-day Oklahoma. When de Soto died, the expedition returned without finding any large supplies of gold. Even before de Soto's death, however, the Spanish had begun to concentrate on settling the area to the south, in present-day Mexico, the Caribbean, and South America.

SECTION REVIEW

1. Identify: Cortés, Doña Marina, Montezuma, Pizarro, Atahualpa, Ponce de León, Pánfilo de Narváez, Appalachees, Cabeza de Vaca, Estevanico.

2. (a) Who were the conquistadores? (b) Why did they explore the New World?

3. What did Cortés hope to gain by conquering the Aztec empire?

4. Were the Spanish efforts to find a fountain of youth successful? Explain.

5. **Critical Thinking** Why would Spain eventually concentrate on settling southern areas of the Americas?

3 Spanish Settlement of the Americas

In December 1492 Columbus and his crew constructed the first Spanish settlement in the New World, a crude fortress built from the timbers of the *Santa María*, which had been wrecked on a reef on Christmas Eve. That first settlement, called La Navidad, or "the birth," in honor of Christmas, and a second, called Isabella, were only temporary outposts, however.

The first permanent settlement, Santo Domingo, was built on the southern side of Hispaniola in 1496. When a tropical storm destroyed Santo Domingo in 1502, the Spanish lost no time rebuilding it.

Designed to resemble a Spanish town, Santo Domingo grew rapidly and became an important base for explorations. Within a few decades, other towns sprang up on Hispaniola, on the islands of Puerto Rico and Cuba, and on the mainland of the Americas.

Governing New Spain

Soon the Spanish faced the task of managing a huge empire. They not only had to oversee explorations, but they also had to find ways to choose sites for towns, transport colonists from Europe to America, distribute land, and organize an economy based on farming and mining as well as trade.

It quickly became apparent that the informal, one-man rule of the conquistadores was inadequate. The rapid growth of New Spain, as the North American part of the empire was called, demanded a more formal system of government. In 1535 Emperor Charles V appointed Antonio de Mendoza (mehn DOH sah) the first viceroy* of New Spain. Mendoza was an able administrator, and the Spanish colony prospered, as did the South American part of Spanish America.

By the middle of the sixteenth century, Mexico City, the capital of New Spain, boasted paved and lighted streets, as well as a police department and public water system. By 1551, universities had opened in the Indies, Mexico, Ecuador, and Peru. Theaters and printing presses were thriving in Spanish America before England began colonizing.

In 1573 Charles's successor Philip II proclaimed the Laws of the Indies in an attempt to exert tighter control over Spain's New World colonies. This royal legislation outlined the way in which Spain intended to govern its New World empire.

The Laws of the Indies dealt with New Spain's political organization and with all other details of colonial life as well. One of the laws indicated, for example, that a town should be built on high ground, surrounded by good farming land, with an abundant supply of water, fuel, and wood. Another told town planners to leave enough open space so that when a town grew it could spread evenly. The laws even contained regulations for planting seeds and raising cattle.

A Plan for Settlement

The Laws of the Indies reveal much about the goals of the Spanish in the New World. They specified that separate settlements be constructed for three main activities: *presidios* (pray SIH dee ohs) for military activities, missions for religious work, and *pueblos* or *villas* for farming, trade, and town life.

The presidios, designed in the shape of a rectangle, were surrounded by high, thick walls. Within the walls were barracks, storehouses, stables, shops, and a few houses for the families of married soldiers.

In time, houses and farms grew up outside the walls of the presidio as colonists moved there for security. Gradually the military communities developed into towns much like the civilian pueblos.

The missions were meant to be centers from which the Spanish could carry on the work of converting the Native Americans to Christianity. Roman Catholic priests ran the missions, and many Native Americans were either persuaded or forced to live there. Usually, the mission community also included a few Spanish settlers and a small garrison of soldiers.

Each of the missions was a self-supporting settlement. Most were farming communities. Many combined farming with the manufacture of pottery, woven blankets, leather, wine, or olive oil, all goods that the mission exported to Spain or sold to other colonists.

Pueblos were usually situated in the middle of a huge tract of farm land. The

---

*viceroy: a person who rules a country or province as the deputy of a king or queen.

Many Spanish missions like this one at San Gabriel became successful economic units. Some Indians farmed the land while others became skilled ranchers and traders.

buildings found in the towns of New Spain were far from simple "frontier" structures. The Laws of the Indies stated clearly that settlers were to build with "the beauty of the town" in mind. Thus, churches, private homes, shops, and other buildings equaled the finest examples of Spanish architecture.

Impact on Native Americans

Many Spaniards migrated to the Americas because of the promise of free or cheap land for farming. They raised crops that were much in demand in Europe: bananas, rice, melons, and wheat. They also began to cultivate crops native to the Americas such as potatoes, tomatoes, maize, beans, pumpkins, squash, and tobacco.

Although farming was a profitable occupation for many Spanish colonists, ranching brought even higher income. Many settlers thus turned to raising horses, pigs, cattle, burros, and sheep on the broad expanses of American land. The vastness of many of these ranches, however, required back-breaking work, usually done by Native Americans.

An early policy of the Spanish government had effectively forced many Native Americans to work on Spanish estates. Successful conquistadores had been granted *encomiendas* (ehn koh mee EHN dahs), the right to demand a tribute or tax from Native Americans living on a given piece of land. Often the conquistador would force the Native Americans to work for him as payment. Eventually they became bound to the land because they had no other way of paying the tax. Work on the encomiendas amounted to a form of slavery. Once a Native American had been enticed or forced to become a laborer, he or she had little chance of becoming anything else.

In those areas of the Americas where gold and silver had been discovered, the Spanish put Native Americans to work in the mines. If labor on the encomiendas was grueling, working in the mines was even more deadly. The dust, dirt, darkness, and disastrous cave-ins combined to produce staggering rates of injury and death among Native American miners.

To make matters worse, the Native Americans proved extremely susceptible to

European diseases carried over by the colonists. Smallpox spread like wildfire through the Americas, killing millions of people. The original population of Mexico, for instance, dropped from over 5 million in 1492 to only one million a century later.

A Misguided Proposal

Eventually, word of the brutal treatment of Native Americans reached Spain. Many Spaniards reacted with concern. Bartolomé de Las Casas (day lahs KAH sahs), a Dominican priest, devoted his life to rescuing the Native Americans. He pleaded the cause of the oppressed to Spanish officials and con-

vinced them to place Native Americans under the protection of the clergy. De Las Casas and other priests were not able to end the Native Americans' enslavement throughout all the colonies, but they did try to relieve some suffering. For example, they allowed many Native Americans to own cattle and raise their own crops. They also replaced some Spanish overseers in the mines with Native Americans.

Although de Las Casas's suggestions may have improved the lot of the Native Americans, they led to the subjugation of another people. To reduce the reliance on Native American labor, de Las Casas suggested that the Spanish import slaves from Africa.

An unknown artist sketched this scene around 1584 at a silver mine and processing plant in South America. The Spanish forced Indians to work long hours in the mines. Note the llamas, used as pack animals.

Africans, he reasoned, had demonstrated their ability to live in the New World on the early voyages of exploration, and they had developed immunity to many European diseases. Furthermore, because their own societies were mainly agricultural, they were skilled farmers.

The implementation of de Las Casas's proposal inaugurated the African slave trade in the New World. The Spanish were soon buying slaves by the shipload from Portuguese traders, who had established contacts years before with African kingdoms.

De Las Casas later realized that his efforts to free one group from slavery had resulted in the equally cruel bondage of another and he bitterly regretted his mistake. To other Spaniards, however, the solution seemed worth the brutal price. American gold and silver, mined by both Native Americans and newly enslaved Africans, catapulted Spain to unprecedented riches. By the mid-sixteenth century, Spain's overseas empire was the most powerful in the world.

SECTION REVIEW

1. Identify: Santo Domingo, New Spain, Antonio de Mendoza, Philip II, Bartolomé de Las Casas.
2. Name the three types of Spanish settlements. What was the main activity of each?
3. How did the Spanish use encomiendas to force Native Americans to work for them?
4. **Critical Thinking** What kinds of problems dealt with in the Laws of the Indies still concern town planners today?

4 The French and English Look North

By the middle of the sixteenth century, Spain had become the strongest nation in Europe. King Philip II ruled not only Spain but also Portugal, the Netherlands, and parts of Italy. Without colonial competitors, Spain dominated the Americas, and its ships monopolized their coastal waters.

The enormous wealth that Spain reaped from North and South America aroused the curiosity and envy of other European nations. The governments of France and England, in particular, began to wonder what the New World might have to offer other enterprising people.

At first, neither the French nor the English had any carefully thought-out plans for exploration or colonization. Their goals were simple: to find as much gold and silver as possible and to discover a fast sea route to Asia.

During the late 1400s and early 1500s explorers employed by England and France, including John Cabot, Giovanni da Verrazano, and Martin Frobisher among others, sailed along the North American coast looking for a likely waterway to the East. (See the map, page 23.) They gathered valuable information about the geography of the area, but found no passage to the Pacific. The only gold and silver they found was on Spanish treasure ships, which they pirated on the high seas.

When it became apparent that their original goals were not to be accomplished, both nations embarked on other, more realistic ventures. Each organized colonies in the northern part of North America and began to exploit what the land had to offer.

An Empire of Fish and Fur

In 1504 fishermen from France sailed into what is today known as the Gulf of St. Lawrence looking for cod. Each year after that they returned. Gradually they realized that they could increase their profits by trading with the Americans they encountered there. In exchange for furs, they supplied the Indians with hatchets, kettles, muskets, and other European goods.

In 1534 the French explorer Jacques Cartier (kahr tee YAY) sailed up the river now called the St. Lawrence. Cartier, like other explorers, was looking for the fabled northwest passage to Asia and hoped that the St. Lawrence River would be that passage. Fur-

Some Native Americans resisted European explorers. This drawing by John White shows a skirmish between Eskimos and an English exploring party headed by Martin Frobisher. White made detailed sketches of Frobisher's expedition.

thermore, local inhabitants had told him that great golden cities lay "just beyond" the horizon. Cartier explored the St. Lawrence as far as present-day Montreal, where he founded an outpost. But the northwest passage and the gold always seemed to stay just beyond the horizon.

Political and religious strife in France prevented the French government from devoting much further attention to colonizing activities until 1560. In that year the head of the French navy sent an expedition to Florida, where he hoped to establish bases from which the French could prey on Spanish commerce. The Spanish, however, retaliated in 1565 when they dispatched an army to the French outpost. The army slaughtered most of the inhabitants.

During the 1590s, when the French government took a renewed interest in North America, it directed its efforts primarily to encouraging the lucrative fur trade. The government granted fur-trading rights to a se-

lect few, including Pierre du Guast (doo GAWST). In 1604 du Guast hired Samuel de Champlain (sham PLAYN) to explore lands he had been granted by the king and to establish a few trading settlements.

Limited French Settlement

Champlain was a knowledgeable sailor, geographer, and superb map maker. His maps, most of which have survived to this day, showed not only the features of the areas he explored but also details of the settlements he founded.

Champlain established one settlement on the Île de Sainte Croix (eel duh saynt KROI), now in the state of Maine. Settlers found the climate so inhospitable, however, that they abandoned it in less than a year. He founded a second settlement, Port Royal, the next year on a sheltered bay in present-day Nova Scotia. Here Champlain left forty-five people to establish a permanent colony.

Champlain himself continued to explore the region, charting the Atlantic coast as far south as Cape Cod. In 1608 he sailed up the St. Lawrence River as far as present-day Quebec (kwee BEHK). There, on a shelf of land overlooking the river, he constructed a massive wooden fortress, which he called the Habitation (ah bee tah SYOHN). Slowly, the city of Quebec grew up around the fortress.

The French government's interest lay primarily in trading furs, not in establishing populous settlements. Thus, they did little or nothing to encourage immigration to New France, as the region was called. Instead, they devoted their efforts to building up trade along the St. Lawrence into the interior of North America.

Over the next hundred years, settlers did trickle in, but there were never enough to sustain a thriving colony. The wealth and success of New France lay not in towns and cities but in the packets of furs from the interior, paddled down the St. Lawrence in 36-foot (11 meter) birchbark canoes.

The Sea Dogs

Relations among the nations of Europe during the sixteenth century were tense. Religious disputes pitted Catholic countries against Protestant countries, as each struggled to win people and lands to its cause.

At the time, Spain was the most powerful Catholic nation in the world. Its resounding success in the New World and subsequent expansion of power heightened existing tensions. England, the leading Protestant nation, was Spain's natural foe.

Gradually, an undeclared war developed between the two. Into the fray stepped the "sea dogs." Eager for plunder and also fiercely loyal to England and its Queen, Elizabeth I, the sea dogs scoured the Atlantic Ocean, pirating Spanish treasure ships. The English government did not officially employ them; nonetheless the crown encouraged their exploits and took a share of the booty.

Sea dogs were involved not only in pirating, but also in transporting slaves to the Americas. One, an adventurer named John Hawkins, was the first English sea captain to engage in the slave trade. In the 1560s Hawkins sailed to Africa several times, picked up slaves from the Portuguese, and transported them to the West Indies. There he exchanged them for gold or rum, which he brought back to England. His days as a slave trader ended when the Spanish scattered his fleet.

Sir Francis Drake, one of the boldest sea dogs, pulled off an especially daring and profitable exploit in 1573. Aided by black slaves who had escaped from the Spanish, he and his crew stole the yearly silver shipment being carried from Peru to Spain over the Isthmus of Panama. Four years later Sir Francis followed Magellan's route around the world, raiding Spanish settlements along the way on the Pacific coast of South America. Because no English ship had sailed those waters before, Drake caught the Spaniards by surprise.

Drake returned to England in 1580 with millions in stolen treasure. King Philip II of Spain demanded that the booty be returned, but Queen Elizabeth saw the matter in a different light. She knighted Drake right on the deck of his ship as a reward. Spain responded to the insult by preparing for war.

In 1588 Philip sent a huge fleet, known as the Armada, against England. The English navy was outnumbered two to one, but Drake and other captains made good use of their smaller, more maneuverable ships. With the help of a storm that scattered the Spanish fleet, the English won a stunning victory. Spain's dominance of Europe was shattered.

The First English Colonies

The English did not long limit themselves to piracy and slave trading. Once their interest in the New World had been aroused, they began to think of more permanent ways to exploit the Americas for England's benefit.

Sir Walter Raleigh, an aristocrat high in the queen's favor, sponsored the first English attempt to found a settlement in North America. He spent much of his personal fortune on the venture. Raleigh also received support from other wealthy investors.

Raleigh envisioned the settlement as more than a way station for pirates and gold diggers. The colonists, in Raleigh's vision,

As war between Protestant England and Catholic Spain loomed, Queen Elizabeth I stalled for time while England built ships. In the meantime English captains known as "sea dogs" preyed on treasure-filled Spanish vessels returning from the New World. Elizabeth hoped to gain a generous share of the booty.

would raise bananas, sugar, and other crops impossible to grow in England's cold climate. They would ship these products back to England along with valuable raw materials such as lumber.

An expedition sponsored by the Virginia Company, as Raleigh and his associates called themselves, sailed from England in 1585. Months later the seven ships, carrying over a hundred men landed on Roanoke (ROH uh NOHK) Island, off the coast of what is today North Carolina.

Roanoke was an appealing location for a settlement because a chain of long, narrow, sandy islands sheltered it from the Atlantic Ocean. The colonists included Joachim Ganz (yoh AH ihm GAHNZ), a mineral expert, and John White, a surveyor and

★ America's Heritage ★

Henry Hudson and Dutch Claims in the New World

By 1600 both Spain and Portugal had bases in the New World. England and France had tried to set up colonies. But all four countries would soon have to reckon with the Netherlands, which had revolted against Spain in the late 1500s.

The 1600s were a time of high achievement for the Dutch. Rembrandt and Jan Vermeer (YAHN vuhr MEER) were great Dutch painters; Christian Huygens (HĪ guhnz) contributed to astronomy and mathematics; Spinoza to philosophy. For trade, the Dutch had formed the East India Company in 1602. Soon Dutch vessels of all kinds were sailing the world's waters. By 1650 the Dutch owned 16,000 ships out of some 20,000 that engaged in European trade.

In the early 1600s, Europeans still hoped to find a northern water route to Asia. To that end the Dutch East India Company sent Henry Hudson and a crew of 20 westward in his ship, the *Half Moon*. Earlier Hudson had sought a passage directly over the North Pole. But the solid ice of the polar seas had made him turn back. On this, his third voyage, in 1609, Hudson reached Newfoundland. Then he sailed south as far as Virginia.

Still searching, Hudson swung north again. On September 2, he sailed into the fine, deep harbor of present-day New York. "This is a very good land to fall in with," reported his mate, "and a pleasant land to see." After spending a few days fishing and picking huckleberries, Hudson journeyed up the broad river that was later named after him.

The *Half Moon* sailed as far north as present-day Albany. On the way Hudson went ashore to visit an Indian village. He was impressed: The village was stocked with "a great quantity of maize or Indian corn, and beans of last year's growth. . . ." But he soon realized that what he had hoped was a strait leading to the Pacific was simply an inland river. Disappointed, he returned home.

His journey was not in vain, though. While Hudson had not found a way through the continent, he had set the stage for New Netherland, the Dutch colony that was to come.

A View of the New World: Using Visual Evidence

The pictures in this textbook, which include drawings, paintings, and photographs, all provide valuable clues to the past. Such pieces of visual evidence can show you what people and places looked like long ago. They can also give you a glimpse of what was happening at a given time and place. Thus they can help you understand the past.

However, the people who made the pictures influence what you see. In order to make the best use of visual evidence, therefore, you must fully analyze it.

Follow the steps below, using the picture on page 33 to practice using visual evidence.

1. **Study the visual evidence to decide what you are seeing.** Look both at the details and at the picture as a whole. (a) Which people in the picture probably lived in the territory shown? Which seem to have arrived recently? How did they come? (b) What does the picture tell you about the territory? About the waters off the coast? (c) Where are Florida, Canada, and Mexico located in this picture? What seems unusual about their location? (d) What area is being shown in this picture?

2. **Analyze the reliability of the visual evidence as a source.** (a) Do you think the artist actually saw all the things shown? Why or why not? (b) Can you tell from the picture where the artist was from? What hints can you find? Whose viewpoint does the picture help you understand? Why? (c) Is this a good source?

3. **Study the visual evidence to learn more about a historical event or period.** Refer to the picture and what you have read in your text to answer the following questions: (a) Describe European activity in the Americas in the 1540s. (b) How did people at that time view the voyage to the Americas? (c) Why do you think the picture appears to be upside down? Why might this view seem natural to a French artist? How might a Spaniard have drawn this picture?

---

artist, who painted watercolors of the new land and its inhabitants. Thomas Hariot, another member of the expedition, was an English scholar and friend of Raleigh. He may have gone as an interpreter, having learned the language of the local people from Indians who had journeyed back to England with earlier explorers.

The 1585 expedition returned to England, but another, including 100 men and 17 women, set out for Roanoke in 1587. Later that year John White returned to England for supplies, leaving behind a prospering colony as well as a granddaughter, Virginia Dare, the first English child born in America. Unfortunately, John White did not return with fresh provisions until 1590, nearly three years later.

In the place where he had left a small but thriving colony, his relief expedition found deserted buildings, rusty armor, grass choking the lanes and paths, and the word "CROATOAN" carved on the door post of the crumbling fort. They saw no sign of the cross, which had been designated as a sign of distress. White also found food buried in the ground, suggesting that the colonists had left willingly, intending to return.

Had the colonists, threatened with hunger and privation, joined the friendly Croatoan tribe nearby? White never found the answer. A storm prevented him from staying to search for the settlers and, to this day, the mystery of the "lost colony" persists.

Roanoke failed as a permanent settlement, but the experience proved to be valuable. Raleigh and his friends realized that a colony could be started with private funds. But they saw that its continued existence depended on more financial support than an

North America in the Desceliers world map of 1546.

informally organized group of investors could provide. Permanent English settlements would have to depend on a different form of sponsorship.

SECTION REVIEW

1. Identify: Jacques Cartier, Samuel de Champlain, John Hawkins, Sir Francis Drake, the Armada, Sir Walter Raleigh, John White.
2. What two goals did most of the early French and English explorers have?
3. What two products became the basis for French activity in the New World?
4. What did the sea dogs accomplish?
5. (a) Why did Sir Walter Raleigh found Roanoke? (b) Did it succeed? Explain.
6. **Critical Thinking** Why might the defeat of the Spanish Armada have fueled England's ambitions for the New World?

Major Events

1492	Columbus's ships land in Americas
1494	Line of Demarcation established
1513	Balboa discovers Pacific Ocean
1517	Protestant Reformation begins
1519	Cortés begins conquest of Aztecs
1534	Cartier explores St. Lawrence River
1535	Charles V appoints first viceroy of New Spain
1585	First English settlement at Roanoke
1588	English fleet sinks the Spanish Armada
1608	Champlain founds Quebec

In Perspective

Columbus's voyage in search of a western route to Asia brought two worlds together. Soon other Europeans were exploring the coast of the Americas for a passage to Asia and going inland to seek gold and silver.

Spanish conquistadores found great wealth among the Aztecs and Incas. Spanish soldiers, missionaries, and settlers followed the adventurers to the New World and began to set up colonies. Spanish accomplishments, however, came at the expense of Native Americans and African slaves.

Spain's growing wealth and power aroused the envy of its European rivals, particularly France and England. French attempts to find a passage through North America and to find gold and silver failed. But during the 1500s the French developed a prosperous trade with Native Americans.

Early English explorers also sought precious metals and a northwest passage. However, most English sailors sought wealth by pirating Spanish ships. The sea dogs enriched themselves while weakening their country's chief rival. In the late 1580s the first group of English settlers arrived in North America. Although their attempt to settle on Roanoke Island failed, they led the way for more lasting settlements later.

Vocabulary

Choose the answer that best completes each of the following sentences.

1. Magellan's fleet was the first to ___, or sail around, the globe. (a) revolutionize (b) circumnavigate (c) rotate
2. The ___ were the Spanish conquerors of the Aztecs and the Incas. (a) encomiendas (b) pueblos (c) conquistadores
3. Settlements devoted to military activity were the ___. (a) presidios (b) pueblos (c) viceroys
4. The ___ were settlements devoted to farming, trading, and town life. (a) villas (b) encomiendas (c) presidios
5. A deputy who represents a monarch in a country or province is a ___. (a) pueblo (b) viceroy (c) provincial
6. The right to demand a tribute or tax from Native Americans living on a given piece of land was a(n) (a) entreaty (b) villa (c) encomienda

Chapter Checkup

1. Why did Queen Isabella finance exploration of the New World by Columbus and other explorers?
2. (a) How did Columbus's discoveries affect the relationship between Spain and Portugal? (b) Why did the Pope intervene? (c) What solution did he offer?
3. (a) What role did the conquistadores play in the colonization of the Americas? (b) Did they achieve their goals? Explain.
4. (a) Describe the Spanish exploration of the area north of present-day Mexico. (b) What were the goals of the explorers? (c) Were they successful? Explain.
5. (a) Why did the Spanish ruler decide to replace the informal one-man rule of the conquistadores? (b) What were the laws of the Indies?
6. (a) What were the three major activities of the Spanish who settled in the Americas? (b) What impact did the settlers have on Native Americans?
7. How did concern about the treatment of Native Americans lead to the introduction of African slavery into the Americas?
8. What were the goals of France, England, and the Netherlands in the New World?
9. How did Sir Francis Drake and other sea dogs help England in its struggle with Spain?
10. (a) What was the fate of the first English colony at Roanoke? (b) Why was it important?

Critical Thinking

1. **Evaluating** What traits did people like Columbus, Cortés, Narváez, Estevanico, Hudson, Cartier, and Drake have in common?
2. **Analyzing** (a) How did Native Americans react to the early groups of Europeans that landed in the New World? (b) How might you explain their reactions?
3. **Comparing** (a) Compare the early experiences of the Spanish, the English, and the French with respect to settling the Americas. (b) How might you explain the similarities and the differences?

Developing Basic Skills

1. **Classifying** Make a chart with two columns. In the first column, list the groups and individuals you read about in this chapter who ventured to the New World. In the second column, list the motives of each. (a) What similarities and differences do you see? (b) What were the most common reasons why people set sail for the New World during the late 1400s and early 1500s?

2. **Researching** Choose one of the explorers of the New World. Research his background and answer the following questions: (a) Where was the person born and raised? (b) What training and experience contributed to his abilities as an explorer? (c) Why do you think he became an explorer?

3. **Map Reading** Study the map on page 21. Then answer the following questions: (a) Which two explorers led expeditions that circumnavigated the globe? (b) Through which continents did the Line of Demarcation run? (c) How did the routes of the Portuguese explorers differ from those of the Spanish and English explorers? (d) Who was the first European explorer to reach India by an all-water route?

4. **Map Reading** Study the map on page 23. Then answer the following questions: (a) What general area was explored by the Spanish? (b) What general area was explored by the English? (c) What general area was explored by the French? (d) Where did Henry Hudson explore? (e) Which European nation was most active in exploring the Americas in the sixteenth century? (f) Why did the search for a northwest passage to India fail?

See page 827 for suggested readings.

Writer's Handbook

Using Question Clues

Before you begin to write the answer to an essay question, you should study the question for clues. Read the following essay question: *How did Spain leave its imprint on the New World in the sixteenth century?* Apply the questions below to the essay question.

1. What does the question word ask you to do? Look for the word that tells you what you are to do with the subject you are writing about. (See Writer's Handbook, page 17.) In the question above, the key word is *how.* The answer requires an explanation of the ways that Spain influenced or changed the New World.

2. What is the scope of the essay? Look for limits on what you are to discuss, such as a time frame, a geographic area, or the number of ideas to be covered. Note in the question above that the discussion is limited to events that took place in the sixteenth century in the Americas.

3. What information do you have that is related to the topic of the question? Since the scope of the essay includes time and geographic limits, you should consult both the chapter time line and maps in addition to the text.

Practice: Apply the questions in this writing lesson to the Critical Thinking questions in this Chapter Review before you begin to write the answers.

3

England's New World

(1607–1732)

Signing the Mayflower Compact

Chapter Outline

1 *A Gamble in Virginia*

2 *The New England Way*

3 *Developing a Colonial System*

The failure of the colony at Roanoke did not end English interest in settling North America. On the contrary, less than 25 years later, in 1607, a group of English men and boys landed at Jamestown. Other men and women soon followed, and by 1732, 13 thriving colonies had been established along the eastern coast of North America.

European settlers came to America for many reasons. Some came in search of wealth, some to start a new life, some to find religious freedom. All took a chance coming to a new land far from the life they had known, and most faced great hardships.

As you will read in this chapter, the founders had a variety of reasons for sponsoring the 13 colonies. Regardless of how the American colonies were founded and who settled them, all proved to be fertile soil for the growth of a strong tradition of representative government that resisted any attempt to deny it.

Royal colonies develop

1600	1620	1640	1660	1680	1700	1720	1740

1607 Jamestown founded

1620 Pilgrims land

1630 Puritans establish Massachusetts Bay

1649 Maryland Toleration Act passed

1682 Pennsylvania founded

1688 Glorious Revolution in England

1712 Carolina divided

1732 Georgia founded

1 A Gamble in Virginia

Sponsoring a colony in an untamed, unknown country thousands of miles from England was a difficult, risky business. The sponsor had to buy ships, pay sailors to transport colonists, persuade settlers—especially laborers and skilled workers—to migrate to America, and outfit an expensive expedition. Raleigh's experience with the colony of Roanoke had shown that individuals, no matter how wealthy, could not do this alone.

Financing the Colonies

The English devised a form of business organization that helped them solve the problem of financing colonies. This organization was known as a *joint stock company*. English merchants had used the joint stock company successfully in trading ventures to Russia, Persia, and the East Indies.

A joint stock company pooled the funds of many investors by selling stock or shares in the company. The amount of risk investors took, as well as the amount of profit they made, depended on the number of shares they owned. In case of bankruptcy, the investors were liable only for the amount of their investment. With the joint stock company, creditors could not seize the investor's personal property as payment for a debt as they could with private individuals or other forms of business organization.

Their ability to muster large amounts of capital and their limited liability permitted joint stock companies to undertake ventures both expensive and risky. Among these ventures was the founding of colonies in the American wilderness.

The Fort on the James

In 1606, 15 years after John White had returned from England to the ghostly emptiness of Roanoke, King James I granted a charter to two companies of English investors. The charter authorized the companies to found colonies in the New World.

One group, the Plymouth Company, included merchants from the port of Plymouth, England. For many years they had sponsored expeditions to the rich Atlantic fishing grounds off Newfoundland. The Plymouth Company's charter gave it the exclusive right to settle land from present-day Maine to New York. (See map below.)

■ *King James I of England gave two companies of investors the right to found New World colonies. Land belonged to the company that settled it first. Which Native American groups lived on land granted to the Plymouth Company? Which groups lived on land granted to the London Company?*

English Land Grants, 1606

IROQUOIS
L. Ontario
L. Erie
VIRGINIA
MOHEGAN
WAMPANOAG
NARRAGANSET
PEQUOT
SENECA
SUSQUEHANNA
Potomac R.
James R.
POWHATAN
Jamestown
TUSCARORA
ROANOKE ISLAND
ATLANTIC OCEAN

Plymouth Company grant, 1606

London Company grant, 1606

Land open to both companies

0   300 Miles
0   400 Kilometers

The London Company acquired rights to the territory stretching from the Potomac River south to what is now North Carolina. According to the agreement between the crown and the investors, the land between the two grants could be claimed by the company that settled it first.

In December 1606, 120 men and boys left London with instructions from the London Company to establish a settlement in what is now Virginia. Four months later 104 survivors landed in North America. After a two-week search for a suitable site, the colonists chose a low, swampy peninsula 30 miles (49 kilometers) upstream from the mouth of the James River.

Their orders from the London Company stated that they were to look for a place well inland on a navigable river. Such a site was thought to have advantages for trade and yet be easier to protect from attack than a location on the coast. The instructions, prepared by men who had never laid eyes on the New World, proved to be disastrous.

The colonists built a fort on the James River and called their settlement Jamestown after the king. The location was easy to defend from attack by local inhabitants, but the marshy peninsula provided a breeding ground for malaria-carrying mosquitoes. Furthermore, the drinking water was brackish, and the unusually damp air rotted the wooden buildings.

Soon Jamestown residents were beset by disease. To make matters worse, most colonists were soldiers or aristocrats unaccustomed to physical work of any kind. Others knew how to make glass, do brickwork, or fashion implements of iron, but virtually no one had the skills needed to survive in the wilderness.

The London Company's goals for the settlement made the shortage of labor for such tasks as growing and hunting food even more acute. They wanted the settlers to continue the search for the northwest passage to China and to look for gold in America.

When the settlers realized that a northwest passage did not exist in that area, they gave top priority to the search for gold. They spent most of their waking hours hunting the precious metal. "No talk, no hope, nor work," recalled Captain John Smith, Jamestown's military expert, "but dig gold, wash gold, refine gold, load gold."

The Jamestown settlers themselves had little incentive to try to make their settlement independent and self-supporting. According to the charter, the London Company owned all the land and was supposed to provide all necessities. Thus, colonists often demanded food from the common food supply while refusing to do any farm work or hunting.

Conditions deteriorated rapidly. The London Company had appointed a council of 13 men to govern the settlement, but the council members quarreled among themselves and seemed incapable of acting. By the end of the first year at Jamestown nearly half of the original 104 settlers had died, and the future of the only English outpost in the New World looked very bleak.

Jamestown Survives

The experiment on the James River might well have ended in its first year if John Smith had not been a member of the colony. Smith, an experienced soldier and intensely independent man, was appalled by the apathy, selfishness, and disorganization he saw around him.

Smith had been expelled from the colony's governing council for fighting with its aristocratic leaders. However, when those who remained could not halt the colony's march toward destruction, they recalled him—this time as president of the council.

He responded to the chaos by taking control of what was left of the colony. He governed sternly, refusing to allow anyone the privilege of not working. Under Smith's leadership, the men of Jamestown marched to work each day as if they were members of a military battalion. They built shelters, cleared the land, and began planting crops. Furthermore, Smith put a stop to the hunt for gold, which had wasted so much of the colony's energy.

From the beginning, Jamestown's residents obtained part of their food supply from the original inhabitants of the area in exchange for English beads and copper. These friendly relations began to cool, however, when Smith demanded more food at his own price. Moreover, the Indians regarded the settlers' clearing of land and planting crops as an invasion of their hunting grounds. The growing hostility sometimes erupted into violence.

Once, a group of Indians seized Smith and threatened his life. Only the intervention of Pocahontas (poh kuh HAHN tuhs), the chief's young daughter, saved Smith. After this incident friendly relations between the English and the Native Americans gradually resumed.

John Smith steered the settlement through its first years, but his efforts alone were not enough to save the colony. The winter after he departed for England, the colonists experienced "the starving time." Food was so scarce that they had to eat shoes, rats, horses, frogs, roots, and insects.

Because of such conditions, the London Company had to resort to extraordinary measures to keep Jamestown populated. At one time company employees kidnapped 100 English orphans and shipped them to the colony. The company gave some English prisoners the opportunity to serve out their sentences in Jamestown, and convinced some settlers to come voluntarily. But by 1617 only 400 of more than 2,000 people who had come survived.

The London Company realized that if the settlement were to last, some family life would have to develop. In 1620 and 1621, two ships brought groups of unmarried women to Jamestown. The company auctioned them off as wives for a product that was beginning to provide the solid economic base the colony needed, tobacco.

Tobacco: The Key to Survival

Ultimately, Virginia's survival depended on two things: its ability to make a profit for the London Company and its ability to attract new settlers. In 1612 a settler named John Rolfe found the key to both when he discovered that Jamestown was an ideal place to grow West Indian tobacco.

The Spanish had first introduced Europeans to tobacco, a native American plant. In the early 1600s the market for tobacco grew as the use of snuff and the habit of smoking spread. The West Indian tobacco that Rolfe adapted to Virginia soil became a favorite with Europeans. Within a few years, tobacco farms dotted the banks of the James River, and the settlers were soon shipping large quantities of tobacco to England at a handsome profit.

Tobacco not only guaranteed the survival of Jamestown, it also encouraged the growth of slavery in the English colonies. Raising tobacco involved back-breaking, unskilled hand labor, the kind of labor the Jamestown settlers found distasteful.

Ætatis suæ 21. A°. 1616.

The daughter of an Indian chief, Pocahontas brought food to hungry Jamestown settlers during "the starving time." Said John Smith, "she was the instrument to preserve this Colony from death, famine, and utter confusion." Later Pocahontas married John Rolfe, and the two of them took Virginia's first tobacco crop to London, where this portrait of her in English costume was painted.

In 1619, just as tobacco cultivation was expanding rapidly, a Portuguese ship arrived at Jamestown with 20 Africans, who were sold either as servants or slaves. Since the Africans came from agricultural societies, they proved to be a boon to the colony.

Slavery did not take hold immediately, though. Until 1670 some blacks and whites worked side by side as servants, and some blacks were free laborers. By the close of the seventeenth century, however, slavery had become entrenched in Virginia.

The First Representative Assembly

Originally, a council of 13 men, each with an equal vote, governed the Jamestown colony. The London Company appointed the council by sending their names to Virginia in a sealed box that was to be opened only upon arrival. However, the council members could not find a competent council leader after John Smith returned to England so the London Company disbanded the council. A governor who had the power to rule in both military and civilian affairs was appointed.

In 1619 the London Company again revised the colony's system of government. When the new governor arrived in Virginia, he instructed the eligible voters to elect 22 burgesses, or representatives, two from each of the 11 areas of the colony. The burgesses, meeting with a council appointed by the governor, would make laws and help administer the colony.

As a representative assembly, the House of Burgesses was part of an English tradition of limiting royal authority and increasing citizen participation in government. In 1215 a group of English nobles forced King John to guarantee them certain rights and privileges, set down in a document known as the Magna Carta, or Great Charter. These rights and privileges benefited mainly the nobles, not the common people, but having the rights listed on paper set a precedent, or tradition, that the king's power was not absolute.

In 1265 the English established a parliament that further limited the power of the monarchy. Parliament consisted of two groups who represented their interests to the king: the House of Lords, made up of nobles and high church leaders; and the House of Commons, a group of gentlemen* elected to represent English counties and boroughs.

Parliament was far from representative of all English people. Yet its existence guaranteed that monarchs could not rule without obtaining the consent of at least some of their subjects.

The London Company's order establishing Virginia's new government in 1619 also came to be called the Great Charter, a Magna Carta in its own right—and with good reason. The House of Burgesses, as the first representative assembly in the New World, established a pattern of government that other English colonies would follow.

SECTION REVIEW

1. Identify: joint stock company, Plymouth Company, London Company, John Smith, Pocahontas, "the starving time," John Rolfe, Magna Carta.

2. List two ways a joint stock company worked better than individual investors for sponsoring colonies.

3. List three problems faced by the first settlers at Jamestown.

4. What steps did John Smith take to help Jamestown survive?

5. (a) What was the House of Burgesses? (b) Who elected its members?

6. **Critical Thinking** Why would many English colonists resist royal laws similar to the Laws of the Indies?

2 The New England Way

Thirteen years after the first English settlers arrived in Virginia, another group of English men and women put down roots on the continent, but this time farther north along the coast. The path followed by these colonists, however, differed from that followed by the Jamestown settlers.

For one thing, the environment of Massachusetts, where the first New England colonists landed, was much more favorable for settlement than the environment of James-town. The climate was dry and healthy. Pure, clear brooks provided a supply of fresh water. Fish and game abounded. Winters were harsh, but just a few years after they arrived, New England colonists were living longer than people in either Virginia or England.

People also had different reasons for migrating to Massachusetts. Most early Jamestown settlers hoped to "get rich quick" and return to England. As a result, early Jamestown had the feel of a frontier "boom town." Flimsy houses of unseasoned wood were thrown up quickly. Ships anchored off shore as floating taverns where colonists all too quickly spent the riches gained from tobacco.

*The title "gentleman" referred to any man who was rich enough to support himself without working. Most often a gentleman's wealth came from land. However, university students, members of the clergy, and army commanders could call themselves gentlemen.

Eventually, the London Company sent women to Virginia, but for years male colonists outnumbered the females. On the other hand, more families with children settled in New England. Furthermore, they came not to make instant fortunes and return to England, but to settle down and begin new lives in the New World.

Search for a More Comfortable Life

Many families migrated to the New World because they were dissatisfied with their lives in England. There a person's social class and place of birth often determined the quality of his or her life.

Among the upper classes, the eldest son inherited family wealth. Younger sons often found themselves without gainful employment upon reaching adulthood. Traditionally, these young men entered the church or the army, or competed for posts at the royal court. With the opening of America, they had other, better prospects.

Lower classes from the rural areas and the cities also found reasons to search for a better life in the New World. As wool became a staple of the English economy, acre upon acre of English farmland was fenced in for sheep pastures. Peasants who had tilled the land for centuries as tenant farmers suddenly found themselves evicted from their homes. Some found employment in rural industries, but most could find no satisfactory work at all.

A middle class of merchants and artisans lived prosperously in England's cities. But life for most city dwellers was characterized by cramped housing, filthy streets with open sewers, frequent fires, water shortages, rampant crime, epidemics, and chronic unemployment.

These conditions influenced many people's decision to make the long and risky journey to the New World. Even more important to earliest immigrants, however, was the New World's promise of the chance to worship in their own way.

The Protestant Reformation

Throughout the Middle Ages, the Roman Catholic Church united Christian believers under the spiritual leadership of the Pope. On the local level, the church was led by priests, who in turn were responsible to their superiors, the bishops and archbishops.

At the beginning of the sixteenth century, Martin Luther, a young German monk, became increasingly distressed by conditions in the church. He was dismayed by the corruption and worldliness that had crept into it, especially the clergy's preoccupation with power and wealth. Most of all, Luther disapproved of certain aspects of Roman Catholic theology. He particularly opposed the church's strong emphasis on good works as a means to eternal salvation. Good works could never save a Christian, Luther argued; faith alone had the power to do that. Luther tried to convince others within the church, but he remained unsatisfied and left the church in 1517.

Martin Luther's actions inaugurated a movement that came to be known as the Protestant Reformation. Soon it spread throughout Europe. John Calvin established a strict version of the new faith in Geneva, Switzerland, and new churches also formed in France and in the Netherlands.

In England Henry VIII declared himself, rather than the Pope, head of the church, provoking a split with Rome. Henry, unlike Luther and Calvin, did not oppose the beliefs of the church. He simply wanted to govern his nation's branch of the church himself—without interference from the Pope. After Henry's death, however, Protestantism flourished in England. Elizabeth, who became queen in 1558, was a Protestant, as were many of her subjects.

But what did being a Protestant mean? Leaders of the reformed churches could not always agree. Luther wanted to base all theology on the Bible, allowing the church to keep only those customs that were specifically permitted by Holy Scripture.

All Protestants agreed, in one degree or another, with Luther's emphasis on scripture, but they often parted company there. Some felt that all church hierarchies should be abolished because the Bible made no mention of them. Others disagreed and felt that the offices of bishop and archbishop should be continued. Still others argued that the only spiritual leaders should be local ministers.

Under Elizabeth, the Church of England felt it was proper to retain the traditional hierarchy of bishops and archbishops. Furthermore, the English church kept many of the Catholic practices, such as not eating meat at certain times.

Some English people believed, however, that the English church had not reformed enough. They objected to church services that incorporated Catholic practices. And they claimed that English priests were still too worldly, superstitious, and ignorant. One Protestant called them "Dumme Doggs, Unskilful sacrificing priestes, Destroyeing Drones." From these strongly dissenting groups came many of New England's colonists.

The Pilgrims of Plymouth Colony

Some dissenters believed that the Church of England remained so impure that true believers should separate from it completely. Those who held this radical position were called Separatists.

When James I succeeded Elizabeth in 1603, the Separatists became alarmed, for the king had vowed to "harry them out of the land." Fearing for their safety and their freedom, many moved to the Netherlands. There the Dutch, known in Europe for their tolerance, allowed the Separatists to worship as they pleased. Yet the Separatists were not satisfied with their new home. They missed their familiar English neighborhoods and customs. When Catholic Spain threatened to seize the Netherlands, which it had ruled earlier, the English Separatist community looked for another haven.

Along with other English people, the Separatists obtained permission from the London Company to start a new settlement in the company's North American territory. In September 1620, 102 men, women, and children, later called Pilgrims, set sail from Plymouth, England, on a small ship, the *Mayflower*.

When they reached the coast of North America, the Pilgrims realized that their course had taken them north of the London Company's lands and, hence, outside its authority. The colonists were thus responsible for governing themselves.

While still on shipboard, the Pilgrims gathered together and drafted an agreement that formed the basis of their community in the New World. Forty-one colonists signed this agreement, called the Mayflower Compact. The compact was not intended to establish a formal government. Rather it was a simple agreement that the settlers would consult each other about matters affecting the community and abide by majority rule.

The first winter at the colony was hard, for the Pilgrims had arrived in December, much too late to plant crops. By the following spring, almost half the settlers had died from cold, hunger, and disease. That more did not perish was due partly to the firm leadership of the young William Bradford. He assumed the governorship of the Plymouth colony during that first winter and led it for many years.

The colony also received invaluable aid from Native Americans, who befriended the

★ Voices of Freedom ★

The Mayflower Compact

The Pilgrims created this short document, the Mayflower Compact, the first step toward self-government in America.

In the name of God, Amen. We, whose names are underwritten, the loyal subjects of our dread [awesome] Sovereign Lord King James by the Grace of God, of Great Britain, France, and Ireland, King defender of the faith, etc.

Having undertaken for the glory of God, and the advancement of the christian faith, and the honour of our king and country, a voyage to plant the first colony in the Northern parts of Virginia. Do by these presents,

solemnly and mutually, in the presence of God, and one another, covenant [contract] and combine ourselves together into a Civil body politick, for our better ordering and preservation and furtherance of the ends aforesaid; and by Virtue hereof do enact, constitute, and frame such just and equal laws, ordinances, Acts, constitution, and officers, from time to time, as shall be thought most meet [suitable] and convenient for the general good of the Colony; unto which we promise all due submission and obedience. In witness whereof we have hereunto subscribed our names at Cape-Cod the eleventh of November, Anno Domini, 1620.

Pilgrims and showed them how to raise corn. When the colonists harvested their first crop in October 1621, they gratefully proclaimed a day of thanksgiving.

The Puritans

While the Pilgrims separated themselves completely from the Church of England, other dissenters, called Puritans, hoped to reform it from within. For a while the Puritans achieved modest successes. Many English congregations simplified their forms of worship. And quite a few Puritans attained positions of power within the English government and universities.

When King James's son, Charles I, assumed the throne, the Puritans found themselves threatened. Charles's religious beliefs had more in common with the Catholic church of Rome than with a "purified" and simplified English church. Also, he felt that the Puritans' objection to a hierarchy threatened not only the church but his own power as well.

In retaliation, Charles and his government denied Puritans the freedom to worship as they pleased and deprived them of leadership positions in the church and the universities. As a result, some Puritans began to look toward the New World.

After much negotiation, a group of Puritans obtained a charter from King Charles to establish a colony in America under the auspices of the Massachusetts Bay Company, a joint stock company Puritans had formed. In 1630 an impressive fleet of 11 ships carrying over 900 colonists arrived in Massachusetts, where an exploratory party had established a beachhead the year before. Under the leadership of John Winthrop, the colony soon began to prosper.

Government at Massachusetts Bay

Meanwhile, persecution of English Puritans continued unabated. The government's hostility to their beliefs led the members of the Massachusetts Bay Company to take an unusual step. Instead of governing from England, as other joint stock companies had, the company moved its headquarters to Boston, its new American settlement.

The company retained the right, under its charter, to make laws for its settlers and to govern them without giving anyone but

This engraving of a service at St. Paul's Cathedral in London around 1618 shows the type of elaborate ceremony the Puritans hoped to escape in the New World.

shareholders a voice in deliberations. But Winthrop and the other leaders did not follow this course of action. They turned the government of the company into a true government of the colony by allowing settlers, not just shareholders, to elect the colony's officers.

Voters chose a legislature, called the General Court, and a governor to direct affairs. In order to preserve the religious character of the colony, however, only male church members were allowed to vote.

Even with this requirement, though, many more citizens could vote in Massachusetts than in England, where only men who owned or rented property worth 40 shillings could vote. As long as a Massachusetts settler was a free man and a church member, he could vote no matter how much his property was worth. Thus, at an early stage, Massachusetts governed itself with a representative assembly.

Despite this genuine advance, Puritans did not believe in democracy. Free men elected leaders, but the leaders' duty was to do God's bidding. Puritans wanted their colony to be a "Bible Commonwealth," run according to their interpretation of scripture. They did not want other religious groups tainting the settlement with "impure" notions. Any such heretics were expelled.

A Search for Tolerance

One of the most prominent "heretics" was Roger Williams, who arrived in Massachusetts Bay in 1630. Williams, like the Puritans, believed that spiritual leaders of the church should keep themselves separate from the worldly affairs of the state. He agreed that ministers should not hold political offices. But Williams went a step further and claimed that the state should have nothing to do with religious matters either. It should not force people to worship in a particular way, as the Puritans were doing in Massachusetts Bay.

In 1635 Massachusetts banished Williams for these opinions, as well as for his belief that the king had no right to grant the settlers lands that already belonged to Native Americans. Williams fled into the wilderness and established what later became the colony of Rhode Island. There he tolerated all forms of religious worship.

Rhode Island soon became a haven for religious dissenters. Among them was Anne Hutchinson, an intellectual and forceful woman who quarreled with Massachusetts leaders over theology and was subsequently banished.

Another group of settlers from Massachusetts Bay founded a town at Hartford, Connecticut, in 1636. Their minister and leader, Thomas Hooker, agreed with the Puritans' theology but felt that John Winthrop and the other magistrates had assumed too much power. Government, Hooker believed, should rest on "the free consent of the people."

Accordingly, in 1639 the settlers in the Hartford area adopted the Fundamental Orders of Connecticut as their new plan of gov-

★ American Profiles ★

Anne Hutchinson: A Voice of Religious Dissent

In March of 1638 the Massachusetts Bay Colony was shaken by a scandal. Anne Hutchinson was on trial. Hutchinson was a strong-minded woman whose religious teaching had won her the support of some of the most important members of the colony. The charge against her was a serious one. She was accused of an attempt to destroy the very foundations of the Puritan Church.

The wife of a wealthy merchant and mother of fourteen children, Anne Hutchinson had come from England a few years earlier. Shortly after her arrival, she began to hold weekly meetings. There she discussed minister John Cotton's sermons with other colonists.

Cotton preached that people could know, on their own, whether or not they were chosen as God's elect. But he held that this knowledge did not free them from the need to lead a godly life.

Anne Hutchinson, however, went much further than Cotton. According to her, people who had received the gift of God's grace might not have to follow the laws that bound other people. Such ideas created a deep rift in the colony. Over seventy men and women sided with Hutchinson against the Puritan authorities. When her followers refused to fight in a war against the Pequot Indians, the very existence of the colony seemed threatened.

Anne Hutchinson was hauled before the Massachusetts General Court and charged with heresy. Although she defended herself ably, the court declared her guilty. She was banished from the colony. With her family, she fled first to Rhode Island and later to New York. There she was killed in an Indian attack. The idea of religious freedom, however, continued to grow in the American colonies.

ernment. While the Fundamental Orders resembled the Massachusetts system closely, they differed significantly in basing their authority on self-government by the people rather than on the divine rule of kings.

While neither Rhode Island nor Connecticut was democratic in the modern sense, both established representative governments of some kind. Both also adopted positions of tolerance and respect for differing religious beliefs.

SECTION REVIEW

1. Identify: Martin Luther, Henry VIII, Separatists, Pilgrims, Mayflower Compact, William Bradford, Puritans, Roger Williams, Anne Hutchinson, Thomas Hooker, Fundamental Orders of Connecticut.

2. Explain why each of the following English subjects might have decided to try a life in the New World: (a) the second son of a wealthy family; (b) a tenant farmer; (c) a city worker.

3. Why did the Pilgrims decide to leave the Netherlands and settle in the New World?

4. (a) What type of government did the Massachusetts Bay Company establish for the colony? (b) Who was qualified to vote?

5. In what way was the founding of Rhode Island similar to the founding of Connecticut?

6. **Critical Thinking** Why did the Puritans think that the clergy should be separate from the worldly affairs of the state?

3 Developing a Colonial System

England's first New World colonies were established by joint stock companies in Virginia and Massachusetts. At first, this method of colonization seemed to hold the solution to the problem of organizing and managing settlements thousands of miles from England.

A company of profit-minded investors could provide the money needed to get the colony off to a good start. Furthermore, because the crown authorized the enterprise by granting the company its charter, the government seemed assured of having some control over colonial affairs. In reality, however, things did not work this smoothly.

A New Approach to Colonization

Although the colony of Virginia thrived, the London Company failed as a profit-making venture. The company mismanaged its business, and the members fought among themselves. Furthermore, as you read, the early colonists, lacking most of the necessities of life, barely survived until tobacco proved to be a profitable crop. In 1624 James I took matters into his own hands. He revoked the company's charter and placed the colony under his personal control.

Massachusetts posed other problems for England. After a few uncertain years the colony thrived, making a profit for the Massachusetts Bay Company. But it acted with more independence than the English government felt a colony should.

Believing that their authority came directly from God, the leaders of Massachusetts ruled church and state with little regard for the king or his ministers. The crown, in turn, found it nearly impossible to impose its will on a settlement of dissenters 3,000 miles away.

With the lessons of Virginia and Massachusetts before them, the English government began to see the need for a more systematic approach to colonization. In an effort to coordinate the settlement of the colonies and to establish uniform standards for them, the crown created a new form of colonial organization, the proprietary colony.

With this method, the king granted territory to a person or small group of persons called *proprietors*. Like feudal lords, proprietors held their domains as absolute and sole owners and acknowledged the sovereignty of the king by making an annual payment of some sort. Proprietors had the right to parcel out their land to other individuals. These tenants did not own the land but held it only as long as the proprietor wished. They also paid rent and taxes to the proprietors, an important source of income.

In most cases the king did limit the authority of the proprietors however. They could institute only those laws that were in accord with the laws of England. And in making laws they usually had to have the consent of the free men of the colony or their chosen representatives.

Maryland: A Proprietary Colony

George Calvert, Lord Baltimore, established the first proprietary colony. One of the original stockholders of the London Company, Calvert envisioned his colony as a refuge for Roman Catholics and as a money-making real estate venture.

Calvert first obtained a grant of land in Newfoundland from James I. When the cold, rough territory proved unsuited for settlement, Calvert moved south. From James's son, Charles I, he acquired the right to 10 million acres (4 million hectares) of Virginia territory around the Chesapeake Bay.

George Calvert died before the grant could be issued, but his son, Cecilius, accepted it in 1632. The Calverts named the new colony Maryland in honor of King Charles's wife, Queen Henrietta Maria.

The first 200 settlers arrived in March 1634. Their only early troubles resulted from border disputes with their Virginia neighbors, which the king brought to a quick end by deciding in Maryland's favor. Relations with neighboring Indians who supplied them with corn were generally friendly.

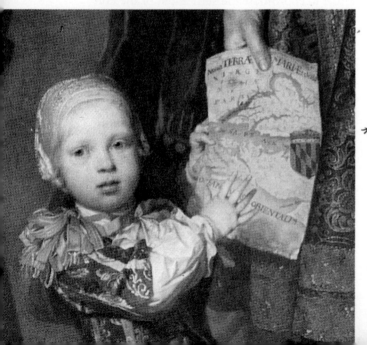

In this detail from a painting, young Cecil Calvert points to a map of Maryland, his family's proprietary colony in the New World.

If their colony was to be profitable, the Calverts knew they had to attract thousands of settlers. Thus, they welcomed Protestants as well as Roman Catholics. In 1649 the colonial assembly passed the Maryland Toleration Act, affirming religious freedom for all Christians.

Land Grants Under Charles II

Charles II made land grants in America primarily as rewards to English nobles who had remained loyal to the monarchy following a revolt against his father, Charles I, in 1642. The leaders of the revolt had executed Charles I in 1649 and abolished the monarchy. Charles II then spent the next 11 years in exile in France until he was restored to the throne in 1660.

The king made an early land grant to his brother James, the Duke of York, in 1664. This grant, stretching from Connecticut to the Delaware Bay, was a bold move on the part of the king because the territory had been settled by the Dutch, who called it New Netherlands. Soon after English forces appeared at the mouth of the Hudson River the inhabitants of New Netherlands, dissatisfied with Dutch rule, surrendered, and the colony was renamed New York. The Dutch retaliated by declaring war on England and harassing English shipping, but New York remained in English hands.

The Duke, who had absolute political power in the colony, appointed a governor and council to administer it rather than go to America himself. He allowed wealthy Dutch landowners to retain their huge estates and gave away equally large tracts of land to his English followers. In matters of religion, James was broad minded. A Roman Catholic himself, he allowed colonists to worship as they pleased.

The area adjoining New York, renamed New Jersey, was originally a part of the Duke of York's grant. He in turn granted the rights to this land to two friends, Sir George Carteret and Lord John Berkeley. Unfortunately, the governor of New York did not hear about the new owners until after he had assigned governmental authority over the area to a group of Puritans. The ensuing legal tangle lasted almost 50 years. The territory was divided into two colonies in 1676 and was not united as New Jersey until 1702.

The Carolinas and Georgia

Charles II made a second gift of land to a group of eight nobles including Sir William Berkeley, the governor of Virginia. In 1663 the group requested and received all the land between present-day Virginia and Florida, bounded on the east by the Atlantic Ocean and on the west by the Pacific.

Settlement of the territory, which was named Carolina after the king and his father, centered around Albemarle Sound, the mouth of the Cape Fear River, and the area that soon came to be known as Charles Towne. Though themselves Anglican, the lords proprietors, as they became known, welcomed colonists of all denominations.

Like the Calverts in Maryland, the lords proprietors of Carolina had the powers of feudal lords. They kept huge estates for themselves and parceled the rest of the land out to tenants, collecting annual rents in return. The proprietors hoped to earn an enormous profit as landlords. Their plan nearly misfired, however, when they tried to impose a strange social and governmental plan on their territory.

Their plan, known as the Fundamental Constitutions of Carolina, was drawn up by the English political philosopher John Locke. The constitution specified that Carolina's society was to be set up along rigid class lines with a hereditary nobility at the top. The proprietors themselves would have titles like Lord Palatine and Lord High Chamberlain.

The first settlers were appalled by the Fundamental Constitutions and rejected all but a few of its provisions. When word of it reached England, immigration to the colony nearly came to a standstill, threatening the proprietors' profit. Eventually a more democratic and realistic government developed.

In 1712 the proprietors divided Carolina into northern and southern parts and gave each its own government. Most settlers in North Carolina moved there from other colonies, especially New England and Virginia, while the first colonists of South Carolina came largely from England or from the plantations of the West Indies. A few were Protestant refugees from France.

Georgia was a third part of the original Carolina grant, and was finally separated from South Carolina in 1732. It was unique among the colonies in being founded neither as a money-making venture nor as a refuge for religious dissenters. A group of proprietors, led by James Oglethorpe (OH gehl thorp), wanted the colony to provide a place where people imprisoned for debt could get a new start in life. Second, they wanted to provide a barrier against the Spanish in Florida.

No more than a few debtors actually migrated to Georgia. But the colony did become a haven for poor shopkeepers and artisans from England and Scotland. Protestant refugees from Switzerland and Germany also found a home there. Roman Catholics, however, were forbidden to settle in Georgia. The proprietors feared that they would side with Catholic Spain in the event of a war.

A Haven in Penn's Woods

When Charles II was in exile, Admiral William Penn had loaned him a substantial sum of money. After Penn died, the king, chronically short of cash, paid the debt in land to Penn's son William.

As a young man, Penn had joined the Society of Friends. Members of the Society were also known as Quakers because their founder, George Fox, directed them to "tremble at the name of the Lord."

The Quakers were a thorn in the side of English authorities. They had no church hierarchy, no regular church building, and no paid clergy. Furthermore, they showed their contempt for the English class system by treating everyone as an equal, and they refused either to take oaths or to fight in wars.

With the Church of England stepping up its persecution of dissenting religious groups, Penn sought a refuge for himself and his fellow Quakers. Pennsylvania, literally "Penn's woods," seemed the ideal place. Penn eventually added more land to his proprietorship by purchasing neighboring territory that would become Delaware.

William Penn, unlike most proprietors, lived in America himself for a while and administered the colony. When he had to be away, he appointed a deputy governor to take charge.

Penn's plan of government was the most democratic in the colonies. Until 1701, it consisted of a legislature with upper and lower houses elected by the freemen of the colony. The upper house proposed laws, and the lower house accepted or rejected

Founding of the Colonies

Colony/Date Founded	Leader	Reasons Founded	Type of Government
New England Colonies			
Massachusetts Plymouth/1620 Massachusetts Bay/1630	William Bradford John Winthrop	Religious freedom Religious freedom	Corporate 1620-1691 Corporate 1630-1691 Both colonies merged 1691; royal 1691-1776
New Hampshire/1622	Ferdinando Gorges John Mason	Profit from trade and fishing	Proprietary 1622-1641; corporate (part of Mass.) 1641-1680; royal 1680-1776
Connecticut Hartford/1636 New Haven/1639	Thomas Hooker	Extend trade; religious and political freedom	Self-governing 1636-1662 Self-governing 1639-1662; royal 1662-65 Both colonies merged 1665; royal 1665-1776
Rhode Island/1636	Roger Williams	Religious freedom	Self-governing 1636-44; corporate 1644-1776
Middle Colonies			
*New York/1624	Peter Minuet	Expand trade	Colony of Dutch West India Co. 1624-1664; proprietary (Eng.) 1664-1685; royal 1685-1776
**Delaware/1638	Swedish settlers	Expand trade	Proprietary 1638-1682; part of Pa. (proprietary) 1682-1704; royal 1704-1776
New Jersey/1664	John Berkeley George Carteret	Profit for founders from land sales; religious and political freedom	Proprietary 1664-1702; royal 1702-1776
Pennsylvania/1682	William Penn	Profit for founders from land sales; religious and political freedom	Proprietary 1682-1776
Southern Colonies			
Virginia/1607	John Smith	Trade and agriculture	Corporate 1607-24; royal 1624-1776
Maryland/1632	Lord Baltimore	Profit for founders from land sales; religious and political freedom	Proprietary 1632-1691; royal 1691-1715 proprietary 1715-1776
The Carolinas/1663 North Carolina/1712 South Carolina/1712	Group of eight proprietors	Profit from trade and agriculture; religious freedom	Proprietary 1663-1712; self-governing until 1719; king buys back North 1719; king buys back South 1729; both royal 1730-1776
Georgia/1732	James Oglethorpe	Profit; haven for debtors; buffer against Spanish Florida	Proprietary 1732-1752; royal 1752-1776

*New York was settled by the Dutch in 1624 and named New Netherlands. It surrendered to the English in 1664.

**Delaware was settled by the Swedes in 1638 and named New Sweden. It was captured and incorporated into New Netherlands by the Dutch in 1655. It was then captured by the English in 1664.

them. Every man who owned a small amount of land or paid taxes was entitled to vote, so a large number of colonists participated in choosing the government.

Movement Toward Royal Colonies

As the colonies grew and prospered, the English crown became increasingly interested in their development. Gradually the king assumed control, creating royal colonies. By 1730 only Pennsylvania and Maryland remained as proprietary colonies.

Colonists usually found royal control preferable to government by the proprietors. For one thing, royal colonies seemed to receive better protection from the English army and navy. Secondly, colonial representatives often had more political power in a royal colony than in a proprietary one.

In a royal colony the king appointed the colony's governor and council, and the eligible voters elected an assembly. The governor controlled trade, appointed judges and other officials, and served as the colony's chief executive.

The council, usually composed of leading colonists, advised the governor and approved official appointments. Furthermore, the governor had to consult the council before he called the assembly into session, issued paper money, or declared martial law. The council functioned as the highest court and as the upper house of the assembly.

The colonial assembly considered itself the guardian of colonial interests. Legislation could not become law until the assembly consented to it. This continued the tradition of representative government that was common to all colonies. The original charters for Massachusetts and Virginia had guaranteed settlers a voice in the colony's government, a tradition that persisted when men and women from Massachusetts founded Rhode Island and Connecticut. Furthermore, the grants to all proprietors, except for the Duke of York, had required them to make laws with the consent of the colonists.

Gradually, the people's right to consent to laws through their representatives grew into the right to initiate, or propose, laws, a trend that continued in royal colonies.

Colonial assemblies also increased their influence in the government because they had to approve the salaries of other officials,

Major Events	
1607	English settlers arrive at Jamestown
1619	House of Burgesses established in Virginia
1620	Pilgrims arrive in North America
1630	Puritans establish Massachusetts Bay
1632	Maryland becomes first proprietary colony
1649	Maryland Toleration Act affirms religious freedom for all Christians in colony
1660	Charles II restored to throne in England
1685	James II establishes Dominion of New England
1688	Glorious Revolution in England

including the governor. They considered this an especially important power, as you will see in Chapter 6.

Persistence of the Representative Tradition

The strength of the representative tradition in the English colonies is most evident in light of the failure of three attempts to bypass it. The first of these was in New York.

Under the Dutch, a director-general had held complete authority in the colony. He ruled without any representative assembly. When the Duke of York assumed control of the colony, he tried to continue the Dutch system. The settlers, however, resisted vigorously and finally forced him to grant them an assembly.

The Fundamental Constitutions of the Carolinas also violated the representative tradition and failed as a result. A third attempt in the 1680s, like the first, involved the Duke of York.

When Charles II died in 1685, his brother, the Duke of York, succeeded to the throne as James II. The new king promptly revoked Massachusetts's original charter. Next, he tightened royal control and discarded the representative assemblies in all colonies north of New Jersey. Then he renamed the area the Dominion of New England.

50

The American colonists greatly resented the action and threatened rebellion, but the English beat them to it. In 1688, the English deposed James II in a revolt called the Glorious Revolution. The New England colonies promptly reinstated the representative assemblies, showing England and the world that, in America at least, representative government would endure.

SECTION REVIEW

1. Identify: George Calvert, Cecilius Calvert, Maryland Toleration Act, Charles II, New Netherlands, William Berkeley, James Oglethorpe, William Penn, Society of Friends.
2. (a) What was a proprietary colony? (b) What role did a proprietor play? (c) What did the tenants have to do in return for use of the land?
3. (a) Why did George Calvert establish Maryland? (b) Who settled there?
4. (a) What was Charles II's motive for granting land in America? (b) Who received the first grant?
5. What two special goals did Oglethorpe have for founding Georgia?
6. (a) Why did William Penn found Pennsylvania? (b) What kind of government did it have?
7. (a) What is a royal colony? (b) Give two reasons why colonists often preferred royal colonies to proprietary colonies.
8. What attempts were made to undermine representative colonial government?
9. **Critical Thinking** What did the settlers' rejection of the Fundamental Constitutions of Carolina demonstrate about their goals?

Chapter 3 Review

In Perspective

English settlement in North America began in earnest in the 1600s. The colony at Jamestown was the first. It was founded by a group of private investors who had formed a joint stock company. Joint stock companies also sponsored the founding of Plymouth and Massachusetts Bay. Unlike the Virginians, the first settlers to New England came in search of religious freedom. This was also the main motive of the founders of Connecticut and Rhode Island, although they were fleeing persecution in Massachusetts, not Europe.

Most of the remaining colonies began as proprietary colonies, set up to make a profit. However, most had other reasons as well. These included religious freedom for Catholics in Maryland and for Quakers in Pennsylvania. The proprietors of the Carolinas tried but failed to establish a rigid social and political system in their colony. Georgia was originally founded as a refuge for debtors and a buffer against the Spanish in Florida.

Although the colonies were founded and settled in different ways, in time they all had representative governments. The belief in democracy had deep roots in English political traditions. It was to be the basis for the movement toward independence, as you will see in later chapters.

Vocabulary

On a separate sheet of paper, write the word or words that best complete each of the following sentences.

1. A business organization that pooled the funds of many investors to finance colonies was a (an) ____.
2. The first representative assembly in the colonies was the ____.
3. Dissenters who wanted to separate completely from the Church of England were the ____.

4. A (An) ____ was a person to whom the king granted territory to hold as sole owner but who acknowledged the sovereignty of the king by making an annual payment of some sort.

5. In a (an) ____ colony the king appointed the governor and council, and the eligible voters elected the assembly.

Chapter Checkup

1. (a) How did the goals and actions of the London Company create problems for the Jamestown colony? (b) How did each of the following contribute to the survival of the colony: John Smith; local Native Americans; the House of Burgesses?

2. (a) Why did the Pilgrims and Puritans immigrate to the New World? (b) How did their attitudes toward the Church of England differ?

3. Describe the role of each of the following in the government of a royal colony: the king, the governor, the council, the assembly.

Critical Thinking

1. Comparing How did the proprietary governments differ from the governments organized under charters?

2. Analyzing How did the colonial governments of New York and Pennsylvania reflect the differing views of their leaders?

Developing Basic Skills

1. Reading a Chart A chart can make comparing data and tracing developments easier. Answer the following questions about the chart on page 48: (a) Which colonies were originally founded by people from nations other than England? (b) Which colonies were founded as proprietary colonies? (c) What were the two most common reasons for founding a colony?

2. Placing Events in Time A time line allows you to see the relationship between events as they happened. Copy the outline of the time line on page 36. Using the information from your text and the chart on page 48, add the name of each colony and the date it was founded. Then answer the following questions: (a) In what 20-year period were the most colonies founded? (b) How many colonies were founded before the Glorious Revolution? (c) What was the last colony founded? Why do you think it was founded so long after the other colonies?

See page 827 for suggested readings.

Writer's Handbook

Rewording an Essay Question as a Topic Sentence

The topic sentence expresses the central idea of a paragraph. It tells the reader what the paragraph is about. In an essay question answer, the topic sentence is often the first sentence in the paragraph. It should indicate what the instruction word is calling for and what ideas will be covered. You can often rewrite the essay question in order to form this type of topic sentence.

Read the following essay question: *Compare how the Spanish and the English governed their early settlements.* A topic sentence based on this question might read: *The English governed their early settlements differently from the way the Spanish governed theirs.* A clear topic sentence is important because the other sentences in the paragraph should develop the idea in the topic sentence. Avoid a topic sentence that is too broad or too narrow. For example, here is a topic sentence that is too broad: *All the nations that established colonies in the New World treated their colonies in different ways.* Here is one that is too narrow: *Spain depended on the conquistadores to establish colonies.*

Practice: Begin your answer for each of the Critical Thinking questions in this Chapter Review with a topic sentence. Underline the topic sentence.

Religion in History

The central role religion has played in American life was demonstrated by the bold and confident Puritans. Persecuted by the English government, the Puritans were lucky to have escaped jail—or even worse. They could have rejected England once they reached America, but their religious beliefs would not allow that. The Puritans felt that they had embarked on a holy mission—to form a society based on God's word as a model for the rebuilding of England. "We must consider that we shall be as a city upon a hill," John Winthrop told his fellow settlers. "The eyes of all people are upon us."

The Puritans believed that God would bless them and make them known around the world. That feeling of a special destiny has been shared by countless others throughout American history. When the colonists took up arms to fight for independence in 1775, one minister proclaimed that "God requires a people, struggling for their liberties to treat such of the community who will not join them, as open enemies, and to reject them as unworthy of the privileges which others enjoy."

Of course, many nations have been guided by religious principles. What made the United States unusual was the importance its citizens placed on religious freedom. More and more, Americans came to insist that the government keep itself separate from religious affairs. "Congress shall

The Pilgrims put their hope for a safe journey in God's hands. Their faith influenced the history of their colony and the role of religion in American life.

make no law respecting an establishment of religion," reads the first sentence in the Bill of Rights.

Religious freedom spread partly because it was supported by English political tradition. But practical circumstances were also important. The Puritans were not the only group to cross the Atlantic seeking religious freedom. Catholics, Jews and other Protestants also wanted to be free to worship as they pleased. With so many different religious groups in America, it made sense to allow each freedom.

Influence on Society   Even though Americans believed strongly that government should stay out of religious affairs, they also held that religion had a legitimate role in shaping society. On the frontier, churches were active in maintaining order. Members could be disciplined for fighting, drinking, gambling, and spreading malicious gossip. In the growing cities, churches encouraged hard work and thrift.

During the nineteenth century, religion sparked devout church groups to social action. Some people campaigned to improve the conditions in prisons. Others worked to obtain political rights for women and to abolish slavery. "Every [church] member must work or quit," said the minister Charles Finney. "No honorary members."

For those who had little power to change society, religion provided a strong anchor in times of distress. The Christian religion was especially strong among blacks in pre-Civil War slave quarters. Black preachers brought the message of God's love for all, and slave songs looked both to triumph in heaven and in the world itself. As one religious song put it, "But some of these days my time will come,/I'll hear that bugle, I'll hear that drum,/I'll see them armies, marchin' along/I'll lift my head and join the song." With the coming of the Civil War and freedom, many blacks did just that.

Religion also played an important part in the lives of countless immigrants. Many immigrants brought with them a strong religious culture. Churches and religious associations helped these newcomers adjust

to their new home. Some congregations helped people in times of sickness and unemployment and set up insurance programs to protect women whose husbands died.

Where so many different religions and denominations existed side by side, getting along was not always easy. Immigrants often found that native-born Americans were hostile to and suspicious of them. It was not until 1960 that a Catholic, John F. Kennedy, was elected President of the United States (although Roger Taney became the first Catholic Chief Justice of the Supreme Court when he was appointed by Andrew Jackson in 1835). The first Jew to hold a position on the Supreme Court was Louis Brandeis, who was appointed in 1919.

Role of Religion Today   Religion continues to have a deep influence on American culture. Churches provide religious worship for their members, support in difficult times, and a strong set of moral beliefs. These beliefs continue to affect American society in many ways. During the 1960s, the Reverend Martin Luther King, Jr., led a nonviolent movement to gain blacks the right to live in a truly integrated society. One leading advocate of the Civil Rights Act of 1964 claimed it would never have been passed without the support of religious leaders.

People both within and outside churches have debated how far politics and religion can mix while keeping the church separate from the state. In the 1980s the Reverend Jerry Falwell and others have spoken for evangelical Christians who hope to promote their values through the political process. Other religious groups are searching for a balance between a level of political action that would nurture moral values and a level that would involve churches too closely in the bustle of everyday politics.

Society faces a number of difficult questions. Should religious leaders run for public office? Should prayer be allowed in public schools? Should government funds be given to religious schools? Where is the line drawn between citizens having the freedom to believe as they choose and imposing those beliefs on other people? These questions, so important in the past, remain important today because religion continues to be such a central part of American life.

1. What underlying belief was the basis of religious influence on colonial American life?
2. How do you think pluralism, or diversity of religious beliefs, has affected American society?

American Profiles Roger Williams

Roger Williams earned a special place in American history as a courageous advocate of religious freedom. Williams grew up in England in the early 1600s. After being ordained an Anglican minister, Williams became part of the growing movement to purify the Anglican Church.

In the summer of 1629, Williams met with Puritan leaders to discuss the Massachusetts Bay enterprise. The next year he and his wife Mary emigrated to New England.

Williams was welcomed by the people of Massachusetts. He taught that people should have complete freedom of conscience and should be allowed to worship God in their own way. He also said that the king could not grant the Puritans ownership of the land because it rightfully belonged to the Indians. Not surprisingly, Williams's ideas brought him into conflict with the church leaders in Boston.

As a result of his differences with these leaders, Williams left Salem for Plymouth, where he spent two years. When he returned to Salem in 1633, Williams insisted that the Puritan church separate itself from the Church of England and that the king's land grant to the colony was invalid.

For a while, Williams was able to stave off opposition from the Puritan leaders because he was strongly supported by his congregation in Salem. But finally, in July 1635, he was brought to trial, accused of rebellious activities against the government and the king. He was ordered to leave the

jurisdiction of Massachusetts within six weeks. An attempt was made to seize him and ship him back to England, but he took shelter among the Indians.

In June 1636 Williams and a tiny band of companions founded the first settlement in Rhode Island. They named it Providence, in honor of "God's merciful providence" to them.

Williams got along well with the local Indians, the Narragansetts. Because he believed that the Indians owned the land, he

Because Roger Williams (1603–1683) was friendly with the Narragansetts, he was able to gain their help for the Massachusetts colonists during the Pequot War. (See page 82.)

paid them for the territory on which he and his followers settled.

Williams allowed people in Providence to follow their own consciences although it made it harder to govern the colony. He believed that people could find the truth only if they were free to search for it without coercion. Williams held that government should never interfere with what people *believed*. It could interfere with their actions, but only when they infringed on the rights of others.

Williams's ideas began to spread slowly. Gradually other colonies developed some forms of religious tolerance, in practice, even if not in principle. Williams's courage in fighting for what he believed to be right had helped gain an important liberty for generations to come.

1. How did Roger Williams's beliefs conflict with the beliefs of the Puritans in the Massachusetts Bay Colony?
2. Roger Williams's colony was not a huge financial success and he died in poverty. Why is he revered and honored today?

Voices of Freedom — Liberty of Conscience

In January 1655 Williams was absent from Providence, Rhode Island, while the colony was experiencing difficulties. He wrote the following letter supporting religious freedom but defining the rights of government to maintain order.

To the town of Providence:
I would never speak or write the slightest bit that suggests an infinite liberty of conscience, which I have always disclaimed and hated. To prevent such mistakes, I shall . . . only propose this case. Many a ship goes to sea, with many hundred souls in one ship, whose welfare and woe is common. The ship's company is a true picture of a commonwealth, or a human combination or society. . . . Sometimes both Catholics and Protestants, Jews, and Turks, may be embarked in one ship. . . . All the liberty of conscience that ever I pleaded for, turns upon these two hinges— that none of the Catholics, Protestants, Jews, or Turks, be forced to come to the ship's prayers or worship, nor denied their own particular prayers or worship, if they practice any.

I further add . . . that notwithstanding this liberty, the commander of this ship ought to command the ship's course. If any of the seamen refuse to perform their duties, or passengers to pay their freight; if any refuse to help; . . . if any refuse to obey the common laws and orders of the ship concerning the peace or safety; if any . . . mutiny and rise up against their commanders and officers; if any . . . preach or write that there ought to be no commanders or officers . . . in such cases, whatever is pretended, the commander or commanders may judge, resist, compel, and punish such transgressors.

I remain studious of your common peace and liberty.

Roger Williams

Adapted from a letter from Roger Williams to the town of Providence, January 1655. From Narragansett Club, *Publications*.

1. What are the two areas of freedom of conscience sought by Williams?
2. How do Williams's views support the idea of separation of church and state?

4

Life in Colonial America

(1650–1750)

Pat Lyon at the Forge *by J. Neagle*

Chapter Outline

1 *The New England Colonies*

2 *The Middle Colonies*

3 *The Southern Colonies*

4 *Colonial Culture*

As colonists put down roots in the New World, they developed ways of life that differed from those in Europe and in other parts of the colonies. Between 1650 and 1750 three distinct styles of life emerged in the New England Colonies of Massachusetts, Connecticut, Rhode Island, and New Hampshire; the Middle Colonies of New York, Pennsylvania, New Jersey, and Delaware; and the Southern Colonies of Maryland, Virginia, North Carolina, South Carolina, and Georgia.

Colonists in each area faced different challenges as a result of varied climates and topographies. As you will read in this chapter, their responses to these challenges affect the way of life that evolved in each region.

In spite of differences, however, certain traditions were growing—a belief in representative government, the growth of religious tolerance, and a concern for education. By the 1750s, an American culture was emerging.

Free press develops

1630	1650	1670	1690	1710	1730	1750	1770

1636 Harvard founded

1647 First public school law passed

1676 Bacon's Rebellion

1691 Massachusetts grants religious freedom

1704 First weekly newspaper founded

1734 John Peter Zenger arrested

1763 Paxton boys revolt

1 The New England Colonies

The weather was harsh in New England. Winters were long and cold, with howling winds, violent storms, and heavy snowfalls. The topsoil was thin, and rocks dropped by ice age glaciers studded the landscape. Inland, dense forests had to be painstakingly cleared before the land could be farmed, while along the coast lay long stretches of barren sand dunes and salt marshes.

One settler wrote to relatives back in England that Massachusetts was "builded upon rocks, sand, and salt marshes." His fellow colonists so resented his bitter remark that they took him to court for slandering a place they believed was next to the promised land.

Farms and Towns in New England

Despite the generally poor soil of the region, many New Englanders earned a living as farmers. Most farmed at a *subsistence* level, producing just enough to feed their families but little more. Some worked the land with the help of slaves, but few farms were large enough to make slave labor profitable.

Running a farm in New England depended largely on cooperative effort. Each member of the family, including the children, had assigned duties, and survival depended on their regular performance. Men were largely responsible for cultivating crops and raising animals, and the women of the household made clothes, utensils, candles, and other necessities, rendering the New England farm largely *self-sufficient*. In other words, a farm family had the resources to get along without help. In spite of this self-sufficiency, families did not live in isolation. Farmers settled in clusters around a town.

Because religion was so important to New England settlers, many of these early towns were founded by the congregations of single churches. The elders of a congregation requested a tract of land from the colonial legislature. If the request was approved, the tract was surveyed and divided into lots. Each family in the community received land on which to build a house, to pasture animals, and to grow crops. In addition, families had the right to cut wood in the communal forest land.

At the center of the settlement stood the meeting house, a plain building used for *town meetings* as well as worship. During a settlement's early years, the elders who planned the town served as its leaders and supervised its expansion. At open town meetings the residents of the town discussed matters of importance such as hiring a new schoolteacher, building or repairing streets, or regulating livestock. They also elected local representatives to the colonial assembly.

A Diverse Economy

While many farm families in New England produced most of their necessities, a large number of residents were less self-sufficient. City dwellers, in particular, depended on trade with other colonies or with England for food, clothing, and other supplies. To pay for such purchases, colonists needed to find a product that could be traded at a profit.

At first furs seemed a likely answer. The forests abounded with raccoon, beaver, and otter, whose pelts were in great demand. However, New England trappers proved to be too skilled for their own good and soon depleted the local fur supply.

The New England forest also provided timber that colonists could ship to England or to other colonies. Gradually the timber industry developed into a major source of income for the region.

In addition to exporting timber, New Englanders used it to build ships. Shipbuilding grew rapidly as fishing became the area's most important commercial activity. Over 5,000 fishermen worked the coastal waters, and New England ports boasted of more than 900 oceangoing vessels. The city of Boston alone had 12 shipyards.

Yet fishing was not the only enterprise that employed New England's ships. The burgeoning shipping industry rapidly took the lead in trade between the colonies, England, and the West Indies.

Shipping could be very profitable, but it was a risky business. Communication was slow, so by the time a cargo arrived at its destination, the product might no longer be needed. The success of New England merchants in this competitive business earned them a reputation as shrewd "Yankee traders."

Women as well as men played an important economic role in New England's towns and cities. They worked as shopkeepers, printers, tavern and hotel keepers, merchants, tinkers, midwives, and shipbuilders. Colonial women often learned new occupations from a male relative, since most colonial businesses operated out of the home. Frequently women would take over the family business when a male relative died.

■ Between 1650 and 1750 North American colonies developed in three regions. According to this map, which colonies made up each region?

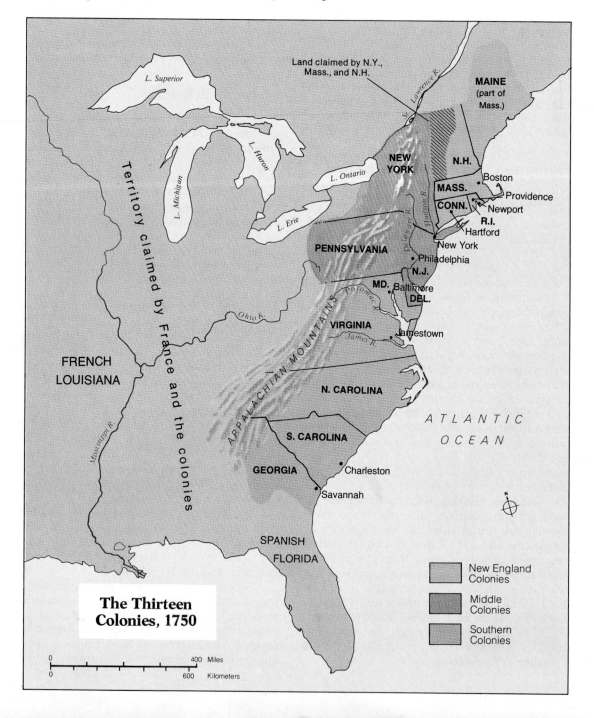

The Thirteen
Colonies, 1750

Social Classes in New England

A rigid class system existed in England, as in the rest of Europe. The royal family and the aristocracy occupied the top, followed by landowners and merchants. Beneath them were shopkeepers, artisans, and small landowners. Lowest on the social scale stood city workers, tenant farmers, and agricultural laborers. These class lines were firm, and movement from one class to another was virtually impossible.

New England society reflected the orderliness of the English class system but not its rigid inflexibility. In colonial New England a person could improve his or her status. Still, most people continued to observe sharp distinctions between classes.

In 1651, for example, the Massachusetts General Court passed a law that officially divided the colony's inhabitants into three classes: "the better class," "those above the ordinary degree," and "those of mean condition." Members of each class were expected to keep to their places and to behave as befitted their station.

As the New England colonies grew, a more democratic spirit began to infiltrate the social system. Members of the lower and middle classes, especially the skilled artisans, grew increasingly prosperous. And with their prosperity came a desire to imitate the upper classes.

Since a person's clothing indicated his or her place in society, dressing like the upper classes was the most popular and widespread form of imitation. Alarmed by such behavior on the part of the lower classes, the Massachusetts General Court expressed its

utter detestation . . . that men and women of mean condition should take upon them the

garb of gentlemen, by wearing gold or silver lace, or buttons . . . or to walk in great boots, or women of the same rank to wear silk or tiffany hoods or scarves which, though allowable to persons of greater estates . . . yet we cannot but judge it intolerable in persons of such like condition.

To stamp out such "intolerable" behavior the court promptly passed a law specifying how much property a family had to own in order to wear "any gold or silver lace, or gold and silver buttons, or any bone lace above two shillings per yard, or silk hoods, or scarfs." The penalty for violating the law was ingenious. A person not only had to pay a fine, but his or her property would be taxed at the rate for the social level being imitated.

Despite such attitudes, social mobility soon became the norm rather than the exception in New England. Everyone except slaves could aspire to and often attain a place in society higher than the one he or she had been born into.

SECTION REVIEW

1. Define: subsistence farming, self-sufficient, town meeting.
2. Why was New England a difficult area in which to settle?
3. How were New England farms self-sufficient?
4. How did church members set up towns in New England?
5. Why was the social system in New England more democratic than in Europe?
6. **Critical Thinking** How did geography influence the New England economy?

2 The Middle Colonies

The largest wave of immigration to New England took place in the 1600s, with most new settlers arriving from England. However, the Middle Colonies did not really begin to grow until the 1700s. People who migrated to this part of North America came not only from England but also from Ireland, Scotland, and the nations of continental Europe.

A Diverse Population

The largest number of non-English settlers came from northern Ireland and Germany. The Scotch-Irish, as those from northern Ireland were known, were the most numerous of the new wave of immigrants. Of Scottish origin, their families had settled in the north of Ireland in the sixteenth century.

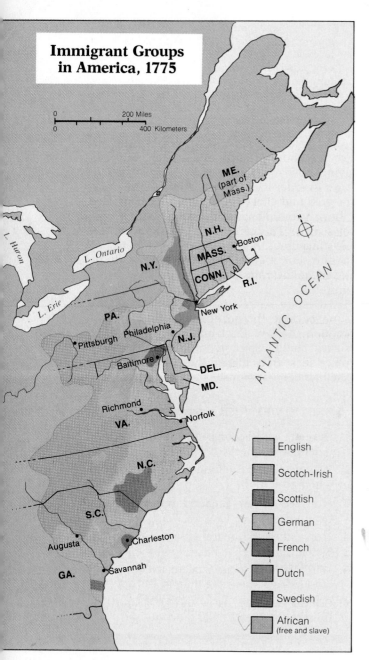

Immigrant Groups in America, 1775

0 200 Miles
0 400 Kilometers

ME. (part of Mass.)
N.H.
MASS. • Boston
N.Y.
CONN.
R.I.
New York
PA.
• Pittsburgh   Philadelphia
N.J.
Baltimore •
DEL.
MD.
Richmond •
VA.   • Norfolk
N.C.
S.C.
Augusta •   • Charleston
GA.   • Savannah

L. Huron
L. Ontario
L. Erie

ATLANTIC OCEAN

■ English
■ Scotch-Irish
■ Scottish
■ German
■ French
■ Dutch
■ Swedish
■ African (free and slave)

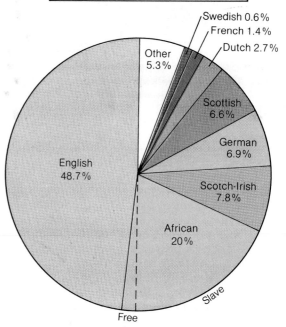

Ethnic Division of Colonial Population, 1775*

Swedish 0.6%
French 1.4%
Dutch 2.7%
Other 5.3%
Scottish 6.6%
German 6.9%
Scotch-Irish 7.8%
English 48.7%
African 20%
Free
Slave

* estimated from 1790 census

■ *By the mid-1770s, only about half of the colonists had English roots. New immigrants brought their own varied cultures. According to the map, where did each group mainly settle?*

During the eighteenth century, about 250,000 Scotch-Irish migrated to the Middle Colonies, especially to Pennsylvania. They left northern Ireland because the policies of the English government and the Anglican church had destroyed their economic well-being and virtually outlawed their Presbyterian religion. Their hatred of England had a profound influence on the future of the colonies.

The second largest group of settlers, the Germans, had been pushed out of their homeland by a series of brutal religious wars between Protestants and Catholics. Invading armies had devastated their homeland, the Rhineland of southwestern Germany. Furthermore, successive crop failures had brought dire poverty and famine to the Rhineland area.

Pennsylvania, with its rich lands, low rents, and widespread toleration, seemed a haven to these immigrants. Eventually, the Rhineland Germans came to be known as Pennsylvania Dutch, from a misuse of the word *Deutsch* (doich), meaning German. These two new groups, when combined with the Swedish colonists in Delaware and the Dutch in New York, made the population of the Middle Colonies the most diverse of English-ruled America.

An Agricultural Economy

The Middle Colonies contained some of the richest farmland on the Atlantic coast of North America. Thus, agriculture became the foundation of the region's economic life. As in other colonies, farmers either adapted European plants and animals to the American environment or used European farming methods to cultivate native American crops.

Although the soil was fertile and capable of yielding abundant harvests, farming was back-breaking work. Farmers used crude wooden plows drawn by teams of oxen to till the soil or did it by hand with a hoe. Harvesting was a grueling task performed by hand with sickle or scythe.

Pennsylvania farms were the pride of the Middle Colonies. On the rich farmlands of the Delaware River Valley, German farmers turned agriculture into a thriving commercial enterprise. These farms produced such large surpluses of wheat, rye, and corn that they were able to feed not only their own people but many people in New England and the Southern Colonies as well. They even shipped some of their products to Europe.

New York's soil was as rich as that of Pennsylvania, but its farms produced considerably less because of the colony's system of landholding. The original Dutch settlers of the area had established an agricultural system based on feudal-style manors.

Some of these manors consisted of hundreds of thousands of acres. Each was owned by one man, called a *patroon*. The patroon divided the lands among tenant farmers who worked their farms but could never own them outright. Furthermore, each year they had to pay the patroon rent and taxes as well as spend time farming his lands.

Few European settlers were willing to put up with such oppressive conditions when they could obtain their own farms in other colonies. Thus, New York's rate of immigration and, consequently, its agricultural productivity, lagged behind that of the other colonies.

Blacks in the North

Although slavery existed legally in the Middle Colonies and in New England, there were far fewer slaves in those colonies than in the South. Farms were smaller and required much less labor. Thus, most northern slaves worked as household servants, and a few worked at skilled and unskilled trades in the towns.

One observer even complained that there was much too much social equality between slaves and their masters in the North. A French traveler remarked that slaves in Pennsylvania "were regarded as being part of the family. They are assiduously cared for when they are sick. They are well fed and clothed."

Free blacks lived primarily in the Middle Colonies and New England; however, their freedom was not complete. Most of the colonies passed laws restricting their activities. In some places, laws limited the number of free black residents. In others, free blacks were allowed to work only at certain occupations. Many free blacks joined the movement to the frontier, where they found more equality and freedom than elsewhere in colonial America.

The Backcountry Frontier

The population of the Middle Colonies grew rapidly and soon expanded westward beyond the established areas of settlement into the backcountry. Pioneers moved beyond the *fall line*, the area in which inland rivers begin dropping toward sea level, and carved farms out of the wilderness.

Expansion continued westward through Pennsylvania to the Appalachian Mountains. The settlers then turned south, following a wide Indian trail that became known as the Great Wagon Road.

In the backcountry nearly all farming was on a subsistence level. Farmers planted crops in small patches between the stumps of newly felled trees rather than on broad, well-plowed fields. When the fertility of one patch was exhausted, the farmers simply cleared another. They supplemented the meager harvests with wild game and plants from surrounding forests.

Separated from the coastal settlements, the people of the backcountry frontier developed a unique way of life. The settlers could often live as they saw fit. They paid no taxes, were subject to few laws, and seldom mixed with others.

Under such conditions, family members depended heavily on one another for basic survival. Although the men generally did

■ Before 1700 settlements clustered along the Atlantic coastline and inland rivers. By 1770 the colonies had spread to the Appalachians and beyond.

Colonial Settlement 1650–1770

ME. (part of Mass.)
Montreal
Falmouth
N.H.
Oswego
Salem
Boston
Ft. Niagara
MASS.
R.I.
N.Y.
Newport
CONN.
Hartford
Ft. Detroit
New Haven
PA.
N.J. New York
Pittsburgh
Philadelphia
Ft. Cumberland
Baltimore
Alexandria
DEL.
VA.
MD.
Richmond
Norfolk
Ft. Chiswell
APPALACHIAN MTS.
N.C.
Charlotte
S.C.
Wilmington
Augusta
Charleston
GA.
Savannah
ATLANTIC OCEAN
L. Michigan
L. Huron
L. Ontario
L. Erie
Ohio R.

Settled before 1650

Settled between 1650 and 1700

Settled between 1700 and 1770

0   200 Miles
0   300 Kilometers

most of the hunting, trapping, and farming, the women were proficient in frontier skills, too. Philip Ludwell, one of the first colonists to leave a full record of rural life, had great admiration for the frontier woman in 1710.

> She is a very civil woman and shews nothing of ruggedness or Immodesty in her carriage, yett she will carry a gunn in the woods and kill deer, turkeys &c., shoot down wild cattle, catch and tye hoggs, knock down beeves [domestic cattle] with an ax, and perform the most manfull Exercises as well as most men in those parts.

Politically, the backcountry settlers were among the most independent in the colonies. They deeply resented the colonial governments, which seemed to be dominated by easterners who ignored their interests. Frustrated by their lack of political influence, these pioneers occasionally resorted to violent revolt.

In 1763, for example, a band of Pennsylvania frontiersmen known as the Paxton boys took matters into their own hands after the colonial government refused to provide protection against Indians who were at war with the settlers. But the Paxton boys ended up destroying a peaceful Indian village instead of fighting the Indians who were actually at war. The woodsmen then stormed off to Philadelphia demanding further protection. They intended to attack the city, but a delegation of city leaders talked them out of it.

In time, conditions in the backcountry improved. Social conditions came more and more to resemble those in the coastal regions. As the pioneers became more prosperous, neat farmhouses replaced rough log cabins. Yet the pioneers did not give up their independence. They continued their tradition of self-sufficiency and repeatedly demonstrated their willingness to take matters into their own hands if necessary.

SECTION REVIEW

1. Identify: Scotch–Irish, Pennsylvania Dutch, Paxton boys.
2. Define: patroon, fall line.
3. (a) What were the two largest groups of non-English settlers in the Middle Colonies? (b) Why did each choose to come to America?

4. (a) Which colony had the most productive farms? (b) Which colony had the least productive farms? Why?

5. (a) In what areas did most free blacks live? (b) Did they have the same freedom as whites? Explain.

6. (a) What was the backcountry? (b) How did settlers make a living there?

7. Critical Thinking Why did a tradition of self-sufficiency and independence develop in the backcountry?

3 The Southern Colonies

Perhaps more than any other area, the South was a region of sharp contrasts. Geographically, it had three distinct areas: the mountainous highlands that formed the western boundary; the rolling hills of the *piedmont region;* and the *tidewater region,* a flat coastal plain with land so low in places that the rivers crossing it flowed backwards with the incoming tides.

The people and ways of life in the South contrasted almost as sharply as its geographical features. While mostly English settlers inhabited the coastal plain, many Germans and Scotch-Irish, a few English, and some French Protestants settled the interior.

Small Farmers of the Southern Backcountry

In many ways the southern backcountry was an extension of the backcountry of the Middle Colonies, and the farmers who settled there had similar problems. In spite of the rich soil, dense forest that had to be cleared by hand made farming a demanding task.

As a result, the farms tended to be small, and families usually lived at a subsistence level. Farmers produced what they needed to live on, with just enough left to trade at the local market for tools and other necessities.

Many farmers, chronically in debt, bitterly resented the wealthy landowners along the coast. As it did in the Middle Colonies, such resentment occasionally erupted into violence. For example, in 1771 a Carolina group calling themselves the Regulators revolted against taxes and their general lack of representation in the colonial legislature. The revolt was put down, but bitterness only increased.

Growth of the Plantation System

The wealthy, aristocratic landowners, who were the objects of backcountry anger, controlled the colonial governments of the South. These powerful magnates, or *planters,* owned the huge plantations that became the region's distinctive type of farm.

The roots of the plantation system went all the way back to the Virginia tobacco boom of the early 1600s. When settlers discovered that tobacco cultivation was most profitable if done on a large scale, they planted huge tracts of land. To tend the crop, planters employed work crews of up to thirty people each.

As the market for tobacco grew, the plantations multiplied. Eventually, planters experimented with other *cash crops,* those grown to be sold at a profit. Along the coasts of Georgia and South Carolina, for example, rice was cultivated.

In the 1740s a woman named Eliza Lucas Pinckney successfully grew *indigo,* a West Indian plant used to make dye. Planters soon began to cultivate this valuable crop. Southerners also started growing some cotton in the eighteenth century. These cash crops produced the largest profit when grown on large plantations.

Life on the Plantation

Plantations usually developed into self-sufficient communities as a result of their large size. Along with one or more cash crops, indentured servants or slaves grew food for all residents of the plantation. Skilled artisans also produced many of the tools and other necessities for the plantation.

Plantation families in Virginia considered dancing an important social grace, as this painting shows.

Life for the planter family centered around the great house, or mansion. Besides gracious and elegant quarters for the family, the mansion usually contained numerous guest rooms, a wine cellar, a large dining room, a variety of parlors, and often a library and music room. Such rooms played an important part in the plantation's social life of elaborate parties and extended formal visits from neighbors and relatives.

Other buildings found on the plantation contributed to its self-sufficiency. These might include a coach house, stables, a dairy, a bakehouse, and a schoolhouse, which often provided quarters for a teacher. A separate workhouse might contain a blacksmith's shop, brickworks, or smokehouses.

The landowner presided over the many plantation activities. He decided what lands would be planted each season and what crops would be grown. He arranged for the shipment and sale of harvested crops, and he purchased items not manufactured on the plantation. Together with his wife, the planter supervised the servants, clerks, overseers, skilled artisans, and slaves.

Although women's legal rights to land ownership were limited, the planter's wife, who was called the plantation mistress, often played a key role on the estate. She organized household activities and supervised the people who worked in the house.

Some women also assumed more direct control of the operations of the plantation.

Eliza Lucas Pinckney, for example, managed both her father's and her husband's plantations in South Carolina when the men were away on business.

Indentured Servants

Because cash crops such as tobacco, rice, indigo, and cotton had to be cultivated on a large scale to be profitable, a plantation's prosperity depended on a correspondingly large supply of labor. At first, such labor was supplied by men, women, and children who came to the colonies as *indentured servants.** Indentured servants agreed to work for a specified period of time in return for the cost of their passage to America. The period of service varied from place to place, ranging from four to seven years. When the term of service was completed, the workers received "freedom dues": clothing, tools, a rifle, and occasionally a parcel of land.

Most of the servants came to the colonies willingly, even eagerly. However, some did not. Throughout the colonial period, the English government sent shiploads of convicts and prisoners of war to the colonies. Orphans, vagrants, poor people, and those considered a nuisance to society were also shipped to America as servants. In some cases, the English government used this method to exile political troublemakers.

Although the life of the indentured servant was hard, the system had its advantages. It often gave men and women the chance to learn a trade or get an education. Indentured servitude also provided an opportunity, not otherwise available, for a poor person to eventually acquire land and become independent.

In the South, however, the planters had claimed most of the good land along the coast. Thus, when an indentured servant became free, the only available land lay in the backcountry. Like other backcountry farmers, the former indentured servants resented the wealth and political power of the planters.

In 1676, the friction between backcountry farmers and coastal planters ex-

*The term "indentured" came to be used because the papers that recorded the agreement were cut or torn with an indentured, or indented, edge so that the two copies, one going to the servant and one to the master, would correspond.

ploded in open warfare. A group of farmers from Virginia felt that the colonial government controlled by planters had not adequately protected them from local Indians, so they marched on the capital. Led by Nathaniel Bacon, a wealthy landowner who sympathized with their cause, the rebels burned the capital at Jamestown and attempted to redistribute large tracts of land. In the middle of the revolt, Bacon died. The uprising, known as Bacon's Rebellion, fell apart, and the governor hanged its leaders, but the friction between planter and farmer remained.

The Growth of Slavery

As plantations expanded, planters found it increasingly difficult to meet their labor needs with indentured servants. The supply of servants rarely met the planters' demand for them. Furthermore, every few years a new group of workers had to be taught the skills needed to run the estate efficiently. And, last but not least, the presence of embittered former servants in the backcountry constantly posed the threat of another Bacon's Rebellion.

Under these conditions, the demand for slave labor grew. As you read in Chapter 3, the first Africans arrived in Jamestown in 1619. Some were probably bought by the local planters as indentured servants, not as slaves. And like white servants, they were freed when their term of servitude had ended.

Gradually, however, temporary servitude became permanent bondage for blacks. There were several reasons for this change. First, slaves provided a constant supply of workers. Moreover, the owner had complete control over this labor force. Because of their color, black slaves found it nearly impossible to run away and blend into the free population.

Slaves did not pose the same social problems as indentured servants because they could never rise out of their bondage and compete with their former masters for wealth and power. The cost of buying a slave was higher than that of purchasing a servant's contract. In the long run, however, slaves came to be cheaper than servants. Servants worked for a limited term, but a slave's bondage to the master was lifelong.

The English government responded quickly to the colonial planters' demand for more slaves. In 1672 it established the Royal African Company to carry on the slave trade. Soon, slave trading developed into a profitable colonial business. Colonists continued to import black Africans as slaves throughout the seventeenth and eighteenth centuries.

The Life of a Slave

The life of bondage for an African slave began on the notorious "middle passage" from Africa to America. On the slave ships, men, women, and children were crammed below deck in spaces sometimes less than five feet high. One observer said they were packed together "like books upon a shelf . . . so close that the shelf would not easily contain one more."

For most of the trip they were chained to each other, making it difficult for one to turn or move without hurting another. In rough seas, the confinement was torturing. With air holes closed off, the heat below deck became so intense as to be intolerable. At such times, large numbers of the slaves would die. Others would contract debilitating, if not fatal, diseases.

Most new slaves worked in the fields, where they performed the tiring, repetitious tasks involved in cultivating tobacco, rice, indigo, and cotton. Some were trained as skilled artisans, becoming carpenters, blacksmiths, sailors, barrelmakers, and millers. A few slaves worked in the great house as cooks, maids, butlers, and nursemaids.

Few slave owners were purposefully brutal to their slaves. But even with the most humane treatment, life as a slave was oppressive and dehumanizing. This was especially true for Africans, who found themselves taken out of their familiar surroundings, deprived of their freedom, subjected to a horrifying trip, and thrust into a totally foreign environment.

All slaves, whether originally from Africa or born in the colonies, had no legal rights, since to most colonists they were merely property—no different from a horse or a plow. An owner had immense power over the lives of his slaves. He could break up a family, selling the members to other planters, or he could force slaves to perform life-endangering work.

As the number of slaves in the South grew, colonial assemblies passed laws to regulate relations between slaves and their owners. Eventually each colony had its own *slave code*. Regulations differed from place to place, but their purpose and effect were the same: to control slaves and prevent uprisings.

Slave codes typically prohibited slaves from leaving a plantation without written permission. A slave accused of a crime could be arrested, tried, and condemned on the testimony of only one witness. While slaves could testify against each other, they could not bear witness against whites. A slave who killed his or her owner—even if the owner had a reputation for exceptional brutality—was hanged, beheaded, or drawn and quartered. But the killing of a slave by a white person was not always a punishable offense.

Resistance to Slavery

The slave codes limited open resistance to slavery by slaves themselves. Running away was seldom successful, since there was nowhere to run, and organized rebellion was rare.

■ Between what years was the growth of slavery most dramatic?

Slave Population in the Colonies 1650–1770

YEAR	North	South	Total
1650	880	720	1,600
1660	1,162	1,758	2,920
1670	1,125	3,410	4,535
1680	1,895	5,076	6,971
1690	3,340	13,389	16,729
1700	5,206	22,611	27,817
1710	8,303	36,563	44,866
1720	14,091	54,748	68,839
1730	17,323	73,698	91,021
1740	23,958	126,066	150,024
1750	30,222	206,198	236,420
1760	40,033	285,773	325,806
1770	48,460	411,362	459,822

Source: *Historical Statistics of the United States*

Millions of Africans were shipped unwillingly to the Americas in slave ships. The diagram shows the "loading plan" for jamming as many chained people into the smallest space possible. The painting, by a British naval officer, is the only surviving sketch from life of the inhuman conditions aboard slave ships.

Some slaves, however, outwardly accepted their status while looking for ways to undermine the system. This might include purposefully working slowly to spite the planter or secretly damaging tools. For some slaves, trying to keep elements of their African cultures, such as names, songs, and religious traditions, and passing them on to their children made life more bearable.

While the vast majority of white colonists accepted slavery, a few protested. Quakers were well known for their opposition to slavery, but others also objected. Samuel Sewall, a New England merchant, commented on the "horrible ... Uncleanness, Mortality, if not Murder, that the Ships are guilty of that bring great crowds of these miserable Men and women."

As a result of protests, some people freed their slaves, and the law provided that their free status be passed on to their descendants. On the whole, however, the infrequent antislavery protests had little effect.

SECTION REVIEW

1. Identify: Regulators, Eliza Lucas Pinckney, Nathaniel Bacon, Royal African Company, "middle passage."

2. Define: piedmont region, tidewater region, planter, cash crop, indigo, indentured servant, slave codes.

3. What problems were faced by farmers in the southern backcountry?

4. What was the advantage of growing crops such as indigo and rice on a large plantation?

5. What did indentured servants hope to gain by coming to America?

6. List three conditions that created a growing demand for slave labor.

7. **Critical Thinking** Why do you think antislavery protests had little effect on the development of slavery?

4 Colonial Culture

With the exception of African slaves, the colonists who first settled on the Atlantic coast of North America were European. They came to America with European ideas, customs, beliefs, and values. During their first grueling and often frightening years in America, they clung firmly to their European ways. To make themselves feel at home in their New World, nearly all the colonists tried to recreate the life they had known in the Old World.

Though the colonists were Europeans, the land in which they settled was not Europe. It was a completely new environment, offering different challenges and opportunities. Gradually, the settlers began to adapt their European ways to their new situation.

By the middle of the eighteenth century, the colonists were developing a distinctively American culture.

Religious Tolerance

The religious denominations of the colonies originated in Europe, but the resemblance ended there. Each European nation had an official, state-supported church to which responsible citizens were expected to belong. Other churches, if not officially outlawed, were nonetheless considered undesirable, and their members often suffered discrimination. Thus toleration of religious diversity in Europe was the exception, not the rule.

★ American Profiles ★

Benjamin Franklin: A Pioneer in Medicine

Medicine in colonial America was a far cry from medicine today. Few doctors had formal training. Some served as apprentices under an established doctor, but many just declared themselves able to practice "physick."

Among Benjamin Franklin's many pursuits was a lifelong interest in medicine and health. Unlike most doctors then, Franklin insisted on observing actual results. And he did not mind admitting when experiments proved one of his theories unsound. For example, he tried applying electricity to stiff or paralyzed joints. When he found little or no improvement, he stopped the treatment.

Franklin also practiced what we call preventive medicine today. When he was only sixteen, he convinced his fellow printing apprentices that they should not drink beer with breakfast.

In an age when the idea of personal cleanliness did not even occur to most people, Franklin urged regular nude bathing in a tub of water. The idea shocked many. He designed and built his own copper bathtub, including a special rack on which he could rest a book and thus read while bathing.

In *Poor Richard's Almanac* he counseled moderation: "He that drinks fast pays slow," and "Early to bed and early to rise makes a man healthy, wealthy, and wise." He championed exercise, especially swimming, for health and also inoculation against smallpox.

Franklin maintained his health practices throughout his long life. But when he fell ill at age 84, he recognized the seriousness of his condition. His daughter, sitting by his bed, wished him many more years of life. "I hope not," commented Franklin. As usual, he was right.

No single church dominated all the colonies. The Puritans' Congregational church was the official, or *established*, church in New England. The Church of England, or the Anglican church, was the established church in Virginia, Maryland, New York, the Carolinas, and Georgia. Regardless of their personal beliefs, citizens paid taxes to support the established church in their colony.

Furthermore, many colonies originated as havens for religious dissenters who resisted any attempt by either the Anglicans or the Puritans to impose their beliefs on the community. Massachusetts, which had managed for so many years to smother dissent within its borders, eventually granted religious freedoms. In 1691 a new charter specified that all religious groups in the colony were free to worship.

Although Protestant denominations gradually extended toleration to each other, they tended to discriminate against Roman Catholics. Even Maryland, which had been founded as a refuge for English Catholics, persecuted them. Laws passed there at the end of the seventeenth century deprived Catholics of political rights and forbade them to hold religious services anywhere but in the privacy of their homes.

Jewish settlers also suffered discrimination, although less than they had in Europe. Most colonies, for example, did not allow Jews to vote.

Still, when compared to Europe at the time, the American colonies practiced a relatively high degree of religious tolerance. This toleration developed mainly out of necessity. With so many different denominations coexisting in the communities, mutual toleration seemed to be the easiest way to get along.

The Importance of Education

Education was often closely connected with religion in colonial America, especially in New England. The early Puritan colonists had emphasized the importance of schooling. They believed that everyone should have access to the "divine truth" found in the Bible. Thus everyone should know how to read. To achieve this goal, the Puritans created a *primer*, an illustrated textbook that taught children how to read and spell while they memorized the tenets of the Puritan faith.

In 1647 Massachusetts passed the earliest public school law in America. It

Few black men and women were able to get a formal education in colonial America, but some managed to do so. Phillis Wheatley was brought from Africa as a slave at age eight. She taught herself English and Latin and began writing poetry, which was widely admired.

stipulated that towns of 50 or more families should maintain a grammar school to prepare young men for college by instructing them in Latin and other classical subjects. Other New England colonies passed similar laws.

Although the Middle Colonies had no tax-supported schools, religious groups founded schools for poor children. Some private schools, mainly for boys, also existed for those who could afford them. In the Southern Colonies tutors who lived with the planters' families customarily taught their children. Others had little access to education.

Although most colonial education was limited to boys, women frequently held classes in their homes for girls and the younger children. At these so-called *"dame schools,"* pupils learned reading and writing, as well as skills like sewing and embroidery. In some colonial cities, artisans also set up evening schools for their workers.

As a result of such efforts, the *literacy rate*, or the proportion of people who could read and write, in the colonies was relatively high, especially in towns and in New England in general. In frontier areas fewer

The Arts in the Colonies: A Practical Approach

In Europe only the wealthy had much chance to enjoy art, music, and literature. Greater opportunity existed in colonial America. However, there the arts were practical and reflected peoples' concerns with day-to-day living.

For example, women made quilts and embroidered or printed designs on the fabric. Colonial artists painted glassware or china. The Pennsylvania Dutch region was especially well known for its stenciled designs.

Stonecarvers and blacksmiths decorated gravestones and weathervanes. Smiths made lanterns and candleholders from tin, pewter, silver, or brass. Silversmiths created tea- and coffeepots, tankards, and serving trays. Paul Revere designed a bowl whose pattern still bears his name.

Furniture was usually made from local woods. Oak and pine were popular when most furniture had bare wood surfaces. These pieces were durable but uncomfortable. Later those who could afford them demanded mahogany or other costly woods. Upholstered furniture became more common. Vegetable dyes colored wood and fabric.

Colonial architecture began to develop around the end of the 1600s. Northerners built wooden houses from local timber. They could get brick, but the lime used to make mortar was in short supply. Brickwork had to be reserved for large fireplaces, used for cooking as well as heating. Glass prices were high, so windows were small. Southerners, on the other hand, used more brick and stone, since clay and lime were not as scarce in their region. Plantation owners sometimes copied grand English manor houses.

Literature followed practical lines too. People read mostly history, diaries, political essays, and sermons. Poetry also had a place. Anne Bradstreet, one of the earliest colonial poets, wrote when she came to New England, "I found a new world and new manners, at which my heart rose."

people could read. People who could not write signed legal documents with an *X*.

Soon after their arrival in the New World, colonists had also turned their attention to higher education for young men, primarily to educate ministers and preachers. Settlers in Massachusetts established the first colonial college in 1636, naming it Harvard after a wealthy colonist who donated land and money to build it. The College of William and Mary was founded in Virginia in 1693, and in 1701 a group of Congregationalists founded Yale.

Boys as young as fourteen could enter college by passing an entrance exam in Greek and Latin. Once there, they studied more Greek and Latin, as well as logic, Hebrew, rhetoric, mathematics, geography, theology, and philosophy. Small amounts of history and botany rounded out the college curriculum.

Cities: Centers of Culture

Although the towns and cities of mid-eighteenth-century America contained less than 10 percent of ·the population, they significantly influenced colonial life. Through the great ports of Philadelphia, New York, Boston, and Charleston, merchants shipped the products of America to England and the West Indies. Towns and cities also served as the focus of a busy trade between the coast and the rapidly growing backcountry.

Cities were the exchange points not only for goods but also for ideas. In Boston, colonists founded the first regular weekly

SKILL LESSON

The Growth of Colonial Cities: Reading Graphs

Graphs are one way to present information visually and to condense a large amount of data. Graphs allow you to see the relationship between two or more sets of data. A line or bar graph can show changes over time. A circle graph points up the relationship of various parts to a whole.

The steps outlined below will help you learn how to read a graph.

1. **Identify the type of information presented on the graph.** Ask yourself: (a) What is the title of the graph? (b) What do the numbers on the vertical axis represent? (c) What do the numbers on the horizontal axis represent? (d) What items are included in the legend, or key? (e) Describe the type of information shown on the graph.

2. **Practice reading the data shown on the graph.** Use the following questions to practice reading the line graph at right: (a) What was the population of New York in 1690? (b) What was the population of Charleston in 1720? (c) In what decade did the population of Boston decline? (d) How much did the population of Philadelphia grow between 1710 and 1720?

3. **Look for relationships among the data presented.** (a) Which city had the largest population in 1690? (b) Which city grew most rapidly between 1700 and 1710? (c) How many more people lived in Boston than in Philadelphia in 1720? (d) Which city grew the least between 1690 and 1700?

4. **Use the graph to draw conclusions about a topic.** Use the line graph and this chapter to answer these questions: (a)

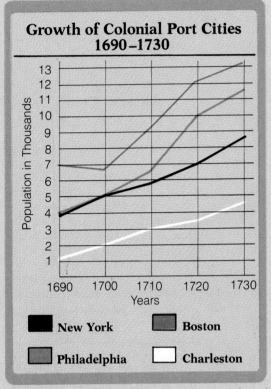

Growth of Colonial Port Cities 1690–1730

The figures above are estimates, except the New York population for 1730, which is from an actual census.

What statement can you make about the population of all four cities between 1690 and 1730? (b) Why do you think port cities were the largest cities in the 1700s? (c) What factors probably contributed to Boston's being the largest port city during this period? (d) Which products were probably shipped out of New York and Philadelphia? Which products were probably shipped out of Charleston?

newspaper in the colonies in 1704. Fifty years later, each of the 13 colonies except New Jersey and Delaware had at least one weekly paper.

The growth of colonial newspapers led to a dispute over freedom of the press. In 1734 John Peter Zenger, publisher of the *Weekly Journal* in New York City, was arrested for libel.* Zenger, who often criticized government officials in his paper, had attacked the governor of New York. Zenger's lawyer argued that his client had not libeled the governor because what he printed had

---

*libel: the act of publishing a statement that unjustly damages a person's reputation.

Major Events	
1636	Harvard founded as first institution of higher learning
1647	First public school law passed in colonies
1676	Bacon's rebellion
1734	John Peter Zenger arrested
1763	Paxton boys revolt

vals, and horse races. Here and there public libraries were established, stocked with books imported from abroad or printed on new colonial presses.

The lives of city dwellers were not typical of most colonists. But the cities served as a focal point for new products and ideas that eventually spread throughout the colonies.

SECTION REVIEW

1. Define: established church, primer, dame school, literacy rate.
2. (a) How did having many religions in the colonies make for religious toleration? (b) Which religions were often not tolerated?
3. (a) Which colony passed the first public school law? (b) Why did the Puritans think that education was important?
4. Compare the education offered to boys with that offered to girls in the colonies.
5. How did cities contribute to the development of colonial culture?
6. **Critical Thinking** Why do you think religion was such an important part of colonial life?

been the truth. The court agreed and freed Zenger.

At the time this seemed like a revolutionary idea, since criticism of the government was generally considered a crime. The principle of freedom of the press was upheld in this case, but years would pass before it was firmly established in America.

Culture also flourished in the cities. By the middle of the eighteenth century, all the major colonial cities had their own theaters. City dwellers also found entertainment at singing societies, traveling circuses, carni-

 ★ ★ ★

Chapter 4 Review

 ★ ★ ★

In Perspective

By the 1700s most of the American colonies had become royal colonies with representative governments. Yet the colonists' way of life differed in the various colonies. In New England a profitable shipping and fishing industry became the mainstay of a thriving economy.

A diverse group of settlers made their homes on the fertile farmland of the Middle Colonies. Agriculture was also the basis of the southern economy, but there the plantation system flourished. Wealthy planters grew cash crops that required a large amount of land and labor. Increasingly, they came to rely on slaves rather than on indentured servants. In the Middle and Southern colonies a different way of life emerged in the backcountry. Socially and politically iso-

lated, the pioneers resented the farmers and planters of the coastal regions.

By 1750, however, the colonists differed more from Europeans than they did from each other. Religious toleration and education were more prevalent in the colonies. In the growing colonial cities, people were able to exchange news and ideas. These shared ideas and values provided the basis for greater unity, as you will read in later chapters.

Vocabulary

On a separate sheet of paper, write the word or words that best complete each of the following sentences.

1. A farm family that had the resources to get along without outside help was ___.

2. In New York, feudal-style manors were owned by ____.

3. ____ were crops grown to be sold at a profit.

4. ____ were laws passed to regulate the relations between slave owners and slaves.

5. The official, or ____, church was supported by tax money.

6. A (An) ____ was a textbook that taught children how to read and spell while they learned the tenets of Puritanism.

Chapter Checkup

1. (a) What was the basis of the economy in New England? (b) What was the basis of the economy in the Middle Colonies? (c) What was the basis of the economy in the Southern Colonies? (d) What factors help account for the different patterns?

2. (a) Describe the social class system in New England. (b) Why did it gradually become less rigid?

3. (a) How did life in the backcountry differ from life along the coast? (b) How can you explain this difference?

4. (a) Why did slavery replace the use of indentured servants on southern plantations? (b) Why did planters come to prefer buying slaves to employing indentured servants?

5. Why were there fewer slaves in the Middle Colonies and New England than in the South?

6. (a) What conditions led to greater religious tolerance in the colonies than in Europe? (b) Were all groups tolerated? Explain.

Critical Thinking

1. **Analyzing** (a) Why was slavery a dehumanizing experience regardless of how a slave was treated? (b) How did slaves try to keep their humanity?

2. **Comparing** (a) How did the position of an indentured servant differ from that of a slave? (b) Why do you think a person would decide to become an indentured servant?

3. **Comparing** (a) How did education for boys differ from education for girls? (b) Why do you think there was a difference?

73

Developing Basic Skills

1. **Ranking** Rank the social systems of each of the following regions from the most rigid to the least rigid: New England towns, Middle Colonies coastal area, Middle Colonies backcountry, Southern Colonies backcountry, Southern Colonies coastal area. (a) Why did you rank them in the order you did? (b) Which areas of the colonies probably had the most rigid class system? (c) How would you account for the different patterns?

2. **Graph Reading** Use the steps you learned on page 71 to read the circle graph on page 60. Study the graph and answer the following questions: (a) What information is shown on this graph? (b) Which were the three largest and three smallest ethnic groups? (c) Based on the graph, what general statements would you make about the ethnic composition of the American colonies?

See page 827 for suggested readings.

Writer's Handbook

Writing a Generalization

As you have learned, sometimes it is possible to rewrite an essay question to form a topic sentence for the answer. When it is not possible to rewrite the question, think about what the information has in common and form a generalization. Your topic sentence would then be that generalization. You will use the information you have to support the generalization in your answer.

Consider this question: *What roles did women play in each of the following areas: New England farms, New England cities, backcountry farms, southern plantations?* One generalization you could make based on the information in the text would be, "Women played important, but varying, roles depending on where they lived in the colonies." You could then complete the paragraph with specific examples.

Practice: Write an appropriate topic sentence for each Critical Thinking question.

5

A Struggle for Empire

(1600–1763)

Battle of Louisbourg

Chapter Outline

1 *The American Colonies: A Vital Part of the British Empire*

2 *Rivalry in North America*

3 *The French and Indian War*

By the first decades of the 1700s, Europeans had made their presence felt not only in the Americas but also around the world. European merchants were trading with Asian nations, as they had dreamed since the 1400s. Missionaries, fur traders, and settlers often followed.

Having discovered the world beyond their doorsteps, the nations of Europe were soon embroiled in a struggle to control it and to obtain a lion's share of its riches. Chief among the competitors for power, wealth, and land were Great Britain, France, and Spain.

Although originally valued far below the fabled lands of Asia, by the 1700s America came to occupy an important position in European imperial designs. As you will read in this chapter, the three European powers claimed large parts of North America in spite of the Native Americans already living there. As American colonies became more important to the British Empire, conflict between the British, French, and Spanish became more likely.

New France expands

1600	1625	1650	1675	1700	1725	1750	1775

| **1602** Vizcaino explores California | **1660** First Navigation Act passed | **1673** Joliet and Marquette explore the Mississippi | **1690s** Spanish missions set up in Arizona, California | **1733** Molasses Act passed | **1754** Albany Congress | **1754–63** French and Indian War |

1 The American Colonies: A Vital Part of the British Empire

The rivalry among European nations involved more than the struggle for political control of far-flung parts of the world. During the late 1600s and the 1700s, commerce also became an arena of fierce, sometimes violent, competition. Colonies became increasingly important in this competition, especially for the British Empire.*

Mercantilism

Behind this fierce rivalry lay an economic theory that has come to be called *mercantilism*, from the word merchant. Under the mercantilist system, each nation attempted to sell more than it bought. In this way, it would preserve or even increase its precious and limited supply of gold. Furthermore, a nation that did not rely on other nations for necessary goods would be less vulnerable in time of war.

A nation could achieve economic independence in several ways. One of the best ways was to have overseas colonies and trading posts. These would increase a nation's self-sufficiency by providing essential raw materials such as precious metals, lumber, agricultural products, cotton, and wool that would otherwise have to be bought from rival nations.

Colonies played a second vital role in the mercantilist system, since they served as markets for goods produced at home. Without colonies, a nation could manufacture only what it could reasonably expect to sell at home and to a few foreign customers. Unsold goods would have to be counted as a loss. With colonial outlets, however, surplus goods could be exported, and manufacturers would have fewer losses and greater profits.

Early in the age of exploration, Sir Walter Raleigh had foreseen the value of mercantilism to a nation. "Whoever commands the trade of the world," he said, "commands the riches of the world and consequently the

Ships like the ones in this 1760 painting of New York Harbor carried valuable cargo between England and the colonies.

world itself." In the late seventeenth century, the crown began to act on Raleigh's advice.

First, as you learned in the preceding chapter, the crown tightened its political control over the colonies. Next, it strengthened its hold on colonial trade. Charles II worked with his ministers to design a strong mercantilist colonial policy that would allow the empire to "command the riches of the world" and then "the world itself."

Regulating Trade

Before the mid-1600s colonial merchants had enjoyed a measure of economic independence. England provided a profitable market for many of their goods. What they could not sell profitably there they traded in the English, French, Dutch, and Spanish islands of the Caribbean, often for an even larger profit.

From the king's point of view, such practices were dangerous. By trading with other nations and their colonies, a colonial merchant deprived the crown of valuable revenues. If such activities occurred on a large scale, England's mercantilist economy, and its status as a world power, would be threatened.

---

*One part of England's transformation into a world power was the unification of England and Scotland into the nation of Great Britain in 1707. After that date, "Great Britain" and "British" were the official terms used to describe the new nation and its residents. Throughout the 1700s, however, these new terms were used interchangeably with "England" and "English."

Unless the American colonies were forced to play their appointed role in the mercantilist system, England's chances of commanding "the world itself" were slim. In 1660 and 1663, therefore, Parliament passed a series of trade regulations called the Navigation Acts. Their purpose was to make sure the colonies traded with England and only with England.

First, colonial merchants were allowed to ship goods only on colonial or English-owned vessels. Three quarters of the crew of such a vessel had to consist of colonial or English sailors.

This regulation was aimed primarily at the Netherlands, England's chief commercial competitor. The Dutch possessed the world's largest merchant fleet, and their ships regularly transported products to and from the English colonies. Every Dutch ship trading with the colonies meant profits for the Dutch and losses for the crown. By prohibiting colonists from using foreign ships, Charles II intended to stop this drain on his nation's economy.

Next, Parliament drew up a list of colonial products, called *enumerated commodities,* that could be shipped only to England. Enumerated articles included sugar, cotton, indigo, ginger, tobacco, and woods used for dye. In later years, the list of enumerated goods was expanded to include other items, such as rice, furs, and naval supplies.

The Navigation Acts also prohibited the colonies from importing products from other European nations unless those products were sent first to England and shipped from there to the colonies. The only exceptions to this rule were slaves, wines, horses, and salt.

This provision guaranteed the crown income from taxes on all products going to and from the colonies, even if the products had been manufactured elsewhere. The taxes imposed on European products would also raise their prices in the colonies. Thus, English industries would be protected from cheap competition. Furthermore, jobs would be created in England to process imports and exports.

Impact on England and the Colonies

For the most part, the trade laws worked, and the mercantile system benefited both England and the colonies. American merchants benefited from laws that excluded foreigners from colonial trade. To compensate the colonists for any profits that might be lost, the crown granted them bonuses for producing certain essential goods. Furthermore, colonial traders welcomed the protection from French and Spanish competitors provided by British forces.

Although most colonists took the trade laws in stride, resistance to the regulations did exist. Some merchants resented the law

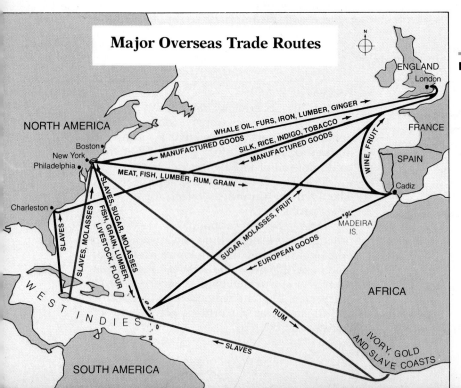

Major Overseas Trade Routes

NORTH AMERICA

Boston
New York
Philadelphia

Charleston

WHALE OIL, FURS, IRON, LUMBER, GINGER
MANUFACTURED GOODS
SILK, RICE, INDIGO, TOBACCO
MANUFACTURED GOODS
MEAT, FISH, LUMBER, RUM, GRAIN
SLAVES, MOLASSES
FISH, GRAIN, LUMBER, LIVESTOCK, FLOUR
SLAVES, SUGAR, MOLASSES
SLAVES
SUGAR, MOLASSES, FRUIT
EUROPEAN GOODS
RUM
SLAVES

WEST INDIES

SOUTH AMERICA

ENGLAND
London

FRANCE

SPAIN

Cadiz

WINE, FRUIT

MADEIRA IS.

AFRICA

IVORY, GOLD AND SLAVE COASTS

■ Overseas trade was an important part of mercantilism. Much of the colonial trade was with England, but colonial merchants also traded with other European nations, Africa, and the West Indies. The slave trade was part of a triangular route (shown on this map in red) between the colonies, the West Indies, and the west coast of Africa.

requiring that goods they imported and exported pass through England. They claimed that it cut into their profits and consumed precious shipping time.

Others were angered by the regulation forcing them to sell enumerated articles only to England. They knew that they could get higher prices for their products in other European countries. Merchants also found that, on occasion, it was cheaper to bribe customs officials than to pay British import and export duties.

The biggest problem with the Navigation Acts arose in the eighteenth century. Increasingly, New England had come to rely on the production of rum, made from molasses, to support its trade. Merchants would ship grain, barrel staves, horses, and fish to the West Indies and bring back molasses.

New England merchants could use the profits from rum to buy English manufactured goods. Or they could ship rum to Africa, buy slaves with it, sail to the West Indies and sell the slaves for more molasses, then return home and make more rum. These patterns of exchange, outlined on the map on page 76, came to be known as the *triangular trade.*

Under the mercantilist system, colonists were supposed to import molasses only from the British West Indies. But the islands there could supply only a small amount of the molasses needed. New England merchants thus made up the difference by importing large amounts from the French, Spanish, and Dutch West Indies.

In 1733, however, the rich sugar planters of the British West Indies convinced Parliament to pass the Molasses Act. The Molasses Act required colonists to pay a stiff duty on all molasses or rum imported from the foreign West Indies. If the duty had been enforced, it would have ruined New England's economy, but New England merchants usually ignored the law or else paid customs officials a small bribe to overlook the foreign molasses. Consequently, the triangular trade routes flourished as much as ever.

By and large the mercantile system worked well—so well, in fact, that as you will read in the next section, it brought the prospering English colonies into conflict with the two rival empires, Spain and France.

SECTION REVIEW

1. Identify: Molasses Act.
2. Define: mercantilism, enumerated commodity, triangular trade.
3. How were colonies an important part of the mercantilist system?
4. Why were the Navigation Acts passed?
5. (a) Did the trade laws work? (b) In what ways could colonists benefit from them?
6. **Critical Thinking** Why do you think the trade routes between the American colonies and their trading partners developed in a triangular pattern rather than a straight line between the American colonies and Britain?

2 Rivalry in North America

England's aggressive mercantilist policies helped transform it from a tiny, self-contained nation into a major world power in less than a century. Step by step, the British strengthened their hold on lands as far from each other as India and North America.

Although British possessions in America were much smaller than those of Spain or France, the British presence grew much more rapidly. At the end of the seventeenth century, 200,000 people lived in British America. By the mid-eighteenth century, the population reached 1,500,000 and was still growing. At the same time, barely 70,000 colonists lived in New France, a territory more than twice the size of the British colonies.

As English settlements expanded, they ran the risk of encroaching on French or Spanish territory. From the start, friction seemed inevitable.

The Spanish Empire

Spain, as you will recall, had established its American colonies years before either France or England and had realized a far greater profit from them. By the eighteenth century, the Spanish empire in America included most of Central and South America, plus what is now Mexico, Florida, the southwestern United States, and California.

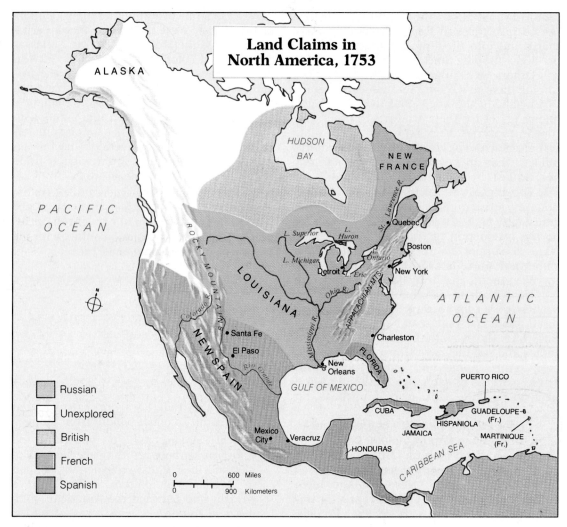

Land Claims in North America, 1753

ALASKA

HUDSON BAY

NEW FRANCE

PACIFIC OCEAN

ROCKY MOUNTAINS

Colorado R.

LOUISIANA

L. Superior

L. Huron

L. Michigan

Quebec

Boston

Detroit

Ontario

Erie

New York

St. Lawrence R.

Ohio R.

APPALACHIAN MTS.

ATLANTIC OCEAN

NEW SPAIN

Santa Fe

El Paso

Rio Grande

Mississippi R.

New Orleans

Charleston

FLORIDA

GULF OF MEXICO

PUERTO RICO

CUBA

JAMAICA

HISPANIOLA

GUADELOUPE (Fr.)

MARTINIQUE (Fr.)

Mexico City

Veracruz

HONDURAS

CARIBBEAN SEA

Russian
Unexplored
British
French
Spanish

0   600 Miles
0   900 Kilometers

■ *France, Spain, Russia, and Great Britain all claimed parts of North America. However, only the English had colonies that grew rapidly. As English colonists moved westward, conflicts with other European nations and with Native Americans increased.*

Since the defeat of the Armada in 1588, however, Spanish power had been declining, and active control of the American colonies had slackened. The amount of money invested by the home country in the New World dwindled, and fewer Spaniards were encouraged to immigrate to America. As a result, the colonies were left to develop largely on their own.

Spanish ships brought fewer soldiers, fewer missionaries, and fewer settlers. Gradually, American-born settlers began to replace Spanish immigrants in positions of authority in the colonies.

The Spanish did continue some explorations of the southwest and Pacific coast during the seventeenth and early eighteenth centuries. Sebastián Vizcaíno (VEES kah EE noh) explored the northern coast of California as early as 1602. He paved the way for later Spanish settlement of the area and gave many places their present names, including San Diego, Santa Barbara, Monterey, and Carmel.

The Spanish founded Santa Fe in present-day New Mexico in 1609, and almost fifty years later established several missions near El Paso. During the 1690s Father Eusebio Francisco Kino helped establish missions in present-day Arizona and California.

Since English settlement was confined to the east coast of North America, however,

SKILL LESSON

Rival Claims in North America: Reading Maps

Maps can provide geographic, social, political, and economic information. Knowing how to interpret the symbols on maps can help you understand American history. Most maps include a title, legend, scale, directional indicator, and topographical features. Follow the steps below, using the map on page 78 to practice using maps.

1. **Decide what is shown on the map.** The title tells you the subject of the map. The legend, or key, tells you what the colors and symbols on the map represent. Colors may be used on a political map to show the extent of political units, such as states, countries, or empires. On a physical map, color may be used to indicate elevation, climate areas, or types of vegetation. There are no standard symbols for all maps. On a thematic, or special purpose, map symbols may be used to show such information as the site of battles, a blockade, trade routes, or mineral resources. (a) What is the title of the map? (b) What is the date of the information? (c) Why is the date essential for this kind of information? (d) What countries' claims are shown on the map? (e) How is each country represented? (f) What information is shown on the map? (g) Is this map primarily a political or a physical map?

2. **Practice reading the information on the map.** The scale, directional indicator, and topographical features also help you read a map. The scale tells you the actual distances, in miles and kilometers, that are represented on the map. Direction is usually shown by an arrow or compass needle indicating which way is north. Some maps have a compass rose that shows all four directions. Topographical features are surface land characteristics such as mountains or rivers. (a) What is the distance in miles and kilometers between Quebec and Charleston? Between Quebec and New York? (b) Which country claimed the territory north and west of British territory? (c) Which mountains bordered British claims? (d) Which two major rivers were part of French territory? (e) Which nations' claims bordered on the Pacific Ocean?

3. **Use the information on the map to draw conclusions about the historical period being studied.** Note the relative size and location of the various claims. Look for a possible relationship between geographic features and political boundaries. Relate what you see on the map with what you know from your reading. (a) Which nation claimed the most territory? (b) What explorations were the basis for Spanish claims? (See Chapter 2.) (c) What explorations were the basis for the French claims? (d) How far west did British settlement extend? Why do you think it stopped there? (e) Where would conflict between the Spanish and British most likely occur? (f) Where would conflict between the French and British be most likely? (g) In 1753, which country claimed the area where you now live?

contacts between the two empires were limited to skirmishes between trading vessels at sea and to friction between Spanish Florida and its English neighbors to the north.

Settlers in Georgia accused Spain of permitting outlaws to cross the Florida border and harass them. Their anxieties were further aggravated in 1738 when the Spanish governor declared that slaves who escaped from servitude in the English colonies could live in freedom in Florida. And the British had always suspected that Spain planned to increase the size of its empire by gaining more territory in the area.

New France

Friction with Spain was an irritation, but only a minor one. France, on the other hand, posed the threat of a major conflict.

During its first years, New France grew slowly. Few French men or women wanted to leave their homeland for the dangers and uncertainties of a wilderness thousands of miles away. Those who wanted to leave, Protestants trying to escape religious persecution, were forbidden to settle in New France.

After 1661, the situation changed. Louis XIV assumed complete control of the French government and launched an ambitious program of empire building. He hoped to make New France into a market for French exports and a source of food for the French West Indies.

Without more French colonists, however, the imperial design would not work. So, for the first time, the French government took steps to encourage people to migrate to North America. It granted large tracts of the best land in New France to army officers and other gentlemen, who in turn rented parts of their land to merchants or peasants.

The land grants improved the rate of immigration to North America somewhat. But the gentlemen-landlords, unused to manual labor, made little or no effort to cultivate their land. Although some of their tenants made farming pay, most resented working land they did not own.

As a result, New France was never able to play the role Louis XIV had envisioned

The Spanish built Mexico City, the colonial capital of Mexico, on the ruins of the Aztec capital of Tenochtitlán. The detail is from a 1728 painting of Mexico City.

for it in his empire. In addition to failing to grow food for the West Indies, the colonies proved incapable of producing enough to feed their own population. The people of New France were forced to depend on the farmers of either the home country or neighboring New England for provisions.

★ American Profiles ★

Coosaponakeesa: Mary Musgrove

Coosaponakeesa, born around 1700, was the daughter of a Creek woman and an English trader. As a young child, she went with her father to South Carolina and learned to speak English.

When Coosaponakeesa was about 18 years old, she married John Musgrove, a fur trader from South Carolina. Then called Mary Musgrove, she later moved with her husband to a trading post on the Savannah River.

At this time James Oglethorpe was trying to establish the colony of Georgia. He wanted to remain friends with the Creeks, who provided trade and a vital buffer against the Spanish in Florida.

From the 1730s until her death in 1760 Mary Musgrove served Oglethorpe as a translator between the colonists and the Creeks. She promoted the trading interests of the Creeks, and she rallied the Creeks in support of Oglethorpe against the Spanish. She also managed to keep strong the English–Creek friendship when the French made efforts to woo the Creeks. By supporting British interests, she played an important part in history.

Expanding French Claims

Although farming failed, two other enterprises succeeded: exploration and fur trading.

In 1673 Louis Joliet (zhoh LYEH) and Jacques Marquette (mahr KEHT), a Jesuit priest, journeyed by canoe down the Fox, Wisconsin, and Mississippi rivers, as far south as the mouth of the Arkansas River. There they encountered Indians who told them that the Mississippi emptied into the Gulf of Mexico, not into the Gulf of California to the west or the Atlantic Ocean to the east, as previously thought. Armed with this information, the explorers decided to turn back rather than to push on to the gulf and risk capture by the Spanish who controlled the territory to the south.

In following years René-Robert Cavelier, Sieur de La Salle (suhr duh lah SAHL), continued the explorations of Marquette and Joliet. By 1682 he had reached the delta* of the Mississippi, just north of present-day New Orleans. There he claimed the surrounding area for the king, naming it Louisiana in his honor.

To consolidate their claims in the New World the French built a string of settlements, missions, forts, and trading posts. From the trading posts, *coureurs de bois* (koo RUHR duh BWAH), literally "runners of the woods," fanned out into the thick forests of New France to trade metal axes, knives, hoes, kettles, woolen blankets, textiles, and weapons to Indian hunters for the furs so valuable to French merchants. To the trading posts came fleets of canoes to take heavy loads of fur over the northern rivers to Quebec and then to Europe.

Impact of the Fur Trade on Native Americans

The fur trade, so lucrative to the French, proved disastrous to many Native American hunters of the northeast. Some tribes competed fiercely with each other for control of rich hunting grounds and for a role in the French trade.

Often, peoples were forced out of lands they had inhabited for centuries. The Iroquois, for instance, drove the Algonquins

The detail of the painting The Habitant Farm *shows the rugged life of French settlers in America. Long, harsh winters challenged the determination and survival skills of families living on the frontier.*

out of their hunting grounds, forcing them eastward to the Atlantic coast. There the displaced Algonquins vented their anger on New England villages and settlements.

As they were drawn into alliances with European powers, Native Americans also became embroiled in European efforts to dominate the North American continent. Frequently, Europeans manipulated existing rivalries between Native American groups to their advantage.

The Huron and the Iroquois, for example, were traditional rivals. The Huron, who had established friendly relations with the French, served as middlemen between other tribes and French traders. The Dutch, eager for a share of the rich fur trade, encouraged their Iroquois allies to attack the Huron. Although the Huron responded forcefully, they were no match for the more numerous and better-armed Iroquois. The Iroquois forced the surviving Hurons to flee westward toward the Mississippi.

81

---

*delta: a deposit of soil at the mouth of some rivers, usually forming a triangular shape.

The English who replaced the Dutch in present-day New York State also profited from the warfare. By pitting the Iroquois against Indian nations that were friendly with the French, they struck a blow at French power in North America. Native Americans would eventually be drawn in on both sides when war broke out between the French and the British in 1754.

The British and Native Americans

Because New France was so sparsely populated, French settlers did not encroach heavily on Indian lands. The British, in contrast, were more numerous and their numbers were growing each year. In addition, the British built permanent settlements rather than temporary trading outposts.

Furthermore, as farmers rather than fur traders, English settlers wanted as much land as possible. More often than not, this involved pushing the Native Americans out of their territory. Sometimes this was done by treaty, but often settlers simply moved into Indian lands and began clearing the forest for planting. Indian reaction to this threat produced recurring violence along the frontier.

In 1636 the Pequot (PEE kwaht) resisted English settlement in the Connecticut Valley. In the so-called Pequot War that followed, colonists attacked and burned a major Pequot town, killing 600 men, women, and children.

Almost 40 years later, in 1675, another war, known as King Philip's War, broke out between Native Americans and colonists in New England. The Indians inflicted heavy losses on the New England militia and destroyed 13 frontier towns, but the Indians were ultimately defeated. After that, settlers in New England generally met little resistance.

Some early English settlers had established harmonious relations with Native Americans. Roger Williams and William Penn, for example, were known for negotiat-

French and Indian fur traders often traveled by water through the wooded wilderness of North America. In this painting, the Indians portage, or carry, their canoes around some rapids.

ing fair treaties and paying for their land. South Carolina fur traders were as successful as the French in their dealings with the original inhabitants of the territory. But in general the competition for land between Native Americans and English settlers led to conflict.

Although individual Indian nations often successfully resisted English expansion for a while, the cultural diversity among tribes made a united effort difficult. As a result, the settlers steadily pushed the Native Americans farther west.

SECTION REVIEW

1. Identify: Louis XIV, Joliet, Marquette, La Salle, coureur de bois, Iroquois, Algonquin, Huron, Pequot War, King Philip's War.

2. Where and why did the English and Spanish compete in North America?

3. (a) What was Louis XIV's design for New France? (b) Did it succeed? Explain.

4. (a) What two French activities in North America were successful? (b) What impact did their activities have on Native Americans?

5. **Critical Thinking** How did the arrival of Europeans disrupt Indian society?

Iroquois chief Ho Nee Yeath Taw No Row, also called John Wolf Clan, visited London in 1710. The Dutch artist John Verelst painted this portrait during the visit.

3 The French and Indian War

The English, French, and Spanish colonies in North America were all extensions of their European governments. Therefore, it was probably inevitable that they would be caught up in conflicts among the great powers. Eventually, these conflicts exploded in a war that determined which nation would control much of North America.

European Conflict in America

Competition for North American territory was part of a larger struggle between Great Britain, France, and Spain for dominance of Europe. Since the defeat of the Armada in 1588, Spain had been the least powerful of the three nations. The power of Britain and France, on the other hand, steadily in-

creased, and a showdown between the two was simply a matter of time.

France and Britain had gone to war in Europe three times since the late 1680s: the War of the League of Augsburg (1689–1697), the War of the Spanish Succession (1702–1713), and the War of the Austrian Succession (1740–1748). Beyond some border skirmishes, colonists were little affected by these wars. However, a fourth war, which came to be known as the French and Indian War, began in North America.

The initial conflict occurred in the Ohio Valley. France claimed the region, but the British colonies had been expanding toward the valley for more than a decade. In fact, Virginia considered the Ohio Valley part of

General Braddock tried to seize Fort Duquesne during the French and Indian War, but his red-coated forces were an easy target for an ambush. After Braddock was killed, Lt. Colonel George Washington led the survivors back to Fort Cumberland.

its territory. Several prominent Virginians had formed the Ohio Company to promote settlement in the area. In 1749 the Ohio Company obtained a 200,000-acre grant (81,000 hectares) from the British government. As settlers moved into the valley, however, they found themselves face to face with the French.

The Albany Congress

In June 1754 representatives from New Hampshire, Massachusetts, Connecticut, Rhode Island, Pennsylvania, Maryland, and New York met in Albany, New York, with representatives from the Iroquois League. Fearing attack by the French and their Indian allies, the colonists wanted to solidify their friendship with the Iroquois and plan a common defense.

In addition to questions about the best way to defend the colonies, the delegates also discussed the possibility of an intercolonial union. They drew up a plan, called the Albany Plan of Union, which was designed to unite the 13 colonies under a single government.

When the Plan of Union was submitted to the individual colonial governments, however, none of them approved it. In the opinion of most colonial legislators, it called for too much control by a central government. Benjamin Franklin, author of the original plan, lamented, "Everyone cries a union is necessary, but when they come to the manner and form of the union, their weak noodles are perfectly distracted."

Early French Victories

While the representatives argued at Albany, the French finished building their forts along the Ohio River. At the same time George Washington, a 22-year-old officer in the Virginia militia, led 150 soldiers into western Pennsylvania to construct forts for the British.

On March 28, 1754, Washington's troops fired on a small party of French soldiers and took them prisoner. Learning from the prisoners that the French were about to move against them, the colonists hastily built a stockade and dubbed it Fort Necessity.

The fort was quickly besieged by a combined force of almost 1,000 French soldiers and their Indian allies. Washington and his small party could not withstand the siege and surrendered on July 3. This was the first of a series of French victories.

The following year, General Edward Braddock took command of British colonial forces. With 2,500 soldiers Braddock began cutting a road through the wilderness of western Pennsylvania to Fort Duquesne (doo KAYN), a French stronghold at the junction of the Allegheny and Monongahela (muh NAHN guh HEE luh) rivers.

When Braddock was within ten miles of the fort, the French launched an ambush. On July 9, just after the red-coated British soldiers had crossed the Monongahela, they were mowed down by musket fire from 100 French troops, 150 Canadian militia, and 800 Indians. Braddock and 900 soldiers perished.

The surviving British troops destroyed their supplies and retreated as fast as they could to the safety of Philadelphia.

That same year an expedition under Governor William Shirley of Massachusetts tried and failed to capture Fort Niagara. A campaign against Crown Point, led by William Johnson, ended in a virtual draw. The British, however, desperately in need of success, proclaimed Johnson the victor and knighted him.

Pitt and British Victories

In 1756 William Pitt became the British secretary of state. He moved quickly to reverse the string of British defeats. Pitt was a vigorous, uncompromising man, confident of his ability to win the war. "I am sure that I can save the country, and that no one else can," he remarked, and he promptly set out to do just that.

Pitt united the previously divided colonies by guaranteeing the colonists payment for military service and supplies. He also dismissed older military commanders and installed more capable young officers. Two of these, General Jeffrey Amherst and General James Wolfe, captured Louisbourg, the most important French Canadian fortress, in 1758. General John Forbes, another Pitt appointee, led an advance on Fort Duquesne. He forced the French to abandon and burn the fort, later rebuilt by the British as Fort Pitt.

In 1759 Pitt planned a three-pronged attack on the French: first, capture Fort Niagara and thus cut off the Great Lakes from the east; second, clear Lake Champlain of French forts; and, third, strike at Quebec itself.

Pitt's plan succeeded. British troops captured strategic French forts, and in early September 1759 General Wolfe and his fleet sailed up the St. Lawrence to Quebec. Fifteen thousand French troops were quartered in the city. At first, Wolfe bombarded the city from the land and the water. When this failed to draw the French into open battle, he boldly ordered his troops to mount a sur-

■ In the French and Indian War both sides fought for control of key western forts. French forts in the Northwest successfully guarded the approaches to Canada against the British until late in the war.

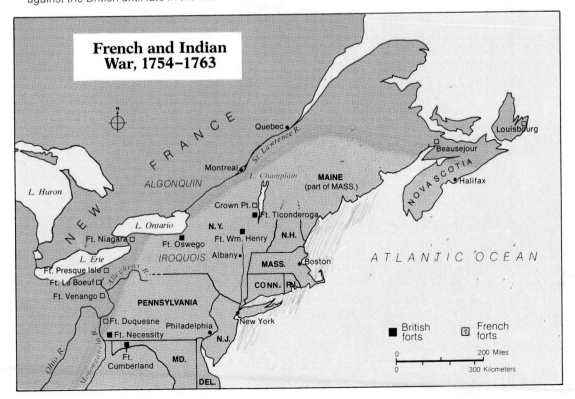

French and Indian War, 1754–1763

prise attack by scaling the cliffs below Quebec during the dead of night.

On September 13, the French commander, Louis Joseph de Montcalm, awoke to find 5,000 British troops arrayed for battle on the Plains of Abraham outside the city. The French marched out to engage them. In the ensuing battle, both Montcalm and Wolfe were killed. On September 17, Quebec surrendered to the British.

Return of Peace

Fighting continued between the major powers and their allies in Europe, but the fall of Quebec signaled the end of the war in North America and the fall of France's New World empire.

According to the Treaty of Paris of 1763, France granted Canada and lands east of the Mississippi River to Great Britain. Spain,

Major Events	
1602	Vizcaíno explores California
1609	Spanish found Santa Fe
1660, 1663	English Parliament passes Navigation Acts
1673	Joliet and Marquette explore Mississippi River
1682	La Salle reaches Mississippi delta
1733	Parliament passes Molasses Act
1754	Albany Congress
1754–1763	French and Indian War

One of the turning points of the French and Indian War was the British victory at Quebec. The British secretly scaled the cliffs by a little-known path, shown at left in this painting by Sigmund Samuel. The surprised French troops were soundly defeated by the invaders.

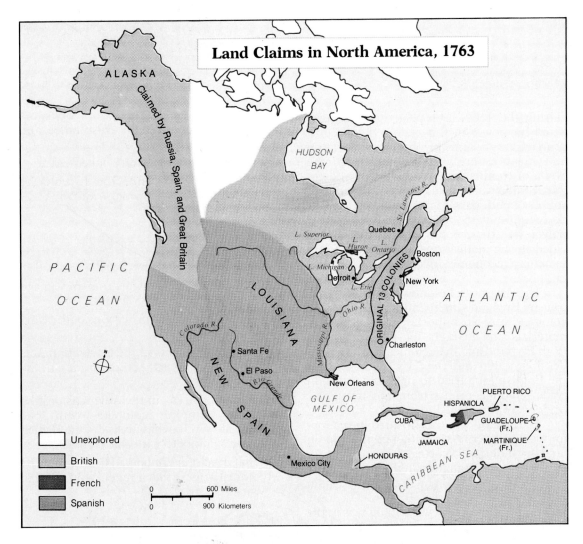

Land Claims in North America, 1763

ALASKA

Claimed by Russia, Spain, and Great Britain

HUDSON BAY

PACIFIC OCEAN

St. Lawrence R.

L. Superior
Quebec
L. Huron
L. Ontario
Boston
L. Michigan
Detroit
L. Erie
New York

ORIGINAL 13 COLONIES

Ohio R.

ATLANTIC OCEAN

LOUISIANA

Colorado R.

Santa Fe

El Paso

Rio Grande

Mississippi R.

Charleston

New Orleans

NEW SPAIN

GULF OF MEXICO

PUERTO RICO

HISPANIOLA

CUBA

GUADELOUPE (Fr.)

JAMAICA

MARTINIQUE (Fr.)

Mexico City

HONDURAS

CARIBBEAN SEA

Unexplored
British
French
Spanish

0   600 Miles
0   900 Kilometers

■ *The Treaty of Paris (1763) drastically changed the areas in North America claimed by the British, French, and Spanish.*

which had entered the war against England in 1762 in alarm at British success, gave up Florida to Britain. In return, Spain received French lands west of the Mississippi. France retained two islands in the Gulf of St. Lawrence and the prosperous sugar-producing islands of Guadeloupe and Martinique in the Caribbean.

The English colonies, which had been confined to the Atlantic coast until 1763, now stretched as far west as the Mississippi River. With the French and the Spanish removed from their flanks, the colonists looked toward a new frontier. Wagons were soon rolling westward.

SECTION REVIEW

1. Identify: Plan of Union, Benjamin Franklin, George Washington, William Pitt, Treaty of Paris.

2. What incident led to war between the French and the British in North America?

3. Why was the Albany Conference held?

4. What two actions of William Pitt helped turn the tide of war in Britain's favor?

5. **Critical Thinking** Why was control of Quebec critical to the outcome of the French and Indian War?

Chapter 5 Review

In Perspective

During the 1600s European nations competed for power in Europe. As these European nations became involved in exploration and colonization around the world, the arena of conflict widened. Colonies and colonial trade were looked on as an important source of national strength and prestige. Underlying the fierce competition for colonial power was the mercantilist theory. It provided strong motivation for monarchs to try to achieve economic independence for their nations.

The American colonies played a major role in England's mercantilist system. The colonies were an important source of raw materials and markets for English goods. Both England and the colonies benefited under this system until the early 1700s. Then as the English king tried to tighten control on trade, colonial profits from the triangular trade were threatened.

As England was transformed into a major world power, it strengthened its hold on land in India and North America. The rapidly growing population in the British colonies in America brought France and Spain into conflict with Great Britain. The only serious area of conflict with Spain was in the region around Spanish Florida. Problems with France, however, erupted into a major war in 1754. Both Great Britain and France allied with Native Americans by exploiting longstanding rivalries. The combined efforts of the British and the colonists defeated the French in 1763. As a result of the Treaty of Paris of 1763, France was all but eliminated from North America. With the departure of the French, the colonists hoped for further expansion to the West.

Vocabulary

On a separate sheet of paper, write the word or words that best complete each of the following sentences.

1. An economic system in which each nation attempted to sell more than it bought was called ___.
2. ___ were colonial products that could be shipped only to England.
3. The pattern of exchange of goods between New England, the West Indies, and England was known as the ___.
4. French fur trappers were called ___.
5. An early plan to unite the 13 colonies under a single government was the ___.

Chapter Checkup

1. Why did the English government want to control trade in the colonies?
2. Describe the major provisions of the Navigation Acts.
3. Explain the effects of the Navigation Acts and the Molasses Act on trade in the 1770s.
4. (a) In what areas in the Americas did the British Empire compete with the Spanish? (b) In what areas did the British Empire compete with the French?
5. What development helped Britain and the colonists win the French and Indian War?

Critical Thinking

1. **Evaluating Information** Sir Walter Raleigh said, "Whoever commands the trade of the world commands the riches of the world and consequently the world itself." Did this seem to have been true for Great Britain in 1763?
2. **Analyzing** Some people have argued that conflict in North America between the English and the French and Spanish was inevitable. Do you agree? Explain.

Developing Basic Skills

1. **Map Reading** Use the map-reading steps you learned in this chapter (page 79) to study the map on page 87. Then

answer the following questions: (a) What information does the map provide? (b) How far west does British territory extend? (c) How far east does Spanish territory extend? (d) Where is French territory located? (e) Which nations would probably be Britain's main territorial rivals in North America after 1763?

2. **Map Reading** One map can provide much information about a historical event or period. If you compare maps, however, you can often gain important insight into historical developments. Compare the maps on pages 78 and 87, and answer the following questions: (a) How did the extent of British territory change between 1753 and 1763? (b) How did the extent of French and Spanish claims change? (c) Which nation gained the most territory east of the Mississippi River? Which lost the most?

See page 828 for suggested readings.

Writer's Handbook

Developing a Topic Sentence

Once you have written a good topic sentence, you must support the sentence with specific, related information. There are several kinds of supporting information that are commonly used to develop a main idea. A paragraph may include one kind or several kinds of support.

Supporting information can include examples, details, facts, reasons, and incidents.

- **Examples** Specific instances that provide evidence to support a generalization.

Topic: The British government passed many measures to tighten its control over colonial trade. *Supporting examples:* For example the Navigation Acts forbade colonial merchants from shipping goods on any but colonial or English-owned vessels. Certain goods, such as sugar, cotton, and tobacco could be shipped to England only. The Molasses Act required the colonists to import rum from the British West Indies only.

- **Details** Descriptive pieces of additional information

Topic: John Verelst's painting of the Iroquois chief Ho Nee Yeath Taw No Row was not unlike a painting of a European monarch. *Supporting details:* The painter used the same kinds of symbols of power and majesty. The chief was dressed in a red blanket draped across his shoulders like a royal robe. In his hand he held a bow—a symbol of his power. His facial expression reflected his pride. The background was a forest scene—a sign of the chief's realm.

- **Facts** Verifiable information that could include evidence such as statistics

Topic: The population of the British colonies increased rapidly. *Supporting facts:* By the late 1600s, there were 200,000 people living in the British colonies. By the mid-1700s, the population had reached 1,500,000. At the same time, the much larger territory of New France had only 70,000 colonists.

- **Reasons** Information that provides the causes for the main idea or explains it

Topic: Colonies were important to a nation's independence. *Supporting reasons:* Colonies provided a source of raw materials so that a nation could be self-sufficient. They also provided markets for manufactured goods.

- **Incidents** Related events or a story that illustrates the main idea

Topic: The British success in the French and Indian War was based on a combination of skill and luck. *Supporting incident:* In order to wage an attack on Quebec, a flotilla of British ships loaded with troops and war materials sailed up the St. Lawrence River. General Wolfe ordered the troops to bombard the city to draw the French into battle. When it seemed as though nothing would dislodge the French, the British spotted a soldier walking along a hidden path to the water's edge. By climbing that path in the dead of night, the British were able to surprise the French and draw them into battle on the plains outside the city.

Practice: For your answers to the Critical Thinking questions in this Chapter Review, underline the topic sentence and identify the type of supporting detail you used.

Unit Two

Creating a Republic

1775 At the Battle of Bunker Hill, American troops showed they could hold their own against the British.

As the split between Britain and the colonies grew, some colonists directed their anger at King George III. This painting shows New Yorkers tearing down a statue of him.

	1760	1765	1770	1775
POLITICS AND GOVERNMENT		**1763** Proclamation limits westward expansion by colonists	**1770** Boston Massacre	
SOCIETY AND CULTURE		**1765** Daughters of Liberty protest the Stamp Act	**1772** Committees of Correspondence formed	
ECONOMICS AND TECHNOLOGY		**1764** Sugar Act passes to raise revenue	**1773** Boston Tea Party held to protest Tea Act	
WORLD EVENTS		**1763** War between France and Britain ends	**1770** Lord North becomes prime minister of Britain	

1765 The Stamp Act required stamps on items such as legal documents, newspapers, and pamphlets.

1775 John Paul Jones was a commander in the Continental Navy, which was formed in 1775.

Many Native Americans, including Joseph Brant, a Mohawk Chief, fought with the British against the colonists.

1788 By ratifying the Constitution, the American states created a nation based on law.

1775	1780	1785	1790

1776 Colonies declare independence from Britain

1783 War for Independence ends

1788 Constitution of the United States is ratified

1777 Vermont is first state to abolish slavery

1786 Virginia law separates church and state

1780s Trade begins with China

1787 Northwest Ordinance controls settlement of western lands

1778 French become allies of American colonies

1789 Revolution breaks out in France

The economy of the new nation would be built on its agriculture and manufacturing, such as glassmaking.

Early in the nation's history, the eagle came to symbolize the United States.

91

6

The Road to Revolution

(1763–1775)

Detail from Patrick Henry Before the House of Burgesses

As a result of its victory in the French and Indian War, Great Britain emerged as the unchallenged ruler of the entire North American continent east of the Mississippi River. Spain controlled the western part of the continent. The French, however, were limited to a few islands in the Caribbean Sea.

Never before had the British Empire been so large. Never before had it seemed so secure. Yet less than two years after the signing of the Treaty of Paris in 1763, many American colonists were openly challenging British authority.

The extent of the empire itself and the British attempts to support it contributed to growing colonial resentment. By 1775 American colonists were exchanging gunfire with British soldiers. Some colonists were even ready to consider a declaration of independence from Great Britain.

Growing split over taxation

1762	1764	1766	1768	1770	1772	1774	1776

1763 Pontiac's Rebellion

1765 Quartering Act passed

1767 Townshend Acts passed

1770 Boston Massacre

1772 *Gaspee* burned

1774 First Continental Congress meets

1775 Fighting at Lexington and Concord

1 Problems of Britain's New Empire

Britain's victory over France won vast new territories, but it also brought a host of new problems. British officials had to come to terms with France's Native American allies. They also had to decide whether to allow settlement of the new lands. Furthermore, if settlers were permitted to move into the area, they would have to be protected from the anger of Native Americans defending their lands. Finally, the crown had to cope with the staggering national debt left by the war.

Each of these problems had to be confronted and solved. Ironically, British attempts to do so created new and potentially more disastrous troubles. Inch by inch the problems drove a wedge between the home country and its American colonies that would eventually split the two apart.

An Uneasy Frontier

The question of settlement of lands west of the 13 British colonies demanded an immediate response. At the end of the war, the region was inhabited by many Indian nations, including the Seneca, Delaware, Shawnee, Huron, Ottawa, and Miami. A small number of French farmers and traders also remained. Neither group had heard of the Treaty of Paris, but they were aware that settlers from the British colonies had begun to filter into the area.

Friction between the newcomers and the older inhabitants developed quickly. And, as if this were not enough, several colonies added fuel to the fire by claiming that their boundaries extended all the way to the Pacific. To back up their claims they promptly built a road over the Appalachian Mountains into the Ohio Valley.

Britain tried to head off open conflict by stationing troops under the command of General Jeffrey Amherst in the disputed territory. General Amherst, however, only provoked the Indians when he allowed settlers to build forts in western New York and present-day Ohio, a violation of treaties with the local tribes.

Amherst also infuriated the Indians by refusing to pay them for their land. The French had long cultivated friendly relations with Native Americans by trading supplies and offering gifts and credit. Amherst had no such intentions. He was determined to force the Indians into submission.

In spring 1763 Amherst harvested the fruits of his efforts, but they were hardly what he expected. Pontiac, an Ottawa chief, led the combined forces of the Seneca, the Delaware, the Shawnee, and other western nations in a rebellion against the British. In May and June, Pontiac's alliance captured British forts in various parts of present-day Michigan, Indiana, Wisconsin, and Pennsylvania. Amherst's forces were able to hold Fort Pitt, Fort Detroit, and Fort Niagara.

For a while the uprising, known as Pontiac's Rebellion, was remarkably successful. But Pontiac's coalition eventually faltered when the Native Americans learned they could expect no more help from the French. By December peace had been restored.

The Proclamation of 1763

Although the uprising failed, the threat forced the British to review their western land policy. The new policy, issued in the Proclamation of 1763, established a boundary between Native American and colonial lands. The boundary line followed the crest of the Appalachian Mountains. According to the proclamation, no colonists were to settle west of the line. Furthermore, colonists already living there were ordered "forthwith to remove themselves." In the future no one could enter the area without permission from British authorities.

The British government had three goals in attempting to control the settlement of the West. First, it wanted to reduce the cost of protecting settlers by eliminating the major source of friction. Next, it hoped to control the colonists more easily by keeping the majority of them between the Atlantic coast and the Appalachians. Finally, the crown wanted to keep revenue from the western fur trade and land speculation in British rather than in colonial hands. To achieve these aims the British stationed 6,000 troops in the western region.

The colonists welcomed reduction of conflict with the Indians but were annoyed

Proclamation of 1763

HUDSON'S BAY COMPANY

NEWFOUNDLAND

NOVA SCOTIA

QUEBEC

MAINE (Mass.)

N.H.

MASS.

N.Y.

R.I.

CONN.

PA.

N.J.

MD.

DEL.

VA.

N.C.

S.C.

GA.

WEST FLA.

EAST FLA.

INDIAN RESERVE

PROCLAMATION LINE OF 1763

APPALACHIAN MTS.

SPANISH LOUISIANA

L. Superior

L. Michigan

L. Huron

L. Erie

L. Ontario

Ohio R.

Mississippi R.

ATLANTIC OCEAN

GULF OF MEXICO

| 0 | | | 600 Miles |
| 0 | | | 900 Kilometers |

■ To reduce friction with Native Americans, the British issued the Proclamation of 1763, forbidding settlement west of a line along the crest of the Appalachians. Settlers in the area were told to move out.

with the rest of the western policy. With the French pushed out of the West, many had looked forward to unchecked expansion into the forests of the frontier. Now, the colonists

learned, their movements were to be tightly controlled.

Furthermore, the colonists grew to resent the presence of so many British troops in America. Successes in the French and Indian War had given the colonists a new sense of confidence. And in 1763 most Americans were convinced that they could do with less, not more, supervision by the crown. The colonists' annoyance increased when they discovered that the British expected them to make a larger contribution to the empire's finances.

The Empire's Empty Treasury

When George Grenville became the British chancellor of the exchequer in April 1763, he encountered a national debt that had grown to staggering proportions during the war with France. Before the war, a normal budget had amounted to about 8 million pounds.* Grenville now faced a figure nearly twenty times that much, around 140 million pounds.

Moreover, Grenville discovered that the American colonies were costing Britain more than they brought in. By smuggling, bribery, or both, the colonists managed to evade British customs duties. Yet salaries for colonial customs officials cost the treasury more than 8,000 pounds a year, four times what the officials collected. Grenville was determined that the colonies would be profitable for the crown. He especially wanted colonists to shoulder some of the burden of Britain's war debt. In cooperation with Parliament he designed a series of measures to bring this about.

In April 1764 Parliament passed the Sugar Act, which cut the molasses duty in half. Grenville thus hoped that the colonists would pay the duty rather than evade it. The Sugar Act, however, also levied new duties on indigo, coffee, wine, cloth, and sugar.

The Sugar Act represented an important departure from previous British policy. For years colonists had accepted Parliament's right to regulate colonial trade for the benefit of the parent country. The Sugar Act, however, was intended not only to regulate trade but also to raise revenue. The colonists interpreted this as a form of taxation, and

*pound: British monetary unit.

they objected even though their taxes were much lower than taxes in England. (The average tax per person in Massachusetts, for example, was one shilling,* while in England it was 26 shillings.)

The colonists objected not because the tax was a burden but because it came from Parliament. None of the colonies sent representatives to Parliament, and Americans firmly believed that British subjects could not be taxed without the consent of their representatives. American representatives sat in colonial legislatures, they argued. If Britain wanted revenue, it should ask those legislatures to raise it.

By raising revenue through taxes passed by Parliament the British threatened their tradition of "no taxation without representation." If such actions went unchallenged, the colonists realized that participation in colonial government might become meaningless.

Growing Pressures

Grenville and Parliament further irritated the colonists with the Currency Act in 1764 and the Quartering Act in 1765. The Currency Act struck another blow at colonial control of public finance. It prohibited the colonial governments from issuing any more paper money and demanded that they recall immediately all the paper money they had issued during the war. Furthermore, the act stated that all taxes and all debts owed to British merchants be paid only in British currency.

Before the act was passed the Americans had always suffered a shortage of silver currency. Trade restrictions, coupled with the need to import many expensive manufactured goods, forced the colonists to pay out more to Great Britain than they received for their products.

The colonists had eased their situation somewhat by printing their own money and paying debts and taxes with it. Colonial currency, however, was valued at much less than British silver coins and was not worth as much in international trade. While the colonists were getting, in effect, a discount on goods, debts, and taxes, the British were losing money. The Currency Act put a stop to this.

---

*shilling: British coin, equal to 1/20 of a pound.

The Quartering Act angered the colonists as much as, if not more than, the Currency Act. The measure required the colonists themselves to help support the several thousand British troops stationed in the colonies. Upon demand, Americans were to provide barracks, candles, bedding, and beverages to any soldiers stationed in their area. Such close personal contact with the army intensified the general ill will the colonists felt toward Britain.

The Stamp Act

When Grenville introduced the Sugar Act, he announced that he planned to institute a stamp tax in the colonies similar to one already in effect in Great Britain. He gave the colonists one year to react to the proposal for a stamp tax and to suggest alternative methods of raising money. Both he and Parliament ignored the colonists' complaints, however, and on November 1, 1765, the Stamp Act went into effect.

The act specified that a stamp be affixed to a wide variety of items. The stamp showed that a tax had been paid on an item. All legal documents were taxed, as well as such things as almanacs, newspapers, pamphlets, playing cards, and dice. The tax on newspapers was a half-penny, that on diplomas two pounds.

The Stamp Act aroused intense anger because of its high visibility. Unlike the duties levied by the Sugar and Molasses acts, the stamp impression could not be overlooked, and there seemed to be no way to avoid paying it.

Adding insult to injury, Grenville planned to try offenses involving the Stamp Act in the Vice-Admiralty Courts, denying violators a trial by jury in regular colonial courts. Furthermore, Admiralty Courts were used mainly for cases involving maritime laws. Using them to try other cases appeared to threaten the colonists' cherished liberties.

A Question of Representation

Perhaps most important, the Stamp Act again raised the issue of "taxation without representation." Unlike the Sugar Act, which at least claimed to regulate trade, the Stamp Act was an outright tax. The British government had assumed powers that the colonists felt belonged to their assemblies. Colonists resented being taxed by a legislative body in which they had no representatives.

British officials replied to the colonists' complaints by claiming that all members of Parliament represented all British subjects. Even though the colonists had not elected specific members of Parliament, their interests were represented there. Thus Parliament could tax them.

Although Americans complained loudly, they did not really want to be represented in Parliament. They knew that at a distance of 3,000 miles (4,800 kilometers), necessary communication between representatives and constituents would be impossible. Americans wanted colonial legislatures to continue to be responsible for tax laws, as they always had been. An editorial in the Providence, Rhode Island, *Gazette* summed up the American position.

> It is really a piece of mockery to tell us that a country, detached from Britain by an ocean of immense breadth, and which is so extensive and populous, should be represented by the British members, or that we can have any interest in the House of Commons.

American Reaction

Before the Stamp Act could even take effect, colonists demonstrated that they would back their principles with action. From Massachusetts to South Carolina, mobs often calling themselves the Sons of Liberty stopped stamped papers from being unloaded. Stamp tax collectors all over the colonies began to wonder if their positions were worth the price of the hot tar and feathers the colonists threatened them with.

On the morning of August 14, 1765, a Boston mob hanged the Massachusetts stamp distributor in effigy. Later they destroyed the stamp tax collector's warehouse, tearing it apart board by board. They chopped off the effigy's head, "stamped" its body, and burned the remains in a bonfire made from the timbers of the collector's building. Next they attacked the stamp collector's house and ransacked the rooms. When the Massachusetts lieutenant governor tried to disperse the crowd, they stoned him and chased him off into the night. Satisfied, the mob finally dispersed at midnight.

Many people in Great Britain objected to the Stamp Act. Here British Prime Minister George Grenville (fourth from left) carries a "coffin" for the Stamp Act's burial.

Colonists also took more responsible action against the Stamp Act. In October 1765 representatives from nine colonies convened a Stamp Act Congress in New York. They drew up a petition to King George and Parliament, stating their position on Parliament's recent actions.

They granted that the colonies were legally subordinate to Parliament and that the British government had the power to regulate colonial trade. They denied, however, that Britain's legislature had the right to tax the colonists; only the colonial assemblies could rightfully do that. Finally, they asked the king and Parliament to repeal the Stamp and Sugar acts.

Colonial merchants backed up the appeal by resolving to boycott British goods. The Daughters of Liberty, a protest group formed by colonial women, aided the boycott by promoting home cloth manufacturing and signing protest petitions.

The boycott did disrupt the British economy, producing the desired effect. In March 1766 Parliament repealed the Stamp Act. Yet stung by colonial insubordination and fearful that repeal might be interpreted as weakness, Parliament passed the Declaratory Act. This legislation denied the claims of the Stamp Act Congress and in effect reasserted Parliament's authority to tax the colonies.

Consequences of the Stamp Act

The Stamp Act had far-reaching consequences. It created colonial unity where dissension had been the rule. The same colonists who had been unable to agree to a plan of union at the Albany Congress in the 1750s stood together against king and Parliament in the 1760s. While accepting Parliament's right to regulate trade, they firmly rejected its right to tax them.

Perhaps even more important, colonial opposition to the Stamp Act brought to the public arena men whose names would haunt the British in the years to come. Among them were cousins Samuel Adams and John Adams in Massachusetts and Patrick Henry and George Washington in Virginia.

One other Virginian would not emerge into the public eye for some time, but he was present during the Stamp Act debates in the House of Burgesses. A young law student, aged 22, he stood outside the legislature, thrilled by what he called Patrick Henry's "torrents of sublime eloquence." Although he was too young in 1765 to participate in politics, 11 years later his own words would stir the people to revolution. His name was Thomas Jefferson.

SECTION REVIEW

1. Identify: Pontiac, Proclamation of 1763, George Grenville, Sons of Liberty, Stamp Act Congress, Daughters of Liberty.
2. What events led to Pontiac's Rebellion?
3. How did the colonists react to the Proclamation of 1763?
4. In what way was the Sugar Act a departure from Britain's former colonial policy?
5. (a) What were the provisions of the Currency Act? (b) Of the Quartering Act? (c) Of the Stamp Act?
6. How did the colonists react to the Stamp Act?
7. What were two important results of the Stamp Act?
8. **Critical Thinking** How did some colonists' view of representative government differ from that of Parliament?

2 The Quarrel Widens

The repeal of the Stamp Act brought universal rejoicing in America, but the same could not be said for Great Britain. The nobility there grumbled that the government had "sacrificed ... gentlemen to the interests of traders and colonists." And the British treasury needed revenue as much as ever. Consequently, the newly appointed chancellor of the exchequer, Charles Townshend, faced the same problems that George Grenville had faced in 1763: making the colonies more profitable and reducing the national debt.

Here a ''Patriotick Barber'' ejects his half-shaven customer from his shop, upon learning he was a British officer. Such cartoons encouraged colonists to defy British rule.

The Townshend Acts

Townshend's task was even more difficult than Grenville's because by 1767 the British economy had plunged into a sharp depression. The depression had bred outbursts of violence and demands that taxes be reduced. Townshend allowed Parliament to cut taxes at home, but this made him even more determined to gain additional revenue from the colonies.

In 1767 Parliament passed new revenue measures, which soon became known as the Townshend Acts. Ultimately, they met the same fate as Grenville's legislation—disastrous failure and repeal.

The Townshend Acts placed small customs duties on glass, tea, paper, paint, and lead, all items that the colonists imported from Britain. The revenues from these duties were to be used to pay the expenses of colonial administration, including governors' and judges' salaries. Because the colonial assemblies traditionally paid these expenses, Townshend's measures looked to them like another attack on their authority.

Townshend thought he could convince opponents of the measures by claiming that

the duties were merely regulations of trade. After all, he argued, the colonists agreed that Parliament had the right to control trade.

Townshend convinced no one. Americans saw the acts for what they were: taxes to raise money, not duties to encourage trade. In fact the measures even hurt British trade because they encouraged the colonists to manufacture goods rather than to import them from England.

As a protest against the Townshend Acts, merchants from Philadelphia, New York, and Boston signed a *nonimportation agreement* in 1768, vowing not to import certain articles rather than pay the tax. Later they were joined by southern merchants and planters. Colonial-made goods suddenly became fashionable, and colonists scorned English luxury items.

Asserting British Authority

Townshend tried to enforce his measures by firing the customs collectors who had been taking bribes. But to no one's surprise, the new officials turned out to be as corrupt as their predecessors. Customs jobs could be quite profitable. Collectors would frequently seize ships and cargoes and sell them at exorbitant prices. The customs official could then pocket a commission amounting to one third the value of the vessel and its contents. The other two thirds of the sale was divided between the governor and the British treasury.

John Hancock, one of Boston's most prominent merchants, experienced typical treatment at the hands of customs officials. After he threw two customs officials off one of his ships for boarding it illegally, they sought revenge. Hancock's sloop *Liberty* carried a cargo of whale oil and tar. The law required that Hancock post a bond as the ship was being loaded, but officials had been allowing the bond to be paid when the ship sailed.

Using one of the hated *writs of assistance*, documents authorizing unrestricted searches, customs officers boarded the *Liberty*, searched the holds, then ordered ship and cargo seized because the bond had not been posted. The incident demonstrated to many colonists the kind of justice Americans could expect from the British government.

Townshend also tried to enforce the irritating Quartering Act, which the colonial legislatures had largely ignored. Since New York was one of the chief offenders, Townshend decided to single it out as an example to the rest of the colonies. He suspended all meetings of the New York assembly until the Quartering Act was obeyed there.

To the rest of the colonies this threat to the political liberty of New York appeared to be a threat to all. They rallied immediately to the support of New York by drafting letters announcing that they would resist every tax imposed by the crown.

Faced with such hostility, Townshend modified the Quartering Act. Instead of requiring the colonists to open their homes to soldiers, he allowed them to provide barracks, unoccupied dwellings, or barns. Even a weakened Quartering Act, however, demanded a greater British presence than the colonists were ready to tolerate.

The Boston Massacre

In response to repeated pleas from Boston customs commissioners for assistance, the British government agreed to send two regiments of troops to Boston. In September 1768 a sullen town watched as the troops came ashore and set up camp on the Boston common. For the next year and a half, the citizens of the city did all in their power short of violence to make the soldiers' lives miserable. They shunned them and taunted them behind their backs.

On March 5, 1770, the friction turned to open conflict. A crowd of several hundred colonists gathered in front of the Boston customs house, where ten British soldiers stood guard. The crowd began jeering and cursing the soldiers, pelting them with oyster shells, snowballs, sticks, and slivers of ice. At least one member of the mob had a cutlass, and another carried a pistol.

Captain Thomas Preston, the commander of the guard, ordered his men to hold steady and not to fire. Unfortunately, someone—whether a soldier or a member of the crowd is unknown—fired a gun, and a volley of shots from British muskets followed. When the shooting stopped, five of the crowd lay dead or mortally wounded on the street. The first to die was Crispus Attucks, a black sailor active in the Sons of Liberty. His wounds killed him almost immediately. The colonial press called the incident the Boston Massacre.

Preston and his troops stood trial in Boston later that year. John Adams accepted the

Boston silversmith Paul Revere made this widely circulated propaganda engraving of the Boston Massacre. The first colonist to be killed was Crispus Attucks, a black sailor, who is not shown in Revere's engraving.

unpleasant duty of defending them in court, in the belief that British soldiers as well as American colonists had the right to a legal defense. Just as crucial was his feeling that the American cause would lose its moral advantage if the soldiers could not get a fair trial in Boston.

Adams obtained deathbed testimony from one of the five men who had been mortally wounded by the British soldiers. The dying man swore that the crowd, not the troops, had been to blame for the Boston Massacre. As a result of this testimony, the worst penalty any of the soldiers received was a branding on the hand.

Repeal at Last

News of the Boston Massacre soon reached Britain, where it contributed to growing concern about the colonies. Clearly, the Townshend Acts were not working. Little tax money flowed to British coffers, and by 1769 the nonimportation agreements had reduced trade at least to some degree. Americans themselves had begun to manufacture paint, glass, paper, and lead products. This new American economic independence represented one of the least desirable developments possible.

Ironically, Charles Townshend had died in 1767 and never saw the problems his taxes had created. In 1770 George III appointed Lord North as prime minister. Both men agreed completely about how to run the colonies. Thus, for the next 12 years, King George would stand firmly behind his prime minister.

Upon taking office, Lord North convinced Parliament to allow the unpopular Quartering Act to expire. Parliament also repealed all the Townshend taxes, except the one on tea, guessing correctly that the repeal would end the American boycott of British goods. The remaining tax on tea guaranteed that at least some money would come into the government's treasury, since the colonists consumed a lot of tea. The tax also served as a reminder that Parliament claimed the right to tax the colonists.

Resistance to Parliamentary measures broke down in America. On the surface, the colonies were calmer than they had been at any time since 1764. Nevertheless, the colonists had been shaken. They had begun, for the first time, to think more clearly about their political rights.

SECTION REVIEW

1. Identify: Charles Townshend, the Boston Massacre, John Adams, Lord North.
2. Define: nonimportation agreement, writs of assistance.
3. Did the Townshend Acts raise revenue? Explain.
4. What was the colonists' reaction to enforcement of the Quartering Act?
5. Why did the British repeal the Townshend Acts but keep the tax on tea?
6. **Critical Thinking** Why was it difficult to obtain reliable testimony about the Boston Massacre?

3 The Roots of Independence

The 1770s began in an atmosphere of deceptive calm. Although Lord North's repeal of the Townshend Acts had taken the edge off colonial anger, suspicion and mistrust remained. For the time being, those feelings were quiet. If new conflicts occurred, however, those suspicions would be awakened and passions would become inflamed once again.

Beginning in 1772, a disturbing series of events convinced Americans that the British were conspiring to take away their rights.

Looking back on these events years later, George Washington would conclude that the evidence of British tyranny had been "as clear as the sun in its meridian brightness."

Tensions Renewed

Early in 1772 the British government renewed its challenge to colonial self-rule. Parliament passed an act stating that the crown would henceforth pay the salaries of royal governors and judges in the colonies, for-

British warships like the Gaspee *patrolled the coastal waters to prevent smuggling. When the* Gaspee *went aground off Providence, Rhode Island, gleeful colonists in Indian disguises rowed out and burned it.*

merly the responsibility of the colonial assemblies. Throughout the 1760s the colonies had staunchly resisted attempts like Townshend's to curtail or remove the responsibility. The colonists realized that the assemblies would have little control over governors and judges who no longer depended on them for their salaries. When Governor Thomas Hutchinson of Massachusetts announced the new law, the reaction was swift and unfavorable.

That same month another incident further heightened tensions. A British warship, the *Gaspee*, patrolled Rhode Island's Narragansett Bay to enforce customs regulations. The *Gaspee* also harassed the local inhabitants. Its captain and crew frequently seized small boats engaged in local trade, cut down orchards for firewood, and stole farmers' livestock. One day, while on a routine patrolling mission near Providence, the *Gaspee* ran aground. That night, the people of Providence burned the ship.

The British government quite correctly believed that the Rhode Island officials would do nothing to round up the offenders, so it appointed a special investigative com-

mission of its own. The commission found no Rhode Islanders willing to testify, and the investigation failed. Nevertheless, the very existence of such a commission made the colonists edgy. They feared that if Britain could bypass the colonial courts, it might shut them down permanently.

These and other incidents (for example, the tarring and feathering of a customs officer on Boston's streets and the seizing of a revenue ship on the Delaware River) increased friction between the British and the colonists. Until 1773, however, there was no clear-cut renewal of old hostilities. In that year, the lull broke once and for all.

The Tea Act

The British East India Company, a private investment company similar to the London and Plymouth companies of the seventeenth century, managed British interests in India. Among these interests was the exporting and marketing of Indian tea.

During the 1760s the European economy had been depressed and the East India

Company's business had declined. This left the company with substantial stocks of unsold tea, much of it originally designated for the American market.

In part, the company's problems resulted from British trade restrictions. The East India Company could sell its tea only to British wholesalers, not on the open market. The wholesalers, in turn, sold the tea to American distributors who then resold it to retail merchants. By the time the tea had reached the colonial market it had been marked up four times.

Dutch tea, on the other hand, was smuggled into the colonies directly from the East Indies. Wholesalers and customs officials were bypassed, making the tea much cheaper than that sold by the East India Company. Needless to say, the colonists preferred it.

In 1773 Parliament tried to boost the company's fortunes by passing the Tea Act. The measure allowed the East India Company to sell its tea directly to American retailers. In addition, the act eliminated Britain's own import tax on tea. When the tea arrived in the colonies, only one duty had to be paid on it, the small tax remaining from the original Townshend Acts. (See page 100.) As a result, East India Company tea would cost no more than Dutch tea.

A Tempest Over Tea

The solution looked good to Parliament. Americans would get cheaper tea and pay more taxes, and the crown would gain revenue. The plan, however, cut most American merchants out of the tea trade.

Soon, colonial tea merchants began to complain about losing business. They warned that other merchants might suffer the same fate before long. All over the colonies the tea tax became a symbol of British oppression. The American spirit of independence had been aroused again.

The enraged colonists acted as quickly as they complained. For the third time since 1763, a colonial boycott went into effect. East India tea rotted on the waterfronts up and down the American coast. Women brewed "liberty teas" from local plants, signed anti-tea declarations, and formed anti-tea leagues.

In Boston, Governor Thomas Hutchinson decided to force the issue. He believed that unless the Tea Act were enforced, British control over the American colonies would end. In December 1773 he ordered East India tea ships in Boston harbor to tie up along the wharves and unload their cargoes.

The Sons of Liberty responded immediately. On the night of December 16, a gang of 30 to 60 men thinly disguised as Indians boarded the East India ships and dumped the tea into the harbor. The incident became known as the Boston Tea Party.

The Intolerable Acts

When Lord North received news of Boston's defiance, he lost all patience. He felt that "New England fanatics," as he called them, were undermining all British authority in the colonies. Both North and George III agreed that the time had come to force the colonists to obey.

Since Boston was the center of colonial resistance, Lord North and the king decided to make an example of Massachusetts. In 1774 they imposed the Coercive Acts, hoping that the retaliation would spread fear

Mercy Otis Warren of Plymouth, Massachusetts was an effective American propagandist who wrote and published many political satires and plays. This 1763 painting is by John Singleton Copley.

throughout the colonies and force them into submission.

First, the acts closed the port of Boston. Second, they revoked the Massachusetts charter, prohibiting the Massachusetts legislature and courts from holding sessions. Military rule was imposed on the colony, and General Thomas Gage, commander of all British troops in North America, became governor of the colony. The acts also forbade town meetings, placing even local government under military control.

More troops arrived in Boston to reinforce the existing garrison. By the time the new arrivals stopped coming, the Boston contingent totaled 4,000 men, one British soldier for every four Bostonians.

Finally, the Coercive Acts revived the old Quartering Act, giving General Gage the authority to house all his troops in Boston, in private residences if need be. Furthermore, any British officials who committed crimes while enforcing the acts would be tried in Britain, not in America. The colonials saw that last provision in particular as a mockery of justice.

The Quebec Act, an attempt to secure the loyalty of the French-Canadians to Britain, soon followed. This act gave the French-Canadians freedom to practice their Catholic faith and expanded the boundaries of Quebec west and south to the Mississippi and Ohio rivers.

The act was not intended to punish the colonies, but the colonists east of the Appalachians regarded the expansion of Quebec's borders as an insult. They felt that Britain had deliberately created an obstacle to westward expansion.

Ultimately, the Intolerable Acts, as the colonists labeled the Coercive Acts and the Quebec Act, helped forge the colonies into a united front. Before a workable alliance between the colonies could be created, however, major differences had to be overcome.

To Submit or Unite?

Thirteen separate and often disparate governments found it difficult to work together, as the Albany Congress of 1754 had demonstrated. Furthermore, the colonies occupied a vast region with varied climate and geography. The economies and social systems of the colonies differed, too, ranging from the

Considered by some the first political cartoon in America, this sketch urged the 13 colonies to unite. Colonial leaders such as Benjamin Franklin felt that only if they worked together could they stand up to British power.

sprawling plantations of the South to the compact farms of New England.

Yet, the forces for unity were stronger than the differences that set the colonies apart. Up and down a territory 1,500 miles long and several hundred miles wide, most colonists spoke a common language and shared common traditions of government. When Parliament and the crown acted to deny what the colonists saw as their "English liberties," Americans began to recognize how much the thirteen colonies had in common.

This sense of unity grew as colonists learned more about the issues of the day. Communication increased as newspapers spread reports of events from colony to colony. In pamphlets writers examined vital issues in depth and called for greater resistance to British tyranny.

Committees of Correspondence

The most effective means of developing a united colonial front proved to be the Committees of Correspondence. First organized by Samuel Adams in 1772 to connect Boston to the rural towns of Massachusetts, committees existed in every colony by 1774.

The Committees of Correspondence kept colonists from north to south and east to west continuously informed of developments in the struggle with Britain. For instance, when the Committees of Correspondence spread the word that the Coercive Acts had closed the port of Boston, the response was instantaneous and supportive. South Carolina sent rice to the beleaguered colony, and Pennsylvania sent flour.

All along, the committees made sure that every incident was reported as an attack on American liberty. One British sympathizer called the committees "the foulest, subtlest, and most venomous serpent ever issued from the egg of sedition."

A decisive step toward unity came in 1774. After the royal governor of Virginia dissolved the House of Burgesses, members of the assembly met in a Williamsburg tavern. They declared that the Intolerable Acts threatened the liberty of all the colonies, and they called for a meeting of delegates from each colony to discuss the legislation. The Committees of Correspondence quickly communicated Virginia's declaration to the rest of the colonies. Soon, colonial assemblies were at work electing delegates to the First Continental Congress.

When the meeting convened in Carpenters' Hall at Philadelphia in September 1774, all 13 colonies except Georgia were represented. As the delegates assembled, they knew their first task was to decide on a response to the Intolerable Acts. Yet another more unsettling question probably lingered in the back of their minds. At some future date, would the colonies have only one recourse left—independence?

★ Voices of Freedom ★

The Local Tavern: A Communication Center

Handbills, pamphlets, and local newspapers told colonists about developments between Great Britain and the colonies. But casual gatherings at local taverns often were even more important. There people also could discuss events and plan possible actions. Below, John Adams describes one conversation he heard at a tavern in Massachusetts in 1774.

Within the course of the year, before the meeting of Congress in 1774, on a journey to some of our circuit courts in Massachusetts, I stopped one night at a tavern in Shrewsbury about forty miles from Boston, and as I was cold and wet, I sat down at a good fire in the bar-room to dry my greatcoat and saddle-bags, till a fire could be made in my chamber. There presently came in, one after another, half a dozen, or half a score substantial yeomen of the neighborhood, who, sitting down to the fire after lighting their pipes, began a lively conversation on politics. As I believed I was unknown to all of them, I sat in total silence to hear them. One said, "The people of Boston are distracted." Another answered, "No wonder the people of Boston are distracted. Op-pression will make wise men mad." A third said, "What would you say if a fellow should come to your house and tell you he was come to take a list of your cattle, that Parliament might tax you for them at so much a head? And how should you feel if he was to go and break open your barn or take down your oxen, cows, horses, and sheep?" "What should I say?" replied the first. "I would knock him in the head." "Well," said a fourth, "if Parliament can take away Mr. Hancock's wharf and Mr. Rowe's wharf, they can take away your barn and my house." After much more reasoning in this style, a fifth broke out: "Well, it's high time for us to rebel.

SECTION REVIEW

1. Identify: *Gaspee*, British East India Company, Intolerable Acts, Committees of Correspondence, Samuel Adams.
2. (a) What was the purpose of the Tea Act? (b) How did the colonists react?
3. What was the purpose of the Coercive Acts?
4. How did effective communication contribute to colonial unity?
5. Why did the First Continental Congress meet?
6. **Critical Thinking** Why do you think that the issue of colonial courts was so important to the colonists?

4 From Protest to Revolution

What could be done about the Intolerable Acts? This question was the first order of business before the Continental Congress, and the delegates had different answers.

The moderates, led by Joseph Galloway and John Dickinson of Pennsylvania, wanted to patch up the quarrel with Great Britain. The radicals, following Samuel and John Adams of Massachusetts, Charles Thomson of Pennsylvania, and Patrick Henry of Virginia, felt the time had come to take a stronger stand. They wanted either to force Britain to agree completely with their demands or to declare total independence.

Defining Relations With Britain

At first the moderates seemed to be making headway at the Congress. Under Galloway's leadership they proposed a union of the colonies under British authority. Colonial legislatures would retain the powers they had before 1763, but Parliament still would be able to pass legislation affecting the colonies. Galloway proposed, however, that Parliament's acts could be vetoed by a "grand council" of American representatives.

Galloway's plan was defeated in a close vote, in large part because of the hard work of Samuel Adams. Adams, complained Galloway, was a man who "eats little, sleeps little, thinks much, and is most decisive ... in the pursuit of his objects."

With the defeat of Galloway's plan, the radicals increasingly dominated the Congress. They no longer accepted the American position of 1765 that Parliament had the right to regulate the trade of the colonies. Instead they accepted a new theory outlined in a pamphlet written by Thomas Jefferson, *A Summary View of the Rights of British America.*

Jefferson argued that just as Parliament had no right to tax the colonies, so it could not legislate for them either. The only connection between the colonies and Great Britain, he asserted, was the king. For Jefferson and the radicals, the British empire was not a single, undivided whole. Rather it was a loose union of more or less independent

Samuel Adams of Boston was a fiery leader of the cause for American independence. He organized the Boston Tea Party and formed the first Committee of Correspondence.

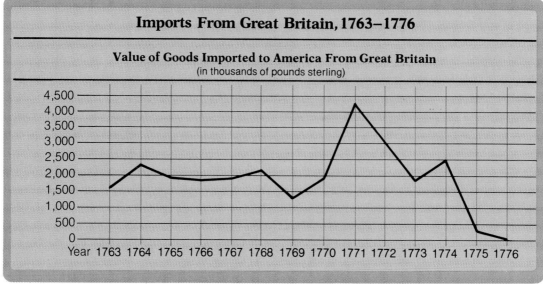

Imports From Great Britain, 1763–1776

Value of Goods Imported to America From Great Britain
(in thousands of pounds sterling)

Source: *Historical Statistics of the United States*

■ *Colonists boycotted British goods in 1765 and 1766 to protest the Stamp Act, in late 1768 and 1769 to protest the Townshend Acts, and again in 1775 and 1776. This graph shows the effects of these boycotts.*

states. Each had its own legislature, which acted as a little parliament, and all were united by a shared loyalty to the king.

The Congress's most significant document, *Declaration and Resolves,* attacked the Coercive Acts and the Quebec Act as well as all revenue measures passed by Parliament since 1763. Citing both "the immutable laws of nature," "the principles of the English constitution," and the original colonial charters, the *Declaration and Resolves* demanded the repeal of all oppressive legislation.

Other Actions

The First Continental Congress also took other decisive actions. Urged on by Samuel Adams, the delegates approved a set of resolutions that had been adopted in Suffolk County, Massachusetts. These resolutions, known as the Suffolk Resolves, called upon the people of Massachusetts to openly disobey the Coercive Acts because they were illegal. The resolutions also recommended that the colonists prepare to defend themselves against possible attack by the British at Boston.

The Congress further voted for an immediate and complete end to trade with Great Britain. To see that this was carried out, the delegates formed a continental Association. Committees were to be set up in every city, county, and town to insure that no colony imported or consumed British goods or exported American goods to Britain. By April 1775 committees were operating in 12 colonies.

Before adjourning on October 26, 1774, the delegates agreed to meet again the following spring. Little did they know that by that time an incident in Massachusetts would set forces in motion that would sever the colonies from Great Britain forever.

Lexington and Concord

Over the winter of 1774–1775, Massachusetts protestors formed a militia, calling themselves *minutemen* because they would be ready to fight on a moment's notice. The minutemen took seriously the Continental Congress's commitment to colonial self-defense. They did not have long to wait for a hostile move by the British troops.

As winter turned into spring, General Thomas Gage, commander of the British forces in Boston, received orders to round up the leaders of the colonial resistance. At first he hesitated, unwilling to provoke open conflict. However, when news arrived that the colonists had an arsenal of weapons and powder at Concord, Gage acted. On April 18 he sent nearly 1,000 soldiers under Major John Pitcairn to seize the arsenal. Pitcairn, who believed that the resistance movement could be smothered easily with a "small action" and the burning of a few towns, looked forward to doing the job.

Pitcairn and his men set out from Boston at night, hoping to surprise the colonists at daybreak. But as the soldiers tramped over the countryside, William Dawes and Paul Revere galloped to villages and farms to warn the minutemen. At sunrise, when the British reached Lexington, 70 minutemen commanded by Captain John Parker waited on the village green. Pitcairn ordered the minutemen to disperse, and Parker gave the order to retreat. Then someone—no one knows who—fired a shot. After a brief skirmish, eight Americans lay dead and ten more lay wounded on the new spring grass.

Only one British soldier received a wound, and that was slight.

Delayed no more than 15 minutes, Pitcairn pushed on to Concord. He entered the village without resistance at eight o'clock but found few of the military supplies he had been sent to seize. To protect his main body of troops while they searched, Pitcairn ordered a covering party to North Bridge, just outside the village center. There, the British met 300 minutemen, and a British trooper fired "the shot heard 'round the world."

After a five-minute exchange of fire, Pitcairn began his retreat. By then, over 3,000 minutemen lined the woods, fields, and stone fences along the road to Boston. Pitcairn's command barely made it back to Lexington. There 1,200 British reinforcements, wisely sent by General Gage, rescued them. By the time the British ran the entire "bloody chute" back to Boston, 73 of their men had been killed, with

Minuteman Amos Doolittle made this detailed engraving of two British commanders scouting the terrain around the Concord cemetery. Their brilliantly clad troops are marching toward the village to face colonial minutemen.

★ **Voices of Freedom** ★

Give Me Liberty or Give Me Death

On March 28, 1775, Patrick Henry addressed the Virginia Convention of Delegates. For almost ten years he had opposed Britain's attempts to impose taxation without representation. As this excerpt shows, by 1775 he had lost all patience with words.

Let us not deceive ourselves, sir. These are the implements of war and subjugation; the last arguments to which kings resort. I ask gentlemen, sir, what means this martial array, if its purpose be not to force us to submission? . . . Has Great Britain any enemy, in this quarter of the world, to call for all this accumulation of navies and armies? No, sir, she has none. They are meant for us; they can be meant for no other. And what have we to oppose them? Shall we try argument? Sir, we have been trying that for the last ten years. . . . Sir, we have done everything that could be done . . . and we have been spurned, with contempt, from the foot of the throne. . . . We must fight! I repeat it, sir, we must fight. . . .

Gentlemen may cry peace, peace—but there is no peace. The war is actually begun! The next gale that sweeps from the north will bring to our ears the clash of resounding arms! Our brethren are already in the field. Why stand we here idle? . . . Is life so dear, or peace so sweet, as to be purchased at the price of chains and slavery? Forbid it, Almighty God! I know not what course others may take; but as for me, give me liberty, or give me death!

---

another 200 wounded or missing. In contrast, the Americans had only 93 casualties.

On April 22 the Massachusetts provincial congress voted to raise 13,600 troops, to be commanded by Artemas Ward. Within a week, Boston was a city under seige. When the Continental Congress gathered again in Philadelphia on May 10, 1775, it had a fight on its hands.

SECTION REVIEW

1. Identify: Joseph Galloway, Thomas Jefferson, *Declaration and Resolves,* Suffolk Resolves, Association, minutemen.
2. Describe the moderates' proposal to the Continental Congress and explain why it failed.
3. How did the radicals' attitude toward Parliament differ from the attitude of most colonists?
4. What information convinced General Gage to act against the colonists?
5. **Critical Thinking** Why was economic independence nearly as important for the colonists as political independence?

Major Events	
1763	Pontiac's Rebellion; Proclamation of 1763
1764	Parliament passes Sugar Act and Currency Act
1765	Quartering Act passed; Stamp Act goes into effect; colonists hold Stamp Act Congress
1766	Parliament repeals Stamp Act
1767	Parliament passes Townshend Acts
1770	Boston Massacre; repeal of Townshend Acts except tax on tea
1772	Rhode Island residents burn the *Gaspee*
1773	Parliament passes Tea Act; Boston Tea Party
1774	Parliament passes Coercive Acts; First Continental Congress meets
1775	First military conflict between British and colonists at Lexington and Concord

SKILL LESSON

Lexington and Concord: Analyzing a Primary Source

Two types of written sources can be used to learn about historical events: primary sources and secondary sources. *Primary sources* are first-hand accounts usually written by a person who was closely involved in the event. They include government documents, letters, diaries, and eyewitness newspaper accounts. *Secondary sources* are second-hand accounts of historical events.

Both types of sources provide factual information, but primary sources also provide insight into the feelings, attitudes, and motives of people. Because the author is closely involved in the event, however, the account may not be accurate. Thus when using a primary source, it is important to analyze its reliability.

Carefully read the document at right. Then use the steps described below to analyze it.

1. **Identify the nature of the document by asking yourself the following questions.** (a) What type of document is it? (b) Who wrote the document? Was he or she closely involved in the event? (c) When was it written?

2. **Decide how reliable the source is.** The following questions will help you judge the reliability of this document. (a) Why did the author write it? (b) What was the author's role in the event described? (c) Was the author British or American? How can you tell? How could that have affected what was reported? (d) Would you say this is a reliable source?

3. **Study the source to learn more about a historical event.** Distinguish between facts and opinions. A *fact* is something that is true and that can be proven. An *opinion* is a judgment that reflects a person's feelings, beliefs, or attitudes. (a) What facts about the fighting at Lexington and Concord can you learn from this document? (b) What was the author's opinion of the colonists' actions at Lexington? What was the author's opinion of British intentions? (c) How would you describe the British feelings toward the fighting?

Report of Lieutenant-Colonel Smith to Governor Gage, April 22, 1775

SIR,—I marched on the evening of the 18th with the corps of grenadiers and light infantry for Concord, to execute your Excellency's orders with respect to destroying all ammunition, artillery, tents, &c, collected there. When I had got some miles on the march from Boston, I detached six light infantry companies. On these companies' arrival at Lexington, they found on a green close to the road a body of the country people drawn up in military order, with arms. Our troops advanced towards them, without any intention of injuring them, further than to inquire the reason of their being thus assembled, and, if not satisfactory, to have secured their arms; but they in confusion went off, principally to the left, only one of them fired before he went off, and three or four more jumped over a wall and fired from behind it among the soldiers; on which the troops returned it, and killed several of them.

While at Concord we saw vast numbers assembling in many parts; at one of the bridges they marched down, with a very considerable body, on the light infantry posted there. On their coming pretty near, one of our men fired on them, which they returned; on which an action ensued and some few were killed. . . .

On our leaving Concord to return to Boston, they began to fire on us from behind the walls, ditches, trees, and continued for, I believe, upwards of eighteen miles; so that I can't think but it must have been a preconcerted scheme in them, to attack the King's troops the first favorable opportunity that offered, otherwise, I think they could not, in so short a time from our marching out, have raised such a numerous body, and for so great a space of ground.

I have the honor, &c,
F. Smith, Lieutenant-Colonel 10th Foot.

In Perspective

In 1763, after its victory in the French and Indian War, Great Britain was the undisputed ruler of North America east of the Mississippi River. The British as well as the American colonists looked forward to a prosperous future. Yet the problems of governing the new empire gradually drove a wedge between the British and the colonists.

One major issue was the settlement of lands west of the 13 British colonies. The colonists hoped to extend into the territory west of the Appalachians. The British were concerned about how they could prevent conflict with the Native Americans who already inhabited the region. Britain's decision to prohibit settlement in the West angered some colonists. Colonists also resented the arrival of more British troops to police the area and keep them out.

An even more serious problem, as far as the British government was concerned, was the need for money to support the empire. Attempts through the Sugar Act, the Stamp Act, and the Townshend Acts to impose taxes to raise money rather than to control trade met with growing resistance in the colonies. Taxation without representation became a troublesome issue.

In the early 1770s tensions increased further as the British government tried to enforce its legislation. The Boston Massacre heightened emotions, but the repeal of the Townshend Acts temporarily eased the unrest. Before long another incident renewed bad feelings. In protest over a tax on tea, angry colonists threw a shipment of tea overboard into Boston harbor. In reaction to the Boston Tea Party, Parliament passed the Coercive Acts. Colonial representatives met at the First Continental Congress to protest the acts and to take the first steps toward economic independence from Great Britain. The first military clash between British troops and colonial militia took place soon afterward at Lexington and Concord. It seemed to be only a matter of time until total independence would be declared.

Vocabulary

Choose the answer that best completes each of the following sentences.

1. An agreement among merchants not to import certain goods was the ___. (a) tariff (b) nonimportation agreement (c) Stamp Act

2. A ___ is a document authorizing unrestricted searches. (a) writ of assistance (b) bill of rights (c) boycott

3. Groups of colonists who wrote to one another concerning the struggle with Britain were the ___. (a) minuteman (b) Vice-Admiralty Courts (c) Committees of Correspondence

4. The First Continental Congress issued the ___ to protest the Coercive Acts and the Quebec Act. (a) Declaration and Resolves (b) Currency Act (c) Suffolk Resolves

5. Massachusetts protestors formed a militia and called themselves the ___. (a) Loyalists (b) minuteman (c) redcoats

Chapter Checkup

1. (a) Why did Pontiac lead the western Indian nations in a rebellion against the British? (b) What impact did the rebellion have on British policy?

2. (a) Describe the measures George Grenville and Parliament took to ease Britain's national debt. (b) How did the colonists react to them?

3. (a) What were the Townshend Acts? (b) How did the British try to enforce them? (c) How did the colonists react?

4. (a) Why did the Tea Act symbolize British oppression to the colonists? (b) What actions did the colonists take to oppose this act?

5. (a) Describe the Coercive Acts. (b) Why did the colonists consider the Quebec Act a threat? (c) How did these so-called Intolerable Acts help unify the colonies?

6. (a) What was the major question facing the First Continental Congress? (b) What actions did it take?

7. (a) How did the position of the moderates at the First Continental Congress differ from the position of the radicals? (b) Which position seemed to dominate by the end of the Congress?

8. How did the Suffolk Resolves probably help set the stage for the outbreak of fighting at Lexington and Concord?

Critical Thinking

1. **Analyzing** (a) Why did the colonists consider the Sugar Act (1764) and the Stamp Act (1765) to be taxation without representation? (b) How did these acts differ from the Molasses Act (1733)? (c) What body did the colonist think had authority to tax them? Why?

2. **Recognizing a Point of View** Look up a definition of the word "massacre" in a dictionary. Why do you think the incident in Boston was called a massacre in the colonial press when only five people were killed?

Developing Basic Skills

1. **Map Reading** Study the map on page 94. Then answer the following questions: (a) What served as a natural boundary for the Proclamation Line of 1763? (b) For whom was the land west of the Proclamation Line intended? (c) What country claimed the territory west of the Mississippi River?

2. **Placing Events in Time** Construct a time line with 1763 as the starting date and 1775 as the ending date. Write in the events that led up to the American Revolution. Then answer the following questions: (a) How long was the Stamp Act in effect? (b) How long were the Townshend Acts in effect? (c) Does the time line support the idea that the colonies were on the road to revolution? Explain.

See page 828 for suggested readings.

Writer's Handbook

Organizing Supporting Detail

Once you have written a topic sentence and gathered supporting information, you must arrange the information in some logical order, or sequence. The common sequences are chronological order, order of importance, comparison and contrast, spatial order, and developmental or topical order. You will study them in more detail in the upcoming Chapter Reviews.

- **Chronological order** Events are arranged in the time order in which they occurred. Chronological order is useful for relating circumstances leading up to a particular event.

- **Order of importance** Ideas are organized from the least significant to the most significant, or vice versa. This order is helpful for developing an argument for or against some action or issue.

- **Comparison and contrast** Ideas or details are organized according to similarities or differences. The ideas can be contrasted item by item, or all of the items of one kind can be compared with all of the items of another kind. This pattern would be useful to show how things were the same or different.

- **Spatial order** Items are organized according to the place they occupy in space, from inside to outside, near to far, left to right, and so on. This pattern is useful for writing a word picture.

- **Developmental or topical order** Information is presented either in some fashion suggested by the topic sentence or according to the writer's judgment. Developmental order is more flexible than the other kinds of orders and can be used when none of the others is appropriate.

Practice: For each of your answers for the Critical Thinking questions in this Chapter Review, underline the topic sentence, identify the kinds of supporting information, and indicate the logical order of organization.

7

A War for Independence

(1775–1783)

Detail from The Battle of Bunker Hill

Chapter Outline

1 *The Revolution Begins*

2 *The Road to Independence*

3 *The Balance of Forces*

4 *Fighting a Colonial War*

5 *Victory for the Americans*

Relations between Britain and its American colonies grew steadily worse during the 1770s. The British seemed determined to maintain their authority, while the colonists vigorously defended their rights. Yet even when fighting broke out at Lexington and Concord, few expected it to become a war for independence.

The decision to declare independence came at the Second Continental Congress, as you will read in this chapter. The Declaration of Independence adopted by the Congress spelled out political and social ideals that would play a major role in shaping the new nation.

Before the American colonies could become truly independent, however, they had to fight a long and often bitter war. These years of sacrifice and determination resulted in victory and the creation of a new republic.

Revolutionary War

1774	1776	1778	1780	1782	1784
1775 Second Continental Congress convenes	**1776** Declaration of Independence; Patriots win at Trenton, Princeton	**1778** French alliance with Patriots	**1780** British win at Charleston	**1781** British surrender at Yorktown	**1783** Treaty of Paris ratified

1 The Revolution Begins

Once fighting had broken out between American colonists and British soldiers, colonial leaders realized the need for a unified and coordinated plan of action. Meeting once again in Philadelphia in 1775, the delegates to the Second Continental Congress took a step far more radical than skirmishing with British troops. The following year they would declare independence from Great Britain.

Declaring independence, however, did not make the colonies independent. The crown was prepared to fight for its American possessions. To achieve their goal, the colonies would have to fight as well. That step demanded that the Americans meet the British with a real army.

The Opening of the Second Continental Congress

On May 10, 1775, less than a month after the outbreak of fighting at Lexington and Concord, the Second Continental Congress convened in Philadelphia. Delegates from each of the colonies except Georgia, who joined the rest a few months later, assembled in the Pennsylvania statehouse, a simple impressive brick building with a white steeple.

The inscription on the steeple's bell reflected the feelings of many delegates: "Proclaim liberty throughout all the land unto all the inhabitants thereof." Over the main entrance to the building, however, was King George III's coat of arms. As the delegates walked into the statehouse, few could have avoided noticing this visible reminder of other sentiments—the colonies' past loyalty to the crown.

The Liberty Bell and the king's coat of arms symbolized the most significant question facing the delegates: where did their loyalties lie? The moderates, led by John Dickinson of Pennsylvania, still wanted to negotiate an agreement with Britain. The radicals, following John and Samuel Adams, clamored for independence.

The radicals had public opinion on their side. Throughout the colonies citizens were forming Committees of Safety to recruit and train local militia, collect funds and supplies, gather information, and disrupt the activities of the king's representatives. One traveler reported, "Wherever you go, you see the inhabitants training, making firelocks, [and] casting mortars, shells and shot."

The radicals also benefited from the superb political skills of Samuel and John Adams. Both worked tirelessly and skillfully to prod the moderates ever closer to independence. In private John Adams complained about the Congress's lengthy debates, but in public he was more than willing to argue, cajole, and then wait. At one point he described America as "a great unwieldy body. It is like a large fleet sailing under convoy. The fleetest sailors must wait for the dullest and the slowest."

The Colonists Take Action

Adams did not have to wait long. Events rapidly drove most of the delegates toward a decision for independence. On the morning of May 10, the same day that the Second Continental Congress convened, Ethan Allen and his band of 83 volunteers, called the Green Mountain Boys, surprised and captured a sleepy British garrison at Fort Ticonderoga in New York. Within a few days, the news reached Philadelphia.

A little over a month later, fighting broke out again. For weeks both the British and the Americans had been pouring troops and supplies into the Boston area, the center of radical agitation. On June 12 the British declared that the city and surrounding area were under military command. When the local Committee of Safety discovered that British troops planned to move onto the heights overlooking the city, they devised a countermove. On the night of June 16, American General Israel Putnam occupied and fortified Breed's Hill and Bunker Hill.

The next morning more than 1,500 British troops launched a frontal attack on the heights, with each soldier carrying a full pack of almost 125 pounds. Positioned securely on the hills, Putnam cautioned his inexperienced troops to conserve their ammunition. "Don't fire until you see the whites of their eyes!" he warned them.

Withering fire from American guns forced the British back twice. Reinforced with fresh troops, the British prepared for a third attack. They threw off their heavy packs, fixed their bayonets, and stormed the heights. But this time they met only sporadic fire. The Americans, with dwindling supplies of powder and no bayonets, had held their ground as long as they could. They were unable to withstand a third British assault.

The British captured the entire area around Charlestown, but they paid a high price for it. Over 1,000 soldiers were killed or wounded, including a number of officers. The Americans lost only 397 soldiers.

The Battle of Bunker Hill was a technical victory for the British but a moral victory for the Americans. Colonial forces had proved they could hold their own against better trained and better equipped troops. Now they could enter the struggle in earnest--and with some hope of winning.

Beginnings of a Continental Army

Two weeks after the battle at Bunker Hill, Massachusetts asked the Continental Congress to take control of the army that had begun to form in the Boston area. Congress then established an army of 20,000 men and unanimously appointed George Washington commander in chief.

Although the forty-three-year-old Washington had limited military experience, he brought a valuable combination of qualities to the job. As a southerner, he broadened colonial support for what had been seen as a New England war. As a natural leader, he knew how to command the respect of the officers and soldiers in the army. And as an early supporter of independence, he had the trust of the delegates to the Continental Congress.

Shortly after his appointment, Washington left Philadelphia for Cambridge, Massachusetts, to take command of an undisciplined force of about 14,000 men. The task he faced would have overwhelmed a lesser man. From a motley group of local militia and volunteers, Washington had to build a continental army. Fortunately, the British, troubled by their heavy casualties at Bunker Hill, remained inactive and gave him time.

Washington also had much to learn. He knew little about directing large groups of soldiers, less about military strategy, and virtually nothing about the use of artillery.

★ Voices of Freedom ★

The Sword of Bunker Hill

The Battle of Bunker Hill was a source of great pride, as you can see in this song.

He lay upon his dying bed;
His eye was growing dim,
When with a feeble voice he call'd
His weeping son to him:
"Weep not, my boy!" the vet'ran said,
"I bow to Heav'n's high will,—
But quickly from yon antlers bring
The Sword of Bunker Hill;
But quickly from yon antlers bring
The Sword of Bunker Hill."

The sword was bro't, the soldier's eye
Lit with a sudden flame;
And as he grasp'd the ancient blade,
He murmured Warren's name:
Then said, "My boy, I leave you gold,—
But what is richer still,
I leave you, mark me, mark me now—
The Sword of Bunker Hill;

I leave you, mark me, mark me now—
The Sword of Bunker Hill.

" 'Twas on that dread, immortal day,
I dared the Briton's band,
A captain raised this blade on me—
I tore it from his hand;
And while the glorious battle raged,
It lightened freedom's will—
For, boy, the God of freedom blessed
The Sword of Bunker Hill;
For, boy, the God of freedom blessed
The Sword of Bunker Hill.

"Oh, keep the sword!"—his accents broke—
A smile—and he was dead!
His wrinkled hand still grasped the blade
Upon that dying bed.
The son remains; the sword remains—
Its glory growing still—
And twenty millions bless the sire,
And Sword of Bunker Hill;
And twenty millions bless the sire,
And Sword of Bunker Hill.

114

Furthermore, his staff, appointed by the Continental Congress, consisted of a few well-meaning but poorly qualified officers. Israel Putnam, or Old Put, as he was known, had Bunker Hill behind him as well as some combat experience during the French and Indian War. But another officer, Artemas Ward, reportedly "had no acquaintance whatever with military affairs."

Two generals, Horatio Gates and Charles Lee, resisted Washington's command because they had had wider military experience as officers in the British Army. In time Washington developed a corps of capable officers: Nathanael Greene, Anthony Wayne, Daniel Morgan, and Henry Knox, among others. At the start, however, poor leadership hampered American efforts.

Military Action in Canada

With their forces and supplies depleted by the battle at Bunker Hill, the British stayed in their Boston quarters during the summer of 1775. While the British waited for reinforcements from across the Atlantic, Washington mounted a siege, placing cannons on Dorchester Heights, strategically located above Boston's harbor. General William Howe, the new British commander, realized that he could no longer defend Boston. In March 1776 he withdrew the British garrison north to Halifax, Nova Scotia.

Meanwhile, the Continental Congress, which was beginning to function as a government for the colonies, learned that Canada's governor, Guy Carleton, was preparing to invade the colonies. Rather than wait for the attack, the Congress decided to act. It ordered American troops to invade Canada.

Marching at a brutal pace through rough northern country, Colonel Benedict Arnold reached Quebec in September 1775. His troops menaced the Canadians throughout the autumn and early winter. In mid-December General Richard Montgomery brought reinforcements, and the troops launched an attack on Quebec.

The Canadians fought valiantly. Montgomery was killed and Arnold wounded. But, instead of withdrawing, Arnold laid siege to the walled city. Hunger, smallpox, and bitter Canadian weather took their toll on his troops. The Canadians, equipped with ample food and supplies, simply bided their time, and the siege, a desperate gamble, ended in failure and frustration.

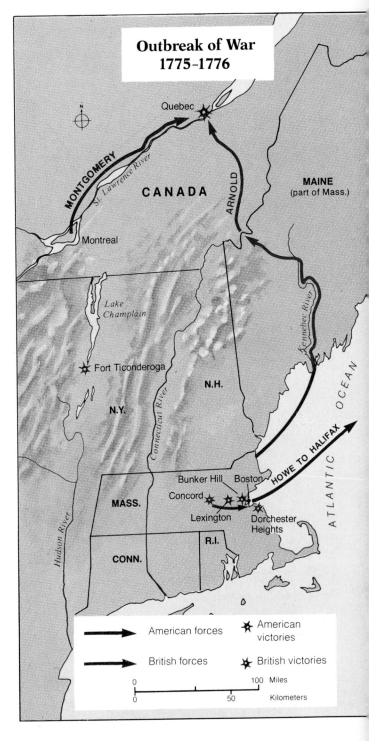

■ American colonists fought the British even before the colonies declared their independence. Ethan Allen's "Green Mountain Boys" captured Fort Ticonderoga in 1775. The Battle of Bunker Hill was also a moral victory for Americans. However, the siege of Quebec failed.

115

SECTION REVIEW

1. Identify: John Dickinson, Committees of Safety, Ethan Allen, Israel Putnam, Bunker Hill, William Howe, Benedict Arnold.

2. Contrast the goals of the moderates with those of the radicals at the Second Continental Congress.

3. What three qualities made George Washington a good commander in chief?

4. What news convinced the Continental Congress to order an invasion of Canada?

5. **Critical Thinking** How could a patriotic song influence people's reactions to an event?

2 The Road to Independence

The Americans' attempt to capture Canada enraged the British. To punish the rebels, they adopted harsher policies. But such tactics only served to swell the radicals' following. The final break came on July 4, 1776. Until that time, the colonists had not really thought of the military actions as a war for independence.

A Harsher British Position

Colonial radicals, favoring independence, found unexpected allies in King George and his ministers. Infuriated by colonial resistance, George III repeatedly refused to make concessions that might have strengthened the position of the moderates. As early as November 1774, he had concluded that "blows must decide whether they are to be subject to the Country or Independent."

In a final attempt to mend the rift, the Continental Congress adopted the Olive Branch Petition on July 8, 1775. Written by John Dickinson, the resolution urged the king to pressure Parliament to repeal the Coercive Acts and to bring about "a happy and permanent reconciliation." Six weeks later George III responded with the Prohibitory Act. In it the king and Parliament proclaimed that a general rebellion existed in the colonies and authorized steps "to bring the traitors to justice." These measures included cutting off all American trade, seizing American ships, and demanding that the rebels formally and publicly repent.

When news of the Prohibitory Act reached the Continental Congress on February 27, 1776, John Adams declared that it was an "Act of Independency, for the King, Lords and Commons have united in sundering this country from that I think forever."

To make matters worse, information soon reached the Continental Congress that the king had hired 10,000 Hessian mercenaries* to suppress the rebellion. The news stunned the delegates, who knew that such troops usually brought looting, plundering, arson, and uncontrolled violence in their wake. Benjamin Franklin remarked with bitter irony on the British need to use German soldiers to crush colonists who were British subjects.

Thomas Paine's *Common Sense*

If George III's harsh statements inflamed Americans, another Briton's words kindled colonial patriotism even more. With the publication of his pamphlet *Common Sense* in January 1776, Thomas Paine helped colonists define their position more sharply and clearly than ever.

Paine, the son of a poor English corset maker, had drifted from one job to another before immigrating to America in late 1774. Over the years, however, Paine had educated himself and had learned to write better than most university-trained men of the day. Using direct and forceful language that aroused his readers, Paine argued that common sense showed that Americans owed allegiance neither to the king of Great Britain nor to any monarchy.

> For all men being originally equals, no one by birth could have a right to set up his own family in perpetual preference to all others for ever. . . . [A monarch is] nothing better than

---

*mercenary: a soldier who fights for pay in a foreign army. The Hessians were from the German state of Hesse.

the principle ruffian of some restless gang. Of more worth is one honest man to society and in the sight of God, than all the crowned ruffians that ever lived.

Declaring Independence

By the spring of 1776 the Continental Congress had begun to adopt resolutions as if it were making laws for an independent nation. Although sentiment in the Middle Colonies still seemed to favor compromise, a decisive break had already been made in New England and the South. Following the lead of these colonies, the Continental Congress approved privateering against British ships, outlawed the importation of slaves, entered into relations with foreign nations, and cut off all trade with Great Britain.

Congress also organized a committee to draft a formal declaration of colonial independence from Britain. Declaring independence seemed a good idea for several reasons. As citizens of an independent nation, captured Americans could demand to be treated as prisoners of war rather than as traitors, subject to the death penalty. Moreover, an independent nation would probably be able to obtain aid from Britain's enemies. Eventually, arguments like these won over all but the most reluctant moderates.

Supported by a congressional resolution stating that "these United States are, and of right ought to be, Independent States," John Adams, Benjamin Franklin, Robert Livingston, Roger Sherman, and Thomas Jefferson set to work on the declaration. Jefferson, who was responsible for most of the draft, later commented, "I turned to neither book nor pamphlet while writing the Declaration."

On July 2, 1776, the committee presented the completed declaration to the Continental Congress. Two days later the delegates adopted it. No opposing votes were cast. Three delegates from Pennsylvania, however, absented themselves, and the New York delegation abstained. Congress then sent the document to the printer.

The Declaration

The Declaration of Independence contained three major sections. The preamble explained the philosophical principles behind the act of declaring independence. The middle section listed specific grievances against the king. The Declaration concluded by stating that the United States of America had severed its ties to the crown and had formed an independent government. (See the Declaration, pages 836–837.)

The preamble had the greatest impact on American society because it established general principles of human rights that applied to all people, not just to the colonists. The beliefs about human rights set forth in the Declaration of Independence were ideals rather than realities in late eighteenth-century America. Yet they helped lay the foundation for a future society based on equal rights for all. Over the years, these ideals encouraged a greater regard for human dignity in nations around the world, stimulating reform movements and political revolutions.

The preamble also justified colonial resistance to Britain in a new way. Earlier, during the Stamp Act crisis, for example, colonists had emphasized the rights they possessed as British subjects, rights guaranteed them by the unwritten British constitution. Now they spoke of natural rights that no human power could take away. Jefferson wrote that people were "endowed by their Creator with certain unalienable rights" and that "among these are life, liberty, and the pursuit of happiness."

People "secure these rights" by forming governments for their protection. Jefferson was guided in his thoughts on this subject by John Locke, a seventeenth-century English political philosopher. Jefferson, like Locke, believed that "governments . . . [derive] their just powers from the consent of the governed." Thus, he argued, the people are the fundamental source of power in any state. This claim ran directly counter to the European theory that kings were the source of power in a state with a God-given right to rule over their subjects.

If the people were the source of government, it followed that they had the right "to alter or to abolish it." However, Jefferson wrote, such a change should be made only when the circumstances truly warranted it, not for "light and transient causes."

The second section of the Declaration of Independence then listed the causes that justified American revolt against British rule. To make the argument as forceful as possible and to cut the ties once and for all,

Jefferson blamed everything on the king. The king, he stated, had refused to allow laws "necessary for the public good" unless the people gave up their "right of representation in the legislature."

The third section of the Declaration officially established a new independent nation. It said that the states had the power to make war, establish alliances, trade with whomever they wanted, and sever all connections with Great Britain. With the adoption of the Declaration of Independence on July 4, 1776, the 13 British colonies ceased to exist. The United States of America were at war.

1. Identify: Olive Branch Petition, Prohibitory Act, Thomas Paine, *Common Sense*.

2. What two actions by King George helped make the colonists more radical?

3. What two arguments won over some delegates reluctant to declare independence?

4. Describe the three major sections of the Declaration of Independence.

5. **Critical Thinking** Compare the attitudes of Thomas Paine and John Locke toward royalty.

3 The Balance of Forces

Early in 1776, John Adams had predicted that Americans would "have a long, obstinate, and bloody war to go through." But few believed that the fighting that had erupted at Lexington in April 1775 would continue for six and a half years. Even fewer realized that it would be the first of over eighty major battles.

Choosing Sides

The crowd outside the Philadelphia statehouse rejoiced when a representative of Congress read them the Declaration of Independence a few days after its passage. People rang bells and lighted bonfires. In New York City, an enthusiastic crowd threw ropes around a statue of King George and pulled it to the ground.

Not all Americans felt the same about independence, though. A significant minority—estimates range from 10 to 20 percent—remained loyal to the crown. They called themselves Loyalists; the Patriots* called them Tories.

Loyalists tended to be among the more well-to-do Americans. They included wealthy merchants, most former officials of the royal government, and ministers of the Church of England. Many farmers and artisans remained "loyal" too, and some large planters sided with the British. Harassed by Patriots, many Loyalists fled to Canada or

This portrait of an unknown free black sailor was painted in 1779.

---

*Patriot: the name by which colonists who wanted independence called themselves.

Paul Cuffe: Another View of Taxation Without Representation

During the Revolutionary War, Paul Cuffe, a free black from Massachusetts, learned that the colonists' persistent cries for "no taxation without representation" had ironic implications for black property owners. Cuffe grew up on an island off the Massachusetts coast. There his father, an African slave who had bought his freedom, owned a farm. Tutored in navigation, Cuffe decided at age 16 to try his hand on a whaling ship.

On his third whaling voyage the Revolutionary War broke out. Cuffe was held by the British for three months as a prisoner of war. After his release, Cuffe and his brother bought a farm in Westport, Massachusetts.

Though the two men were required to pay property taxes on their land, they found that they did not have the same rights as white property owners. "We are not allowed the Privilege of freemen of the State, having no vote or influence in the Election of those that Tax us," Cuffe wrote in a petition to the Massachusetts state legislature, signed by seven other free blacks. As a further protest, the Cuffe brothers stopped paying taxes. In 1780 the Cuffes were jailed for these activities.

Behind bars, they continued their fight for representation. Finally they succeeded in forcing the issue before a local town meeting. Although the Cuffes lost the case, efforts such as theirs helped free blacks win the right to vote in Massachusetts.

Paul Cuffe returned to the sea when the war ended and became a successful trader with his own small fleet of ships. He continued the struggle for equal rights for black Americans throughout his lifetime.

Britain. Others found shelter in cities controlled by the British, such as New York. Most, however, remained in their homes as inconspicuously as possible.

While nearly half of the American people actively participated in the Patriot cause, almost as many—perhaps about 30 to 50 percent—remained neutral. Among them were religious groups such as the Moravians, Quakers, and Mennonites, whose beliefs emphasized pacifism, opposition to the use of force for any reason. Although most managed to stay out of the fighting, the tide of battle sometimes forced them to supply aid to one side or the other.

As a result of such divided loyalties, America found itself in a state of civil war. Many prominent families had members on opposing sides. For example, Benjamin Franklin's son, the governor of New Jersey, sided with the British, causing his father much anguish.

The British population itself was split on the American question. Some prominent members of Parliament publicly supported the Patriot cause. Several leading generals refused to fight in the war and resigned their commissions.

Many Native Americans saw the war as an opportunity to oust colonial intruders. The Iroquois in the North, the Shawnee and Delaware in the western part of the Middle Colonies, and the Cherokee in the South formed key alliances with the British.

The Role of American Blacks

Blacks, both slave and free, tended to support the Patriot cause. A reservoir of black veterans remained from the French and Indian War, and some had already enrolled as minutemen. Black soldiers had also fought at Fort Ticonderoga, Bunker Hill, and Lexington and Concord.

Some women went to war with their Patriot husbands and shared in the battle. Among them was Mary Ludwig Hays, nicknamed Molly Pitcher. She became a legend in the Battle of Monmouth when she took her fallen husband's place to keep a Patriot cannon firing.

As much as they welcomed the support of able-bodied soliders, members of the Continental Congress saw that the participation of blacks posed problems. They worried that blacks would take the idea of freedom too seriously and wondered if such thinking might encourage slaves to revolt.

In November 1775 George Washington, acting with the advice of other generals, recommended that black soldiers be barred from enlisting in the Continental Army. The Continental Congress agreed. In the same month, the British stepped up their efforts to recruit blacks, offering freedom to any slave or indentured servant who would join the British Army.

The British action forced the Americans to reconsider their position, and in January 1777 the Continental Army began enlisting free blacks. A year later Rhode Island raised an entirely black battalion, made up of soldiers both slave and free. Ultimately about 5,000 black soldiers fought for the Patriot cause.

Women's Contribution to the War Effort

Although men were expected to do the fighting, women fought too. Sally St. Clair of South Carolina and Deborah Sampson of Massachusetts disguised themselves as men and enlisted in the Continental Army. When Molly Pitcher's husband fell next to his artillery piece, legend has it that she took his place. Women were also among the most skilled spies in the colonial intelligence network.

Wives often accompanied their husbands' regiments. In camp they cooked, laundered, or sewed during lulls in combat. They collected or prepared medicines and nursed sick and wounded soldiers. Benjamin Franklin's daughter, Sarah Franklin Bache, organized a Daughters of Liberty chapter to make clothing and handle hospital shipments. With many men away fighting, women often had to take over traditionally male jobs. They maintained farms, ran businesses, and worked as blacksmiths, manufacturing the cannons, guns, and shot needed to keep the Continental Army going.

The British Position

Great Britain, the strongest military power in the world at the time, began the war with several distinct advantages. Generals Thomas Gage, William Howe, Henry Clinton, and John Burgoyne had wide-ranging experience in large-scale European wars. They understood military strategy and how to transport and deploy regiments effectively.

For years the British had maintained a huge standing army in the colonies. Redcoats, as British soldiers were called because of their bright red uniforms, were well drilled and fully disciplined. They followed the orders of superior officers unquestioningly, unlike the freewheeling amateur colonial militia. Moreover, the redcoats were fully equipped with artillery, firearms, powder, tents, uniforms, blankets, and the many other necessities of war.

The British regulars were supported by a navy that commanded the seas. The Royal

Navy placed 28 warships equipped with over 500 guns in ports from New York to Halifax, Nova Scotia. Vessels could transport fresh troops from Europe, usually without interference, and shift armies in the colonies by sea, a method considerably more efficient than marching men along dangerous country roads. In contrast, the Americans had no real navy but only privateers.

The British faced disadvantages too, and these ultimately contributed to their undoing. Their chief drawback was the problem of supply, a disadvantage for all foreign-based armies. Fighting in a hostile country, the British had to transport war material 3,000 miles (4,800 kilometers) from ports in England. It took weeks and sometimes months for needed materials and reinforcements to arrive in the colonies. Campaigns often stalled while generals waited for supplies. The farther British troops pushed into the interior, the more problems they faced in transporting supplies.

The British also found it difficult to adapt to the new kind of war being fought in America. Following European custom, the well-trained redcoats lined up in three straight rows, loaded their muskets, and fired across a field at an enemy that was expected to line up in a similar formation. At Lexington, Concord, and other early battles, however, they faced rebel militia who shot at them from behind stone walls and trees.

The British Army could conquer, occupy, and hold cities like Boston, New York, or Philadelphia without difficulty, but in the countryside it was at the mercy of colonial forces. The extent of the land permitted the colonial militia to fall back and vanish into the woods, only to reappear in unexpected locations to ambush British soldiers and supply units. As they gained experience, American officers used this hit-and-run tactic often. These and other guerrilla tactics wore down the British until the Continental Army grew strong enough to defeat them.

The American Position

The colonies began the war with several advantages. As a besieged nation they benefited from the love of a people for their own land. Patriots defending their own farms and cities responded with a fervor that often inspired heroism. Most Americans also knew how to use guns, and in battle American hunting rifles proved more accurate than British muskets. Furthermore, George Washington turned out to be a superb leader. Finally, several foreign countries, especially France, provided valuable aid, as did private citizens from other nations.

The Americans faced problems too. Few soldiers had regular army experience, and volunteers enlisted for short terms. No navy of any significant size existed. And while Americans did not have to transport supplies across an ocean, as the British did, the Continental Army could never get enough food, ammunition, or clothing. The Continental Congress lacked the authority to require states or citizens to provide funds or military service. And most of all, the Americans had to overcome the problem of *localism*, thirteen states going their separate ways instead of acting as one nation.

Maintaining the Military Forces

The development of a navy posed a serious problem for the Americans. Six states owned ships suitable for patrolling inland waterways, but none had vessels like the seagoing British men-of-war. On October 13, 1775, the Continental Congress authorized the construction of a Continental Navy, but one hardship after another befell the effort. For instance, four frigates had to be destroyed before they were finished in order to prevent capture by the British.

Despite these and other problems, the United States did achieve a few notable naval successes. In 1779 Captain John Paul Jones, commanding the *Bonhomme Richard*, named after Benjamin Franklin's book *Poor Richard's Almanac*, engaged the British ship *Serapis* in one of the most savage naval battles of the war. When the British captain called on Jones to surrender his leaking ship, Jones retorted, "I have not yet begun to fight!" Two hours later the British captain surrendered. Jones's feat, however, represented the exception, not the rule. At the end of the war, the American navy consisted of only one or two ships larger than a schooner.

Creating the Continental Army was also difficult. The single greatest task faced by Washington and his staff was that of molding a truly American army from the various colonial militias. Most soldiers' loyalties were to their own states. Few if any felt loyalty to the nation as a whole. If war threatened their home ground, they flocked to its defense. But as soon as the scene of battle shifted, the war became someone else's problem. Soldiers returned immediately to their farms, shops, and families. Those who remained often refused to serve under officers from other colonies.

Generally, each colony took care of its own fighting forces. Colonial governments supplied powder, tents, uniforms, and blankets to their soldiers. Contributing such supplies to the Continental Army was unheard of. It was not unusual for one state militia to refuse to share its provisions and equipment with another—even when it had a surplus.

Washington did everything in his power to discourage the individual colonies from operating as though they were fighting private wars with Britain, but it was an uphill struggle and rarely successful. "I have laboured," he wrote, "to discourage all kinds of local attachments and distinctions of country . . . but I have found it impossible to overcome prejudices."

Political and Financial Localism

Washington's problem with the state militias paralleled the political problems facing Congress. Originally, the Continental Congress had met to deal with a specific threat: the

Coercive Acts. By the time it had approved the Declaration of Independence, the Congress had become a national government. But what powers did it have? How could it enforce its acts? In the beginning no one knew, so the Continental Congress had to move cautiously.

Individual states repeatedly demonstrated concern with local matters and indifference to those affecting the nation as a whole. For example, only states had the authority to draft men into the army. Yet when the Continental Congress requested troops, few states regularly filled their quotas. Early in the war, several states even seemed willing to negotiate separate treaties with foreign nations.

Raising money to finance the war created the worst problems. The states would not surrender power to a central government or grant the Continental Congress authority to tax. The Congress assessed each state a certain sum, but the states either refused to pay or refused to levy the necessary taxes for fear of alienating their people.

Finally Congress authorized a national currency, known as the Continental dollar, but this only contributed to the nation's difficulties. The Continental Congress did not have gold and silver to back up the currency it printed, yet it needed money to support

Both the British and the colonists sometimes found it hard to recruit enough men for their armies. At left is an American recruiting poster. The 1779 British cartoon at right mocks the difficulty British recruiting sergeants had enlisting soldiers.

the war—to buy supplies and pay soldiers. Consequently, Congress simply began to print the money it needed.

Inflation was the result. As more money was printed, its value declined. Eventually even Patriots objected to being paid for supplies in Continental dollars, and the phrase "not worth a Continental" soon became popular. To make matters worse, each of the thirteen states continued to print its own paper money. As a result, 14 different currencies circulated during the war, leading to unavoidable confusion.

SECTION REVIEW

1. Identify: Loyalists, Patriots, Tories, redcoats, John Paul Jones.
2. Define: localism.

3. Describe the policies of the Continental Congress toward the enlistment of American blacks in the army.
4. How did women contribute to the war effort?
5. List the advantages and disadvantages the British forces had.
6. What advantages helped the Americans?
7. What was the single most difficult problem in the creation of the Continental Army?
8. What did the Continental Congress do in order to raise money for the war?
9. **Critical Thinking** Why do you think that the states found it difficult to submit to a central authority?

4 Fighting a Colonial War

The first real test of the newly formed Continental Army came in the months following the Declaration of Independence. Washington had to thrust his hastily trained and poorly armed band of Patriots into combat against the largest military force Britain had ever sent across the seas.

During the last months of 1776, more than 30,000 well-armed British regulars opposed no more than 18,000 Continentals in a series of battles throughout the Middle States. American victories were few and defeats were many, but valuable lessons were learned.

The Continental Army gained both experience and confidence in its powers of survival. Furthermore, Washington and his staff realized that the British were far from being the invulnerable war machine everyone feared they would be. Though their army won skirmish after skirmish, a decisive military victory was always just out of reach.

The New York Campaign

After the British had withdrawn from Boston to Halifax, they decided to strike at New York City. In the summer of 1776, 32,000 British soldiers, led by General Sir William Howe, poured into the city.

Howe, who was sympathetic toward the Americans, believed that the mere sight of such a formidable array of troops would terrify the rebels into surrender. He hoped, if possible, to avoid an armed confrontation and even went so far as to offer the Continental Congress a royal pardon if it would surrender.

To Howe's regret the Congress chose to fight rather than submit. Though he was able to muster a force little more than half as large as Howe's, Washington marched resolutely into battle. War, even with the threat of crushing defeat, seemed preferable to a humiliating surrender.

Despite valiant fighting and skillful maneuvering, Washington's troops could not hold New York and the surrounding area. The British chased them out of Long Island, forced them to abandon strategic positions on Manhattan Island, and pushed them across the Hudson River into New Jersey. Pursued by Lord Cornwallis, Washington beat a hasty retreat southward over the New Jersey plains, finally crossing the Delaware River into Pennsylvania.

As the year drew to a close American morale reached a low point. Thousands of militiamen began to desert the Continental Army. Others, whose one-year enlistments

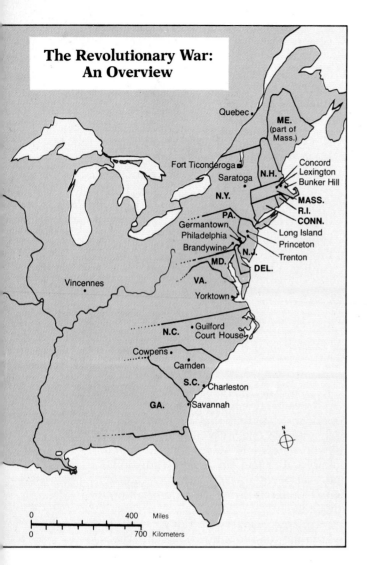

The Revolutionary War: An Overview

■ The Revolutionary War was fought over an enormous land area. This map shows the location of the major battles you will read about in this chapter.

The British, as was customary in eighteenth-century warfare, had settled in for the winter. Their troops occupied various New Jersey towns, including Trenton, just across the river from Pennsylvania.

There a contingent of Hessian mercenaries was celebrating the holidays when Washington pounced on them under cover of night. Groggy with drink, the mercenaries were beaten in forty-five minutes. Washington recrossed the river with 900 prisoners in tow. Four days later, American troops, flushed with success, forged the river again with an army of 5,000.

Although their path was blocked by Cornwallis with an even larger force, the Americans managed to outfox the British and capture Princeton. Had Washington possessed the necessary supplies and equipment, he would have been able to hold the town. Without them, and with an exhausted army, he was forced to relinquish Princeton and take refuge for the rest of the winter in the Morristown hills.

As 1776 drew to a close, the Americans settled into winter quarters with renewed hope. They had suffered defeat, but they had also accomplished one of their principal objectives: to push the British 60 miles (96 kilometers) back from Philadelphia. An Englishman took note of the fact, commenting sadly, "A few days ago they had given up the cause for lost. Their late successes have turned the scale and now they are all liberty mad again."

Saratoga and Philadelphia

During the winter of 1777, the British secretary of war approved a plan to conquer New York and isolate New England. Had the strategy succeeded it would probably have split the United States in two and paved the way for a British victory. Through a combination of chance, poor coordination by British generals, and American persistence, the plan failed. This failure turned the tide of the war firmly in the Patriots' favor.

According to the plan, Lieutenant Colonel Barry St. Leger was to lead a force down the St. Lawrence and then east to the Hudson River. General Howe was to move up the Hudson River to Albany, New York, while another British force, commanded by General John Burgoyne, moved south from Canada to meet him. Instead, Howe decided to

were to expire on January 1, 1777, counted the days before they could rejoin their families. For Washington the situation could not have been bleaker.

Success at Trenton and Princeton

In that desperate hour Washington conceived a bold plan. On the night of December 25, just days before his soldiers' enlistments expired, Washington recrossed the Delaware into New Jersey with 2,400 men.

The Revolutionary War 1776–1777

Legend:
- → American forces
- → British forces
- ✸ American victories
- ✸ British victories

■ *By the end of 1776 Washington's troops had retreated through New York and New Jersey into Pennsylvania. In late December, Washington led a small force across the Delaware River to attack Trenton. Victory there and at Princeton gave the Patriots new heart. In 1777 they defeated the British at Saratoga, a turning point in the war.*

At the start of the war, Washington's poorly equipped and untrained army was no match for the well-drilled British forces. British troops drove the colonials first from one position, then another. A British officer painted this watercolor of the successful British assault on Fort Lee, New Jersey.

seize Philadelphia, the Patriots' capital city. He hoped the move would both demoralize the Americans and encourage the dispirited Loyalists.

Howe successfully occupied Philadelphia, disrupted Congress, and trounced Washington at the Battle of Brandywine. But in the long run his maneuver proved disastrous to the British cause.

St. Leger's forces reached Fort Stanwix, but they retreated when they received word that a large American army led by Benedict Arnold was approaching. General Burgoyne got off to a more promising start. He captured strategically placed Fort Ticonderoga, with its huge arsenal of gunpowder and supplies. But without help from Howe, Burgoyne could not keep up the pace, and a string of crushing defeats followed. Marching south from Ticonderoga, Burgoyne's large, unwieldy army was constantly harassed by the hit-and-run guerrilla tactics of the smaller, more agile American forces. Short of supplies and with no reinforcements in sight, Burgoyne finally withdrew to Saratoga.

The move was ill-advised and Burgoyne knew it, but he had no choice. At Saratoga he was besieged by a crack force under the command of General Horatio Gates and some of the finest officers of the Continental Army. Realizing that he had no alternative but to surrender, Burgoyne ordered his entire army of 6,000 men to lay down their arms on October 17, 1777.

SECTION REVIEW

1. Identify: Sir William Howe, Lord Cornwallis, John Burgoyne, Horatio Gates.

2. What impact did the defeat in New York have on American morale?
3. (a) What new plan did the British devise during the winter of 1777? (b) How did General Howe's actions ruin the plan?
4. Who won the battle of Saratoga?
5. **Critical Thinking** Why was the issue of morale important to the American cause?

5 Victory for the Americans

The victory at Saratoga proved to be a major turning point of the war. It wiped out the British threat from the north and destroyed an entire British army. Even more important, it brought France into the war on the American side.

The French Alliance

France, as a traditional rival of Britain, had decided early in the struggle that support for the Americans was in its own best interest. Before making a commitment, however, French leaders adopted a wait-and-see policy. Knowing that an American alliance would mean war with Britain, the French wanted to be assured of American chances of success before they acted. Saratoga gave them that assurance.

In February 1778 Benjamin Franklin, who had spent more than a year at the French court trying to win friends for the American colonies, negotiated two treaties with France. The first recognized the United States as an independent nation and granted France special trading privileges with it. The second agreement, which was to go into effect only if France and Great Britain went to war, announced that France would give up claims to land in North America east of the Mississippi. The Americans, in turn, agreed to recognize the French right to any lands in the West Indies captured during the war.

The French alliance offered the United States substantial benefits. French naval vessels soon appeared along the American coast, and the new ally dispatched large quantities of supplies and military experts. Even more important, the alliance reduced **British pressure on America. When war broke out with France in June 1778, and**

later with Spain, Great Britain could no longer devote all its military strength to suppressing the American revolution.

Individuals from foreign nations also aided the Patriot cause. After spending a bitter, hungry, and demoralizing winter (1777–1778) camped at Valley Forge, Penn-

■ *During the Revolutionary War, several Indian nations fought with the British. George Rogers Clark led a Patriot force down the Ohio River to defeat the British and their Indian allies.*

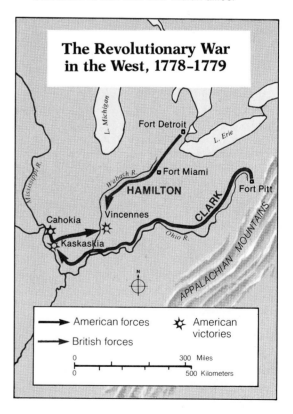

The Revolutionary War in the West, 1778–1779

L. Michigan
Fort Detroit
L. Erie
Mississippi R.
Wabash R.
Fort Miami
Fort Pitt
HAMILTON
CLARK
Cahokia
Vincennes
Ohio R.
Kaskaskia
APPALACHIAN MOUNTAINS
N

→ American forces
→ British forces
✶ American victories

0 300 Miles
0 500 Kilometers

sylvania, Washington's ragged troops were whipped into fighting shape by Friedrich von Steuben. An experienced veteran of the Prussian Army, Baron von Steuben taught the Continentals how to drill, maneuver, and use bayonets like professional soldiers.

From Poland came Thaddeus Kosciusko (kahs ee UHS koh) and Casimir Pulaski (poo LAHS kee). Kosciusko, an able engineer, designed forts along the Delaware River and the first fortifications at West Point. Pulaski served as a cavalry officer.

The War in the West

Although most of the crucial battles of the war took place along the Atlantic coast, significant developments occurred in the area of present-day Ohio, Illinois, and Kentucky. From time to time, Washington sent troops to fight the Shawnee and other western tribes who, as allies of the British, had been attacking frontier settlements.

British power in the West was finally broken by 25-year-old George Rogers Clark, a Virginian who led 175 volunteer frontiersmen against the British and their Native American allies. Clark and his party rescued the Illinois and Ohio settlements.

The War in the South

Having failed in 1777 to crush the revolution by conquering New York and New England, the British developed another battle plan a year later. This time the target was the South rather than the North. The goal, however, remained the same: to crush American resistance once and for all.

Sir Henry Clinton, a cautious strategist, designed the offensive. To execute it he chose Lord Cornwallis, a capable but hotheaded general. Cornwallis, like Howe before him, tended to follow his own instincts even when it meant disobeying orders and changing battle plans in mid-course.

The British based their hope of success on two factors. First, they believed that they could use troop ships to move soldiers from place to place in the South. In this way they would be able to travel more rapidly and efficiently than the Americans, who had to march overland. Second, the British counted on extensive support from southern Loyalists.

On both points, Clinton and his fellow strategists guessed wrong. The British wildly

overestimated the number of Loyalists in the South. Most southerners ardently supported the Patriot cause and provided American forces with constant aid as they trekked over the countryside. The southerners supplied the army not only with food, but also with vital intelligence about British maneuvers. Furthermore, the British had not anticipated the presence of French warships. Although the French could not patrol every inch of the coast, they prevented the British navy from having a completely free hand.

The British captured Savannah, Georgia, in December 1778, and for a year American forces tried to regain it without success. In May 1780 the British won a stunning victory at Charleston, South Carolina. Then, working their way inland, they crushed a Continental force under Horatio Gates at Camden. (See the map on page 128.)

Although the British had won three major victories in the South, they would see few more. Washington relieved Gates of his command and replaced him with the abler General Nathanael Greene. By the time Greene assumed command of the Continental forces, the British had begun to make mistakes that would cost them the war.

Final Victory

Despite mounting evidence that traditional European battle tactics did not work, Lord Cornwallis continued to use them. While Greene harassed the British with small units, Cornwallis massed his troops for a showdown in open battle. Thus, although the redcoats had superior numbers and artillery, they often found themselves standing in battle as stationary targets.

As a result of his devotion to such tactics, Cornwallis received a "very unexpected and severe blow" at Cowpens, South Carolina, on January 17, 1781. Three months later more than a quarter of his army was destroyed by Greene at Guilford Court House, North Carolina. Cornwallis claimed victory at Guilford because Greene withdrew his troops from the field before the close of the battle, but a British observer, hearing of the victory, accurately evaluated its significance. "Another such victory," he commented, "would destroy the British army."

After the "victory" at Guilford Court House, Cornwallis withdrew to Wilmington

The Revolutionary War in the South, 1778–1781

American and French forces
British forces
American victories
British victories

0   150 Miles
0   200 Kilometers

■ *The final stages of the Revolutionary War were fought in the South. British forces won at Savannah, Charleston, and Camden. But Patriot troops continually harried the British Army. After battles at Cowpens and Guilford Court House, General Cornwallis retreated first to Wilmington, then to Yorktown. There he surrendered on October 17, 1781.*

on the North Carolina coast. Battle-weary and discouraged, he wrote to Clinton.

> My present undertaking sits heavy on my mind. I have experienced the distresses and dangers of marching some hundreds of miles, in a country chiefly hostile, without one active or useful friend; without intelligence, and without communication with any part of the country.

For a while Cornwallis's situation seemed to improve. Benedict Arnold, who had deserted to the British, captured and burned Richmond, Virginia. Areas of the state succumbed to isolated British raids, and reinforcements brought Cornwallis's army up to 7,000 men.

Once again, however, Cornwallis erred disastrously. He refused an order by Clinton to send part of his army to New York. Instead, he retreated to the Yorktown peninsula in Virginia and began building fortifications.

Washington, who had just received 5,000 French reinforcements led by the Comte de Rochambeau (roh shahm BOH), immediately recognized Cornwallis's mistake. He realized that the British general had given him the chance he had been waiting for: an opportunity to stage a combined land and sea attack on the major British force.

Rochambeau and Washington marched a French and American force overland from New York to join the Marquis de Lafayette (lah fay EHT) in Virginia. At the same time Admiral de Grasse sailed with thirty ships and 3,000 French marines to Chesapeake Bay. Cut off by land and sea, Cornwallis held out for three weeks. Then, realizing that rescue was impossible, he surrendered his entire army on October 17, 1781.

The battlefield presented an imposing spectacle. The French and the Americans lined up in two facing columns a half mile long. As the British army marched between the victorious troops, the British band played "The World Turned Upside Down." Cornwallis, unwilling to appear, sent his deputy, General Charles O'Hara, who turned his sword over to Washington's deputy, General Benjamin Lincoln. The British soldiers then marched to an open field, where they stacked their muskets.

Clinton still had 16,000 troops in New York, but Yorktown and several French victories in the West Indies brought the war to a close. The defeated British sued for peace.

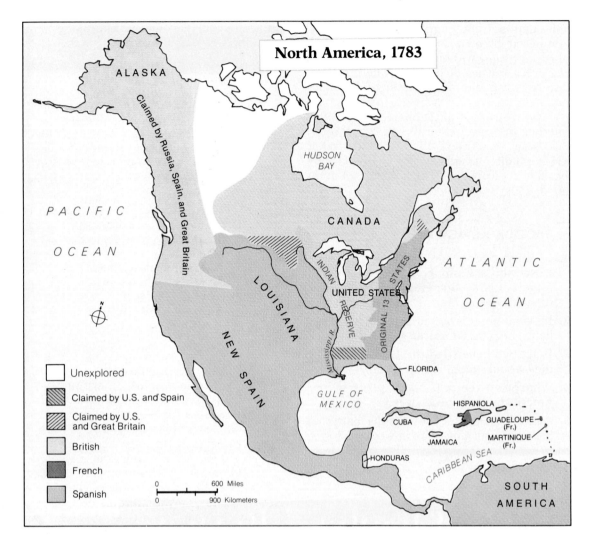

North America, 1783

■ *The Treaty of Paris (1783) ceded to the United States all British land from the Atlantic to the Mississippi and from the Great Lakes to Florida.*

The Peace Treaty

Congress ordered Benjamin Franklin to hold no peace talks without the French, but Franklin began informal, secret talks with the British anyway. When the other peace commissioners, John Adams, John Jay, and Henry Laurens, arrived, formal talks began. In the course of negotiations, the Americans achieved their major goals: British recognition of American independence, and acquisition of all the land from the Atlantic coast to the Mississippi River between the Great Lakes and Florida.

Great Britain also agreed to evacuate military posts in several areas, and the United States won fishing rights off Newfoundland. Britain asked for compensation for the property losses of Loyalists. Although Congress agreed to "recommend" payment, the Loyalists never received compensation from the American government.

Both sides signed the treaty on November 30, 1782. It went into effect two months later and was ratified by Congress on April 19, 1783, eight years to the day after the first shot at Lexington.

How did it all happen? Washington later marveled at the achievement. Who would believe, he said, "that such a force as Great Britain has employed for eight years in this country could be baffled in their plans of subjugating it by numbers infinitely less, composed of men sometimes half-starved, always in rags, without pay, and experiencing every species of distress, which human nature is capable of undergoing." But happen it did!

The Patriots straggled home, one way or another, to neglected farms and happy families. Now there were 13 free states. What kind of nation would they form? Would they be able to work together for the common good of all?

SECTION REVIEW

1. Identify: Baron von Steuben, Thaddeus Kosciusko, Casimir Pulaski, George Rogers Clark, Sir Henry Clinton, Nathanael Greene, Marquis de Lafayette.
2. In what three ways did the French alliance help the American cause?
3. What two beliefs led the British to think they would succeed in the South?
4. What were the two major goals of the Americans at the peace treaty?
5. **Critical Thinking** How was the battle of Saratoga a turning point in world history?

Major Events

1775	British pass Prohibitory Act; Second Continental Congress convenes; Ethan Allen and Green Mountain Boys capture Fort Ticonderoga; battle at Bunker Hill; Continental Army formed under Washington's command; American attack on Quebec
1776	*Common Sense* published; Declaration of Independence signed; New York campaign; Battles of Trenton, Princeton
1777	Battles of Philadelphia, Brandywine, Saratoga
1778	French alliance; British capture Savannah
1780	British victories at Charleston, Camden
1781	Battles of Cowpens, Guilford Court House, Yorktown; British surrender
1783	Treaty of Paris ratified by Congress

 # Chapter 7 Review

In Perspective

After the Second Continental Congress opened in May 1775, fighting between the British and the colonists broke out in New York, Massachusetts, and Canada. The British, by imposing harsh measures, helped convince delegates to the Congress to declare independence in July 1776.

The Americans had to fight a long and difficult war in order to gain independence. Many colonists, however, remained neutral or loyal to Great Britain. Localism also hampered the war effort.

The British had many advantages at the beginning of the war. These included a large, well-trained army and navy. Yet the colonists were defending their homeland, and they had excellent leadership in George Washington. Furthermore, the aid of other European nations, especially France, helped counter British advantages. Tactical errors by British commanders led to final American victory at Yorktown in 1781. When the peace treaty was ratified in 1783, the American states were finally independent. Now they faced the challenge of surviving as a new republic.

Vocabulary

On a separate sheet of paper, write the word or words that best complete each of the following sentences.

1. Groups of citizens who recruited and trained local militia, collected funds, and gathered information were the ___.
2. A request by the Continental Congress urging the repeal of the Coercive Acts was the ___.
3. ___ is the tendency of states to act in their own interests instead of in the interests of the nation as a whole.
4. Colonists who wanted independence called themselves ___.
5. Colonists who supported the king called themselves ___.

Chapter Checkup

1. What was the significance of the Battle of Bunker Hill?
2. (a) What important principle was established in the preamble to the Declaration of Independence? (b) Why has this continued to be significant? (c) What major justifications did the declaration give for independence?
3. (a) Why did the participation of black soldiers in the war pose serious problems for American leaders? (b) What role did American blacks play in the war?
4. (a) Why did Washington decide to attack Trenton? Princeton? (b) What did he and his staff learn from these and other battles throughout the Middle States?
5. (a) What were the terms of the treaties Benjamin Franklin negotiated with the French? (b) Why were the French originally reluctant to form a formal alliance with the United States? (c) Why did they change their minds?

Critical Thinking

1. **Analyzing** (a) According to Thomas Jefferson, what are natural rights? (b) Explain how the theory of natural rights could be used to justify independence.

2. **Evaluating** (a) Why do you think slaves might have decided to enlist in the Continental Army? (b) Why might free blacks have joined?

Developing Basic Skills

1. **Comparing** Make a chart with four columns. In column one list the advantages of the British at the start of the war. In column two list the disadvantages. In columns three and four do the same for the Americans. (a) Who would seem to have the most advantages? (b) Who would seem to have the most disadvantages? (c) Which advantages or disadvantages do you think were the most important to the outcome of the war? Explain.
2. **Map Reading** Study the map on page 129 and compare it with the map on page 87. Describe how the boundary lines changed between 1763 and 1783.

See page 828 for suggested readings.

Writer's Handbook

Chronological Order

As you have learned, events that are arranged in the order in which they occurred are in chronological order. Supporting information can be arranged in time order when you are describing a series of events. For example, you should use chronological order to organize the supporting details for the answer to this question: *What events led up to the issuance of the Declaration of Independence?*

Some words used to show time relationships are: *when, first, later, soon, immediately, then, at last, afterward, meanwhile, as soon as, while,* and *next.*

Practice: (a) Read the subsection "The Colonists Take Action" on pages 113–114. Copy the words and phrases that show the chronological order of the events being described. (b) Write the answer to the essay question in the first paragraph of this lesson. Organize the supporting facts in chronological order.

American Individualism

"What, then, is the American, this new man?" That was the question asked by a Frenchman who visited America around the time of the revolution. Hector St. John de Crèvecoeur (krehv KOR) like many other Europeans, recognized that Americans behaved differently from the people of Europe. Visitors singled out various characteristics in these "new" Americans. But, like Crèvecoeur, many agreed that individualism was one trait that surely set Americans apart from other people.

What is individualism? Americans saw it as self-reliance. They felt that people should count on themselves to get things done in their own way. The rough conditions of early American life encouraged such an attitude. To survive, a backcountry farm family had to master many skills: clearing land, harvesting crops, building furniture, hunting animals, skinning hides, weaving cloth. . . . The list went on and on.

People who relied on themselves in so many different ways also tended to think for themselves. Individualism included the ability to accept the consequences of one's decisions, no matter how dangerous or unpopular they were. Before the revolution, some colonists questioned whether or not the colonies should belong to Britain. The more they considered the issue, the more they concluded that the colonies should be free. So they declared their independence and then had to fight for it.

Even before the skirmish at Lexington and Concord in 1775, Governor Gage of Massachusetts discovered a new spirit among the colonists. He sent someone into the countryside to find out what the people were thinking. The agent stopped at a small house beside the road, where an old man was cleaning his rifle. "I asked him what he was going to kill," the agent reported. "As he was so old, I should not think he could take sight at any game; he said there was a flock of redcoats at Boston, which he expected would be here soon; he meant to try and hit some of them, as he expected they would be very

good marks. . . . I asked him how old he was; he said, 'Seventy-seven, and never was killed yet.' " Here was an individualist, indeed—thinking for himself and willing to fight for his principles.

As the United States expanded westward, the frontier experience enhanced the spirit of individualism. People reveled in the exploits of the likes of Mike Fink—a real-life keelboater along the Ohio and Mississippi rivers. "I can out-run, out-jump, throw down, drag out, and lick any man in the country," he boasted "I'm a Salt-River roarer an' I'm chock full of fight." Similarly, the American cowboy came to be admired as a rugged individualist in the 1870s and 1880s.

Limits on Individualism How far can individualism be pushed? In the 1840s, Henry David Thoreau was so tired of human society, he went off into the Massachusetts woods, built a cabin, and lived alone for two years along the shores of Walden Pond. Thoreau announced that his goal was to simplify his life and go it alone. "I would say to my fellows, once for all, as long as possible live free and uncommitted. . . . I was more independent than any farmer in Concord [the village nearby], for I was not anchored to a house or farm, but could follow the bent of my genius. . . ." His book about his experiences, *Walden*, illustrates individualism taken to its limits. Even Thoreau, however, realized that he could not exist without others. He planned only a temporary stay at Walden Pond.

The pioneers, too, valued the friendship of good neighbors. They may have been individualists, but they also gathered regularly for barn-raisings, quilting bees, or revival meetings. Being an individual did not necessarily mean shutting out the rest of the world.

While tolerant of individualists, American society itself has put limits on them. The leeway to do as one pleases ends where it will infringe on the personal freedoms of others. Some of the best known

The hardy frontier hunters formed the backbone of George Rogers Clark's forces during the Revolutionary War. When the war was over, these rugged individualists once more led the way west.

Western heroes were people who enforced the law, such as Wyatt Earp and Bill Hickok. As the population of the country has increased and people have become more dependent on one another, establishing limits has become more complicated. An inventor with an idea for a new product has the freedom to try to make a fortune from it. But the factories that make the product cannot pollute public waterways. Nor can a producer manufacture a product with total disregard for the safety of the people who will use it.

Individualism Today How much freedom to be individualists do we have today? The balance between individual rights and society's need for protection is still a subject of debate. Most states have laws preventing citizens from driving cars that have bad brakes or are unsafe in other ways. But should people be free not to wear seat belts in a car—even if seat belts reduce the consequences of accidents?

Some states say yes, others no. Should Americans be free to drive while carrying an open bottle of beer in one hand? Do "individualists" have the right to play radios loudly on a downtown street? Should sightseeing planes be free to fly low over national parks like the Grand Canyon? These questions are not easily answered, because Americans, in their individualistic ways, will no doubt continue to disagree on issues that are important to them.

1. How did the need to rely on oneself encourage the development of individualism in early Americans?
2. Why is Henry David Thoreau considered an individualist?
3. Why do you think the rights of the individual must be balanced with the needs of society?

American Profiles   # Ethan Allen

W hat was there about Ethan Allen that earned him a place in history? Of course, he defeated the British at Fort Ticonderoga. But why was he there? The answer lies in the fact that Allen was a person who did things his own way—to the delight of some people and the distress of others.

Allen was born in 1738 in Litchfield, Connecticut. One of a large family, he was devoted to his brothers and worked together with them for most of his life. By the late 1760s, he had moved to the New Hampshire Grants. (At the time, New York and New Hampshire disputed ownership of the Grants, which later became the state of Vermont.)

With his brothers Ira, Heman, and Zimri, Allen joined many of the Grants settlers in refusing to recognize the jurisdiction of New York. They wanted to reorganize the area into the separate province of Vermont. In 1770, Allen took positive action. He formed a militia—the Green Mountain Boys—to press the case by force, if necessary.

In 1771 the new royal governor of New York decided to enforce the colony's claims to the Grants. He offered generous rewards for the capture of the Grants outlaws, and a particularly high price for their popular leader, Ethan Allen.

Although Allen stepped up his attacks on the Yorkers, by the spring of 1775 the Vermont landholders were clearly losing the battle of the Grants. Had the revolution not occurred, it is likely the region would now be part of New York State. But many of the Grants settlers threw their lot in with the revolutionaries and followed Allen, their determined hero, into open rebellion against the British.

At that time, the British fort at Ticonderoga was a strategic stronghold in North America—astride the major north-south water route from Canada into the 13 colonies. To isolate Canada and cut off British supplies to the western colonies, the Committees of Correspondence sent troops

Ethan Allan (1738–1789) was known for doing things his own way. His exploits and legendary strength won him the admiration of many people.

from Connecticut and Massachusetts under Benedict Arnold to capture the fort. In a bold undertaking, 200 militia men led by Ethan Allen spearheaded the fight. The troops and Allen's Green Mountain Boys combined forces on May 8, 1775. By May 10, the rebels had secured the fort, later taking Crown Point to the north.

Soon the Green Mountain Boys were attached to the Continental Army under their own officers. The Americans hoped to capture Montreal.

When expected troops failed to join the invaders, Allen was not discouraged. Perhaps rashly, he led a raid with his own men. The British took him prisoner and threatened to hang him in London. But after a brief stay in a British prison, he was returned to America and held until General Washington himself secured his release.

In the Grants, meanwhile, a revolutionary convention declared Vermont an independent commonwealth in 1777. Once he returned there, Ethan Allen again became an important leader. But Allen did not live to see the fruit of his work. He died in 1789, two years before New York relinquished its claim and Vermont became the fourteenth state.

During his lifetime Ethan Allen was admired by his followers as a colorful leader, a strong supporter of individual liberty, and a fiery defender of the Vermont country. His strong streak of individualism won him the admiration of those who agreed with his stand and the scorn of those who did not. History credits him with championing the rights of settlers of the Vermont country and with securing the victory at Ticonderoga, an invaluable stroke for the American cause.

1. What was the basis of the conflict over the New Hampshire Grants?
2. How does the story of Ethan Allen's adventures resemble a folk tale?

Voices of Freedom

A New Breed of People

French-born Hector St. John de Crèvecoeur traveled widely in the American colonies. He married an American and in 1769 bought a farm in New York.

While passing through England in 1781, Crèvecoeur sold the manuscript of a series of 12 essays he had written describing life in America. These were published as Letters from an American Farmer. *The following reading is taken from the third of these "letters," entitled "What Is an American?"*

What, then, is the American, this new man? He is either a European, or the descendant of a European. . . . He is an American, who, leaving behind him all his ancient prejudices and manners, receives new ones from the new mode of life he has embraced, the new government he obeys, and the new rank he holds. . . . Here the rewards of his industry follow with equal steps the progress of his labor. . . .

Europe contains hardly any other distinctions but lords and tenants. This fair country alone is settled by freeholders, the possessors of the soil they cultivate, members of the government they obey, and the framers of their own laws, by means of their representatives. . . . It is here that the idle may be employed, the useless become useful, and the poor become rich. But by riches I do not mean gold and silver; we have but little of those metals. I mean a better sort of wealth, cleared lands, cattle, good houses, good clothes, and an increase of people to enjoy them. . . .

But how is this accomplished in that crowd of . . . people who flock here every year? . . . Let me select one (newcomer) as an example of the rest. He is hired, he goes to work. Instead of being employed by a haughty person, he finds himself with his equal, placed at the table of the farmer. His wages are high, his bed is not like that bed of sorrow on which he used to lie. If he behaves with propriety, and is faithful, he is embraced and becomes almost a member of the family. . . .

Judge what an alteration there must arise in the mind and thoughts of this man. He begins to forget his former servitude and dependence; his heart involuntarily swells and glows. This first swell inspires him with those new thoughts which constitute an American.

Adapted from *Letters from an American Farmer,* 1782.

1. What did Crèvecoeur believe the newcomers could achieve in America?
2. How would you account for Crèvecoeur's optimistic view of life in the American colonies?

8

An Experimental Era

(1777–1787)

Detail from Exhuming the First American Mastodon *by Charles Willson Peale*

As the newly formed Continental Army struggled against the well-trained British forces, an independent American government took shape. States drafted constitutions and elected legislatures, and they took steps to create a national government. Strong state loyalties made that a difficult task, but by the end of the war the nation's first constitution had been ratified.

As you will read in this chapter, the new government faced difficult challenges boldly. An experimental mood characterized government as it did many other areas of American life. If one idea did not work, people were willing to try another. The new central government had weaknesses that prevented it from solving important political, economic, and foreign policy problems. When the weakness of the central government became obvious, Americans showed that they were willing to experiment again.

Articles of Confederation

1776	1778	1780	1782	1784	1786	1788

1777 Vermont abolishes slavery	**1779** Massachusetts convention drafts a constitution	**1781** Articles of Confederation ratified	**1783** Treaty of Paris ratified	**1786** Shays' Rebellion begins	**1787** Northwest Ordinance passed

1 Making a New Start

The Revolutionary War was a far-reaching event that affected more than the nation's government. It jolted Americans out of their everyday habits. Things that they had taken for granted changed drastically. By the 1780s Americans were ready to experiment in many facets of their lives.

An Experimental Mood

Following the hard-fought struggle for independence, Americans sought practical ways to use their heritage. More Americans began to think that there might be better ways of doing things. As Benjamin Franklin observed, "We are, I think, on the right road to improvement, for we are making experiments." Not only political experiments, he might have added, but experiments that affected all aspects of life.

In education, for example, Americans began to question the teaching of ancient languages such as Latin and Greek. Parents began to demand that their children receive useful, practical educations. Some educators questioned the practice of providing separate schools for boys and girls. Soon the first coeducational schools were founded, and some girls and boys began to go to school together.

Overall, Americans sought to increase their knowledge. They established newspapers and magazines and published more books than ever before. Scientific societies such as the American Academy of Arts and Sciences were founded, and the American Philosophical Society grew in stature.

But behind all the ferment and change was a belief in liberty. And perhaps the most significant American experiments were in the search for liberty and equality.

Steps Toward Greater Political and Social Equality

Political equality became a major goal in the young republic. The newly created constitutions of the state governments seemed to echo Jefferson's words in the Declaration of Independence that "all men are created equal." Most significant, some states extended the right to vote by lowering or eliminating property requirements.

But the echo of political equality was less than perfect. Only "qualified" citizens could vote in elections. To qualify, a person typically had to be male, white, Christian, and a property owner. Despite some criticism of these qualifications, state governments did little to amend them in the early years.

The concern for equality did lead citizens of the new nation to suspect any privilege that made some people seem superior to others. In 1783, for example, a group of former Continental Army officers founded the Cincinnati Society. The society's primary goal was to make the government aware of the needs and wants of veterans, especially officers. Membership was hereditary; only officers and their descendants could belong.

Many people feared that the founders of the Cincinnati Society wanted to establish a new aristocracy. The society was denounced throughout the nation, even though George Washington was its president. The Massachusetts legislature claimed that the society "may be dangerous to the peace, liberty, and safety of the United States." Such intense opposition caused the Cincinnati Society to drop its political activities and become a social club.

Americans greeted other organizations that hinted of aristocracy with similar though less powerful reactions. Such reactions showed that Americans were beginning to think of equality in a social as well as a political context. A popular magazine commented, "The idea of equality breathes through the whole and every individual feels ambitious, to be in a situation not inferior to his neighbor." A Boston newspaper added that the phrase *the better sort of people* became thoroughly contemptible and odious in the estimation of the people."

Some efforts to dissolve social-class barriers proved successful. Changes in inheritance laws broke up large landholdings and redistributed property. In addition, the government sold millions of pounds worth of property confiscated from Loyalists during the revolution. The creation of new opportunities for land ownership accelerated the breakdown of old social barriers.

Limited Opportunities for Women

Although theories and experiments in equality abounded in the United States, inequality for women persisted. Yet some people hoped to remedy the situation. Abigail Adams denounced the lack of female equality, and she warned her husband, John, when he was attending the Continental Congress, "Do not put such unlimited power in the hands of husbands. Remember all men would be tyrants if they could."

Abigail Adams was not the only person who believed that the phrase "all men are created equal" meant "all humans are created equal." Nonetheless, the laws did not provide for such equality. Women had few property rights and no voting rights, in spite of a brief period in New Jersey when they were entitled to vote. The political system was legally restricted to men and remained that way until the twentieth century.

Unlike the political system, the educational system provided some limited new opportunities for women in the 1780s and

Until 1806 women in New Jersey could vote, a right not enjoyed by most American women until 1920.

1790s. A number of New England academies began to admit female students and to allow women to study the same subjects as men. But women continued to face discrimination in higher education.

Lucinda Foote's experience is just one example. At age twelve, Foote proved to a board of examiners that she could do college work, but the report came back saying that she appeared "fully qualified except in her sex, to be received as a pupil of the freshman class of Yale University." Hence, her admission was denied.

Limited Advances for Free Blacks

The revolutionary idea that "all men are created equal" had an impact on black as well as white Americans. Over 50,000 free blacks lived in the United States in the 1780s, most of them in the Middle Atlantic states. Courts in several states began to look more favorably on lawsuits filed by black slaves seeking freedom. North Carolina, Maryland, Kentucky, and Tennessee extended to free blacks the right to trial by jury, the right to compel the appearance of witnesses, and the right to legal counsel.

Furthermore, the first state constitutions in the Northeast did not generally discriminate against blacks in voting rights. In the years following the revolution, free blacks living in the North tended to improve their standard of living due to the high demand for workers. In addition, some formerly all-white churches admitted blacks, although not always with equal membership rights.

In spite of these advances, free blacks in the new nation still suffered discrimination. Most northern states passed laws discouraging black immigration into the region, and areas where free blacks could live were segregated, or set apart from others. In some states in the northern part of the South, the danger of being kidnapped back into slavery remained a reality. States in the deep South, if they allowed free blacks at all, usually deprived them of most civil rights.

Early Actions Against Slavery

Try to picture Thomas Jefferson, sitting at his desk, reviewing the words he wrote in the Declaration of Independence. As his eyes once again scan the phrase "all men are created equal," he turns and looks out the

138

Folk artists captured many vignettes from American life, like the scene on this tea tray. It shows Congregational minister Lemuel Haynes, a Revolutionary War veteran, with one of his congregations.

window at some of the people working on his estate. These people are his slaves. The dilemma did not escape him. Jefferson struggled with the problem of slavery all of his life.

Jefferson was not alone in his concern about slavery. The Continental Congress had banned the slave trade during the Revolutionary War, and all states except Georgia and South Carolina outlawed it by the war's end. Such actions did not end the slave trade however. As you will see in the next chapter, the Constitution protected the slave trade until 1808.

Vermont's constitution, written in 1777, was the first to provide for the complete abolition of slavery. Over the next 20 years, all the northern states either outlawed slavery or devised plans to gradually free slaves within individual state borders, but these changes came slowly.

In the South the problem of slavery proved more difficult. While Jefferson and his fellow Virginians, George Washington and James Madison, opposed slavery in principle, in practice they could not run their plantations without slave labor. Slavery was too important to Southern agriculture. The Virginia legislature, among others, did make the freeing of slaves, called *manumission*, easier. However, sentiment for the abolition of slavery did not gain a strong foothold in the South.

In some states, especially New York and Pennsylvania, groups of citizens banded together to oppose slavery and promote equality. Together with the Quakers, who steadfastly opposed slavery, such societies formed the base from which a strong abolitionist movement would eventually grow. (See Chapter 16.)

Separation of Church and State

Before the Revolutionary War, most colonies officially recognized and supported only one established church. All citizens, whether they belonged to the church or not, had to pay taxes to support it. The Congregational Church was often an established church in the Northeast, and the Church of England, renamed the Episcopal Church after the war, was the established church in the South.

Thomas Jefferson, among others, thought that such partnerships of church and state restricted religious freedom and gave the established church an unfair advantage over others. In 1786 the Virginia legislature passed a bill, sponsored by Jefferson, that effectively separated church and state. "Almighty God hath created the mind free," argued Jefferson. The Virginia law stated that "no man shall be compelled to frequent or support any religious worship, place, or ministry whatsoever." Other southern states also disestablished the Episcopal Church, but in New England, Puritan descendants maintained a favored status for the Congregational Church.

Helping Humanity

During the eighteenth century, many Americans came to believe that society could be improved by human effort. Even before independence, Americans had organized groups to solve problems that individuals could not handle on their own. The large number of volunteer fire departments was one example. In this way the colonists had provided services that their governments had not.

The idealism of the revolution further encouraged Americans to try to improve the lives of their fellow human beings. For example, the treatment of criminals bothered many people. Harsh penalties for crimes, such as execution for robbery, and the appalling conditions in prisons led to the formation of many reform societies. Concerned citizens also formed charitable societies to help the poor, raise money for schools, and

provide aid to new immigrants. One society even existed especially to assist sea captains' widows.

Still other societies were devoted to the economic development of the new nation through transportation and land-use projects. Some encouraged bridge construction and road improvement. Others worked to make rivers passable. George Washington was a member of the Great Dismal Swamp Company, for example, which planned to drain the swamp south of Norfolk, Virginia, and develop the land. The formation of voluntary societies devoted to improving the human condition seemed to encompass all aspects of early American life.

A New National Consciousness

The revolution forced Americans in the 1780s to change the way they thought about themselves. No longer British subjects, they were citizens of a new nation, and they were proud of that fact.

Politicians, philosophers, and ordinary citizens predicted that America would become "a great and mighty empire." According to one New England minister, it would be "the largest the World ever saw, to be founded on such principles of Liberty and Freedom, both civil and religious, as never before took place in the world." Historians wrote about the revolution and the birth of a country. Poets offered lofty praise to their newborn republic.

Assertions of American inferiority by European philosophers brought quick denials. Thomas Jefferson once wrote a scholarly defense of Americans, but not all reactions were so formal. Benjamin Franklin, for example, gave a dinner party in Paris at which a Frenchman, the Abbé Raynal (ray NAHL), argued that the American environment caused plants, animals, and even humans to grow smaller than those found in Europe. Franklin, noticing the height of his dinner guests, asked everyone to stand. The Abbé, who had been so eager to make his point, stood nearly a head shorter than the American guests.

Noah Webster, who would later gain fame for his dictionary, contributed to the new national awareness by experimenting with the American language. Some of his changes survived—"labour" became "labor"—but not all of them caught on. Efforts

Noah Webster: Creating an American Language

Noah Webster's goal in life was to promote the adoption of an American language. He wanted to free Americans from British English as they had freed themselves from the British crown. To this end he published a series of three textbooks: a speller in 1783, a grammar in 1784, and a reader in 1785.

Webster objected to the way certain words had been borrowed from other languages but had not been respelled. The result, he claimed, was a confusing mixture of letters, many of which were not pronounced the way they looked, and others of which were not pronounced at all.

Webster urged Americans to simplify their spelling. For example, he argued that "head" should be spelled "hed"; "bread" should be spelled "bred"; "friend" should be spelled "frend"; "laugh" should be spelled "laf"; and "machine" should be spelled "masheen." Most of Webster's suggestions did not catch on, but his textbooks sold millions of copies.

Webster continued to work for a national language, publishing the first edition of *An American Dictionary of the English Language* in 1828. "A *national language*," he wrote, "is a band of *national union*. Every engine [means] should be employed to render the people of this country *national*; . . . and to inspire them with the pride of national character."

---

by individuals like Webster, along with the pride of creating a nation, helped the people of the United States to begin thinking of themselves as Americans.

SECTION REVIEW

1. Identify: Cincinnati Society, Abigail Adams, Noah Webster.
2. Define: segregated, manumission.
3. (a) What were the typical qualifications for voting in state elections? (b) How had some states extended the right to vote?
4. List three ways the position of free blacks improved after the Revolutionary War.
5. Which state was the first to abolish slavery?
6. How did established churches limit religious freedom, according to Jefferson?
7. Give two examples of ways Americans organized to try to improve society.
8. List three examples of the emerging national consciousness.
9. **Critical Thinking** Why do you think social change accompanied the political change brought about by the American Revolution?

2 The New American States

Although former British subjects were beginning to think of themselves as citizens of a new nation, their chief loyalty was still to their individual states. Even leaders of the struggle for independence felt that way. John Adams referred to Massachusetts as "our country" and called the Massachusetts delegation to the Continental Congress "our embassy." For Thomas Jefferson, "my country" meant Virginia for many years to come. With their own sense of identity and pride, the 13 former colonies assumed their status as independent states and clearly viewed their state governments as more important than the new national government.

Preserving Traditions

The English philosopher John Locke had theorized that when a people overthrow one government, they have to design a new one

141

from the ground up. Yet nothing of that sort happened in the America of 1776.

Instead Americans built on English traditions and their own experiences. Colonial assemblies became state legislatures, many prewar laws remained in effect, and in a few cases the old royal charters became the new state constitutions. By the end of 1776 independent governments were functioning in every state except Georgia and New York.

So few changes were made largely because Americans in general were not displeased with the unwritten English constitution or with the local colonial governments. Their anger had been directed at the king, his representatives, and Parliament for violating English political traditions. The changes they did make were usually to insure that power could not be abused by the new governments as it had been by the old.

State Governments

Each new state government had three branches: an executive branch, a legislature, and a court system. Colonial governors had been the symbol of the British monarchy, and Americans remained suspicious of the office. Accordingly, state constitutions limited the governors' powers.

In most states the governor was elected by the legislature, often for only a one-year term. Usually the governor could not *veto*, or reject, a bill passed by the legislature. Pennsylvania eliminated the position of governor entirely and substituted a council of twelve men as the executive. State judges, like governors, had limited authority. The legislatures, on the other hand, had rather extensive powers, including the power to declare war and conduct foreign affairs.

This faith in representative assemblies had deep roots. Americans had depended on their colonial assemblies to represent their interests since the establishment of the Virginia House of Burgesses in 1619. Not only did the assemblies symbolize the authority of the people, they actively resisted numerous attempts by the king and Parliament to diminish that authority, as you read in Chapter 6. Furthermore, delegates selected by those assemblies had written and signed the Declaration of Independence and had organized the military struggle against the British.

Yet the former colonists did not intend to grant unlimited power to the state legislatures. With the exception of Pennsylvania, each state had a *bicameral* legislature, or one with two houses, a lower house and an upper house. In this way legislative power was divided between two groups that balanced each other.

The lower house was the larger, and voters elected its members directly, usually every year. It generally possessed greater power than the upper house because people believed that it was most responsive to their needs and wishes. Out of tradition, the smaller upper house was intended to be a more cautious body. Accordingly, its members were elected for longer terms, ranging from two to four years.

Some people feared that the upper house might be composed of persons with aristocratic leanings, like the members of the British House of Lords. As a result, some states provided that the lower house elect the upper house. Other states called for direct elections. No longer would governors appoint the upper house as they had in many colonies.

John Adams strongly argued that an upper house should include people of great talent and prestige, an aristocracy based on merit rather than heredity. Adams thought that such people would temper the wilder ideas that the lower houses might receive from the people.

Most state constitutions protected the people from possible abuse by their government by including a bill of rights. This guaranteed certain *inalienable rights* that governments could not take away, including freedom of the press, freedom of religion, and the right to trial by jury.

A Written Constitution Drawn From the People

The content of the new state constitutions reflected colonial experiences under British rule, and so did the actual work of drafting the constitutions. During the colonial period, American rights had been based on the English constitution, but that was not a written document. It consisted of centuries of accumulated laws, judicial decisions, and traditions subject to many interpretations. Americans sought to guarantee their freedoms by putting them in writing, thus hoping to make violations of those rights more difficult.

In most states a provincial congress elected during the Revolutionary War simply wrote a constitution and passed it. Although vague dissatisfaction with this method existed, no one faced the problem squarely until 1778. That year the people of Massachusetts rejected the constitution written by their state legislature. Massachusetts citizens argued that if a legislature could write a constitution, it could also change it whenever it pleased. As a result, nothing could stop a legislature from being as tyrannical as a king.

Instead, Massachusetts devised a system whereby the constitution came from the people. In 1779 its voters elected delegates to a special constitutional convention. The document they drafted was approved the following year by a vote of the people. This system put the constitution beyond the reach of the legislature. The state legislature could not change the constitution without the consent of the people it represented.

Thus Massachusetts helped formulate an important principle of American government: constitutions were to be written by special conventions. The principle gained wide acceptance during the 1780s and was followed in 1787 when a special convention wrote the national constitution in use today.

SECTION REVIEW

1. Define: veto, bicameral, inalienable rights.
2. What changes did Americans make in their new state governments? Why?
3. (a) What were the three branches of the new state governments? (b) Into what two groups were the state legislatures divided?
4. How did Massachusetts protect its constitution from changes by the state legislature?
5. **Critical Thinking** Why might a written constitution be less subject to violation than an unwritten constitution?

3 The First National Government

When the delegates to the Continental Congress declared American independence in 1776, they had to decide what sort of national government would bind the 13 states together. Their task was formidable. The former colonists were staunchly loyal to their own states, and most feared a powerful national government. Yet the delegates knew the new nation needed a government to act for it. A committee, appointed by the Continental Congress, quickly went to work on a constitution.

The Articles of Confederation

The committee completed a draft in a month. But because of fighting on the battlefields, not to mention disputes among delegates trying to protect the rights of their individual states, almost a year and a half passed before the Continental Congress agreed on a final draft of the nation's first constitution. This constitution, known as the Articles of Confederation, was not ratified until 1781. (See page 145.)

The Articles of Confederation proposed a _confederation_, or alliance of independent states. The central government of the confederation was to be composed of a congress. Not surprisingly, the new Congress was much like the existing Continental Congress. On paper, it appeared to be a powerful national government. Congress could declare war and appoint military officers. In foreign affairs it could receive and send ambassadors, sign treaties and alliances, and regulate dealings with Native Americans. In the domestic sphere it could establish post offices, borrow money, and fix weights and measures.

In spite of these specific powers, the Articles of Confederation placed strict limits on the authority of Congress. For example, it could not collect taxes or draft men into the Continental Army. Congress could only request soldiers and money from the states.

With abuses by the British Parliament fresh in their memories, the states were wary of giving too much power to a central authority. To ease this concern, a clause in the

Articles guaranteed that each state would retain its "sovereignty, freedom, and independence" and keep "every power, jurisdiction, and right" not given directly to Congress. This strong *reserved powers* clause protected the rights of the states and made it more likely that the state legislatures would approve the document.

A Question of Fair Representation

The question of representation in the new Congress had caused heated debate in the Continental Congress before it approved the Articles of Confederation. In the Continental Congress each state had one vote regardless of its area or population. The proposed Articles of Confederation contained the same provision. Since the United States was to be a confederation of states, many delegates said, states must have equal representation.

Delegates from states with larger populations strongly objected. They insisted that states with more people deserved more influence and hence more votes. Delegates from less populous states, on the other hand, favored one vote per state, since it gave them equal power.

The majority of delegates eventually accepted the principle of equal representation for each state, with every state having one vote in Congress. Nine of the 13 states had to approve a measure before it became law. Although the representatives of the larger states were not completely satisfied, they recognized the urgent need for a national government because of the ongoing war with Great Britain.

Before the Articles of Confederation could take effect they had to be *ratified*, or approved by the state legislatures of all thirteen states. The Continental Congress submitted the finished document to the states in November 1777, expecting rapid ratification. However, disputes over conflicting state claims to western territories delayed approval until March 1781.

■ *Under the Articles of Confederation, the national government had very limited powers. The states kept important powers, such as the right to tax.*

The Articles of Confederation

No chief executive
No national court system
Laws need approval of 9 of the 13 states
All other powers reserved to the states

Congress could	Congress could not
Declare war and make peace	Levy taxes
Raise an army and navy	Regulate foreign or domestic trade
Make foreign treaties and alliances	Settle disputes among states
Coin and borrow money	Collect state debts owed the central government
Regulate weights and measures	Enforce any of its powers
Establish a post office	
Regulate Indian affairs	

Dispute Over Western Lands

The boundaries of the new states were not clearly defined. Two or more states often claimed the same territory, and a few states claimed land all the way to the Pacific. Some states refused to ratify the Articles of Confederation until their claims were settled. States that had no claim to lands in the West also balked at ratifying the new constitution until the land issue was resolved.

Legislators from Maryland, for example, thought that the vast claims of some states, particularly Virginia, gave them an unfair advantage. What if Virginia sold its western lands to provide income for the state? Then it would not need to tax its citizens. What would prevent people and businesses located in Maryland, which did levy taxes, from flocking to Virginia? Such a situation could rob Maryland of population and revenue. Other states with fixed boundaries, particularly Pennsylvania and New Jersey, urged that all western lands be ceded to the national government. Then, as the land was sold, the revenue would benefit the entire nation and not just a few privileged states.

Such rational arguments, however, were not the only reasons some state legislators wanted the western lands ceded to the national government. A group of individuals, mostly from Maryland, Pennsylvania, and New Jersey, had "purchased" vast stretches of western territory from Native Americans, often illegally.

These land speculators hoped to sell the land to settlers and make a big profit. But first their claims had to be validated. The speculators believed that a national congress would be more cooperative than legislatures outside their own states. Therefore, they pressured their state legislators to refuse to ratify the Articles until the states ceded all western territory to the national government.

Recognizing the need to establish a national government, Thomas Jefferson and other Virginians urged their legislature to cede Virginia's land to the United States. They argued that with all its western lands, Virginia would be too large to govern properly. Virginia agreed to cede its land, but the agreement would take effect only when the government voided all purchases of Native American land. In effect, this action destroyed the speculators' hopes for profits. In

As settlers moved onto the lands of Native Americans, Indian leaders had to decide how to keep the settlers out. The Iroquois chief Ki-on-twog-ky, called Cornplanter, wrote several letters to General Washington complaining about the intruders.

February 1781 Maryland finally approved the Articles of Confederation, the last state to do so.

A New Land Policy

After the Revolutionary War ended in 1783, Congress had to decide how to settle and govern the western lands. Representatives were particularly worried about the vast area ceded by Virginia known as the Northwest Territory. (See the map on page 146.)

Congress passed the Land Ordinance of 1785 in the hopes of raising money. The ordinance provided for the survey and sale of the land. The territory was to be divided into townships. Each township would be subdivided into 36 lots, each one measuring one square mile (2.6 square kilometers), with one

145

The Northwest Territory and Western Land Claims, 1787

CANADA

L. Superior

CLAIMED BY
NEW YORK

MAINE
(Mass.)

L. Huron

L. Ontario

VT.

N.H.

L. Erie

MASS.

NEW YORK

WESTERN
RESERVE
(CONN.)

PA.

R.I.

N.J.

CONN.

L. Michigan

NORTHWEST TERRITORY

MD.

DEL.

Ohio R.

CLAIMED BY
VIRGINIA

VIRGINIA

SPANISH LOUISIANA

CLAIMED BY
N. CAROLINA

APPALACHIAN MTS.

N. CAROLINA

ATLANTIC OCEAN

Mississippi R.

CEDED BY S.C. TO U.S.

S. CAROLINA

CLAIMED BY
GEORGIA

GEORGIA

CLAIMED BY U.S.,
GA., AND SPAIN

SPANISH FLORIDA

GULF OF MEXICO

N

0   400   Miles
0   600   Kilometers

■ *Western land claims created friction among the states. Land ceded to the national government by Virginia and New York became the Northwest Territory.*

sold over a million acres (about 400,000 hectares) of land to the Ohio Company for less than ten cents per acre.

The plan was further complicated by *squatters* who had moved into the new territory and established homesteads without complying with the ordinance or any of its provisions. Congress unsuccessfully tried to clear the Northwest Territory of these unauthorized settlers.

Squatters also presented a problem to land speculators. The Ohio Company, fearing the loss of its legally purchased territory, urged Congress to pass new legislation dealing with the territory. Other eastern interests, viewing the squatters as violent and dangerous, supported the Ohio Company's urgings. As a result, in 1787 Congress passed a second land bill: the Northwest Ordinance.

The Northwest Ordinance

Under the new ordinance Congress would appoint a governor, secretary, and three judges to govern the territory. Residents could elect a representative legislature when the adult male population reached 5,000, but the governor had the power to veto legislative action.

The ordinance gave Congress the authority to divide the entire area into three to five separate territories based on settlement patterns. Once a territory had a population of 60,000 free inhabitants, it could be admitted as a state with all the rights and obligations of existing states. Until such time, the ordinance guaranteed protection of residents' property rights as well as other rights such as trial by jury and religious freedom. The ordinance also prohibited slavery throughout the territory.

Despite continued wheeling and dealing by land speculators, the land ordinance experiment succeeded. Congress had created an orderly system that extended republican government westward with the settlers. New states would be admitted as equals of the original states. The pattern established by the Northwest Ordinance continued to work well for over a hundred years.

Economic Recovery

As with all wars, the American War for Independence had a disruptive impact on the nation's economy. The impact was partic-

lot set aside to support a public school. One provision called for honoring Indian claims, but it was largely ignored.

On paper the plan appeared sound, but in actuality surveyors encountered many difficulties. The terrain was basically uncharted wilderness, with rivers, mountains, and swamps that did not lend themselves to perfect squares. Thus the work progressed slowly and allowed land speculators time to revive their efforts.

One group of New England speculators, calling themselves the Ohio Company, pressed for the suspension of the Ordinance of 1785 so they could purchase a large tract of unsurveyed land. Because Congress desperately needed the additional revenue, it ularly dramatic because the United States had waged this war against its principal trading partner, Great Britain. Merchants were hard hit by the separation from Britain. Some profiteers managed to continue trading during the war and made huge profits, but they were the exceptions.

In New England especially, the merchants suffered terribly. Massachusetts shipyards, turning out 125 ships per year before the war, built only 25 ships per year after the war. The whaling industry was reduced from 150 whaling ships to a mere 24. Some shippers took to privateering and robbed British vessels, but the risks were great and the income sporadic.

After the war foreign trade resumed, but it was not immediately profitable. France expected to gain a large segment of American trade after its wartime alliance with the United States, but it did not. Americans still had a taste for the British products they had traditionally used.

Independence did provide American merchants with the freedom to seek world markets outside the British empire. Merchants pursued these markets with great enthusiasm, taking their trade as far as China. In May 1785 the sailing ship *Empress of China* returned from Canton carrying a

New Bedford and Nantucket were important whaling centers in Massachusetts. The sale of whale oil for lamps was an important part of the economy of these cities.

highly profitable cargo of tea and silks. Before long, ships from Boston, Philadelphia, and Providence began plotting new routes to Asia.

Freed of British trade restrictions, American merchants opened up markets in Asia. In this scene, traders deal with tea merchants in Canton, China. Yankee captains also brought back porcelains, silks, and new kinds of plants.

American industry also profited as a result of the war. The fighting itself created a demand for munitions, guns, clothing, and other supplies. In addition, during the war Americans created new industries to manufacture goods they formerly had imported from Great Britain.

Southern planters survived the war, but not without taking great losses. Exports of tobacco and indigo dropped sharply, while Britain's high import duty prevented South Carolina from selling as much rice as before. Furthermore, Loyalists and British invaders had kidnapped many slaves during the war (almost 25,000 in South Carolina). That meant many southern plantations lacked the labor needed to continue production at pre-war levels.

Small farmers were in a better position. Many grew wealthy providing food for the armies. Farmers who had borrowed large sums of money before the war—and there were many of them—also benefitted from the inflation of the war years. The same was true of debtors who, after the war, paid back their debts with nearly worthless Continentals. These economic dislocations caused a depression in the years following the war, but by 1787 economic recovery was clearly evident. Americans were beginning to build a sound economy.

SECTION REVIEW

1. Identify: Articles of Confederation, Northwest Territory, Land Ordinance of 1785, Northwest Ordinance.
2. Define: confederation, reserved powers clause, ratify, squatters.
3. (a) List the powers given to Congress under the Articles of Confederation. (b) What two crucial powers did it lack?
4. What unsettled dispute delayed the ratification of the Articles of Confederation?
5. What two problems made enforcing the Land Ordinance of 1785 difficult?
6. When could a territory become a state according to the Northwest Ordinance?
7. What groups were hurt economically by the Revolutionary War?
8. **Critical Thinking** What did Benjamin Rush mean when he said, "The American war is over, but this is far from being the case with the American Revolution"?

4 A Need for Further Experimentation

The willingness of Americans to experiment continued even after the formation of the first national government. The problems facing the new republic quickly revealed the weakness of the national government and convinced Americans they had to seek better solutions.

Raising Revenue for the New Government

Since "taxation without representation" had been the major charge against the British Parliament, the authors of the Articles of Confederation tried to guarantee that history would not repeat itself. Consequently, raising money proved to be one of the most serious problems the new national government confronted.

Under the Articles, state legislatures, not the people, elected members of Congress. Thus Congress did not directly represent the people and could not tax them. It could ask the states for money, but only the representatives of the people—the state legislatures—could grant such requests. If the states turned down the request, as they usually did, Congress could do nothing.

Still, the young nation desperately needed money. Without the power to tax, Congress began looking elsewhere. It could continue printing paper money as it had done to help finance the war, but inflation had made the paper Continentals virtually worthless. Dutch bankers loaned some money to the new government. But the sale of western lands turned out to be the best source of revenue.

Yet these sources of income were not nearly enough. On two occasions Congress tried to levy tariffs but failed. Both times the vote was just one short of the number needed for passage. Congress seemed powerless to raise the money it needed.

Economic Disunity

Congress also had little authority to promote economic cooperation among the states. State legislatures protected their economic independence as strongly as they did their political independence.

As the only national currency, the Continental dollar, continued to decline in value, states issued their own money. Businesses and individuals preferred their own state currency to others. Furthermore, states often refused to accept other state currencies at face value. The resulting confusion made trade between states difficult.

Economic rivalry among the states further compounded the difficulty. State legislatures tried to regulate trade with other states, often imposing tariffs. Sometimes one state hoped to make a handsome profit from trade between two other states. New York, for example, taxed goods transported between New Jersey and Connecticut.

Actions like these stifled economic cooperation and unity in the new nation. The Articles of Confederation did not give Congress the power to regulate trade or settle disputes between states. The continuing rivalry seriously threatened the nation's economic development.

Foreign Pressures and Western Intrigues

The lack of unity also threatened the new nation's reputation among European nations. Observing the lack of unity, foreign countries initially refused to enter into trade agreements with the United States. Congress's inability to raise an army—it could only "request troops" from the states according to the Articles—also made the new nation appear weak in the eyes of many Europeans, including the British.

Even though the colonists had defeated Great Britain, King George III was not impressed with American power. He ordered troops in military posts in the Northwest Territory to remain, thus violating the peace treaty. The king knew that the French troops were gone and that the weak central government could not raise or support an army. Ambassador John Adams's heated protests

moved neither the British monarch nor the British troops.

Spain renewed its interest in western American lands after the war. Although many Americans had flocked into the areas that would eventually become Tennessee and Kentucky, the situation there was unstable. Some settlers were squatters with no deeds to their lands. Eastern speculators also claimed vast areas granted to them years before by states like Virginia and North Carolina. Congress had to resolve many conflicting claims, but it made little progress.

In the confusion a group of settlers in the area organized a new state called Franklin in honor of Benjamin Franklin. They petitioned Congress to admit the state to the Union but were refused. At the same time, Spain was trying to separate Franklin from the United States and bring it under Spanish rule. Spain paid secret agents (identified with code numbers) to promote its interests.

Of all the backwoodsmen who helped open the frontier, none was more famous or more likely to spin tall tales about his exploits than Daniel Boone. Boone led the settlers who carved the Wilderness Road through the Cumberland Gap in Kentucky.

Among the agents was the famous frontiers-man Daniel Boone, who apparently took the money but did nothing to earn it.

Spain discovered still another way to pressure the westerners. Spanish forts flanked both sides of the lower Mississippi River, the only practical route for western settlers to ship products to New Orleans and points east. Realizing the river's importance, Spain closed it to American navigators in 1784. If people in the West wanted to use the river, the Spanish declared, they had only to agree to become part of New Spain. Such foreign challenges to American integrity underscored the weakness of the national government.

Weakness at the Center

In the years following the war, the prestige of Congress among Americans steadily declined. The most experienced leaders of the war years were busy elsewhere. George Washington had returned to his Mount Vernon plantation. Thomas Jefferson served as ambassador to France and John Adams as ambassador to Britain. Others, such as Patrick Henry, remained active in state government. Those states that bothered sending representatives to Congress sent poor substitutes for the leaders of the Revolutionary War. It was not unusual for representatives of fewer than nine states to be present, fewer than necessary to act on important matters.

Major Events	
1777	Vermont constitution first to abolish slavery within state; Articles of Confederation submitted to states
1781	Articles of Confederation ratified; American victory at Yorktown
1783	Treaty of Paris ratified
1785	Land Ordinance passed by Congress to organize western lands
1786	Virginia legislature passes bill separating church and state; Shays' Rebellion begins
1787	Northwest Ordinance passed

George Washington showed great foresight in 1780 when he warned, "I see one head gradually changing into thirteen. . . . I see the powers of Congress declining too fast for the consequence and respect which is due to them as a grand representative body of America." Others such as James Madison, Alexander Hamilton, and John Adams saw the nation they had worked so hard to create seemingly break up into 13 stubbornly independent nations.

They saw Congress, the symbol of the national government, becoming a subject of ridicule in the world community and being scorned by state legislatures. They saw a central government so weakened by its inability to raise money that it could not even dislodge troops of the very country that the Americans had defeated in war.

They saw speculators, whose concern was money and not the welfare of the new nation, influencing territorial land policies. They saw the possibility of losing territory in the West to Spain because of jealous bickering among states. These leaders saw many faults in their first experiment. They needed little prompting to try again.

Toward a Constitutional Convention

The opportunity to act came in the fall of 1786. Convinced that the nation was falling into a state of economic anarchy, leaders in Virginia called on the other states to meet in Annapolis, Maryland, to discuss new ways of regulating commerce. Representatives from only five states showed up, but they decided to call another meeting the next year to discuss the broader problem of government under the Articles of Confederation.

If any of the other states doubted that action was needed, they became convinced during the winter when a group of disgruntled farmers from western Massachusetts rebelled against the state government. The farmers had been especially hard hit by a combination of low farm prices and high state taxes. Under the leadership of Daniel Shays, they closed many county courthouses and nearly captured an arsenal at Springfield.

The Massachusetts militia finally quelled the uprising, but it convinced many Americans that they needed a stronger, more effective government. With the reality of rebellion and the threat of anarchy in their

Two Views on Shays' Rebellion

When Shays' Rebellion broke out, John and Abigail Adams were in London, where he was serving as the American minister. Natives of Massachusetts, they were particularly concerned about the disturbances in their home state. In January 1787 Abigail Adams voiced her views on the matter in a letter to Thomas Jefferson, the American minister in France. Soon after, Jefferson expressed his views about the rebellion in a letter to James Madison. Note how Adams's and Jefferson's ideas about the causes of the rebellion differ.

Abigail Adams, January 2, 1787

With regard to the tumults in my native state which you inquire about I wish I could say that report had exaggerated them. It is too true, sir, that they have been carried to so alarming a height as to stop the courts of justice in several counties. Ignorant, restless desperados, without conscience or principles, have led a deluded multitude to follow their standard, under pretense of grievances which have no existence but in their imaginations. Some of them were crying out for a paper currency, some for an equal distribution of property. Some were for annihilating all debts, others complaining that the Senate was a useless branch of government, that the Court of Common Pleas was unnecessary, and that the sitting of the General Court in Boston was a grievance.

By this list you will see the materials which compose this rebellion, and the necessity there is of the wisest and most vigorous measures to quell and suppress it. Instead of that laudable spirit which you approve, which makes a people watchful over their liberties and alert in the defense of them, these mobbish insurgents are for sapping the foundation and destroying the whole fabric at once.

Thomas Jefferson, January 30, 1787

. . . I am impatient to learn your sentiments on the last troubles in the Eastern [New England] states. So far as I have yet seen, they do not appear to threaten serious consequences. Those states have suffered by the stoppage of the channels of their commerce, which have not yet found other issues. This must render money scarce and make the people uneasy. This uneasiness has produced acts absolutely unjustifiable; but I hope they will provoke no severities from their governments. A consciousness of those in power that their administration of the public affairs has been honest may perhaps produce too great a degree of indignation; and those characters wherein fear predominates over hope may apprehend too much from these instances of irregularity. . . .

Even this evil is productive of good. It prevents the degeneracy of government, and nourishes a general attention to the public affairs. . . . Unsuccessful rebellions indeed generally establish the [inroads] on the rights of people which have produced them. An observation of this truth should render honest republican governors so mild in their punishment of rebellions as not to discourage them too much. It is a medicine necessary for the sound health of government.

---

thoughts, state delegates began arriving in Philadalphia in the spring of 1787. A new experiment was under way.

SECTION REVIEW

1. Identify: Shays' Rebellion.
2. (a) According to the Articles of Confederation, who had the power to tax? (b) How could Congress raise money?
3. List three factors that made trade between states difficult.
4. (a) What action did George III take that showed contempt for the new nation? (b) What disrespectful action did Spain take?
5. **Critical Thinking** Which weakness of the Articles of Confederation do you think was most serious? Why?

In Perspective

After the revolution, America entered an experimental age. Steps were taken toward broader political and social equality, but much remained to be done.

Once Americans declared their independence from Great Britain in 1776, they had to learn to govern themselves. The new states quickly adopted state constitutions that showed their belief in government with limited powers. Creating a national government proved more difficult. Throughout most of the Revolutionary War, the nation had no official government because some state legislatures had not ratified the Articles of Confederation. The major stumbling block was the dispute over control of land in the West.

The Articles were finally ratified in 1781. When the war was over, the new government set its land policy through ordinances in 1785 and 1787. Yet the weakness of the central government prevented it from solving crucial economic, political, and foreign policy problems. By 1787 many Americans were ready to experiment again.

Vocabulary

Match each term at left with its definition or description at right.

1. segregated
2. bicameral
3. manumission
4. inalienable rights
5. confederation
6. ratify
7. veto
8. enforce

a. an alliance of independent states
b. natural right of citizens
c. separated on the basis of race
d. the rejection of a bill by a chief executive
e. put into effect
f. a two-chamber legislature
g. the freeing of a slave
h. to approve

Chapter Checkup

1. How was the period after the Revolutionary War an experimental era?
2. (a) Describe a typical state government. (b) What branch had the most power? Why?
3. (a) How were states' rights protected under the Articles of Confederation? (b) Why did the delegates think this was necessary?
4. (a) Describe the national government under the Articles of Confederation. (b) How were representatives allocated among the states? (c) Did everyone agree with this system? Explain.
5. (a) Why were claims to land in the West a problem for states that had none? (b) What effect did such claims have on the ratification of the Articles of Confederation? Why?
6. Compare provisions of the Land Ordinance of 1785 with those of the Northwest Ordinance.
7. Why was economic unity difficult to achieve under the Articles of Confederation?
8. How did foreign nations react to signs of weakness in the United States?

Critical Thinking

1. **Evaluating** Why was the period after the Revolutionary War a time of social and political experimentation?
2. **Using Relevant Information** Did Americans during the 1770s and 1780s consider their state government or national government more important? What evidence can you give to support your answer?
3. **Making Judgments** (a) What weaknesses did the national government have under the Articles of Confederation? (b) Which of these weaknesses do you think was most serious? Why?
4. **Supporting a Point of View** What arguments could have been offered either

for or against maintaining the Articles of Confederation?

Developing Basic Skills

1. **Using Diagrams** Study the diagram on page 144. Then answer the following questions: (a) What branches of government existed under the Articles of Confederation? (b) What powers did Congress have? (c) How did the structure of the national government differ from most state governments?

2. **Researching** Visit a local library or write to your state's secretary of state for information to answer the following questions about your state constitution: (a) When was the constitution ratified? (b) Was the constitution written at a specially elected convention? If not, how was it written? (c) How do the powers of the governor of your state differ from the powers of most governors during the 1780s?

3. **Map Reading** Study the map on page 146. Then answer the following questions: (a) Which states claimed territory beyond their own borders? (b) What country owned Florida and the Louisiana territory? (c) Why was it important that the United States settle the conflicting land claims?

4. **Using Primary Sources** Reread Abigail Adams's and Thomas Jefferson's letters about Shays' Rebellion on page 151 and answer the following questions: (a) Which writer favored the rebellion? (b) According to Abigail Adams who were the leaders of the rebellion? (c) How does Adams think the government should react to the rebellion? Why? (d) According to Thomas Jefferson, what caused Shays' Rebellion? (e) How does he think the government should react to the rebellion? Why?

See page 828 for suggested readings.

Writer's Handbook

Order of Importance

One natural way to arrange reasons or facts is in order of importance. You may emphasize the event that had the greatest effect on later events or led to the most important results. The order of importance is useful for presenting arguments in favor of or opposed to a point of view. When organizing information in order of importance, you have to think about which ideas are essential and should be developed and which ideas are minor and could be merely mentioned.

Transition words are used to show the relationship between ideas and to make the order of ideas clear. Some transition words used to show order of importance include: *first, second, third, even more, even greater, most significant, greatest, more important,* and *most important.*

Practice: Decide which item in each pair was more important to the development of democracy in the new nation. Then write a sentence explaining why the item you chose was of greater importance.

1. **a.** Some states extended voting rights by lowering or eliminating property requirements.
   b. Americans organized a large number of volunteer fire departments.

2. **a.** Most states had a bicameral legislature.
   b. The idea that constitutions were to be written by special conventions gained acceptance.

3. **a.** Virginia gave up its claims to land in the Ohio Territory.
   b. A territory with 60,000 inhabitants could be admitted as a state equal to all others.

4. **a.** In 1786 the Virginia legislature passed a bill that effectively separated church and state.
   b. Noah Webster promoted the adoption of an American language.

5. **a.** Congress refused to admit the state of Franklin into the Union.
   b. Virginia called for a gathering of states at Annapolis, Maryland, to discuss regulating commerce.

9

A More Perfect Union

(1787–1791)

The powerful bald eagle, with its ability to soar high above other birds, was chosen as the symbol of the new republic.

By the spring of 1787, many Americans realized that the Articles of Confederation needed to be changed if the young republic was to survive. The threat of foreign intrigue, economic disruptions, and armed rebellion revealed the weaknesses of the Articles of Confederation.

The delegates to the Constitutional Convention faced a difficult task. Many Americans feared a strong central government, yet they realized that a weak government could not survive. The states wanted to protect their rights, but the delegates knew that the states would have to relinquish some power. Compromise would be necessary. When the delegates completed their work, they had produced a new Constitution, one that would provide a solid and enduring foundation for the new nation.

Constitution ratified

1787	1788	1789	1790	1791

May 1787
Constitutional Convention opens

June 1788
Constitution goes into effect

December 1789
North Carolina ratifies Constitution

May 1790
Rhode Island ratifies Constitution

1791
Bill of Rights ratified

1 Producing a New Constitution

Twelve states responded to Congress's call of February 21, 1787, to send delegates to a convention for "the sole and express purpose of revising the Articles of Confederation." Only Rhode Island declined. Altogether, 55 men journeyed to Philadelphia, where the convention was to be held.

Once gathered, the delegates soon realized that their task would have to go well beyond that of simply revising the Articles of Confederation. They spent much of their time examining and discussing alternatives to the kind of government the Articles had established.

The Delegates

Many of the men who came to Philadelphia had extensive experience in government. Probably the best known and most respected were George Washington and Benjamin Franklin, who was 81 when the convention opened. Other familiar names belonged to younger men, like Alexander Hamilton of New York and James Madison of Virginia, both in their thirties. Madison in particular was exceptionally well educated in history and political theory. He would emerge as one of the chief architects of the Constitution.

Many delegates were surprisingly young. Five men were only in their twenties; another five were in their early or mid-thirties. Despite their relative youth, however, the delegates included two college presidents, three professors, and 28 men who had served in the Continental Congress.

But several well-known and respected Americans were absent from the convention. John Adams and Thomas Jefferson did not attend because both were serving as American ambassadors, Adams in Great Britain and Jefferson in France.

Patrick Henry, an ardent champion of states' rights, suspected that the convention planned to establish a strong central government at the expense of state power. Although named a delegate, Henry stayed away because, as he put it, he "smelt a rat." Samuel Adams, who also declined to attend the convention, shared Henry's suspicions.

The Convention Opens

The delegates convened on Friday, May 25, 1787, and elected George Washington as convention president. His presence, as one delegate noted, helped give the proceedings a "national complexion." When the delegates adopted the rules of the convention, they decided that all debates and discussion should be kept secret so that delegates could speak their minds freely.*

For the next six weeks, through a hot and humid Philadelphia summer, the delegates sat cooped up five or six days a week in a closed and stifling room in the Pennsylvania statehouse. Discussion centered on the disrupted state of affairs within the country. Nearly all present agreed that the nation was heading for disaster under the Articles of Confederation. "Something should be done immediately," argued Gunning Bedford of Delaware. Caleb Strong of Massachusetts agreed that under the Articles, Congress was "nearly at an end. If no Accommodation takes place the Union itself must be dissolved."

The delegates generally agreed as well that the new government must be given clear power to raise taxes, enforce laws, and provide for national defense. It should be a republic, in which citizens elected representatives to make and enforce laws. Finally, the delegates believed that the government of the United States should be based on a written constitution, which they set about drafting.

Within the framework of these principles, however, the delegates faced seemingly countless choices about the nature of the new government. For example, when the debates began, few delegates had a clear idea of what the office of chief executive would be like, although nearly everyone agreed that the nation needed one.

Numerous questions arose. Should the chief executive be an elected president or a monarch chosen for life? Some delegates,

---

*The record of the Constitutional Convention is based on notes taken by delegates. Extracts from James Madison's notes appear on page 158.

The men at the Constitutional Convention wrote a document that has stood the test of time. Among those at the convention were George Washington, presiding, and Benjamin Franklin, seated, second from left.

such as Alexander Hamilton and John Dickinson, favored a monarchy. "The British government was the best in the world," Hamilton argued, and doubted very much "whether any thing short of it would do in America." The delegates finally agreed, however, that the nation should have an elected president.

But this decision only raised more questions. Who should elect the President—the people, the state legislatures, or the Congress? How long should the term of office be? What powers should the President be granted? Delegates debated and agreed on answers to dozens of detailed questions such as these.

The Virginia and New Jersey Plans

Early in the convention, the Virginia delegation presented a plan for the new government. The Virginia Plan, written by James Madison, proposed a national legislature, or Congress, to be divided into two houses, the House of Representatives and the Senate. Voters in each state would elect members of

the House of Representatives. The number of House representatives allotted to each state would be proportional to the size of its population. Larger states would have more representatives than smaller ones.

According to the Virginia Plan, the House of Representatives would select the members of the Senate from candidates suggested by state legislatures. The House would also choose members of the judiciary and a President, who would serve for seven years. Congress would have the power to override state laws and, when necessary, make laws for the states.

Delegates who feared excessive central power objected to the authority that the Virginia Plan gave Congress over state legislatures. The main subject of debate, however, was proportional representation. Delegates from small states like New Jersey protested that such a system would give larger states too much power in the national government. Pennsylvania delegate James Wilson only aggravated the small states' fears when he exclaimed with annoyance, "Shall New Jersey have the same right or influence in the councils of the nation with Pennsylvania? I say no. It is unjust."

After two weeks of debate, William Paterson of New Jersey proposed an alternative plan. The New Jersey Plan suggested that each state, large or small, have an equal voice in Congress. Congress would consist of only one house, to be elected by the state legislatures, not directly by the people.

The New Jersey Plan allowed the central government the authority to raise taxes, regulate commerce, and enforce national laws. But the plan also specified that the states would retain powers not expressly given to the national legislature. This plan, in effect, maintained the major features of the Articles of Confederation, making only minor revisions.

The Great Compromise

The delegates rejected both the New Jersey and Virginia plans. Finally Roger Sherman of Connecticut offered a compromise proposal, which became known as the Great Compromise.

The compromise, like the Virginia Plan, provided that Congress have two houses. Voters in each state would elect members of the House of Representatives for two-year terms. The number of representatives from a state would be proportional to its population. This satisfied the larger states. Each state, regardless of size, would have two representatives in the Senate. As in the New Jersey Plan, this stipulation gave all states an equal voice, at least in one house. This pleased the small states. State legislatures would choose senators for six-year terms.

The Great Compromise marked a turning point. No state wanted to give up some of its power to a national government if its voice in that government would be weak. Sherman's compromise proposal attempted to satisfy both sides in the long dispute over fair representation. Had each side steadfastly held its ground, the convention might have broken up. The willingness to compromise on this crucial issue opened the door for other compromises.

Compromise Between Northern and Southern States

The Great Compromise itself raised another question, one that split northern and southern states. If representation was to be based on the number of people living in the state, should slaves be counted as part of the population? Southern delegates, who wanted to increase their representation in the House, said yes. Northerners, however, argued that because slaves were considered property they should not be counted. Again the delegates compromised. They agreed that only three fifths of the slaves in a state would count toward determining its representation in the House.

Another conflict between northern and southern states involved the slave trade. Many northerners wished to abolish it completely. Southerners objected, claiming that slavery was a necessary part of the southern economy. The delegates finally agreed that Congress could not interfere with the slave trade for 20 years after the Constitution went into effect.

Southern delegates also sought to protect their interest in foreign trade. The South's economy was more dependent on the export of agricultural products than the North's. Southern delegates wanted assurance that northern congressmen would not band together to tax southern exports. Such export taxes would place their tobacco, rice, and cotton at a disadvantage in world trade.

As a consequence, the delegates agreed to prohibit export taxes. Moreover, they required that two thirds of the Senate ratify treaties of any kind, which meant that southern states would have enough power to block unfavorable trade agreements made with foreign countries.

The Convention Ends

By August 6 the delegates had placed most of the fruits of their labor in the hands of a five-member Committee of Detail. Assembling the resolutions, this group produced a document of 23 clauses. Finally, on September 12, the Committee on Style went to work to polish the language.

Five days later, 39 of 42 delegates remaining in Philadelphia signed the document. Two Virginians, Edmund Randolph and George Mason, along with Elbridge Gerry of Massachusetts, abstained. They had concluded that the new Constitution vested too much power in the national government. Alexander Hamilton left the convention early for the opposite reason. He thought the states had retained too much power.

Slavery and the Constitution

Delegates to the Constitutional Convention hotly debated whether the Constitution should abolish the importation of slaves. This excerpt is from James Madison's *Journal of the Constitutional Convention* from August 21, 1787.

Mr. L. Martin [of Md.] proposed to vary article 7, sect. 4 so as to allow a prohibition or tax on the importation of slaves. First, as five slaves are to be counted as three freemen in the apportionment of representatives, such a clause would leave an encouragement to this traffic. Second, slaves [through danger of insurrection] weakened one part of the Union, which the other parts were bound to protect; the privilege of importing them was therefore unreasonable. Third, it was inconsistent with the principles of the Revolution, and dishonorable to the American character, to have such a feature in the Constitution. . . .

Mr. Sherman [of Conn.] . . . disapproved of the slave trade; yet, as the states were now possessed of the right to import slaves, as the public good did not require it to be taken from them, and as it was expedient to have as few objections as possible to the proposed plan of government, he thought it best to leave the matter as we find it.

Col. Mason [of Va.] This infernal traffic originated in the avarice of British merchants. The British government constantly checked the attempts of Virginia to put a stop to it. . . . Maryland and Virginia, he said, had already prohibited the importation of slaves. . . . All this would be in vain if South Carolina and Georgia be at liberty to import. The Western people are already calling out for slaves for their new lands, and will fill that country with slaves, if they can be got through South Carolina and Georgia. . . . He held it essential, in every point of view, that the general government should have power to prevent the increase of slavery.

Gen. [Charles C.] Pinckney [of S.C.] declared it to be his firm opinion that if himself and all his colleagues were to sign the Constitution, and use their personal influence, it would be of no avail towards obtaining the assent of their constituents [to a slave-trade prohibition]. South Carolina and Georgia cannot do without slaves. . . . He contended that the importation of slaves would be for the interest of the whole Union. The more slaves, the more produce to employ the carrying trade; the more consumption also; and the more of this, the more of revenue for the common treasury.

The Constitution required that the voters of each state choose delegates to special state conventions that would meet to decide whether the states should accept the plan for the new government. Once nine out of the 13 states accepted it, the Constitution would go into effect. Before considering the ratification struggle, it is important to look in detail at the new government the convention proposed. (See the Constitution, pages 838–868).

SECTION REVIEW

1. Identify: Virginia Plan, New Jersey Plan, the Great Compromise.
2. Which well-known Americans did not attend the Constitutional Convention? Why?
3. List three principles of government agreed upon by the convention delegates.
4. (a) How would representation have been allocated among the states according to the Virginia Plan? (b) How would it have been allocated according to the New Jersey Plan?
5. What major issue did the Great Compromise resolve?
6. How were slaves to be counted in determining representation for a state?
7. How did the delegates protect the South's interest in foreign trade?
8. **Critical Thinking** How does the name of the United States reflect its early history?

2 Federalism

Central to any government is the question of *sovereignty*, the source of the government's power or authority. The opening words of the Constitution, "We, the people of the United States," suggest that the delegates to the convention in Philadelphia believed that sovereignty in the new government of the United States lay with the people. Yet they disagreed whether this meant the people of the individual states or the people of the nation as a whole. Should ultimate power be given to the states or to the national government?

Debate Over Sovereignty

Many delegates to the Philadelphia Convention considered sovereignty indivisible. It must, they believed, lie completely in one place or another, either with the states or with the national government.

Under the Virginia Plan, the people would have delegated power to the central government, which could veto state legislation. This arrangement satisfied men like Gouverneur Morris of Pennsylvania, who favored the establishment of "a supreme Legislative, Executive, and Judiciary" because he believed "that in all Communities there must be one supreme power and only one."

Under the New Jersey Plan, on the other hand, the states would have remained sovereign, as they had been under the Articles of Confederation. Although the Articles had provided for a national legislature, that body had not been sovereign. It had to depend on state governments to carry out national laws, raise money through taxation, and regulate trade.

A Division of Power

The Constitution solved the conflict over whether sovereignty belonged to the national government or to the states by designing a system of dual, or shared, sovereignty. Under this system, known as *federalism*, governmental authority was divided between national and state governments.

The Constitution gave certain powers exclusively to the national government. These *delegated powers* include the right to coin money, regulate foreign and interstate trade, declare war on another country, and establish a postal system. States were forbidden by the Constitution to do any of these things.

Powers that the Constitution did not specifically grant to the national government were reserved for the states. *Reserved powers* include the right to control trade within a

■ *The federal system created by the Constitution delegated some powers to the federal government and reserved others to the states. Some powers were to be concurrent, or shared, by both the states and the federal government. How do you think experiences under the Articles of Confederation helped shape the way powers were divided?*

System of Federalism

Examples of Delegated Powers

Regulate laws of immigration and
  naturalization
Regulate interstate and foreign commerce
Set standard weights and measures
Create and maintain armed forces
Make copyright and patent laws
Establish postal system
Establish foreign policy
Create lower courts
Print money
Declare war

Examples of Concurrent Powers

Borrow money
Provide for health, safety, and welfare
Administer criminal justice
Set minimum wage
Charter banks
Levy taxes

Examples of Reserved Powers

Create corporation laws
Regulate intrastate commerce
Establish and maintain schools
Establish and maintain local
  governments
Determine eligibility requirements
  for elected state officials
Determine and regulate laws of marriage,
  divorce, and professional licenses

state, to create local governments, and to establish qualifications for voting.

The Constitution granted a third set of powers to both the national and the state governments. Among these *concurrent powers* are the right to support education, enforce laws, and spend money on internal improvements, such as roads, dams, and parks. Finally the Constitution stated that in cases of a disputed claim to authority by states and the national government, federal courts would resolve the conflict.

A True Union

The system of federalism established a new relationship between the states and the national government and between the people and the national government. The Constitution stated that the Constitution and any national laws passed under it were the supreme law of the land. All people had to abide by them, and state legislatures could not change or violate them.

Under the Articles of Confederation, as you know, the people had no direct influence on the national government, nor could the government deal directly with the people. It could only act through the states.

The new Constitution established a direct link between the people and the national government. Voters elected members of the House of Representatives. Moreover, the laws passed by the national government affected the people directly. State legislatures no longer served as intermediaries.

Federalism is the central characteristic of the American political system. The delegates at Philadelphia created a stronger national government because they saw that a true union was necessary. At the same time, they retained significant powers for the state governments, to guarantee that the national government would not become too strong.

SECTION REVIEW

1. Define: sovereignty, federalism, delegated powers, reserved powers, concurrent powers.
2. Would the central or state governments have been sovereign under the Virginia Plan? Under the New Jersey Plan?
3. How did the Constitution solve the conflict over sovereignty?
4. Give one example each of a delegated, a reserved, and a concurrent power.
5. **Critical Thinking** How has federalism protected the right of states to some individuality?

3 Limits to Power

The long and difficult struggle against British tyranny had ended just four years before the Constitutional Convention opened. The delegates wanted to prevent such tyranny in the new government of the United States. Thus they tried to limit the concentration of power in any part of the government. As you read in the previous section, federalism divided power between the states and the central government to prevent either from becoming too powerful. The delegates further sought to define and limit the power of each branch of the national government.

Separation of Powers

The idea of establishing separate branches of government, each with well-defined and limited powers, was not a new one in America. Elected colonial legislatures had existed alongside governors and judges appointed by the king. Furthermore, as you read in Chapter 8, the state constitutions had specified separate executive, legislative, and judicial branches. But the state constitutions usually favored the legislative branch over the executive.

The Articles of Confederation had created a legislature but not a court system or an executive. The experiences of the preceding four years convinced many Americans of the weakness of that system. They also realized that legislatures, as well as executives, could become too powerful. Consequently, the delegates to the Constitutional Convention revived the idea of the *separation of powers.*

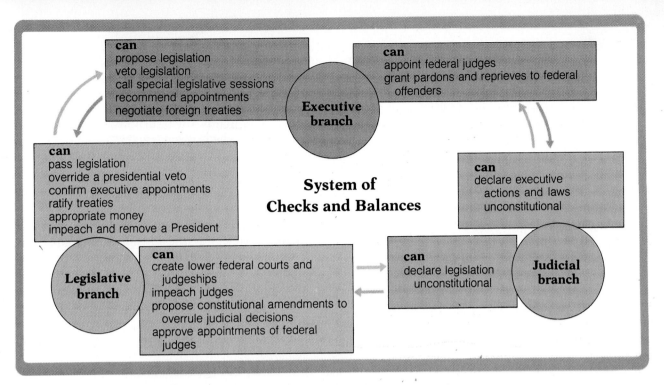

System of Checks and Balances

Executive branch
can
- propose legislation
- veto legislation
- call special legislative sessions
- recommend appointments
- negotiate foreign treaties

can
- appoint federal judges
- grant pardons and reprieves to federal offenders

Legislative branch
can
- pass legislation
- override a presidential veto
- confirm executive appointments
- ratify treaties
- appropriate money
- impeach and remove a President

can
- create lower federal courts and judgeships
- impeach judges
- propose constitutional amendments to overrule judicial decisions
- approve appointments of federal judges

Judicial branch
can
- declare executive actions and laws unconstitutional

can
- declare legislation unconstitutional

■ *The framers of the Constitution wanted to prevent government tyranny. To do so they separated government power into legislative, executive, and judicial branches. Then they set up a system of checks and balances to keep any one branch from becoming too powerful.*

In so doing, they drew on the ideas of Baron de Montesquieu (mahn tuhs KYOO). Montesquieu's views on government, especially those he published in 1748 in *The Spirit of the Laws*, were well known to convention delegates, who often quoted him during the debates.

Montesquieu argued that to function properly a government had to possess legislative, executive, and judicial authority. In other words, the government had to be able to make, enforce, and interpret the laws of the land. To prevent tyranny, Montesquieu continued, these functions should be divided among three branches of government. The powers and duties of each branch should be carefully defined and separated so no branch could gain too much power.

The delegates built Montesquieu's ideas into the Constitution. Legislative, executive, and judicial powers of government were to be kept separate. The main function of the legislature, Congress, would be to make laws. The executive branch, headed by the President, would enforce the laws. The judiciary, or the courts, would interpret the laws and insure that they be applied on a fair and equal basis.

Checks and Balances

To reinforce the separation of powers, the Constitution established a system of *checks and balances* in which each branch of government could check the power of the others. This was based on another of Montesquieu's ideas, designed to prevent any one branch from exceeding its specified powers.

Remembering their quarrel with the king, the delegates in Philadelphia worried especially about the possible abuse of power by the chief executive. Some delegates considered distributing executive authority among several Presidents from different parts of the country. Although they quickly abandoned this plan, the delegates carefully built checks on presidential power into the new government.

The President was given the power to appoint cabinet officers, federal judges, and ambassadors. Such appointments, however, were to be approved by the Senate. The Senate also had to approve any treaties the President negotiated with foreign governments. Congress's sole authority to declare war would limit the President's power as commander in chief of the armed forces.

161

Congress could further check presidential authority by its power to remove a President from office. The House of Representatives could *impeach,* or accuse, a President of "treason, bribery, or other high crimes and misdemeanors." The Senate could then try the President and, upon conviction by a two-thirds majority, remove him or her from office.

Checks on the power of Congress were equally important. Both houses had to agree on a bill before it could be sent to the President. The President could check Congress by vetoing, or rejecting, measures it passed. Congress could override a veto, but both houses had to pass the bill again by a two-thirds majority.

The Supreme Court, with its authority to interpret the laws of the land, could check both the President and Congress by ruling their actions *unconstitutional,* that is, in violation of the Constitution. The President, in turn, appointed judges upon approval by the Senate. Moreover, Congress could impeach and remove judges from office, since the Constitution specified that they "hold their offices during good behavior."

The system of checks and balances resulted from compromises among the delegates, although nearly all agreed on the necessity of curbing excess power. In the end they were satisfied that the combination of federalism, separation of powers, and checks and balances would prevent tyranny by the national government. However, many delegates also feared tyranny by the people. The finished Constitution reflected this concern as well.

Limiting Direct Power of the People

Several factors underlay the belief that the people's direct participation in the national government should be limited. Many delegates argued that representatives whose main business was to run the government were likely to be better educated and informed about issues than the people.

In addition the delegates believed that the people would have a hard time selecting national leaders wisely. Communication was slow and often unreliable. Voters could not possibly be familiar with national candidates and their views. Some delegates feared that large groups of people might be won over by

rabble rousers and inflamed by emotional issues. Representatives, they thought, would be more likely to act slowly, deliberately, and intelligently.

Consequently, the Constitution created a republic in which voters elected representatives to govern the country. Further, as you have seen, voters were to choose only the members of the House of Representatives directly. State legislatures would select members of the Senate.*

The delegates also devised an indirect method of electing the President and Vice-President that is still in effect today. According to the Constitution, states were to choose electors who would vote for President and Vice-President. As a group the electors were called the *electoral college.* The number of electors for each state would equal the state's total number of representatives in Congress.

When the convention adjourned, most delegates felt that they had created a document that balanced the powers of the national government properly. The new government could act with firmness and vigor when needed, but the systems of separation of powers and checks and balances insured that the government would not abuse its power.

SECTION REVIEW

1. Identify: Montesquieu, *The Spirit of the Laws.*
2. Define: separation of powers, checks and balances, impeach, unconstitutional, electoral college.
3. Describe the function of each of the three branches of the new government.
4. Name (a) one way the President can check the power of Congress; (b) one way Congress can check the power of the President; (c) one way the Supreme Court can check the power of Congress.
5. **Critical Thinking** How have attitudes toward popular participation in elections changed over the past two hundred years?

*The Seventeenth Amendment to the Constitution (1913) changed the method of electing senators. After that date, they were to be elected by popular vote rather than by state legislatures.

4 Ratifying the Constitution

Most delegates at Philadelphia were pleased with the government they proposed, but before the Constitution became law it had to be accepted by the people back home. Both supporters and opponents of the new Constitution gathered their forces and planned their arguments for the debates in the state conventions that lay ahead.

Arguments in Favor of the Constitution

Supporters of the Constitution, known as Federalists, argued that the United States needed a strong national government to overcome the clear weaknesses of the Articles of Confederation. The nation, in their opinion, had been in grave danger largely because individual states could reject national policy. According to the Federalists, the new Constitution gave enough authority to the national government to permit it to function effectively. Yet it still protected the rights of the individual states.

Three of the most able Federalists were Alexander Hamilton, James Madison, and John Jay. These men wrote a series of newspaper articles designed to win support for the Constitution in New York State. These articles, known as the *Federalist Papers*, summarized the advantages of a federal union under the Constitution. They remain one of the best discussions of the political theory behind the American system of government.

Opponents of the Constitution

The chief concern of the Antifederalists, or opponents of ratification, was that the new national government would be too powerful. Most thought the states should have retained more authority.

★ Voices of Freedom ★

A Farmer Argues for the Constitution

Many Antifederalists were concerned that the proposed Constitution would not protect the country from tyranny. However, farmer Jonathan Smith urged the Massachusetts convention to ratify the Constitution because he believed it was the only way to prevent tyranny.

Mr. President, I am a plain man, and get my living by the plough. I am not used to speak in public, but I beg your leave to say a few words in this house.

I have lived in a part of the country where I have known the worth of good government by the want of it. There was a black cloud [Shays' Rebellion] that rose in the east last winter, and spread over the west. . . . It brought on a state of anarchy and that led to tyranny. People that used to live peaceably, and were before good neighbors, got distracted, and took up arms against government.

Our distress was so great that we should have been glad to snatch at anything that looked like a government. Had any person that was able to protect us come and set up his standard, we should all have flocked to it, even if it had been a monarch, and that monarch might have proved a tyrant. So that you see that anarchy leads to tyranny; and better have one tyrant than so many at once.

Now, Mr. President, when I saw this Constitution, I found that it was a cure for these disorders. I had been a member of the convention to form our state constitution, and had learnt something of the checks and balances of power; and I found them all here.

Some gentlemen say, don't be in a hurry; take time to consider; and don't take a leap in the dark. I say, take things in time—gather fruit when it is ripe. There is a time to sow, and a time to reap. We sowed our seed when we sent men to the federal convention. Now is the harvest; now is the time to reap the fruit of our labor. And if we won't do it now, I am afraid we never shall have another opportunity.

Source: Jonathan Elliot, *The Debates on the Federal Constitution* (1836), vol. 2, pp. 102–104.

The Antifederalists further believed that the indirect method of electing the President and the Senate removed government too far from the people. They opposed the longer terms of office proposed in the Constitution for similar reasons. Under the Articles of Confederation, congressional elections had been held every year. A longer term of office, argued the Antifederalists, would make representatives less responsible to the voters.

Even more serious in the eyes of many opponents was the lack of a specific bill of rights to protect individual liberties. Antifederalists worried that the new government might become one of tyranny, destroying everything that the colonists had won through the revolution. They urged delegates to state conventions to reject the Constitution.

Battles Over Ratification

State conventions in smaller states like Delaware, New Jersey, and Connecticut quickly ratified the Constitution. Antifederalist forces were weakest in small states, whose interests seemed to be well protected under the Constitution. The key ratification battles came in the more populous states of Pennsylvania, Massachusetts, Virginia, and New York.

In Pennsylvania Federalists showed that they could support their political arguments with tough political tactics. On November 30, 1787, Federalist legislators in the Pennsylvania assembly moved to form a ratifying convention, but before voting the assembly broke for lunch. When Antifederalist legislators refused to return for the vote, the assembly was two votes short of the quorum, or minimum number, needed to conduct business. The speaker of the assembly then sent the sergeant-at-arms out into the streets to find at least two more members and bring them back in. With the doors barred to prevent anyone from escaping, the assembly passed the motion for a convention, which ratified the Constitution on December 12.

Massachusetts delegates convened the next month. There, the Federalists avoided the political shenanigans used in Pennsylva-

The Society of Pewterers carried this banner in a parade celebrating the ratification of the Constitution.

nia. Instead, they hinted to John Hancock, an influential delegate who wavered in his support of the Constitution, that he might win the post of Vice-President in the new government. Hancock's subsequent support helped Massachusetts ratify by a narrow margin in February 1788.

Maryland and South Carolina ratified later that spring. Then all eyes turned toward Virginia, where people expected a lively debate. Virginia delegates included prestigious figures like George Washington and James Madison, who supported the Constitution. On the Antifederalist side, however, stood Patrick Henry, George Mason, and Edmund Randolph, all names well known and respected in Virginia politics.

A real battle loomed until Randolph suddenly announced he would support ratification. His move weakened opposition, and Virginia ratified the Constitution at the end of June. Once news of the Virginia vote reached the New York convention, that state also ratified. New Hampshire's approval had already come in.

With more than the nine votes needed for ratification, Congress, in its last act under the Articles, ordered national elections to be held in January 1789. North Carolina did not ratify the Constitution until December 1789, and Rhode Island not until 1790. But by then the new government was already at work.

165

SECTION REVIEW

1. Identify: Federalists, *Federalist Papers*, Antifederalists.
2. What arguments did the Federalists make in favor of the Constitution?
3. Explain two arguments the Antifederalists made against the Constitution.
4. In which of the states did the key ratification battles take place?
5. **Critical Thinking** How could you have answered the Antifederalist argument that the Constitution was opposed to the interests of state governments?

5 Insuring Individual Rights

No sooner had the Constitution been ratified and the first Congress begun its work than changes were made in the document to insure individual rights. These and future changes were possible because the delegates to the Constitutional Convention had incorporated an amendment process into the final document.

Amending the Constitution

The delegates realized that a method of *amending*, or changing, the Constitution was necessary. They knew the document had to be flexible enough to adjust to conditions they could not foresee. Yet at the same time they wanted to guarantee that any changes would be well considered. Thus the amendment process they devised was a difficult one.

The Constitution provided that an amendment could be proposed at any time by either a two-thirds majority vote of Congress or by a special convention called by two thirds of the state legislatures. That amendment would become part of the Constitution when it had been ratified by three fourths of the states.

It is a testimony to the farsightedness of the men at Philadelphia that in nearly two centuries the Constitution has been amended only 26 times. The first ten amendments were adopted during the first years of the new government, and only 16 changes have been made since 1791.

The Debate Over a Bill of Rights

The first series of amendments involved individual liberties. The question of whether to include a guarantee of citizens' rights in the Constitution had surfaced many times during the convention. Several delegates wanted to clearly specify a list of rights that the government could not violate.

Others, led by Alexander Hamilton and James Madison, replied that there was no need for a bill of rights. The Constitution already protected individual liberties, they argued. One such protection was the right of

This painting Stump Speaking, *by George Caleb Bingham, captures a typically American event, the campaign speech. The Bill of Rights in the new Constitution guaranteed the right to free speech and assembly.*

citizens to obtain a *writ of habeas corpus* (HAY bee uhs KOR puhs), a court order releasing a person arrested without specific charges. Habeas corpus thus protected a person against arbitrary imprisonment.

In addition, the Constitution prohibited state and national governments from passing a *bill of attainder*, a law allowing a person charged with treason or another serious crime to be fined or imprisoned without trial. Such laws had been common in Great Britain. The Constitution also outlawed *ex post facto laws*, or laws that made an act a crime after it had been committed. Finally, the document provided for jury trials in criminal cases.

Madison argued further that listing a set of guaranteed liberties might actually prove restrictive. To specify one set of rights might imply that only those rights and no others

deserved protection. Madison agreed that a bill of rights might be necessary in a government ruled by a king, but not in one, like the United States, in which sovereignty lay with the people.

Despite these arguments, pressure for a bill of rights persisted throughout the ratification struggle. Several states, including Massachusetts and Virginia, ratified the Constitution with the understanding that the new Congress would propose amendments incorporating a bill of rights into the Constitution. Madison, who served in the first Congress as a representative from Virginia, now decided that if there were to be a separate bill of rights, he should draft the document himself.

Congress took Madison's draft and passed it as the first ten amendments to the Constitution. These amendments, known as the Bill of Rights, were then submitted to the states for ratification. Over the next two years, the necessary three-fourths majority of the states accepted the amendments, and the Bill of Rights became part of the Constitution in December 1791.

The Bill of Rights

The ten amendments that make up the Bill of Rights insure the basic freedoms of American citizens. The First Amendment guarantees individual liberties, including freedom of speech and of religion, the right to peaceful assembly, and the right to petition the government. It also protects freedom of the press.

The next three amendments grew out of memories of British rule. The Second Amendment guarantees the right of people to keep and bear arms and thus assured the continued existence of local and state militias. The Third Amendment prohibits the quartering of troops in private homes during peacetime without the owner's consent. Ever since the Boston Massacre, Americans had feared the presence of soldiers in their cities. The Fourth Amendment, recalling the hated writs of assistance used by British customs officials during the 1760s, protects citizens from "unreasonable" searches of their homes or persons and seizure of their possessions.

The Fifth Amendment guarantees *due process* of law. This means that the government cannot act arbitrarily against a person. It must follow a specific open process in which the accused is notified of the charge and is given the opportunity to present a defense in court. Under the Fifth Amendment the government cannot require self-incriminating testimony nor may it try a defendant twice for the same crime.

The Sixth Amendment guarantees a jury trial in criminal cases and the right to be represented by a lawyer. Jury trials in civil cases are required by the Seventh Amendment. The Eighth Amendment forbids judges to set "excessive bail" or to prescribe "cruel and unusual punishments."

The Ninth Amendment assures citizens that the listing of rights in the Constitution does not deny the existence of others not named in that document. This answered the Federalist argument that such a list might restrict individual rights.

The Tenth Amendment was designed to reassure Antifederalists that the power of the national government would be limited. It states that all powers not given by the Constitution to the national government or specifically denied to the states are reserved for the states or for the people.

A Rising Sun

With the addition of the Bill of Rights, the Constitution seemed complete. Yet, the document's flexibility contributed to its greatness. The delegates foresaw that the framework of government would have to accommodate new circumstances. No one, perhaps, knew this better than Benjamin Franklin, who had seen his country grow and change so much over his long career.

When Franklin had first arrived in Philadelphia as a runaway boy many years earlier, the colonies were little more than local settlements along the Atlantic coast. Each colony observed its own customs and tended to go its own way. The colonies were, of course, able to unite on certain things because of a common English heritage and constant trade. Franklin himself had helped to bring the colonies together by improving communication in his post as deputy postmaster. But the colonies had been unable to unite in

Major Events	
1787	Constitutional Convention convenes in Philadelphia; Delaware, Pennsylvania, and New Jersey ratify Constitution
1788	Georgia, Connecticut, Massachusetts, Maryland, South Carolina, New Hampshire, Virginia, and New York ratify Constitution; Constitution goes into effect
1789	North Carolina ratifies Constitution
1790	Rhode Island ratifies Constitution
1791	Bill of Rights ratified as first ten amendments to Constitution

a common cause when Franklin had proposed his Plan of Union in 1754.

Yet Franklin had seen the colonies come together to fight a revolution and later to form a new government under the Articles of Confederation. Finally, at eighty-one, when the infirmities of old age required that he be carried by sedan chair to the convention, he witnessed Americans joining to create a new government.

As the finishing touches were put on the document, Franklin must have thought back over all of the obstacles to unity that he had watched the thirteen colonies overcome. While the delegates were signing the final draft of the new Constitution, Franklin called attention to the presiding officer's high-backed chair. On it was carved a sun.

Artists, he observed, often found it difficult to distinguish in their work a rising from a setting sun. "I have often in the course of the Session . . . looked at that sun behind the President without being able to tell whether it was rising or setting. But now at length I have the happiness to know that it is a rising and not a setting sun."

SECTION REVIEW

1. Define: amend, writ of habeas corpus, bill of attainder, ex post facto law, due process.
2. (a) What are the two ways a constitutional amendment can be proposed? (b) What proportion of the states need to ratify an amendment?
3. Why did Madison object at first to the idea of a bill of rights?
4. **Critical Thinking** Describe one way in which you personally have benefited from the Bill of Rights.

Chapter 9 Review

In Perspective

When delegates from 12 states arrived in Philadelphia in May 1787, few realized that over the next several months they would produce a new constitution. When they had completed their work, however, most felt confident that they had created a fair and workable system of government.

During the convention, the delegates successfully worked out compromises between large and small states and between northern and southern states. The federal system they created was designed to balance power between the national government and the state governments. Within the national government they divided powers among three separate branches and provided careful checks and balances to prevent any branch from becoming too powerful.

The first amendments to the Constitution, the Bill of Rights, were passed soon after the members of the new government took office. These guarantees of individual liberties assured many opponents of the Constitution that the powers of the national government would be limited.

After its ratification, the Constitution remained a plan on paper. The challenge of making it work remained. As you will read in the next chapter, the next 12 years would witness a successful start of that process.

Vocabulary

On a separate sheet of paper, write the word or words that best complete each of the following sentences.

1. The source of a government's power is its ___.
2. ___ is a system of government in which power is divided between the states and the national government.
3. Powers shared by the states and the national government are ___.

168

4. ___ exists in a government where each branch has defined and limited powers.

5. To ___ a President or high federal official is to accuse that person of wrongdoing.

6. A (An) ___ makes an act a crime after it has been committed.

Chapter Checkup

1. (a) Why was the method of allocating representation in the national government such a hotly debated question? (b) How did the Virginia Plan propose to solve the question? (c) How did the New Jersey Plan propose to solve it? (d) What compromise was finally reached?

2. What compromises were made between the interest of the northern and southern states?

3. How was each of the following designed to prevent the abuse of power in the new republic: (a) federalism; (b) separation of powers; (c) checks and balances; (d) the electoral college?

4. (a) What checks were to be placed on the powers of Congress? (b) What checks do the legislative and executive branches have on the judicial branch?

5. Describe the arguments for and against ratification of the Constitution.

6. (a) How were individual liberties protected in the Constitution? (b) Why did many Antifederalists believe that this was not enough protection?

Critical Thinking

1. Making Judgments (a) Why do you think the delegates to the Constitutional Convention decided to make the chief executive a President elected for a limited term of office rather than a monarch chosen for life? (b) Why do you think some delegates still favored a monarch chosen for life?

2. Evaluating Review the limits on the direct power of the people in the Constitution. (a) Which are still in effect today? (b) Why did the delegates want to limit the direct power of the people? (c) Do you think their reasons are still valid?

Developing Basic Skills

1. Classifying Make a chart with three columns. Title the columns Delegated Powers, Reserved Powers, and Concurrent Powers. Using the Constitution, your textbook, and other sources you may have, place each of the following in its appropriate column: voting age, education, an army, fishing regulations, offshore drilling rights, income tax, luxury tax, police protection, motor vehicle regulations, interstate trade regulations, intrastate trade regulations, postal service.

2. Researching Choose any two of the delegates to the Constitutional Convention. Research their personal backgrounds. In an essay, answer the following questions: (a) What similarities do you see in their lives? (b) What differences? (c) Was each a Federalist or an Antifederalist? Why?

See page 828 for suggested readings.

Writer's Handbook

Comparison and Contrast

When you *compare* events or items, you show how they are the same. When you *contrast* elements, you show how they are different. One way to prepare to write a comparison or a contrast is to arrange your information in chart form. For example, if you were contrasting the Virginia Plan and New Jersey Plan with the Great Compromise, you would have a chart with three horizontal columns: Virginia Plan, New Jersey Plan, and Great Compromise. The headings for the vertical columns would be: Number of Houses, Method of Selection of Lower House, Basis of Representation. You could then tell at a glance how the plans were the same and how they were different.

Some words used to compare and contrast include: *but, besides, in addition, however, but . . . also, too, as well as.*

Practice: Make a chart comparing the powers of Congress under the Articles of Confederation and the United States Constitution. Then write the information in paragraph form.

Unit Three

An Emerging Nation

1793 By his second term, George Washington had become a symbol of the new nation.

1797 Abigail Adams spent most of her years as First Lady in Philadelphia, which was the nation's capital until 1800.

	1788	1794	1800	1806
POLITICS AND GOVERNMENT	**1789** George Washington takes office as first President		**1803** *Marbury* v. *Madison* confirms idea of judicial review	
SOCIETY AND CULTURE	**1790** Design of nation's capital at Washington, D.C., begins			
ECONOMICS AND TECHNOLOGY	**1793** Eli Whitney invents cotton gin		**1804** Lewis and Clark begin exploring Louisiana	
WORLD EVENTS	**1789** French Revolution begins		**1804** Napoleon becomes emperor of France	

Washington   Adams   Jefferson

1804 Friendship with Native Americans was a goal of the Lewis and Clark expedition, as this medal shows.

1791 The Bank of the United States was an important part of Alexander Hamilton's economic program.

1812 Battle of the USS *Constitution* and the British ship *Guerrière*.

1820s This painting by George Bingham shows the importance of river travel as Americans moved west.

1806	1812	1818	1824
	1812 War of 1812 with Britain begins		**1823** Monroe Doctrine forbids European interference in the Americas
Early 1800s More women and children work in textile mills			**1820s** More Americans move west of the Appalachians
1807 Fulton travels up Hudson on *Clermont*	**1813** Boston Associates set up first modern textile factory		**1825** Erie Canal from Buffalo to Albany completed
	1812 Britain repeals Orders in Council		**1821** Most Latin American countries have become independent of Spain

The new nation carried on an active foreign trade. This is a carving from an early trading ship.

As industrialization spread, some women worked at jobs such as at this printing press.

10

A Federalist Beginning

(1789–1801)

Salute to General Washington by C. M. Cooke

Chapter Outline

1 *Challenges of the New Government*

2 *A Question of Entangling Alliances*

3 *The Birth of Political Parties*

4 *John Adams's Sacrifice*

To some, the most important question facing the new government of the United States seemed to be what to call the chief executive. The newly elected Senate spent almost three weeks debating the proper form of address.

Although many senators wanted to avoid the traditional titles of royalty, they thought that the President would need an impressive title when dealing with European heads of state. In the end they decided on the democratic-sounding "President of the United States."

The officials of the new government were well aware, however, that they faced greater challenges. They had the Constitution as a guide, but many details of government remained to be worked out. They knew that the decisions they made and the actions they took would set precedents, or examples, for the future. Presidents George Washington and John Adams were also to face unexpected challenges, among them the development of political parties and the threat of war with France.

George Washington's administration

1788	1790	1792	1794	1796	1798	1800	1802
1789 Washington elected first President	**1791** Bank of United States created	**1793** Proclamation of Neutrality	**1794** Whiskey Rebellion	**1796** John Adams elected President	**1798** Alien and Sedition acts passed	**1800** Thomas Jefferson elected President	

1 Challenges of the New Government

Several serious problems faced the nation in 1789. Following election of the Congress and a President, other offices in the government had to be created and filled. President Washington could not handle all the executive duties by himself, so he would have to select advisers. He also had to choose justices for the Supreme Court.

The nation's income was small, its debt large. Paper money issued during the Revolutionary War was virtually worthless. The new nation would have to be put on a firm financial footing. Settlers on the western frontier were demanding that the national government protect them from attacks by Native Americans whose land the settlers had occupied. Finally, the new nation would have to establish credibility with foreign governments.

The First President

When the members of the electoral college unanimously chose George Washington as the nation's first President, they recognized that his popularity and prestige would give the new government much needed respectability. The strength of character Washington had exhibited as commander of colonial forces during the Revolutionary War had earned him the unreserved confidence of the American people.

Washington himself had hoped to retire from public life after the war, preferring the planter's life at Mount Vernon to a political career. However, the organizers of the Constitutional Convention had recalled him in 1787 to preside over the convention. And now he was being called upon again to lead the new government.

As President, Washington was a leader who stood above political conflict and intrigue. He saw himself as an arbiter, or a person who decides disputes, among the various interests within the government and within the nation. To fulfill this role, the President held himself aloof from others. He did not allow this air of dignity to be broken by familiarity. Once when Gouverneur Morris, acting on a wager, slapped the President on the back, the icy stare Washington gave him froze Morris in his tracks.

Setting Up the National Government

The First Congress of the United States, composed of 26 senators and 59 representatives, met in New York City, then the nation's capital. One of its first acts was the organization of the judiciary.

Although the Constitution stated that there would be a Supreme Court, it did not specify how the court should be organized. In the Judiciary Act of 1789 Congress provided that the Supreme Court would consist of a chief justice and five associate justices. President Washington appointed John Jay, who had been head of the Department of Foreign Affairs under the Articles of Confederation, as the first Chief Justice. The Judiciary Act also gave the Supreme Court final jurisdiction over disputes involving the Constitution, federal law, and treaties. Finally, it created thirteen district courts, one in each state, and three circuit courts.

A presidential cabinet also began to take form in 1789. Obviously, the President could not handle all the government's administrative duties by himself, but the Constitution was silent on the details of how to set up the executive branch. Washington frequently sought the advice of members of Congress, especially James Madison, a leader in the House of Representatives. But Presidents would need more formal assistance within the executive branch.

Article II of the Constitution authorized the creation of several unspecified executive departments. In 1789 these included an attorney general, a postmaster general, and secretaries of state, treasury, and war. Washington chose experienced advisers to head them. For example, he selected Thomas Jefferson, former governor of Virginia and author of the Declaration of Independence, as secretary of state. The secretary of war was 39-year-old Henry Knox, chief of artillery during the Revolutionary War.

The most important appointment in Washington's first administration was Alexander Hamilton as secretary of the treasury. As an expert in economics, Hamilton greatly influenced President Washington's policies on important financial questions. The President had personal confidence in Hamilton, since Hamilton had served on his staff during the Revolutionary War.

Only 34 at the time he accepted the treasury position, Hamilton was a man of rare genius and ambition. Born in the British West Indies, he had never developed the intense loyalty to a particular state that characterized so many Americans at that time. Thus he found it easier to think in terms of the nation as a whole.

Yet Alexander Hamilton held some strange opinions for a leader in a democratic republic. An admirer of Great Britain, he had little faith in the principle of equality, as he demonstrated in a speech at the Constitutional Convention when he said,

> All communities divide themselves into the few and the many. The first are the rich and well-born; the other the mass of the people. . . . Turbulent and changing, they seldom judge or determine right. Give therefore to the first class a distinct, permanent share in government.

Hamilton's aristocratic leanings influenced his proposals for solving the economic problems of the new nation, as you will see.

Restoring Public Credit

The most serious problem facing the United States was a huge debt from the war. The government had issued millions of dollars in bonds to support the war effort, and they had not yet been redeemed. Hamilton proposed funding the national debt at its full value of approximately $40 million. *Funding* is a process whereby a government raises or borrows money to pay off a debt. Hamilton planned to raise the money by issuing new bonds. These new bonds would be exchanged at face value for the bonds that had been circulated during the war.

People generally agreed that the debt owed to foreign banks or investors would have to be paid, but disagreement arose over what to do about bonds sold to American

---

★ **America's Heritage** ★

The Creation of a National Capital

When the delegates met in Philadelphia in 1787 to draft a new constitution, they included a provision to set aside an area "10 miles square" to serve as the permanent capital of the republic. Never before had any nation created a totally new capital city.

Offers to host the "Federal Town" poured in from all parts of the country. The choice of a site on the Potomac River was made in 1790. Jefferson and Madison convinced southern congressmen to support Hamilton's Assumption Bill in exchange for locating the nation's capital in the South. (See page 175.)

Pierre L'Enfant, a French engineer who had fought in the Revolutionary War, begged for "a share in the undertaking." And his offer to help create a capital "magnificient enough to grace a great nation" was accepted. Andrew Ellicot and Benjamin Banneker were hired to survey the boundaries of the district.

L'Enfant enthusiastically laid out the plans for a city whose broad avenues would radiate out from the "Grand Edifices." He envisioned a "Congress House," a "Presidential Palace," and a monument that would pay tribute to Washington. Each structure was to be placed on ground that would command the greatest view.

Completing the grand design, however, was not easy. L'Enfant clashed with local landowners over sale of land for the capital and eventually quit in anger, taking his plans with him. But work could continue because Banneker had memorized the original plans.

Finally on June 15, 1800, the long-awaited public offices opened, and the national government moved from Philadelphia to its permanent home, the District of Columbia. Washington, D.C., soon became a symbol of American independence and national unity.

citizens. Most of the soldiers, widows, and other citizens who originally bought the bonds had sold them to speculators, in many cases for only ten to fifteen cents on the dollar. Was it fair, some asked, for the speculators to make a huge profit on the bonds they had purchased for such a low price?

James Madison, for one, objected to full funding. He felt the bonds should be paid off at a reduced rate to speculators, at full value only to the original holders. Madison's position in part reflected the sectional strain that was already developing between the North and the South. Over four fifths of the national debt was owed to northern investors and speculators. Full funding would seem to reward these northern interests at the expense of southerners.

Hamilton disagreed. He believed that purchasers of the bonds deserved a profit since they had supported the government in its darkest times. Besides, the purpose of funding was to restore the nation's credit and reputation. The United States could only do so if it paid its debts in full. Furthermore, Hamilton argued, many of the speculators were wealthy individuals whom the nation would have to depend on for future credit.

Congress passed Hamilton's proposal in February 1790. Some members of Congress who supported Hamilton may have been influenced by their own speculation in war bonds. They stood to make a profit if the bonds were funded in full.

As another step toward putting the new nation on a sound economic foundation, Hamilton proposed that the federal government assume, or take over, all state debts from the Revolutionary War. These totaled over $25 million. Such an action, he argued, would equalize the financial burden of the war. It would also bind the states more firmly to the national government, thus strengthening national unity.

Some states had already paid off their debts, however, so they opposed the *assumption* of state debts. Citizens in Virginia, Maryland, Georgia, and North Carolina did not want to be taxed to pay the debts of another state when they had already paid their own.

Hamilton, Madison, and Jefferson finally worked out a compromise, and Congress passed it. Since southerners owed a proportionately lower debt than northerners, Hamilton offered to appease them by moving the nation's capital from New York to a site on the Potomac River. The prestige and

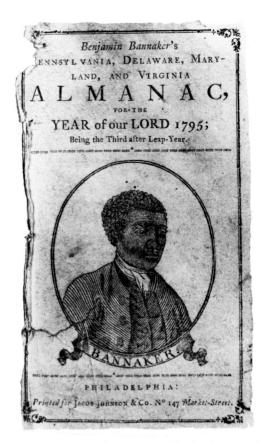

Mathematician and astronomer Benjamin Banneker published highly popular almanacs in the 1790s. He was also a member of the commission that helped design the new capital city of Washington, D.C.

commercial advantages of having the nation's capital in the South appealed to Madison and Jefferson. Thus they agreed to full funding of the national debt and assumption of state debts.

The Bank of the United States

As a second part of his program to build a sound economy, Hamilton proposed the creation of a national bank. The bank would issue United States currency and would help carry out the nation's financial affairs. All federal taxes would be deposited in the bank, whose directors in turn could invest that money.

The government would own one fifth of the stock in the bank, and private citizens could buy the rest. Since stockholders would elect the bank officers, the management of the national bank would be in private hands. Hamilton's goal was to cement the loyalty of wealthy investors to the national government.

In February 1791 Congress passed a bill creating the national bank with little debate. Opponents of the bill, however, fervently urged President Washington to veto it. Madison and Jefferson strongly objected to the bank. They feared that the bank's directors would have too much power over the nation's economy. Together with Attorney General Edmund Randolph, they attempted to convince the President that the bank was unconstitutional.

Jefferson argued that the national government did not have the authority to create such a bank because the Constitution did not specifically authorize it. He cited the Tenth Amendment to the Constitution, which states that "all powers not delegated to the United States . . . are reserved to the states, or to the people." Thus, he concluded, the government had *only* those powers specifically listed in the Constitution. This literal interpretation of the Constitution has become known as *strict construction*.

Alexander Hamilton, on the other hand, favored a *loose construction* of the Constitution. He argued that the government had more powers than were actually listed. He cited Section 8, Clause 18 of the Constitution, which gives Congress the power to make all laws "necessary and proper" to carry out the specific powers listed in the Constitution.* Since the United States had the power to tax, according to Hamilton, it also had the power to create a bank to receive the taxes collected. Hamilton's arguments won the support of the President, who signed the bill into law.

Protecting the Nation's Industries

A third part of Hamilton's economic plan was not so successful. Hamilton wanted to see the nation's manufacturing grow, and he believed that the government should help. He therefore proposed that Congress pass a *protective tariff*. This would place a tax on imported products in order to raise their prices higher than prices on products made in the United States. People would then buy domestic goods. Such a tariff would thereby protect American manufacturers from European competition.

---
*This clause is often called the "elastic clause."

Congress did pass a tariff bill in 1792. However, the tariffs imposed were primarily for revenue, to raise money for the national government, and were lower than protective tariffs would have been.

Much of the opposition to Hamilton's tariff proposals came from the South. Since their economy was mainly agricultural, southerners had to buy more imported manufactured goods than northerners. They felt a protective tariff that raised the prices of those goods was unfair to them.

The Whiskey Rebellion

Finally, Hamilton proposed an excise tax on distilled liquors as another money-raising measure. Congress adopted such a tax in 1791. This measure eventually led to a rebellion in Pennsylvania that threatened the stability of the new nation.

Farmers in the Pennsylvania back country usually distilled their grain into whiskey, because whiskey was less bulky to transport by wagon and brought a higher price. They actually used the whiskey as money, since no stable currency existed yet. Resentment of the excise tax grew steadily as farmers saw their profits dwindle. The farmers finally rebelled in 1794 with cries of "liberty and no excise." They refused to pay any further tax, and some of them tarred and feathered revenue officials.

Although Pennsylvania's governor thought that the state could handle the situation, Alexander Hamilton saw a chance to demonstrate the power of the federal government. President Washington, taking Hamilton's advice, summoned a force of state militia. This show of federal force was overpowering, and the rebellion ended without a shot being fired. Hamilton wanted to punish the leaders, but Washington, with a cooler head, pardoned them.

Alexander Hamilton's economic program contributed to a strong start for the new government by restoring the confidence of both foreign and domestic investors and by building a firm foundation for future economic growth. President Washington's vigorous action against the Whiskey Rebellion also strengthened the national government. It demonstrated the government's authority to act within the borders of a state and clearly showed that the new government would act decisively in times of crisis.

When Pennsylvania farmers rioted against the whiskey tax, President Washington called up the militia to put down the rebellion. Washington personally rode out to review the troops at Fort Cumberland, Maryland, as depicted in this painting by James Peale.

SECTION REVIEW

1. Identify: John Jay, James Madison, Thomas Jefferson, Henry Knox, Alexander Hamilton.

2. Define: funding, assumption, strict construction, loose construction, protective tariff.

3. (a) What was the purpose of the original cabinet? (b) What was the source of the President's power to appoint a cabinet?

4. What were the major provisions of the Judiciary Act of 1789?

5. (a) What was the most serious problem facing the new nation? (b) What was Alexander Hamilton's solution to this problem?

6. (a) Why did Hamilton propose the creation of a national bank? (b) How would it operate?

7. (a) What sparked the Whiskey Rebellion? (b) What action did Washington take?

8. **Critical Thinking** How was operating the new government like sailing an uncharted sea?

2 A Question of Entangling Alliances

When they were part of the British Empire, the colonies had been drawn into European conflicts such as the French and Indian War. Now, even though the nation had achieved independence, it found it was still not totally separated from Europe. During the early years of the republic, Americans faced the danger of being drawn into yet another war.

Divisions Over Foreign Policy

The French people revolted against their king and aristocracy in 1789, the same year the United States adopted the Constitution. Most Americans reacted enthusiastically to the initial news of the French Revolution and the creation of a French republic.

In 1793, however, the French Revolution took a brutal turn. King Louis XVI was beheaded on the guillotine, as were many French nobles. The revolutionaries also replaced Catholicism with the worship of what they called the Supreme Being. This rejection of Christianity outraged pious Americans, and many people were shocked by the violence and bloodshed. Much of the early admiration turned into bitter opposition.

Alexander Hamilton was one person who abhorred the course of the French Revolution. In his opinion, by attacking the upper classes, the revolutionaries were eliminating the very people who were the mainstays of society.

Hamilton also feared that if the United States supported the French Revolution, it would risk war with Great Britain.* Such a development would mean economic disaster. About 90 percent of the nation's revenue came from customs duties, and 75 percent of its imports came from Great Britain. War with Britain would virtually wipe out this major source of income.

Other Americans were less disturbed by the turn of events in France. They believed that liberty often demanded great sacrifice. Thomas Jefferson had been ambassador to France before his appointment as secretary of state. Like many Americans, Jefferson deplored the violence, but he sympathized with the idealistic goals of the revolution. Indeed the French revolutionaries themselves had used Jefferson's ideas in their Declaration of the Rights of Man.

Hamilton and Jefferson tried to convince President Washington to take opposite sides in the war between France and Great Britain. But Washington decided on a more moderate course of action. In April 1793 he issued the Proclamation of Neutrality.

Citizen Genêt

About the same time Washington issued his proclamation, a new French ambassador, Citizen Edmond Genêt (zhuh NAY), arrived in Charleston, South Carolina. Genêt was an arrogant man. Even before he presented his credentials to the President, the Frenchman began outfitting American ships as privateers against England, setting up courts to deal with the ships they captured, and organizing an attack by American frontiersmen on Spanish New Orleans.

Genêt did not bother to consult the American government before undertaking these activities. Yet many Americans found him fascinating and cheered him on his journey to the nation's capital. This popular reception led Genêt to overestimate his influence. He began to believe he was better liked than the President. He told his government, "I live in a round of parties. Old Man Washington can't forgive my success."

When Genêt began organizing pro-French clubs that loudly criticized American neutrality, Washington decided to take action. Even Jefferson, always friendly to the French cause, agreed that Genêt's conduct had become intolerable. President Washington demanded that France recall their ambassador immediately. Genêt might have protested, but he learned that another revolution in France had removed his friends from power and that the new French government had ordered his arrest. Rather than face the guillotine, Genêt retired from public life, married the daughter of New York Governor George Clinton, and lived quietly in New York until his death in 1836.

The Jay Treaty

If Genêt's activities alienated many of France's friends in the United States, the British government was also alienating some of its supporters. Britain still had not withdrawn from its northernmost forts in the United States, although it had agreed to do so ten years earlier. British officials in those outposts reportedly sold firearms to Native Americans who were fighting an effective war against further intrusion into their lands.

Furthermore Britain's navy had begun stopping ships from the United States bound for the West Indies and seizing sailors whom they suspected of having deserted British ships. They then forced these sailors into service in the Royal Navy. In anger many Americans clamored for war with Great Britain.

In 1794 Washington sent Chief Justice John Jay, an experienced diplomat, to London to try to work out the dispute. Conditions did not favor successful negotiations. The British felt they were winning their war with France, so they were not in a con-

---

*By 1793 Great Britain had joined other European nations in a war against France. The British government considered the revolution in France a threat to all monarchies.

ciliatory mood. Jay himself could not negotiate from a position of strength since the United States lacked any real military power. Alexander Hamilton had further weakened Jay's position by telling the British minister about Washington's decision not to enter into an alliance with other European nations.

After learning that it did not have to worry about an American-French alliance, Britain could afford to drive a harder bargain. As a result, the Jay Treaty did not achieve what the United States had hoped for. The British did promise to evacuate their posts on United States soil and to pay damages for the ships they had recently seized. But they made no promises about future seizures or about their relations with Native Americans. Jay had to pledge payment of debts owed to British merchants before the American Revolutionary War.

Although the Jay Treaty avoided war, most Americans were unhappy with it. The pact seemed to be a surrender to Great Britain. The treaty especially offended southerners. Southern planters owed most of the debts outstanding to British merchants. They would have to pay, while northern shipping interests would collect compensation for ships and cargoes that had been seized.

President Washington was not happy with the treaty, but he recognized that the terms were probably the best Jay could negotiate. He recommended that it be ratified, and the Senate consented—barely—with exactly the two-thirds majority required by the Constitution.

A Treaty With Spain

The United States fared better when it negotiated a treaty with Spain shortly thereafter. The Spanish too were at war with France, but the war was not going well for them. Furthermore the Spanish government worried that the Jay Treaty might foreshadow a British-American alliance that one day could be directed against it. Thus when diplomat Thomas Pinckney arrived in Spain to begin negotiations for the Americans, he found the government quite willing to deal with him.

The United States wanted to settle two long-standing disputes with Spain. The border between the United States and Spanish Florida had never been firmly established. In addition Americans wanted to ship cargo down the Mississippi River and deposit it in

New Orleans until it could be picked up by larger, oceangoing ships.

Pinckney negotiated solutions to both problems. Spain allowed the United States access to the Mississippi River as well as the right to deposit cargo in New Orleans. It further agreed to fix the boundary between the United States and Florida at the thirty-first parallel, exactly what Pinckney had been instructed to seek.

Warning Against Permanent Alliances

When President Washington decided not to run for a third term in 1796, he was convinced that his policy of neutrality had been best for the nation. So important was the policy, in fact, that he devoted a lengthy portion of his Farewell Address to it. In the address, which newspapers published in September 1796, Washington warned the nation not to form "permanent alliances." The United States as a young nation would be better off, he said, if allowed to develop on its own.

Washington's warning referred to long-term political alliances that might embroil the United States in European conflicts. He did not oppose economic agreements that would build trade and promote economic growth. His successors would try to maintain a policy of political neutrality but would find it a difficult task.

SECTION REVIEW

1. Identify: Edmond Genêt, Thomas Pinckney.

2. (a) How did Americans first react to the French Revolution? (b) What developments changed their attitude?

3. How did the actions of Edmond Genêt threaten American neutrality?

4. What two promises did Great Britain make in the Jay Treaty?

5. What two problems did Pinckney solve in the treaty he negotiated with Spain?

6. What reason did President Washington give for his warning against permanent alliances?

7. **Critical Thinking** Why was neutrality probably the wisest course for Washington to follow in the war between France and Britain?

Washington's Farewell Address

President Washington's Farewell Address is probably best known for its warning against permanent foreign alliances. However, as you can see in the extracts below, Washington spoke about many challenges facing the young republic.

National Unity

The unity of government which constitutes you one people is also now dear to you. It is justly so, for it is a main pillar ... of your real independence, the support of your tranquillity at home, your peace abroad, of your safety, of your prosperity, of that very liberty which you so highly prize. ... It is of infinite moment [importance] that you properly estimate the immense value of your national union. ... You have, in a common cause, fought and triumphed together; the independence and liberty you possess are the work of joint councils and joint efforts, of common dangers, sufferings, and successes.

The Constitution

The basis of our political systems is the right of the people to make and to alter the constitutions of government. ... The very idea of the power and the right of the people to establish a government presupposes the duty of every individual to obey the established government.

Political Parties

I have already intimated to you the danger of parties in the State. ... Let me now ... warn you, in the most solemn manner, against the baneful effects of the spirit of party generally. ... It serves always to distract the public councils, and enfeeble [weaken] the public administration. It agitates the community with ill-founded jealousies and false alarms; kindles the animosity of one part against another.

The National Government

And remember especially, that for the efficient management of your common interests, in a country so extensive as ours, a government of as much vigor as is consistent with the perfect security of liberty, is indispensable.

3 The Birth of Political Parties

Political parties have become such a familiar part of the American scene that people often assume they have always existed. In the early years of the United States government, however, parties did not exist. In fact, people regarded them as evils to be avoided.

What you know as political parties today were called *factions* in the eighteenth century. The term described a group of people organized to pursue their own private advantages in politics. Faction members in British politics rarely concerned themselves with the interests of the community as a whole.

Thomas Jefferson expressed the general American attitude toward parties when he said, "If I could not go to heaven but with a party, I would not go at all." Even though most Americans shared Jefferson's views, the seeds of political parties were planted during the years of Washington's presidency.

Beginnings of Formal Opposition

James Madison, impressed with Alexander Hamilton's knowledge of economics, had recommended him highly to head the Treasury Department. Yet as the details of Hamilton's economic program emerged, Madison and Thomas Jefferson found themselves disagreeing with many of its main points, as you have seen. Both men tried to persuade President Washington to modify Hamilton's plans, but they were largely unsuccessful.

Jefferson and Hamilton, who came to symbolize opposing sides in the new government, were a study in contrasts. Hamilton dressed well; he was energetic and charming. He had married a woman from a wealthy New York family, and her aristocratic attitude influenced his thinking. Hamilton was knowledgeable and had a well-disciplined mind, yet he wrote in a heavy style that most people could not understand.

In contrast, Jefferson's clothes seldom fit well. He seemed awkward and shy and did not look people in the eye when he talked. His mind seemed less organized than Hamilton's when he spoke, but it was active and curious. His writing, in the Declaration of Independence, for example, had stirred the people to revolution.

Hamilton and Jefferson's political differences were even more significant than their personal ones. Hamilton felt the nation needed a strong central government with its power in the hands of wealthy, well-educated men rather than in the hands of the people. According to Hamilton, the nation's economy should depend less on farming and more on manufacturing, shipping, and commerce.

Jefferson, on the other hand, believed power should be dispersed. He favored democracy because he believed the people were the safest and most virtuous storehouse for power. He believed that universal education would increase the people's ability to govern. Jefferson thought the nation's economy should be based on agriculture.

While Hamilton emphasized a strong central government, Jefferson thought the states should retain authority. Since Hamilton's main concern was that government possess sufficient power to govern, he interpreted the Constitution and its list of governmental powers loosely. As he demonstrated during the debate over the national bank, he felt the Constitution implied powers that it did not specify.

Jefferson, in contrast, was a strict constructionist. He believed the Constitution granted only those powers that it specifically listed. The first two American political parties grew out of the differences between supporters of Hamilton and Jefferson.

Creation of a Party Machinery

In 1791 Jefferson and Madison went to New York, claiming they were going to study botany. The claim was not too preposterous since Jefferson was a well-known naturalist. But their real purpose was to meet with people in New York who also opposed Hamilton.

A small number of families competed for control of New York politics. Governor George Clinton and Aaron Burr led one side. The Schuylers, who were related to Hamilton by marriage, controlled the other.

While Jefferson and Madison were in New York, they struck a deal with the Clinton-Burr faction. This action marked a turning point in national politics. Previously, Jefferson and Madison had opposed Hamilton only on specific policy issues. Now they were taking the first tentative step toward establishing a national party of opposition.

A second step in setting up a party machinery was finding a way to inform the public of the party's point of view. In 1791 the only influential newspaper in Philadelphia, the nation's capital at the time, was John Fenno's *Gazette of the United States*, which consistently praised Hamilton and his economic program. Furthermore Fenno had received printing contracts from the Treasury Department and personal loans from Hamilton himself.

Jefferson had a plan for counteracting Fenno's newspaper. Shortly after returning from New York, he appointed Philip Freneau, a popular poet, to a clerk's position in the State Department. The job, which paid only $250 per year, required little work. But Freneau knew how he was expected to fill his time. He started a newspaper, *The National Gazette*, which published biting attacks on Hamilton. Its praise of Jefferson outdid Fenno's praise of Hamilton.

Madison, Jefferson, and their followers had not originally intended to start a political party, but by 1792 they were consciously referring to themselves as "the Republican party." When the Hamiltonians took the name "Federalists," their action marked the beginning of the two-party system in American politics.

Choosing a New President in 1796

The dispute between Hamilton and Jefferson greatly distressed President Washington since both men were valuable members of his cabinet. The dispute had, in fact, been one of the major factors in Washington's decision to seek reelection in 1792. He hoped that by running he could prevent the split between the supporters of his two cabinet members from developing further. Washington's continued popularity did eliminate the chance of much party activity in that election.

Four years later conditions had changed. Despite Washington's warning against political parties in his Farewell Address, the parties could not be kept out of the election in 1796. When Washington announced his decision not to run for a third term, the two parties became visible and active.

Although both Hamilton and Madison were influential among members of the government, neither had enough support among the people in 1796 to make a serious try for the presidency. The Federalists chose John Adams as their candidate; the Republicans chose Thomas Jefferson. Hamilton, who wanted to continue his influence in the government, feared that John Adams would be too independent if elected. So Hamilton devised a scheme to defeat Adams. First he arranged for Thomas Pinckney of South Carolina to be the Federalist candidate for Vice-President.

In the 1796 election the two parties specifically designated one candidate for President and one for Vice-President. The Constitution, however, did not recognize this distinction. It provided that each elector in the electoral college simply vote for two persons. The candidate receiving the largest number of electoral votes would become President; the one receiving the second largest number would become Vice-President.

Aware of this fact, Hamilton tried to persuade electors from both parties to cast one of their votes for Pinckney for Vice-Pres-

ident. He hoped that Pinckney would thus receive more electoral votes than either Adams or Jefferson. Then Pinckney, the Federalist candidate for Vice-President, would be elected President.

Hamilton's scheme did not work. Adams's supporters recognized the danger and cast their votes for Vice-President almost at random. As a result, Pinckney received only 59 votes. The Federalist John Adams became the second President of the United States with 71 electoral votes. Thomas Jefferson, a Republican, was elected Vice-President with 68 votes.

The outcome of the election had disclosed a flaw in the election process as originally defined in the Constitution. Candidates with opposing views could be elected President and Vice-President. This fact became all the more significant now that the opposing views were represented by distinct political parties.

SECTION REVIEW

1. Identify: Republican party, Federalist party.
2. Define: faction.
3. Contrast Hamilton's and Jefferson's views on who should control the government.
4. List two other ways in which Hamilton's and Jefferson's views differed.
5. What major flaw in the election process did the 1796 election reveal?
6. **Critical Thinking** Why have political parties been called "the lengthening shadows of two great men"?

4 John Adams's Sacrifice

John Adams knew he would face difficult problems when he took office. First, he followed in the shadow of George Washington, already revered as the father of his country. Second, he inherited Washington's neutral foreign policy, which was becoming increasingly difficult to uphold. France had begun to attack American shipping, and members of Adams's own Federalist party were clamoring for war. The President, however, was committed to preventing just such an event.

Adams and the Federalists

Sixty-one years old at the time of his election as President, John Adams already had a distinguished political career behind him. As a lawyer, patriot, delegate to the Continental Congress, and Vice-President under Washington, Adams commanded the respect of all, especially for his fairness and honesty.

Yet honesty did not always serve Adams well in politics. He often told friend and foe alike what he thought, sometimes tactlessly. As a result, he neither commanded great personal loyalty from his subordinates nor encouraged close political friendships.

Nor did Adams and his wife, Abigail, particularly enjoy the cosmopolitan whirl of Philadelphia, the nation's capital from 1790 to 1800. They preferred the simple life on their farm in Quincy, Massachusetts. Adams left for home whenever he could and actually stayed there for 385 days during his four-year term as President. Consequently, he did not control his Federalist party as closely as he might have.

As President, John Adams retained Washington's cabinet, in part because he did not want to slight the former President. But he was also motivated by the difficulty of finding people willing to serve in government. The pay was low, the jobs were hard, and government officials were increasingly subject to personal criticism.

Unfortunately for Adams, Washington's cabinet members were loyal to Alexander Hamilton, the very man who had tried to sabotage Adams's election. The split between President Adams and Hamilton's followers, known as High Federalists, grew as the new administration faced worsening relations with France.

Pressure for War

The French government deeply resented the Jay Treaty (see page 178) because to the French it indicated that the United States favored Great Britain. In reaction France began to seize American merchant vessels sailing for England—300 by the middle of 1797. President Adams sent a mission of three men to France to negotiate an end to this activity.

When the Americans arrived, they were contacted by three secret representatives of the French government, called X, Y, and Z in published reports. X, Y, and Z demanded a loan of several million dollars to the French government, plus a bribe of $250,000 merely for allowing the Americans to talk to the French foreign minister. "Not a sixpence!" cried one of the Americans.

A war fever erupted in the United States at the news of the so-called XYZ Affair. The popular slogan was, "Millions for defense, but not one cent for tribute!" The pro-British Federalists led the cry.

183

American artists tried to find symbols for the patriotism of the new nation. This painting contains several such symbols, including the laurel leaf of victory being placed on George Washington's head, the new flag, the American eagle, and Miss Liberty. Washington's position as a symbol of the new nation made it difficult for his successor, John Adams, to establish his own independence.

The High Federalists saw the crisis with France as an opportunity to crush their Republican opponents. Arguing that the country had to prepare in case of war, they proposed that the United States raise a navy and an army—this in spite of the fact that all the fighting had been at sea. Republicans feared that an army might be used against opponents of the Federalists at home.

The President was under tremendous pressure to declare war, but John Adams had always been an independent man. In this crisis he acted in a way that surprised many people—not the least, the members of his own Federalist party.

Adams wanted to avoid war if possible, but he realized that the country must be prepared in case it came. He resisted the pleas of the High Federalists for an army because concentrating on land forces would leave the American merchant fleet defenseless. Instead he proposed the creation of an American navy.

As of March 1798, the United States had no warships. The small navy of the Revolutionary War had ceased to exist once the war ended. Congress now appropriated money to complete three frigates it had authorized earlier, and in July it issued bonds to pay for 24 more warships. During the summer the first three—the *Constitution*, the *United States*, and the *Constellation*—set sail. The new American ships, larger than comparable vessels in the British and French navies, performed well in skirmishes over the next two years.

As the United States and France neared war in the 1790s, the United States built warships. This print by William Birch shows construction of the Philadelphia.

Avoiding War With France

In the meantime, the High Federalists continued to push for an army and a declaration of war. They persuaded George Washington to return to military duty, but he did so only on the condition that Alexander Hamilton be his second in command. President Adams resisted Hamilton's appointment, but he had to give in when Washington insisted. Adams realized that a declaration of war would increase the Federalists' popularity and perhaps win him a second term. But he knew the country was weak, and he would not gamble with its survival.

After receiving reports that the French might be willing to reopen negotiations, the President decided to make one more attempt. He appointed a new ambassador to France, and, as the Constitution required, submitted the nomination to the Senate.

The High Federalists, who wanted war, not negotiation, brusquely threatened to block Adams's nomination. Adams promptly threatened to resign and leave the presidency to the Republican Vice-President, Thomas Jefferson, if his own party blocked him. The High Federalist senators then agreed to compromise on a three-man delegation to France.

When the delegation arrived in Paris, it found a new French government, headed by Napoleon Bonaparte. Napoleon was more interested in European conquest than in conflict with the United States, so he was willing to compromise. In the Convention of 1800 the French promised that the seas would be free to American shipping. They refused, however, to pay for the American ships and cargoes they had already seized. Still, John Adams had saved the country from expanding a skirmish into a major war.

The Alien and Sedition Acts

Back home the High Federalists were creating another crisis. They introduced a series of acts in Congress, supposedly to prepare the nation for war. When passed by Congress, these laws were among the most repressive ever adopted in the United States.

One law, the Alien Act, attempted to reduce the political influence that foreigners or recent immigrants could have in the United States. It increased the residency requirement for citizenship from five to fourteen years and authorized the President to deport or imprison foreigners during war time. Most recent immigrants voted for Republican candidates when they became citizens. By delaying their citizenship the Federalists hoped to weaken the Republican party.

The Sedition Act had an even more directly political purpose. It provided for the fining or imprisonment of anyone who impeded the progress of the government or defamed its officials. To many people, especially the Republicans, this seemed to be a direct violation of the right of free speech so recently guaranteed in the First Amendment to the Constitution.

The expiration date of the Sedition Act was further evidence of its political nature—March 3, 1801—the day of the next presidential inauguration. The High Federalists hoped that the law would curb Republican criticism over the next three years and thereby guarantee a Federalist election victory in 1800. If the Federalists still lost the election, the law would expire and allow them to attack the new Republican President. While the Sedition Act was in effect the government indicted fifteen Republican newspaper editors, convicting ten.

Republican Resistance

To the Republicans, the Alien and Sedition acts seemed to be a clear abuse of governmental power. Since Federalists controlled the federal courts, Republicans turned to state governments in an attempt to end the persecution stemming from the acts.

In 1798 the Kentucky legislature acted against the Alien and Sedition acts by adopting a series of resolutions written by Thomas Jefferson. In the resolutions Jefferson theorized that since the states had created the federal government, they could *nullify*, or declare invalid, any law it passed. James Madison prepared similar resolutions that were passed by the Virginia legislature.

These resolutions revived the argument about whether the federal government or the states were sovereign. At the time the resolutions had little effect because no other states were willing to adopt such measures. The Alien and Sedition acts eventually expired. The idea of state nullification of federal laws would surface again, however, as you will see in Chapter 13.

Federalist Defeat in 1800

The Federalists faced many problems as the election of 1800 neared. Resentment over the Alien and Sedition acts lingered. The Federalists' agitation against France made them appear to be warmongers, and government preparations for a war that did not occur brought unpopular new taxes.

The taxes sparked violent resistance. In Pennsylvania federal tax assessors were attacked, and an armed band set two tax dodgers free. President Adams sent federal troops and state militia into Pennsylvania to restore order. Although Adams later pardoned all those arrested, the use of federal troops increased resentment.

The Federalists knew they faced a difficult election. They tried to persuade George

Major Events	
1789	Washington elected first President of United States; French Revolution begins
1790	Assumption Bill passed
1791	Bill of Rights ratified; Bank of the United States created
1793	Great Britain declares war on France; Proclamation of Neutrality
1794	Jay Treaty; Whiskey Rebellion
1795	Pinckney Treaty negotiated with Spain
1796	John Adams elected President
1797	XYZ Affair
1798	Alien and Sedition acts passed
1798–1799	Kentucky and Virginia resolutions passed
1800	Thomas Jefferson elected President
1801	John Marshall appointed Chief Justice of Supreme Court

Washington to reenter public life but he refused. The party finally decided to support John Adams for reelection. The Republicans nominated Thomas Jefferson for President and Aaron Burr for Vice-President.

During the bitter campaign, wild charges flowed from both sides. Federalists accused Thomas Jefferson of being an agent of French revolutionaries and atheists. Republicans, in turn, claimed that John Adams was a monarchist who wanted his daughter to marry Britain's King George III.

Tabulation of the electoral vote found Jefferson and his running mate, Aaron Burr, in a tie, each with more votes than Adams. Every Republican elector had cast one of his two votes for Jefferson as President and the other for Burr as Vice-President. In such an event the Constitution stated that the House of Representatives would select the President. The selection was complicated because Federalists had a majority in the House, and many tried to prevent Jefferson's election by voting for Burr. After 35 ballots in over a week's time, the House finally elected Thomas Jefferson.*

*Congress later took steps to prevent the situation from recurring. In 1804 the states ratified the Twelfth Amendment, which required electors to cast their ballots separately for President and Vice-President.

The Adams administration's last major accomplishment was passage of the Judiciary Act of 1801. It created a new system of sixteen circuit courts and reduced the number of justices on the Supreme Court from six to five. President Adams quickly appointed circuit judges to fill the new posts, rather than allow the incoming Republican President to select them. Adams also appointed a Federalist, John Marshall, as the new Chief Justice of the Supreme Court. Marshall was to become one of the most influential persons ever to hold that office.

SECTION REVIEW

1. Identify: High Federalists, XYZ Affair, Napoleon Bonaparte, Convention of 1800, Aaron Burr, Judiciary Act of 1801.
2. Define: nullify.
3. (a) What two French actions led to demands for war by many Americans? (b) What did Adams do to avoid war?
4. (a) Compare the stated purpose of the Alien and Sedition acts with the real purpose. (b) How did the Republicans try to repeal the two laws?
5. Critical Thinking Why did Jefferson refer to his election as "The Revolution of 1800"?

 # Chapter 10 Review

In Perspective

The Federalist's defeat in 1800 marked the end of their era. Although they continued to be a strong opposing voice, they never elected another President. Their belief that an elite group of wealthy and talented men should run the country was out of keeping with growing democratic sentiment.

The Federalists, however, had accomplished a great deal while in power. In just twelve years, they had established a strong national government. Alexander Hamilton's economic program had restored prosperity and the nation had gained some respect abroad.

The creation of political parties was an unexpected development. Yet the two-party system has remained a major part of politics to this day.

Perhaps most important, Presidents Washington and Adams kept the young nation out of war. Yet this became more difficult as time went on.

Vocabulary

Match each term at left with its definition or description at right.

1. funding
2. assumption
3. political party
4. protective tariff
5. nullify

a. group organized for its own political advantage
b. to declare invalid
c. raising or borrowing money to pay a debt
d. designed to reduce imports
e. taking over the debts of others

Chapter Checkup

1. How did each of the following contribute to a strong beginning for the new government: (a) election of George Washington as President; (b) Judiciary Act of 1789; (c) creation of a cabinet?

2. (a) What actions of the British government alienated even pro-British Americans? (b) How did many Americans react to the Jay Treaty?

3. (a) What actions did Jefferson and Madison take in 1791 that led to the creation of political parties? (b) Had they planned to start an opposition political party? Explain.

4. (a) What developments made it difficult for President Adams to continue Washington's foreign policy of neutrality? (b) What steps did Adams take to avoid war?

Critical Thinking

1. **Recognizing a Point of View** (a) Why do you think Washington chose Alexander Hamilton to be secretary of the treasury? (b) How did Hamilton's economic program reflect his political and social views?

2. **Applying Information** (a) How would the Kentucky and Virginia resolutions have repealed the Alien and Sedition acts? (b) Why did the two resolutions have little impact in 1798? (c) Under what circumstances might they have had a greater impact?

Developing Basic Skills

1. **Comparing** Make a chart with three columns. In the first column list the following issues: creation of a national bank, interpretation of the Constitution, the French Revolution, powers of the national and state governments, belief in the people, manufacturing versus farming. In column 2 describe Hamilton's view on each issue. In column 3 describe Jefferson's view on each issue. Based on what you have learned about each man, how might you explain the differences between them?

2. **Using a Primary Source** Study the extracts from George Washington's Farewell Address on page 180 and answer the following questions: (a) Why is this document a primary source? (b) What type of document is it? (c) What does the document tell you about Washington's concerns for the new nation? (d) What can you learn from the document about the United States in 1796?

See page 829 for suggested readings.

Writer's Handbook

Spatial Order

Spatial order is the sensible order to use when describing how something looks. Details are arranged by their location. Usually, you would organize the various items in some pattern, such as left to right, near to far, front to back, and so on. The readers should be able to follow the description in a logical manner as though their eyes were traveling across a scene. Spatial order is helpful when writing an account of a gathering of people, the strategy of a battle, or the visual results of warfare.

Some words to use to show spatial order include: *above, near, beside, in front of, in the distance, beyond, overhead,* and *outside.*

Practice: Look at the picture on page 177 of George Washington reviewing his troops. Write a word picture of the scene.

11

The Republicans in Office

(1801–1815)

Thomas Jefferson *by Rembrandt Peale*

Chapter Outline

1 *Jefferson's Imprint on the National Government*

2 *Expanding the Nation's Boundaries by Treaty*

3 *The Coming of Another War*

4 *A Complex War*

When Thomas Jefferson became President in 1801, he was already well known to most Americans. He had designed the government and educational system of Virginia and had written the Declaration of Independence. And his ideas had been incorporated into the Constitution.

Jefferson had served as George Washington's first secretary of state and as Vice-President under John Adams. As a defender of states' rights and limited government, he had become the most prominent Republican and the Federalists' chief rival.

During his administration, Thomas Jefferson was to preside over the most significant territorial expansion in United States history. He steered the nation along the edge of another European conflict, but his successor, James Madison, would not be able to avoid American involvement. Ironically, the young nation would emerge from that war with reaffirmed vitality and independence.

Western expeditions   **War of 1812**

1794	1797	1800	1803	1806	1809	1812	1815

1795 Treaty of Greenville

1801 Blockade of Tripoli

1803 Louisiana Purchase; *Marbury v. Madison*

1804–1806 Lewis and Clark expedition

1807 Embargo Act passed

1811 Battle of Tippecanoe

1815 Battle of New Orleans

1 Jefferson's Imprint on the National Government

In his spare time Thomas Jefferson conducted scientific farming in Virginia, designed one of the most beautiful homes in the South at Monticello, filled it with intriguing inventions, and played the violin. But his ideas on government concerned Americans most as they awaited the inauguration of their third President. Federalists feared that his election would bring an end to stable and respectable government as they conceived it.

The New President's Style

Jefferson's inauguration was the first to be held in the new national capital, Washington, D.C. Despite this distinction, Jefferson deliberately made the event a low-keyed, almost casual affair. Rather than use the presidential coach, he walked from the boardinghouse where he had been living to the still unfinished Capitol building.

After taking the oath of office he read his inaugural speech in a voice so low that hardly anyone in the chamber could hear him. Then the new President walked back to his boardinghouse for a quiet dinner. When he entered the room, only one of his fellow diners even rose to offer him a chair.

Jefferson consciously made informality a part of his approach to government. The presidency, he felt, should not glorify the person who held the office. Consequently, the new President avoided pomp and ceremony in his duties. People in Washington grew accustomed to seeing the head of their government walking along the street or riding on an old horse as he went about the business of government. Instead of delivering rousing speeches to Congress, he had a clerk read his messages. Instead of holding formal meetings, he conducted as much business as he could at small dinners.

A Policy of Conciliation

Printed copies of Jefferson's inaugural speech quickly found their way into newspapers around the country, and most people liked what they read. This was as Jefferson intended, for he was determined, after the bitter election campaign, to unite the country, not divide it further. In particular, the President wished to assure his opponents that the new administration would not follow a wild course similar to that of the turbulent French Revolution.

To the embittered and defeated Federalists, Jefferson extended a conciliatory, reassuring hand, noting, "We are all Republicans, we are all Federalists." This spirit of acceptance ran throughout the speech.

Jefferson's early actions as President also eased Federalists' fears of an abrupt change in government. The new cabinet appointees, including James Madison as secretary of state and Albert Gallatin as secretary of the treasury, were Republicans, but Jefferson did not routinely dismiss Federalists holding government positions.

The new administration also retained some important Federalist policies. For example, the national government continued to pay off the states' war debts, as Alexander Hamilton had insisted it should do. Jefferson also allowed the Bank of the United States, another of Hamilton's economic measures, to remain in operation.

After his initial gestures of conciliation toward the departed Federalists, Jefferson moved quickly to implement his own Republican principles of government. In doing so he had the support of Republicans in Congress, who had won a majority in both the House and the Senate. He allowed the Alien and Sedition acts to expire and refunded all fines that had been paid under those acts. Under Jefferson's leadership, Congress also restored the former requirements for naturalization that allowed immigrants to become citizens after five years residence.

Conflict With the Judicial Branch

President Jefferson next turned to the task of dismantling the Federalist party's control of the judicial branch of the national government. As one of his last acts in office, President Adams had appointed a number of judges. He hoped this action would leave the Federalists in control of the federal judiciary during the new Republican administration.

Jefferson refused to be bound by these "midnight appointments," as he called them. He instructed the secretary of state, James Madison, not to deliver the official letters of appointment to any of the "midnight judges." The President further convinced Congress to repeal the Federalist-sponsored Judiciary Act of 1801, which had permitted a large number of new appointments to the judiciary.

Jefferson's decision not to honor the "midnight appointments" led to an important decision by the Supreme Court. William Marbury, one of the "midnight judges" appointed by Adams, sued Madison for refusing to deliver his letter of appointment. Part of Marbury's claim rested on a section of the Judiciary Act of 1789 that had set up much of the federal court system.

In the case of *Marbury* v. *Madison* the Supreme Court ruled that the Judiciary Act of 1789 was unconstitutional. Chief Justice John Marshall, a Federalist appointed by John Adams, stated that Congress had exceeded its constitutional authority when it passed the bill. In his decision, the Chief Justice firmly established the principle of *judicial review*, under which the Supreme Court has the power to review a law passed by Congress and reject it if it is considered unconstitutional.

This decision greatly angered Republicans, who thought Marshall was assuming too much power for the judiciary. To them it looked as if the Court could simply veto any legislation by declaring it unconstitutional. The justices had turned the Constitution into "a mere thing of wax," Jefferson complained, which they could shape any way they pleased. He believed this was unacceptable, not just because Federalists controlled the judiciary, but because he feared that Marshall might be upsetting the constitutional balance between the three branches of government.

Yet if the judiciary threatened to become too powerful, Congress itself had power it could use, the impeachment of judges.* Jefferson urged the House of Representatives to impeach certain judges who

_____

*According to the Constitution, the House of Representatives can impeach, or accuse, federal judges of "treason, bribery, or other high crimes." If a two-thirds majority of the Senate votes to convict the judge, he or she is removed from office.

he believed were unfit. The House impeached one federal judge for drunkenness, and the Senate convicted him.

The House of Representatives also began impeachment proceedings against Samuel Chase, a Supreme Court justice. Chase, a Federalist who openly denounced Jefferson's administration in court sessions, was accused of misconduct in office. The Senate, however, refused to convict Chase, arguing that his actions were not within the constitutional meaning of misconduct. In spite of Jefferson's efforts, the Federalists remained strong in the federal judiciary.

Jefferson's Ideas on Government: Laissez-Faire

In his inaugural speech Thomas Jefferson suggested that the key to a "happy and a prosperous" future for America lay in a "wise and frugal [thrifty] government." The role of that government, Jefferson went on, should be confined to preventing people "from injuring one another" and "shall leave them otherwise free to regulate their own pursuits of industry and improvement." The philosophy that Jefferson described has become known by the French term *laissez-faire* (LEHS ay FEHR), meaning noninterference.

As President, Jefferson tried to limit the government's role in people's lives. He reduced the number of positions in the Departments of State and Treasury and cut the federal budget. Congress also repealed the unpopular excise tax on whiskey.

Jefferson took special aim at the military budget, partly because of his belief in laissez-faire, partly because he believed that a large army or navy in peacetime posed a threat to liberty. Consequently, he reduced the armed forces budget to half of what it had been under the Federalists. He confined the navy's role to coastal defense, using small, inexpensive gunboats. Thus the government canceled contracts to build several large oceangoing warships.

Conflict on the Barbary Coast

Cutting the navy proved too hasty an action, however, for its sailors and ships were soon needed against pirates off the coast of North Africa. For years the rulers of the Barbary Coast states of Morocco, Algiers, Tunis, and Tripoli had forced many nations, including the United States, to pay them an annual sum or risk the capture of merchant ships that ventured into the Mediterranean Sea.

Paying tribute irritated the American sense of honor. It was also expensive, since the United States trade in the area was extensive. When the pirates increased their demands in 1801, President Jefferson sent a squadron of eight naval vessels to the Mediterranean to enforce a blockade of Tripoli. When one of the ships, the *Philadelphia*, ran aground, the pirates threw its crew into prison and converted the ship to their own use. Lieutenant Stephen Decatur then sailed another United States ship into Tripoli harbor and burned the *Philadelphia*, depriving the pirates of its use.

Meanwhile, a small force of American marines landed in Tripoli, captured a city, and forced the Barbary leaders to make peace. The United States concluded a victorious treaty with Tripoli in 1805. The Barbary Coast action demonstrated the need to maintain a navy of reasonable size to protect American shipping around the world.

Threats to the Nation's Unity

Throughout his first term, Jefferson worked to conciliate Federalists and to smooth over disputes within the Republican party. He built Republican strength in the former Federalist strongholds of New York and New England. The President also won over some Federalists through his careful appointment policy, removing mostly High Federalists and replacing them with moderate Republicans. As a result, Jefferson won reelection in 1804, with George Clinton as Vice-President, replacing Aaron Burr.

Not everyone had been willing to come under Jefferson's banner during his first administration. Bitter at the resounding defeat of their party in 1800, a small group of High Federalists devised a scheme whereby New England and New York would unite in an independent confederation and *secede*, or withdraw, from the union. They approached Vice-President Aaron Burr. Burr, who had been out of favor with the Republicans since 1800, when he had allowed the Federalists to back his candidacy for President, agreed to join the scheme. (See page 186.) In return he expected the Federalists to support him as a candidate for governor of New York.

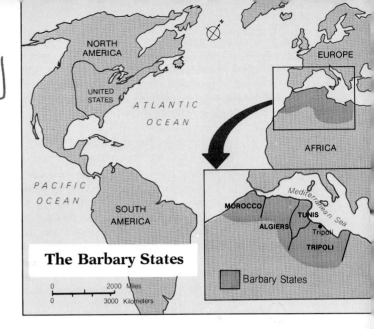

The Barbary States

MOROCCO
ALGIERS
TUNIS
Tripoli
TRIPOLI
Mediterranean Sea

0   2000 Miles
0   3000 Kilometers

Barbary States

■ *For years the Barbary states had forced other nations to pay tribute or have their ships captured. When the Barbary states demanded more money from the United States, President Jefferson sent the small U.S. Navy to blockade the port of Tripoli.*

Before the plot could get very far, Alexander Hamilton exposed Burr's role and called him unfit for public office. Burr responded by challenging Hamilton to a duel. Dueling was illegal, and Alexander Hamilton had publicly opposed the practice, but this time he decided to fight. Hamilton wrote to his wife and eight children that if he backed down from the challenge, he feared people would consider him a coward. Hamilton paid for his decision with his life. In Weehawken, New Jersey, at dawn on July 11, 1804, Vice-President Aaron Burr shot and killed Alexander Hamilton.

Soundly defeated in his bid for the New York governorship and liable for arrest on a charge of murder as a result of the duel, Burr next became involved in a wild conspiracy to take control of land west of the Mississippi River. In 1806 Burr plotted with General James Wilkinson, the commander of American troops in the Louisiana territory, to carve their own country out of Spanish territory in the Southwest.

The details of their scheme were probably no clearer in 1806 than they are to historians today. After a year of plotting, Wilkinson suddenly betrayed Burr and informed Jefferson of the scheme. Burr was arrested, charged with treason, and brought to Virginia to stand trial. But Chief Justice John Marshall, who presided, insisted there was not enough evidence of treason to convict Burr, so he was freed.

In spite of such dramatic dissension, the overall mood of the early years of Jefferson's presidency was one of cooperation and conciliation. His conscious efforts to bring Federalists into his following paid off. But perhaps Jefferson's most popular move came to him unexpectedly. With one stroke of his pen, President Jefferson almost doubled the size of the United States.

SECTION REVIEW

1. Identify: "midnight appointments," *Marbury* v. *Madison*.

2. Define: judicial review, laissez-faire, secede.

3. In what ways was Thomas Jefferson's approach to government informal?

4. (a) How did Jefferson try to gain the good will of the Federalists? (b) What early action showed his Republican principles?

5. What two reasons did Jefferson have for objecting to the Supreme Court's decision in *Marbury* v. *Madison?*

6. (a) Why did the United States pay tribute to the Barbary Coast states? (b) How did the government finally end this piracy?

7. **Critical Thinking** Would Jefferson have favored the role of the federal government today?

2 Expanding the Nation's Boundaries by Treaty

On April 12, 1803, representatives from the United States and France concluded an agreement in which the United States purchased the vast tract of French-owned lands west of the Mississippi River. For this immense territory, the United States paid about $15 million, or less than three cents an acre.

The Louisiana Purchase

Although few Europeans or Americans had explored the Louisiana territory, it had already changed hands several times before it became part of the United States. France, which had originally claimed the area, had given it to Spain as part of the treaty ending the French and Indian War. Then in 1800 Napoleon Bonaparte* secretly arranged for the territory to be transferred back to France.

At about the same time the press of American settlers west of the Appalachian Mountains increased the United States government's interest in the territory. As the number of new settlements in the area of present-day Ohio, Indiana, Kentucky, and Tennessee grew, the question of who owned the territories around the Mississippi River became especially crucial.

Roads in the western territories barely existed, so the Mississippi River and its tributaries served as the main route for trade into and out of the West. The port of New Orleans at the mouth of the river was especially important and, as you will recall, in 1795 Spain had granted American traders the right to use the port for overseas shipment. (See page 179.)

When President Jefferson learned of Spain's secret transfer of Louisiana back to France, he worried that Napoleon might attempt to use the territory as a base to build his own colonial empire in the West. Moreover, the French were again at war with Great Britain. Jefferson feared that if Napoleon closed New Orleans to American shipping, the United States would be forced to join an alliance with Britain against France. Jefferson, like Presidents Washington and Adams before him, wanted to avoid such entangling alliances. The President thus decided to try to gain control of New Orleans for the United States.

He sent Robert Livingston and James Monroe to France with instructions to offer to buy New Orleans and western Florida. Congress appropriated $2 million for the purchase. When Livingston and Monroe made their offer to the French government, its representative, Talleyrand, unexpectedly asked how much the United States would be

*At this time Napoleon was known as the first consul of France. In 1804 he became emperor.

willing to pay for the entire Louisiana territory, stretching from the Mississippi to the Rocky Mountains.

Although the American ambassadors had instructions only to purchase New Orleans, they quickly decided that this was an opportunity they could not pass up. So they agreed on behalf of the United States to buy Louisiana for about $15 million.

Napoleon had decided to sell the whole territory for several reasons. For one thing, he needed money to finance military campaigns in Europe, which he was trying to dominate. Furthermore, his aim of building an American empire had been shattered.

Napoleon had wanted to build this empire around a secure sea base in the Caribbean and had chosen the island of Haiti, a former French possession. In 1791, during the French Revolution, Toussaint L'Ouverture (too SAN loo vehr TYOOR) had led a successful slave rebellion and won Haiti's independence. Napoleon's attempt to reconquer Haiti in 1800 had failed. A combination of Haitian resistance and the devastating impact of yellow fever on the French troops successfully repelled the invasion. Once he had given up his goal of an American empire, Napoleon had little interest in keeping Louisiana.

Throughout the negotiations neither the French nor the United States government had considered the rights of the Native Americans living in the territory. Jefferson had assumed the problem could be resolved later. Napoleon did obtain from the United States the guarantee that French Catholics residing in the area would be given citizenship and the right to worship freely.

A Constitutional Dispute

When President Jefferson received word of the agreement, he faced a dilemma. He favored the purchase, but the Constitution did not specify how the country could acquire new territory or who had the authority to do it. As you know, Jefferson had long argued for a strict construction of the Constitution. His Federalist opponents, on the other hand, had endorsed a loose construction. (See page 176.)

The President first thought about submitting an amendment to the Constitution that would specify how new territory was to be purchased. But that procedure would take time, and the administration was afraid that Napoleon might change his mind and refuse to sell. Jefferson finally decided to base the purchase on his constitutional power to make treaties with foreign nations. He then sent the agreement with France to the Senate for ratification.

Federalists opposed the purchase, arguing that it was a waste of money and would add unreasonably to the national debt. Ironically, the Federalists also reversed their position on interpreting the Constitution. In this case they asserted that because the Constitution did not specifically authorize the President to buy land, he could not do so. Nevertheless, after a brief debate the Senate overwhelmingly approved the treaty. In December 1803 the United States took possession of its new territory.

Exploring the New Frontier

No one in the United States really knew how much land had been bought from France. The treaty that transferred title of the Louisiana Purchase to the United States stated its boundaries in vague terms. Jefferson believed that the United States could now claim all the land draining into the Mississippi River and its tributaries.

Even before the purchase, Jefferson had secretly planned an expedition to explore the territory. Soon after the Senate approved the treaty, he authorized the expedition to begin. Meriwether Lewis, Jefferson's private secretary, and William Clark, younger brother of Revolutionary War General George Rogers Clark, led the exploring party.

The President instructed Lewis and Clark to gather information about the flow of rivers and the availability of natural resources, information that could be used to plan the future commercial development of the region. But Jefferson's natural curiosity and interest in science inspired additional instructions to study the climate, plant growth, and geology of the area.

The Lewis and Clark expedition, consisting of about thirty soldiers and ten civilians, left St. Louis in May 1804. For the next two years they journeyed up the Missouri River to the Great Falls, crossed the Rocky Mountains, and canoed down the Snake and Columbia rivers toward the Pacific.

Along the route Sacajawea (SAHK uh juh WEE uh), a Shoshone woman married to a

French-Canadian explorer, assisted Lewis and Clark as a translator and guide. Her ability to locate edible wild plants fascinated Lewis, who referred to her in his journal as the "snake woman." Sacajawea proved especially helpful when the expedition reached what is now Idaho, the region of the Shoshone nation.

In general, Lewis and Clark dealt cautiously and fairly with Native Americans during their journey. They traveled through the territory of many Indian nations and spent the winter of 1804–1805 in a Mandan village near what is now Bismarck, North Dakota.

In November 1805 the expedition reached the Pacific Ocean, where Clark carved on a tree, "By Land from the U. States in 1804 & 5." The group returned by the same route to St. Louis the following year. Their expedition was an enormous success, and the publication of their journals several years later provided detailed knowledge about the territory.

For decades fur traders, road builders, and settlers referred to the records of the Lewis and Clark expedition as they ventured into the new frontier. Other expeditions that Jefferson organized, especially those led by Zebulon Pike up the Mississippi River and up the Arkansas River to the Rockies, provided further valuable information about the new lands.

■ *After the United States bought the vast Louisiana territory for $15 million, Jefferson was eager to have it thoroughly explored and mapped. Meriwether Lewis and William Clark explored northern parts of the territory. Zebulon Pike explored the Southwest.*

The Louisiana Purchase and Western Expeditions

Claimed by Great Britain, Russia, Spain, and U.S.

BRITISH TERRITORY

SPANISH TERRITORY

SPANISH FLORIDA

Columbia R.
Snake R.
Yellowstone R.
Missouri R.
Great Salt Lake
Colorado R.
Arkansas R.
Red R.
Rio Grande
Mississippi R.
Ohio R.

L. Superior
L. Michigan
L. Huron
L. Ontario
L. Erie
St. Lawrence R.

St. Louis
Santa Fe
Natchitoches
San Antonio
New Orleans

INDIANA TERR.
MICH. TERR.
OHIO 1803
VA.
PA.
N.Y.
VT. 1791
MAINE (part of Mass.)
N.H.
MASS.
R.I.
CONN.
N.J.
DEL.
MD.
KY. 1792
TENN. 1796
N.C.
S.C.
GA.
MISSISSIPPI TERRITORY

UNITED STATES, 1803
- Original states
- New states
- Louisiana Purchase

0   500 Miles
0   800 Kilometers

→ Lewis and Clark, 1804–1806
→ Pike, 1805–1806
--▶ Pike, 1806–1807

194

The Lewis and Clark expedition spent a winter with the Mandan people, who built villages on bluffs above the Missouri River. The women in the foreground of this painting are using bullboats made of buffalo hide stretched over willow frames. The tail was left on the buffalo hide, and a piece of wood was attached to it to keep the round boats from spinning.

SECTION REVIEW

1. Identify: Napoleon Bonaparte, Toussaint L'Ouverture, Meriwether Lewis, William Clark, Sacajawea.
2. (a) Why did Jefferson want to buy Louisiana? (b) Why did Napoleon want to sell?
3. (a) What provisions did the Constitution make for acquiring new territory? (b) How did Jefferson justify his action?
4. **Critical Thinking** How did the Lewis and Clark expedition strengthen the role of the United States on the continent?

3 The Coming of Another War

Like his predecessors, President Jefferson wanted to avoid European entanglements that might push the nation into war. He had stated in his inaugural address that the United States had no interest in what happened in Europe.

The President hoped to devote the full attention of his administration to developing the economic, educational, and cultural institutions that would suit the new nation. But events in Europe dashed his hopes. Jefferson spent much of his second term in office trying to maintain American neutrality. James Madison continued the effort, but it was in vain.

Challenges to Neutrality

During the first decade of the nineteenth century, Europe was caught up in yet another war. Under Napoleon Bonaparte, France conquered nearly all of the continent between 1803 and 1807. Napoleon then turned his sights toward Great Britain. Although France was the undisputed master of the land in Europe, Great Britain ruled the seas.

Both nations used economic as well as military tactics in the struggle. In 1806 and 1807 Napoleon devised what came to be known as the Continental System. He closed

In this 1805 cartoon, King George III of Great Britain and the Emperor Napoleon of France carve up the world between their two nations. Napoleon's army controlled much of Europe, but England's navy dominated the seas.

all European ports to goods from Great Britain and ordered the seizure of all ships carrying such goods, even if they were the ships of neutral nations. The British government responded by issuing the Orders in Council, which prohibited neutral nations from trading with France or its allies. Violators of the orders risked seizure by the British navy.

The United States found itself caught in the middle. France would not allow American ships to trade with Britain, and Great Britain objected to United States trade with France. After 1806 ships bound for European ports were often stopped by the French or the British navies, or sometimes by both, and searched for cargoes destined for the enemy.

By 1807 France had seized five hundred United States ships and Britain had seized nearly one thousand. Such seizures were costly because by the early 1800s the United States had become the largest neutral carrier of goods in the world.

The British practice of *impressment*, or forcing sailors to serve in the Royal Navy, further angered Americans. Many sailors had deserted the British navy because of notoriously bad conditions. The British claimed the right to search American ships for these deserters. Indeed, since conditions on American ships were better than those in the British navy, many British deserters were serving with the Americans.

As the war with France continued, British impressment gangs became increasingly belligerent in their searches. Often they seized *naturalized* American citizens off the ships. These were former British subjects who had become American citizens. By 1811 nearly ten thousand American sailors had been illegally "pressed" into service for Great Britain.

American ships that resisted search and seizure risked damage. In 1807, for example, the British warship *Leopard* fired on the *Chesapeake* when it refused to allow an impressment gang to board. Badly damaged, the *Chesapeake* suffered 21 casualties.

The Embargo

Despite these violations of American rights, President Jefferson tried to find a peaceful way to show France and Great Britain that the United States would insist on respect for its neutrality. He decided to impose an *embargo*, or a complete halt to trade.

Britain and France each wanted to retain United States trade, but only for itself. Thus Jefferson thought that he could pressure the two governments into recognizing the new nation's neutrality by withholding trade benefits from both. Congress agreed and in 1807 passed the Embargo Act, which prohibited virtually all commerce with foreign nations.

The embargo did hurt both Britain and France. Unfortunately, it hurt American merchants too, especially in New England, where many sea captains had been willing to risk the seizure of their vessels for the high profits of wartime trading. The combination of the Embargo Act and the earlier French and British seizures of American ships had a devasting impact on United States exports. (See the graph below.)

President Jefferson had hoped to rely largely on voluntary cooperation from merchants to enforce the embargo, and some merchants did cooperate. Many, however, sought to evade the law. This evasion was most prevalent in New England, where economic survival depended on commerce. The West and South did not feel the effects of the embargo as much since they relied more on domestic trade. Yet some farmers did have a problem with grain surpluses because they could not export their products.

Many merchants who did not violate the embargo were ruined, and pressure mounted for its repeal. In 1809 Congress voted to end the embargo, and Jefferson reluctantly agreed that it had been a failure.

One positive effect of the embargo was not immediately apparent. While the United States was cut off from Europe, American manufacturers began to produce goods that were formerly imported. The embargo thus helped stimulate the development of American industry.

Outbreak of War

Thomas Jefferson decided not to run for a third term in 1808. He chose instead to return to the quiet life of Monticello. His secretary of state, James Madison, easily won election as President over Charles Pinckney, the Federalist candidate. Madison, one of the architects of the Constitution, wanted to continue Jefferson's policy of firm American neutrality.

In 1809 Congress, with Jefferson's and Madison's encouragement, devised a less severe alternative to the embargo, the Nonintercourse Act. This act prohibited trade with Great Britain and France as long as they continued to enforce their orders against neutral shipping, but it allowed Americans to trade with all other nations. The Nonintercourse Act proved to be as unpopular as the embargo because most American trade was with Britain and France.

Madison then announced that if either England or France would remove its restrictions on neutral shipping, the United States would halt its trade with the other nation. Napoleon saw this as an opportunity to trap the United States into siding with France. In November 1810 he announced that France would repeal its decrees against American trade with the British.

Napoleon probably had no intention of following through with his promise, but Madison believed him and did exactly what Napoleon had hoped. In February 1811 the President declared that the United States would continue trading with France but stop all shipments to Great Britain.

The interruption of trade with the United States severely damaged the British economy. In June 1812, following a difficult winter, the British government agreed to repeal the Orders in Council, but it was too late. By the time news of the repeal reached the United States, President Madison had

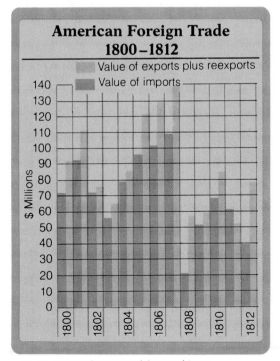

■ French and British seizure of American ships plus a trade embargo imposed by Jefferson in 1807 greatly decreased American foreign trade. President Jefferson imposed the embargo in hopes of keeping the United States out of the war between Great Britain and France.

American Foreign Trade 1800–1812

Value of exports plus reexports
Value of imports

($ Millions; years 1800–1812)

Source: *Historical Statistics of the United States*

lost patience with the policy of neutrality and had asked Congress to declare war on Great Britain.

The declaration passed with overwhelming support from the South and West. Federalists strongly opposed it because they had always been more sympathetic to Great Britain than to France. Representatives from New England and other trading centers—New York, New Jersey, and Delaware—also voted against the war. Despite the disruptions of trade since 1807, many merchants thought a war would be even more damaging to trade. For the second time in thirty years, the United States was at war with Great Britain.

Why War?

Historians have long debated why the United States went to war with Great Britain in 1812. The question is a difficult one since no single incident touched off hostilities. The attack on the *Chesapeake* was the sort of incident that could have started a war, but that happened in 1807, and war was not declared until 1812.

In his war message to Congress President Madison stated that the United States would fight to maintain freedom of the seas. Undoubtedly, Great Britain had violated that freedom. France had also seized American ships, but Madison and a majority of the members of Congress were Republicans, who traditionally sympathized with France.

One factor that contributed to the movement toward war with Great Britain was a growing sense of national pride, particularly strong among westerners. Although the British impressment of American sailors and the seizure of American ships had little direct impact on them, they considered such actions an attack on all Americans, and they clamored for war.

Senator Henry Clay of Kentucky led an especially belligerent group of Republican congressmen from the West, called War Hawks because of their prowar agitation. As intense nationalists, the War Hawks saw war with Great Britain as an opportunity to expand the territory of the United States. They made no secret of their desire to win Canada from Britain and, as one of them put it, "to drive the British from our Continent." The War Hawks also wanted war with Great Britain because they believed that the British were supporting Native Americans who had been resisting settlement of the Northwest Territory.

Western Conflicts

American settlers had encountered resistance from Native Americans in the area west of the Allegheny Mountains since the mid-1700s. As you read in Chapter 6, in 1763 the British had tried to prevent such conflicts by restricting settlement beyond the mountains. After independence, the movement westward grew. Attempts to control settlement such as the Northwest Ordinance had little effect.

In theory the United States government was to obtain Native American land by treaties, then allow settlement. In actuality settlers pushed into whatever region they wanted. When they had taken up the best land in one tract, they expanded farther west without regard for the Indians' rights of possession. Furthermore, many of the treaties the United States did obtain were of dubious validity. Native Americans who signed the treaties often did not represent their nations or did not own the land in question.

Resistance to settlement increased in the late 1780s, especially in the area north of the Ohio River. In 1791 the Shawnee, led by Little Turtle, soundly defeated a force of militia under General Arthur St. Clair. But three years later an army expedition commanded by General Anthony Wayne defeated the Indians in the Battle of Fallen Timbers. The following year in the Treaty of Greenville, Indian leaders ceded a large part of present-day Ohio to the United States. This opened the way for greater settlement of the Northwest Territory, which also meant the acquisition of more Native American land, a total of about 48 million acres (about 20 million hectares) between 1795 and 1809.

Tecumseh and the Prophet

The continued movement of settlers into the Northwest Territory threatened the survival of the Native American nations that inhabited the area. Not only was their land being taken, often by deceit or violence, but their culture was being weakened by the adoption of alien customs.

The anger and frustration produced by this situation led to the emergence of two

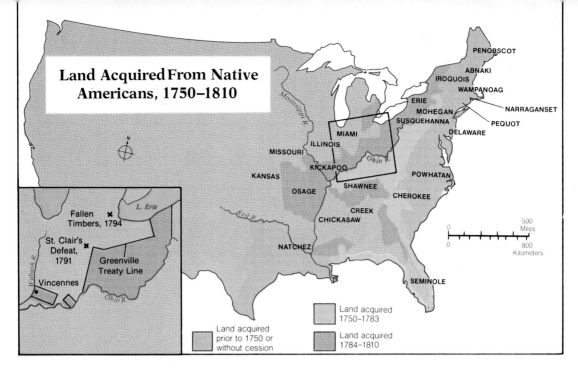

Land Acquired From Native Americans, 1750–1810

Fallen Timbers, 1794
St. Clair's Defeat, 1791
Greenville Treaty Line
Vincennes
Ohio R.
L. Erie

Land acquired prior to 1750 or without cession
Land acquired 1750–1783
Land acquired 1784–1810

500 Miles
800 Kilometers

■ Settlers moving westward took control of more and more Indian land. Indian attempts to resist them failed. In the Treaty of Greenville (1795), Indian nations ceded much of present-day Ohio to the United States.

powerful Shawnee leaders, Tecumseh (tih KUHM suh) and his brother, who was called the Prophet. Their goal was to unite all Indian nations east of the Mississippi to resist further settlement. The Prophet further called on Indians to revitalize their own culture and to give up customs they had adopted from the new settlers.

By 1811 Tecumseh, a skillful orator, had organized a confederation that stretched from the Northwest Territory to Florida. A battle fought at Tippecanoe Creek in Indiana doomed the confederation, however. In November 1811 General William Henry Harrison, the governor of Indiana Territory, led a force of a thousand soldiers against Tecumseh's headquarters by the creek. The battle was a draw, but Harrison's forces destroyed the Indian camp. Westerners considered the battle a great victory, and many Indians became disillusioned with the confederation.

Tecumseh's activities further aggravated the anti-British feelings of westerners, who were convinced that the British were supporting him. When war did break out between the United States and Great Britain in 1812, Tecumseh announced his support for the British. During the war he led his Indian allies against United States forces in the Northwest Territory.

The alliance of the British and the Indians, however, did not dim the War Hawks' enthusiasm. Henry Clay boasted that "the militia of Kentucky alone" could beat the British. Clay would discover that winning another war was not that easy.

SECTION REVIEW

1. Identify: Henry Clay, Battle of Fallen Timbers, Treaty of Greenville, Tecumseh, the Prophet, William Henry Harrison.

2. Define: impressment, naturalized citizens, embargo.

3. What actions did the French and British take against American ships after 1806?

4. How did the step taken by Jefferson to pressure France and Great Britain into recognizing American neutrality affect American merchants?

5. (a) What was the purpose of the Nonintercourse Act? (b) Was it effective? Explain.

6. What did the War Hawks hope to gain from a war with Great Britain?

7. **Critical Thinking** How might an alliance between the British and the Indians have benefited each?

Tecumseh: Who Has a Right to the Land?

Tecumseh tried to convince Indians to stop selling land to the United States government. He argued that the land, like the air, belonged to everyone. In the following speech he protests the Treaty of Fort Wayne (1809) in which two Indian nations sold 3 million acres (1.2 million hectares) of land for a small amount of money.

The Being within, communing with past ages, tells me that . . . until lately there was no white man on this continent; that it then all belonged to red men, children of the same parents, placed on it by the Great Spirit that made them, to keep it, to traverse it, to enjoy its productions, and to fill it with the same race—once a happy race, since made miserable by the white people, who are never contented, but always encroaching. The way—and the only way—to check and to stop this evil is for all red men to unite in claiming a common equal right in the land, as it was at first, and should be yet.

The white people have no right to take the land from the Indians, because they had it first. It is theirs. They may sell, but all must join. Any sale not made by all is not valid. All red men have equal rights to the unoccu-

pied land. The right of occupancy is as good in one place as in another. There cannot be two occupations in the same place. The first excludes all others. It is not so in hunting or traveling; for there the same

ground will serve many, as they may follow each other all day. But the camp is stationary, and that is occupancy. It belongs to the first who sits down on his blanket or skins which he has thrown upon the ground; and till he leaves it no other has a right.

Source: Chauncey M. Depew, ed., *The Library of Oratory: Ancient and Modern* (New York: Globe, 1902).

4 A Complex War

At first, neither Britain nor the United States seemed to take the war very seriously. The British, preoccupied by their fight with Napoleon, tended to view military campaigns in the former colonies as a secondary venture. In the United States opposition to the war continued, especially in the Federalist stronghold of New England. Nearly two years would slip by before the United States could even organize its army into a major fighting force.

A Slow Start

The regular army of the United States numbered fewer than 7,000 soldiers when the nation declared war. Another 690,000 men made up the state militias. Although available for service, the militias were still under

state and local control, and many were reluctant to leave their states. Bringing these units under federal authority required an act of Congress, but Congress moved very slowly.

In addition, the army suffered from an almost total lack of competent leaders. Most of its generals had participated in the Revolutionary War almost 30 years before. It took time and, unfortunately, some defeats in battle to identify promising junior officers and appoint them to command positions.

The navy was in slightly better shape; a number of its officers had gained experience in battles in Tripoli. Still the American fleet remained pitifully small, comprising only 16 vessels when the war began. Again Congress wasted valuable months arguing before it approved the construction of warships. And by the time these were completed, the war had ended.

Ineffective strategy further marred the initial military campaigns of the war. A quick American victory depended on conquering Canada, the center of British power in North America. That objective could most likely have been accomplished with an attack on Montreal to cut off British access to the sea, the same strategy that the British had employed successfully against the French in 1763. However, United States leaders, especially War Hawks, were preoccupied with western Canada and Indian activity on the frontier near Lake Erie. As a result, they never mobilized for a full-scale attack on Canada.

Not surprisingly, the war began with a series of reverses for the United States. In August 1812 General William Hull, a former commander in the Revolutionary War, moved his forces along Lake Erie to Detroit. At Detroit the British tricked Hull into believing that he faced a much larger force of British soldiers and Indian allies than was actually the case. Hull abruptly surrendered his army without firing a shot.

Closer to Montreal, another American campaign failed when the New York state militia refused to cross into Canada to fight. Only at sea were the Americans victorious, when the USS *Constitution* sank the British ship *Guerrière*.

Opposition to the War

The early defeats on land further convinced the Federalists in New England that the war was a mistake and could not be won. Moreover the British navy blockaded the Atlantic coast, which disrupted American trade. This further angered New England merchants. By 1814 foreign trade had fallen over 90 percent from its peak in 1807. Shipbuilding, a major New England industry, dropped 80 percent during the war.

New Englanders were also uneasy about the growing power of the western states. Territorial expansion would mean additional western states, and New England would have even less influence in national affairs.

201

■ Much of the fighting in the War of 1812 took place in the West. Several Indian nations allied with the British in the hope of stopping further settlement.

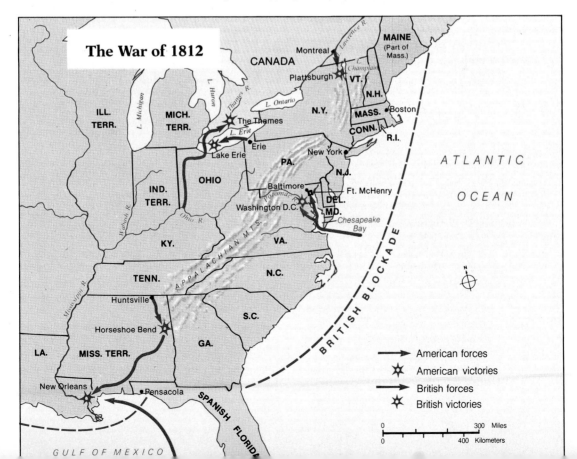

The War of 1812

American forces
★ American victories
British forces
★ British victories

0   300 Miles
0   400 Kilometers

Opposition to the war peaked in the fall of 1814 at the Hartford Convention. Twenty-six delegates from the New England states gathered in Hartford, Connecticut, to protest President Madison's conduct of the war. The delegates issued a long series of demands designed to protect the interests of New England against the South and the West. They threatened to secede and form an independent federation if their demands were not met. However, by the time the results of the Hartford Convention reached Washington, the war was over, and the convention's demands became a dead issue.

The Tide Begins to Turn

By 1813 the American cause appeared more hopeful. In September Captain Oliver Hazard Perry won the first major American victory when his squadron of naval ships defeated a British fleet on Lake Erie. "We have met the enemy and they are ours," Perry reported to General Harrison. Perry's victory gave the United States control of Lake Erie.

Next General Harrison moved a force of recently recruited troops north of Lake Erie into Canada. A month after Perry's victory, Harrison's troops defeated a combined British and Indian force at the Battle of the Thames. The Shawnee leader Tecumseh died during this battle. Without his leadership, the Indian confederation collapsed and ended its alliance with the British.

The following year the British planned an invasion of the United States from Canada. To repel the invasion, the Americans had to win control of Lake Champlain from the 16 British ships that patrolled it. The task fell to Captain Thomas Macdonough.

Macdonough recruited a force of Vermont shipbuilders who constructed ten ships in just 30 days. In September the American force won a decisive victory on Lake Champlain and forced the British to abandon their invasion from the north.

The British, however, had already launched another invasion farther south. This one proved more successful, at least initially. A large British force landed at the mouth of the Patuxent River on Chesapeake Bay and marched toward Washington, D.C. American defenders decided against a fight, and the British entered the city.

Dolly Madison, the President's wife, left the White House hastily, with dinner still on the table, and fled to Virginia. President Madison himself had ridden to the battle front to evaluate the British position, but he soon followed his wife and the cabinet members. After eating the dinner left behind in the White House, British troops burned most of the city and withdrew. Only the quick thinking of Dolly Madison and the efforts of White House servants saved a portrait of George Washington and several important government documents from destruction.

The British then moved up the Chesapeake Bay toward Baltimore. They met strong resistance from a force of volunteers manning Fort McHenry in Baltimore harbor. Despite a three-day bombardment, the British could not take the city.

The heroic defense of Baltimore disheartened the British and inspired the Americans. One person so inspired was Francis Scott Key. A prisoner on a British ship during the bombardment, Key wrote "The Star-Spangled Banner" when he saw that the American flag continued to wave after the bombardment.

Battle of New Orleans

The last battle of the war took place in the South. A British army planned to land at New Orleans, capture the city, and move up the Mississippi River. General Andrew Jackson commanded the United States forces. Jackson already had a reputation as a talented soldier. As major general of the Tennessee militia, he had been fighting against the Creeks in the Southwest since 1813. The so-called Creek War ended in March 1814 when Jackson and 2,000 militia won a decisive victory at Horseshoe Bend. In the resulting Treaty of Fort Jackson, the Creeks ceded two thirds of their land to the United States.

At New Orleans Jackson's men dug trenches for defense and crouched behind bales of cotton for protection. In January 1815 British forces landed and marched forward, expecting the entrenched soldiers to leave their defenses and run. Although far outnumbered, the Americans held their ground and slaughtered the advancing army, inflicting over 2,000 casualties while losing only 21 of their own troops.

It was a great victory for Jackson and his forces, which included the local militia, Kentucky riflemen, the militia from Jack-

Word of the 1814 peace treaty reached the United States too late to prevent the Battle of New Orleans. Led by Andrew Jackson, the outnumbered American troops at left mowed down the advancing British. Jackson is shown near the United States flag in this painting.

son's home state of Tennessee, and two battalions of black soldiers. Many of the latter were veterans of L'Ouverture's revolt in Haiti. (See page 193.) After the battle Jackson congratulated his troops, singling out the black soldiers for special praise.

> I expected much from you but you have surpassed my hopes. . . . Soldiers, the President of the United States shall be informed of your conduct on the present occasion; and the voice of the Representatives of the American nation shall applaud your valor, as your General now praises your ardor.

Free blacks made other contributions to the war effort. Two thousand black men constructed fortifications for the defense of Philadelphia. Free black sailors fought in the Great Lakes battles under the command of Oliver Perry, and two regiments of black volunteers from New York served in the army.

Many slaves also fought for the United States in the war. Others fought for the British, who promised them freedom after the war. Some did win their freedom, but many

were returned to their owners or sold in the West Indies.

A Tentative Victory

Jackson's victory at New Orleans actually came after a peace treaty, the Treaty of Ghent, had been signed in December 1814. But word of the treaty did not arrive in time to prevent the battle. News of the victory added a joyous note to the reading of the treaty in Congress, which quickly approved its terms.

The Treaty of Ghent itself did little more than restore prewar conditions. By late 1814 the British had dropped earlier demands, including the creation of a self-governing Indian nation in the area of Ohio. Furthermore, the war between Britain and France had ended, so the British had already stopped the impressment of American sailors and the search of American ships. The negotiators left other issues, such as border disputes, to be settled later.

Major Events	
1795	Treaty of Greenville
1803	*Marbury* v. *Madison;* Louisiana Purchase
1804–1806	Lewis and Clark expedition
1806–1807	Napoleon enforces Continental System; British enact Orders of Council
1807	Embargo Act passed
1808	James Madison elected President
1809	Embargo Act repealed; Nonintercourse Act passed
1811	Battle of Tippecanoe
1812	War breaks out with Great Britain
1813–1814	Creek War
1814	Treaty of Ghent
1815	Battle of New Orleans

Even though the treaty changed little, many citizens considered the War of 1812 a victory for the United States. The new nation had held its own in a war against a major European power. The final victory in the Battle of New Orleans further stimulated national pride and convinced many Americans that they had won the war.

The war also contributed to the nation's territorial and economic growth. The defeat of powerful Indian nations in the Northwest Territory and the South opened new land for settlement. And the British blockade of American ports encouraged many manufacturers to begin producing items that had been imported earlier.

SECTION REVIEW

1. Identify: Hartford Convention, Andrew Jackson, Creek War, Treaty of Ghent.
2. List three disadvantages the United States faced at the beginning of the war.
3. What two events in 1813 marked a turning point in the war for the Americans?
4. What did black Americans do in the war?
5. **Critical Thinking** Based on the definition of treason in the U.S. Constitution, were the members of the Hartford Convention treasonous? Why or why not?

Chapter 11 Review

In Perspective

Thomas Jefferson began his term as the first Republican President by trying to unite the nation. He kept some Federalist programs, while carrying into effect his own Republican principles, especially the idea of laissez-faire. Jefferson's most important single act probably was the purchase of the Louisiana Territory, which nearly doubled the size of the nation.

The threat of war hung over the last years of Jefferson's presidency. His attempt to force Great Britain and France to recognize American neutrality by imposing an embargo failed, largely because it hurt United States merchants. His successor, James Madison, also failed to maintain American neutrality. In 1812 the United States was at war with Great Britain.

The war began with American defeats, but United States forces soon won important battles on the Great Lakes and in Canada. The heroic defense of Baltimore and the Battle of New Orleans inspired many Americans and convinced them that the United States had won the war. This spirit of nationalism continued to grow over the following decades.

Vocabulary

Match each term at left with its definition or description at right.

1. embargo
2. laissez-faire
3. secede
4. judicial review
5. impressment

a. forcing a sailor to serve in the navy
b. a policy of government noninterference
c. complete trade halt
d. to withdraw from the union
e. power to declare a law unconstitutional

Chapter Checkup

1. (a) What gestures of conciliation did Jefferson make toward the Federalists after his election? (b) How did he try to implement his own principles of government?

2. (a) How did the purchase of the Louisiana territory conflict with Jefferson's interpretation of the Constitution? (b) On what presidential power did he ultimately base his action?

3. How did Jefferson react to the British and French challenges to American neutrality after 1806?

4. (a) What were the provisions of the Treaty of Ghent? (b) What issues were not included in the treaty? Why?

Critical Thinking

1. **Analyzing** How did the principle of checks and balances operate during the dispute between President Jefferson and the Federalists in the judiciary?

2. **Drawing Conclusions** (a) Who favored war with Great Britain in 1812? (b) Who opposed the war? Why? (c) Which group had a right to think they had been right in 1812? Explain.

Developing Basic Skills

1. **Map Reading** Study the map on page 194 and the maps of the United States on pages 812 and 813. Then answer the following questions: (a) What mineral resources have been found in the land that made up the Louisiana territory? (b) How is that land used today, according to the map on page 813?

2. **Graph Reading** Study the graph on page 197 and answer the following questions: (a) In what year was the value of American exports highest? (b) In what year was the value of imports highest? (c) Based on what you read, how would you explain the change in American foreign trade between 1807 and 1812?

See page 829 for suggested readings.

Writer's Handbook

Developmental or Topical Order

Developmental order reflects your own opinion about how the details in a paragraph should be organized. You will use developmental or topical order when the supporting information for a topic sentence does not fit into any of the patterns of organization you have learned about in previous lessons. Suppose you were writing a paragraph to develop the topic sentence: *Thomas Jefferson is known for his many contributions to this country.* You might write: *He helped fashion the future of the nation with the Declaration of Independence. Later, he served as George Washington's secretary of state. When elected President himself, Jefferson oversaw the first of many peaceful transitions of power from a President of one party to a President of another party. Outside of the political arena, he laid the foundation for the Library of Congress and founded the University of Virginia.*

Some words that are used to show developmental organization are: *and, therefore, another, thus, also,* and *consequently.*

Practice: Develop the topic sentence above in your own words.

12

A Growing Nation

(1815–1824)

Deck Life on the Paragon *by Pavel Petrovich Svinin*

Chapter Outline

1 *A Sense of National Unity*

2 *The Industrial Revolution*

3 *Henry Clay's American System*

4 *Building Pathways to the West*

5 *James Monroe and Foreign Affairs*

The War of 1812 stirred a new sense of national pride and unity among Americans. After the war, nationalism burst forth with a fervor never before experienced in the nation's short history.

The growing spirit of nationalism took many forms. Love of country and patriotism were among them, but the new nationalism showed itself in more concrete ways as well. Supreme Court decisions were to strengthen the power of the national government. Industrial development bolstered a sense of national self-sufficiency at a time when better roads, canals, and river transportation were drawing the nation together. In foreign affairs, national pride was to manifest itself in President James Monroe's proclamation to the nations of the world, known as the Monroe Doctrine.

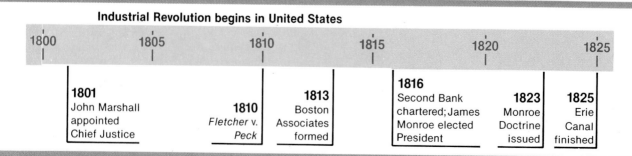

Industrial Revolution begins in United States

1800	1805	1810	1815	1820	1825

1801
John Marshall appointed Chief Justice

1810
Fletcher v. Peck

1813
Boston Associates formed

1816
Second Bank chartered; James Monroe elected President

1823
Monroe Doctrine issued

1825
Erie Canal finished

1 A Sense of National Unity

Political developments after the War of 1812 contributed to America's sense of national identity. For a brief period, the earlier competition between political parties seemed forgotten. Disagreement, however, still lay beneath the surface.

An Era of Good Feelings

As President Madison neared the end of his second term, he took great care to see that the Republicans nominated James Monroe, his secretary of state and fellow Virginian, to succeed him. Despite the objections of some Republican representatives and much grumbling about the "Virginia Dynasty" controlling the presidency, Monroe received the nomination. With the Federalist party now weak and breaking apart, he easily defeated his opponent, Rufus King of New York.

When Monroe was inaugurated in 1817, the nation seemed more united and optimistic than it had ever been. A presidential goodwill tour, which took Monroe to the former Federalist stronghold of New England, demonstrated this change in the American mood. Citizens of Boston warmly received him. One newspaper, the *Columbian Sentinel*, referring to the way in which old political foes greeted each other, called the times the "Era of Good Feelings."

Good feelings seemed to prevail all over the country. Four years later, in 1820 when President Monroe ran for reelection, no one opposed him. Only one electoral vote was cast against him. Monroe's reelection marked the end of the Federalist party. The Federalists, in decline since 1800, had lost most of their remaining support with the American victory in the War of 1812. During the Era of Good Feelings, only a few scattered supporters remained. The country seemed united under one party. the Republican party.

James Monroe: Symbol of Unity

As President, James Monroe became a symbol of the nation's political unity. Over sixty years old when he took office, Monroe was the last President of the Revolutionary War generation. To be sure, men such as Andrew Jackson and John Quincy Adams had been born before 1776, but they were children during the war. Monroe, in contrast, was a young man when Cornwallis surrendered in 1781.

Monroe's perspective was that of the early generation, as his quaint attire showed. He dressed in the fashion of decades past, from white-topped boots and knee-length pantaloons to cocked hat. He even powdered his hair and tied it in a queue at the back. To the postwar generation he was, as one historian observed, "a last nostalgic look at the eighteenth century."

Monroe's mental outlook was equally rooted in the past. Except in the area of foreign affairs, he thought the President had little responsibility for policy making. Monroe believed that the Congress should interpret and enact the public will, and the President should follow.

Nor had he ever fully accepted the idea of political parties. Calling them "the curse of the country," he rejoiced that an era of no parties seemed at last at hand. "The existence of parties," Monroe declared "is not necessary to free government." But political unity turned out to be only an illusion. A new and stronger opposition party would eventually grow out of the ruins of the Federalists.

Marshall and the Supreme Court

Even while the Federalist party was in decline, a leading Federalist, John Marshall, was contributing to the growing sense of national unity.

President John Adams had appointed Marshall as Chief Justice of the Supreme Court in 1801. When Marshall assumed his duties, the Supreme Court lacked both power and prestige. Indeed, John Jay, the first Chief Justice, had resigned because he felt that he had too little to do.

The Supreme Court in the early 1800s rarely met in Washington longer than six weeks a year, and its proceedings attracted little attention. For part of the year, Marshall, like the other justices, rode a federal circuit.

The justices maintained a low public profile. They met in the basement of the Capitol, boarded together, and rarely went

Under the strong leadership of Chief Justice John Marshall, the Supreme Court gained new prestige and power.

out socially. In fact, Justice William Paterson once traveled a full day on the same stagecoach as Thomas Jefferson without either recognizing the other.

Chief Justice John Marshall was a simple man. He was not a legal scholar, but his keen mind helped him get to the heart of legal problems and write clear, forceful decisions. Seldom has a person so dominated the nation's highest court. During his 35 years as Chief Justice, he wrote almost half of the Court's decisions and dissented from the majority opinion only eight times. Even Republican justices appointed by Presidents Jefferson, Madison, and Monroe came under the sway of his forceful personality.

The Court and National Unity

John Marshall was a moderate Federalist who favored strengthening the power of the national government. As Chief Justice from 1801 to 1835, he was able to influence the nation's developing political system.

As early as 1803, in *Marbury* v. *Madison*, the Supreme Court had confirmed the principle of judicial review, the Court's power to decide if a law violated the Constitution. (See page 190.)

In *Fletcher* v. *Peck* (1810) the Court ruled a state law unconstitutional for the first time. The case involved land grants that the Georgia legislature had made to the Yazoo Land Company. The grants had been obtained by bribery and fraud, and a later session of the legislature had tried to invalidate them. In his decision Marshall ruled that the state could not repudiate the grants because they were contracts and the Constitution forbade states to "impair the obligation of contracts."

Nine years later in *Dartmouth College* v. *Woodward* (1819), the Supreme Court again upheld the sanctity of contracts. It overturned an attempt by the New Hampshire legislature to revise Dartmouth's charter, which had been granted during the colonial period. In so doing, Marshall asserted that a contract could not be changed without the consent of both parties, even if one of the parties was a state government. Through these rulings the Court made contractual obligations nearly unbreakable.

In two rulings that increased the authority of the national government, Marshall based his decisions on a loose construction of the Constitution. In the case of *McCulloch* v. *Maryland* (1819), the Court upheld the constitutionality of the second Bank of the United States, which Congress had chartered in 1816. While admitting that the Constitution did not specifically authorize a national bank, Marshall asserted that Congress had to have some leeway in exercising its powers.

> Let the end be legitimate, let it be within the scope of the Constitution, and all means which are appropriate, which are plainly adapted to that end, which are not prohibited, but consistent with the letter and spirit of the constitution, are constitutional.

In *Gibbons* v. *Ogden* (1824) the Supreme Court struck down a New York state law that had awarded a steamboat company a monopoly on passenger service across the Hudson River between New Jersey and New York. The ruling stated that a state can regulate commerce only within its borders. Marshall declared that only Congress could control interstate commerce. In this case the Court reaffirmed its power to overrule a state law. It also guaranteed that the nation would have a unified interstate trade policy. Individual states would not be able to interfere with interstate trade as they had under the Articles of Confederation.

The Supreme Court under John Marshall thus contributed to the growing sense of national unity. Its rulings clarified and affirmed important powers of the national government, especially of the Supreme Court and Congress.

209

SECTION REVIEW

1. Identify: Era of Good Feelings, James Monroe, John Marshall.

2. What incident resulted in the name the "Era of Good Feelings"?

3. Was the Supreme Court powerful before John Marshall became Chief Justice? Explain.

4. (a) What two Supreme Court rulings upheld contracts? (b) What two rulings strengthened the national government?

5. **Critical Thinking** How did the decision in *McCulloch* v. *Maryland* strengthen the federal government?

2 The Industrial Revolution

A period of industrial growth began in Great Britain during the eighteenth century, but it was slow in coming to America. The colonies had depended on Britain for manufactured goods until the Revolutionary War. Local industries finally began to develop after independence and their growth was spurred on by the War of 1812. The British blockade of the Atlantic shore meant that the nation had to rely on itself for many products formerly imported.

The Needs of Industry

Historians often use the term "Industrial Revolution" to describe the economic shift from farming and commerce to manufacturing. The term "revolution" suggests that the changes brought about by the development of manufacturing were so far-reaching that they seemed like a complete overthrow of the old way of life.

In fact, however, the growth of industry was neither violent nor abrupt. It involved many gradual changes. These changes were most evident in three areas crucial to the development of industry: technology, labor, and capital. In the area of technology, inventors found ways to replace manual labor with mechanical devices, which helped speed up the production process.

A new way of organizing labor, known as the *factory system*, developed in Great Britain by the 1770s. Rather than spreading the manufacturing process out over several locations, factories brought workers together under one roof. In textiles, for example, early producers had farmed out wool for women to spin in their homes. Weaving took place in another location and sewing in still another. Textile factories brought the workers to the mill, rather than take wool to individual homes.

Capital, or money for investment, was required for industry to develop. As early as the sixteenth century joint stock companies had worked out fairly simple ways to pool money and lessen the risks of commercial ventures. (See page 51.) But the high cost of new machinery required even larger sums of money.

In Europe corporations had developed to raise the needed capital. Corporations could raise large amounts of money from many small investors. Each investor's personal responsibility for the debts of the corporation did not exceed the initial investment. This idea of *limited liability* made corporations attractive to people who might not otherwise be willing to invest their money.

In spite of these advantages Americans adopted the use of corporations slowly. At first they were formed only for public projects like bridges. Only after the Civil War did the corporation become a dominant business form in the United States. Until then family-owned firms and partnerships were most common.

Technology at Work

The development of the steam engine is an important example of how changes in technology reshaped the manufacturing process. In 1769 James Watt, from Scotland, patented a steam engine. Before the introduction of this new source of power, gristmills were turned by water. But by the 1790s millers had begun using more efficient steam engines to power mills.

A number of other significant inventions came out of Great Britain in the decades after 1760. Advances in the smelting process made iron purer and more durable. James Hargreaves devised the spinning jenny, a means of connecting several spinning wheels together so that they spun eight threads at a time. Improvements on his design soon enabled spinners to produce a hundred threads at once. Other inventions mechanized the process of weaving cloth.

Before long the excitement of the Industrial Revolution began to be felt in the United States. Improved versions of the steam engine appeared. In 1787 John Fitch launched the first steam-powered boat on the Delaware River in Philadelphia. Twenty years later, in August 1807, Robert Fulton traveled up the Hudson River from New York City to Albany in 32 hours aboard the steam-powered *Clermont*, proving to skeptics the practical value of using the steam engine to power new means of transportation.

Another American, Eli Whitney, revolutionized cotton-cloth production with the invention of the cotton gin in 1793. By hand, the average worker could clean the seeds out of one to three pounds of cotton per day. Using Whitney's power-driven cotton gin, the same worker could clean 1,000 pounds a day.

Whitney was the first inventor to introduce *interchangeable parts*, which he originally used in the production of firearms. Traditionally, gunsmiths made each gun by hand, slowly honing the various parts until they fit. Whenever a part broke, a new one had to be custom made. Whitney built a large number of each component part, all exactly alike. Guns could thus be manufactured rapidly by assembling the various interchangeable parts. Repairs could be made just as quickly. As the concept of interchangeable parts spread to other industries,

Early factories were often run by water power. The tall building in this painting of Pawtucket Falls in Rhode Island is thought to be the first American textile mill to use water-powered machinery.

it provided the basis for further industrial development in the United States.

The Spread of Industry to the United States

Not surprisingly, Great Britain, the first country to begin to industrialize, was eager to protect the competitive advantage British goods enjoyed. For this reason it banned the export of industrial secrets and prohibited skilled mechanics who had worked in its more advanced factories from moving to other nations. Initially this slowed American industrial development, but, as you have read, American inventors were at work themselves.

Furthermore, Americans tried to learn the secrets of the British textile industry. Several state legislatures offered large rewards to British mechanics who would supply technical information. In 1789 twenty-one-year-old Samuel Slater, attracted by such offers, slipped away to the United States. He had served as an apprentice in a cotton-spinning factory, and he carried in his head detailed plans of textile machinery.

A wealthy manufacturer, Moses Brown of Providence, Rhode Island, hired Slater to reproduce the machinery and set up a factory. Slater built several improved versions of the machinery he had used in Britain, and in a year he had a factory producing cotton thread. Slater's ideas spread. Seven similar mills were operating by 1800, and by 1815 there were 213 in operation.

In 1813 a group of merchants led by Francis Cabot Lowell formed the Boston Manufacturing Company. With about half a million dollars in capital, these men, known as the Boston Associates, established the first textile factory that combined all the tasks required to turn raw cotton into finished cloth. Like Slater, they relied to a large extent on British technology, for Lowell had smuggled the plans for a power loom into the country. In the following decades, the Boston Associates set up other centers of textile manufacturing in New England. A factory in Lowell, Massachusetts, became the center of their operations.

Labor for the New Factories

Scarcity of labor had been a factor in the economy of the United States from its beginning. With the nation's vast territory, Ameri-

In the 1800s women began to take jobs in industry. The women here work in a book bindery.

cans had found it relatively easy to acquire land for farming, so few were interested in factory work at first. Yet factory owners needed workers. They could not turn to artisans, who had little interest in factory work. Artisans in the United States, like their counterparts in Europe, were used to working at home or in small shops, making quality products by hand. Indeed in the 1820s most products were still made that way. Thus early factory owners looked elsewhere for labor.

In the textile industry, especially, factory owners found most of their workers among women and children. Children held special appeal as textile workers because their small size enabled them to move nimbly around dangerous machinery. Women and children also worked for low wages. One reason was their relative lack of skills compared to artisans who had trained for many years.

Rules at a Mill Boardinghouse

Young women who worked at the textile mills lived in boardinghouses operated by the company. The rules below show how the mill owners tried to regulate the lives of their workers.

Rules and Regulations to be attended to and followed by the Young Persons who come to Board in this House:

Rule first: Each one to enter the house without unnecessary noise or confusion, and hang up their bonnet, shawl, coat, etc., etc., in the entry.

Rule second: Each one to have their place at the table during meals, the two which have worked the greatest length of time in the Factory, to sit on each side of the head of the table, so that all new hands will of course take their seats lower down, according to the length of time here.

Rule third: It is expected that order and good manners will be preserved at table during meals—and at all other times either upstairs or down.

Rule fourth: There is no unnecessary dirt to be brought into the house by the Boarders, such as apple cores or peels, or nut shells, etc.

Rule fifth: Each boarder is to take her turn in making the bed and sweeping the chamber in which she sleeps.

Rule sixth: Those who have worked the longest in the Factory are to sleep in the North Chamber, new hands in the South Chamber.

Rule seventh: As a lamp will be lighted every night upstairs and placed in a lanthorn, it is expected that no boarder will take a light into the chambers.

Rule eighth: The doors will be closed at ten o'clock at night, at which time each boarder will be expected to retire to bed.

Rule ninth: Sunday being appointed by our Creator as a Day of Rest and Religious Exercises, it is expected that all boarders will have sufficient discretion as to pay suitable attention to the day.

Source: Edith Abbott, *Women in Industry* (New York: D. Appleton, 1910).

The Boston Associates, for example, recruited many young, unmarried women from farm families to work in their textile factories. The women usually worked for a few years before they married. Because the company wanted to attract hard-working women from respectable families, it closely supervised their lives. The company provided boardinghouses, educational and recreational facilities, religious instruction, and land for gardening. The workers even published their own monthly magazine.

The women in the Lowell mills worked long hours but, at least in the early years of the company, they were basically well treated. They earned relatively good wages because the company needed to attract workers. The textile mills gave many young women their first chance to work outside the home. Although some observers reported that the Lowell workers were oppressed or unhappy, the women themselves denied it. As their magazine, the *Lowell Offering*, declared, "We are not generally miserable, either in point of fact, or in the prospect of a dreadful future."

Over time, as the factory system spread, factory life became increasingly harsh. When the arrival of large numbers of immigrants provided a cheap labor supply, wages dropped. Those who needed jobs were forced to accept worsening working conditions. Such changes, however, were in the future. At the start, Lowell seemed a symbol of the benefits to be gained by transplanting the Industrial Revolution to America.

A Force for Unity and Division

The growth of industry enabled the United States to free itself from some of its Old World ties. The nation had grown up with an economy based on agriculture and exports. The colonies had exported raw materials to Britain, which in turn had produced manufactured goods and sold them back to the colonies. But by the early 1800s, the United States relied increasingly on local industries to supply manufactured goods. Americans took pride in this growing self-sufficiency, and the development of domestic industry enhanced their sense of national identity.

Industrialization produced divisions as well. Most manufacturing developed in the North, especially New England. The South and the sparsely populated West lagged behind. Northern industrial development did not necessarily hurt the South. The cotton gin, for example, brought major improvements in the South's cotton production. But the North's growing industrialization did foster different ways of life and economic interests among the nation's citizens. Thus the development of industry acted as a force for both unity and division. It nourished a sense of national pride, and at the same time sowed seeds of sectional discord.

SECTION REVIEW

1. Identify: James Watt, James Hargreaves, John Fitch, Robert Fulton, Eli Whitney, Samuel Slater, Francis Cabot Lowell, Boston Associates.
2. Define: factory system, capital, limited liability, interchangeable parts.
3. Describe how two inventions of the late 1700s affected manufacturing.
4. How did American manufacturers learn British industrial secrets?
5. List two reasons why owners of textile factories were anxious to hire women and children as workers.
6. (a) Give one example of how industrialization brought the people of the United States closer together. (b) Give one example of how it also created divisions.
7. **Critical Thinking** How did technological change bring about social change?

3 Henry Clay's American System

During the War of 1812, a group of young men emerged in Congress who challenged the leadership of the older generation. After the war, these younger leaders sought a greater voice in public policy. They were impatient with what they saw as the old-fashioned ideas of Jefferson and Madison. In particular they wanted the federal government to take a greater role in national economic development. With their limitless faith in the country's future, they became the advocates of an economic program for the nation that put national rather than sectional needs first.

Three Dominant Political Figures

Three of these young leaders remained powerful figures in American politics in the coming decades. Daniel Webster was a Federalist from New Hampshire. Henry Clay of Kentucky and John C. Calhoun of South Carolina were Republicans. Clay and Calhoun had first attracted notice as War Hawks during the crisis that led to war with Britain in 1812.

Despite their different backgrounds, all three men championed nationalism at one time or another in their careers. Of the three, Clay was the most consistently nationalistic in his outlook. Webster and Calhoun spoke for nationalism when it benefited their section of the country but opposed it when it did not.

Daniel Webster's dark hair and brows had earned him the nickname "Black Dan." His stocky build helped lend forcefulness to a speaking style that was among the most powerful in the land.

Slim and handsome, John C. Calhoun was an intelligent and eloquent speaker. His knowledge of political theory served him well as a nationalist and as the eventual champion of the South.

Henry Clay was a tall, dashing Kentuckian, full of charm and swagger. His powerful personality enabled him to influence people and mold them into loyal political followers. At times pushy and overbearing, at other times cheerful and accommodating, he quickly set himself up as one of the most powerful political leaders in the nation.

Henry Clay's Design

The Republican party had traditionally opposed strengthening the national government at the expense of state or local governments. In fact, the party had developed out of opposition to Alexander Hamilton's

Daniel Webster was a rising young congressman who challenged older leaders. Along with Henry Clay and John C. Calhoun, he urged the government to take a larger role in developing the national economy.

proposed that the government charter a new national bank to provide a sound and uniform currency, necessary for the smooth operation of business and trade. Finally, he urged a federal program of internal improvements such as better canals and roadways that would aid interstate commerce.

The Tariff of 1816

During the War of 1812 Americans began to manufacture products previously imported from Great Britain. Once peace returned in 1815, quick extinction threatened many new industries. Manufacturers in the United States, lacking the capital and skill of their British counterparts, could not compete with cheaper imported goods.

Clay, like Hamilton earlier, proposed guarding these new industries from foreign competition by means of a protective tariff. By raising the price of imported goods, a protective tariff would make the more expensive American-made products competitive.

Cries for protection from British goods increased when British manufacturers began dumping low-priced goods on the American market in order to get rid of surpluses built up during the European war. This seriously hurt American industry, putting many smaller factories out of business.

Congress finally responded by passing the Tariff of 1816, which raised tariffs on foreign imports by an average of 20 percent. This was enough to protect new and developing American industries from lower-priced competition.

Clay's followers in the Middle Atlantic and western states voiced the strongest support for the tariff. They believed that flourishing commerce as well as tariff revenues would help pay for the roads and canals they needed for trade with the Northeast and the South.

Calhoun also spoke eloquently in favor of the tariff. He thought it was necessary to protect the South's growing cotton industry, and he believed that the South would soon develop its own industrial strength.

Of the three young leaders only Daniel Webster spoke against the tariff. Although some New Englanders wanted it, Webster thundered out his opposition to it. His con-

economic policies, by which the national government had taken an active role in the nation's economic development. Furthermore, Republicans had favored a rural economy rather than an industrial one. But the British blockade during the War of 1812 reduced America's supply of manufactured goods and revealed the danger of relying too heavily on foreign imports. Consequently, many Republicans began to change their thinking and accept some of Hamilton's original economic policies.

Henry Clay brought these ideas together in what he called his American System. Coming from the isolated and less developed West, Clay enthusiastically supported government programs for economic development. He believed that the recent war had shown the United States to be too dependent on foreign imports. The American economy had to become more self-sufficient.

Hence, the cornerstone of Clay's program was a protective tariff to keep American manufacturing growing. Second, Clay stituents in New Hampshire still relied on shipping from Great Britain, which the tariff would hurt. Over the years Calhoun and Webster would reverse their views on the tariff.

Second Bank of the United States

Republicans in Congress had always been suspicious of the first Bank of the United States, which Hamilton had created, so they let its charter expire in 1811. As a result, state banks took charge of issuing *bank notes*, paper money that was supposed to be backed by gold or silver held by the bank.

The bank notes did not remain a stable currency, however. The number of state banks issuing them increased greatly. Since each bank issued its own notes, a wide variety of notes circulated at all times. Whenever the demand for credit rose, as farmers needed to buy land or manufacturers wanted to buy equipment for new factories, the situation worsened. Banks began issuing notes whose value exceeded the amount of gold or silver on deposit. In addition, during the War of 1812, most state banks had stopped redeeming their bank notes for gold and silver at all, and they showed no sign of resuming such payments after the war.

No one could be sure, therefore, exactly how much the various bank notes were worth. Businesses often did not know if the notes they accepted in payment actually matched the price of their goods. The lack of a uniform national currency made interstate commerce extremely difficult.

Clay and others argued that a new national bank was needed. It would provide a more stable means of issuing money and would offer a safe place for the federal government to deposit its funds. Recognizing the problems created by the state banks, President Madison overcame his qualms about expanding the power of the national government. In 1816 he recommended the creation of a new national bank.

In response, Congress chartered the second Bank of the United States for a twenty-year period. Like the first national Bank, its purpose was to serve as a depository for government funds and to stabilize the currency. The Bank soon had a chance to show whether or not it could do its job.

The Panic of 1819

The Bank's charter gave it enough power to regulate the state banking and currency system. Such regulation was badly needed during the period of economic boom after the war as speculation in western land became increasingly popular. But instead of restraining land speculators, the Bank recklessly encouraged them by eagerly extending credit.

In 1819 the national Bank, under a more conservative management, began to call in its loans and to demand gold or silver from state banks in exchange for their notes. State banks, in turn, called in their loans. Since prospective buyers could no longer obtain loans to buy land, speculators could not sell the land in which they had invested. Speculators could not repay their loans, and as a result, western land prices plummeted.

At the same time, European demand for American farm products and textiles began to decline. Southern cotton prices fell. Many planters, already unhappy because of the drop in demand for their products, found their problems compounded because they had speculated in western land.

These events brought on an economic panic. During the Panic of 1819, banks foreclosed on mortgaged farms, business firms went bankrupt, and people lost their jobs, especially in the South and West.

Americans tried to figure out what had caused their troubles, and they blamed the badly managed Bank of the United States. Right or wrong, their choice would have important political consequences in later years.

SECTION REVIEW

1. Identify: Henry Clay, Daniel Webster, John C. Calhoun.
2. Define: bank note.
3. What did Henry Clay, Daniel Webster, and John C. Calhoun have in common?
4. Describe Henry Clay's American System.
5. Why did Webster oppose the Tariff of 1816?
6. What two purposes did Clay think a national Bank would serve?
7. **Critical Thinking** How might the Industrial Revolution in the United States have affected people's attitude toward the role of the federal government?

4 Building Pathways to the West

A major part of Clay's American System was a program of internal improvements paid for by the federal government. Transportation was difficult and costly in much of the United States, especially in the West. Better roads and canals needed to be built and obstacles cleared from rivers and lakes before further economic growth could take place.

Such economic growth was a vital part of the spirit of national unity and pride. John C. Calhoun argued that the lack of adequate transportation weakened the nation. He called on the Congress to "bind the republic together with a perfect system of roads and canals."

Westward Expansion

The postwar wave of migration into the area west of the Appalachian Mountains stimulated the demand for better transportation.

■ *The lure of land drew increasing numbers of pioneers westward. By 1830 the population of the West was slightly larger than that of the South.*

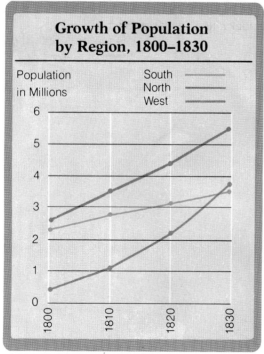

Growth of Population by Region, 1800–1830

Population in Millions

South ——————
North ——————
West ——————

Source: *Historical Statistics of the United States*

High food prices in the East and the availability of rich western farmlands attracted new settlers. As you read in the last chapter, the United States government and individual settlers had used both legal and illegal treaties as well as armed force to push most of the Indian nations out of the area.

Even visitors sensed the size of the migration. "Old America seems to be breaking up and moving westwards," an English visitor observed in 1817. While the pace of westward movement slackened during the Panic of 1819, it picked up again in the economic recovery that followed and reached a peak in the 1830s. By 1840 more than a third of the United States population lived west of the Appalachians. In 1810 only one seventh had.

Most of the migrants came from the older eastern states. Families from New England and the Middle Atlantic region settled around the Great Lakes. Settlers from Kentucky and Tennessee turned to the lands of the old Northwest and the old Southwest. From the southern seaboard states, pioneers poured into the old Southwest and the Ohio River Valley.

The admission of new states to the nation reflected the steady growth of westward expansion. Ohio was admitted as a state in 1803 and Louisiana in 1812. Indiana (1816), Mississippi (1817), Illinois (1818), Alabama (1819), Missouri (1821), Arkansas (1836), and Michigan (1837) followed.

Demand for Better Transportation

As people moved westward the urgent need for better connections with the East and access to its markets became apparent. The difficulty, or in some cases the near impossibility, of transportation plagued the new settlers. In most areas no roads existed at all. In some places the traveler had to go on horseback or on foot.

Where roads did exist, they were crude at best. Following old Indian trails, most roads were too narrow for wagon passage. From winter through spring, the hardpacked dirt turned to mud, and stumps and ruts stood ready to break a wagon's axles.

Westward Movement: Using Statistics

Statistics, or numbers, are frequently used in American history. They provide factual information that helps you understand past events. They can reveal important patterns or trends. Yet you must use statistics cautiously since they present only a partial picture of what happened. The table below, for example, gives data about population growth in several western states. The population statistics, however, do not include Native Americans who lived in those states during the period. If you had not learned previously about the Indian nations in the region, you might assume that the lands were uninhabited before white settlers arrived.

Use the following steps to interpret the statistics below.

1. **Identify the type of information presented in the table.** Begin by asking yourself questions about the different categories of information and how they relate to one another. (a) What time period is covered by this table? (b) What is the interval between years? (c) What do the numbers represent? (d) Describe the type of information presented in the table.

2. **Practice reading the statistics.** (a) What was the population of Mississippi in 1820? (b) What was the population of Ohio in 1800? (c) By what year did the population of Indiana total more than 100,000 people? (d) What was the total population of these western states in 1830?

3. **Look for relationships among the numbers.** With this table you can trace the population growth of each state and compare the population growth of different states. (a) How did Kentucky's population change between 1810 and 1820? (b) How much did Louisiana's population grow between 1810 and 1820? (c) Which state had the largest population in 1810? Which had the largest population in 1830? (d) Which state's population grew the most between 1820 and 1830? (e) How does the population growth in Ohio between 1810 and 1830 compare with that of Tennessee in the same period?

4. **Draw conclusions about a historical event or period by applying what you have learned from the statistics.** Use the table and your textbook. (a) How would you describe the population change in the region between 1790 and 1830? (b) How might you explain the reasons for the change? (c) Why do you think Ohio, Kentucky, and Tennessee had the largest populations? (d) When did each state join the Union? (See page 834.) (e) What is the relationship between statehood and population growth?

Population Growth in the West, 1790–1830

	1790	1800	1810	1820	1830
Ohio	73,600	145,300	230,700	581,400	937,900
Kentucky	35,690	220,900	406,500	564,300	687,400
Tennessee	*	105,600	261,700	422,800	681,900
Mississippi	*	8,800	40,300	75,400	136,600
Indiana	*	5,600	24,500	148,100	343,000
Michigan	*	*	4,760	8,900	31,600
Louisiana	*	*	76,500	153,400	215,700
Illinois	*	*	12,200	55,200	157,400
Missouri	*	*	19,700	66,500	140,400
Arkansas	*	*	1,060	14,200	30,300
Alabama	*	*	*	127,900	309,500

*no data available

The expression, "I'm stumped," is said to have originated from travelers whose vehicles broke down on roads like the one pictured above. Such roads were only partially cleared of tree stumps. At right is a stretch of "corduroy road," with logs laid side by side over a rough or soggy stretch.

Corduroy roads, made by laying tree trunks side by side, offered the best overland route. Yet even on good roads, travel was not easy. One uncomfortable traveler complained about "the noise of the wheels, the rumble of a coach . . . the jerking of the bad roads," and "the most detestable stagecoach that ever a Christian built to dislocate the joints of his fellow man."

Most existing transportation simply did not meet western needs. Settlers wanted a way to send their farm products to the East and bring manufactured goods back to the West. In many cases, the cheapest way for residents of western towns to ship their products to eastern buyers was to float them down the Ohio and Mississippi rivers, around the Florida peninsula, and up the coast. Eager for more direct trade routes, settlers recognized that improved canals and roads could provide faster transportation of bulky goods.

The National Road

Either state governments or private investors paid for the construction of the earliest roads. They then charged a toll to pay for the investment. The federal government first supported construction of a major road during Thomas Jefferson's administration. Authorized by Congress in 1806, the National Road eventually stretched westward from Cumberland, Maryland, to Wheeling, Virginia, and from there through Ohio and Indiana to Vandalia, Illinois.

By the standards of the time, the National Road was of high quality. It was built to withstand the weight of wagons jammed with people moving West. One observant traveler counted 42 children in three wagons during one day's journey and testified to seeing a wagon with 20 passengers on another day.

Yet by modern standards the National Road, like other early roads, was crude and often impassable. In Indiana, for example, where nine tenths of the National Road ran through dense forest, construction plans permitted "rounded and trimmed" tree stumps 9 to 15 inches (about 23 to 38 centimeters) high to remain on the road.

Although President Madison had his doubts about the constitutionality of roads paid for by the federal government, he continued the construction of the National Road. But when Congress tried to distribute money to the states for their own internal improvements, Madison vetoed the measure. Thereafter, local roads and other local improvements became the responsibility of the states.

Canals and Steamboats

The completion of the Erie Canal in 1825, after eight years of construction, opened a new era in transportation. Built by the state of

New York with public funds, the Erie Canal stretched about 350 miles (560 kilometers) from Buffalo to Albany. Goods could then be shipped down the Hudson River to New York City.

The canal allowed New York City to tap the markets of the Ohio River Valley and the Great Lakes region. By using the canal, shippers could cut the cost of transportation from nearly $100 to $5 a ton. Travel time was reduced from 20 days to 8. The success of the Erie Canal made New York City the country's major commercial center.

Shippers used the Erie Canal so heavily that the state recovered its construction costs from tolls in just seven years. The canal's financial success prompted other states to fund ambitious canal-building projects. None, however, matched the Erie's success. The Erie Canal heralded the beginning of the nation's Canal Age.

The adaptation of steamboats to western rivers marked an important advance in American transportation and a new stage in the nation's industrial development. As you read earlier, inventors had improved upon

---

■ Westward expansion created an urgent need for better transportation. Private companies and governments built new roads in the first half of the 1800s. Canals linked river systems, reducing the cost of shipping goods to market and spurring agriculture and industry.

Canals and Roads, 1820–1850

The Erie Canal opened the way to ship goods from the Midwest via the Great Lakes, along the canal to the Hudson River, and then to the port of New York City. Boats had to pass through 82 locks like the one shown in this painting.

James Watt's early steam-engine design. In 1811 Robert Fulton and Robert Livingston built a boat in Pittsburgh and sent it down the Ohio and Mississippi rivers to New Orleans. This trip demonstrated that steamboats could be used in western waters.

Five years later Henry M. Shreve built a steamboat specifically designed to meet the needs of western commerce. Below its towering decks, Shreve's boat had a shallow draft and hull. Designed to operate in shallow water, it could navigate the numerous sandbars and snags of the Mississippi, Missouri, and Ohio rivers. Shreve's boat could also travel at great speeds and carry heavy loads of cargo. When several of his vessels successfully made upstream journeys to Pittsburgh, all doubts about the practicality of his design ended. Steamboats, which cut western freight and passenger rates in half, soon crowded the waters.

Improvements in technology quickened the flow of trade in all directions. Farm products could move eastward along the canals. Manufactured goods bound for the West could come up the Mississippi in steamboats instead of taking the slower route over the mountains. As Calhoun had predicted, internal improvements led to better communications, helping to bind the republic together. This phase of Clay's American System seemed to be working.

SECTION REVIEW

1. Identify: National Road, Erie Canal.
2. Define: corduroy roads.
3. List two ways in which good roads were important to western settlers.
4. (a) Who paid for the earliest roads? (b) When did the federal government become involved?
5. How did the Erie Canal improve trade?
6. **Critical Thinking** How did the American System exemplify the growing spirit of nationalism?

5 James Monroe and Foreign Affairs

Although he tended to follow Congress on domestic issues, President Monroe believed that the President should make foreign policy. In practice, Monroe delegated much of this responsibility to Secretary of State John Quincy Adams.

The choice of Adams as secretary of state was particularly fortunate for the nation. The son of former President John Adams, John Quincy Adams was a skillful and experienced diplomat. An enthusiastic expansionist, he was eager to extend the country's boundaries. And his shrewd grasp of diplomacy enabled him to accomplish many of his goals for the nation.

Foreign Affairs After 1812

Before Adams's appointment, Richard Rush, the acting secretary of state, concluded negotiations with Great Britain concerning the boundary between the Louisiana Purchase and Canada. The Convention of 1818 set the border at the 49th parallel. In the Rush-Bagot Treaty of 1817 the two nations had agreed not to use military ships on the Great Lakes.

Spanish-owned Florida posed another border problem for the United States. Outlaws frequently used it as a haven. Slaves escaping from southern plantations also sought refuge there. In addition, some

■ By 1824, the nation's territory had expanded south and west, and 11 new states had joined the original 13.

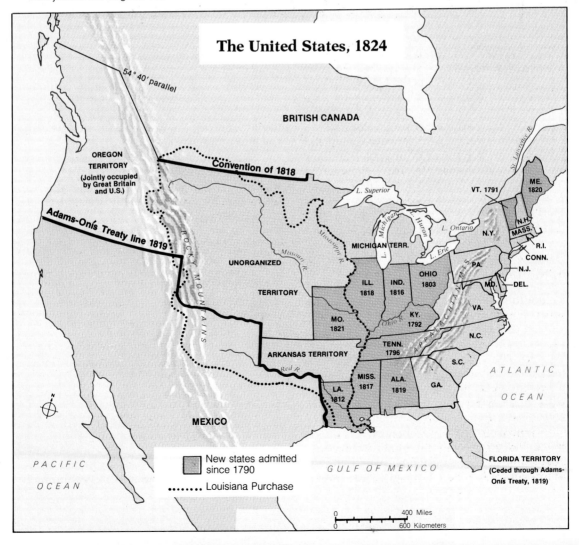

groups of Native Americans raided United States settlements from Florida. The Spanish government seemed unable to control these activities.

In 1818 President Monroe sent a military party under the command of Andrew Jackson into Florida to fight the Seminoles who had made raids into Georgia. Jackson, exceeding his instructions, captured two towns, hanged two British subjects for encouraging Indian attacks, and arrested the Spanish governor.

Although John Quincy Adams knew Jackson had no authority for his actions, the secretary was not displeased. Adams recognized that Jackson's raid had given the United States a stronger bargaining position with Spain. When the Spanish government protested the action, Adams replied that Florida had turned into "a derelict, open to the occupancy of every enemy . . . of the United States, and serving no other earthly purpose than as a post of annoyance."

Plagued by revolts among their own colonies, the Spanish wanted a way out of a difficult situation. In the Adams-Onís Treaty of 1819, negotiated by Adams and the Spanish minister to the United States, Don Luis de Onís, Spain agreed to cede Florida to the United States. In return, the United States dropped its claims of about $5 million against Spain. (See the map on page 221.)

The treaty also formally established the boundary between the Louisiana Purchase and Spanish territory. The western portion of the boundary would extend along the 42nd parallel from the Rockies all the way to the Pacific. This cleared the way for the nation to span the continent.

Other Concerns in the Western Hemisphere

In addition to the trouble in Florida, the Spanish confronted even more serious problems in other parts of their empire. Between 1810 and 1821 most of Spain's colonies in the Western Hemisphere revolted and declared their independence.

Henry Clay had grand visions of trade with these new countries and pressed Congress for immediate recognition of the revolutionary governments. However, President Monroe and Secretary of State Adams feared that such a rash move would endanger negotiations about Florida with Spain.

Consequently, they opposed Clay's efforts in Congress. The United States eventually granted official recognition to the Latin American republics in 1822, when it was clear that they would remain independent.

Most Americans sympathized with the new nations, but most European governments did not. After the defeat of Napoleon in 1812 the governments of Russia, Prussia, Austria, and France formed an alliance. Fearing that revolutionary activity abroad might spread to restless citizens in their own countries, they pledged to suppress any revolutionary movements in Europe. Americans feared that the alliance would not restrict its police efforts to Europe, but that it would try to intervene militarily to restore Spanish control over its former colonies in Latin America as well.

American diplomats also worried about Russian expansion down the coast of Alaska toward Oregon. Secretary Adams told Russia "that the American continents are no longer subjects for any new European colonial establishments." Russia agreed to retract its territorial claims south of the 54° 40′ line.

The British government shared the United States's concern that other European countries might try to seize Spain's former American colonies. In 1823 the British foreign minister proposed that the two countries issue a joint declaration guaranteeing the independence of the new nations.

President Monroe considered the British proposal, but Secretary of State Adams strongly objected. He opposed any agreement that might prevent the United States from annexing new territory. Adams had tried to acquire Texas from Spain earlier, and he still had visions of expansion in that direction.

Furthermore, the intensely patriotic Adams wanted the United States to make a declaration of its own. A joint statement with Britain, he explained, would make the United States appear "to come in as a cockboat in the wake of the British man-of-war." The cabinet finally agreed with Adams's view.

The Monroe Doctrine

With his advisers in agreement, Monroe decided to issue a statement of United States policy concerning European influence in the New World. He chose to make his announce-

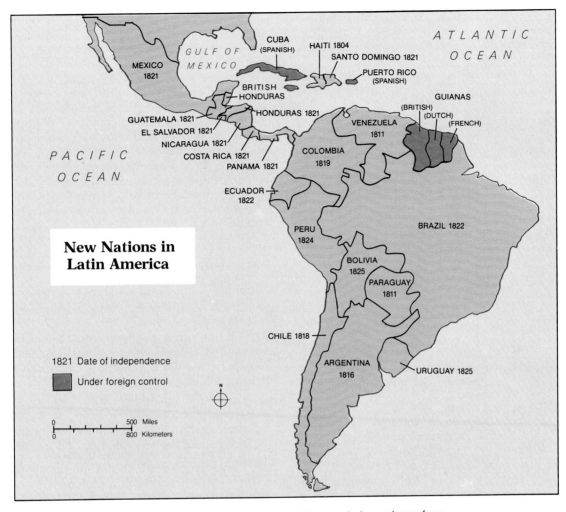

New Nations in Latin America

1821 Date of independence

Under foreign control

0 — 500 Miles
0 — 800 Kilometers

■ *Between 1800 and 1822, most Latin American countries won independence from Spain and Portugal. The Monroe Doctrine warned European powers not to intervene in the new nations.*

ment during his annual message to Congress in December 1823.

Monroe proclaimed that the United States would not interfere in the internal concerns of European countries or in existing European colonies in the New World. It would also oppose all European intervention in the affairs of the independent countries in the Americas. The United States, Monroe warned, would view such intervention as an unfriendly act toward itself. "The American continents," Monroe declared in conclusion, "are henceforth not to be considered as subjects for future colonization by any European powers."

Monroe's message marked the high point of a long period of United States diplo-macy. Beginning with George Washington, Presidents had followed a policy of nonintervention in European affairs. In addition, Americans had always viewed European designs on the New World with suspicion. Monroe's declaration in effect united these principles in a single declaration that Europe and the New World would henceforth refrain from interfering in each others' internal affairs.

Impact of the Doctrine

Monroe's independent actions naturally annoyed the British government. It had wanted a joint declaration, and the President's course denied the British any outward role

223

in setting the policy. Despite their annoyance, the British quietly informed other European governments that they agreed with Monroe's policy.

Without British support, the American declaration would have meant little. The young nation lacked the might to back up its strong words. The British navy, as the European nations well knew, made Monroe's doctrine a reality.

Monroe's message was in tune with the strong nationalist feeling of the time. It showed once again America's pride as a nation. Americans throughout the country warmly applauded and endorsed it. Despite this favorable response, the people soon forgot the Monroe Doctrine. Its greatest significance lay in the future, when a new generation of leaders would unearth it and reestablish it as the country's most basic diplomatic policy.

Major Events	
1801	John Marshall appointed Chief Justice of Supreme Court
1803	*Marbury* v. *Madison*
1810	*Fletcher* v. *Peck*
1811	First national Bank charter expires
1816	Congress passes Tariff of 1816; Congress charters second Bank of the United States; James Monroe elected President
1819	*Dartmouth College* v. *Woodward*; *McCulloch* v. *Maryland*; first major banking crisis
1823	Monroe Doctrine
1824	*Gibbons* v. *Ogden*
1825	Erie Canal completed

SECTION REVIEW

1. Identify: John Quincy Adams, Convention of 1818, Rush-Bagot Treaty, Adams-Onís Treaty.
2. (a) What three problems did Spanish-owned Florida pose for the United States? (b) How did the Adams-Onís treaty solve the problems?
3. (a) How did most Americans feel about the newly independent nations in Latin America? (b) Why were Americans concerned about the new alliance in Europe?
4. **Critical Thinking** How did the Monroe Doctrine reflect American nationalism?

Chapter 12 Review

In Perspective

To President James Monroe, as to many Americans, the years after the War of 1812 were years of national pride and national unity. The country finally seemed to be truly united. Decisions by the Supreme Court under John Marshall added to the sense of unity by strengthening the national government. The Industrial Revolution brought greater economic independence, which enhanced national identity.

The American System, proposed by Henry Clay and supported by young political leaders, reflected the nationalism of the period. Improved transportation strengthened the ties between regions. Finally, in the Monroe Doctrine, President Monroe confirmed American independence and pride.

Yet, as you will read in later chapters, the forces of division as well as unity were at work. Industrialization and westward expansion would eventually help create a sectional split between North and South, a split that would threaten to tear the nation apart.

Vocabulary

Match each term at left with its definition or description at right.

1. bank notes
2. factory system
3. interchangeable parts
4. limited liability
5. capital

a. reduced responsibility for debts
b. paper money
c. method of organizing labor
d. money for investment
e. identical components

Chapter Checkup

1. (a) How did President James Monroe symbolize the Era of Good Feelings? (b) In what ways was he a part of the Revolutionary War generation?
2. (a) Why was labor scarce in the United States in the early 1800s? (b) What groups of people did manufacturers rely on as a result?
3. (a) Explain how, according to Henry Clay, the Tariff in 1816 would help the United States become more self-sufficient. (b) Why did representatives from the West, the South, and the Middle Atlantic states tend to support the tariff?
4. (a) Why did a national bank seem necessary in 1816? (b) How did the second Bank of the United States contribute to the onset of panic in 1819? (c) What other factors contributed to the panic?
5. (a) Why did Secretary of State Adams and President Monroe believe that the President should issue the Monroe Doctrine? (b) How did the doctrine reflect the nationalism of the period?

Critical Thinking

1. **Recognizing Relationships**   Which political, social, and economic developments contributed to the growing sense of nationalism and national unity between 1816 and 1824?

2. **Analyzing a Quotation**   President Monroe stated, "The existence of parties is not necessary to free government." How was his statement a reflection of American political traditions up to that time?

Developing Basic Skills

1. **Inferring**   Review the Supreme Court cases described on pages 208–209. Study the Constitution and decide which clause or clauses the Court might have used to defend its actions.
2. **Map Reading**   Study the map on page 221 and answer the following questions: (a) What is the topic of the map? (b) What treaty established the northern boundary of the Louisiana Purchase? (c) What treaty established the southern boundary of the Louisiana Purchase? (d) How did the Adams-Onís Treaty change the status of Florida?
3. **Researching**   Using library resources, make a list of the government positions held by Henry Clay, John C. Calhoun, and Daniel Webster during their careers. Based on what you learn, why do you think these three men had such an important impact on American politics in the years during and after the War of 1812?

See page 829 for suggested readings.

Writer's Handbook

Writing a Summary

A summary is a short report for which you use only one source of information. The source may be an article, a speech, or a book. A summary contains only the main ideas. To help pinpoint the main ideas of the source, read the material and then ask yourself the following questions: *Who? What? When? Where? Why?* and *How?* After you have written the summary, review the original source to make sure that you have not left out anything important.

Practice: Choose a subsection of this chapter such as "The Monroe Doctrine" and write a summary of it.

Youth in America

When the American republic was launched in the 1790s, it was young in more ways than one. Not only had it existed as a nation for only a few years, its people themselves were youthful. According to the first census in 1790, nearly half of the white men living in the United States were under 16 years of age. The 1790 census collected much less information about free blacks, slaves, and women but, they too were relatively young.

Why was the American population so youthful? In part this youth resulted from an extremely high birthrate. The average American woman bore about seven children during her lifetime, compared with an average today of fewer than two children. Disease took such a high toll that only about half the population lived beyond the age of 45. Today many people live into their seventies or eighties.

In the early nineteenth century, large extended families were common. The new nation had a very high proportion of young people.

Differences From Europe   The young nation was different from the older countries in Europe. Americans' strong belief in democracy influenced how parents dealt with their children. In those early days, visitors commented on the obvious freedom enjoyed by American children. American youngsters seemed more independent and less respectful.

Relations between parent and child became more informal as Americans moved west. A German visitor in the mid-1800s observed a father and his 14-year-old son riding together on a train. "They had long been talking on a footing of equality," he noted. "At last, to while away the time, they began to sing together. . . . There was no attempt at keeping up the dignity of a parent, as might have been considered necessary and proper with us." In 1905, another traveler noted, "Daughters are much with their mothers, and they become their companions younger than they do in Europe."

In fact, youth has long been celebrated in American culture. As a result of the American belief in equality, the young and old are on a more equal footing than they might be in other parts of the world. "Have you reverence enough among your people?" one worried Englishman asked the poet Walt Whitman. "Do the American children respect and obey their parents sufficiently . . .?" Whitman replied, "Your old world has been soaked and saturated in reverence. We are laying here in America the basements and foundation rooms of a new era."

A Young Nation   Politically, younger leaders have often played a key role in directing the nation. Delegates to the Constitutional Convention were remarkably young. Five of them were under 30; Alexander Hamilton was 32; and James Madison, 36. Only four members were over 60. It was the youthful "War Hawks" like John Calhoun and Henry Clay who led the charge into the War of 1812. Teddy Roosevelt, one of the most active Presidents, took office at the age of 42. John F. Kennedy was 43 when he took office in 1961.

When the tide of immigrants to the United States swelled in the late 1800s, the youngest newcomers often led the way in adjusting to American life. Jane Addams, who worked with immigrants in Chicago during the 1890s, pointed out that parents "count upon the fact that their children learn the English language and American customs before they themselves do and act not only as interpreters of the language about them but as buffers between them and Chicago. . . ." Young men often journeyed first to the United States, sending for their wives and families only after settling and finding a job.

In the twentieth century, young people have continued to set the pace in American culture. The 1920s celebrated bold young fliers like Charles Lindbergh and Amelia Earhart, who flew solo across the Atlantic. College campuses were the setting for fads, fashions, and popular literature. The 1960s, too, was a time when youth were prominent. President's Kennedy's Peace Corps sent young volunteers all over the world. Youth were at the center of movements seeking greater civil rights for blacks, Hispanics, and women. Their tastes and lifestyles altered the habits of adults as well.

Enthusiasm and Experience Inevitably, people will question whether Americans have struck the right balance between youth and age. Youth favors new styles, new faces, new experiments. In such a climate, the wisdom that comes with experience can be put aside too easily. "What old people say you cannot do, you try and find that you can. Old deeds for old people, and new deeds for new," proclaimed Henry David Thoreau in *Walden*. But youthful enthusiasm can lead to excess. Those who rush to take up the new and the untried are likely to make the same mistakes their parents did during their own youth.

Indeed, the study of history is one way that young people can temper their enthusiasm for the new with a knowledge of the

This detail of a watercolor shows girls attending an evening school where they learned reading, writing, and homemaking skills.

past. As the philosopher George Santayana once said, "Those who cannot remember the past are condemned to repeat it." Without the guidance of age and tradition, some people worry that youth will have no jumping-off point from which to launch its own experiments.

In coming years, the relation of youth to age will become even more crucial. After World War II, a baby boom among young couples made the population of the United States again more youthful. But those who were children in the 1950s will be the older Americans of the twenty-first century. With advances in medicine increasing longevity, the percentage of older Americans will increase steadily. What responsibilities do the youth of America have to their parents and grandparents? How will society balance the vigor of youth with the experience of age? These are important questions which new generations of Americans will have to answer. Yet a nation that encourages new ideas and new directions will always hold the energy and boldness of youth in high regard.

1. How have Europeans seen the place of youth in American society?
2. Do you think that people can learn from the experience of others? Why or why not?

Catharine Beecher

The Beecher family was one of the most fascinating and talented families of the 1800s. Yet in some ways it was not unlike many other families in that era. Lyman and Roxana Beecher had eight children who survived infancy. After Roxana's death, Lyman married Harriet Porter and had three more children who lived. Because of disease and hardships, it was common for a man to outlive two or more wives and several of his children.

Catharine Beecher (1800–1878), shown later in life, grew up in a large, exceptionally talented family.

Catharine, the oldest child, was born in 1800 on Long Island, New York, where Lyman was the pastor of the Presbyterian church. In the early years, the young family struggled along on the pastor's wages of $300 a year and firewood supplied by the congregation.

Lyman and Roxana decided to open a school to supplement their income. Roxana and her sister Mary, who lived with them, taught English, French, painting, embroidery, and the latest rage—chemistry. Catharine was a somewhat reluctant student. She recalled later, "Oh, the mournful, despairing hours when I saw the children at their sports, and was confined till I had picked out the bad stitches, or remedied other carelessness. . . ."

As the oldest child, Catharine occupied a special place in the Beecher household. Her father, who had grown up in the household of a childless aunt and uncle after his mother died, valued a large and close-knit family. He was attached to his children and devoted a great deal of time not only to their spiritual upbringing but also to entertaining them. In later life, Catharine wrote: "I remember him . . . as a playmate. . . . He taught me to catch fish and I was his constant companion, riding . . . to the villages around, where he went to hold meetings." Catharine recalled, "There was a free and easy way of living, more congenial to liberty and society than to conventional rules." That is not to say there was no discipline. Lyman expected immediate obedience from his children and did not "spare the rod." Any harshness, however, was softened by his obvious affection.

When Catharine was nine, the family moved to Litchfield, Connecticut. Here Lyman Beecher was spiritual adviser to Miss Sarah Pierce's School for "young ladies." As a result, his daughters attended the school free of charge and received an education superior to that of most young women of the time.

Catharine's relatively carefree and happy childhood ended in 1816 when her mother died of consumption. Because she was the oldest, many of the responsibilities for the younger children fell to Catharine. For this reason, it was with both resentment and relief that she welcomed her stepmother the following year.

But the foundation had been laid for this extraordinary family. A contemporary of Lyman Beecher claimed that he was "the father of more brains than any man in America." Catharine Beecher became a noted educational reformer, a writer on morality and religion, an avid promoter of education for women, and the author of a best selling book, *The Treatise on Domestic Economy*. Edward Beecher was the first president of Illinois College. Harriet Beecher Stowe was the author of *Uncle Tom's Cabin*. Henry Ward Beecher was a famous preacher. Isabella Beecher Hooker was an advocate of women's rights. James Beecher was a missionary in China who became a Civil War general. In all, ten of the eleven children of Lyman Beecher pursued professional careers.

1. What advantages and disadvantages did Catharine have as the oldest child?
2. How would you account for the unusually high level of achievement of the Beechers?

Abraham Lincoln's Education

Voices of Freedom

Children who grew up with the young nation learned by "doing." One of the most remarkable examples of this upbringing was Abraham Lincoln. Born in Kentucky in 1809, Lincoln attended a one-room log schoolhouse with a dirt floor and no windows. By the time the family had moved to Indiana, young Abe's formal education was mostly behind him. But Lincoln took every opportunity to satisfy his thirst for learning. His famous biographer, Carl Sandburg, quotes Lincoln: "The things I want to know are in books; my best friend is the man who'll git me a book I ain't read." The reading below is from Lincoln's own account of his childhood, published in 1859.

My father, at the death of his father, was but six years of age, and he grew up literally without education. He removed from Kentucky to what is now Spencer County, Indiana, in my eighth year. We reached our new home about the time the state came into the Union. It was a wild region, with many bears and other wild animals still in the woods. There I grew up. There were some schools, so called, but no qualification was ever required of a teacher beyond readin', writin', and cipherin'. If a straggler supposed to understand Latin happened to sojourn in the neighborhood, he was looked upon as a wizard. There was absolutely nothing to excite ambition for education. Of course, when I came of age I did not know much. Still, somehow, I could read, write, and cipher, but that was all. I have not been to school since. The little advance I now have upon this store of education, I have picked up from time to time under the pressure of necessity.

Adapted from Abraham Lincoln, *Autobiography*, 1859.

1. How did Lincoln seem to have gotten his education?
2. Writing about his youthful experiences, what character traits does Lincoln reveal?

Unit Four

An Era of Expansion

During the early 1800s, Americans became more interested in politics.

1835 Osceola led the Seminoles when they resisted being moved from Florida to Oklahoma.

	1820	1830	1840
POLITICS AND GOVERNMENT	**1821** Stephen Austin founds American colony in Texas		**1838** Southern Indians follow "Trail of Tears" to Oklahoma
SOCIETY AND CULTURE	**1821** Cherokee adopt Sequoyah's alphabet	**1831** *The Liberator* founded to fight for abolition of slavery	
ECONOMICS AND TECHNOLOGY	**1820** Stevens's steam engine is used to pull a train	**1834** Mechanical reaper makes harvesting wheat easier	
WORLD EVENTS	**1821** Mexico wins independence from Spain	**1832** Santa Anna comes to power in Mexico	
	Monroe	Adams	Jackson	Van Buren

1830s The first commercial railroads went into operation in the 1830s.

The cotton gin, invented by Eli Whitney, helped create the Cotton Kingdom in the South.

1844 The telegraph, perfected by Samuel Morse, made communication faster.

Spanish and Mexican influence remained in the Southwest even after the United States had annexed the area.

1840	1850	1860

1848 United States acquires the Southwest and California from Mexico

1848 Convention for women's rights held at Seneca Falls

1856 Wilberforce College founded for black students

1846 Howe invents sewing machine

1851 *Flying Cloud* sails to California in record time

1845 Famine in Ireland brings immigrants to America

1853 Japan allows trade with United States

Harrison   **Taylor**

Slaves feared auctions, such as this one, because families were often broken up.

1848 The discovery of gold at Sutter's Mill led to a gold rush in California.

231

A Democracy for the People

13

(1824–1844)

Andrew Jackson *by Thomas Sully*

Chapter Outline

1 *Emergence of a New Party System*

2 *Rise of the Common People*

3 *Strengthening the National Government*

4 *Hard Times*

The first half of the 1800s was a time of expansion for the United States. The nation moved westward, and its economy grew. It was also a time of important political developments. New political parties evolved, and a growing number of people took an active role in government.

Five Presidents served between 1824 and 1844. Among them, Andrew Jackson, the hero of New Orleans, had the greatest influence, For many Americans, he symbolized the rise of the common people, and he brought increased power and prestige to the office of President and to the national government.

As you will read in this chapter, Jackson's successors would have little opportunity to continue his traditions. A severe economic depression handicapped Martin Van Buren. William Henry Harrison died soon after taking office, and his successor, John Tyler, had little in common with Harrison's party or with Congress.

Age of Jackson

1824	1827	1830	1833	1836	1839	1842

1825
John Quincy Adams elected President

1828
Andrew Jackson elected President

1830
Indian Removal Act

1832
Jackson vetoes Bank bill

1837
Panic begins

1838
Trail of Tears

1841
John Tyler succeeds Harrison as President

1 Emergence of a New Party System

As the Federalist party dwindled and finally disappeared during the Era of Good Feelings, President Monroe had looked forward to a period when the country would no longer be divided by political parties. Yet the young nation, which had grown from 13 colonies with many different peoples and interests, remained too diverse to be fully represented by one political party. By the end of Monroe's second term, a new party system had begun to take shape, one that would allow more people to participate in the government of their nation than ever before.

The Election of 1824

As the election of 1824 approached, the large number of presidential hopefuls revealed the divisions in Thomas Jefferson's old Republican party. Four major candidates emerged, and each of them tended to draw strength from a different section of the country.

Henry Clay, the Kentuckian who was speaker of the House, had support from many westerners. William Crawford, Monroe's secretary of the treasury, drew his following from his native Georgia and other southeastern states. John Quincy Adams, Monroe's able secretary of state, was popular in New England. Andrew Jackson, hero of the battle of New Orleans, was particulary strong in the states of the old Southwest.

The four-way race for the White House, between Jackson, Clay, Crawford, and Adams, resulted in a deadlock. Jackson won more popular votes than any other candidate, but no candidate received the necessary majority of the 261 votes in the electoral college. Jackson had 99 votes; Adams, 84; Crawford, 41; and Clay, 37. Therefore, as provided by the Constitution, the election was to be decided by the House of Representatives, which would choose from among the top three candidates. (See pages 859–860.)

Henry Clay was eliminated; however, he had enough power and influence in the House to determine which of his rivals would be finally chosen. He decided to endorse Adams, whose principles were closest to his own. With Clay's endorsement the House elected John Quincy Adams on the first ballot. Adams then appointed Clay his secretary of state, a position that had often been a stepping stone to the presidency.

Jackson and his supporters were furious. They charged that Adams had been elected by a "corrupt bargain" that placed Adams in the presidency, with Clay set up as his successor. In fact, nothing so dishonest had happened, but the charge proved to be very damaging to both Adams and Clay.

No one believed the "corrupt bargain" charge more fervently than Andrew Jackson. Indignant at the result of the House vote, he resigned from the Senate and returned to Tennessee, where the legislature promptly nominated him for President. The 1828 campaign thus began almost with Adams's inauguration.

■ *Andrew Jackson won the most popular votes in the 1824 election, but he did not receive enough electoral votes to be elected President. The House of Representatives then chose a President from among the top three candidates.*

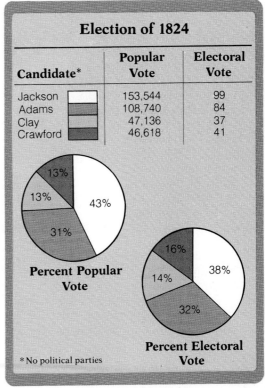

Election of 1824

Candidate*	Popular Vote	Electoral Vote
Jackson	153,544	99
Adams	108,740	84
Clay	47,136	37
Crawford	46,618	41

Percent Popular Vote: 43%, 31%, 13%, 13%

Percent Electoral Vote: 38%, 32%, 14%, 16%

*No political parties

Source: *Historical Statistics of the United States*

John Quincy Adams

John Quincy Adams's presidency never recovered from the cloud of suspicion surrounding his election. This was unfortunate, for President Adams was a man of considerable talent and vision. A nationalist, he took a broad view of the national government's powers. He wanted the federal government to actively encourage economic growth. He even proposed a program to foster the arts, literature, and science by establishing a national university and a national observatory.

Those who wished a more limited role for the federal government were aghast at these proposals. Jefferson accused Adams of trying to establish an aristocracy by plundering the treasury. Even the President's friends considered his proposals impractical. Adams weakened himself more by refusing to use his authority as President to build a strong party. Finally, his cold, reserved personality undercut his leadership still further. He lacked the skill, tact, and warmth necessary to develop a personal following among either politicians or the people.

Parties in the Campaign of 1828

Jackson's great popularity as well as his conviction that Clay and Adams had stolen the election from him, made it certain that he would run again in 1828. Four years earlier all four candidates had called themselves Republicans, but by 1828 the split in the Republican party had taken more definite shape. President Adams's supporters called themselves National Republicans, in order to emphasize the President's commitment to a national program.

Andrew Jackson and his followers wanted to stress their ties to the common people in opposition to the "aristocratic" Adams, so they called themselves Democratic-Republicans. In the next few years these names would undergo further change as party lines became more distinct. The National Republicans renamed themselves the Whigs and Jackson's party became the Democrats. This marked the beginning of the present-day Democratic party.

Party principles, like party names, were not firmly established in 1828. *Party platforms*, or declarations of principles and programs, remained quite vague, and a wide range of opinion existed within each party.

Jackson's political advisers hoped to attract as many voters as possible during the 1828 election campaign. They made few specific promises about what their candidate would do if elected. Instead, they ran Jackson on his popular reputation as "Old Hickory," a nickname acquired for his endurance and determination during the War of 1812.

All across the country, campaign managers used new methods to interest Americans in the election. They held barbecues, served roast ox, organized torchlight parades and bonfires, and provided fireworks displays. Old Hickory, man of the people, was celebrated everywhere.

The campaign of 1828 contained more than the usual amount of mudslinging, even by the standards of the time. Jackson's supporters accused the President of buying "gaming tables and gambling furniture" with government funds. (Actually Adams had installed a chess set and billiard table in the White House basement—with his own money.)

The Adams forces claimed Jackson was an ignoramus from the backwoods who could not spell "more than about one word in four." Even worse, they accused him of murder, circulating handbills with pictures of the coffins of twelve men supposedly executed by Old Hickory.

Jackson Triumphant

The campaign was rough, but it excited Americans as no presidential election had before. Jackson won handily, receiving 56 percent of the popular vote and 178 electoral votes to Adams's 83. In part the victory demonstrated that sectional differences continued to play a major role in American life. Adams won all the New England states but only Delaware and New Jersey outside of New England. Jackson took the South and West.

Although Jackson ran as the candidate of the "common people," many "common people" voted for Adams and many rich men voted for Jackson. Old Hickory received strong support from southern planters and small farmers in the South and West, the sort of people who shared his background and might be expected to favor him. But he also received the votes of many small busi-

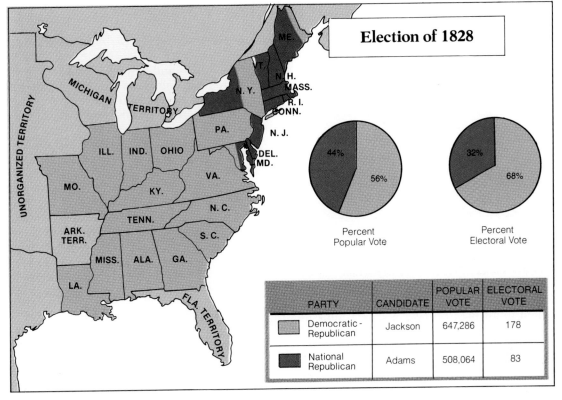

Election of 1828

| Percent Popular Vote | | Percent Electoral Vote | |

PARTY	CANDIDATE	POPULAR VOTE	ELECTORAL VOTE
Democratic-Republican	Jackson	647,286	178
National Republican	Adams	508,064	83

■ *In 1828 Andrew Jackson swept both the popular vote and the electoral vote. In what section of the country was the National Republican party strongest?*

ness leaders, factory workers, and artisans in the large cities. He won Pennsylvania's electoral votes and a majority of New York's. He was, therefore, not simply the candidate of the rural South and West.

Andrew Jackson's inauguration was unlike that of any of his predecessors. Great crowds cheered the general as he slowly journeyed to Washington to assume his new duties. Days before he took the oath of office, people from all over the country began pouring into the capital to witness the event.

A cheering throng witnessed their hero take the oath of office and quietly deliver his inaugural address. After the ceremony, they flocked to the White House to greet the new President. Wild disorder resulted as men, women, and children scrambled for refreshments. Ann Royall, a journalist, commented on the scene.

They clambered upon the satin furniture with their muddy boots. ... Only after disgraceful scenes in the parlors, in which even women got bloody noses, was the situation relieved by

the device of setting tubs of punch on the lawn to lure the new "democracy" out of the house.

To a horrified Supreme Court justice who was present, it seemed the beginning of "the reign of King 'Mob.'" In appearance, anyway, democracy reigned in the White House, and the people had come to power.

SECTION REVIEW

1. Identify: National Republicans, Democratic-Republicans, Old Hickory.

2. Define: party platform.

3. (a) How did John Quincy Adams win the presidency? (b) Why did some claim that his election was the result of a "corrupt bargain"?

4. How did people react to Adams's views of the role of national government?

5. **Critical Thinking** How did the election campaign of 1828 resemble modern election campaigns?

2 Rise of the Common People

Jackson's election and administration have frequently been viewed as the triumph of democracy. His noisy and chaotic inauguration, as well as much of the rhetoric of his supporters, seemed to indicate a victory for the common people. But did Jackson's election mean that the average citizen had achieved power? To what extent did the new political system reflect the emerging power of the people, and to what extent did it remain unchanged?

Old Hickory

Andrew Jackson seemed to personify the aspirations of his era. Of humble origins, he had become a wealthy landowner who owned more than 150 slaves by the time he became President at age 62. He was the first President to rise from a log cabin to the White House, a process that eventually became an American dream.

Jackson lacked formal schooling, yet he was not, as his opponents sometimes claimed, an ignorant, crude frontiersman. He could write forceful, if simple, English, had practiced law, and had wide experience in Tennessee politics.

Old Hickory was an imposing figure. A handsome man with white flowing hair, he stood tall, lean, and erect. His drive and determination impressed everyone who met him. As a former military man, he was used to giving orders and being obeyed. Jackson's quick temper and great self-confidence made him prone to impulsive, energetic action, and he tended to take political disputes personally.

Throughout his life Andrew Jackson endured great pain. When he became President, he carried two bullets in him from frontier duels, and while in office he suffered several major illnesses. Yet he seemed able by sheer force of will to overcome these physical ailments, just as he had overcome other obstacles throughout his career. President Andrew Jackson was not exactly a common man, but he always thought of himself as the champion of the common people.

Political Reform

Political changes during Jackson's administration reflected the popular enthusiasm for democracy. The right to vote was extended to more Americans. During the colonial period, most political thinkers had believed that the right to vote should be given only to property owners, those who had a permanent stake in society. Most states eliminated property requirements during the first half of the nineteenth century and permitted *white manhood suffrage*, that is, voting by all white males.

Democratic changes were also made in the selection of the President. The framers of

President Andrew Jackson enjoyed holding festive public celebrations. This huge cheese was put out for one such occasion. The strong odor of the cheese lingered for months.

The courtrooms of rural America offered entertainment as well as justice. This drawing shows the informality typical of many country courtrooms. Note the children playing in the haylofts at the rear.

the Constitution had originally adopted the idea of presidential electors because they believed that the people themselves would not know enough about the candidates to make a wise choice. (See page 162.) In many states electors had been chosen by the state legislatures, not by the voters directly. However, states gradually moved toward more direct participation by voters. By 1832 every state except South Carolina allowed its voters to choose presidential electors directly.

Political parties, too, became more democratic. Formerly, a party's presidential candidate was usually chosen by a secret party *caucus*, a meeting in which only a few members of Congress had a voice in the decision. By the mid-1830s political parties were holding national nominating conventions in which delegates from all states could participate in the decision. Conventions could still be controlled by party leaders but were now more open and, it was hoped, subject to the voice of the people.

These reforms had an important impact on American politics. All white males were eligible to vote for the first time, and as voters, they had a greater opportunity to influence their government. Furthermore, voters seemed more anxious to use their power. Voting rose from 26 percent of eligible voters in 1824 to 56 percent in 1828 to 78 percent in 1840. Such widespread participation was new in national politics.

Limits to Jacksonian Democracy

Although white men took a greater part in government, other people did not. Women still had no direct political role. Nor did most black Americans. Some states had allowed free blacks to vote, but a number of those states repealed that right during the 1820s and 1830s. Slaves possessed no political rights at all.

Developments in industry and education, some already beginning in the 1820s, would eventually encourage more women to demand a voice in politics. The idea of greater equality for black Americans also gained wider acceptance as the abolitionist movement grew, but such changes evolved slowly. (You will read about these developments later in this unit.) To most white Americans in the first half of the nineteenth century, limiting political activity to white men seemed normal and proper.

A Policy of Indian Removal

Native Americans also had no part in Jacksonian democracy. In fact, by 1840 most Indian nations had been forced to move to land west of the Mississippi River. As you read earlier, attempts by Native Americans to resist the westward movement of settlers had largely failed. Tecumseh's confederation of Indian nations had collapsed when he was killed during the War of 1812. (See page 202.)

The British had insisted in the Treaty of Ghent, signed after the War of 1812, that the United States "restore to such tribes ... all possessions ... which they have enjoyed or been entitled to in [1811] previous to such hostilities." The provision was ignored, however, and settlers continued to push Indian nations westward.

By the mid 1820s about 125,000 Native Americans still lived east of the Mississippi. Chief among them were five southern nations, the Cherokee, Creek, Choctaw, Chicasaw, and Seminole. These were known as the "civilized tribes" because they had adopted many customs of the white settlers. Many were prosperous farmers, and some owned large plantations.

As settlers pressed westward in search of land, however, they eyed the fertile land owned by Indians in parts of western Georgia, North Carolina, Tennessee, Florida, Alabama, and Mississippi. These settlers found an ally in President Jackson.

One of Jackson's goals as President was to complete the removal of Indian nations from east of the Mississippi. His first opportunity to act came soon after he took office. In 1828 the Cherokee living in Georgia tried to safeguard their land by writing a constitution establishing an independent state within the boundaries of Georgia. Stating that the Cherokee were subject to the laws of Georgia, the state government refused to recognize the Cherokee constitution.

The Cherokee appealed to the Supreme Court, which ruled in their favor. Chief Justice Marshall held that the "laws of Georgia can have no force" in Cherokee lands. The Indian nations, he ruled, were "distinct political communities, having political boundaries, within which their authority is exclusive."

President Jackson refused to enforce the Court's decision. "John Marshall has made his decision," Jackson is reported to have said. "Now let him enforce it." The Cherokee were left without legal protection.

238

★ American Profiles ★

Sequoyah: Creating a Written Language

Before 1821 none of the languages of the Indian nations in the United States had a written form. Traditions were passed from generation to generation through oral stories or pictures. In 1809 a Cherokee named Sequoyah decided that his people needed a written language. He believed that a written language would help the Cherokee preserve their culture and independence among the increasing numbers of white settlers.

Sequoyah, who was born about 1760, had been a skilled hunter and trapper before he was crippled in an accident. He worked on an alphabet for 12 years, eventually devising 86 symbols based on English, Greek, and Hebrew letters. In 1821 the leaders of the Cherokee nation accepted Sequoyah's alphabet. Soon Cherokee children were learning to read and write using his system. The Cherokee used the language to publish books as well as a weekly newspaper, *The Cherokee Phoenix.*

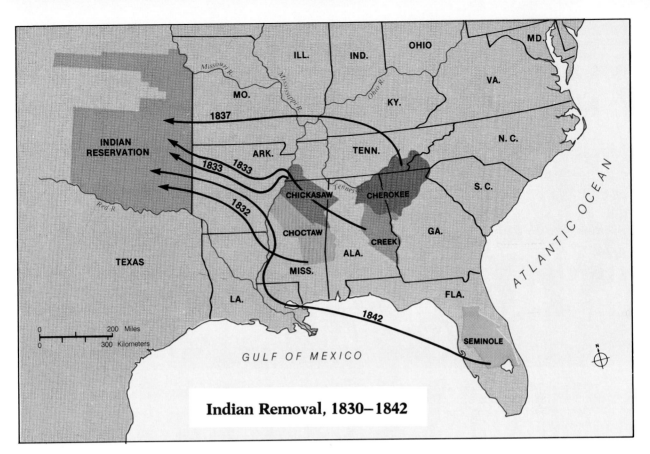

Indian Removal, 1830–1842

■ *The Removal Act of 1830 forced many Indians living east of the Mississippi to leave their land and move to less fertile lands on a western reservation. The five tribes most affected were the Chickasaw, Creek, Choctaw, Seminole, and Cherokee.*

The Trail of Tears

In 1830 Congress passed the Removal Act. This legislation provided funds to negotiate treaties that would force Indians still living in the East to sell their lands and move west. Government officials used these funds to purchase fertile Indian lands in exchange for barren and desolate territory in what is today Oklahoma. White speculators cheated many Indians, buying up their land titles and then reselling them to the government.

With the scales of justice thus tipped against them, southern Indians were forced to embark on what came to be known as the Trail of Tears. In 1838 soldiers drove the remnants of the Choctaw, Creek, and other tribes, as well as over 15,000 Cherokee, west to Oklahoma. An eyewitness, the Reverend Evan Jones, described the scene in the *Baptist Missionary Magazine*.

The Cherokees are nearly all prisoners. They had been dragged from their homes and encamped at the forts and military places, all over the nation. In Georgia especially, multitudes were allowed no time to take anything with them except the clothes they had on. . . . It is a painful sight. The property of many has been taken and sold before their eyes for almost nothing—the sellers and buyers, in many cases, having combined to cheat the poor Indians.

Provided with little or no clothing or shelter, sick, and suffering emotionally after being wrenched from their homes, thousands of Indians died along the way.

Some Indian nations forcibly resisted removal. In the North the Sac and Fox Indians, unhappy with their new lands, crossed the Mississippi River in 1832 and returned to Illinois. Led by Chief Blackhawk, they launched a series of attacks to regain their homelands. But in the Blackhawk War, which followed, United States Army troops and the state militia defeated Indian forces and opened the way for the settlement of the rest of the state.

239

Native Americans who resisted government efforts to force them westward were driven out by the army. This painting by Mary Ann Thompson shows a group of Cherokee moving along what they called the Trail of Tears. Thousands died along the way.

A larger war broke out in Florida, where the Seminole, led by Chief Osceola, refused to leave their homeland. Fugitive slaves who lived with the Seminole aided them in the struggle. The resulting war lasted from 1835 until 1838, when the army finally defeated and removed the Seminole. By 1844 only a few scattered groups of Native Americans remained east of the Mississippi.

SECTION REVIEW

1. Identify: Removal Act, Trail of Tears, Blackhawk, Osceola.
2. Define: white manhood suffrage, caucus.
3. What group of people gained the vote during the early nineteenth century?
4. How had the selection of presidential electors changed by 1832?
5. Which groups were denied political participation under Jacksonian democracy?
6. Which Indian nations were most affected by the Removal Act of 1830?
7. **Critical Thinking** Jackson called the Indians "subjects" of the government and the whites "citizens." What do you think he meant?

3 Strengthening the National Government

Because Jackson had made no specific campaign promises, no one could be sure of the policies he would pursue as President. Old Hickory soon indicated, however, that he intended to lead as firmly in the White House as he did on the battlefield. His actions had far-reaching consequences in two areas especially.

First, because Jackson saw himself as the protector of the common people, he vigorously opposed government policies that protected privileged groups. Second, because he saw himself as the leader of a truly united nation, he asserted federal authority whenever he believed it was needed. Although Jackson did support states' rights, he never allowed them to threaten national unity. Old Hickory was not afraid to challenge state governments on behalf of the federal union.

Jackson's Democratic Approach

The steps Jackson took to organize his administration reflected his democratic temperament. Like other Presidents, he appointed a cabinet, but these men proved to be generally undistinguished. For advice the President turned instead to a small group of editors, officeholders, and old Tennessee associates known as the Kitchen Cabinet.

In filling lower governmental positions President Jackson adopted a policy of removing people who opposed him politically and replacing them with faithful supporters. His political friends naturally approved of this plan, for it opened up many well-paying positions to them. As one Jacksonian leader explained it, "to the victors belong the spoils." This policy became known as the *spoils system.*

The spoils system made good political sense because it strengthened Jackson's party by rewarding party workers. But the President initiated the spoils system for another reason as well. He believed it furthered the ideals of democracy. Jackson believed that officeholders had begun to think of their jobs as personal property rather than as a public trust. Rotation in office would prevent such thinking. He also was convinced that most government jobs were simple enough that any intelligent man could perform them without special training. Thus Jackson attacked the idea of government workers as a special group set apart from the people.

Despite Jackson's promotion of the spoils system, he actually replaced only about one fifth of the federal officeholders. And some of those replacements were for misbehavior rather than for political reasons. Still, his actions set an unfortunate precedent for the future. Government jobs often became simply rewards for faithful political support, having no connection to public service. As you will read in Chapter 22, this frequently led to government corruption.

The Tariff of Abominations

A controversy that arose over tariffs soon put Jackson's democratic approach and his decisive style to a test. Ever since the nation's founding, Congress had placed tariffs on goods imported into the United States, originally to raise revenue. Over the years manufacturers had successfully convinced Congress to raise tariffs repeatedly. These protective tariffs benefited young American industries by raising the price of cheaper European products higher than American-manufactured goods.

In 1828, before Jackson's election, a new law raised tariffs on some items as high as 45 percent and 50 percent of the original European price. Opponents labeled the legislation of 1828 the Tariff of Abominations. Southern planters in particular bitterly objected to this protection for New England manufacturers. Southerners, after all, exported cotton and other raw materials to Europe and in exchange bought many European manufactured goods for their own use. Because the tariff raised the price of the items they bought, southerners protested that it was in effect an indirect tax on their region of the country.

Controversy Over States' Rights

John C. Calhoun of South Carolina, Jackson's Vice-President, was the leading opponent of the tariff and a vigorous one at that. Calhoun had abandoned his earlier nationalistic views and by 1828 had begun to defend a state's right to be free from unwanted national control.

In an unsigned essay called the "South Carolina Exposition and Protest," Calhoun argued that the people of any state could *nullify,* or declare illegal, any federal law they believed to be unconstitutional. If a state convention declared a law null and void within the state, its citizens did not have to obey that law. Calhoun and his supporters were aware that this doctrine could be used to defend slavery from federal interference.

Calhoun had raised an important and familiar issue that had been debated since the Revolutionary War. Was the United States one nation indivisible, with the federal government supreme? Or did the states have final say on how much national authority they would accept, as Jefferson and Madison had suggested in the Virginia and Kentucky resolutions of 1798? The issue had been left unresolved because the Constitution was not specific on the question of sovereignty.

In 1830 Senator Daniel Webster of Massachusetts and Senator Robert Hayne of South Carolina debated whether the states or the federal government had ultimate authority. Hayne supported Calhoun's argument that states had the right to nullify federal laws. Webster replied for the nationalists. An impressive man with booming voice and piercing black eyes, he brought all his debating skills to bear against Hayne.

Webster argued that the federal government, not the states, held final authority under the Constitution and that Calhoun's theory of nullification was illegal and unconstitutional. If any state could disregard a law whenever it wished, chaos would reign and the nation would collapse. The federal government was not the agent of the states, Webster continued, but the agent of the people directly. "It is the people's Constitution, the people's government, made for the people, made by the people, and answerable to the people." His final ringing plea was, "Liberty *and* Union, now and forever, one and inseparable!"

The Nullification Crisis

The dispute over nullification simmered for two years, until Congress passed a tariff bill in 1832 that kept rates high and granted southerners little relief. Voters in South Carolina reacted angrily. A popularly elected convention met in November 1832 and declared the tariff null and void in the state.

This was too much for an old military man like Jackson. He blazed in fury at such defiance of federal authority. "If one drop of blood be shed there in defiance of the laws of the United States," he warned privately, "I will hang the first man of them I can get my hands on to the first tree I can find." Publicly he vowed to uphold the tariff law, and in 1833 he asked Congress to pass a "force bill" allowing him, if need be, to use the military to enforce the new measures.

Despite these threats, Jackson moved cautiously. He did not want to push South Carolina into open rebellion. Consequently he welcomed a compromise tariff bill, proposed by Henry Clay, that would reduce duties to 20 percent over a nine-year period. Since the compromise bill did lower tariffs and since no other southern state supported South Carolina in this dispute, the state's leaders accepted the compromise.

On March 1, 1833, Congress passed Clay's tariff bill, and Jackson signed it. The South Carolina convention then repealed the act nullifying the earlier tariff law. South Carolina's challenge to the national government had failed, and the crisis passed. President Jackson's vigorous actions strengthened both the presidency and the federal government.

Jackson Against the Bank

Another major dispute in Jackson's administration erupted over the Second Bank of the United States. The Bank, originally chartered in 1816, was privately controlled, yet it had immense power. The federal government deposited all its revenue in the Bank, which could then use the money without paying interest. The Bank also issued the only national currency, in the form of bank notes, so it could control how much paper money was in circulation. If the Bank issued large numbers of notes, loans were easier to obtain.

No one was more hostile to the Bank than President Andrew Jackson. To him it was the epitome of special privilege. As a private business, it was responsible, not to the government, but to a small group of stockholders who, he believed, grew rich with public funds. Jackson also argued that the Bank's power made it a corrupting influence in politics. Indeed, the Bank had dispensed favors to government officials, some of whom were even on its payroll.

The Supreme Court had ruled in *McCulloch* v. *Maryland* (1819) that a national bank was constitutional, but President Jackson disagreed. He concluded that Congress had no constitutional power to charter such a bank.

The President was not alone in his opposition. A wide variety of Americans agreed with him, although their reasons differed. Many business leaders, state bankers, and speculators felt that the Bank did not issue enough currency in the form of paper money. They believed that a large supply of money was crucial for rapid economic growth and development.

In contrast, farmers in the South and West along with factory workers in the East thought that the Bank issued too much paper money. They favored a "hard" currency of gold and silver coins. Although some bank notes were backed by gold and silver reserves, some were not. The farmers argued that ordinary citizens had no way of knowing whether the bank notes they received in wages were really worth the amount printed on them. Like Jackson, both groups wanted to see the Bank destroyed.

Victory for the President

The Bank's charter was scheduled to expire in 1836, but the renewal of the charter became an issue in 1832. At that time the Bank's director, Nicholas Biddle, acting on advice from Henry Clay and Daniel Webster, decided to seek an earlier renewal. Clay and Webster felt sure they could get the renewal bill through Congress. If Jackson vetoed it, they would have a ready-made issue for the upcoming presidential election campaign.

Congress granted a new bank charter in March 1832. But President Jackson vetoed the bill, affirming, "The Bank is trying to kill me, but I will kill it!" His veto message attacked the Bank's constitutionality, its size and power, and its tendency to aid "the rich and powerful."

Later that summer, the National Republican party nominated Henry Clay as its candidate for President. As planned, Clay campaigned against Jackson's veto of the Bank. The voters, however, decisively backed Jackson. He won by an electoral college vote of 219 to 49. Taking his victory as a mandate against the Bank, Old Hickory resolved to kill the Bank immediately rather than wait until its charter expired.

First the President ordered all government deposits removed from the Bank. When the secretary of the treasury refused, Jackson fired him and appointed an old supporter, Attorney General Roger B. Taney, to the office. Taney continued to withdraw government funds for normal Treasury Department matters but stopped making deposits. Instead, he began depositing federal revenues in state banks controlled by fellow Democrats. Opponents angrily called them "pet banks."

Biddle responded by refusing to grant new loans and by demanding that existing loans be paid back immediately. With credit unavailable, businesses began to fail, and unemployment rose. Shocked business lead-

President Jackson believed the Bank of the United States was undemocratic. This cartoon shows the President trying to wield a presidential veto against plans to renew the Bank.

ers begged Jackson to end his opposition to the Bank in order to restore public confidence. Jackson refused, blaming the uncertain economic situation on Biddle.

President Jackson eventually won this economic war of nerves. The Bank lost popularity, and Jackson's support grew. After 1836, when its federal charter expired, the Bank continued to operate under a Pennsylvania charter. But the Panic of 1837 (see page 244) weakened it still further, and in 1841 it went out of business.

SECTION REVIEW

1. Identify: Kitchen Cabinet, Tariff of Abominations, Robert Hayne, Nicholas Biddle, pet banks.
2. Define: spoils system, nullify.
3. Why were southerners in particular opposed to the tariff legislation of 1828?
4. How did Calhoun's position and Webster's position on states' rights differ?
5. (a) What action did South Carolina take against high tariffs? (b) Was it successful? Explain.
6. Why was President Jackson opposed to the Second Bank of the United States?
7. **Critical Thinking** How might you counter Jackson's argument that the spoils system furthered democracy?

243

4 Hard Times

As Andrew Jackson neared the end of his second term, he remained as popular as ever. Although he might have used his popularity to run for a third term, Jackson decided to honor the two-term tradition that began with Washington. But he made sure that his influence was felt in the choice of his party's next presidential candidate.

The Election of 1836

The Democrats held their first national nominating convention in 1836, and Jackson took great pains to ensure that his Vice-President, Martin Van Buren, would be the nominee. Van Buren faced bitter opposition from the National Republicans, who renamed themselves the Whigs.*

Whigs agreed on their opposition to Jackson's policies, but they found it difficult to unite on a platform of positive principles. In general, they shared John Quincy Adams's faith that the United States could become a great nation through its wealth and growing industry. Many Whigs supported the goals of Henry Clay's American System and thought federal and state governments should take a more active role in promoting canals, roads, and other internal improvements.

In the North, many merchants and manufacturers supported the Whigs, as did educators, reformers, and commercial farmers. Many southerners also joined the Whigs, including merchants, bankers, and planters who believed that southern prosperity was linked with the expanding commerce of the North.

In 1836, however, the Whigs did not believe they were strong enough to run a single candidate for President. Instead, they decided to run three separate candidates, one popular in each section of the country: William Henry Harrison in the West, Daniel Webster in New England, and Hugh Lawson White in the South. They hoped to prevent Van Buren from winning a majority in the

*They named themselves after the British Whigs, who had opposed King George III during the Revolutionary War, because they claimed that Jackson acted like "King Andrew I."

electoral college and thus, as in 1824, throw the election into the House of Representatives. But the strategy failed. Van Buren won a small majority of both the popular and the electoral vote. Unfortunately for Van Buren, he soon encountered a situation he could not control.

Depression Strikes

As President, Van Buren intended to follow the policies of his popular predecessor, but disaster struck almost immediately. Two months after his inauguration, a severe financial panic soon known as the Panic of 1837, began.

The panic had its roots in land speculation. The prosperity of the previous decade had stimulated the purchase of western land more than ever before. The government held most of the region in public domain and sold it to farmers and investors, over 12 million acres (4.8 million hectares) in 1835 and over 20 million acres (8 million hectares) in 1836. The prospect of high profits brought speculators as well as farmers into the market. Soon speculators were purchasing huge tracts, sometimes by clearly illegal means.

Many of the new landowners in the Southwest grew cotton. For a time this expanded the cotton supply and opened new markets for eastern merchants and manufacturers. Land prices skyrocketed.

Without a powerful national bank to control the money supply, state bank notes flooded the country, many of them not backed by gold or silver. Because of the large amount of money in circulation, state governments began extensive canal and railroad building projects. Banks, merchants, and farmers borrowed money, and banks in turn gave easy credit terms to others.

Shortly before Van Buren's election, President Jackson had tried to slow speculation by issuing a Specie Circular. It stated that public land could be paid for only in gold or silver. The circular convinced prospective land buyers that the boom economy would not last forever. In the climate of economic uncertainty, land sales slowed.

In early 1837 the price of cotton on the international market dropped sharply because of a surplus. For cotton farmers who had mortgaged their farms to buy more land, this drop in prices meant disaster. Without adequate profits from their cotton sales, farmers could not repay their loans. The sagging land market then collapsed.

The resulting depression was one of the most severe in the nation's history. Banks failed by the hundreds, and even some states went bankrupt because of overambitious internal improvement schemes. Unemployment climbed as factories closed.

Many Americans blamed the Democratic administration for the economic hard times, although the administration was not directly responsible for the overspeculation that had caused the panic. Like most citizens, Van Buren did not really understand what caused the crisis. He attributed it to "overbanking" and urged Congress to restructure the Treasury. Congress complied in 1840, but the government did little else to combat the depression.

A Missed Opportunity for the Whigs

The Democrats renominated President Van Buren in 1840, but the continuing economic depression filled the party faithful with gloom. The Whigs, on the other hand, were enthusiastic. They believed that hard times and a popular candidate would insure their victory. They chose General William Henry Harrison of Ohio, a military hero still basking in his victory over Tecumseh at the Battle of Tippecanoe in 1811. To balance the ticket, they nominated John Tyler, a conservative Virginia Whig who favored states' rights, for Vice-President.

The campaign of 1840 was one of the most colorful in the nation's history. With the slogan "Tippecanoe and Tyler Too," the Whigs conducted a spirited and exciting campaign. Having learned the art of mass campaigning from the Democrats, they portrayed Harrison as a simple western farmer, a man of the people who lived in a log cabin and loved hard cider. (Actually, he came from one of Virginia's most distinguished families and lived in a rather elegant house.) People flocked to political rallies, parades, bonfires, and barbecues, where bands and other entertainment helped arouse popular interest.

The Whigs carefully avoided discussing any real issues and made sure that Harrison said nothing of substance. "Let him say not one single word about his principles, or his creed," Nicholas Biddle once advised. "Let him say nothing—promise nothing."

The Democrats sarcastically dubbed Harrison "General Mum," but the Whig strategy paid off. In a large turnout of voters, Harrison won 234 electoral votes to Van Buren's 60. The popular vote was much closer, but the Whigs had elected their first President after 12 years of Democratic control.

The Whigs optimistically looked forward to implementing a vigorous program of economic growth and development based on Clay's American System. But only a month after taking office, the 68-year-old Harrison died of pneumonia. The Whigs were thunderstruck. For the first time, a Vice-President succeeded to the presidency.

As President, Tyler blocked legislation that would have strengthened the national

The 1840 Whig candidate, General William Henry Harrison of Ohio, was nicknamed Tippecanoe for his victory over Tecumseh in 1811. (See page 199.) Harrison's campaign pictured him as a simple farmer living in a log cabin, as you can see in this campaign banner. Actually, he was a wealthy man.

WM. H. HARRISON
THE OHIO FARMER

Major Events

1825	John Quincy Adams elected President
1828	Tariff of Abominations passed; Andrew Jackson elected President
1830	Indian Removal Act
1832	Jackson vetoes new Bank charter; South Carolina "nullifies" tariff
1833	Nullification crisis ends
1836	Martin Van Buren elected President
1837	Panic of 1837 begins
1838	Army drives thousands of southern Indians to Oklahoma
1840	William Henry Harrison elected President
1841	After Harrison's death, John Tyler becomes first Vice-President to succeed to presidency

government at the expense of the states. He opposed federal funding for internal improvement projects and twice vetoed a bill to charter a new national bank.

The Whigs quickly realized that nominating as Vice-President a man so out of sympathy with their policies had been a mistake. For the last years of his presidency, Tyler was literally a President without a party, and Democrats gleefully encouraged his feud with the Whigs. Without effective leadership, national affairs drifted.

SECTION REVIEW

1. Identify: Whigs, Specie Circular, John Tyler.
2. Why did the Whigs run three candidates for President in 1836?
3. How did the drop in cotton prices in 1837 contribute to the depression?
4. What campaign strategies did the Whigs learn from the Democrats?
5. **Critical Thinking** Could the techniques of the campaign of 1840 be used today?

Chapter 13 Review

In Perspective

During the late 1820s two new political parties, the Democrats and the Whigs, gradually evolved from the Republican party of the Era of Good Feelings. Campaign techniques first used by the Democrats in 1828 added new excitement to presidential elections.

Andrew Jackson campaigned as the candidate of the common people in 1828. For some people his election began an era of increased democracy. Political reforms led to greater political participation by white males and gave the average voter a stronger voice in the election process. However, women were denied any voice in government and most blacks were denied basic human rights. During the Jacksonian era,

thousands of Native Americans faced heartbreak and hardship as they were forced to leave their homelands.

President Jackson's battle against the national Bank and his strong position in the nullification crisis strengthened the presidency. The Panic of 1837 resulted in a severe economic depression, which handicapped President Van Buren, who lost to William Henry Harrison in 1840. On Harrison's death, John Tyler became President, but had little sympathy with most Whig goals. Tyler was a strong supporter of national expansion, a process that reached a high point in the mid-1840s, as you will read in the next chapter.

Vocabulary

On a separate sheet of paper, write the word or words that best complete each of the following sentences.

1. A (An) ____ is the declaration of the principles and programs of a political party.
2. To ____ a law is to declare it illegal.
3. A (An) ____ is a secret meeting at which presidential candidates were chosen.
4. Under the ____, an elected official's loyal supporters were given government jobs.
5. ____ is voting by all white males.

Chapter Checkup

1. (a) How did the two parties that emerged during the late 1820s differ? (b) What role did they play in the election of 1828?
2. (a) What reforms increased the political participation of some Americans? (b) Which groups did not participate?
3. (a) Why did John C. Calhoun support a state's right to nullify a federal law? (b) What argument did Daniel Webster use against the principle of nullification?
4. (a) Why did the Whigs nominate Harrison for President? (b) Why did they nominate Tyler for Vice-President? (c) How did their choices backfire?

Critical Thinking

1. **Making a Judgment** Do you think Jackson's presidency was democratic or "the reign of King Andrew"? Explain.
2. **Drawing a Conclusion.** From what you learned about Andrew Jackson, why do you think he agreed with the settlers who wanted the Native Americans removed?

Developing Basic Skills

1. **Map Reading** Study the map on page 239 and answer the following questions: (a) What information is shown on this map? (b) In what states did the southern Indian nations hold land before 1830? (c) How far did each nation have to move from its homeland?
2. **Graph Reading** Study the circle graphs of the 1824 and 1828 presidential elections. (See pages 233 and 235.) Then answer the following questions: (a) Which two candidates ran in both elections? (b) What percentage of the electoral vote did each candidate receive in 1824? in 1828? (c) Based on the election results in 1824, do you think Andrew Jackson had reason to object when John Quincy Adams was elected by the House of Representatives? Why or why not?

See page 829 for suggested readings.

Writer's Handbook

Choosing a Research Topic

When you write a research paper, choose a topic that holds your interest and that you can readily research. Select a number of possible topics then check what resources your library has available. If you discover that there is very little information on a topic, it will probably be wise to eliminate it. If there is a great deal of information on a topic, it is possible that the topic is too broad. For example, the topic *The Life of Andrew Jackson* would be the subject of a book rather than a research paper. A more suitable topic for a paper would be *Andrew Jackson's Indian Policy*.

Practice: Choose two of the following topics and write a sentence describing what aspect of each subject you would like to research.

1. Sectionalism and the Election of 1828
2. Andrew Jackson and the National Bank
3. The "Trail of Tears"
4. The "Civilized Tribes"
5. The Role of Women in the 1820s
6. The Panic of 1837

14

From Sea to Sea

(1820–1860)

Detail of Oregon Trail *by Oscar Berninghaus*

Chapter Outline

1 *The View From West to East*

2 *Oregon and the Fur Trade*

3 *The Republic of Texas*

4 *Surge to the Pacific*

5 *The Challenge of Greater Diversity*

By 1825 the United States had expanded far beyond its original borders, and settlers were moving into the Mississippi River Valley. Although the Louisiana Purchase had extended the nation's boundaries to the Rocky Mountains and beyond, there seemed to be little interest in the territory west of the Mississippi.

Yet within the next 25 years, the United States acquired vast new territory in the West, much of it through war with Mexico. Fur trappers and missionaries opened up the Oregon territory, prospectors streamed to California, and settlers moved into Texas and other parts of the Southwest.

The new territories added to the geographic diversity of the nation, ranging from rugged mountains to deserts and rain forests. The people who lived in the newly acquired areas, especially Native Americans and Mexicans, contributed to the ethnic diversity of the United States.

Expansion to the Pacific

1820	1825	1830	1835	1840	1845	1850	1855	1860

1821 Austin founds colony in Texas

1830 Joseph Smith founds Mormon Church

1836 Texas wins independence

1846 Mexican War begins

1849 Gold Rush begins

1853 Gadsden Purchase

1 The View From West to East

Because the United States evolved from the English colonies along the Atlantic seaboard, thinking of the nation's growth as westward expansion to the Pacific Ocean may seem quite natural. Yet Native Americans had been living in the West, as they had in the East, for thousands of years. Their perspective was bound to differ from that of settlers from the east coast.

Spain's perspective also differed. The Spanish had established a claim to vast areas of North America almost 100 years before the first English settlers arrived in Jamestown. By the time settlers from the former English colonies became interested in the western part of North America, Spanish culture and institutions flourished in many areas there.

The Spanish in California

In 1800 New Spain, the northernmost Spanish province in the Americas, extended as far north as present-day Montana and as far east as the Mississippi River. Spain, however, paid little attention to its lands north and east of the Gila River and the Rio Grande. For the most part, only small settlements were established in order to prevent other European nations from claiming territory too close to Spanish lands.

In the mid-eighteenth century Spanish authorities took a renewed interest in the northern part of New Spain. They learned that Russian seal hunters and traders were moving south from Alaska into California. In 1769 the Spanish sent an expedition under Don Gaspar de Portola (POR TOH lah) to reassert Spanish authority in Upper California, the area north of the California peninsula.

Portola marched first to San Diego, where he built a stockade. Then he continued north to Monterey. On November 2, 1769, while exploring this area, he discovered San Francisco Bay. (Ships had passed the entrance to the bay for years without sailors realizing that it was the opening to a great inland harbor.)

A group of Franciscan friars led by Father Junípero Serra (SEHR rah) accompanied Portola's expedition. They intended to establish missions to convert the California Indians to Christianity. From San Diego northward a chain of missions was set up along the California coast, where they prospered, forming the backbone of the Spanish government's attempt to settle California. In 1776, the same year that the English colonies declared their independence from Great Britain, Misión Dolores was founded where San Francisco now stands.

The Mission System

The missions claimed virtually all the land in California. The friars who ran the missions either convinced or compelled local Indians to live on mission land, where they worked as farmhands or herders and were converted to Christianity. By 1830 approximately one tenth of the 300,000 California Indians lived on mission lands. They raised cattle, horses, and sheep, cultivated grapes and wheat, and built irrigation facilities. As a result of Indian labor, many of the missions were self-sufficient.

In return for Indian labor, the friars offered food, clothing, and shelter. In the Spaniards' eyes, their greatest contribution to the local Indians was the gift of Christianity. Many Indians accepted conversion, and over the years their own customs and traditions faded. Furthermore, even though the missionaries started with good intentions, many eventually came to view the Indians mainly as a pool of cheap labor. Working conditions then became harsher.

Although the Spanish established a few forts in California, the missions remained the main political and economic symbol of Spanish control until 1821. In that year revolutionaries in New Spain successfully threw off Spanish rule and declared Mexico an independent nation. California remained isolated from the fighting but accepted the authority of the new Mexican nation.

Impact of Mexican Independence

In 1833 the Mexican Congress passed the Secularization Act, which altered the economic and political administration of California. It opened church lands to settlement by other Mexicans and decreed that Indians were no longer under the protection or control of the church. Any semblance of real

Wealthy landowners in New Spain often controlled vast tracts of land. The clothing of the landowners at center reflects the traditions of Spain. Spanish language and customs left a permanent stamp on the American Southwest.

freedom for the Indians, however, was short-lived.

The Mexican government granted large portions of valuable mission land to Mexican citizens, who were eager to exploit the profits to be made from farming and ranching. Vast ranches quickly replaced the missions as the main economic unit in California.

For manual labor, the *rancheros,* or ranch owners, turned to the local Indian populations, just as the missionaries had earlier. Although technically the Indians were free, most rancheros forced them to work and hunted them down if they tried to escape.

Hard work and alien customs took a tremendous toll. The *mortality rate,* or death rate, among Indians working on California ranches was four times as high as among Mexicans in California and twice as high as the mortality rate among slaves in the southern United States. By 1848 about 20 percent of the California Indians had died.

The independence of Mexico opened up the territory to traders from the United States for the first time. The ranches of California, with their vast cattle herds, offered a new market for enterprising Yankee merchants, who soon dominated the lucrative cattle-hide trade in California. In 20 years one Boston firm alone exported half a million hides. Still, until the mid-1840s, developments on the east coast of North America had little impact on life in California.

Arizona and New Mexico

The Spanish made several attempts during the eighteenth century to establish settlements in the area of present-day Arizona. The Yuma and Apache Indians of the area, however, defended their homelands fiercely, and by 1830 the Spanish had abandoned several mines and missions, leaving only a few outposts.

Farther east, in New Mexico, the Spanish established more permanent settlements. About 44,000 Spanish settlers lived along the Rio Grande from El Paso to Taos as sheep ranchers. As in California, a few rich families owned vast herds, numbering as many as a million sheep, which were tended by local Indians.

The Spanish also founded more missions in New Mexico than in Arizona, partly because the Pueblo and Zuni offered less open resistance than the Apache and Yuma. Yet many Indians in New Mexico did resent Spanish attempts to impose an alien religion and way of life on them.

Traders from the United States appeared in Santa Fe, the capital of New Mexico, as early as 1804, but the Spanish threw them in jail and confiscated their goods. Spain wanted to discourage foreign interest in its territory. But when Mexico declared its independence in 1821, the new government welcomed American traders as a way of increasing its own prosperity. The first successful trading expedition from Missouri reached Santa Fe the same year. The traders returned home triumphant; they dumped bags full of Spanish dollars on the sidewalks while onlookers watched in amazement. Soon the Santa Fe trade flourished.

Texas

In the 1720s the Spanish had claimed all of present-day Texas and had driven out the few French colonists living there. Yet a hundred years later only 4,000 Spanish settlers resided in Texas, making a living primarily by cattle ranching. Although the Catholic church established a few missions in Texas, the Indians there, such as the Comanche and Apache, were nomadic and resisted any attempts to force them to adopt Spanish ways.

Here and there, a few farmers from the United States had crossed the Sabine River into eastern Texas. But the area remained sparsely settled. In the 1820s the newly independent Republic of Mexico wanted to make its northern province, Texas, more prosperous and secure. To do that, the Mexican government knew it would have to attract many new settlers.

In 1820 an American named Moses Austin requested and received permission to found a colony of 300 people in Texas. Austin died before he could begin the trip, but his son Stephen took over the project. Stephen Austin appeared particularly ill suited for the task. He was sensitive and well educated and might have seemed more at home in a university than on the frontier. But he was tolerant, fair, and honest and displayed careful judgment and considerable diplomatic talent.

Austin founded his new colony in December 1821. Each family received about 250 acres (about 100 hectares) for farming and stock raising. Austin's colony thrived in large part because of his skill in choosing people. By 1824 he had settled 2,021 persons in his colony, the center of which was the little town of Austin. This marked the beginning of an ever-increasing flood of American settlers into Texas.

Oregon

The land north of Upper California extending to Vancouver Island and the coast of present-day British Columbia had been claimed not only by Spain but by Russia, Great Britain, and the United States as well.

In 1818 the United States and Great Britain agreed to a joint occupation of the Oregon country, the area north of the 42nd parallel and south of latitude 54° 40′. The British and the Americans would be free to settle and trade there. Both, however, generally ignored the rights and interests of the territory's original inhabitants, as Europeans had done since they first landed in the Americas. By 1825 Spain and Russia withdrew their claims to these lands.

For many years only a few Europeans or Americans came to settle in Oregon, and their main interest was the fur trade. Since furs bought from the Indians could be sold at tremendous profits in China, Yankee traders from New England stopped along the Oregon coast frequently—so frequently, in fact, that the Indian name for white man in many areas was "Boston."

The Yankee traders in Oregon were among a small number of Americans who lived in the West. Up until the mid-1820s, if you had viewed the history of North America from the west coast looking east, the conflicts and trials of the United States would have played a minor role. Soon, very soon, that situation would change.

SECTION REVIEW

1. Identify: Don Gaspar de Portola, Father Junípero Serra, Secularization Act, Stephen Austin.
2. Define: ranchero, mortality rate.
3. What development renewed Spanish interest in northern New Spain?
4. What political function did the missions serve for the Spanish in California?
5. What did California Indians do on mission lands and on Spanish ranches?
6. (a) Where did the Spanish establish settlements? (b) Where was this most difficult?
7. **Critical Thinking** What qualities do you think Austin looked for in his settlers? Why?

2 Oregon and the Fur Trade

The role of the United States in the far West changed partly because Americans began to learn more about the country beyond the Mississippi River. Before 1820, Americans knew little about the area except for information reported by the Lewis and Clark expedition. During the 1820s, however, word began to trickle back about the vast and fertile lands of Oregon, beyond the Rocky Mountains. Those who spread the word and blazed the trails that later pioneers would follow were enterprising fur traders known popularly as "mountain men."

The Mountain Men

Rocky Mountain streams abounded in beaver, and the resourceful and hardy mountain men could make a fortune trapping the animals and trading their pelts. Yet they led a lonely, often dangerous existence. Grizzly bears and other potentially dangerous animals populated the forests; an accident could strand a mountain man far from help. Furthermore, many of the Native Americans

in the territory, particularly the Blackfeet, resented the trapping on their hunting grounds and frequently attacked the outsiders.

These outsiders were a diverse group. French-Canadian trappers had begun to probe the Rockies as early as the 1770s. By the 1820s the mountain men included not only French-Canadians but also British, Irish, and Mexicans as well as white and black trappers from the United States. James Beckworth, a black mountain man from the United States, became a chief of the Crow Indians. Louis Vasquez, half French and half Spanish, became a mountain man in 1822 and was one of the founders of Denver, Colorado. At least one "mountain man" was a woman. Marie Dorion, an Iowa Indian, became famous throughout the United States for her feats of survival.

While the trappers made money from their labor, the traders who bought the furs and sold them in the East made the biggest profits. Two of the largest trading companies were John Jacob Astor's American Fur Company and the Rocky Mountain Fur Com-

Forts doubled as trading posts in the Northwest. Here a fur buyer deals with several trappers, including Native Americans, at Fort Walla Walla in Oregon country. The heavy demand for beaver pelts led to overtrapping, and by the 1830s beaver were becoming scarce.

pany. In its 12 years of operation, the latter alone purchased furs worth nearly $500,000, an enormous sum at that time. Other smaller companies eagerly joined the search for furs, competed with each other, and recruited their own mountain men.

The competition between the companies, however, led to drastic overtrapping of streams and rivers. After 1832, with the beaver population greatly reduced, the fur trade fell into serious decline.

Early Settlers in Oregon

As the heyday of the mountain man ended, the day of the pioneer began. Former mountain men and employees of fur companies told of the beautiful and rich land that lay beyond the Rockies, in Oregon country.

Tales of rich land were not all that lured settlers westward. Easterners heard rumors that Indians in the West wanted to learn about Christianity and the Bible. The Indian tribes actually had their own rich religious traditions, and few had even heard of Christianity. But churches sent missionaries to Oregon in response to the reports.

The best-known missionaries were Jason Lee, sent by the Methodists in 1834; Marcus and Narcissa Whitman, Presbyterians who led a band of settlers west in 1836; and Henry and Eliza Spalding, who accompanied the Whitmans. None of the missionaries had much success converting Native Americans to the Christian religion, but they nevertheless wrote home urging friends to join them.

Gradually more and more Americans made their way to Oregon, settling in the Willamette Valley near the missionaries' homes. Families wrote descriptive letters back East, which newspapers often published.

Booklets appeared extolling the virtues of Oregon, often exaggerating wildly. Many Americans spoke the way one Missouri farmer did to his family when he announced his decision to move West.

> Out in Oregon I can get me a square mile of land. And a quarter section for each of you all. Dad burn me, I am done with this country. Winters its frost and snow freeze the body; summers the overflow from Old Muddy drowns half my acres; taxes take the yield of them that's left. What say, Maw, it's God's country.

The Way West

The Oregon Trail, developed by earlier traders and trappers, became the most famous route to Oregon country. It began at Independence, Missouri, followed the Missouri and the Platte rivers to southern Wyoming, crossed the Rockies at South Pass, and took a northern cutoff to the Columbia River, which it followed to the Willamette Valley. In all, the trail stretched for about 2,000 miles (about 3,200 kilometers), and the journey took four to six months.

In the early 1840s growing numbers of people responded to the publicity about Oregon. The pioneers traveled along the trails to Oregon in caravans of covered wagons. Safety and prudence required such organization. One danger was Indian attack. Indians did not often attack the wagon trains that crossed their lands, but the settlers wanted to be prepared in any case.

Another problem was the land itself. Beyond central Nebraska, streams ran dry in the summer, and the grass grew thin where it grew at all. For pioneers used to wooded, well-watered country, the experience was frightening. When the wagon trains drew into a circle for the night, it was as much to keep the precious livestock from wandering away to find more grass as it was for protection.

Each wagon train winding westward established its own government, complete with a code of laws and officials to enforce them. The experience of literally forming their own government proved valuable preparation for the settlers once they arrived on the Pacific coast, where government was limited, at times even nonexistent.

Self-Government: The First Organic Law

As you read earlier, Great Britain and the United States had agreed to a joint occupation of the Oregon country in 1818. But when the settlers arrived in the Willamette Valley, the only government authority they found was the British Hudson's Bay Company, which was hardly equipped to deal with a flood of permanent settlers. Americans thus grew dissatisfied with the vague arrangement of joint occupation.

After 1842, when Americans began to outnumber the British, they drew up their

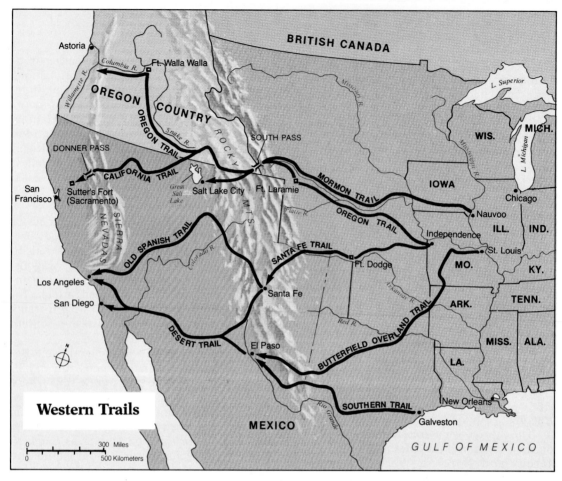

Western Trails

0 ___ 300 Miles
0 ___ 500 Kilometers

■ *The way west to Oregon and California stretched some 2,000 miles. Much of the land on the way was arid or mountainous or both. Wise pioneers, therefore, traveled with an experienced guide over one of the trails shown on this map.*

own framework of government, the First Organic Law. It outlined a temporary government for the Oregon Territory, which continued in force for the next few years.

By 1845 about 5,000 Americans had settled in Oregon, most of them from northern states. They opposed the introduction of slavery in Oregon, but many also objected to the immigration of free blacks. In an effort to discourage such immigration the First Organic Law provided that any black entering Oregon would be whipped.

Even under such harsh conditions, a few blacks did arrive and some prospered. George Washington Bush, for one, led a company of black settlers to Oregon. He and his family became wealthy wheat farmers, known for their kindness toward poorer white settlers. Bush and his company were also known for their willingness to shoot in

self-defense, so the antiblack provisions of the Oregon law were never enforced.

The Americans looked forward to the day when Oregon would become a territory of the United States and then a state.

SECTION REVIEW

1. Identify: Oregon Trail.
2. What was the goal of the mountain men?
3. List two reasons pioneers settled in Oregon.
4. (a) What was the First Organic Law? (b) What purpose was it to serve?
5. **Critical Thinking** What contribution to western settlement did the mountain men and missionaries share?

3 The Republic of Texas

Just as the increasing number of immigrants from the United States into Oregon caused problems for the Hudson's Bay Company, so the tide of settlers in Texas caused problems for Mexico. By the end of the 1820s about 20,000 Americans lived in Texas, compared to only about 4,000 Mexicans. Furthermore, the potential for conflict was high. Many differences existed between Mexican and American ways of life.

Clash of Two Cultures

Natural tensions arose between Mexicans and Americans because of basic cultural differences. Most Mexicans spoke Spanish; most Americans spoke English. The American settlers were overwhelmingly Protestant, while most Mexicans were Catholic. And the Mexican government permitted public worship only in Roman Catholic churches.

Political differences also contributed to the conflict. Settlers from the United States had strong democratic traditions. The background of the Mexicans was quite different. Under the old Spanish empire, government had been undemocratic. Provincial officials and local mayors were appointed by the crown, not elected by the people.

When Mexico became independent, its government did adopt a constitution and formed legislatures in each of its states. However, Texas was part of a larger state, and Texans sent only one representative to the legislature. Consequently they had little influence on the government of Mexico.

Furthermore, Americans found it difficult to become accustomed to the Mexican judicial system. A single judge sitting in Saltillo, the state capital, ruled on court cases. The plaintiff and defendant did not testify personally before the judge, nor was a jury present. A system that depended so heavily on one person's opinion did not seem just to Americans.

A further point of friction was slavery. Most Americans who settled in Texas were southerners. Some brought slaves along, and others expected to acquire them there. The Mexican government had abolished slavery in Texas in 1827 and later throughout Mexico. Yet since enforcement was lax, American settlers continued to bring slaves. Even though Mexican authorities revoked the ban on slavery in Texas a few years later, the American colonists still believed slavery would not be secure as long as Texas remained under Mexican rule.

Beginning of Conflict

The Mexican government had its own reasons for distrusting the American colonists. It suspected that the settlers wanted to bring Texas into the United States. The United States government, after all, had already attempted to purchase Texas twice, in 1826 and 1829.

To strengthen its hold on Texas, the Mexican government established new military garrisons in the province and fortified already existing ones. To American-born Texans, those actions looked like the beginning of military rule. Then, in the summer of 1832, a revolution in Mexico brought to power a new and vigorous leader, General Antonio de Santa Anna. Many American settlers had supported Santa Anna's struggle. They hoped that he would grant them a greater role in the government of Texas. Most were willing to remain loyal to Mexico despite their foreign background as long as the Mexican government allowed them a measure of freedom.

Santa Anna, however, proved to be less liberal than he had first appeared. In October 1834 he abolished the Mexican constitution and legislatures and set himself up as dictator of all Mexico. Rumors spread north from Mexico City: Santa Anna, some said, intended to disenfranchise American Texans, abolish local governments, and drive all Americans out of Texas. Santa Anna was sending troops north, said others.

When Santa Anna, hearing of discontent in Texas, actually did send reinforcements to the Mexican garrisons, a group of Americans led by the fiery William B. Travis decided to act. They captured a Mexican garrison at Anahuac (AHN ah wahk) on June 30, 1835.

Struggle for Texan Independence

Stephen Austin rallied the American settlers behind the goal of independence for Texas. When a Mexican force reached Gonzales,

Americans from all over the countryside rushed to the town, fiercely attacked the Mexicans, and forced them to withdraw.

A convention representing all American settlements met in November 1835 at Austin. The delegates issued a Declaration of Causes justifying their decision to take up arms. They appointed Sam Houston, a popular figure in Texas, as commander of their forces, and they established a provisional government. The following year, on March 2, 1836, Texas declared its independence as the Republic of Texas.

True independence, however, would come only with military victory. During February and March of 1836, the Mexican army pushed northward, laying siege to a small Texas garrison of less than 200 men in the Alamo, an abandoned mission in San Antonio. The defenders of the Alamo included William B. Travis, commander; Jim Bowie, second in command; and Davy Crockett, the best known of a large number of United States volunteers who had come to Texas to join the fight. All of the defenders were killed when the fort fell to the Mexicans on March 6. Their heroic actions had given the Texas revolutionaries time to form an army and had provided the rallying cry, "Remember the Alamo."

With the Americans now aroused and united, volunteers flocked to Sam Houston's army. Houston, however, realized that his new recruits were too inexperienced to fight. So despite the criticism of rasher men, he temporarily retreated in order to get his army into fighting shape before challenging Santa Anna.

On April 21, 1836, Houston ended his retreat. Although outnumbered two to one, he led an attack on Santa Anna's army near the San Jacinto (SAHN jah SEEN toh) River. Catching the Mexicans by surprise, the Texans routed their foes in 15 minutes and cap-

★ America's Heritage ★

The Siege at the Alamo

Fewer than 200 Americans held the Alamo for 12 days against almost 4,000 Mexican troops. The heroism of this defense can be seen in the following message from Commander William B. Travis.

Fellow Citizens and Compatriots:

I am besieged by a thousand or more of the Mexicans under Santa Anna. I have sustained a continued bombardment for twenty-four hours and have not lost a man. The enemy have demanded a surrender; otherwise the garrison is to be put to the sword if the place is taken. I have answered the summons with a cannon shot, and our flag still waves proudly from the walls. *I shall never surrender or retreat.*

Then, I call on you in the name of liberty, patriotism, and of everything dear to the American character to come to our aid with all dispatch. The enemy are receiving reinforcements daily. Though this call may be neglected, I am determined to sustain myself as long as possible and die like a soldier who never forgets what is due to his own

honor and that of his country. *Victory or death.*

William B. Travis

Source: Henderson Yoakum, *History of Texas* (New York: 1856).

tured Santa Anna. While a prisoner, Santa Anna signed two treaties, one granting Texas its independence and another setting the Rio Grande as its southern boundary.

Texas: An Independent Republic

In the fall of 1836 the Republic of Texas held its first presidential election, choosing Sam Houston by an overwhelming majority. But for most Texans independence was not the ultimate goal. In this same election, all but 61 of 6,000 voters voted in favor of annexation to the United States. President Sam Houston ardently shared their desire.

In the United States feelings were mixed. President Andrew Jackson favored annexation, but he shrewdly recognized the grave difficulties of such a move. Annexing Texas would mean war with Mexico. Furthermore, many northerners feared what they saw as the growing power of the South. Texas had been settled mostly by southerners. If it were admitted as a state, the northerners argued, the South would be strengthened. In the end, Jackson refused to support the annexation of Texas, but he did formally recognize its independence.

Heavy American immigration to the new republic during the late 1830s continued to swell its population. The Texas government encouraged this immigration by offering free land to settlers. It also granted land to speculators who agreed to establish settlements. The economic depression that began in 1837 brought hard times to the United States (see page 244), and many people pulled up stakes and moved to Texas.

Although most of the settlers were white southerners, other Americans moved to Texas. Among them were free blacks who were also attracted by the offer of land. Some, such as Greenburg Logan, came in the early 1830s and fought valiantly for Texan independence. But Logan found life difficult after independence. Severely wounded in the war, he applied to the legislature for tax relief but was refused. Aaron Ashworth, another free black who moved to Texas in the early 1830s, became a successful rancher. By 1850 he owned over 2,500 head of cattle.

The population of Texas soared from 30,000 in 1836 to 142,000 ten years later. Cotton was the major cash crop, and the economy flourished. The city of Houston, in 1838

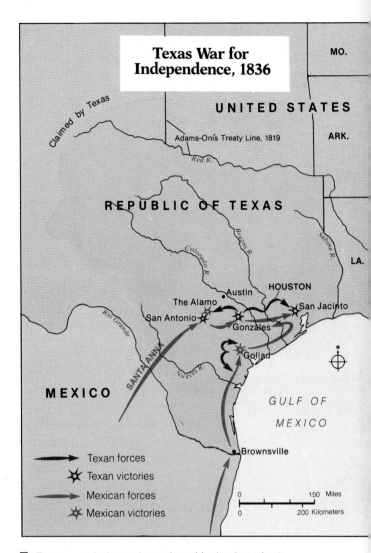

Texas won independence from Mexico in a short but bitter war. Texan forces eventually overwhelmed the Mexican Army near the San Jacinto River and took Santa Anna prisoner.

a small village with tree stumps blocking the main streets, grew in typical fashion. Only a year later it included a courthouse, a jail, two theaters, a statehouse, 12 stores, and 47 saloons. Five years later it had 40 stores, three hotels, several newspapers, schools, four churches, a cotton press, an iron foundry, grist- and sawmills, and two packing houses.

Texas continued to grow and to press for annexation. But the United States government remained reluctant to take the step until 1845.

This painting shows an early farm in Texas a few years after the family had settled there. Work on a fancier house often had to wait while barns were built, corrals made, crops planted, and livestock tended.

SECTION REVIEW

1. Identify: Antonio de Santa Anna, William B. Travis, Declaration of Causes, Sam Houston, "Remember the Alamo."
2. (a) What were two cultural differences between Mexicans and the Americans in Texas? (b) List three political differences that existed between the two peoples.
3. What action by Santa Anna led to military conflict between Mexicans and Americans?
4. What were the provisions of the two treaties signed by Santa Anna in 1836?
5. (a) Why was Jackson reluctant to annex Texas? (b) What did he finally do?
6. **Critical Thinking** Mexicans outnumbered Texans 120 to 1. How do you account for the victory of the Texans?

4 Surge to the Pacific

The American movement to the far West, which had begun in the 1820s and had gathered momentum in the 1830s and early 1840s, reached a peak between 1844 and 1846. Americans had settled in areas beyond the territorial limits of the United States, and this situation was bound to give rise to tensions, as the story of Texas shows. Although most of the immigrants liked the new land they had moved to, they still thought of themselves as Americans. Many hoped that their territory would eventually be incorporated into the United States.

Manifest Destiny

From the days of the first English settlements, American colonists had felt a deep sense of mission about their society and its future. The New England Puritans, for example, tried to establish a society that would set an example for the world. In Pennsylvania the Quakers called their colony the Holy Experiment. Those people who carved farms and villages out of the wilderness were often sustained by a strong sense of the rightness of their actions. And they were moving ever westward.

The American Revolution added a strong political element to this sense of mission. The United States, many Americans believed, had become the torchbearer of liberty in the world. Its system of government was a shining example of how a republic ought to conduct its affairs. Americans in the nineteenth century continued to believe in the superiority of their way of life. When they heard tales of mountain men or listened to accounts of Yankee merchants in California or read letters from pioneers in Oregon and Texas, many naturally assumed that one day all those lands would become part of the United States.

In 1845 a New York editor, John O'Sullivan, neatly summarized those ideas. He wrote that it was America's "manifest destiny to overspread and to possess the whole of the continent which Providence has given us for the development of the great experiment of liberty and federated self-government entrusted to us." Americans quickly took up the new phrase "manifest destiny." It stood for both their faith in American institutions and their desire for expansion. In the 1840s the attitude of the United States government, led by President John Tyler, reflected those widely held sentiments.

Annexation of Texas

When their first efforts to join the United States failed, Texans decided that the next best thing would be to strengthen their independent republic. Mirabeau Bonaparte Lamar, who followed Sam Houston as president, hoped to extend the boundaries of Texas to the Pacific. The British government, seeing a chance to erect a powerful barrier against further United States expansion, actively encouraged Texas to maintain its independence.

In 1841 Sam Houston was reelected president. Two years later he opened negotiations with American officials about the possibility of annexation to the United States. President Tyler eagerly welcomed Houston's overture. As you read in Chapter 13, Tyler had lost most of his political authority because of disagreements with his party, and he hoped to regain his popularity by expanding the nation's boundaries.

The President signed a treaty of annexation with the Texans in April 1844. Many senators were uncertain of public support for the treaty and feared that war with Mexico would result. Consequently, the Senate refused to ratify the treaty.

The supporters of expansion, however, were undaunted. In 1844 the Democrats nominated James K. Polk of Tennessee, an enthusiastic expansionist, as their presidential candidate. Polk soundly defeated Henry Clay, his Whig opponent. Interpreting the results as a victory for expansionist sympathies, President Tyler decided to try again to annex Texas before he left office. He urged Congress to admit Texas by a joint resolution rather than a treaty. *

The Democrats mustered enough votes in Congress to approve annexation, and Tyler signed the joint resolution on March 1, 1845. In December 1845, after Texas voters had approved the proposal, Texas joined the United States as the twenty-eighth state.

The annexation brought new problems. Texas claimed that its borders extended south to the Rio Grande, as specified in the treaty that Santa Anna had signed in 1836. The Mexican government strongly disagreed. It argued that the Texas border should be the Nueces (noo AY says) River, some 200 miles (320 kilometers) to the north. The Mexicans claimed that virtually no Americans lived south of the Nueces and that the Republic of Texas had not previously tried to govern that territory. But the United States insisted that the Rio Grande was the border. Mexico broke off diplomatic relations with the United States in March 1845. Further troubles appeared likely.

The Division of Oregon

For a time war threatened in Oregon as well. Although the United States had agreed with Great Britain to a joint occupation of Oregon Territory north to latitude 54° 40′, the expansionists who wrote the Democratic party platform of 1844 brushed Britain's claims aside. "Our title to the whole of the Territory of Oregon is clear and unquestionable," their platform proclaimed. They ignored a previous offer by the United States to divide the territory along the 49th parallel. "Fifty-four Forty or Fight!" became a rousing slogan.

The British government was alarmed by that slogan, and its alarm increased when Polk won the election. The British knew that in Oregon itself the 5,000 American settlers

---

*A joint resolution would require only a simple majority in both houses rather than the two-thirds vote in the Senate needed to ratify a treaty.

greatly outnumbered the 750 British. Furthermore, heavy American immigration and depleted fur catches had already convinced the Hudson's Bay Company to move its headquarters away from the Columbia River north to Vancouver Island. The American settlements were left to flourish unchecked.

Despite his expansionist beliefs and his party's slogan, President Polk did not want to fight Great Britain. He secretly renewed the earlier American offer to divide the territory. The British government decided that the disputed territory was not worth a war and agreed to divide the Oregon country at the 49th parallel. The United States Senate approved the treaty in June 1846.

Attempts to Acquire California

Like most believers in the manifest destiny of the United States, President Polk had a vision of the country stretching from the Atlantic to the Pacific Ocean. From the beginning, his ultimate aim had been the acquisition of California, with its excellent harbors at San Diego and San Francisco.

By 1845 only about 700 United States citizens lived in California, a small number compared to the 5,000 in Oregon. Most of the settlers had traveled along the same overland trails as the Oregon settlers, splitting off once the Rockies had been crossed and moving into the Sacramento and San Joaquin river valleys.

During the 1830s and early 1840s, under Presidents Jackson and Tyler, the United States had tried unsuccessfully to purchase California from Mexico. President Polk tried again in 1845. As you read, Mexico broke off relations with the United States in March 1845 over the issue of the southern border of Texas. When Polk sent diplomat John Slidell to Mexico City to try to continue discussions about the Texas border, he authorized Slidell to offer to buy California for $25 million and New Mexico for $5 million. However, the Mexicans adamantly opposed the further division of their country. The government refused to receive Slidell and he returned home.

The Bear Flag Revolt

Having failed to buy California, President Polk decided to try other methods of acquiring the territory. He encouraged Thomas Larkin, the American consul at Monterey,

California, to quietly support those Mexican Californians who desired annexation to the United States.

Before Larkin could proceed, an extravagant and swashbuckling American named John C. Frémont arrived in California with plans of his own. Frémont, a United States Army captain, had become famous as the "Pathfinder" for his earlier exploration of the Sierra Nevada mountain passes. He claimed to be in California on a simple mission of scientific exploration for the United States. But he had brought with him a band of 60 frontiersmen, which made the Mexican government suspicious.

Before Frémont could take any action, another group of Americans impulsively attacked the unprepared town of Sonoma. On June 15, 1846, the rebels proclaimed the formation of the California Republic and raised their new flag over the plaza in Sonoma. The flag featured a grizzly bear and a lone star. This so-called Bear Flag Revolt signaled the beginning of the struggle to seize control of California from Mexico.

Frémont rushed to the support of the revolt. Taking command of the rebel forces, he drove the Mexican governor's troops out of northern California. He soon learned, however, that war had broken out between the United States and Mexico. The final conquest of California was to be the responsibility of United States military forces, not of the Bear Flag insurgents alone.

The War With Mexico

The spark that had finally touched off war between the United States and Mexico was ignited by the continuing dispute over the southern border of Texas. After the Slidell mission had failed, President Polk ordered General Zachary Taylor and an army of 1,500 troops to cross the Nueces River and take up a position along the Rio Grande. Tensions between Taylor's army and the Mexican authorities, who viewed his act as nothing less than an invasion of their country, remained high.

In the spring of 1846 Polk decided that if the United States was to acquire the territory it wanted and settle the Texas border dispute, a fight with Mexico was inevitable. As he was working on a war message to Congress, word arrived that on April 25, Mexican troops had crossed the Rio Grande and clashed with Taylor's force. Sixteen Ameri-

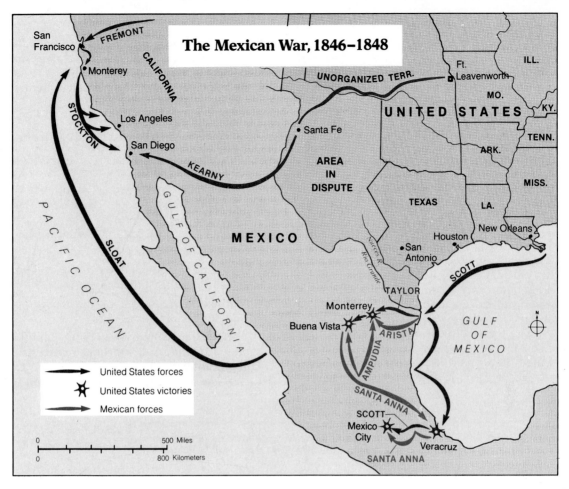

The Mexican War, 1846–1848

San Francisco
Monterey
FREMONT
CALIFORNIA
STOCKTON
Los Angeles
San Diego
KEARNY
SLOAT
PACIFIC OCEAN
GULF OF CALIFORNIA
MEXICO
UNORGANIZED TERR.
Ft. Leavenworth
UNITED STATES
Santa Fe
AREA
IN
DISPUTE
TEXAS
San Antonio
Houston
New Orleans
Nueces R.
Rio Grande
SCOTT
TAYLOR
Monterrey
Buena Vista
ARISTA
AMPUDIA
SANTA ANNA
SCOTT
Mexico City
Veracruz
SANTA ANNA
GULF OF MEXICO
ILL.
MO.
KY.
TENN.
ARK.
MISS.
LA.

United States forces
United States victories
Mexican forces

0   500 Miles
0   800 Kilometers

■ *Many Americans in the 1840s were convinced that the United States would eventually span the continent. A dispute between the United States and Mexico over land claimed by Texas helped trigger the Mexican War in 1846.*

can soldiers were killed or wounded in the skirmish. In response to this news, Polk finished his message and sent it to Congress. Asserting that Mexico had "shed American blood on American soil," he asked for a declaration of war, which Congress quickly passed.

Mexico eagerly accepted war. It was confident that its army could defeat the Americans and end what it considered aggressive designs on its territory. Sentiment among Americans was by no means unanimous. Since the territory to be gained from Mexico lay to the south and west, most Americans in southern and western states enthusiastically supported the conflict. Northeasterners, on the other hand, tended to view the fighting as merely another way for southerners to extend the institution of slavery westward.

President Polk's plan was to attack on several fronts at the same time in hopes of winning a quick victory. In the summer of 1846 General Stephen W. Kearny marched from Fort Leavenworth to establish one front at Santa Fe, which he captured without firing a shot. Leaving part of his army behind, he then marched to California. There, in conjunction with American naval forces, he subdued scattered Mexican resistance. By January 1847 the United States controlled New Mexico and California.

General Taylor in the meantime had carried the war into Mexico. He crossed the Rio Grande and won a series of victories climaxing with the Battle of Buena Vista. Taylor's victory in this battle ended the war in northern Mexico.

The final offensive against Mexico was led by Major General Winfield Scott. Under

Scott, American forces landed near Veracruz and began a slow and difficult march toward the capital, Mexico City. On September 14, 1847, they successfully captured the city, ending Mexican resistance.

The Treaty of Guadalupe–Hidalgo

With their armies defeated and their capital occupied, Mexico's leaders had no choice but to agree to American terms. Under the Treaty of Guadalupe-Hidalgo (GWAH duh LOOP ay ih DAHL goh), the United States acquired California and the New Mexico territory. Mexico also recognized the Rio Grande as the border of Texas. In return for this territory, the United States paid Mexico $15 million and assumed responsibility for existing Mexican debts to United States citizens.

The treaty almost completed American expansion across the continent. In 1853 the United States paid Mexico $10 million for a strip of land south of the Gila River in Arizona and New Mexico. Known as the Gadsden Purchase, this land provided a route for a southern transcontinental railroad. With the Gadsden Purchase, the struggle to realize manifest destiny seemed to be over.

SECTION REVIEW

1. Identify: manifest destiny, James K. Polk, "Fifty-four Forty or Fight," John C. Frémont, Zachary Taylor, Stephen W. Kearny, Winfield Scott, Gadsden Purchase.

2. Describe the dispute over the southern border of Texas in 1844.

3. What action did President Polk take after the failure of the Slidell mission?

4. What were the terms of the Treaty of Guadalupe-Hidalgo?

5. **Critical Thinking** Why was Polk willing to make a boundary compromise with Britain but not with Mexico?

■ *This map shows the growth of the United States from sea to sea. State boundaries are shown, but in 1853 Missouri, Louisiana, Iowa, Texas, and California were the only states west of the Mississippi.*

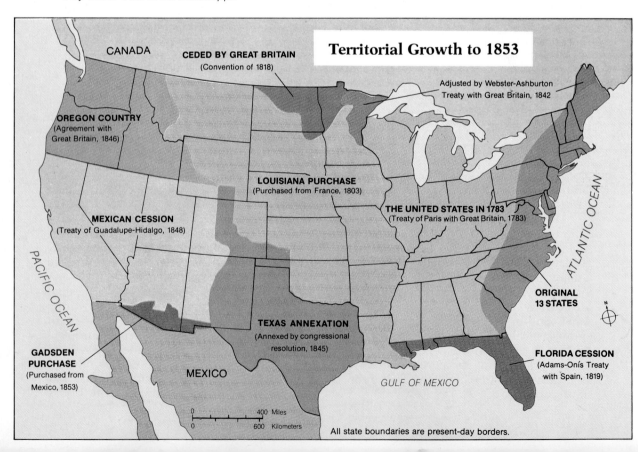

Territorial Growth to 1853

CANADA

CEDED BY GREAT BRITAIN
(Convention of 1818)

Adjusted by Webster-Ashburton
Treaty with Great Britain, 1842

OREGON COUNTRY
(Agreement with
Great Britain, 1846)

LOUISIANA PURCHASE
(Purchased from France, 1803)

MEXICAN CESSION
(Treaty of Guadalupe-Hidalgo, 1848)

THE UNITED STATES IN 1783
(Treaty of Paris with Great Britain, 1783)

PACIFIC OCEAN

ATLANTIC OCEAN

ORIGINAL
13 STATES

TEXAS ANNEXATION
(Annexed by congressional
resolution, 1845)

GADSDEN
PURCHASE
(Purchased from
Mexico, 1853)

MEXICO

FLORIDA CESSION
(Adams-Onís Treaty
with Spain, 1819)

GULF OF MEXICO

0   400 Miles
0   600 Kilometers

All state boundaries are present-day borders.

5 The Challenge of Greater Diversity

One of the central features of the United States since its founding has been the diversity of cultural groups living within a single nation. With the expansion of the nation to the Pacific, the United States acquired not only new territory but also hundreds of thousands of new residents to whom English culture and customs were foreign. These residents formed two major groups: Native Americans with a wide variety of cultures and Mexicans who shared a combined Spanish and Native American heritage.

Continuing Tensions

As you read earlier, the differences between Mexican and American cultures had created friction when Texas had been part of Mexico. This friction continued in the newly annexed areas. Many Americans, imbued with the spirit of manifest destiny, assumed that any inhabitants already living in an area would benefit from the government of the American republic.

Yet Mexicans, without moving an inch, suddenly found themselves living in a nation that was foreign to them, a nation that considered them "foreigners." Residents of New Mexico, for example, remained suspicious of American intentions. "The Americans say they have come for our good," one irate New Mexican declared. "Yes, for all our goods." Such resentment flared up in a rebellion at Taos, New Mexico, in 1847, which the United States Army subdued.

In California the wealthier Mexican landowners, desiring order and stability, generally welcomed United States rule. Other residents, however, shared the resentment of the New Mexicans and organized a rebellion of a thousand people. American forces defeated the rebels and offered generous terms of surrender, which were accepted.

The situation for Native Americans remained complex. The Mexican government had regarded the California Indians as Mexican citizens. When it surrendered territory to the United States, Mexico insisted on guarantees of the land rights of all Indians living there. The United States agreed to the guarantees in the Treaty of Guadalupe-Hidalgo. But there were no provisions to allow Native Americans full rights as United States citizens, and the nation's previous record of keeping promises to Indians had been poor.

A Sanctuary for the Mormons

While people with different cultures had to learn to live side by side in the new territories of California and New Mexico, a religious group from the East known as the Mormons developed another way of coping with diversity. They used the spaciousness of the land to evolve their own way of life in isolation.

In 1830 a farmer named Joseph Smith founded a new religion in Palmyra, a village in western New York. He based its teachings on a revelation that he claimed was given him through a set of golden tablets. Smith's followers assumed the name still used: The Church of Jesus Christ of the Latter Day Saints.

Joseph Smith was an energetic man who convinced many people to adopt his new religion. But some of the doctrines of the religion, such as the communal ownership of property, angered local residents. Such opposition forced Smith and his followers to move first to Ohio, then to Missouri, and finally to Illinois.

Everywhere the Mormons went, they met hostility. The situation worsened in 1843, when Smith officially revealed a teaching that permitted men to marry more than one woman. Tensions mounted near the Mormon settlement in Nauvoo, Illinois, until in 1844 a mob killed Smith and his brother.

Leadership of the Mormons fell to Brigham Young. A year after the murders, Young decided that his flock should move to the Great Salt Lake Basin, in present-day Utah, a sparsely populated area that was then still Mexican. Under Young's capable leadership, the final migration began in the summer of 1847. Wave after wave of faithful recruits followed, swelling the population of Utah. At last they seemed safe from interference.

In Utah they established a church-centered government that emphasized community and cooperation more than individual effort. Families were assigned land and not permitted to abandon it. They made the desert bloom with a remarkable system of irrigation. By moving to an isolated location, the Mormons were relatively free to develop a different life away from the conflicts of their earlier history.

Gold in California

The discovery of gold in the foothills of the Sierra Nevadas complicated life in California. The influx of large numbers of people increased tensions among the diverse cultures of the state. The result in the early days was frequently one of conflict. This "gold rush" was to be an early test of the nation's ability to accommodate different cultures and rapid change.

The first discovery of gold occurred at Sutter's Mill in January 1848. Soon gold fever gripped California, Oregon, and other western areas, and the rush was on. Sailors deserted their ships and flocked to the diggings. As many as two thirds of the able-bodied men in Oregon left for California.

Soon others joined the rush to California's gold fields. Beginning in 1849, men and women poured into California from all parts of the United States, as well as from Europe, Australia, South America, and China. About 80,000 people came to California that year, many by sea, more by overland trail.

The first miners to arrive found considerable deposits of gold. Moreover, they found them in places easy to mine, like dry gulches and former creek beds. In those early days some did, indeed, strike it rich, but few made large fortunes.

Deposits that could be dug up easily in dry gulches or shallow streams were soon picked clean. Then heavy machinery, which required a large capital investment and a large labor force, became necessary. Thus individual frontier prospectors gradually gave way to large mining companies. The miners became simply workers, toiling long hours for a wage.

Gold Rush Society

Society in early mining camps was unique. Towns sprang up overnight with names like Wildcat Bar, Skunk Gulch, Git-up-and-Git, and Ground Hog Glory. Without accepted social restraints, life went on at a hectic pace. Drinking and gambling abounded, along with racing, singing, and dancing.

Though the population of the mining camps consisted chiefly of young men, women were not absent. They came as workers and as shopkeepers. They laundered, cooked, entertained in saloons, ran boardinghouses, and sold food supplies. Those women who were merchants and landladies often prospered because of high California prices. Supplies were scarce, and demand was so great that shopkeepers in San Francisco could charge 50 to 75 cents for a loaf of bread that cost 5 cents in New York.

The miners governed themselves informally. They drew up codes, held their own trials, and carried out the punishments, including whipping, branding, and even ear cropping. Such crude justice was perhaps inevitable, since camps and towns grew so quickly. But it often had undesirable consequences. In a rough-and-tumble world where fortunes were at stake, it was easy for the majority of Yankees from the United States to overlook the rights of other immigrants as well as the rights of Californians of Mexican or Indian origin.

The "Conquered" Californians

Whatever the intentions of the United States government, the California miners ignored the rights of the Indians as spelled out in the Treaty of Guadalupe-Hidalgo. As far as the miners were concerned, the Native Americans were in the way and had to be removed.

The timeless lure of gold drew thousands of prospectors to California. The men in this early photo are using a sluice to separate out the gold.

The California Indians were generally peaceful and lived in small groups, often numbering only a few dozen people. Consequently they could offer little resistance. They were driven off their lands and many fell ill or starved to death. Individual Indians were casually murdered; whole villages were massacred. The California Indian population, which had numbered over 200,000 in 1848, plunged to roughly 17,000 by the 1870s.

English-speaking miners generally regarded the Mexicans in California as a conquered people and treated them as such. If a dispute arose over land rights, miners' courts customarily ruled against Mexican claims. To make the court rulings stick, vigilante groups drove Mexicans from the gold fields. When California became a state in 1850, its legislature passed a law taxing foreign miners; "foreigners" included Mexicans, no matter how long they had lived in California.

Chinese Arrive in California

Like many other immigrants, the Chinese arrived in California expecting to make their fortune and then return to their native land. The first Chinese immigrants, who came after 1847, were treated with respect. California needed laborers, and the Chinese were hardworking and honest. But as their numbers increased, they encountered bitter hostility.

English-speaking miners found Chinese customs foreign and unsettling. Because

Major Events	
1818	United States and Great Britain agree to joint occupation of Oregon
1821	Mexico declares independence from Spain; Stephen Austin founds American colony in Texas
1830	Joseph Smith founds Church of Jesus Christ of the Latter Day Saints
1836	Texas wins independence
1843	First Organic Law drawn up by Americans in Oregon
1845	Polk becomes President; Texas admitted as twenty-eighth state
1846	Oregon divided along 49th parallel; Bear Flag Revolt; Mexican War begins
1848	Treaty of Guadalupe-Hidalgo; gold discovered at Sutter's Mill
1853	Gadsden Purchase

their appearance and behavior seemed so different, the Chinese became easy targets of mockery and abuse. Perhaps more important, their economic success aroused some

 ★ American Profiles ★

Fatt Hing: A Chinese Pioneer

Fatt Hing was an aspiring 19-year-old who helped support his family as a fish peddler on the wharves of Kwanghai, China. When he first heard tales of the "mountains of gold" in California, he decided to seek such a fortune. Amidst a tearful farewell from his family, he was smuggled aboard a Spanish ship destined for San Francisco.

After a strenuous journey lasting three months, the California coast became visible on the horizon. Fatt Hing and hundreds of others watched anxiously as their ship approached the dock. Weary but happy, Fatt Hing was greeted by a group of fellow Chinese. These earlier Chinese pioneers had set up a company that served as an orientation center for more recent arrivals. Fatt Hing was assured of food, shelter, friendship, and work. If lucky, he was told, he would not have to remain in California long.

Fatt Hing was lucky. He quickly found a job in the mines, and he was permitted to keep half of the gold he mined. After two years Fatt Hing returned to his home in China. His family watched breathlessly as he opened the parcels of gold. In the short time that Fatt Hing had combed the hills of California, he earned enough money to marry and buy land for a farm. Fatt Hing eventually returned to California, and like many Chinese made it his home.

Based on material in B. L. Sung, *Mountain of Gold: The Chinese in America* (New York: Macmillan, 1967).

resentment. By patience and hard work, the Chinese were often able to make mining claims profitable after more wasteful miners had abandoned them.

Faced with prejudice and hostility, the Chinese relied on one another for aid and protection. They regulated their own affairs, often transferring traditional Chinese institutions to America. Frequently forced out of the mines, the Chinese often did the back-breaking work scorned by other groups. Their contributions to the developing California economy were vitally important. They farmed, irrigated, and reclaimed vast stretches of land, and, in the 1860s, built the western part of the first transcontinental railroad, as you will read later.

Black Americans in California

Before 1850 it was unclear whether slavery would be allowed in California once it became a state. Consequently many slaveholders brought slaves to California. Some slaves later earned their freedom by working in the gold fields. Free blacks also came to the gold fields to make their fortunes. They numbered 1,000 by 1850 and were soon the wealthiest black community in the country.

Black Americans faced prejudice and discrimination in California, as they did in many other parts of the West. One law, for example, denied free blacks the right to testify in trials involving whites, but black Californians organized against that law and won its repeal in 1863.

The rapid influx of people to California made it essential that the issue of statehood be settled quickly. By 1850, California had passed the peak of its gold rush, and Californians looked forward to becoming a state. Yet the diverse groups in California still needed to learn how to live together.

SECTION REVIEW

1. Identify: Joseph Smith, Brigham Young, Sutter's Mill.
2. What impact did the gold rush have on California Indians?
3. How did English-speaking miners react to the Chinese gold seekers?
4. What problems did black Americans face in California?
5. **Critical Thinking** Did the discovery of gold help or harm California? Explain.

★★★ Chapter 14 Review ★★★

In Perspective

Between 1825 and 1850, the United States expanded its territory from Texas and the Rocky Mountains to the Pacific Ocean. It negotiated with Great Britain for half of the Oregon country and conquered nearly half of Mexico.

In the process, the United States became a transcontinental nation and the strongest power in the Western Hemisphere. Its new domains were rugged and varied. They also contained valuable resources, as the California Gold Rush showed.

The new territories were also diverse in their people. In addition to the Indians and Mexicans already living there, the California Gold Rush attracted a variety of Americans and immigrants from around the world. Significant among these immigrants were the Chinese, the first large group of Asians to enter the United States.

Grand as the territorial gains were, they brought serious problems. After the Mexican War, Latin Americans viewed the United States with suspicion. It was unclear whether the diverse groups of people in the West could live together without open conflict. Furthermore, as you will read in Chapter 17, acquiring territory added to the bitter quarrel between North and South over whether slavery would be allowed in the new lands.

266

Vocabulary

On a separate sheet of paper, write the word or words that best complete each of the following sentences.

1. Mexican ranch owners, or ___, used Indians as laborers on their land.
2. The ___, or death rate, of the Indian workers was very high.
3. Enterprising fur traders in the Oregon country were known as ___.
4. An agreement reached by both houses of Congress that requires only a majority vote is a (an) ___.
5. ___ was the belief that the United States should extend to the Pacific.

Chapter Checkup

1. (a) How did the arrival of the Spanish affect Native Americans in California? (b) Did their lives change much after Mexican independence? Explain.
2. Describe the role each of the following played in the American settlement of Oregon: (a) mountain men; (b) fur-trading companies; (c) missionaries.
3. Why did tensions exist between Mexican and American settlers in Texas?
4. (a) What is the meaning of the phrase "manifest destiny"? (b) Was this attitude a new one among Americans? Explain.
5. (a) Why did Mormons decide to start a new life in Utah? (b) Were they successful? Explain.

Critical Thinking

1. **Analyzing** (a) What challenges did mountain men face that most people in the early 1800s did not? (b) What personal characteristics might have helped in that type of life?
2. **Comparing** (a) In what ways were the American Revolution and Texans' struggle for independence similar? (b) In what ways were they different?

Developing Basic Skills

1. **Map Reading** Study the map on page 254. (a) Why was the journey to Oregon and California difficult? (b) How might you explain the route of the Oregon Trail?
2. **Comparing** Make a chart with four columns. In the first column write: Louisiana, Florida, Texas, Oregon, Mexican Cession, Gadsden Purchase. In the second column write the date each territory was acquired. In the third column write the name of the country or countries from which it was acquired. In the fourth column describe how each territory was acquired. To complete this chart refer to earlier chapters in this book.

   Use your chart and the map on page 262: (a) Which method of acquiring territory was most common? (b) From which country did the United States acquire the most territory? (c) Would you agree or disagree with the statement: The greatest expansion of the borders of the United States took place between 1845 and 1848.

See page 829 for suggested readings.

Writer's Handbook

Determining Your Purpose

Before you decide on the exact topic of a research paper, you should consider your purpose for writing the paper. The most common purposes for a history research paper are to inform or to persuade your audience. Possible topics for a paper designed to inform are *The Effect of the Mission System on the Indians of California* or *The Events Leading to the Independence of Texas*. Possible topics for a paper designed to persuade are *Why the United States Had/Did Not Have the Best Claim to Oregon* or *Why the United States Was/Was Not Justified in Annexing Texas*. If you choose a controversial topic, it is important that you present the topic in a balanced and fair manner.

Practice: Based on the information in Chapter 14, write three possible topics for a research paper that informs and three possible topics for a paper that persuades.

The Different Worlds of North and South

15

(1820–1860)

Camden and Amboy Railroad With the Engine Planet in 1834 *by Edward Henry*

Chapter Outline

1 *The Growth of Industry in the North*

2 *Life in the Industrializing North*

3 *Economic Growth in the South*

4 *Life in the South*

5 *The Slaves' World*

By the middle of the 1800s, many people believed that the North and the South were two different worlds. The North seemed to be a world of factories, machines, and industrial workers, while the South seemed to be a world of large plantations, poor white farmers, and slaves. Such views reflected only the surface of life in the North and South, but they did represent important aspects of each region's economic development.

As you will read in this chapter, industry continued to expand in the North, and a railroad network emerged. Growing industry attracted large numbers of European immigrants. Industrialization also changed the southern economy. The invention of the cotton gin, in particular, greatly expanded cotton production. Although most white southerners did not own slaves or work on plantations, the "cotton kingdom" affected daily life in the South.

Rise of cotton kingdom					Growth of immigration			
1820	1825	1830	1835	1840	1845	1850	1855	1860

1825 Erie Canal opens

1831 Nat Turner's rebellion

1834 McCormick patents reaper

1839 Goodyear develops vulcanized rubber

1844 Morse perfects telegraph

1853 Perry opens trade with Japan

1 The Growth of Industry in the North

One of the most important developments that contributed to the growing differences between North and South was the Industrial Revolution. The first manufacturing firms had established themselves in the North, and new industries and factories continued to grow there. The North improved its transportation network by leading the way in railroad development and construction. Technological innovations also changed the shape of agriculture in the North, making commercial farming much more common.

The Spread of Industry

Early industries, such as textile manufacturing, continued to expand during the first half of the nineteenth century. In 1800 seven textile mills operated about 2,000 cotton spindles. By 1830 over 2 million spindles were operating, and by 1860 there were more than 5 million, most in New England.

The machinery for textile mills and other factories was made from iron, and the iron industry grew with the increased demand. In the 1820s iron foundries in Pittsburgh began using new techniques to refine the impurities out of iron. The switch from charcoal to anthracite coal for fuel after 1840 further improved the production of iron. The increased use of anthracite coal in turn stimulated the growth of mining operations in Pennsylvania and elsewhere.

Technology developed in other areas as well. In 1839 Charles Goodyear developed a method for vulcanizing rubber so it could withstand extremes of heat and cold. This allowed the manufacture of heavy-duty drive belts to help run machinery. In 1844 Samuel F. B. Morse perfected the telegraph. Messages that had taken days to deliver now took seconds, and the speed of American life and work increased to meet the change. Elias Howe's sewing machine, invented in 1846, made the mass production of clothing possible.

By 1860 over 74,000 manufacturing facilities employed almost one million people in the North. In contrast, in the South 20,000 factories employed only 110,000 workers. In 1859, for the first time, the value of the products of American industry exceeded the value of the products of American agriculture. Manufacturing would continue to grow most rapidly in the North, and it would affect the quality and style of life there.

Improved Transportation

As you read in Chapter 12, advances in transportation had encouraged the growth of trade and industry, especially the use of steamboats on western rivers and the construction of canals like the Erie Canal. Although the use of steamboats increased in the period before 1860, canal construction was slowed by the Panic of 1837. The depression forced many northern states to reduce their support for internal improvements, including canals. By that time also, railroads were becoming an alternative to water transportation.

The principles of railroad technology—the steam engine and carts drawn on rails—had been available since the beginning of the nineteenth century. Experiments using steam engines to tow cars on rails began soon after 1800 in both Great Britain and the United States. In 1820 a steam locomotive invented by John Stevens of New Jersey successfully pulled five cars over a short stretch of track.

Despite Stevens's work, government officials continued to favor canals because of the problems early railroads experienced. The first wood-burning locomotives belched great quantities of smoke and sparks into the air and onto the passengers. The first rails, which were made of wood covered with a strip of iron, frequently broke under heavy loads. Soft roadbeds and weak bridges added further hazards to railroad travel.

Still, promoters believed in the future of railroads. "The time will come," one boasted, "when people will travel in stages moved by steam engines . . . almost as fast as birds fly, fifteen or twenty miles an hour."

Gradually engineering skills caught up with this optimism. Engineers learned to construct sturdier bridges and solid roadbeds. They replaced the wooden rail with a T-shaped cast-iron rail. Such improvements made railroad travel safer, faster, and more efficient. Soon Americans looked as hopefully to the railroad as they had to the canal.

Expanding the Railroad Network

The first commercial railroads in the United States went into service in the 1830s. By 1840 the nation had 2,818 miles (4,509 kilometers) of railroad track. In the next decade, railroad construction rapidly expanded, so that by 1850 there were over 9,000 miles (14,400 kilometers) of track. The 1850s witnessed an even more startling increase to 30,626 miles (49,003 kilometers) by the end of 1860. In less than two decades, the railroads had gone from a novelty to a major means of transportation. (See the map below.)

At first railroads acted as *feeder lines* to the water transportation system. Trains hauled freight to a river or canal, where the load was transferred and transported by water to its final destination. Shipments by water still dominated the country's transportation network in 1850.

As railroads continued to expand, however, *trunk lines* developed. These were heavily traveled routes that linked major cities. Shorter side roads along the route served as feeder lines, just as smaller rail-

roads had fed into canals and rivers. Merging railroads into great trunk lines was difficult. Varying gauges, or widths, of track, different equipment, and rivalry between competing lines all slowed the process of consolidation. But once established, the trunk lines cut shipping costs and time. By 1860 the nation, particularly the North and the West, was crisscrossed by a series of major lines and affiliated branch lines.

The South made enormous strides in the 1850s toward building a railroad network. Richmond, Charleston, and New Orleans were linked to Memphis, and Atlanta was rapidly emerging as a railroad center. But despite this progress, the North had much more track and many more trunk lines than the South. New York and Chicago were major railroad centers, and all the major northern cities were linked by one or more trunk lines. Thus the railroad joined the Northwest with the Northeast, while the South tended to remain isolated.

The railroads encouraged the growth of industry in the North by making it possible to distribute goods cheaply and quickly from a central point of manufacturing. Raw materials could also be moved to factories more easily.

■ *A flurry of railroad building in the 1850s greatly expanded train service. According to this map, which cities were becoming major rail centers?*

America's Merchant Marine

Steam power came to dominate land transportation with the railroad and river transportation with the steamboat. Ultimately it would dominate ocean commerce as well, but not before Yankee ingenuity had enjoyed a triumphant "golden age" of sail.

You read earlier about American sailors and merchants traveling all over the world, buying hides in Spanish California, trading for furs with coastal Indians in Oregon, and sailing across the Pacific to Asia for tea, silk, and other luxuries. New England merchants had controlled shipping in the colonies, and the northern section of the United States continued to dominate foreign trade in the nineteenth century.

Trade with China grew in the 1840s and 1850s. When the British forced China to grant them special trading privileges in 1844, the United States was able to win the same guarantees. By 1860 Americans carried more than half the trade going to and from Shanghai.

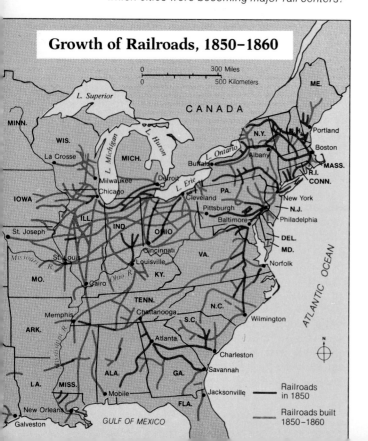

Growth of Railroads, 1850–1860

Railroads
in 1850

Railroads built
1850–1860

Japan was closed to American trade until Commodore Matthew Perry sailed to Japan with a fleet of United States warships in 1853. Here the commodore presents gifts (including a miniature train) to the Japanese government.

Japan remained closed to American merchants until 1853 when President Millard Fillmore sent Commodore Matthew Perry to Japan with a fleet of warships. Through a combination of vague threats of war and diplomatic skill, Perry secured commercial privileges for the United States in Japan.

In foreign trade speed was a considerable advantage. American merchants began designing sleek sailing vessels known as *clipper ships*. The ships were long and narrow, with tall masts towering almost 200 feet (60 meters) into the air and great canvas sails that strained to catch every gust of wind.

And race the clipper ships did! In 1851 Donald McKay, their most well-known designer, built the *Flying Cloud*, which sailed from New York to San Francisco in 89 days; another ship made the trip from Boston to Liverpool, England, in 12 days. With the advantage of speed, America's merchant marine prospered.

By the mid-1850s, however, steam power finally caught up with the clipper ships. On the heavily traveled routes to Europe, English steamships proved to be superior in both speed and cargo capacity. The construction of a railroad across Panama ended the need for long trips around South America for the California trade.

Impact on Northern Agriculture

You have already read that many of the railroads and canals linked the West and the East. Improved transportation made it more profitable for western farmers to ship their cash crops, such as wheat, to the East. In turn, farmers could afford to buy more manufactured goods, which stimulated eastern industry. Industrial innovations changed life for northern farmers in other ways as new inventions made farming more efficient.

A Virginia farmer, Cyrus McCormick, had worked for some time on a mechanical reaper to harvest wheat. In 1834 he finally solved the difficulties that made earlier versions impractical. The reaper was not an elegant-looking machine. When it was exhibited in England, the London *Times* ridiculed it as a "cross between an Astley chariot, a wheelbarrow, and a flying machine." Still, it worked. With a reaper, farmers could harvest many more acres of wheat with much less labor than before.

Another important invention was John Deere's steel plow, introduced in 1837. The deep root system of the midwestern prairie was almost impossible to plow with the traditional cast-iron plow. Deere's plow solved this problem and allowed farmers to put many more acres into production at less cost.

The impact of these inventions was not felt immediately. Farmers only gradually adopted new methods, and many could not afford expensive machinery. McCormick patented his reaper in 1834. Yet 13 years passed before he produced 100 machines for trial marketing. And it was not until the 1850s that the reaper came into general use.

The new machines offered northern farmers the opportunity to increase profits, but they needed money to buy the machines in the first place. As a result, subsistence farming gradually gave way to more specialized farming, by which farmers raised cash crops for sale in distant markets.

With continued improvements in transportation and farming equipment, northern agriculture developed a distinct character. Wheat production increased in the West, with its fabulously fertile black soil. Farmers in eastern states such as New York concentrated more on fruits and vegetables, which could be shipped swiftly to cities. By the end of the 1850s agriculture in the North differed from that in the South. As you will read later in this chapter, the South focused on subsistence farming or on cotton planting.

SECTION REVIEW

1. Identify: Charles Goodyear, Samuel F. B. Morse, Elias Howe, Matthew Perry, Donald McKay, Cyrus McCormick, John Deere.
2. Define: feeder lines, trunk lines, clipper ships.
3. How were early trains improved?
4. Which regions had the most developed railroad network by 1860?
5. What was the major activity of the merchant marine?
6. **Critical Thinking** How did the expansion of the United States affect its view of the importance of Asia?

2 Life in the Industrializing North

The coming of industry to the United States and its continuing development after 1820 changed not only the way the country organized its economy but also the way people lived and worked. This change was most visible in the North, which was turning out 90 percent of the country's manufactured goods by 1860. The expansion of industry brought increased demand for labor, and many of the workers came from Europe. By the 1840s immigration was as important a factor in the North's development as factories and industrial technology.

The New Factory as a Work Place

You read earlier how the factory system developed in the 1820s. (See page 209.) At first, factory work seemed to be an improvement over farm life. Farm work was toilsome and difficult, and the typical work day ran from dawn to sunset. This was especially true in New England, where the soil was thin and rocky and farms were unprofitable. There-fore women and children frequently worked in factories to help support their families.

Factory owners such as the Boston Associates had tried to provide good working conditions for their workers. However, the expense of programs like that at the Lowell Mills and increased competition from new factories eventually led manufacturers to try to cut costs by lowering wages.

Working conditions also worsened during the 1830s as the attitude toward workers changed. One factory manager remarked, "I regard my workpeople just as I regard my machinery. So long as they can do my work for what I choose to pay them, I keep them, getting out of them all I can."

When the reputation for bad working conditions spread around a New England town, mill owners had to try to recruit more workers from the countryside. This often meant describing an idyllic but false picture of factory life to farm women, promising "that the work is so very neat, and the wages such, that they can dress in silks and spend half their time in reading." "Now is this

In small towns and rural areas across the nation, one of the most welcome visitors was the traveling peddler. A peddler brought not only goods but also news and gossip. Many peddlers eventually established shops or warehouses as factories began turning out more and more products.

true?" fumed one angry woman. "Let those girls who have been thus grossly . . . deceived answer."

Artisans were also affected by the development of new industries. Shoemakers, for example, sewed their boots by hand, but now manufacturers could cut costs by stitching with the new sewing machines. Factory-made boots were cheaper, and shoemakers lost business, as did many other artisans. A hatmaker who could earn $12 a week in 1835 earned only $8 a week ten years later.

Worker Attempts to Organize

As early as the 1790s, workers in the United States had tried to organize to protect their rights. Their early efforts had limited success. The courts ruled that *strikes*, or work stoppages, were illegal because they were conspiracies to do economic harm to manufacturers and the public.

During the 1820s, however, as industry grew in the North, workers in major cities of the Northeast made further attempts to band together. Most of these workers were artisans who practiced skilled crafts, such as shoemaking, typography, carpentry, or cabinetmaking.

Workers' associations, or *unions*, as they began to be called, objected first and foremost to the long work hours. They proposed a ten-hour day, working from 6:00 A.M. to 6:00 P.M. with two hours off for meals. Workers called strikes in several cities to achieve their goal, but only in New York City were they successful. Elsewhere, employers either forced workers back to their jobs through court action or hired nonunion workers to take the places of the strikers.

Still the movement gradually expanded. Workers from different cities recognized the benefits of coordinating their efforts and in 1834 organized the National Trades Union. Other representatives of labor held a national convention in the same year. By this time about 300,000 workers belonged to some sort of labor organization, although most of them had not banded together on a national level.

Early Political Action

Workers also tried to improve their position through political action. Beginning in the late 1820s, they organized local *work-ingmen's parties*, which campaigned to improve the status of workers. Since most workers could not fulfill property requirements for voting, the parties demanded universal white manhood suffrage. To provide their children with better opportunities, they advocated free public education.

Workers had economic grievances too. In most states in the 1820s, a person could be thrown into jail for not paying a debt. Naturally such debtor laws worked primarily against the poor. In 1830 five sixths of the persons in the jails of northern states were debtors, most of them owing less than $20. Workingmen's parties campaigned to abolish all debtor imprisonment laws.

For all their efforts, the early unions and workingmen's parties were unable to gain the leverage they wished. The Panic of 1837, in particular, seriously weakened the early workers' movement. The depression threw thousands of people out of work. The jobs that remained were eagerly sought by workers desperate to make a living. Under such conditions employers easily found people willing to work for lower wages. The workingmen's parties disappeared and the unions were virtually destroyed.

Still, many of the political reforms succeeded even though the workingmen's parties did not. By the mid-1840s, virtually all states had abolished debtor imprisonment laws and provided for universal white male suffrage. Other reformers joined with labor to create or improve the state public school systems, as you will read in Chapter 16.

Workers also won an important legal victory in 1842 in *Commonwealth* v. *Hunt*. That case arose when a group of Boston bootmakers banded together to try to hire only union men. The employers took the workers to court, where union members were convicted of having formed a "criminal conspiracy" to injure their employers and the public. The Massachusetts supreme court overturned the conviction and for the first time ruled that labor organizations were not illegal. Yet the movement to organize workers grew slowly. In 1860 less than one percent of the nation's labor force was organized.

Other Workers

Only a small number of American workers, mostly skilled artisans, were involved in the early labor movement. Workers in the new factories, including women textile workers, generally did not participate. Attempts by these workers to organize were seldom successful. For example, in 1834, when the owners of the Lowell factories cut women's wages by 15 percent, a thousand women walked off the job. One of the leaders, reported a Boston newspaper, "mounted a stump, and made a flaming . . . speech on the rights of women," but the strike failed and the women returned to work.

Another group of laborers who remained outside the early labor movement were free blacks. Northern states had eliminated virtually all slavery by 1820,* but much prejudice remained against free blacks, and jobs were difficult to find. For example, Frederick Douglass, who had escaped from slavery in Maryland, was a skilled ship's caulker. Nevertheless he could not find work at his trade in the shipyards of New Bedford, Massachusetts. When he searched for a job there, he was told that if he was hired, he would drive white workers away. Turned away from his trade, Douglass supported himself by working as an unskilled laborer, a coachman, and a waiter.

Under such circumstances, free blacks were willing to work almost anywhere, often for very low wages. Consequently white workers feared that black laborers would undercut wages and take their jobs. In many cases blacks worked as strikebreakers and often had to fight striking white laborers to stay at work.

Though most black workers were unskilled, some became doctors, lawyers, ministers, and undertakers who served the needs of the black community. Frederick Douglass, in fact, complained that his son could more easily find work in a lawyer's office than in a blacksmith's shop.

An Increase in Immigration

One group of workers who helped make life in the North distinct from life in the South were European immigrants. There had al-

---

*All northern states had passed emancipation laws by 1804, but some of these laws called for gradual emancipation, so there were still slaves in the North after 1804.

ways been a steady flow of immigrants to the United States, but beginning in the mid-1840s the number increased dramatically. The South, with its system of slave labor, was generally unattractive to these immigrants, but the North, with its expanding economy and need for workers, seemed truly a land of opportunity.

Steamship companies, which could load their vessels with immigrants for the return voyage to the United States, and manufacturers, who were looking for cheap labor for their factories, actively promoted this image of America. This promotion was effective. Between 1845 and 1854 almost 3 million people from northwestern Europe migrated to the United States. However, the immigrants were not told about the competition for jobs and housing they would find in the United States.

Immigrants came for many reasons. In the British Isles, Scandinavia, and southwestern Germany, the enclosure system had converted peasant farms into pastures to raise wool for textile mills. Deprived of their homes, many peasants sought a better life in America. Miners left the coal pits of Wales for higher wages in the mines of Pennsylvania.

Roughly three fourths of the new immigrants came from Germany and Ireland. One cause of immigration from Germany was a revolution that swept the continent of Europe in 1848. Revolutionaries wanted to replace the European monarchies with demo-cratic governments, but they failed. Many German supporters of the revolution were forced to flee. They were attracted to the United States by the American traditions of freedom and republican government.

The main cause of the Irish exodus to America was a famine caused by a blight that wiped out the potato crop. For the two thirds of the Irish population affected by the famine between 1845 and 1850, the choice was stark: move or starve. Ireland was part of Great Britain, and support of the starving Irish peasants would have been a heavy public expense to the British government. So it was relieved at the massive exodus.

The Irish needed great courage to leave their homeland. Because of the famine, many began the trip in poor health and suffered greatly during the voyage. Hundreds died en route, and many arrived penniless in eastern cities. In fact, Boston became a major destination for the Irish precisely because the fare from Liverpool was cheaper than to any other American city. Although most Irish had been farm workers back home, few could buy land in America. Instead, they tended to take manual jobs, working on canals or railroads or in New England factories.

German farmers were often luckier. Many had been able to save money before they left Europe. When they arrived in the United States, they could move west and buy good farm land. German immigrants also

★ **American Profiles** ★

Carl Schurz: Crusader for Democracy

Carl Schurz was a German who immigrated to the United States in 1852. His life both in Germany and in the United States reveals him as a courageous crusader for democratic ideals.

While a student at the University of Bonn, Schurz emerged as a leader in Germany's student movement and as a champion of political democracy. During the Revolution of 1848, Schurz fought as an officer in the revolutionary army.

When this struggle met with defeat, Schurz sought political asylum in Switzerland. He might have remained there forever but for his loyalty to an old friend and university professor imprisoned in Germany. Risking his own life, Schurz reentered Germany and liberated his friend. From there he sought sanctuary in France but was soon expelled because of his political background. During a brief interlude in England, he met and married Margarethe Meyer.

Carl and Margarethe Schurz set sail for the United States in August 1852. He soon mastered the English language and became a noted speaker against slavery. Schurz embraced the American political system and served his new country well. He would take an active role in the Civil War and would be elected to the United States Senate in 1868. The passion that Carl Schurz brought to his life stands as a reminder of the deep feelings that drove many immigrants to the United States in their search for freedom.

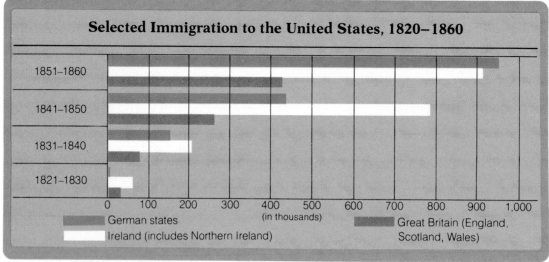

Selected Immigration to the United States, 1820–1860

- German states
- Ireland (includes Northern Ireland)
- Great Britain (England, Scotland, Wales)

(in thousands)

Source: *Historical Statistics of the United States*

■ *Immigration increased sharply after 1830. From what country did the greatest number of immigrants arrive between 1841 and 1860?*

included merchants, artisans, and intellectuals, many of whom settled in midwestern cities such as Cincinnati, St. Paul, St. Louis, Chicago, and Milwaukee.

Like the earliest settlers in the American colonies, most immigrants of the 1840s and 1850s arrived from Europe in search of freedom and a better life. They worked hard to achieve their goals, and most became United States citizens as soon as they legally could.

Negative Reaction to Immigrants

Some Americans viewed the large influx of immigrants with alarm. They began to campaign against what they considered to be harmful consequences of immigration. These people were known as *nativists* because they championed the virtues of native-born Americans and their way of life.

Much of the nativist dissatisfaction sprang from economic causes. Immigrants competed for jobs and, with the increase in the labor supply, wages declined. Furthermore, when native-born workers went on strike for higher pay, immigrants were often hired as strikebreakers.

Also important were social, religious, and political tensions between new immigrants and persons born in the United States. Nativists resented the immigrants' tendency to cluster together. Immigrants

settled in areas where other people from their homeland lived. In these ethnic neighborhoods they continued to value old customs. They worshiped in their own churches, formed their own social institutions, and continued to speak their native language. As a result, immigrants did not always *assimilate* quickly into American society. That is, they did not merge into society by adopting American cultural standards and values. They continued to seem "foreign" rather than "American."

Furthermore, most of the Irish immigrants and many of the Germans were Catholics. This aroused concern among some Americans because the United States had been a predominantly Protestant country since its founding.

Nativists also pointed with alarm to the high rate of poverty and crime among new immigrants, especially in eastern cities. They blamed these conditions on the nature of the immigrants without considering the difficult circumstances immigrants faced.

The new immigrants seemed to be a political threat to nativists. After five years, immigrants could become naturalized citizens and be eligible to vote. And they began to vote in significant numbers. By the 1850s, immigrants outnumbered people born in the United States in several cities, including New York, Chicago, Milwaukee, and St. Louis.

Immigrants were a sizable minority in many other cities, such as Philadelphia and Cincinnati. As both major political parties appealed increasingly to the new voters, nativists began to put forward their own political candidates.

The Know-Nothings

During the 1840s in many areas of the North, nativists organized secret societies. Members pledged to oppose foreign influence by voting for candidates who were sympathetic to nativist beliefs and by refusing to vote for an immigrant or a Catholic. In a few cities these secret societies enjoyed some success.

Nativism became a national movement in the mid-1850s with the emergence of the Know-Nothings, who were so named because they were sworn to answer inquiries about the order by saying, "I know nothing." The Know-Nothings began in 1845 as a secret organization called the Supreme Order of the Star-Spangled Banner. The order rapidly spread through the North and showed considerable strength in the South. It soon dropped its secrecy and became a political party.

Calling themselves the American party, the former Know-Nothings nominated Millard Fillmore for President in 1856. But the party lacked sectional balance. Nativism was most popular in the North, where most immigrants had settled. As you will read in

Chapter 17, the issue of slavery in the territories flared in the 1850s. The Know-Nothings in the North split over whether to take an antislavery stand, and the party rapidly lost support.

Nativism itself was soon overshadowed by the growing conflict between the North and the South. However, the underlying hostility toward immigrants, on which the Know-Nothings had built their strength, did not disappear. In future years it would surface again. Immigration and the tensions between immigrants and the native born had become a significant feature of northern society.

SECTION REVIEW

1. Identify: National Trades Union, *Commonwealth* v. *Hunt*.
2. Define: strike, union, workingmen's party, nativist, assimilate.
3. How did the growth of industry affect the earnings of artisans?
4. What types of workers tried to organize unions in the 1820s and 1830s?
5. List three goals of workingmen's parties.
6. What attracted immigrants to the North?
7. **Critical Thinking** Why did immigrants initially try to preserve their traditional way of life?

3 Economic Growth in the South

Although the impact of early industrialization was greatest in the North, it also affected the economy of the South. As you will read, some industries developed in southern cities, but for the most part new factories were located in the North. In the South the Industrial Revolution had the greatest impact on agriculture.

Changes in Southern Agriculture

Such improvements in transportation as the steamboat and the railroad affected the South as well as the North. Since the South had an extensive system of navigable rivers, the steamboat provided cheap, convenient

transportation. This enabled farmers in the interior to ship products to the coast. After 1850 railroads developed in the South, but, as you read, the railroad network grew more slowly in the South than in the North.

The most significant development for the southern economy was the invention of the cotton gin. Eli Whitney invented the cotton gin in 1793 while working as a tutor on a Georgia plantation. This machine, which separated cotton seeds from fibers, transformed cotton production.

Before the introduction of the cotton gin, workers had to separate the seeds from the fiber by hand. This was a slow process, often requiring one worker a whole day to separate one pound (about .45 kilogram) of cotton. For cotton production to be profitable, planters needed to grow a strain of cotton with long fibers that could be separated fairly easily from the seeds. This type of cotton would grow only on the Sea Islands, off the coast of Georgia and South Carolina.

Cotton grown inland was a short-fiber variety, called short-staple cotton, that was more difficult to separate by hand. Because it required more labor, it was less profitable. Consequently most cotton production had been confined to the coastal region. The cotton gin, however, made it much easier to separate the seeds from the fiber whether the fiber was long or short. With the improved cotton gins available in the early nineteenth century, a worker could separate up to 1,000 pounds (about 450 kilograms) of cotton a day. This development greatly ex-

panded the area where cotton could be grown profitably.

At the same time, the growth of the textile industry in the North and in Great Britain stimulated the demand for cotton. Southern farmers rushed to fill the demand by cultivating more land for cotton production.

Rise of the Cotton Kingdom

Gradually, the soil in the southern states along the Atlantic coast became depleted and farmers looked westward.* The large tracts of fertile unused lands in Alabama, Mississippi, and Louisiana appeared increasingly attractive. After the War of 1812, farmers flocked to those areas. By 1860 cotton production had expanded westward into Texas. Large portions of the South had become part of a cotton kingdom.

The map on page 279 shows the expansion of the cotton kingdom to the new states of the South. Since cotton required a growing season of at least 200 frost-free days a year, cotton growing was limited to the southernmost portion of the region.

The cotton boom had human dimensions too. Cotton was picked by hand, and the chance to make big profits depended on having a large labor force. As a result, slavery spread westward along with the cultivation of cotton.

By the 1840s cotton was a central part of the economy of the South. In the late 1790s, only about 10,000 bales of cotton were produced each year; in 1840 a million and a half bales were produced. That amounted to over 60 percent of all the cotton produced in the world and over 60 percent of the value of all American exports, from both North and South. Clearly cotton had become king.

Other Southern Crops

Because cotton could not be grown in the northern sections of the South, farmers there often depended on other cash crops. Tobacco had been exported since 1619, and it continued to be planted in Virginia, North Carolina, and Kentucky. However, the large plantations of colonial days gradually gave way to smaller tobacco farms.

■ *These two graphs show the relationship between cotton and slavery in the first half of the nineteenth century. As the production of cotton became more profitable, the demand for slaves increased.*

Cotton Production, 1800–1860
Slave Population, 1800–1860

Bales of Cotton (in thousands)

Years

Number of Slaves (in thousands)

Years

Source: *Historical Statistics of the United States*

---

*With land plentiful and cheap, Americans in both the North and the South had traditionally used land wastefully. Once minerals in the soil were depleted, a farmer could move on to new land.

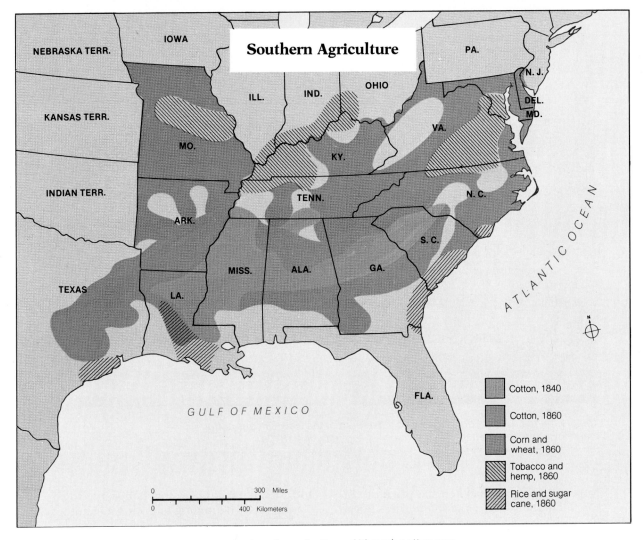

Southern Agriculture

Cotton, 1840

Cotton, 1860

Corn and wheat, 1860

Tobacco and hemp, 1860

Rice and sugar cane, 1860

■ The southern economy was predominantly agriculture. Although cotton was
"king," rice, tobacco, and sugar cane were also important.

While the typical tobacco farm in Virginia or North Carolina needed only two field hands to raise five and a half acres of tobacco, other southern crops required large plantations if they were to make a profit. The rice growers along the South Carolina and Georgia coasts and the sugar growers of Louisiana and Texas needed many workers to raise their crops. They also used expensive irrigation and drainage systems, and sugar growers needed machinery to grind the sugar cane. Since small farmers simply could not afford the costs, the plantation system dominated the sugar- and rice-growing areas.

In addition to the major cash crops of cotton, rice, and sugar, the South led the nation in livestock production, including hogs,

oxen, horses, mules, and beef cattle. Much of this livestock was raised in areas that were unsuitable for growing crops, such as the pine woods of North Carolina.

Early Industry in the South

As cotton became increasingly important to the economy of the South, many southerners began to realize how much they depended on the banks and factories of the North. Southern planters often borrowed money from northern banks to expand their plantations, and many of their farm tools and machines came from northern factories. Northern textile firms bought the cotton and wove it into cloth; northern shippers often hauled the raw cotton from the South to the

The great French artist Edgar Degas left this record of the New Orleans cotton market. Cotton was the nation's single largest export by the 1840s.

North or to Europe. When the price of cotton fell in the 1840s, some southerners began to establish factories in order to make the South more independent.

William Gregg of South Carolina led the movement to bring industry to the South. He built a successful textile mill in Graniteville, South Carolina, and operated it in the same benevolent manner that had characterized the early Lowell mills.

Gregg landscaped the grounds with shrubbery and flowers and set up cottages for working families, each with a large garden for the workers' children. He began the first compulsory school in the South and personally punished any boy or girl he caught playing hooky. In his more cheerful moments he held picnics for students. Wages for workers were low but compared favorably with wages in northern mills.

Manufacturers in Richmond, Virginia, made good use of the coal and iron ore in the area. The Tredegar Iron Works led production in the South, making railroad equipment, cannons for the United States Navy,

and steam machinery for Louisiana sugar plantations. The milling of flour was another leading form of southern manufacturing.

Yet by and large the South remained dependent on the North for industrial goods. Industrialization changed the South in the first half of the nineteenth century, but it did so chiefly by making cotton king.

SECTION REVIEW

1. Identify: Eli Whitney, William Gregg.
2. Which single invention had the biggest impact on the southern economy? Why?
3. What attracted many southern farmers to the land in Alabama, Mississippi, and Louisiana?
4. What factors help explain why rice and sugar were most often raised on plantations rather than small farms?
5. **Critical Thinking** How did the early success of cotton in the South hinder that region's economic development?

4 Life in the South

Although the southern economy revolved around farming, the daily lives of southerners varied. Few southerners lived in the grand style of wealthy planters. For most people, life meant hard work and simple joys.

Small Farmers

The great majority of white southerners, perhaps 75 percent, were small, independent farming families who owned their own land and possibly a few slaves. A description of a Virginia county in 1838 would apply to the whole South: "If we have very few rich men, we have, on the other hand, not many that are poor: the great mass is composed of the 'middle interest,' the bone and sinew of every country."

Such farmers could be found throughout the South but especially in the hilly regions of eastern Tennessee, northern Georgia, Alabama, and Mississippi and on the poorer soils of the coastal regions. Most were subsistence farmers who raised corn, oats, wheat, or sweet potatoes for food. They also sometimes planted an acre or two of cotton or tobacco to sell for cash.

In many ways these men and women were frontier people. Proud and hardworking, they lived simply. They learned to overcome their isolation by gathering together whenever they could, and they had a genius for turning work into play. Routine, time-consuming jobs, such as corn shucking, quilting, log rolling, and house raising became occasions for games and parties. For example, log rolling involved lifting logs off fields that were to be planted in the spring. A farmer's neighbors would gather from nearby farms and turn the job into a weight-lifting contest, followed by a cookout and a square dance.

Poor Whites

About 10 percent of the southern population consisted of "poor whites." They lived on land that for the most part could not support cash crops: backwoods, hills and mountains, sandy-soiled pine-barrens forests. Occasional travelers passing a backwoods cabin might well be deceived by seeing only a few acres of corn, a patch of sweet potatoes and other vegetables, perhaps a cow or two, three small horses, and a pack of hounds.

Yet this scene hid the family's greatest source of income: the herds of wild cattle or razorback hogs that fed off grass and forest land. Some poor whites were content to manage a small herd only large enough to sustain their families. Others tended several hundred head of cattle or hogs and drove them to market for a tidy profit.

Herdsmen usually considered it beneath them to farm. As a result, women not only had to do such household chores as weaving and making lye soap, but they also had to tend the vegetable patch and perhaps a small field of tobacco. Life in these areas was hardest for the women.

A monotonous diet and lack of medical care meant that the poorest of these people suffered from malnutrition. Furthermore, the hookworm parasite, which could be easily picked up in these areas, often sapped their energy.

Free Blacks

By 1860 about 260,000 free blacks lived in the South. Many of them were the descendants of slaves freed during the revolutionary era. Most free blacks lived in or around the cities and towns of the northern sections of the South, over one third residing in Maryland alone.

Most blacks worked as domestic servants or hired themselves out as agricultural laborers. Some were skilled workers, such as shoemakers and blacksmiths. They had a virtual monopoly on certain occupations, including barbering. A handful were merchants, hotel keepers, and planters who owned their own black slaves.

The life of a free black in the South was not easy. In the towns and cities, white workers and artisans resented them for competing for jobs, just as white laborers did in the North. Planters generally suspected free blacks of being potential leaders of slave insurrections. Moreover, the mere presence of blacks who were free and prospering struck many white southerners as a threat to the institution of slavery.

As a result of these fears, southern legislatures severely restricted the rights of free blacks. Though they had to pay taxes, as did other free persons, they could not vote, just as they were denied the ballot in most northern states.* Blacks normally could not testify in court, were sometimes required to have a white guardian, and were subject to curfew laws. Their rights of movement and assembly were severely curtailed, and they lived in constant danger of being illegally kidnaped and sold into slavery. Yet many of the harsh laws against free blacks were not enforced; and the status of free blacks in the South was in fact little worse than in the North.

The Planters

At the top of southern society were the planters, with their often elegant homes, gracious manners, and huge landholdings worked by slaves. Southern planters set the social style of the region, and they dominated its politics as well. Small farmers envied them, sometimes resented them for their power, but almost always hoped some

---

*After 1822 free blacks could vote only in Massachusetts, New Hampshire, and Vermont.

day to gain enough land and slaves to join them.

To be considered a planter, a farmer had to own at least 20 slaves, for then one could purchase a cotton gin and hire an overseer to supervise the slaves. Few achieved this goal. Out of 8 million southerners, fewer than 50,000 families owned more than 20 slaves, and only 10,000 owned more than 50 slaves.

Many planters tried to recreate the lifestyle of English country gentlemen. They built airy, spacious brick mansions faced with white columns, purchased elegant furniture and imported silver tea sets and other luxuries from Great Britain. They usually hired tutors to teach their children. The wealthiest planters also maintained town houses in cities like Charleston. Farther to the west in the newer farming regions, plantation life was much less refined, even among prosperous planters.

Planters had to work hard in order to succeed. A plantation was a large and difficult business. Planters had to make critical decisions about planting, harvesting, and marketing their crops. They had to be acquainted with the world market for cotton, sugar, or rice. A planter's wife often helped

Wealthy southern planters built elaborate country homes such as this one in Louisiana. The red building at right is the sugar refinery on the Olivier Plantation. The elegant clothing shown typified the lives on many plantation owners.

in the management of the business. She supervised the household servants, cared for the sick, both black and white, and supervised such domestic industries as weaving cloth, making soap, and sewing clothes.

Planters with large landholdings preferred to break them down into smaller plantations, since it was impractical for fields to be more than an hour's walk from the slave quarters. In such cases, the planters hired overseers to supervise the day-to-day operations of their individual plantations. Most of the overseers were ambitious small farmers and younger sons of planters who hoped to gain sufficient capital to enter the planter class themselves. Occasionally trusted slaves were made overseers, but this was the exception rather than the rule.

Though planters remained a minority among white southerners, they left an indelible stamp on the sectional character of the South. Their aggressive economic development of southern lands established cotton as king and commercial agriculture as a way of life.

SECTION REVIEW

1. How did most white southerners make a living?
2. (a) Where did most free blacks live in the South? (b) What work did they do?
3. How did planters differ from other farmers?
4. **Critical Thinking** What did a Virginian in 1838 mean when he called the middle class "the bone and sinew of every country"?

5 The Slaves' World

By 1860 slaves made up over one third of the population of the South. Slaves worked at many jobs and under a variety of conditions. Life on one plantation might differ greatly from life on a neighboring plantation. A slave who worked in the main house would have different experiences than one who worked in the cotton fields or the blacksmith shop. Yet slaves were united by the fact that they were another person's property. They could be bought and sold, and they were denied even the most basic human rights.

Work

The vast majority of slaves, both men and women, worked in the fields, cultivating, planting, and harvesting crops. Slaves also worked as servants in the plantation houses and as skilled artisans. The conditions under which they worked varied greatly. If slaves worked for a small landowner, they might be in close daily contact with their owner, working side by side, sharing the same tasks and often the same food. Most slaves, however, worked as field hands on large plantations.

On many rice and hemp plantations and on the Sea Island cotton plantations, slaves worked under the *task system*. Slaves had specific jobs or tasks to complete each day. If they completed their jobs before the end of the day, they had free time to devote to personal pursuits.

The *gang system*, used on tobacco, sugar, and short-staple-cotton plantations, was more common. Under this system slaves worked together as gangs in the field under the supervision of an overseer, sometimes aided by a black driver who helped maintain discipline. These slaves normally worked from sunrise to sunset, with a two-hour rest period in the middle of the day.

Slavery could be physically harsh and brutal or relatively mild, depending on the type of plantation and especially on the temperament of the owner. But regardless of their attitudes toward their slaves, most planters believed that slaves needed the threat of physical punishment to force them to work long hours for limited rewards.

Living Conditions

Large-scale planters typically grouped their slave quarters together not far from the main house. Southern farm magazines frequently advised planters to provide slaves with good housing. Some of the planters

This young mother and her baby are being auctioned from the steps of a Missouri courthouse. Members of a slave family could be sold to different owners. They could be sold "down the river" to a rice or sugar plantation, where working conditions were the worst of all.

holiday feast, the usual slave diet was "hog and hominy," pork and corn. Seafood, dairy products, and other meats were rare but fruits and vegetables were often provided in season.

Importance of Family Life

Nothing provided critics of slavery with a more compelling case than the breaking up of slave families. State governments in the South did not recognize the legality of slave marriages. Although some planters tried to maintain slave families, it was by no means uncommon for families to be broken up and individual members sold, often to planters hundreds of miles away.

Family life was of great importance to slaves. By providing badly needed emotional support, the family could help make life under slavery bearable. Slaves who were sold to new owners often ran away from their new plantations in an attempt to rejoin their kin.

On some plantations, slaves used their garden plots and free time to hold their families together. By growing their own vegetables or hunting their own food, slave families quietly but firmly asserted their competence. By providing for their children's needs without the planter's direction, slave parents showed themselves worthy of their children's respect.

Preserving Human Dignity

Equally important to the slaves' sense of dignity were religion, holiday celebrations, and the remnants of African culture they managed to preserve. For slaves, Christianity proved to be sometimes a comfort, sometimes a hindrance. On one hand, planters often supervised the slaves' religious life, making sure the sermons they heard emphasized meekness and obedience.

On the other hand, slaves used Christianity to hold their community together. While masters emphasized Christian teachings of obedience, slaves stressed the importance Jesus attached to marriage, the family, and people's obligations to one another. In addition, they developed an important body of music, the spirituals, which protested slavery as much as it provided comfort.

Christmas was an important time for slaves. It provided them with a rare good

responded by building decent brick or frame cabins for their slaves and by providing ample firewood for fuel. However, most planters ignored the advice of the farm journals. Typically, slave cabins had one room and dirt floors and were crudely built. An Alabama doctor concluded, "One of the most prolific sources of disease among negroes is the condition of their houses. . . . Small, low, tight, and filthy, their houses can be but laboratories of disease."

Clothing and food were hardly better. Slaves commonly received a regular allotment of clothing that was too scanty to carry them through the year, and cases of frostbitten feet were fairly common in the colder areas of the South. Despite an occasional

meal and important free time. They used this time to celebrate another year's endurance and to visit each other. The holiday thereby reinforced their sense of community.

Many slaves relied on traditions from their African homelands to shape their distinctive culture. Because slave importation had been prohibited in the United States after 1808, few slaves had direct ties or contacts with Africa. Yet some African customs were passed down by word of mouth from older slaves to their children and grandchildren.

Such oral traditions played an important part in slave life. For example, slaves often followed the West African custom of naming children after their grandparents. The tradition of extended families, by which parents, grandparents, aunts, uncles, and other relatives were considered part of the immediate family, also had roots in Africa.

Most important, the oral traditions kept alive the memory of an African past when their ancestors had been free. This historial sense held out the hope that it was possible to resist slavery and that someday slavery would end.

The Slaves' Reaction to Slavery

Trying to preserve human dignity through family life, religion, holidays, and cultural traditions was one way slaves learned to live in a society that denied them their most basic rights. But there were other reactions to slavery.

Many slaves adopted an outwardly cheerful and carefree manner, professing loyalty to their masters. For some, especially house servants, that loyalty may have been sincere, especially when a master treated them kindly. But many slaves used this carefree face as a mask to hide their resentment. By pretending to be happy they developed countless ways to exasperate their masters and escape punishment.

Some slaves became adept at a sort of day-to-day resistance to slavery: slowing down work, stealing extra food, breaking tools, destroying crops, and pretending sickness or disability. Slaves aptly called this type of resistance "puttin' on old Massa."

Escape was another, more extreme reaction to slavery. The chances of success were slim. Runaways were tracked with

Despite the fact that laws usually did not recognize slave marriages, family ties remained strong and deep among slaves. The family in this early photograph worked on a South Carolina plantation.

285

Two Views of Slavery: Analyzing Conflicting Sources

Primary sources provide important information about historical events and developments. But even two eyewitnesses can provide very different pictures of what happened. Two descriptions of slavery are presented below. The first was written by Sir Charles Lyell, a British traveler who visited a plantation in Georgia in the 1840s. The second was written by Solomon Northup, a free black who was kidnapped in New York and sold into slavery on a Louisiana plantation.

1. **Review the contents of each source.** (a) What does the writer say about the working conditions of slaves? (b) What does the writer say about the type of food given slaves? (c) What does the writer say about the use of whippings by slave owners?

2. **Compare the sources.** (a) On which aspects of slave life do the accounts seem to agree? (b) On which do they disagree?

3. **Evaluate the reliability of the sources.** (a) How might the aristocratic background of Sir Charles Lyell affect his attitude toward southern planters and toward slavery? (b) How might the fact that Solomon Northup was kidnapped and sold into slavery affect his description of slavery?

4. **Study the sources to draw conclusions about a historical event or development.** (a) Would you consider either account an accurate description of slavery? Why or why not? (b) What conclusions would you make about slavery based on the two accounts?

Sir Charles Lyell

The laborers begin work at six o'clock in the morning, have an hour's rest at nine for breakfast, and many have finished their assigned task by two. In summer they go to bed in the middle of the day, then rise to finish their task, and afterward spend a great part of the night in chatting, preaching, and psalm-singing. The laborers are allowed Indian meal, rice, and milk, and occasionally pork and soup. As their rations are more than they can eat, they either return part of it at the end of the week, or they keep it to feed their fowls, which they usually sell, for cash, to buy molasses and other luxuries. When disposed to exert themselves, they get through the day's task in five hours, and then amuse themselves in fishing. . . . The sight of the whip was painful to me as a mark of degradation, reminding me that the lower orders of slaves are kept to their work by bodily fear. That the whip is rarely used, and often held for weeks over them, merely in terror, is no doubt true on all well-governed estates.

Solomon Northup

An hour before day light the horn is blown. Then the slaves arouse, prepare their breakfast, fill a gourd with water, in another deposit their dinner of cold bacon and corn cake, and hurry to the field again. It is an offense invariably followed by a flogging to be found at the quarters after daybreak. Then the fears and labors of another day begin; and until its close there is no such thing as rest. With the exception of ten or fifteen minutes, which is given them at noon to swallow their allowance of cold bacon, they are not permitted to be a moment idle until it is too dark to see, and when the moon is full, they often times labor till the middle of the night. They do not dare to stop even at dinner time, nor return to the quarters, however late it be, until the order to halt is given by the driver. Finally, at a late hour, they reach the quarters, sleepy and overcome with the long day's toil. All that is allowed them is corn and bacon, which is given out Sunday morning. Each one receives, as his weekly allowance, three and a half pounds of bacon, and corn enough to make a peck of meal. That is all.

dogs, and slaves knew little about the countryside beyond their own plantation. Yet in the 1850s perhaps as many as 1,000 slaves tried to run away each year.

Sometimes slaves would run away as a temporary protest. They would hide in swamps or woods and often not return for months. This was one of the few means of active protest available to slaves in the deep South, where the great distances from the free states made successful flight all but impossible.

Slave Revolts

The slave's ultimate protest was violent revolt, something whites constantly feared. Rumors of slave conspiracies surfaced periodically, yet in reality few slaves revolted. This is hardly surprising, since the odds were overwhelmingly against the slaves. Slaves had few weapons and were under constant surveillance. The threat of discovery by whites or betrayal by slaves loyal to their masters was always present. As a result, only a handful of slaves ever participated in a revolt.

Nevertheless, there were several important slave revolts in the nineteenth century. The revolt of 1791 in Haiti, where Toussaint L'Ouverture successfully established a black republic (see page 193), served as an inspiration for many slaves, some of whom had come from Haiti.

In 1800 Gabriel Prosser was caught leading a conspiracy to make Virginia a black republic. In 1811 between 300 and 500 slaves marched on New Orleans in well-organized companies, but they were easily defeated by the militia. Denmark Vesey, a free black carpenter in Charleston, was plotting a major uprising when he and his associates were betrayed by a slave and arrested in 1822.

In 1831 Nat Turner, a slave preacher, led a full-scale revolt in Southhampton County, Virginia. Inspired by reading the Bible and by his vision of black and white angels fighting, he led a group of about 70 armed slaves in a bloody revolt. By the time the authorities had crushed the uprising, the rebels had killed over 60 whites. The state militia responded by killing scores of blacks, including many who had no part in the revolt. Turner himself was captured and executed.

The Defense of Slavery

The Turner revolt sent shock waves of fear throughout the South. As you will read in the next chapter, that anxiety, as well as the rise of abolitionist activity in the North, led many white southerners to change their attitudes toward slavery.

At the time of the Revolutionary War, many considered slavery a "necessary evil." They felt guilty about owning slaves and sometimes freed them in their wills. But following Nat Turner's rebellion in 1831, southern legislatures began to enact harsher slave codes that limited the actions of free blacks as well as slaves even further. The codes also made it more difficult for planters to free their slaves.

These attempts to strengthen the institution of slavery accompanied a growing conviction among many southerners that slavery was a positive good. They noted that the ancient civilizations of Greece and Rome had been based on slavery. Many slave

Major Events	
1793	Eli Whitney invents cotton gin
1825	Opening of Erie Canal
1831	Nat Turner's rebellion
1834	Cyrus McCormick patents the mechanical reaper; National Trades Union organized
1837	John Deere introduces steel plow
1839	Charles Goodyear develops method to vulcanize rubber
1844	Samuel Morse perfects telegraph; China grants United States special trading privileges
1845	Famine begins in Ireland
1846	Elias Howe invents sewing machine
1848	Revolutions in Europe
1853	Commodore Perry secures trading privileges for United States in Japan

owners pointed out that the Constitution protected a person's property. Furthermore, some argued, slavery was an economic necessity in the South, where planters depended on large labor forces. The defenders of slavery also insisted that slavery benefited the slaves.

Some writers defended slavery by comparing the lives of slaves with the lives of workers in northern factories. One of those writers was George Fitzhugh, a Virginia planter. He claimed that slaves received better treatment than northern workers because slave owners formed a genuine bond of affection with their slaves much like that between parents and children. A plantation, Fitzhugh asserted, was like a little community in which each person had certain responsibilities that contributed to the good of the entire community. Northern factory owners, on the other hand, felt no responsibility for workers who became sick, disabled, or aged.

While writers like Fitzhugh wrote perceptive critiques of northern society, they generally compared the luckiest of the slaves with the most unfortunate workers in the North. The supporters of slavery failed to recognize the cruel indignity of one person's being owned by another. That many slaves managed to retain their dignity and humanity in the face of such an institution is a tribute to their strength and perseverance.

SECTION REVIEW

1. Identify: "puttin' on Old Massa," Nat Turner.
2. Define: task system, gang system.
3. (a) Which plantations used the task system? (b) Which used the gang system?
4. What Christian teachings were most important to slaves?
5. What effect did Nat Turner's revolt have on southerners' attitudes toward slavery?
6. **Critical Thinking** How was the poorest northern worker better off than the best treated slave?

★★★ Chapter 15 Review ★★★

In Perspective

The early 1800s brought economic growth to both the North and the South. Industrial expansion was greatest in the North, as was the development of railroad systems. As industry spread in the 1830s, working conditions grew worse. Skilled workers tried to improve conditions by organizing unions and workingmen's parties but with limited success. The influx of European immigrants in the 1840s greatly expanded the labor supply in the North. This helped create antiimmigrant sentiment among some Americans.

In the South the invention of the cotton gin and increased demand for cotton caused a boom in cotton production. Large plantations were used in cotton growing and also for other crops, such as sugar and rice. While most southerners were small farmers, planters influenced much of southern life.

Most slaves lived on plantations, but their working and living conditions varied. Even under the best conditions, however, slaves were still the property of others. They often relied on family life, religion, holidays, and cultural traditions to retain a sense of human dignity.

As the economies of the North and South developed in different ways, sectional differences grew. Slavery and especially its spread westward became an increasingly divisive issue in the nation, as you will read in the next two chapters.

Vocabulary

On a separate sheet of paper, write the word or words that best complete each of the following sentences.

1. A ___ is a work stoppage.
2. The ___ is a means of organizing labor according to the job to be done.

3. ____ are persons opposed to unlimited immigration.

4. ____ are heavily traveled routes that link major cities.

5. Workers form ____ in order to bargain for better conditions.

Chapter Checkup

1. (a) How were early problems in the development of the railroads overcome? (b) What impact did the railroads have on the economy of the North?

2. (a) How did factory work change during the 1830s? (b) How did workers try to improve conditions?

3. (a) How did the invention of the cotton gin affect the nature of cotton growing in the South? (b) What impact did expanding textile mills in the North and Great Britain have? (c) What impact did the rise of the cotton kingdom have on slavery?

4. (a) How did the life of small farmers in the South differ from that of poor whites? (b) How did the life of planters differ from that of other southern farmers?

5. Explain how each of the following affected the conditions under which slaves worked: (a) the size of a plantation; (b) the crop grown; (c) the temperament of the slave owner.

Critical Thinking

1. **Analyzing** (a) Why do you think most railroads in the early 1800s ran east and west rather than north and south? (b) What effect do you think this had on the settlement of the West?

2. **Comparing** (a) What problems did free blacks face in the North? (b) What problems did they face in the South? (c) In what way were the problems similar? (d) In what way were they different?

Developing Basic Skills

1. **Map Reading** Study the map on page 279 and answer the following questions: (a) What information is shown on this map? (b) In what areas was cotton growing most prevalent in 1840? (c) In what part of the South was cotton not grown? How might you explain that?

2. **Researching** Find out more about the life of one of the inventors you read about in this chapter. Study the person's personal background and the circumstances surrounding his invention. Did his inventions bring him success?

See page 829 for suggested readings.

Writer's Handbook

Considering Areas for Research

A major part of your success in writing a research paper will depend on your ability to find the information you need. Often, you will be able to find information on a topic listed under more than one subject. For example, suppose that you are writing a research paper about the effect of the cotton gin on southern agriculture. After you have exhausted sources listed under the topic *cotton gin,* you should consider the period of time you are studying, the geographic location, and other related subjects. You might research the history of agriculture in the South, United States history in the early nineteenth century, Eli Whitney, inventions, technological history, slave labor, or the eco-nomic history of the United States.

If you cannot think of any related topics, look in an encyclopedia for an article on your topic. Often, an article in an encyclopedia will provide a bibliography as well as a list of other entries in the encyclopedia on related subjects.

Practice: List two other possible areas of research for each of the following topics. *The Expansion of Industry in the Early Nineteenth Century; Early Railroads in the East; The Contributions of the Clipper Ships; The Labor Movement in the Early 1800s; The Reaction of Americans to Immigrants, 1840–1860; Southern Society Before the Civil War; Slave Revolts.*

American Ingenuity

In the 1830s, John Deere's neighbors in Illinois knew him as blacksmith with an inventive mind. If they had a practical problem, they took it to Deere. One recurring problem they had was how to plow the soil. The Illinois prairie was covered with thick grass that broke the cast iron blade of the farmers' plows.

Deere knew that hardened steel would do the job, so he reshaped the blade of an old steel saw and attached it to a plow. Hitching his plow to a team of horses, Deere cut twelve smooth, straight furrows. Not once did he have to stop to clean the plow blade!

Word of Deere's success spread quickly. Soon he was selling so many steel plows that his backyard business grew into a major industry. Deere's ingenuity made him rich.

Isaac Singer is seen at a demonstration of his sewing machine.

Inventive Americans   Simple ingenuity—the knack for figuring things out—seems to have been part of the American character from the start. Long before Deere built a plow to cut prairie sod, Thomas Jefferson had adapted the English plow to the soil of Virginia. By 1855, the Patent Office in Washington, D.C., had issued 372 patents just for improvements to the plow!

Why were Americans so adept at inventing and improving? For one thing, there was so much to *do* in the New World. In Europe, houses, churches, and streets had existed for hundreds of years. But Americans had to build everything from scratch. And while the new nation was rich in natural resources, it was always short of labor. This prompted Americans to look for ways to get a job done as quickly and easily as possible.

When Alexis de Tocqueville visited America in the 1830s, he commented on how well Americans understood "the purely practical."

Tocqueville noted that Americans saved their highest praise for practical inventions. "Every new method that leads to a shorter road to wealth, every machine that spares labor . . . seems the grandest effort of the human intellect."

Age of Invention   By the mid-1800s, Americans were astonishing the world by producing one invention after another. In the 1840s alone, Yankee ingenuity created the telegraph, the sewing machine, vulcanized rubber, and an improved printing press. This flood of inventions did not come from research laboratories or great universities. Instead, most were invented by ordinary people who improved the tools and machines they worked with ten hours a day, six days a week. For every well-known inventor like John Deere, there were thousands like Walter Hunt whom few people remember. Yet anyone who has used a safety pin owes Hunt thanks for his 1849 invention.

According to Thomas Edison, genius was "1 percent inspiration and 99 percent perspiration." Edison's favorite invention was the phonograph.

Walter Hunt may not be famous, but at least he profited from his invention. Not all inventors were so lucky. Before the Civil War, many slaves were craft-workers—ironworkers, wheelwrights, and so on. Laws in many southern states kept slaves from getting credit for inventions. After the Civil War, black inventors at last had the protection of the law. In 1872, Elijah McCoy created a special cup that oiled engines automatically. The saying "the real McCoy" may have come from customers who would buy only McCoy's invention, not a copy.

The industrial boom after the Civil War nearly doubled the rate of patents being issued. At the same time, Americans began to approach technology in a more systematic way. In 1861, the Massachusetts Institute of Technology began to train students in engineering and other practical sciences. The Morrill Land Grant Act of 1862 helped states create new universities that specialized in improving agriculture.

As industry became more scientific, businesses began to take research and development seriously. Thomas Edison was a pioneer in the area, building his "invention factory" in Menlo Park, New Jersey, in 1876. When other industrialists saw useful and profitable inventions pouring forth from Menlo Park, they followed suit.

A Practical Philosophy In the late 1800s, an American philosopher, William James, pioneered a new philosophy based on practicality. He called his philosophy pragmatism. To James, most philosophers had wasted their time debating whether abstract ideas were true or false. James believed that an idea had to be judged on the basis of its practical results—the truth of an idea could be tested by experience.

Pragmatism had a wide influence. In the 1890s, John Dewey set out to reform public schools, which he felt were teaching abstract ideas that had little to do with real life. Dewey told a story to prove his point. "When I was visiting in the city of Moline [Illinois] a few years ago, the superintendent told me that they found many children every year, who were surprised to learn that the Mississippi River in the textbook had anything to do with the stream of water flowing past their homes."

Dewey believed students should learn by doing. While studying colonial America, for example, students at Dewey's "laboratory school" in Chicago cleaned cotton, spun wool, and built a weaving loom. "You can concentrate the history of all mankind into the evolution of the flax, cotton, and wool fibers into clothing," Dewey said. Dewey's ideas had a lasting impact on American education.

Today, much research is carried on in gleaming laboratories at universities or corporate research and development departments. Yet the individual inventor is not obsolete. Not long ago, a computer "hacker" named Steven Jobs along with two or three other computer experts built a small electronic machine in a garage. A few years later the world knew that machine as the Apple II, the personal computer used in millions of homes, schools, and businesses.

Is it possible that Americans are too practical for their own good? Tocqueville worried, 150 years ago, that Americans were so practical they would ignore important issues. But a blend of the practical and the ideal holds promise for society today.

1. How did the American approach to technology become more systematic after the Civil War?
2. How do the ideas of William James and John Dewey reflect American practicality?

American Profiles ## Cyrus McCormick

Cyrus Hall McCormick was a leader among the gifted industrialists of his era. He developed a machine that revolutionized farming in the 1800s. He also introduced to American industry practices such as buying on credit that have remained important to this day.

Cyrus McCormick was born in 1809 on a farm in Virginia's Shenandoah Valley. Cyrus's father, John McCormick, was a part-time inventor, who had developed a new type of mill to grind wheat. But his efforts to build an efficient, horse-drawn reaper had failed. John McCormick encouraged his son to take up the project.

Cyrus worked on a mechanical reaper enthusiastically. In 1831, he and his father tested the new machine successfully in a Virginia wheatfield. For a fee of $30, Cyrus patented the McCormick reaper and set out to make his fortune manufacturing it for local farmers.

Although his invention was a great advance, Cyrus McCormick sold only a few reapers in Virginia, where there was still a slave economy. Deeply in debt, he decided to go west in the 1830s. Labor was scarce on the vast prairies of Illinois and beyond, and the gently rolling terrain was ideally suited to the mechanical reaper.

McCormick needed to build a factory near his potential customers. At the time, Chicago was little more than a way station on Lake Michigan. But McCormick saw that the town lay between the opening West and the commercial East. With a $25,000 loan from the mayor of Chicago, he set up his factory. Rail lines fanning out from Chicago carried McCormick's reapers to farmers, and wheat poured back to Chicago to be shipped east. Both Chicago and Cyrus McCormick prospered.

As an inventor, McCormick was clearly a practical man. He stayed ahead of the competition by constantly improving his reaper. As an entrepreneur, however, McCormick was brilliant. For example, he let cash-poor farmers buy his reaper by putting a little money down and paying the rest in installments. If times were hard, McCormick let customers stretch out their

With $60 in his pocket, Cyrus McCormick (1809–1884) arrived in Chicago to start manufacturing his reaper. Two years later he was a millionaire.

payments. At the time, most companies insisted on payment in full.

Unlike other manufacturers, McCormick also gave a written guarantee with his product. He refunded the money of dissatisfied customers. But McCormick showed that integrity was indeed practical. By 1880, the McCormick reaper works in Chicago was shipping 50,000 reapers a year to farmers all over the world.

When McCormick died in 1884, he was a rich man. Unlike many wealthy industrialists of the Gilded Age, however, McCormick was mourned by farmers and working people. They admired him for his business ethics as well as his success.

---

1. How did McCormick's marketing techniques differ from those of his competitors?
2. How did McCormick show that "integrity was indeed practical"?

Voices of Freedom

Celebration of the Railroad

In 1847, the famous Whig Senator Daniel Webster spoke at a celebration marking the completion of the Northern Railroad in his native New Hampshire. Webster described the changes that had transformed rural New Hampshire.

In my youth and early manhood, I crossed these mountains along all the roads or passes which lead through or over them. . . . At that day, one [had to] traverse this wilderness on horseback or on foot. . . .

It was difficult to persuade men that it was possible to have a passable carriage road over these mountains. . . . As far as I now remember, my first speech after I left college was in favor of what was then regarded as a great and almost impractical internal improvement, to wit, the making of a smooth, though hilly, road from [the] Connecticut River to the Merrimack River.

But a vastly greater [achievement] was now approaching, the era of steam. This is the invention which distinguishes this age. The application of steam to the moving of heavy bodies, on the water and on the land, towers above all other inventions of this or the preceding age. . . .

Fellow citizens, can we without wonder consider where we are and what has brought us here? Several of this company left Boston and Salem this morning. . . .

They have treaded all the valleys and gorges, and here they now are, at 2 o'clock at the foot of the Cardigan Hills. . . . By the way, if they had thought fit they might have brought us a few fish taken out of the sea at sunrise this morning, and we might here enjoy a fish dinner.

Fellow citizens, this railroad may be said to bring the sea to your doors. You cannot, indeed, snuff its salt water, but you will taste its best products, as fresh as those who live on its shores. . . . I cannot conceive of any policy more useful to the great mass of the community than the policy which establishes these public improvements. Let me say that in the history of human inventions there is hardly one so well calculated as that of railroads to equalize the conditions of men. The richest must travel in the cars, for there they travel fastest. The poorest can travel in the cars, while they could not travel otherwise, because this mode of conveyance costs but little time or money.

Adapted from *The Works of Daniel Webster*, 16th edition, Boston, 1872, Vol. II. Reprinted in *Annals of America.*

---

1. What did Webster consider the greatest achievement of the age?
2. According to Webster, how did this development encourage the growth of democracy?

16

A Land of Idealism

(1820–1860)

The Country School *by Winslow Homer*

Chapter Outline

1 *The Reforming Impulse*

2 *Social Reform*

3 *A Campaign for Women's Rights*

4 *The Battle Against Slavery*

5 *Flowering of an American Culture*

In 1840 the American writer and philosopher Ralph Waldo Emerson rode to Boston to satisfy his curiosity about a meeting of people who called themselves the Friends of Universal Reform. He found many different groups—some with strange names and a variety of goals.

"If the assembly was disorderly, it was picturesque," remarked Emerson. "Madmen, madwomen, men with beards, Dunkers, Muggletonians, Come-outers, Groaners, Agrarians, Quakers, Abolitionists, Calvinists, Unitarians, and Philosophers—all came and seized their moment, if not their hour, to chide, or pray, or preach, or protest."

During the mid-1800s the United States seemed to be filled with reformers ready to change the world. Women's rights, the abolition of slavery, better education for all Americans, humane treatment of the mentally ill—all these problems and more the reformers set out to conquer.

Growth of public education

1820	1825	1830	1835	1840	1845	1850	1855	1860

1821 Troy Female Seminary founded

1831 *Liberator* founded; Nat Turner's revolt

1839 Liberty Party founded

1848 Seneca Falls Convention

1856 Wilberforce College founded

1 The Reforming Impulse

Although agitation for reform was especially strong in the period between the War of 1812 and the Civil War, the idea of remaking society for the better had strong roots in the political and religious heritage of the nation.

Political Ideals

The United States began its history with a revolution, one that freed Americans from British rule and proclaimed that all men were created equal. The Constitution of the new country, especially the Bill of Rights, established that an individual had certain rights under the law that could not be violated.

Reformers believed that those principles of individual liberty and equality had not been fully carried out. If all people were created equal, why did slavery continue to exist? And why did women have fewer rights than men? Reformers who were concerned with applying the principles of individual liberty and equality saw many areas in which to work.

Some reformers worked for the improvement of the public school system. How could a republic function properly, they argued, if its citizens were not well educated? How might prisons rehabilitate inmates so they would return to society as productive members of their community? What sort of treatment did the mentally ill deserve? Reformers believed they were moving the country closer to its ideals.

Religious Influence

When settlers first arrived in Massachusetts Bay during the 1630s, John Winthrop reminded them that they would be "as a city upon a hill" with the "eyes of all people . . . upon us." He encouraged the new colony to conduct itself as a shining example to the rest of the world. It had a mission to demonstrate how a "godly community" ought to live.

This religious vision of America persisted over the years. It inspired many of the Revolutionary War generation to believe that the young republic would be an example to the world, not just in politics but also in religion.

In the nineteenth century the religious community continued to grow just as the nation did. Many different denominations, such as the Congregationalists, Presbyterians, Baptists, and Methodists, founded churches in the new settlements and spread their own religious beliefs. All shared the dream that one day the United States would be a Christian commonwealth, where sin was unknown and virtue reigned. Combined with the political ideals of equality, liberty, and democracy, this religious conviction spurred many reformers.

Reforming Personal Lives

Some reformers tried to improve American life by convincing individuals to lead holy and upright lives. By changing personal habits, religious leaders hoped to improve the nation as a whole. Frequently they tried to achieve this goal by holding *revivals*, so called because these meetings attempted to revive a religious spirit in people who were not taking their religion seriously. Revivals had been held in America as early as the 1740s, but it was in the nineteenth century that they became more frequent.

Revivals often took place in the countryside. Several thousand people would come from miles around to a clearing in the woods, set up tents, and listen to preachers for several days.

At a large "camp meeting," six or seven ministers might preach at the same time to different crowds of people. "The noise was like the roar of Niagara," recalled one preacher. "The vast sea of human beings seemed to be agitated as if by a storm. . . . Some of the people were singing, others praying, some crying for mercy. . . ." On the frontier, where churches had not yet been established, revivals proved to be an effective method of spreading religion and exhorting people to reform their lives.

The effort to reform personal lives took many forms. For example, different Protestant denominations put aside their differences and formed organizations to promote Christianity. The American Bible Society made Bibles available at very low cost. Other societies published inexpensive religious pamphlets designed to reform personal morals. In 1836 alone, one such society sold over 3 million copies of their publications.

The Temperance Movement

One of the most widespread movements to improve individual lives was the campaign against alcoholic beverages, which came to be known as the *temperance movement.* For many Americans during the early nineteenth century, no social event—from dances and house raisings to weddings and funerals—was complete without a large amount of alcohol.

At first reformers in the temperance movement urged only that Americans reduce the amount of liquor they consumed. But beginning in the late 1820s, more and more reformers advocated total *abstinence,* refraining from all alcohol. They convinced some state legislatures to impose taxes on liquor and to allow local communities to prohibit the sale of alcoholic beverages.

The movement eventually led, in the early 1850s, to the passage of *Maine laws,* so named because Maine was the first state to enact one. These laws prohibited the sale of all alcoholic beverages. Many people opposed such drastic measures, however, so most states that adopted such laws soon repealed them.

Whatever the results, many reformers continued their efforts to improve personal morals. And their efforts soon extended to the area of social reform, where they tried to change not only personal behavior but also social institutions.

SECTION REVIEW

1. Identify: Maine laws.
2. Define: revivals, temperance movement, abstinence.
3. What did reformers believe about individual liberties and equality?
4. What was the purpose of revivals?
5. How did some state legislatures respond to the temperance movement?
6. **Critical Thinking** How can people's religious beliefs affect the type of society they strive for?

2 Social Reform

Reformers gradually came to believe that they needed to do more than change personal behavior. Even if citizens were virtuous and upright, reformers argued, the public could not vote intelligently if there were few schools to provide them with a proper education. Prisoners could not be expected to reform themselves if they were treated viciously and kept in filthy, cramped surroundings. Reformers decided that some of the institutions of American society also needed reforming.

Educating the Young

Colonial Americans, especially in New England, had placed great emphasis on educating the young. Those influenced by Puritan beliefs thought a person should be able at least to read the Bible. Therefore, New England colonial legislatures required each town to maintain a public school, with all families but the poorest paying fees to support it. Although similar laws still existed in the nineteenth century, public support for town schools had decreased. Buildings had fallen into disrepair, and teachers were not as well trained.

In other areas of the country the situation was worse. Free education did exist in the Middle Atlantic states but only for those who declared themselves paupers. Geography contributed to educational problems in the South. Because of isolated farms and poor roads, the community effort needed to support public schools was slow to materialize. Large plantation owners, who had the influence to make changes, had little interest in public education because they generally hired tutors for their children.

In the West residents of new communities faced a variety of problems that slowed the establishment of schools. Even when towns set up schoolhouses, they were often crude, desolate buildings, poorly ventilated, and inadequately heated. They were frequently located on the most worthless site in the town. "For the sheepfold and cow-house, sheltered situations are carefully selected," complained one reformer, "but a bleak hill-top, swept by the winter blast, or a sandy plain, scorched by a dogday sun, will do for a school." Inside, schools were equally unappealing, with a few rough benches and desks, bare walls, no blackboards, and few windows.

The quality of teachers around the country varied, but almost all were poorly paid and had received little education themselves. Even good teachers faced difficult conditions. Sometimes as many as 80 children of all ages crowded into a gloomy room. Some students were learning to read, some were studying arithmetic, others geography—all at the same time. Students who got too rowdy received a crack on the knuckles from the teacher's rod, or worse.

Beginnings of Educational Reform

The lack of good public education concerned many reformers, chief among them, Horace Mann. Mann gave up a promising career as a lawyer to become Massachusetts' first superintendent of education in 1837. For 12 years he pleaded, argued, lectured, and goaded the state government into improving the schools. Every year he issued an annual report demanding better school buildings, better textbooks, and less physical punishment of students.

A dedicated reformer, Mann was enthusiastic about his work. He even devoted his vacations to work as he toured the country visiting schools. But Mann believed that the effort was worth the price. In his opinion a democratic republic needed well-educated citizens. "If we do not prepare children to become good citizens," he declared, "then our republic must go down to destruction, as others have gone before it."

During Mann's term as superintendent, education made important strides in Massachusetts. State appropriations for education doubled, teachers' salaries increased, and the school year was lengthened by one month. The state also established three schools to train teachers.

Public Education

In other states, reformers followed Mann's lead as they struggled to establish free public education for all students. This movement met with strong opposition, however. For

one thing, all taxpayers would have to contribute to state-supported schools. Some taxpayers asked, "Why should we have to pay school taxes even if we have no children?" Parents who sent their children to private schools, a common practice, wondered why they should have to pay both tuition at a private school and taxes to support a public one.

Some parents also objected to the fact that reformers wanted education to be *compulsory*, that is, all children would have to attend until a certain age. They argued that this deprived parents of control of their own children. Furthermore, farm families as well as many factory workers depended on their children's labor to help support the family. If the government required children to attend school, they would not be able to work.

In spite of such opposition, most northern states followed the lead of Massachusetts and established free public elementary schools by the 1850s. In the South public education grew slowly although some people worked to improve conditions there.

Fewer high schools existed, partly because young people usually began work at an early age. Again Massachusetts led the way. By 1860 there were nearly 100 public high schools in that state, compared to about 200 in the rest of the nation. Private high schools continued to provide education for many young people.

Even with these achievements, much remained to be done. For example, although the Constitution guaranteed the separation of church and state, many public school teachers openly promoted Protestant Christianity, and schools often used textbooks written with an anti-Catholic bias. As a result, many Catholics hoped to establish their own parochial schools in which the education would include instruction in the Catholic faith as well as other subjects.

Black children found even less opportunity for public education. Most towns simply ignored the educational needs of black Americans or emphatically barred black students from the public schools. Where public schools existed for blacks, as in New York City and Boston, they remained segregated and were less well financed than schools for whites.

Women who wanted to continue their education beyond the basics of reading and writing met with little success at the beginning of the nineteenth century. "We don't pretend to teach the female part of the town anything more than dancing, or a little music perhaps," commented one New Hampshire resident.

Higher Education

Private colleges dominated the field of higher education. At first they offered few courses, but as the desire for wider and better education grew, the colleges responded by broadening their curriculums. Instead of studying only the classics, college students of the 1820s and 1830s learned about literature, history, political science, economics, and, increasingly, science. The number of colleges also grew as many religious denominations established their own schools and as more states supported colleges. By 1860, 16 states financed some type of higher education.

Colleges, like most elementary and high schools, were primarily for white males. A few private colleges, such as Oberlin, Harvard, and Dartmouth, did admit a small number of black students, and three colleges especially for black students were founded. For example, in 1856 the African Methodist Episcopal church founded Wilberforce College in Ohio, named after William Wilberforce, a noted English abolitionist.

Oberlin College admitted women in 1837, becoming the first coeducational college. For the most part, however, higher education for women was limited to a few academies or seminaries. (See page 300.)

Reforming the Prisons

Punishment for criminal offenses had been severe in the colonial period. The death penalty was generally imposed for serious offenses, and some form of pain or humiliation for minor ones. Virginia's colonial legislature made 27 offenses capital crimes, punishable by death. Other states designated fewer capital crimes, but listing 10 or more such offenses was common. As late as 1817, public floggings took place in Philadelphia.

In the early nineteenth century imprisonment gradually replaced physical punishment, but this created new problems. The first prisons were makeshift. Prisoners often ran short of clothing. Prison officials crowded men, women, and children together in small rooms, giving them poor and insufficient food. Prisons even charged inmates fees during their stay in jail, while jailers made extra money by selling rum to the prisoners.

These wretched conditions led reformers to press for change. In the 1820s, New York and Pennsylvania led the way by establishing new penitentiary systems based on isolation. In New York's Auburn system, for example, prisoners slept alone in a cell. They worked together during the day, but they could not talk to other prisoners or even exchange glances. Reformers hoped that if criminals were isolated from their old environment and given a regular occupation and a strict schedule, they would develop good habits. Yet the system placed a severe psychological strain on prisoners since it denied them the normal benefits of society. For all the changes, the new systems succeeded in "reforming" few of their inmates.

Helping the Mentally Ill

Most people understood little about mental illness in the nineteenth century. Men, women, and children who suffered from mental illnesses were locked up, sometimes in jails or poorhouses. They often received inadequate care and little medical attention. The condition of these people went largely unnoticed until the 1840s when Dorothea Lynde Dix, a Boston school teacher, began to campaign for better treatment of the mentally ill.

In 1841 Dix was invited to teach a Sunday-school class at a jail in Cambridge, Massachusetts. Among the inmates at the jail were mentally ill people dressed in rags and housed in unheated quarters. Dix was shocked at what she saw. She then visited every institution in the state where the mentally ill were housed and wrote a report detailing the mistreatment she discovered. She urged that such people be treated as patients who were ill, not as criminals.

Dix convinced the Massachusetts lawmakers to improve care for the mentally ill. She also carried her crusade to the rest of the nation, finding success among other state legislatures. In response to her appeals, 15 states established special hospitals for the mentally ill. Dix failed to win support from the national government, however. In 1854 she campaigned for federal land grants to support hospitals. Congress passed such a bill, but President Franklin Pierce vetoed it. Still, Dorothea Dix had called the public's attention to a long-ignored problem.

Dorothea Dix crusaded for better medical care and proper facilities for the mentally ill. Her campaign led 15 states to establish hospitals for their care.

conditions he saw in the growing industrial society.

Most of these utopian communities ultimately failed to reach their goals. Often a strong leader organized and ran the community in its early days. Then, when the leader departed, the remaining members split into factions and the community dissolved. Furthermore, founding entire communities took a large amount of money, and many groups failed to find substantial support, especially in the first crucial years of existence.

It is perhaps the nature of utopians, and all reformers, that their dreams and hopes often exceed the concrete results of their efforts. Yet even if reforms in the areas of prisons, treatment for the mentally ill, and education had not perfected American society, at least reformers had forced Americans to ask questions about their society. They had held up to the public the political and religious ideals of the nation and demanded that their fellow citizens come closer to fulfilling those ideals.

Creating an Ideal Society

Some reformers were not content to reorganize or improve one particular institution, such as prisons or schools. Rather, they wanted to remake society entirely. Since they could not make over the entire country, these reformers founded their own *utopian*, or ideal, communities as a demonstration of how a new system might work.

Some groups based their utopian communities on religious principles. One such group, the Shakers, hoped to isolate themselves from what they considered a corrupt society, supporting themselves by farming while working to attain perfection. Other communities, such as Robert Owen's New Harmony in Indiana, were more concerned with economic principles. In New Harmony, Owen hoped to eliminate many of the harsh

SECTION REVIEW

1. Identify: Horace Mann, Dorothea Dix.
2. Define: compulsory education, utopian.
3. List three problems of public education in the early 1800s.
4. What are two reasons some people opposed free public education?
5. What gradually replaced the physical punishment of criminal offenders?
6. (a) How were the mentally ill usually treated in the early 1800s? (b) What did Dorothea Dix accomplish on their behalf?
7. **Critical Thinking** How does free public education for all promote equality?

3 A Campaign for Women's Rights

During the 1840s and 1850s women took an increasingly active part in reform movements. Yet women themselves suffered many forms of legal discrimination. They could not vote, and in many states they could not own property, make a will, or file a lawsuit. If a woman worked outside the home, the law gave her husband the wages she brought home. Consequently, some reformers gradually turned their attention to rights for women.

Early Strides in Education

As you read earlier, women had limited educational opportunities in the early nineteenth century. Early attempts to establish college-level education for women widened these opportunities and contributed to growing demands for full legal rights.

As early as 1821, Emma Willard, a pioneer in the field of education, established the Troy Female Seminary in Troy, New York. Her father had given her a good basic education, but like other intelligent women, she had been unable to continue her education because no college would admit women. Her seminary successfully instructed students in mathematics, physics, history, and geography, proving that women could master such subjects as easily as men. Willard's goal was to train women teachers who in turn could teach others.

For many years seminaries were the only institutions in which women could attain a higher education. Many of the seminaries were small and existed only as long as their benefactors lived. Mary Lyon, however, dreamed of establishing a permanent college for women. During the 1830s she began a campaign to raise funds for such a college. Her work was slow and contributions were small, but she prevailed. In 1836 the cornerstone of Mount Holyoke Female Seminary was laid in South Hadley, Massachusetts. The name of the school hid Lyon's true intent. She realized that many people opposed a college education for women, so she carefully avoided calling the school a col-

★ Voices of Freedom ★

Sojourner Truth: Equality for Women

Sojourner Truth was born a slave in New York State in 1797. She ran away in 1826 just one year before she would have been freed according to New York law. Originally named Isabelle Baumfree, she took the name Sojourner Truth about 1843 because she believed her calling was to journey around the country, boldly speaking the truth about slavery, women's rights, and other causes. At a women's rights convention in 1851, she responded with powerful words to a man who claimed that women were inferior to men.

That man over there says that women need to be helped into carriages, and lifted over ditches, and to have the best place everywhere. Nobody ever helps me into carriages, or over mudpuddles, or gives me any best place! And ain't I a woman? Look at me! Look at my arm! I have ploughed, and planted, and gathered into barns, and no man could head me! And ain't I a woman? I could work as much and eat as much as a man—when I could get it—and bear the lash as well! And ain't I a woman? I have borne thirteen children, and seen them most all sold off to slavery, and when I cried out with my mother's grief, none but Jesus heard me! And ain't I a woman?

Then they talk about this thing in the head; what's this they call it? That's it, honey [intellect]. What's that got to do with women's rights? If my cup won't hold but a pint and yours hold a quart, wouldn't you be mean not to let me have my little half?

Then that little man in black there, he says women can't have as much rights as men, 'cause Christ wasn't a woman! Where did your Christ come from? *Where did your Christ come from?* From God and a woman! Man had nothing to do with Him.

If the first woman God ever made was strong enough to turn the world upside down all alone, these women together [here] ought to be able to turn it back, and get it right side up again! And now they are asking to do it, the men better let 'em.

lege. Despite its name, Mount Holyoke was the first women's college in the United States.

Resistance to Women Reformers

Many women shared in the general reforming spirit of the age. But women who tried to campaign for such causes, especially when they tried to speak in public, discovered that most male reformers did not want their help. Reforming, the men felt, was not a woman's occupation. "The power of woman is her dependence," lectured one group of Massachusetts ministers. A woman who gives up that dependence on men to become a reformer "yields the power God has given her for her protection, and her character becomes unnatural."

Some women vigorously rejected the status of "second-class" reformers. Sarah and Angelina Grimké, for example, led the fight for full female participation in the antislavery reform movement. The two sisters were from South Carolina, where their father was a slave owner. They left home because of their opposition to slavery. At first they lectured only to other women, but soon they began speaking to mixed audiences. To their dismay they found that the men would often boo and shout them down.

The Grimkés persisted, however. "To me," said Sarah Grimké, "it is perfectly clear that whatsoever it is morally right for a man to do, it is morally right for a woman to do." When some abolitionists asked them to give up the cause of women's rights, Angelina asked, "What *then* can *woman* do for the slave, when she herself is under the feet of man and shamed into *silence?*"

In 1840 the antislavery movement in the United States split into two groups. One of the issues was whether women should be allowed to participate in movement activities. Later that year in London, the World Anti-Slavery Convention voted to exclude the female delegates from the United States.

The Seneca Falls Convention

Frustrated by such restraints, women reformers began to see the need to campaign for their own rights as well as for the rights of others. In 1848 Lucretia Mott and Elizabeth Cady Stanton, two of the delegates who

Elizabeth Cady Stanton worked to gain for women such basic rights as legal ownership of their own property. Stanton helped found the women's movement in the United States. She is shown here with one of her seven children.

had been rejected by the London antislavery conference, called a convention for women's rights in Stanton's home town, Seneca Falls, New York. Stanton and Mott wanted to publicize the need for women's rights and to create a program for action.

In calling the meeting, Stanton drafted a proclamation modeled after the Declaration of Independence. "We hold these truths to be self-evident: that all men and women are created equal," it began. And it continued, "The history of mankind is a history of repeated injuries and usurpations on the part of man toward woman, having in direct object the establishment of an absolute tyranny over her."

Over 250 women and about 40 men attended the meeting. Stanton introduced nine resolutions. All passed unanimously except one calling for women's suffrage, which won a small majority. So began the long struggle for women's rights, which Stanton led throughout her lifetime.

Stanton was soon joined by Susan B. Anthony, who brought tremendous energy and organizational skills to the struggle for women's rights. In the years after the Seneca Falls Convention, advocates of women's rights held annual meetings and petitioned state legislatures to try to change laws. Despite such activity, the movement remained small until after the Civil War.

Since higher education for women was limited, Maria Mitchell taught herself astronomy. In 1847 she discovered a comet, and later she taught astronomy at Vassar College.

Advances of American Women

Slowly women's role in American life expanded. As schools such as the Troy Female Seminary and Mount Holyoke graduated qualified teachers, women were accepted into the teaching profession.

Elizabeth Blackwell applied to medical school at Geneva College, New York, and was voted in almost as a joke. But she surprised her male classmates and graduated at the head of the class. In 1850 she began practicing medicine in New York City as the first woman doctor. Blackwell founded the first school of nursing in the United States in 1857, to teach a profession that women would enter in increasing numbers.

Americans also accepted women as authors and editors. Margaret Fuller edited a noted philosophical magazine and wrote several books. Her work, *Woman in the Nineteenth Century*, published in 1845, played an important part in the women's rights movement. Fuller argued that women were as capable as men and were able to do the same type of work.

Louisa May Alcott enjoyed considerable success with her children's books, including *Little Women*. Harriet Beecher Stowe excited nationwide controversy with her anti-slavery book, *Uncle Tom's Cabin*, as you will read later. (See page 317.) Many other women wrote essays and poetry for local newspapers or published tracts on popular moral crusades of the day.

However, despite the accomplishments of individual women, the legal status of women changed little. In some states women did gain the right to control their own property after they married, but the women's suffrage movement gained no headway. Women still remained outside the political process. Yet the reformers had publicized their cause well and did not abandon it. The questions of women's rights would be debated but could no longer be ignored.

SECTION REVIEW

1. Identify: Emma Willard, Sarah and Angelina Grimké, Lucretia Mott, Elizabeth Cady Stanton, Susan B. Anthony, Elizabeth Blackwell, Margaret Fuller, Louisa May Alcott, Harriet Beecher Stowe.
2. What goal did Mary Lyon have for Mount Holyoke Seminary?
3. How did people respond to women reformers?
4. What was the Seneca Falls Convention?
5. **Critical Thinking** Why was the women's movement weak in the early 1800s?

4 The Battle Against Slavery

Many problems captured the attention of reformers during the first half of the nineteenth century, but the most far-reaching reform movement of the period was the crusade to abolish slavery. But Americans, both black and white, who opposed slavery did not agree on how it should be abolished.

A Gradual Approach

Opposition to slavery did not suddenly appear in the early nineteenth century. Some Americans from both northern and southern states had long opposed slavery and favored emancipation of the slaves. When the nation abolished the slave trade in 1808, many believed that slavery would soon die out. Others worked actively to abolish it. Such activity took many forms. One was to stimulate public discussion of the subject. Newspapers concerned with ending slavery sprang up in the North and in parts of the South, such as Tennessee and North Carolina.

During the 1820s Benjamin Lundy published the *Genius of Universal Emancipation* in Ohio. It became one of the most influential antislavery newspapers. Through his newspaper, Lundy proposed a program of gradual emancipation that included stopping the spread of slavery to new states, abolishing the slave trade within the borders of the United States, and urging slave states to free their slaves gradually. In 1829 Lundy hired an assistant editor, William Lloyd Garrison, a man who held a more radical viewpoint and who would eventually become a leader in the drive to abolish slavery.

The Colonization Movement

Even though many white Americans in both North and South admitted the evils of slavery, few could imagine blacks assuming a full and equal part in American society. As a result of such feelings, some abolitionists endorsed a program in which freed slaves would move to Liberia, a country in Africa founded in 1822 by former American slaves.

The American Colonization Society, established in 1817, tried to carry out the program but found it impractical. The society could afford to send only a small number of blacks to Liberia each year. In 1830, for example, the society sent only 259 free blacks to Liberia, bringing the total to about 1,400. Furthermore, the society failed to convince many plantation owners to free their slaves. Slave owners claimed that such a move would create too great an economic hardship.

Opposition from many free blacks eventually doomed the colonization movement. A free black, Paul Cuffe (see page 119), had been one of the originators of the idea. He thought that blacks would have a better chance of making a good life for themselves if they lived where they did not face discrimination. Cuffe personally took 38 black settlers to Africa in 1815. But many black Americans became disillusioned with the idea of colonization. In 1831 a convention of free blacks meeting in New York City declared that the United States, not Africa, was their home.

> The time must come when the Declaration of Independence will be felt in the heart, as well as uttered from the mouth, and when the rights of all shall be properly acknowledged and appreciated. God hasten that time. This is our home, and this is our country. Beneath its sod lie the bones of our fathers; for it, some of them fought, bled, and died. Here we are born, and here we will die.

Radical Abolitionism

By the 1830s some opponents of slavery believed that a more radical approach was needed. Gradual abolition seemed less and less likely. Whitney's cotton gin had enlarged the cotton kingdom in the South, and the planters' dependence on slave labor seemed greater than ever. Furthermore, as you read in Chapter 15, the fear created by Nat Turner's rebellion in 1831 hardened many southerners' attitude about slavery. Some who had once apologized for owning slaves now praised the institution. Abolitionists saw little hope that slave owners would voluntarily free their slaves.

William Lloyd Garrison symbolized the change within the abolitionist movement. While he worked with Lundy, Garrison tried to tone down his more radical ideas. But in 1831 he established his own antislavery paper, *The Liberator*, in Boston.

In *The Liberator* Garrison proclaimed his doctrine with vigor: slavery was a sin, and the nation had to be purged of this evil immediately and without compensation to slave owners. The first issue of the paper testified to Garrison's fierce unwillingness to compromise. "I *will be* as harsh as truth, and as uncompromising as justice. ... I am in earnest—I will not equivocate—I will not excuse—I will not retreat a single inch—*and I will be heard.*"

Yet even Garrison recognized that immediate emancipation was unlikely. "We have never said that slavery would be overthrown by a single blow," Garrison admitted privately, "that it ought to be, we shall always contend."

Garrison enjoyed support among many free blacks in the North and great notoriety in the South. In 1832 he organized the New England Anti-Slavery Society and helped found the American Anti-Slavery Society. Although he favored immediate emancipation,

Garrison opposed the use of violence to end slavery.

Other abolitionists contributed to the growing radicalism of the movement. Theodore Weld, an intensely religious young man, spoke eloquently about the moral evils of slavery. In 1834 Weld led a revival among the students at Lane Seminary in Cincinnati. When most of the students eagerly converted to the doctrine of immediate emancipation, the more conservative trustees of the seminary suppressed all antislavery agitation on campus. Weld and many of his students then began traveling from town to town, effectively organizing abolitionist sentiment.

David Walker's *Appeal to the Colored Citizens of the World*, published in 1829, advocated a more radical position than Garrison or Weld. A free black born in North Carolina and living in Boston, Walker appealed to slaves to rise up and free themselves. Walker's *Appeal* did not lead to revolts among slaves, but it created a sensation among many slave owners and among moderate and conservative whites in the North.

Division Among Abolitionists

Although radical abolitionists united in their desire to see slavery ended immediately, they did not agree on tactics. One dispute arose over whether women should participate in the movement. As you read earlier in this chapter, abolitionists split over this issue in 1840. William Lloyd Garrison's outspoken support for women's participation alienated many abolitionists.

Garrison's position on political action also divided the radical abolitionists. He opposed all political activity as a way to achieve emancipation. Garrison argued that the Constitution favored slavery and that political institutions were corrupt. Consequently, he believed nothing could be gained by trying to work within the system.

Instead Garrison sought to expose the evils of slavery in his newspaper, in lectures and public discussions, and through letter-writing campaigns. In this way he believed the American people would be convinced to support the abolition of slavery.

Many abolitionists supported this approach, including the Grimké sisters, Theodore Weld, Sojourner Truth, and Frederick Douglass. Sojourner Truth, who became well known as an antislavery speaker, greatly aided the abolitionist movement with her impassioned pleas for equality. Frederick Douglass emerged as the most important black leader of the abolitionist movement. Tall and broad-shouldered, his commanding presence was matched by a keen intelligence and powerful speaking voice. During the 1840s Douglass lectured in the United States and Great Britain against American slavery. In 1847 he began publishing an antislavery newspaper, the *North Star*, in Rochester, New York. Douglass also actively protested discrimination against free black Americans.

Black abolitionist groups generally supported Garrison's approach to abolitionism. Black Americans had actively opposed slavery long before most white reformers became involved. By 1830, 50 black antislavery groups existed, and they became increasingly important over the next three decades.

Political Opposition to Slavery

Those who disagreed with Garrison found leadership in Arthur and Lewis Tappan, two wealthy New York City merchants who first broke with Garrison over the inclusion of women in the movement. The Tappans concentrated on achieving change through political activity and found that many radical abolitionists had similar views. In 1839 the Tappans and James Birney, a former Kentucky slave owner converted to abolitionism by Theodore Weld, helped found the Liberty party. In 1840 and again in 1844 Birney ran for President on the Liberty party ticket.

In 1848 the Free Soil party replaced the Liberty party as the nation's most important antislavery political party. The support enjoyed by the Free Soil party among both politicians and voters resulted largely from its more moderate platform. Instead of demanding the abolition of slavery in the South, Free Soilers wanted to stop the expansion of slavery into new territories. Most Free Soilers demonstrated little concern for the rights of blacks. Many, in fact, wanted to keep all blacks, free as well as slave, out of the territories.

The Underground Railroad

Some abolitionists took direct action against slavery by working for the "underground railroad." This was not an actual railroad but rather a network of men and women who

Frederick Douglass:
A Denunciation of the Slave Trade

The slave trade was an important target of abolitionists. Although importing slaves was banned after 1808, smuggling continued. The slave trade increased as the cotton kingdom pushed westward. Frederick Douglass was a slave for 21 years. After his escape in 1838, he became a noted abolitionist speaker. Below is an excerpt from a speech Douglass made in New York in 1852.

To me the American slave trade is a terrible reality. When a child, my soul was often pierced with a sense of its horrors.

The flesh-mongers gather up their victims by dozens, and drive them chained, to the general depot at Baltimore. When a sufficient number has been collected here, a ship is chartered to convey the forlorn crew to Mobile, or to New Orleans.

In the deep, still darkness of midnight, I have been often aroused by the dead, heavy footsteps, and the piteous cries of the chained gangs that passed our door.

Fellow-citizens, this murderous traffic is, today, in active operation in this boasted republic. I see the bleeding footsteps; I hear the doleful wail of fettered humanity on the way to the slave-markets where the victims are to be sold like horses, sheep, and swine. . . . My soul sickens at the sight.

helped slaves escape to the North or to Canada. These "conductors" led slaves, or "passengers," along back-country roads called "tracks." Farm wagons often served as "trains." Homes along the way where slaves could find food and shelter were called "stations."

The success of the railroad depended on the cooperation of many blacks and whites and on the heroic actions of such individuals as Harriet Tubman. An escaped slave herself, Tubman risked her life time after time, returning South to lead 300 fugitive slaves to the North. Her courage made her a legend among abolitionists and slaves, who called her the "Black Moses." Slave owners also knew her, and they offered a $40,000 reward for her capture.

Reaction to Abolitionism

The arguments of the radical abolitionists attracted only a small number of supporters to the abolitionist cause. In fact, their uncompromising attitudes and fiery rhetoric aroused opposition in both the South and the North.

Abolitionist agitation led more southerners to actively defend slavery. For one thing, Garrison began publishing his newspaper in 1831, the same year as Nat Turner's rebellion. Furthermore, his critique of slavery included strident attacks on the South and southerners. Southern postmasters struck against abolitionism by refusing to deliver abolitionist material. The state of Georgia even offered a reward of $5,000 to anyone who brought Garrison to the state for trial.

In the North more moderate abolitionists feared the consequence of the "immediate emancipation" advocated by Garrison. Moreover, although white northerners might abhor the institution of slavery, most did not want free blacks living in their communities. Many white workers feared that free blacks might take their jobs by working for lower salaries.

When abolitionists spoke throughout the North, they were frequently booed and

305

treated roughly. In 1835 a Boston mob dragged Garrison through the streets with a rope around him. Authorities probably saved his life by throwing him in jail. Two years later Elijah P. Lovejoy, a New England abolitionist, established an antislavery newspaper at Alton, Illinois. A mob, aided by local authorities as well as "gentlemen of property and standing," destroyed the press and killed Lovejoy. Even people who were not abolitionists were shocked by the suppression of free speech and free press. Lovejoy became a martyr all across the North, and sympathy for the abolitionist cause grew.

Despite the antislavery agitation of the 1830s and 1840s, black Americans saw scant hope that they would be freed. More to their dismay, they found that even abolitionists were patronizing. "Too many," noted one black reformer, "... best love the colored man at a distance."

More and more black leaders began to heed David Walker's early call for stronger action. Henry Highland Garnet, a former Maryland slave, had seconded Walker's appeal in 1843. "Brethren, Arise, Arise! . . . Rather die like free men than live as slaves." In 1851 Frederick Douglass openly broke with Garrison's pacifism, and many others joined him. "The time is come," announced a group of blacks in 1854, "when our people must assume ... the battle against caste and Slavery; it is emphatically our battle; no one else can fight it for us. . . ."

The calls for abolition continued through the 1850s, and increasingly Americans saw that the question of slavery seemed to be approaching a crisis. It highlighted the many social and economic differences between the North and South. The nation would soon find itself engulfed in a controversy that would test its ideals and reforming spirit as well as its identity as a nation.

SECTION REVIEW

1. Identify: William Lloyd Garrison, Theodore Weld, David Walker, Frederick Douglass, Sojourner Truth, underground railroad, Harriet Tubman, Elijah P. Lovejoy.
2. What three steps did Benjamin Lundy propose for the gradual emancipation of slaves?
3. What three factors helped to end the colonization movement?
4. What developments by the 1830s led some abolitionists to believe a more radical approach was needed?
5. What two disputes split the radical abolitionists?
6. How did the goal of the Liberty party differ from that of the Free Soil party?
7. **Critical Thinking** What economic weapons might have been used to encourage slaveowners to give up slavery?

5 Flowering of an American Culture

The efforts of reformers in the first half of the nineteenth century reflected the tradition of idealism in American society. Most looked optimistically toward the future. While they argued that American society was far from perfect, they believed in the possibility of changing life for the better, of aspiring toward the ideal. Many American artists and writers also believed in the idealism of the period, and through their art they helped create a truly unique American culture.

The American Landscape

During the early 1800s American painters became increasingly interested in the wild, natural beauty of the land. Many painted lavish

landscapes that glorified the rugged grandeur of American lakes, rivers, forests, and canyons. The nationalism of these painters is seen in their ideal portrayals of America.

George Caleb Bingham grew up in Missouri and painted scenes of everyday life there, known as genre paintings. His paintings of river life captured the harmony of nature on the American frontier.

Artists in the East also found beauty in the American landscape. Their view was often more nostalgic than that of western painters because in much of the East, settlement and growing industrialization were beginning to infringe on nature. A group of painters including Thomas Cole and Asher Durand became known as the Hudson River

The Hudson River School of painters in the early 1800s tried to capture the beauty of the rugged American landscape. The Oxbow, *by Thomas Cole, done in this style, shows the Connecticut River.*

School. Their landscapes of the Catskill Mountains and Hudson River area revealed a love of nature and a confidence felt by many Americans during the early 1800s. Such characteristics were also found in much American literature.

Reflections on Life in a Changing America

Ralph Waldo Emerson and Henry David Thoreau greatly influenced American writers, thinkers, and reformers during the period before the Civil War. Emerson himself did not join reform organizations, but he acted as a philosophic observer, commenting on the spirit of the times in essays and lectures. His optimism and belief in progress encouraged reformers.

Thoreau absorbed many of Emerson's ideas and developed them further. Emerson, like many Americans, believed in the self-reliance of the individual. Thoreau became a proponent of this individualism, refusing to be associated with institutions of government and industry that he considered corrupt. In 1845 his distaste for the artificial

Major Events	
1817	American Colonization Society founded
1821	Troy Female Seminary established
1829	David Walker's *Appeal to the Colored Citizens of the World* published
1831	Antislavery paper *The Liberator* established; Nat Turner's revolt
1836	Mary Lyon founds Mount Holyoke Female Seminary
1837	Horace Mann becomes first superintendent of education in Massachusetts
1839	Liberty party founded
1848	Seneca Falls Convention
1856	Wilberforce College founded

and complex nature of the growing industrial society led him to retreat to a cabin at Walden Pond outside Boston, where he lived alone for two years.

His refusal to conform to "corrupt" society led Thoreau to a principle of civil disobedience. He refused to pay taxes during the war with Mexico because he believed the war was immoral, arguing that individuals must be guided by their own conscience.

A Flourishing American Literature

The works of Emerson and Thoreau were part of a growing volume of American literature. Many writers of the period shared the reformers' vision of what America should be like, although they were often less optimistic about the chances of improving society. Literature also reflected the nationalism of the first half of the nineteenth century. This nationalism was most obvious in the increasing use of American themes. James Fenimore Cooper's tales of life on the American frontier and Washington Irving's "Rip Van Winkle" and "The Legend of Sleepy Hollow" are among the earliest examples.

Nathaniel Hawthorne used the history and culture of New England as the background for his novels *The Scarlet Letter* and *The House of Seven Gables.* Hawthorne's works and Herman Melville's *Moby-Dick,* dedicated to Hawthorne, became American classics and earned American authors a place in world literature. The poetry of Edgar Allan Poe and Henry Wadsworth Longfellow earned respect for American verse.

More than any other writer, the poet Walt Whitman captured the idealistic spirit and hopefulness of the early nineteenth century. His vibrant and visionary language virtually bursts from the page. Whitman's lines in *Leaves of Grass* take in every sort of scene, every kind of American.

> A southerner soon as a northerner, a planter nonchalant and hospitable
> A Yankee bound my own way . . . ready for trade . . . my joints the limberest joints on earth and the sternest joints on earth,
> A Kentuckian walking the vale of the Elkhorn in my deerskin leggings
> A boatman over the bays or along coasts . . . a Hoosier, a Badger, a Buckeye . . .
> In all people I see myself, none more and not one barleycorn less,
> And the good or bad I say of myself I say of them.

SECTION REVIEW

1. Identify: George Caleb Bingham, Ralph Waldo Emerson, Henry David Thoreau, James Fenimore Cooper, Washington Irving, Nathaniel Hawthorne, Herman Melville, Edgar Allan Poe, Henry Wadsworth Longfellow, Walt Whitman.

2. How did American landscape paintings reflect a sense of nationalism?

3. **Critical Thinking** How do artists and writers benefit society?

Chapter 16 Review

In Perspective

The years between 1820 and 1860 were years of intense reform. Reformers had a vision of what they thought the nation should be like, and they tried to convince Americans to change in order to reach that ideal.

Horace Mann led the movement to improve public education in the United States, and Dorothea Dix campaigned for better treatment of the mentally ill. Reformers also tried to improve the prison system. Women were active in reform movements and soon began to demand their own rights.

Opposition to slavery increased during this period. Abolitionists often disagreed among themselves, and their actions created great resentment in the South as well as strong opposition among some people in the North. However, their efforts helped keep the issue before the public. Although few artists or writers actively participated in reform movements, many shared the idealistic vision of America.

Vocabulary

On a separate sheet of paper, write the word or words that best complete each of the following sentences.

1. ___ were spirited religious meetings to renew people's faith.
2. Under a system of ___, children are required to attend school.
3. The ___ was a campaign against the use of alcoholic beverages.
4. A (An) ___ community is ideal or perfect.
5. ___ is refraining from the consumption of alcohol.

Chapter Checkup

1. Describe the political and religious roots of the reform spirit of the early nineteenth century.
2. Describe the state of public education in New England, the Middle Atlantic states, the South, and the West.
3. (a) What type of education existed for black Americans in the early nineteenth century? (b) What type of education existed for women?
4. (a) What role did women play in the abolitionist movement? (b) How successful was that movement during the 1840s and 1850s?

5. How did literature and painting assume a unique American character in the first half of the nineteenth century?

309

Critical Thinking

1. **Evaluating** Why do you think it was effective for individuals like Sojourner Truth and Frederick Douglass to speak out against slavery?
2. **Analyzing** Reread the extract from Walt Whitman's poem on page 308. How does the poem reflect the idealism and optimism of many Americans of the time?

Developing Basic Skills

1. **Relating Past to Present** (a) Describe the legal position of women in the early nineteenth century. (b) How is woman's legal position different today?
2. **Using a Primary Source** Reread Frederick Douglass's speech about the slave trade on page 305 and answer the following questions: (a) What type of document is it? (b) Was the author closely involved with the events described? Explain. (c) Why did Douglass make this speech? (d) What can you learn about the slave trade from this document?

See page 829 for suggested readings.

Writer's Handbook

Sources of Information

Some of the most common research aids are the library card catalog, *The Readers' Guide to Periodic Literature*, newspaper indexes, and specialized reference books. The card catalog is an alphabetical list of books in the library arranged by subject, title, and author. *The Readers' Guide to Periodic Literature* is an index to articles in 170 different magazines. It is particularly helpful in finding information on current events. A newspaper index lists articles according to subject. Since news events are usually covered by many newspapers on the same day, any newspaper index can be a guide to finding articles in other newspapers. The index for *The New York Times* begins in 1851. Specialized reference books include in-depth information on such topics as definitions of terms, biographies, and statistics. You will learn more about these reference tools in later Chapter Reviews.

Practice: List one possible source of information for each of the following: Horace Mann; the women's rights movement in the 1840s; current educational reforms; the complete works of Walt Whitman; the number of slaves in 1850; *Maine* laws. Explain each choice.

Unit Five

A Nation Torn Apart

1852 Southerners were enraged by the portrayal of slavery in the novel and play, *Uncle Tom's Cabin.*

Abraham Lincoln is shown here with his young son, Tad.

	1850	1855	1860
POLITICS AND GOVERNMENT	**1850** North and South reach compromise over slavery in territories		**1857** Dred Scott decision by Supreme Court shocks northerners
SOCIETY AND CULTURE		**1854** Pro- and antislavery groups rush to settle Kansas	
ECONOMICS AND TECHNOLOGY		**1850s** Cotton becomes critical to southern economy	
WORLD EVENTS		**1853** United States begins trade with Japan	**1858** United States and China sign friendship treaty

Fillmore   Pierce   Buchanan

Slaveowners used tags such as these to identify their slaves.

The Fugitive Slave Law of 1850 required all citizens to help recover runaway slaves.

So much Confederate money was printed during the war that the South suffered terrible inflation.

Drummer boys were the youngest "soldiers" on both sides of the Civil War.

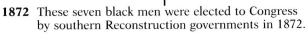

1860	1865	1870	1875
1860 Southern states begin to secede from the Union	**1865** General Lee surrenders at Appomattox	**1871** Congress outlaws the Ku Klux Klan	
	1863 President Lincoln issues the Emancipation Proclamation	**1870** Fifteenth Amendment guarantees the right to vote	
	1862 Ironclad ships battle at Hampton Roads	**1869** Transcontinental railroad complete	
1861 Czar of Russia abolishes serfdom		**1871** A unified German state is created	

Lincoln   Johnson

1872 These seven black men were elected to Congress by southern Reconstruction governments in 1872.

The diary kept by Mary Boykin Chesnut of South Carolina revealed the horrors of the war for southern women.

17
The Cords of Union Broken

(1820–1861)

Detail from The Underground Railroad

In 1850 Senator Daniel Webster of New Hampshire predicted, "Secession! Peaceable secession! Sir, your eyes and mine are never destined to see that miracle." Webster knew Americans well. By 1860 the nation stood on the brink of civil war.

Strong sectional jealousies pitted North against South. The institution of slavery was a major source of disagreement. Abolitionists wanted to end slavery in the South. Other citizens wanted to stop the spread of slavery into the territories. Southerners saw each attempt to control slavery as a threat to their way of life.

Southern states eventually concluded that they had no future within the Union. But the newly elected President, Abraham Lincoln, saw the preservation of the nation as his duty. So Webster's prediction came true. Peaceable secession proved impossible as the flames quickly grew into the inferno of civil war.

Attempts to balance slave and free states

1820	1825	1830	1835	1840	1845	1850	1855	1860

1820 Missouri Compromise	**1832** South Carolina threatens to secede	**1836** Arkansas enters as slave state	**1837** Michigan enters as free state	**1850** Compromise of 1850	**1854** Kansas-Nebraska Act	**1859** John Brown raids Harpers Ferry

1 Attempts to Resolve Conflicts Between North and South

During the first half of the nineteenth century, debates in Congress reflected the growing strain between the North and the South. Much of the tension arose from disagreements over western territories that wanted to join the nation as new states. Should Congress prohibit slavery within the territories and later admit them as *free states*, states in which slavery was prohibited? Or should Congress allow slavery within the territories and admit them as *slave states*, states in which slavery was permitted?

How Congress answered these questions could determine the balance of political power between North and South. The North, with its larger population, had more votes in the House of Representatives, since the number of representatives from each state depended on its population. But in the Senate each state had two senators. By 1819 there were 11 free states and 11 slave states. Thus, while southerners did not control the Senate, they could usually block legislation detrimental to their region. Neither the South nor the North wanted the balance in the Senate to tip in favor of the other.

The Missouri Compromise

In December 1818 Missouri, which had been part of the Louisiana Purchase, sought admission to the Union as a slave state. This request threatened the balance of power in the Senate. Northern members of Congress offered a counterproposal: admit Missouri as a slave state on the condition that no more slaves be brought into the state, and that all children of slaves be freed when they reached age 25. That way, Missouri would eventually become a free state.

Debate flared as northerners and southerners accused each other of trying to seize additional power and influence. Seventy-six-year-old Thomas Jefferson, observing the crisis from his plantation in Virginia, foresaw great danger to the Union: "This momentous question, like a firebell in the night, awakened and filled me with terror."

Henry Clay exercised his talents as a compromiser and, after long hours of negotiating, persuaded Congress to adopt a measure known as the Missouri Compromise. By admitting Missouri as a slave state and

Maine, formerly part of Massachusetts, as a free state, Congress preserved the balance between free and slave states. The Missouri Compromise further provided that in the remaining portion of the Louisiana Purchase slavery would be prohibited forever north of latitude 36°30′, the southern boundary of Missouri, and would be permitted south of that line. Southerners accepted this limitation since plantation agriculture was unlikely to develop north of that line, and there would be less need for slaves. (See the map on page 314.)

Most Americans breathed a sigh of relief when Congress adopted the Missouri Compromise in 1820. Concerned citizens hoped that the slavery question had been settled to everyone's satisfaction and that it would gradually disappear. But the question persisted, and rivalry between North and South increased.

A Delicate Balance

Whenever a new state requested admission to the Union, the problem of maintaining a balance between the North and the South resurfaced. In 1836 and 1837 Arkansas and Michigan joined, the former a slave state, the latter a free state. But in 1845 Florida and Texas both entered as slave states. Additional free states (Iowa in 1846 and Wisconsin in 1848) soon restored the balance.

The outbreak of war with Mexico in 1846 raised a new problem, however. A victory over Mexico would add extensive territory to the United States. Since the Missouri Compromise applied only to territories in the Louisiana Purchase, a disturbing question arose: what would the status of slavery be in the new territories?

On a steamy Washington night in August 1846 Representative David Wilmot of Pennsylvania proposed an answer to the question. Congress was debating an appropriation for the purchase of land in the Southwest in connection with negotiations with Mexico. In a surprise move, Wilmot added a provision that would ban slavery forever from any territory acquired from Mexico.

Suddenly the congressmen, who had been wearily fanning themselves, plunged

The Missouri Compromise, 1820

CANADA

OREGON COUNTRY

UNORGANIZED TERRITORY

PACIFIC OCEAN

ME.

VT.

N.H.

MASS.

N.Y.

R.I.

CONN.

MICH.

TERR.

PA.

N.J.

DEL.

MD.

ILL.

IND.

OHIO

VA.

MO.

KY.

N.C.

Missouri Compromise line 36° 30'

TENN.

S.C.

ARKANSAS TERR.

MISS.

ALA.

GA.

NEW SPAIN

LA.

FLA. TERR.

ATLANTIC OCEAN

GULF OF MEXICO

0   500 Miles
0   800 Kilometers

Free states and territories

Slave states and territories

■ The Missouri Compromise proposed by Henry Clay admitted Missouri as a slave state and Maine as a free state, thus maintaining a balance between slave and free states. The compromise also prohibited slavery in the Louisiana Purchase north of 36°30' latitude.

into a heated debate that threatened the long history of sectional compromise. The House passed the amendment, known as the Wilmot Proviso, but two days later the Senate defeated the measure. When the United States finally acquired the southwestern territory from Mexico in 1848, the peace treaty said nothing about slavery. The unsuccessful Wilmot Proviso had reopened the question of slavery in the new territories.

Positions on the Slavery Issue

As debate over the issue of slavery in the territories continued, various groups proposed remedies to the problem. David Wilmot's solution, which sought to exclude slavery from all territory gained from Mexico, represented the extreme northern position. Moderates from both North and South had long argued that slavery would eventually die out, but many northerners saw that slavery was spreading. In their opinion only firm legislative action would control it, so they supported the Wilmot Proviso.

John C. Calhoun, now a grizzled and gaunt old man, represented the extreme southern position. Slaves were personal property, he declared. The Fifth Amendment to the Constitution specified that no person could be deprived of "life, liberty, or property without due process of law." Yet slave owners could be deprived of their property if they moved to a territory where slavery was forbidden. Therefore, Calhoun concluded, slavery should be permitted in all territories.

Between the extreme positions lay two moderate solutions. One group of moderates proposed that the Missouri Compromise line of 36°30' be extended west to the Pacific Ocean. Slavery would be prohibited north of the line but allowed south of it. President James Polk supported this solution. Senator Stephen Douglas of Illinois championed the idea of *popular sovereignty*. He proposed that the voters of each territory decide whether or not to allow slavery within the territory, regardless of where it was located.

Over the years the two moderate positions gradually lost support, and by the end of the 1850s the more extreme positions had become dominant.

Emergence of the Free Soil Party

During the election campaign of 1848, both the Democratic and Whig parties wanted to avoid the question of slavery in the territories, but many Democrats and Whigs in the North demanded a vigorous position against the expansion of slavery. Consequently they joined with members of the Liberty party (see page 304) and formed the Free Soil party. As you read in Chapter 16, the basis of the Free Soil party was its opposition to slavery in the territories. Despite some abolitionist and free black membership, the party did not advocate the abolition of slavery in existing states, North or South. In fact, many Free Soilers did not want any blacks, slave or free, in the territories.

In 1848 the Free Soilers nominated former President Martin Van Buren for President. The Democrats nominated Lewis Cass, a senator from Michigan who advocated popular sovereignty. The Whigs nominated Zachary Taylor, a hero of the Mexican War and a wealthy slave owner from Louisiana. Taylor had not taken a stand on the slavery question, but many assumed that he would support the South's position.

Taylor won the election in both the northern and the southern states. The Democrats and the Whigs had maintained their positions as national parties in 1848, but Van Buren won nearly 10 percent of the popular vote, receiving all his support from the North. The emergence of a political party whose strength lay in only one section of the nation showed that the issue of slavery in the territories was widening the split between South and North.

The Compromise of 1850

Although in 1848 the Democrats and Whigs had evaded the question of slavery in the southwestern territories, they were soon forced to address the issue. The discovery of gold had brought thousands of people to California, and in 1849 Californians requested admission to the Union as a free state. Since there were now 15 free states and 15 slave states, southerners opposed the admission, but northerners favored it.

When Congress convened in December 1849, the question of California's statehood was the subject of heated debate. Other issues also contributed to a bitter mood. Many northerners objected to the selling and buying of slaves in the nation's capital and wanted it ended. Southerners, in turn, demanded a more effective fugitive slave law to prevent abolitionists from helping slaves escape.

As the debate continued, tempers flared and the very existence of the Union seemed to be at stake. Henry Clay, who had earned the nickname "The Great Compromiser" during his long career, stepped forward to propose a solution that he hoped would satisfy both sides. Clay suggested that California be admitted as a free state but that the rest of the southwestern territory be open to slavery by popular sovereignty. Slave trade would be abolished in the District of Columbia, but Congress would officially declare that it had no power to abolish the slave trade between existing slave states. Finally, Congress would pass a strong fugitive slave law.

For six months Clay used all the bargaining skills and persuasive eloquence at his command to win support for the compromise. He received important support from Daniel Webster, his long-time rival, who believed that without a compromise the United States would be torn apart. When he addressed the Senate, Webster began, "I wish to speak today, not as a Massachusetts man, nor a northern man, but as an American. . . . I speak today for the preservation of the Union."

But John C. Calhoun, while strongly advocating the South's position, made the most dramatic warning about danger to the Union. Gravely ill, with only a month to live, Calhoun sat one last time in his Senate seat, staring fiercely ahead, too sick to read his speech, while Senator James Mason of Virginia read it for him.

"It is a great mistake to suppose that disunion can be effected at a single blow," Calhoun argued. "The cords which bind these states together in one common Union are far too numerous and powerful for that." Yet one by one these cords were being broken. "Already the agitation of the slavery question has snapped some of the most important, and has greatly weakened all the others. . . ." If controversy continued, he warned, the break-up of the United States would be inevitable.

Calhoun's stern warning, combined with the pleas of Webster and Clay, persuaded many members of Congress that the threat to the Union was real and that they should compromise once again. President Taylor vigorously opposed Clay's plan, but in the summer of 1850 he died suddenly. His successor, Millard Fillmore, supported the compromise, and in September Congress passed

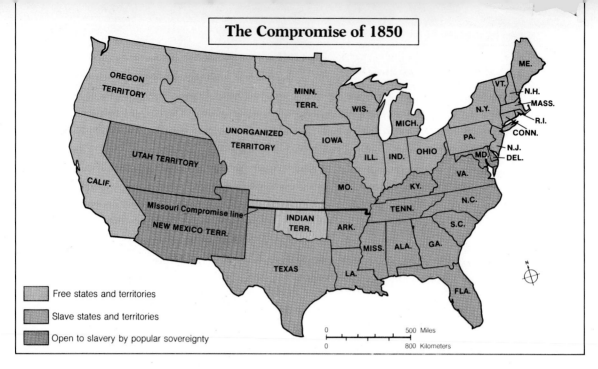

The Compromise of 1850

Free states and territories

Slave states and territories

Open to slavery by popular sovereignty

■ According to the Compromise of 1850, California was to be admitted to the Union as a free state. In the remainder of the southwestern territory acquired from Mexico, residents could decide whether to allow slavery.

it. For the moment it appeared that compromise had succeeded one more time.

SECTION REVIEW

1. Identify: David Wilmot, Stephen Douglas, Zachary Taylor.
2. Define: free state, slave state, popular sovereignty.
3. What were the two major provisions of the Missouri Compromise?
4. (a) What were the extreme northern and southern positions on slavery in the new territories? (b) What were the two moderate positions?
5. Compare the ways in which northerners and southerners would benefit from the Compromise of 1850.
6. **Critical Thinking** What do you think Calhoun meant by "the cords which bind these states together"?

2 A Faltering Compromise

Most Americans hoped that the Compromise of 1850 would settle the questions dividing the North and the South. Yet portions of the compromise weakened it, and developments in Kansas soon revived the issue of slavery in the territories.

The Fugitive Slave Law

To southerners the new Fugitive Slave Law, part of the Compromise of 1850, represented only what was due them. They claimed that the Constitution permitted them to hold slaves as property and that fugitive slaves were either runaways or stolen property and should be returned.

But many northerners bitterly resented certain provisions of the Fugitive Slave Law. For example, a person accused of being a fugitive slave had to stand trial before a special commissioner, not a judge. No jury heard the case, and the accused could not even testify in his or her own behalf. Furthermore, the commissioner received a $10 fee if he sent the accused fugitive back to slavery and only $5 if he freed the person.

This, angry northerners pointed out, amounted to little less than a bribe to insure that the accused was declared a runaway slave. Finally, the law required all citizens to assist in capturing a fugitive slave.

The new law terrified free blacks in the North. It permitted the retrieval not only of newly escaped slaves but of anyone who had ever fled from slavery. Thus a slave who had escaped many years earlier faced the prospect of being thrown in jail and returned to a former master in the South. Furthermore, the flimsy protections against incorrect identification meant that free blacks were in danger of being falsely claimed by slave owners as fugitives.

Newspapers throughout the North denounced the Fugitive Slave Law as "an outrage to humanity," "a hateful statute of kidnappers," and something that should be "resisted, disobeyed at all hazards." When slave owners from the South sent agents north in search of escaped slaves, abolitionists organized open resistance. Free blacks also set up vigilance committees to protect themselves against kidnappers.

Hatred of the Fugitive Slave Law was one reason for the immense popularity of Harriet Beecher Stowe's novel *Uncle Tom's Cabin,* published in 1852. With a brilliant grasp of the tensions slavery produced in American society, Stowe created scenes and images that haunted the imagination: the desperate flight to freedom of fugitive slaves,

Antislavery forces in the North printed posters to warn free blacks and fugitive slaves about the danger of being captured under the new Fugitive Slave Law.

the break-up of slave families and marriages, the cruel effects of slavery on blacks and whites alike. Southern leaders protested that slaves were treated much better than *Uncle Tom's Cabin* suggested, but thousands of

★ Arts in America ★

The Republic

Politicians were not the only Americans who feared for the fate of the United States in 1850. Poet Henry Wadsworth Longfellow expressed his faith in the republic in this excerpt from *The Building of the Ship.*

Thou, too, sail on, O Ship of State!
Sail on, O UNION, strong and great!
Humanity with all its fears,
With all the hopes of future years,
Is hanging breathless on thy fate!
We know what Master laid thy keel,
What Workmen wrought thy ribs of steel,
Who made each mast, and sail, and rope,
What anvils rang, what hammers beat,

In what a forge and what a heat
Were shaped the anchors of thy hope!
Fear not each sudden sound and shock,
'Tis of the wave and not the rock;
'Tis but the flapping of the sail,
And not a rent made by the gale!
In spite of rock and tempest's roar,
In spite of false lights on the shore,
Sail on, nor fear to breast the sea!
Our hearts, our hopes, are all with thee,
Our hearts, our hopes, our prayers, our tears,
Our faith triumphant o'er our fears,
Are all with thee—are all with thee!

Source: Henry Wadsworth Longfellow, *Complete Poetical Works* (Boston, 1893).

northerners who read the book or saw the play came away determined to oppose the Fugitive Slave Law.

The Fugitive Slave Law increased sectional tensions because it affected northerners directly. Confronted with the plight of a slave seeking freedom, more and more northerners, even those previously immune to abolitionist appeals, sympathized with the fugitive. Nothing else stirred northern sensibilities in quite the same way.

Growing Political Division

Despite controversy over the Fugitive Slave Law, political leaders tried to minimize tensions during the presidential election of 1852. Both Whigs and Democrats accepted the Compromise of 1850, but the superficial similarities of the party platforms hid serious disagreements.

Disputes between northern and southern factions severely disrupted the Whig party, but northern Whigs finally pushed through the nomination of another war hero, General Winfield Scott, for President. Southern and northern Democrats quarreled too but avoided a split by nominating a little-known New Hampshire politician, Franklin Pierce. With the Whigs badly divided, Pierce won the election easily.

Northerners soon discovered, however, that President Pierce sympathized with many southern goals. In particular, Pierce hoped to obtain Cuba from Spain. If Cuba joined the United States, it would surely be as a slave territory and ultimately as a slave state.

In 1854 three of Pierce's diplomatic ministers, meeting in Ostend, Belgium, issued a manifesto, or declaration, in which they suggested that the United States try to buy Cuba from Spain. If that failed, the so-called Ostend Manifesto proclaimed boldly, Americans might be justified in seizing the island by force. President Pierce repudiated the statement, but northerners branded the act another attempt to expand slavery.

The Kansas–Nebraska Act

The question of slavery in the territories became an issue again in 1854 when Senator Stephen Douglas of Illinois introduced a bill in Congress to organize the vast Nebraska territory west of Iowa and Missouri. Douglas wanted to establish a transcontinental railroad by extending the existing lines from Chicago to the Pacific. The senator felt that such a route would be possible only if the Nebraska territory was organized.

According to the Missouri Compromise of 1820, slavery was prohibited in the Nebraska lands. But by 1854 a number of prominent southern senators had come to support John C. Calhoun's position that slavery ought to be permitted in all territories. Those senators refused to support Douglas's bill unless it allowed slavery within the Nebraska territory.

Douglas then proposed, and Congress passed, a compromise bill that divided the area into a Nebraska and a Kansas territory. The Kansas-Nebraska Act repealed the Missouri Compromise and in its place applied the doctrine of popular sovereignty. The people of each territory, rather than Congress, would decide whether to permit slavery.

Senator Douglas believed that popular sovereignty was the only democratic solution to the slavery question, but many northerners vehemently protested the repeal of the Missouri Compromise. They argued that the act created the possibility that any territory could be opened up to slavery.

Conflict Over Kansas

Most Americans assumed Nebraska would eventually become a free state because it was too far north for plantation agriculture. In addition, many thought Kansas would become a slave state because it was located directly west of Missouri, which was a slave state. But since the question of slavery would be decided by the voters, the final result remained uncertain.

Some abolitionist groups encouraged antislavery settlers to move to Kansas, hoping that the vote would go against slavery. The New England Emigrant Aid Society, for example, sent about 650 settlers to Kansas in 1854. Although the numbers were small, Missourians heard rumors that "mobs" of abolitionists were moving to Kansas. They feared that if slavery was not permitted in Kansas, their own slaves could easily escape across the border. Consequently proslavery elements encouraged settlers from Missouri to move to Kansas.

When the first elections to the territorial legislature were held in March 1855, about

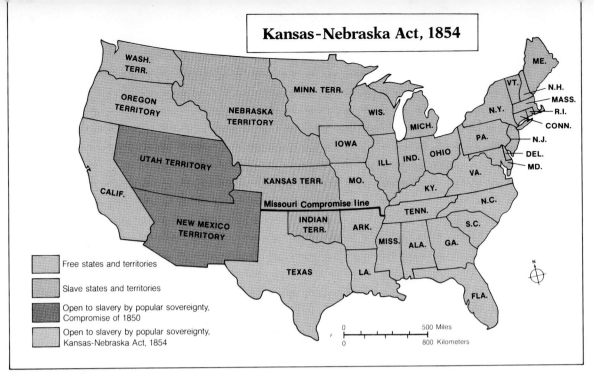

Kansas-Nebraska Act, 1854

WASH. TERR.

OREGON TERRITORY

MINN. TERR.

ME.

VT.

N.H.

MASS.

R.I.

CONN.

N.Y.

WIS.

MICH.

PA.

N.J.

DEL.

MD.

NEBRASKA TERRITORY

IOWA

UTAH TERRITORY

ILL.

IND.

OHIO

VA.

CALIF.

KANSAS TERR.

MO.

KY.

N.C.

Missouri Compromise line

NEW MEXICO TERRITORY

INDIAN TERR.

ARK.

TENN.

S.C.

MISS.

ALA.

GA.

TEXAS

LA.

FLA.

Free states and territories

Slave states and territories

Open to slavery by popular sovereignty, Compromise of 1850

Open to slavery by popular sovereignty, Kansas-Nebraska Act, 1854

0   500 Miles
0   800 Kilometers

■ *The Kansas-Nebraska Act repealed the Missouri Compromise by allowing slavery in territories north of the Missouri Compromise line if the voters wanted it.*

8,000 settlers lived in Kansas. Proslavery voters outnumbered antislavery voters by more than a thousand and could have won the election fairly. But several thousand angry Missouri "border ruffians" crossed into Kansas and voted illegally, giving the proslavery forces a lopsided victory.

Northerners promptly claimed the election had been stolen. They became even more incensed when the territorial legislature passed harsh proslavery laws. One law made it a crime to declare slavery illegal in Kansas; another ordered the death penalty for anyone who helped an escaped slave. In response to these actions antislavery settlers in Kansas refused to recognize the authority of the territorial government and established a rival free-state government at Lawrence, Kansas.

Chaos soon reigned throughout the territory, with two separate governments proclaiming authority and armed bands roaming the countryside. Finally, in May 1856 three events made the Kansas issue the focus of national attention. On May 21 a mob of Missourians acting as a sheriff's posse charged into Lawrence, looted and burned several houses, threw two printing presses into the river, and bombarded the Free State Hotel with cannon.

On May 22 Senator Charles Sumner of Massachusetts delivered a speech denouncing the violence in Kansas. Sumner charged that slave owners, including some of his colleagues in the Senate, were responsible. The next day Congressman Preston Brooks of South Carolina, a cousin of one of South Carolina's senators, attacked Sumner with a cane as he sat at his Senate desk. The injured Massachusetts senator was unable to resume his duties in the Senate for three years, and he never fully recovered.

On the night of May 24 a little-known Kansas antislavery agitator named John Brown took vengeance for the Lawrence attack into his own hands. Brown and a group of followers massacred five southern men and boys at a proslavery settlement at Pottawatomie Creek, Kansas, even though the victims had had nothing to do with the Lawrence raid.

The three violent events, following one another so closely, demonstrated how badly the Compromise of 1850 had failed. One of its major elements, the Fugitive Slave Law, had outraged the North. The question of extending slavery to the territories, which the compromise was supposed to settle, had been raised more violently than ever on the battleground of "Bleeding Kansas."

SECTION REVIEW

1. Identify: *Uncle Tom's Cabin*, Franklin Pierce, Ostend Manifesto, John Brown.
2. (a) How did southerners justify the Fugitive Slave Law? (b) What aspects of the law especially angered northerners?
3. Describe the Kansas-Nebraska Act.
4. (a) What was the outcome of the first territorial elections in Kansas? (b) What led to the establishment of a free-state government?
5. **Critical Thinking** Why was the Compromise of 1850 less successful than the Missouri Compromise?

3 Rise of Sectional Politics

The Whigs and Democrats as national political parties had been important "cords" binding the Union together since the mid-1830s. They had traditionally received support from both southern and northern states. However, growing sectional strains, aggravated by events in Kansas, divided the national parties and gave rise to a new political party.

Birth of the Republican Party

Citizens who opposed the expansion of slavery into the territories, known as *free soilers*, could find little hope in either the Whig or the Democratic party.* By the mid-1850s the Whigs had been seriously weakened by disputes between northern and southern factions; and the Democratic President, Franklin Pierce, had shown that he was sympathetic to the South.

During the summer of 1854, conventions of free soilers met in several northern states, hoping to form a new political party. At one such convention in Jackson, Michigan, the delegates for the first time called themselves Republicans. In the course of the next year, a sizable number of former Whigs, Democrats, and Free Soilers joined the Republicans, who were convinced that they could become a major party opposing the extension of slavery into the territories.

The Republican party grew rapidly. By 1856 they had elected some of their candidates to Congress and won several state elections. That same year they made their first bid for the presidency, nominating John Frémont, the impulsive, swashbuckling military leader who had encouraged the Bear Flag Revolt in California.

The Democrats chose James Buchanan of Pennsylvania. Buchanan supported the Kansas-Nebraska Act and popular sovereignty, but he remained vague about how or when the people of Kansas and Nebraska would decide the question of slavery. The remnants of the Whig and Know-Nothing parties both nominated former President Millard Fillmore in separate conventions, but the contest was between Frémont and Buchanan.

Republicans knew they had no chance in the South; most southern states did not even allow the names of Republican candidates on the ballot. But because the North had a majority of the electoral votes, the Republicans thought Frémont could win. When the ballots were counted, Buchanan had won—but only by a narrow margin.

The 1856 election demonstrated just how divided the nation had become. Buchanan carried every southern state except Maryland. Frémont carried every free state except Pennsylvania, Indiana, Illinois, New Jersey, and California. Increasingly, the Democrats spoke for the South, the Republicans for the North.

The Dred Scott Decision

A few months after Buchanan's victory, the Supreme Court rocked the nation with a major proslavery decision in the case of *Dred Scott* v. *Sandford*. Dred Scott had been a slave in Missouri. His owner served in the army for several years and took Scott with him to Illinois, a free state, and to Minnesota, a free territory. Eventually Scott's owner returned to Missouri.

---

*Both the Liberty and Free Soil parties had remained active for only a short period of time.

When Scott's owner died, some abolitionists aided Scott in suing for his freedom, claiming that he was free by virtue of his residence in Illinois and Minnesota. After a series of trials and conflicting judgments in the lower courts, the case finally went to the United States Supreme Court.

The Supreme Court faced two major questions in this decision. First, was Scott entitled to bring suit in a federal court? Slaves had no right to sue, and it was not even clear whether free blacks were United States citizens and as such had the right to sue. The Constitution itself did not specifically define the qualifications for citizenship. The second question was whether Scott's residence in a free state and a free territory had made him a free man.

The Court ruled that persons of African descent, whether slave or free, could not be citizens of the United States, and therefore Scott could not sue in a federal court. Missouri law, it concluded, should determine Scott's status, and according to Missouri law Scott was a slave.

The Court went further, ruling that the Missouri Compromise was unconstitutional because it had prohibited slavery north of 36°30′. Under the Fifth Amendment, the Court declared, Congress had no power to deprive anyone of property without due process of law. Because slaves were property, Congress could not forbid owners to take them into free territories—which was, in effect, what the Missouri Compromise had done.

The Dred Scott decision shocked a great many northerners, even moderates. First, it affirmed the most extreme southern position, that slavery could not be outlawed in any territory. Second, the decision marked the first time the Supreme Court had ruled a major piece of federal legislation unconstitutional. Only once before (*Marbury* v. *Madison*, see page 190) had it ruled any law unconstitutional.

Republicans were especially incensed. Above all, their party stood for the principle that Congress had the right to keep slavery out of the territories. And now the Supreme Court had, in effect, ruled that the party's goals were unconstitutional.

Northern Democrats, led by Stephen Douglas, also felt the shock. The Court by implication had ruled against the doctrine of popular sovereignty. If Congress had no power to prohibit slavery in the territories, then neither could it delegate that power to a territorial legislature.

A Senate Race With National Implications

As controversy enveloped the country, national attention focused on the 1858 Senate race in Illinois, in which the Democratic and Republican candidates skillfully debated the issues that divided the country.

The Democratic candidate, Senator Stephen Douglas, was the more well known of the two men. Douglas was just over five feet tall, with a large head and broad shoulders. A scrapper who loved an argument, he had a burning, energetic drive. Few could match his debating skills on the Senate floor, where he had helped Henry Clay push through the Compromise of 1850 and had vigorously defended the doctrine of popular sovereignty.

★ Voices of Freedom ★

Dred Scott v. *Sandford*

The text of the Dred Scott decision, as expressed here by Chief Justice Roger B. Taney, stated that the Constitution protected a citizen's property, including slaves.

[T]he rights of property are united with the rights of person, and placed on the same ground by the fifth amendment to the Constitution, which provides that no person shall be deprived of life, liberty and property, without due process of law. And an Act of Congress which deprives a citizen of the United States of his liberty or property, merely because he came himself or brought his property into a particular Territory of the United States, and who had committed no offense against the laws, could hardly be dignified with the name of due process of law. . . .

And no word can be found in the Constitution which gives Congress a greater power over slave property, or which entitles property of that kind to less protection than property of any other description.

Stephen Douglas (left) was a leader of the Democratic party in 1856. His opponent for a seat in the Senate, Abraham Lincoln (right), became nationally known after debating Douglas.

Douglas's Republican opponent was a respected lawyer named Abraham Lincoln. Born in Kentucky, Lincoln had moved with his family to Indiana and then to Illinois, where he combined his law practice with a career in politics, first as a Whig and then as a Republican.

At six feet four inches, Lincoln was as tall and lanky as Douglas was short and stocky. Self-educated and unpretentious, the Republican candidate combined a folksy, backwoods manner with a keen legal mind that instinctively sought out the logic of a situation in its clearest, simplest terms. Lincoln appeared awkward and homely and lacked a polished speaking style, but he had a sharp sense of humor, an easy manner with all sorts of people, and a compelling eloquence.

He had sounded his campaign theme in his speech accepting the nomination for senator. Beginning with the biblical observation that "a house divided against itself cannot stand," Lincoln stated his case:

> I believe this government cannot endure, permanently half slave and half free. I do not expect the Union to be dissolved; I do not expect the house to fall; but I do expect it will cease to be divided. It will become all one thing, or all the other.

The Lincoln–Douglas Debates

As the lesser-known of the two candidates, Lincoln challenged Douglas to a series of debates during the campaign. In seven memorable appearances the "Little Giant," as people called Douglas, squared off against "Honest Abe." Cheering crowds, bands, and torchlight parades accompanied their appearances, and the debaters faced the controversial issue of slavery squarely and directly. Newspapers across the country reprinted the candidates' words, and citizens argued over who was more persuasive.

Lincoln argued that the major philosophical difference between Republicans and northern Democrats like Douglas was the Republican belief that the institution of slavery was morally wrong. Douglas, Lincoln pointed out, had said he did not care whether slavery was accepted or rejected in the territories. Although Lincoln believed that blacks and whites might not be equal, he maintained that blacks were entitled to "all the natural rights enumerated in the Declaration of Independence, the right to life, liberty, and the pursuit of happiness."

Douglas sought to defend the doctrine of popular sovereignty as fair and workable. At a debate in Freeport, Illinois, Lincoln pressed Douglas to reconcile his doctrine of popular sovereignty with the Dred Scott decision. The Supreme Court had ruled that slavery must be allowed in every territory. Was there any legal way, Lincoln asked, that the residents of a territory could exercise popular sovereignty and prohibit slavery?

Douglas replied that since slavery could not exist without a slave code to protect it, the people of a territory could simply refuse to enact a slave code. Douglas's solution, soon known as the Freeport Doctrine, gained him the support of many voters. In the election, he defeated Lincoln by a narrow margin.

The senator's victory cost his party dearly. The Freeport Doctrine impressed northern Democrats, but southerners considered it an act of treachery. From their point of view, Douglas was encouraging setlers in the territories to stop slavery from spreading. This drove a deeper wedge between northern and southern Democrats and further weakened the Democrats as a national party.

SECTION REVIEW

1. Identify: Dred Scott, Abraham Lincoln, Freeport Doctrine.

2. Define: free soiler.
3. What issue led to the creation of the Republican party?
4. How did the election of 1856 reveal divisions in the nation?
5. In the Supreme Court's opinion, why was Dred Scott still a slave?
6. **Critical Thinking** Why does a lesser-known candidate stand to gain more by participating in a campaign debate?

323

4 The House Divided

The 1850s had begun with a concerted effort to put aside the differences that separated North and South. Yet by 1859 the country had been split apart in many ways. At the center of the conflict was slavery, the issue that would not go away. As the presidential election of 1860 approached, the nation resembled a powder keg waiting for a spark to ignite it.

Harpers Ferry

John Brown struck the spark. Brown, a Kansas abolitionist, had shocked the South and much of the rest of the nation by leading the massacre at Pottawatomie Creek. He seemed to be a strange, violent man with a flair for the dramatic. After his raids in Kansas, Brown returned east and began raising money for a mysterious mission. Concealing the details, he would only hint at his plan.

Some of the more radical abolitionists financed Brown's activities, knowing that he planned a raid on southern plantations to free slaves and begin a rebellion. When Frederick Douglass heard about the plan, he warned that it would not succeed. As an escaped slave, Douglass knew conditions in the South firsthand and recognized that the plan was impractical, but Brown would not change his mind.

On the night of October 15, 1859, Brown led a band of 18 men to the federal arsenal at Harpers Ferry, Virginia, seized its weapons, and waited for slaves to rise in rebellion and join him. But Brown had made several mistakes. Few slaves lived in the area of Harpers Ferry, and they were unlikely to stake their lives on the leadership of a man they had never heard of. Furthermore, Brown lingered at Harpers Ferry until all avenues of escape were cut off. A day after the attack, United States troops led by Colonel Robert E. Lee easily subdued the raiders.

Brown's military conduct was amateurish, but he carried himself with dignity and calm when he was brought to trial for treason. Even his southern jailer and guards were impressed. Brown's dignity also won him sympathy in the North—and he knew the strategic value of martyrdom. On December 2, state authorities hanged Brown from a scaffold in Charlestown, Virginia, following his conviction.

A Charged Atmosphere

In the North church bells tolled in mourning. Black bunting hung on windows, and sympathizers held mass prayer meetings in New York, Boston, and Philadelphia. John Brown's death proved more effective in mobilizing antislavery opinion than his actions had. Despite the show of sympathy, however, many northern leaders, including Republican party members, repudiated Brown's actions and dismissed him as a lunatic.

In the South, however, such words had little effect. Southerners heard about the church bells and prayer meetings and read some abolitionist speeches calling for slave insurrections. Increasingly they came to believe that their security could be maintained only by *seceding*, or withdrawing, from the Union. One Virginia newspaper noted that there were "thousands of men in our midst who, a month ago, scoffed at the idea of a

In this painting by the black artist Horace Pippin, the fierce abolitionist John Brown is hauled to his execution in 1859. At right, a black woman turns away in despair as Brown rides his own coffin to the gallows. Pippin's mother told him she had watched Brown's execution.

dissolution of the Union as a madman's dream, but who now hold the opinion that its days are numbered."

In Washington tensions had grown so high that senators and representatives often went to legislative sessions armed, and some claimed that spectators in the galleries carried weapons too. When a pistol accidentally fell from the pocket of a New York congressman during one heated debate, a shooting fray nearly erupted. "The only persons who do not have a revolver and a knife," reported one South Carolina senator, "are those who have two revolvers."

The 1860 Conventions

In this atmosphere of increasing suspicion and distrust, the presidential nominating conventions assembled. The Democrats met in Charleston, South Carolina. Some southerners, determined to defeat Stephen Douglas and the northern Democrats, demanded that the party endorse a federal code to protect slavery in all territories. When the convention rejected this platform, those delegates walked out.

Unable to agree on a nominee, the convention finally adjourned, to reassemble six weeks later in Baltimore, Maryland. There the delegates quickly nominated Douglas. A group of southern Democrats then held their own convention, adopted the original southern platform, and nominated John Breckinridge of Kentucky to head their ticket.

A new party, the Constitutional Union party, also held a convention in 1860 and nominated John Bell of Tennessee for President. The Constitutional Unionists denounced the sectionalism of the other parties. They hoped to rally conservatives in both South and North around a vague platform that supported the Constitution and one Union.

The Republican convention met in Chicago in the Wigwam, a building specially constructed for the event. Hundreds of enthusiastic Republicans squeezed inside while a crowd of as many as 20,000 people cheered outside.

The leading contender for the nomination as the convention opened was William H. Seward of New York. Seward, however, had a reputation as a radical, and party leaders worried that he could not win. As they searched for a more moderate candidate, their attention focused on Abraham Lincoln, whom all factions of the party found acceptable. In addition, Lincoln came from Illinois, a state Republicans needed to carry in 1860. He received the nomination on the third ballot.

In 1860 the Republicans sought to broaden their platform. They endorsed a protective tariff, which was popular in the industrial areas of the Northeast, and a homestead law, granting free land to settlers, which was popular throughout the West. Moreover, their statements about slavery were less shrill than in 1856, although the party continued to insist that Congress ban slavery from all territories.

The Election of 1860

The presidential campaign of 1860 revealed just how close to disunion the country was. Lincoln's supporters did not campaign in the South, and his name was not even on the ballot in ten southern states. Breckinridge, on the other hand, had virtually no support in the North. Only Douglas, weary but determined, campaigned actively in both northern and southern states, warning of the dire consequences of disunion. A month before the election, Douglas knew his chances were lost, and he predicted that Lincoln would be elected.

On November 6, the voters confirmed Douglas's prediction. Lincoln received 39 percent of the popular vote and carried every northern state except New Jersey. Breckinridge swept the deep South and divided the border states with Bell and Douglas. Although Douglas finished last in the electoral college, he received more popular votes than anyone except Lincoln.

Lincoln's election marked a dramatic change in American politics. He was the first President to be elected by a sectional party with its strength entirely in the North. To

southerners the future was particularly alarming. A man had been elected President who was not even on the ballot in their part of the country. The North had simply outvoted them. Since the South now had only one third of the total white male population of the United States, many southerners concluded that the only way they could continue to play a role in any national government was to secede and form a government of their own. (See map on page 326.)

The Secession Crisis

South Carolina, which had threatened to secede during the nullification crisis of 1832 (see page 238), again took the strongest action. Its legislature called a convention and, on December 20, 1860, the convention adopted an ordinance of secession, stating that South Carolina was no longer part of the Union but was now a free and independent state. By the end of February 1861, the six states of the deep South had followed South Carolina's lead. (See map on page 324.)

In February delegates from the seceded states met in Montgomery, Alabama, and formed the Confederate States of America. As their frame of government they adopted most features of the United States Constitution, making only a few changes. They stressed the "sovereign and independent character" of each individual state, and they made it clear that slaves could be held as property.

On February 18 Jefferson Davis of Mississippi was inaugurated as the President of the Confederate States. Davis, a former United States senator, read his inaugural address while new military companies clad in red, green, and gray battle jackets paraded with new bayonets on their rifles.

In the North, meanwhile, James Buchanan watched these developments with an increasing feeling of powerlessness. He was a *lame duck* President, serving until his successor's inauguration. The Democrats had not renominated him, and the voters had rejected his policies by electing Lincoln. So Buchanan did little.

In December 1860 Congress made one last attempt to hold the Union together. Senator John Crittenden of Kentucky proposed that the Missouri Compromise line be restored and applied to all territory then part of or later acquired by the United States. He also suggested that an "unamendable"

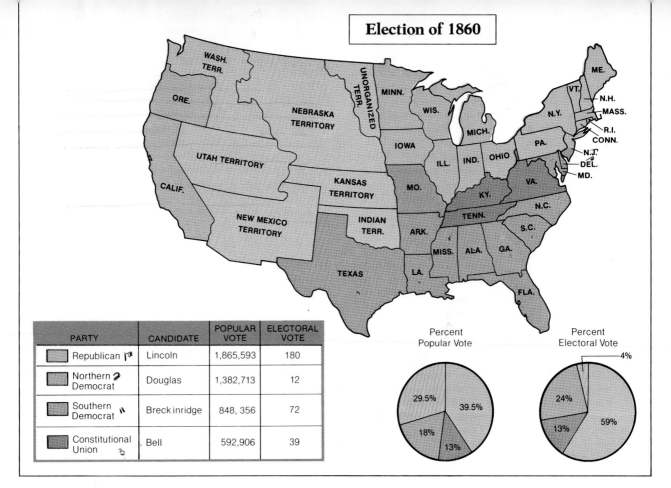

Election of 1860

PARTY	CANDIDATE	POPULAR VOTE	ELECTORAL VOTE
Republican	Lincoln	1,865,593	180
Northern Democrat	Douglas	1,382,713	12
Southern Democrat	Breckinridge	848,356	72
Constitutional Union	Bell	592,906	39

Percent Popular Vote

29.5% 39.5% 18% 13%

Percent Electoral Vote

4% 24% 13% 59%

■ *The deep divisions of the nation were shown in the election of 1860. Lincoln carried every northern state except New Jersey, while Breckinridge swept the deep South. Bell, Douglas, and Breckinridge split the border states.*

amendment be added to the Constitution to forever guarantee the right of slavery in states south of the compromise line. But Republicans refused to support these or any other compromise proposals, so Crittenden held no hope of getting them passed. The breach between North and South had become too wide for compromise.

Fort Sumter

When Abraham Lincoln became President in March 1861, the seceded states hoped that the North would allow them to depart in peace. Across the South, Confederate forces seized federal arsenals and forts. Only Fort Sumter, on an island outside Charleston Harbor, and three forts in Florida remained in federal hands.

Lincoln was determined to hold the Union together. Yet he faced a delicate situation. The northern section of the South, including the key state of Virginia, had rejected secession and remained in the Union.

If Lincoln used force rashly, he would risk losing the border states.

Events finally forced Lincoln to act. Major Robert Anderson, the commander of Fort Sumter, reported that his supplies were running low. Confederate forces were ready to take the fort, and he could not hold out much longer unless resupplied. Lincoln was determined not to surrender federal authority without a fight, yet he did not want the North to be guilty of starting a civil war. After much deliberation, he notified Confederate officials that he would not reinforce the fort with either arms or men. He promised to send only food.

In Charleston, Confederate General P.G.T. Beauregard demanded that Major Anderson surrender Fort Sumter. Anderson told the Confederates that he would withdraw on April 15 if he did not receive supplies or other orders.

But southern suspicion of northern intentions ran high. At four-thirty on the morn-

Causes of the Civil War: Analyzing Interpretations

Historians may interpret events differently even if they study the same sources. Their environment affects their *frame of reference,* or the way they view a historical event. Two views of the causes of the Civil War are printed here. The first was written by Frank Owsley in 1930, the second by Arthur Schlesinger, Jr., in 1949.

1. **Identify the interpretation.** (a) What does Owsley seem to think was the basic cause of the Civil War? (b) What does Schlesinger seem to think was a major cause?

2. **Decide how a person's frame of reference affects his or her interpretation.** To complete this step, you need to know about the time period in which the historian lived. The years after 1929 were ones of severe economic depression in the United States. After the Allies had defeated Germany in 1945, Americans were horrified to learn about the Nazi concentration camps. Use this background information to answer the following: (a) Can you find any evidence that concern about the nation's economy may have influenced Owsley's interpretation? (b) How might the discovery of the existence of Nazi concentration camps have affected Schlesinger's interpretation?

3. **Decide which interpretation you think is most accurate.** (a) How did the economy of the North and the South help cause the war? (b) How did the moral aspects of slavery help cause the war? (c) What other factors were important?

Frank Owsley

[S]lavery as a moral issue is too simple an explanation. . . . Complex though the factors were which finally caused war, they all grew out of two fundamental differences which existed between the two sections: the North was commercial and industrial, and the South was agrarian. . . . Herein lies the irrepressible conflict, the eternal struggle between the agrarian South and the commercial and industrial North to control the government either in its own interest or, negatively, to prevent the other section from controlling it in its interests. . . . The irrepressible conflict, then, was not between slavery and freedom, but between the industrial and commercial civilization of the North and the agrarian civilization of the South.

Arthur Schlesinger, Jr.

It was the moral issue of slavery, for example, that gave the struggles over slavery in the territories or over the enforcement of the fugitive slave laws their significance. . . . To say that the Civil War was fought over the ''unreal'' issue of slavery in the territories is like saying that the Second World War was fought over the ''unreal'' issue of the invasion of Poland. The democracies could not challenge fascism inside Germany any more than opponents of slavery could challenge slavery inside the South; but the extension of slavery, like the extension of fascism, was an act of aggression which made a moral choice inescapable. . . . Human slavery is certainly one of the few issues of whose evil we can be sure. It is not just ''a very ancient labor system,'' it is also a betrayal of the basic values of our Christian and democratic tradition. No historian can understand the circumstances which led to its abolition until he writes about it in its fundamental moral context.

ing of April 12, Confederate batteries opened fire on the fort. All day long the Confederates kept up the bombardment while fashionable ladies and gentlemen of Charleston watched from the shore. On April 13, his ammunition gone, Anderson accepted Beauregard's terms of evacuation and marched out of the fort.

The tension of waiting was broken. Both sides had chosen war to achieve their goals. The attack on Fort Sumter boosted morale in the South, and because Lincoln's cautious

Major Events	
1820	Missouri Compromise
1846	Wilmot Proviso proposed
1849	California seeks admission to Union
1850	Compromise of 1850
1852	*Uncle Tom's Cabin* published; Franklin Pierce elected President
1854	Kansas-Nebraska Act
1856	James Buchanan elected President
1859	John Brown leads raid at Harpers Ferry
1860	Abraham Lincoln elected President; South Carolina secedes from Union
1861	Confederate States of America formed; Fort Sumter falls

diplomacy had forced the South to fire the first shot, the North rallied behind the cause of Union with a sense of moral outrage.

SECTION REVIEW

1. Identify: Harpers Ferry, Constitutional Union party, Confederate States of America, Jefferson Davis, Fort Sumter.
2. Define: secede, lame duck.
3. (a) What effect did John Brown's death have in the North? (b) What effect did it have in the South?
4. Why did Republican party leaders choose Abraham Lincoln as their presidential candidate in 1860?
5. How did the election of 1860 add to southern desires to secede from the Union?
6. **Critical Thinking** Would war necessarily have been avoided if Lincoln had allowed the Confederate states to secede?

Chapter 17 Review

In Perspective

From the 1820s through the 1850s attempts were made to resolve conflicts between the North and the South. The Missouri Compromise worked as long as the balance between slave and free states was maintained. After 1848, the question of slavery in the territories became a major issue.

The Compromise of 1850 admitted California as a free state but allowed slavery in the rest of the Southwest. Many northerners opposed the strong fugitive slave provision of the compromise. The Kansas-Nebraska Act allowed the status of slavery in those territories to be decided by popular vote. This led to violence in Kansas and further divided the nation.

Sectional strains divided both the Whigs and the Democrats. The Republican party emerged in opposition to the extension of slavery to the territories. When Lincoln was elected president in 1860, many southerners thought they had no choice but to secede.

John C. Calhoun's stern prophecy of 1850 was fulfilled in 1861 when one nation became two. Whether they would remain separated would be decided by four years of bitter fighting and heroic sacrifice.

Vocabulary

On a separate sheet of paper, write the word or words that best complete each of the following sentences.

1. In a ＿＿ state, slavery was not allowed.
2. ＿＿ was a method by which voters would decide whether or not to allow slavery in a territory.
3. ＿＿ opposed the spread of slavery into the territories.
4. South Carolina ＿＿, or withdrew, from the Union.
5. A ＿＿ is an official who is serving until a successor takes office.

Chapter Checkup

1. (a) Why did California's request for admission to the Union cause heated debate in Congress? (b) What problems did the Compromise of 1850 try to solve?

2. (a) How was the question of slavery to be decided in the Kansas and Nebraska territories? (b) How did that method differ from the one established by the Missouri Compromise?

3. How did the Dred Scott decision affect the status of slavery in the territories?

4. (a) Why were there two Democratic candidates for President in 1860? (b) How did the election results show the sectional split?

Critical Thinking

1. **Analyzing** Why did John Brown's death create more sympathy for abolitionism than did his actions at Harpers Ferry?

2. **Comparing** In what way was the Constitution of the Confederate States of America similar to the Articles of Confederation? (See page 143.)

Developing Basic Skills

1. **Map Reading** Based on the maps on pages 314, 316, and 319, how did the following affect the status of slavery in the territory west of Iowa and Missouri: Missouri Compromise, Compromise of 1850, Kansas–Nebraska Act?

2. **Placing Events in Time** On a time line write the events that led to the split between South and North. (Review Chapters 13 through 17.) Does the time line support the belief that a division of the nation was becoming increasingly likely?

See page 830 for suggested readings.

Writer's Handbook

Using a Cataloging System

A library card catalog has subject, title and author cards. The call number classifies a book according to the Dewey Decimal System or the Library of Congress System. Under the more commonly used Dewey Decimal System, history and geography fall in the 900s.

Practice: Study the catalog author card and answer the following questions:

1. What is the title of the book?
2. When was the book published?
3. Does the book include a bibliography?
4. What is the call number of the book?
5. Is the book illustrated?

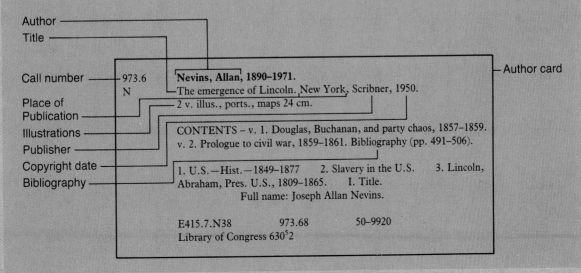

Author
Title
Call number — 973.6 N
Place of Publication
Illustrations
Publisher
Copyright date
Bibliography

Author card

Nevins, Allan, 1890–1971.
The emergence of Lincoln. New York, Scribner, 1950.
2 v. illus., ports., maps 24 cm.

CONTENTS – v. 1. Douglas, Buchanan, and party chaos, 1857–1859. v. 2. Prologue to civil war, 1859–1861. Bibliography (pp. 491–506).

1. U.S.—Hist.—1849–1877   2. Slavery in the U.S.   3. Lincoln, Abraham, Pres. U.S., 1809–1865.   I. Title.
Full name: Joseph Allan Nevins.

E415.7.N38   973.68   50–9920
Library of Congress 630⁵2

18

Divided by War

(1861–1865)

Confederate soldier, Private Edwin Jenson

Chapter Outline

1 *Preparing for War*

2 *War Begins*

3 *Freedom*

4 *Behind the Lines*

5 *An End to the War*

With the fall of Fort Sumter, a war fever swept the divided nation. Throughout North and South a similar scene repeated itself: wives, sweethearts, and children cheered as volunteers marched down the streets carrying an assortment of weapons, extra clothes, cooking utensils, and 'perhaps some cakes or cookies from home. "So impatient did I become for starting," wrote one eager Arkansas youth, "that I felt like a thousand pins were pricking me . . . and I started off a week in advance of my brothers."

Most Americans thought the conflict would be brief and decisive, but it stretched into four years of bloody combat. In the end more Americans died in the Civil War than in any war the nation has fought before or since.

Confederate victories in East		Union moves toward victory		
1861	1862	1863	1864	1865
1861 Firing on Fort Sumter; Battle of Bull Run	**1862** Battles of Fort Henry, Fort Donelson, Shiloh, Antietam; Homestead Act passed	**1863** Emancipation Proclamation; Battles of Vicksburg, Gettysburg, Chickamauga	**1864** Lincoln reelected; Sherman marches to sea	**1865** Grant takes Richmond; Lee surrenders

1 Preparing for War

The guns at Fort Sumter began the war, but it took a great while for the North and the South to prepare for military conflict. The Union had just inaugurated a new President, Abraham Lincoln, who held responsibility for pursuing the war. He had to oversee the calling of troops, the organizing of supplies, and the raising of money.

The South faced similar problems, with the added disadvantage that their Confederate government was only a month old. For President Jefferson Davis and his administration, the tasks of organization and preparation were even greater.

The Border States

As the two sides prepared for war, one major question loomed above all others. On whose side would the unaligned states fight? Seven states had not yet committed themselves to either the Union or the Confederacy.

President Lincoln forced a decision on the question three days after the attack on Fort Sumter. On April 15, 1861, he issued a call to the state governors for 75,000 militiamen. Those states that had not seceded had to decide whether to send soldiers to fight the Confederacy or join it. Virginia, Arkansas, Tennessee, and North Carolina seceded; Maryland, Missouri, and Kentucky wavered.

The situation in Maryland was tense. If Maryland joined the Confederacy, the Union capital, Washington, D.C., would be surrounded by Confederate territory. After Confederate sympathizers attacked Union troops in Baltimore, President Lincoln decided to act. On April 27 he sent federal troops to occupy the city, proclaimed martial law in Maryland, and suspended *habeas corpus*, the right not to be imprisoned without a trial. He then jailed the most blatant Confederate supporters, including some state legislators.

With the major opposition in prison, the Maryland legislature defeated a resolution to secede. Although the state remained in the Union, many of its citizens continued to sympathize with the Confederate cause.

At first Kentucky tried to remain neutral, but Lincoln's careful personal diplomacy toward his home state fostered sympathy there for the federal government. A Confederate invasion of the state in September 1861 gave Kentucky's pro-Union legislature an excuse to throw its support to Lincoln, ending the state's neutrality.

In Missouri sporadic fighting occurred between groups favoring opposing sides until a decisive battle in 1862 secured the state for the Union. Three critical states had sided with the Union. (See the map on page 332.)

The South's Position

When the war began, each side was confident of victory. Southerners believed they were fighting a war for independence similar to the Revolutionary War. They did not intend to carry the war to the North. Their aim was to defend their homeland. The North faced the difficult task of invading. Northern lines of supply would have to be much longer than Confederate supply lines and would thus be more open to attack.

Soldiers from the rural South had the additional advantage of being generally more experienced than many northerners in the use of firearms and horses. The southerners often hunted game and felt at home in the outdoors. Furthermore, Confederate military leaders were among the best in the nation. Many had been trained at the United States Military Academy at West Point, including talented men like Robert E. Lee, Thomas "Stonewall" Jackson, and Joseph Johnston.

Despite these advantages the South faced major problems. The Confederate Constitution limited the authority of the central government over individual states. Governor Joseph Brown of Georgia, for example, insisted that Georgia troops be commanded only by Georgia officers. Moreover, the South carried the burden of defending slavery, which made it more difficult to enlist European nations as allies.

The North's Position

The North had a larger population, providing almost four times as many potential soldiers, and many more factories than the

332

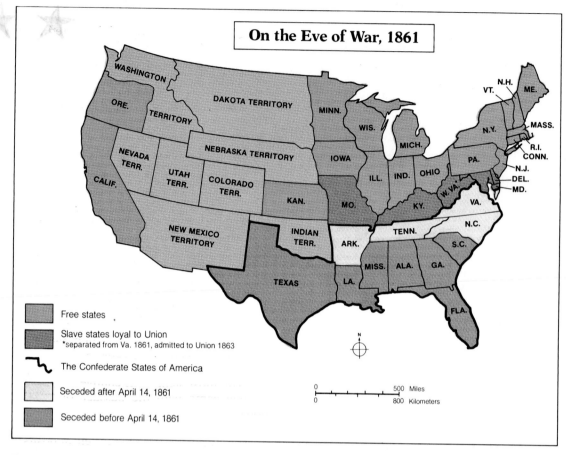

On the Eve of War, 1861

Free states

Slave states loyal to Union
*separated from Va. 1861, admitted to Union 1863

The Confederate States of America

Seceded after April 14, 1861

Seceded before April 14, 1861

■ *In early 1861, seven states had not yet chosen sides in the struggle. Arkansas, Tennessee, North Carolina, and Virginia seceded after the fall of Fort Sumter. Maryland, Kentucky, and Missouri remained in the Union.*

South. Massachusetts alone produced more manufactured goods than the entire Confederacy. A good railroad network and control of the country's navy and almost all its merchant marine added to the strength of the North.

Before the impact of superior numbers and greater supplies could be felt on the battlefield, however, the North had to convert its industries from peace- to wartime production. The North put its superior resources to use slowly and thus lost some of its advantage.

President Lincoln first offered the command of the Union army to Robert E. Lee, a Virginian, but Lee chose to serve with the Confederacy. Like the South, the North had many able military men trained at West Point, but Lincoln and his advisers knew little of their abilities and made several false starts before finding a commander able to win the war.

Civil Leadership

Civil leaders as well as military commanders played a vital role in the war effort. When the Civil War began, few people in Washington knew Abraham Lincoln well. Many suspected he was not up to the job of commander-in-chief. Lincoln's own attorney general wrote that the President "lacks will and purpose, and, I greatly fear, he has not the power to command."

But Lincoln proved his critics wrong. He extracted the best from his cabinet and demonstrated exceptional political skills. For example, he had the ability to maintain public morale through regular contact with the citizens. Several days a week, he opened the White House to the public and talked with anyone who wanted to see him.

Jefferson Davis, the Confederate President, appeared more distinguished and more experienced than Lincoln. He had served in the House of Representatives, the Senate, and as secretary of war under President Pierce. He was hard working and dedicated. As a graduate of West Point and a veteran officer of the Mexican War, he seemed well equipped to lead the Confederacy.

Yet precisely because of his devotion, President Davis often overworked. He labored over details of military strategy best left to others. He quarreled often with the Confederate Congress and vetoed 38 bills. (All but one of the vetoes were overridden by the Congress.) Lincoln, in contrast, vetoed only three bills.

Mobilizing for War

At the beginning of the war, each side hoped to raise an army of volunteers, but responses were inadequate. The Union army tried to encourage enlistment by offering *bounties*, sums paid to recruits signing up for service. Bounties were especially appealing to the poor, but some unscrupulous men took advantage of the system by *bounty jumping*. They would enlist, collect a bounty, then desert and reenlist somewhere else, collecting another bounty.

In 1863 the United States passed its first national draft law, requiring military service of males between the ages of 20 and 45. A person with money, however, could hire a substitute or pay a fee of $300 to exempt himself from military service.

The Confederacy had passed its draft law earlier, in 1862. At first, men between the ages of 18 and 35 were eligible for the draft; the range was later extended to age 45. The Confederate law allowed paid substitutes until 1863, when that provision was repealed. The most hated provision of the Confederate draft law exempted one man from each plantation that had 20 or more slaves.

Disillusioned participants on both sides soon came to feel that the Civil War was "a rich man's war and a poor man's fight." Such dissatisfaction was one cause of desertion, a problem that plagued both the Union and the Confederate armies.

Paying for the War

Southern leaders did not levy taxes to support the war because they feared that heavy taxation would erode popular support. Instead, they raised two fifths of their income

by selling bonds that could be cashed in after the war. The remaining source of income for the Confederacy was the printing press. The Confederate government simply printed money, even though there was no gold or silver to back it. Eventually that practice led to runaway inflation.

Like the South, the North was reluctant to raise money by imposing taxes. In August 1861, however, it levied the first income tax in the nation's history and imposed new sales taxes and taxes on manufactured goods. Only the tax on manufacturers raised much money, but the sales and income taxes established precedents for future legislation. The North also raised money by selling bonds.

By 1862 the war was costing the North almost $1.75 million a day. To raise further funds, Congress passed the Legal Tender Act, which authorized the government to issue paper money. Since the new bills were printed in green ink, people soon came to call them greenbacks.

The most significant change in northern finance came with the passage of the National Bank Act in 1863. The act raised additional war bonds by requiring new national banks to invest one third of their deposits in federal bonds. At the same time, it forced state banks to stop printing their own notes, allowing only national banks to issue paper money.

The new requirements created the nation's first truly centralized banking system. Since they wanted to continue issuing bank notes, over 800 state banks became national banks and invested their deposits in United States war bonds.

Diplomacy During the War

When the war began, both the Union and the Confederacy hoped for foreign assistance. Because of Great Britain's strong navy and large industrial capacity, both sides were especially eager to win its support.

British opinion about the war was divided. Despite President Lincoln's refusal to interfere with slavery where it already existed, many British reformers and ordinary citizens supported the North because of the slavery issue. On the other hand, many people in Britain supported the Confederacy's wish to be recognized as an independent state. Much of the British nobility, especially, identified more with southern planters than with northern factory workers.

Early in the war, Jefferson Davis banned cotton shipments to England, hoping that shortages would force the British to recognize the Confederacy. British textile mills, however, had a surplus of cotton when the war began, and the ploy failed. In the end, Great Britain chose to remain officially neutral, refusing to commit itself to either South or North. As the war continued and neither side gained a clear upper hand, Europeans generally decided to stay neutral. The war between North and South remained a civil war.

SECTION REVIEW

1. Identify: National Bank Act.
2. Define: habeas corpus, bounty, bounty jumping.
3. Which border states sided with the Union?
4. What goal were southerners fighting for?
5. What two major advantages did the North have over the South as the war began?
6. What were Jefferson Davis's qualifications as President of the Confederacy?
7. (a) What methods did the Union use to raise an army? (b) What methods did the Confederacy use?
8. (a) What methods did the Confederacy use to raise funds during the war? (b) What methods did the Union use?
9. **Critical Thinking** Why has the declaration of neutrality by the Kentucky legislature been termed a "vain dream"?

2 War Begins

As both sides mobilized for war, few leaders realized how long or how devastating the conflict would be. Northerners thought that victory would be theirs once they captured Richmond, Virginia, the capital of the Confederacy. Southerners believed that if they pushed back northern invasion attempts often enough, the North would give up. In fact, the struggle would be a turning point in the history of combat, foreshadowing the more deadly warfare of the twentieth century.

The New Shape of War

The large number of soldiers involved in any given battle distinguished this war from previous American conflicts. In the War of 1812 and the Mexican War, there were never more than 14,000 or 15,000 soldiers opposing each other in a single battle. In the war between the Union and the Confederacy, battles involving more than 100,000 soldiers were not uncommon, and the number of casualties was correspondingly high. At least 540,000 Americans lost their lives.

More efficient weaponry was responsible for many of the deaths. Old rifle balls were replaced by cone-shaped Minié bullets, which were about twice as accurate. Thus trenches became necessary for defense. Bayonets lost much of their usefulness because soldiers could shoot one another from a distance long before they could get close enough for hand-to-hand combat. The Union manufactured artillery pieces that could fire projectiles weighing up to 300 pounds (135 kilograms). With few factories, the Confederacy had to import or capture most of its field artillery. Nevertheless it was able to bring these deadly weapons to bear.

Medical practices amidst difficult battlefield conditions were also responsible for much suffering and death. Sanitation was poor, and water was often contaminated. Doctors were in short supply. Antiseptics were unknown, so wounds and incisions often became infected. Painkillers were neither easy to come by nor particularly effective. One Confederate officer wrote that his men had as much to fear from their own doctors as they did from Union troops.

Northern Strategy

At the outbreak of war General Winfield Scott, a hero of the Mexican War, supervised all Union forces. Old and in ill health, Scott nonetheless retained a keen mind. Unlike most people, he realized that the war would not be over in 90 days.

Scott suggested a grand war strategy to President Lincoln. The navy should set up a complete blockade of Confederate ports from Norfolk, Virginia, to Galveston, Texas. Union forces should split the Confederacy into three parts at the Appalachian Mountains and the Mississippi River and then use Union naval superiority to isolate and strangle each weakened section.

People ridiculed Scott's scheme, calling it the "anaconda," after a huge South American snake that kills its prey by crushing, but the course of events would prove the value of Scott's strategy. The Appalachians and the Mississippi did divide the Confederate States into three regions, which became the theaters of the war.

West of the Mississippi, in Louisiana, Arkansas, and Texas, Confederate defenders under the command of Edmund Kirby-Smith kept northern forces at bay. But this far-western theater remained isolated from the main conflicts and influenced the final outcome of the war very little. Most of the action centered in the western theater (the area between the Appalachians and the Mississippi) and in the eastern theater (the area around Virginia and Maryland).

The First Battle of Bull Run

Implementing Scott's plan would take time, and northerners were demanding bold action to end the war quickly. To satisfy this demand President Lincoln sent Union troops to fight a Confederate army camped in northern Virginia near Washington. On a pleasant afternoon on July 21, 1861, northern picnickers and newspaper reporters settled on a hill overlooking a small stream called Bull Run. They waited for Union troops to advance, expecting to see a decisive Union victory.

The battle did not go according to expectations. Both Union and Confederate troops were inexperienced and poorly prepared. Furthermore, neither Union General Irvin McDowell nor Confederate General P.G.T. Beauregard was accustomed to commanding large forces.

At first Union troops fought well. But their advance was blocked by men under the command of General Thomas J. Jackson, who stood "like a stone wall" awaiting relief. (It was for this brave stand that Jackson earned the nickname "Stonewall.") When

Neither side expected a long struggle at the beginning of the war, and some families joined the soldiers in camp. You can see some of the daily routines of camp life in this photo of a Pennsylvania soldier and his family.

Confederate reinforcements arrived, General McDowell tried an orderly retreat, but his men bolted and ran. The green southern troops, in turn, were too surprised to press their advantage.

When the nation learned of the Confederate success, dismayed northerners realized that an easy victory was not in sight. Southerners rejoiced and felt confident about the war's eventual outcome.

War at Sea

Because the South was primarily an agricultural region, it had always depended on northern and European sources for manufactured goods. With the start of the war,

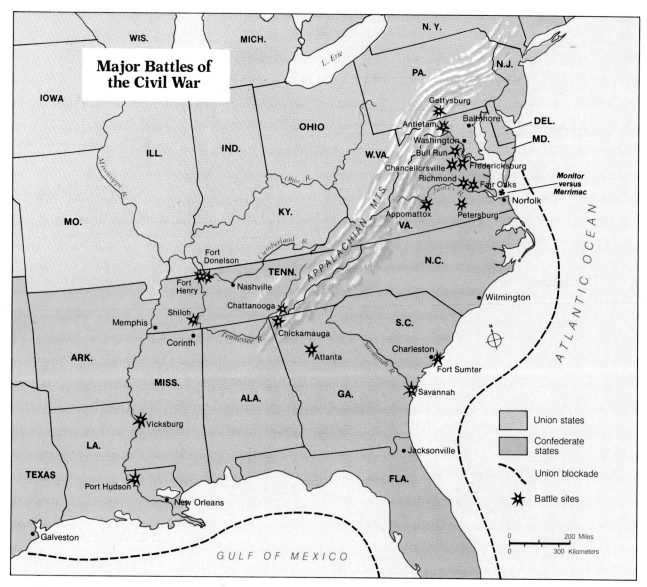

Major Battles of the Civil War

WIS.

MICH.

N. Y.

IOWA

OHIO

PA.

N.J.

ILL.

IND.

W.VA.

Gettysburg

Antietam

Baltimore

DEL.

MD.

Washington

MO.

KY.

Bull Run

Chancellorsville

Fredericksburg

Richmond

Fair Oaks

Monitor
versus
Merrimac

Appomattox

VA.

Norfolk

Petersburg

Fort
Donelson

TENN.

Fort
Henry

Nashville

N.C.

Wilmington

Shiloh

Chattanooga

Memphis

Corinth

Chickamauga

S.C.

ARK.

Atlanta

Charleston

MISS.

ALA.

GA.

Fort Sumter

Savannah

Vicksburg

LA.

Jacksonville

TEXAS

Port Hudson

FLA.

New Orleans

Galveston

GULF OF MEXICO

ATLANTIC OCEAN

	Union states
	Confederate states
---	Union blockade
✸	Battle sites

0   200 Miles

0   300 Kilometers

■ *This map shows the broad extent of the Civil War, while the smaller maps on the following pages show details of individual campaigns. Most battles were fought in the South.*

trade with Europe became even more crucial because the North was no longer a source of supply. Consequently the North began to implement Scott's anaconda strategy by blockading the southern coast. The Union navy tried to cut off all imports by patrolling major southern ports and wherever possible capturing the ports themselves.

Before the war, approximately 6,000 ships a year entered southern ports; in the first year of the blockade, the number dropped to 800. As the war continued, the Union blockade became even more effec-

tive. Still, loopholes existed. Enterprising southerners living along the coast sometimes successfully "ran" the blockade.

The small Confederate fleet of seagoing cruisers also damaged Union trade. In less than four years the *Alabama* and the *Florida*, built for the Confederacy in Great Britain, destroyed 257 northern ships.

Both sides recognized the importance of the navy in the war, and both worked to produce the newest and strongest ships possible. This led to the use of armorplating to strengthen ship hulls. The Confederacy was first to put a fully ironclad ship into service: the reconditioned *Merrimac,* a 40-gun warship abandoned by Union forces near Portsmouth, Virginia.

Armed with iron plate 4 inches (10 centimeters) thick and renamed the *Virginia,* the ironclad quickly proved superior to wooden warships. On March 8, 1862, it sank one Union ship at Hampton Roads, drove another aground, and forced a third to surrender. The *Virginia* seemed capable of defeating the entire Union navy.

The Union countered with its own ironclad, the *Monitor.* It did battle with the *Virginia* on March 9. When neither ship could seriously damage the other, they disengaged and the battle was a draw. Eventually Confederates were forced to destroy the *Virginia* before it fell into enemy hands. The *Monitor* later sank in heavy seas off the North Carolina coast.

General Grant in the West

While the Union blockade pressured the southern coast, a little-known Union general, Ulysses S. Grant, carried out another part of Scott's anaconda plan in the western theater. The plan called for Union forces to take control of the Mississippi River, but the Confederates had fortified it well. Grant saw that he could reach the heart of the Confederacy by pushing south along the Cumberland and Tennessee rivers. (See the map at right.)

Two Confederate forts stood in Grant's way: Fort Henry on the Tennessee and Fort Donelson on the Cumberland. President Jefferson Davis, recognizing Grant's intentions, dispatched General Albert Johnston to coordinate Confederate defenses. In early February 1862 Grant captured Fort Henry with a flotilla of Union gunboats. Johnston was forced to withdraw to Nashville, leaving 15,000 troops to guard Fort Donelson.

Grant sent gunboats against Fort Donelson, but the Confederates withstood the attack. Grant then surrounded the fort and prepared for a siege, correctly gauging that the Confederates were low on supplies. When the Confederates tried to break out and rejoin Johnston's army, Grant pushed them back into the fort, demanded unconditional surrender, and got it.

General Grant next pushed south along the Tennessee River but was surprised on April 6 by Confederate forces under Gener-

als Johnston and Beauregard. The ensuing melee, which took place near a country meetinghouse called Shiloh, was the largest battle to date in North America. Johnston and Beauregard nearly routed the Union forces, but Grant held on until reinforcements arrived on April 7. The outnumbered Confederates, who had lost General Johnston in the battle, retreated to Corinth, Mississippi. By the end of May, Union forces had driven the Confederates out of Corinth.

The anaconda plan was having its effect in the West. Grant had penetrated south along the Tennessee River. Flag Officer David Farragut took New Orleans in April and continued up the Mississippi. Union gunboats also captured Memphis, leaving Vicksburg the only remaining Confederate stronghold on the river.

■ *Part of the Union's strategy was to gain control of the Mississippi River. A first step was to seize Fort Henry and Fort Donelson, shown on this map. By the spring of 1863, Vicksburg was the only remaining Confederate stronghold on the Mississippi.*

The Eastern Peninsular Campaign

The Union's eastern campaign did not go as well. After the defeat at Bull Run, Lincoln appointed General George B. McClellan commander of the Army of the Potomac. McClellan's first task was to transform raw recruits into able soldiers. This he did well. Discipline and organization replaced the confusion of Bull Run, and the troops respected McClellan. But the general seemed reluctant to engage in battle. "If McClellan does not want to use the army," said President Lincoln, "I would like to *borrow* it."

In March 1862, after almost a year of training, McClellan decided that his men were ready for combat, and he began to plan an attack on Richmond. He intended to move most of his army by steamboat down the Potomac River to the Chesapeake Bay, put them ashore on the peninsula between the York and James rivers, and move up the peninsula to attack the Confederate capital from the southeast. (See the map on page 339.) The success of the operation depended on surprise and speed. But after he landed McClellan moved cautiously, giving Confederate forces ample time to prepare.

On May 31 General Joseph E. Johnston attacked McClellan at Fair Oaks Station. When Johnston was wounded in the indecisive battle, Jefferson Davis ordered Robert E. Lee to take command of Johnston's forces, the Army of Northern Virginia. Lee would keep that command until the end of the war.

Robert E. Lee and George B. McClellan had attended West Point together. Remembering McClellan's caution, Lee devised a brilliant plan to keep the Union general from pressing too quickly toward Richmond. He sent Stonewall Jackson on a series of rapid marches against Union troops in the Shenandoah Valley of Virginia. Jackson's diversions were so successful that President Lincoln believed that Washington, D.C., was threatened. As a result, troops earmarked for McClellan were sent instead to deal with Jackson, and McClellan never received the reinforcements he had ordered.

Confederate General Robert E. Lee (right), in a photograph taken by Mathew Brady, was a military genius. General Lee grew up in a wealthy Virginia family. General Ulysses S. Grant (left), with his stubby beard and casual dress, seemed the opposite of the aristocratic Lee. Yet he was the man President Lincoln would choose to lead the faltering Union armies.

Between June 26 and July 2, 1862, Lee and Jackson kept McClellan off balance in a series of encounters known as the Seven Days' Battles. With the help of the dashing cavalry of J.E.B. "Jeb" Stuart, the Confederates not only prevented McClellan from taking Richmond, but forced him to withdraw to the James River. By taking the offensive, Lee had saved Richmond. Disgusted by McClellan's failure to take the Confederate capital, President Lincoln ordered him back to Washington and temporarily relieved him of his command.

Union generals planned another attack on Richmond in August, but once again Lee and Jackson outwitted them, at the Second Battle of Bull Run on August 28 and 29. Union General John Pope found his forces surrounded, and he retreated in defeat. Reluctantly Lincoln allowed McClellan to resume his command.

Antietam

President Lincoln had reason to be concerned. In September General Lee crossed the Potomac on a bold offensive into Maryland. The Confederates knew that a successful campaign in enemy territory would be a great blow to northern morale.

Expecting McClellan to be slow, as before, Lee divided his army. He sent Stonewall Jackson to capture the federal arsenal at Harpers Ferry, Virginia, while he marched into western Maryland. But McClellan had an incredible stroke of luck. One of his men stumbled upon three cigars dropped by an unknown Confederate messenger. They were wrapped in a dispatch containing Lee's battle plan.

This time McClellan did not delay. He mobilized his forces and attacked Lee at Antietam Creek on September 17, hoping to defeat him before Jackson returned. Reinforcements arrived from Harpers Ferry in time to prevent a complete Confederate rout, but Lee was forced to retreat across the Potomac into Virginia.

The battle of Antietam may have marked the bloodiest single day of the war. Lee lost 11,000 men, McClellan, 13,000. The Union army had not decisively defeated Lee, but it had forced him back to Virginia. Limited though it was, the Union victory had more than just military importance, as you will read later.

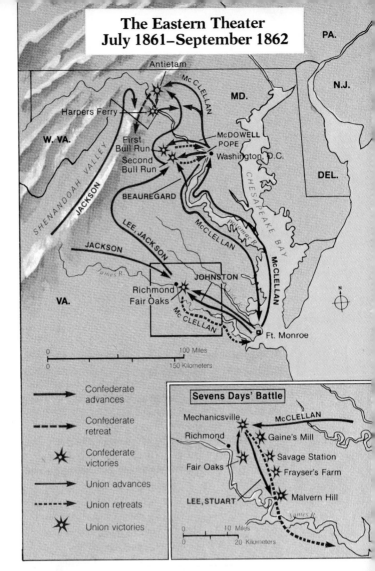

The Eastern Theater July 1861–September 1862

→	Confederate advances
⇢	Confederate retreat
✸	Confederate victories
→	Union advances
⇢	Union retreats
✸	Union victories

Sevens Days' Battle

■ During the early Virginia campaigns, Confederate forces under General Robert E. Lee outmaneuvered and outfought Union forces.

SECTION REVIEW

1. Identify: Stonewall Jackson, the *Virginia*, the *Monitor*, Ulysses S. Grant, George B. McClellan, Robert E. Lee.

2. How did warfare in the Civil War differ from warfare in earlier wars?

3. (a) What was Scott's war strategy? (b) What were the three theaters of the war?

4. How did General Lee prevent Union forces from taking Richmond?

5. Who won the battle of Antietam?

6. **Critical Thinking** What was the strategic importance of the battle between the *Monitor* and the *Merrimac*?

3 Freedom

As the battles raged and the soldiers died, many people questioned why the war was being fought. Southerners justified their resistance as a war for independence. They were fighting to preserve the southern way of life, which included slavery. Northerners remained less sure of their goals. First and foremost, they were fighting to preserve the Union; that seemed clear enough. But were they preserving a union that would continue with or without slavery?

Pressure for Emancipation

President Lincoln argued that union, not slavery, was the war's primary issue. "If I could save the union without freeing any slave I would do it," he announced in August 1862, "and if I could save it by freeing all the slaves I would do it; and if I could save it by freeing some and leaving others alone I would also do that."

Early in the war Lincoln handled the slavery issue cautiously, in part because he did not want to lose the support of the border states. As the war continued, however, more and more northerners began to favor an end to slavery. Pressure for emancipation came from several sources: abolitionists, fugitive slaves, and radical Republicans in Congress.

Abolitionists found increasing support in the North. "It is hard to realize the wondrous change which has befallen us abolitionists," wrote a reformer named Mary Grew. "After thirty years of persecution . . . abolitionists read with wonder . . . respectful tributes to men whose names had hitherto been used as a cry wherewith to rally a mob."

The question of what to do about fugitive slaves led the President to reconsider his policy. After the war began, thousands of slaves left southern plantations and fled behind Union lines. At first, in an attempt to conciliate the border states, Lincoln urged military commanders to return runaway slaves to their masters. But public sentiment in the North opposed such action.

In the spring of 1861 General Benjamin Butler declared fugitive slaves who had come into his camp to be *contraband* of war and not returnable to their masters. There-

after Lincoln allowed Union generals to use their discretion in dealing with fugitive slaves.

Although the President still proceeded cautiously, Congress passed antislavery measures in the spring and summer of 1862. One law abolished slavery in Washington, D. C., and the territories. Another made Butler's contraband policy legal and forbade Union officers to return fugitive slaves. The bill also allowed the President to recruit blacks for the army. The most vocal support for these laws came from a group of radicals in the Republican party led by Senator Charles Sumner of Massachusetts and Congressman Thaddeus Stevens of Pennsylvania.

The Emancipation Proclamation

Lincoln recognized the growing call for abolition and was willing to respond. But he hesitated to act until Union forces had won a victory, so that emancipation would be seen as a bold, new policy. The Union showing at Antietam gave Lincoln the opportunity he had been waiting for. On September 22, 1862, he issued a preliminary proclamation that all slaves in territories still in a state of rebellion on January 1, 1863, would be freed.

On January 1, 1863, the Emancipation Proclamation was issued. It applied only to Confederate states still at war. It did not affect slaves in areas occupied by Union troops or slaves in border states still loyal to the Union. In effect, it did not apply to any slaves within the immediate reach of the Union.*

The President had hoped that the threat of emancipation would pressure southern slave owners to surrender in order to safeguard slavery. Although that goal was not realized, the proclamation dramatically changed the character of the war. The war had become a battle for freedom as well as for union.

Rights of Black Americans

The Emancipation Proclamation did not free any slaves in the Union, nor did it have any direct influence on free blacks in the North.

---

*Slavery was abolished completely by the Thirteenth Amendment to the Constitution, ratified in December 1865.

However, the President's decision to issue the proclamation did advance the struggle for equal rights for black Americans.

When war began in 1861, free blacks suffered severe discrimination in northern states. Only in New York and most of New England could black males vote, and in New York they had to meet a property requirement not applied to whites. Only in New England could black and white children attend the same schools. In many major cities, including Philadelphia and New York City, blacks rode on segregated public transportation, if they were allowed to ride at all. Black Americans everywhere faced discrimination in housing and employment.

With the outbreak of the Civil War, many abolitionists turned their attention to securing equal rights for blacks in the North. Advances were slow but meaningful. Even in New York City, where workers feared an influx of black labor from the South, reformers made progress. Increased support from social and political leaders led to the integration of public transportation in New York City before the end of the war. Reformers throughout the North also succeeded in opening many more public schools to black children.

After the war, several actions effectively nullified the Dred Scott case's denial of citizenship to black Americans. For example, in 1865 John Rock, a black attorney from Boston, was admitted to practice before the Supreme Court. Both the State and Justice departments established rules clearly stating that blacks were entitled to citizenship. The movement for black rights continued, gaining strength because of blacks' participation in the war.

Black Soldiers

From the onset of the war, many blacks volunteered as cooks, drivers, carpenters, and scouts for the Union army, not only out of patriotism but also to be recognized as full partners in the nation and the war effort. Until the summer of 1862, federal law prohibited blacks from becoming soldiers, but when Congress repealed that law, blacks enlisted in the Union army.

Frederick Douglass explained why: "Once let the black man get upon his person the brass letters, *U. S.*; let him get an eagle on his button, and a musket on his shoulder and bullets in his pocket, and there is no

Parker Robbins was a sergeant-major of a Union cavalry regiment. Later he became a representative from North Carolina.

power on earth which can deny that he has earned the right to citizenship in the United States." By the end of the war 180,000 blacks had fought in the Union army and 29,000 in the navy.

Although they were allowed to enlist, black soldiers suffered discrimination. Their term of enlistment was longer than whites', and they were paid less. The army assigned them to all-black regiments mostly under the command of white officers. Medical care, bad enough even in the best circumstances, was even worse in the black units. The weapons black soldiers carried were often ones discarded by white troops. If taken prisoner by the Confederates, black soldiers (unlike white soldiers) faced enslavement or execution by hanging or firing squad.

In spite of such difficult conditions, the bravery of black soldiers under fire became well known. In the summer of 1863, for example, the all-black 54th Massachusetts Regiment led an assault on Fort Wagner in Charleston Harbor. Under heavy artillery barrage, nearly a hundred soldiers forced their way into the fort and engaged the Confederate troops in hand-to-hand combat. The

54th suffered great casualties in the battle, but such displays of courage won black soldiers a degree of acceptance among many white Americans.

SECTION REVIEW

1. Define: contraband.
2. What did President Lincoln believe was the main reason to fight the Civil War?
3. What were three sources of pressure on President Lincoln to end slavery?
4. Which areas of the nation were affected by the Emancipation Proclamation?
5. **Critical Thinking** How do you think the issuance of the Emancipation Proclamation affected European attitudes toward the Civil War?

4 Behind the Lines

The war affected everyone, not just the troops on the front lines. Civilians behind the lines grew food crops and manufactured military equipment to support the war effort. They maintained transportation networks to move troops and supplies, and they tended the wounded. Governments in both the South and the North faced opposition to the war and the economic hardship it caused.

Discord in the North

The government of a nation at war counts on the loyalty and support of its citizens. Yet the Constitution of the United States guarantees Americans the right of free speech and open dissent. Did northerners who opposed Lincoln's handling of the war, then, have the right to speak out? At what point would political opposition to the war become treason? These were questions President Lincoln and his administration had to consider.

Throughout the North, a few citizens vocally supported the Confederacy. This was especially true in the Union border states and in sections of the Old Northwest originally settled by southerners. Other northerners simply opposed the war, demanding an armistice and peace negotiations. Loyal Republicans called opponents of the war *copperheads,* after the poisonous snake of the same name.

Lincoln believed that in time of war a President had special powers not available in peacetime. In order to preserve the Union, he felt justified in violating civil liberties guaranteed by the Constitution. At the beginning of the war, to prevent Maryland from seceding, he had denied habeas corpus to citizens of that state. On January 1, 1863, he denied habeas corpus to all persons who resisted the draft, discouraged enlistment, or were suspected of being "guilty of any disloyal practice affording aid and comfort to rebels."

Resistance to the draft was especially strong in large cities like New York, where many immigrant workers belonged to the Democratic party and had little sympathy for Republicans. Workers resented being drafted for what they considered to be a "rich man's war" when those who could afford to pay the exemption fee remained home. Some white workers resented competition from free blacks for jobs; consequently, they had little interest in fighting a war to free the slaves.

Resentment and frustration boiled over in July 1863, when a mob of workers in New York City attacked Union army recruiters. The mob then looted the homes of several wealthy citizens, burned a black orphanage, and lynched several blacks who were unfortunate enough to be caught in the vicinity. Federal troops were called in from Gettysburg to quell the disturbance.

Opposition to the draft and to the war continued until the war was over. Between 1863 and 1865 military authorities arrested and imprisoned more than 13,000 people for alleged disloyalty of one kind or another.

The Northern Economy

The Civil War stimulated economic growth in the North and accelerated the industrialization that had begun before the war. Between 1860 and 1865, for example, woolen mills producing uniforms for Union troops almost tripled their profits.

The war also spurred the growth of agriculture in the North. To meet the army's demands, farmers stepped up food production. Grain farmers purchased over 165,000 mechanical reapers during the war, simultaneously increasing grain supplies and freeing men for fighting.

Congress also came to the aid of farmers in 1862. The Homestead Act gave 160 acres (64 hectares) of western land to any citizen who agreed to occupy and improve it for five years. The Morrill Act gave states land grants to endow colleges of agriculture. To increase their support among midwestern farmers, Republicans worked for the creation of a cabinet-level Department of Agriculture, which Congress established in 1862.

Inflation accompanied the expansion of industry and agriculture. Wartime demand for goods increased prices by 50 percent between 1860 and 1862. Wages, however, failed to keep pace, increasing by only 10 percent. People could buy fewer goods with their weekly earnings than before the war. Thus, although the war stimulated the North's economy, individual citizens faced economic hardship.

Hardships in the South

Although life behind the lines was disrupted in the North, suffering in the South was far worse. Most of the fighting took place in the Confederacy, so the destruction of property and crops was greater. As the war progressed the Union blockade became increasingly effective, forcing many southerners to do without basic manufactured goods such as new clothing.

Factories in the North continued to supply Union armies with new equipment. But the South lacked the industrial capacity to carry on a long war. When locomotives broke down, they often could not be replaced or repaired because of a lack of parts. When track was destroyed, it could be replaced only by borrowing track from less important branch lines.

Shortages like these seriously hurt the war effort. Troops and supplies could not be moved, and food could not be distributed. In 1863, although Confederate farmers in the Shenandoah Valley had reaped good harvests, famine threatened Richmond and there were riots for bread.

Astronomical inflation was caused by the lack of a firm backing for Confederate currency. In 1863 a Confederate official noted that boots cost $200, coats $350, and shoes $125. Food was expensive, too, when it was available. Two chickens cost $30, potatoes $25 per bushel, and butter $15 per pound (0.45 kilogram). In 1863, flour sold for $275 a barrel; by the end of the war, that price had soared to $1,000.

Divisions in the Confederacy

The government of the Confederacy faced political as well as economic problems. Not all southerners supported the war. The draft, for example, was as unpopular in the Confederacy as in the Union. Small farmers, especially, objected to the exemptions for planters.

Pro-Union sentiment was widespread in the northern reaches of the South, the mountains, and the poorer sections of the Confederacy. In 1861 residents in the western sections of Virginia, who had traditionally opposed the eastern part of the state, organized a pro-Union government. In 1863, the area was formally admitted to the Union as the state of West Virginia.

President Davis, like Lincoln, attempted to suspend habeas corpus in order to deal with dissenters. Such efforts led some of Davis's critics to denounce him as a dictator. Yet others thought he was not decisive enough. Davis's most outspoken critic was his own Vice-President, Alexander H. Stephens. Stephens remained in his native state of Georgia for a substantial part of the war, refusing to serve in Richmond.

The unwillingness of some state governors to give up any authority to the central government also handicapped President Davis. For example, the governor of Alabama would not allow the central government to collect taxes in his state. Governor Joseph Brown of Georgia hindered the Confederate government at every turn. He even considered making a separate peace treaty with the Union.

Women in the War

Women, although not allowed to fight, nevertheless contributed greatly to the war effort. In the North and the South, women formed aid societies as soon as the war began. The Union's Sanitary Commission, for example, collected over $15 million worth of supplies. In the Confederacy, the Society of Center Ridge, Alabama, contributed "422 shirts, 551 pairs of drawers, 80 pairs of socks, 3 pairs of gloves, 6 boxes and a bale of hospital stores, 128 pounds of tapioca, and $18 for hospital use" in one month.

More informally, volunteer women operated "refreshment saloons" in the North, and "wayside homes" in the South, in which communities donated food, drink, and medical care to soldiers who were passing through. Women aided in the purchase of military hardware as well. "Ladies Gunboat Funds" were common in the Confederate states.

Women played an increased role in agriculture, especially in the South where labor was short. They often harvested crops and supervised the day-to-day operation of farms and plantations. In the North more and more women found employment in the federal government as clerical jobs were opened to them.

Nursing became an important activity for many women in both the South and the North. At first people did not consider nursing male soldiers proper work for women. The work was considered too unpleasant and difficult. Nevertheless, women stepped in to help.

In 1861 the Union government named Dorothea Dix superintendent of women nurses. She was efficient and warmhearted, but some men resented her skill as a tough administrator. Clara Barton, a school teacher, was not appointed to any official post, but she set immediately to work organizing care for the sick and wounded. She served behind Union lines and on the battlefields of some of the fiercest conflicts of the war.

Black women also took an active role in the northern war effort. They worked in hos-

★ Voices of Freedom ★

Diary of a Confederate Nurse

Kate Cumming served the Confederate cause as a nurse. In the excerpt below, she describes her first encounter with wounded soldiers after the battle of Shiloh.

April 11—Miss Booth and myself arrived at Corinth to-day. As I had never been where there was a large army, and had never seen a wounded man, except in the cars, as they passed, I could not help feeling a little nervous at the prospect of now seeing both. When within a few miles of the place, we could realize the condition of an army immediately after a battle. As it had been raining for days, water and mud abounded. Here and there were wagons hopelessly left to their fate, and men on horseback trying to wade through it. As far as the eye could reach, in the midst of all this slop and mud, the white tents of our brave army could be seen through the trees, making a picture suggestive of any thing but comfort. . . .

The crowd of men at the depot was so great that we found it impossible to get to our place of destination by ourselves. . . . I met Mr. George Redwood of Mobile, who kindly offered to pilot us. . . . We are at the Tishomingo Hotel, which, like every other large building, has been taken for a hospital. The yellow flag is flying from the top of each. Mrs. Ogden tried to prepare me for the scenes which I should witness upon entering the wards. But alas! nothing that I had ever heard or read had given me the faintest idea of the horrors witnessed here. . . . Certainly, none of the glories of the war were presented here. Gray-haired men—men in the pride of manhood—beardless boys—Federals and all, mutilated in every imaginable way, lying on the floor, just as they were taken from the battlefield; so close together that it was almost impossible to walk without stepping on them. I could not command my feelings enough to speak, but thoughts crowded upon me. O, if the authors of this cruel and unnatural war could but see what I saw there, they would try to put a stop to it! . . . What can be in the minds of our enemies, who are now arrayed against us, who have never harmed them in any way, but simply claim our own, and nothing more!

pitals and on battle lines, and they helped re-settle former slaves who had fled from the South. Sojourner Truth continued her effective public speaking, turning her oratory against all those copperheads who hoped to conclude peace without abolishing slavery. Charlotte Forten and Mary Peake taught former slaves to read and write. Harriet Tubman helped slaves to escape and acted as a spy behind Confederate lines. The work of women was indispensable to the war effort of both the South and the North.

345

SECTION REVIEW

1. Identify: copperheads, Homestead Act, Morrill Act, Clara Barton.
2. How did war help the northern economy?
3. Why was there greater destruction of property in the South than in the North?
4. What areas of the South were pro-Union?
5. How did women contribute to the war effort?
6. **Critical Thinking** How does a war create a strain on civil rights?

During the Civil War, Susie King Taylor served with the Union army as a nurse and teacher.

5 An End to the War

As the war dragged on—longer than either side had expected—the North's superior resources began to make a difference on the battlefield. The Union's naval blockade squeezed tighter around the South, and the likelihood of southern victory became more and more remote. But still the Confederacy fought on.

Confederate Victories

After the battle of Antietam, General Lee's forces retreated through the Shenandoah Valley. Once again, General McClellan failed to pursue or attack; he encamped and sent requests for supplies. On November 7, 1862, President Lincoln removed McClellan from command and replaced him with General Ambrose E. Burnside.

Burnside was supposed to move on Richmond by way of Fredericksburg, Virginia. On December 13, he ordered his men to make six frontal assaults across open ground near Fredericksburg. Confederates under Lee pushed them back with withering fire.

The following spring the effective combination of Lee and Jackson outwitted Union General Joseph Hooker at Chancellorsville, Virginia. On May 3, 1863, Hooker tried to outflank the Confederates. But Lee and Jackson routed the Union forces in ten minutes. Although the Confederates won the battle, they suffered a severe loss. An edgy Confederate sentry fired into the night, hitting Stonewall Jackson twice in the arm. One of the Confederacy's ablest generals died the next day from a resulting blood clot.

Gettysburg

Victories at Fredericksburg and Chancellorsville inspired the Confederacy, but the Union showed no sign of giving up. General

Lee and President Davis hoped that another Confederate move into the North would break the Union's resolve. Thus Lee led his army into Pennsylvania and into the battle that would be the turning point of the war.

Fighting began unexpectedly at Gettysburg, Pennsylvania, when advance detachments of Lee's army met a cavalry division of the Union army commanded by General George Meade. On July 1 Confederates drove the Union forces out of the town, but Meade's army managed to set itself up on the strategically located Cemetery Ridge nearby. Lee's forces took up position across the way on Seminary Ridge.

The curve of Cemetery Ridge made it easy for Union troops to defend it along the crest. Lee's plan was to attack around both ends of the ridge and close in on the Union forces from behind. On July 2 Confederates led by General Richard S. Ewell took the northern slope of Culp's Hill. But Union forces repelled the attack on the southern end at Little Round Top. If Confederates had occupied that hill, they could have directed their artillery fire up and down the main Union line. The next day Union forces drove Ewell off Culp's Hill.

Lee then decided to attack the Union forces at their center, but Meade anticipated this move. When 15,000 Confederates in three lines began their march across three quarters of a mile of open field, Union troops were ready and opened up a devastating fire. Still the Confederates pushed on. Through clouds of gunsmoke, General George Pickett led one last valiant attempt to storm the lines. About 100 Confederates actually breached the Union embankments temporarily, but Meade's forces held the ridge.

Lee had no choice but to take his exhausted and diminished army back south toward the Potomac. General Meade let him go, passing up an opportunity to pursue and capture the Confederates as they withdrew to Virginia. Nevertheless, the battle of Gettysburg marked the beginning of the end for the Confederacy.

Vicksburg and Port Hudson

At about the time that Lee was moving toward defeat at Gettysburg, General Ulysses S. Grant began a campaign to secure Union control of the Mississippi River between Vicksburg, Mississippi, and Port Hudson,

Louisiana. Vicksburg was situated on a heavily fortified bluff overlooking the Mississippi and the swamplands of the Yazoo River. Grant spent the first three months of 1863 unsuccessfully trying to outflank Confed-

■ Following Confederate victories at Fredericksburg and Chancellorsville, General Lee marched into Pennsylvania. At Gettysburg, however, the Confederate army suffered heavy losses in a battle that became a turning point.

The Eastern Theater December 1862–July 1863

	Confederate advances
	Confederate retreat
	Confederate victories
	Union advances
	Union victory

erate General John Pemberton in the Yazoo swamps. Failing to do so, Grant adopted a bolder strategy.

In April Union troops marched unnoticed south of Vicksburg while a fleet of Union gunboats floated silently downstream past Vicksburg, their engines and lights turned off. The gunboats then ferried the Union troops to the east bank of the Mississippi River.

Grant's men, carrying only four days' rations, marched east across Mississippi into enemy territory. After a series of small victories, they captured the state capital of Jackson on May 14. Grant then abruptly reversed his march and headed back to Vicksburg, arriving only 18 days after he had left. Union forces now surrounded Vicksburg. After a six-week seige the Confederates surrendered on July 4, 1863—the day after the Battle of Gettysburg ended.

On July 9 Port Hudson fell to Union forces. Two black regiments, spurred on by the heroism of Captain Andre Callious, were instrumental in the victory. The fall of Vicksburg and Port Hudson placed the entire Mississippi River in Union hands. The western grip of the anaconda was now firm. The Confederacy's position was becoming steadily more desperate.

Grant Takes Command

With the western front largely secure, Union troops moved to split the Confederacy even further by pushing eastward. In September Union armies under General William Rosecrans secured the strategic railroad center at Chattanooga, Tennessee. Mistakenly thinking that Confederate General Braxton Bragg's force was retreating to Atlanta, Rosecrans proceeded east and almost lost his entire army when Bragg's force counterattacked at Chickamauga on September 19 and 20. However, General George Thomas held off the Confederates long enough to allow Rosecrans to retreat to Chattanooga.

The next spring when Union forces began to march east again, Lincoln placed Grant in charge of all Union armies. Grant devised a three-pronged attack to destroy his opposition. One Union army would march into the fertile Shenandoah Valley, defeating enemy forces and laying waste to the land so that no crops would grow until after the war. General Philip E. Sheridan completed this

The Western Theater January–December 1863

→ Confederate advance	→ Union advances
▪▪▶ Confederate retreat	▪▪▶ Union retreat
✳ Confederate victory	✳ Union victories

▪ General Grant, in a swiftly executed maneuver, sent ships and troops to surround Vicksburg. With the fall of Vicksburg and Port Hudson, the Union controlled the river.

mission in October 1864. Two other armies would be led by Grant himself and by General William Tecumseh Sherman.

Grant and Sherman were alike in several ways. Both men wore stubbly, shortcropped beards, dressed sloppily, and possessed an indomitable will to win. Both were willing to take any steps necessary to achieve victory. They intended to wage total war, defeating not only the opposing military forces but the civilian will to resist as well. Sherman's army was to march from Chattanooga to Atlanta, and Grant's was to march from Washington to Richmond.

347

Sherman's March to the Sea

General Sherman outfitted his 100,000 soldiers with only the most basic supplies. On May 6, 1864, they left Chattanooga. As the Union army proceeded it lived off the land, leaving destruction behind. General Sherman described the march: "We have devoured the land and our animals eat up the wheat and corn fields close. All the people retire before us and desolation is behind. To realize what war is one should follow our tracks."

Progress was slow, because Confederate forces under General Joseph Johnston and General John Hood opposed Sherman at every turn. Finally, on September 1, 1864, Sherman forced the Confederate army to abandon Atlanta.

Until the capture of Atlanta Lincoln had expected defeat in his bid for reelection because of public frustration over the war. The

Democrats had adopted a platform calling for an armistice and had nominated General McClellan to oppose Lincoln. Even some Republicans had been urging immediate peace with the South. News of the fall of Atlanta rallied popular support for Lincoln and insured his reelection.

In mid-November General Sherman prepared to set out for Savannah, on the coast. Before leaving, he ordered his troops to set fire to Atlanta, destroying much of the city. Sherman's army arrived at Savannah on December 10, having left a path of devastation 60 miles (96 kilometers) wide. On December 21 Savannah fell.

Throughout the campaign Sherman's army had destroyed any supplies that might have been used to feed Confederate soldiers, wrecked railroad lines, and ruined cotton gins and mills. They dealt the South a devastating blow, which left southerners with bitter memories long afterward.

■ *General Sherman's "March to the Sea" left a wide path of destruction in Georgia. His army lived off the land, seizing whatever it needed.*

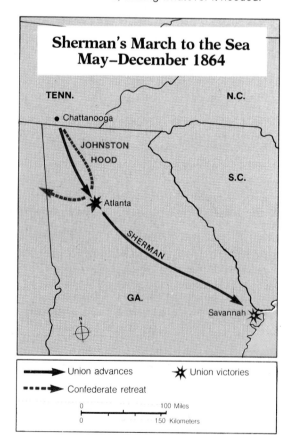

Capturing Richmond

Grant led the third part of his plan himself. Early in May 1864 troops under his command arrived in the Wilderness, a wild area near Fredericksburg, Virginia, where he began the first of three unsuccessful efforts to defeat Lee's much smaller army.

Both sides suffered heavy casualties over the next two months. Grant lost nearly 60,000 men, Lee nearly 30,000. Although Grant's casualties were greater, the Union had reserves to replace them. The Confederacy did not. Lee's army was forced to retreat to Petersburg, a few miles south of Richmond, where the Confederates dug a network of trenches, built heavy fortifications, and prepared for a siege.

Grant and Lee fought each other for nine more months. The siege of Petersburg lasted from the summer of 1864 through the winter of 1865. Faced with encirclement and cut off from his lines of supply, Lee finally withdrew his forces on the night of April 2, 1865. Grant pursued. With the battlements of Petersburg behind him, the Union commander moved into Richmond the next day and took the Confederate capital.

Appomattox: A Sad Peace

One week later, Lee's army was trapped near the small town of Appomattox Court House. Realizing that further resistance would lead only to greater loss of life among his troops, Lee sent a soldier carrying a white towel as a flag of truce to arrange a conference with General Grant.

On April 9, 1865, Lee and Grant met to discuss the terms of surrender. Robert E. Lee wore a full-dress uniform with ceremonial sash and sword. Ulysses S. Grant appeared, characteristically untidy, in a private's shirt, his collar unbuttoned. They talked about their days before the Civil War, when they had both served in the United States Army. Then Grant suggested generous terms of surrender:

> Officers and men paroled ... arms and material surrendered ... officers to keep their side arms, and let all the men who claim to own a horse or mule take the animals home with them to work their little farms.

One of Grant's aides recalled that General Lee "gazed sadly in the direction ... where his army lay—now an army of prisoners. He thrice smote the palm of his left hand slowly with his right fist in an absent sort of

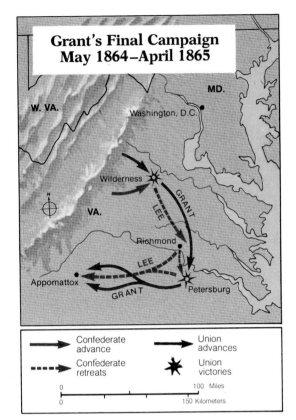

Grant's Final Campaign May 1864–April 1865

Legend:
→ Confederate advance
⇢ Confederate retreats
→ Union advances
✶ Union victories

0 — 100 Miles
0 — 150 Kilometers

■ Union strategy in 1864 was to crush Confederate resistance between two fronts. While Sherman's troops marched through Georgia, Grant faced Lee in Virginia. Finally, at Appomattox, General Lee surrendered.

way." As the Union soldiers saw Lee mount and ride away toward his men, they began cheering. Grant immediately ordered them to stop. "The war is over," he told them, "the rebels are our countrymen again."

SECTION REVIEW

1. Identify: William Tecumseh Sherman.
2. (a) What victories in late 1862 and early 1863 encouraged the Confederates? (b) Why did Lee invade Pennsylvania?
3. What did the capture of Vicksburg and Port Hudson mean for the Union?
4. How did General Sherman try to destroy the Confederates' ability to resist?
5. What convinced Lee to surrender?
6. **Critical Thinking** Based on the terms of surrender, what kind of treatment might the South have expected after the war?

Major Events	
1861	Battle of Bull Run
1862	Battles of Fort Donelson, Fort Henry, Shiloh; Union capture of New Orleans; Confederacy passes draft law; battle of Fair Oaks; Department of Agriculture formed; Homestead Act; Morrill Act; Seven Days' Battle; Second Battle of Bull Run; battles of Antietam, Fredericksburg
1863	Emancipation Proclamation; National Bank Act; Union passes draft law; battle of Chancellorsville; West Virginia admitted as state; battles of Vicksburg, Port Hudson, Gettysburg, Chattanooga, Chickamauga
1864	Wilderness Campaign begins; siege of Petersburg begins; Sherman takes Atlanta; Lincoln reelected President; Sherman's March to the Sea
1865	Grant takes Richmond; Lee surrenders at Appomattox

At the end of the war, General Lee's troops had one final duty: to furl the Confederate flag for the last time.

Chapter 18 Review

 ★ ★ ★ ★ ★ ★

In Perspective

After the shelling of Fort Sumter, both the United States of America and the Confederate States of America faced the task of preparing for war. The Union had important material advantages, but citizens of the Confederacy were ready to fight for their independence. Confederate troops won the first battle of the war. Yet, by April 1862 General Grant had pushed as far as Corinth, Mississippi. In the East General Lee repelled McClellan's attempt to take Richmond but lost at Antietam Creek.

The Emancipation Proclamation, issued on January 1, 1863, changed the purpose of the war for many northerners. Although the proclamation did not directly affect free blacks or slaves in the Union, it did contribute to the struggle for greater rights.

The war affected all aspects of life. Both sides were faced with opposition to the war, resentment over the draft, and inflation. Yet economic growth was stimulated in the North, while the Confederacy suffered greater hardships as the war progressed.

Confederate armies fought gallantly during the last two years of the war, but the superior numbers and supplies of the Union army gradually wore them down. Robert E. Lee finally surrendered to Ulysses S. Grant in April 1865. The war was over, but the task of reuniting the nation was just beginning.

Vocabulary

On a separate sheet of paper, write the word or words that best complete each of the following sentences.

1. Loyal Republicans called opponents of the Civil War ___.

2. ___ is the right not to be imprisoned without a trial.

3. A sum paid to a recruit for signing up for military service was a (an) ____.

4. During the Civil War, the term ____ referred to a slave who had fled behind Union lines.

5. ____ was a system of enlisting, collecting a bounty, deserting, reenlisting, and collecting another bounty.

Chapter Checkup

1. (a) List the advantages and disadvantages of the Confederacy. (b) List the advantages and disadvantages of the Union.

2. (a) Describe General Scott's war strategy. (b) Why was it called the anaconda? (c) Was the strategy most successful in the West or in the East?

3. (a) Why did Lincoln finally decide to issue the Emancipation Proclamation? (b) Whom did it affect directly?

4. (a) Compare the discontent about the war felt in the North with that felt in the Confederacy. (b) How did Presidents Lincoln and Davis try to deal with it?

5. (a) What impact did the war have on the northern economy? Why? (b) How did it affect the southern economy?

Critical Thinking

1. **Analyzing** Why did it take the North, with its many advantages, four long years to defeat the South?

2. **Determining Cause and Effect** Why were there more casualties in the Civil War than in previous American wars?

Developing Basic Skills

1. **Comparing** Compare Abraham Lincoln, Jefferson Davis, Ulysses S. Grant, George B. McClellan, Robert E. Lee, and Stonewall Jackson. (a) What characteristics did each have that helped him be a good leader? (b) What characteristics did each have that weakened him?

2. **Classifying** Make a chart with two columns, titled Western Theater and Eastern Theater; and three rows, titled Confederate Victory, Union Victory, and Neither. Write the name of each battle you read about in the appropriate box. Then answer the following questions: (a) Which side won the largest total number of battles? (b) How does the chart help you explain the outcome of the Civil War?

See page 830 for suggested readings.

Writer's Handbook

Using *The Readers' Guide*

To find information in magazines and journals, you need an index to periodicals. *The Readers' Guide to Periodical Literature* lists subjects and authors alphabetically according to date.

To interpret the entries, study the labels on the sample from *The Readers' Guide*.

Practice: Use the sample entry from *The Readers' Guide* to answer the following questions.

1. What is the title of the article by J. Skow?

2. Under what subject heading does it appear?

3. In what magazine was it published?

4. What is the date of the magazine?

5. On what pages does the article appear?

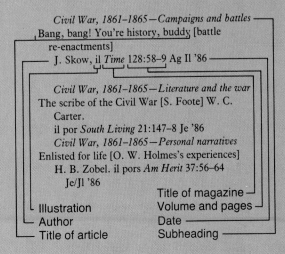

19

A Difficult Reunion

(1865–1877)

Ruins on Carey Street, Richmond, Virginia

In 1865 both northerners and southerners looked back on the four years of civil war with mixed feelings of sadness and pride. Their nation had been ripped apart by the war, families had been separated, and many men and women had suffered hardship, injury, and death. But both sides could claim their share of heroes and tales of glory.

In contrast, the 12 years following the war were to produce few heroes. The truce at Appomattox led to a period of peace in which national leaders were determined to reunite the country. However, that task would prove to be a difficult one.

Although the Union had been preserved by the war, problems remained. The status of the former Confederate states had to be decided. Four million slaves had been freed, but they faced a difficult adjustment to freedom. The postwar period was called Reconstruction, but the scars of the war were slow to heal.

Radical Reconstruction

1865	1867	1869	1871	1873	1875	1877

1865
Freedmen's Bureau set up; Lincoln assassinated

1867
Reconstruction Acts passed

1870
15th Amendment passed

1871
Ku Klux Klan Act passed

1874
Democrats gain House majority

1876
Rutherford B. Hayes elected President

1 Beginning of Reunion

After four years of fighting, many Americans hoped to take up life where they left off before the war. But the war brought political, economic, and social changes in its wake, leaving great problems unsolved. The task of reunion would be a difficult one.

Effects of War

The human consequences of the war would haunt the nation for many years. Over 360,000 Union soldiers and 258,000 Confederate soldiers had lost their lives, as had many civilians. Thousands of veterans were permanently disabled. The war also left a legacy of bitterness and resentment. Confederates had lost their struggle for independence and seen much of their land laid waste by Union armies. Furthermore, many southerners feared retribution by the victorious North.

Beginning life anew was severely hindered by the economic dislocation caused by the war. The North had remained prosperous during the war, yet it faced serious problems in the postwar years. The Union dismissed 800,000 men from the army, and these men needed jobs. At the same time, factories that had been making arms and ammunition laid off many employees because the government canceled its orders. These abrupt changes produced a recession.

By the late 1860s manufacturers began to expand their factories and build new ones. Veterans found work as the demand for labor rose, and the northern population enjoyed a boom period that lasted until 1873. While disruptions in the North were temporary, the war had devastated the South. Union armies had destroyed factories and railroads, forcing banks to close and disrupting the structure of business. Atlanta, Charleston, Columbia, and Richmond were burned-out shells of cities. And the fighting had disrupted agriculture.

Some wealthy planters found their fortunes gone and their plantations destroyed. Small farmers and poor whites were even more severely affected. One traveler in Alabama reported, "I visited four families, within fifteen minutes' ride of town, who were living in the woods, with no shelter but pine boughs, and this in mid-winter."

Freedmen

The Civil War had begun as a war over the right of secession, but when it was over about 4 million slaves had been freed. To former slave owners, emancipation meant billion-dollar property losses. Moreover, it had a great impact on social relationships. In both the North and the South, white Americans were reluctant to accept blacks as equals. The Thirteenth Amendment to the Constitution, ratified in December 1865, abolished slavery, but it did not change people's attitudes. Few southern whites could think of blacks in any status other than as slaves, and many were afraid that newly freed slaves might seek revenge. Generous behavior on the part of most blacks did little to relieve such fears.

Former slaves, called *freedmen*, faced severe problems as the war ended. Since teaching slaves to read and write had been illegal in most states, few freedmen were literate. Although most were skilled in farming, they owned no land and had no money to buy any. Few people could afford to hire them, and in any case, going to work for a former master seemed too much like slavery.

In March 1865 Congress established the Freedmen's Bureau to aid freedmen and refugees. The bureau issued clothing and over 15 million rations of surplus army food to freed slaves and poverty-stricken whites. It provided over $5 million in educational funds and sent agents to organize schools for black children and adults. The agents sought work for the freedmen and attempted to prevent their exploitation by employers. The bureau also provided medical care for over a million people.

The Freedmen's Bureau was created to alleviate some of the immediate effects of the war, but the federal government had to face difficult questions concerning the legal status of the freedmen and of the former Confederate states.

Early Steps of Reconstruction

Even before the end of the war, President Lincoln had begun to consider how to bring the seceded states back into the Union. From the beginning, the President had believed

Even before the war ended, the federal government set up the Freedmen's Bureau to help freed slaves adjust to their new lives. One activity of the bureau was opening schools for former slaves.

that states had no legal right to secede from the Union. When he first summoned troops after the fall of Fort Sumter, Lincoln treated the southern rebellion as an insurrection. The Confederacy, he argued, was only a group of individuals who were resisting federal authority, not states that had actually seceded. The Constitution gave the President, as commander-in-chief, power to quell insurrections; thus Lincoln believed it was his responsibility to restore harmonious relations with the South as soon as possible.

As early as December 1863 Lincoln had proclaimed a plan of reconstruction for those areas of the South that had come under Union control. He offered a pardon to Confederates on the condition that they swear an oath to support the Constitution and the Union. When 10 percent of the state's citizens who had voted in the 1860 election subscribed to the oath and formed a loyal government and when the state abolished slavery, the President promised to recognize its government and readmit it to the Union.

Lincoln believed that the process of reconstruction should work gradually and patiently because, he argued, "we shall sooner have the fowl by hatching the egg than by smashing it." By the spring of 1864 Louisiana and Arkansas had reorganized their governments according to Lincoln's 10-percent formula.

One group of Republicans in Congress, known as the Radicals, believed the President's plan treated the South far too leniently. Even moderate Republicans argued that Lincoln had overstepped his authority by issuing a plan of reconstruction without seeking the advice and consent of Congress.

In July 1864 moderate Republicans joined forces with the Radicals to pass a bill outlining their version of reconstruction. The Wade-Davis Bill stipulated that a majority of white males had to take an oath of allegiance before the state could be reorganized. Furthermore, those who wished to vote or take a more active role in the new governments would have to swear that they had never voluntarily supported the Confederacy. Finally, the Wade-Davis Bill required that southern state governments repudiate, or refuse to honor, old Confederate debts, abolish slavery, and repudiate their act of secession. Lincoln refused to sign the Wade-Davis Bill because he did not wish to place such severe restrictions on the seceded states.

The President Assassinated

Whether Lincoln's moderate plan could have succeeded is unknown. On April 14, 1865, little more than a month after his second inauguration, the President attended a play at Ford's Theater, seeking some relief from the strains of his office. During the play, an unstable former actor, John Wilkes Booth, crept into the President's box and fired a bullet into the back of his head. The President died next day. The nation was horrified. Rumors flashed across the country, and Confederate leaders were unjustly accused of masterminding the plot.

The army and Secret Service tracked Booth down and trapped him in a barn near Bowling Green, Virginia. When Booth refused to surrender, his pursuers set the barn on fire. Booth was shot, probably by himself, but, in any case, he did not escape. Authorities hung four alleged accomplices and imprisoned four others. Although the assassins were caught and rumors of wider conspiracy quieted, these actions could not compensate for the loss of Lincoln. His firm leadership and ability to compromise with so many groups within the Union would be sorely missed.

A New President, a New Plan

Vice-President Andrew Johnson, now thrust into the presidency, had been born in North Carolina and had moved to Tennessee as a young man. Johnson was a Democrat in the mold of Andrew Jackson, and he bore little love for the rich and aristocratic planters. He had been governor of Tennessee and had represented the state in both the House of Representatives and the Senate before the war broke out.

When Tennessee seceded in 1861, Johnson bitterly opposed the move. Consequently, President Lincoln appointed him military governor of the occupied areas of Tennessee during the war. In 1864 the Republicans offered Johnson the vice-presidential nomination. As a pro-Union Democrat from a state of the upper South, he attracted badly needed votes to help Lincoln win reelection.

As President, Johnson first appeared to take a harsh attitude toward the South. He promptly offered rewards for the capture of Jefferson Davis and other Confederate officials, vowing that "treason must be made infamous and traitors must be impoverished." Senator Benjamin Wade, a Radical Republican, rejoiced, "By the gods there will be no trouble now in running the government."

The Radical Republicans soon discovered, however, that Johnson's intentions differed from theirs. He quickly recognized the governments that had organized themselves according to Lincoln's plan. Then in May 1865 the President announced requirements for the readmission of the remaining states. These were stiffer than Lincoln's conditions but were more moderate than those of the Radical Republicans.

Johnson demanded that all former Confederate states disavow their acts of

★ Voices of Freedom ★

Lincoln's Second Inaugural Address

When President Abraham Lincoln delivered his second inaugural address on March 4, 1865, Confederate armies were still holding out. (See Chapter 18.) But Lincoln was looking ahead to reuniting the nation, as you can see below.

. . . Fondly do we hope, fervently do we pray, that this mighty scourge of war may speedily pass away.

Yet, if God wills that it continue until all the wealth piled by the bondsman's 250 years of unrequited toil shall be sunk, and until every drop of blood drawn with the lash shall be paid by another drawn with the sword, as was said 3,000 years ago, to still it must be said, "The judgments of the Lord are true and righteous altogether."

With malice toward none, with charity for all, with firmness in the right as God gives us to see the right, let us strive on to finish the work we are in, to bind up the nation's wounds, to care for him who shall have borne the battle and for his widow and his orphan—to do all which may achieve and cherish a just and lasting peace among ourselves and with all nations.

Source: John G. Nicolay and John Hay, eds., *Complete Works of Abraham Lincoln* (New York: 1905) vol. 11, p. 47.

secession, repudiate their war debts, and ratify the Thirteenth Amendment. By the winter all the former Confederate states except Texas had moved to obtain Johnson's recognition. But some states were reluctant to fulfill all the President's terms. For example, several state legislatures repealed their acts of secession but would not condemn them. South Carolina refused to repudiate its war debt, and Mississippi refused to ratify the Thirteenth Amendment.

Even more troubling to many Republicans, southern legislatures indicated that they had no intention of giving freedmen equal rights. One state convention echoed the sentiments of many white southerners when it announced that theirs was a "Government of White People, made and to be perpetuated for the exclusive political benefit of the White Race" and that blacks ought not to be considered citizens.

President Johnson was eager to bring all the states back into the Union, however, and he recognized the new southern governments. The states immediately elected representatives to Congress, often selecting wartime leaders.

When Congress convened in December 1865, Johnson announced that his plan had worked, and he urged Congress to seat the southern representatives. Congress refused. Instead, a majority of Republicans, the moderate wing and the Radicals, voted to set up a Joint Committee on Reconstruction to determine if the southern states were truly "reconstructed." Soon Congress would challenge the President for control of Reconstruction.

SECTION REVIEW

1. Identify: Freedmen's Bureau, Wade–Davis Bill, John Wilkes Booth, Andrew Johnson, Joint Committee on Reconstruction.
2. Define: freedmen.
3. List a problem faced by the North and one faced by the South after the war.
4. What did the Freedmen's Bureau do?
5. What was Lincoln's 10-percent plan?
6. **Critical Thinking** How did the priorities of President Johnson and the Radical Republicans differ?

2 Congress Takes Over

Andrew Johnson could direct the course of Reconstruction as long as the Radical Republicans in Congress did not have the two-thirds majority needed to override a veto. Gradually, however, many moderate Republicans joined the Radicals, and Congress took control of Reconstruction.

The Radical Position

Some Radical Republicans believed that the former Confederate states had forfeited their statehood when they seceded and had returned to the status of territories. As with new territories, the Radicals insisted, the southern states should be "under the exclusive jurisdiction of Congress." Therefore Congress, not the President, should decide when the states were ready to be readmitted to the Union. This argument was one basis for the Radical Republican opposition to the moderate plans of Lincoln and Johnson.

The Radicals' demand for a harsh policy toward the South also reflected their desire to retain a Republican majority in Congress. The newly elected representatives and senators from the southern states were mostly Democrats. If the Republicans agreed to seat them, the Republicans risked losing their majority and with it their power.

Furthermore, some Radical Republicans disapproved of Johnson's plan simply because they felt it was too lenient. Representative Thaddeus Stevens, one of the most outspoken Radicals, strongly protested presidential pardons of former Confederates. "Did any respectable Government ever before allow such high criminals to escape with such shameful impunity? . . . No sir; they have not been punished as they deserve. They have exchanged forgiveness with the President, and been sent on their way rejoicing." Stevens advocated confiscation of all plantations and division of the land among the freedmen.

Although hate and revenge played a part in the motivation of some Radical Republicans, not all were concerned with political gain or vengeance. Many had been fighting for the freedom of slaves long before abolitionism became popular and long before the Republican party came to dominate Congress.

These Radicals believed that unless black Americans received their full rights as citizens in the South and the North, every battle of the war had been fought in vain. "We must see to it that the man made free by the Constitution ... is a freeman indeed," explained one Radical, "that he can go where he pleases; work when and for whom he pleases ... and that he walks the earth, proud and erect in the conscious dignity of a free man."

The Black Codes

When the Joint Committee on Reconstruction (see page 356) met early in 1866, its members heard testimony about conditions in the South. This convinced many moderate Republicans that a more severe Reconstruction plan was needed. Among the most disturbing reports were those of laws designed to limit the activities of freedmen.

Such laws, known as Black Codes, were similar in many ways to former slave codes (see page 66), but they did provide freedmen with certain basic rights. They allowed blacks to sue and be sued and to buy and sell property. Ex-slaves who had been married informally could now make their marriages legal. The Black Codes also provided guidelines to protect young blacks who worked as apprentices. Employers were required to supply food, clothing, and training in a craft.

But the protection of certain rights could not hide the fact that the Black Codes explicitly limited the rights of black citizens by setting many restrictions. While the Constitution guaranteed the right to bear arms, the codes denied that privilege to black Americans. Blacks could not meet together after sunset. They could not marry whites. If any were found idle or unemployed, they were fined for vagrancy and faced imprisonment or hard labor for a year.

Southern state legislatures passed most of the Black Codes in the fall and winter of 1865 and 1866. Many southerners were still convinced that former slaves might rise in revolt or that, at best, they would be unable to contend with their sudden freedom.

Congress reacted to the Black Codes by trying to protect the rights of freedmen. In February 1866 it passed a bill to extend the work of the Freedmen's Bureau for an indefinite period and increase its authority. President Johnson vetoed the bill. He vetoed a second Freedmen's Bureau bill later in the year, but moderate Republicans joined the Radicals to override the veto.

In April Congress passed the Civil Rights Act, over the President's veto. The act provided that blacks could become United States citizens and possess all the legal rights of citizens. Thus Radicals hoped to secure rights for black Americans even if state laws tried to abridge them.

A Guarantee of Citizenship

Like any law passed by Congress, the Civil Rights Act was subject to review by the Supreme Court. Since the Court had ruled in the Dred Scott case that blacks were not citizens (see page 321), Republicans feared that the Court might declare the Civil Rights Act unconstitutional. Congress therefore proposed a constitutional amendment guaranteeing citizenship to black Americans.

At the heart of the Fourteenth Amendment was the simple and direct statement that "All persons born or naturalized in the United States ... are citizens." Any person who had held a national or state government position before the Civil War and who had given "aid or comfort" to the Confederate cause was forbidden to hold public office unless pardoned by Congress. In addition, all Confederate debts were cancelled, and no former slave owners could be reimbursed by any government, state or national, for the loss of their slaves by the act of emancipation.

Some Radicals wanted to include a provision guaranteeing all males, black and white, the right to vote. But many Republicans hesitated to go that far. At the time, only a few northern states permitted blacks to vote, and Republicans feared an angry reaction from their white constituents if blacks received the vote. The amendment did provide, however, that if states did not allow black males to vote, they would lose a proportionate number of seats in the House.

The Fourteenth Amendment was passed in June 1866 and sent to the states for ratification. By July 1868, enough states had approved the measure to make it part of the Constitution. Although the Fourteenth Amendment guaranteed citizenship to black Americans, they did not explicitly gain the right to vote in all states until the Fifteenth Amendment was ratified in 1870. The Fifteenth Amendment stated that no citizen could be denied the right to vote "on account of race, color, or previous condition of servitude."

The Beginning of Radical Reconstruction

When Republicans in Congress first proposed the Fourteenth Amendment in the summer of 1866, the split between them and President Johnson became irreparable. Johnson scorned the Fourteenth Amendment, urging southern legislatures to reject it as an invasion of states' rights.* To counter Radical influence, the President actively campaigned for candidates who supported his policies in the fall congressional elections. Unfortunately for Johnson, his speeches cost him support. When his audiences heckled him, he often lost his temper and responded with vulgar, vindictive language.

Outbreaks of racial violence in Memphis and New Orleans in which many blacks were killed reinforced the growing popular mood against the President. The riots convinced many northerners that Johnson's lenient policies had not worked and that stronger measures were needed to protect the freedmen.

The election results were a disaster for Johnson and a triumph for the Republicans. The Republican party won majorities in every northern state legislature, every northern governor's race, and over a two-thirds majority in both houses of Congress, assuring them of enough votes to override any presidential veto.

With control of Congress assured after the 1866 elections, Radical Republicans devised their own program for Reconstruction, passing the Reconstruction Act in March

---

*Every state government Johnson had recognized, except for the one in Tennessee, did reject the Fourteenth Amendment the first time it was considered.

1867. All former Confederate states except Tennessee, readmitted in July 1866 after it ratified the Fourteenth Amendment, had to meet a new set of requirements for readmission to the Union. Each state had to adopt a state constitution that disqualified former Confederate officials from holding office and granted black citizens the right to vote. The states also had to ratify the Fourteenth Amendment.

Until they were readmitted, the former Confederate states would be under military control. The Reconstruction Act divided the states into five military districts, each commanded by an army general. The commanders became responsible for organizing the state constitutional conventions and were required to register blacks and loyal whites to vote for convention delegates. In this way Congress tried to prevent state conventions from rejecting parts of the plan as Johnson had originally encouraged. The President vetoed the Reconstruction Act and several supplementary acts that followed it. But Congress easily overrode his vetoes, and Radical Reconstruction went into effect.

A Showdown Between the President and Congress

Although Congress had wrested control of Reconstruction from the President, it still feared that Johnson would try to execute as little of the plan as possible. Consequently Congress passed several laws that limited the President's freedom to act. One of these, the Tenure of Office Act, stated that any office-holder appointed by the President, with the advice and consent of the Senate, could not be dismissed without the Senate's consent. The Radicals hoped, thereby, to protect their sympathizers in the administration.

When Congress recessed in the summer of 1867, President Johnson decided to test the constitutionality of the act by removing Edwin Stanton, an ally of the Radicals, as Secretary of War. Stanton refused to leave, barricaded the doors of his office, and continued to issue orders. Johnson also angered Republicans by dismissing commanders of the military Reconstruction districts who sympathized too openly with Congress.

During 1867 many Radical Republicans came to believe that if Reconstruction were to succeed, Johnson would have to be removed from office. But the only way Congress could remove a President was to impeach and convict him for "high crimes and misdemeanors" committed while in office.* A congressional committee appointed to investigate the President's actions searched in vain for evidence of such crimes. Nevertheless, the Radicals proceeded with a plan of impeachment, claiming that Stanton's firing was serious enough to warrant action.

On February 24, 1868, the House of Representatives voted to impeach. President Andrew Johnson stood trial in the Senate from March 25 to May 26.

Much was at stake beyond the immediate issue of Reconstruction. Because Congress had no specific evidence to substantiate its charge of "high crimes and misdemeanors," it was essentially trying to dismiss a President simply because he disagreed with it. In the final tally 35 senators voted for conviction, 19 against, one vote short of removing the President from office.

Johnson served out his term, but the impeachment effort had undermined his power. Although Congress had not convicted him, it came close enough to demonstrate that it was determined to remain in absolute charge of Reconstruction.

Facsimile of a ticket to the impeachment trial of President Andrew Johnson.

SECTION REVIEW

1. Identify: Thaddeus Stevens, Black Codes, Civil Rights Act, Reconstruction Act, Tenure of Office Act.

2. Why were Radical Republicans harsh toward former Confederate states?

3. (a) What rights did the Black Codes extend to black Americans? (b) What rights did they deny black Americans?

4. What were the major provisions of the Fourteenth and the Fifteenth Amendments?

5. Why did Congress try to impeach President Johnson?

6. **Critical Thinking** On what grounds do you think Johnson considered the Reconstruction Act of 1867 unconstitutional?

---

*As you learned in Chapter 9, the House of Representatives can vote to impeach, or accuse, a President of committing "high crimes and misdemeanors." If a two-thirds majority of the Senate votes to convict a President, he or she is removed from office.

3 The Reconstruction South

When the Radical Republicans imposed their own version of Reconstruction in 1867, citizens in southern states began the process of writing constitutions and electing state governments. Black voters participated for the first time in these elections. Republicans dominated the new state governments, which quickly fulfilled Congress's requirements for Reconstruction. Most former Confederate states had been readmitted by July 1868 and all had by 1871. But rebuilding the southern economy would prove more difficult.

The Difficulty of Rebuilding

The devastation caused by the war made southern economic recovery difficult. Efforts to rebuild were further handicapped by a lack of cash. Confederate money was worthless after the war, and United States currency did not filter into the South as rapidly as it was needed. Planters and small farmers who were deeply in debt at the end of the war looked for a way to borrow money and begin all over again. However, many found that difficult to do.

Since land was the chief item of value left in the South, many planters and farmers were forced to sell their land in order to survive. Others bought supplies on credit from merchants at high prices and high interest rates. Farmers promised to repay the loan when the crops were harvested. Each year, more planters and farmers found themselves going deeper into debt to the merchants.

Poor white and black farmers who owned no land of their own had to work on other people's lands either as tenants or as sharecroppers. *Tenants* rented land from a large landowner and supplied their own seed and supplies. Tenants might sell their crops and pay their rent in cash, but many paid "in kind" by giving the landowner a portion of the crop. *Sharecroppers* farmed a piece of land and shared the crops they raised with the landowners. Usually, one third of the crop would go to the landowner, one third to the sharecropper, and one third to whoever provided the seeds, fertilizer, mules, and other farming equipment.

Many freedmen became sharecroppers with the hope of being able to buy their own land one day. But few realized that dream. Instead, like many other southerners, they became locked into a system of debt that promised little more than year-to-year survival.

New Forces in Southern Politics

Politics in the South during Radical Reconstruction differed greatly from that of prewar days. The Fourteenth Amendment and congressional reconstruction acts had barred former Confederate officials from taking part in state governments and had opened up participation to black citizens. Two groups, which conservative southerners called carpetbaggers and scalawags, also influenced southern politics.

Carpetbaggers were those northerners who had settled in the South after the war and supported Radical Reconstruction. Southern whites viewed them as unscrupulous intruders from the North who were seeking only personal gain. All carpetbaggers, however, did not fit that description. Some were Union soldiers who had remained in the South after the war. Others had moved South to help freedmen face their new problems.

Scalawags were white southerners who supported Radical Reconstruction. Many had been southern Unionists during the war and continued their support for the Union. Although some southerners supported the Radicals in hopes of political or financial favor, many did so because they thought it was in the interest of the South. One such person

With the southern economy in ruins, fields unplanted, and many homes burned to the ground, many southern families moved west to rebuild their lives.

A lawyer and a scholar, Representative Robert Brown Elliot of South Carolina was a southern black leader. Here he argues for a civil rights bill in the House of Representatives in 1874.

was James Longstreet, one of Lee's best generals and a successful business leader after the war. He argued that in the long run it was best for the South to cooperate with the Radicals in order to regain economic stability.

The influence of carpetbaggers and scalawags varied from state to state. In Mississippi the carpetbaggers controlled politics. In Tennessee the scalawags did. In no state, however, did blacks control the government, although they played a part in all.

Black Americans held offices previously denied them, but their influence was far less than conservative whites claimed. Only in South Carolina did blacks win a majority in one house of a legislature, and in no state did they win the governorship. Hiram R. Revels and Blanche K. Bruce, both of Mississippi, were the only two black Americans elected to the United States Senate during the Re-

construction period. Like most blacks elected to office following the Civil War, they served with pride and dignity.

Actions of the Reconstruction Governments

The southern state governments during Radical Reconstruction achieved a number of genuine improvements for their states. Legislatures passed laws giving black citizens equal civil and political rights. For the first time, southern states established free public education for all children. New laws improved care in prisons and provided centers for the care of mentally and physically handicapped persons.

But the Radical Reconstruction governments faced many problems. Since most of

This cartoon illustrates southern resentment of Reconstruction. The South bears the burden of a heavy carpetbag full of weapons. Riding the carpetbag is Ulysses S. Grant, President during much of the Reconstruction period.

the South's experienced political leaders had been Confederates, the Reconstruction governments sometimes suffered from inexperience and incompetence. New officeholders often found it difficult to handle their jobs, since they had little preparation.*

---

*In the years before the war, southern legislatures were dominated by wealthy planters who had denied educational and political opportunities to lower- and middle-class whites and to all blacks.

Corruption also plagued the Reconstruction governments. One state legislature, for example, awarded $1,000 to the speaker of the house to cover a lost bet on a horse race; and billed the state for hams, perfume, clothing, champagne, and a coffin.

Although such corruption gave the Reconstruction governments a bad reputation, bribery and graft were characteristic of governments throughout the nation after the Civil War, as you will read in Chapter 22. But this was scant consolation to conservative white southerners. They resented northerners who came to the South and prospered while many southerners lost their land. As former Confederates, they were naturally bitter when they saw southern Unionists come to power in the new governments. And they reacted with fear and skepticism toward their former slaves, who now were voting and holding office in governments once controlled by the wealthy whites.

SECTION REVIEW

1. Identify: Hiram R. Revels, Blanche K. Bruce.
2. Define: tenants, sharecroppers, carpetbaggers, scalawags.
3. What conditions contributed to a shortage of cash in the South?
4. What new groups entered southern politics after the War?
5. List two problems that plagued Reconstruction governments in the South.
6. **Critical Thinking** Why were any southern governments after the war likely to become scapegoats?

4 Unfinished Business

With the passage of the Reconstruction Acts in 1867, the Radical Republicans reached the peak of their influence. They had defeated President Johnson's conservative Reconstruction program and neutralized his power by bringing impeachment proceedings. They had forced the southern states to call new constitutional conventions, elect new governments, and give black Americans the right to vote. But over the next ten years

Radical Reconstruction steadily lost ground and finally collapsed completely.

A Changing Political Climate

Radical Reconstruction faltered in the South partly because the national leadership of the Republican party changed. Representative Thaddeus Stevens died in 1868, and Benjamin Wade lost his seat in the Senate in 1869. Other Radicals retired from public life.

Radical Republicans hoped to restore their falling influence by nominating General Ulysses S. Grant for President in 1868. In a close election, Grant defeated the Democratic nominee, Governor Horatio Seymour of New York. Once in office, however, President Grant proved much less sympathetic to the Radicals' cause than they had hoped. He was also ill prepared for the presidency.

As a military leader, the General had been hard driving, stubborn, and thorough. As a political leader, he lacked any real experience. Consequently, he often depended on the advice of others and rewarded many of his friends with appointments in the new administration. Several members of his cabinet swindled the government of millions of dollars.

By 1872 one group of Republicans, disillusioned with the corruption, split with the Grant administration. Calling themselves Liberal Republicans, they nominated New York Tribune editor Horace Greeley to run against Grant in his bid for reelection. The President, however, still retained much of his personal popularity and the worst of the scandals had not yet been exposed. Consequently, he won the 1872 election by a greater margin than he had in 1868.

The North's Declining Interest in Reconstruction

The war remained an important issue in the 1868 election and even in 1872. Republicans frequently reminded northern voters about the lives lost and money spent to win the war. But as the 1870s progressed, passions cooled. Northerners increasingly believed that the arguments and ill feelings of the past should be forgotten and that southerners should be allowed to run their own governments—even if that meant blacks might lose the rights they had so recently gained.

Furthermore, reports of corruption among carpetbaggers and scalawags shocked and disillusioned many Republicans who had supported the Reconstruction governments. They were also disheartened when some black officials, often through inexperience, became involved in the corruption. The longer Grant stayed in office, the more people focused their attention on the issue of corruption in government, both state and national. They grew less concerned with the older issues of Reconstruction.

Many northern business leaders argued for an end to Reconstruction. They believed that the Radical governments were preventing the South from expanding economically. Northern manufacturers wanted to invest in the South, but only if they could count on stable governments free from turmoil. "We have tried this Reconstruction long enough," concluded one business leader. "Now let the South alone."

Ending Radical Rule

A majority of white southerners had always resented the Republicans' attempt to reconstruct the South. Over the years they worked to regain control of the state governments from the Republicans. Some, particularly among the upper classes, believed that the best way to return to power was to accept the Radicals' changes, gain the goodwill of the new black voters, and woo them away from the Republicans into the Democratic party.

When Wade Hampton, a wealthy South Carolinian, ran for governor of his state in 1876, he campaigned among blacks, telling them, "We want your votes; we don't want you to be deprived of them. . . . if we are elected, as far as in us lies, we will observe, protect, and defend the rights of the colored man as quickly as any man in South Carolina."

But a large number of white southerners rejected this strategy. Poor white farmers, who were having trouble making a living in the war-torn South, feared economic competition from blacks. Blacks had been viewed as slaves for so many years that many white southerners, both rich and poor, resented the freedmen's right to vote and hold office. Consequently, these groups were determined to drive scalawags and carpetbaggers from office and to end the influence of blacks in elections.

Pressure and intimidation were among the tactics used. Newspapers might publish the names of southern whites sympathetic to Reconstruction, and the sympathizers were then snubbed by their neighbors. Landowners could pressure black tenant farmers to vote Democratic or not at all.

Other people resorted to force or the threat of it. In some areas, groups banded together in informal military groups or rifle clubs. They drilled conspicuously in areas where blacks lived or sent armed pickets to prevent blacks from registering to vote.

The Ku Klux Klan used floggings, hangings, and other acts of violence to frighten blacks and their white supporters. This newspaper cartoon gives a warning to carpetbaggers.

Secret organizations such as the Ku Klux Klan and the Knights of the White Camelia were formed with the purpose of ending Radical Republican rule in the South. The Klan tried to keep black and white Republican voters from the polls by burning houses and whipping, shooting, or hanging blacks and sympathetic whites. Dressed in white robes and hoods, the Klan often rode at night, breaking up Republican meetings. Moderate southerners condemned such violence and even some leaders of the Klan felt its organization had gone too far, but the Klan's campaign of intimidation kept many potential Republican voters away from the polls.

In 1870 and 1871 Congress passed the Force Act and Ku Klux Klan Act, outlawing the use of force to prevent people from voting, and authorized President Grant to use federal troops to enforce the laws. Under such pressure the Klan's activities diminished, but the threat of violence lingered. One by one, the southern states voted out the Radical Republican governments and replaced them with conservative ones. By 1876 only Louisiana, Florida, and South Carolina retained their Radical governments.

The Hayes–Tilden Compromise

The election year of 1876 found the Republicans in disarray. In 1874 southerners elected enough Democrats to Congress to give that party a majority in the House of Representa-

tives and a near-majority in the Senate. The Grant administration had been marred by scandal after scandal. With the issue of corruption so prominent, both parties nominated for President men with reputations as reformers. The Republicans chose Rutherford B. Hayes, an Ohio lawyer, and the Democrats selected Governor Samuel Tilden of New York.

In the election Tilden received 250,000 more popular votes than Hayes, but he was one vote short of the necessary 185 electoral votes. Hayes had only 165 electoral votes. The remaining 20 electoral votes, from the states of Florida, Louisiana, and South Carolina, plus one from Oregon, were claimed by both sides.

The Oregon vote eventually went to Hayes, but the decision in the other states was not easy. Florida, Louisiana, and South Carolina were the only states in the South still dominated by Republicans. Tilden had won a majority of the popular vote in each

Major Events	
1863	Lincoln proclaims 10-percent plan for Reconstruction
1864	Wade-Davis Bill proposed
1865	Congress establishes Freedmen's Bureau; Appomattox; Abraham Lincoln assassinated; Andrew Johnson becomes President; Thirteenth Amendment ratified
1866	Civil Rights Act passed; Fourteenth Amendment proposed
1867	Reconstruction Acts passed
1868	House of Representatives impeaches President Johnson; Fourteenth Amendment ratified; Ulysses S. Grant elected President
1870	Fifteenth Amendment ratified; Force Act passed
1871	Ku Klux Klan Act passed
1876	Rutherford B. Hayes elected President

state, but the Republican-controlled state election boards ruled that he had received his majority through fraud and intimidation of black voters. In the heat of the election dispute, rival Republican and Democratic electors claimed victory, voted for their candidate, and sent in their ballots.*

The nation now faced a terrible dilemma. Which electoral votes from these states should be counted? Congress finally named an electoral commission to decide the issue, consisting of seven Republicans, seven Democrats, and one independent. At the last minute, however, a Republican replaced the independent, and Hayes had the votes he needed to win the election.

---
*According to the Constitution, the electors of each state send a list of their votes to the President of the Senate, who counts the votes in the presence of both the House and the Senate.

Democrats were outraged, especially in the South. It seemed as if Hayes had stolen the election. Although there was some talk of a new civil war, conservative southerners in Congress negotiated a compromise with the Republicans. In return for their support, Hayes promised federal aid to construct new railroads and to control floods along the Mississippi River. Most important, he pledged to remove the last federal troops remaining in the South and to bring Reconstruction to a swift close.

The End of Reconstruction

Rutherford B. Hayes was inaugurated as President on March 5, 1877. In April the last federal troops withdrew from South Carolina and Louisiana, and Democratic governors replaced Republican incumbents. The

■ The election of 1876 was one of the closest in American history. As the table and graphs indicate, Tilden won the most popular votes. However, election irregularities led to a dispute about electoral college votes. Eventually, these votes went to Hayes.

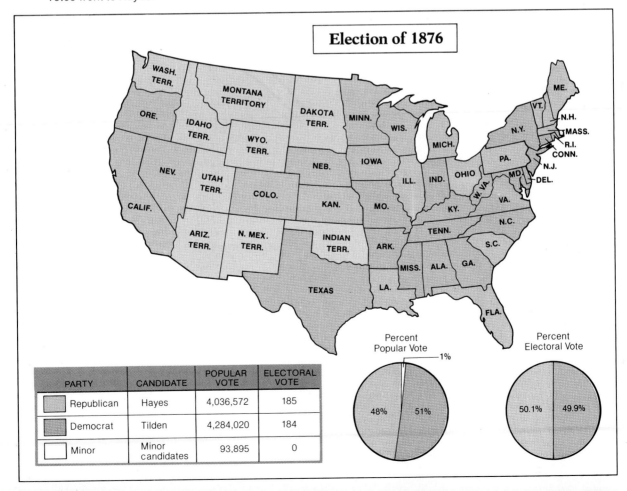

Election of 1876

PARTY	CANDIDATE	POPULAR VOTE	ELECTORAL VOTE
Republican	Hayes	4,036,572	185
Democrat	Tilden	4,284,020	184
Minor	Minor candidates	93,895	0

Percent Popular Vote — 1%, 48%, 51%

Percent Electoral Vote — 50.1%, 49.9%

Republican government in Florida had been defeated even before the inauguration.

Although Reconstruction was over, much of what it had started remained unfinished. The South had not recovered economically for blacks or whites. Neither civil nor political equality for black Americans was yet a reality in the South or North. In fact, in subsequent years many of the advances made in the early years after the war would be lost.

Nonetheless the postwar events had laid the foundation for change. The states had ratified two amendments, granting black Americans full rights of citizenship and the right to vote, at least in theory. Many years would pass before these rights would become a reality, but the amendments set standards toward which the country could aim. In later years, they would become levers for freedom.

SECTION REVIEW

1. Identify: Ku Klux Klan, Force Act, Ku Klux Klan Act, Rutherford B. Hayes, Samuel Tilden.

2. How did the death of Thaddeus Stevens and the defeat of Senator Benjamin Wade affect Radical Reconstruction?

3. Why did northern business leaders seek an end to Reconstruction?

4. Did the tactics used in the South to discourage blacks from voting succeed? Explain.

5. What did Rutherford B. Hayes agree to in exchange for support from conservative southerners?

6. **Critical Thinking** How might qualities that benefited Grant as a general have limited his success as a President?

Chapter 19 Review

In Perspective

The Civil War left scars that remained for decades. Lincoln's moderate plan for reuniting the Union died when he was assassinated. Johnson's plan to recognize the Confederate state governments quickly was challenged and eventually defeated in Congress.

The Radical Republicans thought Johnson's plan was too lenient. When they won a two-thirds majority in Congress in 1866, they were able to override any presidential veto. Their attempt to remove President Johnson from office failed, but it weakened his presidency.

Many black Americans voted for the first time in the elections of new state governments under the Radical Reconstruction program. Although handicapped by inexperience and corruption, the new governments did institute important reform measures.

As support for the Radical Republicans faded, some white southerners used fear tactics to prevent blacks and white Republicans from voting. Over time more conservative state governments replaced those set up under Radical Reconstruction. Reconstruction ended in 1877 when President Hayes ordered the removal of federal troops from the South. As you will read, reconstruction left many problems to be faced by future generations.

Vocabulary

Match each term at left with its definition or description at right.

1. freedmen
2. scalawags
3. carpetbaggers
4. sharecroppers
5. tenants

a. northerners who supported Radical Reconstruction
b. former slaves
c. people who rented farm land
d. owed some crops to the landowner
e. southerners who supported Radical Reconstruction

Chapter Checkup

1. (a) Why did Lincoln believe it was his responsibility as President to reunite the nation? (b) Describe Lincoln's plan for Reconstruction. (c) Why did he favor a moderate approach?

2. (a) What was the Radical Republicans' attitude toward the legal status of former Confederate states? (b) Why did they favor harsher requirements for readmission?

3. (a) Why did Congress propose the Fourteenth Amendment to the Constitution? (b) What was its major provision? (c) What other provisions did it contain? (d) What was the major provision of the Fifteenth Amendment?

4. (a) Why did many planters and farmers go into debt after the war? (b) How did many poor whites and freedmen make a living after the war?

5. (a) What were the achievements of the Reconstruction governments in the South? (b) What problems did they have?

Critical Thinking

1. **Analyzing** Do you think the Radical Republicans believed in a strict or loose interpretation of the Constitution? Give specific examples to support your answer.

2. **Predicting** How might the history of Reconstruction have been different if Lincoln had not been assassinated?

Developing Basic Skills

1. **Comparing** Make a chart with three columns. In one column list the provisions of Lincoln's Reconstruction policy. In column two list the provisions of Johnson's policy. In column three list the provisions imposed by the Radical Republicans. (a) Which policy seemed the least severe? (b) Which policy seemed the most severe? (c) Based on what you read, how would you explain the differences?

2. **Map Reading** Study the election map and graphs on page 365. (a) Which candidate received the most electoral votes? (b) Which candidate received the most popular votes? (c) In which states were the votes disputed? (d) Why do you think most southerners voted for the Democratic candidate?

See page 830 for suggested readings.

Writer's Handbook

Using an Index for Old Newspapers

Newspapers provide up-to-the-minute information about current affairs. Most libraries have bound copies of the index to the *New York Times* and back copies of the newspaper on microfilm. Larger libraries may have a complete collection of the *New York Times* since it began publication in 1851.

The *New York Times* index has changed over the years. The sample below is from 1876. To understand how to use the index, study the labeled sample. A sample of the current index is in the Chapter 20 Review. (See page 391.)

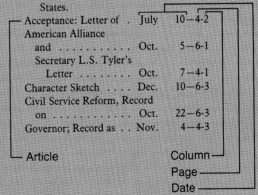

Practice: Use the sample index to answer the following questions.

1. What is the subject of the first article?

2. What is the date, page, and column of the article about Hayes's record as governor?

3. What is the subject of the article about R. B. Hayes in the December 10, 1876, issue of the *New York Times*?

Equality in America

We hold these truths to be self-evident, that all men are created equal. . . ." That phrase from the Declaration of Independence is breathtakingly simple, yet at the same time extremely complex. Certainly it was complex when the nation was embroiled in the issue of slavery.

The Debate Over Equality   In their debates over slavery in 1858, Abraham Lincoln and Stephen Douglas struggled to define the "equality" referred to in the Declaration. Douglas argued that equality could not apply to blacks because the writers of the Constitution had permitted slavery to continue. The phrase "all men are created equal" must include only white men, Douglas concluded.

Lincoln replied that the Declaration's notion of equality was not a statement of fact. It was a goal—an ideal to work toward. As an example, he recalled a saying of Jesus: *As your Father in Heaven is perfect, be ye also perfect.* "The Savior, I suppose, did not expect that any human creature could be perfect as the Father in

The career of Hiram Revels reflected the impact of the Civil War on the issue of equality. He was the first black lawyer admitted to try cases before the United States Supreme Court. He was also a United States senator and a college president.

Heaven," said Lincoln, "but He . . . set that up as a standard, and he who did most towards reaching that standard, attained the highest degree of moral perfection. So I say in relation to the principle that all men are created equal, let it be as nearly reached as we can."

Lincoln and Douglas were neither the first nor the last to argue the meaning of equality. The debate has long been a central part of American history. For many years after the Declaration was written, the phrase "all men are created equal" did not mean that women, blacks, or Indians had the same rights as white men. In fact, in the years after the Revolution, only white, property-holding adult males had full equality before the law. And, even for those who had the same legal rights, factors such as education and wealth could limit the realization of equality.

What should be done about those conditions? How much should they be changed to make all Americans equal? James Fenimore Cooper, the novelist of the early nineteenth century, readily accepted the Declaration's guarantee of the right to "life, liberty, and the pursuit of happiness." But in his view, in practice, equality "can only mean a common misery."

The Continuing Struggle   But what if people could not compete equally because of past discrimination? Unlike Cooper, some Americans argued that society should step in to alter such situations. After the Civil War, for example, Radical Republicans argued that it was not enough to free blacks from slavery. If blacks had been deprived of property for years, how could they be expected to compete with whites who had long owned property?

To solve this problem, Thaddeus Stevens proposed that the government break up the estates of the leading rebels. "Give, if you please, 40 acres to each adult freedman," he urged. "This subdivision of the lands will yield ten bales of cotton to one that is made now, and he who produced it will own it and feel himself a man."

Young black women learned basic skills at freedmen's schools throughout the South.

In the end, Congress failed to provide land for the freedman. As Frederick Douglass lamented, "The government . . . felt it had done enough for him. . . . He was free from the old plantation, but he had nothing but the dusty road under his feet."

Women, too, challenged notions of equality in the 1800s. In its Declaration of Sentiments, the Seneca Falls Convention of 1848 rephrased the principle of equality in the Declaration of Independence: "We hold these truths to be self-evident: that all men and women are created equal." Women's rights crusaders concentrated their efforts on the right to vote. However, even after women finally were granted that right in 1920, the debate over equality for women was not ended. For women, as well as for blacks, immigrants, and minority ethnic groups, equality was still a goal—not a reality.

A New View of Equality The civil rights movement of the 1960s, sometimes referred to as the "second Reconstruction," marked a new chapter in the ongoing debate over the meaning of equality. President John F. Kennedy reminded Americans, "This nation . . . was founded on the principle that all men are created equal. . . . Every American ought to have the right to be treated as he would wish to be treated."

The civil rights movement resulted in legislation designed to end the discrimination that had threatened equality for so many years. In particular, the Civil Rights Act of 1964 prohibited discrimination on the basis of race, sex, or ethnic origin.

Yet the civil rights movement of the 1960s raised the same question as Reconstruction had in the 1860s: Was it enough simply to grant equal rights? Should society step in and guarantee equal opportunity as well? As President Lyndon Johnson argued, "You do not bring a person who for years has been hobbled by chains and liberate him, bring him to the starting line of a race and then say, 'You are free to compete with all the others,' and still justly believe you have been completely fair."

In effect, the debate over civil rights during the 1960s brought into focus a new view of equality. This view went beyond granting everyone the right to run in the race *(equal rights)*. It went beyond giving the disadvantaged a head start in the race *(equal opportunity)*. Indeed, it went so far as to suggest that everyone should have the chance to finish the race at the same time *(equal results)*. Equality of results has proven to be the most controversial definition of equality.

The strong support for equality in the Declaration of Independence ensured that the Americans would never stop seeking to define its meaning as broadly as possible. Like the nation's founders, Americans today are committed to the principle of equality. They will continue to debate its meaning and seek its reality for years to come.

1. How did Abraham Lincoln define equality?
2. Why do you think the civil rights movement of the 1960s has been referred to as the "second Reconstruction"?

American Profiles

The Grimké Sisters

Angelina and Sarah Grimké were key figures in the nation's struggle for equality. Their efforts in both the antislavery and women's rights movements in the 1830s fueled a furious national debate that consumed the middle part of the nineteenth century.

The Grimké sisters were born in Charleston, South Carolina—Sarah in 1792 and Angelina in 1805. They enjoyed the advantages of growing up in a wealthy, prominent southern family.

At age 29, Sarah moved to Philadelphia. Eight years later, she persuaded Angelina to join her and adopt her Quaker beliefs. Both sisters felt the need "to do God's work on earth." By 1834, they had found purpose in the abolition movement.

Mob violence against abolitionists in Boston in 1835 stirred Angelina to write a letter to William Lloyd Garrison's abolitionist paper *The Liberator*. Readers were surprised that a woman from the South had taken such a strong stand against slavery. Recognizing the influence the Grimkés might have on the public, the American Anti-Slavery Society asked them to participate in its campaign. Angelina and Sarah became the only women in the "Group of Seventy," a select team of speakers trained to spread the abolitionist message.

The Grimkés began their first tour of New England in the summer of 1837. At first, they addressed only women in "parlor meetings." Their powerful oratory, however, soon attracted large crowds, including men, and their meetings were rescheduled in churches and large halls.

At the same time, the Grimkés drew much criticism. The Massachusetts Congregational clergy voiced disapproval of women speaking out in public on controversial issues and urged that the churches close their doors to the Grimkés.

The Grimkés responded to this criticism by writing *Letters on the Equality of the Sexes*, one of the first essays on women's rights. In it, Angelina declared,

Sarah Grimké (1792–1873) and Angelina Grimké (1805–1879) were among the first women to give public lectures in the United States. They spoke out in favor of abolition and women's rights.

"[Women's rights] is part of the great doctrine of Human Rights and can no more be separated from Emancipation than the light from the heat of the sun; the rights of the slave and woman blend like the colors of the rainbow."

In 1838, Angelina married Theodore Weld, an abolitionist leader. In the following years, the sisters limited their abolitionist and women's rights activities to correspondence and pamphleteering. As war fever grew, however, the sisters resumed more active roles as abolitionists. In 1863, Angelina addressed the convention of the "Loyal Women of the Nation" in New York, speaking once again with her old dramatic fire.

After the Civil War, the Grimkés continued the struggle for the causes they had pioneered before the war. They realized that equality for blacks and women would not be gained easily or quickly. Their work for black equality was limited to help for individuals, but they once more took public roles in the struggle for women's rights. At their deaths, the same newspapers that had criticized them in the past praised their courage and determination in the fight for human rights.

1. Why were the Grimkés an important symbol to the abolitionist cause?
2. How did the Grimkés support the abolitionist movement?
3. Why do you think the Grimkés and their contributions have continued to gain prominence even after their deaths?

Celebrating Emancipation

Emancipation marked the first meaningful step for blacks in their search for equality. On the day the Emancipation Proclamation was issued—January 1, 1863—Union Colonel Thomas Higginson held a formal celebration at his headquarters on the Sea Islands of Georgia. In this account of the celebration, Higginson reveals the joy and hope of the newly freed slaves present at the event.

The colors were presented to us by the Rev. Mr. French, a chaplain who brought them from the donors in New York. All this was according to the program. Then followed an incident so simple, so touching, so utterly unexpected and startling, that I can scarcely believe it on recalling, though it gave the keynote to the whole day. The very moment the speaker had ceased, and just as I took and waved the flag, which now for the first time meant anything to these poor people, there suddenly arose, close beside the platform, a strong male voice (but rather cracked and elderly), into which two women's voices instantly blended, singing, as if by an impulse that could no more be repressed than the morning note of the song-sparrow, "My Country, 'tis of thee, / Sweet land of liberty, / Of thee I sing!"

People looked at each other, and then at us on the platform, to see whence came this interruption, not set down in the bills.

Firmly and irrepressibly the quavering voices sang on, verse after verse; others of the colored people joined in; some whites on the platform began, but I motioned them to silence. I never saw anything so electric; it made all other words cheap; it seemed the choked voice of a race at last unloosed. Nothing could be more wonderfully unconscious; art could not have dreamed of a tribute to the day of jubilee that should be so affecting; history will not believe it; and when I came to speak of it, after it was ended, tears were everywhere. . . . Just think of it!—the first day they had ever had a country, the first flag they had ever seen which promised anything to their people, and here, while mere spectators stood in silence, waiting for my stupid words, these . . . souls burst out in their song, as if they were by their own hearths at home! When they stopped, there was nothing to do for it but to speak, and I went on; but the life of the whole day was in those unknown people's song.

Adapted from Thomas Wentworth Higginson, *Army Life in a Black Regiment* (Boston, 1882).

1. What was the occasion for the celebration?
2. What incident did Higginson consider the highlight of the celebration?
3. Why did Higginson motion to whites on the platform to stop singing?

Unit Six

Transforming a Nation

The Homestead Act, which offered land to settlers, encouraged many Americans to move onto the Great Plains.

By the 1800s most immigrants to the United States were arriving from eastern and southern Europe.

	1865	1870	1875	1880	1885
POLITICS AND GOVERNMENT		**1872** Crédit Mobilier scandal is first one of Grant presidency		**1883** Civil Service Act passed	
SOCIETY AND CULTURE		**1869** Wyoming is first state to grant women the right to vote		**1881** Tuskegee Institute founded for black students	
ECONOMICS AND TECHNOLOGY		**1870** Rockefeller founds Standard Oil	**1876** Invention of telephone revolutionizes communication		
WORLD EVENTS		**1867** Alaska is purchased from Russia		**1882** United States and Korea sign a trade agreement	

The Plains Indians respected nature and believed that the arrival of settlers from the East threatened their way of life.

Garfield

1878 Thomas Edison invented the phonograph, which was patented in 1878.

During the Gilded Age, wealthy people indulged in elaborate decorations as seen in this Tiffany lamp.

1898 Theodore Roosevelt led his Rough Riders up San Juan Hill in the Spanish-American War.

1885	1890	1895	1900	1905

1887 Dawes Act tries to bring Indians into American mainstream

1899 Open Door notes try to keep China open to trade

1889 Addams founds Hull House

1893 Columbian Exposition celebrates American progress and industry

1887 ICC set up to regulate railroads

1894 Coxey's Army protests the government's silver policy

Late 1800s Spheres of influence set up in China

1895 Cubans rebel against Spanish

1900 Boxer Rebellion breaks out in China

The steel industry grew rapidly in the late 1800s. This painting shows steelworkers at lunch time.

As railroads expanded, they offered more comforts to passengers, including a reclining chair seat.

20

The Western Frontier

(1865–1914)

Pioneer Woman *by Harvey Dunn*

Chapter Outline

1 *Visions of the West*

2 *Opening of the West*

3 *Tragedy for the Plains Indians*

4 *The Cattle Frontier*

5 *The Sodbusters' Frontier*

In July 1806 Zebulon Pike led an exploration party through what is now Kansas and eastern Colorado. Pike reported that he had seen enormous tracts "where the wind has thrown up the sand in all the fanciful forms of the ocean's rolling waves, and on which not a speck of vegetable matter existed." He argued that the land could not support farming and therefore should be left to the Indians. Fourteen years later Stephen Long explored the area that was to become Nebraska and Oklahoma and labeled it the "Great American Desert."

Until the 1860s that label stuck. Pioneers crossed the area to reach the lush lands of Oregon or the gold fields of California, but few stopped along the way. However, after the Civil War, a growing number of people began to settle the huge region between the Mississippi River and the Sierra Nevadas.

Western cattle boom

1865	1875	1885	1895	1905	1915

1869 Transcontinental railroad completed

1876 Battle of Little Big Horn fought

1887 Dawes Act passed

1889 Oklahoma land rush

1907 Oklahoma becomes state

1912 New Mexico, Arizona become states

1 Visions of the West

The United States began as a nation with a frontier reaching along the Appalachians and into the Ohio Valley. Gradually the frontier line was pushed westward. By the Civil War American settlement had advanced west of the Mississippi River and into Texas, Iowa, and eastern Kansas and Nebraska. In these areas, with their rich soil and moderate rainfall, farming was profitable. But the Great Plains farther west provided new challenges.

Life on the Great Plains

The Great Plains stretch from about the 98th meridian to the Rocky Mountains. Less than 20 inches (50 centimeters) of rain falls on these vast plains each year, compared with up to 40 inches (100 centimeters) a year in the East. The land is treeless, except for occasional timber in the river bottoms.

West of Denver, Colorado, the Rockies spring abruptly out of the plains. Beyond the mountains extends the Great Basin, where Death Valley and the Mojave (moh HAH vee) Desert are located. The frontier of 1860 was bounded on the west by the high peaks of the Sierra Nevadas and the Cascades. Beyond these two ranges lay the rich valleys of California and Oregon, which were already being settled.

As you read in Chapter 1, before the arrival of European explorers many Plains peoples had been nomadic. On foot they hunted buffalo and other game. Horses had been extinct in the Americas for thousands of years, but early Spanish explorers and settlers brought their mounts from Europe. Over the years some horses had strayed and multiplied. Gradually herds of wild horses traveled north from Mexico onto the Great Plains. During the 1700s Plains Indians began to tame and ride horses, and by the 1780s most groups had become accomplished at riding.

The Kiowa, Sioux, Crow, Comanche, Cheyenne, Arapaho, Blackfeet, and other Indian nations could thus roam hundreds of miles on horseback to hunt buffalo. With more successful hunts, the Plains Indians prospered, and their population tripled, reaching about 150,000 by the mid-nineteenth century. Despite this growth, the vast plains remained sparsely settled. Most of the Indians hunted only enough buffalo to supply basic needs without destroying the herds.

These shaggy animals supplied most of the necessities of life. The carcass provided fresh meat. What excess meat could not be eaten was dried for use during winter. Women prepared buffalo hides to make teepees and clothing. Sinew was made into thread and bowstrings, bones into tools, and horns into eating utensils. Dried buffalo dung became fuel and the rough side of the tongue a hairbrush.

Native American Vision of the West

The Indians of the Great Plains believed that the natural world was in close harmony with the supernatural spirits who governed it. Only by maintaining a proper relationship with the many spirit-gods of the plains would the Indians be rewarded with success in hunting and in war. Accordingly, the purpose of Indian religious rituals was to bring the lives of the participants into harmony with the spiritual world.

Since they revered nature, the Plains Indians disturbed the land and its creatures as

For the Kiowa, as for other Plains people, vast buffalo herds provided food, clothing, and shelter. Kiowa warrior Two Hatchets, shown here, typifies the dignity of the Plains Indians.

little as possible. Any wasteful or harmful use of the natural environment disturbed their vision of a balanced world. But their way of life, resting on a precarious balance with nature, changed drastically with the arrival of immigrants from the East, immigrants who had a different vision of the West.

New Visions of the West

On the Fourth of July, 1868, William Gilpin, the first territorial governor of Colorado, stood up in the rough frontier town of Denver and delivered an enthusiastic oration on the future of the West. For Gilpin the Great Plains were not the Great American Desert, as some called them. He brushed aside the problem of limited rainfall by claiming that artesian wells, bored deep into the ground, would transform the plains into a garden.

Gilpin accepted the belief, common in his era, that once crops had been planted, the new vegetation would change the climate and encourage rain. Gilpin predicted that the land would eventually support a billion people.

In the year after this address, a young man who was to reject Gilpin's vision began his own trek westward. John Wesley Powell was a rough, striking figure and a magnetic leader. Fighting as a volunteer in the Civil War, he had lost his right arm at the elbow in the battle of Shiloh. Undaunted, he returned to active service and rose to become a major.

In 1869, as a trained geologist, Powell was poised to lead a scientific expedition down the Colorado River through the Grand Canyon. He was not deterred by the frailty of his boats or the swirling canyon rapids. As he mapped the Grand Canyon and studied the surrounding areas, Powell built his own vision of how the land should be treated.

The West, he claimed, was a mixture of natural environments shaped by the amount of rainfall in each locality. One overriding fact remained: water was scarce throughout. While a farmer in the rainy East could make an adequate living on a farm of 160 acres (64 hectares), Powell predicted that in the arid West, over 1,200 acres (480 hectares) of unirrigated land would be needed.

With water so scarce, Powell foresaw the need for cooperation among western settlers. In the East a farmer had a legal right to do whatever he wanted with a river flowing through his property. In the West, Powell warned, the use of water would somehow have to be regulated and shared.

Beginning in 1860s the vision of the Native Americans would be challenged and then destroyed by miners, railroad builders, ranchers, and farmers who came west with their own dreams and hopes. Many of the first pioneers shared Gilpin's vision of unlimited resources, but gradually more settlers came to accept Powell's view that cooperation would be needed to overcome the hardships people would face.

SECTION REVIEW

1. Identify: William Gilpin, John Wesley Powell.
2. List one climatic and one topographical feature of the Great Plains.
3. How did the Plains Indians make use of the buffalo?
4. How did the Plains Indians treat the land?
5. (a) What was the Native American view of the West? (b) What was Gilpin's vision? (c) What was Powell's vision?
6. **Critical Thinking** How would you account for the different views of the West held by the Indians, Gilpin, and Powell?

2 Opening of the West

Before the 1860s the only American settlers to see the Great Plains, the Rocky Mountains, the Great Basin, and the Sierra Nevadas and Cascades beyond were traveling to California or Oregon. Those settlers considered the land worthless and crossed it as quickly as possible. But in the late 1850s and early 1860s new gold and silver strikes in the Rockies attracted a growing number of Americans to the West. The completion of a transcontinental railroad in 1869 made it easier for people to travel there.

The New Mining Frontier

Miners who had flocked to California during the Gold Rush of the late 1840s set out to find new strikes in the late 1850s. From California they pushed east into the Sierra Nevadas and the Rocky Mountains. Thus the mining frontier was unusual in American history, since it moved from the west coast eastward.

Most of the first strikes were made in the late 1850s and early 1860s. Nearest to the original California fields were the mines of western Nevada. In the next 20 years the Comstock Lode near Virginia City, Nevada, yielded over $300 million in gold and silver, the richest mining strike in history.

To the north, miners discovered valuable mineral deposits in the Columbia and Fraser river valleys. They also made strikes in Idaho and Montana along the Bitter Root and Salmon River mountain ranges. Farther east in Colorado, mining towns such as Denver, Boulder, and Colorado Springs grew up near gold strikes. (See the map on page 386.)

Even more than the earlier California mines, these deposits required large corporations to extract the mineral riches. In strikes like the Comstock Lode, the richest deposits lay well underground, trapped in quartz veins that could not be mined without costly tools. Only organized investors with large sums of money for rock-crushing machinery and drills that could bore down a thousand feet (300 meters) or more could take advantage of the new finds.

From Mining Camps to Towns and Cities

The discovery of mineral riches brought thousands of people to the West. Towns sprang up throughout the area as rumors of gold or silver strikes spread. If little gold and silver was found, people quickly left, leaving behind a ghost town of empty buildings.

Sometimes towns were built in anticipation of a big strike even before gold was discovered. In 1858 when Denver was founded along the South Platte River, only a few ounces of gold had been found in the Colorado streams. Yet farsighted planners had already bought up town space and begun laying out streets and erecting cabins. When rich deposits were found the following year, Denver prospered. By 1860 it had its own lending library, two newspapers, one theater,

a schoolteacher, and a barber who encouraged miners to "get your beards mowed."

Although most miners were men, enterprising women also profited from the new strikes. With only a few dollars to her name a woman could open a boardinghouse in a western boom town and make a tidy fortune. Cooking and baking jobs could bring rich rewards too. One ambitious baker reported that in less than a year she had baked and sold $18,000 worth of pies.

Frequently the rapid growth of towns led to disorder and lawlessness. Makeshift governments tried to establish order, but miners often organized vigilante committees, self-appointed enforcers of the law. Singling out the worst desperadoes and outlaws, vigilante groups gave them speedy trials and frequently lynched them.

Informal methods of government gradually gave way to more formal arrangements. In 1861 Colorado, Dakota, and Nevada were organized as territories; Idaho and Arizona followed in 1863 and Montana in 1864. Although boisterous mining towns would continue to spring up through the mid-1870s, the process of more permanent settlement had begun.

Transportation Opens the West

When news of gold strikes in Colorado first reached the East in 1859, transportation between the two regions was limited. Few railroads extended west of the Mississippi River. (See the map on page 386.) Without a good system of transportation linking West and East, the growth of the West would be severely limited.

In the 1850s the first stagecoach lines began offering service between East and West. John Butterfield's Overland Express looped south through Texas and New Mexico, then up the California coast. The firm of Russell, Majors, and Waddell followed a more central route along the Platte River and across the Rockies to San Francisco.

Travelers who could afford the $200 fee and were willing to wait 10 days to reserve a place on the stage could travel from Missouri to California in about 20 days. Passengers rode packed three abreast in an elegant coach complete with broad iron "tire" wheels that didn't sink in the sand. The bumpy ride nonetheless was exhausting and grimy.

Temporary lodging was available at the way stations where stage drivers changed horses, but few passengers cared to stop. The station huts offered only a few bunks covered with old rags and buffalo robes. The floors, grumbled one traveler, were "much like the ground outside, only not nearly so clean."

Mail service also improved. The Pony Express, established in 1860, delivered a letter from St. Louis to San Francisco in ten days at a cost of up to $10 an ounce. Eighty riders sped east and west along a route almost 2,000 miles (3,200 kilometers) long, working in relays to bring the mail through. But the Pony Express lasted less than two years. In 1862 wires had been strung across the plains, and messages could be transmitted instantly using the telegraph, invented by Samuel Morse in 1832.

Linking East and West by Rail

Observing the rapid growth of eastern railroads in the 1850s, many westerners concluded that their region would benefit greatly if rail service could be extended to the Pacific. A train could carry hundreds of passengers and large amounts of freight.

However, building a transcontinental railroad posed major problems. Most lines in the East were operated by small companies. The sums of money needed to build a railroad stretching across the nation were beyond the means of most private investors, especially since that route meant cutting through both the Sierra Nevadas and the Rocky Mountains.

In 1862 the government stepped in to encourage the railroad companies to build a transcontinental line. It offered railroad companies land in the West as an incentive. The United States government had acquired the western lands through treaties and purchases from Native Americans. (See the map on page 382.) Land that belongs to the nation and not to individuals is called *public domain*. For every mile (1.6 kilometers) of track laid, Congress granted the railroad companies 20 square miles (52 square kilometers) of land plus a 400-foot-wide (120-meter) right of way. In addition, Congress agreed to loan money for every mile of track completed.

The laying of the first section of track for the transcontinental railroad in 1863 started one of the great races in American history as two companies competed for the

For two years the riders of the Pony Express galloped across the West. Stations were located every 10 to 20 miles along the route. A rider would stop at a station just long enough to exchange his exhausted horse for a fresh mount. This painting by Frederic Remington is titled The Coming and Going of the Pony Express.

By 1869 railroad tracks connected the west coast with the Midwest. Much of the back-breaking work of hacking out a railbed through the Sierra Nevadas was done by crews of Chinese workers. The workers in this painting cheer one of the first trains along a track they have built.

government grants and loans. Union Pacific crews laid their first tracks on Nebraska flatlands as they moved westward. Starting in Sacramento, California, and moving east, the workers of the Central Pacific had to break through the high Sierra Nevadas. In the first four years, the Central Pacific laid only about 100 miles (160 kilometers) of track.

Charles Crocker, in charge of the Central Pacific crews, was determined to conquer the difficult route. He supervised about 10,000 Chinese laborers who had been hired by the Central Pacific when few other workers were willing to take on the perilous task of bridging the mountains.

Facing solid granite walls, the Chinese workers had to cart away mounds of rubble, using only baskets and wheelbarrows. The work was so difficult that progress sometimes dwindled to a mere 8 inches (20 centimeters) a day. When winter came to the Sierra Nevadas, Crocker ordered his workers to dig tunnels through 40-foot (12-meter)

snowdrifts in order to lay track on the frozen ground. Without the strength and endurance of the Chinese workers, the transcontinental railroad would have taken much longer to build.

To the east, the Union Pacific relied largely on Irish Americans, many of whom were Union veterans of the Civil War. Crossing the flat plains from Omaha, the work went quickly. As much as 3 miles (5 kilometers) of track might be laid between sunrise and sunset.

Every 60 miles (about 100 kilometers) the workers threw up a temporary town. As soon as the next stretch of track was complete, they pulled the buildings down, loaded the wood on a flatcar, and built a new town farther down the line. The towns included shacks for the men to live in as well as saloons, dance halls, and gambling tents for entertainment.

By 1868 the crews of both companies had reached the flat ground of the Utah plains, and the pace of laying track increased. Since each company was anxious to lay more track than the other, thereby receiving more government land and loans, the crews raced past each other without meeting. They continued putting down track until Congress ordered them to join at Promontory Point, Utah. When the last symbolic gold and silver spikes had been driven on May 10, 1869, the first transcontinental railroad was complete and the whole nation celebrated.

Settlement Follows the Rails

In time, five major railroads linked West and East. By 1893 the Southern Pacific railway ran from New Orleans across Texas and along the Mexican border into California. The Santa Fe connected Missouri with southern California. The Northern Pacific and the Great Northern spanned the upper Midwest to Washington and Oregon. (See the map on page 386.)

The railroad routes greatly influenced the course of development in the West. Towns grew quickly along the tracks. Railroads brought new settlers and insured them of supplies and a way to take their products to eastern markets. The largest towns and cities developed at the crossroads of major railroad lines. In southern California, for example, Los Angeles began its spectacular growth only after the Santa Fe and Southern Pacific railroads met there.

All across the West, the railroad signaled growth and prosperity for new settlements. With travel and transportation of goods made easier, it was not long before miners were followed by farmers and ranchers.

SECTION REVIEW

1. Identify: Comstock Lode, Pony Express, Union Pacific Railroad, Central Pacific Railroad.
2. Define: vigilante, public domain.
3. Where were discoveries of gold and silver made in the 1850s and 1860s?
4. List disadvantages of stagecoach travel.
5. What did the federal government offer railroad companies as an incentive for laying track in the West?
6. **Critical Thinking** Are railroads as important for transportation and communication today as they were in the 1800s? Explain.

3 Tragedy for the Plains Indians

In 1830 when Andrew Jackson implemented his policy of removing all Native Americans to lands west of the Mississippi River, he expected conflict between the two cultures to end. But after 1840 the United States extended its boundaries to the Pacific. Wagon trains crossed the plains to reach Oregon and California. The mining frontier moved into Indian territory, and railroads crossed Native American hunting grounds. As more easterners recognized the value of the West, pressure on the Plains Indians increased.

Outbreak of Warfare on the Plains

In 1851 representatives of the United States government and the major Plains Indian nations met near Fort Laramie in Wyoming. They hoped to find a way for the Indians and the new settlers to live peacefully. In exchange for promises of yearly payments in money and goods, the Indian leaders agreed to confine their hunting to specified regions with definite borders.

By containing the Indians in certain areas, government representatives hoped to reduce the chances of conflict among Indian nations and between Indians and settlers. Government agents would also use the provision to negotiate with Native American nations individually.

The agreement of 1851 worked poorly because neither the United States government nor the Indian leaders could enforce it. The chiefs who signed the agreement could not prevent members of their nations from hunting where they wished, and arriving settlers consistently ignored Indian land claims.

When thousands of miners came to Colorado in the gold rush of 1859, the chance of conflict with Native Americans increased. Miners claimed land that less than a decade before had been promised "forever" to the Cheyenne and Arapaho nations. When United States agents forced Indian leaders to forfeit their land, many Indian nations declared war. In 1865 the Sioux went to war when the United States government announced it was going to build a road through Sioux hunting grounds to the mining towns of Bozeman and Virginia City.

The warfare was bitter. The Plains Indians were fighting for their homeland and their way of life against people who had consistently broken promises to them. Consequently, Indians attacked settlements and army supply trains. In 1866 Sioux in the Big Horn Mountains led a surprise attack on a detachment of troops led by Captain W. J. Fetterman, killing all 82 soldiers.

The new American miners and settlers believed that they had a right to the land. Most felt that they would make better use of its resources than Indian hunters had. Easterners were outraged by Indian ambushes, which they considered unfair, and were horrified by stories of Indians torturing captives.

United States government troops often struck back mercilessly at the Indians. In 1864, for example, Colonel John Chivington ordered his soldiers to slaughter 450 Cheyenne men, women, and children at Sand Creek, Colorado, after the Cheyenne had been guaranteed protection. "I have come to kill Indians," Chivington declared tersely, "and believe it is right and honorable to use any means under God's heaven to kill them."

Outcome of the Wars

The conflicts in the West convinced the government that a new Indian policy was needed. In 1867 and 1868 government agents demanded that the Plains nations give up even more land and move to *reservations*, areas specifically set aside for them, The Indians of the southern plains were expected to move to a poor, unproductive tract in Oklahoma. The northern nations were to be confined to the Black Hills area of the Dakota territory. Major Indian leaders agreed to the demands, but since many Indians did not, warfare on the plains continued.

Yet even the Indians who agreed to move to the reservations were not allowed to live peacefully. In 1874 miners discovered gold in the Black Hills. Thousands of prospectors rushed into the area to stake claims. The outraged Indians fought back. When Colonel George Custer led a detachment of 265 men into the heart of Sioux country in June 1876, he found himself outmaneuvered. Led by Crazy Horse, Sitting Bull, and Rain-in-the-Face, a Sioux force of 2,500 killed every one of Custer's men at Little Big Horn.

The Sioux had won the battle, but they lost the larger campaign. The U.S. Army could mount too many men with too many modern weapons for the Indians to withstand a prolonged war. In the autumn of 1876 the Sioux surrendered.

A few nations continued to resist in the following years but without real hope. In 1877 Chief Joseph led the Nez Percé (NEHZ puhr SAY) of Oregon and Idaho in a brilliant defensive campaign crossing a thousand miles (1,600 kilometers) before he was forced to surrender in Montana. The Apaches of

Fact and legend merge in the tales of Calamity Jane, a sharpshooter and frontier woman whose real name was Martha Jane Canary Burke. At one point during the Indian wars she worked as a scout for General George Crook.

Arizona, led by their determined chief, Geronimo, held out until 1886.

Individuals on both sides commented on the tragedy. Chief Joseph put aside his weapons wearily. "I am tired of fighting," he declared sadly.

> Our chiefs are killed. . . . The little children are freezing to death. My people, some of them, have run away to the hills and have no blankets, no food. . . . Hear me, my chiefs, I am tired; my heart is sick and sad. From where the sun now stands, I will fight no more forever.

General Philip Sheridan, the Civil War veteran who led many campaigns against the Indians after the war, was also aware of the injustice of the conflict. "We took away their country and their means of support, broke up their mode of living, their habits of life, introduced disease and decay among them, and it was for this and against this that they made war. Could anyone expect less?"

A Vanishing Way of Life

Sheridan had correctly perceived that the Indians had lost more than a few battles and a great deal of land. They were losing a whole way of life. One of the most devastating blows to the Plains nations was the destruction of the buffalo herds.

As you have read, the buffalo played a central role in Plains Indian culture. Beginning in the 1860s, however, the herds began to dwindle. As railroad crews laid tracks

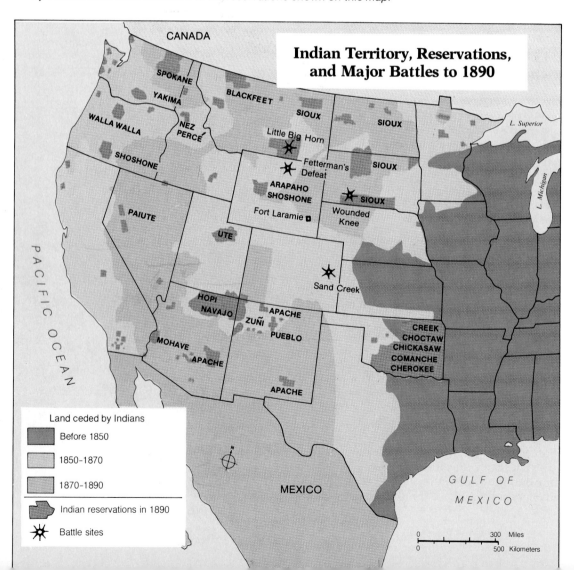

■ The United States government had promised large tracts of western land to Native American tribes. However, most of that land was ceded back to the government. By 1890 Indians were restricted to the reservations shown on this map.

Indian Territory, Reservations, and Major Battles to 1890

CANADA

SPOKANE
YAKIMA
BLACKFEET
SIOUX
SIOUX
L. Superior
WALLA WALLA
NEZ PERCE
Little Big Horn
SHOSHONE
Fetterman's Defeat
SIOUX
ARAPAHO
SHOSHONE
SIOUX
L. Michigan
PAIUTE
Fort Laramie
Wounded Knee
UTE
Sand Creek
HOPI
NAVAJO
ZUÑI
APACHE
PUEBLO
MOHAVE
APACHE
CREEK
CHOCTAW
CHICKASAW
COMANCHE
CHEROKEE
APACHE
PACIFIC OCEAN

Land ceded by Indians

	Before 1850
	1850–1870
	1870–1890
	Indian reservations in 1890
✳	Battle sites

MEXICO

GULF OF MEXICO

0   300   Miles
0   500 Kilometers

across the prairie, thousands of animals were slaughtered to provide food. Buffalo hunting also became a fashionable sport for easterners, who would sometimes organize expeditions and shoot the herds from the comfort of train cars.

Then, in the 1870s, merchants discovered that buffalo hides could be sold in the East as fashionable robes or turned into belts to drive machinery. Commercial hunters shot thousands of the animals, skinned them right on the prairie, and hauled off the hides on large wagons. Out of the 13 million animals on the plains in 1860, only a few hundred remained by the end of the century.

With the buffalo nearly gone, Plains Indians could no longer support themselves as they had before. Driven onto reservations, they were forced to depend on the government for food. Unfortunately, the corruption that became widespread in government after the Civil War also affected Indian policy.

Money meant to purchase food supplies often went directly into the pockets of corrupt government agents. Food supplies that did find their destination were often spoiled. "No branch of the national government is so spotted with fraud, so tainted with corruption . . . as this Indian Bureau," concluded one member of the House of Representatives in 1869.

Calls for Reform

Others spoke out against the evils of the reservation system. Susette La Flesche, an Omaha Indian, campaigned vigorously on behalf of Native Americans. Her father had been chief of the Omaha when treaties had reduced his nation's hunting grounds to a small reservation on the Missouri River. In the 1870s, La Flesche drew attention to Indian grievances through her writing and by conducting lecture tours.

One of the people La Flesche influenced was Helen Hunt Jackson. Jackson was incensed by the Indians' plight, and she wrote a book, *A Century of Dishonor* (1881), which vividly outlined the history of broken treaties between the United States and the Indians.

Partly in response to such calls for reform, Congress passed the Dawes Act in 1887. The legislation was an attempt to bring Indians into the mainstream of American life by breaking up traditional Indian organizations. Reservation land was no longer to be held by the tribe in common but was parceled out in 160-acre (64-hectare) lots to families and individuals. Those Native Americans who accepted land became full citizens of the United States. Congress provided additional funds to support schools that would teach Indian children "the white man's way of life."

The creators of the Dawes Act failed to appreciate the strength of Indian traditions. Furthermore, white citizens eager for additional land often tricked Indians into selling their lots for a small price. The result was that once again Indian land ended up in white hands.

Reformers who supported the Dawes Act hoped the Indians would also give up their religion, but the Indians resisted. Looking back to their days of freedom, some of the Sioux on Dakota reservations began to practice a religious ritual known as the Ghost Dance. The dance celebrated the sacred customs of the past and hailed the time when the Sioux would return to the freedom of those days.

Settlers near the Sioux reservations feared that another uprising was in the making. In 1890 they summoned the cavalry. At Wounded Knee, South Dakota, the soldiers arrested a group of several hundred Indians

At left is Tom Torlino, a Navajo youth, before he was sent to a school for Indians run by whites. At right, after attending the school for only a few months, all traces of his Navajo heritage seem to have vanished.

and disarmed the men among them. In a moment of confusion a shot was fired, and the cavalry turned their machine guns on the defenseless Sioux. By the time the guns had ceased firing, over 290 men, women, and children had been killed or wounded.

For many Indians, the shootings at Wounded Knee symbolized the sad fate of their people. Although some Native Americans made the transition to "the white man's way of life," many others continued to cling with determination to the Indian vision of what the West should be. Unable to return to life on the plains as they had known it and unable or unwilling to adapt to a new culture, they had neither hope nor opportunity.

SECTION REVIEW

1. Identify: Little Big Horn, Chief Joseph, Geronimo, Susette La Flesche, Helen Hunt Jackson, Dawes Act, Ghost Dance, Wounded Knee.
2. Define: reservation.
3. (a) Why did Plains Indians declare war after 1859? (b) What led to new fighting in 1874?
4. How were buffalo herds destroyed?
5. What was the Dawes Act?
6. **Critical Thinking** Based on their experiences, how would the whites and the Indians view one another?

4 The Cattle Frontier

As the mining frontier spread from the west coast eastward into the mountains, another wave of settlement, mainly from Texas, pushed northward onto the plains. The new settlers sought to take advantage of the prairie grass and public lands. Fortunes could be made there, not by panning gold, but by raising cattle.

The New Cattle Country

As you read in Chapter 14, the Mexicans and the Spanish before them had established cattle ranches in the Southwest. The countryside there had been so hospitable, in fact, that many cattle had thrived untended. A type of cattle known as the Texas longhorn roamed freely across the plains. By 1860 some 5 million longhorns grazed in Texas.

Despite the abundance of cattle, ranching developed slowly there. The Texas longhorn was a tough and ill-tempered creature, its wiry frame providing very little tender meat. In addition, few buyers existed. Texans could not sell outside of local areas since they had no way of transporting the beef to distant markets.

The railroads opened up those markets for Texas beef. As the population in the East grew, the demand for meat rose, and the railroads provided a quick way to ship it east. Cattle that could be purchased for $3 to $5 a head in Texas could be sold at the nearest railhead or shipping point for $30 to $50 each. A rancher who marketed a herd of 3,000 steers could make a profit of $100,000 in one year.

In 1866 the closest railheads lay over a thousand miles (1,600 kilometers) to the north, but that did not stop enterprising Texans. In the following years they drove their cattle north, looking for the best route across prairie country. Their successful search began the era of the "long drives" and the cattle boom. In 1867 the first herds reached the new depot of Abilene, Kansas. As the rails pushed west, new cattle centers sprang up at Ellsworth and Dodge City, Kansas. (See the map on page 386.)

The Long Drive

The men who drove the cattle along these trails soon earned a place in the folklore of the nation. The cowboys, as they were called, borrowed much of the Spanish vaquero's outfit; and the cowboy vocabulary incorporated many Spanish terms, including lariat, corral, hombre, and bronco. Vaquero even became translated as "buckeroo." Cattle drives attracted a large number of black and Mexican Americans. On the long drives, one out of every seven cowboys was black, and nearly one in five was Mexican.

Every year Texas ranchers drove their cattle to railheads hundreds of miles away. The detail of the painting at left shows cowhands driving a herd along the Chisholm Trail. Herds were often on the trail for two or three months. Many of the cowhands on the long drives were blacks or Mexican Americans. Yet in the folklore of the West, those cowhands were often ignored or forgotten.

Every spring, a rancher would select about 16 to 18 men to ride herd over some 3,000 cattle, about one cowboy for every 175 animals. A chuck wagon would follow with its cook and a wrangler who looked after the extra horses. For such demanding work, each cowboy had about eight mounts, so he would always have a fresh one. The horses had distinctive names such as Gold Dollar, Julius Caesar, Pop Corn, or Snakey.

The long drive often took two or three months to complete. Cattle walked in a long thin line along the trail, with the cowboys spread out in pairs over the line. Moving the men and animals at the required pace of 20 to 25 miles (32 to 40 kilometers) a day, the herd manager signaled his crew using arm motions borrowed from Plains Indian sign language. At night the herd would be gathered together along the side of the trial. Such work was hard indeed. Cowboys often sat in the saddle for 16 to 18 hours a day.

The Cattle Boom

The cattle business grew rapidly after 1867. Railheads became bustling centers where cattle were herded into yards and then shipped east, and where cowboys had a chance to let off steam after their grueling ride. In 1867, Abilene, Kansas, consisted of only a dozen log huts with dirt roofs. The town was so poor that the saloonkeeper tended a colony of prairie dogs that he sold to an occasional tourist. By 1870, when 300,000 cattle were shipped through Abilene, the town had become a bustling business center.

It was not long before cattle ranchers decided to expand their grazing range. As the buffalo vanished from the plains, ranchers began grazing cattle there. Routes like the Goodnight-Loving Trail opened up grazing areas in Colorado and Wyoming. (See the map on page 386.)

385

Ranchers let their cattle run wild across the prairie, identifying them with a distinctive mark, or brand. Twice a year the cattle were rounded up, and new calves were given the owner's brand mark with a hot iron.

By 1880 about 4.5 million cattle grazed on the plains from Kansas to Montana. The profits from ranching were so handsome that ranching became a field for speculation. Investors came from the East and as far away as Britain and other European nations. All of them viewed the cattle business as the latest bonanza, the newest way to get rich quick. But the bonanza was not to last.

From Boom to Bust

Several developments contributed to the end of the cattle bonanza. As the number of cattle multiplied, the plains were overgrazed

and the grasses died. Ranchers quarreled over land and water rights, often violently, and cattle rustlers, or thieves, proved to be a nagging problem.

Competition for grazing land led to other problems. Fencing had been limited on the plains as long as fencing materials—wood or stone—were scarce. When barbed wire was marketed in 1874, ranchers began stringing up fences to keep their cattle in. But ranchers were not the only people who found a use for barbed wire.

Conflict arose with other groups who wanted to use the land for their own purposes. Sheep ranchers brought their herds to the prairie, but sheep tended to crop the prairie grass so close to the ground that cattle could not eat it. Farmers also moved onto the plains and began fencing in land. Bitter range wars erupted over who had the

■ *Railroads, mining, and cattle grazing helped open the Great Plains for later settlement, as indicated on this map.*

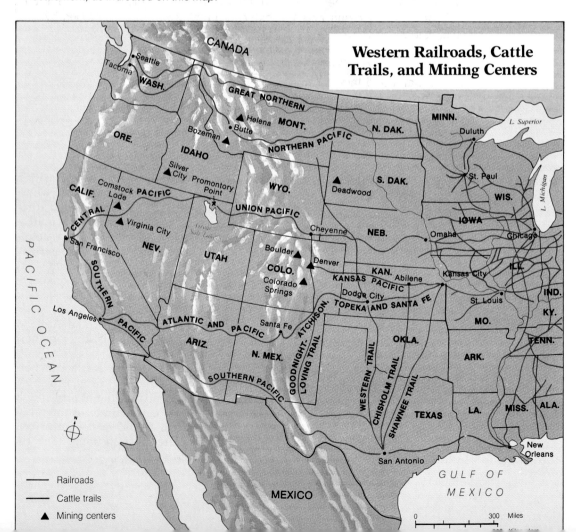

★ America's Heritage ★

Spanish Roots of the American Cowboy

No other figure has so completely captured the American imagination as the cowboy. Thousands of novels and films describe this legendary figure. The independence and courage of the cowboy have become part of the American character. Yet the roots of the American cowboy go back to the Spanish settlers of Mexico and the Southwest.

Between 1600 and 1845 the lands that became Texas, New Mexico, Arizona and southern California were settled by Spaniards and later by Mexicans, who raised cattle on the open range. These settlers developed a way of life suited to this land. This way of life helped form the character of the American cowboy.

Spanish words and customs were borrowed and adapted. The lands where livestock was raised, *ranchos* (RAN chohz) in Spanish, became American ranches. And the *vaqueros* (vah KEHR ohz), who tended the *vacas* (VAH cahz), or cows, became cowboys. The special saddle with a horn used by the vaquero became the "western" saddle of the cowboy. He draped his *riata* (ree AHT ah), or lariat, over the horn and tied the rope to it after throwing his *lazo* (lasso).

The American cowboy adopted the vaquero's clothing, which was well adapted for his work. He wore a wide-brimmed *sombrero* (sahm BREHR oh), in Spanish "a hat that provides shade," to protect his face from the hot sun. Special high-heeled, pointed-toe boots helped balance the cowboy when he used his lariat to lasso a calf during the roundup. The boots also kept his feet from slipping too far into the stirrups. The cowboy used the vaquero's leather *chaparrerjos* (CHAP ah RAY hohs), or chaps, to protect his legs from thorny chaparral bushes.

The vaqueros tested their skill in horsemanship, cattle roping, and branding at annual roundups, when the cattle were brought together from the open range for branding. The western rodeo of today has its roots in those roundup contests.

Vaqueros often sang and played the guitar in the evenings on the open trail. They sang for their own entertainment and to calm the cattle, who might be made nervous by the sounds of wild animals. Their songs were running accounts of the adventures of the vaquero. English-speaking cowboys adopted this custom and created their own ballads, many of which are still popular today.

right to use the land or control valuable water holes.

The weather delivered the biggest blow to the ranchers, however. The severe winter of 1885–1886 killed off large numbers of cattle. The following summer was extremely dry, and cattle suffered poor grazing. The winter of 1886–1887 whipped the plains with blizzards and subzero temperatures even more severe than the previous year. By the time warmth returned to the land 80 to 90 percent of all cattle lay dead.

Many ranchers and speculators were ruined. Those who survived the disaster discovered that the cattle business had changed. Many ranches went from individual ownership to management by large corporations such as the Union Cattle Company of Wyoming. Furthermore, with the spread of barbed wire, ranchers no longer let their animals roam free. Instead they purchased and fenced land, drilled wells to guard against dry weather, and provided hay for cattle during difficult winter months.

The cattle frontier had gone the way of the other boom economies. The days when individuals could make huge fortunes on the Great Plains had passed. Ranching remained an important part of the West, but it became more of a business and less of an adventure.

SECTION REVIEW

1. Identify: Texas longhorn, long drives.
2. (a) How did railroads contribute to the growth of cattle ranching? (b) How did ranchers move cattle to the railhead?
3. List two ways competition for grazing land contributed to an end of the cattle bonanza.
4. **Critical Thinking** How has the cattle frontier been depicted in folklore?

387

5 The Sodbusters' Frontier

While miners and ranchers were staking their claims to the West, another group was not far behind: the farmers. The farming frontier expanded rapidly, especially after 1870. Rising prices on the world grain market lured farmers into the Dakotas, western Nebraska, Kansas, and western Texas. The first to arrive usually settled in the more fertile river valleys, but eventually other farmers tried their luck on the rolling plains.

Encouraging Settlement

In 1862 Congress passed the Homestead Act to encourage farmers to settle the West. The act provided that any citizen (or immigrant who intended to become a citizen) could purchase 160 acres (64 hectares) of public land for a small registration fee. By 1900, 600,000 farmers had claimed homesteads.

Despite government incentives, only about 20 percent of the homestead land was purchased directly by small farmers. Most was bought up by speculators who evaded the provisions of the Homestead Act. They purchased large parcels of land, then divided and resold the land to individual farmers at higher prices.

The Homestead Act was impractical in many areas. As John Wesley Powell had foreseen, a 160-acre (64-hectare) farm might be fine in the East, where rain was plentiful. However, in the West the costs and risks of farming were greater, and much larger tracts of land were needed to make a profit. Nonetheless, farmers came West. Many were encouraged by the Homestead Act. Others came in response to appeals from railroads.

As you read earlier, the government had given railroads large sections of land along their western routes. This land could not be bought under the Homestead Act, but the company executives knew that the success of their lines depended on attracting settlers. With more towns and farms in the West, passenger travel and freight shipping would increase. Consequently, the railroads advertised throughout the East, sold their land, and then provided transportation west.

The railroads advertised in Europe also. From the Scandinavian countries especially, thousands of families emigrated to areas of Minnesota and the Dakotas. Many German and Irish immigrants joined American settlers in Nebraska and the Dakotas.

When railroads worked together with the settlers to develop an area, both the region and the railroad prospered. One of the most successful and responsible attempts was led by James J. Hill, president of the Great Northern Railway. Towns and farms grew up quickly along his Dakota rail line.

Adapting to the Plains

Life on the dry, nearly treeless plains differed greatly from what the settlers had left behind in the East. They had to learn new skills to meet the challenges of their new land.

With little wood available, families relied on other materials to build houses. At first they used the land itself, tough sod held together by the tight weave of prairie-grass roots. Settlers cut bricks of sod, then arranged them into walls three feet (one meter) thick. The roof began with tarpaper, if available, then a layer of sod. Eventually sunflowers and grass might grow from the roof of the hut.

New techniques and inventions made farming the plains easier and more profitable. Among them were deep wells, dry farming, and improved machinery. Drilling deep wells allowed farmers to reach water several hundred feet into the ground. Windmills powered the pumps by harnessing the steady winds of the plains. Most wells supplied enough water to irrigate an acre near the house where the family could raise its own vegetables.

Dry farming enabled farmers to grow cash crops like wheat. Newly developed steel-tipped plows could cut through dense root networks that would have broken iron or wooden plows. With these plows, farmers were able to reach moisture lying deeper in the ground, which then rose gradually to the roots of the crops. The soil had to be broken up often to prevent the moisture from evaporating too quickly, especially after rains.

To make the large western farms profitable, farmers depended on machinery. Threshing machines were constantly being

To build a shelter on the often treeless Great Plains, early settlers carved out chunks of the earth itself. Tough prairie grass growing year after year undisturbed had created a thickly matted crust called sod. Squares of sod were cut, then used like bricks to make sod houses, or "soddies." The Kansas homesteaders in this photo have lined up the family and their prized possessions for a traveling photographer.

improved, and mechanical binders quickly tied wheat into bundles. Using improved machinery, a wheat farmer could harvest in three hours what originally took 61 hours to do. The time spent harvesting corn, oats, and hay also dropped dramatically.

Farm Life on the Plains

New farming techniques and labor-saving inventions made it possible for western farmers to survive, but life for most settlers still posed severe trials. Each season of the year held its special threat to the farmer.

Spring brought welcome warmth, but along with melting snow might come floods that washed away houses and livestock. In the summer temperatures soared over 100° Fahrenheit (39° Celsius) for weeks while hot winds blasted the plains. Moderate temperatures in the summer might mean grasshopper plagues. The grasshoppers ate everything: crops, food, clothing and even tree bark. The summer heat broke in autumn but by then the grasses were so dry that one spark could send thousands of acres into flames.

But the pioneers dreaded winter most. Cruel winds swept ice, dust, and snow across the plains. Settlers could awake to find their food frozen and snow on the furniture. Animals suffered even more.

Few of those who came to the plains could withstand the strains of farm life for long. Some moved on westward; others retreated back east. "From Kansas, where it rains grasshoppers, fire, and destruction," read the sign on one returning wagon.

Of course, life was not always so harsh, and many prairie farmers prospered. Still, farm families were isolated, living far from friends and neighbors. Under such conditions, all settlers pitched in to make life bear-

Major Events	
1851	Fort Laramie agreement
1860	Pony Express established
1862	Homestead Act passed
1863	Construction of transcontinental railroad begins
1867–68	Plains nations ordered onto reservations
1869	Wyoming grants women voting rights; first transcontinental railroad completed
1874	Barbed wire marketed
1876	Battle of Little Big Horn
1881	*A Century of Dishonor* published
1887	Dawes Act passed
1889	Oklahoma land rush

389

able. Women worked alongside men. Some, like Elinore Stewart from Wyoming, homesteaded their own farms. Women's contribution to life in the West was evidenced by the fact that 11 western states and territories, led by Wyoming in 1869 and Utah in 1870, granted women the vote before any states east of the Mississippi.

Almost from the start, churches and schools played an important part in western settlement. Church members joined together to recreate the patterns of community life left behind in the East or in Europe. Before the schools were built, most rural families relied on the churches and Bible reading to educate their children.

Soon, however, communities erected schools. These were usually one-room buildings with rows of hard benches where a teacher taught six to eight grades under one roof. Both the church and the school were centers of community life where farm families could gather and find relief from the isolation and hard work of life on the plains.

The Closing Frontier

As farmers spread across the plains, fewer areas remained to be settled. The last major land rush took place in central Oklahoma in 1889. This land had belonged to Cherokees, Creeks, Seminoles, and other southeastern nations since the 1830s, when Andrew Jackson's removal policy forced them from their eastern homes. In 1885 the United States, pressured by settlers, bought the land back.

The government made homesteads free to citizens, but these could be claimed only after noon on April 22, 1889. About 100,000 "boomers" lined up on the border in wagons, buggies, horses, and trains, waiting to rush in and stake claims. When the cavalry fired the official opening volley, all went charging in, only to find that others had gotten there sooner, having evaded the army border patrols. Between the "boomers" and "sooners," the entire district was parceled out in the space of a few hours.

The following year, the superintendent of the 1890 census announced that, for the first time in the history of the United States, settlements had spread so far that "there can hardly be said to be a frontier line."

One by one, the western territories became states: Nebraska in 1867; Colorado in 1876; North Dakota, South Dakota, Montana, and Washington in 1889; Idaho and Wyoming in 1890; Utah in 1896; Oklahoma in 1907; and New Mexico and Arizona in 1912.

SECTION REVIEW

1. (a) What was the purpose of the Homestead Act? (b) What were the provisions?
2. List three techniques that made farming on the plains easier and more profitable.
3. How did schools and churches contribute to community life on the plains?
4. **Critical Thinking** How might the existence of a frontier affect society?

 # Chapter 20 Review

In Perspective

Indian nations had lived on the Great Plains for thousands of years. Few of the early European settlers to arrive in North America tried to make a permanent home on the open plains. After the Civil War, however, interest in the interior of the country grew. Discoveries of gold and silver deposits attracted miners eastward from California.

The growth of railroads further opened up the West. Cattle ranching became profitable because cattle could be shipped east by rail. New techniques and inventions enabled farmers and ranchers to adapt their methods to the harsh environment of the plains.

Most of the Plains Indians believed in a close relationship with nature. They hunted buffalo and other game without disrupting their environment. The influx of miners, cattle ranchers, and farmers destroyed the buffalo herds and led to conflict with the Indians. The United States government tried to confine Indian nations to reservations. When the Indians resisted, many years of warfare followed. Overwhelmed by the size and weaponry of the army, the Indians suffered defeat.

Vocabulary

Match each term at left with its definition or description at right.

1. vigilante
2. reservation
3. public domain
4. sodbuster
5. long drive

a. cattle trail
b. prairie farmer
c. land set aside for the Indians
d. land held by the nation
e. self-appointed law enforcers

Chapter Checkup

1. (a) What are the Great Plains? (b) How did the introduction of horses in the 1700s affect the Plains Indians? (c) What role did the buffalo play in their lives?

2. (a) Where was the new mining frontier of the 1850s and 1860s? (b) How did this frontier contribute to the growth of western towns and cities?

3. (a) What efforts were made to improve the reservations? (b) Were the efforts successful? Explain.

4. Describe how each of the following contributed to the end of the cattle bonanza: (a) increased numbers of cattle; (b) barbed wire; (c) sheep ranches; (d) farmers; (e) climate.

Critical Thinking

1. **Analyzing** How did the disappearance of the buffalo symbolize the end of a way of life for the Plains Indians?

2. **Comparing** How were the mining bonanzas and cattle bonanzas similar?

Developing Basic Skills

1. **Map Reading** Study the map on page 386. (a) What cities developed along railroad lines? (b) What cattle centers developed along railroad lines? (c) What major cattle trails led to these centers? (d) How did the railroads contribute to the growth and prosperity of the West?

2. **Map Reading** Study the map on page 382. Then answer the following questions: (a) What lands did the Indians cede to the federal government between 1850 and 1870? (b) What lands did they cede to the government from 1870 and 1890? (c) What happened to Native Americans between 1860 and 1890?

See page 830 for suggested readings.

Writer's Handbook

Using an Index for Current Newspapers

The *New York Times Index* for current newspapers is more complex than the index for older newspapers you learned about on page 367. To become acquainted with how to use a current index, study the labeled sample below.

Practice: Answer the following questions based on the information in the labeled sample.

1. What is the date, section, page, and column of the article about the meeting of American Indian tribal leaders?

2. What is the length of the article?

3. How is the information in this article related to the subject matter in Chapter 20?

21

An Age of Industry

(1865–1914)

Fireworks at the opening of the Brooklyn Bridge in New York City

Between 1865 and 1914 the United States was transformed from a largely rural nation to one of the leading industrial powers in the world. The Brooklyn Bridge, completed in 1883, symbolized the change. Its 16-inch steel cables supported a bridge 1,595 feet long, making it the longest suspension bridge in the world at that time.

Steel was one of the foundations of industrial growth. Such growth was fueled by other inventions and by innovations in business organization.

The impact of industry on the nation was uneven. Manufacturing was most common in the Northeast and Midwest, but industry also began to flourish in the South. While economic growth meant vast fortunes for some business leaders, factory workers faced long hours, hazardous conditions, and low pay. Consequently, workers began to organize to improve their lot.

Growth of union movement

1865	1875	1885	1895	1905	1915

1869 Knights of Labor founded

1872 Westinghouse invents air brake

1876 Bell invents telephone

1881 AFL founded

1886 Haymarket riot

1892 Homestead strike

1904 AFL grows to 1 million members

1 The Ties That Bind

As you read in Chapter 20, the transcontinental railroads and the telegraph helped open the West for settlement after the Civil War. Advances in transportation and communication also helped stimulate the nation's industrial growth.

Communication by Wire

In 1844, when Samuel Morse succeeded in sending coded messages over an electrical wire, he revolutionized communication. By 1860 telegraph wires connected the West with the East. The merger in 1866 of the Western Union Telegraph Company, which handled communications in the West, with the American Telegraph Company, which dominated eastern communications, created a nationwide telegraph network.

The telegraph greatly speeded the pace of business. For example, store owners and manufacturers could order supplies by telegraph almost instantaneously. But the telegraph did more than speed the delivery of messages. It provided a new source of employment for women, who were hired as telegraphers. It also helped make rail transportation safer and more efficient. The telegraph allowed stationmasters to coordinate the movement of trains. (The railroads had permitted Western Union to string wires parallel to their tracks in exchange for free telegraph service.)

More changes in communication were to come. In 1858 financier Cyrus Field and other investors spent $1.5 million to lay an underwater telegraph cable across the Atlantic. Although the cable broke shortly after the first few messages had been transmitted, Field did not give up. In 1866 he laid a new and improved cable, which provided almost instant communication across the Atlantic.

In 1876 Alexander Graham Bell, a Scotsman who taught speech to the deaf in Boston, transmitted the human voice over wires with his new "speaking telegraph." A year later, the first intercity phone conversation took place between Boston and New York, and that same year Bell organized the Bell Telephone Company.

Soon Bell Telephone was laying cable from business to business and from city to city. After 1885 American Telephone and Telegraph, which had been organized by the directors of Bell Telephone, combined 100 local telephone companies and provided business and government with long-distance service. By the mid-1880s over 300,000 of Bell's "electrical toys" were in use in the United States. Most of them were business phones, however. Not until rates were reduced in 1900 did many private households acquire telephones.

Transportation by Rail

Although advances in communication were important, they took a back seat to the achievements of railroad builders. Transportation was the key to industrialization. To succeed as an industrial nation, the United States needed to be able to quickly move freight and passengers to all parts of the country. In 1860, despite impressive progress since 1850, that could not be done.

The American rail system in 1860 consisted of about 30,000 miles (48,000 kilometers) of track. But much of it was in the East, and no railroad bridge yet crossed the Mississippi, Ohio, or Hudson rivers. Furthermore, a large number of small companies controlled various sections of track, which were often not interconnected. Richmond, Virginia, for example, was the last stop for six separate rail lines.

Even if local rail lines had been connected, one company's cars often would not have been able to travel on another company's track. No standard gauge, the distance between the rails, had been agreed upon, so the trains of one company did not fit on the track of another. Consequently, shippers who wished to send freight over a long distance had to have their freight loaded and unloaded all along the way. Each link in the journey required new freight charges, additional paperwork, and delay.

Consolidation of Railroads

After the Civil War, railroad builders took vigorous action to create a more efficient and economical system of rail transportation by *consolidating, or combining, small lines.* Owners of large lines often purchased smaller lines or tried to drive them out of business.

The development of the New York Central illustrates one method of consolidation. In 1866 the New York Central connected Albany and Buffalo. Other railroad lines ran east from Albany to Boston and New York City and west from Buffalo to Chicago. Commodore Cornelius Vanderbilt hoped to unite these lines into one company. He had already made a fortune with a steamship line on the Hudson River, hence his nautical title.

Vanderbilt quickly bought up most of the railroad lines linking New York and Chicago, but the strategically located New York Central held out. In the winter of 1867, to end the stalemate, Vanderbilt suddenly refused to let passengers and freight transfer from the New York Central line to his lines. With freight and passengers stranded, the New York Central vainly appealed to the New York State legislature for protection against Vanderbilt.

The New York Central finally surrendered, and Vanderbilt promptly went to work acquiring the feeder lines that joined his New York-to-Chicago trunk line. At the time of his death in 1877, he controlled 4,500 miles (7,200 kilometers) of integrated railroad connecting New York City and the Great Lakes region.

Progress Along the Rails

Consolidating small railroad lines often led to more efficient rail service despite the rough competition between railroad builders. The rail system also improved in other ways. By 1886 the railroads had adopted a standard gauge. Since trains were able to run longer distances without stopping, passengers and freight were moved more quickly.

Rates also decreased. By the end of the century, passenger fares had been cut in half, and freight rates dropped even more. Furthermore, rail companies had worked out arrangements allowing the freight cars of one line to use the tracks of another. Goods loaded on a car in Chicago, for example, stayed on the same car all the way to New York, and shippers paid only one fare for the whole distance.

Many railroads replaced iron rails with steel rails that could support the weight of new, more powerful locomotives. New signals along the track improved safety. Many major lines began to install a second set of tracks, so that traffic could move in both directions at the same time.

By 1883 efficient shipping had become so important to the nation's economic life that the American Railway Association divided the country into the four time zones that exist today: Eastern, Central, Mountain, and Pacific. Before the zones were created, each town kept its own time, which often varied by several minutes from the time kept in a neighboring town. These variations had made it difficult for the railroads to establish uniform schedules. The creation of the zone system simplified scheduling and improved efficiency.

Railroad tycoon Cornelius Vanderbilt is pictured in this cartoon as a modern colossus towering over his domain. But as the cartoon indicates, Vanderbilt was only one of several men who held the reins of the rapidly expanding rail network.

The new railroads advertised heavily to attract riders. The Erie Railway, for instance, stressed the fabulous scenery at Niagara Falls.

Persistent Problems

Progress brought growing pains. Most of the railroads were heavily in debt. Constructing railroads required large amounts of money. To raise money, owners of railroad lines issued *bonds*, certificates that earn interest and are redeemed on a given date, and sold *stock certificates,* shares of ownership in a company.

Some of the stock certificates sold, however, were not actually backed by the companys' *assets*, that is, their property and cash. Such certificates were known as *watered stock* because selling them was similar to a trick used by some ranchers of having their cattle drink large amounts of water before being weighed for sale. Furthermore, railroad owners often did not have the money to pay the interest on bonds or to redeem them.

The burden of a large debt was complicated by cutthroat competition. Despite efforts to consolidate lines, in some areas many lines continued to compete for the same customers. A manufacturer wanting to ship freight from Atlanta to St. Louis, for example, could choose from 20 different carriers.

Rival railroad lines thus engaged in rate wars, even if they were forced to operate at a loss. Since owners had already paid for their tracks, engines, and freight cars, running at a loss seemed to be better than not running at all. The situation became so competitive that companies resorted to some illegal practices to solve their problems.

To attract a large volume of business, railroads secretly offered rebates to their largest customers. The *rebate* was a discount on the normal shipping charge. Because such reductions were not offered to all shippers, rebating was illegal. Small shippers complained, but the practice continued.

Where several railroads competed for business, *pooling* was sometimes practiced. Under a pooling arrangement, railroad managers from competing companies would agree that each line would carry a certain portion of the total volume of freight, thus assuring that they all could stay in business. They would also pledge not to cut prices in order to undersell their rivals.

Pooling, rebates, and other questionable practices, such as charging less per mile for a long haul than for a short haul, led state and federal governments to regulate railroads, as you will read in Chapter 22. In spite of the abuses, however, a nationwide rail system developed and became an essential part of the national economy. Improved communications and transportation strengthened the ties that bound the nation together.

SECTION REVIEW

1. Identify: Samuel Morse, Alexander Graham Bell, Cornelius Vanderbilt.
2. Define: consolidate, bonds, stock certificates, assets, watered stock, rebates, pooling.
3. What impact did the telegraph have on business in the United States?
4. List two ways rail transportation in 1860 was inadequate.
5. List four ways railroads improved after the Civil War.
6. (a) How did railroad companies raise money? (b) What methods did they use to attract more business?
7. **Critical Thinking** Why did the spread of railroads lead to the creation of a system of time zones?

2 Innovations and Inventions

One reason for the tremendous growth of the American economy between 1865 and 1914 was the remarkable ability of industry to innovate. Some inventions, such as Bell's telephone, gave birth to whole new industries and radically changed American life. Others, like manufacturer Levi Strauss's use of rivets to strengthen the stress points of blue jeans, seemed small but proved to be of lasting importance. In the 1880s and 1890s Americans patented over 21,000 inventions a year—more than ten times the yearly average number during the 1850s. "America has become known the world around as the home of invention," observed the commissioner of the patent office.

Steel: A Foundation for Industry

No invention contributed more to the spread of industry in America than the discovery of how large quantities of steel could be made cheaply and easily. Steel is a form of purified iron. Long valued because it was stronger than iron, steel was difficult to make. Before the 1860s steel was made by heating iron to high temperatures that could be created only in small furnaces. The process was slow, required a large amount of coal to heat the furnace, and produced only a small amount of steel.

In 1859, however, Henry Bessemer, in England, and William Kelly, in the United States, independently discovered a better way to make steel. The *Bessemer process*, as it came to be known, began by heating iron in a large furnace. Blasts of cold air were then blown through the heated iron, causing the impurities to burn.

The "air boiling" technique invented by Bessemer and Kelly produced strong and durable steel. The Bessemer process reduced the amount of coal needed to produce one ton of steel from seven tons to one ton. It also speeded the manufacture of steel.

The process revolutionized industry. Before 1867, when the first Bessemer steel was produced, United States manufacturers were turning out fewer than 2,000 tons (1,820 metric tons) of steel a year. By the end of the nineteenth century, 7 million tons (6.4 million metric tons) were produced annually.

Much of the earliest Bessemer steel was rolled into train tracks, which lasted ten times longer than the old iron rails. But other industries soon began to discover uses for the cheap steel. New "skyscrapers," soaring 20 stories and more into the air, required steel girders to support their great weight. In 1879 plans for the Brooklyn Bridge called for the use of steel beams. Steel nails, screws, needles, pins, bolts, barrel hoops, and barbed wire were only a few of the everyday uses of steel.

Inventions Create New Industries

While the Bessemer process was reshaping many existing industries, other inventions made entirely new businesses possible. Alert business leaders rushed to take advantage of new technology.

The invention of the Bessemer process for refining iron into steel revolutionized industry. The use of Bessemer converters, shown above in a Pennsylvania plant, permitted the development of a large-scale steel industry. Because steel was stronger and more durable than iron, it spurred many other technical advances, such as the construction of steel bridges and steel-frame buildings.

For example, Gustavus Swift and Philip Armour introduced refrigeration to the meatpacking* industry in the late 1800s. They established firms in Chicago, midway between the cattle raised on the Great Plains and the cities of the East. Cattle were shipped from the West to the Chicago meatpacking plants, where they were slaughtered and cut into sides of beef. Refrigeration allowed Swift and Armour to store the beef in warehouses and to ship it East on railroad cars even in warm weather. This procedure, in effect by the 1880s, provided an efficient and inexpensive way to ship fresh meat.

The use of refrigeration in rail cars and meatpacking plants changed the national economy and the eating habits of many Americans. It made possible the marketing of the most perishable products and increased the availability of important sources of food. "Through the wages I disburse and the provisions I supply," boasted Armour, "I give more people food than any man living." The new packing facilities also provided thousands of jobs. Large, centralized facilities took the place of small, local meat packers who could not compete.

Some new industries were created around inventions designed to improve rail travel. In 1864 George Pullman designed a sleeping car that eventually saw widespread

■ Americans—both native-born and immigrant—used what they called Yankee ingenuity to devise better ways of making things. This chart shows the number of inventions filed with the United States Patent Office in the decades before 1900.

United States Patents Issued 1861–1900

Five-Year Periods	Number of Patents
1861–1865	20,725
1866–1870	58,734
1871–1875	60,976
1876–1880	64,462
1881–1885	97,156
1886–1890	110,358
1891–1895	108,420
1896–1900	112,188

Source: *Historical Statistics of the United States*

*The term "meatpacking" was used in the days before refrigeration when beef was salted and packed in wooden barrels. Today meatpacking refers to the processing and distribution of fresh and frozen meat.

use. In 1868 George Westinghouse created a successful business by marketing his new air brake. The brake enabled locomotive engineers to stop all cars on a train simultaneously, eliminating the need for individual brakemen on each car. The results were increased passenger safety and comfort, as well as longer and faster trains.

Other inventions helped business prosper. Christopher Sholes, a printer, developed a typewriter that was first sold by the Remington Arms Company in 1875. The machine greatly improved business communication. In 1852 Elishu Otis developed the first passenger elevator. Frank Sprague, an engineer trained at the United States Naval Academy, helped to perfect the modern elevator, making movement from story to story in skyscrapers possible.

Thomas Edison's electrical inventions, especially the incandescent light bulb, opened the way for new industries. In 1882 the generators of the Edison Illuminating Company supplied enough power to light the New York Stock Exchange and several other large buildings in Manhattan. Both Edison's and George Westinghouse's companies worked to expand the electrical power industry. By 1900 local power companies were bringing electricity to many urban areas, and electric cars and trolleys had been introduced. Electrical machinery was beginning to replace steam-powered engines in many heavy industries.

A New Philosophy for Business

The innovations and inventions that sparked industrial growth allowed many business leaders to earn huge fortunes. By 1900 there were over 4,000 millionaires in the United States, compared with only a few before the Civil War.

The rich were not shy about displaying their wealth. Many of the new millionaires built large mansions and competed with each other to see who could sail the longest yachts, ride in the fanciest private railroad

★ American Profiles ★

Thomas Alva Edison: The Wizard of Menlo Park

Few people have contributed more to the growth of United States industry or the comfort of the American people than Thomas Alva Edison. Born in Ohio in 1847 and basically self-taught, Edison was one of the leading figures in the technological development of the United States during the late 1800s. At the time of his death, the former newsboy and telegraph operator held over 1,300 United States and foreign patents.

Edison's first inventions were connected with the telegraph industry. He devised a transmitter and receiver for the automatic telegraph, a system for transmitting four messages at the same time, and an improved stock ticker system.

Among his hundreds of other major inventions were the phonograph, the incandescent lamp, and electrical power machinery to bring electricity to homes and factories, an experimental electrical railroad, the storage battery, synchronization of motion pictures and sound, the mimeograph machine, an ore separator, and an electric safety lantern.

Edison built and staffed a research laboratory in Menlo Park, New Jersey. This research laboratory was devoted entirely to inventive work. It is considered by many to be his most important contribution to technology. Edison called his all-purpose research laboratory an "invention factory," and inventions poured from it in an unending stream. He made a business out of invention itself, hiring a staff of workers including distinguished physicists, engineers, clockmakers, and machinists. He boasted that he could turn out a minor invention every ten days.

In the 1890s large companies began to follow Edison's lead and established their own research laboratories. Among the first and most important were the laboratories of Bell Telephone, Eastman Kodak, and General Electric. No longer did lone inventors pursue experiments at a workbench in some factory or barn. Modern research requires abundant good instruments, a group of expert helpers, and rigorous experimentation. Since the creation of Edison's "invention factory," United States corporations have generated a flood of technological developments that have transformed society.

cars, or purchase the fastest racehorses. Reports of spectacular parties became a regular feature of newspaper social pages. At one such affair the lobby of a hotel was turned into a small lake complete with gondolas. The emergence of a wealthy class of industrialists was accompanied by the development of theories to explain the success of those industrialists.

Andrew Carnegie, a millionaire steel mill owner (see page 401), vigorously defended the accumulation of wealth. The wealthy, Carnegie insisted in a magazine article written in 1889, had a right to make money and a responsibility to spend it properly. Carnegie argued that the millionaire should be a "trustee for his poorer brethren, bringing to their service his superior wisdom, experience, and ability to administer, doing for them better than they would or could do for themselves." This Gospel of Wealth, as Carnegie called it, commanded the wealthy to donate their money to worthy causes.

Some philosophers applied the theories of English biologist Charles Darwin to defend the accumulation of wealth. Darwin believed that there was a constant struggle in nature in which only the fittest members of a species survive. Thinkers who applied Darwin's concept of survival of the fittest to society became known as social Darwinists. Most influential among the social Darwinists was William G. Sumner, a professor of political and social science at Yale University.

Sumner and the other social Darwinists argued that the struggle for survival occurred in the business world and should not be checked by government regulation. Firms led by the "fittest" would drive their weak competitors out of business. As a result, the social Darwinists argued, society would find itself led by the strongest, wisest, and most able citizens.

Related to social Darwinist thought were the ideas of *laissez-faire economics*, a school of thought that rejected government involvement in the economy. Herbert Spencer, a social scientist from England whose ideas were well known in the United States, maintained that the economy worked best when it was free of government regulation. Government regulation, the supporters of laissez-faire argued, would upset the balance between supply and demand and plunge the economy into chaos.

The probusiness philosophy was accepted by rich and poor alike. Millions of people read the dime novels of Horatio Alger, which told over and over again the rags-to-riches stories of young men who worked hard in factories and then by "pluck and luck" got the breaks that brought them fame and fortune.

Thus the ideas of the late nineteenth and early twentieth centuries reflected the spirit of the age. Bessemer-produced steel, electric devices, and other inventions changed the patterns of day-to-day life. Americans found in the ideas of Carnegie, Sumner, Spencer, Alger, and others, a philosophy that justified the change.

SECTION REVIEW

1. Identify: Gustavus Swift, George Pullman, George Westinghouse, Thomas Edison, Gospel of Wealth, social Darwinism.

2. Define: Bessemer process, laissez-faire economics.

3. How did the Bessemer process affect the production of steel?

4. What impact did the use of refrigeration have on the meatpacking industry?

5. List four inventions that helped create new industries in the 1800s.

6. **Critical Thinking** What is the assumption about the poor underlying Carnegie's Gospel of Wealth?

3 New Ways of Doing Business

The size and production of industrial firms greatly increased in the years following the Civil War. For example, Pittsburgh steel mills that produced a maximum of 600 tons (546 metric tons) of steel per week in 1870 produced twice as much ten years later. United States industry produced $1.8 billion worth of goods in 1860 and almost $10 billion worth by 1890. Such growth required a new approach to business. Business leaders sought better organization and looked for ways to raise money and reduce competition.

The Rise of the Corporation

Before the Civil War, most businesses were owned and run by individual proprietors or by partners. Proprietorships and partnerships are well suited to small-scale operations in which a few employees produce simple goods or services. After the Civil War, as industries grew larger, such forms of business proved inadequate, and they were discarded in favor of the corporation.*

Several factors made the corporate form preferable to the proprietorship or partnership. One is the matter of responsibility for losses. Proprietors and partners are generally responsible for the debts of their business. Failure of the business could result in financial ruin for each investor.

Corporate organization eliminates this problem. A person who invests, or buys stock, in a corporation is responsible only for the amount he or she actually invests. The liability of the investor in the event of corporate failure is thus limited.

Other advantages of the corporation are its special legal status and its permanence. A corporation is recognized by a state government, which issues a charter defining the corporation's rights and activities. Unlike proprietorships and partnerships, the corporation is, for legal purposes, a "person" in its own right. A corporation may buy and sell property or sign contracts without directly involving its owners, the stockholders.

The survival of a corporation, unlike that of a proprietorship or partnership, does not hinge on the life of the owners. A corporation granted a charter by the state could "live" forever.

Because of such factors, corporations have less difficulty attracting investors and raising *capital*, or money used in a business, than do proprietorships and partnerships. Thus, after the Civil War, the executives of more and more companies decided to incorporate. The corporate form became common among manufacturers of iron, steel, brass, aluminum, textiles, and chemicals.

New Sources of Capital

With railroad construction booming, new industries springing up, and established manufacturers enlarging their operations, business needed new sources of capital to finance and maintain a rapid rate of growth. Commercial and savings banks, which had been in existence before the Civil War, expanded to meet the demand. Between 1860 and 1900 the number of commercial banks in the United States rose from 1,500 to 12,000. Deposits in savings banks soared from about $149 million to $2.5 billion.

The money that people deposited was used to finance the construction of railroads and other businesses. In addition, banks spurred the growth of business by extending credit even when they did not have deposits on hand to cover all their loans. Life insurance companies provided another source of capital. By investing millions of dollars in railroad construction and by supplying mortgages to farmers, textile manufacturers, and other businesses, life insurance companies contributed extensively to economic expansion.

Gradually corporations raised additional capital by selling more and more shares of stock to the public. Although a corporation might be worth millions of dollars, the price of each of its shares of stock might be relatively low. Thus the average person could afford to invest in stocks. The widespread ownership of corporate stock increased the amount of investment capital available to business.

Seeking Better Organization

As corporations grew larger, the need for better internal organization became clear. Before the Civil War, large factories employing hundreds of workers had only a few executives to manage the bookkeeping and direct operations.

Gradually, however, corporations began to set up separate departments to handle each major activity: purchasing raw materials, manufacturing, marketing the finished product, and coordinating finances. An executive was put in charge of each department. The size and complexity of the corporate administration grew almost as quickly as the business itself.

As corporations expanded, they continued to search for ways to survive and prosper in the booming, competitive economy. Andrew Carnegie and John D. Rockefeller were two men who successfully pioneered new forms of business organization that helped make economic expansion possible.

*You read about early corporations in Chapter 12. See page 209.

The Incorruptible Cashier

Until the 1870s merchants had no way to figure their exact income or profit. Rather than keeping a detailed record of sales and receipts, clerks made change from their own pockets or from an open cash box. The owner might ask clerks to enter cash transactions in an account book, but carelessness, illiteracy, and dishonesty often stood in the way of accurately recorded income.

James Ritty ran a cafe in Dayton, Ohio, during the 1870s. He was surprised that although business was brisk, he did not seem to be making a profit. Ritty suspected that it was because his employees were helping themselves to the open cash box. His health was ruined by worries over his apparent losses in business. So Ritty took a trip to Europe to recover. One day while visiting the ship's engine room, he noticed a machine that automatically recorded each revolution of the propeller shaft. He wondered whether a similar machine might record each sale in his cafe, and he rushed home to find out.

Ritty devised a simple cash register based on the principles he had discovered in the engine room and patented it in 1879. The first model machine was soon improved so that the amount could be displayed to both the clerk and the customer. Ritty believed that publicly showing the amount the clerk should put in the cash box would reduce the temptation to steal. He was so pleased to have found a machine that would keep clerks honest that he called his invention the "incorruptible cashier."

Later developments included a mechanism that recorded each day's transactions on a paper roll so that the owner could check on the amount of money in the cash box and also check the number of transactions. Later still, a cash drawer and a bell that rang every time the drawer was opened were added. Now the clerk had to record the sale in order to have access to the cash drawer. At the same time all the transactions were added and recorded for the owner. The bell announced that a brisk business was being done. In this way James Ritty's incorruptible cashier, devised to keep his clerks honest, helped develop modern merchandising methods.

Andrew Carnegie and the Vertical Integration of Steel

The career of Andrew Carnegie closely resembled Horatio Alger rags-to-riches stories. Born in Scotland in 1835, Carnegie came to America at age 13. He began working in a textile mill for $1.20 a week. Then he took a job as a telegram messenger. Carnegie worked long hours and studied Morse code at night. Soon Carnegie became a skilled telegrapher.

Luck favored Carnegie when Thomas Scott, superintendent of the Pennsylvania Railroad, hired the young man as his assistant. Scott introduced Carnegie to other industrial leaders and helped him invest the savings from his salary. Although Carnegie's annual salary was only $2,400, shrewd investments quickly made him a millionaire.

While traveling in England, Carnegie saw the revolutionary Bessemer process for making steel and realized its potential. Although the United States was in the midst of an economic depression in 1873, Carnegie began building the largest steel plant in the country, at Homestead, Pennsylvania, near Pittsburgh. Using the Bessemer process, Carnegie was able to produce steel rails inexpensively and sell them for half the price charged by his competitors.

But Carnegie was not satisfied with this initial success. In 1880 the steel and iron business was highly competitive, with over a thousand separate producers. Carnegie realized that his steel plant was vulnerable to people and forces he could not control. Carnegie's business depended on mining companies to remove iron ore from the ground. Ships and rail lines were needed to move the ore to a plant to be converted to pig iron. Other railroads then transported the pig iron to the Homestead plant for the production of steel.

To insure a steady supply of raw material and a dependable transportation network, Carnegie bought mining companies, rail lines, ore ships, and pig iron plants until

401

he had a hand in each of the industries critical to steel making. The control of all the steps required to turn a raw material into a finished product is known as *vertical integration*. Vertical integration eliminated Carnegie's dependence on owners of independent mines, railroads, and shipping lines. This gave Carnegie an advantage in the competition with other steel companies.

John D. Rockefeller and the Standard Oil Trust

While Carnegie was vertically integrating his steel operation, John D. Rockefeller was trying to eliminate competition in the oil business. The first major oil drilling in the United States took place in 1859 near Titusville, Pennsylvania. At that time oil was valued because it could be used to make kerosene, an efficient and cheap fuel for lamps. When news of the first successful wells spread, a boom in oil drilling began.

Rockefeller correctly understood that oil was relatively valueless until it was re-

fined, or purified. Thus he concluded that the refinery business was the key to success in the industry. During the Civil War, Rockefeller entered the oil-refining business and in 1870 formed the Standard Oil Company.

Rockefeller believed that the savage competition of his era was wasteful and destructive. Unlike Carnegie, however, Rockefeller at first chose not to expand his business vertically. Instead of buying drilling companies, rail lines, and warehouses, Rockefeller concentrated on acquiring other refineries. Expansion in one area of production is known as *horizontal integration*.

Rockefeller often used ruthless methods to eliminate competition. Because the railroads needed Rockefeller's business, railroad executives agreed to give rebates to Standard Oil freight. Weakened by higher freight rates, rivals of Standard Oil were further hurt by Rockefeller's relentless price cutting. Standard Oil would lower oil prices to capture a competitor's customers and then raise prices after the competitor was driven out of business. As a result of Rocke-

After the first successful oil well was drilled at Titusville, Pennsylvania, in 1859, prospectors scrambled to locate more oil nearby. The hillside of Pioneer Run, Pennsylvania, in 1865 bristled with derricks and drillers' shanties.

feller's tough methods, Standard Oil controlled over 90 percent of American refining capacity by 1879.

To tighten his control over the industry, Rockefeller also accumulated the stock of other oil companies under trust agreements. In a *trust*, stockholders of independent companies agree to exchange their shares of stock for trust certificates issued by a giant firm such as Standard Oil. The holders of trust certificates receive *dividends*, or shares of the company's profit, but lose the right to participate in the management of the firm.

Eventually, Standard Oil embarked on a plan of vertical integration. It bought barrel companies and railroads and began to manufacture and install its own pipelines. By such methods Standard Oil acquired a virtual *monopoly* of the oil industry, that is, the company had almost total control of the market for oil.

Other large businesses quickly saw the advantage of operating as a trust and followed the example of Standard Oil. In the 1880s trusts appeared in such areas as sugar refining, whiskey distilling, and the manufacture of cottonseed and linseed oils.

Free Enterprise in an Age of Growth

Since the founding of the nation, the economy had been based on the idea of free enterprise. *Free enterprise* is a system in which private individuals make economic decisions such as what products to make, how much to produce, where to sell products, and what prices should be.

Some people in the late 1800s believed that leaders of the giant corporations were abusing the free enterprise system. These critics especially objected that the creation of monopolies eliminated competition, a central part of free enterprise. To end the abuses, critics began to demand government regulations, as you will read in the following chapter.

Historians and economists have continued to debate the consequences of the economic changes of the last half of the nineteenth century. Part of the debate centers on the character and aims of the business leaders of the period. Some historians, who label those business leaders robber barons, charge that men like Carnegie and Rockefeller ruthlessly drove small companies out of business and exploited workers.

Other historians use the term industrial statesmen to describe the leaders of American business. They believe that people such as Carnegie and Rockefeller should be praised for their innovative business methods as well as their generous financial support of hundreds of schools, libraries, and museums.

Another area of debate is the issue of the efficiency of the giant corporation. Critics of the large corporation charge that big firms discourage technological change rather than discard existing equipment. Some critics maintain that the big businesses that grew up after the Civil War polluted the environment and wasted raw materials.

The defenders of big business argue that large corporations invented and perfected technological breakthroughs that revolutionized American life. They maintain that the growth of giant corporations in the late 1800s brought lower production costs and prices, higher wages, and a better quality of life for millions of Americans.

Although the merits of post–Civil War business practices are still the subject of debate, there is no question that nineteenth-century business leaders transformed American life, taking the nation from the "horse and buggy" to the automobile age. Under their leadership Americans attained a standard of living higher than that of any other people on earth.

SECTION REVIEW

1. Identify: John D. Rockefeller.
2. Define: capital, vertical integration, horizontal integration, trust, dividend, monopoly, free enterprise.
3. List three advantages of corporations over proprietorships and partnerships.
4. What sources of capital were available to business people in the last half of the 1800s?
5. What methods did John D. Rockefeller use to eliminate competition in the oil industry?
6. (a) List one criticism of big business in the late 1800s. (b) List one defense of big business.
7. **Critical Thinking** What qualities did Carnegie and Rockefeller have in common?

4 The Growth of Industry in the South

Before the Civil War, the southern economy was largely agricultural, and the South had relatively few factories. As the region struggled to recover from the devastation of war, many southerners believed that the way to prosperity lay with industry. They envisioned a "New South" economically similar to the industrial North. And indeed the South had many natural resources and agricultural products, including coal, iron ore, timber, sugar, and cotton, that could fuel industry.

The Rise of the "New South"

No one expressed the idea of the "New South" better than Henry Grady, editor of the Atlanta *Constitution*. In spreading the idea of southern industrialization, Grady liked to tell the story of a poor Georgia cotton farmer's funeral. The farmer had been buried in a pine forest in Georgia. His pine coffin, however, had been manufactured in Cincinnati. Although an iron mine stood not far from the cemetery, the coffin's iron nails were made in Pittsburgh. The cotton coat the farmer was buried in came from New York, his trousers from Chicago. Concluded Grady, the "South didn't furnish a thing on earth for that funeral but the corpse and the hole in the ground!"

Grady's story pinpointed the South's dilemma. Though rich in natural resources, the South produced few of the manufactured goods it consumed. Along with other southerners Grady argued that an important first step toward attracting industry was the improvement of the southern railroad network. Southern states encouraged northern financiers to invest in southern lines, offering free land as well as access to the natural resources of the region. As a result, southern railroads grew at a pace faster than the national average.

The South also had changed the gauge of its track to conform to the national standard. On one day at a prearranged signal, 8,000 workers for the Louisville and Nashville railroad moved the rails of over 2,000 miles (3,200 kilometers) of track 3 inches (7.5 centimeters) closer together. For the first time, rail freight was able to move directly between North and South.

Agricultural Industries

Many southerners realized that the best way to begin industrializing was to build plants geared to use agricultural goods, such as cotton and tobacco, that the South was already producing. After the war, a number of textile mills were built to weave cotton thread. The early mills were organized much like the old plantations. The factory owner provided the workers with housing, stores, churches, and schools, as well as jobs. Most of the textile workers were women and children. Wages were low, 75-hour work weeks were common, and decent housing was rare. But a small garden plot and a steady cash income put mill workers slightly ahead of most southern agricultural workers.

Nevertheless, by 1880 the entire South was still producing fewer textiles than the state of Massachusetts. During the 1880s the industry grew as southerners purchased the latest machinery for use in new textile factories. "Every little town wanted a mill," noted one observer. "If it couldn't get a big one, it would take a small one."

The American Cotton Oil Trust built factories in the South to extract oil from cotton seeds. Cottonseed oil was the essential ingredient in soap and cosmetics and was used as a substitute for butter and olive oil. The remaining cotton pulp was used for fertilizer and cattle feed.

The southern tobacco industry also grew rapidly after the Civil War. In 1865 Washington Duke returned from General Lee's army to his farm in North Carolina to find only one tobacco barn remaining. He and his son James soon began to market Duke's Mixture. Using innovative advertising techniques, James Duke sold cigarettes in the North as well as the South. He also purchased exclusive rights to the cigarette-rolling machine invented by James Bonsack, also a southerner.

With each machine turning out 100,000 cigarettes a day, Duke revolutionized the tobacco industry. Taking advantage of railroad rebates and lowered production costs, he bought out several competitors and in 1890 formed the American Tobacco Company. Like John D. Rockefeller, who served as his model, Duke established a mammoth trust

Within a decade of the Civil War, Charleston, South Carolina, had regained much of its prewar vitality. In the background of this 1872 painting are the masts of ships docked at the Charleston port. Many of the products of new southern industries were shipped to northern factories for the final steps of the manufacturing process.

that eventually controlled 90 percent of the nation's tobacco industry.

Mining and Lumbering

Southern industry was not restricted to the use of agricultural products. Mineral industries also grew. Local deposits of iron ore and coal made steel production cheaper in Alabama than in Pennsylvania. Pig iron was first produced in Birmingham, Alabama, in 1876. Steel production began in Birmingham in 1880, and by 1900 the population of the city had risen from 3,000 to 26,000.

Oil refining developed in Texas and West Virginia. Coal mining grew in West Virginia and Alabama, copper mining and granite and marble quarrying in Georgia and Tennessee. Forest-related industries also flourished. Many forests in the North had been depleted, and by 1895 the southern yellow pine was competing with the northwestern white pine in total production of

lumber. Some southern factories began to manufacture cypress shingles, and hardwood furniture was produced in High Point, North Carolina.

A Dependent Economy

By 1900 the South had made progress toward a more balanced economy. It had its own textile factories, consolidated railroads, and giant companies such as the tobacco trust. But the growth of the North and West had been even more spectacular. The South continued to lag behind. In fact, it had a lower percentage of the nation's factories in 1900 than it had in 1860.

Many factors contributed to this lag. To raise money, southerners often had to borrow from large northern banks. Consequently, northern bankers exerted control over many southern industries and reaped much of the profits. Furthermore, many of the industries in the South produced only raw materials. These were sent to factories in the North for final processing—and from final processing came the greatest profits.

When southern factories did produce finished goods, northern railroad owners charged them higher rates to ship the products. This made it difficult for southern products to compete with those made in the North. At the same time, the rates for shipping raw materials to the North were deliberately set low.

During the late 1800s, much of the wealth of the South went North. By 1900, Henry Grady's dream of a New South had begun to take shape, but years were to pass before the dream became a reality.

SECTION REVIEW

1. **Identify:** Henry Grady, Washington Duke.
2. How did southern railroads improve after the Civil War?
3. List three ways southern industries used agricultural products grown in the South.
4. **Critical Thinking** How was the economic policy of the North toward the South similar to mercantilism?

5 Workers Organize

An expanding economy increased the need for factory workers. Many workers moved from rural areas to industrial cities like Chicago, Buffalo, and Pittsburgh. Large numbers of immigrants from Europe joined them. Low wages, long hours, dangerous factories, unhealthy working conditions, and periodic unemployment were common. To correct those problems, workers found it increasingly necessary to band together.

The Work Force

The industrial work force was made up of individuals from a variety of backgrounds. The majority of workers were white American men, many of whom had left the farm for the city hoping to better their lot. A small number of factory workers were black. When black Americans turned from rural labor to the urban factories, however, they were often turned away or given the hardest and lowest-paying jobs. Employers frequently hired blacks and immigrants to replace striking workers.

Women played an increasingly important role in the labor force. By 1890 approximately one million women were working in factories. They made up at least half of the work force in textile mills and tobacco factories and outnumbered men in the garment manufacturing trade. Women also worked in shoemaking, food processing, packaging, and other industries that did not require heavy physical labor. However, a few industries requiring heavy labor, such as tin plate mills and print shops, occasionally hired women. No matter what the work, women received less than half the wage of a man for the same job.

Between 1865 and 1900, over 13.5 million immigrants came to the United States. (See page 438.) Without their contribution to the work force, the national economy would never have expanded as rapidly and vigorously as it did. In 1870 about one third of all factory workers in America were foreign born. The immigrants tended to settle near and work with people of their own nationality. Thus different ethnic groups tended to specialize in different industries. Many Slavs, for example, took jobs in the steel mills of Gary, Indiana; Jews often worked in New York City's garment industry.

Because immigrants were new to the country and because their standard of living in Europe had often been lower than that of many Americans, they often accepted unpleasant, dangerous, and poorly paid jobs that Americans preferred to turn down. With immigrants so eager for work, employers found they could offer them less than the standard wage. In the steel industry, immigrants might expect to earn $12 a week, compared with $22 a week for white native-born workers.

Working Conditions

Working conditions varied from industry to industry, but most factories were badly lighted, poorly ventilated, and hazardous. Facing stiff competition, owners refused to pay for expensive safety features that would raise the price of their products. Textile workers inhaled the dust and fibers that filled the air in the mills. Workers in cigarette factories had to endure tremendous heat and the stench of tobacco. Coal miners deep underground faced the perils of explosions and cave-ins. Garment workers, who often did their work at home, crouched over tables in dimly lighted apartments, straining their eyes to see if the seams were properly sewn.

Among the most demanding and dangerous occupations were jobs in the steel mills. At Andrew Carnegie's Homestead plant, men toiled 12 hours a day, 6 days a week. In the furnace room Bessemer converters belched fire and sparks. The metal floors were so hot that when water was poured on them they sizzled. Men routinely worked close to molten steel, sometimes within inches of it. Inevitably, such conditions took their toll in human life. In one year during the late 1800s, industrial accidents killed 195 workers in the steel factories of Pittsburgh.

Wages and the Economy

Despite difficult working conditions, the economic situation of the average laborer improved between 1870 and 1900. Average wages rose more than 10 percent during that period. Buying power increased because consumer prices declined. This picture is somewhat deceptive, however. The statistical averages hide wide variations in pay among workers in different occupations and in different parts of the country. Even those whose wages increased found it difficult to support a family.

"A family of workers can always live well," commented a man familiar with the textile industry in Massachusetts, "but the man with a family of small children to support, unless his wife works also, has a small chance of living properly." Some families found their situation so desperate that they were forced to send their children to work. In Pennsylvania, for example, 10-year-old boys commonly worked in the mines. At the turn of the century, almost 2 million American children between the ages of 10 and 15 were at work.

Furthermore, workers' gains were subject to the uncertainties that plagued the industries. Competition was often fierce, and many companies went out of business suddenly, leaving workers without jobs. The depressions of 1873, 1882, and 1893, threw many people out of work. During 1873 and 1874 in New York City, for example, between one fourth and one third of the workers

New inventions often created new types of jobs, including jobs for women. Office clerks had traditionally been men. With the introduction of the typewriter, however, women began to replace men on office staffs. These typists worked for an insurance company.

Business Cycles, 1865–1900

Upward Business Trends

Downward Business Trends

+20%
+10%
-10%
-20%

1865   1870   1875   1880   1885   1890   1895   1900

■ Times of prosperity
■ Times of depression or recession

■ *The ups and downs of the economy were felt more sharply as the nation industrialized and more people worked for wages. Which years were most prosperous? In which years did severe depressions strike?*

were jobless. National unemployment figures soared from 4 percent in 1890 to 11.7 percent during the depression of 1893. Because there was no system of unemployment insurance, depressions were times of great distress.

The Knights of Labor

Low wages, periodic unemployment, illness, and accident threatened a worker's well being. Some workers escaped these misfortunes by moving on to better jobs. Others tried to band together to achieve common goals.

The organization known as the Knights of Labor was formed in 1869 as a secret brotherhood of skilled workers. Under the leadership of Uriah Stephens, a garment cutter, the society supported idealistic goals, chief among them the hope that all laborers would unite within "one big brotherhood." The Knights also advocated an eight-hour day for workers and equal pay for men and women.

In 1879 the Knights elected Terence V. Powderly as their leader. To strengthen his union, Powderly removed its veil of secrecy and opened its ranks to women, blacks, immigrants, and unskilled laborers. This was the first attempt to organize all workers.*

---

*Earlier unions had been restricted to skilled workers, as you read in Chapter 15. (See pages 273–274.)

Powderly tried to keep the organization free of politics, and he opposed the use of strikes, or work stoppages. He believed the Knights of Labor should campaign for social and economic reforms: the eight-hour day, improved safety in factories, and compensation for on-the-job injury. Under Powderly's leadership, membership increased from 9,000 in 1879 to approximately 115,000 by the end of 1884.

The Knights' greatest gains came in the following year. Despite Powderly's no-strike policy, railroad workers belonging to the Knights went on strike against tycoon Jay Gould's southwestern railroads to protest a pay cut. They forced Gould to restore the cut. Thousands of laborers, impressed by the successful railroad strike, joined the Knights of Labor. By mid-1886 membership had soared to a peak of 700,000.

The Haymarket Riot and the Decline of the Knights

Worker discontent, which had swelled the ranks of the Knights of Labor, led to an incident that, paradoxically, contributed to the downfall of the organization. In 1886, 80,000 Chicago workers went on strike in support of an eight-hour day. During the strike several workers were killed by the police in a disturbance near the McCormick Harvester Works. To protest these deaths, a group of *anarchists*, people who oppose all organized government, planned a rally for May 4.

Rain fell and a little more than a thousand people gathered in Haymarket Square to hear anarchist speakers denounce the police and the industrialists. When the police moved in to break up the meeting, a bomb was thrown, killing one police officer and six other people in the crowd. In the riot that followed, seven police officers and four civilians were killed.

Eight anarchists were convicted of conspiracy to commit murder in the bomb-throwing incident. Four were hanged, one committed suicide, and three were sentenced to long terms in prison.

The Haymarket riot turned the public sharply against labor organizations. Even though Terence Powderly and other officials of the Knights of Labor deplored the Haymarket bombing, their reputations were tarnished by it. Because the Knights and the anarchists both supported the eight-hour day, the two groups became linked in the mind of the public.

Weakened by the Haymarket incident and violence during an unsuccessful railroad strike in 1886, the Knights of Labor declined. By 1890 membership had dropped to 100,000. During the rest of the decade members either left the labor movement or joined the rising American Federation of Labor.

The American Federation of Labor

The American Federation of Labor (AFL) was founded in 1881. Its first president was a London-born cigarmaker named Samuel Gompers. Gompers believed that the Knights of Labor should not have tried to include unskilled workers in their unions. Membership in the AFL was restricted to skilled workers, who had special training. Unskilled workers, blacks, and women were not allowed to join. Recent immigrants, particularly those from Asia, were also excluded from AFL unions.

Workers did not join the American Federation of Labor directly. Individuals joined a local *craft union*, a union of persons practicing the same occupation. Each local union was affiliated with organizations on the state and national levels. The AFL was a federation of self-governing national unions. Each union was independent and had its own treasury but followed general AFL policies.

The AFL kept its goals specific and realistic. "Our organization does not consist of

idealists," insisted one AFL leader. "We are going on from day to day. We are fighting only for immediate objects—objects that can be realized in a few years." The AFL favored the eight-hour day and worked for *collective bargaining*, the right of unions to represent workers as a group.

Unlike the Knights of Labor, the AFL regarded strikes as an acceptable tactic. And unlike anarchists and other radicals, the AFL rejected schemes to reorganize society. Its moderate philosophy attracted a growing number of workers. From 150,000 members in 1886, the AFL grew to 500,000 members by 1900 and reached more than a million by 1904.

Tension Between Labor and Management

Most company owners and managers were hostile to unions. Owners felt that they had the right to bargain with each worker individually. "If I wanted boiler iron," explained one railroad official, "I would go out on the

Terence Powderly opened the Knights of Labor to unskilled workers, blacks, immigrants, and women. In this drawing, Powderly (center) is introduced to the Knights' annual convention at Richmond, Virginia, by delegate Frank Farrell (left).

market and buy it where I could get it cheapest, and if I employ men, I would do the same." Unions, he argued, interfered with his rights.

For their part, union officials were skeptical of claims that employers had workers' best interests at heart. A few industrialists tried to provide their workers with such benefits as libraries and recreational facilities, but even those employers did not recognize the right of unions to exist. Consequently suspicion and distrust persisted on both sides.

With labor and management mutually antagonistic, violent strikes were not uncommon. The most serious strike erupted at Carnegie's Homestead steel plant in 1892. Angered by an unexpected wage cut, the Amalgamated Association of Iron and Steel Workers refused to accept the company's offer.

With a strike threatening, Henry Clay Frick, the plant manager, took action. He closed the plant, put up a wire fence around it, and hired 300 Pinkerton guards. When the Pinkerton guards rafted down the Monongahela River and tried to land at the plant, furious union workers attacked them. Gunfire erupted. Before the battle was over, seven Pinkerton men and nine workers lay dead.

In response to the violence, the Pennsylvania National Guard surrounded the plant and arrested the strikers. Gradually workers began to return to the steel mills, but no Amalgamated men were given their jobs back, and wages fell by about 50 percent.

Since the steel workers' union at Homestead had been the American Federation of Labor's largest union, the entire AFL suffered from this stunning defeat. The conflict set back the union movement in the steel industry for the next 20 years. The AFL continued to organize other industries, but the Homestead strike made it clear that unions faced a difficult battle for recognition.

Efforts to form labor organizations were slowed by public distrust of unions. In this 1886 cartoon, the Knights of Labor and trade unions are pictured careening toward lawless disorder. In the background, the less militant Brotherhood of Locomotive Engineers is shown, by contrast, as orderly and lawful.

Common Occupations in the Late 1800s

Occupation	Number of Males	Number of Females	Total
Farmers (self-employed, managerial)	5,055,130	226,427	5,281,557
Hired hands (farm)	2,556,958	447,104	3,004,062
Servants, waiters	238,152	1,216,639	1,454,791
Carpenters	618,044	198	618,242
Railroad workers	460,771	1,442	462,213
Miners	386,862	376	387,238
Wagon drivers, teamsters	368,265	234	368,499
Teachers, college professors	101,278	246,066	347,344
Dressmakers	836	292,668	293,504
Salespeople	205,943	58,451	264,394
Blacksmiths	209,521	60	209,581
Tailors	123,516	64,509	188,025
Bookkeepers, accountants	131,602	27,772	159,374
Physicians, surgeons	100,248	4,557	104,805
Lawyers	89,422	208	89,630
Clergy	87,060	1,143	88,203
Barbers, hairdressers	82,157	2,825	84,982
Sailors	76,823	51	76,874
Guards, police, detectives	74,350	279	74,629
Nursery workers, gardeners, florists	70,186	2,415	72,601

■ *Women who joined the labor force in the late 1800s were concentrated in certain occupations, as can be seen in this table.*

Reaction to Unions

Employers were not the only Americans who were unsympathetic to unions. Courts frequently issued *injunctions,* orders prohibiting a given action, to stop strikes. Furthermore, courts held that strikers could be held personally responsible for economic losses that employers suffered during a strike.

The press in many local communities sided with the employer during labor-management disputes. Newspaper publishers, who depended on local businesses for advertising revenue and who were employers themselves, often editorialized against what they saw as the unjustified demands of labor.

Furthermore, much of the public opposed unions. Despite the moderate positions of most American unions, people often considered them radical organizations. This belief was probably influenced by the activity of socialists in some European nations. Despite differing views, socialists believed that wealth derived from labor should be evenly distributed among the workers and that society as a whole, not profit-seeking individuals, should make economic decisions. In 1877 the Socialist Labor party was formed

Major Events

Year	Event
1844	Morse invents telegraph
1852	Otis invents passenger elevator
1859	Oil drilling begins in Pennsylvania; Bessemer process invented
1864	Pullman designs sleeping car
1869	Knights of Labor founded
1872	Westinghouse invents airbrake
1876	Bell invents telephone
1879	Edison invents incandescent light bulb
1881	American Federation of Labor founded
1883	Country divided into four time zones
1886	Haymarket riot
1892	Homestead strike

in the United States, but it remained small and had little influence.

The idea of collective bargaining also seemed foreign to many Americans. The tradition of individualism was strong, and people believed that individual effort was the way to advancement. The generally negative attitude of the public slowed the growth of unions.

SECTION REVIEW

1. Identify: Knights of Labor, Terence Powderly, American Federation of Labor, Samuel Gompers.

2. Define: anarchists, craft unions, collective bargaining, injunction.

3. (a) What were the goals of the Knights of Labor? (b) Who could join?

4. How did the Haymarket riot of 1886 affect the Knights of Labor?

5. (a) What were the goals of the American Federation of Labor? (b) Who could join?

6. How did much of the public react to unions in the late 1800s?

7. **Critical Thinking** How did industrialization affect the relationship of employees and employers?

Chapter 21 Review

In Perspective

Many of the dramatic changes that transformed American life between 1865 and 1914 were the result of increasing industrialization. Corporate mergers and inventions in communication and transportation helped create a truly national economy. Increasingly, business people saw the entire nation as their market.

Nothing forged the nation together more than the railroads. Evolving from many independent lines to a more centralized system controlled by a few giant companies, the railroads brought consumers and producers closer together. The telegraph and later the telephone also put Americans in closer touch with each other.

These feats in transportation and communication paved the way for the consolidation of industry. Taking advantage of new inventions, enterprising industrialists expanded old businesses and created new ones. Many businesses, old and new, were consolidated into large, powerful units. Trusts, vertical integration, and horizontal integration served to make such large businesses more efficient and powerful.

Workers began to organize to improve working conditions and work for common goals. The Knights of Labor, which had

enjoyed initial success, declined after the Haymarket riot of 1866. Although many Americans disapproved of labor unions, the American Federation of Labor, which stressed practical goals, grew during the late 1800s.

"The day of combination is here to stay," John D. Rockefeller concluded. Many people were convinced that he was right, but some also began to wonder whether the government had an obligation to regulate the new concentrations of industrial power, as you will read in Chapter 22.

Vocabulary

Match each term at left with its definition or description at right.

1. assets
2. rebates
3. pooling
4. dividend
5. monopoly
6. injunction

a. discount on normal charges
b. total control of an industry
c. order prohibiting an action
d. share of profits
e. property and cash
f. apportionment of volume of business

Chapter Checkup

1. What technological developments in communication helped stimulate industrial growth?

2. Explain how each of the following helped stimulate American industry: (a) Bessemer process; (b) refrigeration; (c) air brake; (d) typewriter; (e) incandescent light bulb.

3. (a) Describe free enterprise. (b) Why did some critics of giant corporations believe that those corporations were abusing the free enterprise system?

4. Why did the growing industry of the South fail to bring that region's economy up to the level of the northern economy?

5. (a) What conditions convinced many American workers to join unions in the late 1800s? (b) What attempts were made to create a national labor organization? (c) Were they successful? Explain.

Critical Thinking

1. **Supporting an Opinion** Do you agree with John D. Rockefeller's observation that the United States was entering a period of combination? Cite specific examples to support your answer.

2. **Evaluating** Of all the inventions you read about in this chapter, which do you think had the greatest impact on the daily lives of Americans? Why?

Developing Basic Skills

1. **Comparing** Make a chart with two columns and four rows. Label one column Knights of Labor and the other American Federation of Labor. Label the rows Date Founded, Goals, Types of Members, and Approved Tactics.

    Complete the chart. Then answer the following questions: (a) How did the membership of the organization differ? (b) What goals did both organizations have in common? (c) What goals were different? (d) Do you think any of the factors you analyzed may have made the AFL more likely to be successful? Explain.

2. **Comparing** Review the description of vertical and horizontal integration on page 402. Then answer the following questions; (a) What segments of an industry does a company control if it is vertically integrated? (b) What segments of an industry does a company control if it is horizontally integrated? (c) How might each give the company an edge over competition?

See page 830 for suggested readings.

Writer's Handbook

Using Specialized Reference Books

Specialized reference books provide detailed information about a particular subject area. Some valuable specialized reference books in United States history are listed below. Most of these books are available only in the reference section of your library.

Dictionary of American History—basic information about topics in American history

Encyclopedia of American History—description of events in American history in chronological order

United States Government Manual—comprehensive information on the agencies of the legislative, executive, and judicial branches

Statutes at Large—information about laws passed each year

Leading Constitutional Decisions—information about significant Supreme Court cases

Statistical Abstract of the United States—current economic and social statistics

Historical Statistics of the United States—economic and social statistics from colonial times to the present

Practice: In one of the specialized reference books mentioned above, find additional information related to a subject discussed in Chapter 21. Identify the source and write a brief paragraph explaining what you have learned.

22

Politics and Reform

(1867–1900)

The Lost Bet *by Joseph Klir*

Chapter Outline

1 *Political Corruption in a Gilded Age*

2 *Attempts at Reform*

3 *Politics in the New South*

4 *The Populist Crusade*

5 *The Decline of Populism*

Throughout the 1800s, American political campaigns had been colorful and exciting. Yet, important political issues were far from the minds of most people.

One issue that did concern many Americans was the prevalence of corruption at all levels of government. Efforts to reform corrupt political practices began in earnest during the 1880s. Some people also demanded that government regulate the unfair business practices of the giant trusts that developed during this period.

A national political movement known as Populism drew on the reform spirit and on the discontent of farmers in the West and South. Since many farmers thought that they were not well represented by the two major political parties, they formed a third party. The Populist movement was short-lived, yet the Populists were to pave the way for later generations of reformers.

Farmers organize

1865	1870	1875	1880	1885	1890	1895	1900

1867
The Grange founded

1872
Crédit Mobilier scandal

1877
Munn v. *Illinois*

1881
Garfield assassinated

1887
Interstate Commerce Act passed

1892
Populist party formed

1896
Plessy v. *Ferguson*

1 Political Corruption in a Gilded Age

The rapid industrialization of the years following the Civil War brought problems as well as material progress. The fortunes of industrialists gave them immense influence over many aspects of life, especially politics. Some industrialists, such as Andrew Carnegie, used their wealth to try to improve society, but others were mainly interested in increasing their fortunes and power.

Bribery and Politics

In 1877 Collis P. Huntington, builder of the Central Pacific Railroad and director of the Southern Pacific line, had a problem. His archrival, Thomas Scott of the Pennsylvania Railroad, had placed a bill before Congress that would break Huntington's control of rail routes to southern California. Huntington's solution was to bribe key members of Congress. "It costs money to fix things," he explained. To Huntington, bribery made good sense. "If [another] man has the power to do great evil, and won't do right unless he is bribed to do it," he said, "it is a man's duty to go up and bribe the judge."

Many industrialists openly showed their contempt for society and the law. Cornelius Vanderbilt, when told that some of his ac-

tions were against the law, snorted, "Law! What do I care about the law? Haven't I got the power?" Indeed, with his huge private fortune and railroad empire, Vanderbilt did have the power.

The lure of power and riches tarnished Congress and the presidency. Votes, political favors, and political offices were bought and sold. Representatives of wealthy special interests bribed members of Congress to pass legislation that benefited those interests. Cabinet members and other high-ranking officials took advantage of their positions to make fortunes for themselves.

The climate of corruption also infected small businesses and governments at the state and local levels. The author Mark Twain believed that such corruption constituted the underside of public life, the brass under a thin layer of gold. He labeled the era the Gilded Age, and the nickname stuck.

Wheeling and Dealing in Congress

Congress itself helped confirm the popular notion that politicians were corrupt and interested only in enjoying the spoils of victory. Of the two houses of Congress, the

Giant trusts were popularly considered the "bosses of the Senate," as this cartoon shows. What famous speech is parodied in the sign on the wall?

Senate was by far the most powerful. In part, this was because senators faced reelection only every six years, unlike members of the House of Representatives, who faced it every two years. Some senators had been in office for several decades and had accumulated enormous reserves of power and influence. Many were political bosses in their home states, and they could reward supporters with a wide range of appointments and favors.

Many senators were also personally wealthy, so many in fact that the Senate became known as a "rich man's club." The country, remarked one prominent observer, had a "government of the people, by the people, for the benefit of the Senate."

The House of Representatives demonstrated less influence partly because it conveyed the impression of being a rather disorderly place. Representatives often sat with their feet propped on their desks, smoking cigars or spitting tobacco juice. Members might be seen reading newspapers or writing letters instead of attending to business. Representatives who wanted to listen to a speech had to crowd close to the podium in order to hear the proceedings. Nevertheless, some members emerged as effective legislators and prominent national figures.

Despite its tarnished reputation, Congress had a high opinion of itself. As you read in Chapter 19, the impeachment of President Andrew Johnson was a sign that Congress had decided to assert authority over the executive branch of the government. In the years after Reconstruction, the presidency remained weak and Congress became stronger. Congressional leaders firmly defended their responsibility to propose and make laws. The President, they believed, should only enforce laws passed by the legislative branch.

The Presidency in the Gilded Age

Acting under the shadow of the Congress, the Presidents who served during the Gilded Age did not achieve great distinction. Rather, the men who occupied the White House during the late 1800s tended to be colorless figures who were good politicians but not inspiring leaders. Although some of the Presidents during this period saw the need for reform and were often behind important changes, they basically agreed that the presidency was less powerful than the legislative branch.

Even if a President had wanted to lead vigorously, he would have found it difficult to do so. The executive staff was small. Without additional help, a President was in no position to take the initiative on legislative issues. Moreover, no President between 1865 and 1897 had the advantage of having his own party in control of both houses of Congress throughout his full term of office.

Finally, Presidents were thwarted by the widespread political corruption of the period. Although most of them were personally honest, they were often surrounded by unsavory politicians interested only in personal gain.

Scandals During the Grant Years

The worst examples of corruption at the national level took place during the administration of Ulysses S. Grant (1869–1877). Grant was an honest, able military general, but loyalty to his friends led him to appoint people who eventually betrayed his trust.

The first major scandal came to light in 1872. A newspaper, the New York *Sun*, reported that officials of the Union Pacific Railroad had enriched themselves by creating a company called the Crédit Mobilier. The Crédit Mobilier was supposedly a construction company. As such, it received contracts from the Union Pacific to lay track on the transcontinental route. On the strength of these contracts, Crédit Mobilier raised additional money by selling shares of stock.

Much of the stock, which paid high dividends, was sold to members of Congress at bargain prices. In return, the stockholding legislators voted funds for Union Pacific construction. The Union Pacific then paid the Crédit Mobilier according to the contracts, but the firm never laid a foot of track. The company existed merely to make money.

Other investigations revealed that at least five members of Grant's cabinet had engaged in corrupt practices. The most serious offender was Secretary of War William Belknap, who was involved in many of the shady dealings used by white traders to cheat Native Americans who lived on reservations. (See page 383.)

When Grant's secretary of the treasury resigned over another scandal, his replacement uncovered what came to be known as

the Whiskey Ring. The federal government was supposed to collect an excise tax on every bottle of whiskey sold. But hundreds of distillers had bribed treasury officials in order to avoid paying those taxes. Even the President's personal secretary was involved. Though Grant ordered investigators to "let no guilty man escape," the President protected his secretary from punishment.

The scandals of the Grant administration damaged the office of the presidency. Much of the public came to agree with Mark Twain that corruption in politics was indeed a hallmark of the Gilded Age. Yet the scandals also made some people more determined to reform political life, and the reformers were soon to gain prominence.

SECTION REVIEW

1. Identify: Crédit Mobilier, Whiskey Ring.
2. What attitude did some wealthy industrialists, such as Collis P. Huntington, have toward bribery?
3. (a) According to congressional leaders after Reconstruction, what were their two responsibilities? (b) In their opinion what was the President's job?
4. What impact did scandals during Grant's administration have on the presidency?
5. **Critical Thinking** Why and how does power shift between Congress and the President?

2 Attempts at Reform

The widespread political corruption of the Gilded Age eventually convinced some Americans that reform was needed. The resulting reform efforts were not limited to attacks on bribery. Reformers also turned their attention to the abuse of power by giant railroads and trusts.

The Mugwumps

One strong movement for reform came from within the Republican party. These reform-minded Republicans were nicknamed Mugwumps, an Indian term meaning big chief. The Mugwumps believed in laissez-faire economics and clean politics. They opposed the "spoils system" that had begun under President Andrew Jackson. (See page 241.) The spoils—federal, state, and local offices—were being handed out, not for merit, but simply as rewards to loyal party workers. The Mugwumps argued that this *patronage system*, the practice of giving out government jobs as favors, should be replaced by a civil service in which job applicants would be tested to determine their fitness for particular jobs.

Among the Mugwumps were the editors of well-known journals: E. L. Godkin of *The Nation* and George W. Curtis of *Harper's Weekly*. They wrote editorials urging reform and exposés of corrupt political machines. One of the most effective publicists was *Har-*per's cartoonist Thomas Nast, whose caricatures of greedy trusts and wicked political bosses were popular throughout the nation.

The Mugwumps, however, were paid little attention by most politicians, who realized that the average American did not share the Mugwumps' distaste for the rough and tumble of politics. Nevertheless, the Mugwumps eventually achieved partial success in their crusade to clean up American politics.

Chipping Away at the Spoils System

Most Mugwumps would not have predicted that the three Republican Presidents who followed Ulysses S. Grant would advance the cause of reform. Yet Presidents Hayes (1877–1881), Garfield (1881), and Arthur (1881–1885) each took steps to reform the old patronage system.

As you read in Chapter 19, President Rutherford Hayes was elected to office in 1876 by a political deal. In that deal Republican politicians agreed to end Reconstruction in return for Democratic help in resolving the disputed presidential election. (See page 365.) But Hayes soon surprised Republican party leaders by appointing a noted reformer, Carl Schurz, to the cabinet as secretary of the interior. "Hayes has passed the Republican party to its worst enemies," grumbled one old-line Republican.

President Hayes also launched an investigation into the administration of the customs house in New York. The customs house, in charge of collecting duties on imports unloaded at the port of New York, had the reputation of being one of the most corrupt organizations in the nation. The investigation revealed that over 200 officials in the customs house were receiving salaries without doing any work. High officials were lining their pockets with some $1.5 million in duties each year. Although influential Republicans bitterly fought the investigation, the President dismissed two senior customs house employees.

Hayes's successor, James Garfield, no sooner assumed office in 1881 than he found himself in the middle of a spirited struggle over patronage between two rival factions of the Republican party. One group was the "Half-breeds," so called because of their half-hearted commitment to Reconstruction, and the other was the "Stalwarts," who had supported a tough policy of Reconstruction. Each tried to convince Garfield to reward their own loyal followers with the lion's share of political offices.

The efforts of the two groups ended abruptly on July 2, 1881 when a mentally unstable office seeker, Charles Guiteau, shot President Garfield. Guiteau was bitter because he had not received a government appointment. For nearly two months the President clung to life. His death in September left the nation shocked at the evils of the patronage system and eager to accept reform of some sort.

The Civil Service Act

When Vice-President Chester Arthur succeeded Garfield, few suspected that he would take any action toward reform. Arthur was an elegant, easy-going man with expensive tastes. He was also one of the customs house officials dismissed by President Hayes. Yet as President, Arthur rose to the demands of his new office and pushed for civil service legislation.

Reacting to public outcry, Congress passed the Civil Service Act in 1883, and President Arthur promptly signed it into law. The act classified approximately 15,000 federal jobs as civil service positions, to be given only to applicants who had passed a competitive examination administered by a Civil Service Commission. Furthermore, the act prohibited firing of civil service employees for political reasons.

Although the new legislation did not abolish the spoils system overnight, it was an important step. For the first time many federal employees did not hold office simply because they belonged to a certain political party. The Civil Service Act allowed Presidents to expand the list of civil service jobs. Over the years they did exactly that—not always out of idealism, but because it was a way to keep their appointees from being dismissed by a new President. By 1897 over half of the approximately 175,000 federal employees held civil service jobs.

Cleveland and Reform

The presidential election of 1884 offered a reformer to the public, but not Chester Arthur. Although Mugwumps had been surprised and delighted by Arthur's support for reform, old-line Republicans were angered. They refused to renominate him and instead chose James G. Blaine, a Maine senator who led the Half-breed faction of the party.

The reform candidate in 1884 was Grover Cleveland, the Democratic governor of New York. Cleveland had won a national reputation defying the political bosses in New York City, speaking his mind, and running an honest administration. During the campaign, each side blasted the other with accusations of dishonesty and immorality. Cleveland survived and went on to win the election. For the first time in 25 years, a Democratic President would be living in the White House.

President Cleveland's administration was often a stormy one. A man of principle, he worked diligently to satisfy the Mugwumps and appoint competent officeholders, but he angered many members of his own party who wanted their share of the spoils. In 1888 Cleveland lost a bid for reelection to Republican Benjamin Harrison, the grandson of President William Henry Harrison. When Harrison proved to be an undistinguished President, however, the voters reelected Cleveland to a second term in 1892.

Although Cleveland was interested primarily in reform of the civil service, perhaps the most significant piece of reform legislation passed during his first term concerned regulation of the railroads.

Regulating the Railroads

As you read in Chapter 21, cutthroat competition among railroads had resulted in practices such as rebates and pooling. (See page 395.) Small shippers complained that the railroads discriminated against them by giving their larger rivals lower rates. Often, too, railroads charged higher rates for hauling freight short distances than they did for long hauls.

As early as 1837, a few state governments had acted to regulate railroads, but not until the 1870s did many states establish regulatory commissions. Midwestern states, such as Iowa and Illinois, had strong commissions that enforced strict regulations. In other states, such as Massachusetts and Alabama, the commissions had only advisory power but were still influential.

The railroads did not accept regulation willingly. Their lawyers questioned whether states had the power under law to regulate the railroad business. In 1877, in the case of *Munn* v. *Illinois*, the Supreme Court ruled that the Constitution permitted state regulation of railroads. But the Court later reversed itself in the case of *Wabash, St. Louis, & Pacific Railway Company* v. *Illinois* in 1886. Only Congress, the justices stated, had the power to regulate commerce between the states. Railroad freight crossing state lines, the Court held, could not be regulated by state commissions.

Under the leadership of Representative John Reagan of Texas and Senator Shelby Cullom of Illinois, Congress responded to increased demands for reform by passing the Interstate Commerce Act in 1887. The act outlawed rebating and pooling. The railroads were ordered to establish "reasonable and just" rates and to refrain from charging short-haul customers higher rates than long-haul customers. A five-member Interstate Commerce Commission (ICC) was established to investigate complaints and take action by filing suit in the courts.

The Interstate Commerce Act proved difficult to enforce in the courts. Favored by skilled lawyers and judges who believed the government had limited regulatory power, the railroads were able to blunt the force of the act. Between 1887 and 1906 the ICC lost almost every railroad regulation case brought before the Supreme Court. Yet the Interstate Commerce Act set an important

precedent. In the years ahead many federal commissions would be established to regulate other large industries; and as the Supreme Court became more sympathetic to the regulation of business in later years, the power of the ICC increased.

Attacking the Trusts

Pressure for reform also led Congress to curb the economic power of trusts. Although John D. Rockefeller had proclaimed that "the day of combination" had come to stay, many Americans viewed trusts with suspicion. They charged that the size and power of trusts gave them an unfair advantage, which hindered the operation of the free

Trusts were complicated legal arrangements that concentrated control of an industry in the hands of a few people. As this 1889 cartoon shows, some people thought trusts were undermining traditional American liberties.

enterprise system. Large trusts could afford to drive smaller companies out of business by lowering prices and then raising them again. This enabled many to become monopolies, free to charge as high a price as they wanted for a product.

By ruthless use of monopoly power, trusts violated the public's sense of fair play. Cartoonists portrayed trusts as octopuses greedily grasping for still more economic control. In 1888 public demand for regulation of trusts had grown so great that both Republicans and Democrats endorsed the idea.

During President Benjamin Harrison's administration, Congress passed the Sherman Antitrust Act. The 1890 law prohibited monopolies, stating, "Every contract, combination in the form of trust or otherwise, or conspiracy in restraint of trade or commerce . . . is hereby declared illegal." It thus became a crime for one corporation to eliminate all competition.

The Sherman Antitrust Act sounded uncompromising, but enforcing it proved difficult. To sidestep the law, corporations devised a substitute for the trust known as the *holding company*. Instead of merging separate companies into a trust, a holding company gained control of member companies by buying their stock. The "held" companies remained separate entities and business went on as usual, but the holding company controlled them just as effectively as a trust could. In the first five years after passage of the Sherman law, 25 new holding companies came into being.

Furthermore, government officials hesitated to challenge the powerful trusts, and no commission like the ICC existed to respond to complaints. Another blow was dealt to the effectiveness of the Sherman Act in 1895 when the Supreme Court narrowly interpreted the legislation in the case of *United States* v. *E. C. Knight Company*. This was the first Supreme Court case involving the act.

The suit against the E. C. Knight Company charged the company with furthering monopoly by selling out to the American Sugar Refining Company. With the purchase of Knight's sugar-refining facilities the American Sugar Refining Company became one of the strongest monopolies in the country. Yet the Court ruled that the sale did not violate the Sherman Antitrust Act because Knight refined all its sugar at plants within one state. The act, the Court held, prohibited the restraint of "trade or commerce." Since the E. C. Knight Company was not involved in shipping, it could not be prosecuted under the existing law.

With industry assured that the Supreme Court would interpret the antitrust legislation narrowly, the number of holding companies and monopolies continued to grow throughout the 1890s.

★ Voices of Freedom ★

United States v. E. C. Knight Company

Reformers hoped that the Sherman Antitrust Act of 1890 would curb the power of giant trusts. In the case of *United States* v. *E. C. Knight Company*, however, the Supreme Court ruled that the act could be enforced only if a company were involved in trade between states or with foreign nations. The extract below, from the opinion of Chief Justice M. W. Fuller, states the Court's position.

It was in the light of well-settled principles that the act of July 2, 1890, [Sherman Antitrust Act] was framed. Congress did not attempt thereby to assert the power to deal with monopoly directly as such; or to limit and restrict the rights of corporations . . . in the acquisition, control, or disposition of property; or to regulate . . . the price . . . at which such property or the products thereof should be sold. . . .

What the law struck at was combinations, contracts, and conspiracies to monopolize trade and commerce among the several states or with foreign nations; but the contracts and acts of the defendants related exclusively to the acquisition of the Philadelphia refineries and the business of sugar refining in Pennsylvania, and bore no direct relation to commerce between the states or with foreign nations. The object was manifestly private gain in the manufacture of the commodity, but not through the control of interstate or foreign commerce.

The Radical Reformers

Reform of the civil service, railroads, and trusts was achieved by politicians who wished to work within the established economic system. Even the Mugwumps accepted the basic idea of laissez-faire; but others during this period demanded more far-reaching reform.

One such reformer was Henry George, a self-taught economist whose book *Progress and Poverty* sold over 2 million copies. George believed that labor should be the basis of all wealth a person accumulated. Under the existing system, land rose in value simply because a railroad ran near it or a town sprang up. Land speculators thus made large profits without any labor. George proposed that Congress enact a single tax on land as a means of controlling what he considered illegitimate profits.

Edward Bellamy attracted considerable attention in 1888 with his novel *Looking Backward.* The novel pictured a utopia in 2000 A.D. in which the government ran all industry with great wisdom. Under such a system, Bellamy predicted, the "evils" of competition would no longer exist and people would live in harmony. Bellamy's followers urged that his proposals be enacted into law.

Henry Demarest Lloyd aroused public opinion against the trusts when he published *Wealth Against Commonwealth* in 1894. Lloyd concentrated his attack on Rockefeller's Standard Oil Company, marshaling facts and providing vivid examples of the trust's ruthless business practices.

These critics of American society were often widely read, but their proposed solutions were seldom accepted either by politicians or by most Americans. Still, the reformers focused public attention on problems that later political movements would deal with more effectively.

SECTION REVIEW

1. Identify: Mugwumps; Civil Service Act; *Munn* v. *Illinois;* Interstate Commerce Act; Sherman Antitrust Act; *United States* v. *E. C. Knight Company.*
2. Define: patronage system, holding company.
3. According to the Mugwumps, how should government employees be selected?
4. In what way did the Civil Service Act make the hiring and firing of government employees less political?
5. (a) How did the railroads discriminate against small shippers? (b) How did they discriminate against short-haul shippers?
6. What important precedent was set by the Interstate Commerce Act?
7. **Critical Thinking** How did the growth of industry lead to the expansion of the federal government?

3 Politics in the New South

The end of Reconstruction in 1877 brought significant political changes to the South. As you read in Chapter 19, Democrats had gradually gained control of southern state governments. (See page 364.) During the last part of the century, the Democratic party in the South achieved such strength that Republican opposition all but disappeared. At the same time, many of the gains made by black Americans during Reconstruction gradually eroded.

Conservatives in Control

The Democrats, also known as Conservatives, who came to dominate southern politics after the end of Reconstruction were not the same group of wealthy planters who had been in control before the Civil War. Many of the Conservatives were industrialists who strongly supported Henry Grady's vision of a New South.

Like most business leaders in the North and West, southern industrialists opposed interference with their business activities by either state or national government. But southerners had a special reason for supporting laissez-faire. They had just experienced Radical Reconstruction, which to them was the height of government interference. The Conservative leaders of the southern states thus framed new constitutions severely limiting the power of state governments to regulate economic affairs.

The Conservatives enjoyed widespread support, but they were not totally unopposed. Other southerners occasionally tried to vote them out of office, primarily because of scandals that rocked the Conservative governments from time to time. Graft and bribery flourished in the South as they did in the North. Whenever evidence of corruption came to light, independent candidates ran for office, and Republicans tried to win back southerners to their party.

Despite such attempts, Conservatives were seldom voted out of office. Republicans, tainted by the war and Reconstruction, would be politically crippled in the South for many years to come. The domination of the region's political affairs by Democrats gave rise to the expression the "solid South."

The Rise of Jim Crow

When President Hayes toured the South in 1877, he told black citizens that their "rights and interests would be safer" if southern whites were "let alone by the general government." Hayes was, in effect, advocating a laissez-faire policy toward race relations. The federal government would maintain that policy for the next 75 years.

For their own part, southern Conservatives adopted what they felt was a moderate policy toward black citizens. The white politicians did not regard former slaves as their equals but believed that blacks should have some limited rights, and they courted black political support.

Throughout the 1880s and early 1890s many blacks in the South continued to vote and hold minor political offices. They served as justices of the peace, constables, and occasionally as representatives in state legislatures. Southern blacks faced less social discrimination than blacks living in the North. Public transportation remained integrated, as did theaters, bars, soda fountains, parks, and cemeteries.

During the 1890s, however, southern state governments moved to deprive black Americans of their political rights and to segregate them from whites. Conservative politicians were partly responsible for the shift in policy. As you will read in the following section, many rural southern reformers challenged Conservative political dominance. To gain support from the reformers, the Conservatives abandoned their moderate racial policy, and racial hatred became a major plank in Conservative platforms.

Difficult economic conditions also strained relations between whites and blacks. Falling farm prices and tightened credit during the depression of 1893 plunged white southern farmers into a desperate mood. Many turned their resentment toward blacks, demanding that they be segregated and denied the right to vote.

Although the Fifteenth Amendment to the Constitution guaranteed black Americans the right to vote, between 1890 and 1907 southern states one by one adopted laws making it all but impossible for black citizens to exercise that right. Rigid residency requirements for voting effectively *disenfranchised*, or denied the vote to, many sharecroppers who changed residences often. Literacy tests and *poll taxes*, fees paid in order to vote, further reduced the number of blacks who could vote, since many were unable to read or too poor to pay the tax.

However, these voting restrictions worked against poor whites as well as blacks. Consequently, many southern states adopted so-called *grandfather clauses*. These clauses allowed individuals to satisfy voting requirements if their father or grandfathers had been eligible to vote in 1867. Because blacks had not been allowed to vote at that time, they could not qualify under the grandfather clauses. (The Supreme Court declared such clauses unconstitutional in 1915.)

Southern legislatures also passed laws establishing strict social segregation. Blacks were forbidden to mingle with whites in railroad cars, buses, trolleys, passenger terminals, and other public facilities. Laws required blacks to drink from separate water fountains and sit in separate sections in theaters.

These Jim Crow* laws, as the segregation codes were called, received important support in 1896 when the Supreme Court decided the case of *Plessy* v. *Ferguson*. In that case, the Court ruled that segregation was legal as long as blacks were given "equal but separate" facilities. In other words, a state could require that blacks and whites sit in separate railroad cars if the railroad provided equal accommodations for members

---

*Jim Crow was a black stage character, created by a white song-and-dance man in 1830. The character conveyed an unfavorable impression of black people.

of both races. Despite the Court's ruling, however, the facilities for blacks, though separate, were rarely equal.

Sparked by racial hatred, lynch law and mob rule competed with justice in many parts of the United States. During the 1890s almost 200 people a year were lynched in the nation. Four fifths of the lynchings took place in the South, and most lynching victims in all areas of the country were black. Mark Twain, for one, was so shocked by the violence that he wrote an essay titled, "The United States of Lyncherdom."

The Black Response

Faced with segregation and violence, black Americans searched for a solution to their plight. Some looked to the West as a land of opportunity. In the years following 1877, approximately 200,000 blacks moved West, many homesteading in Kansas or Oklahoma.

Blacks who chose to remain in the South pursued a variety of occupations. The majority continued to be sharecroppers and tenant farmers. Others worked at skilled trades such as carpentry, masonry, plastering, and painting, but even fewer opportunities existed in these areas than before the war. A few blacks overcame the difficulties of raising capital and founded their own businesses. Most notable was the North Carolina Mutual Life Insurance Company,

organized in 1898. It soon became the largest black-owned business in the world.

Black Americans increasingly relied on each other for support in these difficult times. Black schools and churches, established during Reconstruction, continued to grow during the 1880s and 1890s. Fraternal lodges, mutual aid societies, and groups like the National Negro Business League, an association of black business people founded in 1900, all responded to the needs of black citizens.

Booker T. Washington and Practical Education

One of the most prominent black leaders during these years was Booker T. Washington. Born a slave, Washington was determined to improve his economic status after the war. He enrolled at Hampton Normal and Industrial Institute of Virginia, a school established by the Freedman's Bureau to help blacks learn trades, such as teaching and mechanics.

Washington decided to spread the Hampton ideal of practical education. In 1881 he founded the Tuskegee Institute in Alabama. Tuskegee attracted hundreds of young blacks seeking vocational training. Tuskegee also sponsored the research of the distinguished black scientist George Washington Carver. Carver, who began teaching

Thousands of blacks moved west in the late 1800s to escape racial segregation and violence. This family homesteaded a farm in Kansas in 1885.

Booker T. Washington attended the Hampton Institute in Virginia. The institute was founded after the Civil War to provide a practical education for newly freed blacks. Above, Hampton students work in a science laboratory.

at Tuskegee in 1896, discovered hundreds of uses for southern agricultural products.

Throughout his career, Booker T. Washington insisted that conditions in the South made political equality for blacks an impossible goal. He suggested that blacks ignore social equality and focus on achieving economic success. "Through the dairy farm, the truck garden, the trades, and commercial life . . . the negro is to find his way to the enjoyment of all his rights," he advised. Even without the vote, Washington noted, blacks had that "little green ballot," money, which could be deposited at the teller's window, where "no one will throw it out or refuse to count it."

Washington's message of conciliation and compromise found its fullest expression in a speech he gave before an Atlanta business convention in 1895. He assured white business and political leaders that blacks were loyal to the southern way of life. Because of that loyalty, Washington maintained, black citizens should have a chance to earn a decent living in the South. Washington's speech, in which he abandoned social and political equality and asked for prosperity, is often referred to as the Atlanta Compromise.

W.E.B. Du Bois Answers

While Booker T. Washington advocated a policy of adjustment to segregated society, another black leader recommended vigorous protest against Jim Crow laws. William E. B. Du Bois grew up in Massachusetts and studied at Fisk and Harvard universities. He was the first black to graduate from Harvard with a Ph.D. degree. Du Bois began teaching economics and history at Atlanta University in 1896, about the time that Washington's views were receiving wide publicity.

The young Du Bois disagreed with Washington's advice to black Americans. Blacks, he argued, should fight for the right to vote and the right to enjoy equality of opportunity. In a book entitled *The Souls of Black Folks*, published in 1903, Du Bois attacked Washington for abandoning the goal of equal rights. "Negroes must insist continually," Du Bois maintained, "that voting is necessary to proper manhood, that color discrimination is barbarism, and that black boys need education as well as white boys."

Inspired by Washington, Du Bois, and others, southern blacks made slow but genuine economic progress. By 1900 one out of five owned a home, and the combined worth of black farms totaled almost $500 million. While less that 5 percent of blacks could read in 1865, approximately 56 percent were literate in 1900. By 1915 blacks in the South owned 30,000 businesses, including grocery and drug stores, dress shops, sawmills, banks, and insurance companies.

Yet there was no denying that the aspirations of black Americans in the South and the North were stifled by segregation and discrimination. The road to full political and social equality stretched far into the future.

SECTION REVIEW

1. Identify: "solid South," Jim Crow laws, *Plessy* v. *Ferguson*, Booker T. Washington, Atlanta Compromise, W.E.B. Du Bois.

2. Define: disenfranchise, poll tax, grandfather clause.

3. List three ways in which southern blacks were discouraged from voting.

4. List four ways in which Jim Crow laws discriminated against blacks in the South.

5. What kind of training was offered at Tuskegee Institute?

6. According to W.E.B. Du Bois, in his book entitled *The Souls of Black Folks*, what rights should black Americans fight for?

7. **Critical Thinking** How would Booker T. Washington's ideas be received today? Why?

4 The Populist Crusade

As long as the economy continued to prosper, reformers' demands for change had little appeal. In the mid-1880s, however, the economic problems of farmers in the West and the South sparked what came to be known as the Populist movement. Beginning as local alliances of farmers, it eventually grew into a nationwide third party that challenged the traditional two-party system.

Roots of Discontent

Farmers in the 1870s and 1880s found it increasingly difficult to make a living in the United States. Most were producing more than ever before, but the prices they received were declining. The increased production of American farmers was accompanied by a similar growth of agricultural production in Australia, South America, and Canada. With so much food on the world market, prices dropped. Some farmers realized that overproduction was a major cause of low prices. Mary Lease, a fiery Kansas reformer, expressed their frustration.

> We were told two years ago to go to work and raise a big crop, that was all we needed. We went to work and plowed and planted; the rains fell, the sun shone, nature smiled, and we raised the big crop they told us to; and what came of it? Eight-cent corn, ten-cent oats, two-cent beef, and no price at all for butter and eggs—that's what came of it.

Farmers suffered further when credit was hard to get, as it was during the 1880s and 1890s. They needed to borrow money to buy seed and machinery, then pay back their debts once crops were harvested and sold. A poor crop often meant farmers could not pay back their loans. In the West, especially, farmers had borrowed extensively to buy the large tracts of land needed to make farming profitable. Consequently, in all parts of the country farmers bore the burden of debt.

Being in debt was a special hardship during these years because the economy was experiencing *deflation*, that is, the price of goods and services was dropping. As a result, the dollar of 1886 bought more than that of 1876. Farmers who borrowed money one year and paid it back several years later found that the money they paid back was worth more than the money they had borrowed.

Furthermore, most farmers were angry at the railroads that shipped their grain to market. The farmers claimed, quite rightly in many cases, that the rates the railroads charged in the West, where they had a monopoly, were two or three times higher than rates charged in the East.

These hardships were aggravated by several natural disasters that struck during the late 1880s. Hard winters and summer droughts destroyed cattle and crops in the

425

All but the very young members of farm families worked to make ends meet. Several generations of women in this Alabama family are spinning and weaving.

West. In the South floods in the lower Mississippi Valley ruined much land.

Organizing for Action

By the 1870s farmers had begun banding together to deal with their problems. In 1867 Oliver Kelley founded an association known as the Patrons of Husbandry, popularly called the *Grange*. Kelley's organization grew slowly at first, but by 1874 over 14,000 local grange associations had been started.

Kelley considered his organization a social one, designed to overcome the isolation and loneliness of rural life, but soon Grangers began to campaign for political causes. In midwestern states their influence helped to create state railroad commissions that came to regulate freight rates.

The Grange also acted to boost farm profits. Most farmers sold their harvested grain to distributors, who for a fee stored the grain in giant elevators and arranged to ship it to market. Grangers tried to eliminate the distributors by forming cooperatives. The cooperatives built their own grain elevators and marketed the grain themselves without charging a large fee for profit. Stores were established to buy farm machinery and sell it to members at low prices.

The Grange was strongest in the Midwest and in Kentucky and Missouri. But even in these areas, the organization became less active in the late 1870s as the economy recovered from the depression of 1873. As conditions worsened again in the mid-1880s, other protest organizations grew rapidly, especially in the South and the West.

The Northwestern Farmers' Alliance, established in 1880, represented farmers in the Midwest. Its largest membership was in the Dakotas and Kansas. Most prominent among the southern groups was the Southern Farmers' Alliance. The alliance had existed in Texas since 1875, but after 1886, under the direction of Charles W. Macune, an energetic Methodist preacher, it spread throughout the South. At its height, the alliance claimed as many as 3 million members, including small landowners and tenant farmers. At the same time, a separate Colored Farmers' National Alliance represented the interests of over a million black farmers.

The alliances adopted many of the Grangers' techniques. They organized cooperatives to purchase equipment and market crops. They began newspapers and lecture bureaus to spread their ideas. Increasingly, reformers in both the South and the West came to believe that if farmers were to prosper, political action was needed to change national policies.

The Ocala Platform

In 1889 a large part of the Northwestern Alliance joined with the Southern Alliance to form the National Farmers' Alliance. The following year, the organization met in a convention at Ocala, Florida, and created a program for political reform. The Ocala Platform, as it was called, outlined the reformers' major goals.

Chief among these was the demand that the government help the farmers out of their credit bind. Farmers had to sell their crops at harvest time in order to pay back loans for seed and machinery. If prices were low at that time, farmers could not make enough money to pay back the loans and their debts grew.

The Ocala Platform suggested that the government set up regional subtreasuries that would lend farmers up to 80 percent of the local market value of their crops. Thus farmers would receive the cash they needed and be able to store their agricultural products in warehouses or granaries until the market price rose.

The Ocala Platform advocated government action to discourage deflation. The government, it maintained, should increase the amount of money in circulation. It could do this in part by minting silver coins. The increase in the money supply would tend to inflate the currency and would work to the advantage of debtors.

The Ocala Platform also argued that government actions were unfairly burdening the farmer and landowner while aiding wealthy manufacturers. High tariffs protected domestic manufactured products from competition with cheaper European goods. Farmers then had to pay higher prices for the protected products. Yet they were forced to sell their agricultural products in the international market without any government protection similar to the tariff.

Furthermore, most government taxes were based on the amount of land a person owned. The Ocala Platform recommended that wealth, not land, be taxed. It proposed a *graduated personal income tax*, that is, the tax rate would be proportional to a person's income. Persons with higher incomes would pay a higher rate. Finally, the Ocala Platform

called for strict regulation of the railroads. If regulation failed to work, the National Farmers' Alliance recommended that the government take over the railroads and run them fairly.

Birth of the Populist Party

During the 1890 elections members of the National Farmers' Alliance worked to elect representatives to Congress. In the South, where the Democratic party dominated, farmers demanded that Democratic candidates publicly support reform measures in return for the farmers' votes. In the West many farmers decided to form their own independent parties.

Candidates sympathetic to agrarian reform enjoyed great success in the election of 1890. In the South the farmers' movement helped elect four governors, 44 representatives, and three senators. In the West, Kansas and South Dakota each elected a reform senator, and Nebraska and Kansas elected several reform representatives.

However, southern reformers were shocked to find that of all the "reform" Democrats they elected, only Tom Watson of Georgia continued to support agrarian reform once in office. Watson, a fiery rebel, left the Democratic party and formed his own "People's Party." A number of western reformers in Congress also backed Watson and began to put together a third-party national organization.

The Populist party, as the new party was generally called, met in Omaha, Nebraska, in 1892 to nominate a presidential ticket. This was no ordinary convention. From all over came farmers, cattle ranchers, miners, small-town newspaper editors—virtually anyone who was tired of the old parties and looking for change.

Many of the convention delegates appeared in broad-brimmed hats and dusty boots. Their leaders had nicknames like "Sockless Socrates" Simpson of Kansas, "Calamity" Weller of Iowa, and "Cyclone" Davis of Texas. But regardless of how rustic these people appeared to eastern reporters, their demands for action were clear.

The Populists finally agreed on two former Civil War generals as candidates, James B. Weaver of Iowa for President and James G. Field of Virginia for Vice-President. Throughout the campaign, the Populists

Kansas orator and author Mary Lease was among the most articulate spokespersons for the Populist cause. Populists represented a broad segment of American society, including farmers, small-town businesspeople, and others who felt squeezed by the power of large monopolies.

continued to support the platform formulated at Ocala.

Democrat Grover Cleveland won the election of 1892 and returned for a second term as President after being out of office four years. Yet the Populists did surprisingly well for a new party. Their national ticket received over a million popular votes and 22 electoral votes (from Kansas, Colorado, Idaho, Nevada, and North Dakota). As 1893 began, there were high hopes that the demand for reform would continue to grow.

SECTION REVIEW

1. Identify: National Farmers' Alliance, Ocala Platform, Populist party.
2. Define: deflation, Grange, graduated personal income tax.
3. List three problems faced by American farmers in the last half of the nineteenth century.
4. Name four reform goals outlined in the Ocala Platform.
5. How was the election of 1892 significant for the Populist party?
6. **Critical Thinking** How was the Populist crusade similar to the labor movement?

5 The Decline of Populism

The pressure for reform that surfaced in the 1892 elections grew even stronger when depression struck the nation the following year. The Populists looked forward to still greater success in the 1896 elections. Yet within five years of their surge in 1892, the Populist movement would exhaust itself.

The Depression of 1893

Within a few days of his inauguration in 1893, President Grover Cleveland found himself face to face with a financial collapse that sent the nation into the worst depression it had yet experienced. The collapse began when the Philadelphia and Reading Railroad went bankrupt. Panicked investors sold stock, and prices fell on the New York Stock Exchange. Worried bank officers demanded that loans be repaid, but companies were in no position to make good on their debts. One by one, other major railroads declared bankruptcy, including the Erie, the Union Pacific, and the Santa Fe.

The situation at the end of 1893 was grim. About 500 banks had failed and 1,500 businesses had gone bankrupt. Nearly 3 million workers were left unemployed by the business failures. Men and women who still had jobs had to accept drastic cuts in their wages.

President Cleveland strongly believed that the depression had been caused by allowing silver to circulate as part of the currency. Most economists today believe that government silver policies did little to either harm or benefit the economy, but Cleveland's belief and the actions he took provoked a political tempest.

Controversy Over Silver

The silver question had been the subject of heated debate for many years. Until 1873 the United States government had minted gold and silver coins and had printed paper money backed by gold and silver. In 1873 Congress passed the Coinage Act, which declared that henceforth gold alone would be minted and used to back paper money. The act effectively reduced the amount of money in circulation and thus contributed to the deflation of the period.

Farmers, as you have read, were hurt by deflation, and they demanded that silver be minted in order to increase the supply of money. Silver miners in the West also wanted to see the government buy silver for coins. This was especially true after discovery of new deposits in the 1870s drove down the price of silver.

In 1878 Congress responded to such demands by passing the Bland-Allison Act, which required the government to buy a set amount of silver each year to be minted into coins. Then in 1890, partly in reaction to pressure from the National Farmers' Alliance, Congress passed the Sherman Silver Purchase Act. The act increased the amount of silver that had to be purchased yearly and allowed the treasury to issue paper money backed by silver.

The Sherman Silver Purchase Act had a limited impact on the money supply, but Cleveland blamed its passage for the onset of depression in 1893. He believed that a currency based on both silver and gold, resulted in a decline in the value of gold. In his opinion, this decline in turn weakened the confidence of the business community, discouraged new investment, and created unemployment. Like many business people of the day, he maintained that a *gold standard*, or currency based solely on gold, was necessary for a healthy economic climate.

Consequently, President Cleveland wanted to do away with the Sherman Silver Purchase Act, which he once called a "dangerous and reckless experiment" in monetary reform. In 1893 Cleveland achieved his goal when Congress repealed the Sherman Act. Yet the depression continued.

Coxey's Army

As the depression deepened in 1894 with no relief in sight, more and more people blamed the President's policies. Among Cleveland's most vocal critics was an Ohio stone-quarry owner named Jacob Coxey. Over the years, Coxey had prospered, but now, like the Populists, he believed that something had to be done for the millions of unemployed. He proposed that the government begin a massive road-construction program to provide work relief. If the treasury issued $500 million in new money, Coxey argued, it would create inflation, stimulate the economy, and pay for the road construction.

Cleveland rejected all such schemes, as did Congress. Coxey angrily retorted that if Washington would not listen, he and his supporters would "send a petition to Washington with boots on." Over 500 followers

A hostile cartoonist in 1891 labeled the Populists "A Party of Patches." The cartoonist portrays the Populist party as a hastily stitched patchwork of dreamers and dangerous radicals. Several Populist leaders are shown floating along in the ramshackle balloon.

A PARTY OF PATCHES.
Grand Balloon Ascension—Cincinnati, May 20th, 1891.

marched from Massillon, Ohio, Coxey's home town, to Washington, D. C. Along the way, sympathetic crowds turned out to cheer the marchers, who became known as Coxey's Army.

When Coxey's Army arrived in Washington, it did not receive a pleasant welcome. The violence of labor strikes like the one at Carnegie's Homestead plant (see page 410) had led some government leaders to fear that revolution might be at hand. Although Coxey's intentions were peaceful, police arrested him along with other leaders and dispersed his followers.

The question of coining silver was a hotly contested issue at the Democratic convention of 1896. President Cleveland was committed to the gold standard, but western and southern Democrats demanded the unlimited coinage of silver. William Jennings Bryan warned against the gold standard. "You shall . . . not crucify mankind upon a cross of gold," he declared. Cartoonists—both for and against Bryan—had a field day with the "cross of gold" image. This cartoon attacks Bryan for using a Biblical image to make his point.

THE SACRILEGIOUS CANDIDATE.

The Democrats Divide

Coxey's march demonstrated the depth of public discontent. President Cleveland also found growing opposition within his own party. Many southern and western Democrats disagreed with Cleveland's commitment to the gold standard. The President's low standing was reflected in the comment of Democratic Governor "Pitchfork" Ben Tillman of South Carolina: "I haven't got words to say what I think of that old bag of beef."

When the Democratic presidential nominating convention met in 1896, southern and western Democrats angrily outvoted Cleveland's eastern supporters. The party platform adopted many of the Populists' goals, including unlimited coinage of silver, a lower tariff, and an income tax.

In the midst of the debate on this issue, a dramatic orator from Nebraska, William Jennings Bryan, held the delegates spellbound. "We have petitioned and our petitions have been scorned; we have entreated, and our entreaties have been disregarded; we have begged, and they have mocked when our calamity came. We beg no longer; we entreat no more; we petition no more. We defy them!"

Referring to Cleveland's support of the gold standard, Bryan thundered, "You shall not press down upon the brow of labor this crown of thorns, you shall not crucify mankind upon a cross of gold!" The delegates roared their approval.

Bryan was nominated as the presidential candidate over the strong objections of Cleveland's supporters. Though only 36 years old, the Nebraskan was already well known throughout the South and West as the leading spokesman for the prosilver faction. He supported the Democratic party platform wholeheartedly.

The Populist party now faced a difficult choice. Many members had hoped to succeed as an independent third party, but the Democrats had stolen much of their thunder by nominating Bryan. Populist leaders wondered whether they too should support him. At their own convention, many Populists wanted to nominate a different candidate, but finally Tom Watson persuaded the delegates to place Bryan at the top of their ticket as the man most likely to have a chance against the Republicans. Thus Bryan was the candidate of two parties.

The Election of 1896

With the Democratic party divided, the Republicans sensed victory. They picked Senator William McKinley from Ohio as their presidential candidate. McKinley's first-ballot victory at the convention was the product of careful groundwork laid by Marcus "Mark" Hanna, a coal, iron, and shipping tycoon from Cleveland, Ohio.

The campaign that followed presented the voters with a dramatic contrast in style and policy. "Billy" Bryan moved at a hectic pace, traveling 18,000 miles (28,800 kilometers) to make over 600 speeches. He appeared before almost 5 million people. Always his themes reflected the Populist creed: regulate the railroads, curb the power of monopolies, and establish a currency backed by silver. The Bryan campaign gained the endorsements of reformers Henry George and Edward Bellamy, as well as labor leaders Eugene V. Debs of the Railway Union and Samuel Gompers of the AFL.

McKinley, for his part, remained in his home town of Canton, Ohio, throughout the campaign. Occasionally he read speeches from his front porch to admirers who came to town to hear him. Such speeches contained quiet assurances that the nation's economic system was sound and that the gold standard was best for the country.

Meanwhile, Mark Hanna worked hard behind the scenes to round up campaign contributions from the trusts, railroad owners, large banks, and industrialists. Hanna raised well over $3 million, ten times as much as Bryan's campaign had. With so much money at his disposal, Hanna sent Republican speakers across the country to stump for their candidate. He distributed some 250 million pieces of literature.

McKinley won the election by 600,000 popular votes. Bryan carried the South and most of the West, but McKinley took the populous Northeast. Bryan failed to capture the northern labor vote. Without support from the industrial sections of the country, the southern and western coalition had been unable to carry a presidential election.

The Populists' Fate

Bryan's defeat marked the end of the Populist movement. In part, the party declined because of a failure of morale. The agricultural reformers had done their best, carrying

Major Events	
1867	The Grange founded
1872	Crédit Mobilier scandal uncovered
1875	Southern Farmers' Alliance founded in Texas
1877	*Munn v. Illinois*
1878	Bland-Allison Act passed
1880	Northwestern Farmers' Alliance established
1881	President Garfield assassinated; Tuskegee Institute founded
1883	Civil Service Act passed
1886	*Wabash, St. Louis, & Pacific Railway Company v. Illinois*
1887	Interstate Commerce Act passed
1889	National Farmers' Alliance formed
1890	Sherman Antitrust Act passed; Sherman Silver Purchase Act passed
1892	Populist party formed
1893	Severe economic depression begins; Sherman Silver Purchase Act repealed
1894	Coxey's Army marches on Washington
1895	*United States v. E. C. Knight Co.*
1896	*Plessy v. Ferguson*

every state west of the Mississippi and in the South. Yet they had fallen short. Furthermore, the Democrats had lured many Populists back into the Democratic party.

Improved economic conditions also hurt the Populist movement. In the first three years of McKinley's term, prosperity slowly returned to the nation. A wheat crop failure abroad in 1897 stimulated demand for United States farm exports. Gold discoveries in Alaska helped expand the treasury's gold reserves. Ironically, the increase in the gold supply inflated the currency—which was exactly what the silver campaigners had been demanding. With conditions improving, the Populist drive lost its momentum.

Prosperity made McKinley's business principles appear sound. On the President's recommendation, Congress passed the Gold Standard Act of 1900 to put the nation back on the gold standard. The quiet acceptance of gold as the single basis of currency signaled the end of the long-standing controversy. Few people objected when Congress passed even higher tariff rates for industry in the Dingley Tariff Bill of 1897. In the next decade, other voices of reform would be raised, but by the time prosperity returned and the nineteenth century ended, the Populists' dramatic moment on the national scene had passed.

SECTION REVIEW

1. **Identify:** Coinage Act, Bland-Allison Act, Sherman Silver Purchase Act, Coxey's Army, William Jennings Bryan, William McKinley, Mark Hanna.
2. **Define:** gold standard.
3. According to President Cleveland, what caused the depression of 1983?
4. Which two parties nominated William Jennings Bryan as their candidate in 1896?
5. What happened to the Populist movement after Bryan's defeat in 1896?
6. **Critical Thinking** How was the election of 1896 a victory for the Hamiltonian view of society over the Jeffersonian view?

Chapter 22 Review

In Perspective

The years after the Civil War were a time of political corruption in much of the nation. The lure of great wealth tarnished the reputations of both Congress and the presidency, particularly during President Grant's administration.

The abuses of power and wealth eventually led to reform efforts. The Civil Service Act, the Interstate Commerce Act, and the Sherman Antitrust Act were passed to curb some major abuses in government and industry. The last two laws proved difficult to enforce, however. Both the railroads and the giant trusts found ways to evade the new regulations.

In the South the conservative Democrats consolidated their control of state governments. During the 1890s southern state governments began to pass laws that discriminated against blacks. In reaction, thousand of blacks moved west to homestead. Others sought self-improvement as encouraged by Booker T. Washington. Followers of W.E.B. DuBois thought they should fight for their rights.

American farmers, burdened by debt and falling farm prices during the late 1800s, began to organize to improve their lives. First they founded the Grange and then the National Farmers' Alliance. Eventually in 1892 farmers became part of a major third-party movement. The Populist party saw some success in the 1892 elections, and in 1896 many of their proposals were adopted by the Democrats. Many Populist political and economic goals were eventually enacted into law.

Vocabulary

On a separate sheet of paper, write the word or words that best complete each of the following sentences.

1. The practice of giving out government jobs as favors was the ____.
2. A (An) ____ was a corporation that owned stock in other corporations in order to control them.
3. People denied the vote were ____.
4. ____ results in lower prices for goods and services.
5. A (An) ____ is paid for the right to vote.

Chapter Checkup

1. (a) What was the reputation of the Senate and the House of Representatives during the Gilded Age? (b) Why was Congress, with such a reputation, able to dominate the presidency? Give examples.

2. (a) How did state governments try to regulate railroads in the 1870s? (b) How did the Supreme Court rule on the states' power to regulate railroads in 1875? In 1886? (c) What were the provisions of the Interstate Commerce Act?

3. (a) How did Booker T. Washington urge southern blacks to respond to segregation? Why did he favor this response? (b) What response did W.E.B. Du Bois recommend? Why did he favor such action?

4. (a) Why did farmers find it increasingly difficult to make a living in the late 1800s? (b) What organizations did they form to deal with their problems? (c) What methods did these organizations use to help farmers?

5. (a) Why did farmers and miners favor the coinage of silver? (b) How did Congress react to pressure from the two groups? (c) Why did Cleveland favor a gold standard?

Critical Thinking

1. **Analyzing** (a) Why did Mark Twain label the decades after the Civil War the Gilded Age? (b) In what ways do you think it was a Gilded Age? Give examples.

2. **Evaluating** Why do you think the views of Booker T. Washington were more popular among white southerners than the views of W.E.B. Du Bois?

Developing Basic Skills

1. **Analyzing Political Cartoons** Political cartoons are valuable pieces of historical evidence. By analyzing them, you can learn more about the political issues of a historical period. Study the cartoon on page 419 and answer the following questions: (a) Which economic development is the cartoon illustrating? (b) What impact does the cartoonist think this development is having on the people of the United States? (c) Do you think the cartoonist favors or opposes trusts? Why?

2. **Comparing** Make a chart with three columns. Label the first column Reform Actions. Label the second column Purpose and the third column Degree of Success. List the reform actions you learned about in this chapter in the first column. In the second column describe the problem the action was to solve. In the third column note how successful each of the actions was in the late 1800s. Then answer the following questions: (a) What problems were the reformers trying to solve? (b) How successful were they? (c) Why do you think this was the case?

See page 830 for suggested readings.

Writer's Handbook

Evaluating a Source of Information

The quality of your research will depend in large part on the accuracy and impartiality of your sources. To help evaluate a book, check the author's educational background and area of interest. This information often can be found on the dust jacket or back cover of the book. Look at the date of publication on the copyright page. Recent books may have the benefit of more up-to-date research. Also look at who published the book. Major publishers and university presses are usually careful about the quality of the books they publish. Note whether the book cites sources and includes a bibliography.

Your library is a good source of information about periodicals. The publication, *Magazines for Libraries*, reviews magazines for quality and possible bias.

If you are consulting a newspaper, you will want to use a newspaper of record such as the *New York Times*, the *Washington Post*, the *Saint Louis Post-Dispatch*, or the *Los Angeles Times*. A newspaper of record reports major events in detail and carries the full text of important speeches and press conferences.

Practice: Using the guidelines above, review a magazine or book from your library. Tell why you think this book or magazine would or would not be a good source of historical information for a research paper.

23

Toward an Urban Age

(1865–1914)

Washington St., Indianapolis, at Dusk
by Theodore Groll

Chapter Outline

1 *Beginning of an Urban Age*

2 *Immigrants and Cities*

3 *An Urban Way of Life*

4 *A Changing Society: Problems and Prospects*

When Indianapolis became the capital of Indiana in 1825, its population was less than 1,000. With the completion of the National Road in 1830 and the construction of railroads during the 1850s, the population of the city grew, reaching over 18,000 by 1860.

Like many American cities, Indianapolis experienced its most dramatic growth during the last half of the nineteenth century. It served as a market for nearby farms and as a center of new industry. By 1900 nearly 170,000 people lived there.

Many American cities expanded rapidly during the late 1800s as the United States entered an urban age. Transportation, industry, and immigration were among the factors that contributed to urban growth. Developing cities were to provide jobs, entertainment, and excitement for millions of Americans. Yet they were also the source of new, often bewildering, social and political problems.

			"New" immigration increases				
1865	1875		1885	1895		1905	1915
1869 Tweed Ring in New York City	**1871** Chicago becomes boom town	**1882** Chinese Exclusion Act passed	**1889** Jane Addams founds Hull House	**1893** Columbian Exposition opens		**1900** New York City grows to 3.5 million people	**1910** 8 million women hold jobs

1 Beginning of an Urban Age

Although cities had played an important role in the development of the nation since colonial days, before the Civil War most Americans lived on farms or in villages. After the war, that pattern shifted so rapidly that bewildering new problems faced the nation.

The Rapid Growth of Cities

The explosive growth of cities was fueled by the expansion of industry in the late nineteenth century. Manufacturers built new plants in cities, where large numbers of workers could be found. Cities could provide transportation facilities needed to move raw materials and finished products. The additional jobs in turn drew increasing numbers of people to urban centers.

In 1880 less than 25 percent of all Americans were living in cities. Then between 1880 and 1900 the urban population doubled. New York City grew from less than 2 million residents in 1880 to nearly 3.5 million in 1900. The population of Chicago more than tripled, rising from 440,000 to 1.7 million. The tilt toward the cities was sharpest in the Northeast, as people left farms for city jobs. In the last 20 years of the nineteenth century, 60 percent of the rural townships of the Northeast lost population.

By 1900 nearly 40 percent of the 70 million people living in the United States resided in cities. Philadelphia had a population of more than a million. St. Louis, Boston, and Baltimore had populations exceeding 500,000. Smaller cities like San Francisco, Milwaukee, Cleveland, and Detroit were growing rapidly. The majority of Americans still lived in rural areas, but the trend was away from the country and toward cities. That trend would continue well into the twentieth century.

Urban growth was further spurred by the arrival of men and women from abroad. In the last half of the nineteenth century, immigrants poured into American cities. By 1890, 68 percent of Chicago's population were foreign born and another 10 percent were American-born children of immigrants. Indeed Chicago perhaps more than any other city symbolized the growth of an urban America.

Chicago: Symbol of an Urban Age

Early in 1893, a crew of 7,000 workers led by architect Daniel Burnham labored around the clock through the rain, sleet, ice, and snow of a Chicago spring to meet a May 1 deadline. At times their workhorses floundered belly deep in mud. The hectic pace paid off, however, and on May 1, 1893, a fair marking the four-hundredth anniversary of Columbus's discovery of the New World was ready for the public.

Congress had awarded Chicago the honor of playing host to the Columbian Exposition, which was billed as a celebration of American progress and industry. The choice of Chicago was apt, for Chicago typified both the vitality and the problems of America's developing cities.

■ *The total population of the United States grew rapidly in the late 1800s. As the graph indicates, the population of cities and towns grew faster in the 1880s and 1890s than did the population of rural areas.*

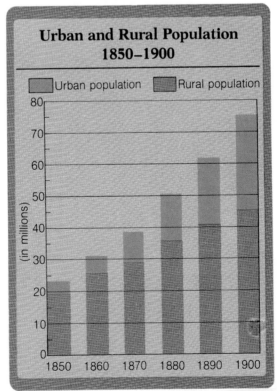

Urban and Rural Population 1850–1900

Source: *Historical Statistics of the United States*

SKILL LESSON

Urban Growth: Interpreting Thematic Maps

As you have learned in Chapter 5 (see page 79), maps are a valuable source of information for the study of American history. Many of the maps you have studied in this text have been general reference maps. They provide basic information such as the location of cities, rivers, or states. Other maps show the distribution of such things as population, rainfall, or crop production. These special maps are called *thematic maps*. The key is particularly important on a thematic map because it explains the meaning of symbols used. To practice using thematic maps, study the maps below and on page 437. Then follow these steps.

1. **Decide what is shown on the maps.** (a) What is the topic of the maps? (b) What do the circles represent? (c) What do the areas shaded orange represent?

2. **Read the information on the maps.** (a) How many cities appear on the 1860 map?

(b) On the 1900 map? (c) Which cities had a population between 1 and 5 million in 1860? (d) In 1900? (e) Which of the cities that appear on both maps grew in population between 1860 and 1900? (f) Which areas of the country were industrialized in 1860? (g) To which areas had industry spread by 1900? (h) Which cities are located on important waterways?

3. **Draw conclusions about the historical period being studied.** Use the text and the maps to answer the following questions: (a) What relationship is there between industry and urban growth? (b) What relationship can you see between the location of cities and important waterways? (c) In which areas of the country did cities develop between 1860 and 1900? (d) In which areas was there little urban growth? Why?

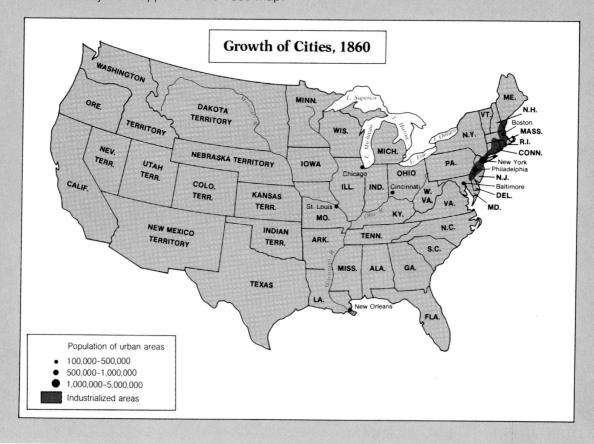

Growth of Cities, 1860

Population of urban areas
- 100,000–500,000
- 500,000–1,000,000
- 1,000,000–5,000,000
- Industrialized areas

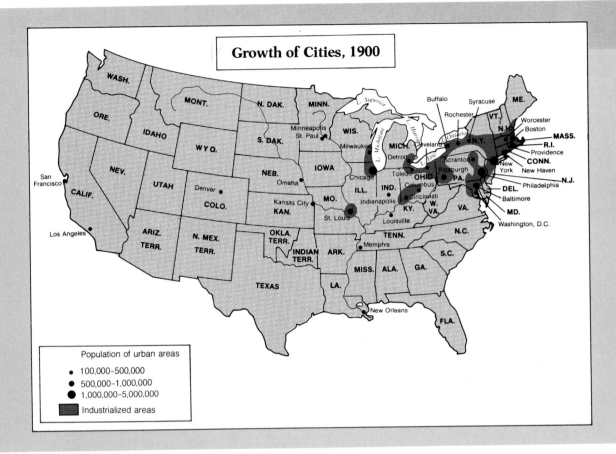

Growth of Cities, 1900

Population of urban areas
- 100,000–500,000
- 500,000–1,000,000
- 1,000,000–5,000,000

Industrialized areas

Chicago, located on the southern shore of Lake Michigan, had grown rapidly. A central geographic location had made the city a transportation hub. Railroads connected the city with the rest of the nation. Ships moved raw materials and finished products in and out of the port on Lake Michigan. The excellent transportation network and access to raw materials attracted industry. Each new industry in turn lured to the city manufacturers and people seeking jobs.

Pioneering industrialists and manufacturers in Chicago made fortunes in meatpacking, merchandising, and steel. More than 200 self-made millionaires lived in grand style in mansions lining the lake front.

Gradually manufacturing and industry pushed the city outward, and politicians began to annex nearby towns, extending the city boundaries. Communities that had been independent were absorbed into Chicago. When the city's transportation system reached these outlying areas, some wealthy residents and members of the small middle class moved out of the central city, leaving the downtown section to the poor and to commerce and industry.

Problems of a Growing City

Chicago's rapid growth created problems as well as fortunes. In contrast to the stately mansions on the lake front were the crowded tenements of the Chicago slums. There the poor citizens of the city lived in squalid conditions, often without even the most basic necessities, such as running water. Diseases like typhoid regularly raged through entire neighborhoods.

Tens of thousands of immigrants clustered in separate ethnic neighborhoods. Some sections became all Polish, some all Bohemian, Greek, Russian, or Chinese. Black Americans also moved to Chicago from the South and settled in neighborhoods of their own.

Rich and poor alike endured some of the problems created by the city's rapid growth. As late as 1890, only one third of Chicago's streets were paved with cobblestones. When rain fell or snow melted, the streets became quagmires of mud. The droppings of thousands of horses pulling wagons, trolleys, and carriages also fouled the city streets. Grease, sewage, and dead animals floated

437

Chicago, 1871

Area of city
Railroad lines

LAKE MICHIGAN

Brickton (Park Ridge)
Elgin
Evanston
Cicero
Chicago
Aurora
South Chicago
Hammond

0 20 Miles
0 30 Kilometers

■ *By 1871, Chicago was a boom town of 300,000 people. By 1900 it had become the major shipping point for the entire Midwest, and its population had surged to 1.7 million.*

like most cities of the day, operated on graft and payoffs. (See page 450). A bribe bought a city contract. Chicagoans nicknamed the members of their city council the "gray wolves." In a popular vaudeville skit, a hostess looked at several city officials sleeping at her feet after an evening's partying. She asked her husband, "Will I wake them?" "Leave them be," he replied. "While they sleep the city's safe."

In 1893, when the Columbian Exposition was amazing 27 million visitors to Chicago, a concerted effort by Americans to deal with the problems of their cities seemed long overdue.

SECTION REVIEW

1. Name two reasons manufacturers built plants in cities.
2. Where was urban growth the fastest?
3. What two means of transportation made Chicago a transportation hub?
4. **Critical Thinking** How were the problems of cities in the late nineteenth century similar to problems of cities today?

down the Chicago River. So many chemicals had to be dumped into the river to purify it that wealthy residents refused to drink from the city water supply.

Rapid urban growth also offered rich opportunity for corrupt politicians. Chicago,

2 Immigrants and Cities

In 1886 France presented the United States with a statue to honor the American spirit of liberty. Joseph Pulitzer, an immigrant from Hungary, promptly launched a campaign in his newspaper to collect nickels and dimes from children and adults to build a base for the statue. Nearly 120,000 people contributed. For millions of immigrants the Statue of Liberty at the entrance to New York Harbor symbolized a welcome to a new life. Most newcomers began that life in America's cities.

The Pull of America

In the five decades after the Civil War a flood of immigrants reached the United States. From 1865 until the turn of the century, 13.5 million people arrived from abroad. Not until the 1920s, when Congress began setting immigration quotas, would the numbers dwindle.

Wars, famine, religious persecution, and overpopulation all prompted people to leave Europe and seek a better life in the United States. Some people left their homelands in search of political or religious freedom. Some left because, in spite of their skills or education, they were unable to find work. In many rural areas of Europe, small plots of land had been so often divided among children and grandchildren that the plots were too small to farm profitably. Younger sons and daughters had to look elsewhere if they wanted to farm their own land.

From the United States came letters that told of a better life. Friends and relatives who had already made the trip wrote home saying that work was available for all and that no one starved in America. One Polish immigrant wrote to relatives back in Europe, "We eat here every day what we get only for Easter in our country." But the passage to that new life was a difficult one.

Passage to the United States

Passage to the United States often cost a life savings. Hotel operators, railroad and steamship companies, and especially ticket agents sometimes cheated immigrants shamelessly. Most of the newcomers bought the cheapest steamship ticket for accommodations in steerage. That gave them space in the noisiest, least comfortable part of the ship, near the engines and the rudder. Packed in like cattle, steerage passengers had little to eat and endured filthy conditions. Consequently, outbreaks of disease were common.

The crowded steerage frequently contained a diverse group of people. Many were poor farmers. Some were schoolmasters unable to find work in Europe, skilled artisans looking for wider opportunities, or musicians and artists eager to see the world. Young men and women with a spirit of adventure were willing to risk traveling into the unknown. At journey's end, there was yet another ordeal to be overcome. A person could be shipped back if he or she failed to pass the medical inspection administered at the port of entry.

After 1890, Ellis Island in New York Harbor served as port of entry for most immigrants. The processing was a dehumanizing, humiliating experience for many. Long lines of people were tagged according to the language they spoke—one color for Greek, another for Italian, another for Armenian, Czech, and so on. Patiently, men, women, and children moved toward the dreaded moment before the immigration inspector.

With hundreds of immigrants to process daily, the overworked inspectors had just two minutes to ask 32 questions and to complete a medical inspection. A newcomer who was found to have a contagious disease would be detained and possibly shipped back home. Furthermore, a person whose last name was Bratkowski might emerge from the processing with the name Brown because the immigration official did not want to struggle with the foreign spelling.

The "New" Immigration

Before the 1880s most immigrants to the United States, some 85 percent, had arrived from Great Britain, Canada, Germany, and Scandinavia. Many of them had been Protestants, and a number spoke English. During the 1880s a dramatic shift occurred. In that decade an average of 500,000 immigrants arrived each year. The new immigrants came increasingly from southern and eastern Europe, from Italy, Poland, Russia, Hungary, and Bohemia.

Between 1865 and 1900, about 13.5 million immigrants arrived in the United States. Most traveled the cheapest way possible: on the steerage decks of jam-packed steamships. The deck of the S S Permland is shown here.

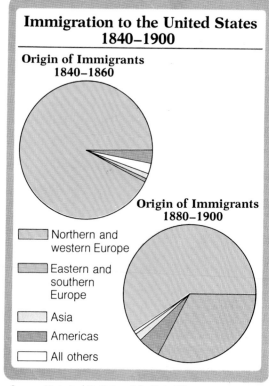

Immigration to the United States 1840–1900

Origin of Immigrants 1840–1860

Origin of Immigrants 1880–1900

- Northern and western Europe
- Eastern and southern Europe
- Asia
- Americas
- All others

Source: *Historical Statistics of the United States*

■ *Before 1880 nearly all immigrants to the United States came from the British Isles and northern Europe. These two circle graphs show the dramatic shift that began after 1880 as more immigrants began to arrive from eastern and southern Europe.*

People in this "new" immigration differed from Americans and from the "old" immigrants from northern and western Europe. The newcomers were often Catholic or Jewish. Their religion, language, and customs made them seem quite strange to many Americans.

The largest number came from Italy. Millions left the impoverished southern part of the country because of drought, economic disaster, and cholera. Three out of four were men whose families stayed behind. Some of these men planned to earn money in the United States and then return to Italy.

In the next largest group were Jews from eastern Europe, mainly Russia. More than 3 million arrived in the United States between 1880 and 1920. The Jewish arrivals fled Europe, not just because of economic hardships, but also to escape religious persecution. For 30 years Jews in Russia and Po-

land had been victims of *pogroms*, violent attacks against Jewish neighborhoods. A Russian Jew reflected on his past sufferings:

> Sympathy for Russia? How ironical it sounds. Am I not despised? Am I not urged to leave? ... Do I not rise daily with ... fear lest the hungry mob attack me ... It is impossible that a Jew should regret leaving Russia.

Jewish immigrants, unlike many Italian immigrants, did not plan to return home. Whole families came to America together.

More than a million Slavs from Russia, the Ukraine, Poland, Croatia, Serbia, Bulgaria, and Bohemia made up the third-largest group of immigrants. Other immigrants arrived from Greece, Portugal, Armenia, and Turkey, and from China and Japan.

Patterns of Settlement

Most of the new immigrants settled in American cities, especially the industrial centers and ports. By 1900 two thirds of the foreign-born people in the United States lived in cities. One third of the residents of Boston and one fourth of the residents of Philadelphia were immigrants. In New York City four out of five residents were either foreign-born or were the children of immigrants.

Italians often became subway workers in New York, stockyard workers in Chicago, miners in Illinois, Michigan, and Minnesota. Those who could afford to buy land often planted small gardens, orchards, or vineyards.

More than two thirds of the Jewish immigrants arrived as skilled workers. They entered New York's clothing industries by the thousands. By 1917, 70 percent of all the workers in the garment trades were Jewish. Other Jewish immigrants became bookbinders, teachers, and store owners.

Poles and other Slavs often moved to midwestern cities or to coal mining towns in Pennsylvania or the Midwest. Germans and Scandinavians frequently bought farms in Iowa, Nebraska, and the Dakotas. Chinese and Japanese immigrants settled on the west coast, usually in California. The influx of immigrants from eastern and southern Europe and from Asia in the late 1800s brought an outburst of nativism, or hatred of foreigners, which was similar in many ways to that of the 1840s. (See Chapter 15.)

Reaction Against Immigrants

Some native-born Americans feared and resented the new immigrants. Their languages, religions, and customs seemed especially strange to Americans who traced their heritage to northern and western Europe. The newcomers also competed for jobs. Desperate to find work, immigrants were often willing to accept lower wages and worse working conditions than American-born workers.

When economic conditions worsened, antiforeign feelings became stronger. Groups such as the American Protective Association urged Congress to bar immigration from certain countries. The American Protective Association, founded in 1887, attracted a million members and preached against Roman Catholic immigrants.

Immigrants faced attacks by some American newspapers. One editorial, for example, charged that the country was being

★ America's Heritage ★

Emma Lazarus and *The New Colossus*

The campaign to raise money to build a pedestal for the Statue of Liberty, a gift from the French, seemed to reach a snag in 1883. The statue was almost completed and ready to be shipped from France, but the pedestal was not nearly finished. The Pedestal Fund Committee then organized a temporary art exhibition to raise funds. Prominent New Yorkers lent paintings, and a number of artists and writers contributed their drawings and letters to be auctioned. After some urging, Emma Lazarus wrote a poem for the occasion.

Emma Lazarus, the daughter of a prominent New York Jewish family, was a crusader for ethnic tolerance. She had worked tirelessly to help the refugees who were streaming into New York City in ever-increasing numbers. She did not usually write patriotic works. But to her, the Statue of Liberty, facing toward the Old World, held out a message of hope to all those uprooted from the land of their birth. Emma Lazarus called her poem "The New Colossus." (The brazen giant referred to in the first line is the Colossus of Rhodes, which once stood in the harbor of Rhodes and was known as one of the seven wonders of the ancient world.)

> Not like the brazen giant of Greek fame,
> With conquering limbs astride from land to land;
> Here at our sea-washed, sunset gates shall stand
> A mighty woman with a torch, whose flame
> Is the imprisoned lightning, and her name

> Mother of Exiles. From her beacon-hand
> Glows world-wide welcome; her mild eyes command
> The air-bridged harbor that twin cities frame.
> "Keep, ancient lands, your storied pomp!" cries she
> With silent lips. "Give me your tired, your poor,
> Your huddled masses yearning to breathe free,
> The wretched refuse of your teeming shore.
> Send these, the homeless, tempest-tost to me
> I lift my lamp beside the golden door!"

The statue became a symbol of a new land waiting for immigrants, a land full of promise for a new beginning.

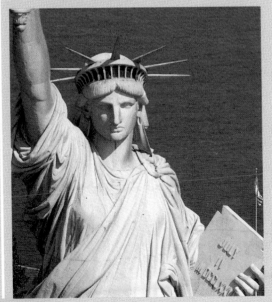

subjected to "an invasion of venomous reptiles ... long-haired, wild-eyed, bad-smelling, atheistic, reckless foreign wretches, who never did a day's work in their lives."

New immigrants also encountered discrimination. Jewish immigrants, for example, were denied entrance to the nation's better universities, and it was difficult for Jews to get office jobs in New York City. In California, Chinese immigrants were subject to physical attacks. Gangs of ruffians routinely terrorized Chinese residents. In the summer of 1877 gangs burned 25 Chinese laundries in San Francisco. Congress yielded to the anti-Chinese feelings in 1882, passing an exclusion act that stopped immigration from China.

Contributions to American Society

Although much attacked, the new immigrants made valuable contributions to American life. They helped build and staff the booming new industries. They laid track, built roads, stitched clothing, made shoes, packed meat. Each group brought to America the traditions of homelands much older than the United States. They added a sparkling diversity to American life.

Immigrants brought to the cities their foods, their songs, their theater, and their literature. Foreign-language newspapers were published in many cities. The immigrants formed choral groups, literary societies, sewing clubs, theater groups, and sports clubs.

When the first attempts were made to start symphony orchestras and opera companies in the growing cities, most of the musicians and virtually all the conductors were foreign born. Italian, German, and Jewish immigrants filled the audiences to hear music they remembered from Europe. Immigrants helped shape the look and feel of nearly every city and made a lasting mark on the evolving urban culture.

Immigrants from southern and eastern Europe provided much of the labor needed to maintain the pace of American industrialization. These workers are laying track near Union Square in New York City.

SECTION REVIEW

1. Define: pogrom.
2. List three reasons many Europeans decided to immigrate to the United States in the years after the Civil War.
3. (a) Where did the largest group of new immigrants come from? (b) Who made up the second-largest group?
4. Where did most immigrants settle?
5. (a) How did bad economic conditions contribute to antiforeign feelings among some Americans? (b) What other factors contributed to these feelings?
6. **Critical Thinking** How has your community been enriched by immigrants?

3 An Urban Way of Life

"We cannot all live in cities," newspaper editor Horace Greeley commented, "yet nearly all seem determined to do so." Young people, he said, were looking for " 'hot and cold water,' baker's bread, the theatre, and the streetcars."

As Greeley noted, the city's lure was not just jobs. It included comforts like piped-in hot water and entertainment like vaudeville. There was always something new to marvel at and talk about: a new steel bridge, a skyscraper, or the latest crime reported in detail in the newspapers. New kinds of stores opened, new sports were played, and other activities unfolded in cities before spreading into rural areas.

Urban Transportation

The urban centers of the east coast had developed as "walking cities." Everything of importance was within walking distance of everything else. Only the rich rode to work in carriages. Everyone else walked. The horse trolley, the electric trolley, and finally the electric railway changed that way of life.

With the new modes of transportation, cities began to expand.

The electric trolley, with its fixed overhead wire, could go twice as fast and carry three times as many passengers as the horse-drawn trolley. By 1895, 800 trolley lines were operating in the United States. The placement of lines for trolleys and electrified railways affected the direction of a city's growth. Shops, housing, and businesses followed the transit lines out from the center of the city.

The new means of transportation did more then take workers to and from the job.

★ American Enterprise ★

Advent of the Streetcar

During the early part of the 1800s, movement in cities was largely limited to the distance one could go on foot. Only those who could afford private carriages were able to travel much beyond the city's boundaries. Poorer citizens lived in crowded tenements within walking distance of their work. Then, about the time of the Civil War, omnibuses, large vehicles that anyone could board for a fee, came into use. The omnibuses, which had come from Europe, were drawn by horses along rails set upon the cobblestone city streets. Americans, coining a new word, called them "streetcars."

Although an improvement, the horse-drawn streetcars were slow, and their range was limited to the power of the horse. Not until the invention of the electric motor did the streetcar really become an effective means of transportation.

One of the most important pioneers of the electric streetcar was Stephen Dudley Field. He had worked with Edison to provide an electric railway at the Chicago Railway Exposition in 1883. Field's most serious problem was how to transmit electricity from a central power station in a crowded city to a moving streetcar without endangering the lives of people in the streets. The problem was solved when a way was found to transmit power along a wire from an overhead trolley. Americans, coining a new phrase, called the electric streetcars "trolleys."

The first extensive trolley system in the United States was built by Frank Julian Sprague in Richmond, Virginia, in 1888. It was an extraordinary feat of organization. Sprague had worked with Thomas Edison and had developed several electrical devices of his own. Leaving Edison, Sprague set up his own company and in 1887 contracted to set up an electric streetcar in Richmond in only 90 days. Sprague had to build 80 motors, equip 40 cars, lay 12 miles of track, and install overhead trolley wires along the whole route. He also had to build and equip an adequate central power plant. Incredibly, Sprague fulfilled his contract!

As new electric trolleys began to extend from cities in all directions, real estate developers went into action. They began promoting "streetcar suburbs" as part of the American way of life. The American dream of owning a home was made possible by the electric streetcar.

People could now easily go for a picnic, to a library, or to the new department stores. With the electric trolley, urban working people gained greater mobility.

Department Stores

A new kind of store had emerged in American cities, the all-purpose department store where a shopper could browse and buy a wide variety of goods. Instead of keeping the best merchandise out of sight, to be brought out only for wealthy customers, these stores invited everyone to look, touch, and buy.

R. H. Macy in New York, John Wanamaker in Philadelphia, Jordan Marsh in Boston, and Marshall Field in Chicago pioneered such stores. They were widely copied elsewhere. The principle was to sell a larger volume of goods at slightly lower prices than smaller shops offered. Department stores also offered credit, free delivery, and a marked price. Shops of an earlier era often did not display prices. Instead customer and salesperson had dickered over the amount to be charged.

F. W. Woolworth took the single-price idea a step further. All goods in his store were marked with a fixed price, usually under a dime. His goods were so inexpensive that people were tempted to buy things they did not need. In Woolworth's new "five and tens" employees were kept busy stocking shelves with goods, rather than trying to sell customers a particular item.

Mass-Circulation Newspapers

Advertising from department stores helped pay for the mass-circulation newspapers that developed in the late nineteenth century. Such advertising brought in enough money to allow publishers to sell their papers cheaply. As circulations grew, advertisers were willing to pay well to reach a million or more readers with a single advertisement.

The mass-circulation newspapers attracted readers with news of crime, sports, and gossip. No paper was more flamboyant than Joseph Pulitzer's New York *World*. Pulitzer bought the newspaper in 1883 and promptly changed the tone and lowered the price. He called it a "people's paper" and charged two cents a copy. Pulitzer was master of devising stunts to attract more readers. Once he sent a reporter, Nellie Bly, on a race around the world and had readers guessing the exact number of days, hours, and minutes her journey would take.

Changing the Face of Cities

As more people and businesses moved to the cities the price of land rose sharply. Innovative architects built upward, gaining more usable space from small parcels of land. One of the first to do so was Louis Sullivan, a Chicago genius who began using steel as the skeleton for the tall buildings known as skyscrapers. (See Chapter 21.) In 1889 Sullivan designed the first all-steel skeleton building, the Auditorium Building in Chicago. A year later, the 26-story World Building was completed in New York. Other Sullivan buildings soon went up in St. Louis and Buffalo. The "race to the skies" in downtowns across the nation was on in earnest.

Retailers, too, sought a new kind of building in which to display their wares. The Cast Iron Palace in New York featured a huge first floor ideal for browsing. Patrons rode to upper floors on the newly invented elevator. Through plate-glass windows shop-

The first five-and-dime store was opened in 1879 in Lancaster, Pennsylvania, by F.W. Woolworth. By the early 1900s F.W. Woolworth and Charles Woolworth had a chain of stores.

This advertising poster depicts an evening of music in a Victorian parlor. Advertisers sought to market goods for the expanding middle class.

pers indulged in a new pastime, window-shopping.

Daniel Burnham was among the first to urge cities to plan their future growth. He spearheaded the development of a long-range plan for Chicago, setting aside park land on the lakefront. Other cities hurried to build parks before all downtown land was paved over. Frederick Law Olmstead designed Central Park in Manhattan and Prospect Park in Brooklyn. Olmstead's parks were laid out to give visitors a sense of being in the country. In this period, communities began to set aside land for botanical gardens, and several started zoos.

Music, Theater, and Art

With so many people, the cities could support leisure activities unavailable in most rural areas. Between 1862 and 1900, New York, Chicago, Pittsburgh, Cincinnati, and Philadelphia established symphony orchestras. In 1883 the Metropolitan Opera House opened in New York.

It was the heyday of vaudeville, with stand-up comedians, singers, dancers, and jugglers. Tickets to plays cost between 25 cents and $1.50, and people crowded the box offices. Plays ranged from fine Shakespearean works to popular but forgettable melodramas. Leading performers from Great Britain toured American cities to wild acclaim from audiences.

An increasingly literate public flocked to new public libraries. Over a period of years, Andrew Carnegie donated $60 million to establish libraries across the country. By 1900 there were about 9,000 public libraries in the United States. Many were in the small towns that still dominated much of the country. Several cities started museums of fine arts beginning in the 1870s. The new museums collected paintings and sculpture from all over the world.

Many of the best American artists, like James McNeill Whistler, preferred to live in Europe. At home, however, major talents were producing important works of art. In Maine, Winslow Homer painted scenes of the coastline, capturing the flickering of sunlight on water. Thomas Eakins, who taught at the Pennsylvania Academy of Art, painted realistic, often harsh, portraits of people and landscapes. His works, largely unsold in his lifetime, were vivid renderings of the new industrial age.

445

Eakins and some of the artists who followed him were called the American Realists because they portrayed the harsh life around them. This group and the American impressionist painters found few buyers in nineteenth-century America. In the early years of the twentieth century, however, their work began to draw international admiration.

Sports

The big-city newspapers, with their crisply written sports news, brought spectator sports such as baseball, football, and basketball into the mainstream of American life.

The exact origin of baseball is unknown, although popular myth credits Abner Doubleday with invention of the sport in Cooperstown, New York, in 1839. During the Civil War the game spread when Union soldiers from New York taught soldiers from other parts of the country how to play. At that time the pitcher threw the ball underhand, the catcher caught it on the first bounce, and none of the players wore gloves.

The first professional baseball team was the Cincinnati Red Stockings. In 1876 eight teams organized the National League of Professional Baseball Clubs. A rival American League was started some years later, and in 1903 the first World Series was held.

Basketball was invented in Springfield, Massachusetts, by Dr. James Naismith, who was looking for an indoor winter sport for young boys in his Young Men's Christian Association (YMCA). The first games in the United States were played in 1891 or 1892. Basketball became a popular sport and soon spread to other nations.

Games of football using various rules from British soccer and rugby had been played in North America since colonial days. College students began playing the game before the Civil War, and its popularity increased once the war was over. By the 1890s football games between Harvard, Yale, and Princeton were drawing huge crowds. In 1895 seven colleges in the Midwest began to organize what eventually became the Big Ten conference.

The wide variety of entertainment available in urban areas made them exciting for thousands of new residents. All the glitter, however, could not hide the problems that accompanied the rapid growth of the cities.

Boxing matches as well as football, baseball, and basketball games drew large crowds in the late nineteenth century. Thomas Eakins, who painted this scene, was a leader of the group of painters known as the American Realists.

SECTION REVIEW

1. Identify: F. W. Woolworth, Joseph Pulitzer, Louis Sullivan, Winslow Homer, Thomas Eakins, American Realists, Abner Doubleday, James Naismith.
2. How did the electric trolley and electrified railway lines affect city growth?
3. List two ways department stores differed from the shops of earlier eras.
4. How did newspapers like the New York *World* try to attract readers?
5. **Critical Thinking** What attracts people to cities today?

4 A Changing Society: Problems and Prospects

Although there was much that was entertaining and exciting in the cities, there were also crushing problems. Nearly every city needed more sewers, better water systems, more roads, and more trolley lines. Disease and crime were widespread, and the cities lacked facilities to deal effectively with either. The cities also had to provide schools to educate a diverse group of children and deal with a dozen other urgent problems.

Exposing Urban Problems

Observers of life in American cities documented a wide range of urban problems, including street gangs, illiteracy, fire hazards, and unsanitary conditions giving rise to contagious diseases. Increasingly, reformers gathered facts and figures to bring to public attention. They believed that exposing terrible conditions was the first step in eliminating them.

Grim statistics were indeed revealed. For example, in one section of Chicago, in one year alone, 60 percent of all babies died before reaching 12 months of age. One New York social worker counted 1,231 people living in just 120 rooms in that city. Another was unable to locate a single bathtub in over 3 city blocks of tenements.

In 1890 *How the Other Half Lives*, written by a young New York reporter, Jacob Riis, was published. In the book Riis described in detail the wretched lives of people living in the city slums, including the horrid stench, everpresent filth, and blocked fire escapes. Reformers like Riis helped create a public demand for decent living conditions for all.

Jane Addams and the Settlement House Movement

In several cities, hardheaded idealists were already at work. They moved into slum neighborhoods and established settlement houses, community centers that offered a wide range of services to slum residents. The best known of the settlement houses was Hull House in Chicago, founded in 1889 by Jane Addams and a group of other young well-educated women.

On a trip to England, Addams had visited the founders of Toynbee House, a community center in the London slums. Impressed with the British achievements,

Reformers who visited crowded city slums were appalled at the conditions they found. To arouse the public to action, they published reports on disease, crowding, and other problems. Photos such as this one by Jacob Riis inspired public demand for stronger health laws and other reforms.

Addams spearheaded the purchase of a decaying mansion in one of the worst neighborhoods in Chicago and began Hull House.

Hull House provided a nursery and kindergarten for the children of working mothers. Adult education classes in English, nutrition, and health were offered. In time a gymnasium was added for young people. There was also a theater group.

The women of Hull House documented the urgent problems of the neighborhood. Then, armed with facts, the reformers worked to get new laws passed. Alice Hamilton, a physician working from Hull House, treated the neighborhood's sick. She soon realized that laws were needed to control the spread of disease, and she became an effective crusader for health legislation. Florence Kelley researched the harmful impact of industrial jobs on young children and became a national spokeswoman for effective child-labor laws. She also served briefly as chief factory inspector for Illinois.

By 1895 there were at least 50 settlement houses in American cities. The first settlement house operated by the Catholic church opened in 1898 in an Italian neighborhood of New York. Two years later Brownson House opened in a Mexican section of Los Angeles.

Settlement houses became testing grounds for ideas about how to improve urban living. The houses attracted a dedicated group of professional people. College professors and researchers came to visit and discuss ideas with social workers, teachers, and nurses. From the friendships and alliances forged there came the first effective group of urban reformers in the United States.

Despite their many successes, these reformers realized that private efforts were not enough. "Private beneficence," said Jane Addams, "is totally inadequate to deal with the vast numbers of the city's disinherited." Government action, the reformers believed, was necessary to correct harmful conditions.

Women: New Opportunities and the Struggle for Rights

Influenced by the settlement house movement, many college-educated women chose professions, such as teaching or social work, that enabled them to serve the poor. Opportunities in other professions, however, remained limited. For example, Iowa in 1869 was the first state to allow women to practice law, but it was not until 1920 that women could practice law in all states. Despite restrictions and discouragement, there were 1,000 women lawyers and 7,000 women physicians by the turn of the century.

Other opportunities also opened for women after the Civil War. Large numbers of clerical jobs were created by the invention of the typewriter, telegraph, and telephone. Women increasingly took such jobs, replacing men as office workers. The rise of department stores also created new jobs. By 1900 about 500,000 women worked in clerical and sales jobs.

By the turn of the century women had gained a firm position in the working world. The number of women who held jobs outside the home rose dramatically, from 4 million in 1890 to 8 million in 1910. Paralleling these developments were strides toward greater legal equality for women.

Increasingly in the late 1800s state legislatures passed laws giving married women control over their own property. Before 1900,

The wistful eyes of this child underscore the task facing urban reformers. The dimly lighted slum in which he lived was overcrowded and probably lacked running water. Typically, the boy and his brothers and sisters could expect to begin working in a "sweatshop" in another year or two.

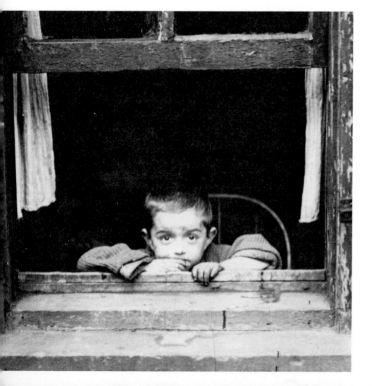

four western states—Wyoming, Colorado, Utah, and Idaho—had given women the right to vote in state elections. For most American women, however, the vote remained only a dream.

Turning that dream into reality continued to be a difficult struggle. Little headway had been made since the Seneca Falls Convention in 1848. (See page 301.) During the early twentieth century, women like Alice Paul and Carrie Chapman Catt would continue the struggle for women's suffrage, as you will read in Chapter 26.

The Growth of Public Education

For many Americans before 1870 education meant a one-room school and a *McGuffey's Reader*. The average adult in 1870 had attended school for four years, and about one in five could not read or write. At the time there were only 160 public high schools in the entire nation.

In the period after the Civil War schools were built at a rapid rate. Dozens of new colleges and universities opened. The new graduates helped staff thousands of new classrooms. By 1900 the concept of free public schools for all citizens was widely accepted, and there were 6,000 public high schools in the United States.

In the cities, however, traditional methods of teaching, such as drills and memorizing, did not work for many children. A child who spoke no English could make little sense of what was happening in the classroom. A frequent visitor to Hull House, Professor John Dewey of the University of Chicago thought he had a solution.

Dewey urged schools to move away from the rote-learning routines. He and his wife, Harriet, tested their ideas at an experimental school at the university. Students in the school could work in a kitchen, a carpentry shop, or a sewing room, as well as in classrooms. Under Dewey's system, children actively participated in education.

Dewey's ideas were part of a broad movement to tailor education to fit the needs of the children being taught. The movement, often called progressive education, was part of a larger reform movement called progressivism. (You will read about progressivism in Chapters 25 and 26.)

Progressive teachers had three main goals. First, they believed that school pro-

Born into a wealthy Illinois family, Jane Addams turned her enormous energies and talents to improving conditions in the Chicago slums. Hull House, which she helped found, became a model for other settlement houses. It offered education, medical care, English classes, sports, and other practical help for residents of the neighborhood in which it was located.

grams should be widened to include teaching about health, jobs, family, and community life. Second, they wanted to apply new discoveries in science and psychology to classroom teaching. Third, they argued that teaching techniques should suit the kinds of children in the classroom. The reformers hoped to adapt and improve the education of children living in a more urban and industrial society than their parents had grown up in.

Other Humanitarian Efforts

As you read in Chapter 21, during the nineteenth century, many Americans argued that government had no right to interfere in their lives. This belief in laissez-faire extended to the area of social reform as well as economics. Religious leaders had usually shared this view. But late in the century the depth of social problems in the growing cities convinced some Christians that churches had to become actively committed to social reform.

These activist clergy developed what was called the Social Gospel. They argued that before churches could save souls, they had to improve the daily lives of the wretchedly poor. The Social Gospel was most prominent among Protestants.

Catholics also became more active in social reform. In 1889 an Italian nun, Frances Xavier Cabrini, arrived in the United States with a small group of nuns to work among Italian immigrants. Before her death in 1917, Mother Cabrini, as she was known, founded 70 hospitals throughout North and South America.

During the late 1800s a number of organizations were founded to deal with social problems in a systematic way. These included the Salvation Army and the Red Cross. William Booth, a Methodist minister, established the Salvation Army in London in 1878. Its purpose was to help house and feed the poor. An American branch of the Salvation Army was established a year later. Living in the poorest city slums, members of the Salvation Army established soup kitchens for the poor and homeless.

The Red Cross had been founded in Europe in 1859 originally to aid soldiers wounded in war. Clara Barton, who had served as a nurse during the Civil War, helped establish the National Society of the Red Cross in the United States in 1881. It provided needed social services in the growing urban areas.

Governing the Cities

In the late nineteenth century growing cities continued to be governed as they had been for over a century. Most had to have permission from state legislatures before passing important municipal laws. City governments, like state and national governments, suffered from the political corruption of the era. Andrew White, president of Cornell University, wrote, "With few exceptions, the city governments are the worst in Christendom—the most expensive, the most inefficient, and the most corrupt."

The governments White was describing were often run by a group of men known as political bosses. The bosses controlled what was called the "machine" or the "club." The machine offered city jobs and contracts to those who had the right connections. A well-placed bribe could win a company a contract to pave the streets, build schools, or operate trolley lines. "Boodle," payoffs in return for contracts or official favors, was a way of life in many cities.

Yet the machines did more than take bribes and offer favors. The politicians often

An all-female company of the newly formed Wyoming State Guard prepares to celebrate statehood in 1890. Wyoming was one of the first states to permit women to vote.

Major Events

1883	Pulitzer buys New York *World*; Metropolitan Opera House opens in New York City
1889	Jane Addams founds Hull House; Hazen Pingree elected as reform mayor of Detroit
1890	Jacob Riis's *How the Other Half Lives* published
1893	Columbian Exposition opens in Chicago

provided important services for poor city residents. An unemployed slum dweller could turn to the boss or one of his "ward heelers" for help in finding a job or for a loan to pay the rent. The machine sometimes offered English lessons or legal advice to immigrants and helped them apply for citizenship. Food baskets were often given away on holidays. In return for such assistance, the boss was assured of the votes of most poor and immigrant city dwellers.

Perhaps the most notorious political boss of the era was William Marcy Tweed of New York City. Boss Tweed held no political office, but he controlled the Democratic political machine, popularly known as Tammany Hall. In three years, from 1868 to 1871, a group of Boss Tweed's associates, known as the Tweed Ring, robbed the city of over $20 million, perhaps as much as $200 million. Such pilfering provided more than enough money to keep the machine running "smoothly."

As cities grew larger during the last years of the century, many public-minded citizens came to realize that a better system of urban government was needed.

The Good-Government Movement

In city after city reformers like Jane Addams teamed up with honest business people in an attempt to make urban government more efficient and more honest. The reformers often began by tackling specific abuses such as undependable garbage collection. Each small success increased the reformers' authority and encouraged stronger drives for better city government. Extension of water and sewer lines, improved building codes, better sanitation facilities, and more fire and police protection were all demanded. Essential to the reformers' goals was the destruction of the "invisible government" of the political machines.

Reformers scored a major victory when Detroit elected Hazen Pingree as mayor in 1889. Mayor Pingree forced the transit authority to lower streetcar fares. Under his leadership the city built more public parks and schools. When an economic depression struck, he started a relief program for the unemployed. Samuel M. "Golden Rule" Jones, Toledo's reform mayor, brought in professional city planners to help direct city operations. Cleveland elected Tom Johnson, called the "best mayor of the best-governed city in the United States."

Many of the reformers believed that cities should be run by professionals using business methods. They brought a new, well-educated group into city government, but the new officials sometimes overlooked the poor, whom the bosses had routinely "taken care of." Where the reformers succeeded, the middle and upper classes generally took control of the cities. Nevertheless, imperfect as it was, the reform movement at city level signaled the dawn of a major era of reform. The urban reformers led the way for the national progressive movement, which helped restore idealism to public life.

SECTION REVIEW

1. Identify: Jacob Riis, Jane Addams, Hull House, John Dewey, Social Gospel, Frances Xavier Cabrini, William Booth, William Marcy Tweed.

2. What services were offered by Hull House?

3. (a) What type of job opportunities opened for women in the late 1800s? (b) In which states had women won the right to vote in state elections?

4. Name the three main goals of progressive education.

5. (a) What did political machines offer the urban poor? (b) What characteristics of the machines led reformers to demand a better system of urban government?

6. **Critical Thinking** What services do people today expect to receive from city governments?

In Perspective

By 1914 the United States was becoming a nation of cities. Although most Americans continued to live in small towns or rural areas, cities grew dramatically between 1865 and 1914. They were the centers of the industrial development of the last half of the nineteenth century. Immigrants from Europe and Asia poured into the United States in the 1880s and 1890s. They were driven by difficult conditions in their homelands and attracted by the promise of a better life in America.

A new way of life was developing in the cities, characterized by electric trolleys, department stores, and skyscrapers. City dwellers could choose a wide variety of entertainment—from vaudeville to museums and baseball games. Yet despite the attractions, the growing cities suffered great problems.

Reformers like Jane Addams worked to improve such conditions. Settlement houses throughout the nation offered valuable services to urban dwellers. Other reformers sought to improve education and to clean up corrupt city governments. Although many problems remained, urban reformers introduced a new strain of idealism in American life that would lead to further reforms, as you will read in Chapter 25.

Vocabulary

Choose the answer that best completes each of the following sentences.

1. "Boodle" referred to (a) the part of the ship that most immigrants traveled in; (b) payoffs in return for contracts or official favors; (c) neighborhoods in which immigrants settled.
2. In city government, a machine was (a) the organization of political bosses who controlled city jobs and contracts; (b) an unemployed slum dweller on welfare; (c) an organization of city reformers.
3. Violent attacks against Jewish neighborhoods are (a) mugwumps; (b) potlatches; (c) pogroms.
4. Nativism is (a) hatred of foreigners; (b) an exaggerated loyalty to one's ancestors; (c) a study of a people's national heritage.
5. A term referring to city life is (a) suburban; (b) urban; (c) rural.
6. An ethnic neighborhood is one in which (a) people who share the same language, customs, and cultures live; (b) there is a wide diversity of cultures and races; (c) young, upwardly mobile people are replacing older, poorer inhabitants.

Chapter Checkup

1. What developments in the last half of the 1800s helped spark the growth of cities?
2. (a) What attracted industry to Chicago? (b) What problems did Chicago face as a rapidly growing city?
3. (a) What attracted immigrants to the United States in the late 1800s? (b) How was their journey difficult?
4. (a) How did the "new" immigrants of the 1880s and 1890s differ from earlier immigrants to the United States? (b) How did these differences contribute to antiforeign feeling among some Americans?
5. Explain how each of the following affected life in the cities: (a) electric trolleys; (b) department stores; (c) mass-circulation newspapers.
6. (a) What types of problems arose in the new urban areas? (b) How did settlement houses attempt to solve these problems?
7. (a) How did the growth of industry and cities help create new job opportunities for women? (b) How did women's legal rights increase during this period?
8. (a) What role did political machines play in the government of many cities? (b) Why did reformers want to change city governments?

Critical Thinking

1. **Relating Past to Present** (a) Why do you think many young people were attracted to city life in the late 1800s? (b) Would they probably be attracted by the same things today?

2. **Identifying Relationships** (a) How did humanitarian groups like the Salvation Army and the Red Cross try to improve the lives of city residents? (b) How do the activities of such groups reflect the American tradition of voluntary action to improve society?

Developing Basic Skills

1. **Relating Past to Present** Make a list of the problems you read about in this chapter that faced the cities in the late 1800s. Using sources in your school or public library, decide whether each problem still exists in many cities today. Why do you think some have been solved and others not?

2. **Researching** Visit the library to learn about the history of a city near where you live. Then answer the following questions: (a) Did the city grow rapidly during the late 1800s? Why or why not? (b) Did many "new" immigrants settle in the city? (c) If so, where did they come from?

See page 831 for suggested readings.

Writer's Handbook

Skimming and Scanning

How can you choose the best sources and find the most useful information without reading each entire book that you find? The answer is to skim and scan.

Look at the table of contents and the index to see if a book contains any of the topics that you need. Suppose that you were researching Jane Addams and the settlement house movement. You would look for key words such as "Jane Addams," "settlement houses," "reformers," "Hull House," "Chicago," and "charity." Using the page numbers in the index or table of contents, turn to the part of the book that is indicated. Look at headings to get an idea of the main topics of each passage. Glance over the material, looking for the key words that will tell you whether or not that section will be helpful. This technique is called skimming.

When you find a passage that contains the key word clues, read it quickly to see if handles the topics in a way that is useful to your research. Reading a selection quickly is called scanning. Skimming and scanning let you preview books without reading them in depth.

Practice: Skim and scan the following paragraph to answer the questions:

1. Which of the following does the author mention: party nominations, personal popularity, Thomas Nast, state senate, felony charges, Samuel J. Tilden?

2. Does this passage contain information about the type evidence that was used against Tweed?

3. Does this passage tell when and where Tweed died?

Boss Tweed (1823–1878) was a bookkeeper whose stint as a volunteer fireman gave him influence in local city politics. Tweed worked his way up until he controlled party nominations and party patronage and was the absolute power in city government. Through control of city finances, he made himself and his friends wealthy men. Tweed's generosity toward the poor helped him maintain his personal popularity even when evidence of his corruption was printed in the *New York Times*. Finally, Thomas Nast's effective political cartoons aroused public feeling. Tweed was tried and convicted on felony charges. After he served a year in prison, he was arrested on new charges and fled abroad. He was extradited to the United States in 1876 and died in prison two years later.

Mobility in America

The story of the movement of people is a common thread woven through the annals of history. The migration of the American people has been part of this pattern. Americans are mobile. They move not only from place to place (physical mobility), but also from one level of society to another (social and economic mobility).

Land of Opportunity According to the social historian Max Lerner, there have been three kinds of physical mobility in American history: migrations across the oceans, migrations across the country to new frontiers, and the "internal crisscrossings" of people from farms to cities and cities to suburbs. All three kinds of physical mobility have been closely linked to social and economic mobility. People have moved, in large part, to better their own lives or those of their children. As one turn-of-the-century Italian immigrant freely admitted, "If I could have worked my way up in my chosen profession in Italy, I would have stayed in Italy. But repeated efforts showed me that I could not. America was the land of opportunity, and so I came. . . ." Millions of others who migrated "across the oceans" did so for the same reason.

America was viewed as a land of opportunity as early as the 1600s. Indentured servants came to Massachusetts in the same ships as did Puritan settlers. Up and down the Atlantic coast, indentured servants were working to pay off their debt and then move on in search of land.

Many people who came to America left societies that still bore the imprint of feudalism. These societies accepted the idea that a person's social status and occupation were inherited. In America differences existed between the rich and the poor, but they were thought to be accidental, not the result of essential differences in people. No better symbol of this belief could be found than Thomas Jefferson's order to replace the rectangular table in the White House with a round one. He did not want to decide which of his official guests should sit at the head of the table and which at the foot. No better testing ground for this belief existed than the American frontier. There a person's rank was based on talent and ability, not on birth. The upper ranks of society were open to anyone willing and able to work.

Westward Migration In the early 1800s, Americans moved steadily westward from the Atlantic coast. One English visitor said Americans seemed to suffer from "a disease of locomotion." Others thought this motion was temporary. The superintendent of the 1850 census claimed, "When the fertile plains of the West shall have been filled up, and men of scanty means cannot by a change of location acquire a homestead, the inhabitants of each State will become comparatively stationary."

States competed with one another for ambitious immigrant laborers. This poster advertised the benefits of moving to California.

Industrialization spurred physical and social mobility. Many people took advantage of the new means of travel—the railroad.

But already other forces were at work to keep people moving. In the mid-1800s, a swelling stream of northern European immigrants was carried on the canals, roads, and railroads that were beginning to connect the older cities of the East with the West. By the time the census of 1890 showed that the frontier was closed, the country was in the midst of an industrial revolution. As economic and political problems disrupted southern and eastern Europe, booming industries in the United States welcomed millions of immigrants to fill their need for workers.

The American Dream Would the American dream of opportunity and a better life be fulfilled for these millions of Italians, Jews, and eastern Europeans? The expanding economy made it a possibility. As one New York banker said, "A man here may be a common day laborer, but if he

has the right material in him, there is no reason why he should not occupy the best place in the nation." To a native-born American the idea that success could be earned was ordinary, but such was not always the case for the immigrant. Mario Puzo, author of *The Godfather,* writes of his own experience: "My mother wanted me to be a railroad clerk. And that was her highest ambition; . . . when I let everybody know that I was going to be a great writer . . . she quite simply assumed that I had gone off my nut. . . . Her peasant life in Italy made her believe that only the son of the nobility could possibly be a writer."

As millions of southern and eastern European immigrants were setting their sights on the American dream, a great internal migration was beginning to take place. Thousands of black men and women were leaving small farms in the South to search for a better life in the urban North. During the industrial expansion caused by World War I, many migrants envisioned a future bright with promise. One wrote, "I should have been here 20 years ago. . . . It's a great deal of pleasure in knowing that you have got some privilege. My children are going to the same school with the whites and I don't have to [bow] to anyone. I have registered—Will vote the next election." But when the war was over, black workers who had been welcomed when they were needed began to see that welcome fade. Then the depression hit. It was not until World War II that many blacks saw a renewal of opportunity for economic and social mobility.

Mobility has helped form the American character. Unlike many Europeans, Americans who have achieved positions of power and influence have remained proud of their humble origins. The idea of "pulling up stakes" has become part of our national experience. And as a nation we have made "change" and "progress" have almost the same meaning.

Today we are in the midst of new migrations. No longer do the majority of immigrants come across the Atlantic. Recent arrivals are far more likely to have crossed

the Pacific Ocean or the Caribbean Sea. The South now competes with the West for migrants from the older urban areas. Yet these urban areas are themselves receiving new migrants—people who have returned to the cities to pursue new job opportunities. Americans continue to move to find a "better life."

1. What are the three kinds of physical mobility identified by Max Lerner?
2. How have different groups exemplified these types of mobility?
3. How do you think that the size and natural wealth of the United States have helped shape the American character?

American Profiles — Sarah Breedlove Walker

Like many Americans, Sarah Breedlove Walker was determined to achieve a better life. Through hard work and ingenuity, she overcame her humble beginnings and realized the American dream of wealth and fame.

Sarah Breedlove was born in Louisiana in 1868 to former slaves. An orphan at age 7 and a widow and mother by age 20, she learned very early to cope with poverty and responsibility. Sarah Breedlove left Louisiana in 1888 and settled in St. Louis, Missouri. For many years, she worked as a maid, cook, and laundress—often for as little as $1.50 a day—to support herself and her child.

In her early thirties, however, Breedlove became concerned about financial security for her old age. According to one account, she thought of a money-making idea while balancing a basket of laundry on her head. Why not develop hair care products for blacks? For several years she considered the idea and in her spare time developed formulas for salves and soaps.

At age 37, Sarah Breedlove uprooted herself again. She chose Denver, Colorado, as the place to start a hair care business. Married to C.J. Walker, a newspaperman, she manufactured and marketed her hair preparations under the name of Madame C.J. Walker.

Door-to-door sales in the Denver area proved successful. Soon she added cosmetics and toiletries to her line of products. Soaring profits enabled her to expand her business nationwide. Within a short period of time, she had established Walker schools of beauty culture across the country. From an initial investment of $1.25, Mrs. Walker was on her way to becoming the first black woman millionaire.

Walker's success did not end there. She took profits from her business and invested in real estate. She acquired valuable property in the West and the South and a fashionable mansion near New York City.

A more comfortable life was not the only satisfaction that Mrs. Walker derived from her newly gained wealth. In an interview two years before her death, Mrs.

Sarah Walker (1867–1919) is seen here at the wheel of her automobile. Walker's rise from a laundress to a millionaire was a powerful testimony to her own determination and American opportunity.

Walker said that she wanted money not for herself but to benefit others. She made generous donations in support of education and civil rights for blacks and willed two-thirds of the profits of her company to charities.

Mrs. Walker died in 1919 at age 51. The story of her rise from poverty was an inspiration to other struggling Americans.

Her success proved that upward mobility in the United States was a reality.

---

1. What were some of Mrs. Walker's goals during her lifetime?
2. How was physical mobility related to Mrs. Walker's economic success?

An American Journey

In the late 1800s some newly arrived immigrants followed a pattern of migration already familiar to many native-born Americans: they set out from eastern cities to the sparsely inhabited West. Among them were Polish immigrants, Isadore and Anna Solomon. In 1876 the Solomons left the East to open a general store in a primitive town in New Mexico. Their store was an immediate success, and the Solomons soon started a bank, a newspaper, and a hotel. The following is an account by Anna Solomon of the family's first months in New Mexico.

We sold everything we possessed except our three children and started on our journey for New Mexico. We had a very hard trip. . . .

When we reached La Junta, the end of the railroad in those days, [we] had to travel by stage, packed in like sardines day and night for six days. . . . When we got [to Las Cruces], I was tired out to death. . . . I lived [there] with the children for four months while my husband looked around for a location for our business. He finally found a place, and this is where we have been living now for thirty years.

When we were going to leave Las Cruces, we bought a two-seated wagon called a buck board, and a pair of horses. Into this we put a tent, some bedding, our cooking utensils, our provisions, our clothes, our children, ourselves. . . . It took us several days and nights to get there. How often I was frightened thinking I saw Indians. . . .

Now we had to start the housekeeping, but we had no furniture, no cooking stove, and nothing else that belongs to the comfort of the human race. [So] we cooked outside on the ground. We had a stove and other very necessary things coming from Las Cruces, being sent by an ox team with two loads of goods for the store that we were going to put up. But the wagons broke down on the road, and we had to send someone to repair them. They got here after three months. Until then we had no bed to sleep in, no stove to cook in, no table to eat off, no flour to bake bread. For three months I baked bread out of corn meal in a Dutch oven.

[Meanwhile] I took sick with chills and fever and my baby, Rose, also took sick. We had some very dark and sad times, but that did not hinder us from doing a good deal of business. We also started building—at first a bedroom, then a store. When that store was finished I felt like the Queen of England.

Adapted from Kenneth Libo and Irving Howe, *We Lived There Too* (New York: St. Martin's/Marek 1984).

---

1. What hardships did Anna Solomon encounter in setting up a home for her family in New Mexico?
2. How did the lives of the Solomons typify the quest for the American dream?

Becoming a World Power

(1865–1900)

Battle at Manila Bay *by F. Fetherston*

Chapter Outline

1 *The Dream of Expansion*

2 *The Spanish-American War*

3 *Responsibilities of Empire*

During the first half of the 1800s, the area of the United States doubled, stretching from the Atlantic Ocean to the Pacific. Although the nation bought Alaska from Russia in 1867, the decades after the Civil War were generally years of isolation from world affairs. Domestic concerns captured the attention of most Americans.

Gradually, toward the end of the century, concern about international developments increased. The economic growth of the period fueled interest in new markets, and many Americans began to dream of territorial expansion. Such dreams, however, led to conflict with other nations and eventually to war with Spain.

When the United States acquired territory as a result of that war, the nation encountered the responsibilities of an overseas empire. Its response to those responsibilities was to have a major impact on future relations with nations in Latin America and Asia. Whether Americans favored an empire or not, most were aware that by 1900 the United States was becoming a world power.

Growing interest in world affairs

1865	1870	1875	1880	1885	1890	1895	1900

1867
Alaska purchased

1871
Britain pays *Alabama* Claims

1880s
U.S. trade abroad increases

1889
Samoa agreement signed

1893
Queen Liliuokalani overthrown

1895
Cuba revolts against Spain

1898
Spanish-American War; Hawaii annexed

1 The Dream of Expansion

In the years immediately following the Civil War, the attention of most Americans was focused on economic growth, settlement of the West, and the new entertainments of the Gilded Age. Most of the population had little interest in events beyond their shores. The New York *Sun* even suggested that the Department of State, which was responsible for foreign relations, had "outgrown its usefulness" and should be abolished.

With little concern about foreign relations, most Americans did not feel their country needed a large navy or army. The United States Navy had dwindled to a handful of rotting sailing ships following the Civil War. At the same time the European powers were building new steam-powered battleships. The powerful army of the Civil War was gradually reduced to only 25,000 soldiers. There were signs, though, that the United States was about to become a leading actor on the world stage.

Early Signs

William H. Seward, secretary of state under Presidents Lincoln and Johnson, believed that the United States should become the center of a vast *empire*, a system of territories governed by one nation. If the United States was to attain this goal, Seward decided, it had to prevent other nations from gaining influence in North America.

During the Civil War, France had set up a puppet government in Mexico backed by French soldiers. In 1866 Seward moved 50,000 United States troops to the Mexican border, making United States opposition to French intentions clear. The French eventually withdrew from Mexico.

Then, in 1867, Seward bought Alaska from Russia for just $7.2 million. Thereby he eliminated French and Russian influence in North America, and he acquired a huge territory for the United States. The secretary of state also hoped to buy the Virgin Islands. He negotiated a treaty with Denmark to buy the islands, but the Senate refused to ratify it. In 1867 most Americans, including members of Congress, were not interested in such ambitious overseas projects, so Seward dropped his plans.

During President Grant's administration a proposal to take over the island of Santo Domingo in the Caribbean and a scheme to annex Canada attracted little support. A Philadelphia newspaper expressed the popular mood when it stated, "The true interests of the American people will be better served . . . by a thorough and complete development of the immense resources of our existing territory than by any rash attempts to increase it."

When it came to pressing financial claims, however, the United States showed determination. For example, the government demanded that Great Britain pay for about 100,000 tons (about 91,000 metric tons) of shipping destroyed during the Civil War by Confederate ships like the *Alabama* that were built in British shipyards. In 1871, after years of argument, the two countries signed

Before the discovery of gold in the Yukon, the purchase of Alaska from Russia in 1867 had been ridiculed by many as "Seward's Folly." However, by 1898, when this photograph was taken, prospectors were racing to Alaska. The two women prospectors in this photograph faced a hazardous journey over treacherous mountain passes to reach the Klondike.

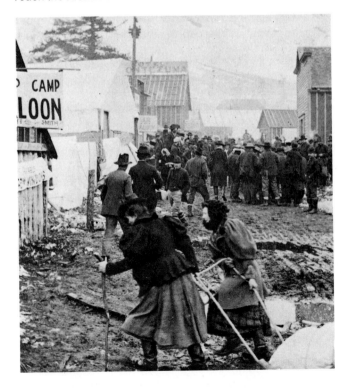

the Treaty of Washington. Under that treaty, an arbitration court ordered the British to pay $15.5 million in damages for the so-called *Alabama* Claims.

During the 1880s the dream of empire began to surface again. The same economic growth that had preoccupied Americans since the Civil War inspired new dreams of overseas expansion. By 1880 the United States was producing more food and manufactured goods than could be used at home. As a result, Americans began to export more to other countries.

Exports increased from $450 million in 1870 to $853 million in 1880. By the early 1890s they exceeded $1 billion. Slowly but surely the United States began to penetrate world markets previously dominated by European nations. Such competition increased the likelihood of conflict with these nations.

A Rationale for Expansion

As Americans began to take a new interest in overseas markets and territories, three men offered reasons for such expansion: historian Frederick Jackson Turner, naval officer Alfred Thayer Mahan, and Congregationalist minister Josiah Strong.

Frederick Jackson Turner was a young professor of history at the University of Wisconsin during the 1890s. He maintained that the availability of free land in the West had enabled poor or restless Americans to move West and prosper. With the free land on the western frontier rapidly disappearing, he feared that Americans without much land might become rebellious. Indeed, labor unrest and political turmoil between 1870 and 1900 seemed to suggest that Turner was right.

The answer, according to Turner, was to channel the energies of Americans toward the expansion of trade abroad. Increased foreign trade would create jobs that might give ambitious people the same opportunity for success the frontier had once provided. Turner's ideas appealed to many Americans, including Theodore Roosevelt and Woodrow Wilson. As President, both Roosevelt and Wilson tried to expand American influence abroad, as you will read in Chapter 27.

Admiral Mahan also believed that the expanding industrial capacity of the United States required new markets abroad. Mahan preferred to see the expansion of trade rather than the acquisition of colonies. Even

if the United States was not interested in more territory, he believed it needed a stronger navy. In Mahan's opinion, a powerful navy was essential to protect trade routes, especially since competition for trade might lead to conflicts with world powers.

Mahan urged the government to rebuild the navy and add modern steam-powered battleships. He also believed that the United States should build a canal across Central America and annex Hawaii. Hawaii would be an important naval base in the Pacific, and the canal would allow American ships to pass quickly between the Atlantic and Pacific oceans.

Josiah Strong envisioned an American Christian empire that would spread across the Pacific into Asia. He argued that the "white race," represented by the United States, had been divinely chosen to "civilize" the rest of the world. Strong had his own interpretation of Charles Darwin's theory of the "survival of the fittest." (See page 399.) In Strong's opinion, the white race was the "fittest" and thus the American empire would survive and prosper.

Strong stressed American territorial expansion, while Mahan and Turner were more interested in the expansion of trade. The ideas of all three influenced both the public and politicians as the United States took its first steps toward gaining greater influence in the Pacific.

A Foothold in the Pacific

Americans had traded with Asian nations since the eighteenth century. This trade had increased in the early 1800s. In 1844 the United States had signed a commercial treaty with China, and in 1858 Commodore Matthew Perry opened trade with Japan. (See page 271.) In 1882 the United States signed a treaty opening trade with Korea.

In the 1880s the United States began to show interest in the Pacific island of Samoa (sah MOH ah), where the fine harbor of Pago Pago (PAHNG oh PAHNG oh) could serve as a naval base and commercial harbor. Germany and Great Britain, however, also realized the value of the harbor. For several months in 1889 German and United States sailors eyed each other nervously from gunboats anchored at Pago Pago. A powerful storm sank the ships of both countries just as tensions were at their highest, and the threat of war soon eased.

Public sentiment in favor of expanding United States influence abroad was strong. In this proexpansion cartoon, McKinley appears to be fitting Uncle Sam for a larger set of clothes. Opponents of expansion, at left, try to convince Uncle Sam to take diet medicine.

Great Britain, the United States, and Germany finally agreed in 1899 to share control of Samoa, with the United States obtaining the harbor at Pago Pago. The events in Samoa had demonstrated the growing danger of conflicts with other powers.

Hawaii

Although agreeing to cooperate with the other powers in Samoa, the United States wanted sole control of Hawaii. Europeans and Americans had first learned of the Hawaiian Islands in 1778 after British sea captain James Cook had come ashore there for fresh water and to trade with the Hawaiians. The islands had originally been settled by visitors from the Polynesian islands in the Central and South Pacific 2,000 years before. The individual islands were ruled by local chiefs until 1795, when King Kamehameha (kah MAY hah MAY hah) unified Hawaii.

During the nineteenth century, Hawaii attracted traders from China, France, Spain, and the United States. Americans, especially, valued the islands as a stopover for the growing trade with China. Missionaries also settled in the islands. Many of their descendents became prosperous sugar growers who dominated the islands' economy and the government of King Kamehameha.

In 1891 Queen Liliuokalani (lih LEE oo OH kuh LAH nee), a strong nationalist, came to the throne. She tried to restore the power of the Hawaiian monarchy and reduce the privileges of foreign merchants, but the foreigners in Hawaii organized her overthrow in January 1893. With the help of a detachment of United States Marines, they then organized a new government.

President Benjamin Harrison supported an annexation treaty with the new Hawaiian government. However, Grover Cleveland, who succeeded Harrison in 1893, was outraged at the high-handed actions of the American sugar growers and the role of the marines in the revolt. Consequently, he withdrew the treaty from the Senate. Americans who favored annexation of Hawaii grew increasingly concerned that another nation might seize the islands. Finally, in 1898, during President McKinley's administration, Congress passed a joint resolution annexing Hawaii to the United States.

461

Queen Liliuokalani, who ruled from 1891 to 1893, was the last Hawaiian monarch. A strong nationalist, she tried to reduce the power of foreign merchants in the islands.

Latin America and the Caribbean

Since President James Monroe had issued the Monroe Doctrine in 1823, Americans had maintained a special interest in Latin America and the Caribbean. The Monroe Doctrine stated that the United States would oppose all European intervention in the affairs of independent nations in the Americas. (See page 222.)

Latin America became especially important in the late 1800s. Merchants and manufacturers valued the region's raw materials. Military leaders considered many areas to be strategically important. The navy was interested in Panama as a possible location for a canal across Central America. Such a canal could allow warships to pass between the Atlantic and Pacific without circling South America. It would also benefit the growing trade with Asia.

The French were the first to attempt to build a canal across Panama. In 1878 Ferdinand de Lesseps (leh SEHPS), a Frenchman who supervised the construction of the Suez Canal, announced plans to build a canal. Citing the Monroe Doctrine, President Hayes condemned the French plans. Despite the protest France went ahead with the canal project, which soon became a disaster. Malaria killed 20,000 of the canal workers, and financial problems plagued de Lesseps's company. Work on the canal stopped in 1889. (You will read about the eventual construction of the canal in Chapter 27.)

Meanwhile, south of Panama, a border dispute between Venezuela and the British colony of Guiana (gee AH nah) brought the United States close to war in 1895. The boundary between Venezuela and Guiana had long been contested. The discovery of gold in the disputed area increased the stakes and the tension. Britain rebuffed President Cleveland's offer to mediate the dispute. It also dismissed any claim that the Monroe Doctrine gave the United States the right to meddle in Britain's South American affairs.

Enraged by the insult to the Monroe Doctrine, President Cleveland threatened war if the British seized territory to which they had no right. Both sides seemed to be gearing up for a fight, but the British had more serious worries about German threats to their interests in Africa. As a result, the British wanted to avoid conflict with the United States. In 1897 after Great Britain agreed to have an independent commission settle the boundary dispute, the crisis ended. The events in Panama and Venezuela showed that Americans still considered the Monroe Doctrine a vital force in United States policy toward Latin America.

SECTION REVIEW

1. Identify: William H. Seward, Frederick Jackson Turner, Alfred Thayer Mahan, Josiah Strong, Queen Liliuokalani.

2. Define: empire.

3. How did Secretary of State Seward end Russian influence in North America?

4. According to Admiral Mahan, why was a strong navy essential?

5. According to Josiah Strong, what was the mission of the United States?

6. (a) Which nations wanted to control Samoa? (b) What agreement was made about the island?

7. Who dominated the Hawaiian government before Queen Liliuokalani?

8. **Critical Thinking** How were industrialization and expansionism interrelated?

2 The Spanish-American War

The United States had become increasingly involved in world affairs in the late 1800s, but it had not yet assumed a place among major world powers. The collapse of the Spanish empire in Latin America and Asia offered the United States the opportunity to develop an overseas empire. As the Spanish empire crumbled, expansionists in the United States were eager to pick up the pieces.

Moving Toward War

Although activity in foreign affairs during the 1880s and early 1890s had brought the United States close to war several times, actual battle had been avoided. The successful outcome of the disputes in Samoa, Venezuela, and Hawaii, along with growing naval strength, had made American citizens and their leaders confident.

This confidence in the nation's power, however, threatened to develop into *jingoism*, an intense national pride. Jingoists often advocated a more warlike foreign policy during the 1890s. In 1891 they demanded war with Chile after two United States sailors were killed and 17 injured during a riot in Valparaiso, Chile. President Harrison ordered the navy to prepare for war. Faced with American threats, the Chilean government offered compensation, and the crisis ended.

Near Florida, however, lay a trouble spot that eventually would lead to war: Cuba. Americans had invested money in Cuba since before the Civil War, mainly in the rich sugar plantations. There had even been talk of annexing the island, although it still belonged to Spain.

In 1895 Cuban hatred of Spanish rule and frustration with falling sugar prices led to a revolt. Choosing repression instead of reform, Spain sent a new governor, General Valeriano Weyler (WAY ee lair) to Cuba in 1896. He treated rebel prisoners brutally and imposed a policy of reconcentration on the Cuban people. *Reconcentration* meant that people in the towns and villages were marched into detention camps where they would be guarded by Weyler's soldiers. Inhuman conditions in the camps outraged Americans. Anti-Spanish feeling was fanned by a group of Cubans in New York who spread publicity for the rebel cause.

Rebel publicity was fed to two New York City newspapers, Joseph Pulitzer's *World* and William Randolph Hearst's *Journal*. In overstating Weyler's atrocities and playing down those of the rebels, these publishers gave birth to a new form of newspaper writing, called *yellow journalism*. They purposely tried to whip up the emotions of their readers. Paying little attention to the facts, the yellow press tried to sell newspapers by featuring screaming headlines and sensational stories, with Spain portrayed as the villain.

In the battle for readers in New York, Pulitzer and Hearst tried to outdo each other with more spectacular reports of Spanish

In the fierce competition for newspaper readers, popular dailies headlined sensational news and scandals. This cartoon satirizes the "mudslinging," or name calling, that was typical of the yellow journalism of the day. The tall figure is President McKinley.

Lola Rodríguez de Tió: Poet and Patriot

Lola Rodríguez de Tió was a true daughter of Cuba and Puerto Rico. Her poems and speeches inspired many Latin Americans seeking freedom from the despotic rule of Spain in the late 1800s. Born in Puerto Rico in 1843, Lola Rodríguez was educated by her father, who nourished her poetic skill and her independent spirit. She was the first Puerto Rican woman to deliver a public speech on the island and the first to join in the literary and political discussions that took place among the men of her native town.

After marrying Bonocio Tió Segarra, a journalist and poet, Lola Rodríguez de Tió joined the struggle for Puerto Rican independence from Spain. In 1887, when a cruel Spanish governor unleashed a reign of terror in Puerto Rico, the poet appealed for help to the Spanish government. The tyrant was put out of office and the political prisoners were freed, but the Tió family was sent into exile.

They fled to Cuba, where their home became a meeting place for Cuban nationalists. But the family was forced to flee from Cuba after Lola Rodríguez de Tió recited her well-known poem, "A Cuba." The Spanish authorities considered the poem subversive. The Tiós then settled in New York. Lola Rodríguez continued to recite her patriotic poems and to work for Cuban independence from Spain. After the Spanish–American War, she returned to Havana, where she received a hero's welcome.

Lola Rodríguez de Tió published three books of verse. Her poems spoke of friendship, of patriotism, of her love for children, and of the natural wonders of the island of her birth. The works are praised as literary masterpieces throughout the Spanish-speaking world. These two verses, in Spanish and English, were published in 1876.

Es libre aquel que lo quiere,
Hombre llámese, o mujer,
Que aspirar puede al derecho
Quien reconoce el deber

Niega todo lo que quieras,
Si negar es tu desgracia,
Mas, no me niegues tres cosas
El alma, Dios y la patria.

Freedom comes if you want it,
Be you called a man or woman,
If you can aspire to justice
If you recognize duty.

Deny all that you like,
If denying is your misfortune,
But do not deny me three things:
Spirit, God and nation.

cruelty in Cuba. Hearst was so confident of his ability to sway public opinion that he told one photographer who was heading for Cuba, "You supply the pictures. I'll supply the war." Influenced by the yellow press, many Americans clamored for a war to liberate Cuba from Spanish rule. Sympathies might have been on the side of the rebels in any case, since the Cuban revolt could be compared to the Revolutionary War in the United States. Such natural sympathy, however, was intensified by the yellow press and jingoists calling for overseas expansion.

On the Brink of War

When riots erupted in Havana, the Cuban capital, in 1898, President McKinley ordered the battleship *Maine* into the harbor to protect United States citizens and property. On February 15, 1898, a huge explosion destroyed the battleship, killing 260 sailors. An investigation failed to reveal who had sunk the *Maine*, but people in the United States blamed Spain. An enraged public called for war. (See pages 466–467.)

After the sinking of the *Maine*, the United States wavered on the brink of declaring war for several months, but President McKinley opposed war. In March 1898 McKinley proposed a cease-fire to halt fighting between Spanish troops and Cuban rebels. He offered to mediate talks between Spain and Cuba but clearly indicated that the outcome should be Cuban independence. Spain rejected McKinley's peace plan.

War fever in the United States continued to run high. Expansionists, such as Ad-

miral Mahan and Assistant Secretary of the Navy Theodore Roosevelt, foresaw a victory over Spain as the beginning of an empire for the United States. Many social reformers, labor leaders, and religious leaders favored a war as a moral crusade to improve conditions in Cuba. Millions of ordinary citizens, outraged by the sinking of the *Maine* and by Weyler's atrocities, also demanded war against Spain.

Most business leaders, on the other hand, except the few with large holdings in Cuba, opposed war. Industrialists believed that war would disrupt the United States economy, but they were not powerful enough to hold back the tide of war. In April 1898 Congress recognized Cuban independence from Spain. Spain responded by declaring war against the United States. The next day Congress declared war on Spain.

War in the Pacific

Fighting did not immediately break out in Cuba, however. The Spanish–American War began on the other side of the world, in the Philippine Islands, which were also controlled by Spain. The United States had begun preparations in the Philippines two months before the declaration of war. On February 25, Assistant Secretary of the Navy Theodore Roosevelt had sent a message to Commodore George Dewey, commander of the United States fleet based in Hong Kong. If war was declared, Roosevelt said, Dewey's mission would be to destroy the Spanish fleet at Manila Bay in the Philippines.

When war broke out, Dewey steamed out of Hong Kong toward Manila Bay. At dawn on May 1, Dewey's guns opened fire, sinking the entire Spanish fleet with just one American casualty. Having made contact with Filipino rebels led by Emilio Aguinaldo (AH gwee NAHL doh), Dewey asked for troops to conquer the Philippine Islands. McKinley sent 11,000 troops and additional naval support. On August 13, 1898, rebel and United States forces took Manila.

Even hardened antiexpansionists in the United States admired Dewey's victory. The expansionists were especially thrilled by the stunning naval performance in Manila Bay. Those who dreamed of empire believed that they were seeing the dawn of a new age of American expansion.

War in the Caribbean

While American forces were crushing the Spanish in the Philippines, preparations were under way for an invasion of Cuba. Anxious to fight in what Secretary of State John Hay called a "splendid little war," 200,000 men volunteered to join the army.

During the spring of 1898, 17,000 troops gathered at a military base in Tampa, Florida. The army, however, was not equipped to launch an invasion. Soldiers bound for Cuba were issued heavy woolen uniforms, while cavalry troops waited in vain for horses. Despite this confusion, the invasion force sailed on June 14. (See the map on page 469.)

Among these troops was the spirited Theodore Roosevelt. He had resigned his desk job in the Navy Department so that he could be second in command of a volunteer unit called the Rough Riders, filled with a motley crew of cowboys, college students, and adventurers. Roosevelt came to symbolize national enthusiasm for the fight against Spain.

■ *The sea battle between the United States and Spain ended quickly in the Pacific, when ships under Admiral George Dewey steamed south from Hong Kong to strike the Spanish at Manila. The Americans sank the Spanish fleet stationed in the Philippines.*

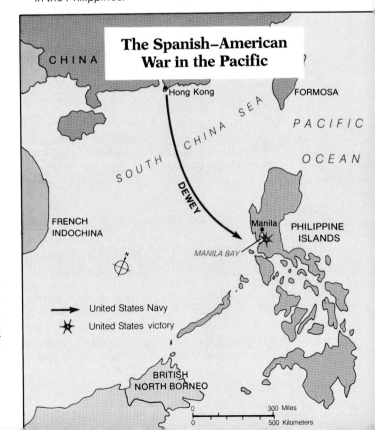

The Spanish–American War in the Pacific

CHINA

Hong Kong

FORMOSA

SOUTH CHINA SEA

PACIFIC OCEAN

DEWEY

FRENCH INDOCHINA

Manila

PHILIPPINE ISLANDS

MANILA BAY

→ United States Navy

★ United States victory

BRITISH NORTH BORNEO

0 300 Miles

0 500 Kilometers

SKILL LESSON

Sinking of the *Maine:* Recognizing Propaganda

Propaganda is a deliberate attempt to manipulate the truth about people or events to further one's own cause or damage an opposing cause. Propaganda often includes many accurate facts, but the propagandist distorts the facts to fit the impression he or she wants to convey.

Many types of historical evidence may contain propaganda. Thus it is important to recognize propaganda. Propaganda, for example, may have influenced the outbreak of the Spanish-American War. Two pieces of evidence about the sinking of the *Maine* are reproduced here and on page 467. One is the dispatch the captain of the *Maine* sent to the secretary of the navy immediately after the incident. The second is the front page of a newspaper.

1. **Identify the facts.** A fact is something that is true or that can be proven. An opinion is a judgment that reflects a person's feelings, beliefs, or attitudes. (a) List the facts in Captain Sigsbee's message. (b) What opinions can you identify in his message? (c) List the facts in the *World* report. (d) Is any of the information in the report based on opinions? Give examples.

2. **Identify distortions of fact.** (a) What does Captain Sigsbee say about the cause of the explosion? (b) What does the *World* imply about Sigsbee's opinion of the cause?

3. **Analyze the emotional appeal.** (a) Does Captain Sigsbee seem interested in arousing public opinion against the Spanish? (b) What effect might the picture of the explosion in the *World* report have on the public? Why? (c) What impact might the use of the word enemy in the third headline have on the reader? (d) Find three other words that are likely to have an emotional appeal. What emotion is each likely to arouse?

4. **Reach conclusions.** Use your text and the two documents to answer the following questions: (a) What overall message is conveyed by the author of the *World* report? (b) Why might the author want to present a distorted account of the incident? (c) What effect do you think reports such as the one in the *World* had on the outbreak of the war?

Message From Captain Sigsbee to the Secretary of the Navy, February 15, 1898

Maine blown up in Havana Harbor at nine-forty tonight and destroyed. Many wounded and doubtless more killed or drowned. Wounded and others on board Spanish man-of-war and Ward Line steamer. Send lighthouse tenders from Key West for crew and the few pieces of equipment above water. No one has clothing other than that upon him. Public opinion should be suspended until further report. All officers believed to be saved. . . . Many Spanish officers, including representatives of General Blanco, now with me to express sympathy.

By the end of June, United States troops had established a beachhead near Santiago on the eastern tip of Cuba. Again inefficiency hindered the war effort. Many soldiers died from food poisoning after eating badly preserved meat. Finally, on July 1, troops engaged the Spanish defenders of Santiago. In a bloody fight the United States forces attacked the ridges surrounding the city. Roosevelt's Rough Riders and black soldiers of the 9th Cavalry charged up San Juan Hill. Under withering fire, they suffered heavy casualties, losing over 1,500 men. The Spanish army, however, was demoralized and short of ammunition, and the Americans took the hill.

Then, on July 3, the United States Navy sank the Spanish fleet in a lopsided battle in

863,956
WORLDS CIRCULATED YESTERDAY

The World.

863,956
WORLDS CIRCULATED YESTERDAY

"Circulation Books Open to All."   "Circulation Books Open to All."

VOL. XXXVIII. NO. 13,310   NEW YORK, THURSDAY, FEBRUARY 17, 1898   PRICE

MAINE EXPLOSION CAUSED BY BOMB OR TORPEDO

Capt. Sigsbee and Consul-General Lee Are in Doubt---The World Has Sent a Special Tug, With Submarine Divers, to Havana to Find Out---Lee Asks for an Immediate Court of Inquiry---Capt. Sigsbee's Suspicions.

CAPT. SIGSBEE, IN A SUPPRESSED DESPATCH TO THE STATE DEPARTMENT, SAYS THE ACCIDENT WAS MADE POSSIBLE BY AN ENEMY.

Dr. E. C. Pendleton, Just Arrived from Havana, Says He Overheard Talk There of a Plot to Blow Up the Ship---Capt. Zalinski, the Dynamite Expert, and Other Experts Report to The World that the Wreck Was Not Accidental---Washington Officials Ready for Vigorous Action if Spanish Responsibility Can Be Shown---Divers to Be Sent Down to Make Careful Examinations.

Santiago Harbor. This blow ended Spanish resistance in Cuba.

With Spain dislodged from Cuba, the United States turned to the Spanish-held island of Puerto Rico. American troops landing in Puerto Rico during late July met little opposition and quickly conquered the island. On August 12, 1898, the defeated Spanish signed a truce.

Results of the War

In the peace treaty signed on December 10, 1898, the United States acquired Puerto Rico, the Philippines, and Guam, an island in the Pacific Ocean. Cuba became an independent nation. The United States Senate ratified the treaty in 1899. Although most Americans were pleased by the newly won

467

The 10th Cavalry was one of the regiments sent to fight the Spanish in Cuba in 1898. John J. Pershing, who may be one of the white officers in this painting, had served earlier as an officer with the black regiment on the western frontier. When war broke out with Spain, Lieutenant Pershing wangled a transfer back to the 10th Cavalry. Pershing's nickname, "Black Jack," came from his years with the regiment.

status as a great power, they were soon to learn that power brought with it great, and sometimes troublesome, responsibilities.

SECTION REVIEW

1. Identify: Valeriano Weyler, William Randolph Hearst, the *Maine*, George Dewey, Theodore Roosevelt.

2. Define: jingoism, reconcentration, yellow journalism.

3. What methods did the yellow press use to stir up hatred against Spain?

4. What effect did the sinking of the *Maine* have on public opinion in the United States? Explain.

5. What effect did Dewey's victory in Manila Bay have on Americans?

6. (a) List the territories that the United States acquired as a result of the Spanish-American War. (b) What status did Cuba achieve as a result of the War?

7. **Critical Thinking** Who benefited from the sinking of the *Maine*?

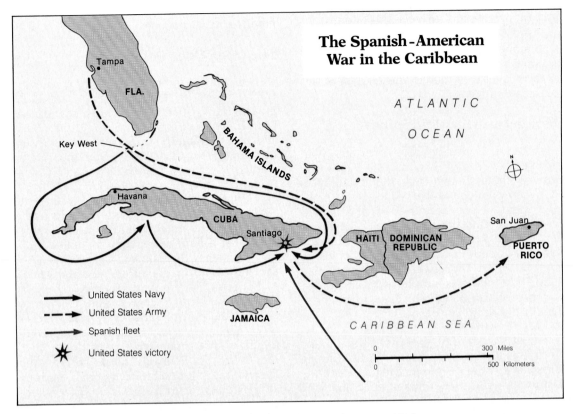

The Spanish-American War in the Caribbean

■ *In the Caribbean the United States Navy sank a Spanish fleet in a one-sided battle. American ground troops met and defeated the Spanish in pitched battles in Cuba. Moving on to Puerto Rico, the Americans met little opposition from Spanish troops there.*

3 Responsibilities of Empire

The United States emerged from the Spanish-American War with far-flung overseas holdings. The nation now had colonies in the Pacific and Latin America, and its navy patrolled the waters of the Atlantic and Pacific. The easy victory over Spain made Americans confident that the United States could continue to expand. While some Americans were thrilled by the challenge of empire, others were troubled by the responsibilities.

The Cuban Problem

The conclusion of the war with Spain did not end United States involvement in Cuba. After the war, the island was in chaos: government was at a standstill, sanitation almost nonexistent, and disease rampant. In response to these conditions, President McKinley installed a military government to administer the island. Under the leadership of General Leonard Wood, the Americans worked to wipe out yellow fever and improve Cuban education and agriculture.

In 1900 Cubans began to draft a constitution, but President Theodore Roosevelt insisted that the Cubans include a document known as the Platt Amendment. Cuba would thereby agree not to make treaties or loans that might threaten its newly won independence. The United States would be allowed to establish two naval stations on the island. Finally, Cuba had to recognize the right of the United States to send troops to Cuba in order to preserve life, liberty, or property.

The United States pulled the army out of Cuba in 1904 but intervened again in 1906 and 1917. Cuba was at least technically an independent nation, but the United States had assumed control of the Philippines. This was to raise questions about the United States role as an imperial power.

Debate Over the Philippines

At the end of the Spanish-American War, President McKinley was not sure how the United States should treat the Philippines. He paced the floor of the White House night after night before deciding that the United States must rule the Philippines. The President argued that the Filipinos "were unfit for self-government" and that Americans had a duty to "uplift and civilize and Christianize them." He said this despite the fact that a majority of the population had been Christian for hundreds of years.

Most Americans probably shared McKinley's view that governing the Philippines was the responsibility of the United States. But some people insisted that colonialism was wrong. They maintained that the annexation of the Philippines violated Americans' belief in liberty. Some were also concerned that an overseas empire would drag the country into war with other powers. Other critics argued that the Constitution made no provision for governing colonies.

The American debate over annexation was complicated by a Filipino rebellion. Filipino nationalists had revolted against Spanish rule during the Spanish-American War. The revolutionaries led by Emilio Aguinaldo had hoped that an American victory over Spain would bring independence to the Philippines. But while the Senate debated the peace treaty ending the Spanish-American War, President McKinley had ordered American troops to occupy all the islands. Aguinaldo then rebelled against the United States.

The Senate ratified the treaty making the Philippines an American colony, but the war for independence continued. For three years Filipino nationalists fought a fierce battle against the foreign troops. Finally, in 1901, the United States declared that the Filipino revolt had been crushed. The war against Aguinaldo's rebels had lasted longer and cost more men and money than the original war against Spain in 1898. The long and bitter struggle showed that determining how

American power ought to be used was not going to be easy.

The Open Door Policy

United States interest in Asia, especially China, grew after the annexation of the Philippines and Guam. Americans saw these islands as stepping stones to China. Missionaries wanted the opportunity to convert the Chinese to Christianity, and merchants wanted to take part in the profitable China trade.

These hopes were threatened in the late 1800s by the great powers who sought to divide China into *spheres of influence*, or areas of control. Taking advantage of Chinese military weakness, Russia had seized Port Arthur in the north, Japan claimed the island of Formosa, Britain held Hong Kong off of China's southern coast, and Germany claimed the port of Kiachow. These spheres of influence restricted United States participation in the China market.

After the Spanish-American War the United States decided to try to open China to all nations on an equal basis. In 1899 Secretary of State John Hay sent letters, known as the Open Door notes, to the nations already involved in China.

Hay asked these powers to respect three principles: no power would prevent others from trading in a sphere of influence; tariffs in China would be collected by the Chinese, not by foreign nations; and no power would ask for harbor or railroad duties in its sphere that discriminated against the other powers. Most of the nations were neutral to the Open Door letters, but Hay announced that the Open Door policy was in effect since none of the nations had rejected it outright.

In the spring of 1900, a group of Chinese nationalists known as the Boxers rebelled against the Europeans, hoping to expel all foreigners from China. They killed more than 200 foreigners and attacked buildings owned by foreign governments in Peking. These hostilities, known as the Boxer Rebellion, lasted for more than a month until troops from several European countries and the United States arrived to repress the Boxer uprising.

After the siege of Peking ended, Hay sent another series of Open Door notes to the European powers and Japan. He hoped to prevent them from reducing China to a

group of colonies as a reprisal for the Boxer Rebellion. This second series of notes not only upheld the principles of the first but stressed that the United States believed in maintaining an independent China.

Only Great Britain, France, and Germany accepted the second Open Door notes. However, the other powers, fearing that any attempt to divide China might lead to an open war, also observed Hay's policy. As a result, the United States gained access to trade with China.

The Fruits of Expansion

After 1900 the United States would annex few new territories, but it continued to extend its political and economic influence. Expansion had absorbed the national energy much as Frederick Jackson Turner had predicted. It provided new markets and sources of raw materials for American industry, which was rapidly becoming the largest and most efficient in the world. These markets and raw materials provided more jobs and investment opportunities for Americans. Expansion also increased United States involvement in international affairs.

In the meantime, another consequence of expansion became clear. The United States had been founded on the principle of self-government. Yet annexation often meant ruling without the consent of the governed. Expansionists justified colonial rule by insisting that the people who had been annexed were "not fit for self-government." But others maintained that colonialism was wrong because it violated the ideals of liberty and self-rule.

In some areas United States influence meant better education, improved health care, and more stable government than that which had prevailed before. The hard fact remained, however, that the United States had become a colonial power, like Great Britain at the time of the Revolutionary War.

Major European powers set up spheres of influence in a weak and divided China. When a group of Chinese militants called the Boxers tried to drive all foreigners out of China in 1900, the United States dispatched marines to rescue Americans trapped in Peking. Below, allied troops mass for an attack on the Boxers.

Major Events

1867	Purchase of Alaska from Russia
1871	The *Alabama* Claims
1889	Great Britain, United States, and Germany agree to share control of Samoa
1893	Queen Liliuokalani overthrown
1895	Venezuelan border dispute; Cuban revolt against Spain begins
1896	Weyler becomes Spanish governor of Cuba
1898	Sinking of the *Maine;* Spanish-American War begins; Dewey sinks Spanish fleet in Manila Bay; Battle of San Juan Hill; destruction of Spanish fleet in Santiago harbor; Hawaii annexed; treaty signed
1899	Filipino rebellion against United States; Hay sends Open Door notes
1900	Boxer Rebellion erupts

By 1900 the United States had taken its place among the international powers. One French diplomat observed, "The United States is seated at the table where the great game is played, and it cannot leave it." Indeed, Theodore Roosevelt and Admiral Mahan had no desire to see their nation abandon the contest. They could rejoice that in just over a century the United States had grown from a colony to a major world power.

SECTION REVIEW

1. Identify: Platt Amendment, William McKinley, Emilio Aguinaldo, John Hay, Open Door notes, Boxer Rebellion.
2. Define: spheres of influence.
3. (a) Which nations had spheres of influence in China? (b) What effect did the spheres of influence have on United States attempts to do business with China?
4. What was the purpose of Hay's second Open Door note?
5. **Critical Thinking** Was the philosophy of the Open Door Policy compatible with that of the Monroe Doctrine?

Chapter 24 Review

In Perspective

Immediately after the Civil War, Americans had little interest in foreign affairs. Yet Secretary of State Seward exhibited vigor in United States foreign policy by his protest of French domination of Mexico and his purchase of Alaska from Russia. By the late nineteenth century, Americans had renewed their dream of expansion.

It was the Spanish–American War in 1898 that transformed the United States into a world power. Outraged by stories of Spanish atrocities in the Cuban war for independence and by the sinking of the *Maine,* Americans clamored for war against the Spanish empire. As a result of the war, the United States acquired Puerto Rico, Guam, and the Philippines. Cuba enjoyed limited independence under American protection.

Now a world power, the United States assumed huge responsibilities. Aguinaldo's rebellion against United States rule in the Philippines showed that colonization carried with it grievous problems. But most Americans believed that expansion was good for the United States and for the people in the colonized region.

Vocabulary

On a separate sheet of paper, write the word or words that best complete each of the following sentences.

1. A (An) ____ is a system of territories governed by one nation.

2. ___ is intense national pride.

3. ___ was a system of control of Cuba's civilian population.

4. ___ is a term used for sensational newspaper writing.

5. A (An) ___ is an area of one country under the economic and political control of another country.

473

Chapter Checkup

1. (a) What was the attitude of most Americans toward foreign affairs after the Civil War? (b) How did that attitude change by the 1880s? (c) What developments influenced the change?

2. Explain how each of the following contributed to the outbreak of the Spanish–American War: (a) jingoism; (b) General Weyler; (c) yellow journalism; (d) sinking of the *Maine*.

3. (a) Why did President McKinley install a governor in Cuba after the Spanish–American War? (b) What conditions did the Platt Amendment place on Cuba?

4. (a) Why were Americans interested in China during the late 1800s? (b) What action did Secretary of State Hay take to try to improve the United States position in China?

Critical Thinking

1. Evaluating William G. Sumner (see page 399) was one American who opposed the annexation of the Philippines. He argued that the notion of a civilizing mission was dangerous because it would lead the United States down the path of intervention and war. Do you think the developments in the Philippines between 1899 and 1901 tended to confirm or refute Sumner's argument? Cite specific evidence to support your answer.

2. Making a Judgment (a) What reasons did President McKinley give for maintaining control of the Philippines after the Spanish–American War? (b) Do you think his rationale was justified? Why or why not?

Developing Basic Skills

1. Relating Past To Present Make a list of territories acquired by the United States between 1865 and 1901. Locate each area on the map of the world on pages 806–807. Then answer the following questions: (a) What is the present-day status of the area? (b) How does the present status differ from that of the late 1800s? (c) Choose one of the areas and research its history since 1900. Then write a report explaining how control of the area has changed.

2. Ranking Review the developments leading to the Spanish–American War. Then rank them according to which you think was most important in the eventual outbreak of the war. Explain.

See page 831 for suggested readings.

Writer's Handbook

Bibliography Cards for Books

To prepare a working bibliography, make out a separate bibliography card for each book or periodical you use. Write the full name of the author or editor, last name first. Write *ed.* after a name to indicate editor. If there are two authors, write only the first author's name—last name first. If there are three or more authors, write the name of the first and add *et al.* Underline the title and subtitle. Note the edition number and volume number, if there is more than one. Include the city of publication, publisher's name, and the date of publication. Write the call number of the book in the upper right corner of the card.

973
B

Burner, David *et al.* *America: A Portrait in History.* 2nd ed. Englewood Cliffs, N.J.: Prentice-Hall, Inc., 1978

Practice: Write a bibliography card for your textbook. Use the call number 973.

Unit Seven

Entering a Modern Age

Scientist George Washington Carver promoted the interests of black Americans.

1904 After work began, cutting the canal across Panama took ten grueling years.

	1900	1904	1908
POLITICS AND GOVERNMENT	**1900** La Follette is governor of Wisconsin	**1904** Roosevelt Corollary justifies intervention in Latin America	
SOCIETY AND CULTURE	**1903** Ida Tarbell exposes Standard Oil		**1909** NAACP founded
ECONOMICS AND TECHNOLOGY	**1903** Department of Commerce and Labor created	**1906** Pure Food and Drug Act bars use of harmful additives	
WORLD EVENTS		**1904** War breaks out between Japan and Russia	

McKinley   Roosevelt

Conditions in crowded cities were one target of reformers in the early 1900s.

The campaign to prohibit the sale of alcohol eventually led to passage of the Eighteenth Amendment in 1917.

1912 Some Woodrow Wilson supporters tried to identify him with George Washington as this song sheet shows.

1918 American soldiers helped stop a German counteroffensive at the Second Battle of the Marne.

1912	1916	1920

1913 Federal Reserve system created to regulate credit supply

1917 United States enters war on side of the Allies

1916 Interstate shipping of items produced by children is forbidden.

1920 Women win right to vote

1911 Triangle Factory fire leads to factory safety regulations

1918 War Industries Board organizes industry in support of the war

1911 Mexican Revolution begins

1914 War begins in Europe

1919 Treaty of Versailles ends the war

Taft	Wilson	Harding

1919 President Wilson and other Allied leaders hammered out the Treaty of Versailles to end the war.

1917 Posters like this encouraged Americans to conserve food so soldiers would have enough.

25

The Progressives

(1900–1909)

Theodore Roosevelt as portrayed in a political poster

Chapter Outline

1 *Voices for Change*

2 *Reform of State and City Government*

3 *Theodore Roosevelt Takes Charge*

4 *The Square Deal in Action*

In 1900 the United States was emerging from a period of rapid material growth. While many people did not share in the prosperity, it was a time of brimming national confidence and energy. Rapid change, however, had left parts of American society in disorder. In the cities, particularly, crowding, disease, and other ills abounded. Political corruption was common.

As the century began, the reformers who had worked to establish settlement houses in the 1880s and to defeat corrupt city bosses in the 1890s joined in a broad crusade. Those reformers shared a belief that progress was possible, and from that belief came the label "progressive."

Most historians date the progressive era from 1901 to 1917, from the start of Theodore Roosevelt's presidency to the entry of the United States into World War I. In this period the progressives were to achieve major reforms in the economy and the politics of the nation.

Square Deal

1900	1902	1904	1906	1908	1910
1901 McKinley assassinated	**1902** Roosevelt intervenes in coal strike	**1904** Roosevelt elected; *Shame of the Cities* published	**1906** Pure Food and Drug Act passed	**1908** William Howard Taft elected President	**1909** NAACP founded

1 Voices for Change

Although a few reform measures had been passed in the late nineteenth century, severe problems remained. Political corruption, monopolies, and poverty persisted, and many Americans continued to face political and economic inequality. By 1900 a new generation of reformers, known as progressives, resolved to right many of these wrongs.

Who Were the Progressives?

Kansas newspaper editor William Allen White joked that progressivism was simply Populism that had "shaved its whiskers, washed its shirt, put on a derby, and moved into the middle class." White correctly observed that progressivism was basically a middle-class movement. Progressive reformers were typically city dwellers and college-educated professionals. They sympathized with the downtrodden but were not among them.

Some progressives began their careers in the settlement houses. There social workers met with reform-minded reporters, professors, teachers, doctors, nurses, and business people. These middle-class individuals formed the core of the progressive movement.

Progressivism was a diverse movement. It included Democrats and Republicans, as well as members of smaller political parties. Some reformers were mainly concerned about corruption in government and the need to make government more responsive to the needs of the people. Many progressives worked to pass laws against unsafe working conditions, spoiled food, and slum housing. Others battled to pass legislation that would regulate the business practices of the powerful monopolies. But all progressives shared the belief that the United States needed to be reformed and the confidence that it could be.

The Muckrakers

The first step in reforming society was exposing the conditions that needed reform. Often that meant writing about grim details people would rather ignore. For example, Upton Sinclair charged in his book *The Jungle*, published in 1906, that the meatpacking industry slaughtered diseased cattle and injected the meat with dyes to disguise its color. Such reports disturbed many people, including President Theodore Roosevelt. In a Washington speech Roosevelt compared journalists like Sinclair to a man in a story who raked muck, or manure. That man, Roosevelt explained, was so intent on raking muck that he would not look up when he was offered a crown. Muckraking writers, declared Roosevelt, were similarly obsessed with wretched things.

Muckraking journalism had actually begun some years before Roosevelt labeled it. In 1902 Lincoln Steffens wrote a series of articles exposing corruption in city government. The articles were collected in a book and published in 1904 under the title *The Shame of the Cities.* In his article on Philadelphia, Steffens charged that voting lists in that city contained the names of "dead dogs, children, and non-existent persons," who voted for the party in power.

Muckraking journalists had a wide variety of concerns. John Spargo's book, *The Bitter Cry of Children* (1906), documented the poverty that resulted in hundreds of thousands of children going to school hungry. Ray Stannard Baker, who joined the staff of the muckraking *McClure's* magazine in 1897, wrote articles exposing the terror of lynching. Ida Tarbell's *History of the Standard Oil Company* (1903) cataloged the ruthless tactics John D. Rockefeller used to build his oil monopoly.

Although the muckrakers were not the first reformers to put their thoughts into print, they were the first to reach a vast American audience. Advances in printing and paper production made it possible for magazines to expand their circulation nationwide. Now the average American could read about corruption in high places and sickening conditions in meatpacking plants.

The muckrakers did not provide their readers with many solutions, but they did inform the public of urgent social and economic problems. Once aware, a growing number of Americans became involved in reform efforts, hoping to correct the evils the muckrakers had exposed.

Ida Tarbell was one of the most influential journalists of the progressive era. Her history of the Standard Oil Company showed how the Rockefeller company had used rebates and price cuts to drive competitors out of business.

Organizing for Change

Despite their concern about injustice, many progressives were unconcerned about the plight of black Americans. A large number of progressives, like many white Americans of the period, believed that white people were superior to people with darker skin. Southern progressives often worked to strengthen Jim Crow laws. (See page 422.) Progressives in the North usually ignored the existence of segregation and discrimination.

But some progressives were outraged by the suffering inflicted on black Americans. After antiblack rioting erupted in Springfield, Illinois, in 1908, a group of progressives issued a declaration urging the creation of an organization to protect the rights of blacks. Among the signers of the declaration were the muckraking journalists Lincoln Steffens and Ray Stannard Baker; Jane Addams of Hull House; John Dewey, the founder of progressive education; and W.E.B. Du Bois, a historian and outspoken advocate of black rights.

In 1909 this group of white and black reformers founded the National Association for the Advancement of Colored People (NAACP). Du Bois edited the association's official journal, *The Crisis*, but most of the officers during the early years of the organization were white. Represented by lawyers

Historian and author W.E.B. Du Bois was one of the founders of the National Association for the Advancement of Colored People in 1909. He is shown below in his office at the NAACP journal, The Crisis.

The Niagara Movement: A Declaration of Principles

In July 1905 a group of black teachers, ministers, lawyers, and other professionals met near Niagara Falls, New York, to protest discrimination against black Americans. Led by W.E.B. Du Bois, the group, which became known as the Niagara Movement, demanded political, economic, and social equality. The participants in the Niagara Movement were among those who founded the National Association for the Advancement of Colored People. A portion of the group's Declaration of Principles is printed below.

The members of the conference, known as the Niagara Movement, assembled in annual meeting at Buffalo, July 11, 12, and 13, 1905, congratulate the Negro Americans on certain undoubted evidences of progress in the last decade, . . . the buying of property, the checking of crime, the uplift of homelife, the advance in literature and art, and the demonstration of constructive ability in the conduct of great religious, economic, and educational institutions.

At the same time, we believe that this class of American citizens should protest continually against the curtailment of their political rights. We believe in manhood suffrage; we believe that no man is so good, intelligent, or wealthy as to be entrusted wholly with the welfare of his neighbor.

We believe also in protest against the curtailment of our civil rights. All American citizens have the right to equal treatment in places of public entertainment according to their behavior and deserts.

We especially complain against the denial of equal opportunities to us in economic life. . . . Common-school education should be free to all American children, and compul-

sory. High-school training should be adequately provided for all, and college training should be the monopoly of no class or race in any section of our common country. . . .

We demand upright judges in courts, juries selected without discrimination on account of color, and the same measure of punishment and the same efforts at reformation for black as for white offenders. . . .

We plead for health—for an opportunity to live in decent houses and localities, for a chance to rear our children in physical and moral cleanliness. . . .

We urge upon Congress the enactment of appropriate legislation for securing the proper enforcement of those articles of freedom, the Thirteenth, Fourteenth, and Fifteenth Amendments of the Constitution of the United States. . . .

At the same time we want to acknowledge with deep thankfulness the help of our fellowmen from the Abolitionist down to those who today still stand for equal opportunity and who have given and still give of their wealth and of their poverty for our advancement.

And while we are demanding, and ought to demand, and will continue to demand the rights enumerated above, God forbid that we should ever forget to urge corresponding duties upon our people:

The duty to vote.
The duty to respect the rights of others.
The duty to work.
The duty to obey the laws.
The duty to be clean and orderly.
The duty to send our children to school.
The duty to respect ourselves, even as we respect others.

This statement, complaint, and prayer we submit to the American people and to Almighty God.

Source: Cleveland *Gazette,* July 12, 1905.

who donated their time, the NAACP defended black citizens who had been arrested on questionable evidence. The organization investigated race riots and lynchings and fought for a federal antilynching law. By 1914 the NAACP had offices in 50 cities and a national membership of 6,000.

Advances for Workers

Workers endured hard conditions at the beginning of the twentieth century. In 1900 laborers in the steel industry worked 12 hours a day, 7 days a week. Textile workers, many of them women and children, worked from

60 to 84 hours a week. Unemployment insurance was unheard of, and workers injured on the job received no disability pay. Few employers offered retirement pensions. Child labor and unsafe machinery were common in many plants.

Labor unions had grown slowly since the 1880s. Only 3 percent of the workers belonged to unions in 1900. By 1910 the figure was just 5 percent. The American Federation of Labor (AFL), the nation's largest labor organization, consisted of skilled artisans such as printers, brewers, and carpenters. Unskilled workers were rarely organized in AFL unions. (See page 409.) Furthermore, long-time AFL president Samuel Gompers was suspicious of government efforts to improve labor conditions. If workers were well organized, Gompers argued, they would not need to be protected by government regulation.

The progressives entered the vacuum left by the AFL and fought with impressive results for legislation to protect working people. Between 1912 and 1917, 12 states passed minimum wage laws for women. Progressives also successfully pushed for state-sponsored insurance plans to cover industrial accidents. Thirty states had some kind of industrial accident insurance system by 1917. Laws that barred children from working at night were passed in many states. After a tragic fire at the Triangle Shirt Waist Factory in 1911 killed more than a hundred workers, a number of state legislatures tightened factory safety regulations.

Women in the Progressive Era

By 1910 women held nearly one fourth of all jobs in the United States. Although the majority of women working outside the home were employed as maids and cooks, more and more were moving into office jobs, factory work, and professions such as teaching and nursing.

The so-called New Woman who worked outside her home was most visible and vocal in the settlement houses. Many of these women became highly skilled organizers and advocates of reforms. Among the most successful was Florence Kelley, formerly of Hull House.

Kelley took over leadership of the National Consumers League, originally founded by a group of New York women in 1890. The league urged consumers to boycott companies that had unsafe working conditions and to buy only products that carried the league's white label. Members of the league and other progressive women campaigned for shorter working hours for women and children and for better working conditions. Oregon was the first state to pass a law limiting the working day for women to ten hours.

Although women could not vote in most states, they were involved in a wide range of political and economic issues. The General Federation of Women's Clubs, which had almost a million members in 1910, concerned itself with factory conditions, political corruption, and law enforcement. Many clubs limited their activity to discussing these problems, but some pressed for state and local reform. This helped broaden many women's political knowledge and experience and helped prepare them for the successful suffrage campaign you will read about in the following chapter.

Muckraking journalists and progressive reformers drew public attention to the grim living conditions of workers in booming new industries. Pittsburgh steelworkers lived in the bleak and grimy neighborhood shown below.

SECTION REVIEW

1. Identify: muckraker, Lincoln Steffens, Ida Tarbell, NAACP, Florence Kelley.
2. Which groups of people formed the core of the progressive movement?
3. List three concerns of the progressives.
4. What did the early NAACP accomplish?
5. List four types of legislation passed to protect working people.
6. **Critical Thinking** How were the progressives fighting extremes of wealth and poverty?

2 Reform of State and City Government

Appalled by the corruption and waste in city and state administration, most progressives believed that strong measures were necessary to save local government. One strategy they proposed was to make government more responsive to the will of the people. A second strategy was to employ experts, such as engineers and social workers, to make government more efficient. Greater democracy and efficiency emerged as two pillars of progressive reform.

Agenda for Government Reform

Progressives proposed several ways to make governments more responsive to the people. These included primary elections, the initiative, the referendum, and the recall election.

Until the beginning of the twentieth century political party leaders had traditionally chosen candidates for state and local government office. In some areas a political machine (see page 450) controlled the selection process. To make the process more democratic, progressives urged that *primary elections*, or elections to pick party candidates, be held before general elections. Voters would have a chance in the primary elections to choose among several candidates for the party nomination. Wisconsin adopted the primary in 1903. By 1916 all but three states had adopted the primary election.

Once voters elected members of a city council or a state legislature, the people had little influence on the government until the next election. Under established procedure only members of the legislature could introduce a bill, which meant that citizens could not submit their ideas to the legislature directly. To give voters a greater voice in law making, the progressives proposed a device called the *initiative*. It allowed citizens

to initiate, or propose, a bill by collecting a required number of signatures from registered voters.

Progressives also thought voters should have a way to vote directly on some issues. In a vote called a *referendum*, proposals would appear on the ballot at an election. South Dakota, Utah, and Oregon adopted the initiative and referendum by 1902.

Another progressive proposal, the *recall election*, would allow voters to remove elected officials before they completed their terms. When a required number of voters signed a petition asking for a recall, a special election would be held to decide whether the official stayed in office. By 1914, 11 states had provided for recall elections.

Efficiency, as well as democracy, was an important consideration in progressive proposals for the reform of local government. One device for improving efficiency was the *city manager*, a professional administrator hired by an elected board of trustees to run a city government. Progressives believed that a professional manager with no political ambition would be more efficient than elected officials who had no training in municipal administration. The first city manager was hired in Staunton, Virginia, in 1908, and by 1914 the idea had spread to many cities.

La Follette and the Wisconsin Idea

Many cities and states experimented with progressive ideas for reform, but Wisconsin took the lead. When voters there chose Robert La Follette as governor in 1900, progressives had elected someone who would test their full program on a state-wide scale. Nicknamed "Battlin' Bob," La Follette was a tough-minded progressive who believed firmly in the need for greater democracy and

John Sloan was one of a group of painters that critics ridiculed as the "Ash Can School." Sloan painted the reality of urban life in the early 1900s, as seen in this view of New York City's Greenwich Village. Urban living conditions were among the concerns of progressive reformers.

efficiency in government. His far-reaching reforms of state government came to be known as the Wisconsin Idea.

Under La Follette's leadership the Wisconsin legislature established the direct primary in state elections. But Governor La Follette realized that good government needed more than a voting public. Complicated problems, he believed, needed to be solved by experts. Borrowing heavily from the University of Wisconsin faculty, La Follette recruited economists, engineers, and social workers to help him solve state problems.

La Follette's experts drafted legislation and sat on government commissions. His railroad rate commissions, for example, lowered rates and, as a result, increased the volume of freight traveling across the state. To the benefit of shippers and railroads alike, La Follette's experts made railroading more efficient.

The Wisconsin Idea was so successful that it became a national model, a so-called "laboratory for democracy." Several important progressive ideas became law in Wisconsin, including the creation of a tax system based on a person's ability to pay. The legislatures also passed laws strengthening the civil service and protecting natural resources. "Battlin' Bob" La Follette was elected to the United States Senate in 1906, where he continued as a major progressive spokesman.

Progressives in Other States

Although Wisconsin served as a model for progressive reform, progressives were active in every section of the country. In New Jersey, Woodrow Wilson, a former president of Princeton University, became a skillful reform governor. He won passage of laws establishing state regulation of railroads and utilities, the direct primary, and a system of industrial accident insurance.

California Governor Hiram Johnson successfully challenged powerful railroad interests who had controlled the state government. In New York Governor Charles Evans Hughes exposed corruption in the life insurance business. In the South Jeff Davis of Arkansas, Hoke Smith of Georgia, and "Pitchfork" Ben Tillman of South Carolina tried to weaken the influence of big business in state and local politics.

The progressives battled waste and corruption on many fronts. But one man eventually captured the national imagination as a brash fighter for reform. He was the hero of San Juan Hill: Theodore Roosevelt.

SECTION REVIEW

1. Identify: Robert La Follette, the Wisconsin Idea, Woodrow Wilson.
2. Define: primary election, initiative, referendum, recall election, city manager.
3. What were two main pillars of progressive reform?
4. How did Governor La Follette try to make use of experts to solve state problems?
5. **Critical Thinking** How did the progressives' ideas of democracy and government compare with Andrew Jackson's?

As governor of Wisconsin and United States senator, Robert "Battlin' Bob" La Follette never backed away from the fight for progressive causes.

3 Theodore Roosevelt Takes Charge

On September 6, 1901, President William McKinley was shot while attending a reception in Buffalo, New York. When he died on September 15, Vice-President Theodore Roosevelt became President. As President Roosevelt made progressivism a national force. The White House, Roosevelt observed, was a "bully pulpit," from which he lectured the nation on the need for constructive political changes.

Roosevelt's Background

Theodore Roosevelt became President by accident, yet he was well qualified for the job. He had not only the necessary intelligence and the energy, he also had broad experience in government on the city, state, and national level. Roosevelt provided wonderful copy for the mass circulation newspapers of the day. Indeed, everything "Teddy" did seemed larger than life, whether he was leading a cavalry charge in the Spanish-American War or crusading as the New York City police commissioner.

This vigorous man began life as a sickly child suffering from asthma. His father, whom he admired greatly, urged young Teddy to overcome his physical weakness through exercise, to build his body to match his active mind. Shortly after graduation from Harvard University, Roosevelt began his political career as a member of the New York State legislature. Then tragedy struck. His young wife died in childbirth only hours after the death of his mother. At the end of his elected term, Roosevelt quit politics—he thought permanently. He bought two ranches in North Dakota, where he often worked on horseback for 12 hours a day.

483

Eventually, though, Roosevelt returned to public service, becoming a commissioner of the United States Civil Service, then commissioner of the New York City police force. He served as assistant secretary of the navy during President McKinley's first term. As the Spanish-American War loomed, Roosevelt recruited cowboys, polo players, mounted policemen, and college athletes into a cavalry troop nicknamed the Rough Riders.

Emerging from the war as a hero, Colonel Roosevelt was elected governor of New York. With typical gusto, he set out to reform the state. In fact, it was partly to get him out of New York that the state's Republican leaders engineered Roosevelt's nomination for the vice-presidency. They considered the position a powerless one. Mark Hanna, who dominated the Republican Party, was less than pleased. "Don't you realize there is but one heartbeat between the White House and this madman?" he exclaimed.

Prosecuting the Trusts

When Theodore Roosevelt succeeded to the presidency, many Republican leaders feared that he was a radical determined to remake society. In fact the President believed firmly in the free enterprise system. He welcomed the growth of industry, but he wanted government to have the authority to regulate the practices of giant corporations. He was called a trust buster, but Roosevelt opposed only what he called "bad" trusts: those that used ruthless competitive tactics. In his view, government had to protect the public from irresponsible elements in the business community.

The President's first opportunity to apply his ideas on the regulation of business came in 1902 when he confronted the Northern Securities Company. The Northern Securities Company had been created in 1901 by the merger of three railroads: the Great Northern; the Northern Pacific; and the Chicago, Burlington and Quincy. It monopolized a significant portion of the national railroad system.

In 1902 Roosevelt ordered the attorney general to bring suit against the Northern Securities Company, charging it with violating the Sherman Antitrust Act. (See page 420.) The act had been ineffective since the 1895 Supreme Court decision in *United States* v. *E. C. Knight Company*. The Northern Securities case was Roosevelt's invitation to the Court to revive the act.

In *Northern Securities Company* v. *United States* (1904) the Supreme Court ruled that the Northern Securities Company had violated the Sherman Antitrust Act, and it ordered the break-up of the company. Roosevelt's victory prompted him to move against other trusts. The beef, oil, and tobacco trusts were all prosecuted by the government during his presidency.

Despite these prosecutions, monopolies became more prevalent during the Roosevelt years. Robert La Follette questioned whether Roosevelt deserved to be called a trust buster. Roosevelt, La Follette charged, did not bust enough trusts, nor did he prevent new trusts from forming. In fact, although Roosevelt prosecuted more trusts than previous Presidents, the two Presidents who followed him were to prosecute even more.

The Supervision of Business

Roosevelt was not an enemy of big business. He accepted large businesses as an important part of the modern economy and thought that many combinations made good economic sense. However, the President did move against industrialists when he thought they acted irresponsibly, as in the 1902 strike by anthracite coal miners in Pennsylvania. The union asked for a shorter working day and better wages, but the coal operators flatly refused to negotiate.

Summer passed as coal supplies around the country dwindled. Schools and hospitals began to run out. Even after the union agreed to let an arbitrator settle the issues, the operators refused to negotiate. The arrogant attitude of the owners outraged both the President and the public.

The situation was ready-made for Roosevelt's drive to establish the government's right to control harmful business practices. He threatened to send troops in to run the mines if the coal owners refused to negotiate with the union. Other Presidents had used troops in labor disputes, but in support of employers, not workers. The coal mine operators backed down, and Roosevelt was hailed as a champion of working people.

In another effort to increase government supervision of business practices,

Roosevelt convinced Congress to establish the Department of Commerce and Labor in 1903. The department's first job was to assemble facts about American business. Within the department, the Bureau of Corporations publicized information about industry. Roosevelt believed that if the activities of an industry were open to public scrutiny, the business would stay honest.

In expanding government regulation of business, Roosevelt encountered strong opposition within the Republican party. "Old-guard" Republicans traditionally represented business interests. These politicians believed that government interference would weaken the free enterprise system. Thus Roosevelt moved somewhat cautiously in his first years as President, a job he had inherited rather than won on his own.

President in His Own Right

Although Roosevelt prosecuted several important trusts during his first term in office, he did not institute his overall program for reform. He wanted to win an election, to show popular support for his ideas. Roosevelt displayed all his political skills as he planned for the 1904 election. He used presidential appointments to gain supporters and consolidate his control over the party. The Republican convention nominated Roosevelt for President and Charles W. Fairbanks of Indiana for Vice-President.

Since the Republicans were running as reformers, the Democrats tried to attract conservative voters. They nominated Judge Alton B. Parker of New York. Parker's campaign was listless, and Roosevelt won by more popular votes than any previous President. He received 336 electoral votes, compared to Parker's 140, and took a stunning 2.5-million lead in the popular vote.

The election of 1904 made Roosevelt the unchallenged leader of his party. More im-

While some reformers wanted to ban all corporate trusts, Roosevelt made a distinction between "good trusts" and "bad trusts." He ordered the Department of Justice to bring suit against trusts he considered harmful. Roosevelt was the subject of many political cartoons, such as this one.

portant, he and his programs received a clear vote of approval from the people. With typical energy, Roosevelt rushed to put his reform program into effect.

SECTION REVIEW

1. Identify: *Northern Securities Company* v. *United States.*
2. What big business did Roosevelt oppose?
3. What action did Roosevelt take to settle the 1902 coal miners' strike?
4. What was the first task of the Department of Commerce and Labor?
5. **Critical Thinking** How could government regulation strengthen rather than weaken the free enterprise system?

4 The Square Deal in Action

During the 1904 presidential election campaign, Theodore Roosevelt had promised, "I shall see to it that every man has a square deal, no less and no more." Roosevelt's plans for reform quickly became known as the Square Deal. With a combination of per-

suasion, patronage, and skillful use of public outrage, he prodded Congress to pass legislation increasing government authority to regulate business. The President won passage of laws on food, drugs, railroad rates, and the protection of natural resources.

Meat Inspection

"These rats were nuisances," Upton Sinclair wrote in *The Jungle*, "and the packers put out poisoned bread for them; they would die, and then rats, bread, and meat would go into the hoppers together.... The meat would be shoveled into carts, and the man who did the shoveling did not trouble to lift a rat out even when he saw one." Sinclair's book, published in 1906, generated enormous public support for laws requiring strict federal inspection of meatpacking plants.

One of the interested readers of *The Jungle* was the President. Although he regarded some of Sinclair's charges as unfounded, Roosevelt accepted the fact that unsanitary conditions existed in the meatpacking industry. He remembered that during the Spanish-American War hundreds of American soldiers had died from eating tainted meat. Consequently, he pressed Congress to pass a strong meat inspection law.

Albert Beveridge of Indiana piloted a rigorous bill through the Senate. The legislation gave the secretary of agriculture broad authority to settle disputes between government inspectors and meatpackers. It also outlawed misleading labels and dangerous chemical preservatives. The House of Representatives, however, proved friendlier to the meatpackers and passed a weaker bill. At that point Roosevelt stimulated public concern by publicizing a report supporting many of Sinclair's charges. The President encouraged the Republican leaders of the House and Senate to work out a compromise bill.

Reformers were not completely satisfied with the final meat inspection law. For example, it gave the courts, rather than the secretary of agriculture, final authority in disputes between inspectors and meatpackers. But the Meat Inspection Act of 1906 did provide for the enforcement of health and sanitary standards in all phases of the interstate meatpacking industry. Roosevelt thus achieved some but not all of what the reformers wanted. He also reasserted government authority to regulate an industry that ignored the public interest.

The Pure Food and Drug Act

Evidence of other harmful practices in the food and drug industries led to another major piece of legislation in 1906. Canned foods, argued Harvey Wiley of the Department of Agriculture, were being contaminated with dangerous chemical additives. Unfortunately for American consumers, the food industry had repeatedly blocked the passage of corrective legislation introduced up to that point.

While Wiley was exposing the dangers of canned food, Samuel Hopkins Adams was publishing muckraking accounts of misleading advertising in the nonprescription drug industry. Without any proof, companies often claimed that their products cured a wide variety of ailments. Finally, prodded by Roosevelt, Congress passed the Pure Food and Drug Act in 1906. The act barred the use of harmful additives in foods and forbade the use of misleading statements in the advertisement of drugs.

Controlling the Railroads

Farmers and owners of small businesses had long demanded new legislation to tighten government regulation of the railroads. The Interstate Commerce Commission, established in 1887, had been stripped of most of its power by a series of Supreme Court decisions. The Elkins Act, passed in 1903, barred rebates, but railroads were still free to set ruinous shipping rates.

Advertisements for patent medicines, or nonprescription drugs, were affected by the Pure Food and Drug Act of 1906. False and misleading advertising was prohibited, but advertisers still appealed to people's desire to be attractive.

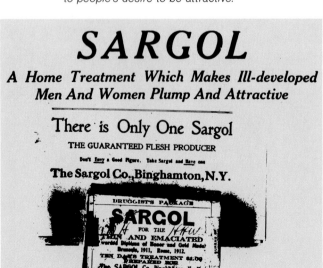

SARGOL

A Home Treatment Which Makes Ill-developed Men And Women Plump And Attractive

There is Only One Sargol

THE GUARANTEED FLESH PRODUCER

Don't Envy a Good Figure. Take Sargol and Have one

The Sargol Co., Binghamton, N.Y.

DRUGGISTS PACKAGE

SARGOL

FOR THE THIN AND EMACIATED

Awarded Diploma of Honor and Gold Medal
Brussels, 1911, Rome, 1912.

TEN DAYS' TREATMENT $1.00
PREPARED BY
The SARGOL Co., Binghamton, N. Y.

The Need for "Pure" Food

By 1900 muckracking writers and government investigators began uncovering conditions in the food industry that threatened the health of Americans. Some of the problems resulted from a lack of sanitary standards or the greed of dishonest merchants, but many occurred because of the demands of a growing urban population for processed foods. For example, it was common knowledge in large cities that milk was diluted. All that dealers needed to boost two quarts of milk to a gallon of milk was access to a water pump. And to improve the color, they often added molasses, chalk, or plaster. Furthermore, milk from diseased cattle was distributed widely.

Some farmers bought garbage from city governments to feed to their cows. Butter and cheese were made from every imaginable part of the animal. A popular jingle described conditions.

Things are seldom what they seem;
Skim milk masquerades as cream;
Lard and soap we eat for cheese;
Butter is but axle grease.

Rising concern led to the passage of laws in some states regulating the preparation of food products. Action on the national level came when Theodore Roosevelt sponsored the Meat Inspection and the Pure Food and Drug acts of 1906. Since then the federal government has continued to enforce standards for food production.

Roosevelt and progressives in Congress proposed a bill that would give the Interstate Commerce Commission the power to nullify unreasonable freight rates. The House approved the measure, known as the Hepburn Bill, but conservatives in the Senate opposed it. President Roosevelt then threatened to lower import tariffs if the bill was not passed. Since the conservatives believed high tariffs were vital to industry, they voted for the bill.

The Hepburn Act, passed in 1906, gave the Interstate Commerce Commission the power to act on complaints from shippers by setting maximum freight rates. Although the railroads could challenge commission decisions in court, they had to charge the new rate while the issue was being decided. The act also placed other transportation facilities such as ferries and oil pipelines under the supervision of the Interstate Commerce Commission.

Conserving Natural Resources

As an outdoorsman and one-time cattle rancher, President Roosevelt loved the American wilderness. Once in 1903 he camped out in a grove of giant sequoias with conservationist John Muir. "I stuffed him pretty well regarding the timber thieves, and the destructive work of the lumbermen, and other spoilers of the forest," said Muir. The next night, while the two camped out, four inches of snow fell. It was, proclaimed the exuberant Roosevelt, the "grandest day of my life." Roosevelt took Muir's words to heart, lashing out at those who would "skin the land, and abandon it when impoverished . . . to the point of worthlessness."

Although Roosevelt loved the forest, he did not share Muir's belief that all the wilderness should be simply left alone. Roosevelt's views on conservation resembled those of Gifford Pinchot, chief of the United States Forest Service. Pinchot believed that forests could serve many purposes. They could be used for recreation, but they could also provide vital wood for lumber and wood products. Planned harvests of trees, Pinchot argued, would enable lumber companies to use the forests without destroying them.

The President urged a balanced conservation program. He supported the Forest Homestead Act in 1906, which allowed the secretary of the interior to open up certain forest lands for agricultural use. Then, in 1907, he slowed the destruction of American forests by barring the cutting of trees on 150 million acres (60 million hectares) of government timberland. Roosevelt also promoted conservation by creating five national wilderness areas.

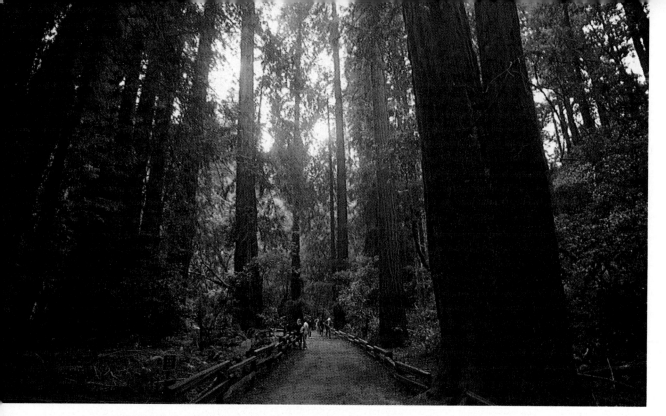

In 1908 Muir Woods National Monument was created by President Roosevelt on land donated to the United States government. The preserve, near San Francisco, was named in honor of John Muir and is known for its giant redwoods.

Major Events	
1900	Robert La Follette elected governor of Wisconsin
1901	McKinley assassinated; Theodore Roosevelt becomes President
1902	Roosevelt intervenes in anthracite coal strike
1903	Congress creates Department of Commerce and Labor
1904	*The Shame of the Cities* published; Roosevelt elected for second term
1906	Upton Sinclair's *The Jungle* published; Hepburn Act passed; Meat Inspection Act passed; Pure Food and Drug Act passed
1908	William Howard Taft elected President
1909	NAACP founded

Agenda for Further Reform

"You have no idea," wrote progressive Senator Albert Beveridge in 1906, "how profound, intense, and permanent the feeling among the American people is that this great reform movement shall go on." President Roosevelt hoped to take advantage of the broad support.

In 1908 he created three groups to consider the problems of farmers and the need to protect national resources. Forty-four governors attended the National Conservation Congress and agreed that such meetings should be held regularly in the form of an annual governors' conference. The National Country Life Commission and the Inland Waterways Commission drafted documented reports, but their activity came to a standstill when Congress refused to provide funds. Many members of Congress feared that executive agencies had gained too much power under Roosevelt.

Roosevelt was discovering that a President whose term was drawing to a close had less influence than a newly elected chief executive. He was further handicapped by the onset of financial panic and depression in

1907. The split between Roosevelt and the conservative wing of his party deepened because conservatives blamed the panic on Roosevelt's antibusiness speeches and actions. They said his trust busting had destroyed confidence in American business.

In response, Roosevelt denounced the "malefactors [evildoers] of great wealth" and promised to continue his campaign against "speculation, corruption, and fraud." Executives of large companies, he said, had opposed "every measure for honesty in business that has been passed during the last six years."

In quick order Roosevelt proposed a series of reform measures that further alarmed conservative Republicans. In messages to Congress in December 1907 and January 1908, the President proposed inheritance and income taxes, more regulation of interstate commerce, and federal investigation of labor disputes. He called for an eight-hour work day and workers' compensation. He also suggested federal regulation of the selling and buying of stock.

Roosevelt's two speeches outlined an ambitious reform agenda for the future and further underscored the growing split between progressives and conservatives in the Republican party.

Passing the Reins to Taft

Following a tradition that began with George Washington, Roosevelt chose not to run for a third term. He did plan, however, to pick his successor. His choice was Secretary of War William Howard Taft. Taft had been a respected judge and had served admirably as governor-general of the Philippines. The Republican convention nominated Taft on the first ballot, with James S. Sherman of New York for Vice-President. The party platform had some progressive planks but was more conservative than Roosevelt or Taft would have liked.

The Democrats tried to regain the presidency by appealing to progressive sentiments. They nominated William Jennings Bryan, who ran a strongly antitrust and pro-labor campaign. However, Bryan did not rekindle the fiery support he had received in his earlier races. In the end Taft won partially because people identified him with Roosevelt. He carried 52 percent of the popular vote and won in the electoral college by a vote of 321 to 162.

William Howard Taft, a lawyer and judge, accepted the Republican nomination for the presidency with some reluctance. His ambition was to be appointed to the Supreme Court. Taft became the only person in history to serve as President of the United States and later as Chief Justice of the Supreme Court.

With the White House securely in Republican hands of his own choosing, Roosevelt embarked on a hunting safari in Africa that kept him out of the country for more than a year. He left behind a record of leadership and dynamism that set high standards for future Presidents. The presidency not only regained the prestige it had lost since the Civil War, but it was becoming the most powerful branch of the federal government. Furthermore, Theodore Roosevelt gave momentum to the progressive movement, which was to dominate the next decade of national politics.

SECTION REVIEW

1. Identify: Upton Sinclair, Meat Inspection Act, Pure Food and Drug Act, John Muir, Gifford Pinchot, William Howard Taft.

2. How did President Roosevelt contribute to passage of the Meat Inspection Act?

3. How did Roosevelt convince Senate conservatives to vote for the Hepburn Act?

4. How did Pinchot's attitude toward the wilderness differ from Muir's?

5. What actions by Roosevelt helped split the progressive and conservative wings of the Republican Party?

6. **Critical Thinking** What do you consider the most important achievement of the Roosevelt administrations? Why?

Chapter 25 Review

490

In Perspective

Progressivism was a reform movement that began around 1900. The core of the movement was formed primarily by members of the middle class. Political corruption, contaminated food, and unhealthy living and working conditions were among the concerns of the progressives. Crusading journalists known as muckrakers publicized scandalous practices. They alerted the public to the issues and paved the way for reform.

Although many progressives were indifferent to the plight of black Americans, some whites joined with blacks to organize the NAACP in 1909. Many progressives sought to improve the conditions of the workers. They urged passage of minimum wage and factory safety laws. They wanted state legislatures to pass child labor laws and to provide state-sponsored industrial accident insurance. Women were active in the progressive movement even though they could not vote in most states. The progressives believed that government should be made more democratic and more efficient.

President Theodore Roosevelt brought progressivism to national government. He filed lawsuits against major trusts. During his second term in office, Congress passed laws establishing federal regulation of the meat-packing, drug, and railroad industries. Roosevelt also took steps to protect forests from destruction. Roosevelt chose William Howard Taft to succeed him. Taft easily won election in 1908.

Vocabulary

Choose the answer that best completes each of the following sentences.

1. A writer who exposed corruption and bad business practices was called a (a) suffragist; (b) muckraker; (c) initiator.

2. Party candidates were chosen by means of (a) primary elections; (b) recall elections; (c) popular assemblies.

3. A professional administrator who is hired to run a city government is (a) a city manager; (b) a council member; (c) an executive director.

4. A means for people to propose bills to the legislature is the (a) referendum; (b) popular poll; (c) initiative.

5. An election to decide if an official will stay in office is (a) a primary election; (b) an open election; (c) a recall election.

6. A direct vote by the people on issues is (a) a referendum; (b) an initiative; (c) a poll.

Chapter Checkup

1. (a) What belief did most progressives share? (b) Did all progressives pursue the same reform goals? Explain.

2. (a) Who were the muckrakers? (b) How did they contribute to the growing reform efforts of the early 1900s?

3. (a) How did progressive attitudes toward the plight of black Americans differ? (b) What action did concerned progressives take to protect the rights of blacks?

4. (a) How did progressives try to improve conditions for workers? (b) Were they successful? Explain.

5. Describe the purpose of the following: (a) primary election; (b) initiative; (c) referendum; (d) recall election.

6. How did Theodore Roosevelt try to increase government supervision of business?

7. (a) Why did Americans feel there was a need for federal guarantees of the purity of food and drugs? (b) How did Congress respond to that need?

8. (a) What was Theodore Roosevelt's attitude toward the conservation of natural resources? (b) What actions did he take?

Critical Thinking

1. **Making a Judgment** (a) How did Theodore Roosevelt's actions as President increase the role of federal government in the national economy? (b) Do you think his actions were good for the country? Why or why not?

2. **Drawing a Conclusion** (a) Why do you think some people were angry about the muckrakers' activities? (b) Are there any journalists today whom you think might be called muckrakers? Explain.

Developing Basic Skills

1. **Relating Past to Present** Visit your local library to find out whether the initiative, referendum, or recall election is allowed in your state. If any of them are, write a report about their use. Include information about the number of times each has been used and the issues involved.

2. **Classifying** Make a chart with three columns. In the first column list the pieces of legislation you read about in this chapter. In the second column describe the problem or issue the law dealt with. In the third column describe how the law tried to solve the problem. When you have completed your chart, answer the following questons: (a) Which of the new laws reflected the concerns of the progressives? (b) Do you think progressives were satisfied with all the measures? Why or why not?

See page 831 for suggested readings.

Writer's Handbook

Bibliography Cards for Other Sources

You should prepare the bibliography cards for a working bibliography as you go along. The information that you need for a magazine or journal card can be found in the *Readers' Guide* listing. The information you need for an encyclopedia or a newspaper article will be available only from the publication itself.

> Rose, Jonathan. "The Sorry History of Drug Abuse in the U.S." *Scholastic Update*. 117 May 10, 1985: 19.

> 032 Enc
> Mowry, George E. "Theodore Roosevelt." *Collier's Encyclopedia*. 1985 ed.

On each card you prepare, write the full name of the author, last name first. Write the title of the article in quotation marks followed by the name of the publication, which should be underlined. For magazines, include the date of publication and the page numbers of the article. For newspapers, include the date, edition, section, and page numbers. For journals include the volume, the year of publication in parentheses, and the page numbers. For encyclopedias, write the edition and the year of publication. If the article is unsigned, begin the card with the title of the article.

Practice: Prepare bibliography cards for the following items.

1. An article entitled Muckrakers, written by David M. Chalmers, published in the 1983 edition of Encyclopedia Americana by Grolier in Danbury, Connecticut.

2. P. Robbins's article The Speech That Saved Theodore Roosevelt's Life, published in the February, 1984, issue of American History Illustrated, Vol. 18, page 6.

3. An article entitled The Making of a Best Seller, 1906, by C. P. Wilson, published in The New York Times Book Review, Vol. 90, December 22, 1985, page 1.

Self-Improvement

As the horse-drawn coach jolted along a dirt road, young Theodore Roosevelt glanced around him. He was, in his own words, "a sickly boy, with no natural bodily prowess." He shared the coach with two other boys about 12 years old, "but very much more competent and also much more mischievous." The boys teased Roosevelt and before long a fight broke out. Roosevelt discovered that either could "handle me so as not to hurt me much and yet to prevent my doing any damage."

The experience changed Roosevelt's life. "I made up my mind," he wrote, "that I would not again be put in such a helpless position." Through his own efforts, the sickly boy built himself into a hardy, powerful adult. Although he was "a painfully slow and awkward pupil," he spent years becoming an expert boxer and wrestler. He also learned to ride and took up hiking, fishing, and hunting.

Roosevelt never forgot his struggle to overcome physical illness. Throughout his life, he encouraged Americans to challenge themselves with rigorous exercise. Not only was "the strenuous life" good for the body—it was good for the spirit as well. Good health in individuals would also help the country, Roosevelt believed.

Theodore Roosevelt's quest for self-improvement reflected a long American tradition of striving for personal perfection. In the 1600s the Puritans in Massachusetts stressed that people should work to eliminate sin from their lives. A career was not work for its own sake, but a calling to do God's work. In that spirit, Jonathan Edwards, whose preaching helped inspire the Great Awakening in 1738, wrote in his spiritual diary, "*Resolved,* never to lose one moment of time, but to improve it in the most profitable way I possibly can."

Striving for Perfection By the mid-1700s Benjamin Franklin had transformed that religious ideal into a more worldly "Project for Arriving at Moral Perfection." In it, Franklin described 13 virtues that he wished to develop in himself. They included frugality, industry, justice, moderation, cleanliness, and tranquility. Each week, Franklin concentrated on nurturing one of the virtues. At night he noted in a book any offenses he was guilty of that day. At the end of 13 weeks, he started over.

Although few Americans have been as systematic as Franklin in seeking self-improvement, the values he upheld have had a wide influence on society. William Holmes McGuffey, a nineteenth century educator and minister, published illustrated readers to teach reading and develop honesty, thrift, charity, and courage in schoolchildren. Over 122 million copies of McGuffey's *Eclectic Reader* were sold from 1836 to 1920. A true education to McGuffey involved moral improvement as well as mastery of the three R's.

A Need for Books In the early 1820s and 1830s, the public school system was

The accommodations at camp meetings were not luxurious, but people bent on self-improvement returned year after year to reform and to improve their lives.

PHYSICAL CVLTVRE

William Muldoon
Horace Fletcher
Charlotte Perkins Gilman
Daniel Carson Goodman
Bernarr Macfadden

The costumes have changed but the activities remain the same. Physical fitness was in vogue in the early 1900s as people tried to improve themselves.

teaching Americans to read. However, many educated adults could not afford books to satisfy their thirst for knowledge. To fill this gap, several experiments in adult education were carried out. One was the lyceum movement founded by Josiah Holbrook. The lyceums began as local study groups and later presented lectures and debates. Holbrook hoped to provide "numerous cheap and practical tracts," which would be circulated to "branch lyceums, schools, academies, taverns, steamboats, and private families." The link between books and self-improvement was growing.

Meanwhile there was another force creating a need for some form of community education for adults. The nation was industrializing and the growing cities were beset with problems of crime, alcoholism, and delinquency. Reformers saw education as a means of raising the level of morality and civic responsibility of the population. In the 1830s the combination of these forces led to the first tax-supported institution for the informal education of adults—the public library. It was organized to provide continuing education for adults.

Chautauqua Movement The quest for self-improvement took many forms. In the late nineteenth century a new movement developed, offering continuing education to adults. The Chautauqua movement was named after the lake in western New York State where its organizers first held meetings. It began as a program for training Sunday school teachers, but expanded in scope over the years.

By the 1880s, hundreds of men and women spent their summers in tents and cabins by the shore of Lake Chautauqua, improving their minds. They studied Hebrew, Latin, Greek, chemistry, music theory, and Shakespeare, among other courses. They listened to lectures on such timely topics as "The Importance of Science to the Religious Thinker," "Nature's Mechanics," and "Teaching in the West." Chautauquans improved their physical health with swimming, tennis, and other sports.

Soon summer institutes modeled on Chautauqua were being held all around the country. The creators of Chautauqua also began a program of home reading, so that those unable to go to camp could participate at home. One home reader began the program when he was 71 years old. At age 86, he wrote to the founders to say, "My vision has been wonderfully enlarged. I have learned something of the sciences. . . . In all these, to me, new revelations I have enjoyed more of life in the last fifteen years than in all the years before." Over the years, millions of Americans have found that the Chautauquas gave them a vision of a better, more fulfilling life.

Not all movements for self-improvement have been as positive as the public library system or the Chautauquas. At times the quest for self-improvement has led some Americans to try ridiculous schemes for instant results. In the 1920s, followers of French philosopher Emile Coué believed

494

they would reach perfection simply by chanting, "Day by day in every way I am getting better and better." Others have tried cure-all diets, special baths, and different forms of mysticism. But most Americans realize that there is no quick route to self-improvement. They would agree with Benjamin Franklin, who wrote in 1758, "There are no gains without pains."

1. What were two underlying causes for the development of the public library system?
2. How would you account for the popularity of the Chautauqua movement?
3. Do you agree with Benjamin Franklin's view that "there are no gains without pains"? Why or why not?

American Profiles # Ernest Thompson Seton

Ernest Thompson Seton, explorer, artist, and writer, was one of the best-known naturalists of his time. A gifted artist, he wrote and illustrated a series of popular wildlife books that drew attention to the nation's vanishing wilderness. Perhaps most important of all, he founded an outdoor organization called the Woodcraft Indians, which later became the Boy Scouts of America. Through the Woodcraft Indians, Seton pioneered a way for young Americans to improve themselves through outdoor activities.

Ernest Thompson Seton was born in London in 1860. At age 6 he moved to Lindsay, Ontario, where his family started a farm. As a boy, Seton loved to listen to an old hunter who lived nearby tell about stalking bear and killing wolves. Slowly, however, he learned a different feeling for the animals of the deep Canadian woods. Seton was interested in observing wild animals, not killing them. His dream "was to be with and study the wild creatures of the world about me."

Several obstacles threatened to keep Seton from reaching his dream. When he was 10, the farm at Lindsay failed, and his family moved to Toronto. Seton did not want to leave the birds and animals he loved. "But the spirit power, the will power, was driving," he discovered, "and each year showed that even in the city the wild things came."

Seton's father presented another obstacle. His father wanted him to give up nature study and become a painter. Seton obeyed his father, working hard and winning a scholarship to art school in London. But the lure of the wilderness drew him back to North America. He traveled widely, sketching birds and animals and writing nature stories. Through hard work, he had made a career that combined his skill as an artist with his love of nature.

With money from his first book, Seton set up a nature sanctuary outside New

---

Ernest Thompson Seton (1860–1946) helped found the Boy Scouts of America and wrote the first Boy Scout manual.

York City. Here he intended to live and experiment with wildlife conservation. But the sanctuary was threatened by local teenagers, who broke down the outer fence and killed Seton's animals. Friends urged Seton to call the police. Instead, he invited the youths, who attended a nearby school, to spend a weekend camping out in the sanctuary. His offer to the students was greeted with a stony silence, but 42 boys showed up on Friday afternoon.

From this incident, Seton saw that outdoor experience could help city youths, and he organized the Woodcraft Indians. Soon chapters had opened all across the country, with young boys learning the skills and crafts of the outdoors. For each skill they perfected, the "Indians" earned a feather. Seton's group became part of the Boy Scouts, which had begun in England,

in 1902. The feathers earned by Seton's Indians became the merit badges of the Boy Scouts. Scouting has given young people a chance to improve themselves.

Seton struggled hard to reach his goals. As one of 14 children, he expected and got little financial help from his parents. He worked hard to achieve success, and then used his success and love of the outdoors to benefit others. The key, he believed, was determination. "All things are possible to him that wills," he told a friend, "for will is the greatest power under the sun."

1. What obstacles did Seton overcome to achieve his goals?
2. How did Seton use nature study to help young people improve themselves?

The Woodcraft Indians

In the following passage, Ernest Thompson Seton describes his first outing with the boys who had vandalized his sanctuary.

Now we set out on what was destined to be an epoch-making outing for the village boys, for myself, and for thousands of boys elsewhere. . . .

The boys wanted to wear feathers. I said: "Certainly, but remember, after the manner of the Indians. The good old Indian did not wear just any feather. . . . Each feather was conferred by the Council as the decoration for an exploit. I will give you a hundred exploits, each of which will entitle the doer to a feather. . . ."

I allowed a feather for all . . . who could walk four miles in an hour, or run 100 yards in eleven seconds. The only cheap one was for swimming. All who could swim one hundred yards, no matter how slowly, got the swimming feather.

In the second department, called Campercraft, I allowed honors to all who could light a campfire with rubbing sticks,

could measure the width of a river without crossing it, etc.

The third department was nature study, and honors were allowed to all who could name correctly twenty-five trees, fifty flowers, fifty birds, etc. . . .

[The outing's] success far exceeded my highest expectations. Rough and wild boys may defy the teacher, and scoff at the opinions of their elders; but they cannot scoff at the public opinion of their playmates. . . .

In the final outcome, there was not one of these a bad boy. All turned out well, and are high-class citizens today.

Adapted from *Trail of an Artist/Naturalist: Autobiography of Ernest Thompson Seton,* (Greenwich, CT: Devin-Adair, 1940).

1. How did Seton adapt the ways of the Indians to his organization?
2. Why do you think Seton's methods worked to instill pride in the boys?

26

Reform Continues

(1909–1919)

Portrait study of Woodrow Wilson
by Sir William Orpen

Chapter Outline

1 *The Ordeal of William Howard Taft*

2 *Choosing a New President*

3 *Reform at High Tide*

4 *Amending the Constitution*

Launched nationally by Theodore Roosevelt and continued less enthusiastically by William Howard Taft, the progressive era reached its high point under President Woodrow Wilson. Even as the progressive tide ran strongest, cautious voices warned that government regulation and other progressive ideas could be dangerous.

Elihu Root, a senator from New York, warned that the "habit of undue interference by government in private affairs breeds the habit of undue reliance upon government at the expense of individual initiative, energy, enterprise, courage."

Despite such doubts, progressives pressed for reform. They were instrumental in adding four amendments to the United States Constitution between 1913 and 1920. Although progressives did not achieve all their goals, they made fundamental changes in American government and politics.

Reform movements

1908	1910	1912	1914	1916	1918	1920

1909 Payne-Aldrich Tariff passed

1910 Mann-Elkins Act passed

1912 Progressive party formed; Wilson elected President

1913 16th, 17th Amendments ratified

1916 Child Labor, Workingmen's Compensation acts passed

1919 18th Amendment ratified

1920 19th Amendment ratified

1 The Ordeal of William Howard Taft

William Howard Taft faced many dilemmas. He was a conservative at heart but had been hand-picked for the Republican nomination by a progressive, Theodore Roosevelt. Taft had wanted to be a Supreme Court justice but had been pushed toward the presidency by his ambitious wife, Helen. As President, Taft hated the political deals that were part of his job. He was a quiet individual, serving in the shadow of the boisterous Roosevelt. While the presidency had been an exciting challenge for Roosevelt, it was somewhat of an ordeal for Taft.

Taft and the Tariff

Taft had consistently supported the reduction of tariffs on imported goods, an important part of the progressive program. As long as tariffs protected American products from foreign competition, manufacturers could charge high prices. Progressives considered this practice unfair to consumers. In his campaign Taft pledged to reduce the tariff, and upon taking office in 1909 he called a special session of Congress to do so.

During that session Republican Representative Sereno Payne sponsored a tariff-reduction bill, which the House passed. But the Payne bill ran into trouble in the Senate. There Senator Nelson Aldrich of Rhode Island added so many amendments to the bill that it actually raised the tariff on 500 frequently used items.

Instead of fighting to reverse the increases, Taft drifted into agreement with the Aldrich amendments. Thus the Payne-Aldrich Tariff Act of 1909 cut tariffs on a few items, but its main effect was to further insulate domestic manufacturers from foreign competition. When Taft called the tariff "the best bill that the Republican Party ever passed," progressives were dismayed. Progressive disaffection with Taft would soon extend to other issues.

The Fight Against Cannon

Throughout the first decade of the twentieth century and for many years before, the House of Representatives had been dominated by Representative Joseph G. Cannon of Illinois. As speaker of the house, Cannon made committee appointments, which were extremely important to representatives. If, for example, a representative from a farm state wanted to sit on a committee that drafted farm legislation, only Cannon could put him there.

Furthermore, under the rules of the House, the speaker had the right to appoint a majority of the members of the Rules Committee. That committee determined when bills would be debated by the entire House. Cannon, a conservative, had often used his power to block reform legislation.

Taft disliked Cannon personally and opposed his extreme conservative views. In 1909 when rebellious House Republicans proposed to strip Speaker Cannon of some of his power, Taft pledged to support them. Led by George Norris of Nebraska, House progressives began the struggle to change the rules of the House. They assumed that Taft would stand with them, but once again the President disappointed them.

Conservative Republicans promised to cooperate with Taft on other issues if he would support Cannon's reelection as speaker in 1910. The President agreed, but despite Taft's inaction, progressives from both parties were able to gather enough votes to pass rules limiting the speaker's power.

Conservation

Taft's action on the conservation of natural resources also disappointed many progressives. Although President Taft set aside more national park and forest land than Roosevelt had, he emerged as a villain to those who favored conservation.

The trouble began in 1910 when Taft's secretary of the interior, Richard A. Ballinger, issued an order allowing the government to sell certain wilderness areas in Wyoming and Montana. As a conservation measure these areas had been withdrawn from sale during the Roosevelt administration. Ballinger, who doubted the legality of Roosevelt's ban on the sale, repealed it.

Gifford Pinchot, the chief of the United States Forest Service, was enraged by the

Throughout his presidency, William Howard Taft worked under the shadow of Theodore Roosevelt. Comparisons between the two were made frequently. In this 1910 cartoon, Taft knits himself into a hopeless tangle of unsolved problems. Roosevelt turns a disapproving eye on the man he picked to succeed him.

repeal. He charged that Ballinger was trying to enrich corporations interested in exploiting the resources of the area. Angry at the attack on his administration, Taft fired Pinchot.

The Ballinger-Pinchot controversy was a political disaster for Taft. The public came to doubt the President's commitment to conservation. Popular outrage against Ballinger forced Taft to ask for his resignation. Theodore Roosevelt resented Taft's treatment of Pinchot and was impatient with the President's seeming indifference to conservation. The controversy widened a growing gap between Taft and Roosevelt supporters within the Republican party.

Continuing Progressive Reform

President Taft's battles with Republican reformers obscured the achievements of his administration. He had supported several new conservation laws and had set aside more public lands for conservation than Roosevelt. Furthermore, although Roosevelt was known as a trust buster, Taft's administration prosecuted more trusts.

President Taft was an unlikely opponent of trusts. As a judge he had a probusiness reputation, and as President he filled his cabinet with prosperous corporation lawyers. Yet Taft did not favor the trusts. Taft's attorney general filed 90 antitrust lawsuits, compared to 44 during the Roosevelt administration. Cases against Standard Oil and the American Tobacco Company resulted in the reorganization of those giant firms. Despite Taft's willingness to enforce antitrust laws, many progressives in Congress favored more far-reaching measures against monopolies.

President Taft took other progressive actions as well. He supported the Mann-Elkins Act of 1910, which allowed the Interstate Commerce Commission to regulate railroad rates on commission members' initiative even without complaints from shippers. The act also gave the ICC power to regulate telegraph companies.

The Department of Commerce and Labor was split into two separate departments under Taft, and Taft fulfilled another progressive objective by creating a Children's Bureau in the Labor Department. He also approved new safety regulations for mines and railroads. During his administration Congress established an eight-hour workday for government employees and increased the number of government jobs filled by the Civil Service, further limiting patronage positions. Yet Taft lacked the skill to turn these actions into political gains. Republican progressives saw Theodore Roosevelt as their leader.

Return of the Rough Rider

Progressive Republicans asked Roosevelt for support in the congressional elections of 1910. They felt that Taft and the conservatives were working to crush progressivism in the Republican party. Roosevelt, recently returned from his hunting trip in Africa, entered the fray.

In a speech at Osawatomie, Kansas, on August 31, 1910, Roosevelt advocated a New Nationalism. This program contained a full package of progressive reforms. It urged stringent federal regulation of business, the enactment of social welfare laws, and a curb on the power of courts to nullify regulatory legislation. Fired with enthusiasm, Roosevelt attacked "local selfishness" and championed

a strong national government committed to the public welfare.

Conservative Republicans shuddered at what sounded to them like a deeply radical program, and they deserted progressive Republican candidates in droves. With the Republicans badly split, the Democrats scored major gains in 1910. They won control of the House of Representatives for the first time in nearly 20 years. They also won many important governorships, including that of New Jersey, where Woodrow Wilson trounced the Republican opposition. Disunity would continue to plague the Republican party during the presidential election of 1912.

SECTION REVIEW

1. Identify: Payne-Aldrich Tariff, Joseph Cannon, Richard Ballinger, Mann-Elkins Act, New Nationalism.
2. (a) Why did progressives oppose high tariffs? (b) How did they react to Taft's acceptance of the Payne-Aldrich Tariff?
3. What position made Joe Cannon powerful in the House of Representatives?
4. List three ways President Taft continued progressive reform.
5. **Critical Thinking** Are any of the issues that troubled the Taft administration still issues today?

2 Choosing a New President

In March 1912 Theodore Roosevelt said of President Taft, "I have never been so disappointed in any man." Frustrated on the political sidelines, Roosevelt attempted to win the Republican nomination. His move further split the Republican party and helped put a Democrat in the White House for only the third time since the Civil War.

The Progressive Rebellion

As the 1912 election approached, Robert La Follette of Wisconsin challenged Taft for the Republican presidential nomination. La Follette drew strong support from Republican progressives. When La Follette's health failed, Roosevelt decided to take up the challenge. Taft refused to step aside for his for-

mer friend and sponsor, and the fight was on. Often the fight turned rowdy as Republican delegates at state conventions shouted, punched, and hurled chairs at each other.

President Taft controlled the Republican party apparatus that ran the national nominating convention held in June 1912. With skillful maneuvers, Taft filled the convention with loyal delegates. Roosevelt claimed fraud, and his supporters left the hall. The remaining delegates nominated Taft on the first ballot.

Roosevelt and his fellow progressives promptly launched a new political party, which they named the Progressive party. The new party held its own presidential nominating convention in Chicago in August. The delegates quickly nominated Roosevelt and greeted his fiery acceptance speech with thunderous applause. Roosevelt announced that he felt "as strong as a bull moose," so that animal became the party symbol. Now the Republican elephant and Democratic donkey had to contend with a fighting-mad bull moose.

The Progressive party platform called for the initiative and referendum (see page 481), women's suffrage, and direct presidential primaries. On the question of trusts, the Progressive party rejected suggestions that large monopolies be broken up. Instead the platform called for government regulation of the activities of large corporations. The party also urged passage of a minimum wage, unemployment insurance, and workers' compensation insurance. The platform clearly reflected the New Nationalism Roosevelt had outlined in 1910.

The point of this 1912 cartoon seems to be that the Progressive, or "Bull Moose," party was little more than a forum for Theodore Roosevelt. Yet the creation of the Progressive party did more than provide Roosevelt with a way to run for reelection. It also brought together leading reformers from both major political parties.

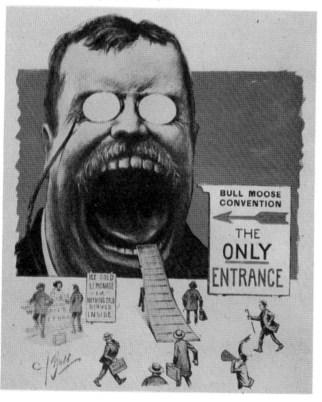

New Freedom v. New Nationalism

Confident because of the split in Republican ranks, the Democrats looked forward to victory in 1912. The Democratic convention nominated Woodrow Wilson, a progressive who had been president of Princeton University and governor of New Jersey. Wilson was an attractive candidate, intelligent, honest, and dedicated to reform. It soon became apparent that the election was a two-way race between Wilson and Roosevelt. Taft had little chance for reelection.

Wilson championed what he called the New Freedom. The New Freedom demanded the break-up of the giant trusts because, Wilson believed, they choked off competition. He feared that increasing government regulation would make the government too powerful. In his opinion, competition was the best way to promote individual opportunity. Roosevelt, on the other hand, insisted that the federal government should be powerful enough to police even the largest trust. The issue of the trusts dominated the presidential campaign of 1912.

The Socialist Challenge

Taft, Wilson, and Roosevelt were not the only candidates running for the presidency in 1912. Eugene V. Debs, founder of the American Railroad Union, was the presidential candidate of the Socialist party.

The Socialist party was founded in 1901, with Debs as one of the prime architects. The party contained diverse elements. Moderate socialists, content with city-government ownership of the utility industries, were often called gas-and-water socialists. More radical socialists, including Debs, favored government ownership of all large-scale business. In this way Debs differed from Roosevelt, who believed that government should supervise monopolies, and Wilson, who believed they should be broken up.

The goal of government ownership of industry was too extreme for most Americans, but the Socialist party platform contained other planks that broadened its appeal. For example, it supported the right of workers to join labor unions.

Debs had first run for President in 1900. He ran again in 1904 and received four times as many votes as in 1900. In 1912 he made his most impressive showing: almost 900,000

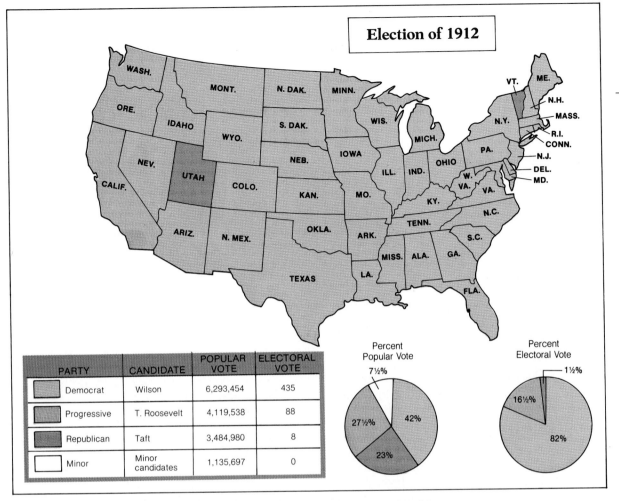

Election of 1912

PARTY	CANDIDATE	POPULAR VOTE	ELECTORAL VOTE
Democrat	Wilson	6,293,454	435
Progressive	T. Roosevelt	4,119,538	88
Republican	Taft	3,484,980	8
Minor	Minor candidates	1,135,697	0

Percent Popular Vote

7½% 42% 27½% 23%

Percent Electoral Vote

1½% 16½% 82%

■ *In the 1912 election Republican strength was split between party candidate William Howard Taft and ex-President Theodore Roosevelt, who ran as a Progressive. As the table and graph show, Democrat Woodrow Wilson won a stunning victory in the electoral college. The popular vote was much closer.*

votes, or 6 percent of the total popular vote. Debs's increasing popularity was linked, in part, to the reform spirit of the period. Awakened to social injustices by journalists and other writers, much public dissatisfaction spilled over into support for the socialists. However, the Socialist party was unable to build on its gains in the 1912 election. By the 1920s its popular support had largely evaporated.

A Democratic Victory

Taft and Roosevelt split the Republican vote in the 1912 presidential election, and Woodrow Wilson won handily. He received only 42 percent of the popular vote but won a majority in the electoral college. (See the graphs above.) Democrats also won control of the House and the Senate and 21 governorships.

If the election of 1912 was a defeat for Roosevelt's Progressive party, it was not a defeat for reform. The three reform candidates—Wilson, Roosevelt, and Debs—received almost 11 million of the 15 million votes cast. Reform would be on the national agenda for the next four years.

SECTION REVIEW

1. Identify: Progressive party, New Freedom, Eugene V. Debs, Socialist party.
2. What led Theodore Roosevelt to leave the Republican party in 1912?
3. How did the attitudes of Wilson and Roosevelt toward trust differ?
4. **Critical Thinking** For whom would you have voted in 1912? Why?

3 Reform at High Tide

Many people looked skeptically at the scholarly professor elected President by less than half the voters. They wondered if a man who had spent most of his life in the academic world could withstand the demands of national politics.

Any such doubts soon vanished. In his own way Wilson was every bit as forceful as Roosevelt. An excellent leader, he knew how to inspire people. He believed that the President should be the voice of the highest national ideals. Of the President he said, "Let him once win the admiration and confidence of the country, and no single force can withstand him, no combination of forces can easily overpower him."

Tackling the Tariff

Progressives had been outraged over the Payne-Aldrich tariff passed under President Taft. They looked to Woodrow Wilson, who shared their goal of lowering tariffs. Wilson opposed high tariffs because he believed that American industry would become more efficient if it were faced with greater foreign competition. Competition would force American industrialists to improve their products and lower their prices. Wilson maintained that such actions would benefit the economy of the United States.

Soon after taking office in 1913 Wilson called Congress into special session to reduce tariff duties. To dramatize the moment, the President appeared in Congress to deliver his message personally. No President since John Adams had done so, and the action riveted public attention on the tariff issue.

Under strong pressure from Wilson, the House passed a bill removing the tariff from many items and lowering duties on others. But the Senate proved less cooperative. Lobbyists for such industries as lumber, steel, and wool, which would face greater competition under the proposed legislation, urged senators to vote against it. Probusiness newspapers supported the attacks on the tariff bill.

Wilson did not back away from the fight. As the hot Washington summer wore on, he kept up the pressure on wavering senators. Finally Wilson prevailed, and on October 3, 1913, he signed the Underwood-Simmons Tariff Act. The act substantially lowered the duty on imports for the first time since the Civil War, and many believed that it would lower the cost of living for the average citizen.

To replace revenues lost by cutting tariffs, the Underwood-Simmons Tariff Act included a provision that drew little debate at the time but would have a lasting effect on ordinary citizens. It enacted a graduated income tax, a system of taxing personal incomes by which people who had higher incomes paid proportionately higher taxes.

The Federal Reserve Act

After the passage of the Underwood-Simmons Tariff Act, Wilson pushed through other economic reforms. One such reform was the creation of the federal reserve system. The financial panic of 1907 had convinced many Americans that government action was needed to insure a reliable supply of credit. A small group of bankers seemed to control the national money supply, and they were often unable or unwilling to extend credit.

President Wilson believed that government should regulate the supply of credit. He declared that "control must be public, not private, [and] must be vested in government itself, so that the banks may be the instruments, not the masters, of business and individual enterprise and initiative." After a long struggle in Congress, Wilson's banking bill was passed.

The Federal Reserve Act, signed by Wilson on December 23, 1913, transformed the banking system. It divided the nation into 12 districts and established a federal reserve bank for each district. National banks within a district deposited monetary reserves in the federal reserve bank. This money could then be used to increase the credit supply.

The Federal Reserve Board, headquartered in Washington, D.C., controlled the system of banks. The board set interest rates on loans made by the federal reserve banks to member banks. By lowering interest rates, the Federal Reserve Board made loans easier to obtain, which thereby increased the money supply. By raising rates, the board, in turn, could tighten the money supply. President Wilson hoped that the Federal Reserve Act would increase competition in the business world by making it easier for investors to obtain credit.

Attacking the Trusts

As a candidate, Wilson seemed to favor the break-up of all large trusts. As President, he embarked on a more moderate course, but he did support two pieces of legislation that sought to control monopolies.

The Federal Trade Commission Act, passed in 1914, provided for the creation of the Federal Trade Commission (FTC). The purpose of the FTC was to preserve competition by preventing one firm from destroying another through unfair business practices. The commission would investigate complaints of unfair practices such as misleading advertising. If the commission found that a complaint was justified, a "cease and desist" order would be issued. Such an order would bar the firm from continuing the misleading advertising.

The Clayton Antitrust Act, also passed in 1914, was designed to strengthen the Sherman Antitrust Act. (See page 420.) The new law prohibited pricing policies that might destroy competition and outlawed the purchase of stock in competing firms. It also made the use of interlocking directorates illegal. The *interlocking directorate* was the practice of allowing the same individuals to serve on the boards of directors of various firms in the same industry. The practice had been used to create monopolies.

The Clayton Antitrust Act, unlike the Sherman Antitrust Act, stated that labor unions could not be prosecuted under antitrust laws. Furthermore, it recognized the right of workers to strike and picket. Samuel Gompers, president of the American Federation of Labor, considered the act a major victory for workers.

A Mixed Record on Social Issues

At the beginning of his administration Wilson was hesitant to foster social legislation. His main interest had been economic fairness. He had repeatedly opposed legislation that benefited only certain groups of people, but pressure from the progressive wing of his party made him more willing to support social-reform bills. These included the Seaman Act of 1915, establishing minimum standards for the treatment of merchant sailors, and the Adamson Act of 1916, establishing an eight-hour work day for railroad workers.

The elimination of child labor was a key progressive goal. These young waterboys worked at the Homestead, Pennsylvania, steelworks. School ended at the eighth grade or earlier for many young people.

In 1913 department store owner Rodman Wanamaker financed an expedition to visit more than 200 Native American groups. The purpose of the expedition was to promote Native American citizenship and make a photographic record of Native American life. President Wilson recorded a speech to be played at ceremonies such as this one in Pauma, California.

Congress passed the Workingmen's Compensation Act in 1916. It provided financial assistance to federal civil service employees who became disabled. The Child Labor Act, signed by the President in 1916, banned from interstate commerce any goods produced by child labor. The President also signed the Farm Loan Act in 1916, which made it easier for farmers to get loans.

Wilson resisted pressure to increase restrictions on immigration even though many progressives favored the idea. Social workers, for example, wanted to restrict immigration because they believed it contributed to urban problems. Labor unions wanted to reduce the number of immigrants who competed for jobs. Twice the President vetoed bills that would have restricted immigration. But in 1917 Congress overrode his veto and passed a bill requiring immigrants to pass a literacy test.

As you read in Chapter 25, some progressives were concerned with the problems of black Americans, but many were not. During his campaign for President Woodrow Wilson had promised "absolute fair dealing" to black Americans. But when he took office his actions disappointed black leaders. For example, he approved the policy of official segregation in the federal government. Ac-cording to this policy, black employees were forced to use separate rest rooms, and in some offices screens were placed between black and white employees.

In 1913 a group of black leaders went to the White House to talk to Wilson about segregation in government employment. After listening to their protest the President told them that "segregation is not humiliating but a benefit, and ought to be so regarded by you gentlemen." Throughout his presidency, Wilson did not change his attitude toward segregation in government.

SECTION REVIEW

1. Identify: Underwood-Simmons Tariff Act, Federal Reserve Act, Federal Trade Commission, Clayton Antitrust Act.
2. Define: interlocking directorate.
3. What action could the Federal Reserve Board take to increase the money supply?
4. Name two practices outlawed by the Clayton Antitrust Act.
5. What social reform legislation was passed during Wilson's administration?
6. **Critical Thinking** How did Wilson's reforms reflect the growing industrialization of the United States?

4 Amending the Constitution

The framers of the United States Constitution purposely made the document difficult to change. To amend the Constitution both houses of Congress must pass a proposed amendment by a two-thirds majority. Although there are four ways to ratify an amendment, the most typical procedure is ratification by the legislatures in three fourths of the states. Since the first ten amendments, the Bill of Rights, were ratified in 1791, only five amendments had been added to the Constitution by 1912. Yet between 1913 and 1920 the Constitution was amended four times. The new constitutional amendments reflected the reform spirit of the progressive era.

The Income Tax

In 1895 the Supreme Court had ruled that an income tax was unconstitutional, but the progressives continued to push for one. An income tax would fulfill two of their goals. First, it would provide revenue to pay for progressive reforms. Second, a graduated income tax would place the greatest tax burden on those who had the highest incomes. The progressives believed that such a system would be fairest.

Many Americans opposed an income tax, however. Some believed that the government had no right to take away money that people earned. Others objected to the way the federal government spent tax revenues. They disapproved of such plans as workers' compensation insurance.

During President Taft's administration, progressives proposed an income tax to replace revenue lost by a reduction in tariffs. Taft favored an income tax, but he thought that the Supreme Court would again strike it down. Consequently, the only way to enact a federal income tax was to amend the Constitution.

In July 1909 Congress passed the Sixteenth Amendment, granting Congress the power to lay and collect taxes on incomes. By February 1913 three fourths of the states had ratified the amendment. Later that year the Underwood-Simmons Tariff Act imposed a graduated income tax.

Direct Election of Senators

Until 1913 voters did not choose United States senators directly. As specified in the Constitution, state legislatures elected the senators who represented the states in Congress. However, the election of senators by state legislatures was accompanied by many problems. Interest groups could "buy" seats in the Senate by bribing legislators. And political machines controlled some state legislatures, placing the election of senators in the hands of machine bosses.

Progressives believed that the direct election of senators would end these abuses and make the system more democratic. With people voting for senators directly, bribery would be eliminated. A special interest group might try to bribe a whole legislature, but it could not pay off the entire electorate.

Progressive efforts to change the constitutional procedure for electing senators met with rapid success. In May 1912 Congress passed the Seventeenth Amendment, requiring direct election of senators. A year later the required number of states had ratified the amendment, and it too became part of the Constitution.

Prohibition

The progressives favored the direct election of senators because they thought it would reduce corruption. A similar impulse aided the movement to outlaw liquor. Advocates of *prohibition*, the ban on the sale of alcoholic beverages, believed that liquor was a corrupting influence. They argued that excessive drinking ruined families and caused industrial accidents. Saloons were seen as centers of immorality and corruption.

The drive to eliminate alcoholic beverages from the United States had begun many years earlier as a moral crusade. The roots of prohibition reached far back into Protestant New England. As early as 1851, Maine had voted itself "dry," banning the sale of alcoholic beverages. (See page 296.) By 1917 there were 26 other dry states, although many permitted the sale of weaker beverages such as beer.

Spearheading the temperance crusade was the Women's Christian Temperance Union, headed by Frances Willard, and the Anti-Saloon League. Both groups urged a ban on the sale and manufacture of all alcoholic beverages. The prohibitionists helped create the moral climate that made prohibition possible, but many people believed a law against drinking would never succeed. Theodore Roosevelt, although sympathetic to temperance arguments, thought such a law would be unenforceable and would only lessen respect for laws in general.

The outbreak of war in Europe in 1914, however, strengthened the temperance movement. After the United States entered the war in 1917, prohibitionists argued that a ban on alcohol would increase industrial efficiency. Furthermore, they claimed that grain used for making alcohol could be used as food for soldiers instead. Congress passed the Eighteenth Amendment, prohibiting the manufacture, sale, and transportation of liquor, in December 1917. It was ratified in January 1919.

Women's Suffrage

As you read in Chapter 23, women at the turn of the century were entering the work force in greater numbers than ever before.

Women dominated the crusade to ban the use of alcohol. Saloons around the nation were shut down because of the prohibition amendment. This former saloon at the Majestic Hotel in New York City became a library. Note the books on top of the "bar."

★ American Profiles ★

Carrie Chapman Catt: A Victory for Women

Carrie Chapman Catt, born in Wisconsin in 1859, was influenced by the frontier atmosphere of her youth. She developed a strong sense of independence and purpose. After graduating from Iowa State College in 1880, she accepted a position as principal at a nearby high school. Within two years she had become superintendent of schools, an unusually responsible post for a woman at that time. Catt later worked for a year on a San Francisco newspaper before returning to Iowa, where she became active in the women's suffrage movement.

Catt became an accomplished speaker for women's suffrage on both the state and national levels. She became president of the National American Woman Suffrage Association in 1900. In four years she built an efficient nationwide organization with a healthy treasury.

In 1916 the association adopted a strategy, proposed by Catt, that led to the passage of the Nineteenth Amendment. Association members worked to win women the right to vote in individual states. As a result of their efforts the number of so-called suffrage states increased dramatically in 1917 and 1918. These victories convinced President Wilson to actively support the amendment, which was passed by Congress in June 1919. Yet Catt's work was far from over. In the summer of 1920 she spent two months campaigning in Tennessee, the final state needed for ratification. The Tennessee legislature approved the amendment in August 1920, and women's suffrage was won.

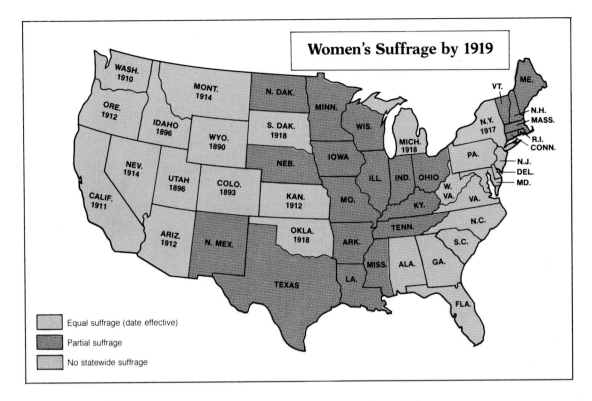

Women's Suffrage by 1919

WASH. 1910
MONT. 1914
ORE. 1912
IDAHO 1896
WYO. 1890
N. DAK.
S. DAK. 1918
MINN.
WIS.
NEV. 1914
UTAH 1896
COLO. 1893
NEB.
IOWA
MICH. 1918
CALIF. 1911
KAN. 1912
ILL.
IND.
OHIO
W. VA.
PA.
ARIZ. 1912
N. MEX.
OKLA. 1918
MO.
KY.
VA.
N.C.
ARK.
TENN.
S.C.
TEXAS
LA.
MISS.
ALA.
GA.
FLA.
VT.
ME.
N.H.
MASS.
N.Y. 1917
R.I.
CONN.
N.J.
DEL.
MD.

☐ Equal suffrage (date effective)
☐ Partial suffrage
☐ No statewide suffrage

■ *By 1919 women in most states could vote in state and local elections. As the map shows, women had full suffrage in 15 states, mostly in the West. Only 11 states had no women's suffrage.*

Their growing economic independence nourished demands for political rights. Women's experience in state and national progressive reform movements also prompted them to demand the right to vote. Women reformers had learned that without the vote they lacked the power needed to bring about political change.

Some women believed that women should have the right to vote because they were morally superior to men. They argued that women in politics would raise the moral standards of public life. Suffragists asserted that without the right to vote, women were powerless against people who made and enforced laws affecting them.

By 1912 the impact of changed social roles and the general spirit of reform had allowed the suffrage movement to flourish. Two groups led this movement. One was the National American Woman Suffrage Association, headed by Carrie Chapman Catt. In state after state the association pressured legislatures to extend suffrage.

A young Quaker, Alice Paul, and the Woman's party she helped found introduced a more militant approach to the campaign for the right to vote. On the day of Wilson's inauguration, Paul organized a spectacular parade through Washington, D. C., to demonstrate support for women's suffrage. When Wilson refused to support a constitutional amendment granting women the right to vote, Alice Paul and the Woman's party began picketing the White House every day. She and other pickets were jailed and, when they went on a hunger strike, were force-fed. The resulting publicity dramatized the suffrage crusade.

While Congress stalled on suffrage, states in the West and Midwest voted it in one by one. By 1919, 15 states permitted full women's suffrage, and many other states allowed women to vote in local or state elections. Only 11 states, mostly in the East and South, did not allow women to vote at all. (See the map above.) After a major effort by both suffrage organizations, Congress passed the Nineteenth Amendment in 1919. It was ratified by the states in August 1920.

The Nineteenth Amendment marked the last major reform of the progressive era. During this period reformers had struggled to make politics less corrupt and more

Major Events	
1909	Payne-Aldrich Tariff Act passed
1910	Ballinger-Pinchot controversy; Mann-Elkins Act passed
1912	Progressive party formed; Woodrow Wilson elected President
1913	Sixteenth Amendment, authorizing income tax, ratified; Seventeenth Amendment, establishing direct election of senators, ratified; Underwood-Simmons Tariff Act passed; Federal Reserve Act passed
1914	Federal Trade Commission established; Clayton Antitrust Act passed
1919	Eighteenth Amendment, prohibiting manufacture and sale of liquor, ratified
1920	Nineteenth Amendment, giving women right to vote, ratified

democratic. They had sought economic justice for workers, farmers, consumers, and owners of small businesses. Congress had accumulated an impressive record of legislation, and the Constitution had been changed in important ways. But by 1917, war loomed. Americans turned away from reform and paid closer attention to foreign affairs.

SECTION REVIEW

1. Identify: Women's Christian Temperance Union, Anti-Saloon League, Carrie Chapman Catt, Alice Paul.
2. Define: prohibition.
3. What two reasons did progressives have for favoring an income tax?
4. According to progressives, how would the direct election of senators reduce corruption?
5. What tactics did Alice Paul use to bring attention to the suffrage movement?
6. **Critical Thinking** Which of the amendments passed between 1913 and 1920 do you think had the greatest effect on society? Why?

Chapter 26 Review

In Perspective

William Howard Taft had been chosen for the Republican presidential nomination by the progressive-minded Roosevelt, but, as President, Taft disappointed many progressives. Although he instituted a number of reforms, Taft alienated progressives over issues such as the tariff and conservation.

Impatient with Taft's policies, Theodore Roosevelt tried to win the Republican nomination in 1912. When he failed, he founded his own political organization, the Progressive Party. With the Republicans split, the Democratic candidate, Woodrow Wilson, won easily.

During Wilson's presidency, Congress continued to pass progressive legislation. It lowered the tariff, established federal control of the banking system, and strengthened antitrust laws. It also acted to improve working conditions.

Far-reaching constitutional changes occurred during the progressive era. Amendments were ratified authorizing an income tax, establishing the direct election of senators, extending suffrage to women, and banning the manufacture and sale of alcoholic beverages. By 1917, however, the attention of most Americans was turning from domestic reform to world affairs.

Vocabulary

On a separate sheet of paper, write the word or words that best complete each of the following sentences.

1. A (An) ____ is a system of taxation by which people with higher incomes pay proportionately higher taxes.

2. ___ is the ban on the sale of alcoholic beverages.

3. The ___ movement sought to gain for women the right to vote.

4. A (An) ___ barred a company from continuing deceptive advertising.

5. A (An) ___ is the practice of allowing the same individuals to serve on the boards of directors of various firms in the same industry.

Chapter Checkup

1. In what ways did Taft continue progressive reform? Give specific examples.

2. What reform measures did the Progressive party platform call for?

3. Describe the system established by the Federal Reserve Act.

4. (a) What four amendments to the Constitution were ratified between 1913 and 1920? (b) Describe the content of each.

Critical Thinking

1. Analyzing What developments between 1850 and 1920 do you think contributed to the eventual success of the women's suffrage movement?

2. Comparing Compare Wilson's New Freedom and Roosevelt's New Nationalism. Which of the two do you think was a better way to approach the giant trusts?

Developing Basic Skills

1. Analyzing Read the text of the Sixteenth, Seventeenth, Eighteenth, and Nineteenth amendments on pages 862–863. (a) Which amendment or amendments changed part of the original Constitution? (b) Which constitutional clause or clauses were altered?

2. Comparing Make a chart with three columns. In column 1 list the actions of President Roosevelt that reflected progressive goals. (See Chapter 25.) In column 2 list the actions of President Taft that reflected progressive goals. In column 3 list the actions of President Wilson that reflected progressive goals. Which President do you think best represented the progressive era?

See page 831 for suggested readings.

Writer's Handbook

Preparing the Final Bibliography

The final bibliography is an alphabetical list of the sources you used to prepare your research paper. Since you wrote the author's last name first on each bibliography card, you can organize your bibliography by putting the cards in alphabetical order. Unsigned articles are alphabetized according to the first word of the title of the article. When you have more than one source by the same author, arrange them alphabetically by title. The author's name is written out only once. From the second entry on, three short dashes replace the author's name. Study the sample entries for style and punctuation.

Angle, Paul McClelland. _Crossroads: 1913._ Chicago, Rand McNally, 1963.

Johnson D.E. and J.R. Johnson. "Three Hats in the Ring." _American History Illustrated_, November 19, 1984, pp. 12-17.

DiBacco, Thomas V. "Taxing Time." _Christian Science Monitor_. March 18, 1986, p. 14.

Practice: Arrange, capitalize, and punctuate the following bibliography entries.

1. An article entitled Carrie Chapman Catt, by Edna Lamprey Stantial, published in Collier's Encyclopedia, 1985 edition.

2. A book by Paolo Enrico Coletta entitled The Presidency of William Howard Taft, published in 1973 by the University Press of Kansas in Lawrence.

The United States in World Affairs

27

(1900–1916)

Detail from Across the Canal at Culebra *by Jonas Lie*

Chapter Outline

1 *The Growth of American Power Abroad*

2 *The Panama Canal*

3 *The United States and Asia*

4 *Woodrow Wilson and Moral Diplomacy*

By 1900 the United States was becoming an important actor in world affairs. American territory included the Philippines, the Hawaiian Islands, Puerto Rico, and Guam. The United States also exercised a protectorate over Cuba and was involved in China. Yet, the United States had little experience in the complicated art of international diplomacy. It had asserted its power in Latin America under the provisions of the Monroe Doctrine, but challenging the power of Great Britain, France, Germany, Japan, and Russia would test American leaders.

Theodore Roosevelt gladly accepted the test. He wanted the United States to exercise authority in Latin America and Asia. The construction of the Panama Canal was symbolic of his efforts. Roosevelt's successors, William Howard Taft and Woodrow Wilson, based their actions on different theories, but they continued to pursue an active foreign policy.

Wilson's "moral diplomacy"

1900	1902	1904	1906	1908	1910	1912	1914	1916

1901
Hay-Pauncefote Treaty signed

1904
Roosevelt Corollary issued

1906
U.S. troops restore order in Cuba

1908
William Howard Taft elected President

1911
Mexican Revolution begins

1912
Woodrow Wilson elected President

1915
Panama Canal opens

1 The Growth of American Power Abroad

As President, Theodore Roosevelt pushed for greater American involvement in world affairs. He established policies that continued throughout the progressive era. Indeed, echoes of Roosevelt's foreign policy would be heard throughout most of the twentieth century. Roosevelt actively promoted commerce abroad. He championed the Monroe Doctrine and stood ready to meet any challenge to the national interest. He expressed his faith in action in 1900 when he said, "I have always been fond of the West African proverb, 'speak softly and carry a big stick, you will go far.'"

Advancing American Commerce

Americans needed new markets where they could sell their industrial and agricultural products, which were pouring forth in quantities never before seen anywhere in the world. The people of the United States lived in a country of extraordinary mineral wealth and vast fertile farmland. Those natural endowments, coupled with a great talent for inventing labor-saving machines and organizing businesses to produce on a grand scale, had given the United States the potential to become the richest nation on earth.

To realize this potential, businesses in the United States needed to be able to buy and sell goods abroad. President Roosevelt encouraged companies to sign contracts with buyers in Europe and Asia. To insure that American business would be able to compete successfully in the struggle for world markets and to safeguard national interests, the President prodded the navy to add new steam-powered warships to its growing fleet. United States merchant ships would be protected by modern, well-equipped naval vessels.

Policing the Western Hemisphere

Roosevelt's "big stick" policy expressed a view, held by many Americans, that it was the "mission" of "superior" countries such as the United States to carry out the "most regrettable but necessary international police duty which must be performed for the sake of the welfare of mankind." In 1902,

when British, German, and Italian warships blockaded Venezuela and fired on one of its seaports, the United States took the opportunity to initiate this "international police duty."

The situation in Venezuela was typical of that in a number of Latin American countries at the turn of the century. After overthrowing Spanish rule, Venezuela had been unable to establish a stable system of government. In an effort to advance their own interests, Great Britain, Germany, and Italy had loaned money to Venezuela. When the Venezuelans failed to repay the loan, the European powers decided to use force.

Venezuela asked the United States to intervene and settle the dispute. Germany and Great Britain in turn requested that President Roosevelt himself serve as mediator. Roosevelt accepted eagerly.

During the discussions, a German ship fired on a Venezuelan village. Roosevelt warned the Germans that he would not hesitate to use force to prevent them from seizing territory in Venezuela or anywhere else in the Caribbean. Roosevelt proposed that the issue be taken to the Permanent Court of Arbitration at The Hague in the Netherlands. Despite initial German opposition to the suggestion, the case was eventually decided at The Hague.

The Venezuelan incident was of great significance to the United States. It reinforced the Monroe Doctrine, since Great Britain, Germany, and Italy had followed the wishes of the United States. Interpreting the incident as a sign of the danger that could result from European intervention in the Western Hemisphere, Roosevelt began to formulate a new policy for the Caribbean.

Action in the Dominican Republic

The United States faced another problem in the Caribbean in 1903. Like Venezuela, the Dominican Republic had fallen into debt to European financiers. President Roosevelt was reluctant to get involved because, as he told Secretary of War Elihu Root, "If we intend to say 'Hands Off' to the powers of Europe, sooner or later we must keep order ourselves."

Nevertheless, Roosevelt believed that the Dominican Republic should honor its financial obligations. He also believed that the European powers would intervene if the United States did not. Still, the President claimed he had no plans to take on the Dominican Republic as a colony. "I have about the same desire to annex it as a gorged boa constrictor might have to swallow a porcupine wrong end to," he remarked.

In 1905 Roosevelt persuaded Dominican officials to submit to United States control of their national finances. Forty-five percent of Dominican customs revenues would be returned to the Dominican government for internal expenses. Fifty-five percent would go toward paying the foreign debts.

Roosevelt submitted his agreement to the Senate for ratification as a treaty. But the Senate was opposed to United States supervision of Dominican debts and refused to ratify the treaty. Roosevelt then signed an executive order, which did not require Senate approval, and put his financial plan into action.

The Roosevelt Corollary to the Monroe Doctrine

In December 1904 Roosevelt took advantage of the Dominican situation to announce a new Latin American policy known as the Roosevelt Corollary to the Monroe Doctrine. The President asserted the right of the United States to exercise "international police power" in Latin America.

The use of power by the United States had taken a new turn. Whereas the Monroe Doctrine had been designed to prevent European intervention in the Americas, the Roosevelt Corollary justified intervention by the United States. Countries such as Argentina, Brazil, and Chile, all strong enough to

Like many Americans of his time, Roosevelt believed that United States officials had a moral duty to act as "international police" for less-developed areas of the world. Would you say that the cartoonist of this 1905 cartoon agreed or disagreed with Roosevelt?

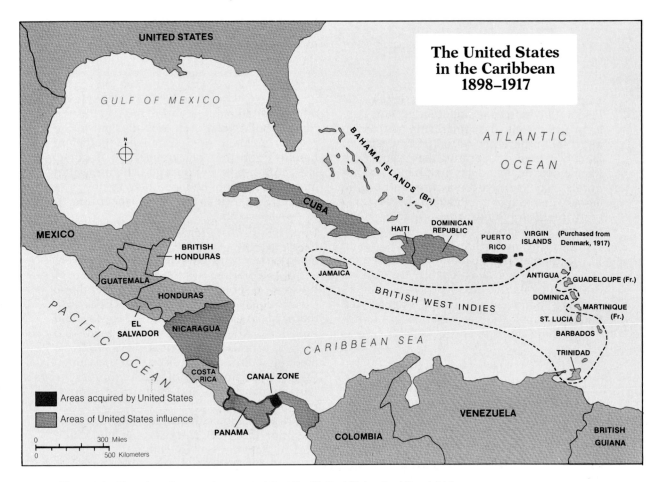

The United States
in the Caribbean
1898–1917

UNITED STATES

GULF OF MEXICO

N

MEXICO

BRITISH
HONDURAS

GUATEMALA

HONDURAS

EL
SALVADOR

NICARAGUA

COSTA
RICA

CANAL ZONE

PANAMA

PACIFIC OCEAN

BAHAMA ISLANDS (Br.)

CUBA

HAITI

JAMAICA

ATLANTIC

OCEAN

DOMINICAN
REPUBLIC

PUERTO
RICO

VIRGIN
ISLANDS

(Purchased from
Denmark, 1917)

ANTIGUA

GUADELOUPE (Fr.)

DOMINICA

MARTINIQUE
(Fr.)

ST. LUCIA

BARBADOS

BRITISH WEST INDIES

CARIBBEAN SEA

TRINIDAD

VENEZUELA

COLOMBIA

BRITISH
GUIANA

■ Areas acquired by United States

Areas of United States influence

0   300 Miles
0   500 Kilometers

■ In 1904 Theodore Roosevelt asserted that the United States had the right to
exercise "international police power" over the neighboring Caribbean area. By
1917 the United States controlled several areas, including Puerto Rico, part of the
Virgin Islands, and the Panama Canal Zone.

take care of their own affairs, did not face intervention, but weaker nations did.

In 1906 a rebellion broke out in Cuba.
Roosevelt sent Secretary of War William
Howard Taft to stop the fighting and set up a
new temporary government. Backed by
5,000 troops, American civilians governed
Cuba for 28 months. Yet, Roosevelt said,
"The United States wishes nothing of the Cubans save that they shall be able to preserve
order among themselves and therefore to
preserve their independence." When order
returned, the Americans withdrew.

President Taft later used the Roosevelt
Corollary to justify American intervention in
Nicaragua and Honduras. Taft sent troops to
impose civil order and used United States
funds to pay debts owed European investors. He then forced the Nicaraguans and
Hondurans to repay the United States. De-

spite claims by Roosevelt, and later by Taft,
that United States intervention was in response to concern over European intentions,
distrust of the United States grew steadily in
Latin America.

SECTION REVIEW

1. Identify: Roosevelt Corollary.

2. What role did the United States Navy play
   in American trade abroad?

3. How did the Roosevelt Corollary change
   the meaning of the Monroe Doctrine?

4. How did the United States react to the
   1906 rebellion in Cuba?

5. **Critical Thinking** Why do you think President Roosevelt was able to carry out his
   foreign policy?

513

2 The Panama Canal

Ever since 1513 when Balboa sighted the Pacific Ocean from a mountain peak in Panama, Europeans and Americans had recognized the importance of the narrow strip of land, or isthmus, separating the Atlantic and Pacific oceans. American merchants and admirals alike yearned for a canal to be built across the Isthmus of Panama. By avoiding the trip around South America, ships could shorten the journey from New York to San Francisco by more than 7,500 miles (about 12,000 kilometers). A canal would reduce the cost of shipping and enable the United States to avoid the heavy expense of maintaining separate navies in the Atlantic and Pacific oceans.

Early Plans

As early as 1850, under the terms of the Clayton-Bulwer Treaty, the United States and Great Britain had agreed to joint control of a future canal in Panama or Nicaragua. Later the French made a separate agreement with Colombia, which controlled Panama. In 1882 a French company led by engineer Ferdinand de Lesseps began digging a canal in Panama. After eight years, however, de Lesseps gave up. His company lacked money and adequate tools, and many of his workers had died of tropical diseases.

In 1898 the Spanish-American War rekindled American interest in building a canal. The battleship *Oregon* had to steam from San Francisco all the way around South America to the fighting in Cuba. Congress then saw the strategic importance of an interocean canal, but the Clayton-Bulwer Treaty limited American ability to act.

"I Took the Canal Zone"

In 1901 President Roosevelt negotiated a new agreement with Great Britain, the Hay-Pauncefote Treaty. It gave the United States the sole right to build, operate, and fortify a canal across Panama or Nicaragua. A commission of experts recommended the Panama route. Congress authorized the President to negotiate with Colombia the purchase of the land for the canal.

When Colombia rejected the President's offer and demanded more money for the right to build, Roosevelt took his fight to the press. He called the Colombians "inefficient bandits" and the "blackmailers of Bogota." His comments encouraged Panamanian nationalists, who had revolted against Colombia 53 times in 57 years, according to Roosevelt's count.

From their rooms in the Waldorf-Astoria Hotel in New York City, a group of Panamanian conspirators plotted another revolt, with United States knowledge. The leader of the plot, a French citizen named Philippe Bunau-Varilla (byoo NOH vah REEL yah) met with Secretary of State John Hay and President Roosevelt. Roosevelt made no specific promises, but Bunau-Varilla left the meeting with the impression that the United States would not help Colombia suppress the Panamanian rebels and might even support the rebellion.

Not by coincidence, a United States warship, the USS *Nashville*, steamed into port in Panama on November 2, 1903. The Panamanians revolted the following day. United States troops blocked the advance of the Colombian army, and on November 3 Panama declared independence from Colombia. The United States officially recognized the new nation two days later.

Less than two weeks after that, the Panamanian government granted the United States a larger canal zone than the Colombians had proposed but on the same terms. Years later Roosevelt bragged, "I took the Canal Zone and let Congress debate."

Digging the Big Ditch

With the Canal Zone in hand, the United States set about completing the task undertaken by de Lesseps some 20 years earlier. British author James Bryce called the building of the Panama Canal "the greatest liberty Man has ever taken with Nature."

The operation began in 1904, when Colonel William C. Gorgas attacked the problem of disease in the isthmus. Gorgas, a physician, had wiped out yellow fever in Cuba after the Spanish-American War. Now he would try to destroy the mosquitoes that spread yellow fever and malaria and the rats that carried bubonic plague. Gorgas and his workers drained swamps, cut down brush, and destroyed grassy marshes where the mosquitoes bred. By 1906 his work was almost complete.

Roosevelt placed Colonel George W. Goethals, an army engineer, in charge of construction. In seven years, a work force of 43,400, including laborers from the West Indies, Italy, and Spain and clerical and construction workers from the United States, removed 211 million cubic yards (278 million cubic meters) of earth before finishing the "big ditch." Crews dug the Gaillard Cut, dammed the Chagres River to form Gatun Lake, and constructed three pairs of locks to lift and lower ships from one water level to another.

On August 5, 1914, the passenger-cargo ship SS *Ancon* made the first complete trip through the canal. The words on the official seal of the Canal Zone had at last come true: "The Land Divided, the World United." On July 12, 1915, President Woodrow Wilson formally proclaimed the opening of the Panama Canal. At a cost of thousands of lives and $400 million, the United States had provided its navy with easy access between the Atlantic and Pacific. As an emerging world power, the nation now had greater ability to extend its influence in Asia.

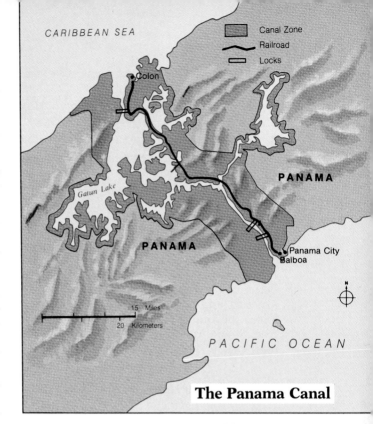

The Panama Canal

■ Carving a canal through the dense jungle of Panama took about ten years and the work of about 43,000 laborers. A series of locks raised and lowered water levels for ships moving through the canal. The opening of the canal let both merchant and navy ships move quickly between the Atlantic and the Pacific.

515

Technological advances in medicine and industry made the building of the Panama Canal possible. Yellow fever had to be controlled, and swamps had to be drained. This photograph, taken at the Culebra Cut, shows the extent of the earth-moving task and the type of machinery used to accomplish it.

SECTION REVIEW

1. Identify: Clayton-Bulwer Treaty, Hay-Pauncefote Treaty, William C. Gorgas.
2. List advantages of a canal across Panama.
3. What was the United States response to the revolt in Panama?
4. How did the Colombian government react to the United States offer to buy land for a canal?
5. **Critical Thinking**   How did Theodore Roosevelt use presidential powers to secure the Panama Canal Zone?

3 The United States and Asia

President Roosevelt, like President McKinley before him, was not interested solely in Latin America and islands in the Pacific. He too looked beyond Hawaii and the Philippines to Asia. So did American businesses looking for markets and outlets for investment.

United States Interests in China

President Roosevelt did not think the United States had any vital interests in China, but he knew that the country had been previously involved there and might become so again. For example, John D. Rockefeller's Standard Oil Company had made huge investments in China, and the American China Development Company had engaged in railroad construction there. Roosevelt thus championed the Open Door policy, begun under President McKinley. (See page 470.) He believed that no nation seeking investment opportunities in China should be shut out.

Roosevelt hoped that competition between Japan and Russia for influence in China would keep China free of Russian domination. In that case, he thought, American businesses would be free to pursue their interests in China without direct involvement by the United States government. The rivalry between Japan and Russia, however, soon erupted into war.

■ *Many foreign powers claimed territory in Asia. The map below shows the possessions of Britain, France, the Netherlands, the United States, and Japan. Several countries controlled trade in their "spheres of influence" in China.*

In 1905 war between Russia and Japan flared over control of the Chinese province of Manchuria. The personal intervention of President Theodore Roosevelt helped produce a peace treaty between the warring nations. This 1918 Japanese lithograph shows a Russian city in Manchuria.

The Russo–Japanese War

Japan, a densely populated island kingdom with few natural resources, needed raw materials to fuel its growing industry. Nearby Manchuria, in northern China, seemed the best source. However, Russia wanted to exclude Japan from China and seal off Manchuria for itself. Great Britain, long the most powerful European nation trading in Asia, attempted to maintain stability in China. In 1902 Britain signed a secret treaty with Japan, agreeing to cooperate in restricting Russian expansion into Manchuria.

For more than a year tensions between Russia and Japan ran high. Then, in February 1904, Japan launched a surprise torpedo attack on the Russian fleet anchored at Port Arthur in Manchuria. The Japanese followed their initial success with more victories. But by the spring of 1905, both nations were exhausted from the fighting and eager to make peace.

President Roosevelt invited Russia and Japan to send representatives to a peace conference at Portsmouth, New Hampshire. There, largely through Roosevelt's diplomatic efforts, the two nations worked out an agreement that ended the war.

The Treaty of Portsmouth, signed in September 1905, recognized the Japanese victory, the first for an Asian nation over a European power. Japan was awarded Port Arthur, the southern half of Sakhalin Island, control of the Manchurian railroads, and, in effect, control of Korea. In turn, Japan gave up its demand that Russia pay for war damages. Manchuria remained part of China.

To satisfy United States interests, Japan and Russia pledged that China would be kept open to trade with all nations. Through the Treaty of Portsmouth, the United States maintained the Open Door in China. Never before had an American president played a central role in an international crisis. Roosevelt won the Nobel Peace Prize for his efforts.

The Nobel Peace Prize

In 1906 Theodore Roosevelt became the first American to win the Nobel Peace Prize. The Nobel Peace Prize—together with Nobel prizes in the fields of physics, chemistry, medicine, literature, and economics—was established in 1901 by Alfred B. Nobel, the inventor of dynamite.

Nobel was born in Sweden in 1833 and educated in St. Petersburg, Russia, where he worked with his father in the development of explosives. He grew up with severe misgivings about his family's business, so closely tied to the miseries of war. Bothered by the destructive nature of dynamite, Nobel became a pacifist, a person opposed to war.

Upon his death, Nobel left $9 million. The income from his fortune is used for annual prizes to people who make outstanding contributions to society in science and the humanities. The Nobel Peace Prize is awarded annually in Oslo, Norway. Other prizes are awarded in Stockholm, Sweden.

Japanese-American Relations

Roosevelt's efforts at Portsmouth impressed Europeans and Americans alike but won the friendship of neither the Russians nor the Japanese. The Russians blamed Roosevelt for their losses in the Treaty of Portsmouth. The Japanese still wanted Manchurian raw materials, and they feared that fewer of those resources would flow into Japanese factories as more nations took advantage of the Open Door policy.

Faced with these tensions, Roosevelt sent Secretary of War Taft to Japan. Taft exchanged full recognition of Japanese control over Korea for a pledge by the Japanese to leave the Philippine Islands under United States control.

Shortly after the Korea-Philippine agreement had been reached, agitation against Japanese immigrants flared up on the west coast of the United States. Many Americans resented the Asian newcomers because they competed for jobs and seemed so different. In 1906 the San Francisco Board of Education placed all Asian pupils in a special school. Japan sent a formal protest to the United States government, and Roosevelt intervened to soften what the Japanese regarded as a racial insult.

The President denounced the San Francisco school board action as a "wicked absurdity." He offered to bring the entire board to Washington to discuss the matter. A delegation of eight board members visited the White House and reached a compromise. The school board returned the Japanese children to their regular schools, and Roosevelt took steps to restrict further Japanese immigration.

During this crisis, nationalists on both sides of the Pacific called for war. Although the President had no intention of using military force, he wanted to make sure that no one interpreted his actions as a sign of weakness. Consequently, in 1907, Roosevelt undertook a dramatic demonstration of military strength.

The President sent the entire United States battle fleet on a cruise around the world. Congress objected to the expense of the voyage and questioned its value, but the fleet sailed on. When the Great White Fleet, as it was known, entered Japanese waters, leaders there were duly impressed by the second-largest navy in the world. Only the British had a larger fleet. Welcoming parties for the Americans seemed to be a sign of improved Japanese-American relations.

By the time the fleet returned to the United States in 1909, Secretary of State Elihu Root and Japanese Ambassador Takahira (tah kah HEE rah) signed a pledge settling most of the differences between the two countries. Both nations agreed to preserve stability in the Pacific, mutually respect territorial claims, maintain the Open Door in China, and use peaceful methods to protect Chinese independence.

Dollar Diplomacy in Asia

In 1909 William Howard Taft succeeded Roosevelt as President. He decided to modify Roosevelt's foreign policy by "substituting dollars for bullets." Taft tried to avoid military confrontations to further United States interests in Asia. Instead, he encouraged financial investments in China in the hope that an economic presence would "give the voice of the United States more authority in that country." President Taft was interested in commercial ventures that would advance United States foreign policy.

Taft's "dollar diplomacy" had little impact on Asian affairs, however. The United States did not make investments large enough to tip the balance of power there, and Taft would not resort to military intervention. Dollar diplomacy, however, did play a larger role in Latin America.

SECTION REVIEW

1. Identify: Treaty of Portsmouth, "dollar diplomacy."
2. How did President Theodore Roosevelt help end the Russo–Japanese War?
3. What development led to increased friction between Japan and the U.S.?
4. How did President Taft hope to promote United States interests in Asia?
5. **Critical Thinking** Do you think Roosevelt's foreign policy was based on idealism or realism? Why?

4 Woodrow Wilson and Moral Diplomacy

Woodrow Wilson, who was elected President in 1912, had little interest in world diplomacy. "It would be the irony of fate if my administration had to deal chiefly with foreign affairs," he remarked to a friend upon taking office. An unstable world order, indeed, forced Wilson to devote much of his energy to foreign affairs.

Instead of continuing the policies of Roosevelt and Taft, Wilson and his secretary of state, William Jennings Bryan, believed in a "moral diplomacy." They were determined to use negotiation and arbitration in dealings with other nations. They hoped that colonial empires would be replaced by independent nations with democratic governments. Stating that "the force of America is the force of moral principle," Wilson set out with missionary zeal to promote democracy, maintain the peace, and secure American economic interests abroad.

Moral Diplomacy in Action

In 1913 and 1914 Secretary of State Bryan set in motion a plan for achieving world peace through a series of "cooling-off" treaties. Under the terms of the treaties, 29 countries agreed to submit international disputes to a permanent international committee for investigation and arbitration. While the committee made its inquiry, the nations agreed to refrain from acts of war and from building up arms for a one-year period.

Bryan and humanitarian groups hailed the treaties as a great stride toward world peace. But Theodore Roosevelt and other proponents of military strength believed they were unenforceable and therefore meaningless.

In Asia Wilson pursued the policy of moral diplomacy by terminating United States participation in a China railway consortium organized by President Taft. A group of British, French, German, American, and later Russian and Japanese bankers had been formed to lend $125 million to China for construction of the Hukuang (hoo KWAHNG) Railroad. Sensing the threat to Chinese independence, President Wilson ordered United States bankers to withdraw.

Some suspected Wilson of ordering the bankers out for fear that Japan and Russia would dominate the consortium. Wilson's supporters endorsed the decision for preserving the Open Door policy, winning Chinese good will, and rejecting dollar diplomacy.

Moral Diplomacy Falters

Relations with Japan, in contrast, posed a number of problems for the concept of "moral diplomacy." In California, legislators seeking favor with local agriculture and labor groups had enacted a law prohibiting noncitizens from owning land in the state. Japanese immigrants were most specifically affected by the law, and they filed an angry protest in Washington.

President Wilson played down the issue and ignored the racist overtones of the California law. He thus failed to enforce national treaty obligations to treat Japanese immigrants fairly. Only after public outrage in Japan had risen to fever pitch did the President act. He dispatched the secretary of state to California, but Bryan could not persuade the state legislature and governor to discontinue their policy.

Japanese-American relations worsened in 1915. While the European powers were preoccupied with the war that had broken out in 1914, Japan presented 21 demands to China. In effect, by agreeing to the demands, China would become a Japanese protectorate. The United States objected to such a violation of the Open Door policy, however, and Japan eased its pressure on China, at least for the moment.

Reversals in Latin America

Although President Taft had not been able to make dollar diplomacy work in Asia, he was able to apply it more freely in Latin America. There, the United States faced little competition from the European nations that had long-standing interest in Asia.

Concern for the security of the Panama Canal undermined Woodrow Wilson's wish to abandon Taft's dollar diplomacy and promote democratic government in Latin America. Wilson and Bryan reasoned that to make the canal secure, the United States should encourage friendly relations with nearby countries. However, the instability of many of those countries frustrated such plans.

The outgoing Taft administration had drafted a treaty giving the United States a permanent option to build a second canal across Nicaragua. For this and other privileges, the United States was to pay Nicaragua the small sum of $3 million. Forsaking moral principles, Bryan not only supported the treaty but added a new provision authorizing the United States to intervene in Nicaraguan internal affairs.

In the Dominican Republic, Bryan began with moral principle. But when peaceful methods failed to end a civil war there, Wilson sent in the United States Marines. In 1916 the marines began a full-scale military occupation of Santo Domingo, the capital.

Events in Haiti turned out no better. In 1915 a series of revolutions and assassinations of high government officials rocked the country. In July 1915 United States Marines landed to restore order and to protect United States property and banking interests. The marines' efforts at "pacification" met with such stiff resistance from Haitian soldiers that a bloody war followed. To end the bloodshed the Haitian government signed a treaty in September establishing a United States protectorate over Haiti.

Although Wilson had hoped to aid the Latin American nations and prepare them for democracy, he failed. Instead, he created an "American lake" in the Caribbean and inspired hatred rather than friendship.

Civil War in Mexico

The United States maintained an interest in the affairs of all of Latin America, but interest in Mexico was especially strong. The two nations shared a common border, and the states of California, Arizona, Texas, and New Mexico had close cultural ties with Mexico dating back to Spanish settlement of the region some 400 years before. Yet political unrest in Mexico finally led Wilson to substitute military power for moral diplomacy.

In 1911 the dictatorial government of Mexico was overthrown. Two years later General Victoriano Huerta (WEHR tah) seized power from the new revolutionary government. A group led by Venustiano Carranza (kahr RAHN zah) opposed the Huerta regime. A bloody civil war raged in Mexico, and for a time Wilson adopted an attitude of "watchful waiting." He hoped that Mexico would adopt a constitutional government serving the needs of all Mexicans and that the new government would be friendly to the United States.

However, the civil war dragged on, and Huerta proclaimed himself military dictator of Mexico. First Wilson banned arms shipments to Mexico. Then he offered to mediate the dispute between Carranza and Huerta. Somewhat indiscreetly, he even offered to support the Carranza faction if it would guarantee the orderly establishment of constitutional government. Carranza refused.

In April 1914 Mexican soldiers in Tampico, Mexico, arrested members of the crew of the USS *Dolphin*. Although the sailors were promptly released with an apology, Wilson used the incident to push for United States entry into Mexican internal affairs.

Without waiting for congressional approval, the President ordered the navy to capture the port of Vera Cruz before a German ship could land a cargo of arms for Huerta's forces. The Mexicans resisted, and in the battle that followed, 126 "Huertistas" and 19 Americans died. The minor importance of the *Dolphin* arrests, contrasted with the severity of Wilson's reaction, brought outcries of horror from Huerta, his rival Carranza, and newspaper editors throughout the world.

Wilson and Bryan averted war by allowing Argentina, Brazil, and Chile to mediate the crisis. At a conference in Niagara Falls, New York, Carranza's delegation again resisted Wilson's attempt to direct the outcome of the Mexican struggle. In July 1914, a month before World War I began in Europe, Huerta accepted defeat. In August, Carranza took over the government in Mexico City.

United States Involvement

The dispute might have ended had not Francisco "Pancho" Villa (VEE yah), a Mexican revolutionary, led a revolt against Carranza. In October 1915 the United States recognized the Carranza government. Villa, in retaliation, began a series of anti-American raids. In January 1916 he removed 17 United States citizens from a train in Mexico and had them shot. In March, Villa and his band crossed the Rio Grande and set fires in Columbus, New Mexico, killing 19 Americans.

The Carranza government agreed to permit United States soldiers to enter Mexico to

Major Events	
1901	Hay-Pauncefote Treaty
1902	Venezuelan crisis
1903	Panama declares independence and grants canal zone to United States
1904	Construction of Panama Canal begins; Roosevelt Corollary to Monroe Doctrine issued
1905	United States supervises finances of Dominican Republic; Russo-Japanese War; Treaty of Portsmouth
1906	United States troops restore order in Cuba
1908	William Howard Taft elected President
1911	Mexican Revolution begins
1912	Woodrow Wilson elected President
1914	United States Navy captures Mexican port of Vera Cruz; Panama Canal opened to traffic
1915	United States Marines sent to Haiti
1916	United States troops enter Mexico to search for Pancho Villa; United States Marines sent to Dominican Republic

Pancho Villa's raids into the United States provoked a strong reaction in 1916. United States cavalry troops under General John Pershing pursued Villa and his followers for hundreds of miles across Mexico.

pursue Villa. The Wilson government organized a punitive expedition under Brigadier General John Pershing to capture Villa dead or alive. Far exceeding the spirit of the agreement, 6,000 troops pursued Villa over 300 miles (480 kilometers) into Mexico.

In April 1916 Carranza demanded an end to the United States "invasion." Wilson refused to recall the troops. Villa fueled growing war fever in the United States when he suddenly swung north to attack Glen Springs, Texas. Casualties on both sides and the capture of American troops posed a serious threat to peace.

Neither Carranza nor Wilson wanted war, however. Carranza had pressing domestic problems to deal with, and the war in Europe occupied the attention of Wilson. In July 1916 a joint commission was convened to resolve matters, and early the following year Wilson ordered American troops out of Mexico.

As the United States withdrew from Mexico, Americans turned their attention to the war that had begun in Europe in 1914.

They realized that their nation had undergone remarkable changes since 1898. United States troops and ships were stationed in Asia and Latin America. American business interests spanned the globe. The United States still sought peace, but it had become too much a part of the world community to ignore the outbreak of war in Europe.

SECTION REVIEW

1. Identify: "moral diplomacy," Victoriano Huerta, Venustiano Carranza, Francisco "Pancho" Villa, John Pershing.

2. What was the purpose of the "cooling-off" treaties negotiated in 1913 and 1914?

3. In which two Latin American countries did Bryan and Wilson resort to the use of troops during 1915 and 1916?

4. **Critical Thinking** Why do you think Mexicans referred to the United States as the "Colossus of the North"?

Chapter 27 Review

In Perspective

The Spanish–American War marked the entrance of the United States onto the world stage. In the decades that followed, the nation took an increasingly active role in world affairs. President Theodore Roosevelt believed that the country had an international police duty, which he tried to carry out in Venezuela, the Dominican Republic, and Cuba. Roosevelt's assertion that the United States had a right to intervene in Latin America became known as the Roosevelt Corollary to the Monroe Doctrine. One benefit of the growing influence of the United States in Latin America was construction of the Panama Canal, which began under Roosevelt and was completed under Woodrow Wilson.

The United States had a less direct interest in Asia during the early twentieth century, but Roosevelt maintained the Open Door policy by helping negotiate an end to the Russo-Japanese War. Discrimination against Japanese immigrants in California disrupted relations between the United States and Japan under Roosevelt and Wilson, but both Presidents were able to preserve peace in the Pacific.

Woodrow Wilson and his secretary of state, William Jennings Bryan, brought moral zeal to American foreign policy. They wanted to maintain world peace and encourage the establishment of democratic governments for all people. Wilson also became involved in the affairs of Latin American nations. Soon the United States would look beyond the Western Hemisphere as a major war raged in Europe.

Vocabulary

On a separate sheet of paper, write the word or words that best complete each of the following sentences.

1. ____ is negotiation and arbitration to attain foreign policy goals.
2. Roosevelt's ____ policy advocated the use of force to attain foreign policy goals.
3. The ____ policy guaranteed all countries equal access to Chinese trade.
4. Financial investments with foreign policy goals are called ____.
5. To take the territory of another country as one's own is to ____ it.

Chapter Checkup

1. (a) What was the Roosevelt Corollary to the Monroe Doctrine? (b) How did Roosevelt apply his corollary in Cuba? (c) How did Taft apply it in Nicaragua and Honduras?
2. (a) Why did the United States want to construct a canal across the Isthmus of Panama? (b) What steps did Theodore Roosevelt take to gain control of the canal zone for the United States?
3. (a) Why did Russia and Japan go to war in 1905? (b) What was the outcome of the war? (c) What role did the United States play in ending the conflict? (d) What did the United States gain as a result of the peace treaty?
4. (a) In what three Latin American countries were Wilson and Bryan unable to carry out their "moral diplomacy"? (b) What action did they take in each case?

Critical Thinking

1. **Comparing** Compare Roosevelt's "big Stick," Taft's "dollar diplomacy," and Wilson's "moral diplomacy." (a) How did the *theory* behind each phase differ? (b) Based on what you learned in this chapter, do you think the policies differed in *action?* Explain.

2. **Recognizing Relationships** Domestic events and foreign affairs have often influenced one another in United States history. Describe one example of this between 1900 and 1916.

Developing Basic Skills

1. **Placing Events in Time** Review Chapter 24 and what you have read in this chapter. Construct a time line of United States actions in world affairs from 1860 to 1916. Then answer the following questions: (a) In which decades did the United States acquire new territory? (b) In which decades did the United States intervene militarily in other nations?
2. **Map Reading** Study the map about foreign influence in Asia on page 516. (a) Which nations claimed spheres of influence in China? (b) Which nations claimed territory in Asia? (c) Based on the map, where might you expect conflict to occur?

See page 831 for suggested readings.

Writer's Handbook

Writing a Preliminary Thesis Statement

The thesis statement is the main idea of a paper stated in a declarative sentence. Writing this statement helps limit your topic and guide your research. Of course, you may have to revise your preliminary thesis because you cannot find the information to support it or because you find evidence that your thesis is incorrect.

A possible thesis statement for a paper on the United States in world affairs is: *The Roosevelt Corollary marked a major change in United States foreign policy toward Latin America.*

Practice: Write a possible thesis statement for each of the topics below.

1. Theodore Roosevelt's Role in Obtaining the Canal Zone
2. Woodrow Wilson and Moral Diplomacy
3. The United States and the Mexican Civil War

28

The World at War

(1914–1919)

Machine Gunner *by Harvey Dunn*

Chapter Outline

1 *War in Europe*

2 *The Home Front*

3 *The United States in the War*

4 *Search for a "Just Peace"*

Europe had not experienced a major war since 1815, so Americans were shocked in the summer of 1914 when war broke out between Germany and Austria-Hungary on one side and Great Britain, France, and Russia on the other. "This dreadful conflict of the nations came to most of us as lightning out of a clear sky," Robert Page wrote his brother Walter, the American ambassador in London. "The horror of it all kept me awake for weeks, nor has the awfulness of it all deserted me."

Americans had reason to be horrified. This war was like no other. Modern technology—poison gasses, submarines, tanks, airplanes, machine guns—had greatly enhanced the ability of human beings to slaughter one another.

What would be the role of the United States as this tragedy unfolded? Many Americans hoped that the broad Atlantic would keep the flames of war from their shores. But their hopes were in vain.

United States at war

1914	1915	1916	1917	1918	1919
1914 War begins in Europe	**1915** Germans sink *Lusitania*	**1916** Germany suspends submarine attacks	**1917** U.S. enters war; Espionage Act passed	**1918** Fourteen Points announced; Germany surrenders	**1919** Treaty of Versailles signed

1 War in Europe

On June 28, 1914, in Bosnia, a province of Austria-Hungary, a young nationalist assassinated Archduke Francis Ferdinand of Austria. The young man belonged to a group that wanted to unite Bosnia with the independent nation of Serbia, now part of Yugoslavia. Few people expected a world war to result from this act.

War Begins

By 1914 the major powers of Europe had arranged themselves in competing alliances. On one side was the Triple Alliance of Austria-Hungary, Germany, and Italy. On the other side was the Triple Entente (ahn TAHNT) of France, Great Britain, and Russia. This system of alliances helped turn the archduke's assassination into a major war.

Austria-Hungary responded to the assassination by issuing a stiff ultimatum to Serbia. The Austrians claimed that the Serbs were behind the attack. Not satisfied with the Serbian reply and spurred on by Germany, Austria-Hungary declared war on Serbia. Russia, competing with Austria-Hungary for power in southeastern Europe, backed the Serbs and declared war on Germany. Russia's ally France supported this move. Then, on August 1, 1914, Germany declared war on Russia and two days later on France.

The Central Powers, as Austria-Hungary and Germany were called, anticipated a swift and total victory. They planned to march rapidly west to defeat France, then swing east to defeat Russia. The shortest route to France was through Belgium, a neutral nation. Germany requested permission to move troops through Belgium and offered King Albert payment for any resulting damages. The Belgian monarch refused the German request, stating, "Belgium is a nation, not a road."

Nevertheless on August 3, German forces invaded Belgium. The next day Britain, committed to defend Belgium, declared war on Germany. Within weeks Turkey joined the Central Powers, and Japan united with Britain, France, and Russia, which were known as the Allies.

A valiant defense by 200,000 Belgian soldiers failed to stop the Germans but delayed their progress long enough for the Allies to mobilize. The year 1914 ended with the German advance halted in France and a stalemate in the east. On both the eastern and the western battlefronts, opposing armies dug an extensive network of trenches from which enemy lines could be fired on. On both sides thousands of soldiers died to advance just a few yards.

Despite the slaughter early in the war, most European leaders expected quick and easy victories. They had no idea how costly the war would be or how long it would last.

American Neutrality

President Woodrow Wilson and most of his advisers favored the Allies. Wilson considered Germany a "lawless" nation. In

---

■ Most European nations participated in the war as either Allied Powers or Central Powers. According to the map, which nations remained neutral?

Allies
Central Powers
Neutral nations

Europe During the War

addition, Germany had posed the greatest threat to United States interests in Latin America. But like most American policymakers, Wilson believed that the Allies could win without United States military involvement. Thus the President adopted a policy of formal neutrality. He urged Americans to be "impartial in thought as well as in action." He wanted the United States to shine as the light of reason in a world gone mad with violence and hate.

However, few Americans could remain calm, much less neutral. The United States was a nation of immigrants with strong emotional ties to the countries of their ancestors. The majority of Americans shared language and ancestry with the British. Traditional friendship with France also drew the United States to the cause of the Allies.

Many Americans, however, favored the Central Powers. Eight million German Americans viewed the war as a defense of German soil against French and Russian aggression. Some 4 million Irish Americans, bearing an ancient antagonism toward the British, generally sided with the Central Powers. Similarly, American Jews, harboring strong anti-Russian sentiments, tended to sympathize with the German cause.

Supporters of both the Central Powers and the Allies used propaganda to try to influence public opinion in the United States. Because most of the major newspapers backed the Allies, supporters of the Central Powers concentrated their efforts in German, Irish, and other immigrant newspapers. They tried to persuade Americans that the Allies had caused the war and that Germany was fighting to save Western Europe from a so-called "Slavic peril."

Allied propaganda probably had a greater impact on American thought. After the invasion of neutral Belgium, the British flooded the United States with stories of German atrocities against Belgian civilians. The Germans were more easily portrayed as aggressors, for most of the fighting was on Allied soil.

German experiments with such new weapons as submarines and poison gas struck Americans as brutal and immoral. Furthermore, many Americans believed that the Allies were fighting to defend civilization. They viewed the Germans as militaristic and authoritarian, believing in total obedience to authority rather than individual freedom.

Economic Impact

American economic ties to the Allies made strict neutrality unlikely. At first, war jolted the United States economy. For example, cotton exports to Germany and Austria stopped completely. But a deluge of war orders from the Allies soon created a boom.

Almost overnight a new munitions industry sprang up. Within three years, the United States sent $1 billion worth of arms and explosives to the Allies. Under the pressure of Allied orders, American steel, copper, oil, grain, and food production increased. Trade with the Allies grew from $500 million in 1914 to $3.5 billion in 1917.

At the same time a British naval blockade disrupted trade with the Central Powers. To make the blockade effective, the British navy mined the North Sea. The British also blocked United States trade with neutral Holland and Denmark and forced American ships into port for inspection. President Wilson protested these actions, but he could do little to make his protest effective.

The British, in turn, tried to soften the impact of the blockade on the United States economy. For example, they prevented a slump in the cotton market by purchasing the cotton that would normally have been sold to Germany. In light of such activities the Germans considered the United States a silent partner of the Allies. Wilson maintained, however, that the United States was not actively pursuing a pro-Ally policy and thus was not violating neutrality.

The Submarine Controversy

Although the American reaction to the British blockade was mild, the German use of a new weapon, the submarine or U-boat provoked outrage. In 1914 and 1915 while the German navy was bottled up in the North Sea by the British blockade, the Germans used submarines to attack Allied ships.

The submarine complicated the question of neutral rights in wartime. International law required that a ship give warning before an attack in order to allow the crew to escape. But submarines were slow on the surface and vulnerable to ramming, so they could not risk surfacing to warn their targets.

Early in 1915 the Germans warned that any ships entering a war zone around Great

Britain risked an attack without warning. However, President Wilson refused to compromise American honor or interrupt trade by declaring the zone off limits to shipping. When Americans began losing their lives in submarine attacks, the American public became incensed.

On March 28, 1915, a German torpedo sank the British liner *Falaba* in the Irish Sea, and one American was drowned. Then, six weeks later, on May 7, a German submarine torpedoed the *Lusitania*, a sleek British passenger ship. Among the 1,200 passengers who died were 128 Americans.

The United States was still neutral in 1915 when a German submarine sank the British passenger liner Lusitania. At bottom the flag-draped body of one of the 128 Americans who died in the attack is carried to a temporary morgue in Queenstown, Ireland. Below is the front page of the New York Times report of the disaster.

LUSITANIA SUNK BY A SUBMARINE, PROBABLY 1,260 DEAD;
TWICE TORPEDOED OFF IRISH COAST; SINKS IN 15 MINUTES;
CAPT. TURNER SAVED, FROHMAN AND VANDERBILT MISSING;
WASHINGTON BELIEVES THAT A GRAVE CRISIS IS AT HAND

SHOCKS THE PRESIDENT

Washington Deeply Stirred by the Loss of American Lives.

BULLETINS AT WHITE HOUSE

Wilson Reads Them Closely, but Is Silent on the Nation's Course.

HINTS OF CONGRESS CALL

Loss of Lusitania Recalls Firm Tone of Our First Warning to Germany.

CAPITAL FULL OF RUMORS

Reports That Liner Was to be Sunk Were Heard Before Actual News Came.

The Lost Cunard Steamship Lusitania
X Where the First Torpedo Struck.   XX Where the Second Torpedo Struck.

SOME DEAD TAKEN ASHORE

Several Hundred Survivors at Queenstown and Kinsale.

STEWARD TELLS OF DISASTER

One Torpedo Crashes Into the Doomed Liner's Bow, Another Into the Engine Room.

SHIP LISTS OVER TO PORT

Makes It Impossible to Lower Many Boats, So Hundreds Must Have Gone Down.

ATTACKED IN BROAD DAY

Passengers at Luncheon—Warning Had Been Given by Germans Before the Ship Left New York.

Only 650 Were Saved, Few Cabin Passengers

QUEENSTOWN, Saturday, May 8, 4:28 A. M.—Survivors of the Lusitania who have arrived here estimate that only about 650 of those aboard the liner were saved.

President Wilson demanded that the Germans end submarine attacks on unarmed ships. The Germans eventually apologized, but they continued their attacks. After the French steamer *Sussex* was torpedoed in March 1916, Wilson issued another protest to the Germans. The Germans did not want to push the United States into the war on the side of the Allies, so they agreed to suspend the unannounced submarine attacks.

Peace and the Election of 1916

Submarine warfare and the relationship of the United States to the European powers became a major political issue at home. Former President Theodore Roosevelt attacked President Wilson for his restraint in the face of German provocation and maintained that the United States should prepare the army and navy for a war.

Wilson disliked the prospect of a large standing army in peace time, and he resisted Roosevelt's efforts to marshall public opinion behind a major program of preparedness. Yet he could not ignore the possibility that the United States might become involved in the war. In 1916 the President doubled the size of the regular army and urged the construction of a "navy second to none."

As the presidential election of 1916 approached, however, the nation still seemed to favor peace. The Republicans nominated Charles Evans Hughes for President. Hughes was a respected justice of the Supreme Court and a former reform governor of New York.

Democrats labeled Hughes a "war candidate" in spite of his moderate position on the war. At the same time they portrayed Wilson as the candidate who would keep the nation out of the war. "Wilson and Peace with Honor, or Hughes with Roosevelt and War?" they asked the voters.

The election was close. Hughes went to bed election night convinced he had won, while glum Democrats awaited the final count. By morning, late returns from the South and West insured that Wilson would remain in the White House. He won 49.4 percent of the popular vote, compared to 46.2 percent for Hughes. The American desire for peace brought Wilson victory, but peace would not last long, for the tragedy in Europe was deepening.

The End of Neutrality

Wilson had long hoped to negotiate an end to the war in Europe. Twice he sent his trusted friend and adviser Colonel Edward House to mediate between the opposing sides, and twice House failed. In late 1916 Wilson once again hoped the senselessness of the slaughter might bring European leaders to the peace table.

In December the President worked on a diplomatic note pledging the United States to end the war and help keep the peace. Before he had finished his draft, the Germans announced they were ready to negotiate an end to the war. Confident of victory, they demanded territory from Belgium, France, and Luxembourg, in addition to concessions along the Baltic Sea and in Africa. Such demands were unacceptable to the Allies.

In January 1917 Germany unleashed its submarine fleet to sink all ships, enemy or neutral. German officers anticipated victory before the United States could enter the war. Wilson broke off diplomatic relations with Germany in response to these actions, but he hesitated to do more. However, the loss of American lives and ships to German submarine attacks moved the United States closer to war.

In early March news of a document known as the Zimmerman Telegram ended the President's reluctance. The government made public a note from German Foreign Minister Arthur Zimmerman to the German minister in Mexico instructing the minister to urge Mexico and Japan to join the Central Powers if the United States entered the war. With such a direct threat to United States security, Wilson knew the country could not remain neutral much longer.

Later the same month events in Russia removed Wilson's last doubts about entering the war. A revolution there overthrew the autocratic Czar and set up a constitutional government. Now the President could more easily claim that the Allied cause was more just. He asked Congress for a declaration of war on Germany, which it voted on April 6. The United States was officially at war.

SECTION REVIEW

1. Identify: Central Powers, Allies, *Lusitania*, Charles Evans Hughes, Zimmerman Telegram.

2. What policy did President Wilson follow when war first broke out in Europe?

3. (a) How did the Central Powers and Allies try to influence American public opinion? (b) Which effort was more successful?

4. (a) How did Wilson react to German submarine attacks on unarmed ships? (b) What was the German response?

5. What three events eventually led to United States entry in the war?

6. **Critical Thinking** How could you have predicted Roosevelt's reaction to the war in Europe?

2 The Home Front

When the United States declared war, President Wilson and his advisers had no idea how desperate the Allies were. Americans were shocked to learn that the Allies were down to their last reserves. Missions from the Allied countries begged for massive supplies of men and materials. To save the Allies, the United States devoted its resources and patriotic fervor to winning the war. The nation soon demonstrated that it had an abundance of both.

Raising an Army

Even before the United States entered the war, Congress had hotly debated the best way to raise an army. Should volunteers be recruited, or should all able-bodied men of a certain age be drafted? President Wilson favored the draft as the most rational and democratic means. Still, his selective-service bill triggered a long debate in Congress. Not until May 7, 1917, was Wilson able to sign the

Clubs for servicemen, called canteens, were set up in many cities as recreation centers for soldiers who would soon be leaving to fight in Europe. Women volunteers worked at canteens such as this one in Newark, New Jersey.

bill, which set the minimum age of draftees at 21.

Some officials feared the draft would lead to riots as it had during the Civil War, but patriotic appeals sparked a massive response among men eligible for the draft. By June 5, 1917, almost 10 million men between the ages of 21 and 31 had registered without protest of any kind. Through voluntary enlistments and the draft, the American military had almost 5 million soldiers under arms by November 1918.

Black Americans responded as enthusiastically as whites. Unfortunately, many of them encountered the same segregation and discrimination in the armed forces that they knew at home. Of the 371,000 black soldiers in uniform, only a few thousand ever went into combat. Those who did served in all-black units. The rest, also limited to segregated units, were restricted to menial duties.

For the black soldiers overseas, Europe proved a marked contrast to life at home. The French, for example, had no history of racial conflict. They treated black soldiers much like their white comrades. When a black regiment demonstrated great courage, the grateful French government awarded two of its members, Henry Johnson and Needham Roberts, the Croix de Guerre (CRAH duh GAIR), or War Cross, a high military honor.

Wartime Industry

The declaration of war caught the nation short of supplies. On hand were just 600,000 rifles, about 2,000 machine guns, and less than a thousand artillery pieces. The initial effort to increase production of military supplies was chaotic. American military leaders competed with the Allies and private industry to purchase equipment and material.

By the summer of 1917 President Wilson knew that bold action was necessary to create some order. He established the War Industries Board (WIB) to spur industrial production and coordinate activities. However, problems still remained. Soldiers in training lacked adequate clothing and shelter, rail transportation was snarled, and steel production was falling.

Then on March 4, 1918, the President appointed Wall Street genius Bernard Baruch as chairman of the WIB. Wilson gave Baruch sweeping powers to organize industry. The WIB established strict controls over scarce materials like steel, set prices, and standardized production.

Similar efforts brought order to the railroad and shipping industries. The energetic and resourceful Edward Hurley left the Federal Trade Commission to build an adequate merchant marine. The President appointed William Gibbs McAdoo, his son-in-law and an able lawyer, to head the United States Railroad Administration. McAdoo spent almost half a billion dollars to improve track and equipment and organized all the rail lines into a single national network.

The government supported the massive mobilization of citizens through increased taxes and bonds. Amidst fanfare, parades, and patriotic appeals, the government organized four Liberty Loan drives to sell war bonds. When citizens bought bonds, they were loaning the government money in exchange for a promise to repay the loan with interest at a future date.

Workers During the War

The effort and support of American workers was central to the successful mobilization of industry. In April 1918 President Wilson created the National War Labor Board to unify labor policies. The board served as an arbitrator of disputes between management and labor. The board sometimes sided with industrialists, but more often it favored workers. The mandatory mediation produced an unusual period of cooperation between employers and workers.

Wilson threw the full force of the federal government behind workers' rights, resulting in impressive gains for labor during the war. Active government support for the right of workers to organize and bargain collectively resulted in a jump in union membership. The American Federation of Labor grew from just over 2 million members in 1916 to nearly 3.3 million in 1920.

The federal government also worked to improve working conditions. In some cases it insisted on an eight-hour workday. It set standards for the employment of women and children, and it demanded that employers pay fair wages. Despite the rapid inflation of the war years, real income rose 14 percent in 1917 and 20 percent more in 1918.

Increased demand for workers to produce war materials opened up new economic opportunities for women. Many women found jobs in steel mills, and 100,000 worked in munitions factories. For the first time government agencies opened their doors to women lawyers and doctors.

Most of the new opportunities lasted only as long as the war. By 1920 the percentage of women who worked outside the home was lower than it had been in 1910. One union spokesman expressed the attitude of many when he declared that "the same patriotism that induced women to enter industry during the war should induce them to vacate their positions after the war."

Black Americans also found new job opportunities during the war. Blacks had been moving north in growing numbers since 1900. In the five years after 1914 the chance to find work in war industries attracted about 500,000 black Americans to northern cities. Yet the opportunities of wartime were short-lived. Once the war ended, many black workers were thrown out of work or had to accept lower-paying jobs.

Producing Food

When the United States entered the war, the people of France, Britain, and Italy,* along with their armies, were facing starvation. Thus increasing American food production became a top priority. To get the job done, President Wilson appointed Herbert Hoover, an engineer and self-made millionaire, as head of the Food Administration. Hoover was known worldwide as the man who had organized a massive food relief program to Belgium during the German invasion. The Lever Act, passed in August 1917, gave Hoover full authority over food production, distribution, and farm supplies.

The top food priorities were wheat, pork, and sugar. Poor harvests kept wheat supplies low, but voluntary restraints by Americans freed adequate supplies for the Allies. Meatless and breadless days brought the spirit of sacrifice home to the nation. "Victory gardens" in back yards stretched available produce.

The results were staggering. Without rationing or great sacrifice, the United States almost tripled the amount of food sent to the Allies. Before the war an average of 7 million tons (.63 million metric tons) of food crossed

*Italy entered the war on the side of the Allies in 1915.

The call to arms left thousands of jobs unfilled at home. Women stepped forward to do work previously considered suitable only for men. These young women are delivering ice. Other women worked in factories, mills, and offices.

the Atlantic each year. By 1919 the figure topped 18.6 million tons (16.9 million metric tons).

Influencing Public Opinion

President Wilson wanted Americans to know that they were fighting for a just cause. The President told the nation: "The world must be made safe for democracy. . . . We have no selfish ends to serve. We desire no conquest, no dominion." To solidify public support for the war effort, the President created the Committee on Public Information (CPI) and appointed journalist George Creel to head it.

Creel showed remarkable resourcefulness and zeal in converting any remaining hostility to the war into patriotism. He enlisted over 150,000 lecturers, writers, actors, artists, and scholars in a gigantic propaganda campaign. Their message was that the war was being fought for freedom and democracy. They also warned that disloyalty, spying, and sabotage threatened the war effort.

The CPI successfully spurred the sale of Liberty Bonds, reduced job absenteeism, and raised morale, but it also stirred up fear and suspicion. German-Americans especially became the victims of hate campaigns. Schools banned the teaching of the German language. People renamed sauerkraut "liberty cabbage" and called German measles "liberty measles."

Critics of the war among pacifist and socialist ranks suffered verbal and physical abuse. Socialist leader Eugene V. Debs was imprisoned for criticizing the war in a speech. Dissent had become the same as treason.

Legislation passed during the war also stifled dissent. For example, the Espionage Act of 1917 imposed fines up to $10,000 and jail sentences up to 20 years for aiding the enemy or obstructing recruitment. The law

★ American Enterprise ★

Backing the War Effort

During 1917 and 1918, as the trickle of American soldiers to the French battlefront became a flood, Congress established the Committee on Public Information to mobilize American support for the war effort. Artists, advertisers, poets, historians, photographers, educators, and actors were enlisted in the campaign. Key to that campaign were some 75,000 "four-minute" men. These were local volunteers who stepped onto the stages of the nation's movie houses and in four-minute talks encouraged audiences to back the war effort and to conserve food and fuel.

Four times during the course of the war, the government asked the American people to lend it billions of dollars, and the people responded. Pressure to buy Liberty Bonds was great. Neighbors knocked on doors to encourage each other to buy bonds. Those who bought bonds received Liberty Buttons, which they wore proudly on their lapels. Over $18 billion was raised through the sale of Liberty Bonds.

If to an adult "doing your bit for the country" meant buying a Liberty Bond, to a child it meant growing vegetables in the school playground and buying "thrift stamps" for a quarter each. Five million children joined the United States School Garden Army and turned school yards, public parks, and private estates into vegetable plots. By selling vegetables, children earned money to buy thrift stamps. A filled thrift card bought a war savings stamp worth $5, and a filled war savings card bought a $50 Liberty Bond.

At home parents sang the same songs as their sons at the front. They showed their pride by hanging out a red and white service flag with a blue star sewn in it for each family

member at war. Occasionally one would see a flag with a gold star, for a son who had died at the front. Rarely had the American people been so united in their dedication to sacrifice for a common goal: to make the world safe for democracy.

gave sweeping authority to the postmaster general to confiscate material considered disloyal. The Sedition Act passed in 1918 imposed punishment for any expression of disloyalty to the American government, flag, or military uniforms.

SECTION REVIEW

1. Identify: War Industries Board, Bernard Baruch, William Gibbs McAdoo, National War Labor Board, Herbert Hoover, Committee on Public Information, George Creel.

2. What actions did the War Industries Board take to mobilize industry?

3. List two ways the government improved conditions for American workers during the war.

4. How did the American public help increase food production during the war?

5. What was the purpose of the Committee on Public Information?

6. **Critical Thinking** Why are civil liberties endangered when dissent is treated as treason?

3 The United States in the War

Because mobilization proceeded slowly at first, American troops were unable to rush to the aid of the battle-weary British and French armies. Although the United States officially entered the war in the spring of 1917, by March 1918 fewer than 300,000 American fighting men were in Europe. Reinforcements arrived more quickly after that, however, and the Germans felt the impact of the United States presence. At sea, the United States Navy provided vital help almost immediately.

War at Sea

The British navy dominated the surface of the oceans but was not very effective against German submarines, which continued to disrupt Allied shipping. Unescorted merchant vessels were easy targets for U-boats, even in areas patrolled by the British. U-boat attacks were destroying Allied ships faster than the shipbuilding industry could produce them. American fighting forces and war supplies would be of no value if they could not safely cross the Atlantic.

Admiral William S. Sims convinced the British to use the *convoy* to reduce the danger of submarine attack. In convoys, destroyers and other warships escorted merchant vessels across the ocean, providing some defense against U-boats. With the United States supplying many of the destroyers, the method proved effective. Convoys transported American soldiers to Europe without the loss of a single life. They also delivered supplies to the Allies and American

forces more quickly than had been anticipated, further strengthening the war effort.

American industry strained to produce warships, especially destroyers and sub chasers. The effort was so successful that by the end of the war, the United States Navy had grown to include over half a million sailors and 2,000 ships.

The American Expeditionary Force

President Wilson chose General John J. Pershing to lead American troops, known as the American Expeditionary Force. General Pershing angered Allied military leaders by insisting that American soldiers go through a period of training before heading for Europe. This delayed the arrival of large numbers of American combat troops until 1918.

Pershing also demanded that the American Expeditionary Force keep its own identity and not be used merely to reinforce the French and British armies. Allied leaders, desperately needing more troops, resented his attitude. Developments on the battlefield soon led to greater cooperation, however.

The first years of the conflict had consisted mostly of trench warfare. Both sides dug defensive trenches, often within a hundred yards of each other, maintained devastating artillery barrages, and mounted occasional infantry charges. The loss of life was great, with little territorial gain by either army. This situation changed in early 1918.

In November 1917 a second revolution within a year forced Russia to drop out of the war. As a result German officials focused their attention on the western front. In the spring of 1918 they launched an all-out attack on the Allied lines, breaking the defensive pattern of the war. Allied leaders appointed Field Marshall Ferdinand Foch of France commander of all Allied forces in Eu-rope. Pershing quickly agreed to cooperate with Foch.

In May 1918 German troops moved to within 50 miles (80 kilometers) of Paris before Allied resistance stiffened. A combined force of French and American troops

■ *For more than four years and at incredible loss of human life, fighting seesawed over the western front in Europe. Although the United States declared war in 1917, large numbers of United States troops did not reach France until 1918, when an Allied counteroffensive finally defeated the Central Powers.*

The Western Front 1914–1918

Major battle sites
Farthest German advance, 1914
Farthest German advance, 1918
Allied counteroffensive, 1918
Armistice line, 1918

After Russia abandoned the war on the eastern front because of revolution at home, German armies massed their strength on the western front. At first Allied forces reeled backward. Then they began a massive counteroffensive. United States forces were assigned the section between Meuse and the Argonne Forest, shown here. One tenth of them were killed or wounded in the savage fighting.

stopped the Germans and drove them out of Belleau Wood. American troops also assisted the French army in stopping a German offensive near Rheims. By autumn, enough American soldiers had arrived to allow Pershing to control his own fighting force, the American First Army. He quickly mounted offensives against German lines in the south.

American successes in that sector allowed the British and French to gain control over the other areas of battle. By early November an Allied victory was assured. On November 11, 1918, German delegates met with Marshall Foch and signed an armistice. The war was over.

The arrival of American troops and supplies had helped turn the tide of battle. The "Yanks," as the American soldiers were known, not only provided the Allies with a numerical advantage but raised the spirits of the exhausted British and French soldiers. Although the United States effort had been vital and over 100,000 American soldiers had died, the other Allies had contributed even

more. Britain lost nearly a million people, France 1.5 million, and Russia 1.7 million.

Diplomacy and War

As early as 1914 President Wilson had suggested the outlines for what he termed a "liberal" peace. He believed that disarmament would end the military competition among industrial powers and that public diplomacy would end the system of secret alliances that had contributed to the outbreak of war. Wilson urged rejection of territorial gains and payment of huge penalties, or *reparations*, by the losers. This policy, he claimed, would lead to a more permanent peace.

In 1916 Wilson explained that the United States wanted a peace treaty that guaranteed the *territorial integrity* of nations, that is, one that protected their boundaries. The peace should also guarantee the right to *self-determination*, or independence; freedom of the seas; and protection from aggression. These were grand ideas, but until the

535

Woodrow Wilson: A Proposal for Peace

In early 1917 President Wilson was still hopeful that peace could be negotiated between the Allies and the Central Powers. He outlined proposals for that peace in a speech to the Senate on January 22, 1917. The final part of Wilson's speech is printed below.

I am proposing, as it were, that the nations should with one accord adopt the doctrine of President Monroe as the doctrine of the world: that no nation should seek to extend its polity over any other nation or people, but that every people should be left free to determine its own polity, its own way of development—unhindered, unthreatened, unafraid, the little along with the great and powerful.

I am proposing that all nations henceforth avoid entangling alliances which would draw them into competitions of power, catch them in a net of intrigue and selfish rivalry, and disturb their own affairs with influences intruded from without.

I am proposing government by the consent of the governed; that freedom of the seas which in international conference after conference representatives of the United States have urged with the eloquence of those who are the convinced disciples of liberty; and that moderation of armaments which makes of armies and navies a power for order merely, not an instrument of aggression or of selfish violence.

These are American principles, American policies. We could stand for no others. And they are also the principles and policies of forward-looking men and women everywhere, of every modern nation, of every enlightened community. They are the principles of mankind and must prevail.

United States entered the war, Wilson had little influence. The contribution of American troops and goods in ending the war strengthened the President's diplomatic position.

Early in 1918, with his country actively involved in the war, Wilson gave a speech in which he proposed a plan for peace called the Fourteen Points. The first five points called for open treaties, freedom of the seas, free trade, arms reductions, and impartial adjustment of colonial claims. Points six through thirteen dealt with national self-determination and the realignment of borders that had been changed during or prior to the war. The fourteenth point was essential to Wilson's personal vision of world peace. It called for the establishment of an international organization to settle disputes between nations and prevent future wars.

As the war neared an end, the President tried to guarantee a peace built around his Fourteen Points. Responding to pressure from Wilson, German Kaiser Wilhelm II stepped down on November 9. The Germans then established a democratic government in an attempt to win more lenient treatment from the victorious Allies. Now Wilson had to persuade Allied leaders, and many Americans, to accept his version of peace.

SECTION REVIEW

1. Identify: Fourteen Points.
2. Define: convoy, reparation, territorial integrity, self-determination.
3. What turned the tide of the war in 1918?
4. What was Wilson's "liberal" peace?
5. **Critical Thinking** How had industrialization changed the nature of war?

4 Search for a "Just Peace"

When the fighting stopped, attention turned to negotiations for a peace treaty. Widespread enthusiasm for the Fourteen Points among the European people convinced Wilson that the delegates to the peace conference would use the plan as a guide. Although Allied leaders agreed with Wilson's overall ideas, they objected to specific details. They wanted to punish Germany and prevent it from ever becoming a major power again. Wilson also faced opposition in the United States.

Resistance at Home

Some of the domestic opposition to Wilson's plans for peace had political roots. The Republicans did not want the Democrats to use the peace to win votes in the upcoming election. Furthermore, many Americans questioned whether the United States should join a world organization, as called for in the fourteenth point. Avoiding involvement in European affairs had been a long-standing American tradition. People felt that now that the German threat was over, the United States should return to that tradition.

The President's own actions contributed to the growing opposition to his peace plan. President Wilson tried to increase popular support at home for his version of the peace by making the 1918 congressional elections a referendum on his policies. The effort backfired. Republicans gained control of both houses of Congress. Republican leaders insisted that the election results repudiated Wilson's foreign policy.

The President lost support in an already hostile Congress when he named the members of the negotiating team that would go to Paris. His appointees were all able men, experienced in diplomatic affairs, but he included no influential Republicans. Republicans in Congress, therefore, looked on any treaty as a Democratic one, open to partisan attack.

Wilson also stirred up opposition when he decided to lead the delegation to Paris himself. No President had ever traveled abroad on a diplomatic mission. Many Americans felt that the President should stay home and help the nation deal with the problems of readjusting to peace.

A new difficulty arose when other countries at the conference demanded that the negotiations be secret. Secrecy alienated American reporters who were trying to keep their readers informed about the progress of the peace talks. Furthermore it seemed to violate the first of Wilson's Fourteen Points, which called for open agreements. Despite such concerns, President Wilson left for Europe in December 1918 with high hopes.

The Versailles Peace Conference

President Wilson visited several countries before the peace conference, which began in January 1919 at Versailles, near Paris. Wildly enthusiastic crowds greeted him in London, Paris, and Rome. Wilson considered his reception evidence of great popular support for his ideas among the people of Europe.

When the war ended, Americans celebrated in the streets. This impressionistic painting by Gifford Reynolds Beal captures the joyful spirit of the day.

An American Experience in the World War: Analyzing Fiction as Historical Evidence

Novels, short stories, and other works of fiction can be used as historical evidence. An excerpt from *Three Soldiers*, a novel by John Dos Passos, is printed below. Dos Passos finished the novel in the spring of 1919. He was disillusioned about the war because idealism had been tarnished by the harsh realities of modern warfare. Use the following steps to analyze the excerpt as historical evidence.

1. **Identify the nature of the document.** (a) What type of document is it? (b) Who wrote it? (c) When was the document written?

2. **Analyze the document as an historical source.** (a) What was the author's attitude about the war? (b) Does the attitude seem to have influenced his description of the event? Explain.

3. **Study the source to learn about an historical event.** (a) What can you learn about the war by reading this excerpt? (b) In what ways is the excerpt limited as historical evidence?

John Dos Passos

Chrisfield ... looked at the stars in the black sky that seemed to be going along with the column on its march. Or was it that they and the stars were standing still while the trees moved away from them, waving their skinny shattered arms? He could hardly hear the tramp of feet on the road, so loud was the pandemonium of the guns ahead and behind. Every now and then a rocket would burst in front of them and its red and green lights would mingle for a moment with the stars. But it was only overhead he could see the stars. Everywhere else white and red glows rose and fell as if the horizon were on fire.

As they started down the slope, the trees suddenly broke away and they saw the valley between them full of the glare of guns and the white light of star shells. It was like looking into a stove full of glowing embers. The hillside that sloped away from them was full of crashing detonations and yellow tongues of flame. In a battery near the road, that seemed to crush their skulls each time a gun fired, they could see the dark forms of the artillerymen silhouetted against the red glare. Stunned and blinded, they kept marching down the road. It seemed to Chrisfield that they were going to step any minute into the flaring muzzle of a gun.

Actually, few Europeans fully understood the American President's plan for peace. Rather, they saw him as a great leader, the head of the nation that had helped end the terrible war engulfing their countries. Their reception, however, only strengthened Wilson's determination to make the peace treaty fit his plan.

In Paris, Wilson encountered equally determined men. Prime Minister David Lloyd George of Britain, Premier George Clemenceau of France, and Prime Minister Vittorio Orlando of Italy all had clear ideas of what they wanted in the treaty. They sought to protect the interests of their own countries and punish Germany for the damages the Allies had suffered in the war. The Treaty of Versailles, which they forced Germany to sign on June 28, 1919, reflected these goals.

Austria-Hungary had collapsed, and the treaty recognized several new nations created out of the old empire. (See the map on page 539.) France acquired the province of Alsace-Lorraine, from Germany, as well as mining rights in the Saar Valley and the right to occupy the Rhineland for 15 years. George, Clemenceau, and Orlando convinced Wilson to agree to demands that Germany pay huge reparations to France and Great Britain and that the treaty include a clause blaming Germany for the war.

Although much of the treaty seemed a violation of Wilson's original goals, he agreed to it because it included the Covenant, or constitution, of the League of Nations. Wilson believed that such an international body could prevent future wars through negotiation.

The President was aware, however, that a significant number of Republican senators opposed the idea of a League of Nations. In fact, during the negotiations, 39 Republican senators—enough to block ratification of a treaty—had signed a petition stating that the treaty was unacceptable. The senators, led by Henry Cabot Lodge of Massachusetts, especially objected to Article 10 of the Covenant of the League of Nations. That article guaranteed the territorial integrity of member states and called for possible economic and military sanctions against violators. These senators did not want an international body making foreign policy decisions for the United States.

Wilson negotiated changes in the original covenant in order to make it more acceptable to the Senate. In its final form, the covenant allowed voluntary withdrawal from the league, made participation in sanctions optional, and recognized the importance of the Monroe Doctrine in the Western Hemisphere. With the revised treaty in hand, the President returned to the United States to try to win ratification from the Senate, a step requiring the votes of two thirds of the 96-member body.

Defeat of the Treaty

On July 10, 1919, Woodrow Wilson personally delivered the 264-page Treaty of Versailles to the Senate. Democrats gave him a loud ovation. The Republican majority sat in silence.

Wilson's effort to revise the treaty failed to satisfy the Republicans. They resented the fact that Republicans had not participated in the negotiations, and some charged that Wilson was using the treaty to win a third term. Most Americans probably favored the treaty and American participation in the League of Nations although German and Irish Americans, along with many liberals, thought the treaty was too harsh on Germany.

In the Senate opposition and support for the treaty broke along party lines. All but 4 of the 47 Democrats stood loyally with Wilson. While some of the 49 Republican senators leaned toward the strict isolationist thinking of William Borah of Idaho and Hiram Johnson of California, most sup-

Europe After the War

TERRITORY LOST BY
- Austria-Hungary
- Bulgaria
- Germany
- Russia

■ The map of Europe after the peace conference looked very different from the map five years earlier. (See page 525.) Many new nations were created as the old empires of Austria-Hungary and Russia collapsed.

ported a series of amendments to the treaty proposed by Henry Cabot Lodge.

Senator Lodge wanted to "Republicanize" the treaty so that the Democrats could not use it to their political advantage. More important, he believed that the League of Nations was a threat to the sovereignty of the United States. His goal was to prevent United States involvement in the internal affairs of other nations and to protect the authority of Congress to declare war.

Wilson refused to accept all but the mildest changes in the treaty. Failing to gain senatorial support, he decided to go directly to the American people. Early in September he embarked on a cross-country trip to explain the treaty. In Omaha, Nebraska, he warned, "I can predict with absolute certainty that within another generation there will be another world war if the nations of the world do not concert . . . to prevent it." The crowds were friendly and enthusiastic, but the enthusiasm did not change Senate votes.

539

The trip destroyed the President's fragile health. On September 25 Wilson collapsed. A week later he suffered a stroke that paralyzed his left side. For weeks he lay near death, and for months he remained almost helpless in bed.

Major Events	
1914	War begins in Europe
1915	German submarine sinks *Lusitania*
1916	Germany suspends unannounced submarine attacks
1917	Germany resumes submarine attacks; Zimmerman Telegram; United States enters war; Espionage Act passed
1918	Fourteen Points announced; War Industries Board created; National War Labor Board created; Sedition Act passed; Germany surrenders
1919	Treaty of Versailles signed
1920	Senate rejects treaty

In November 1919 the treaty, carrying Lodge's amendments, was defeated in the Senate. Wilson had ordered Democrats to vote against the treaty as long as it contained Lodge's amendments. In March 1920 another amended version of the treaty came before the Senate, and again it failed to pass. President Wilson was so opposed to Lodge's changes that he was willing to see the entire treaty defeated rather than accept them. By rejecting the Treaty of Versailles, the Senate dashed Woodrow Wilson's dream of a new world order. The League of Nations began its peacekeeping mission with the United States.

SECTION REVIEW

1. Identify: Treaty of Versailles, League of Nations, Henry Cabot Lodge, Article 10.
2. List two actions by President Wilson that stirred up opposition to his plans for peace.
3. What action did the Senate finally take concerning the Treaty of Versailles?
4. **Critical Thinking** How could the fact that 1920 was an election year have affected the chances for the ratification of the treaty?

★ ★ ★ Chapter 28 Review ★ ★ ★

In Perspective

When war broke out in Europe, President Wilson urged Americans to remain neutral, but neutrality was hard to achieve. A common heritage with Great Britain and skillful Allied propaganda influenced American attitudes toward the war. Even before the United States entered the war, most Americans were friendly to the Allies. After a long series of provocations, Wilson asked Congress to declare war on Germany in April 1917.

The United States now turned its full attention to the war effort. Millions of men were drafted, and industry soared to unprecedented production heights. Congress created a War Industries Board to coordinate war production and a National War Labor Board to unify labor policy. Joining the Allied forces, the United States helped defeat Germany.

President Wilson did not want the victorious Allies to inflict a harsh peace settlement on Germany. But the European Allied leaders demanded a peace treaty that would punish Germany. The Treaty of Versailles deprived Germany of territory and forced the nation to make reparation payments to the victors. President Wilson agreed to the Treaty of Versailles because it contained a provision for the establishment of the League of Nations, but he was unable to persuade the Senate to ratify the treaty.

540

Vocabulary

Match each term at left with its definition or description at right.

1. neutral	**a.** independence
2. convoy	**b.** protected boundaries
3. reparation	
4. territorial integrity	**c.** a protective escort
	d. payment of costs of war
5. self-determination	**e.** nonaligned

Chapter Checkup

1. (a) How did the German use of the submarine complicate the question of neutral rights? (b) How did Wilson react to the sinking of unarmed ships by German submarines? (c) Why did the Germans agree to stop unannounced attacks in 1916?

2. (a) How did the government try to mobilize industry to support the war effort? (b) What actions did the government take to win the effort and support of American workers?

3. (a) Briefly describe President Wilson's Fourteen Points. (b) Which parts of the Treaty of Versailles seemed to contradict the Fourteen Points? (c) Why was Wilson willing to accept the treaty despite such contradictions?

4. (a) How did Wilson alienate many Americans even before the peace conference began? (b) Why did most Republican senators oppose the treaty? (c) What was the purpose of Senator Lodge's amendments to the treaty?

Critical Thinking

1. **Evaluating** (a) How did black Americans, women, and workers in general benefit during the war? (b) Why do you think this occurred during wartime and not earlier?

2. **Supporting an Opinion** (a) What do you think the union official meant by his comment that "the same patriotism that induced women to enter industry during the war should induce them to vacate their positions after the war"? (b) Do you agree with him? Why or why not?

Developing Basic Skills

1. **Map Reading** Compare the two maps on pages 525 and 539. (a) Which new independent countries existed after the war? (b) Which nation no longer existed after the war? (c) Which nations lost territory? (d) Which nations gained territory?

2. **Using a Primary Source** Read the excerpts from President Wilson's foreign policy speech on page 536. (a) Why is this document a primary source? (b) What can you learn about Wilson's goals for peace by reading the document? (c) How does this primary source differ from a diary account?

See page 831 for suggested readings.

Writer's Handbook

Preparing a Preliminary Outline

A preliminary outline helps you focus on areas of research. The first steps in preparing a preliminary outline are to write down the title and thesis statement of your paper. Then formulate questions about the topic. Using the questions as a guideline, draw up a simple outline. Study the following example.

Title: The United States Home Front Mobilizes for War

Thesis statement: Once the United States entered World War I, the nation marshalled its human and material resources to help the Allied effort.

1. The government builds up the armed forces.

2. The government organizes industry.

3. Industry responds.

4. The government encourages public participation.

5. The public responds.

Practice: Choose a topic from Chapter 28 and prepare a preliminary outline.

Unit Eight

The Roaring Twenties

Ben Shahn's tribute to immigrants highlights Albert Einstein, shown with the violin case, among the unknown masses.

Because of the work of jazz singers, such as Ruby Green, the 1920s are often called the Jazz Age.

	1918	1920	1922	1924
POLITICS AND GOVERNMENT		**1919** Fear of radicals leads to the Red Scare	**1921** Veterans Bureau created to handle veterans' claims	
SOCIETY AND CULTURE		**1920** First commercial radio station broadcasts	**1922** Willa Cather's *One of Ours* is published	
ECONOMICS AND TECHNOLOGY		**1919** Strikes in steel and coal industries		
WORLD EVENTS	**1918** Armistice ends fighting in the war	**Early 1920s** Severe inflation hits Germany	**1922** Mussolini comes to power in Italy	

Wilson · Harding ·

Farmers did not share in the prosperity of the Roaring Twenties.

The automobile, shown in this 1920s advertisement, helped transform American society.

Boom Town, by Thomas Hart Benton, caught the spirit of the general economic growth of the 1920s.

1932 This Hoover poster warns against changing Presidents during a crisis.

1924	1926	1928	1930	1932
1924 Fall indicted in Teapot Dome scandal	**1926** Revenue Act slashes taxes on high incomes			**1931** Bonus Army leaves for Washington
1924 Congress cuts immigration from southern and eastern Europe	**1927** *Jazz Singer* is first talking movie		**1930** Grant Wood's *American Gothic* depicts a farm couple	
	1926 Hurricane ends the Florida land boom	**1929** Stock market crash leads to the Great Depression		
	1926 Germany joins the League of Nations		**1930** Depression spreads in Europe	

Coolidge   Hoover

By the late 1920s, millions of Americans were speculating on Wall Street.

1932 As the depression deepened, pressure grew for more government action.

A Search for Peace and Prosperity

29

(1919–1928)

Flag Day *by Childe Hassam*

Chapter Outline

1 *The Rocky Road to Peacetime*

2 *The Politics of Normalcy*

3 *Calvin Coolidge and the Business of America*

When the World War ended on November 11, 1918, Americans jubilantly looked forward to better times. After a period of fighting abroad and new government regulations at home, many yearned for calmer, more familiar times. Instead, they entered a decade of startling, bewildering change. The 1920s opened with labor unrest, social turmoil, and widespread panic about the possible effect of the Russian Revolution on the United States.

In such turbulent times, voters turned to politicians who promised calm and a return to prewar order. Business became the symbol of that order. Americans seemed worn out by crusades for peace abroad and reform at home. Many were far more concerned with gaining a bigger share of the "good life" for themselves.

Yet while newspapers wrote of rich movie stars and fancy new cars, many Americans struggled just to earn enough to eat. The prosperity of the Roaring Twenties masked underlying economic problems.

Politics of "normalcy"

1918	1920	1922	1924	1926	1928
1919 Labor unrest; Red Scare begins	**1920** Warren G. Harding elected President	**1923** Calvin Coolidge succeeds Harding	**1924** Immigration Act passed	**1926** Revenue Act passed	**1928** Coolidge vetoes McNary-Haugen bill

1 The Rocky Road to Peacetime

Before Americans could enjoy the fruits of victory, they had to solve the problems caused by war. Millions of veterans needed work. Factories had to switch from the production of war supplies and equipment to the production of consumer goods. The heated emotions of war needed time to cool.

Returning to Normal

When the war ended in 1918, President Woodrow Wilson asked for a rapid end to government ownership and operation of industries such as railroads, and Congress quickly agreed. However, the President concentrated his efforts on persuading the Senate to consent to the Versailles Treaty. (See page 539.) The country had no plan for easing soldiers and sailors back into civilian life or for avoiding economic dislocation.

The armed forces discharged 4 million men after the war. Hundreds of thousands of wartime employees were also cut from government payrolls. Soon thereafter many factories shut down to retool for peacetime production, so fewer jobs were available. Consequently unemployment climbed to almost 5 million in 1921.

Veterans who could not find work thought they deserved more help from the government. They demanded bonuses to make up for the wages they lost while in uniform. Some veterans received disability benefits, pensions, or hospitalization costs. However, Congress refused to grant the bonuses.

Consumers meanwhile went on a spending spree, buying goods that were unavailable during the war. Since the war began, prices had soared, doubling the cost of living between 1913 and 1920. Inflation pushed the retail price of a new Model T Ford from $360 in 1918 to $480 in 1920. Between 1920 and 1922 the country slid into a recession that was particularly hard on farmers. The price of wheat, for example, sank from a wartime high of $2.26 a bushel to less than $1 a bushel in 1922.

The end of the war also meant an end to peaceful relations between factory owners and workers. During the war the government had encouraged high wages and collective bargaining. In a spirit of patriotism, management and labor had worked to solve problems without strikes.

Rising prices and unemployment after the war fueled workers' demands for higher wages. Employers refused, and many unions went on strike. Workers in the clothing, textile, telegraph, and telephone industries won higher pay, but unions in other industries met with less success.

Some employers charged that union leaders were radicals who wanted to undermine the United States economy. Unions argued that factory owners were greedy and insensitive to the needs of workers. The nation was entering a period of industrial strife.

Postwar Labor Unrest

The first serious postwar confrontation between labor and management occurred in the steel industry. In 1892 the Homestead strike had temporarily ended attempts to unionize the steel industry. (See page 410.) After the war, the American Federation of Labor decided to launch a second organizing effort.

In September 1919 a newly formed steel workers' union demanded higher wages, one day's rest out of seven, and an end to the 12-hour work day. When steel mill owners refused to negotiate, the union called a strike. Within a week 365,000 workers across the country had walked out. When violence erupted, local police and state militia helped steel companies break the picket lines. Companies hired strikebreakers to replace the union workers. After 20 deaths and the loss of $100 million in wages, the union called off the strike on January 9, 1920. It had won no concessions.

A strike in the coal industry was more successful. The United Mine Workers, led by John L. Lewis, also went on strike in 1919. Attorney General A. Mitchell Palmer secured a court order against the strike. Lewis urged the miners to return to work, but they refused. Finally the government ordered a 14-percent wage increase, and the strike ended.

Two strikes in particular convinced many Americans that radical foreign forces might be causing the labor unrest: a general strike in Seattle, Washington, and a police strike in Boston, Massachusetts.

• In 1919 the Central Labor Council of Seattle called a *general strike*, a strike of the members of all unions, in support of striking shipyard workers. The call for a strike by all union members, not just by workers in a single industry, alarmed many Americans. They considered the general strike a radical tactic imported from Europe. When Seattle Mayor Ole Hanson used troops to crush the strike, he became a national hero.

The strike by Boston police seemed even more alarming to most citizens. Police officers walked off the job in September 1919 after the police commissioner fired 19 officers who had tried to join the AFL. With no police protection, looting broke out despite efforts by volunteer groups to maintain order. Actual damage was small, but shock waves of fear rumbled across the nation. Massachusetts Governor Calvin Coolidge was widely admired for condemning the strike as a threat to public safety.

These strikes and hundreds of others hardened the public attitude toward unions. Union membership sank from more than 5 million in 1920 to about 3.6 million in 1923. Employee associations sponsored by management, called *company unions,* became more common, and collective bargaining became rarer.

The Red Scare

As you read in Chapter 28, after the November 1917 revolution Russia signed a cease-fire agreement with Germany. (See page 533.) The revolution had been led by the Bolsheviks, a group of radical communists. Communists believe in control of all property by the community as a whole or by the government. After the war the Russian Bolsheviks, called Reds, advocated worldwide revolution. To many people the labor unrest of the postwar years, typified by the strikes in Seattle and Boston, raised the threat of revolution in the United States.

Terrorist incidents created further anxiety. A package containing a bomb arrived in the Seattle mayor's office after the general strike. Similar packages—set aside for insufficient postage—were found in a New York post office addressed to known opponents of organized labor or immigration. One bomb sent to Senator Thomas Hartwick of Georgia exploded, injuring his maid. Another device exploded when a terrorist tried to plant it on Attorney General Palmer's front porch.

For many people those acts of terrorism, combined with labor unrest, confirmed the fear of communist revolution, and a period known as the Red Scare began. Many Americans could not see the difference between a few criminal terrorists and peaceful protestors or strikers. During 1919 and early 1920 socialists and other radicals were frequently harassed by individual citizens and local authorities. Immigrants, especially those from eastern Europe, were often the targets of such harassment. Some Americans believed these immigrants to be agents of the Russian Bolsheviks.

In response to public demands for action, Attorney General Palmer organized a series of raids to arrest suspected communists. In January 1920 over 6,000 people in 33 cities were seized. Almost none had committed any crime. Of those arrested, about 550 were deported. The raids revealed no plots to overthrow the government.

At first people responded enthusiastically to Palmer's actions, but eventually a growing number of Americans became concerned about violations of constitutional rights. Some public officials, such as former Supreme Court Justice Charles Evans Hughes, spoke out against Palmer's tactics. Furthermore, people lost their enthusiasm for such raids as it became obvious that no revolution had broken out. By late 1920 the Red Scare had faded.

Restrictions on Immigration

One of the underlying causes of the Red Scare had been a negative reaction to immigrants. As you read in Chapter 23, many Americans believed that the "new immigrants" from southern and eastern Europe and Asia would not fit into American society.

During the war, antiforeign feelings had been fueled by government warnings about foreign secret agents. Once the war had ended, a new flood of immigrants entered the country, causing further concern. Workers worried that immigrants would compete for jobs and drive wages down.

In the turbulent postwar period, antiforeign feelings erupted in a campaign to restrict immigration. The cartoonist whose work appears above clearly shared such sentiments. The "Black Hand" referred to in the cartoon was a European terrorist group.

In 1920 the Massachusetts trial of two Italian anarchists accused of murder during a payroll robbery revealed the depth of public concern. Nicola Sacco and Bartolomeo Vanzetti were convicted and sentenced to death even though the evidence against them was far from conclusive. Public opinion was split on the verdict. Many people, including several distinguished lawyers, believed the anarchists had been convicted because they were Italian and held unpopular political views. An equally vocal group argued that the executions would be a warning to other radicals. After many futile appeals, the two were put to death in 1927.

Congress responded to public demands for immigration restriction by passing the •Emergency Quota Act of 1921. Annual immigration from Europe was restricted to a fixed quota, set at 3 percent of the population of a particular nationality living in the United States in 1910. When the Emergency Quota Act failed to reduce the flow of south-

ern and eastern European immigrants substantially, Congress passed the Immigration Act of 1924.

The new law lowered the quota from 3 to 2 percent and changed the base year from 1910 to 1890, when few southern and eastern Europeans were living in the United States. This provision substantially reduced the number of new immigrants from those regions. The act dealt even more harshly with the Japanese, barring them from the United States as "aliens ineligible to citizenship."

By 1929 Congress had reduced the annual quota of immigrants to about 152,000. Of this total, 132,000 were permitted from northern Europe and only about 20,000 from the rest of the world outside of the Western Hemisphere. Since the complicated quota system did not count black Americans, it effectively barred immigration from Africa. The new laws, however, did not limit immigration from the Western Hemisphere, which had increased sharply in the early 1900s.

547

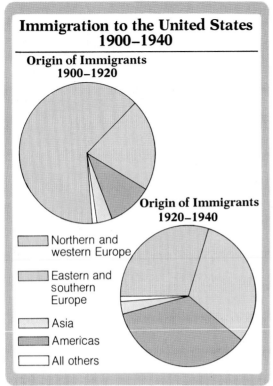

Immigration to the United States 1900–1940

Origin of Immigrants 1900–1920

Origin of Immigrants 1920–1940

- Northern and western Europe
- Eastern and southern Europe
- Asia
- Americas
- All others

Source: *Historical Statistics of the United States*

■ *New immigration laws drastically changed the pattern of immigration to the United States. The graph at top shows the percentage of immigrants from various areas before the new laws went into effect. The new laws set no limit on newcomers from the Western Hemisphere. As the graph at bottom shows, more than one third of all immigrants between 1920 and 1940 came from Mexico, Canada, and other nations in the Americas.*

Black Americans Are Disillusioned

The war had raised the aspirations of many black Americans as new job opportunities opened in war industries. Between 1917 and 1925 about 600,000 blacks migrated to northern industrial cities. Black veterans returned from Europe with a new sense of pride. Having served their country, they demanded better jobs and fair treatment.

The postwar years were a time of disillusionment for many blacks. They faced discrimination in northern cities and suffered greatly from the widespread unemployment of the period. White workers resented blacks competing for jobs. Tension between blacks and whites further increased in northern cities when blacks tried to move into all-white neighborhoods.

In 1919 racial tensions sparked riots in over 20 cities, including Washington, D. C.; Omaha, Nebraska; and Chicago, Illinois. The Chicago riot erupted when a black youngster swimming in a "white" area of Lake Michigan was attacked by a group of angry whites. Before the riot ended, over 500 people were injured and 38 were killed. In Washington, D. C., a mob outside the White House gates attacked black soldiers who were still in uniform.

The intolerance of the period was reflected by the revival of the Ku Klux Klan. The new Klan was formed in Georgia in 1915, and the organization spread quickly from the South to parts of the Midwest and West. While the original Klan, founded after the Civil War, had terrorized freed slaves and whites who sympathized with them, the

■ *The exodus of black Americans from the South, which began after the Civil War, picked up momentum around 1900. Most blacks moved north and west for better jobs. Some, however, left because of segregation.*

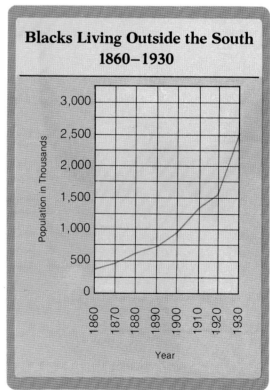

Blacks Living Outside the South 1860–1930

Population in Thousands

3,000
2,500
2,000
1,500
1,000
500
0

1860 1870 1880 1890 1900 1910 1920 1930

Year

Source: United States Bureau of the Census

After the World War, a revived Ku Klux Klan attacked blacks, Jews, Catholics, and immigrants, among others. Although the political strength of the Klan declined after 1924, the group staged a large parade in Washington, D.C., in 1925.

new Klan had a broader goal: to preserve the United States for white, native-born American Protestants. Consequently, the Klan attacked not only blacks, but also immigrants, Catholics, and Jews.

By 1923 the organization claimed 4 million members and had become a political force in Texas, Oregon, Georgia, Oklahoma, Alabama, and especially Indiana. Klan-supported candidates were elected to governorships in Oklahoma and Oregon. The political power of the Klan declined after 1924, however, as the corruption and illegal activities of many of its leaders became known.

SECTION REVIEW

1. Identify: A. Mitchell Palmer, Calvin Coolidge, Bolsheviks Red Scare.
2. Define: general strike, company union.
3. Which nationalities were affected by the new legislation restricting immigration?
4. Why were black veterans disillusioned?
5. How did the new Ku Klux Klan differ from the post–Civil War Klan?
6. **Critical Thinking** Why can economic problems lead to social unrest?

2 The Politics of Normalcy

After the war years and the turbulent postwar period, Americans looked forward to a time of tranquility. Warren G. Harding, elected President in 1920, made popular a phrase that came to signify what the public wanted. He called it normalcy.

The Election of 1920

Republicans were confident of victory in the presidential election of 1920. With the Democratic party badly split over the Versailles Treaty, the Republicans thought that all they needed to win was an attractive candidate. Deciding on such an individual, however, proved to be difficult. The nominating convention, meeting in Chicago, was divided. Finally a group of party leaders gathered in a smoke-filled room at the Blackstone Hotel and chose Senator Warren G. Harding of Ohio. "This Harding's no world beater," they admitted, "but . . . he's the best of the bunch." The convention delegates agreed and selected Governor Calvin Coolidge of Massachusetts for Vice-President.

The Democratic presidential nominating convention took 44 ballots before choosing Governor James Cox of Ohio as their candidate. Franklin D. Roosevelt, Wilson's assistant secretary of the navy, was selected as the Democratic vice-presidential candidate.

In the first national election in which women had full suffrage, Harding polled a record 16 million votes, compared to Cox's 9 million. As one Democrat admitted, "It wasn't just a landslide, it was an earthquake." The President-elect urged the country to seek "not heroism but healing, not nostrums but normalcy." No one had heard the word "normalcy" before, but everyone knew what Harding meant.

The Harding Administration

Harding's inauguration began 12 years of Republican leadership. Throughout the 1920s Republicans controlled both the presidency and Congress.

The affable Harding fit the image of President. Distinguished, gray-haired, and handsome, he cut an impressive figure. Once a small-town politician and newspaper editor, he had risen to the United States Senate. But as President, Harding often felt the job was beyond him, and he nearly worked himself to death trying to meet the demands of the office. Unfortunately, he was probably correct when he said, "I knew this job would be too much for me." His problems often resulted from the questionable appointments of some of his poker-playing friends to major government positions.

During the election campaign Harding had promised to recruit the best minds in the country for his administration, and a few appointments did fulfill the promise. As secretary of state he named former Supreme Court Justice Charles Evans Hughes. Henry C. Wallace, the new secretary of agriculture, was a leader in the movement for farm reform. As secretary of commerce Harding appointed Herbert Hoover, an internationally admired engineer and humanitarian. The man who dominated Harding's administration, however, was Treasury Secretary Andrew Mellon, who had made a fortune as a banker and industrialist.

A Businesslike Economic Program

Andrew Mellon shared the probusiness orientation of the Harding administration. He favored a high tariff that would protect American business from foreign competition. Consistent with Mellon's views,

The great German physicist Albert Einstein was honored by President Harding on a visit to the United States. Einstein (at left) is shown in this photograph with his wife, Elsa Einstein, the President, and Dr. Charles Walcott, secretary of the Smithsonian Institution. In 1933 the Einsteins moved permanently to the United States.

Congress passed the Fordney-McCumber Act in 1922, raising tariffs to a new high.

Mellon also believed that taxes on large incomes should be reduced. If taxes were lowered, he argued, the wealthy would have more money to invest. More investment would create more jobs, which would mean more income for middle- and lower-income people. Mellon believed wealth would "trickle down" and improve the standard of living for everyone. A majority of Congress agreed with Mellon's reasoning. The Revenue Act of 1921 and other new tax laws slashed taxes on higher incomes.

In his drive to promote efficiency and economy in government, Mellon instituted a much-needed budgeting process for government departments. Working with the new budget director, Charles Dawes, Mellon reduced the national debt and balanced the budget. Government expenses fell from $6.4 billion in 1920 to $2.9 billion in 1927.

The determination to cut costs led to conflict with the American Legion and other veterans' groups. Congress had formed the Veterans Bureau in 1921 to handle claims for hospitalization and administer a program of veterans' insurance. Many veterans believed they deserved more government assistance and better medical treatment.

Twice Congress passed "bonus bills" to compensate veterans for the money they could have earned instead of serving at low pay in the armed forces. But President Harding vetoed the bills because he thought they were too expensive. In 1924 a bill giving the average veteran about $1,000 worth of life insurance was passed over President Coolidge's veto. However, the money was not to be paid for 20 years.

Corruption in Government

Although President Harding was honest, his administration was riddled with swindlers and corrupt officials. Attorney General Harry Dougherty and his friend Jesse Smith made fortunes selling government favors, immunities from prosecution, and pardons. The head of the Veterans Bureau, Charles Forbes, sold shipments of bandages, drugs, and bedding and pocketed the money while veterans lay in hospitals desperately short of supplies. Theft at the Veterans Bureau was just one scandal that shook President Harding's administration.

Who Says a Watched Pot Never Boils?

Dishonesty and corruption were common in the Harding administration. This 1924 cartoon refers to the Teapot Dome scandal, which involved the leasing of valuable government-owned oil fields.

In 1921 Secretary of the Interior Albert B. Fall convinced the secretary of the navy and President Harding to transfer control of oil reserves at Teapot Dome, Wyoming, and Elk Hills, California, from the Department of the Navy to the Department of the Interior. Once in control of the oil, Secretary Fall leased the reserves to two oil men, Harry F. Sinclair and Edward L. Doheny. In exchange for the oil reserves Sinclair and Doheny "loaned" Fall about $400,000.

Fall's sudden increase in wealth attracted attention. A Senate committee began an investigation in 1924, and a grand jury indicted Fall for bribery. He was eventually convicted, sentenced to one year in prison, and fined $100,000. Albert Fall was the first cabinet officer in history to be sent to prison. Doheny and Sinclair were acquitted on the bribery charge. Sinclair later went to jail for contempt of court and contempt of the Senate.

President Harding never learned the full extent of the corruption in his administration. He died of a heart attack on August 2, 1923. The task of restoring faith in government fell to Calvin Coolidge.

SECTION REVIEW

1. Identify: Warren G. Harding, Andrew Mellon, Harry Dougherty, Albert Fall.

2. Define: normalcy.

3. Name two ways Mellon tried to promote efficiency and economy in government.

4. What led to Fall's bribery conviction?

5. **Critical Thinking** Did Harding's administration reflect the influence of the progressives or the conservatives in the Republican party? Why?

3 Calvin Coolidge and the Business of America

Calvin Coolidge took the oath of office, administered by his father, a justice of the peace, in the living room of the Vermont farmhouse that five generations of Coolidges had called home. Because the new President rarely smiled and spoke little, he struck people as cold. Once a college student told Coolidge she had bet her roommate she could get him to say more than three words. "You lose," was the reply. Yet Coolidge proved able to restore national confidence in government.

No man was more committed to the business community. As the economy improved during the 1920s, Coolidge became more convinced that the United States should be guided by business principles. Thrilled by the prosperity that developed during his administration, Coolidge proudly proclaimed that "the business of America is business."

The Election of 1924

As the 1924 election neared, the Republicans nominated Coolidge without difficulty, but the Democrats battled for 17 days in a July heat wave before agreeing on a candidate and a platform. Millions of Americans listened on the radio to the struggle between the rural followers of William Jennings Bryan and the urban supporters of the Tammany Hall politicians from New York.

The most hotly contested issue at the Democratic convention was a proposed plank in the party platform condemning the Ku Klux Klan. The plank was defeated by just one vote out of more than a thousand cast. After 103 ballots the Democrats finally nominated John W. Davis, a corporate lawyer closely associated with Wall Street banking interests. Both parties thus chose candidates with a business orientation.

Farmers, social reformers, socialists, and progressives rallied behind the Progressive party candidacy of Robert La Follette of Wisconsin. La Follette supported government ownership of the railroads, the abolition of child labor, and the right of unions to organize and engage in collective bargaining. The Progressive party platform attacked "the control of government and industry by private monopoly."

Americans voted overwhelmingly to "keep cool with Coolidge," who won 35 states. Davis won 12 states, and La Follette won one: Wisconsin. A few progressive voices continued to argue for government regulation of the economy, but in the 1920s they fought lonely battles.

Business Under Coolidge

Coolidge did not disappoint those who wanted a President sympathetic to business interests. In 1925, for example, he appointed William E. Humphrey to chair the Federal Trade Commission. (See page 503.) The new chairman condemned the FTC as "an instrument of oppression" of the business community, and under his leadership the FTC systematically refused to investigate various monopolistic agreements.

Coolidge appointed other friends of business to run the Interstate Commerce Commission and the Federal Reserve Board, agencies that had been created to regulate business practices. (See pages 419 and 502.)

A View of Business in the 1920s

When President Calvin Coolidge proclaimed that "the business of America is business," he was expressing the opinion of many people. Seldom in American history had the business community been so admired as during the 1920s. The extent of that feeling can be seen in the following excerpts from an article written by Edward E. Purinton in 1921.

Among the nations of the earth today America stands for one idea: *Business*. . . . Through business, properly conceived, managed, and conducted, the human race is finally to be redeemed. . . .

What is the finest game? Business. . . . The fullest education? Business. The fairest opportunity? Business. . . . You may not agree. That is because you judge business by the crude, mean, stupid, false imitation of business that happens to be located near you.

The finest game is business. The rewards are for everybody, and all can win. There are no favorites. And in this game there is no "luck." The speed and size of your winnings are for you alone to determine. And your slogan is not "Down the Other Fellow!" but rather "Beat Your Own Record!" or "Do It Better Today!"

The fullest education is business. A proper blend of study, work, and life is essential to advancement. . . . In the school of business, moreover, you teach yourself and learn most from your own mistakes. What you learn here you live out, the only real test.

The fairest opportunity is business. You can find more, better, quicker chances to get ahead in a large business house than anywhere else on earth.

The President's appointments provoked progressive Senator George Norris of Nebraska to remark:

The effect of these appointments is to set the country back more than twenty-five years. It is an indirect but positive repeal of congressional enactments, which no administration, however powerful, would dare to bring about by any direct means. It is the nullification of federal law by a process of boring from within.

Critics charged that Coolidge's appointments were intended to destroy the effectiveness of the regulatory agencies.

The Revenue Act, signed by President Coolidge in 1926, was also favorable to business. The act drastically slashed tax rates on high incomes while making only modest rate cuts for middle incomes.

Coolidge's probusiness program appeared to be a great success as the nation enjoyed a period of dazzling prosperity. Between 1921 and 1929 the output of industry nearly doubled. Profits and wages grew, and unemployment was low. Not everyone became rich, but more people could afford to buy more products than ever before.

The Farm Problem

Farmers did not share in the general prosperity of the 1920s. They faced high expenses and low prices for farm products. During the war American farmers had increased the number of acres they planted in order to increase production. Prices soared because of the great demand from Europe. But when the war ended and European farmers returned to work, the demand for American produce fell and so did prices.

Prices rose gradually during the 1920s, but expenses rose faster. Railroad shipping rates, taxes, seed prices, and interest rates spiraled. Farmers bought expensive machinery and chemical fertilizer in order to increase production. Unfortunately for farmers, the resulting surplus of farm produce kept prices low. Increased harvests in nations such as Canada and Australia contributed to worldwide overproduction.

To improve their position, farmers banded together in farm bureaus, which in turn joined the American Farm Bureau Federation. Farmers also formed cooperatives to store, market, and ship their produce. But overproduction continued to glut the market, and prices continued to fall.

553

Major Events	
1915	Ku Klux Klan reorganizes
1917	Bolsheviks take power in Russia
1918	War ends
1919	Strikes in steel industry and coal mines; Seattle general strike; Boston police strike
1919–1920	Red Scare
1920	Warren G. Harding elected President
1921	Emergency Quota Act passed
1923	President Harding dies; Vice-President Calvin Coolidge becomes President
1924	Immigration Act passed; Albert Fall indicted in Teapot Dome scandal; Coolidge elected President

Farmers also sought assistance from the federal government. Legislators from agricultural districts voted together as a "farm bloc" to promote measures that would help farmers. One such proposal was the McNary-Haugen bill.

The purpose of this legislation was to establish a government-supported two-price system for some farm products, such as wheat and corn. The farmer would receive a parity price regardless of the market price. *Parity* meant that a farmer's purchasing power would remain constant even if market prices dropped.

President Coolidge vetoed the McNary-Haugen bill in 1927 and again in 1928. The overall prosperity of the 1920s hid the severity of the farm problem as well as other flaws in the economy.

SECTION REVIEW

1. Identify: McNary-Haugen bill.
2. Define: parity.
3. Who supported the Progressives in 1924?
4. What factors caused farm expenses to rise during the 1920s?
5. **Critical Thinking** How did the Democrats' difficulties benefit Coolidge?

Chapter 29 Review

In Perspective

Returning to normal after the war was not easy. High prices and unemployment contributed to a rising number of strikes. Partially because of these strikes and the successful Bolshevik revolution in Russia, many Americans began to fear a revolution in the United States. During the so-called Red Scare, many immigrants were arrested. Anti-immigrant feelings led to laws restricting immigration from southern and eastern Europe, Asia, and Africa. Black Americans also faced discrimination and violence during the postwar years.

By 1921 when Warren G. Harding was inaugurated, the heated emotions of wartime had cooled, and people looked forward to a time of peace and prosperity. Under both Harding and Coolidge, the government followed probusiness policies. Harding's administration was marred by scandals, but President Coolidge restored national confidence. He was encouraged by the general prosperity of the period, but, like many Americans, he overlooked the problems of farmers. As you will read in the following chapter, the prosperity of a growing number of people helped earn the new decade its nickname: the Roaring Twenties.

Vocabulary

On a separate sheet of paper, write the word or words that best complete each of the following sentences.

1. A (An) ___ is a strike by members of all unions in a particular place.
2. ___ is a system of price supports for farm products.
3. ___ were a group of radical communists.
4. A (An) ___ is a management-sponsored employee association.
5. ___ was a term coined by Harding to describe the need of the country.

Chapter Checkup

1. (a) What economic problems did Americans face when the war ended? (b) How did these problems increase tension between employers and workers?
2. (a) What developments contributed to a rise in antiforeign feeling after the war? (b) How did Congress respond to that feeling? (c) How did the Emergency Quota Act of 1921 and the Immigration Act of 1924 affect the number of immigrants who came to the United States?
3. How did Andrew Mellon reflect the pro-business orientation of the Harding administration? Give examples.
4. (a) What did farmers do to improve their situation in the 1920s? (b) Were they successful? Explain.

Critical Thinking

1. **Analyzing** List the actions taken during the administrations of Harding and Coolidge that would be considered probusiness. Describe how you think each action would help the growth of business and industry.
2. **Interpreting Evidence** Review the description of the presidential campaign and election of 1924. (See page 552.) How might you use the election as evidence that the progressive era was over?

Developing Basic Skills

1. **Graph Reading** Study the graphs on immigration on page 548 and compare them with the graphs on page 440. Then answer the following questions: (a) From which region did the largest percentage of immigrants come between 1900 and 1920? (b) How would you describe the change in the origin of immigration to the United States since the 1840s?
2. **Comparing** You have read about a rise in antiforeign feelings during three periods of American history: during the 1840s (see pages 276–277); after 1880 (see pages 441–442); and during the 1920s. Review what you have learned and answer the following questions: (a) What groups were the objects of antiforeign feelings during each period? (b) In what ways were the three outbreaks of antiforeign feeling similar? (c) In what ways were they different?

See page 832 for suggested readings.

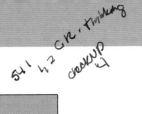

Writer's Handbook

Taking Notes

If you have followed the suggestions in the previous lessons, you are now ready to begin serious note-taking. Compare your bibliography cards with your preliminary outline and select the sources that you think will be most relevant. Use a separate note card for each source and for different subjects from the same source. Write the subject in the right-hand corner so that you will be able to organize the cards according to your outline. In the upper left-hand corner write the title, author, and publishing information that you will need for footnotes. Record the pages from which you have obtained each fact, idea, or quotation. Write notes on the front of the card only.

Practice: Write a sample note card on the subject "American culture." Use your textbook as the source.

30

Life in the 1920s

(1920–1929)

A flapper on the cover of McClure's magazine

Chapter Outline

1 *A Decade of Material Progress*

2 *The Jazz Age*

3 *Behind the Facade*

Life in the United States was never the same after the World War. Before the war people still hitched their horses to posts outside the general store, scrubbed their clothes over washboards, and read by flickering gaslights. After the war gas pumps replaced hitching posts, washing machines replaced scrub boards, and electric lights replaced gas flames. Farmers bought tractors to replace their workhorses. Women cut their hair short and abandoned the long, restrictive skirts they had worn before.

The 1920s was a breathless decade with many names: the Roaring Twenties, the Jazz Age, the Flapper Era, the Golden Twenties. Most of all it was a time of rapid and exciting change as movies, radios, electricity, vacuum cleaners, and dozens of other inventions altered everyday life.

One symbol of the decade was the automobile. Henry Ford's pioneering efforts to mass-produce a low-priced car allowed many Americans to buy one. The extensive use of private cars transformed American society.

Jazz Age

1920	1922	1924	1926	1928	1930

1920
First radio station starts broadcasting

1922
Sinclair Lewis writes *Babbitt*

1925
Countee Cullen writes "A Song of Praise"

1926
Gertrude Ederle swims English Channel

1927
Lindbergh flies Atlantic

1928
Iron lung developed

1929
Museum of Modern Art opens in New York City

1 A Decade of Material Progress

For many Americans, the 1920s meant a better life. Factories poured out a seemingly endless stream of goods, and more people than ever before could afford to buy them. Industrial innovations and improved technology increased productivity and added to the nation's material wealth.

A Surge of Electrical Power

The output of electricity soared after 1900 as a result of new production methods that allowed power plants to burn less coal while generating more power. Between 1902 and 1929 the production of electric power increased by 19 times. Before the war, 20 percent of American homes had electricity. By the end of the 1920s, 70 percent were equipped with electric power.

Abundant electricity allowed Americans to enjoy a wide range of electrically powered consumer goods. Electric refrigerators, vacuum cleaners, and electric stoves transformed American homes during the 1920s. Total sales of major household appliances more than doubled during the decade, while sales of portable appliances jumped from $71 million to $106 million. Electricity not only made home life more pleasant, it made industrial production more efficient.

More Efficient Industry

Although the number of industrial workers remained the same, production of goods in the United States increased 25 percent between 1921 and 1928. The growing use of electrically powered equipment was partially responsible. In 1914, 30 percent of American factory machinery was electrically powered. By 1929 that figure had risen to 70 percent. Electric power enabled a worker to do more in less time. Between 1920 and 1929 output per working hour went up 35 percent, twice the increase of the previous decade.

Scientific management also made industry more efficient. The leading advocate of scientific management was Frederick W. Taylor. He believed that employers should systematically study the performance of their workers in order to find ways to increase efficiency. As chief engineer at the Midvale Steel Company during the 1880s, Taylor studied the productivity of individual workers. He observed the number of steps a worker took and how often the worker picked up a particular tool.

Taylor conducted experiments to determine how much workers should be able to lift and carry. Then he devised plans to increase the efficiency of workers and machines. He might suggest the use of a smaller shovel or the repositioning of a machine control panel. At the Midvale plant Taylor was able to boost output by 300 percent with no increase in the work force.

News of Taylor's success spread rapidly, and many firms, including the Bethlehem Steel Company, sought his advice. Although

Improved technology and management methods combined to increase the productivity of business in the 1920s. The text of this 1925 advertisement noted that the product used "up-to-date machinery so located that every manufacturing process follows in logical order."

Taylor died in 1915, other "efficiency experts" emerged to continue his work. By the 1920s Taylor's methods were widely practiced in American industry.

Henry Ford

Henry Ford was one industrialist who learned Taylor's lessons well. After working as chief engineer for the Edison Illuminating Company, Ford turned his attention to the manufacturing of cars. After he organized the Ford Motor Company in 1903, he revolutionized the automobile industry. Ford applied electric power and scientific management to the production of an item the public wanted to buy.

In 1914 Ford introduced an electrically powered assembly line at his Highland Park, Michigan, plant. On the *assembly line* workers stood at their work stations while unfinished cars moved past them on a conveyor belt. Each worker performed one simple task on each car as it moved by. Ford's efficiency experts determined what each individual task should be and how long

it should take. The Model T, Ford's first car, rolled off the new assembly line in record numbers.

Before the introduction of the assembly line, each car had taken 14 hours to build. But in Ford's new Highland Park plant a car could be assembled in an hour and a half. As other automobile manufacturers instituted Ford's techniques, the industry prospered. The number of cars produced annually soared from 4,000 in 1900 to 4.8 million in 1929.

Ford knew how to sell cars. He believed that more people would buy a car if the price was low. With his efficient assembly lines, Ford could produce cars inexpensively. In 1914 a new Model T sold for $400. A decade later Ford had reduced the price to $260. Although the Model T came in only one color—black—people flocked to Ford showrooms.

The Impact of the Automobile

About 9 million automobiles were registered in the United States in 1920. By 1930 registra-

Dozens of new products appeared on the market in the 1920s, but none was more sought after than the automobile. By 1928, when this photo was taken in Maryland, a new phenomenon had entered the American scene: the traffic jam.

tions had more than tripled. The millions of new cars created new demands. In 1920 highways were often nothing more than rutted dirt roads, and driving was often hazardous. Congress passed the Federal Highway Act of 1921 to encourage road building. State governments imposed taxes on gasoline to raise money for highway construction. Between 1921 and 1929 surfaced road mileage in the United States almost doubled. When the Bronx River Parkway opened in New York in 1927, visitors came from Europe to study it. The parkway was an American innovation in highway construction: a limited-access road that wound through a parklike setting.

With good roads, car owners no longer found it necessary to live close to their jobs in the city. The new mobility caused a boom in the growth of suburbs. During the 1920s the population of Shaker Heights, a suburb of Cleveland, increased tenfold. The population of Scarsdale, a New York City suburb, almost tripled during that same period.

The effects of growing suburbs rippled through the economy. Homes, schools, churches, libraries, and post offices had to be built to meet the needs of suburban residents. New construction provided work for many thousands of carpenters, bricklayers, masons, and other skilled workers.

Automobile production generated economic growth in other fields. New jobs opened up in industries that supplied materials used to build cars. These included the rubber, steel, and glass industries. Roadside food stands and motels were built to serve motorists. By 1930 one out of nine workers had a job related to the automobile industry. Each new industry generated jobs, providing more money to spend on goods such as sewing machines, refrigerators, and, of course, cars.

Scientific Breakthroughs

Although the automobile industry was the most spectacular sign of progress during the 1920s, technological breakthroughs affected hundreds of other industries. Many new inventions transformed American life.

During the war, shortages of natural fibers had forced Americans to rely on *synthetics*, or chemically produced fibers. Research in chemistry during the 1920s created

additional synthetic fibers. Celanese was developed as an alternative to silk and rayon, an earlier silk substitute. Synthetics wrinkled less easily than natural fibers and were thus popular among busy people who had little time for ironing. A new plastic called cellophane was developed as an alternative to wrapping paper.

Telephoto, a process for sending pictures by wire, was invented during the 1920s, and the first transcontinental photo was sent in 1925. The first transatlantic telephone service between New York and London also began during the decade. Although commercial television was not available in the United States until the late 1940s, researchers performed successful experiments with television during the 1920s. The first televised transmission of pictures occurred in 1927. The following year researchers broadcast the first drama on television.

Advances were also made in medicine. Improvements in anesthesia made surgery safer and less painful. Phenobarbital, a sedative, was first used for the control of epileptic seizures. In 1928 the iron lung was developed to help polio patients breath. A year later a British researcher, Dr. Alexander Fleming, discovered penicillin.

The life expectancy of Americans increased from 49 to 59 years between 1910 and 1930. Infant mortality dropped by two thirds. Deadly diseases such as tuberculosis, diptheria, and smallpox were brought under control. Advances in science and medicine combined with major technological breakthroughs to improve the quality of life for many Americans.

SECTION REVIEW

1. Identify: Frederick W. Taylor, Henry Ford.
2. Define: scientific management, assembly line, synthetics, telephoto.
3. What impact did Frederick Taylor's studies have on output at Midvale Steel?
4. How was Ford able to keep the prices of his Model T low?
5. List three scientific advances in the 1920s.
6. **Critical Thinking** What industry other than the automobile industry has had a major impact on society? Explain.

2 The Jazz Age

Novelist F. Scott Fitzgerald called the period between the war and 1929 the Jazz Age. "My candle burns at both ends," wrote poet Edna St. Vincent Millay, offering an image that captured the restless spirit of the 1920s. This was the decade in which American jazz captured world acclaim and Hollywood became the international film capital. American playwrights, novelists, and poets created enduring works esteemed on both sides of the Atlantic. Americans searched for fun and escape—and many thought they found it.

The American Sound

Of all the music that poured from the new radios, none was more uniquely American, more original, or more typical of the 1920s than jazz. Born in the South, perhaps in New Orleans, jazz blended West African rhythms, black work songs and spirituals, minstrel songs, and European harmonies. Jazz also had roots in the ragtime rhythms of composers such as Scott Joplin and in another kind of music created in the United States, the blues. Musicians improvised on a theme to make jazz what it was: flexible, alive, and everchanging.

The first great jazz musicians were black. They included composer "Jelly Roll" Morton, singer Bessie Smith, and trumpet player, singer, and great improviser Louis Armstrong. Jazz transcended color, however, and musicians of all backgrounds adopted it, adding to the repertoire. In 1917 the all-white Original Dixieland Jazz Band became the first jazz group to make recordings with a large record company.

The Harlem Renaissance

Jazz spread from New Orleans to Chicago to the area of New York City known as Harlem. There Duke Ellington led a jazz band that performed in the well-known Cotton Club. Harlem was home to many black musicians, poets, and novelists. During the 1920s, their work produced a flowering of creativity that became known as the Harlem Renaissance.

Much of the poetry of the Harlem Renaissance protested the prejudice of the era. Langston Hughes, probably the best-known figure of the Harlem Renaissance, proudly reminded his readers of black Americans' African heritage.

Poet Countee Cullen was a Harvard graduate and New York City schoolteacher. One of his earliest poems, "A Song of Praise" (1925), was filled with black pride. Pride was also an important theme in the poetry of Claude McKay. Although McKay lived in Europe during much of the Harlem Renaissance, his powerful verse cast a penetrating light on the problem of discrimination in the United States.

Other figures of the Harlem Renaissance wrote scholarly books and articles about black Americans. Carter G. Woodson, a pioneer in the field of black history, established the *Journal of Negro History* in 1916. The *Journal* published articles on every aspect of black life and history. W.E.B. Du Bois (see page 424) wrote about the history of black people and advanced the idea that the fate of blacks in America and Africa was linked.

Marcus Garvey, who came to New York from Jamaica in 1916, drew widespread attention when he urged American blacks to return to Africa to establish a nation there. Garvey's weekly paper, *Negro World*, spread the message of racial pride and tried to popularize the idea of returning to Africa. Although he attracted a large following, Garvey never established an American black community in Africa. His plans collapsed after the failure of several business ventures.

The Movies

The motion picture became a popular pastime during the 1920s. Movie theaters began to appear as early as 1903. After the war Hollywood, a suburb of Los Angeles, emerged as the movie capital of the world.

Early films did not identify the actors, but movie studios soon discovered that the public had clear favorites and would buy tickets to see them again. The age of the movie star had begun, as Clara Bow, John Barrymore, Mary Pickford, Charles Chaplin, and Lillian Gish became celebrities. With Barrymore or Gish on the marquee, a studio could be almost certain of success.

Izzy and Moe: Prohibition Agents

The doorman at a New York speakeasy, or illegal nightclub, peered through his peek hole. Outside, a fat man clutched a pail of dill pickles. Though the doorman did not recognize the fellow, he opened the door. Who could suspect a person carrying pickles? The pickle salesman, however, was a federal prohibition agent. As such, he was charged with enforcing the Eighteenth Amendment to the Constitution, which prohibited the manufacturing, buying, and selling of alcoholic beverages.

Isadore "Izzy" Einstein stood five feet, five inches tall and weighed 225 pounds. His partner, Moe Smith, was a bit taller and heavier. They frequently made newspaper headlines as the zaniest and most effective prohibition agents in the country.

Izzy, particularly, was a master of disguise. He could move through New York's diverse neighborhoods easily, for he spoke five languages well, four others not so well. On the waterfront, he would dress as a fisherman, lugging along a string of fish.

Between them Izzy and Moe made more than 4,000 arrests. In their five-year career they seized $15-million worth of alcohol and much equipment for making alcohol. Few agents could approach their record of success.

By the mid-1920s, bootlegging, the illegal manufacture and sale of alcohol, was a billion-dollar-a-year business. About half a million people were involved in bootleg operations. Fleets of boats brought alcohol across the Great Lakes from Canada. Rumrunners from Cuba landed easily on the long coastline of Florida. Cars with "booze" hidden in false bottoms crossed the Mexican border. Thousands of homemade stills turned out home-brewed concoctions. Fifteen hundred federal prohibition agents were charged with shutting down these diverse operations. They were expected to patrol the entire country.

Because they were so effective, Izzy and Moe were often sent to other cities. On the road, Izzy timed how long it took a stranger (himself) to find and buy an illegal drink. His report: New Orleans, 35 seconds; Pittsburgh, 11 minutes; Atlanta, 17 minutes; Washington, D.C., one hour. His experience showed that while Americans may have voted for Prohibition, millions did not want it applied to their own lives. When Izzy wrote a book about his exploits, he dedicated it "to the 4,392 persons I arrested, hoping they bear me no grudge for having done my duty."

Until 1927 movies were silent; that is, they had no sound track. Audiences read subtitles to follow the plot, and a theater organ or piano provided background music. Americans roared with laughter at the antics of Laurel and Hardy. They thrilled to the fearless exploits of Douglas Fairbanks in *The Three Musketeers* (1921) and adored the romantic Rudolph Valentino in *The Sheik* (1921). The "western" achieved popularity early in the silent era. Actors such as Tom Mix and William S. Hart played tight-lipped heroic

561

cowboys who outsmarted and outfought outlaws.

Despite early popularity, attendance at the silent films began to taper off by the mid-1920s. People were listening to the radio instead. Then, on October 6, 1927, the first talking movie was released, *The Jazz Singer*, starring Al Jolson. The great success of *The Jazz Singer* signaled the end of the silent era. Charlie Chaplin's *City Lights*, made in 1931, was among the last of the great silent movies. Audiences delighted in the new "talkies." Attendance at the movies rose from 60 million paid admissions per week in 1927 to 110 million per week in 1929. Even so, the movies did not dim the popularity of the radio.

Radio

Experimental radio stations had begun to broadcast around 1915, but before 1920 radio was mainly limited to "ham operators" with earphones and crystal sets. The first commercial broadcasting station, WWJ in Detroit, went on the air on August 20, 1920.

The first radios were cumbersome devices. Sounds could be heard only through earphones attached to wires. Rapid technological advances soon modified radio design, however. Within a few years of this photograph, radios had become common in millions of American homes.

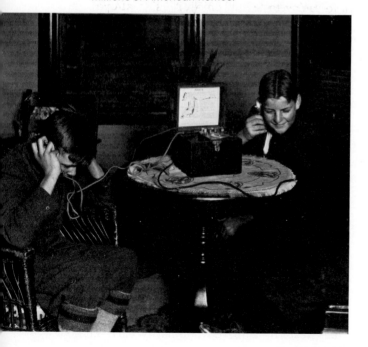

On November 2, 1920, KDKA in Pittsburgh broadcast the presidential election returns. But few heard the news of Harding's election on the radio, which was still a novelty in American homes.

By 1921 the new invention had attracted enough interest to fill Madison Square Garden in New York with people listening to radio reports from Arlington National Cemetery on the burial of the "unknown soldier" from the war. Also in 1921, those who had sets could hear blow-by-blow accounts of the heavyweight fight between Jack Dempsey and the French war hero Georges Carpentier. A year later listeners were tuning in to a radio broadcast of the World Series.

President Harding had a radio installed in the White House. Millions listened to the 1924 Democratic convention and the heated debates over candidates and whether to condemn the Ku Klux Klan.

The popularity of radio spread across the United States with stunning speed. Two years after the first commercial broadcast, annual sales of radios totalled $60 million. In 1929 Americans spent $843 million on radios. By 1930 one home in three had a radio. The government began assigning wavelengths to stations in 1927.

A new style of life developed as families clustered around the radio after dinner to listen to their favorite programs. Classical music was a mainstay of early radio programming, which also included comedy series, popular music, news reports, and broadcasts of sports events.

A Time for Heroes and Fads

Bringing nearly immediate reports of news into millions of homes, radio helped create instant heroes and fads. After Gertrude Ederle became the first woman to swim the English Channel in 1926, New York City, her home town, gave her a ticker tape* parade. A year later Charles A. Lindbergh received an even larger parade.

In May 1927 Lindbergh flew from New York to Paris in 33 hours, making the first solo nonstop flight across the Atlantic. Presi-

---

*Offices in the Wall Street area were equipped with ticker tape machines, devices that record telegraphed stock quotations on strips of paper or tape. During a ticker tape parade, office workers would throw shreds of ticker tape out of windows.

Charles Lindbergh's solo flight across the Atlantic to Paris made the modest young captain an instant hero. This ticker tape parade in New York City was one of several parades in his honor.

dent Coolidge sent a warship to bring the pilot and his plane home. When Lindbergh returned to New York City he received a tumultuous welcome. Newspapers estimated that street cleaners swept up 1,800 tons (about 1,600 metric tons) of paper after Lindbergh's ticker tape parade. Lindbergh was widely regarded as a hero, since his feat combined bravery and skill. To many he embodied the values of courage and modesty.

Other heroes emerged from the movies, as millions felt they personally knew glamorous stars like Greta Garbo, Mary Pickford, and Douglas Fairbanks. Comedians Buster Keaton and Charlie Chaplin, in their gentle satires of the newly mechanized society, touched the lives of thousands. Young people tried to copy the dress, hairstyles, and mannerisms of the stars. Sports greats such as auto racer Barney Oldfield, tennis player Helen Wills, and boxer Jack Dempsey achieved glory and captured the imaginations of many.

In 1927 fans listened to their radios breathlessly as Babe Ruth hit one homerun after another to set a record of 60 homers in one season. Fans filled major league baseball stadiums to see Ruth, Ty Cobb, and other stars. College football, with stars like Red Grange, also drew thousands of spectators. Sports events of all kinds, from horse and auto racing to tennis, enjoyed rising attendance. The number of golf courses tripled in the decade.

Magazines, newspapers, and radio stations looked for amusing stories and publicized dozens of fads from sitting on flagpoles for days to playing the Chinese game Mah Jong. Crossword puzzles also became a rage. Golfers studied the *Psychology of Golf* while insurance salespeople pored over the *Psychology of Selling Life Insurance*. A Frenchman, Emile Coué (ay MEEL koo AY), filled auditoriums with his lectures on how to find contentment. His formula, simplified, consisted of repeating, "Day by day in every way I am getting better and better."

A Modern Kind of Art

On February 17, 1913, a huge art show opened at the Sixty-ninth Regimental Armory in New York City. The Armory Show was organized by the Association of Painters

The Flapper: A Symbol of the Roaring Twenties

A popular song described her as having "turned-up nose" and "turned-down hose." She was, the singer said, a "flapper, yes sir, one of those." And then he asked wistfully, "Has anybody seen my gal?" If there was a single symbol of the Roaring Twenties, it was the flapper, the restless young woman who always liked to be moving on and trying something new. She shocked her elders in a dozen ways, with her clothes, her slang, her dances, and her refusal to follow traditional rules.

Clothes were the outward expression of her defiance of tradition. Compare a young flapper to the young women of ten years earlier. The older girl dressed in skirts to her ankles, over several layers of petticoats. Under all that she wore a rigid corset to achieve an "hourglass" figure. Her sleeves were long and her neckline high. Her long hair was caught up modestly in braids or a bun.

The flapper refused to wear petticoats or to squeeze into a corset. She shortened her skirts right up to the knee, revealing, not traditional dark cotton stockings, but flesh-colored silk hosiery. Frequently, she rolled the stockings down to her knees. She "bobbed" her hair short for comfort and simplicity. And, while the well-bred woman of an earlier generation rarely "painted" her face, the flapper wore bright red lipstick.

Yet the flapper was more than just a giddy symbol of the jazz age. She also symbolized the new social freedom of women. A 1922 letter to the *Daily Illini*, a college newspaper, noted:

> The word flapper to us means, not a female atrocity who smokes, swears, delights in pictures like *The Sheik,* and kisses her gentlemen friends good night. . . . We always think of the flapper as the independent . . . young woman, a typical American product. . . . Any real girl . . . who feels pugilistically inclined [ready to fight] when called the "weaker sex" . . . and who wants to get into things herself, is a flapper.

The most common image of the flapper, however, was that of a zany young woman such as the one shown below, being serenaded by musicians at the Washington Zoo.

and Sculptors and had for its motto "The New Spirit." The exhibition was the first major display of modern art in the United States.

While traditional European and American artists tried to represent reality in a fairly photographic way, modern artists did not let realism limit what they put on the canvas. Much of modern art was abstract. For example, Pablo Picasso, a Spanish artist, painted his figures in geometric shapes: cubes, spheres, and cones. The new styles provoked howls of protest. An abstract painting by Marcel Duchamp titled *Nude Descending a Staircase* became the object of endless jokes. One skeptic parodied Duchamp's work by painting *The Rude Descending a Staircase*, a rather jumbled picture of the New York subway at rush hour.

Although modern art remained controversial, during the 1920s many American artists and critics began to accept the new form. In 1929 the Museum of Modern Art opened in New York City. Under the direction of Alfred H. Barr, Jr., the museum began to bridge the gap between European and American art. It displayed not only paintings and sculpture but also the work of architects, designers, photographers, and filmmakers. It thus helped the public understand that these fields too were "art."

While the museum tried to define trends in art, individual painters pursued their own private visions, sometimes far outside the "modern" framework. Edward Hopper's landscapes captured both the isolation of rural farmhouses and the lonely anonymity of industrial cities. Grant Wood also painted scenes of rural America, including his memorable portrait of a somber farm couple, *American Gothic* (1930). Georgia O'Keeffe celebrated urban landscapes of skyscrapers in her early paintings and later turned to southwestern themes.

The variety of entertainment Americans enjoyed during the 1920s reflected the restless spirit of the decade. Movies and radio made use of new technology, and many musicians and painters tried to capture the mood of the growing cities. Yet the world of entertainment and fads was only part of life during the Roaring Twenties.

SECTION REVIEW

1. Identify: Harlem Renaissance, Langston Hughes, Marcus Garvey, Gertrude Ederle, Charles Lindbergh.
2. What types of music provided the roots of jazz?
3. What characteristics made Charles Lindbergh a hero to many Americans?
4. What type of art was exhibited at the Armory Show of 1913?
5. **Critical Thinking** How did the radio accelerate social change?

3 Behind the Facade

The glamor of the Roaring Twenties shone from movie screens and blared from radio speakers. However, not all Americans were caught up in the excitement. Many rejected the glitter and the changing values, defending a more traditional way of life. Large numbers of Americans were bypassed by the material prosperity of the decade. One group of disillusioned American writers saw conformity and corruption behind a facade of material progress.

In Defense of Traditional Values

Millions of Americans, especially those living in small towns and rural areas, believed that the rapid social and economic changes of the Roaring Twenties were destroying a way of life. To counteract what they considered an immoral force, these people worked to strengthen and defend their own values.

Church membership grew throughout the 1920s, and books on religion multiplied. Revival meetings attracted large audiences. All over the nation people went to church socials, rodeos, and country fairs—pastimes far removed from city speakeasies, private clubs where alcohol was sold illegally.*

---

*As you read in Chapter 26, the Eighteenth Amendment had banned the manufacture, sale, and transportation of alcoholic beverages. The amendment was in effect throughout the 1920s, but it was frequently ignored even by otherwise law-abiding citizens.

The fads and fancies of the Jazz Age attracted publicity, but the traditional life of much of rural America continued with little outward change. Painter Grant Wood captured the serenity of the countryside in this painting, Stone City, Iowa.

To many Americans, Henry Ford represented the strength of traditional values. He was widely admired for his rise from modest origins, his organizational ability, and his vast fortune. Because Ford championed the values of honesty and thrift, he was a hero to many Americans.

Changes for Women

Henry Ford praised the 1920s as a time of great opportunity. Yet that opportunity was more a promise than a reality for American women. Women had won the right to vote with the ratification of the Nineteenth Amendment in 1920. (See page 507.) Many reformers believed that this victory would usher in an age of complete equality, but they were wrong. Women did not concentrate their political efforts on women's rights causes or candidates. The League of Women Voters, for example, supported a wide range

of reform measures, not just "women's" issues.

Some young women expressed a new sense of social freedom by cutting their hair short and wearing loose-fitting, comfortable clothes. Homemakers also found some of their tasks simplified by new electrical appliances and by a trend to smaller houses and apartments. However, few women achieved economic independence in the 1920s. Although more women were working outside the home, they received far from equal treatment in the job market. Most women held jobs with low pay and little prestige.

Those Prosperity Missed

Although prosperity was symbolic of the 1920s, not all Americans enjoyed economic well-being. As you read in Chapter 29, farmers found it increasingly difficult to make a living after the war. Southern agriculture was particularly hard hit. The boll weevil destroyed millions of acres of cotton. New synthetic fabrics decreased the demand for cotton and lowered cotton prices. Black sharecroppers* suffered terribly during these years.

Because of the depressed economy and rigid racial segregation in the South, almost a million blacks fled to the North during the 1920s. Yet few found greater prosperity in northern cities. Black workers were excluded from most labor unions and often limited to the lowest-paying jobs when they could find them.

Native Americans and Mexican immigrants were also deprived of the prosperity of the 1920s. The authors of the Dawes Act, passed in 1887, had hoped to see Indians assimilated into the general population. (See page 383.) Reservation land was to be divided up among individual Indians to encourage farming.

In actuality, however, Native Americans lost over 60 percent of the land they had owned before 1887, and what acreage remained was often unsuitable for farming. Furthermore, the Dawes Act had weakened Indian culture and traditions. A 1926 report on conditions among Native Americans revealed that a majority were "extremely poor" and that they suffered from poor health and inadequate education.

In 1900 there were about 100,000 people of Mexican birth living in the Southwest. From 1911 to 1920, the Mexican Revolution disrupted the Mexican economy and sparked an exodus to the United States. By 1930 more than a million Mexicans had crossed the border.

Mexicans were attracted to the United States by the availability of jobs in the vegetable fields and orchards of the Southwest. As the area became industrialized, the immigrants took factory jobs. By 1930, 180,000 Mexican-Americans worked in agriculture while 150,000 were employed in industry.

Mexican agricultural workers lived under difficult conditions. As *migrant workers*, they traveled from farm to farm, employed by farmers only as long as necessary to bring in a crop. Migrant workers usually received low wages and could find only squalid hous-

---

*As you read in Chapter 19, sharecroppers farmed a piece of land and shared the crops they raised with the landowners.

ing. In the cities Mexican Americans were crowded into dilapidated, poverty-stricken districts. Like most blacks and Native Americans, Mexican Americans shared little of the material wealth of the 1920s.

The Lost Generation

Some of the best writers of the 1920s took a critical look at prosperity and material progress. In books, plays, and poetry, this Lost Generation, as they were known, described a society that congratulated itself on progress while stifling dissent and creativity.

No writer was more scathing than Sinclair Lewis, author of *Main Street* and *Babbitt*, novels about fictitious Midwestern communities. George Babbitt, the main character of the second novel, illustrated all the traits Lewis disliked. Babbitt was boorish, smug, and determined to make everyone else think and act as he did. When Lewis won the Nobel Prize for Literature in 1930, however, he remarked that it should have gone instead to another American writer, Willa Cather. Cather, a former magazine editor, wrote novels stressing the importance of moral values. She had won a Pulitzer Prize in 1922 for *One of Ours*.

F. Scott Fitzgerald, author of *The Great Gatsby* and *This Side of Paradise*, attacked the transparent values of the period and

Major Events	
1913	Armory Show of modern art
1914	Henry Ford introduces assembly line
1920	First radio broadcasting station goes on the air
1926	Gertrude Ederle swims English Channel
1927	Charles Lindbergh flies Atlantic Ocean; first televised transmission of pictures; *Jazz Singer* is first talking movie
1928	Iron lung developed
1929	Museum of Modern Art opens in New York City

spent a great deal of his career in Paris. There he mingled with other talented American *expatriates*, people who had given up their homeland to live abroad, such as Ernest Hemingway. In his books Hemingway explored the disillusionment of people who had believed the war had been fought for the betterment of humanity.

The brilliant American poet T. S. Eliot moved permanently to London, where he wrote, but for some years he had to earn a living as a bank clerk. Others of the Lost Generation remaining in the United States often clustered in places where conformity was not expected, such as Greenwich Village in New York City. Wherever they lived, talented Americans produced enduring literature during this period. Eugene O'Neill wrote 18 plays during the 1920s. Theodore Dreiser wrote *An American Tragedy*. Eliot produced *The Waste Land*, and John Dos Passos wrote *Manhattan Transfer*.

Most of the great writers of the period were deeply concerned about the quality of American life. They believed that Americans had become obsessed with wealth and material progress. These writers believed that

conformity was burying the tradition of individualism. They saw vitality in American life but believed that Americans were wasting their energies on frivolous, meaningless pursuits. Some great literature was produced in reaction to the new values of the Roaring Twenties.

SECTION REVIEW

1. Identify: Sinclair Lewis, Willa Cather, F. Scott Fitzgerald, Ernest Hemingway, T. S. Elliot.
2. Define: migrant worker, expatriate.
3. Did achieving the right to vote usher in an age of equality for women? Explain.
4. What groups missed the prosperity of the 1920s?
5. What did the name Babbitt come to mean as a result of Sinclair Lewis' novel *Babbitt*?
6. **Critical Thinking** How could material progress benefit a society? How could it harm a society?

Chapter 30 Review

In Perspective

The 1920s were years of impressive material progress. The use of electricity grew rapidly, and industry became more efficient. Productivity increased, especially in the automobile industry, in which Henry Ford introduced the assembly line and efficient manufacturing methods. The period saw the beginning of the automobile age, leading to the rapid growth of suburbs and of industries that supplied materials for automobile manufacture.

Jazz, a uniquely American music, flourished and gave the decade its flavor. The period also saw a flowering of black culture known as the Harlem Renaissance. By the end of the 1920s silent movies, popular early

in the decade, were being replaced by "talkies." Radio was a novelty in 1920, but by 1930 it had become a major part of American life. The new form of mass communication helped popularize heroes and fads.

Not everyone participated in the social changes of the Roaring Twenties, however. Millions of Americans continued to believe in traditional values and traditional ways of life. Many people were also denied the prosperity of the decade. Farmers, blacks, Native Americans, and Mexican Americans frequently suffered economic hardship. Some of the best American writers of the 1920s were critical of the materialism they saw in American society. As you will read in the following chapter, their pessimistic visions became reality for much of the nation as the decade drew to a close.

Vocabulary

Match each term at left with its definition or description at right.

1. scientific management
2. assembly line
3. synthetic
4. telephoto
5. expatriate

a. person who has given up his or her homeland
b. process of sending pictures by wire
c. chemically produced fiber
d. system whereby workers specialize
e. survey of performance to increase efficiency

Chapter Checkup

1. (a) How did the use of electricity change between 1900 and 1930? (b) How did that change affect American home life? (c) How did it affect industry?
2. What were the themes of much of the writing of the Harlem Renaissance?
3. Explain how each of the following missed the prosperity of the 1920s: (a) black Americans; (b) Native Americans; (c) Mexican Americans.

Critical Thinking

1. **Supporting a Point of View** (a) How did the writers of the Lost Generation describe American society? (b) What do you think influenced these writers' opinions? (c) Do you think most Americans agreed with them? Explain.
2. **Identifying Supporting Details** (a) How might you explain the stunning growth in the popularity of radio during the 1920s? (b) What evidence of that growth can you cite?

Developing Basic Skills

1. **Using Primary Sources** Works of art and literature can be important sources of information about a historical period. Studying a painting or a poem, for example, can help you understand the artist's view of the time in which he or she lived. Choose an artist or writer who was active during the 1920s and study one of his or her works. Write a report in which you explain what you learned about the 1920s from the work.
2. **Relating Past to Present** Consider the role that television plays in contemporary society. (a) In what ways do you think radio played a similar role in the 1920s? (b) How has the role of radio in American society changed since the 1920s?

See page 832 for suggested readings.

Writer's Handbook

Using Quotations

Some of the notes that you take while researching your topic will probably include direct quotes. That is, you may find a reference made by an authority or material from a primary source that you would like to report exactly as it appears. In order to be accurate, you have to indicate whether you have used all or part of a quote. Do this by using ellipses (. . .). The quote below is from an interview given by Charles Lindbergh after he arrived in Paris in 1927.

Ellipsis at the beginning: ". . . no sooner had my plane touched the ground than a human sea swept toward it."

Ellipsis in the middle: "I appreciated the reception which had been prepared for me, . . . but no sooner had my plane touched the ground than a human sea swept toward it."

Ellipsis at the end: "I appreciated the reception which had been prepared for me. . . ."

Note that there are four dots in an ellipsis at the end of a quote because one represents the period at the end of the sentence.

Practice: Quote a passage from your textbook. Use an ellipsis at the beginning of the passage, in the middle, and at the end, as in the sample.

Sports in America

On July 21, 1921, some 91,000 spectators poured into Boyle's Thirty Acres in Jersey City, New Jersey, to see Jack Dempsey knock out "Gorgeous" Georges Carpentier in the fourth round. That was boxing's first million dollar gate—the first time Americans had spent $1 million to watch a single sporting event. Again that year crowds broke records to see the New York Yankees' Babe Ruth hit 59 home runs and the New York Giants beat the New York Yankees in the World Series. Each Saturday afternoon in the fall tens of thousands of fans flocked into huge new college football stadiums to cheer on their heroes. The United States had entered the Golden Age of Sports.

Americans had not always had such a passion for games. In the colonial era, Puritan ministers preached against "gaming," or playing game for stakes. "The path of amusement can become the broadway to destruction," warned the *New York Magazine* in the 1700s. James Fenimore Cooper, the nineteenth-century novelist, still felt it necessary to caution that time devoted to games and relaxation was time "misspent."

Disapproval of idleness and games reflected the realities of life in pre-industrial America. Faced with obtaining the necessities of life by their own hand, Americans had little time for recreation. Work was the key to survival. "Contests" and "bees" such as corn huskings and log rollings were fun and provided sport, but work, not recreation, was their main purpose. "I have never been so happy in my life," wrote the French immigrant, Crèvecoeur, in the 1700s, "as when I have assisted at these simple merriments, and indeed they are the only ones I know. Each returns home and is satisfied, and our work is done."

With the onset of the Industrial Revolution in the mid-1800s a higher standard of living and more leisure time transformed Americans' dim view of recreation. Foreign travelers reported that ordinary

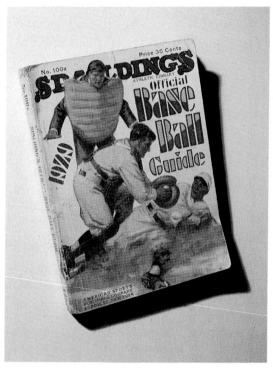

Guides, like this one, helped fans keep track of their favorite players as spectator sports became an important part of the American scene.

Americans were much taken with "amusements, spectacles, and distractions." Moralists now worried that with less physically demanding labor people would lose their "muscular vigor." "Who, in this community, really takes physical exercise?" one concerned writer asked in 1858. He urged his readers to take up the strenuous activities of their childhood.

Development of Sports in America
The rapid growth of factories and cities after the Civil War further spurred the development of sports. By the late 1800s, football, baseball, ice hockey, track and field, golf, and tennis had taken root. To keep active in winter, Americans even invented an indoor sport—basketball. Newly formed associations set up rules for amateur and professional sports. *Strike, ball,*

and *foul* took on new meanings. Newspapers fueled public interest with vivid reports of the latest games. "The craze for sports, contests, and 'events' is a feature of the modern world," one writer of the 1880s observed.

The sports craze kept pace with the rapid spread of industry. By the 1920s, the average American family spent only half of its income for the necessities of life, and the average work week was down to 48 hours. The stage was set for a new era—the Golden Age of Sports. Record numbers of people participated in sports. Even greater numbers of Americans became spectators at sports events.

Sports Express American Values
Sports was looked on as a training ground for life. In 1911 Albert Spaulding, a former baseball player and an organizer of the National League, claimed that the person who achieves as an athlete "has within him the elements of pronounced success in other walks of life." He proclaimed baseball the "national game" because "it is the exponent of American courage, confidence, combativeness; American dash, discipline, determination; American energy, eagerness, enthusiasm; American pluck, persistency, performance; American spirit, sagacity, success; American vim, vigor, virility."

For some, sports were expressions of traditional values. Roderick Nash, a historian, claims that during the 1920s sports provided "living testimony of the power of courage, strength, and honor of the self-reliant individual." "The athletic hero," he explains, "was the twentieth-century equivalent of the pathfinder or pioneer."

Equally important, sports provided a common ground for *all* individuals to achieve. In 1947, Jackie Robinson became the first black athlete to play in the major leagues. This breakthrough marked the beginning of racial integration in many other sports as well. A significant gain for women came in the Educational Amendment Act of 1972. It signalled that schools would have to devote more money to women's sports than they had in the past.

Sports Today Americans still have a passion for sports. And they still embrace

Although prejudice was still an obstacle for black athletes, Jesse Owens thrilled the world at the 1936 Olympic Games where he won three gold medals.

sports as an antidote to the problems of society. In the 1980s Americans have made great strides in achieving physical health through sports. Popular magazines feature articles on the "fitness craze" and shopping malls all over the country have stores devoted solely to sporting goods. But some old and new questions still remain. How can schools best integrate sports and study? Have sports become too commercial? Should we expect professional athletes to serve as role models? These and other questions deserve attention because the influence of sports and sports figures on American life cannot be ignored.

1. How did Americans view recreation before the Industrial Revolution?
2. Why were sports considered important in industrial America?
3. How can emphasis on sports benefit or harm a society?

American Profiles The 1927 Yankees

Many outstanding athletes and teams stood in the sports spotlight during the 1920s. None, however, won greater fame and success than the New York Yankees of 1927. That season, the "Bronx Bombers" and its "Murderers' Row" of power hitters captured the hearts and minds of Americans with their spectacular feats on the baseball field.

The stars of the team were baseball legends George Herman "Babe" Ruth—the "Bambino"—and Lou Gehrig—the "Iron Horse." Ruth's batting average of .356, 164 runs batted in, and 60 home runs stunned Yankee opponents and thrilled Yankee fans. Gehrigs' statistics were equally impressive: a batting average of .373, 175 runs batted in, and 47 home runs.

Other power hitters, including Bob Meusel, Earl Combs, and "Push-em-up" Tony Lazzeri, contributed to the Yankees' reputation as the "Window Breakers." At the season's end, Yankee players led the American League in home runs, triples, doubles, hits, slugging average, total bases, and runs batted in.

To the delight of their fans, the Yankees frequently unleashed all of their power in a single inning—usually the eighth inning, as one sportswriter pointed out. In an onslaught that was dubbed "five o'clock lightning," the Yankees often came from behind to soundly defeat their bewildered opponents.

Yankee power hitting translated into a Yankee winning season. Maintaining first place from their second game to their last, the Yankees boasted a sensational record in October: 110 victories, a winning percentage of .714, and a finish 19 games ahead of the second place Philadelphia Athletics. As the American League champions, the Yankees faced the Pittsburgh Pirates in the 1927 World Series.

Some baseball historians claim the series was over before it began. During batting practice before the first game, the Yankees demoralized the Pittsburgh nine by belting one long drive after another into the outfield seats. Paced by the awesome hitting of Ruth and Gehrig, the unstoppable Yankees won the series in four straight games.

The World Series was a dramatic end to one of the greatest seasons achieved by any team in American sports. Other Yankee teams went on to win championships, but none has outshone the "Bronx Bomb-

The 1927 New York Yankees have been called the greatest baseball team of all time.

NEW YORK YANKEES 1927

ers" of 1927. That team and its heroes still serve as a wonderful example of the magic, the fantasy, the spectacle of American sports.

1. How did the 1927 New York Yankees capture the imagination of the public?
2. What American values did the 1927 New York Yankees reflect?

Voices of Freedom

Red Grange—Sports Hero

During the 1920s, newspapers heightened the public's passion for sports by portraying athletes as heroes. In this colorful account of a college football game, sports reporter Harry Cross hails the extraordinary Red Grange, halfback for the University of Illinois.

Philadelphia, Oct. 31, 1925—The golden yellow headgear of Red Grange of Illinois flashed over Franklin Field this afternoon while 65,000 spectators, gathered from all over the East saw him almost singlehandedly defeat Pennsylvania's great eleven by a score of 24 to 2. The speed, cleverness, and uncanny intuition of any other football player have never made such an impression on the Eastern gridiron as Grange's meteoric flights over a slippery, muddy field today.

The East has heard of the great achievements of this football player and has taken them with a grain of salt. They did not believe that he could be as great as the Middle West said he was. But he is. That is the strange part about it. Red Grange is human. He is not a myth. He dashes and dodges over the gridiron with a speed of foot and an alertness of mind which set him high up on a pedestal among this generation of football players.

Three times this afternoon Grange raced majestically through the Pensylvania eleven to touchdowns. Not only that, but he carried the ball thirty-six times in today's battle and gained 363 yards in his mad dashes. Twice did Grange gallop 60 yards. Once he left the Quakers trailing 40 yards behind him and another time he raced 24 yards through a compact defense before he was dragged into the mud from behind.

One of the assets of this irrepressible Grange is mental. He thinks quicker than the players who try to stop him. He is a flash at picking openings and his real skill begins when the tacklers of the opposition begin to twine their arms about him. This afternoon Pennsylvania tacklers dropped off Grange like the leaves fall from a tree in autumn. . . .

His left arm is a rod of steel. When he shoots it out straight at the onrushing opposition, they bowl over like so many tenpins. And how the boy can keep his feet! . . . In every scrimmage which marked Pennsylvania's downfall, Red Grange was the last player to go down. The other players . . . piled about him, but there he stood, the last contestant on his feet, and he did not topple over until the last inch had been gained.

Pennsylvania suffered terrible shock in the humiliation of the Red and Blue this afternoon. This eleven was triumphantly pointed toward an Eastern and even a national championship. It was proud of its strength and boastful of its achievements. It . . . was so certain that the wet and muddy field today would be Grange's undoing that it was prepared for nothing but the sweetness of victory. It tasted nothing but bitterness.

©1925 by The New York Times Company. Reprinted by permission.
Adapted from "Grange Shows the East," by Harry Cross.

1. According to Cross, what qualities does Grange have?
2. How does Cross capture the excitement of Grange's performance?
3. Does television capture the excitement of sports events as well today?

31

From Prosperity to Despair

(1928–1932)

A cover from Vanity Fair *magazine*

For many Americans the 1920s seemed a decade of unending prosperity. Yet in the fall of 1929 the United States plunged into a prolonged economic depression that shattered the lives of millions of Americans. The depression continued throughout the 1930s and did not end completely until the United States entered a second world war in 1941.

Before 1929 most Americans believed that with an education, hard work, and a little luck, they could get ahead. At the very least, their children could get ahead. However, the long, bleak years of depression dimmed that optimism.

Millions of people eager for work were unable to find jobs. Feet shuffling with embarrassment, they stood in endless lines for bread and soup. They begged for work—any work, at any salary. By 1932, the worst year of the Great Depression, one in four Americans in the labor force was jobless.

Great Depression begins

1928	1929	1930	1931	1932
1928 Herbert Hoover elected President	**1929** Stock market crashes	**1930** Bank failures, unemployment increase	**1931** Bonus Army begins march on Washington	**1932** RFC created; Franklin D. Roosevelt elected President

1 The Bubble Bursts

The glitter of the Roaring Twenties hid economic problems that lay beneath the surface of general prosperity. Workers were finding it more difficult to make a decent living. Farmers were suffering from low prices. More and more people were borrowing money to finance get-rich-quick schemes. Signs of these problems were evident by 1927, but few observers noticed.

Signs of a Slowdown

Although the wages of industrial workers grew during the 1920s, they did not keep up with rising prices or the rising production of goods. Thus workers found it increasingly difficult to buy the very products they made. As a result, demand for some goods began to decline, and production slowed down. Manufacturers invested less money in new plants and equipment. As factories cut back production, workers were laid off. The cutbacks lowered workers' income still further. In 1929 a study of working families in Muncie, Indiana, revealed that in 40 percent of the families, a worker had been laid off at least one month that year.

Some industries, such as textiles and soft-coal mining, had been in a state of decline for many years. For workers in those industries, the prosperity of the 1920s was just something they read about in the newspapers. The words on a tombstone in a Pennsylvania mining town lament the plight of many workers:

For forty years beneath the sod
With pick and spade I did my task
The coal king's slave, but now, thank God,
I'm free at last.

Even in prosperous industries there were signs of economic slowdown. By 1929 construction was growing at a slower pace than earlier in the decade. Production in the automobile industry, which had been one of the fastest-growing industries of the decade, began to decline. Conditions in agriculture were even more disturbing.

One third of American families lived on farms during the 1920s, and they faced grim economic conditions throughout much of the decade. It was becoming increasingly expensive to run a farm. Like most Americans, farm families wanted modern appliances and a car. But their expenses rose much faster than the prices they received for their products. The very efficiency of the farmers contributed to their financial problems, since overproduction kept prices low. (See page 553.)

As the 1928 presidential election neared, most people saw the farm problem as the one major economic difficulty facing the country. They had not yet noticed the other warning signals.

The Election of 1928

Had he run for reelection, Calvin Coolidge might have won easily. However, he surprised nearly everyone by announcing in his typically concise fashion, "I do not choose to run for President in 1928."

Republicans had little difficulty choosing Herbert Hoover to replace Coolidge. Secretary of Commerce Hoover had the popularity, the experience, and the confidence of party leaders. He had made a fortune as a consulting engineer on projects all over the world. Hoover had also directed a massive famine-relief program in Europe in the wake of the war. Through his efforts, millions of people were fed. As secretary of commerce for eight years, he had actively promoted the development of United States business. To many Americans, Hoover represented several ideals: he was a self-made man of wealth, an efficiency expert, and a humanitarian.

At their convention in Houston, Texas, Democrats picked a candidate who offered a vivid contrast to the businesslike, restrained Hoover. They chose the outspoken four-time governor of New York, Al Smith. The son of Irish immigrant parents, Smith grew up in New York City. He differed from Hoover in his background, style, and beliefs.

Smith's initial rise in politics had been through the New York City Tammany Hall political machine. A Roman Catholic, he attracted the support of many of the "new immigrants" from southern Europe who had settled in cities. In contrast, Hoover, born in West Branch, Iowa, seemed to represent traditional small-town Protestant America.

The positions of the two candidates were also quite different. Hoover believed in what he called the "rugged individualism" of Americans. He recognized that farmers were suffering, but he felt that their problems could be solved by their own efforts and through cooperation. Government, he claimed, should not meddle in farmers' problems. Hoover also opposed government interference in business.

By contrast, Al Smith stood for public ownership of some electric power companies. Furthermore, the Democratic platform urged strong government action to help farmers. As the first Roman Catholic to be nominated for the presidency by either party, Smith became the focus of a savage anti-Catholic campaign. His pledge to end Prohibition also drew fierce attacks from "dry" forces who wanted it continued.

On election day the popular Hoover swept 40 of the 48 states, including Smith's own New York. Hoover's victory reflected the voters' belief that the nation was healthy and, in general, prosperous. During the campaign, Hoover capitalized on this belief when he declared, "We in America today are nearer to the final triumph over poverty than ever before in the history of any land."

Get-Rich-Quick Fever

When people made quick fortunes during the 1920s, newspapers told their stories. Soon many people who read these stories believed that they too might stumble onto a pot of gold. They thought that the quickest way to get rich was to speculate in land or stocks.* The object was to buy a piece of land or a stock at a low price, wait for the price to rise, and then sell the stock or property for a handsome profit.

People speculated in land all across the country as the building of suburbs drove land prices skyward. But nowhere was the land boom as big as in Florida. The suitability of the warm Florida climate for vacation resorts attracted many speculators. People bought any land available, including swamps, in the hopes of making a big profit. And indeed the value of Florida land soared. Those who had bought early made huge profits. But a devastating hurricane roared through Florida in 1926, ending the land boom there.

If investing in land seemed too risky, speculators could always turn to the stock market. Only a small percentage of the population actually bought stocks during the 1920s. One estimate put the number of investors at about 1.5 million. However, their success stories fascinated people everywhere. Investors often paid little attention to what the companies issuing the stocks actually earned. Inexperienced investors assumed that prices would simply keep rising no matter how well the companies did.

To attract investors, many brokers sold shares of stock *on margin*. That is, the investor paid only part of the selling price in cash and borrowed the rest on margin from the stock broker. The broker in turn borrowed money from banks and corporations in order to cover loans made to investors. If the investor could not repay the loan, the

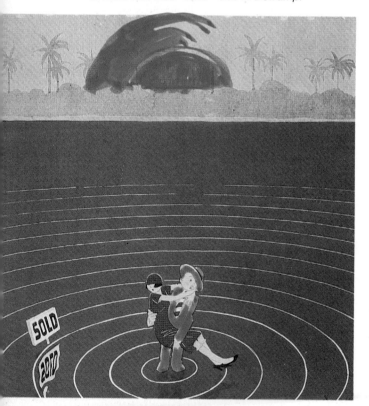

Among the many get-rich-quick schemes of the 1920s was speculation in Florida land. This 1925 drawing for the cover of Life magazine mocks a couple who bought Florida land sight unseen, only to learn that their "land" was in a swamp.

---

*As you learned in Chapter 21, stocks are shares of ownership in a corporation.

SKILL LESSON

The Land Boom in Florida: Using Historical Photographs

Like other visual evidence, historical photographs provide information about the past. Photography, which was developed by Louis Daguerre in France in 1839, has become an important record of events for students and historians. Along with painting, photography has expanded our knowledge of ordinary people and everyday events.

Although a photograph is a real-life picture of a scene, you must analyze it as you would any visual evidence. By their choice of subjects, lighting, and camera angle, photographers can influence what you see. Photographers may choose a scene that appeals to them or that they think will make the most interesting picture. Merely by making these choices, they affect what you will learn.

Use the steps below to analyze each of the photographs on this page.

1. **Study the photograph to identify the subject.** Look at the overall picture and at the details. (a) What do you see in each of the pictures? (b) Which details in the picture at the left do you think are important for someone studying about the Florida land boom?

Which details in the picture at the right do you think are important for someone writing about how the hurricane affected people in Florida?

2. **Analyze the reliability of the photograph as a source of information.** (a) How does the angle from which the photograph at the left was shot affect the impression the picture gives? (b) What elements in the photograph at the right give a clue to the power of the hurricane? (c) Would the photograph have been as effective if it had not included the people who lived in the house? Why or why not? (d) How soon after the hurricane do you think this picture was taken?

3. **Study the photograph to learn more about the historical period.** Refer to the photographs and what you have read to answer the following questions. (a) What do you think Florida looked like before the building boom? (b) How do you think the building boom affected the economy of Florida? (c) Why was a hurricane so damaging to Florida's economy?

Land development attracted hundreds of thousands of people to Florida in the 1920s. In 1921 alone seven new counties were formed.

Hundreds of people were killed in two major hurricanes that devastated parts of Florida in 1926 and 1928.

broker took the stock. Investors had to pay interest on the loan, but if the price of the stock went up, the buyer could repay the loan and interest and still make a profit.

The Crash

For a while, the system seemed to work. Stock prices rose steadily during the 1920s. In March 1928 prices began to soar, and the number of shares traded rose sharply. There seemed little reason for the upswing since business profits and prices of goods had leveled off the year before. But the boom continued through the summer of 1929.

By September stock prices were 400 percent higher than they had been five years earlier. Some cautious investors began to sell their stocks. There were fewer buyers, and prices edged downward. In early October, prices slid badly as orders to sell outnumbered orders to buy.

A flood of sell orders hit the New York Stock Exchange on October 24. Prices tumbled. Brokers put out *margin calls* to cover loans. That is, the brokers asked investors who had bought on margin to put up more money to cover their loans on stocks that were now worth less. Some investors were unable to put up the extra money and lost their stocks. The margin calls produced more selling as investors tried desperately to raise money. Banks and other creditors, meanwhile, called in their loans to brokers.

On October 29 orders to sell at any price swamped the stock market. There were almost no buyers. The value of stocks crashed downward on the worst day in stock market history. Fortunes vanished in hours.

Business leaders and bankers met hurriedly to find ways to avert a panic. In an attempt to restore public confidence in the economy, John D. Rockefeller announced, "My son and I have for some days been purchasing some common stocks." When he heard this, comedian Eddie Cantor replied, "Sure, who else has any money left?"

SECTION REVIEW

1. Identify: Al Smith.
2. Define: on margin, margin calls.
3. What was one sign of economic slowdown during the 1920s?
4. How did Hoover and Smith differ on the question of government help for farmers?
5. What two types of investments attracted many speculators during the 1920s?
6. **Critical Thinking** How did the attitude of government toward business contribute to the conditions that led to the crash?

★ American Enterprise ★

The Nation's Marketplace

The New York Stock Exchange is often called the nation's marketplace because it is the largest center in the world for buying and selling stock in American and foreign businesses. It was organized in 1792 on Wall Street in New York City. Each year investors trade billions of shares of stock through the New York exchange and other stock exchanges.

Corporations sell stock to raise money. When investors buy stock, they are entitled to a share in the profits of the corporation and a voice in how the business is run. To buy stock a person places an order with a stockbroker, who handles the transaction. The transaction is recorded and relayed to brokerage firms through a nationwide communications network.

Stock prices often reflect the state of the economy. If business conditions are good, stock prices tend to rise, creating a bull market. If conditions are poor, stock prices tend to drop, creating a bear market. During the bull market of the 1920s stock prices rose so high that they no longer reflected the state of the economy or the value of the corporations in which stockholders were investing. Much of the stock had been bought on margin, and when brokers began to demand repayment of the loans, investors had to sell at a big loss. The resulting panic led to the great stock market crash in 1929.

2 The Grim Years Begin

The stock market crash did not cause the depression that followed, but it did mark the end of the apparent prosperity of the 1920s. Few escaped the effects of the economic collapse. For major corporations and millions of individuals, fear and failure became as commonplace as optimism and prosperity had been only a short time earlier.

The Causes of the Depression

Many factors contributed to the onset of a wide-ranging economic depression. One cause was a sharp imbalance between supply and demand. For a free enterprise system to operate effectively, the supply of products should equal the demand for those products. But demand had begun to fall during the late 1920s.

American industry had mastered mass production techniques and was supplying a growing number of products. Yet demand was not growing as rapidly as supply. As you read earlier in this chapter, workers' wages had not kept up with prices. Consequently, workers could not afford to buy the goods being produced. The continued weakness of agriculture also meant that farm families could afford to buy few products.

Furthermore many of the items produced in such abundance were durable goods. *Durable goods* are products designed to last several years before being replaced, such as automobiles, refrigerators, stoves, and tractors. By 1929 many people either owned the goods they wanted or could not afford to buy any more, even on credit. Thus the demand for such goods decreased.

Business inventories, or lists of unsold goods on hand, crept upward in 1928 and 1929. In response factories cut back production and laid off some workers. Each person laid off represented another family unable to buy durable goods that year. Job layoffs therefore cut consumer demand still further.

The frailty of the banking system also contributed to the economic collapse. Despite the federal reserve system (see page 502), many individual banks were unable to survive the economic slowdown. Banks had loaned large amounts of money to speculators. In the wake of the stock market crash, some banks failed when borrowers could not pay back their loans. Each bank closing shook the confidence of depositors in other banks, and people began withdrawing their money. Each withdrawal further decreased the money supply. Nearly 5,000 banks failed between 1929 and 1932.

The onset of depression in the United States had international repercussions. Faced with harsh economic troubles of their own, European investors withdrew their money from the United States. A key Vienna bank failed in 1931, indicating a worldwide economic breakdown. The collapse of the German economy came next. The Great Depression had begun.

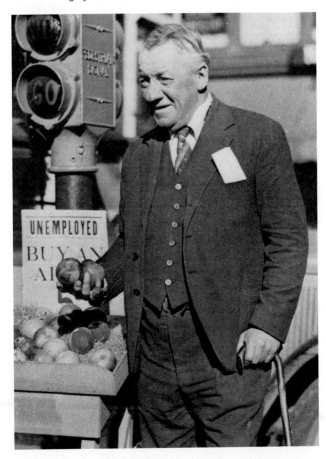

The ripple effects of economic collapse wiped out many fortunes. Fred Bell, who had been rich before the depression, was photographed selling apples on a San Francisco corner in 1931. The image of a once-prosperous person peddling apples became an enduring symbol of the Great Depression.

Economic Collapse

The spread of depression in the United States was swift and relentless. In 1930, 26,355 businesses failed. Two million fewer cars rolled off the assembly lines than in 1929. Industrial areas suffered first, as payrolls dropped by one third. Employers tried to save money by reducing the work week. They cut the work week to three days, then two, then one. Finally, they laid workers off.

The unemployed workers bought little more than necessary food. Old clothes were patched, mended, or darned. Families fell behind on credit payments for radios, cars, and homes. In time, many lost their cars and houses. People who fell behind on rent were evicted. Construction of new housing came to a halt, throwing still more people out of work.

Bank failures wiped out the savings of hundreds of thousands of individuals who thought they had provided for emergencies. People who had deposited money in savings accounts throughout their entire careers found that their banks had closed. Frequently their money was gone.

For those who were poor when the depression began, life became much more desperate. Poet Langston Hughes noted that the depression took everyone down a peg or two, but that blacks had fewer pegs to fall.

Impact of the Collapse

The United States had experienced depressions before, but the Great Depression seemed to be the worst. For the first time in history, newspapers, magazines, and radio, carried the images of joblessness and homelessness to every corner of the nation. Furthermore, during earlier depressions, more people had lived on farms, where they could at least grow some of their own food. But in

Painter Isaac Soyer captured the soul-crushing despair of being out of work and out of hope in this painting, entitled Employment Agency.

CON-
CLUSIONS
BASED
ON
DATA

Index of Common Stock Prices 1920–1932

Source: *Historical Statistics of the United States*

■ *There are many ways to measure changes in the national economy. The graphs above and the two on the following page show pieces of the economic pattern between 1920 and 1932. The first graph traces the climb in the price index of common stocks in the 1920s, the sharp break in 1929, and the plummet after the crash. An index is a way to measure economic change. The index of common stocks is a weighted average of the prices of selected stocks. The numbers along the vertical axis of the graph are benchmarks for measuring price movements.*

Gross National Product 1920–1932

Source: *Historical Statistics of the United States*

■ *The gross national product, or GNP, is the total dollar value of all goods and services produced by a country in one year. It is considered a good measure of overall economic health.*

1930 millions depended on industrial jobs for their livelihood. When the factories closed there was no job, no food, and no land on which to grow any.

The depression did not just undercut people's standard of living. It also sapped their sense of personal worth. Americans traditionally valued hard work and believed that the individual was responsible for his or her own welfare. By 1930, 4 million Americans were out of work. By 1932 the figure had risen to 12 million, almost a quarter of the work force.

But such statistics tell little of the misery of broken people looking hopelessly for a job. Men and women lost their identities as carpenters, masons, secretaries, bookkeepers, or auto workers. Whole families scavenged at the city dump and in restaurant garbage cans. Many men, unable to find work, left their families to roam the land seeking work.

New suburban houses built during the boom years stood empty while thousands of families were homeless. People moved into condemned buildings, took over abandoned railroad boxcars, built shacks of tin, cardboard, or orange crates. Everywhere there were lines—lines of people waiting to apply for a job, lines of people waiting for free soup, lines of people waiting for donated clothing.

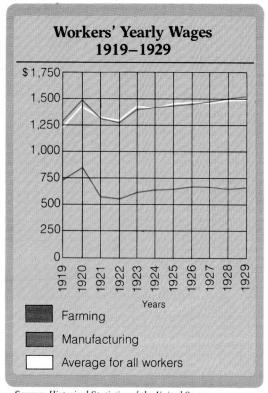

Workers' Yearly Wages 1919–1929

Farming
Manufacturing
Average for all workers

Source: *Historical Statistics of the United States*

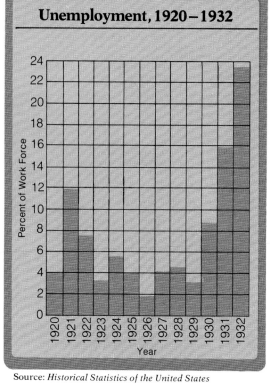

Unemployment, 1920–1932

Percent of Work Force

Year

Source: *Historical Statistics of the United States*

■ *Most workers earned more as the 1920s progressed. But farmers did not share this prosperity because of falling world prices for farm products. Farm workers earned less in 1929 than they had ten years earlier. Another way of measuring a nation's economic health is to look at the percentage of people who cannot find work. Note the rise and fall in unemployment in the 1920s, then the steep jump in unemployment after 1929. By 1932 nearly one out of every four workers was jobless.*

SECTION REVIEW

1. Define: durable goods, business inventories.
2. How were supply and demand imbalanced in the late 1920s?
3. How did the crash affect banks?
4. **Critical Thinking** How do the graphs on pages 581 and 582 show a relationship between the GNP and unemployment?

3 Failure of Traditional Remedies

In the first years of the depression, President Hoover believed he should provide moral leadership and bolster public confidence in the economic system. He stood steadfastly by his belief that government should not intervene directly in the economy. Government-sponsored relief programs, in the President's opinion, would undermine people's self-reliance.

An Initial "Hands-Off" Policy

The President's advisers believed that depression was an inevitable part of the economic cycle and so was recovery. Thus they urged Hoover to allow the depression to proceed without government intervention. Andrew Mellon believed that the depression was a good thing. "People will work harder,

SKILL LESSON

The Economy of the Roaring Twenties: Synthesizing Pieces of Evidence

To make the best use of historical evidence, you must be able to synthesize, that is, put pieces of evidence together to form a whole.

To practice the skill of synthesizing, use the graph of the index of common stock prices on page 581; the graph of workers' average yearly wages on page 582; the picture on page 576; and the quotation at right, published in 1927. Follow the steps below:

1. **Analyze each piece of evidence.** (a) According to the graph on page 581, what was the index of common stock prices in 1925? (b) How had it changed by 1929? (c) According to the graph on page 582, how did the average yearly income of farm workers change between 1922 and 1929? (d) Which group of workers had the largest increase in yearly wages between 1921 and 1929? (e) What economic development is portrayed in the picture on page 576? (f) What did the writer predict about business cycles?

2. **Compare the pieces of evidence.** (a) If you looked only at the graph of stock prices between 1925 and 1929, what would you conclude about the economy of the 1920s?

(b) Would the data about the wages of farm workers confirm that conclusion or conflict with it? (c) Does the picture give you the same impression of the economy of the 1920s as the quotation does? Explain.

3. **Synthesize the evidence in order to draw conclusions.** (a) Were the 1920s generally a period of economic prosperity? Explain. (b) What economic problems can you identify? (c) Write a paragraph describing the economy of the 1920s.

From "This Prosperity"

Business has attained a degree of stability in this country that is quite beyond any previous precedent. It is wholly probable that the old abrupt business cycles, with their rapid ascents from depression, to recovery, and on up to prosperity in about two years, and their still more rapid descents through general decline back down to depression again in about another year, are things of the past. The country is now too wealthy, and our credit supplies are too ably administered through the Federal Reserve System, to permit a return to those . . . recurring conditions.

---

live a more moral life, . . . and enterprising people will pick up the wrecks from less competent people."

Despite such advice, President Hoover did try to turn the economy around. He realized that many people had lost confidence in the economy, and he wanted to restore public morale. Hoover tried to convince Americans that conditions were improving. In May 1930 he stated, "We have now passed the worst, and with continued unity of effort we shall rapidly recover." A month later the President announced that the "depression is over."

In another effort to bolster confidence, Hoover invited business leaders to the White House for a series of economic conferences. He urged businesses to expand rather than

cut back. Hoover obtained a promise from those who attended the conferences that they would not reduce wages and prices. However, such agreements failed to survive worsening conditions. By September 1931 most major industries had begun to cut wages in order to maintain profits.

The President also suggested spending public funds on public-works projects such as dams and highways. Such projects, he argued, would increase employment and put money back into the economy. By the end of Hoover's presidency, the federal government was spending $500 million more a year on public works than it had in 1928.

Hoover urged state and local governments to spend more money on public works as well. However, the depression had

sharply cut revenue from state and local taxes. Thus few governments had extra money for public-works projects. President Hoover insisted that federal public-works projects be funded only to the extent that there was cash to pay for them. He rejected the advice of some experts that the government should borrow money to pay for projects that would create jobs.

Believing that the business cycle would correct itself, Hoover maintained a "hands-off" policy in the beginning of the depression. But the public did not share the President's faith in the economy. In the 1930 elections. voter discontent returned the Democrats to control in the House of Representatives for the first time since 1916.

The Reconstruction Finance Corporation

Pressures for more government action mounted, and Hoover responded in late 1931 by proposing a government agency that could stop bank failures and business closings. Congress created the Reconstruction Finance Corporation (RFC) in 1932. The RFC had power to make loans to banks, railroads, and insurance companies. In addition, Congress went beyond the President's intentions and gave the RFC the right to lend money to local communities for public-works programs.

The RFC did not work the way the President or Congress had hoped. RFC officials were reluctant to loan the money that Congress had given the agency. Banks that did receive loans often used the funds to strengthen their own finances rather than extend credit to the community. The RFC virtually ignored the congressional goal of financing public works.

The creation and operation of the RFC reflected Andrew Mellon's "trickle-down" theory. If the problems of business and industry were solved, the theory held, then benefits would trickle down to ordinary people. But there was little time for the "trickle-down" theory to work as conditions rapidly worsened.

The winter of 1931–1932 was the third winter of depression. "Men are sitting in the parks all day long and all night long, hundreds and thousands of them, muttering to themselves, out of work, seeking work," said William Green, a labor leader from Detroit.

In New York hundreds of homeless people rode the subways all night long that winter because it was warmer than sleeping on a park bench.

By December 1931, 800,000 were jobless in New York City. In Detroit some 223,000 people had no jobs. In Chicago 40 percent of all workers were jobless. Social workers tried valiantly to find money to feed the unemployed and to force government to act. "Have you ever seen the uncontrolled trembling of parents who have gone half starved for weeks so the children may have food?" demanded Lillian Wald of the Henry Street Settlement House in New York.

A Question of Relief

Although President Hoover opposed any direct relief action by the federal government, he urged a massive effort to provide relief through private, voluntary agencies. Organizations such as settlement houses, the Salvation Army, the YMCA, community chests, church groups, and others worked relentlessly to feed and shelter the jobless millions. But sheer numbers of unemployed overwhelmed the effort.

The system of public relief that existed in the first years of the depression was strictly on a local level. Neither the states nor the federal government took part. In rural areas and in some cities and towns, no public relief was available at all. Local poverty relief had been designed to take care of small numbers of people who were unable to work. The system had not been intended to handle the needs of millions.

Furthermore, just when communities needed more money for relief, income from taxes was shrinking. Some cities responded by reducing the amount of relief per family. By the winter of 1931–1932, for example, New York City was able to give each family on relief just $2.39 a week. Many areas did not have even that much to offer.

After more than two years of depression, many city treasuries were empty. By 1932 about 100 cities had run out of funds. In that year only about one in four unemployed received any kind of relief. What they did receive was primarily food. Yet 12 million Americans were jobless, and the number was growing monthly. Those who did have jobs sometimes worked for five or six cents an hour.

At a national conference of social workers in Milwaukee, Wisconsin, Jacob Billikopf, executive director of the Federation of Jewish Charities, warned that private efforts, however valiant, were failing. Government, he said, "will be compelled, by the cruel events ahead of us, to step into the situation and bring relief on a large scale."

The Bonus Army

As the cry for government action increased, jobless veterans took to the road to dramatize their demands. After the war, Congress had voted veterans a bonus to be paid in 1945. In 1931 Congress voted to let veterans borrow up to 50 percent of the value of their bonuses, but President Hoover vetoed the bill.

In protest, a group of veterans from Oregon set out on a widely publicized journey to Washington, D.C., to demand their bonuses immediately. As they traveled eastward, hundreds and then thousands of other veterans joined them. About 17,000 reached the capital city in the spring of 1932. Most camped in makeshift tents or shacks on the Anacostia Flats, a swampy area near the Potomac River. Some set up camp in abandoned warehouses and government buildings nearby. Wives and children joined many of the veterans.

The House of Representatives voted to give the veterans their bonuses immediately, but the Senate overwhelmingly rejected the bill. Discouraged, some of the "bonus marchers" returned home, but thousands decided to stay in Washington. They vowed to camp there until the government gave them their money.

The presence of such a large group of protestors did little to improve the image of the Hoover administration. Despite the fears of Hoover and his advisers, the veterans were largely peaceful. Much of the calm could be attributed to the tireless actions of Washington Police Chief Pelham Glassford, a former brigadier general. Some of the vet-

Across the United States men, women, and children stood in lines. They stood in lines at factories or employment offices, hoping to get a job. Like the people in this rural soup line, they stood in line for food. Most early relief efforts were private, church-sponsored, or run by local government.

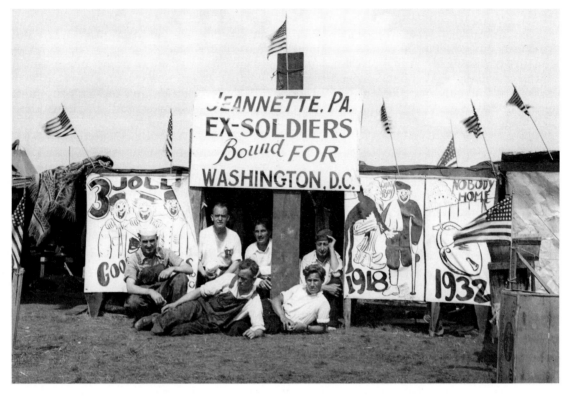

Many jobless veterans hoped that the federal government would make early payment of long-promised World War bonuses. When President Hoover vetoed a bonus bill, thousands of veterans joined a "March on Washington." The signs and placards of these Pennsylvania veterans tell their story.

erans had served under Glassford in the war, and he still considered them "his boys." Daily he rode through the bonus camp on his motorcycle, helping people locate food, shelter, and medicine. When food ran out, he spent his own money to buy more.

President Hoover refused to meet with march leaders. When a fight broke out between marchers and local police, the President ordered the army to tear down the veterans' camp. Under the command of General Douglas MacArthur, cavalry troops used tear gas to clear out the veterans and their families. Newspaper and magazine photos and movie newsreels of the event shocked the public. The scene convinced many that the Hoover administration was incapable of handling the spreading misery of the depression.

The Election of 1932

President Hoover had taken more government action to try to alleviate economic problems than Presidents had in any pre-

vious depression. Yet because of the widespread misery in 1932, Hoover became the object of anger and scorn. People living in shanty towns called their communities Hoovervilles. Empty pockets turned inside out were called Hoover flags. Day-old newspapers were known as Hoover blankets.

The President became gloomier as time went on. One observer noted, "If you put a

Major Events	
1926	Hurricane hits Florida
1928	Herbert Hoover elected President
1929	Stock market crashes
1932	Reconstruction Finance Corporation created; Bonus Army arrives in Washington, D. C.; Franklin D. Roosevelt elected President

Presidential Election Results, 1928 and 1932

	Party	Candidate	Popular Vote	Percent of Popular Vote	Electoral Vote
1928	Republican	Herbert Hoover	21,391,993	59	444
	Democrat	Alfred Smith	15,016,116	41	87
1932	Republican	Herbert Hoover	15,758,901	40	59
	Democrat	Franklin Roosevelt	22,809,638	58	472
	Minor	Minor candidates	881,951	2	0

■ *The decline of Herbert Hoover's popularity can be seen clearly in this table comparing the 1928 and 1932 presidential elections. In 1928, with the nation enjoying unparalleled prosperity, Hoover swamped his Democratic opponent. Four years later, with joblessness and bank failures at all-time highs, Hoover's bid for reelection was buried in a landslide of votes for Franklin Roosevelt.*

rose in Hoover's hand, it would wilt." The delegates to the Republican nominating convention knew that Hoover's reelection would be almost impossible, but they stood by him and renominated him for a second term.

Democrats at their convention in Chicago had little doubt that Hoover could be defeated, and several well-known leaders sought the nomination. By the fourth ballot the delegates had agreed on the governor of New York, Franklin Delano Roosevelt. A distant cousin of Theodore Roosevelt, the candidate bore a name recognized by most Americans.

A popular and progressive governor, Roosevelt had acted quickly and compassionately when the depression hit. New York was the first state to set up a relief plan for the unemployed. Roosevelt initiated a program that created jobs on land conservation projects, and he proposed a plan for unemployment insurance.

Once nominated, Roosevelt broke tradition by flying to the convention to deliver an acceptance speech in person. "I pledge myself," he told the delegates, "to a new deal for the American people."

During the election campaign, Hoover was dreary and pessimistic while Roosevelt radiated charm and confidence. Roosevelt did not outline a specific program, but he insisted that something needed to be done:

The country needs bold, persistent experimentation. It is common sense to take a method

and try it. If it fails, admit it frankly and try another. But above all, try something.

A majority of Americans agreed with him. Roosevelt won the election by a landslide, with 57 percent of the popular vote. Hoover carried only six states, all in the Northeast.

Roosevelt's support had come from city dwellers, immigrants, workers, and farmers. As the Democratic candidate, he also won the "solid South," where Democrats had been in control since the end of Reconstruction. These groups began to form a coalition of voters that would make the Democrats a majority party for the first time since the Civil War.

SECTION REVIEW

1. Identify: Reconstruction Finance Corporation, Bonus Army, Franklin Delano Roosevelt.

2. What did President Hoover think he should do at the onset of the depression?

3. How did Congress go beyond Hoover's intentions when it created the RFC?

4. What did the Bonus Army want from the federal government?

5. What was Hoover's attitude during the election campaign of 1932?

6. **Critical Thinking** How did American reaction to hardship reflect faith in the democratic institutions?

In Perspective

By the late 1920s the economy showed signs of imbalance, especially in agriculture, but few people were aware of them. Most Americans looked forward to a bright and prosperous future when they overwhelmingly elected Herbert Hoover President in 1928. Speculation in land or stock seemed an easy way of assuring the future. However, such speculation also contributed to the end of prosperity. When stock prices began to fall in late 1929, the flood of orders to sell led to a stock market crash. The economy of the United States slipped into a deep depression. Businesses and banks closed, and people lost their jobs, their cars, and even their homes.

President Hoover opposed federal government interference in the economy, but he did propose the Reconstruction Finance Corporation to halt business and bank failures. He also urged local agencies to provide relief, but the problem was too severe for their meager resources. As the depression deepened without any sign of ending, more and more people blamed Hoover and demanded government action. In 1932, 57 percent of the voters cast their ballots for Franklin D. Roosevelt.

Vocabulary

Choose the answer that best completes each of the following sentences.

1. The practice of buying stock by which the buyer uses some of his or her own money and borrows the rest from a broker is buying on (a) the cuff; (b) margin; (c) review.

2. A request by a broker for an investor to put up more money to cover a loan for the purchase of stocks that are now worth less is a (a) margin call; (b) credit call; (c) stock option.

3. Products designed to last several years before being replaced are (a) perennial goods; (b) consumable goods; (c) durable goods.

4. Lists of unsold goods on hand are (a) clearance items; (b) stock lists; (c) business inventories.

5. The total dollar value of all goods and services produced in a country in one year is the (a) gross national product; (b) annual production inventory; (c) national industrial register.

Chapter Checkup

1. What were the signs of economic problems underlying the prosperity of the 1920s?

2. Describe the personal and political differences between Herbert Hoover and Al Smith, the presidential candidates in 1928.

3. (a) How did speculators try to "get rich quick" during the 1920s? (b) What ended the Florida land boom? (c) How were investors able to buy stocks without paying the full price?

4. Describe how each of the following contributed to the onset of depression: (a) imbalance of supply and demand; (b) production of more durable goods; (c) rising business inventories; (d) bank closings.

5. (a) How did the onset of the depression affect many people? (b) Why did this depression seem worse than earlier depressions?

6. (a) What did President Hoover's advisers urge him to do? (b) How did Hoover try to restore public confidence? (c) What type of public-works programs did he support?

7. (a) What powers did Congress grant the Reconstruction Finance Corporation? (b) How did it carry out those powers?

8. (a) Who did Hoover think should be responsible for providing relief? (b) Why were private agencies and local governments unable to provide enough relief?

9. (a) What was the Bonus Army? (b) What did it hope to accomplish?

Critical Thinking

1. **Analyzing** (a) How was the Reconstruction Finance Corporation an example of the "trickle-down" theory? (b) Why did Hoover support that theory?

2. **Evaluating** Why do you think almost 60 percent of American voters cast their ballots for Franklin Roosevelt in 1932?

Developing Basic Skills

1. **Using Primary Sources** In the library, look at copies of a newspaper from October 1929. What evidence can you find that the stock market was collapsing?

2. **Using Statistics** Study the table on page 587. (a) How many electoral votes did Roosevelt receive in 1932? (b) How many popular votes did the Democratic candidate receive in 1932? (c) How many more popular votes did Hoover receive in 1928 than in 1932? (d) How might you explain this change?

See page 832 for suggested readings.

Writer's Handbook

Deciding When to Document

There are certain circumstances in which you must document, or identify, the sources of the information that you include in a research paper. Generally these include: (a) any direct quotation, even if it is only a phrase; (b) the summary of an author's ideas; (c) statistical facts; (d) a fact that is not common knowledge or a fact that is disputable. By citing sources, you give the proper credit to a person for the work he or she has done. You also provide valuable information for readers if they want to do further research themselves.

There are times that documentation is not necessary. You do not have to identify the source of any fact that is generally known, even if you did not know the fact yourself. Basic biographical information about a public figure, such as his or her birthplace, education, public offices, and accomplishments, is usually considered general knowledge. A rule of thumb is that a fact that appears undocumented in several sources need not be documented.

It is not necessary to document proverbs and quotations that are familiar. For example, you need not document the adage, "A stitch in time saves nine," or the quotation, "The business of America is business."

Practice: Copy the items from the following list that would require documentation in a research paper.

1. The date of the 1929 stock market crash
2. The gross national product for 1930
3. The economist John Kenneth Galbraith's theory of the cause of the depression
4. A passage from Herbert Hoover's inaugural address
5. The names of Al Smith's parents
6. The amount of money invested in real estate in Florida in 1922
7. A person's account of how the depression affected her life
8. The fact that thousands of people were homeless during the depression

Unit Nine

A Time of Trial

1933 Parades, songs, and posters were used to build support for the National Recovery Administration.

WPA murals often emphasized the theme of self-improvement and hard work.

	1933	1935	1937	1939
POLITICS AND GOVERNMENT	**1933** New Deal begins with "first hundred days"		**1936** Supreme Court rules AAA unconstitutional	
SOCIETY AND CULTURE	**1933** CCC provides jobs for young men	**1935** Social Security Act creates pensions for the elderly		
ECONOMICS AND TECHNOLOGY	**1933** TVA created	**1935** WPA puts people to work on public works projects		**1938** Economy takes a plunge
WORLD EVENTS	**1933** Hitler and the Nazis come to power in Germany	**1936** Civil War breaks out in Spain		

1932 The drought that lasted until 1936 turned farmland into dust.

1936 In this 1936 presidential campaign memento, the glass bottle represents the TVA. President Roosevelt is shown as the cork.

590

1940 The British defense against German attack created sympathy for Britain among Americans.

"above and beyond the call of duty"

1941 Dorie Miller received the Navy Cross for his valor at Pearl Harbor.

1939	1941	1943	1945
1939 Executive Office of the President created	**1941** Japanese attack U.S. ships at Pearl Harbor		**1944** Allies begin invasion of France
1939 *The Grapes of Wrath* portrays life in the Dust Bowl	**1942** Japanese Americans on Pacific coast are relocated inland		
	1942 War Production Board created to manage the economy		**1945** Atomic bombs dropped on Japanese cities
1939 Germany invades Poland and World War II begins		**1943** Allies invade Italy	**1945** Germany surrenders

1939 Hollywood movies, such as *Gone With the Wind,* helped Americans escape from the depression.

Women Ordnance Workers took jobs in arms factories to support the war effort.

"THE GIRL HE LEFT BEHIND IS STILL BEHIND HIM She's a **WOW**

32

A New Deal

(1933–1935)

Franklin Delano Roosevelt *by Ellen Emmet Rand*

Chapter Outline

1 *The Roots of the New Deal*

2 *The First Hundred Days*

3 *Critics of the New Deal*

4 *The Second New Deal*

When Franklin D. Roosevelt took the oath of office in March 1933, the nation's situation could not have been bleaker. The banking system was near collapse. One quarter of the population had virtually no income, and their desperation was frightening.

In January 1933 several hundred jobless people surrounded a restaurant in New York City, demanding to be fed free of charge. In February 5,000 unemployed people besieged the County-City Building in Seattle, demanding help for themselves and their families. Over one million Americans, one quarter of them under age 21, roamed the country looking for work.

In his acceptance speech at the Democratic nominating convention, Franklin Roosevelt had promised "a new deal for the American people." Now he and his administration faced the overwhelming prospect of implementing that new deal to revive the stricken country.

New Deal

1932	1933	1934	1935	1936
1932 Franklin D. Roosevelt elected President	**1933** Civilian Conservation Corps created	**1934** National Youth Administration established	**1935** Works Progress Administration formed; Social Security Act passed	**1936** Agricultural Adjustment Act declared unconstitutional

1 The Roots of the New Deal

The policies and programs that comprised the New Deal reflected the diversity of the people who framed it. A new breed of government workers streamed into Washington as the Hoover administration drew to a close. Social workers, sociologists, economists, political scientists, and lawyers came with highly varied learning, experience, and plans for action. Their goal was to pull the nation out of economic crisis, and their leader was President-elect Franklin D. Roosevelt.

Franklin D. Roosevelt

Like his distant cousin Theodore, Franklin Roosevelt came from a background unusual for a professional politician. As a boy, Franklin grew up in the genteel atmosphere of Hyde Park, New York, amid the rolling country estates lining the Hudson River. There his strong-willed mother taught him that the wealthy and privileged had an obligation to help those less fortunate than themselves.

Roosevelt studied history and government at Harvard College and law at Columbia University. In 1905 he married Anna Eleanor Roosevelt, niece of then President Theodore Roosevelt.

Bored with the idea of a Wall Street law practice, the young Roosevelt was attracted to a potentially more exciting career: politics. In quick succession, he became a New York State senator, assistant secretary of the navy during the war, and Democratic candidate for Vice-President in 1920. After the Democrats lost the 1920 election, Roosevelt returned to private life.

The following summer, as the family vacationed at Campobello in New Brunswick, Canada, Franklin Roosevelt was stricken with polio. At the age of 39, his legs paralyzed, he thought his political career was over.

Eleanor Roosevelt and her husband's devoted political adviser Louis Howe thought differently. They convinced Roosevelt not to give up his active life. Buoyed by their faith in him and his own courage, Roosevelt worked to overcome his physical limitations. After years of grueling exercise and therapy, he was able to walk with the help of heavy metal braces clamped to his nearly useless legs.

In 1928 Franklin Roosevelt ran for governor of New York at the request of Democratic presidential candidate Al Smith. Roosevelt won, even though the national Democratic ticket was defeated. The stock market crashed during his first year in office. As governor Roosevelt saw all too clearly the human suffering caused by the Great Depression. He believed that the government should do what it could to end the depression and relieve the suffering.

Roosevelt had learned early that his wealth obliged him to help others. His illness gave him a sense of compassion for victims of adversity. Those experiences and his belief that government should aid people in need all shaped his political philosophy. That philosophy was one of the bases of the New Deal.

Ideas for Action

In politics, Roosevelt was above all an activist. Although he had no specific program, he had promised a "new deal" during the 1932 campaign. (See page 587.) Once elected, Roosevelt sought bold ideas for action. Many of the ideas on which the New Deal was based were not new. They reflected the aims of progressives early in the century: conserving natural resources, breaking down monopolies, regulating business, and improving working conditions. Like the progressives, the architects of the New Deal wanted to preserve democracy and the free enterprise system.

The lessons learned during the World War also influenced the development of the New Deal. To fight the war, government planning agencies had worked with business and agriculture to coordinate the efficient production of food and manufactured goods. (See page 530.) Many of Roosevelt's advisers thought that similar federal agencies should be set up to fight the war against economic depression.

Still more ideas came from a group of advisers called Roosevelt's brain trust, so named because several of them had taught at universities. These professors of economics, social planning, and law, led by Raymond Moley and Rexford Tugwell, helped Roosevelt chart the course of the early New Deal. They stressed the value of centralized planning to avoid overproduction and wasteful competition.

Roosevelt's cabinet members also contributed to the New Deal programs. The new secretary of the interior, Harold Ickes, had been a progressive Republican and a leader of reform politics in Chicago. Henry A. Wallace, another progressive Republican, led the fight for new farm programs as secretary of agriculture. Roosevelt called on Frances Perkins, a labor relations specialist, to take the post of secretary of labor, making her the first woman ever to hold a cabinet position.

Frances Perkins, the first woman cabinet officer, served as secretary of labor under Roosevelt. Previously, as chairwoman of the New York State Industrial Board, she had won reduction of the work week for women in New York from 54 to 48 hours. Here, the secretary of labor greets workers.

Although Roosevelt began the New Deal with few concrete plans, he had a wealth of ideas from which to choose. Furthermore the goals of the new President and his administration were clear: to provide relief for the unemployed as quickly as possible, to help bring about the recovery of the nation's weakened economic structure, and to enact reforms to correct the conditions that had contributed to the economic crisis.

A New Beginning

On inauguration day, March 4, 1933, Herbert Hoover and Franklin Roosevelt rode together in an open car down Pennsylvania Avenue toward the Capitol. The months since the November election had strained relations between the two men. Hoover had asked Roosevelt for a pledge to carry out certain policies that the Republican President thought essential. Roosevelt, who rejected his predecessor's economic policies, had refused. As they rode along, they barely spoke to each other.

When they spoke to the country at large that day, they expressed opposite points of view. Upon leaving office, Hoover had lamented privately, "We are at the end of our rope. There is nothing more we can do."

Roosevelt, on the other hand, voiced confidence, optimism, and promise for the country in his inaugural address. "First of all," he began, "let me assert my firm belief that the only thing we have to fear is fear itself—nameless, unreasoning, unjustified terror which paralyzes needed efforts to convert retreat into advance." Promising a dramatic change in economic policy, the President concluded, "The nation asks for action and action now. We must act and act quickly."

SECTION REVIEW

1. Identify: brain trust, Harold Ickes, Henry A. Wallace, Frances Perkins.

2. How might Roosevelt's being stricken with polio have affected his attitude toward fighting the Great Depression?

3. List sources of ideas for the New Deal.

4. **Critical Thinking** Why do you think Franklin Roosevelt attracted progressive Republicans to his administration?

2 The First Hundred Days

The Roosevelt family had barely moved into the White House when the new President plunged into action. He knew that he had to move quickly to convince the American people that their nation could indeed be saved from total economic disaster. During the first three months of his administration Roosevelt drafted and convinced Congress to pass 15 major pieces of legislation. The new laws established agencies to fight every aspect of the Great Depression. This period of frenzied action came to be called "the hundred days."

Relieving the Banking Crisis

During the four months between Roosevelt's election and his inauguration the national banking system neared total collapse. Fearful of repeated bank failures, people withdrew their money and hoarded it in mattresses, under floorboards—anywhere but in the banks. As the money flowed out, the banks failed. The governor of Michigan had ordered all the banks in Detroit closed in an attempt to save them. Similar action was planned in the major banking centers of Chicago and New York.

Roosevelt decided that his first step must be to halt the crippling bank failures. Within hours of his inauguration he declared a national "bank holiday." With this action he closed all the banks in the country for an indefinite period. This "holiday," he believed, would stop people from withdrawing their money and thus prevent still more bank failures.

At the same time, the President ordered his secretary of the treasury to draft an emergency banking bill to save the banking system. Five days later the bill was read to a special session of Congress, called by the new President. With shouts of approval, Congress passed the Emergency Banking Relief Act almost unanimously.

The new law allowed the reopening of banks that had sufficient funds to satisfy depositors' withdrawal requests. Essentially sound banks would be allowed to borrow federal funds to reopen. Those banks judged unsound would remain closed.

A few nights later Roosevelt went on nationwide radio with the first of many *fireside chats*, informal talks he made to the American people. In clear and convincing terms he described the measures the Emergency Banking Relief Act provided. He urged his listeners to return their money to the reopened banks. "I can assure you," he said, "it is safer to keep your money in a reopened bank than under the mattress."

During those first days Roosevelt presented other proposals to Congress. He sent the legislature a government economy bill that would reduce the salaries of all federal employees and cut veterans' pensions. Two days later Congress passed the bill despite the vehement opposition of veterans. The President also submitted a proposal to legalize the sale of beer and light wines. Again Congress agreed, this time over the opposition of the prohibitionists. *

The speed with which the new administration converted proposals into action excited many Americans. Will Rogers, the popular humorist, summed up Roosevelt's first week in office: "The whole country is with him, just so he does something."

Relieving the Employment Crisis

Over 13 million people were out of work in 1933. Those unemployed desperately needed money for the barest essentials of food, clothing, and shelter. During the first months of the new administration Congress passed two major acts to provide financial assistance and jobs.

The first was the Civilian Conservation Reforestation Relief Act. It had the dual aims of conserving natural resources and putting young people to work. The act set up the Civilian Conservation Corps (CCC), which enlisted unemployed single men between the ages of 18 and 25. In forestry camps all over the nation the new work force planted trees, dug reservoirs, built bridges, and developed parks. The federal

---

*Later in 1933, the Twenty-first Amendment to the Constitution, repealing the earlier prohibition amendment, was ratified.

One of the most successful New Deal programs was the Civilian Conservation Corps, which provided jobs and training for men between the ages of 18 and 25. Members of the CCC planted 17 million acres of forests, built dams, and created parks. The CCC also offered medical care for its members. This corpsman is learning the use of a surveyor's transit.

government paid for the men's housing, clothes, and food, so part of their salary could be sent home to help their families. By the end of the 1930s, more than 2.5 million young men had served in the CCC.

Next Congress passed the Federal Emergency Relief Act (FERA) to provide immediate "relief" payments to the unemployed. The FERA allocated money to local and state welfare agencies, which distributed it to the unemployed.

Roosevelt appointed Harry Hopkins, who had administered a New York State relief program, to head the FERA. Hopkins moved to Washington, D.C., set up a desk in a federal office building, and distributed $5 million in his first two hours on the job. But in spite of his energetic efforts, Hopkins felt that the program was inadequate. He be-

lieved that to rebuild their lives and self-respect, the unemployed needed jobs, not handouts.

President Roosevelt agreed with Hopkins that the major task of the government was to get Americans back to work. As a result Roosevelt authorized Hopkins to establish the Civil Works Administration (CWA). The CWA offered jobs rather than relief. Within a few months it employed over 4 million people.

Hopkins displayed a genius for creating jobs. Working for the CWA, construction crews built roads, athletic fields, and airports. Opera singers toured rural areas giving concerts, and archaeologists excavated prehistoric mounds. Despite such achievements, the CWA drew a great deal of criticism. Some people accused the agency of spending funds on unnecessary "make-work." Concerned that the country might grow overly dependent on the CWA, the President ended the program early in 1934.

Planning for Agricultural Recovery

Depression, unfortunately, was not unfamiliar to American farmers. As you read in Chapter 31, farm profits had fallen steadily throughout the 1920s. Much of the problem resulted from chronic surpluses of such crops as wheat, corn, and cotton. As farm prices fell, farm costs rose. Farmers planted more crops to try to cover costs, creating larger surpluses and going further into debt to buy seed and machinery.

The Roosevelt administration decided that something extraordinary had to be done to break the vicious cycle of production surpluses, falling prices, and decreasing farm income. The President's economic advisers thought that if the size of major crops could be reduced, their prices would rise. The administration proposed that farmers reduce their production to specified levels.

In return for the farmers' cooperation, the government would pay them for the crops they did not plant. The money for those payments would come from a special tax collected from the mills and packing houses that prepared agricultural products for the consumer.

By April 1933 the Department of Agriculture had prepared a draft of these proposals for Congress. There was little time to waste. Farmers were growing desperate as more and more faced bank foreclosures of the mortgages on their farms. In Iowa a group of farmers had forced their way into a courtroom and nearly lynched a judge who had authorized banks to foreclose the farmers' mortgages. Moreover, spring had come and farmers were beginning to plant their crops. As one Agriculture Department official put it, "We were racing against the sun."

Even so, it was May before Congress passed the Agricultural Adjustment Act, forming the Agricultural Adjustment Administration (AAA). By that time over 40 million acres (16 million hectares) of cotton had been planted. Another surplus was expected.

Roosevelt and Congress decided to pay the farmers to plow under, and thus destroy, part of their crops. Agriculture agents traveled across the South in the late spring and summer of 1933, convincing farmers to sign up for the plow-under campaign. One of the biggest difficulties was convincing the mules. They had been taught to walk between rows of cotton; now they had to learn to trample the cotton plants.

Since there was also a surplus of pork, the AAA bought and destroyed 5 million pigs. It was bitterly ironic that sources of food and clothing were destroyed while thousands of Americans were hungry and poorly clothed. Secretary of Agriculture Henry Wallace, himself a farmer, regretfully pointed out that "to destroy a standing crop goes against the soundest instincts of human nature." Yet the plan seems to have worked—for the farmers at least. In later years farmers limited production as planned. Bad weather also reduced production. As a result prices and farm income rose.

Planning for Industrial Recovery

Like agriculture, industry was also trapped in a downward economic spiral. One fourth of the labor force had no jobs at all. Those fortunate enough to be employed found their wages steadily reduced as employers cut costs to lower prices. Competition for sales was fierce since a growing number of people could not afford to buy manufactured products. Falling consumer purchasing power further decreased the demand for goods, which lowered production, which caused still more unemployment, which further reduced buying power. There seemed no end to the plunge.

The administration decided to take major action, as it had with agriculture. Several members of the brain trust urged that government and industry cooperate to provide overall planning of industrial production. They suggested that the War Industries Board, which had set priorities and production quotas during the World War, be used as a model.

In June 1933 Congress passed the National Industrial Recovery Act to establish a similar agency to fight the depression. The major provision of the act established trade associations in each industry to draft codes regulating production, prices, and working conditions within the industry. Section 7A of the act forbade employers to interfere with attempts by workers to organize unions. It also guaranteed labor unions the right to bargain with employers about wages, hours, and working conditions.

The administration hoped that cooperative action would stabilize production, end the price cutting that forced business to cut wages and lay off workers, and establish decent standards of wages and working hours. The National Recovery Administration (NRA) was created to enforce the codes.

The National Industrial Recovery Act also established the Public Works Administration (PWA), headed by Secretary of the Interior Harold Ickes. Like the CWA, the new agency tried to stimulate employment by spending large sums of money on public works projects. The PWA started slowly, but PWA workers eventually built a municipal auditorium in Kansas City; the Triborough Bridge in New York City; a water supply system in Denver; a deep-water port for Brownsville, Texas; new schools in Los Angeles; and two aircraft carriers for the navy.

With all the fanfare of a national crusade, the NRA, under the colorful leadership of former army general Hugh Johnson, began functioning during the summer of 1933. The agency emblem was a Blue Eagle over the slogan "We Do Our Part." To show they were following NRA codes, business people stamped the symbol on their products and posted it in store windows, on factory doors, and on delivery trucks.

Huge parades were held in several cities to dramatize the Blue Eagle crusade and to urge Americans to buy only products stamped with the symbol. In New York City a quarter of a million people, ranging from

The Fireside Chats

When Franklin D. Roosevelt was inaugurated in March 1933, the American people were ready to welcome a friendly voice. In the depths of what seemed to be an endless economic depression, people throughout the country were seeking assurance that the nation could be set back on its feet.

To Franklin Roosevelt, radio broadcasts seemed ready-made for this purpose. He could sit in his study and give "fireside chats" that explained government policies to Americans everywhere. Secretary of Labor Frances Perkins described the chats:

> When he talked on the radio, he saw them [the people] gathered in the little parlor, listening with their neighbors. He was conscious of their faces and hands, their clothes and homes. His voice and his facial expression as he spoke were those of an intimate friend. After he became President, I often was at the White House when he broadcast, and I realized how unconscious he was of the twenty or thirty of us in that room and how clearly his mind was focused on the people listening at the other end. As he talked his head would nod and his hands would move in simple, natural, comfortable gestures. His face would smile and light up as though he were actually sitting on the front porch or in the parlor with them. People felt this, and it bound them to him in affection.
>
> I have sat in those little parlors and on those porches myself during some of the speeches, and I have seen men and women gathered around the radio, even those who didn't like him or were opposed to him politically, listening with a pleasant, happy feeling of friendship. The exchange between them and him through the medium of the radio was very real. I have seen tears come to their eyes as he told them of some tragic episode. . . . I have also seen them laugh. . . . [T]he laughter of those gathered around radios of the country was a natural, sincere, and affectionate reaching out to this man.

Roosevelt's fireside chats gave the American people new hope. The broadcasts created the impression that the head of a vast and powerful nation had the people's interests at heart and was working to improve their lives.

---

factory workers to stock brokers to actors, marched down Fifth Avenue behind the NRA Blue Eagle.

But the NRA needed more than fanfare to succeed. Before long, problems appeared. The extension of NRA regulation resulted in codes for the production of hair tonic, shoulder pads, dog leashes, and musical comedies. More important, many businesses simply ignored the codes. Industrialist Henry Ford had refused to cooperate with the NRA from the start. Labor leaders complained that the NRA kept wages too low. The NRA had helped to stop the price-cutting, wage-cutting cycle in large industries, but enforcing its numerous codes became increasingly difficult.

Remaking a Region: TVA

In a time of bold experimentation perhaps no program was more daring than the Tennessee Valley Authority (TVA), which Congress authorized during the frantic first hundred days of Roosevelt's presidency. The TVA was to transform the entire Tennessee River Valley from a backwater of poor farms into a rich and productive region. Never before had a nation embarked upon a conservation and social planning effort on such a grand scale.

The area, extending over parts of seven states, had been victimized by careless use of resources resulting in frequent flooding. Loggers had cut down most of the trees in the area, loosening the soil and causing massive erosion. Heavy rainfall regularly swelled the Tennessee River, which flooded crops. Such conditions made farming difficult. Personal income in the region was half the national average, and living conditions were abysmal.

The TVA changed the face of the area. Engineers built a series of dams along the length of the Tennessee River and its tributaries. Then the TVA constructed hydroelectric power plants to supply electricity to homes and farms in the valley and to attract industry and new jobs. The dams also helped control flooding and conserve water for future use. (See the map on page 600.)

The TVA channeled some of the newly created power into the manufacture of fertilizer, selling it to farmers at cost. With fertilizers, farmers improved the land and were able to increase harvests. The TVA also planted millions of trees in the valley to stop erosion. Finally, the authority introduced many educational, recreational, and health services into the region to improve economic and social conditions.

The TVA was the subject of heated controversy. Power companies in the area objected to government production and sale of power. The companies argued that such government competition was unfair. Other critics objected to "social planning" by the TVA. They maintained that the federal government had no right to interfere in the region and that problems there were matters of state and local concern. Despite such criti-

The whirlwind creation of new agencies and programs during "the hundred days" aroused deep fears among those who believed the President was destroying traditional values. This illustration for a 1934 cover of Vanity Fair magazine shows Roosevelt wearing the symbol of the National Recovery Administration, the Blue Eagle, and riding roughshod over the nation. Many people thought that New Deal programs gave government too much power over business.

cism, the mammoth project transformed the region and continues in operation today.

Other Hundred Days Measures

The legislation passed during the first hundred days of Roosevelt's administration was not part of a unified plan for recovery. Rather, each law passed or agency created represented an attempt to solve a particular problem or to change a particular condition plaguing the depression-ridden nation.

The Truth-in-Securities Act tried to end the wild stock market speculation that had helped bring on the crash. This law required full public disclosure of all relevant financial information about corporation stocks. Misrepresenting such information became a criminal offense.

The Glass-Steagall Banking Act reformed the national banking system. It

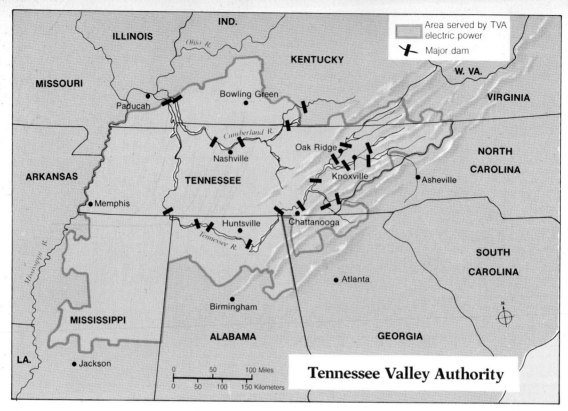

■ *The vast Tennessee Valley Authority project affected seven states, harnessing the power of the Tennessee River and others nearby. In addition to electricity, TVA dams created lakes that spurred recreational development in the region. The map shows the major TVA dams and the total area provided with electric power.*

created the Federal Deposit Insurance Corporation (FDIC), which to this day insures savings accounts against bank failure. The law provided that in the event an FDIC-insured bank failed, the government would reimburse the depositors. Depositors began to put money back into banks instead of taking it out.

The Farm Credit Administration (FCA) was established to provide low-interest loans for farmers, to enable them to pay their debts and keep their farms. During the mid-1930s the FCA helped as many as 300 farmers a day save their farms from foreclosure and bankruptcy.

The Home Owners' Loan Corporation (HOLC) performed a similar service for home owners. It provided owners with low-interest loans that could be repaid over a long period of time, thus reducing monthly payments. The HOLC helped almost 1,000 families a day keep their homes during the mid-1930s.

The hundred days ended in the early hours of June 16 as Congress adjourned. The weary legislators expressed the hope that their efforts would bring the depression to a swift conclusion. But the economic crisis of the nation would not be easily solved.

SECTION REVIEW

1. Identify: Harry Hopkins, Blue Eagle.
2. Define: fireside chat.
3. How did President Franklin Roosevelt try to relieve the banking crisis?
4. What were the two aims of the Civilian Conservation Reforestation Relief Act?
5. (a) What was the purpose of the Federal Emergency Relief Act? (b) How did the purpose of the Civil Works Administration differ from that of the FERA?
6. (a) What was the main provision of the National Industrial Recovery Act? (b) What was the main purpose of the Public Works Administration?
7. List three actions of the Tennessee Valley Authority.
8. **Critical Thinking** How did Roosevelt's economic policies differ from those of Herbert Hoover?

Through the building of a series of dams such as the Fontana Dam, above, the TVA generated electrical power, provided jobs, and helped attract new industry to the economically depressed region.

3 Critics of the New Deal

A noted political writer, Walter Lippman, praised the first hundred days of the New Deal: "At the end of February, we were a [collection] of disorderly panic-stricken mobs and factions. In the hundred days from March to June we became again an organized nation confident of our power to provide for our own security and to control our own destiny."

But not all Americans shared Lippman's enthusiasm for the New Deal. Some critics firmly believed that the government was interferring too much in people's lives. Others believed that the administration should take more drastic steps to aid the American people. Many critics had originally supported Roosevelt. Now they spoke against the New Deal in growing numbers.

Demands for Stronger Action

One of the first of Roosevelt's earlier supporters to attack the New Deal was Senator Huey Long of Louisiana. The Kingfish, as he was called, felt that Roosevelt's New Deal had done nothing to redistribute the nation's wealth more evenly. He proposed his own plan for the future, expressed in the motto "Share Our Wealth."

Long suggested that the government confiscate "the swollen fortunes" of the rich and tax 100 percent of all income over $1 million a year. The senator wanted the money redistributed to provide every American family with a house, a car, education for the children, a pension for the elderly, and an income of $2,000 to $3,000 a year. Long's idea attracted millions, especially among the poor. He decided to challenge Roosevelt for the presidency, but in 1935 he was shot and killed by a young man, for reasons never clearly understood.

Another vocal critic of Roosevelt and the New Deal was Father Charles Coughlin, known as the radio priest. Each week he told at least 10 million radio listeners that the depression was the fault of an international conspiracy of bankers. Before the 1932 election, Coughlin backed Roosevelt, telling his listeners that they could choose "Roosevelt

601

or ruin." Eventually, however, Coughlin lost his enthusiasm for the New Deal, believing that stronger actions should be taken against "banking and money interests." Soon he was using his radio programs to attack Roosevelt and his programs.

Dr. Francis E. Townsend, a retired California physician, wanted the government to help older citizens. He proposed that the government pay every person over age 60 a monthly pension of $200. In return, the recipient would agree to retire, freeing a job for someone else. The pensioner would also agree to spend the entire $200 within the month, thereby further stimulating the economy. Like Long and Coughlin, Townsend had many supporters, and Townsend Clubs sprang up all over the country.

Roosevelt and his advisers knew that they could not ignore the supporters of such

critics as Long, Coughlin, and Townsend. "In normal times, the radio and other appeals by them would not be effective," said Roosevelt, "However, these are not normal times; the people are jumpy and very ready to run after strange gods." Furthermore, the rise of dictators in Italy and Germany (see page 627) had shown to what extremes nations might go. Consequently, the planners of the New Deal began to reconsider their positions regarding taxation, banking, and aid to the elderly.

The Conservative Reaction

While Long, Coughlin, and Townsend wanted the government to do more, many critics wanted it to do less. These conservatives were convinced that the new laws were a threat to individual liberty. Many business people, especially, thought they were being paralyzed by excessive taxes and regulations. They argued that the government had no right to tell them how to run their businesses. Raymond Moley, who had been a member of Roosevelt's brain trust, bitterly criticized administration policies that he thought undermined the free-enterprise system.

In 1934 two prominent Democrats helped to found the American Liberty League because of their objections to some aspects of the New Deal. Members of the league believed that the government had a duty to encourage private enterprise and to protect private ownership and use of property. They charged that New Deal programs were undermining private enterprise with heavy taxation and government planning and regulation. Among the many well-known members of the American Liberty League was Roosevelt's one-time political ally, Al Smith.

Attack by the Supreme Court

Administration officials had based the legislation of the first hundred days on the view that the depression was a national emergency, similar to war, which justified an expansion of government power. They believed the government should use that power to revitalize the nation's economic and social well-being.

From the outset, however, many of Roosevelt's advisers worried that the Su-

Cartoonists and critics often made fun of the many "alphabet agencies" created by the New Deal. In his first campaign, Roosevelt had promised to try new remedies to end the depression. If those remedies failed, he said he would abandon them and try others. Can you supply the full names of the programs labeled by letters in this cartoon?

preme Court might find the expansion of federal power unconstitutional. Their concerns proved justified. On May 27, 1935, the Supreme Court handed down a decision involving a Brooklyn, New York, chicken processor who had been convicted of violating an NRA code. In *Schechter* v. *United States*, the Court declared unanimously that since the federal government had no power to regulate intrastate* commerce, the National Industrial Recovery Act was unconstitutional.

In 1936, the Court struck down the Agricultural Adjustment Act. The Court ruled that Congress had violated the Constitution when it levied a tax to pay farmers for cutting back production because it had taken "money from one group for the benefit of another."

In the same session the Court declared three other New Deal laws unconstitutional. In each case the Court ruled that under the New Deal the federal government had gone beyond the limits of constitutional authority. Roosevelt complained that the Supreme Court decisions reflected a "horse and buggy," or old-fashioned, definition of what the Constitution allowed, but the decisions stood.

SECTION REVIEW

1. Identify: Huey Long, Charles Coughlin, Francis E. Townsend, American Liberty League, *Schechter* v. *United States*.

2. What did Huey Long think should be done with tax money from the rich?

3. What group of people was Francis Townsend especially concerned about?

4. List two New Deal laws the Supreme Court declared unconstitutional.

5. **Critical Thinking** Why do you think the depression led to the development of some extreme proposals?

---

*intrastate: within the boundaries of one state.

4 The Second New Deal

The Supreme Court decisions striking down key legislation ended the period known as the first New Deal. During that time, relief and recovery measures were uppermost among administration priorities. Some reform measures had been passed—the Truth-in-Securities Act and the Glass-Steagall Banking Act, for example—but the main emphasis had been on relief and recovery.

Roosevelt believed that to achieve national economic health, the causes as well as the symptoms of the depression had to be treated. In this spirit, he and Congress launched a "second hundred days" of legislative action. From July into September 1935, Congress passed a series of far-reaching reform acts, but it did not end efforts to provide relief.

Works Progress Administration

As the New Deal entered its third year, widespread unemployment continued to resist solution. Twenty million people still relied on public assistance and welfare to survive. Roosevelt decided that only a massive public works program could provide the jobs needed to bring about economic recovery. Yet Congress had grown more cautious about passing New Deal programs Roosevelt proposed. After some pressure from the administration, it passed the Emergency Relief Appropriations Act, which created the Works Progress Administration (WPA).

Roosevelt named Harry Hopkins, former head of the Civil Works Administration, to head the new agency. Hopkins distributed huge sums of money to provide jobs and get money into circulation. As with the CWA, Hopkins was accused of creating "make-work" projects that would not benefit the country in the long run. "People don't eat in the long run," Hopkins replied with exasperation. "They eat today."

The WPA immediately put people to work on a wide variety of construction projects. WPA workers built or improved 2,500 hospitals, 5,000 schools, 13,000 parks and playgrounds, and 1,000 airports. But such projects employed only construction workers. Hopkins set about providing jobs for other workers as well.

Soon the WPA established several projects for people in the arts. The Federal Theatre Project hired actors, actresses, and directors to put on plays, vaudeville shows, and circuses across the country. Entertainers often traveled to remote rural areas where people had never seen a theater production. The Federal Writers Project employed authors to write historical and geographical guides for every state in the nation. The Federal Art Project hired artists to paint murals in public buildings.

Despite providing work for nearly 3 million people, the WPA fell far short of meeting the goal of providing work for all the able-bodied unemployed. Nearly 3 million families were still on relief, and youngsters in such households often had to quit school to look for a job. In so doing, young people lost the opportunity for an education and more often than not wound up on the unemployment rolls.

An extension of the WPA, the National Youth Administration (NYA) attacked that problem. The NYA offered young people a way to stay in school and earn money by providing part-time jobs in and around their schools. The agency helped 600,000 students work their way through college and another 1.5 million stay in high school.

Reforming Labor Relations

Organized labor had won a victory when Congress passed the National Industrial Recovery Act. Section 7A of that law had banned interference with union organizing. It had had guaranteed collective bargaining. When the law was declared unconstitutional, section 7A was struck down with it.

Senator Robert F. Wagner of New York had become the leading advocate for workers in Congress. In 1935 he introduced a new bill to guarantee workers' rights to organize and bargain collectively. The bill also banned as unfair certain practices employers used to discourage employees from organizing. Such practices included firing

★ American Profiles ★

Mary McLeod Bethune

Soon after his inauguration, President Franklin Roosevelt called together a group of black Americans to advise him on programs and policies. Among the members of this so-called Black Cabinet was Robert C. Weaver, who later served as secretary of the Department of Housing and Urban Development, and Ralph Bunche, who later won a Nobel Peace Prize. Mary McLeod Bethune, a well-known educator, also served in the Black Cabinet.

Bethune had been an adviser to President Coolidge. Roosevelt asked her to serve on the committee that helped establish the National Youth Administration (NYA) in 1934. The NYA made it possible for thousands of hard-pressed high school and college students to continue their educations. In 1936, when the Division of Negro Affairs of the NYA was established, Bethune was appointed to direct it. She was the first black American to head a government agency.

Bethune served as director of the NYA from 1936 to 1944. In 1945 she served as a consultant on interracial understanding at the San Francisco Conference of the United Nations. Mary McLeod Bethune worked tirelessly in government service and education. She received many honors, including in 1935 the Springarn Medal for outstanding achievement, awarded annually by the NAACP. She is pictured below in the 1950s.

workers who joined unions or infiltrating unions with company spies.

Many business people opposed the bill vehemently, insisting that it defined unfair action by management but said nothing about unfair action by labor. Nevertheless Congress passed the National Labor Relations Act in July 1935. The Wagner Act, as it was known, established the National Labor Relations Board (NLRB) to administer the law. The NLRB had the authority to determine when enough workers in an industry desired union representation. In such matters the business community often accused the NLRB of consistently favoring labor over management.

Regulating the Utilities

The Roosevelt administration had watched with growing concern the increasing monopoly of the *utility companies.* By the 1930s, gigantic holding companies had taken complete control of gas and electricity distribution in various sections of the country. The holding companies could effectively close out competition in those areas. Thus they could set rates at any level, knowing that customers had nowhere else to go for power.

To break this monopoly and lower customer rates, Roosevelt urged Congress to pass the Public Utilities Holding Company Act. Under this act, the government could forbid holding companies from owning more than one utility company in any one part of the country. The government could dissolve any holding company that could not prove that it was servicing a local area efficiently.

When the legislation was introduced, the powerful utilities mounted a million-dollar campaign to defeat it. But Congress passed it nonetheless. The Public Utilities Holding Company Act ended most of the large empires and put the rest under direct supervision of government agencies.

Providing Social Security

For Secretary of Labor Frances Perkins, providing security against poverty in old age and against wage loss during unemployment was a top priority. In fact, Perkins was so

concerned that she had refused to take her cabinet post until Roosevelt accepted her ideas for a program of old age and unemployment insurance. Once in office, she mobilized support for the program and, with the help of Senator Wagner, guided the legislation through Congress.

In September 1935 Congress passed the last piece of legislation of the second hundred days: the Social Security Act. The act created a national system of pensions for the elderly, supported by payments from employers, employees, and the federal government. It also established state-run insurance programs to provide unemployment compensation for people who lost their jobs. Finally, the act granted states money to provide support for the handicapped and dependent children.

Criticism of the Social Security Act was varied. Some people thought the bill did not go far enough in providing for the unemployed or the elderly. They argued that too many workers were not eligible to take part. Other people were alarmed by the idea of a public rather than a private insurance

Major Events	
1932	Franklin Roosevelt elected President
1933	National bank holiday ordered; Emergency Banking Relief Act, Civilian Conservation Reforestation Relief Act, Federal Emergency Relief Act, Agricultural Adjustment Act, and National Industrial Recovery Act passed; Tennessee Valley Authority formed
1934	American Liberty League formed
1935	Supreme Court declares National Industrial Recovery Act unconstitutional; Works Progress Administration formed; National Labor Relations Act, Public Utilities Holding Company Act, and Social Security Act passed
1936	Supreme Court declares Agricultural Adjustment Act unconstitutional

The Social Security Act created a separate fund in the federal treasury for old age and disability benefits. Critics said that Social Security was the first step toward socialism. To some, the idea of issuing a number to identify each citizen was an attack on the American tradition of individualism.

program. One business leader believed it would ruin the nation "by destroying initiative, discouraging thrift, and stifling individual responsibility." Despite the criticism, the Social Security Act continues as law today.

SECTION REVIEW

1. Identify: Robert F. Wagner.
2. Define: utility company.
3. (a) What problem led to creation of the Works Progress Administration in 1935? (b) How did the WPA try to solve it?
4. What did the National Youth Administration accomplish?
5. What rights did the Wagner Act guarantee to workers?
6. (a) What groups of people were affected by the Social Security Act of 1935? (b) Describe its major provisions.
7. **Critical Thinking** How are the services provided by utility companies different from those provided by other types of companies?

Chapter 32 Review

In Perspective

During the presidential campaign of 1932, Franklin Roosevelt promised the American people action. He did not have a specific plan for action, but he had a wealth of ideas, experiences, and advisers on which to rely. During the first hundred days, the administration produced a flood of legislation aimed at providing immediate relief and recovery from the Great Depression. These laws were designed to end bank closings, distribute money for food and clothing, and provide jobs for millions of unemployed. The AAA and NRA were created to further the recovery of agriculture and industry.

The early New Deal encountered considerable opposition. Some critics thought the programs did not do enough to help the American people. Others argued that the actions of the government threatened the free-enterprise economic system. In 1935 the Supreme Court ruled several New Deal laws unconstitutional.

Legislation passed during the second hundred days primarily concerned reforms, although the Works Progress Administration was another attempt to relieve widespread unemployment. Organized labor won important rights in the Wagner Act. The elderly and unemployed gained some protection from financial ruin through the Social Security Act. The government had acted as Roosevelt had promised in 1932, but whether its actions would end the Great Depression remained to be seen.

Vocabulary

On a separate sheet of paper, write the word or words that best complete each of the following sentences.

1. The ___ was a nickname for a group of Roosevelt's advisers.
2. The closing of banks for an indefinite period was referred to as the ___.
3. ___ commerce is commerce within the boundaries of one state.
4. The ___ were Roosevelt's radio broadcasts that explained government policies.
5. A (An) ___ is a company that distributes gas and electricity.

Chapter Checkup

1. Explain how each of the following contributed to the ideas of the New Deal: (a) progressivism, (b) lessons from the world war, (c) cabinet members.
2. (a) What two pieces of legislation did Congress pass during the first hundred days to provide immediate relief to the unemployed? (b) Describe the provisions of each act.
3. Explain why each of the following criticized the New Deal: (a) Huey Long, (b) Charles Coughlin, (c) Francis E. Townsend, (d) Raymond Moley
4. (a) What legislation made up the second hundred days? (b) What was the main purpose of that legislation?

Critical Thinking

1. **Comparing** (a) What advances did organized labor make during the New Deal? (b) How did those advances compare with the situation of labor during the early 1920s? (See Chapter 29.) (c) How might you explain the difference?
2. **Supporting an Opinion** (a) Why did some critics fear that the New Deal programs would undermine the free-enterprise system? (b) Do you think their concern was justified? Explain.

Developing Basic Skills

Due FDAY

1. **Classifying** Make a chart with three columns. In the first column list the New Deal laws described in this chapter. In the second column describe the problem or problems each law tried to solve. In the third column list the groups of people each law affected.

   After completing your chart, answer the following questions: (a) Which problem generated the largest number of laws? (b) What groups of people were affected by the New Deal legislation? (c) Which group was probably affected most? Explain.

2. **Relating Past to Present** Find out whether the Works Projects Administration sponsored any projects near where you live. (You may be able to learn about WPA projects from the local chamber of commerce or local historical society.) How do you think the WPA contributed to your community?

See page 832 for suggested readings.

Writer's Handbook

Avoiding Plagiarism

Plagiarism is copying information word for word or paraphrasing information without giving credit to the original source. Proper documentation can mean the difference between plagiarism and a well-written paper.

Practice: Compare each of the paragraphs below with the first paragraph in the Chapter Opener on page 592. Which paragraph is an example of plagiarism? Why?

1. Franklin D. Roosevelt was sworn in as President of the United States in March 1933. At that time the banking system was practically collapsing and one quarter of the population was unemployed. The people were desperate.

2. When Franklin Roosevelt took office in March 1933, he was faced with major concerns for the welfare of the nation. The people's confidence was at a low ebb: not only was one quarter of the population unemployed, but people's savings were threatened by the weak condition of the banking system.

33

The New Deal Continues

(1936–1939)

Years of Dust *by Ben Shahn*

Chapter Outline

1 *New Deal Gains and Losses*

2 *Further Reform*

3 *Life During the New Deal Years*

The situation in the United States seemed brighter in 1936 than it had in 1933. The bread lines had disappeared. The flood of bank closings had slowed to a trickle. Six million jobs had reopened in private industry. Farm income had increased. Nevertheless, 10 million American workers were still unemployed, and nearly 4 million more remained on government relief.

By 1936 the feeling of hopelessness and panic that had contributed to Franklin Roosevelt's election in 1932 had subsided. When Roosevelt was first inaugurated in March 1933, one leading senator had said, "Whatever laws the President thinks he may need to end the depression, Congress will jump through a hoop to put through." Now, three eventful years later, Congress was through hoop jumping. Roosevelt would meet more resistance to his New Deal in the years to come. Yet the New Deal was to continue, especially in the area of reform.

Renewed growth of organized labor

1935	1936	1937	1938	1939	1940

1935
Congress of Industrial Organizations founded

1936
Franklin D. Roosevelt reelected

1937
National Housing Act passed; recession begins

1938
Food, Drug, and Cosmetic Act passed; Fair Labor Standards Act passed

1939
Hatch Act passed; Executive Office of President created

1 New Deal Gains and Losses

In November 1936 the New Deal faced a nationwide test at the polls. Voters would have a chance to register their approval or disapproval of New Deal programs. In 1934 state and congressional elections had indicated approval. The Democrats had gained 20 new seats in the Senate and 18 in the House. Roosevelt and his administration seemed to have little cause for worry as the 1936 election approached. But support for the New Deal faltered in the months following the election.

The Election of 1936

The Republican party chose Governor Alfred M. Landon of Kansas to oppose Roosevelt in the election. Landon had an impressive political record. In 1934, when Democrats won widespread victories in state and congressional elections, he had been the only Republican governor in the nation to win reelection.

Landon represented the moderate wing of the Republican party, which accepted many of the New Deal efforts to use government power to fight the Great Depression. However, Landon's campaign attracted those who shared the strong anti-Roosevelt feeling held by some members of the business community. Such critics thought that Roosevelt's programs threatened the free-enterprise system. The family of millionaire J. P. Morgan, Jr., for example, asked visitors not to mention the President's name in Morgan's presence, fearing that his blood pressure would rise dangerously.

Roosevelt met such antagonism head on. At a campaign speech in Madison Square Garden in New York, he lashed out against his critics in business and financial circles. "Never before in all our history have these forces been so united against one candidate as they stand today," he told the cheering crowd. "They are unanimous in their hate for me—and I welcome their hatred."

When Landon opened his campaign, his criticism of the New Deal was moderate. He did not call for an end to Roosevelt's programs. Instead, he argued that Republicans could manage those programs more effectively, waste less money, and achieve longer-lasting results. But when this strategy brought little support, Landon stepped up his attack. By November, he was denouncing the Social Security Act as "unjust, unworkable, stupidly drafted, and wastefully financed."

The day before the election, Roosevelt's campaign manager accurately predicted that the President would carry every state except Maine and Vermont. Roosevelt won 61 percent of the popular vote, Landon 37 percent. The Union party, formed by followers of Father Coughlin, Dr. Townsend, and the late Huey Long, won 2 percent of the popular vote. Roosevelt and the New Deal seemed to have received an overwhelming vote of confidence from the people.

The Roosevelt Coalition

Much of the success the New Deal enjoyed at the polls stemmed from the Democratic coalition Roosevelt had carefully built since his election in 1932. Each group in the coalition had its own reasons for backing the Democratic party.

Before 1936 the Democrats had been the smaller of the two major parties. They drew membership from two very different sources. One source was the "solid South," where distaste for the Republican party remained since the Civil War and Reconstruction. The other source was the political machines of many big eastern and midwestern cities. Those party organizations could deliver votes for Democratic candidates with the regularity of well-oiled machinery. The votes came mainly from the immigrant groups that had most recently settled in the cities.

To that base Roosevelt added organized labor. The Wagner Act (see page 605) had given workers the right to organize without opposition from management. Consequently, organized labor not only voted Democratic in strength, but also became a major source of campaign funds.

Roosevelt and the New Deal were also able to attract black Americans to the Democratic party. Abraham Lincoln had issued the Emancipation Proclamation, and for years black voters had remained loyal to the Republicans, "the party of Lincoln." However, under the New Deal, the government began taking an active interest in the conditions of black life. Eleanor Roosevelt, especially, tried to see that New Deal programs did not discriminate against black Americans. Blacks were also brought into important government positions. (See page 604.)

Finally, Roosevelt attracted scholars to the Democratic party. Their number may have been small, but they had significant influence. As teachers, university professors, and writers, they helped mold public opinion by publicizing and popularizing Democratic party ideas and candidates. The coalition, first formed in 1936, was to strengthen the Democratic party and make it the majority party for decades to come.

An Attack on the Supreme Court

Roosevelt opened his second term as President with a spectacular announcement. In February 1937 he asked Congress to redesign the federal judiciary. He argued that there were too few federal judges, resulting in long delays before cases could be heard. Therefore he wanted more judges appointed.

The heart of the problem, Roosevelt said, was the Supreme Court. He believed the Court needed not only more justices but also younger ones. He recommended that the President have the power to appoint one additional justice for every justice on the Supreme Court aged 70 or over who refused to retire. The maximum number of justices on the Supreme Court would be increased from nine to fifteen.

Unfortunately for Roosevelt, his plan was recognized as an attack on the Supreme Court. As you have read, the Supreme Court had struck down several key pieces of early New Deal legislation. (See page 602.) The President feared that the Social Security Act and the Wagner Act might also fail to survive a court test.

The Court loomed as a major roadblock to the administration's plans. Four justices usually supported New Deal measures, but they were neutralized by the "Four Horsemen," as the conservative justices were known. The fate of most cases rested with Justice Owen Roberts, who often voted with the conservatives. Roosevelt thought the appointment of additional justices would create a sympathetic majority.

Roosevelt's political instincts had failed him, however. He was accused of trying to

Roosevelt's plan to increase the number of justices on the Supreme Court was widely seen as an attack on the Court itself. This cartoon shows Roosevelt asking Secretary of the Interior Harold Ickes for money from the Public Works Administration (PWA) to carry out his plan.

"pack" the Court, and opposition came from all sides. Critics of the New Deal who had worried all along that Roosevelt was out to destroy constitutional government in the United States saw their suspicions confirmed. Even supporters of Roosevelt on other issues began to desert him on this one. Upon hearing of Roosevelt's court plan, one supporter of the New Deal in Congress turned to reporters and said, "Boys, here's where I cash in my chips."

Few people believed the President's claim that he sought only to improve the Court's efficiency. Chief Justice Charles Evans Hughes pointed out that there was no significant delay in cases coming before the Court. He insisted that an increase in the number of justices might actually delay decisions. After a six-month battle, Roosevelt finally accepted defeat and withdrew his proposal for court reform.

The Supreme Court fight cost the President congressional and public support and badly divided the Democratic party. At the same time, however, there were two unexpected results. First, the Court suddenly began upholding New Deal legislation. Justice Roberts voted with the President's supporters to uphold all the key provisions of the Social Security Act as well as the Wagner Act and a minimum-wage law in the state of Washington.

Second, the retirement of one of the conservative justices gave Roosevelt the opportunity to make his first appointment, without the need for reorganization. By the end of his presidency, the President had appointed a total of eight associate justices and one chief justice. Looking back on the court fight of 1937, Roosevelt always claimed that although he had lost the battle, he had won the war.

The Economy Takes Another Plunge

The turmoil over court reform had barely begun to subside when the Roosevelt administration found itself deep in another crisis. During 1935 and 1936, the economy had slowly but steadily improved. By early 1937 several of Roosevelt's key advisers believed that many of the New Deal programs to stimulate economic recovery could wind down.

Those advisers believed that the government should reduce heavy expenditures in public works and employment programs. Now it was time to allow private enterprise to complete the recovery without federal aid. As Secretary of the Treasury Henry Morgenthau, Jr., later said, "this was the moment . . . to strip off the bandages, throw away the crutches, and see if American private enterprise could stand on its own feet." The President agreed that the time was right to cut government spending. Congress drastically reduced WPA programs and allocated no funds for new programs.

Meanwhile two other developments reduced the total amount of private spending in the economy. First, the Federal Reserve Board had raised interest rates, increasing the cost of loans for new factories and equipment. Thus, companies began to cut back. Second, new social security taxes on employers and employees left less money for business and consumer spending.

The combination of reduced government spending and the inability of private business to take up the slack resulted in a severe economic recession in the fall and winter of 1937–1938. Unemployment increased by 4 million in a seven-month period. Large inventories piled up in warehouses as reduced wages and loss of jobs decreased consumer spending. Across the nation, the economic collapse was actually sharper than in the first months of the Great Depression. Nearly all of the gains in employment and production were wiped out.

Despite the severe conditions, Roosevelt at first hesitated to act. He hoped private business could reverse the downward trend of the economy without the stimulus of renewed government spending for jobs and relief. By March 1938, however, the President decided that the government had to resort to deficit spending in order to stimulate the economy. *Deficit spending* is the practice of spending more money than is taken in

611

■ *This chart of the percentage of people out of work between 1932 and 1945 shows a rise in employment between 1933 and 1937. It seemed for a time that the end of the Great Depression was in sight. But with another recession in 1937 and 1938, joblessness rose again. How did World War II affect unemployment?*

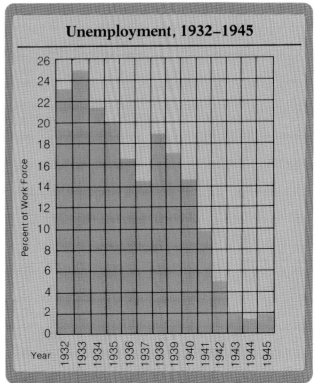

Source: *Historical Statistics of the United States*

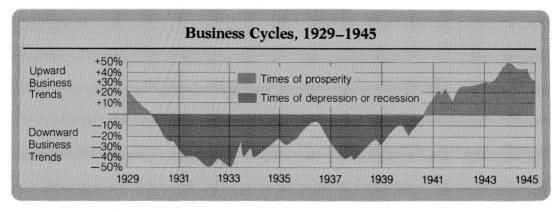

Business Cycles, 1929–1945

Upward Business Trends

+50%
+40%
+30%
+20%
+10%

Times of prosperity

Times of depression or recession

Downward Business Trends

−10%
−20%
−30%
−40%
−50%

1929 1931 1933 1935 1937 1939 1941 1943 1945

■ *This chart traces fluctuations in the business cycle between the stock market crash of 1929 and the end of World War II in 1945. Economic recovery from the Great Depression seemed near in 1936, but the deep slump of 1937–1938 signaled a new recession. As the chart shows, the depression did not finally end until the United States geared up for war production in 1941.*

from taxes. The recession of 1937–1938 showed the extent to which the New Deal policies of the previous five years had failed to bring about full recovery.

SECTION REVIEW

1. Identify: Alfred M. Landon.
2. Define: deficit spending.

3. What was Alfred Landon's original attitude toward the New Deal?
4. Describe the Democratic coalition of 1936.
5. What happened to the economy in the fall and winter of 1937–1938?
6. **Critical Thinking** Why do you think even Roosevelt's supporters opposed his plans for the Supreme Court?

2 Further Reform

As Roosevelt entered his second term, he continued to press for reform. The intended beneficiaries of such reform were primarily those hardest hit by the Great Depression: workers, farmers, and the poor.

The Growth of Organized Labor

The passage of the Wagner Act in 1935 was taken as a clear signal by labor unions to go ahead with further organization. The American Federation of Labor began a massive drive to recruit a million more workers into labor unions and thus increase its bargaining power.

For some union leaders in the AFL, the recruiting drive did not move fast enough. Furthermore, they thought that the AFL was concentrating too much on unions for skilled workers such as pipe fitters, machinists, and printers. Those leaders wanted to form

unions in large industries—such as steel, textile, and automobile manufacturing— which employed great numbers of unskilled laborers.

At the head of that faction was John L. Lewis, president of the United Mine Workers. At the 1935 AFL convention, he argued in favor of *industrial unions*, unions that would represent every worker in an entire industry, not just workers in skilled crafts. Many AFL leaders opposed this idea. In the heated debate that followed, Lewis punched William "Big Bill" Hutcheson of the Carpenters' Union and knocked him down. Lewis may have won the fist fight, but he did not win AFL support for his plan. As a result he and several other AFL union leaders formed a rival group of unions, later called the Congress of Industrial Organizations (CIO).

The CIO proceeded to organize workers in whole industries, as Lewis had demanded.

The organizers came into conflict with employers who resisted labor unions in spite of the Wagner Act. In response to such resistance, workers in the Goodyear tire factory in Akron, Ohio, developed a new type of action, the *sitdown strike*. One night at exactly 2:00 A.M., the workers stopped the production line. Then they sat down next to the idle machines and refused to leave the factory until their employers recognized the union. The employers chose not to use force to remove the workers because of the potential destruction of factory property.

Soon sitdown strikes spread to other industries. A common tactic of plant managers was to turn off the heat to force sitdown strikers out of the factory. Often the workers sang, danced, and roller-skated to keep warm. Even gravediggers in Kansas City and Chicago used the new sitdown tactic.

Strikes began to achieve success in the automobile industry. In 1937 a six-week sitdown strike closed several General Motors plants in Flint, Michigan. The company called in the police and the National Guard, but the union held out. Eventually General Motors recognized the United Automobile Workers as the employees' union, the first in the industry.

The steel industry proved even more difficult. Union organizers recalled the bloody battles of the early 1920s, when the steel industry had defeated several strikes for better working conditions. Unexpectedly, in 1937 the huge U.S. Steel Corporation agreed to recognize the Steel Workers Organizing Committee of the CIO. Other steel companies refused to follow that example, however, and violence resulted. In what became known as the Memorial Day Massacre, police shot and killed ten strikers at the Republic Steel Plant in Chicago. The National Labor Relations Board then stepped in and forced the steel industry to negotiate with the union.

Total union membership grew from fewer than 3 million in 1933 to nearly 9 million in 1939. Organized labor had clearly attained more economic and political power under the New Deal than ever before in history.

The Fair Labor Standards Act

Large numbers of workers were still unorganized by the union movement. For millions of laborers working conditions remained dismal. Shoe factory workers in New

Passage of the Wagner Act in 1935 opened the way to more aggressive labor organizing techniques. Unions made major efforts to organize automobile workers on an industrywide basis. In 1937 auto workers used a new technique, the sitdown strike. The strike closed General Motors for six weeks before the company agreed to recognize the United Auto Workers as its employee union.

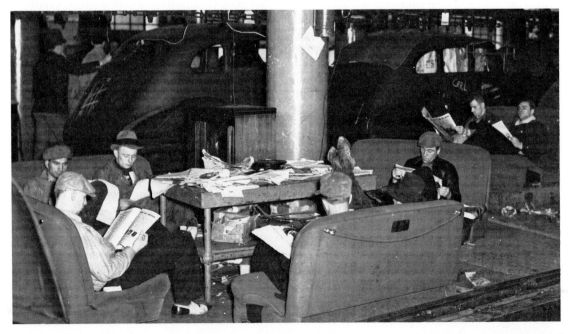

England earned only $853 per year. Cotton factory workers in the South averaged less than 40 cents an hour. Most worked 12 hours a day, six days a week throughout the year.

In 1937 Roosevelt urged Congress to pass a bill to improve wages and conditions for all workers in the country. He wanted a federal wages-and-hours law that would "put a floor below which wages shall not fall, and a ceiling beyond which the hours of industrial labor shall not rise."

Such a bill met with strong opposition, especially from business owners who felt that government was once again threatening private enterprise. Farmers also objected because they felt they could not pay workers as much as industries did. Only by agreeing to exclude a wide range of workers, such as agricultural laborers and domestic servants, did the supporters of the bill save it.

Finally, in June 1938, Congress passed the Fair Labor Standards Act. The act established minimum wages and maximum hours of work in a number of industries whose products were shipped across state lines. It also banned child labor under age 16 in industries engaged in interstate commerce. Furthermore, the act established a precedent for federal legislation to improve working conditions.

The Dust Bowl

Suffering severe hardships since the end of the World War, many farmers found it nearly impossible to survive the Great Depression. Then, in the midst of the economic disaster, large sections of the Midwest from Texas to the Dakotas suffered a drought from 1932 to 1936. Vast stretches of grassland and crops lay scorched and withered. The skies darkened as clouds of dust, thousands of feet across, arose from the sun-dried land, giving the area a new name, the Dust Bowl.

The clouds blew across the plains, so thick that train engineers were unable to read signal lights. Winds dropped trails of grit and dirt everywhere. As far east as Cleveland and Memphis, people had to mask their faces with handkerchiefs to protect themselves from the "black blizzards." Red snow fell on New England, and sailors in the Atlantic found traces of Nebraska soil.

Many midwestern farmers watched helplessly as their land was blown away and what was left of their farms was taken over by banks and land companies. Thousands of families sadly loaded their possessions into old cars or trucks and headed west.

Over a million "Okies" or "Arkies," so named because they came from Oklahoma and Arkansas, made the weary trek along Highway 66 toward the Pacific coast. They sought work in the orchards, orange groves, and lettuce fields of Washington, Oregon, and California. For many, however, the end of the journey brought, not work, but eviction by sheriffs and self-appointed vigilantes of western towns. Westerners had their own unemployment problems and wanted no outside competition.

Tenant Farming and Sharecropping

The poverty of the Okies and the Arkies was matched by that of another farming group: the tenant farmers and sharecroppers of the southern cotton belt. Too poor to buy land of their own, these farmers rented a few acres, from which they struggled to obtain a meager living. Each spring they borrowed enough money from a bank or the landowner to plant a crop, usually cotton, in the field. When the crop was harvested in the fall, the farmers used it to pay off the loan, keeping what was left over for themselves. With worsening economic conditions, there was almost nothing left. Each year the farmers were driven deeper into debt.

The early farm policies of the New Deal actually worsened the plight of tenants and sharecroppers. By reducing the number of acres in production in order to cut surpluses, the Agricultural Adjustment Act forced these people off the land they worked. Unlike the landowners, who were paid for agreeing not to produce, the tenants and sharecroppers received nothing in return.

Agricultural Reforms

The Roosevelt administration grew increasingly aware of the problems of rural poverty and searched for new ways to overcome it. One attempt had been the Resettlement Administration (RA), established in 1935 to resettle poor farmers on good land and provide sufficient equipment and advice for them to make a fresh start. But the program received little support and was hampered by lack of funds. As a result the RA resettled only 4,441 families, compared to the projected goal of 500,000.

In 1937 the Farm Security Administration (FSA) replaced the Resettlement Administration. The FSA extended loans to help tenants and sharecroppers buy farms and equipment. By 1940 short-term loans were made to more than 800,000 farm families and long-term farm-purchase loans to another 13,600. One other New Deal action helped ease the drudgery of life for many farmers. The Rural Electrification Administration loaned money for building electric power lines, thus extending electricity to isolated rural areas.

Soil conservation became another New Deal priority. The President himself inspired one way to attack drought. At his urging, the Forest Service planted a "shelter belt" of trees across the open plains. These trees blocked wind, held moisture and soil, and provided a refuge for animals.

In 1936 President Roosevelt signed the Soil Conservation and Domestic Allotment Act. Provisions of the act encouraged farmers to stop growing soil-depleting crops like corn, tobacco, cotton, and wheat on part of their land. They were to substitute soil-enriching land cover such as grass and soybeans to revive the fertility of the soil. In addition, farmers would receive payments from the government to compensate them for lost crops.

A New Agricultural Adjustment Act

When the Supreme Court struck down the Agricultural Adjustment Act in 1936, the government lost a way of limiting farm surpluses. As the four-year drought ended, surpluses began to reappear, threatening the gains farm prices had made earlier. Secretary of Agriculture Henry Wallace ironically complained that if there was a good harvest "we would be sunk." To solve the new farm problem and help alleviate future difficulties, Congress passed the second Agricultural Adjustment Act in 1938.

Under the new act the government could once again call on farmers to limit their crops. But payments for such limitations could not come from the processing tax that had caused the first Agricultural Adjustment Act to be struck down. Money would come instead from congressional appropriations. Crop production could be limited either through crop allotments—set amounts that each farmer was allowed to grow—or by taking land out of production

for soil conservation. The second Agriculture Adjustment Act also insured wheat farmers against drought losses.

Finally, the act put into practice Wallace's plan for an "ever-normal granary." Under this plan, crop surpluses would not be sold on the open market. Instead the government would buy the crops and store them for use in times of poor harvests. In this way farm products would be available in steady supply.

Other New Deal Reforms

In Roosevelt's second inaugural speech he had stated that one third of the nation was still "ill-housed, ill-clad, and ill-nourished." The National Housing Act was passed in 1937 to do something for the ill-housed. The act provided loans to stimulate the construction industry to provide new housing for low-income families in rural and urban communities. It also created the United States Housing Authority, which in only a few years helped fund more than 150,000 new housing units.

To give consumers better protection in the marketplace, Congress passed the Food, Drug, and Cosmetic Act in 1938. It was a much stronger piece of legislation than the 1906 Pure Food and Drug Act. For the first time manufacturers were ordered to list the ingredients of certain products on the package. The new law also required that new drugs be rigidly tested before they could be sold.

In 1939 Congress passed the Hatch Act to prevent abuses of power by government officials. The need for such an act came to light as a result of scandals connected with the WPA. Some officials had granted people relief payments only in return for promises to vote for Democratic candidates. One series of newspaper stories charged that a Kentucky senator's reelection had been "bought with WPA votes." The Hatch Act forbade government employees, except those in policy-making positions, from actively participating in political campaigns.

One reform few people noticed at the time was to have far-reaching consequences in later years. In 1939, in response to the growing demands on the presidency, Roosevelt issued Executive Order 8248, by which he created the Executive Office of the President. The new office included administrative assistants, press secretaries, budget officers,

The FSA Photographs: Faces of Rural America

Crops froze in the California pea fields in the spring of 1936. Photographer Dorothea Lange recalled the scene:

I saw and approached the hungry and desperate mother as if drawn by a magnet. . . . She asked me no questions. . . . I did not ask her name. . . . She said that they had been living on frozen vegetables from the surrounding fields, and birds that the children had killed. She had just sold the tires from the car to buy food.

The photograph Lange took of that mother and her children (below) is one of the best known in an extraordinary collection. Lange and ten other photographers worked for the Historical Section of the Farm Security Administration (FSA). Their assignment was to create a pictorial record of life in rural America during the Great Depression.

Dorothea Lange, Walker Evans, and Ben Shahn, better known as a graphic artist and painter (his lithograph *Years of Dust* appears on page 608), were among the individuals hired for the project.

FSA photographers shot pictures during frigid New England winters, when their cameras sometimes froze. They recorded cotton pickers in Mississippi, the laughter of an elderly midwestern couple, and a thousand other scenes of rural life. Yet it was the stark images of sharecroppers in wretched shacks, of dusty migrant families, and of the haunted eyes of fathers and mothers unable to feed their children that left the strongest impressions on viewers. These photographs, available free to newspapers and magazines, helped awaken city people and Congress to the urgency of rural suffering. In an era before television, the FSA collection brought home the reality of desperate poverty.

Arthur Rothstein

Dorothea Lange

Dorothea Lange

legal counsels, and other assistants. Later Presidents were to add more positions, and the Executive Office became an important part of the executive branch of government.

SECTION REVIEW

1. Identify: John L. Lewis, Congress of Industrial Organizations, Farm Security Administration, second Agricultural Adjustment Act.

2. Define: industrial union, sitdown strike.
3. What type of workers did John L. Lewis want to organize?
4. What were the two major provisions of the Fair Labor Standards Act?
5. What two disasters affected many farmers in the Midwest during the 1930s?
6. **Critical Thinking** What are arguments for and against the Hatch Act?

3 Life During the New Deal Years

Nearly everyone who lived through the Great Depression would carry vivid memories of the hardships for the rest of their lives. Those memories would be passed down to children and grandchildren in the form of advice about family budgets, borrowing and spending money, and the importance of financial security.

The depression upset traditional ideas about the "American dream." People who had worked hard all their lives and saved their money to provide a secure future lost everything when a bank closed or a business failed. Hard-working people lived in poverty because of forces over which they had no control. Children watched as shock and helplessness overpowered their parents. "I remember how, after dinner, my father would just lie on the couch in utter despair, night after night for hours," recalled one adult many years later.

The Search for Entertainment

Americans everywhere needed diversion from daily worries. Talking pictures and radio were popular sources of entertainment. Many people could afford a radio. Movie theaters charged only 25 cents and gave away free dishes one night a week.

The 1930s were the golden years of the American film industry, and Hollywood, California, was its headquarters. Before the New Deal, many movies questioned traditional values. Gangsters were frequently movie heroes. In films such as *Little Caesar*, *Public Enemy*, and *Scarface*, gangsters combined ambition, hard work, and loyalty in order to get ahead in a chaotic world. Those

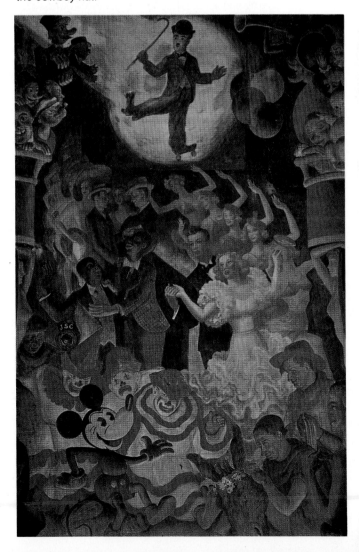

This 1937 mural, entitled Comedy, *was painted by John Steuart Curry. Curry included familiar faces from movies and cartoons as well as portraits of popular radio personalities. Will Rogers appears in the cowboy hat.*

who were normally expected to uphold law and order, including police, lawyers, and politicians, were often shown as dishonest and corrupt. Social disorder was even the subject of movie comedies such as the Marx Brothers' *Duck Soup* and Mae West's *She Done Him Wrong*.

With the coming of the New Deal, Hollywood moved in a new direction. Comedies with stars like Cary Grant, Katharine Hepburn, and Irene Dunne showed how even when the world seemed totally confused, the social order still worked. New dramas made heroes of federal government agents who relentlessly stalked criminals. Lavish musicals, film versions of the classics of literature, and huge epics such as Margaret Mitchell's Civil War story *Gone With the Wind* gave audiences a chance to escape, for a few hours at least, from the troubles of the real world.

The Great Depression had badly shaken Americans' faith in their society. Many Hollywood directors and producers set out to restore that faith and rebuild confidence in the value of hard work, perseverance, and moderation. Walt Disney's cartoon character Mickey Mouse embodied the ideals of initiative and enterprise. In the *Three Little Pigs*, Disney used an old story that captured the purposeful spirit of the New Deal. When the pigs in the cartoon sang "Who's Afraid of the Big, Bad Wolf?" many in the audience recognized the big, bad wolf as a symbol of the depression.

Director Frank Capra introduced Americans to populist-style heroes in *Mr. Smith Goes to Washington*, starring James Stewart, and in *Mr. Deeds Goes to Town* and *Meet John Doe*, starring Gary Cooper. Capra's heroes struggled against corrupt power. They met humiliation and frustration, but with the help of "ordinary" people, they accomplished their missions.

Like the movie industry, the radio broadcasting industry thrived during hard times. As the depression forced vaudeville theaters to close, talent flooded the airwaves. Such stars as George Burns, Gracie Allen, Jack Benny, Mary Livingston, Ed Wynn, and Fred Allen offered listeners comic relief. With so many people out of work and at home, daytime radio serials drew large audiences. These popular shows were called soap operas because soap companies often sponsored them.

Art Reflects the Times

The cruelty of the depression years was powerfully portrayed by American artists and writers. One of the best-known novels of the 1930s was John Steinbeck's *Grapes of Wrath*. In it the author traced the painful and heartbreaking migration of Okies and Arkies westward to California.

Dorothea Lange captured pitiful Dust Bowl scenes in photographs later published in *An American Exodus*. Photographer Margaret Bourke-White vividly portrayed rural poverty in the South in *You Have Seen Their Faces*, as did photographer Walker Evans and writer James Agee in *Let Us Now Praise Famous Men*. Richard Wright's novels *Uncle Tom's Children* and *Native Son* opened many Americans' eyes to what it meant to grow up as a black youth during the Great Depression.

Because of WPA-supported projects in literature, painting, and sculpture, many writers and artists were able to carry on their work. Often the work reflected the search for common themes that could bind the country together.

The past was given new emphasis as writers compiled histories of each state and wrote biographies of figures such as Benjamin Franklin and Abraham Lincoln. Painters used walls of public buildings for giant murals of farmers at work in the countryside and construction workers erecting huge projects in the cities. Federal funds enabled the sculptor Gutzon Borglum to continue carving the massive heads of Washington, Jefferson, Lincoln, and Theodore Roosevelt on Mount Rushmore in the Black Hills of South Dakota.

Black Americans and the New Deal

For black Americans the depression worsened an already intolerable situation. They continued to be victims of racial discrimination in both the North and the South. Many could live only in segregated areas, and most were paid less for their work than whites were paid.

Blacks who had jobs in industries in the North found themselves the objects of the "last hired, first fired" employment policy. They were often the first to be laid off in any cutback. Black tenant farmers and sharecroppers in the South frequently lost their

In the process of creating jobs, the Works Progress Administration (WPA) became a patron of the arts on a grand scale. The WPA gave jobs to writers, photographers, sculptors, and painters. This mural by William Gropper captures the monumental scope of such WPA projects as dam building.

land as a result of surplus reduction policies. (See page 614.) Furthermore, lynching of blacks increased during the tense early years of the depression. Over 60 blacks lost their lives to lynch mobs between 1930 and 1934.

President Franklin Roosevelt denounced the lynchings as "collective murder," but he refused to encourage a bill in Congress that would have made lynching a federal crime. Southern legislators controlled key committees in the House and Senate, and the President needed their support for his economic programs. "I did not choose the tools with which I must work," he told black leaders who urged him to support the bill. "If I come out for an anti-lynching bill now, they will block every bill I ask Congress to pass, to keep America from collapsing. I just can't take that risk."

Black Americans witnessed some improvement during the New Deal, however. As you have read, Eleanor Roosevelt, as well as Harry Hopkins and Harold Ickes, tried to prevent discrimination against blacks in the relief and job programs of the New Deal. Thousands of young black men received the opportunity to learn a trade through the Civilian Conservation Corps. More blacks than ever before were appointed to impor-

tant government positions during the New Deal. Although no legislation was passed to protect civil rights or end discrimination, the New Deal offered black Americans greater hope for political and social improvement than they had had before.

Attempts to Improve Life for Native Americans

During the 1930s John Collier directed the Bureau of Indian Affairs. Collier was deeply committed to assisting Native Americans in the West and Southwest. With the support of President Roosevelt, he worked to extend the benefits of New Deal relief and job programs to Indians.

Under Collier's leadership, the sale of land originally granted to Indians was stopped. In addition, a special Indian Emergency Conservation Work group was established under the CCC. The group employed Indians in programs of soil erosion control, irrigation, and land development.

By improving agriculture, Collier helped to improve Native Americans' economic position in their local communities. The Indian Reorganization Act of 1934 was a further effort to better Native American life. Funds were set up to provide scholarships for

619

promising students and to help Indians set up their own businesses.

Expulsion of Mexican Americans

As you read earlier, hundreds of thousands of Mexicans had been migrating to California and the Southwest since the early 1900s. (See page 567.) Most of these people labored as migrant workers or found jobs in local industries or in coal and copper mines. As much of the country became the Dust Bowl and as factories and mines closed during the depression, many Americans who had been happy about the influx of cheap labor now saw the Mexican workers as serious competition for the few remaining jobs.

Popular unrest in the region convinced government officials to adopt a deportation policy whereby thousands of families were uprooted and sent back to Mexico. The majority of those families had children born in the United States. The children were therefore American citizens, but the government refused to honor their rights.

Small Gains for Women

During the 1920s women had made some economic gains, entering the work force in greater numbers and holding jobs with higher status and incomes. But when depression struck, women were often forced out of their jobs, and men were hired to replace

them. It was argued that since men were the "breadwinners" in the average family, they should have what jobs were available. Many companies refused to hire a woman if her husband had a job.

In 1932 Franklin Roosevelt appointed Mary Dewson, an officer of a national consumers' organization, to coordinate women's activities in the presidential campaign and later in the administration. She urged Roosevelt to support the rights of women in two ways. First, Dewson persuaded the President to appoint women to important posts in the administration. The most notable was Secretary of Labor Frances Perkins. Roosevelt also appointed the first women to serve as minister to a foreign nation, as director of the United States mint, and as judge in a circuit court of appeals. Mary Dewson also worked for equal treatment of women in New Deal programs.

Eleanor Roosevelt was the most visible champion of women's rights during the New Deal. After her husband was elected President, she began holding her own press conferences—for women reporters only. Since her activities and statements frequently became front-page news, her press conferences gave women reporters a chance to publish major stories before male reporters. The First Lady had her own syndicated newspaper column, called "My Day," and her own radio program. She was also active in the League of Women Voters and the Women's Trade Union League.

The efforts of such women as Mary Dewson, Frances Perkins, and Eleanor Roosevelt showed American women that they might gain more political, social, and economic equality by supporting the New Deal.

Impact of the New Deal

After 1938 the New Deal lost most of its momentum. Americans began to turn their attention to events in Europe and Asia that were propelling the world toward war. The depression seemed to be under control, but it had not ended. Six million Americans were still unemployed.

Yet the New Deal had profoundly affected American life and government. For one thing, Franklin Roosevelt had shown Americans that a democratic republic could survive a severe crisis without becoming a dictatorship. Through the New Deal, the government had taken a moderate course. It

Eleanor Roosevelt was a niece of Theodore Roosevelt and a distant cousin of her husband, Franklin. She became an outspoken advocate for the jobless, the disadvantaged, and minorities. A tireless traveler, Roosevelt is shown here speaking in Tennessee.

had preserved the free enterprise system by reforming it.

New Deal programs had greatly increased the size and scope of the federal government. The government had assumed a much larger role in the economy. Government regulation of big business and the control of monopoly did not originate with the New Deal, but the banking, securities, and public utility legislation of the period expanded the concept. For the first time, in the United States at least, the government had acted as an employer of the unemployed and a sponsor of work projects.

People's views about the responsibility of government had also changed during the New Deal. Before the 1930s, most people viewed government assistance to the needy as charity, something that humiliated those forced to accept it. But the New Deal fostered the idea that people were entitled to public assistance when they became victims of economic conditions over which they had no control.

SKILL LESSON

A View of the New Deal: Analyzing Oral Evidence

A tape-recorded oral account of an event can be a valuable historical document. It can help you understand how historical events affect people and can give you insight into what it was like to live during a specific time. The extract at right is transcribed from part of an interview with David Kennedy in the late 1960s. Kennedy had served on the Federal Reserve Board during the New Deal. At the time of the interview he was the chairman of the board of a major company. Follow the steps below to analyze the document.

1. **Identify the source of the document.** (a) Who was interviewed? (b) When did the interview take place?

2. **Decide how reliable the evidence is.** (a) What was the person's role in the events being described? How might his role affect his interpretation? (b) How long after the event did the interview take place? How might that affect his account? (c) How might the person's position at the time of the interview affect his account?

3. **Study the evidence to learn more about an historical event.** (a) How does the person think President Roosevelt may have helped the nation early in the New Deal? (b) How did his attitude toward Roosevelt change? Why? (c) What can you learn about the effect of the New Deal from this document?

David Kennedy

Roosevelt gave us quite a bit of hope early. He probably saved us from complete collapse in that sense. But he did not answer the things. Many of his programs were turned on and off, started and stopped . . . shifting gears. Because we had never been in anything like this.

Planning had not been done. So they'd go out and sweep the mountains and clean up the debris, and then the wind comes along and blows it back again. It gave some work. But the people that got the money in some ways were benefited and in other ways were hurt. They didn't like to see the waste. . . . They had mixed reactions. . . .

I was enthusiastic when Roosevelt came in. I thought: We're in serious trouble. Something has to be done, and here's a man that's going to do it. I voted for him his first term and his second. After that, I voted against him. It wasn't just on the two-term basis, although that was important. The packing of the Supreme Court and the fact that we were not making the progress I thought our country was capable of making . . . I became terribly disenchanted.

He was a dramatic leader. He had charm, personality, poise, and so on. He could inspire people. But to me, he lacked the stick-to-it-iveness to carry a program through.

Source: Studs Terkel, *Hard Times* (New York: Avon, 1970).

Before 1933 most Americans considered the federal government remote from their lives. By 1939 it was hard to find anyone who did not have a friend or relative who owed a job, house, farm, education, or some other benefit to a New Deal program. Defenders of the New Deal pointed to that fact with pride. Never before, they argued, had people had security against old age or unemployment.

However, critics charged that the growth of the federal government threatened American values and traditions. The ideals of individual initiative and free enterprise, they argued, were being undermined.

Debate about whether the changes brought about by the New Deal were good for the nation has continued. Yet few people deny that the New Deal had a major effect on government, the economy, and society.

Major Events

1935	Congress of Industrial Organizations founded
1936	Roosevelt elected for second term
1937	Roosevelt proposes redesign of judiciary; Farm Security Administration established; National Housing Act passed; severe recession begins
1938	Second Agricultural Adjustment Act; Food, Drug, and Cosmetic Act; and Fair Labor Standards Act passed
1939	Hatch Act passed; Executive Order 8248 issued

SECTION REVIEW

1. Identify: John Steinbeck, Dorothea Lange, Margaret Bourke-White, Walker Evans, James Agee, Richard Wright, John Collier, Mary Dewson.
2. List two ways black Americans were affected by the New Deal.
3. What was the main activity of the Indian Emergency Conservation Work Group?
4. What impact did the depression have on Mexican workers in the United States?
5. What government posts did women hold in Roosevelt's administration?
6. **Critical Thinking** How did artists and writers contribute to an understanding of the effects of the depression?

 # Chapter 33 Review

In Perspective

In 1936 over 60 percent of American voters indicated their support for Franklin Roosevelt by electing him to a second term. Soon, however, even some of his strongest supporters questioned his attempt to "pack" the Supreme Court. A severe recession in 1937 and 1938 revealed that although New Deal programs had temporarily relieved unemployment, the problems underlying the depression had not been solved.

During his second term, Roosevelt continued to support reform measures that benefited workers and farmers. The Congress of Industrial Organizations helped unskilled workers organize for the first time. Farmers were especially hard hit during the 1930s because of a severe drought, but several new laws were designed to improve conditions for them.

The Great Depression devastated the lives of millions of Americans, and many sought escape through movies and radio. Artists documented the effect of the depression, and many chose themes that would encourage economic recovery. In some ways the reform spirit of the New Deal improved conditions for black Americans, women, and Native Americans, but many Mexican workers were forced to return to Mexico. Although the New Deal did not end the depression, it did result in rapid growth in the size and influence of the federal government.

Vocabulary

On a separate sheet of paper, write the word or words that best complete each of the following sentences.

1. ____ represent everyone in a particular industry.
2. ____ is the practice of spending more money than is taken in.
3. Fluctuations between times of prosperity and times of depression or recession are called _Business cycle - Slump_
4. The term, the ____, referred to the area in the Midwest beset by drought during the Great Depression.
5. During a ____, workers refuse to leave the work place until their demands are met.

Chapter Checkup

1. (a) What groups comprised Roosevelt's coalition in the 1936 election? (b) How had the Democrats won the support of organized labor and black Americans?
2. (a) How did drought from 1932 through 1936 affect midwestern farmers? (b) What actions did the Roosevelt administration take to try to alleviate the problems of farmers?
3. Why was the Great Depression a difficult time for many black Americans?
4. How did John Collier try to improve the conditions for Native Americans?
5. How did the onset of the depression affect women working outside the home?

Critical Thinking

1. **Analyzing** (a) How did movies and radio help Americans cope with the effects of the Great Depression? (b) What values did many movies try to reinforce? (c) What impact do you think the efforts of filmmakers had on people at the time?
2. **Supporting a Point of View** Many observers believed that President Roosevelt's plan to add justices to the Supreme Court would have upset the system of checks and balances. Do you agree or disagree with that view? Why?

Developing Basic Skills

1. **Using Visual Evidence** The painting on page 619 was done as a WPA project. (a) What is shown in the painting? (b) How does the painting reflect the goals of the New Deal? (c) What message do you think the artist was trying to convey to people living during the Great Depression?
2. **Collecting Evidence** In this chapter you have read an oral history. (See page 621.) Talk with someone you know who lived during the 1930s and ask what life was like during the Great Depression. Write a report about what you learned.

See page 832 for suggested readings.

Writer's Handbook

Organizing Note Cards

To organize the information you have gathered for your research paper look at the subject you have written in the corner of each note card. Correlate the cards with the divisions in your preliminary outline. Choose those cards that support your thesis statement and are related to the outline topics. Decide on the order of supporting information you will use under each topic. (See page 111.) Arrange your cards in that order.

Practice: Imagine that one of the subheadings in an outline you have prepared for a paper on the New Deal is "New Deal Reforms." Which of the following notecard topics would correlate with that subhead? Explain your choices.

1. Fair Labor Standards Act
2. "black blizzards"
3. Hatch Act
4. Supreme Court
5. sitdown strike
6. Agricultural Adjustment Act
7. National Housing Act
8. Executive Order 8248

Prelude to Another World Conflict 34

(1920–1941)

The front page of the New York Times, September 1, 1939, as war begins in Europe

Between 1920 and 1941 most Americans were preoccupied with events at home. During the Roaring Twenties the desire to "get rich quick" and to take part in the gaiety of the age seemed more important than distant events in Europe and Asia. During the Great Depression of the 1930s, millions of Americans had to concentrate on simply surviving from day to day. They read about political turmoil in Germany, but such developments seemed far removed from the burdens of their own lives.

Japanese aggression in Asia and the rise of dictatorships in Italy and Germany threatened world peace. Yet even after war broke out in Europe in 1939, Americans still hoped to avoid the conflict. Eventually, however, actions by Japan were to end American isolationism.

Aggression in Europe and Asia

1921	1925	1929	1933	1937	1941

1921 Washington Naval Conference

1924 Dawes Plan adopted

1928 Kellogg-Briand Pact signed

1931 Japan invades China

1933 Hitler seizes power in Germany

1936 Germany invades Rhineland; Spanish Civil War begins

1939 Germany invades Poland; World War II begins

1941 Japan attacks Pearl Harbor; U.S. enters World War II

1 American Diplomacy From Harding to Hoover

Americans were weary of foreign involvements after the World War, and the Presidents they elected during the 1920s shared those feelings. President Harding shunned a major American role in world affairs. He remained true to his promise that "normalcy" would be restored during his administration. His successors in the White House, Calvin Coolidge and Herbert Hoover, were also hesitant to plunge the United States into the complexities of world affairs.

Despite a deep distrust in foreign affairs, the American people did accept some policies requiring cooperation with other nations. Limited cooperation emerged as a major theme of United States foreign policy during the 1920s.

Isolation Versus World Cooperation

During the 1920s most government officials and many citizens were *isolationists*, that is, they believed that the United States should avoid alliances and entangling agreements with other nations. Isolationism kept the United States from joining the League of Nations. (See page 540.) Rather than sign the Treaty of Versailles, which contained a provision for league membership, the United States negotiated a separate peace treaty with Germany in 1921.

President Harding was also hostile to membership in the League of Nations. The United States, Harding declared in 1923, "does not propose to enter [the league] now by the side door, or the back door, or the cellar door."

No matter how strong the isolationist mood, the United States could not stand aloof from world affairs. After the World War, Japan had begun building a powerful navy to support its goal of creating a Pacific empire. Great Britain and the United States opposed such actions. As a result all three nations became involved in a naval arms race, competing to build more battleships and cruisers.

In 1921 President Harding asked representatives of nine Asian and European nations to meet in Washington to discuss ways to ease tensions in the Pacific. American Secretary of State Charles Evans Hughes startled the delegates when he proposed a limit on construction of large warships for ten years. The delegates to the Washington Naval Conference finally agreed that for every five large ships the United States or Britain owned, Japan could have three, and France and Italy could have one and three fourths.

Japan resented its inferior position under the new treaty. Therefore the United States, Britain, and France offered a Four Power Treaty. Along with Japan, they agreed to respect each others' rights in the Pacific and to refer any future disputes to a conference. The delegates also signed a Nine Power Treaty in which they formally accepted the Open Door policy toward China.

The Washington Naval Conference seemed to be an important step toward peace. It eased the arms race and tensions in the Pacific. Soon, however, all the agreements came undone. Nations avoided them by building smaller warships and submarines. Japan also continued to strive for a Pacific empire.

As international tensions increased in the late 1920s, United States Secretary of State Frank B. Kellogg and French Foreign Minister Aristide Briand proposed a pact to try to guarantee peace. In 1928, 15 nations signed the Kellogg-Briand Pact, outlawing war except in cases of self-defense. Eventually, most other nations joined the pact, but there was no military or political organization to enforce it. Senator Carter Glass of Virginia said the treaty was worth no more than a postage stamp, but he voted with 84 other senators to consent to it.

During the 1920s the United States also participated in many League of Nations conferences on international trade, communications, and transportation. Still, United States tariff policy showed the strength of isolationist sentiments. The Fordney-McCumber Act of 1922 had raised most tariff rates. During the first years of the Great Depression, the Hawley-Smoot Act of 1931 raised rates even more. Those highly protective tariffs disrupted world trade and made the depression worse for all nations.

The United States in the World Economy

The United States took a direct role in the world economy in 1923 when Germany, devastated by wild inflation, failed to make reparation payments to France.* In reaction French troops occupied the Ruhr region of Germany, threatening the delicate balance of power. In 1924, to help Germany pay reparations to France, the United States proposed the Dawes Plan, named after banker Charles G. Dawes.

According to the plan, the United States would lend money to Germany. Germany would then use the loan to pay reparations to France and the other Allies. The Allies, in turn, would be able to repay their wartime debts to the United States by drawing on the reparations received from Germany. The Dawes Plan rescued Germany from economic ruin and enabled the Allies to repay the United States.

Despite isolationist sentiment and high tariffs, the 1920s was a period of growing international trade and investment for the United States. The nation emerged from the World War with a strong economy. Many factories and farms in Europe had been destroyed during the war, but United States industry and agriculture was undamaged.

Exports soared in 1919 and 1920 and then slackened as the national economies of Europe recovered. Nonetheless, in 1925 the volume of United States exports was almost double what it had been in 1913. Investment abroad also grew as American companies built manufacturing plants in Europe and established an interest in Middle Eastern oil fields.

Policy Toward Latin America

United States policy toward Latin America was not one of isolationism. Unstable conditions in several Latin American nations prompted the United States to send in troops to restore order. During the early 1920s United States soldiers were stationed in Panama, the Dominican Republic, and Honduras. The marines, in Nicaragua since 1912, withdrew in 1925. But when civil war broke

---

*As you read in Chapter 28, reparations were penalty payments that Germany was to make to the Allies for war damages.

out in 1928, the marines were sent back to Nicaragua to fight antigovernment forces and enforce a free election.

By the end of the decade, the pattern of military intervention was coming to an end. Under fire from progressives in his own party, President Coolidge placed less emphasis on armed intervention in Latin America. Developments in Mexico tested Coolidge's ability to deal with a Latin American neighbor without resorting to force.

In 1927 the Mexican congress passed a law limiting United States ownership of Mexican oil resources to 50 years. President Coolidge appointed Dwight W. Morrow, a prominant banker, to negotiate with the Mexican government. Morrow was instructed "to keep us out of war." The resulting agreement allowed United States corporations to retain oil properties acquired before 1917. Morrow's success encouraged the United States to continue this more peaceful approach to Latin American affairs.

In 1928 Undersecretary of State J. Reuben Clark drew up a memorandum stating that the United States did not have a right to intervene militarily in the affairs of Latin American nations. Officially released by the Hoover Administration in 1930, the Clark Memorandum was warmly received throughout Latin America. Within a short time President Hoover demonstrated that he meant to honor the principle of nonintervention. He refrained from sending troops to El Salvador in 1932 when that country failed to repay some debts. He also agreed to withdraw troops from Haiti.

War in Asia

Developments in Asia threatened world peace when, in 1931, Japanese troops began to occupy the northern Chinese province of Manchuria. China petitioned the League of Nations for help. The league considered an economic boycott against Japan and asked the United States to participate. The Hoover administration refused, and the league took no action. Manchuria fell in January 1932, and Japan set up a "puppet" state, that is, one controlled by Japan. In February the Japanese air force bombed Shanghai, killing many civilians.

Japanese aggression outraged Americans, but the United States did not want to become involved in a war on the other side of the world. Unable to make even mild threats, Secretary of State Henry L. Stimson issued a statement, known as the Stimson Doctrine. He declared that the United States would refuse to recognize Japanese territorial gains in China. Although the Stimson Doctrine was a declaration of American opposition to Japanese aggression, no proposals for concrete action against Japan were included.

Most Americans, fearing that the United States would be drawn into an Asian war, supported President Hoover's cautious policy toward Japan. Only a minority of the population, known as *internationalists,* wanted the United States to abandon the policy of isolation and take a more active role in world affairs. They warned that American inaction would encourage hostile acts by aggressive powers.

SECTION REVIEW

1. Identify: Kellogg-Briand Pact, Dawes Plan, Clark Memorandum, Stimson Doctrine.
2. Define: isolationist, internationalist.
3. What were two results of the Dawes Plan?
4. What agreement was reached with Mexico with respect to oil rights in Mexico?
5. **Critical Thinking** How does the policy of the United States toward Nicaragua today compare with its policy in the 1920s?

2 International Challenges During the 1930s

The Great Depression dominated the lives of nearly all Americans during the 1930s. People concentrated on immediate problems such as jobs, food, clothing, and shelter. They paid little attention to international events. But aggressive acts by Germany, Italy, and Japan eventually forced the United States to become involved in world affairs.

Rise of Totalitarian Dictatorships

By the mid-1930s dictators had established totalitarian governments in Italy and Germany. In a *totalitarian state* the government is supreme and individuals have few rights. All constitutional representation and political opposition is forbidden.

Benito Mussolini had established himself as dictator of Italy in 1922. His followers, known as Fascists, suspended elections and crushed all opposition. Mussolini put the Italian economy under strict government supervision and began to modernize the armed forces. To his people, he held out the promise that Italy would become a great power in the Mediterranean region and in Africa.

The military gradually assumed control of Japan after 1930, and Emperor Hirohito became little more than a figurehead. The aggression in Manchuria was only the beginning of an effort to secure markets and raw materials essential to a powerful empire.

Adolf Hitler and his National Socialist, or Nazi, party came to power in Germany in 1933. The Nazis had grown increasingly popular during the 1920s and early 1930s because of Hitler's fierce attacks on the Treaty of Versailles. He expressed the feelings of many Germans who believed that Germany had been unfairly punished by the treaty. Other Germans supported Hitler because he promised to keep the communists out of power.

Once in power Hitler and the Nazis established totalitarian control of Germany. One of their earliest actions was to secretly begin building up the German military in preparation for aggressive expansion.

Economic Issues

Totalitarian dictatorships won much support during the 1930s because of the worldwide depression. Industry was virtually at a standstill. Many nations had erected high tariff barriers to protect their failing businesses from foreign competition. But the collapse of international trade only made the depression worse.

President Roosevelt and Secretary of State Cordell Hull believed that the depression in the United States and the rest of the world could be eased by reviving international trade. American exports had

By 1933 Adolf Hitler controlled the German government. This German poster shows him holding a flag with the Nazi symbol, the swastika.

American products, and exports increased only modestly.

Economic considerations also played a part in the decision to grant diplomatic recognition to the Soviet Union in 1933. The United States had refused to recognize the Bolshevik government after the revolution in 1917. Some Americans believed that recognition of the Soviet Union would result in greatly increased trade with that country. The expectations of vigorous trade, however, did not materialize.

The worldwide depression also affected the repayment of wartime debts. During the war the Allies had borrowed almost $10 billion from the United States. According to the Dawes Plan of 1924 the Allies paid their debts to the United States by collecting reparation payments from Germany. The reparation payments, as you have read, were partly financed by United States loans to Germany. When the depression struck, the United States stopped aid to Germany, and Germany slowed its reparations payments to the Allies. The Allies consequently found themselves unable to pay their debts to the United States.

In 1931 President Hoover suspended all debt payment for a year. But when payments again came due, many of the debtor nations were still unable to fulfill their obligations. The United States eventually collected about one quarter of the money owed by the Allies. Americans resented the Allies for not paying for their full share of the war effort. (Only Finland met its obligations.) This resentment helped strengthen isolationist sentiment during the 1930s.

The Isolationist Impulse

United States foreign policy continued to be dominated by isolationism during the 1930s. From 1934 to 1936 Senator Gerald Nye of North Dakota chaired a congressional committee investigating the United States entry into the World War in 1917. The committee's findings strengthened isolationist feelings and influenced foreign policy.

Nye claimed that the United States had been drawn into the war in Europe by international bankers. They feared that France and Britain would be unable to repay bank loans because of the expense of the war. The Nye committee charged that the bankers lobbied powerfully for the United States to enter the war. The committee further alleged

dropped 50 percent between 1929 and 1933. Roosevelt and Hull wanted to reverse the trend as quickly as possible.

One strategy was to *devalue* the currency, that is, to reduce the value of the dollar in relation to other currencies. As a result, American products would be less expensive on the world market. In the hopes of stimulating exports, the President began a policy of devaluing the dollar in 1933, but the devaluation had little impact on trade.

In another attempt to improve foreign trade, Roosevelt pressed for lower tariffs. Congress responded by passing the Trade Agreements Act in 1934. Under the act the President had the power to lower existing tariffs as much as 50 percent for nations agreeing to lower import taxes on United States goods.

Roosevelt had hoped that lower tariffs abroad would enable the United States to increase exports. If exports increased significantly, economists argued, industrial production would rise and unemployment would fall. But because of the worldwide depression, there was little demand for that, anticipating increased profits, munitions industries also pressed for American entry into the war. With each new allegation more people were won over by the isolationists.

Taking advantage of the growing isolationist feeling in the country, congressional isolationists introduced legislation banning arms sales and loans to nations at war. The Neutrality Act of 1935 authorized the President to bar arms sales to warring nations. President Roosevelt soon invoked the act, refusing to sell arms to Italy or Ethiopia. The two nations were at war following the Italian invasion of Ethiopia earlier in 1935. However, Italy was in a stronger military position and was able to continue purchasing food and gasoline, which were not covered by the act. Consequently the act worked against Ethiopia.

In 1936 Congress extended the neutrality legislation to include loans to belligerents. However, developments in Spain soon tested the policy of neutrality. In 1936 civil war broke out between supporters of the republican government and fascists led by Francisco Franco. Franco received military support from Germany and Italy, while the republicans received aid from the Soviet Union. Despite widespread American sympathy for the republican government, President Roosevelt asked for strict neutrality. A joint resolution of Congress in January 1937 banned United States aid to either side.

In 1937 isolationists extended presidential authority to bar shipment of nonmilitary goods. The new law also banned travel by Americans on the ships of belligerents. Thus a powerful isolationist impulse shaped the foreign policy of the United States during the 1930s. As Germany, Italy, and Japan became more aggressive, however, that policy was to be challenged.

The Good Neighbor Policy

Faced with aggressive dictatorships in Europe and Asia, President Roosevelt tried to secure the friendship of the Latin American nations. In his inauguration speech in March 1933, Roosevelt proclaimed that the United States would follow "the policy of the good neighbor."

In late 1933 Secretary of State Cordell Hull attended the Seventh Pan-American Conference in Montevideo, Uruguay. At the conference Hull supported the principle that "no state has the right to intervene in the internal or external affairs of another." In 1934 Roosevelt implemented the "good neighbor" policy by withdrawing the marines from Haiti and nullifying the Platt Amendment, which had restricted Cuban independence.

The "good neighbor" policy benefited the United States. In 1936 when President Roosevelt traveled to Buenos Aires, Argentina, to attend the Inter-American Conference for the Maintenance of Peace, he received an enthusiastic welcome. In his address to the conference Roosevelt stressed the unity of the United States and Latin America. He informed his listeners that nations outside the Western Hemisphere seeking "to commit acts of aggression against us will find a hemisphere wholly prepared to consult together for our mutual safety and our mutual good." The friendship of Latin American nations proved to be important for the United States when war broke out.

As the threat of war in Europe grew, most Americans hoped the United States would not become involved in the conflict. As this 1938 cartoon shows, many Americans recalled the battle casualties of World War I and the failure of European nations to pay war debts.

The Good Neighbor Policy

Latin American nations had long been critical of United States military intervention in the region. Resentment was still strong in the early 1930s even though Presidents Coolidge and Hoover had reduced the United States' military role there. President Roosevelt announced the "good neighbor policy" in his first inaugural address. In a speech in 1936, he spoke of the success of that policy.

We seek no conquest: we stand for peace. In the whole of the Western Hemisphere our good neighbor policy has produced results that are especially heartening. . . .

Throughout the Americas the spirit of the good neighbor is a practical and living fact.

The twenty-one American republics are not only living together in friendship and in peace—they are united in the determination so to remain.

To give substance to this determination a conference will meet on December 1, 1936, at the capital of our great southern neighbor Argentina, and it is, I know, the hope of all chiefs of state of the Americas that this will result in measures which will banish wars forever from this vast portion of the earth.

Peace, like charity, begins at home; that is why we have begun at home. But peace in the Western world is not all that we seek.

It is our hope that knowledge of the practical application of the good neighbor policy in this hemisphere will be borne home to our neighbors across the seas.

SECTION REVIEW

1. Identify: Benito Mussolini, Adolf Hitler, Nye committee, "good neighbor" policy.

2. Define: totalitarian state, devalue.

3. What issue helped Hitler gain popularity in Germany?

4. What did Roosevelt hope to accomplish by devaluing the dollar?

5. List two ways that President Roosevelt implemented the "good neighbor" policy.

6. **Critical Thinking** Would the United States be likely to try to remain isolated from European affairs today?

3 The Threat of War

The League of Nations, the treaties signed at the Washington Naval Conference, and the Kellogg-Briand Pact had all been designed to promote peace and cooperation. But they did not prevent aggressive acts by Italy, Japan, and Germany. Italy invaded and conquered Ethiopia in 1935 and 1936, and Japan conquered much of northern and eastern China in 1937. In the meantime Germany began to expand into central Europe.

Japanese Militarism in Asia

United States policy toward Japanese aggression in Asia changed little after Franklin Roosevelt was inaugurated. In 1934 Congress passed the Tydings-McDuffie Act, promising the Philippine Islands complete independence within a decade.* The United States appeared ready to withdraw from a military or political role in Asian affairs.

Japan renewed attacks on China in 1937, seizing Peking, Shanghai, and other cities. Because of American sympathy for China, President Roosevelt did not invoke the Neutrality acts, which meant that both sides could buy arms from the United States. Although the President hoped his action would help China, the Japanese were able to acquire more war materials because they had more merchant ships to carry arms.

---

*As you read in Chapter 24, the United States had taken control of the Philippines after the Spanish-American War.

In 1931 Japan invaded and captured the Chinese province of Manchuria. In 1937 the Japanese attacked China again, overwhelming the ancient capital of Peking and the port city of Shanghai, where this photograph of Japanese troops was taken.

In a major speech in Chicago in 1937 the President warned Americans that unless nations acted positively "to preserve world peace," armed conflict anywhere in the world would affect all nations. Comparing war to a highly contagious disease, Roosevelt urged a "quarantine" of armed conflict wherever it might break out.

Despite Roosevelt's efforts to alter isolationist sentiments in the country, events two months later demonstrated that he had not succeeded. On December 12, 1937, Japanese bombers attacked and sank the American gunboat *Panay*, on patrol on the Yangtze River in China. Two crew members were killed in the *Panay* incident. The United States took no action. Instead the government accepted a Japanese apology and payment of $2 million for damages.

So many Americans feared that a similar incident would lead the country into war that many supported the Ludlow Amendment to the Constitution. That amendment would have required a national vote before the United States could enter a war, except in case of invasion. The proposed amendment failed by a narrow margin in Congress. The near passage of the amendment was evidence of a strong desire to avoid war.

Germany on the March

Once, when an adviser suggested to Adolf Hitler that he not anger other European powers, Hitler boasted that they would "never act! They'll just protest. And they will always be too late." Events proved Hitler correct. Throughout the 1930s he accelerated military preparations for expansion.

In 1936 German soldiers marched into the Rhineland, German territory located between the Rhine River and the French and Belgian borders. In so doing, Germany violated the Versailles Treaty. The French viewed the German troops as a threat but did not want to start a war over the Rhineland. Therefore, France offered no resistance, and the German army remained.

The policy of meeting Hitler's demands became known as *appeasement.* To avoid war, Britain and France allowed Germany to acquire new territory in Europe. Sooner or later, the European leaders believed, Hitler would gain enough and end his conquests.

In 1938 Germany annexed Austria to the Third Reich* without resistance from the

---

*The Third Reich was the name of the German state under the Nazis.

Austrians or the rest of Europe. Later that year Hitler demanded that Germany take possession of the Sudetenland, the western section of Czechoslovakia. He argued that the Sudetenland should be part of Germany because 3 million Germans lived there.

At a conference in Munich, Germany, in 1938, British Prime Minister Neville Chamberlain claimed he had found a formula for "peace with honor" and "peace for our time." The French and British agreed to allow Germany to take the Sudetenland. Italy and Germany in turn joined Britain and France in a pledge that none of the four would ever make war on the others. Czechoslovakia protested vigorously at the loss of its territory but was powerless to resist the German action.

At Munich Hitler had assured Chamberlain that he had no interest in more territory in Czechoslovakia or anywhere else in Europe. Yet in 1939 Hitler annexed the remainder of Czechoslovakia without resistance. In the same year Italy conquered Albania.

Hitler had decided that if he was to continue seizing European land, he would have

The appeasement policy of European leaders at Munich cost Czechoslovakia land the Germans wanted. This cartoon, showing Hitler as the taxi passenger, appeared in 1938.

TAKE ME TO CZECHOSLOVAKIA, DRIVER

YES SIR!

to protect Germany from a war with the Soviet Union. In August 1939 the foreign ministers of the Soviet Union and Germany signed a nonaggression agreement. The Molotov-Ribbentrop Pact, named after the foreign minister of each nation, proclaimed that neither side would make war on the other. Secret provisions divided Poland between the two nations and guaranteed that Germany would not interfere if the Soviet Union invaded Finland.

Early Preparations

Chamberlain may have forecast peace, but Britain and other European countries had begun preparing for war. The United States, meanwhile, had almost no military force. Following the end of war in 1918, Congress had ordered drastic reductions in the size of the armed forces. Hitler had such disdain for United States military might that he mocked, "The inferiority and decadence of this allegedly new world power is evident in its military inefficiency."

The United States did make some attempts to expand the army and navy in the mid- and late 1930s. For example, President Roosevelt authorized the construction of additional cruisers and aircraft carriers. And in 1935 Congress increased the size of the army to 165,000 personnel. Despite such actions, however, the United States remained unprepared for war.

President Roosevelt was more concerned with diplomacy than with weapons. After the Munich Conference with Hitler, he searched for ways to alter the neutrality acts so the United States could aid allies in case of war. Roosevelt especially urged Congress to repeal the restrictions on selling arms. "I've fired my last shot," Roosevelt told Senate leaders in 1939. "I think I ought to have another round in my belt." But Congress refused to honor the President's request, and the neutrality legislation remained in effect.

The War Begins

At dawn on the morning of September 1, 1939, German airplanes, tanks, and infantry invaded Poland. Britain and France had committed themselves to the defense of Poland following the German occupation of Czechoslovakia. Thus, two days after the invasion of Poland they declared war on

Aggression in Europe 1935–1939

■ *In 1935 Italy under Mussolini invaded Ethiopia. Then between 1936 and 1939 Hitler sent the German army to win control of several areas bordering Germany. Said Hitler of the other European powers: "They'll just protest. And they will always be too late." The areas shown in yellow on the map were occupied by Germany before war officially began on September 1, 1939.*

Germany. After several weeks of German *Blitzkrieg,* or lightning war, Poland surrendered on October 6, 1939. Meanwhile, Soviet troops had invaded eastern Poland. The two nations then divided Poland into German and Soviet zones. One month later the Soviet Union invaded Finland, an act that especially outraged Americans since Finland had been the one nation that had continued to repay its previous war debts.

An overwhelming majority of Americans sympathized with the Poles, Finns, British, and French. A public opinion poll in the fall of 1939 showed that 84 percent of Ameri-

cans supported the Allies, as Britain and France were called. Only 2 percent supported Germany. Roosevelt issued a proclamation of neutrality two days after the outbreak of war but commented that Americans need not "remain neutral in thought."

Even while declaring neutrality, Roosevelt made further efforts to repeal restrictions on arms sales to nations at war. Isolationists in Congress fought the proposal. Finally, a compromise called cash-and-carry allowed the United States to sell arms to the Allies as long as they paid cash and transported the materials on their own ships. At the same time, Roosevelt assured isolationists that there was not "the remotest possibility of sending the boys of American mothers to fight on the battlefields of Europe."

German Victories

After the occupation of Poland, there was a lull in the fighting. Newspapers in the United States began to write about the "phony war." However, in April 1940 the Germans attacked and overran Norway and Denmark. One month later, German forces invaded neutral Belgium and the Netherlands before pushing on to France. Mussolini entered the war by attacking France from the south. "The hand that held the dagger," said Roosevelt, "has struck it into the back of his neighbor."

French forces and British support troops buckled before the crushing Nazi Blitzkrieg. Retreating to the coast of France, the British Army was just saved from destruction at Dunkirk. Hundreds of small boats rushed across the English Channel to evacuate the exhausted forces from the beaches. France surrendered to Germany on June 22, 1940.

Britain now stood alone. Neville Chamberlain, the prime minister who had carried out the ill-fated policy of appeasing Hitler, resigned. Winston Churchill, a longtime critic of appeasement, succeeded him. As Britain braced itself for attack, Churchill told his people he could only offer them the prospect of "blood, toil, sweat and tears." He inspired the British and won the admiration of Americans by pledging "to wage war, by sea, land and air, with all our might and with all the strength God can give us."

In the United States, preparations for war began in earnest. Congress authorized huge sums of money to modernize the army and navy. Within five months over $17 billion was appropriated for defense.

In 1940 Prime Minister Churchill pleaded with Roosevelt for ships to reinforce the British Navy. Roosevelt at first hesitated. But in September, as German submarine attacks on British shipping continued, he agreed to a deal. In exchange for a 99-year lease on naval and air bases in Newfoundland and the Caribbean, the United States transferred 50 old but usable destroyers to the British fleet. Roosevelt called the destroyer agreement "the most important action in the reinforcement of our national defense that has been taken since the Louisiana Purchase."

SECTION REVIEW

1. Identify: *Panay* incident, Ludlow Amendment, Neville Chamberlain, Winston Churchill.
2. Define: appeasement, Blitzkrieg.
3. How did the United States help China after the Japanese attack in 1937?
4. How did the United States prepare for the possibility of war in 1939 and 1940?
5. **Critical Thinking** Why did Roosevelt's reaction to war in Europe differ from Wilson's reaction to World War I?

4 Between Peace and War

Night after night during the summer of 1940, German planes rained bombs on British cities. The British evacuated thousands of children to the northern parts of the island nation. Those who remained in London spent long nights in the subway stations below the streets to escape the bombs. The armed forces prepared for a German invasion. The Royal Air Force took to the skies to defend the country and, at a terrible cost of life and aircraft, managed to fight off the German planes. In the United States people listened to nightly radio broadcasts by Edward R. Murrow and other war correspondents reporting directly from London. Americans wondered how much longer the United States could stay out of the war.

A Third Term for Roosevelt

Meanwhile a presidential campaign had begun in the United States. The Republicans nominated Wendell Willkie, a corporate executive from Indiana. Willkie had come to national attention during the early years of the New Deal. As president of Commonwealth and Southern, a public utilities holding company, he had led the fight against the policies of the Tennessee Valley Authority regarding electrical power.

Franklin Roosevelt had dominated the Democratic party for the previous eight years. No successor to his leadership had emerged, and the President seemed the likely choice to oppose Willkie in the election. Yet the "third-term issue" bothered some Democrats. Never before had a President served more than two terms. Roosevelt, citing the crisis in Europe and his established relations with European leaders, had announced his decision to run again. By the summer of 1940 the international situation overshadowed the third-term issue, and the Democrats renominated Roosevelt. He chose Secretary of Agriculture Henry Wallace as his running mate.

Willkie opposed many aspects of the New Deal, but he was an internationalist who approved of many of Roosevelt's foreign policy actions. He supported increased aid to Britain, including Roosevelt's destroyer deal. (See page 634.) Willkie also approved of the Selective Service Act, which instituted the first peacetime draft of young American men. The act went into effect in the fall of 1940. As the presidential campaign continued through the fall, Willkie had increasing trouble finding an issue on which to challenge Roosevelt.

Late in the campaign, Willkie began accusing Roosevelt of maneuvering the country into war. The President responded with his old promise. He told an audience in Boston, "I have said this before, but I shall say it again and again: Your boys are not going to be sent into any foreign wars." Roosevelt easily won election to an unprecedented third term with 54 percent of the popular vote.

Lend-Lease

During 1940 Britain had been buying supplies from the United States under the cash-and-carry arrangement, but by the end of the year the British treasury was running out of money. Despite sympathy for Britain, many Americans, including members of Congress, hesitated to support loans of money. They hoped that Hitler's aggression could be stopped without dragging the United States into war.

Shortly after the election, President Roosevelt proposed a solution: the United States would lend Britain whatever supplies it needed to wage war against Germany. He compared his idea to that of helping neighbors whose house was on fire. If the neighbors needed your garden hose to put out the fire, Roosevelt pointed out, you would not waste time arguing about the cost of the hose or how it would be paid for. You would simply give your neighbors the hose and tell them to return it after the fire.

In early 1941 Congress passed the Lend-Lease Act by a large margin. The act gave the President the authority to sell, exchange, lend, or lease war materials to any country whose defense he deemed vital to the defense of the United States. Roosevelt told the

By 1940 all of England's allies had been crushed by the German war machine. Hitler assumed that Britain too would yield quickly. But Prime Minister Winston Churchill vowed, "We shall fight on the beaches . . . and in the streets. . . . We shall never surrender." Between September 1940 and May 1941 German planes bombed London nightly. Below, Churchill inspects the wreckage of the House of Commons.

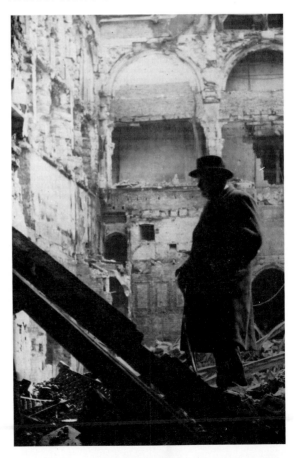

country that the United States must now become the "arsenal of democracy."

During 1941 a growing volume of war supplies left Atlantic coast ports for Britain. But getting the supplies across the ocean proved difficult. "Wolf packs" of German submarines sank many ships throughout the spring of 1941. Some advisers urged Roosevelt to order navy destroyers to escort and protect the British ships as they made the dangerous voyage across the Atlantic. But the President rejected such a drastic step. Instead, he extended the area of the Atlantic in which United States Navy ships would cruise on patrol.

However, in July 1941, faced with continued German attacks on vessels carrying lend-lease supplies, Roosevelt announced that United States warships would accompany British freighters as far as Iceland. At Iceland the British Navy would take responsibility for escorting the merchant vessels to British ports. Soon an undeclared naval war had erupted on the Atlantic. During September and October German submarines attacked the American destroyers *Reuben James* and *Kearny*. The United States was on the brink of war.

End of Isolationism

In May 1940, when the German Blitzkrieg struck France, Roosevelt had proclaimed that the European conflict created an "unlimited national emergency" for the United States. The President urged an all-out effort to strengthen national defense. Internationalist groups, which had long believed that the country should prepare for war, were pleased by the proclamation.

A vocal group of isolationists, however, continued to mount vigorous arguments against involvement in foreign military and political affairs. The America First Committee led the opposition to the Lend-Lease Act and all other aid to the Allies. As events worsened in Europe, the isolationist position became increasingly unpopular.

Most Americans wanted to see Germany defeated but without direct United States participation. Thus policy makers continued to seek a middle road between isolationism and war. However, international events soon engulfed the ongoing debate. In June 1941 Germany launched a surprise attack on the Soviet Union. German troops pushed deep into Soviet territory. They soon held Stalingrad and Leningrad under siege and were threatening Moscow.

The United States immediately extended the Lend-Lease Act to include the Soviet Union. Roosevelt and Churchill agreed that even if Stalin's government was in many ways as oppressive as that of Hitler, it was nonetheless essential to help the Soviet Union ward off the German invasion.

Britain and the United States continued to move toward an alliance, although the United States remained officially neutral. Military leaders of the two countries met secretly in Washington, D.C., to plan a joint strategy to be followed if the United States did enter the fighting. In August 1941 Roosevelt and Churchill met aboard a warship off the coast of Newfoundland. They talked extensively about the crises in Europe and Asia. Roosevelt still refused to commit fighting forces, but he and Churchill did agree on a statement of "certain common principles" on which they based "their hopes for a better future for the world."

In this statement, the Atlantic Charter, the United States and Britain agreed to seek no territorial gain and supported "the right of all peoples to choose the form of government under which they will live." The United States and Great Britain urged all nations to cooperate economically to raise the general standard of living in the world. They also proposed the disarmament of all aggressor nations after the defeat of Nazism and "the establishment of a wide and permanent system of general security." But while Roosevelt and Churchill met, the danger of a wider war in Asia grew.

Embargo Against Japan

Relations between Japan and the United States had worsened steadily since 1937. (See page 631.) Despite American support for China, Japan continued to import 90 percent of its scrap metal and 60 percent of its oil from the United States. President Roosevelt hesitated to cut off the trade for fear that Japan would invade Southeast Asia in order to obtain supplies there.

When France and the Netherlands fell to Germany in the spring of 1940, their Asian colonies were open to Japanese attack. In September Secretary of State Cordell Hull informed Japan that the United States would not tolerate Japanese military presence in European colonies in Asia. However, before the month ended, Japan had established military bases in French Indochina (now the nations of Vietnam, Cambodia, and Laos). The United States responded on September 26 by placing an embargo on the export of scrap metal, oil, and aviation fuel to Japan. The following day Japan announced that it had formed a military alliance with Germany and Italy.

Thereafter the United States increased aid to China in the hope of stemming Japanese aggression. War loomed closer in the summer of 1941. On July 25 Japan established more bases in French Indochina. The next day the United States froze all Japanese bank accounts in American banks, preventing Japan from buying any goods from the United States.

In November 1941 Secretary of State Hull met in Washington, D.C., with Japanese diplomats. The Japanese asked the United States to end aid to China and restore full economic relations with Japan. Hull countered with a proposal that Japan withdraw its troops from China and Indochina. In exchange the United States would end the economic embargo on Japan. The talks continued without agreement.

While their diplomats met with Hull, the Japanese prepared for an attack against the United States. On November 25 Japanese aircraft carriers set out for Pearl Harbor, the American naval base in Hawaii.

Pearl Harbor

On Sunday, December 7, 1941, Japanese carrier-based airplanes attacked the United States fleet at Pearl Harbor. The United States Navy was taken by surprise. Despite many warnings, military leaders had believed that Japan would attack southeast Asia rather than Pearl Harbor. Thus no special precautions had been taken. Most of the fleet was caught at anchor. Among the large ships based at Pearl Harbor, only the aircraft carriers were not docked at the time of the attack.

The attack on Pearl Harbor was a catastrophe for the United States. Nineteen ships, including six battleships, sank or suffered severe damage. Japanese planes destroyed over 150 aircraft still on the ground. Over 2,300 American soldiers and sailors died.

The next day, a visibly grim and shaken President addressed a special joint session of Congress. The hall was silent as Roosevelt described the "sudden and deliberate attack" on United States forces by Japanese airplanes on a day "which will live in infamy." Roosevelt asked Congress to declare that a state of war had existed between the United States and Japan since the hour of the attack. Congress passed a declaration of war with only one negative vote. Several days later Germany and Italy declared war on the United States. Congress immediately passed a declaration of war against the two European powers.

Major Events	
1921	Washington Naval Conference
1922	Mussolini seizes power in Italy
1924	Dawes Plan
1928	Kellogg-Briand Pact
1930	Hawley-Smoot Act; Clark Memorandum
1931	Japan invades China
1932	Stimson Doctrine
1933	Hitler seizes power in Germany; Roosevelt announces Good Neighbor Policy
1935	First Neutrality Act passed
1936	Germany occupies Rhineland; Spanish Civil War begins
1938	Munich Conference
1939	Molotov-Ribbentrop Pact; Germany invades Poland; World War II begins
1940	Bases-for-destroyers agreement with Britain; Roosevelt elected to third term
1941	Lend-Lease Act; United States embargo on supplies to Japan; Japan attacks Pearl Harbor; United States enters World War II

On Sunday morning, December 7, 1941, a surprise Japanese air raid destroyed the United States fleet at Pearl Harbor. Fifteen ships were put out of commission or sunk, and over 150 planes were wrecked. Luckily, the aircraft carriers stationed at Pearl Harbor were not in port. The United States immediately declared war on Japan.

SECTION REVIEW

1. Identify: Wendell Willkie, Lend-Lease Act, Atlantic Charter.

2. How were the positions of Roosevelt and Willkie on foreign policy similar?

3. What development led Roosevelt to propose the policy of "lend-lease"?

4. Why was trade with the United States important to Japan?

5. Where did United States military leaders think the Japanese would attack?

6. **Critical Thinking** Was the entry of the United States into World War II inevitable? Explain.

Chapter 34 Review

 ★ ★ ★   ★ ★ ★

In Perspective

During the 1920s most of the American public and elected officials shared isolationist feelings. Yet the United States participated in many international conferences and signed the Kellogg-Briand Pact. During the 1930s the nation tried to insulate itself from a troubled world by passing a series of neutrality acts.

When war broke out in Europe in September 1939, the United States stayed out of the fighting but began building up the army and navy. Germany quickly conquered much of Europe, and soon Britain stood alone against the onslaught. President Roosevelt increased aid to Britain, and later the United States Navy was deployed as far as Iceland to protect British ships carrying lend-lease supplies.

In the Pacific, Japan was waging war on China and extending its influence in Asia. The United States futilely tried to halt Japanese aggression by imposing an economic embargo. Tensions between the two nations increased during 1941, and on December 7, 1941, Japan bombed the United States naval base at Pearl Harbor, Hawaii. The United States was now engaged in a second world war.

Vocabulary

Match the term at left with its definition or description at right.

1. isolationist
2. internationalist
3. appeasement
4. totalitarian state
5. devalue

a. giving in to demands to avoid conflict
b. country where state is supreme
c. favors limited foreign involvement
d. reduction of the value of the dollar
e. favors helping victims of foreign aggression

Chapter Checkup

1. (a) How did the United States show a willingness to support world cooperation during the 1920s? (b) How did the country become directly involved in the world economy in 1924?

2. (a) How did the Nye committee investigation contribute to feelings of islolationism during the mid-1930s? (b) Describe the legislation passed as a result of the isolationism of the period.

3. (a) What actions by Japan between 1930 and 1937 alarmed the United States? (b) How did the Hoover administration react? (c) How did Franklin Roosevelt react? (d) Was Roosevelt able to counter the isolationist mood of the country at that time? Explain.

4. (a) What was the Lend-Lease Act? (b) How did it allow the United States to help Britain?

Critical Thinking

1. **Evaluating** How do you think the mood of the Roaring Twenties (see Chapters 29 and 30) may have contributed to the feeling of isolationism during that decade?

2. **Supporting an Opinion** No President had ever served more than two terms, yet Franklin Roosevelt was elected for a third term in 1940. Why do you think that happened? Cite specific evidence to support your answer.

Developing Basic Skills

1. **Comparing** Review the events that led to United States entry into the World War in 1917. (See Chapter 28.) How did entry into World War II differ? Were there any similarities? Explain.

2. **Analyzing Political Cartoons** Study the cartoon on page 629. Then answer the following questions: (a) What is the subject of the cartoon? (b) The cartoon is titled "A Good Time for Reflection." What do you think Uncle Sam is reflecting on? (c) Based on the cartoon, how do you think the cartoonist viewed the threat of war in Europe? (d) Would you consider this cartoon isolationist, internationalist, or neither? Explain.

See page 832 for suggested readings.

Writer's Handbook

Writing a Topic Outline

Once you have organized your notecards and classified them according to topics, you should prepare a topic outline. A topic outline helps you to focus on the main idea and the supporting details. Look at the portion of a topic outline below. The main topics are identified with Roman numerals. Subtopics are labeled with capital letters.

I. Introduction
II. Isolation Versus World Cooperation
   A. Washington Naval Conference
   B. Nine Power Treaty
   C. Kellogg-Briand Pact
   D. League of Nation conferences
   E. Fordney-McCumber Act of 1922
   F. Hawley-Smoot Act of 1931
III. The United States in the World Economy
   A. Dawes Plan
   B. Foreign trade

Practice: Complete the topic outline based on the information in Section 1 of Chapter 34.

35

The Second World War

(1941–1945)

Detail of Tank Breakthrough at St. Lô *by Ogden Pleissner*

Chapter Outline

1 *A World War*

2 *On the Home Front*

3 *The Allies on the Offensive*

4 *Wartime Diplomacy and Politics*

5 *Victory*

Rarely had Americans faced a crisis so united in spirit and purpose as during the months following the Japanese attack on Pearl Harbor. The four years of war that followed demanded the full energy of United States military forces, the American economy, and the American people.

    The United States and its allies encountered defeat and disappointment in the first year after Pearl Harbor. But by 1943 they seemed to have stemmed the tide of German and Japanese advances. For the first time they sensed victory. But the Allies faced two more years of brutal fighting on Pacific Islands, in eastern Europe, in Sicily and Italy, in France and Germany. The effect of the war would be felt for decades to come.

Allies on the offensive

1941	1942	1943	1944	1945

1941
Executive Order 8802 issued

1942
Japanese relocated; Battles of Coral Sea, Midway

1943
Allies invade Italy; Teheran Conference

1944
Allies invade France; bombing of Japan begins

1945
Yalta, Potsdam Conferences; Germany, Japan surrender

1 A World War

No war in history covered as much of the earth, cost as many lives, or caused as much destruction as World War II. Over 50 nations took part before the war ended.

The Allies Against the Axis Powers

Early in the war 26 nations, calling themselves the United Nations or Allies, had joined forces to fight the Axis powers. The Axis powers included Germany, Italy, Japan, and four other nations. The major powers among the Allies were the United States, Great Britain, and the Soviet Union. By the end of the war the Allies numbered 49 nations. (See the chart below.)

Because of the vast distance between the Pacific and Europe, World War II was actually two separate wars. In the Pacific war the United States, Great Britain, Australia, and New Zealand were pitted against Japan. The fighting stretched for 5,000 miles (8,000 kilometers) from Alaska in the north to Java in the south, and for 7,000 miles (about 11,000 kilometers) from Hawaii in the east to India in the west.

The war in Europe and Africa consisted of three major fronts, or battle zones. Savage fighting took place on the eastern front, where the Soviet Union faced Germany, Bulgaria, Finland, Hungary, and Romania. On the southern front United States, British, and

■ *Few nations remained neutral in World War II, as this chart shows. The date in parentheses after a country's name is the year in which it entered the war.*

Allies and Axis Powers

Allies

Argentina (1945)	Ethiopia (1942)	New Zealand (1939)
Australia (1939)	France (1939)	Nicaragua (1941)
Belgium (1940)	Great Britain (1939)	Norway (1940)
Bolivia (1943)	Greece (1940)	Panama (1941)
Brazil (1942)	Guatemala (1941)	Paraguay (1945)
Canada (1939)	Haiti (1941)	Peru (1945)
Chile (1945)	Honduras (1941)	Poland (1939)
China (1941)	India (1939)	San Marino (1944)
Colombia (1943)	Iran (1941)	Saudi Arabia (1945)
Costa Rica (1941)	Iraq (1943)	South Africa (1939)
Cuba (1941)	Lebanon (1945)	Syria (1941)
Czechoslovakia (1941)	Liberia (1944)	Turkey (1945)
Denmark (1940)	Luxembourg (1940)	U.S.S.R. (1941)
Dominican Republic (1941)	Mexico (1942)	United States (1941)
Ecuador (1945)	Mongolian People's	Uruguay (1945)
Egypt (1945)	Republic (1945)	Venezuela (1945)
El Salvador (1941)	Netherlands (1940)	Yugoslavia (1941)

Axis Powers

Albania (1940)	Italy (1940)
Bulgaria (1941)	Japan (1941)
Finland (1941)	Romania (1940)
Germany (1939)	Thailand (1942)
Hungary (1940)	

Neutral Nations

Eire (Ireland)
Portugal
Spain
Sweden
Switzerland

Australian troops fought the Germans and Italians in North Africa and Italy. On the western front, the greatest air-sea-land military operation in history involved 3 million people to plan and carry out an invasion of Europe across the English Channel.

Dark Days of 1942

After the Japanese attack on Pearl Harbor, Admiral Ernest King and General Douglas MacArthur proposed that the United States concentrate its armed forces to defeat Japan. But President Roosevelt had already accepted the British view that the Allies must defeat Germany and Italy first.

The United States entered the war short of almost all critical war materials. Some early military training was conducted with broom handles for rifles and airplanes made of plywood. German and Japanese submarines were sinking ships faster than the Allies could build them.

Furthermore, in the first years of the war, the Japanese had conquered many of the islands in the western Pacific and a considerable area of eastern and southern Asia. By early 1942 Chinese resistance was severely strained, India was threatened from east and west, and Australia was preparing for a Japanese invasion.

The war in the Pacific seemed nearly lost, and the Allies found little cause for optimism in Europe. Germany had conquered most of western and eastern Europe before the attack on Pearl Harbor. In the spring of 1942, Hitler's armies renewed their onslaught against the Soviet Union. They drove deep into Soviet territory, threatening oil fields in the south and advancing on the capital, Moscow. Moreover, the British defense of Egypt was near collapse. Germany and Italy were close to controlling North Africa, the Suez Canal, and the oil fields of the Middle East.

The War in North Africa

In 1942 American Generals George C. Marshall and Dwight D. Eisenhower urged the Allies to undertake an invasion of France across the English Channel no later than the spring of 1943. They were afraid the Soviet Union might be driven from the war. The Soviets were enthusiastic, hoping that such an invasion would force Hitler to divert some of his troops from the eastern to the western

front. The British agreed reluctantly, but as the Allies suffered defeat after defeat, Prime Minister Winston Churchill proposed an alternative strategy: an invasion of North Africa, followed by advances into the Mediterranean area. The strategy was named Operation Torch.

In November 1942 combined British and United States forces under the command of General Eisenhower landed on the coast of French North Africa in Morocco and Algeria. The troops easily defeated soldiers of Vichy (VEE shee), France,* who were stationed in North Africa. Reaching Tunisia, the Allies met stiff resistance from the German Afrika Korps, led by Field Marshall Erwin Rommel. After initial setbacks, the Allied troops drove the Germans north toward the Mediterranean Sea. In May 1943 the greatly outnumbered Axis forces in North Africa surrendered.

Allied victory in North Africa opened the Mediterranean Sea to Allied shipping and made an invasion of southern Europe possible. Even more important, for the first time the Allied countries heard good news about the war. Though the Allies had suffered 70,000 casualties, the Germans and Italians had lost over 250,000 soldiers and much valuable equipment.

A Holding Action in the Pacific

The Japanese had followed the attack on Pearl Harbor with what seemed an endless string of victories. Guam, Wake Island, and Hong Kong fell within three weeks. Singapore fell two months later. In May 1942 American and Filipino defenders surrendered the Philippine Islands. General Douglas MacArthur led the defense of Bataan and Corregidor, but when the situation became hopeless he was evacuated. Before he left, however, he promised the people of the Philippines, "I shall return." Meanwhile, Japanese forces advanced from Indochina into Burma, threatening India to the west and Australia and New Zealand to the south.

The adoption of a "beat Hitler first" strategy did not mean abandoning the Pacific theater. Fortunately, the United States aircraft carriers then stationed in the Pacific had survived the attack on Pearl Harbor.

---

*After France fell to Germany in 1940, some French officials decided to cooperate with the Germans. They formed a government at Vichy, in southern France.

The war in North Africa was often fought in blistering desert heat. Here, officers of a tank destroyer battalion consult their maps in Tunisia. American forces launched highly successful hit-and-run attacks with half-track personnel carriers such as the one in the photo. The speedy half-tracks waited until enemy tanks were near, fired off a barrage, then raced away faster than the lumbering German tanks could follow.

Relying on the aircraft carriers, a naval task force engaged a Japanese fleet in the Coral Sea near Australia in early May 1942. After a three-day battle the Japanese fleet fled northward, but only after severely damaging the aircraft carrier *Lexington* and sinking two other American ships.

One month later, the United States Navy won a major victory at Midway Island in the central Pacific. The navy destroyed four Japanese carriers, several smaller ships, and 253 planes. It lost the carrier *Yorktown*, a destroyer, and 150 planes. Later that summer United States Marines began a hard-fought struggle for control of Guadalcanal in the Solomon Islands. The island was secured by February 1943.

By early 1943 United States forces had stopped Japanese advances through the Pacific and Southeast Asia. Allied troops had driven the Axis powers out of North Africa.

Finally, Soviet soldiers and civilians, aided by one of the worst winters in history, had halted the German advance into their country. For the first time in the war the Allies sensed eventual victory.

SECTION REVIEW

1. Identify: Allies, Axis powers, Dwight D. Eisenhower, Douglas MacArthur.

2. In what two areas was most of World War II fought?

3. What happened in 1942 that made the Allied situation in the Pacific desperate?

4. List two reasons why the Allied victory in North Africa was significant.

5. **Critical Thinking**   Why do you think Germany and Japan had success in the early days of the war?

2 On the Home Front

The Japanese attack on Pearl Harbor united the American people as nothing had before. Although no fighting took place in the United States after Pearl Harbor, the war became a fact of life for everyone. Most families had a father, brother, sister, or other relative in the armed services. News of the war filled newspaper headlines and radio waves. Industries idled by the Great Depression sprang back to life, and economic prosperity returned. The war would demand sacrifices, but Americans faced the struggle united.

Building the Armed Forces

After declaring war; Congress swiftly set out to build up United States fighting forces. Six million men and women volunteered for service. Almost 10 million men were drafted. Women enlisted in the Women's Auxiliary Army Corps, the Women Appointed for Voluntary Emergency Service in the Navy, the Women's Auxiliary Ferrying Squadron, the Women's Reserve of the Coast Guard Reserves, and the Women Reserve of Marine Corps.

Training took place at posts and bases across the nation. At one time the army alone had to provide housing for over 5 million personnel. Training for a worldwide war was not easy. Soldiers might have to fight in jungles on Pacific islands, in African deserts, or in European countryside. To meet this challenge, the armed forces were soon providing soldiers with a wide variety of equipment, clothing, and combat training.

Organizing for Wartime Production

The war had to be won as much on the production lines of industry as on the battlefields. President Roosevelt announced staggering production goals for 1942: 60,000 airplanes, 45,000 tanks, 20,000 antiaircraft guns, and 8 million tons (7.3 million metric tons) of merchant shipping. United States industry and workers met the demands and sometimes surpassed them. Even higher goals were achieved in 1943 and 1944.

To manage and control the economy, Roosevelt created the War Production Board. The first task of the board was to supervise conversion from a peacetime to wartime economy. Factories that had manufactured shirts redesigned assembly lines to make mosquito netting. Model-train producers made bomb fuses. Metal weather-stripping factories switched to producing mortar shells. Kitchen sink assembly lines were retooled to produce cartridge cases. After 1942 all manufacture of civilian automobiles halted as auto makers changed to full-time production of tanks, trucks, armored personnel carriers, and aircraft.

In an attempt to control inflation, Roosevelt established the Office of Price Administration (OPA). The OPA set price ceilings on most items, including rents, since housing was scarce throughout the war. The agency also supervised a rationing system for such items as gasoline, tires, coffee, canned food, and meat by allotting a certain number of coupons per item per family.

By 1943 industry was fully mobilized for war. Under James Byrnes, the Office of War Mobilization coordinated the activities of all wartime agencies. The War Manpower Commission made the critical determination of where in the economy workers were most needed. The problem of peace between labor and management occupied the War Labor Board. The board contributed to the growth of union membership by enforcing the provisions of the Wagner Act. (See page 605.) The board allowed wage increases to offset rising prices and at the same time tried to limit inflation. The wages of most Americans climbed steadily from 1941 to 1945.

To pay for the war, the government raised taxes, especially on the incomes of high-salaried workers. In addition, it borrowed huge amounts of money by selling war bonds. Spectacular drives employing movie stars and comic book heroes such as Batman and Dick Tracy were mounted to sell bonds and bolster patriotic spirit.

The Return of Prosperity

The improvements in the United States economy during the war were staggering. Between 1939 and 1945 the gross national product rose from $91.1 billion to $213.6 billion. During 1942 alone, war production rose over 300 percent. The United States produced more than Germany, Italy, and Japan combined. In 1939 American aircraft manufacturers employed about 47,000 workers to make 5,900 planes. Five years later, 2.1 million workers were producing almost 100,000 planes annually. The output of the shipbuilding industry grew from one million tons (.91 million metric tons) in 1941 to 19 million tons (17.3 million metric tons) in 1943.

Not only was such production crucial to the Allied war effort, it also ended the depression as demand for manufactured goods skyrocketed. As industries geared up, unemployment decreased dramatically. Growing demand for agricultural products also brought farmers a level of price stability and prosperity they had not experienced since 1919. Between 1940 and 1945 crop prices doubled. Production increased even though farm population and acreage declined.

Resisting Government Controls

Various groups in the labor force believed that the controls set by the War Labor Board were unfair. In January 1943 miners in Alabama struck. John L. Lewis, president of the United Mine Workers, asked union members to return to the coal fields while he negotiated with the War Labor Board. Negotiations continually broke down, and the miners called further strikes.

In May the President seized the mines. He threatened to send soldiers to replace the miners and warned that he would draft the striking miners. The miners, however, refused to be intimidated. By November negotiations had broken down again, and a fourth strike had taken 530,000 men out of the mines. The government was forced to agree to some of the union's demands. The 11-month struggle won the miners a pay raise of $1.50 per day.

Other challenges came from business. Montgomery Ward, a large mail-order firm, refused to recognize its workers' union. When the workers went on strike, the War Labor Board ordered Sewell Avery, the company president, to negotiate with the union. Avery ignored the order. President Roosevelt then invoked the wartime Smith-Connally Act, which gave him power to seize any strike-bound plant necessary to the war effort. Newspapers across the country ran a front-page picture of two soldiers carrying Avery out of his office after he refused to leave. For the rest of the war, the government ran the company.

Changes in Daily Life

Family separation, frequent movement from one place to another, and worry about men and women fighting overseas were concerns shared by most Americans during World War II. Such experiences gave Americans a common sense of purpose. The "V for Victory" became a familiar symbol. It was displayed on buildings, sketched in store windows, and broadcast in Morse code as the sign-on and sign-off signal used by radio stations. Back yards became "victory gardens" to stretch the food supply. Scrap-rubber and scrap-iron collection drives were held to bring in scarce materials.

Americans grew accustomed to saving ration coupons and standing in long lines to buy scarce items. Newspaper, magazine, and radio advertisements urged Americans to sacrifice luxuries and make do with less, all for the war effort. Instead of urging people to buy more, industries mounted campaigns explaining that certain purchases would best be put off until after the war. One tire manufacturer asked consumers to conserve rubber by driving less, using the slogan, "Hitler smiles when you waste miles."

The role of women changed dramatically during the war, though in many cases only temporarily. Women joined the various military services by the hundreds of thousands. They piloted bombers across the Atlantic Ocean to bases in Europe, repaired airplanes and land vehicles, drove trucks, operated radios, and did clerical and technical work of all kinds.

As the demand for workers rose, women joined the civilian work force in record numbers. By the end of the war, one out of every three workers in industry and business was a woman. Traditional barriers against the employment of women in such industries as steel and shipbuilding fell before the ever-increasing demand for more workers. Songs and stories praised the women who kept American production lines moving.

As factories worked around the clock to produce the ships, planes, uniforms, ammunition, and hundreds of other items needed for war, women assumed jobs formerly open to men only. Below, a woman works on a bomber in California. One aircraft company popularized a mythical worker called "Rosie the Riveter."

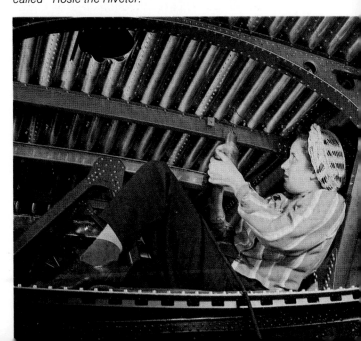

Changes in clothing, appearance, and hair styles reflected new work roles. More basic, however, was the impact on how people felt and thought. Many women began to believe that they could pursue a career and have a family at the same time. Women became more aware of the wide range of roles available to them.

Black Americans During the War

The war years produced a mixed record in the long struggle of black Americans for economic, political, and social equality. The increase in war production provided black Americans good jobs in unprecedented numbers. Some 2 million blacks worked in aircraft factories, steel mills, and shipyards. In both North and South blacks experienced improved levels of social acceptance and economic well-being. Lynchings stopped almost completely. Black and white leaders joined to form the Southern Regional Council to fight prejudice and misunderstanding.

The need for workers in expanded war industries opened jobs to groups that often had been excluded: blacks, migrants, teenagers, senior citizens, and the handicapped. The number of black women in industry, for example, rose 11.3 percent during the war. The woman in this photo is stitching a parachute.

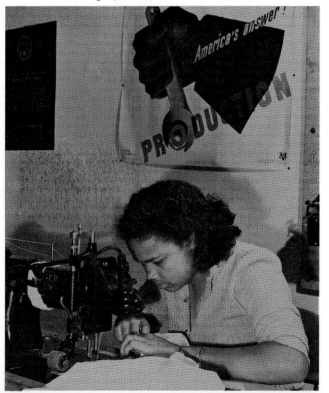

Yet discrimination and racial tension had not disappeared. In 1941, before the United States entered the war, A. Philip Randolph, head of the Brotherhood of Sleeping Car Porters, threatened to lead a march on Washington, D.C., to protest prejudice against black workers. In response President Roosevelt issued Executive Order 8802. The order banned discrimination in all government agencies, in job training programs, and in all companies doing business with the federal government. It also established the Fair Employment Practices Committee to insure equal treatment for blacks and other minorities in war industries.

During much of the war, however, official policy established all-black units of soldiers or sailors commanded by white officers. In the navy most blacks were designated as porters. In huge training camps in the South, black soldiers on leave had to contend with segregated eating places, movie houses, and recreational facilities.

In the North increased migration of southern blacks to northern industrial cities aggravated housing shortages. White workers continued to resent black competition for jobs. In one instance street car workers in Philadelphia went on strike to protest the upgrading of black workers to motormen. The President sent in army troops to maintain operation of vital war industries in the city.

Sometimes resentment flared into violence. In Detroit efforts to move blacks into a federal housing project named after Sojourner Truth, the black abolitionist, aroused anger among whites. In the summer of 1943 isolated violent incidents erupted into a riot. Before police and federal troops restored order, 25 blacks and 9 whites lay dead.

Other Victims of Discrimination

Mexican Americans continued to face discrimination, especially in the cities of the Southwest. Like many recent immigrants before them, Mexican Americans were frequently crowded into run-down urban areas, suffered high unemployment rates, and met hostility from long-time residents.

Young Mexican Americans became the object of frequent violent attacks in Los Angeles. During the early 1940s, young Mexican American men adopted a flamboyant style of dress, sporting "zoot" suits and wearing their hair long and slicked back into "duck tails." In July 1943 groups of sailors and soldiers home on leave roamed the streets, beating up the "zooters," tearing their clothes, and cutting their hair.

Newspaper and radio reports blamed the violence on the zooters. However, a citizens' committee appointed by California Governor Earl Warren revealed the truth about the riot and the need for improved housing for Mexican Americans.

Italian Americans and German Americans also felt the sting of discrimination from fellow citizens during the war. Some of them changed their names to conceal their families' country of origin. Yet the problems suffered by the European immigrants were not nearly as severe as those experienced by Japanese Americans.

Japanese Americans Lose Their Liberties

Because of the attack on Pearl Harbor, Japanese Americans were the target of great bitterness. Since most of them lived on the Pacific coast, in small, easily identifiable communities, they were especially vulnerable to systematic discrimination.

In February 1942 defense officials labeled Japanese Americans living on the Pacific coast "a menace which had to be dealt with." Military leaders insisted that Japanese Americans be moved away from the coastal areas where, officials warned, acts of sabotage could be committed. President Roosevelt and the Justice Department supported this demand and granted the War Department full authority to relocate thousands of innocent people.

With little or no warning, Japanese Americans were moved to huge inland internment camps. Two thirds of those evacuated were American-born citizens. They had to sell their homes, businesses, household goods, and most of their personal possessions for whatever prices they could get. For most of the war, the Japanese Americans were detained in the isolated camps. Home was a wooden barracks, with but one room per family.

In 1944 the Supreme Court upheld the forced relocation of the Japanese Americans as a justifiable wartime measure. The following year, when Allied victory appeared certain, the people were allowed to return to their communities to rebuild their shattered lives.

After the surprise attack on Pearl Harbor, many people feared a similar attack on the west coast of the continental United States. In this atmosphere of fear, Americans of Japanese descent on the Pacific Coast were labeled a menace to national security. In the spring of 1942, the government uprooted 112,000 Japanese Americans and moved them to temporary camps inland, where they were forced to remain for three years.

SECTION REVIEW

1. Identify: War Production Board, Office of Price Administration, Office of War Mobilization, War Manpower Commission, War Labor Board, A. Philip Randolph, Executive Order 8802.

2. Give two examples of how industry converted to wartime production.

3. How did conditions for workers improve during the war?

4. What type of work opened up to women as a result of the war?

5. How did opportunities for black Americans increase as a result of the war effort?

6. **Critical Thinking** How did the war help bring the United States out of the depression?

3 The Allies on the Offensive

During 1942 and early 1943 the Allies had worked to stop the advances of the Axis powers in Europe and the Pacific. Meanwhile the Allies developed strategies for counterattack and the mobilization of people and industry in support of the war effort. In 1943 the Allies were prepared to take the offensive against Italy and Germany in Europe and against Japan in the Pacific.

The Invasion of Italy

As you have read, the United States commanders had originally wanted to attack Europe by crossing the English Channel into France. (See page 642.) But they finally agreed with the British that Italy was the weakest point in the Axis empire. While continuing air attacks on German cities,* the Allies began an invasion of Italy.

In July 1943 paratroopers of the 82nd Airborne Division parachuted into Sicily in

---

*Allied air attacks on German cities began in the summer of 1942 from bases in Britain. The attacks increased in intensity during 1943 and 1944. By 1945 the Allied air war had nearly paralyzed German transportation and destroyed many vital war industries. Yet German war production increased until almost the end of the war. The Allies lost over 158,000 pilots and crew members and over 40,000 planes in the air war over Germany.

■ *By the time the United States entered the war at the end of 1941, Axis powers controlled virtually all of western Europe and North Africa. Arrows indicate the important Allied campaigns between 1942 and 1945. By 1943 Soviet troops were attacking the Axis powers from the east. The vast invasion along the coast of Normandy in 1944 was the beginning of the final assault on Germany.*

World War II in Europe and North Africa, 1942–1945

the first large-scale Allied airborne assault of the war. The attack suffered from bad weather and poor coordination between army assault forces and naval bombardments of the island. However, the invasion of paratroopers and forces landed from seaborne transports succeeded.

From Sicily, Allied forces pushed on to the Italian mainland, assaulting Salerno in September 1943. In the face of the successful Allied invasion, Mussolini was overthrown. The new Italian government surrendered to the Allies and offered to join in the fight against Germany.

The actual conquest of Italy, however, proved long and difficult. Hitler ordered German troops in Italy not to surrender. Bitter and costly fighting marked almost every mile up the Italian peninsula. At Monte Cassino, in central Italy, the Germans stopped the Allied advance. The Allies responded with another amphibious landing in January 1944 at Anzio, near Rome. It took six months of fighting before Rome finally fell to the Allies. The Allies then continued north, but German forces in Italy did not surrender until the war had nearly ended.

The Eastern Front

For almost three years the most bitter fighting of the war took place in the Soviet Union on the eastern front. To help his embattled nation survive the German onslaught, Soviet Premier Joseph Stalin had asked for three things from his allies: massive supplies, recognition of his territorial demands in eastern Europe, and the establishment of a second front in western Europe. He had been disappointed on all three.

Churchill and Roosevelt feared that the Soviet Union might make a separate peace with the Axis powers. But during the winter of 1941–1942 Soviet troops halted the German advance outside Moscow. A year later they ended the 900-day German siege of Leningrad.

The Allies meanwhile had found a way to deliver critical supplies to the Soviet Union. German submarines had made it impossible to send ships to the northern Soviet port of Archangel. Consequently, the United States and Great Britain shifted their supply operations to a much longer but safer route that went north through the Persian Gulf and across Iran.

By the summer of 1943 the Red Army, as the army of the Soviet Union is known, had gone on the offensive. It soon recaptured the Ukraine, the Crimean peninsula, White Russia, and eastern Poland. By capturing Romania, Bulgaria, and Hungary during a four-month period in 1944, the Soviets forced Hitler's Balkan allies to surrender. The Soviet offensive helped the British and Americans launch the largest single military operation in history. With the opening of a successful second front and the supply operations, only Stalin's territorial demands threatened to drive the Allies apart.

The Cross-Channel Invasion

In early 1944 the Supreme Allied Command made final plans for the long-awaited cross-channel invasion from England into France. General Eisenhower, summoned from the Italian front, was appointed supreme allied commander of the European theater of operations. The attack, code-named Operation Overlord, was scheduled for the late spring of 1944.

The success of Overlord depended on three conditions. First, the Allies had to build up an enormous reserve of supplies for the invasion: ammunition, trucks, food, construction equipment, medical supplies, tanks, artillery, and countless other items. Complete artificial harbors, constructed out of concrete, had to be towed across the channel and used for the landing and for unloading supplies. The second condition was secrecy. The Germans expected an attack but did not know when or where it might come. The third condition was clear weather. An unexpected storm or fog would make paratroop landings behind German lines and amphibious landings on the beaches all but impossible.

At 6:30 A.M. on June 6, 1944, the largest amphibious invasion in history began. Nearly 6,000 Allied ships ferried 60,000 men and their supplies across the channel and onto beachheads in northern France. The invaders met with heavy resistance. At one beachhead, American casualties in the first assault groups on the beach were 60 percent.

Six weeks passed before landing areas were fully secured. By that time, other Allied troops had moved into northern France and captured the port of Cherbourg, which would serve as a major receiving point of

On June 6, 1944, American, Canadian, and British forces stormed ashore along the French coast. Despite heavy bombarding to weaken German positions before the amphibious landing, Allied losses in the first waves were staggering. At left, the First Infantry wades ashore at Omaha Beach in Normandy. At right, a French farmer offers prayers and flowers beside the body of an American soldier killed in 1944.

supplies for the rest of the war. On August 25 the rapidly advancing Allied armies liberated Paris after four years of German occupation.

General Eisenhower did not believe the Allies had sufficient supplies to launch a single drive into the heart of Germany. Instead he decided to move along a broad front. In August he ordered an invasion across the Mediterranean into southern France. As the winter of 1944–1945 approached, Eisenhower's armies had recaptured most of western Europe. Now they planned the final assault on Germany.

Taking the Offensive in the Pacific

While the Allies attacked Europe from the south, the east, and the west, an equally important war raged in the Pacific. There, Allied forces were under the command of General MacArthur and Admiral Chester Nimitz. The two men disagreed on the best "road to Tokyo." MacArthur preferred a South Pacific route, pushing northward from Australia through New Guinea and the Phil-

ippines and on to Japan. Nimitz favored an advance toward Japan via the islands of the central Pacific.

The military commanders finally decided to follow both strategies. They succeeded with a *leapfrogging* technique. Rather than take Japanese-held islands one by one, the Allies decided to invade a few strategically placed islands, bypassing others. The theory was that the Japanese would not be able to supply their forces on islands that the Allies had leapfrogged. Isolated, these islands would have to surrender.

In 1943 and 1944 the United States Marine Corps, with naval support, assaulted the islands of Tarawa (tuh RAH wuh), Kwajalein (KWAHJ uh lihn), Wake, and Guam in the central Pacific. Meanwhile, MacArthur's troops captured New Guinea in the south. Fierce Japanese resistance resulted in heavy Allied casualties. At Tarawa, for example, casualties in some marine units reached 50 percent. But the technique of amphibious landings—requiring close coordination among air bombings, naval support, and troop movements—steadily improved.

In October 1944 General MacArthur's forces began an invasion of the Philippine Islands. MacArthur himself landed on the island of Leyte (LAY tee), where he proclaimed, "People of the Philippines, I have returned." In the battle of Leyte Gulf, which followed, the United States Navy sank an entire Japanese fleet. By late 1944, United States bombers had begun steady aerial attacks on the islands of Japan itself.

651

■ By 1942 the situation in the Pacific seemed desperate. Japan controlled much of China, the nations of eastern and southern Asia, and a string of Pacific islands. Although neither side realized it at the time, the Battle of Midway in 1942 was a turning point. At Midway the United States Navy, crippled by the destruction of much of the fleet at Pearl Harbor, nevertheless stopped the Japanese fleet. For the next two years Allied forces attacked Japanese-held islands in a "leapfrog" pattern. At times casualties in the difficult amphibious landings numbered as many as half the troops involved.

World War II in the Pacific 1942-1945

Allied nations
Under Japanese control
Maximum extent of Japanese control, 1942
◼—1943—▶ Allied advances

In the Pacific, the war was fought inch by inch, island by island, often against Japanese snipers who were prepared to die rather than surrender. Besides the Japanese, there were other enemies: savage heat, jungle fevers, malaria, fungus infections. Above, Americans storm a beach in the Solomon Islands in June 1943.

SECTION REVIEW

1. Identify: Joseph Stalin, Operation Overlord, Cherbourg, Chester Nimitz.
2. Define: leapfrogging.
3. What events led to the overthrow of Benito Mussolini in Italy?
4. List the three operations necessary for the success of Operation Overlord.
5. **Critical Thinking** Study the maps on pages 648 and 651. Why do you think the Soviet Union did not declare war on Japan until the last days of the war?

★ America's Heritage ★

The Code That Was Never Broken

One of the most important weapons of a nation during wartime is a good communications system. Information on deployment of troops and instructions to commanders in the field must be transmitted quickly and efficiently. To maintain secrecy, military messages are sent in code. But there is always a risk that the enemy will break the code.

During World War II, the United States military used a code system that was virtually foolproof. The Marine Corps recruited a group of Navajos to work as code talkers, using their own language instead of an artificial code. Because Navajo was still an unwritten language, few people other than the Navajo themselves were able to speak it. It was also extremely difficult to learn.

About 350 Navajo code talkers worked in the Pacific theater during the war. They were a familiar sight in command posts or huddled over radio sets in combat zones, transmitting messages. The code talkers assigned the names of birds, fish, and animals to military terms and then transmitted the code words in Navajo. A member of the team on the receiving end translated the Navajo words into English. Calls to headquarters for airplanes or artillery were thus transmitted rapidly and accurately in complete secrecy. The Japanese were unable to break the Navajo "code," which helped Allied forces advance from the Solomons to Okinawa and achieve eventual victory over Japan.

4 Wartime Diplomacy and Politics

During the war, Allied leaders conferred frequently through correspondence and occasionally in person. They made broad policy decisions, which were relayed to military officers around the world. At home politics continued. In 1944 presidential elections took place against the backdrop of war.

The Big Three Confer

By the fall of 1943 the Allies were confident that they would win the war. Therefore, they began planning for the postwar period. The foreign ministers of Britain, the Soviet Union, and the United States met in Moscow in October 1943. They discussed plans for the creation of a new organization of nations to maintain international peace and security. Membership in the organization was to be open to all nations, no matter how large or small.

In November 1943 Roosevelt boarded the battleship *Iowa* for a long journey to Cairo, Egypt. There he and Churchill met with Chinese President Chiang Kai-shek (jyahng ky SHEHK) to discuss plans for supply lines through Burma and a new Chinese military offensive against Japan. Stalin did not attend because the Soviet Union was not at war with Japan.

From Cairo, Roosevelt and Churchill flew to Teheran, capital of Iran, for their first face-to-face meeting with Soviet Premier Joseph Stalin. Although the Big Three, as the leaders of the United States, Britain, and the Soviet Union were known, made only tentative plans, the Teheran Conference influenced the shape of the postwar world.

Discussions began on the strategy for final defeat of the Axis powers. Stalin and Roosevelt insisted on final commitment to Overlord. Stalin, in turn, promised a spring offensive to coincide with the cross-channel landing. Furthermore, he promised to enter the Pacific war once Germany surrendered. The three leaders also discussed the planned international organization and the postwar fate of Germany.

At the end of the conference, the three leaders declared, "We leave here, friends in fact, in spirit, and in purpose." The Teheran meeting represented the high point of Allied good will. A troubled road lay ahead.

Diplomatic discussions after the Teheran Conference continued to focus on postwar settlements. Economic ministers meeting in Bretton Woods, New Hampshire, in 1944 drew up plans for the International Monetary Fund and the International Bank. These organizations were designed to aid in postwar recovery and to finance long-range improvements in nonindustrial and war-ravaged countries. At Dumbarton Oaks, in Washington, D.C., delegates from the United States, Britain, China, and the Soviet Union made further plans for the creation of an international peace-keeping organization, to be known as the United Nations.

The Election of 1944

At the height of the war, Americans began to ask if their President would seek a fourth term in office. "All that is within me cries to go back to my home on the Hudson," Roosevelt told reporters in the summer of 1944. Nevertheless, citing the need for continuity in leadership during the war, Roosevelt decided to run again.

The President had almost no opposition within his party. However, the Democrats did have some difficulty selecting a candidate for Vice-President. After rejecting Henry Wallace as too liberal and several other candidates as too conservative, the nominating convention settled on Senator Harry S. Truman of Missouri.

The Republicans selected New York Governor Thomas E. Dewey, who had come to prominence as a strong district attorney, to oppose Roosevelt. Dewey chose to avoid international issues in the campaign. Instead he focused on the failure of Democratic economic policies. Only the war, he charged, had ended the depression. A peacetime economy would require better management than a Democratic administration could provide, Dewey told American voters.

Although the strain of his years in office had aged Roosevelt noticeably, the President made special efforts during the campaign to show he was still in good health. At one point he spent an entire day in New York City campaigning from an open car during a rain storm. Roosevelt's popularity remained high, and a majority of voters did not want to change leaders during the war. As a result, Roosevelt won election to an unprecedented fourth term as President with 54 percent of the popular vote and 432 of 531 votes in the electoral college.

The Meeting in Yalta

In February 1945 Roosevelt, Churchill, and Stalin met for the second and last time at the winter resort of Yalta in the Soviet Union. They continued their discussions of strategy in Asia, postwar settlements in Europe, and plans for the United Nations. Above all Roosevelt wanted a firm commitment from Stalin to enter the war against Japan. The island campaigns in the Pacific had made clear that many hundreds of thousands of Americans would be killed or wounded in an assault on Japan.

At Yalta, Stalin again agreed to declare war on Japan three months after the surrender of Germany. In return, Roosevelt and Churchill agreed to Stalin's demands for postwar control of the Kurile Islands and southern Sakhalin Island, Japanese territories off the Pacific coast of the Soviet Union. The Soviet Union would retain control of the province of Outer Mongolia in northern China. It would also maintain shipping rights in the harbor of Port Arthur and control over railroads in Manchuria.

The leaders agreed that free elections should be held as soon as possible in the countries that Germany had occupied during the war. Germany would be divided into four zones of occupation, governed by American, British, French, and Soviet forces. April 1945 was set as the month for a conference of the United Nations in San Francisco. There they were to draw up a charter for a permanent peace-keeping organization.

By April 1945 the Red Army already occupied much of eastern Europe as it prepared for the final attack on Germany. (See page 649.) Roosevelt's and Churchill's vision of world peace rested on the hope that Stalin would honor the spirit of the Yalta agreements and allow free elections in the occupied nations. Churchill would later comment, "Our hopeful assumptions were soon to be falsified. Still, they were the only ones possible at the time."

SECTION REVIEW

1. Identify: Chiang Kai-shek, the Big Three, United Nations, Harry S. Truman, Thomas E. Dewey.

2. What was discussed at Teheran?

3. What issue did Dewey emphasize in the election of 1944?

4. What did the Big Three decide at Yalta about the fate of Germany after the war?

5. **Critical Thinking** Why do you think Roosevelt was in a stronger position to influence the allies than Wilson had been?

5 Victory

In the final year of the war in both Europe and the Pacific, Allied forces drove steadily toward victory over Germany and Japan. Allied armies battled across France and into Germany. Allied airplanes bombed major cities in the enemy's homeland. Naval and marine forces inched closer to Japan. By 1945, as the United States entered its fourth year of war, victory seemed near. But neither Germany nor Japan was willing to sue for peace. It was clear that the price of victory would be high indeed.

Ending the War in Europe

In December 1944 German troops launched one last counteroffensive in the Ardennes Forest along the border of Belgium and Luxembourg. In the Battle of the Bulge, the Germans, with the advantage of surprise, broke through Allied lines and surrounded American soldiers at the small town of Bastogne. Despite heavy casualties and what appeared to be certain defeat, when asked to surrender, Brigadier General Anthony C.

McAuliffe replied, "Nuts." The Allies stopped the German advance although the Battle of the Bulge slowed the Allied invasion of Germany by six weeks.

The German war machine was disintegrating. In the east the Soviets pushed across Poland, Czechoslovakia, and Hungary into Germany. Allied bombers pounded Berlin, Hamburg, and other German cities. One particularly severe fire bombing leveled the entire center of the city of Dresden. In March a small American force captured a key bridge across the Rhine River. Soon Allied armies crossed the Rhine and began the final conquest of Germany.

At that point General Eisenhower had to decide whether to concentrate his forces for a swift advance across Germany to meet the Red Army near Berlin or to spread his armies out to pursue German troops in the southern provinces. Churchill urged Eisenhower to push on to Berlin. The British prime minister did not trust Stalin's promise for free elections in postwar Europe. He wanted the United States and Britain to occupy as much of Germany and eastern Europe as possible before the war ended.

However, Eisenhower believed that the military goal of defeating Germany as completely as possible should outweigh postwar political considerations. The general permitted his field commanders to move slowly but thoroughly as they conquered Germany. Shortly before the war ended, American and Russian troops met at the Elbe River, nearly 100 miles (160 kilometers) west of Berlin.

The Third Reich was now in almost total ruin. The Nazi dictator had committed suicide in Berlin on April 30. One week later, on May 7, General Eisenhower accepted Germany's unconditional surrender, effective the next day, thereafter known as V-E Day.

The joy accompanying the end of the war in Europe was clouded. As Allied troops moved across Europe, they liberated huge concentration camps at Buchenwald, Dachau, Bergen-Belsen, and Auschwitz. Within these horrible camps, the Nazis had carried out their policy of genocide against European Jews. *Genocide* is the systematic destruction of a race of people. The Nazis had starved, tortured, and murdered about 12 million civilians in the concentration camps, including over 6 million Jews. One third of the Jewish population of Europe perished under the Nazi regime.

No rumors of the horrors of Nazi concentration camps could match the scenes Americans found when they liberated the prisoners. Above, at the Buchenwald concentration camp in Germany, United States troops talk to newly freed prisoners. The gaunt man at right was healthier than many of the starving prisoners who survived the camps.

President Truman Takes Office

On April 12, less than one month before the Germans surrendered, President Roosevelt died at his vacation resort in Warm Springs, Georgia. Americans mourned his loss with the greatest outpouring of grief since the death of Abraham Lincoln.

On the afternoon of April 12, Eleanor Roosevelt informed Vice-President Harry S. Truman that her husband had died. Shocked, Truman asked if there was anything he could do for her. "Is there anything we can do for *you?*" she replied. "For you are the one in need of help now."

Certainly Truman had not been prepared for the responsibilities of the office he now assumed. He had no information about the atomic bomb that American scientists were developing. Truman knew little of the Yalta agreements, and he had never been in the secret map room of the White House.

"I felt," Truman admitted, "like the moon, the stars, and all the planets had fallen on me." Nevertheless, Truman, a veteran of Missouri and national politics, moved quickly to take up the unfinished business of Roosevelt's administration.

One of Truman's first acts was to announce that the United States would participate in the United Nations conference in San Francisco later that month, as planned. With Truman's approval, the conference drafted and adopted the Charter of the United Nations. Congress consented to United States membership in the world organization in July 1945.

Meanwhile, planning of the final offensive against the Japanese continued. Hard-won battles on the islands of Iwo Jima (EE woh JEE muh) and Okinawa (OH kuh NAH wuh) brought United States forces within striking distance of Japan. The final assault on the home islands promised to be bitter and bloody, with heavy casualties almost certain. At Iwo Jima and Okinawa, Japanese fighter pilots had employed *kamikaze* tactics, sacrificing their lives by deliberately crashing their planes into Allied ships. There was every reason to think the Japanese would put up an even more desperate struggle if the United States were to invade Japan.

A New Weapon

In July 1945 President Truman went to Potsdam, near Berlin, for a final meeting of the Big Three to discuss postwar settlements in Europe and to plan the final attack on Japan. While at Potsdam, Truman received word that American scientists had successfully detonated an atomic device. On July 16, a blinding light illuminated the early morning sky over the New Mexico desert. Windows cracked over 75 miles (about 120 kilometers) away.

The explosion of the atomic device in New Mexico was the result of a massive research effort known as the Manhattan Project. Between 1942 and 1945, the United

Large American aircraft carriers could launch 300 airplanes—planes that sometimes flew bombing raids over Tokyo. The carriers were therefore prime targets for Japanese kamikaze pilots. A kamikaze pilot would dive at a ship, firing as his plane zoomed to its inevitable crash. In this painting a kamikaze plane is hit before it can strike the carrier Hornet. About one in four kamikaze pilots hit his target.

The city of Hiroshima, Japan, was leveled when an American bomber dropped the first atomic bomb ever used in warfare. A second bomb was dropped on Nagasaki before the Japanese agreed to unconditional surrender.

States government had spent over $2 billion to design and build three atomic bombs. The project required 37 factories and laboratories in 19 states and Canada. It employed over 120,000 people, including many of the most respected nuclear physicists from the United States, Britain, and Canada as well as scientists from throughout Europe who had fled Nazi tyranny.

For President Truman, news of the successful nuclear test came as a great relief. The discussions with Stalin over Poland, Germany, and other difficult postwar problems now seemed less pressing. American leaders had tried to compromise with Stalin because they believed the United States would need Soviet help to defeat Japan. Now that the United States had the atomic bomb, Soviet help became less crucial.

Truman told Stalin about an unspecified new American weapon, and Stalin encouraged him to use it. In the declaration that emerged from the Potsdam Conference, the Allies warned the Japanese that they faced complete destruction if they did not agree to unconditional surrender. Unaware of what the warning really meant, the Japanese ignored it.

On August 6, 1945, the *Enola Gay*, a specially fitted B-29 bomber, dropped an atomic bomb on Hiroshima, Japan, leveling the city. Three days later a second atomic bomb was dropped on Nagasaki. Over 150,000 Japanese died in the two explosions. Thousands more civilians were injured by the radiation from the bomb. In the face of these disasters and the Soviet entry into the war on August 8, the Japanese surrendered on August 14.

The Legacy of World War II

World War II brought unequaled destruction to the nations of the world. Over 55 million civilians and soldiers died in the conflict, nearly 30 million in the Soviet Union alone. About 290,000 Americans died, and 670,000 were wounded. Three military dictatorships had been defeated, but a terrible price had been paid.

The war also changed the map of the world. Former colonial powers, such as France, the Netherlands, Germany, Italy, Japan, and Great Britain, found their empires in ruin. Nations formerly under imperial rule in Asia and Africa were seeking independence and would soon enter the world community as free states. The Soviet Union had become the dominant power in Europe and a powerful force in the rest of the world. The United States had demonstrated that it had the most powerful military force in the world.

World War II revealed the enormous potential of science and technology to either advance civilization or destroy it. The mushroom clouds over Hiroshima and Nagasaki would linger in memory as the dreaded symbols of a new age. But if put to peaceful use, science and technology could improve the

Major Events	
1941	Executive Order 8802 issued
1942	War Department relocates Japanese Americans; Battle of Coral Sea; Battle of Midway; Operation Torch begins
1943	Siege of Leningrad ends; Allies secure Guadalcanal; Axis forces in North Africa surrender; Allies invade Italy; Teheran Conference
1944	Allies begin cross-channel invasion of Europe; United States invades Philippines; Roosevelt elected for fourth term; bombing of Japan begins; Battle of the Bulge
1945	Yalta Conference; Roosevelt dies; Truman becomes President; United Nations founded; Germany surrenders; Potsdam Conference; United States drops atomic bomb on Hiroshima and Nagaski; Japan surrenders

human condition. Better communication and transportation systems could be used either to control people or to liberate them.

Americans entered the postwar era hopeful that their arsenal of weapons and their good will could serve the cause of peace. These hopes were soon tested. Questions about boundaries and free elections that had divided the Allies during the war threatened the peace they had struggled so painfully to achieve. A new era of confrontation was dawning.

SECTION REVIEW

1. Identify: Manhattan Project.
2. Define: genocide, kamikaze.
3. What did General Eisenhower think the most important Allied goal was in 1945?
4. What discovery clouded the joy over German surrender?
5. **Critical Thinking**   In Japanese culture surrender was considered a disgrace. How do you think this belief affected Japanese conduct of the war?

 # Chapter 35 Review

In Perspective

When the United States entered World War II, the future appeared bleak for the Allies. The German army was driving deep into the Soviet Union, and the Japanese were nearly in control of the Pacific and eastern Asia. Allied victories in North Africa and a United States holding action in the Pacific gave the Allies some hope by early 1943.

The American effort on the home front was crucial to ultimate success in the war. Industrial production increased dramatically, and the Great Depression came to an end. The war affected the lives of all Americans. Women assumed a larger role in the civilian labor market. Black Americans also found new opportunities in industry, but black civilians and soldiers continued to face

discrimination. Because of fear of sabotage, Japanese Americans living on the Pacific coast were removed from their homes and jobs and relocated at inland camps.

By 1943 the Allies had begun to take the offensive against the Axis powers. United States and British troops invaded Italy, and Soviet forces moved into eastern Europe. In June 1944 the Allies began the cross-channel invasion of France. The Japanese suffered and inflicted heavy casualties as they relinquished control of Pacific islands. A final German counteroffensive failed, and in early 1945 the Allies marched into Germany. By May the Germans had surrendered, but the war in the Pacific continued until the United States dropped atomic bombs on Hiroshima and Nagasaki in August, ending the war in the Pacific.

Vocabulary

On a separate sheet of paper, write the word or words that best complete each of the following sentences.

1. Another name for battle zones is ___.
2. Japanese-Americans were detained in ___ during World War II.
3. The technique of seizing only strategic islands held by Japan was called ___.
4. ___ is the systematic destruction of a race of people.
5. ___ attacks were suicide attacks by Japanese airplane pilots.

Chapter Checkup

1. (a) Why was 1942 a dark year for the Allies? (b) How did Operation Torch improve the Allied situation in Europe? (c) Why did the Allied position in the Pacific improve by early 1943?
2. Explain how the war affected each of the following groups: (a) organized labor, (b) women, (c) black Americans, (d) Mexican Americans, (e) Italian and German Americans, (f) Japanese Americans.
3. (a) Why did the Allies decide to invade Italy? (b) Were they successful? Explain.
4. (a) Describe Operation Overlord. (b) Was it successful? Explain.
5. (a) Where did diplomatic conferences between Allied leaders take place during the war? (b) What topics did the Big Three discuss at these conferences?

Critical Thinking

1. **Supporting an Opinion** The war that lasted from 1914 to 1918 is usually called World War I, while the war that lasted from 1939 to 1945 is called World War II. Would you agree that World War II was actually more "worldwide" than World War I? Explain.
2. **Comparing** (a) How were Japanese Americans treated during World War II? (b) How does their treatment compare to the way German Americans were treated during World War I? (c) How might you explain the difference?

Developing Basic Skills

1. **Comparing** Review how the government mobilized industry during World War I. (See Chapter 28.) (a) In what way was the effort during World War II similar? (b) In what way was it different? (c) How might you explain the similarities and differences?
2. **Analyzing Fiction as Historical Evidence** World War II has been the topic of many fictional stories in novels, movies, and television shows. Review the steps for analyzing fiction on page 538. Then write a report about the story you have read or seen about the war. Be sure to answer the following questions in your report: (a) What type of source did you use? (b) When was it written or produced? (c) What do you know about the author or creators? (d) What can you learn about World War II by using this source? (e) How is the source limited as historical evidence?

See page 832 for suggested readings.

Writer's Handbook

Writing and Revising a First Draft

There are a few general thoughts to keep in mind when you are ready to revise your first draft. Ask yourself if the introduction leads into the thesis logically. Does each paragraph develop one idea related to the thesis and are the paragraphs organized in a logical order? Is all the information relevant? Are direct quotes smoothly incorporated into the text? Does the conclusion reinforce the thesis? Is your language appropriate and have you explained any unfamiliar technical terms?

Practice: Rewrite the paragraph below to improve the organization and style.

In October 1944, Genral MacArthur who had said "I shall return," returned to the Philippines. In two humongous battles, Japan's sea power was done in. This took place at the battle of the Philippine Sea and the battle for Leyte Gulf. Japan's air force was now reduced to kamikazes who could not turn the tide. MacArthur liberated Manila in February 1945.

Volunteerism

On December 7, 1941, Japanese airplanes bombed the United States fleet at Pearl Harbor. The next day, President Roosevelt asked Congress to declare war on Japan and began to ready the nation for the battles ahead.

The government had the power to draft soldiers, levy taxes, and order factories to produce war materials. But winning the war depended on Americans giving whole-hearted support to the struggle, and this the government could not order. On December 9, President Roosevelt spoke to the American people over the radio. "We are now in this war," he said. "We are all in it—all the way. Every single man, woman, and child is a partner in the most tremendous undertaking in American history." Roosevelt asked Americans to help voluntarily in whatever way they could.

The Volunteer Spirit Americans responded generously to the President's plea. The nation faced a critical shortage of rubber, vital for many military uses. Roosevelt asked Americans to turn in "old tires, old rubber shoes, bathing caps. . . ." Within a few weeks, Americans had dug some 450,000 tons of scrap rubber from their attics, garages, and basements. The scrap rubber was boiled down and made into tires for jeeps and airplanes.

Even children did their part for the war effort. War industries were constantly short of iron, steel, aluminum, and copper. So, all around the country, children organized groups like "Uncle Sam's Scrappers" and the "Tin Can Colonels." They scoured their neighborhoods for old cans, car parts, and other scrap metal. By 1945 scrap scavengers were supplying much of the steel and half the tin and paper needed for the war effort. Millions more Americans helped the government finance the war by buying war bonds—some $49 billion worth from 1941 to 1945.

The volunteer spirit Americans showed during World War II had its roots deep in American history. As far back as 1717,

Gathering scrap metal was just one of the many ways volunteers helped out during World War II.

Boston had set up a volunteer fire department. During the Revolution, Americans had overwhelmingly favored using voluntary state militias rather than a standing army organized by the federal government. So great was the response of Tennesseans to the call to arms during the Mexican War that Tennessee ever since has been known as the "Volunteer State."

By the 1800s, the new nation had thousands of voluntary groups. When Alexis de Tocqueville visited the United States in the 1830s, he noted, "Americans of all ages, all conditions, and all dispositions constantly form associations. . . . The Americans make associations to give entertainments, to found seminaries, to build inns, to construct churches, to diffuse books, to send missionaries to the antipodes [places exactly opposite on the Earth]; in this manner they found hospitals, prisons, and schools."

Women's Role Women took a leading role in the voluntary associations of the mid-1800s. By then, mass-produced goods eased the housekeeping duties of middle-class women. Many women found that volunteering gave them a chance to do challenging and rewarding work. Women thus made up the leadership as well as the rank-and-file of literary societies and temperance, antislavery, and women's suffrage groups.

During the Civil War, women of all social and economic classes on both sides pitched in to help. Women organized thousands of aid societies to collect money, make blankets, bullets, and other gear, and care for wounded soldiers. At first, both the Union and Confederacy refused to allow women nurses to work near the battle line. But as the bloody war dragged on,

sheer necessity forced both armies to change their policies. Women worked in field hospitals just out of cannon range, and even helped take wounded men from the field after battles.

Clara Barton set the model for selfless volunteerism during the Civil War by risking her life helping the wounded on both sides of the fray. From her experience aiding both the Union and Confederacy, Barton realized the need for a relief organization that would have access to both sides during wartime. The American Red Cross, founded in 1881, met this need. As president of the Red Cross, Barton fought for an international agreement designating the Red Cross as a neutral agency. Today, Red Cross volunteers are often the only people allowed to visit prisoners in totalitarian countries.

In today's fast-paced world, many functions once carried on by volunteers are now performed by professionals. Nurses, firefighters, and police are usually salaried employees. Major charities have staffs of paid professionals. Yet, the voluntary spirit is very much alive in the United States today. Business organizations such as the Lions, Rotary, and Kiwanis and fraternal organizations like the Knights of Columbus, Elks, and Shriners are supported by volunteer work and countributions, as are Little League and 4-H. Citizen action groups like Common Cause or the American Enterprise Institute and professional societies from the Police Benevolent Association to the American Historical Association have flourished as well. As Tocqueville foresaw, Americans have continued to nurture their democracy, not only through participation in government, but through the variety of their voluntary associations as well.

War puts unusual strains on a society. During World War II, volunteers helped provide food for the home front while the United States sent tons of food to Europe.

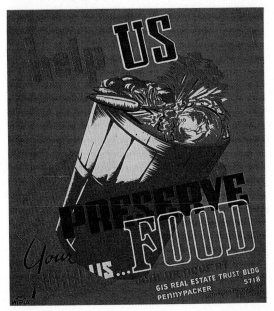

1. How did Americans display a spirit of volunteerism during World War II?
2. What special contributions have American women made as volunteers?
3. How can volunteer work benefit the volunteer as well as society?

Lillian Gilbreth

There is a saying, "If you want something done, ask a busy person." No better example could be found to support this idea than Lillian Moller Gilbreth. Lillian Gilbreth was the mother of 12 children, holder of several Ph.D.s, and a world-famous efficiency expert who ran her own business. Yet like many other Americans, she found an astounding amount of time for volunteer work.

Lillian Moller grew up in Oakland, California. She studied psychology at the University of California, where she was the first woman to speak at a commencement. Not long after, on a visit to Boston, Lillian met Frank Gilbreth. They were married in 1904.

At the time, Frank Gilbreth was a pioneer in the field of scientific management. He was constantly seeking more efficient ways to use time and labor. The Gilbreths made their home a laboratory for experiments in efficiency. A "Family Council" of parents and children managed day-to-day business, since the Gilbreths believed democracy increased cooperation. The council assigned all the household chores. Other jobs, like painting or repairing, went to the child who bid the lowest price. Two of the Gilbreth children later told the story of their unusual upbringing in the book *Cheaper by the Dozen.*

In 1924, Lillian's efficiency was put to the ultimate test. That year her husband died, leaving her with 11 surviving youngsters to raise alone. Lillian Gilbreth had to convince clients that she could carry on without her husband. Soon, she confirmed her own reputation as an expert in scientific management.

In the 1930s, Gilbreth became concerned with problems faced by the handicapped. She found that houses, furniture, and appliances were not built with the needs of the handicapped in mind. Gilbreth designed a model kitchen for the handicapped and wrote *Normal Lives for the Disabled,* which suggested ways for dis-

The volunteer activities of Lillian Gilbreth (1878–1972) spanned several decades and included service on the New Jersey Board of Regents and a national committee of the Girl Scouts of America.

abled people to do housework. She also donated her talents to help several groups that did physical rehabilitation.

Despite her heavy work schedule, Gilbreth made time to do other volunteer work as well. She helped churches and libraries in her community and was an educational adviser to the Girl Scouts of America. In the first years of the Great Depression she served on the Emergency Committee for Unemployment Relief formed by President Roosevelt. During World War II she was a consultant on education to the Office of War Information. Following the war, she served as a member of the Civil Defense Advisory Commission. In 1966 she was the first woman to receive the Hoover medal for distinguished public service by an engineer.

Lillian Gilbreth remained an active writer and lecturer well into her eighties. Today, many of her ideas about rehabilitating the handicapped are still studied. Most of all she is remembered as a woman whose full, active life combined business, scholarship, family, and public service.

1. What did Lillian Gilbreth do to help the physically handicapped?
2. In what ways is Lillian Gilbreth an example of the spirit of volunteerism?

Voices of Freedom

Entertaining the Troops

World War II brought the voluntary spirit in the United States to a peak. The United Service Organizations (USO) put together touring companies of actors, comedians, bandleaders, singers, and dancers to entertain the armed forces overseas. The following account of one of these traveling shows is from the New York Times of April 2, 1944.

The stage is a rough board affair, supported by freshly hewn logs. On it a girl, dressed in a simple cotton dress like those you see on the boardwalk . . . on a summer afternoon, is singing. Behind her two other entertainers are sitting on camp stools and to the right an accordionist pumps his arms. . . .

The scene is in New Guinea. It is hot—115 degrees in back of the stage, 130 plus under the arc lights that are powered by a mobile Army generator standing nearby. . . . The accordion's tones swell to a crescendo for the closing phrases. The singer's last note is cut short by a roar that breaks across the jungle stillness. A thousand pairs of hands are clapping. Men are shouting and whistling.

The singer and the performers with her in New Guinea make up an overseas company of the Camp Shows branch of the United Service Organizations. At the present time, eighty such companies are out of the country, giving shows in bomb-damaged opera houses in Italy, in rickety Nissen huts in North Africa, in storage barns in Alaska and the Aleutians, in jungles, deserts, mountain hideouts—in fact, wherever American boys are stationed.

Camp Shows over the past two and a half years has built a far-flung global circuit . . . . Camp Shows' job—with the help of the Hollywood Victory Committee—is primarily one of finding talent and molding it into variety-type shows. The talent falls into two classifications. First there are the paid USO Camp Show performers, hired from theaters, vaudeville companies, night clubs, and shows. . . . In the second class are Broadway, Hollywood, and radio volunteers who offer their services for a minimum of six weeks. . . .

Letters flood . . . into USO-Camp Shows from soldiers and sailors in the fighting zones and from their parents at home attesting the gratitude of the servicemen for the "live shows." There is not an actor who has returned who has not had mail and telephone calls from parents in all parts of the United States to tell how much their sons liked their performances.

©1944 by The New York Times Company. Reprinted by permission.

1. Why would members of the armed forces be so responsive to the live shows?
2. What motivated Americans to such a high degree of volunteerism during World War II?

Unit Ten

The United States in a Changing World

As suburbs grew in the 1950s, more and more people took trains to work in the cities.

1964 The Beatles were one of the British rock groups that revolutionized American music.

	1945	1955	1965
POLITICS AND GOVERNMENT		**1950** McCarthy makes charges about communists	**1963** John Kennedy assassinated
SOCIETY AND CULTURE	**1947** Jackie Robinson is first black player in major league	**1956** *The Organization Man* analyzes bureaucracies	
ECONOMICS AND TECHNOLOGY	**1946** Strikes in steel, automobile, railroad industries		**1962** John Glenn orbits the earth
WORLD EVENTS		**1949** Communists win control of China	**1956** Hungarians revolt against Soviet control
	Truman	Eisenhower	Kennedy

1950 United States troops fought in Korea as part of a United Nations force.

1963 Martin Luther King, Jr., led a huge demonstration in Washington, D.C., to demand an end to discrimination.

1972 Richard Nixon's visit to China opened the door for improved relations.

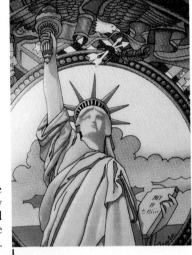

1986 The centennial of the Statue of Liberty showed the renewed patriotism of the late 1980s.

| 1965 | 1975 | 1985 | PRESENT |

1974 Richard Nixon resigns as President in wake of Watergate

1984 Reagan reelected President

1965 Voting Rights Act allows federal officials to register voters

1981 Sandra Day O'Connor appointed to Supreme Court

1973 Alaskan Pipeline is approved

1980 Inflation rate is 13.5 percent

1986 Congress passes major tax reform bill

1967 Six-Day War breaks out

1975 Helsinki Accords spell out human rights standards

1986 Nuclear accident occurs at Chernobyl plant in Soviet Union

Johnson   Nixon   Ford   Carter   Reagan

1984 Ronald Reagan was easily renominated at the Republican National Convention.

Lasers are instrumental in many scientific advances, from medicine to music.

The Postwar International Scene

36

(1945–1960)

A 1946 atomic bomb test in New Mexico

At 7:00 P.M. on August 14, 1945, President Harry Truman announced the unconditional surrender of Japan. Across the nation millions of Americans poured into the streets to celebrate. Two million people danced and cheered in Times Square in New York City, where the celebration lasted until dawn. In St. Louis people knelt quietly at 2:00 A.M. for a prayer service. Everyone rejoiced that the war was over.

Behind the outpouring of joy, however, hung doubts about the future. The explosions of atom bombs at Hiroshima and Nagasaki cast a shadow over the victory celebration. Incredible destruction in Japan and many European nations created concern about their future. Americans grew increasingly worried about the intentions of the Soviet Union.

Korean War

1945	1947	1949	1951	1953	1955	1957	1959	1961

| **1945** United Nations founded | **1947** Truman Doctrine, Marshall Plan announced | **1949** NATO founded; communists win in China | **1952** Dwight D. Eisenhower elected President | **1955** Summit Conference in Geneva | **1956** Suez crisis begins; Hungarian revolt | **1959** Castro wins power in Cuba | **1960** U2 shot down over U.S.S.R. |

1 The Postwar World

After World War I, the United States had tried to withdraw from foreign affairs. At the end of World War II, however, the nation was a major world power with awesome responsibilities. Both allies and enemies had been devastated by the war, leaving only the Soviet Union and the United States to compete for world leadership.

Roots of Conflict in Europe

From the moment the Bolsheviks seized power in 1917, most Americans had viewed the Soviet Union with a mixture of mistrust and fear. World War II had brought the Soviet Union and the United States together as Allies, but deep suspicions lingered on both sides.

Soviet Premier Joseph Stalin had doubted his allies' willingness to assist the Soviet Union during the war. He believed that the British and Americans had purposely delayed the cross-channel invasion in order to prolong the Soviet struggle against Germany. He was also angered by their refusal to acknowledge that the Soviet Union needed a buffer zone of friendly states near its borders to protect it against future German attack.

Many Americans, including some officials in the Department of State, doubted that the United States could trust the Soviet Union. Some believed that the Soviets had a plan for worldwide revolution and unlimited territorial expansion. Soviet actions after the war seemed to justify such concern.

In 1944 and 1945 the Red Army had driven German troops out of Soviet territory and continued to pursue them west. (See page 649.) As a result the Soviet Union emerged from the war in control of much of eastern Europe. During the wartime conferences, Stalin had agreed to allow free elections in Poland once the war was over. Instead, the Soviets installed a communist-dominated government and crushed all opposition. A similar fate befell other eastern European nations over the next three years. The Red Army maintained order, and Soviet-backed communists organized governments.

Another conflict arose over the future of Germany. During the war Britain, France, the United States, and the Soviet Union had agreed to divide Germany into four zones. (See the map below.) The capital city, Berlin, was similarly divided into four sectors. But Berlin itself was located deep in the Soviet zone, and the agreement among the Allies did not guarantee free access to Berlin through Soviet-controlled territory. Soviet actions in Berlin and the rest of eastern Europe were soon to emerge as major points of conflict between the United States and the Soviet Union.

The United Nations

The Allies knew that the end of the war would not result in an end to international conflict. Even as war raged they had planned

■ *At the end of World War II, the Allied powers divided Germany into four zones of occupation. Although the German capital, Berlin, was in the Soviet-occupied zone, all four Allies shared control of the city.*

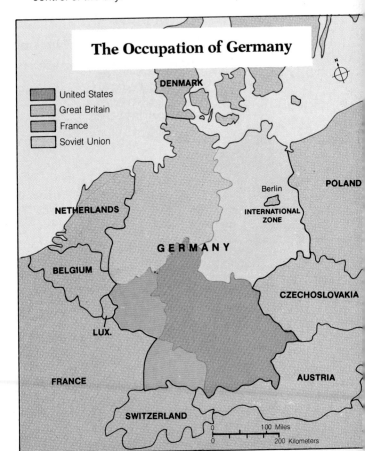

The Occupation of Germany

United States
Great Britain
France
Soviet Union

DENMARK

NETHERLANDS

BELGIUM

LUX.

GERMANY

Berlin

INTERNATIONAL ZONE

POLAND

CZECHOSLOVAKIA

FRANCE

AUSTRIA

SWITZERLAND

0   100 Miles
0   200 Kilometers

for an international peace-keeping organization. (See page 653.) In April 1945 representatives of 50 nations met in San Francisco and adopted a charter for such an organization, the United Nations (UN). Member states pledged to seek peaceful solutions to international disputes. The UN would try to prevent wars and try to stop those that did break out. UN members also pledged to work together to eliminate hunger, disease, and illiteracy.

According to the UN charter, six major bodies make up the United Nations. (See the diagram below.) All member nations belong to the General Assembly, which discusses world problems and recommends action to members or other UN organizations.

The Security Council is the UN body most directly responsible for maintaining world peace. Originally representatives of 11 nations made up the Security Council, but that number has since grown to 15. Five major powers—the United States, Great Britain, France, the Soviet Union, and China—have permanent seats on the council. The remaining members are elected for two-year terms by the General Assembly.

The Security Council investigates conflicts between nations and recommends solutions. It can organize a peace-keeping force made up of troops from member nations. However, the council has no power to enforce its decisions. Furthermore, any permanent member of the Security Council can veto council resolutions. The Soviet Union used the veto frequently during the early postwar years.

UN Action in the Middle East

The first case to come before the Security Council involved a confrontation between the Soviet Union and the United States over Iran. During the war, Soviet, British, and American troops had occupied Iran to guard its vital oil fields and protect the main supply route to the Soviet Union. When the war ended, the Soviets encouraged rebellion in

■ Representatives of 50 nations met in San Francisco in 1945 to adopt the Charter of the United Nations. The diagram shows the six major bodies of the United Nations, which has its headquarters in New York City.

The United Nations

Security Council
investigates situations that threaten the peace and develops UN policies

Secretariat
is responsible for the administrative work of the UN, headed by the secretary-general

General Assembly
discusses issues and recommends actions

Economic and Social Council
promotes human rights and works for improved economic and social conditions

International Court of Justice
rules on international legal disputes

Trusteeship Council
administers territories that were not self-governing when the UN was established

Iran, and Soviet troops prevented the Iranian government from restoring order.

With strong support from the United States, Iran brought a complaint before the UN Security Council. As the council debated, the Soviet Union refused to remove its troops even though Britain and the United States had already done so. Finally, in April 1946, after forcing an oil concession from the Iranians, the Soviets withdrew and the crisis ended.

The UN also tried to settle a crisis in Palestine, a territory administered by Great Britain since World War I. British rule became increasingly unpopular after World War II, both among the Arabs, who made up a majority of the population, and among resident Jews. Many European Jews had settled in Palestine during the 1930s as a result of Nazi persecution.

In 1947 a UN commission recommended that Palestine be divided into an Arab and a Jewish state. In 1948 the British withdrew, and the Jewish residents of Palestine proclaimed the nation of Israel. President Truman immediately recognized Israel. But neighboring states vowed to resist, and war broke out. The UN eventually arranged an armistice in 1949, which restored an uneasy peace to the area.

Turmoil in Southern Europe

World War II plunged much of southern Europe into political and economic turmoil. After the Allies drove the Nazis out of Greece in late 1944, a bitter civil war erupted between supporters and opponents of the Greek monarchy. A truce in January 1945 ended the fighting temporarily, but civil war broke out again in 1946. Meanwhile the Greek economy was in ruin, and starvation was widespread.

Major opponents of the Greek monarchy were communists who received aid from Yugoslavia, a communist nation bordering Greece. The Greek monarchy received aid from Britain. Fear on the part of United States officials that communists might seize power in Greece was heightened when it became apparent that Britain could not continue to aid the Greek government for long.

Communists also became a political force in Italy after World War II. Difficult economic conditions made many Italians desperate for reform, and some turned to the Communist party. In the 1946 parliamentary elections the Communist party won 104 of 556 seats.

East Asia Transformed

The end of the war brought dramatic changes to East Asia, especially Japan, Korea, and China. After the war, the United States Army, under the command of General Douglas MacArthur, occupied Japan. General MacArthur drafted a constitution for Japan that called for representative government and left the emperor powerless. Traditional educational practices, family-controlled land trusts, state-supported religion, and the large standing army were abolished. MacArthur intended to demilitarize Japan, that is, to end the influence of the military on Japanese society and government.

Japan had been the most powerful nation in Asia for decades. The defeat and demilitarization of Japan left a power vacuum in East Asia. As a result, the United States and the Soviet Union competed for influence there. Korea, which had been under Japanese control since 1910, became a major area of conflict. A wartime agreement between the United States and the Soviet Union provided that Korea would be divided along the 38th parallel. The Soviet Union was to disarm Japanese troops in the northern zone, and the United States was to do the same in the southern sector. The two powers agreed that national elections would be held to unify the country.

After the war the Soviet Union installed a communist government in its zone and refused to cooperate in national elections. An American-born Korean, Syngman Rhee (SIHNG muhn REE), was elected president in the south. In effect, by 1948 Korea had become two nations: North Korea backed by the Soviet Union and South Korea backed by the United States. The stage was set for further conflict.

Civil war had raged in China since the early 1930s. Mao Tse-tung (MOW zuh DUNG) led communist forces against the nationalist government of Chiang Kai-shek. During World War II, Chiang had used his best troops against the communists rather than concentrating on Japan. Once the war was over, the civil war became more bitter. The communists had an army of 500,000 troops, less than one fourth the strength of the nationalist army. The nationalist army was also more modern, largely trained and equipped by the United States. However, the government of Chiang Kai-shek was plagued by widespread corruption. That weakened the nationalists' ability to fight and drove many Chinese to support the communists.

In December 1945 President Harry Truman sent General George C. Marshall to China to work for the unification of China under a government acceptable to both sides. Shortly after Marshall's arrival a cease-fire was declared, and negotiations between the nationalists and the communists began. But neither side was willing to compromise. The civil war continued, and Marshall returned to the United States in January 1947.

SECTION REVIEW

1. Identify: United Nations, Security Council, General Assembly, Mao Tse-tung, Syngman Rhee.
2. What agreement did the Allies reach about the fate of Germany after World War II?
3. What role did the UN play in the creation of Israel?
4. What were the two opposing forces in the Chinese civil war?
5. **Critical Thinking** Why do you think the United States did not return to the isolationism that followed World War I?

2 A Cold War Begins

The events of the early postwar years in eastern and southern Europe and in East Asia contributed to growing tension between the United States and the Soviet Union. In 1946 Bernard Baruch, an elder statesman and presidential adviser, used the term "cold war" to describe that tension. That same year in a speech in Fulton, Missouri, Winston Churchill described an "iron curtain" that had fallen between the nations of western and eastern Europe.

The Truman Doctrine

United States policy toward the Soviet Union after World War II drew on the ideas of George Kennan. Kennan had served as a diplomatic officer in the United States embassy in Moscow and had become a leading expert on the Soviet Union. His wartime dispatches from Moscow contained many warnings about Soviet ambitions.

Kennan attributed Soviet actions largely to Stalin's fear that "hostile capitalist" nations would encircle the Soviet Union. In Stalin's view, Kennan continued, the Soviet Union would have to overthrow all western governments to prevent such encirclement. Kennan argued that the United States should "contain" aggressive Soviet actions by applying counterforce at strategic political and geographic locations.

Events in Greece and Turkey soon gave the Truman administration an opportunity to apply such a "containment" policy. In February 1947 the British informed the United States they could no longer afford to assist the Greek monarchy. As you have read, Greece was in the midst of a civil war. (See page 669.) President Truman feared that British withdrawal would mean victory for the communist forces. Political unrest in neighboring Turkey made that nation desperate for foreign assistance as well. Furthermore the Soviet Union was demanding part of Turkish territory.

Encouraged by Under Secretary of State Dean Acheson, Truman decided to ask Congress for $400 million in aid to Greece and Turkey. In what became known as the Truman Doctrine the President declared before a joint session of Congress that "it must be the policy of the United States to support free peoples who are resisting attempted subjugation." In his speech Truman formally recognized a cold war between democratic nations and those under communist domination. Economic and military aid, he said, would be the major weapons of the United States.

George Kennan objected to the administration's application of containment. The unrest in Turkey was not caused by communists, he argued, and military aid might be

The Truman Doctrine

On March 12, 1947, President Harry S. Truman was before a joint session of Congress to seek aid for Greece and Turkey. United States military experts had told the President that the Greek government might fall to communist revolutionaries if it did not receive assistance. Turkey was facing territorial demands by the Soviet Union. A portion of Truman's speech is printed below. The policy he proposed became known as the Truman Doctrine.

I believe that it must be the policy of the United States to support free peoples who are resisting attempted subjugation by armed minorities or by outside pressures. I believe that we must assist free peoples to work out their own destinies in their own way. I believe that our help should be primarily through economic and financial aid, which is essential to economic stability and orderly political processes.

Should we fail to aid Greece and Turkey in this fateful hour, the effect will be far-reaching to the West as well as to the East. We must take immediate and resolute action. . . .

The seeds of totalitarian regimes are nurtured by misery and wants. They spread and grow in the evil soil of poverty and strife. They reach their full growth when the hopes of a people for a better life has died. We must keep that hope alive. The free peoples of the world look to us for support in maintaining their freedoms. If we falter in our leadership, we may endanger the peace of the world—and we shall surely endanger the welfare of our own nation.

Great responsibilities have been placed upon us by the swift movement of events. I am confident that the Congress will face these responsibilities squarely.

---

unnecessarily provocative. However, Truman and Acheson disagreed with Kennan because they were eager to take a forceful stance in the growing cold war. The Truman Doctrine proved to be effective in both Greece and Turkey. Bolstered by American aid, the Greek monarchy defeated the uprising against the government, and order was restored in Turkey.

The Marshall Plan

In 1947 Secretary of State George C. Marshall returned from a trip to Europe greatly concerned. He had seen nations and people badly in need of economic and material assistance. "The patient is sinking while the doctors deliberate," he warned.

With its attention now focused on western Europe, the Truman administration moved quickly. The Europeans needed financial assistance to rebuild their devastated economies. Marshall urged European leaders to draw up a plan for recovery. He purposely did not exclude the Soviet Union or the eastern European nations, which had become known as the Soviet bloc.

In June 1947 a Soviet delegation arrived in Paris to meet with delegations from Great Britain and France. Three days later the Soviets left, refusing to accept the French and British plan for a program for recovery in Europe as a whole. Within a week the Soviet Union had devised a plan to create an economic bloc in eastern Europe. Meanwhile, representatives from 16 other nations met in Paris to work out a recovery program, which was completed by September. They requested $16 billion in American aid over a period of four years.

In presenting the program to Congress, President Truman pointed out that such aid would have many benefits for the United States. Stronger economies would help the nations of western Europe resist any domestic communist threat. Economic recovery would also strengthen their military capacity. Furthermore, Truman noted that the demand for American exports would increase, thereby improving the United States economy.

For the United States, the key to the European Recovery Plan, or Marshall Plan, as it was known, was the economic recovery of Germany. "Without a revival of German

671

production," Marshall told Congress, "there can be no revival of Europe's economy." Though fearful of a strong Germany, other European nations agreed, since they would also benefit from the aid. In four years over $12 billion went into rebuilding western Europe.

The Marshall Plan became the crowning achievement of the containment policy. As prosperity returned to Europe, the likelihood of communist victories subsided. But the decision to help rebuild western Germany was to lead to conflict with the Soviet Union.

The Berlin Blockade

Germany, as you have read, had been divided into four zones of Allied occupation after the war. (See page 667.) Britain, France, and the United States worked closely in the administration of the western sectors of the country, while the Soviet government administered the eastern section. By June 1948, after fruitless discussions with the Soviet Union over the unification of Germany, the United States, Britain, and France decided to merge the western zones and establish the area as an independent nation. The unified zones would become the German Federal Republic, known today as West Germany.

On June 24, 1948, the Soviet Union responded to the division of Germany by denying all road, rail, and river access to West Berlin, thereby cutting off supplies to more than 2 million residents. Berlin, located in the Soviet zone, was highly vulnerable to a blockade. The Soviets hoped that the blockade would drive the other Allies out of Berlin and lay the basis for the unification of Germany under Soviet influence.

President Truman reacted strongly to the Soviet challenge in Berlin, ordering a massive airlift to supply West Berlin during the blockade. Each day for 321 days, the Berlin airlift delivered thousands of tons of supplies to the western sector of the city. In May 1949, convinced of American determination to preserve the independence of West Berlin, the Soviet Union ended the blockade.

Growing Commitment

In March 1948 Britain, France, Belgium, the Netherlands, and Luxembourg had signed the Brussels Treaty, stating that if any of the five was the victim of military attack, the others would offer assistance. Although originally opposed to a military alliance with European nations, many members of the United States Congress changed their minds

When the Soviet Union closed off all road, rail, and river traffic to West Berlin in 1948, the United States launched an airlift to supply the encircled city. An American cargo plane delivering food and other vital supplies to West Berlin is seen here above the walls of Berlin buildings bombed during World War II.

after the Berlin blockade. They saw that such a union would be of political as well as military benefit.

In April 1949 representatives of the Brussels Treaty nations, joined by Denmark, Norway, Portugal, Italy, Iceland, Canada, and the United States, signed a mutual defense treaty creating the North Atlantic Treaty Organization (NATO).* The treaty stated that an attack on any one of the NATO nations would be considered an attack on all of them. The Soviet Union later formed an opposing alliance, the Warsaw Pact, with Albania, Bulgaria, Czechoslovakia, East Germany, Hungary, Poland, and Romania. (See the map on page 674.)

United States membership in NATO represented a break with an isolationist past. It was the first time that the United States had joined a peacetime alliance committing the country to the defense of Europe. Possession of nuclear weapons made the United States the most important member of the alliance. As a result, the commander of NATO military forces was always an American general.

A successful foreign policy contributed to Truman's reelection in 1948. In his inaugural address, however, he tried to balance public concern about military issues by announcing a "bold new program" to provide economic aid to newly independent nations. After 18 months of debate Congress agreed to provide $27 million in aid. The aid program thereafter was modest, but it had some effect. For example, American assistance helped the Iranians wipe out malaria.

Challenges to Postwar Confidence

Two events in late 1949 underscored the realization among Americans that the tension of the cold war was to dominate international affairs for years to come. The first of these occurred in China. Each month of 1949 brought news of another victory of Mao Tse-tung's communist forces over the nationalist armies of Chiang Kai-shek. By the end of the year, the communists had taken control of mainland China and established the People's Republic of China. The nationalists had retreated to the island of Formosa, now known as Taiwan.

European concern about Soviet aggression after World War II was a major reason for the founding of NATO. This French poster shows the Soviet military threatening Europe. The figures in the background are Soviet citizens being sent to Siberia. Stalin is the small figure in the center.

Mao's victory provoked a storm of criticism against the Truman administration. Critics charged that Truman had "lost" China by concentrating military and economic aid to Europe. More aid to the nationalists, some Americans insisted, would have saved Chiang's regime. The defeat of the Nationalist Army weakened American confidence in the way President Truman was applying the policy of containment.

Truman refused to recognize the communist government on mainland China. Instead the United States government recognized the nationalists on Taiwan as the legitimate government of China. In 1950 the United States began providing military protection for Taiwan.

Another event in 1949 dampened American hopes for a quick end to the cold war. In September, President Truman announced that the Soviet Union had successfully tested an atomic device. United States monopoly on atomic power was over. As Senator Arthur Vandenberg of Michigan grimly put it, "This is now a different world."

---

*Turkey and Greece joined NATO in 1952, West Germany in 1955.

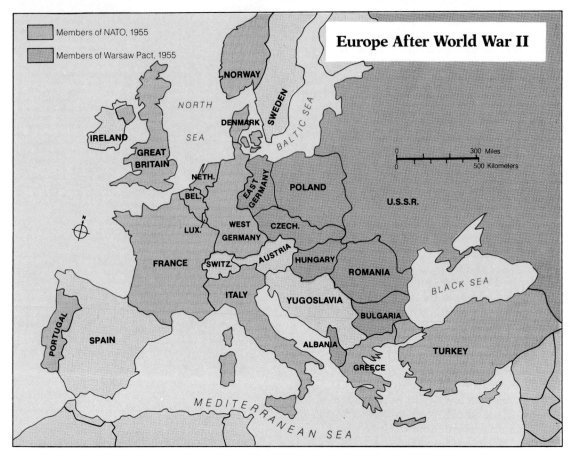

Members of NATO, 1955

Members of Warsaw Pact, 1955

Europe After World War II

NORWAY

NORTH

SEA

SWEDEN

BALTIC SEA

DENMARK

IRELAND

GREAT
BRITAIN

300 Miles

500 Kilometers

NETH.

EAST GERMANY

POLAND

BEL.

U.S.S.R.

LUX.

WEST
GERMANY

CZECH.

FRANCE

SWITZ.

AUSTRIA

HUNGARY

ROMANIA

BLACK SEA

ITALY

YUGOSLAVIA

BULGARIA

PORTUGAL

SPAIN

ALBANIA

TURKEY

GREECE

MEDITERRANEAN SEA

■ *The United States joined with nations of western Europe in 1949 to create NATO. NATO countries agreed that an attack on one was an attack on all. Countries under Soviet influence later formed the Warsaw Pact. As the map shows, few countries in Europe remained outside the two alliances. Compare this map with the map of Europe after World War I on page 515. What countries were independent in 1918 but not in the 1950s? What happened to them?*

Responding to criticism at home and to the Soviet nuclear test, President Truman authorized full-scale work on the development of the even more powerful hydrogen bomb. Over the next two years the United States began rebuilding its conventional, or nonatomic, forces, such as land armies, weapons, and air power. All of them had been greatly reduced after World War II. Many of the rebuilt forces were committed to the NATO command in Europe.

President Truman further authorized the National Security Council, which consisted of the heads of defense and intelligence agencies, to undertake a full examination of possible foreign policy strategies. In 1950 the council produced the classified document NSC 68. It described the future of the world as "an indefinite period of tension and danger." The authors of NSC 68 argued that the United States must com-

mit itself to whatever military steps necessary to protect the noncommunist world and to meet "each fresh challenge promptly and unequivocally." NSC 68 provided the basis for United States foreign policy through much of the 1950s and 1960s.

SECTION REVIEW

1. Identify: Truman Doctrine, Marshall Plan, NATO.

2. Define: containment.

3. According to General Marshall, what was the main purpose of the Marshall Plan?

4. What two events in 1949 increased cold war tensions?

5. **Critical Thinking** How did the Truman Doctrine thwart the Soviet Union's hopes for a warm water port?

3 The Korean War

In the midst of President Truman's re-examination of cold war policies after the events of 1949, the United States faced a major crisis in Asia. A communist invasion of South Korea tested American commitment to the policy of containment.

The War Begins

As you have read, after World War II Korea was divided into a northern zone dominated by the Soviet Union and a southern zone tied to the United States. Negotiations on the unification of Korea had been unsuccessful. On June 11, 1950, the South Korean government arrested several delegates from the north. And on June 25, 1950, North Korea invaded South Korea.

An emergency meeting of the United Nations Security Council later that day passed a resolution condemning the invasion and demanding immediate withdrawal of North Korean forces. Two days later, the council recommended United Nations action to aid South Korea. Both votes in the Security Council passed because the Soviet representative was not present to veto the resolutions. The Soviet Union was boycotting the council to protest the failure of the UN to grant membership to the People's Republic of China.

On the same day that the UN voted to provide military aid to South Korea, President Truman ordered United States planes and ships to back up the South Korean army. Three days later, on June 30, Truman ordered United States troops into the Korean fighting. A week later the UN voted to establish a joint UN fighting force under the command of a general chosen by the President of the United States. Truman selected General Douglas MacArthur. About four fifths of the UN force under MacArthur consisted of United States troops.

The goal of the United Nations action, as described by President Truman, was to drive the North Koreans out of South Korea. But United States troops rushed in from bases in Japan were poorly prepared to fight, and the South Koreans lacked vital equipment. Consequently, Soviet-supplied North Korean troops pushed farther south. By August 1950

When North Korea attacked South Korea, the United Nations condemned the action. The United States and other UN countries sent troops to help the South Koreans. Here, North Korean prisoners under American guard file through a Korean field.

the North Koreans had captured virtually all of South Korea. In September, however, MacArthur directed a surprise landing at Inchon, behind North Korean lines. Within two weeks, UN forces had recaptured almost all of South Korea.

According to the original objectives of the war, the United Nations–United States mission was complete. But the momentum of MacArthur's assault now began to take over. In October, under MacArthur's orders and with the approval of both Truman and the UN General Assembly, UN forces crossed the 38th parallel into North Korea. As MacArthur pushed north, the UN revised

■ *When North Korea attacked South Korea, a United Nations force came to the assistance of the south. A North Korean advance drove deep into South Korea. Then UN troops under General Douglas MacArthur landed at Inchon, far behind North Korean lines. From there they recaptured most of South Korea. When the forces continued north across the 38th parallel, however, the People's Republic of China entered the war in support of North Korea.*

Line of farthest North Korean advance, September 1950

Line of farthest UN advance, November 1950

Line of farthest North Korean–Chinese advance, January 1951

Armistice line

CHINA

Yalu River

NORTH

KOREA

SEA OF JAPAN

• Pyongyang

N

38th parallel

Panmunjom

• Seoul
Inchon

YELLOW

SEA

SOUTH

KOREA

The Korean War

150 Miles

0

0

200 Kilometers

• Pusan

its aims, calling for "the establishment of a unified, independent, and democratic Korea."

The invasion of North Korea brought disastrous consequences. Communist China had warned that it would not "sit back with folded hands" if United States troops marched into North Korea. American leaders paid little attention to such warnings, believing that China would never intervene. The American leaders were wrong. In late November hundreds of thousands of Chinese soldiers crossed the Yalu River into North Korea and forced United Nations troops to retreat with heavy losses across the 38th parallel.

A Clash Between Truman and MacArthur

The Korean conflict was now, in General MacArthur's words, "an entirely new war." How that war should be fought became the focus of a controversy between General MacArthur and President Truman. Truman and most of his advisers decided to revive the original objectives of the war: restoring the boundary between North and South Korea. They now supported the strategy of limited war. In a *limited war* the United States would seek specific objectives rather than total victory over North Korea. Limited war also meant that nuclear weapons would not be used.

Truman reasoned that a major land war in Asia to defeat North Korea and China might provoke Soviet retaliation in Europe or elsewhere in Asia. MacArthur, however, did not accept the concept of limited war. In war, he declared, "there is no substitute for victory." He believed that political decisions made in Washington hampered his ability to conduct the war. MacArthur wanted to extend the war into China by bombing bases in Manchuria.

Relations between MacArthur and Truman grew steadily worse. By March 1951, after United Nations forces had recovered most of South Korea, Truman was ready to seek a negotiated peace. MacArthur, however, wanted to advance into North Korea again. Ignoring the President, MacArthur issued a public statement demanding total North Korean surrender. The statement undercut Truman's attempt at negotiations. Because of MacArthur's insubordination, President Truman removed the general from command and ordered him back to the United States.

MacArthur returned home to a hero's welcome, and he received a standing ovation when he addressed a joint session of Congress. A congressional committee began investigating Truman's dismissal of MacArthur. For a time, feelings ran high in support of the general, but Truman successfully defended his decision. The long-standing tradition of civilian control of the military in the United States was reaffirmed.

Cease-Fire

Negotiations to work out a cease-fire in Korea began in July 1951. They continued for the next two years while the fighting went on. During the presidential election campaign of 1952, the Republican candidate, General Dwight D. Eisenhower, pledged that if elected he would personally go to Korea and get the stalled peace negotiations moving again.

Eisenhower won the election and visited Korea within a few weeks of his victory. By then both sides were eager for a cease-fire. Only the problem of what to do about prisoners of war remained. The two sides finally agreed to turn the prisoner-of-war issue over to an international commission.

A cease-fire ending the hostilities in Korea was signed on July 27, 1953. The agreement restored the 38th parallel as the boundary between North and South Korea and provided for a demilitarized zone along that boundary. Relations between North and South Korea remained tense, with periodic conflicts in the demilitarized zone, but these incidents never erupted into war. Over 54,000 Americans and 3,000 soldiers from other United Nations countries had lost their lives in the Korean War. The UN force had successfully repelled the invasion of South

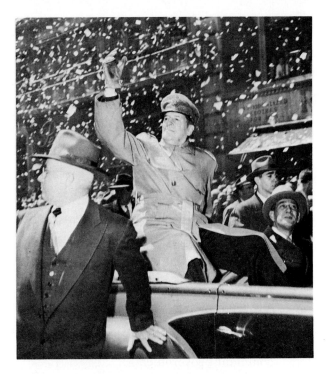

Dismissed as commander in Korea by President Truman, General Douglas MacArthur returned to a hero's welcome in New York City.

Korea, and the United States had shown it meant to stop armed aggression.

SECTION REVIEW

1. Identify: 38th parallel.
2. Define: limited war.
3. What action did the UN take when North Korea invaded South Korea?
4. What issue led to conflict between President Truman and General MacArthur?
5. **Critical Thinking**   Do you think that the military should be under civilian control? Why or why not?

4 New Directions in Foreign Policy

With the end of the Korean conflict, the cold war continued under new leadership in both the United States and the Soviet Union. In the United States, a new President, Dwight Eisenhower, began his term by rejecting many of the policies of his predecessor. Two months after Eisenhower took office Soviet Premier Joseph Stalin died. After an intense political struggle, Nikita Khrushchev (nuh KEET uh kroosh CHAWF) emerged as premier of the Soviet Union. New leadership offered the opportunity to reduce tension between the United States and the Soviet Union.

A Different Approach

John Foster Dulles was secretary of state under President Eisenhower. Dulles believed that communism was an immoral system of government. He rejected the containment policy of the Truman administration because that policy tolerated Soviet power where it already existed. The secretary of state believed the object of United States foreign policy should be not merely to contain communism but to destroy it.

Dulles's foreign policy was guided by two principles. First, he believed that the United States should encourage the "liberation of the captive peoples" in eastern Europe by widespread use of political pressure and propaganda. Radio broadcasts to eastern European countries by the Voice of America and Radio Free Europe urged people in those nations to overthrow their communist governments.

Second, Dulles proposed a new military strategy of *massive retaliation*. Instead of merely supporting local efforts to fight aggression, as in Korea, Dulles believed that the United States should make clear its determination to retaliate directly against the Soviet Union or China with nuclear weapons if necessary. During the 1950s the United States and the Soviet Union began an *arms race* to accumulate sophisticated nuclear arsenals. However, neither the policies of Dulles nor the arms race prevented efforts to reduce tensions by the late 1950s.

A "Thaw" in the Cold War

After the death of Stalin in 1953, Soviet policy underwent several changes. First, Soviet leaders began to concentrate on improving living conditions within the Soviet Union. They hoped to impress nations in Asia, Africa, and Latin America with the superiority of communism as an economic system. In addition, the Soviet leadership now stated that war between the Soviet Union and the West* was unnecessary. In their opinion peaceful competition between the two

---

*The United States, nations of western Europe, and other nations opposed to Soviet expansion were often referred to as the "West" or the "western powers." The Soviet Union and its allies became known as the "East" or the "eastern powers."

would demonstrate the superiority of the Soviet system.

New directions in Soviet policy offered an opportunity for a "thaw" in the cold war. President Eisenhower resisted the advice of those who condemned any negotiations with the Soviets. Cautiously he moved to relax tensions between the two powers.

The first indication of the thaw was a summit conference held in Geneva, Switzerland, in 1955. President Eisenhower met with the leaders of the Soviet Union, Britain, and France to begin discussions about European security and disarmament. The western powers wanted Germany to be reunited. The Soviets resisted, fearing the threat of a powerful reunited Germany, especially if it was allied with the West.

There was some agreement on the issue of disarmament, however. Both East and West had come to realize the terrible danger of nuclear destruction that threatened the entire world as long as the arms race continued. Thus, discussions of banning the testing of nuclear weapons continued after the Geneva meeting. In 1958 the Soviet Union, the United States, and Britain suspended the testing of nuclear weapons as efforts continued for a permanent halt to the arms race.

The high point of the thaw in American-Soviet relations came in the summer of 1959 when Nikita Khrushchev made a two-week visit to the United States. The Soviet leader toured factories, attended a midwestern barbecue, discussed raising corn with an Iowa farmer, and visited Hollywood.

Khrushchev concluded his tour with a lengthy series of talks with President Eisenhower at Camp David, the presidential retreat outside Washington. The two leaders agreed to hold a summit meeting the following year. Hopes for a further relaxation of tensions ran high as the "spirit of Camp David" warmed Soviet-American relations.

A Setback to Peaceful Relations

The spirit of Camp David was soon destroyed by what became known as the U-2 incident. A U-2 is a high-altitude plane specially equipped to take photographs of ground activities. For example, U-2 planes could take pictures of convoys of Soviet troops and missile locations. American U-2s began making flights over the Soviet Union in 1956.

In 1960, ten days before the planned Paris summit conference, Khrushchev announced that a U-2 had been shot down over the Soviet Union. The pilot had been captured and had admitted that his job was to photograph Soviet military facilities. Several days later President Eisenhower stated that he had authorized the U-2 flights in the interest of national security.

In an effort to save the summit conference, Eisenhower announced that he had suspended U-2 flights, but Khrushchev was not satisfied. The Soviet leader arrived in Paris and demanded an apology. Eisenhower refused, and the summit collapsed.

SECTION REVIEW

1. Identify: Nikita Khrushchev, John Foster Dulles.
2. Define: massive retaliation, arms race.
3. What was the high point of the thaw in the cold war in the late 1950s?
4. What effect did the U-2 incident have on the thaw?
5. **Critical Thinking**   How does the present United States policy toward the Soviet Union compare with the policy after World War II?

5 The Challenge of Nationalism

Nationalism emerged as a powerful force during the 1950s. In Africa, the Middle East, and Asia nationalist groups sought to free their nations from the colonial rule of the British, French, and Dutch. Many of those colonies did win independence. Throughout the postwar period the United States and the Soviet Union competed for influence in the newly independent nations.

The United States and the Soviet Union also faced growing nationalism in neighboring countries. The Soviets were challenged by the people of eastern Europe who were unhappy living under foreign domination. In Latin America resentment of the United States exploded in violence and revolution.

The Hungarian Uprising

In 1956 anti-Soviet nationalism erupted in two eastern European nations. Relaxation of some political and economic controls within the Soviet Union encouraged the people of eastern Europe to demand more freedom for themselves. In Poland workers rioted against Soviet rule and won greater control of their own government.

Encouraged by the Polish example, Hungarian nationalists demanded that pro-Soviet Hungarian officials be replaced, that Soviet troops be withdrawn, and that non-communist political parties be legalized. Hungarian students and workers organized huge demonstrations in support of these demands.

Soviet tanks and troops moved swiftly into Hungary to crush the uprising. The western powers provided refuge for those Hungarians who escaped, but they sent no direct aid. Some Americans regarded the inability of the United States to help the Hungarians as proof that Secretary of State Dulles's demand for the "liberation" of eastern Europe was not a practical policy.

War in Southeast Asia

After the defeat of Japan, the French returned to their colonial territories of Vietnam, Cambodia, and Laos in Southeast Asia. But Vietnamese forces led by Ho Chi Minh (hoh chee mihn) continued the long and costly war for independence that they had been waging since the 1930s.

By the late 1940s the French considered withdrawing from Southeast Asia. Since Ho Chi Minh was a communist as well as a nationalist, however, the United States urged France to continue the war. For almost five years the United States contributed money and supplies to the French war effort. But even with the aid, France was unable to defeat Ho's guerrilla forces.

Meanwhile Ho's armies continued to grow in strength and popular support. In May 1954, after a month-long siege, the

After Soviet troops crushed a 1956 revolt in Hungary, some 200,000 Hungarians fled the country. The Hungarians above escaped across a river into Austria by a makeshift bridge consisting of a log and a guiderope.

remaining French force surrendered at Dien Bien Phu (dyehn byehn foo). President Eisenhower, fearing another land war in Asia like the Korean conflict, refused to commit United States troops to the fighting. He also rejected Dulles's advice to use nuclear weapons against the Vietnamese. Instead, an international conference in Geneva in 1954 divided Vietnam into two regions, with the promise that elections to reunify the country would be held later.

A communist government led by Ho Chi Minh took control of North Vietnam. In South Vietnam the United States supported the government of Ngo Dinh Diem (noh din ZEE em). Diem resisted holding elections to unify the two Vietnams, and the country remained divided.

The United States replaced France as the leading western power in Southeast Asia. Many justified American presence there by what became known as the domino theory. According to this theory, if one nation accepted communism, neighboring nations would topple like a set of falling dominoes. United States policy was to prevent the first domino from falling.

To prevent communist expansion in Asia, the United States sponsored the creation of the Southeast Asia Treaty Organization (SEATO).* Under the terms of this alliance the United States pledged to aid nations threatened by aggression. Furthermore, in 1955 the United States began to send military advisers to help train the South Vietnamese armed forces. The United States also pledged to come to the aid of Taiwan if it were attacked by mainland China.

The Middle East

Gamal Abdel Nasser, who became president of Egypt in 1956, was a strong nationalist. Like other Arab nationalists, Nasser opposed the existence of Israel. (See page 669.) In the first year of Nasser's leadership, the United States withdrew support from construction of a dam it had offered to build in Egypt. Nasser reacted by seizing control of the Suez Canal, which was important for western economic and military interests. Britain and France threatened military action against Egypt, expecting the United States to join them. Dulles and Eisenhower opposed such action.

In the midst of the Suez crisis, Israel, in reaction to frequent Arab raids along its border, attacked Egypt. With the outbreak of war, Britain and France began bombing Egyptian targets, claiming that they were protecting the canal. The United States

---

*The original members of SEATO included the United States, Great Britain, France, Australia, New Zealand, Thailand, Pakistan, and the Philippines.

pressed Britain and France to stop the fighting before the war became a larger conflict. In the United Nations, the United States sponsored a resolution condemning the attack on Egypt. Faced with combined UN and United States pressure, Israel and its allies ended their invasion. Eventually the Suez Canal reopened under Egyptian control.

Although the Soviet Union had not been directly involved in the Suez Crisis, it had offered military and economic aid to Egypt. The threat of further Soviet activity in the Middle East could not be ruled out. To cope with that threat, President Eisenhower announced that the United States would offer financial support to Middle East countries that requested help against communist aggression. This policy became known as the Eisenhower Doctrine. In 1958 the Eisenhower Doctrine was used to justify the landing of United States marines in Lebanon as a show of force to end civil war there.

Revolution in Latin America

By the 1950s dictators had taken power in many Latin American countries. The United States government had maintained friendly relations with those dictators in the hopes that they would provide a strong defense against the possibility of revolution. Many Latin Americans resented the dictatorial rule of their leaders and believed that the dictators had been installed to protect the investments of United States corporations.

In 1958 a visit by Vice-President Richard Nixon to Peru and Venezuela revealed the depth of anti-American feeling. Angry mobs threw stones and eggs at the Vice-President and attacked his limousine. United States marines were alerted for possible intervention, but the Vice-President returned to Washington before serious violence occurred.

In 1959 a young lawyer named Fidel Castro led a successful revolution against the dictatorial regime of Fulgencio Batista (bah TEES tah). President Eisenhower recognized the new government a week after Castro took power. During the following months, however, Castro's policies resulted in increasingly tense relations with the United States. The Cuban economy was heavily dependent on the United States. For example,

Americans owned 80 percent of the Cuban utilities industry, 40 percent of its sugar plantations, and 90 percent of its mineral resources.

Castro believed that any attempt to strengthen the Cuban economy would have to begin by lessening the control of American private enterprise. In June 1960 the Cuban government seized several American- and British-owned oil refineries. President Eisenhower retaliated by reducing the quota of Cuban sugar exports to the United States. Relations worsened during the summer and fall of 1960, when the Cuban government seized more American businesses. In October President Eisenhower placed an embargo on trade with Cuba.

Major Events	
1945	United Nations founded
1947	Truman Doctrine and Marshall Plan announced
1948	State of Israel proclaimed; Soviet Union blockades Berlin
1949	NATO founded; Berlin blockade ends; Soviet Union tests atomic device; communists win civil war in China
1950	Korean War begins
1952	Dwight D. Eisenhower elected President
1953	Cease-fire in Korean War
1955	Summit conference in Geneva
1956	Hungarian uprising; Suez crisis begins
1959	Cuban revolution; Khrushchev visits the United States
1960	U-2 incident
1961	United States breaks off relations with Cuba

During this period Cuba was establishing close ties with the Soviet Union. In July 1960 Premier Khrushchev proclaimed that the Soviet Union would protect Cuba from any military attack by the United States. The Soviets began to supply Cuba with growing amounts of economic and military aid. By the end of 1960 Cuba was clearly moving into the Soviet camp. President Eisenhower broke off diplomatic relations with Cuba on January 3, 1961, 17 days before his term of office ended.

Between 1945 and 1960 the United States had strengthened its relationship with the industrialized nations of Europe and Asia. However, in the competition with the Soviet Union for the allegiance of other nations, the results were less certain. Furthermore, the arms race between the two powers continued to threaten the entire world.

SECTION REVIEW

1. Identify: Ho Chi Minh, Dien Bien Phu, domino theory, Fidel Castro.
2. What led the United States to encourage France to stay in Vietnam?
3. What action did France and Britain take when Israel invaded Egypt in 1956?
4. What disrupted relations between the United States and Cuba?
5. **Critical Thinking** How might Dulles's foreign policy have encouraged the Hungarian uprising?

Chapter 36 Review

In Perspective

International developments after World War II presented many challenges to the United States. Eastern Europe had fallen under Soviet influence, and communist movements in Greece and Italy challenged the governments in those countries. In China communist forces were struggling to seize power. By 1946 a cold war had broken out in Europe. President Truman declared that the United States would block further communist expansion. To enforce the policy of containment, the United States sponsored the Marshall Plan, organized the Berlin airlift, and joined NATO.

In Asia, the policy of containment was tested when North Korea invaded South Korea in 1950. After early defeats, the combined United Nations–United States force drove back the invaders. In 1953 a cease-fire restored the prewar border between North and South Korea. Dwight D. Eisenhower became President shortly before the end of the Korean War. During his administration, tensions between the United States and the Soviet Union relaxed until the U-2 incident.

Nationalism became an important international force during the 1950s. It contributed to a Hungarian uprising against Soviet control and the continuation of the Vietnamese war against France. Soviet influence increased in Egypt and Cuba as nationalists in those nations reacted against the western powers. Competition between the United States and the Soviet Union was to continue both in developing nations and in other parts of the world, as you will read in Chapter 38.

Vocabulary

On a separate sheet of paper, write the word or words that best complete each of the following sentences.

1. ____ is a policy of applying counterforce at strategic political and geographic locations to avoid the spread of influence by the Soviet Union.
2. ____ is fought for specific objectives rather than for total victory.
3. ____ is a military strategy in which the United States would retaliate directly against the Soviet Union or China with nuclear weapons if necessary.
4. The ____ is the competition between the United States and the Soviet Union to develop the most powerful nuclear arsenal.

5. The ____ was an idea that if one Asian nation became communist, neighboring nations would follow.

Chapter Checkup

1. (a) What were the goals of the United Nations? (b) What was the main responsibility of the Security Council? (c) What action could the council take to achieve that goal? (d) How were its actions limited?

2. (a) What was the Marshall Plan? (b) In what way was it a part of the policy of containment? (c) Was it successful? Explain.

3. (a) How did the United States react to the North Korean invasion of South Korea? (b) Why did the goal of the UN and the United States change in October 1950? (c) What was the consequence of the invasion of North Korea?

4. (a) What led to a "thaw" in the cold war during the late 1950s? (b) What resulted from the 1955 summit conference between Khrushchev and Eisenhower? (c) What ended the thaw?

5. (a) What was the first reaction of the United States to the revolution led by Fidel Castro in Cuba? (b) Why did the American attitude toward Castro change?

Critical Thinking

1. Defending an Opinion Would you agree with Senator Vandenberg that after the Soviets exploded their first atomic weapon, it was "now a different world"? Why or why not?

2. Evaluating Do you think the policy of containment was generally successful between 1947 and 1960? Why or why not?

Developing Basic Skills

1. Map Reading Locate the original members of the NATO alliance on the map on page 674. (Include the nations that joined in 1952 and 1954.) Then locate the mem-

bers of the Warsaw Pact. How do you think that alignment of nations contributed to the fact that nations opposed to Soviet expansion are often called the West and pro-Soviet nations are called the East?

2. Using Visual Evidence Study the photograph on page 677. Then answer the following questions: (a) What is being shown in the photograph? (b) How might a supporter of General MacArthur interpret the meaning of the photograph? (c) What issue led to a dispute between President Truman and MacArthur? (d) How was the dispute resolved? (e) What constitutional provision was reinforced by that outcome?

See page 833 for suggested readings.

Writer's Handbook

Proofreading Your Paper

After you have revised your first draft, you should proofread it for spelling, capitalization, and punctuation errors. Listed below are the standard proofreading symbols.

Symbol	Meaning of symbol
b̲	Capitalize a letter.
Ⱦ	Lower-case a letter.
op̂ꞃn	Insert or change a letter or punctuation mark.
ℐℯ	Delete a word, letter, or punctuation mark.
wa͡s	Close up a space.
and͟i͟n	Add a space.
(o)f	Transpose letters.
⁋This	Begin a new paragraph.
⊙	Add a period.
⋀	Add a comma.
Truman̓s	Add an apostrophe.
sto͟p͟never	Keep what is crossed-out.

Practice: Rewrite this paragraph making the changes indicated: The United states replaced Frnace as the leading Western power in Southea st Asia. many justified America presence there by what became known as the domino theory According to this theory if one nation accepted communist, neidhboring nations would topplelike a set of falling dominose.

A Search for Stability

(1945–1960)

The Kansas City Spirit *by Norman Rockwell*

Chapter Outline

1 *From War to Peace*

2 *The Cold War at Home*

3 *Stability Under Eisenhower*

4 *A Deceptive Calm*

American entry into World War II ended the Great Depression as orders for munitions and other war supplies revitalized industry. Yet no one was certain whether the return to peace would mean continued prosperity.

Once the war ended, Americans sought greater stability, as they had after World War I. Economic and political concerns plagued the early postwar years. The Cold War intruded upon American life and fed suspicions that some Americans were disloyal to their country. But by the mid-1950s many Americans thought they had found stability under President Dwight Eisenhower.

Despite the outward calm, the 1950s proved to be a time of important social change. Black Americans' demands for full equality were to grow during the period. Furthermore, a reevaluation of the educational system would lead to greater emphasis on science and mathematics in American schools.

Eisenhower administration

1945   1947   1949   1951   1953   1955   1957   1959   1961

1947
Taft-Hartley
Act passed

1948
Truman
reelected

1950
McCarthy
charges communists in
government

1952
Dwight D.
Eisenhower
elected
President

1954
Brown v.
*Board of
Education of
Topeka*

1957
Troops sent to
Little Rock;
Sputnik
launched

1960
John F.
Kennedy
elected
President

1 From War to Peace

When World War II ended on August 14, 1945, Americans burst into demonstrations of joy and relief. But clouds loomed on the horizon. What could Americans expect from their new President? Would he follow the path of Franklin Roosevelt and extend New Deal benefits? Or would he end the reforms, as many Roosevelt critics urged? Above all, Americans feared that the end of wartime spending might mean a return to the high unemployment of the depression years.

Economic Issues

During World War II unemployment fell to an extreme low of 1.9 percent. The war brought high wages, but there were few consumer products to buy. Americans had saved a total of $44 billion during the war, and now they were eager to spend.

Such anticipation would turn to frustration, however. Throughout the war the government had established ceilings to keep prices and rents reasonable. As soon as Congress lifted the controls, rapid inflation struck. Prices soared upward as customers bought goods in short supply. Many people were willing to pay an extra dollar to get a scarce steak or offer an extra month's rent for an apartment. By 1948 prices were 48 percent higher than in 1945.

An almost unending string of strikes slowed the conversion from war to peace. As inflation cut into buying power, workers demanded large wage increases. When employers resisted their demands, the workers went out on strike. In January 1946 the steel, automobile, meatpacking, and electrical appliance industries were idled by strikes. Even gravediggers walked out. The nation seemed almost paralyzed.

Truman was especially angered when railroad workers walked off their jobs in May 1946. "What decent American would pull a strike at a time like this?" the President asked. Truman's efforts to resolve the dispute between railroad workers and management failed to produce a settlement. He then stunned the nation by asking a joint session of Congress for emergency power "to draft into the armed forces of the United States all workers who are on strike against their government."

Under that pressure the union quickly came to an agreement to end the strike. Liberals and conservatives alike condemned the President's abuse of the draft system. Senator Robert Taft of Ohio called the threat an offense against the Constitution, and labor leaders never quite forgave Truman.

Yet Truman had worked hard to smooth the conversion to peacetime. In 1944 Congress had passed the Servicemen's Readjustment Act, sometimes called the GI* Bill of Rights. It granted veterans a variety of benefits. A year of unemployment insurance provided income for veterans unable to find work. Those who attended college after the war received financial aid. The act also entitled veterans to government loans for building homes and starting businesses.

In the spirit of the New Deal, President Truman asked Congress to make "maximum employment, production, and purchasing power" a formal government responsibility. Conservative members of Congress opposed the request as an attempt to revive New Deal spending programs. As a result, the Employment Act passed in 1946 did little to spur employment. It did, however, make full employment a national goal. The act also established a Council of Economic Advisors to guide the President on economic matters. Unemployment rose to about 6 percent during the late 1940s but did not return to the levels of the Great Depression.

The Eightieth Congress

By the 1946 congressional elections, many voters were tired of inflation, shortages, and strikes. They blamed the President for their problems. One critic joked, "To err is Truman." Republicans referred to the President's problems in their campaign slogan, "Had enough?" and won a majority in both houses of Congress.

Most members of the Eightieth Congress, which convened in January 1947, believed that much of the New Deal legislation had undermined personal initiative and private enterprise. As a result, Truman faced a

---

*GI refers to a member of the United States armed forces. The term originated in soldiers' jokes that they, like their equipment, were "government issue."

hostile Congress. The legislature refused to pass bills to provide federal funds for public housing or education and rejected a federally financed medical insurance plan.

The most far-reaching action of the Eightieth Congress was passage of the Taft-Hartley Act. Enacted in 1947 over Truman's veto, the act reflected antiunion feeling generated by the epidemic of postwar strikes. According to the act, the attorney general could apply for a court order to delay for 80 days any strike endangering health or safety. Other provisions banned union contributions to political campaigns and the *closed shop*, in which all workers are required to be union members. Sponsors of the bill believed that closed shops denied workers the right to work without joining a union.

The Election of 1948

The Republicans expected victory in the presidential election of 1948. Their stunning gains in the 1946 congressional elections and Truman's sagging popularity indicated that the President could be defeated easily. The Republicans again nominated Governor Thomas E. Dewey of New York. Truman won the Democratic nomination.

Truman's candidacy was badly hampered by a split within his party. Southern Democrats, angry at Truman's support for civil rights legislation (see next column), broke with the Democratic party and established the States' Rights party. They nominated Governor Strom Thurmond of South Carolina for President. Meanwhile, other Democrats, unhappy with Truman's containment policy, formed a new Progressive party. The Progressives turned to Henry Wallace, Vice-President during Franklin Roosevelt's third term. Truman supporters feared that the candidacies of Thurmond and Wallace would draw Democratic voters away from the President.

Yet Truman refused to give up. In a vigorous campaign, he traveled over 20,000 miles (32,000 kilometers) and made nearly 300 speeches in eight weeks. He attacked what he called the "do-nothing" and "good-for-nothing" Eightieth Congress. Condemning that Congress as the "worst in history," Truman lashed out at the Republicans for opposing his social legislation.

On election day few doubted that Dewey would be the next President. Into the night Dewey supporters celebrated the anticipated victory. A Chicago *Daily Tribune* headline proclaimed, "Dewey Defeats Truman." But when all the votes were counted, Truman emerged as the victor with 49.5 percent of the popular vote compared to 45 percent for Dewey. He had managed the political upset of the century.

The Fair Deal

After the election the President declared, "Every segment of our population and every individual has the right to expect from his government a fair deal."

The Fair Deal Truman proposed would have extended the New Deal with a broad package of reform. He successfully worked for the passage of the National Housing Act of 1949, a measure that helped finance low-income housing. Also in 1949 Congress passed an amendment to the Fair Labor Standards Act (see page 614), raising the minimum hourly wage from 40 cents to 75 cents. The most important piece of Fair Deal legislation was probably the Social Security Act of 1950. That law increased the number of people covered under the old-age insurance provisions of the Social Security Act of 1935.

But Truman failed to accomplish some major objectives. Congress refused to repeal the Taft-Hartley Act and again rejected bills to provide federal aid to education and establish federally financed health insurance. Bills to ban the poll tax* and discrimination in employment were also defeated.

Extending Civil Rights

Although Truman was unable to persuade Congress to pass civil rights legislation, he did try to use his influence as chief executive to lessen discrimination against black Americans. Racial segregation persisted after World War II. In the North there was much *de facto segregation*, that is, segregation that existed in fact if not in law. In the South, Jim Crow laws separated black and white public facilities. Blacks could not sit at the counters in most coffee shops. They attended segregated schools and movie theaters and were

---

*As you read in Chapter 22, poll taxes were fees a person had to pay in order to vote. They had been used to prevent poor blacks from voting.

Jackie Robinson was the first black baseball player on a major league team. He played infield for the Brooklyn Dodgers.

restricted to separate sections on buses and in other public facilities.

Yet some change was apparent. In 1947, for example, Jackie Robinson became the first black man to play on a major league baseball team. Blacks had previously been allowed to play only in all-black leagues. During and after the war there were also some public demonstrations against segregation in dining and recreational facilities.

In September 1946 representatives from an antilynching organization visited the President to protest violence against blacks. The President publicly condemned lynchings, declaring that Americans could not tolerate "acts of intimidation and violence in our . . . communities."

Truman also created the President's Committee on Civil Rights. In 1947 the committee issued a report entitled *To Secure These Rights.* The report called for "the elimination of segregation from American life." Although the committee had no authority to enforce its suggestions, it did inform the public of the injustice of segregation.

In 1948 Truman issued a directive banning segregation in the armed forces. The executive order proclaimed that it was "the policy of the President that there shall be equality of treatment and opportunity for all persons in the armed services." Desegregation of the military proceeded slowly during the late 1940s, but by 1951 most units in the Korean War were integrated.

In order to reduce discrimination in employment Truman reaffirmed Franklin Roosevelt's executive order banning discrimination in firms doing business with the federal government. Early in 1952 the President created the Committee on Contracts Compliance to investigate instances in which employers receiving government contracts had discriminated against minorities. The committee, however, lacked enforcement powers, and it proved ineffective in curbing discrimination. Nonetheless, President Truman's actions in support of greater civil rights contributed to a movement that would grow stronger in the 1950s and 1960s, as you will read later in this chapter and the next.

SECTION REVIEW

1. Identify: Taft–Hartley Act, Thomas E. Dewey, States' Rights party, Progressive party.

2. Define: closed shop, de facto segregation.

3. How did American workers react to post-war inflation?

4. What did the GI Bill of Rights provide?

5. List three measures of the Fair Deal.

6. What did President Truman do to reduce racial discrimination in employment?

7. **Critical Thinking** What means does a President have to overcome an uncooperative Congress?

2 The Cold War at Home

The cold war that developed between the United States and the Soviet Union after World War II divided much of the world into opposing blocs. It also began to divide Americans at home. Many people resented the New Deal, the strikes by labor unions, and other dislocations caused by the war. Some blamed national problems on people they considered subversive or disloyal to the country.

A Question of Loyalty

As the cold war intensified, many Americans grew increasingly intolerant of anyone who was sympathetic toward communism or the Soviet Union. Although the Communist party in the United States was small and had little influence, people worried that it might harbor Soviet spies.

In 1947 President Truman recognized public concern about communism and created the Loyalty Review Board. The purpose of the board was to guarantee the "unswerving loyalty" of all employees of the federal government. Truman created the board even though he personally did not believe that any government employees were disloyal to the nation. When the board revealed that some people of "doubtful loyalty" were on the federal payroll, critics charged that Truman had been unmindful of the dangers of communism.

Other investigations increased public concern about the potential influence of communists in the United States. The House of Representatives had created the Un-American Activities Committee (HUAC) in 1938 to investigate possible subversive activity by fascists or communists. After the war it focused on communist activity. The committee held hearings on alleged communist

activity in the movie industry in 1947. Although there was rarely any solid evidence, the hearings tarnished the reputations of a number of writers, producers, and performers. The committee also pressed filmmakers to adopt a "blacklist" barring employment to anyone suspected of being a communist.

In 1948 HUAC began an investigation of disloyalty in government. Whittaker Chambers, a former member of the Communist party, testified that a state department official, Alger Hiss, had belonged to the party during the 1930s. Chambers also charged that Hiss had given him official state department documents to pass on to Soviet agents. Chambers then led investigators to his farm, where he had hidden microfilmed documents in a pumpkin.

In 1950 Hiss was convicted of perjury, or lying under oath, because he had denied to the committee that he knew Chambers. Hiss's conviction convinced many Americans that President Truman had been too hasty when he had dismissed claims that communists had infiltrated the government.

But nothing generated more concern about internal security than the charge that some Americans had secretly helped the Soviets build an atomic bomb. Dr. Klaus Fuchs, a British subject, had been a member of the research team that developed the atomic bomb at Los Alamos, New Mexico. In February 1950 British authorities arrested Fuchs and charged him with sending atomic secrets to the Soviet Union. Fuchs pleaded guilty and agreed to reveal the workings of the Los Alamos spy ring.

The Fuchs case led to the arrest of Ethel and Julius Rosenberg, both American citizens, in the summer of 1950. The Rosenbergs were charged with passing atomic secrets to

Soviet agents. A jury found them guilty of spying, and they were executed in 1953. The widely publicized cases of Hiss and the Rosenbergs increased public anxiety and contributed to the rise to prominence of a Republican senator from Wisconsin.

McCarthyism

Senator Joseph R. McCarthy of Wisconsin seized on American fear about disloyalty in government and almost overnight became the most controversial senator in the nation.

Much of the controversy surrounding McCarthy stemmed from the scope of his accusations. In a speech delivered February 9, 1950, in Wheeling, West Virginia, McCarthy claimed that he had the names of 205 state department employees who were members of the Communist party. The charge provoked a furor. Later McCarthy said he meant there were "205 bad security risks" in the department. Then he claimed that 57 employees were communists. In subsequent speeches he used different numbers. It was impossible for the state department to refute such a variety of accusations.

For four years Senator McCarthy continued to denounce his enemies. He charged that the Democratic party had been guilty of "twenty years of treason." He called for

Truman's impeachment, maintained that General George C. Marshall had been "an instrument of the Soviet conspiracy," and hinted that President Eisenhower was not sufficiently anticommunist.

McCarthy's influence was so great during the early 1950s that people came to use the term "McCarthyism" to refer to his technique of making sweeping accusations, frequently without evidence. Although his investigations revealed little anti-American activity, he persuaded millions that he was protecting national security. Even though he was unable to prove most of his accusations, the publicity he created ruined the reputations of many scholars and other public figures for years to come.

McCarthy's Fall

McCarthy's recklessness, which had been his source of strength, eventually caused his downfall. When his assistant, David Schine, was drafted into the army in 1954, McCarthy allowed his top aide, Roy Cohn, to press the army to make Schine an officer. The army rebuffed Cohn's efforts. Soon a major controversy developed over the Schine case. In April 1954 the Senate held hearings to air the differences between McCarthy and the army. The Army-McCarthy hearings were

689

Senator Joseph McCarthy charged that communists had infiltrated many areas of American life. In 1954 he accused the army of misconduct. Here, McCarthy (with map) testifies in the Army-McCarthy hearings. At left is the army counsel, Joseph Welch. The televised hearings diminished McCarthy's popularity, and in December 1954 the Senate censured him for "conduct unbecoming a member."

televised and ran for a total of 187 hours. On some days as many as 20 million people watched the hearings.

McCarthy claimed that there were many communists at the Fort Monmouth, New Jersey, army base. He charged that the army was holding Schine as a "hostage" to discourage an investigation of Fort Monmouth. This time McCarthy had gone too far. Television cameras focused on McCarthy's abrasive manner. The army's lawyer, Joseph Welch, subjected the senator's case to intense examination. For many Americans, McCarthy emerged from the hearing as a bully, not a hero.

In December 1954 the Senate passed a resolution condemning McCarthy for "conduct unbecoming a member." The censure resolution eroded McCarthy's popular appeal and his national political force.

SECTION REVIEW

1. Identify: House Un-American Activities Committee, McCarthyism.
2. List two developments that created public concern about communism in the United States.
3. How did Joseph McCarthy rise to national prominence?
4. What led to McCarthy's decline?
5. **Critical Thinking**   How was McCarthy's reaction to communists similar to the Red Scare? How was it different?

3 Stability Under Eisenhower

Senator McCarthy's accusations of treason in high places and the seemingly endless war in Korea undermined President Truman's popularity. He decided not to run again in 1952. Voters wanted someone who could bring stability, prosperity, and peace to the nation.

Victory for the Republicans

In 1952 the Democratic party nominated Governor Adlai E. Stevenson of Illinois for President and Senator John J. Sparkman of Alabama for Vice-President. The Republicans chose Dwight D. Eisenhower as their presidential candidate and Senator Richard M. Nixon of California as his running mate.

The race was uneven from the start. Stevenson was virtually unknown outside Illinois, and the public considered him too intellectual. Opponents labeled Stevenson an "egghead." Eisenhower, on the other hand, was a national hero. He had commanded the United States forces in Europe during World War II and the American occupation forces in Germany after the war. From 1948 to 1951, Eisenhower served as president of Columbia University. He also possessed great personal appeal.

The Republicans, who had not won a presidential election since 1928, fought a hard campaign. They reminded voters that Truman had once scoffed at the charge that communists filled important posts in the federal government. They also blamed the Democrats for the stalemate in Korea. Eisenhower promised to break the deadlock by going to Korea personally.

Eisenhower won by a landslide, receiving nearly 34 million votes compared to 27 million for Stevenson. Four years later, in 1956, Eisenhower ran against Stevenson again and beat him by an even larger margin.

As President, Eisenhower took a moderate political course. He condemned two of McCarthy's assistants, but he refused to denounce McCarthy personally until the Wisconsin senator had passed the height of his power. While Eisenhower resisted demands to dismantle New Deal programs, he also refused to work for new social legislation.

Government and the Economy

President Eisenhower and the Republican-controlled Congress tried to reduce the government's role in the economy. Congress limited federal aid for public housing and ended the wage and price controls established by the Truman administration. Furthermore, Congress transferred offshore oil fields, previously under federal control, to state control. The secretary of agriculture reduced federal aid to farmers.

The American people generally prospered during the Eisenhower years. Unemployment hovered at about 5 percent. Industrial wages increased somewhat, but inflation lowered purchasing power. Nonetheless, inflation was not as serious as in the years immediately following the war. The gross national product, the total of goods and services produced during a given year, climbed upward until 1957, when the economy was hit by a serious recession, or economic downturn.

Eisenhower's handling of the 1957–1958 recession reflected his belief that the government should not control the economy. When unemployment reached 6.8 percent in 1958, the Democrats called for New Deal–style public works projects to stimulate the economy. But Eisenhower refused to aid the economy with federal money.

In a 1958 speech, delivered after economic recovery had begun, the President declared that it was wrong to believe "that when the economy starts to slow up, only a vast outpouring of . . . tax dollars will pump us out of trouble." He maintained that increased federal spending would create a false prosperity and increase inflation. "Huge programs," he argued, "would have only enfeebled the economy." Eisenhower survived Democratic criticism as the economy slowly recovered. By 1959 unemployment had returned to 5 percent.

Life in the 1950s

One of the most profound social changes in the 1950s was the rapid growth of suburbs. Several factors encouraged that growth. A postwar "baby boom" created a need for new housing, while the prosperity of the period enabled many people to buy their own homes. The GI Bill of Rights also provided federal aid for veterans seeking home-loan mortgages. Furthermore, a massive postwar road-building program linked suburban homes to city jobs.

During the 1950s the suburbs became increasingly self-contained. While suburban residents of the 1920s had depended on the city for entertainment and shopping, the postwar suburban dweller could find a vast array of goods and services in nearby shopping plazas.

After the war, most of the women who had entered the work force returned to being homemakers. Managing a home in the

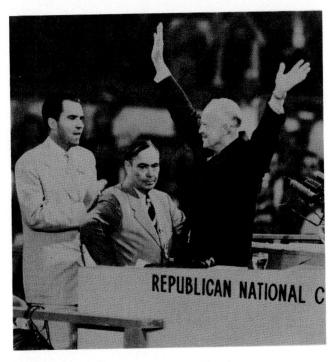

Presidential candidate Dwight David Eisenhower, the five-star general who had commanded United States armies in Europe during the war, accepts the cheers of the 1952 Republican convention. Nominated as his running mate was a young California congressman, Richard Nixon (at left).

suburbs and raising a family became the goal of many women during the 1950s. The popular culture of the period reinforced their view of women's role in society. Some commentators argued that women could not compete with men in the business world. Others blamed a rise in crime among young people on the fact that more mothers were working outside the home.

Newspapers, magazines, and especially television had an impact on the perception of women's role in society. Since the beginning of national network broadcasting in 1946, the popularity of television had risen dramatically. During the 1950s almost 7 million television sets were sold each year. Most commercials showed only women doing domestic tasks. Popular programs such as *Father Knows Best* seldom portrayed them with other careers. The view that women should only be homemakers was reinforced through the decade.

Religion played an especially important part in American life during the 1950s. Church membership grew twice as fast as the population. The Reverend Norman Vincent Peale wrote a best seller, *The Power of*

691

After two decades of depression and war, the United States went on a building binge in the 1950s. Millions of new homes were built, spilling suburban development into former farmlands. Techniques of mass production helped produce suburbs like Levittown, New York, shown here. Levittown had 17,477 low-priced houses, all with the same floor plan. With the GI bill, veterans could buy such homes with low down payments that allowed millions to become homeowners.

During the Battle of Britain in World War II, nightly radio reports by Edward R. Murrow had brought the sounds of the war to Americans. With the rapid spread of television in the 1950s, Murrow emerged as one of the most respected television reporters. He was among the first to make television documentaries on American life.

Positive Thinking, which stressed the need for religion in a successful life. Religion on television was also influential. For example, Bishop Fulton J. Sheen hosted a popular program, and the Reverend Billy Graham led a television crusade that gave his ministry national attention.

The growing religious feeling among many Americans was one indication of their search for stability and peace. Religious faith became closely linked with patriotism. As President Eisenhower stated, "our government makes no sense unless it is founded in a deeply felt religious faith." In 1954 Congress added the words "under God" to the Pledge of Allegiance to the Flag.

SECTION REVIEW

1. Identify: Adlai E. Stevenson.
2. What was Eisenhower's attitude toward the government's role in the economy?
3. List two factors that encouraged the growth of suburbs after World War II.
4. What was the goal of many American women during the 1950s?
5. **Critical Thinking** Why do you think both Democrats and Republicans wanted Eisenhower as their presidential candidate?

4 A Deceptive Calm

For most Americans the 1950s was a period of general stability. Yet beneath the surface calm, developments were occurring that would greatly affect the future. Black Americans increased their demands for civil rights. Young people adopted a new music that shocked many parents. Social critics lamented the national emphasis on conformity. And an impatient public demanded a more rigorous education for American youth.

Early Steps Against Segregation

In the 1896 case of *Plessy* v. *Ferguson* the Supreme Court had ruled that "separate but equal" facilities for blacks and whites were constitutional. (See page 422.) That decision had provided the legal basis for segregation. During the 1940s the National Association for the Advancement of Colored People had begun to attack the "separate but equal" principle by suing segregated colleges and universities. As a result the University of Texas and the University of Oklahoma as well as several other southern colleges admitted black students. However, elementary and secondary schools remained segregated.

In the early 1950s the NAACP filed suit against the Board of Education of Topeka, Kansas, on behalf of Linda Brown. The board had denied Brown admission to an all-white school. The case reached the Supreme Court in 1954.

Brown's lawyer, Thurgood Marshall, charged that public school segregation violated the "equal protection" clause of the Fourteenth Amendment to the Constitution. He maintained that segregation deprived black children of an equal educational opportunity. Separate could not be equal, the NAACP argued, because segregation in itself lowered the morale and motivation of black students.

In *Brown* v. *Board of Education of Topeka*, the Supreme Court ruled that "separate educational facilities are inherently unequal." "The doctrine of 'separate but equal,'" it held, "has no place in public education." A year later the Court ordered school integration to proceed "with all deliberate speed."

The Court's decision sparked an angry reaction among many southern officials who considered the ruling a threat to state and local authority. President Eisenhower believed

★ Voices of Freedom ★

Brown v. *Board of Education of Topeka*

In 1954 the Supreme Court reversed the 1896 ruling in *Plessy* v. *Ferguson*, which had stated that separate facilities for blacks and whites were legal if they were equal. In this excerpt from *Brown* v. *Board of Education of Topeka* Chief Justice Earl Warren presents the opinion of the Court.

Compulsory school-attendance laws and the great expenditures for education both demonstrate our recognition of the importance of education to our democratic society. It is required in the performance of our most basic public responsibilities, even service in the armed forces. It is the very foundation of good citizenship. Today it is a principal instrument in awakening the child to cultural values, in preparing him for later professional training, and in helping him to adjust normally to his environment. In these days, it is doubtful that any child may reasonably be expected to succeed in life if he is denied the opportunity of an education. Such an opportunity, where the state has undertaken to provide it, is a right which must be made available to all on equal terms.

We come then to the question presented: Does segregation of children in public schools solely on the basis of race, even though the physical facilities and other "tangible" factors may be equal, deprive the children of the minority group of equal educational opportunities? We believe that it does.

that the government should not try to force integration, but in 1957 he decided he had to intervene.

The governor of Arkansas had called in the National Guard to prevent a group of black students from attending Little Rock Central High School. In reaction to the governor's open defiance of federal authority, President Eisenhower sent troops to Little Rock, and the students entered the school. Resistance to school integration remained strong in some parts of the country, but the Supreme Court ruling was a significant step toward greater equality.

Black citizens also increased their use of organized public protest against continued segregation. In December 1955 Rosa Parks, a

In 1957 black students tried to enroll in formerly all-white public schools in Little Rock, Arkansas. The governor called out the National Guard to stop them. In response, President Eisenhower sent federal troops to protect the students. Below, federal troops are shown guarding the first black students (on bottom stairs at left) to attend Central High.

Under segregation, blacks had to sit in the back of public buses if whites needed a seat. One day in 1955 Rosa Parks refused a bus driver's order to give up her seat. She was promptly arrested. The arrest led to a yearlong boycott of the bus system by black citizens in Montgomery, Alabama. In 1956, after the Supreme Court ruled against segregation on public transportation, Rosa Parks, shown above, sat in the front of a Montgomery bus.

black woman, was arrested for refusing to move from the "white" section of a bus in Montgomery, Alabama. Black citizens quickly organized a boycott of the bus line. The Reverend Martin Luther King, Jr., led the year-long boycott. He advocated *civil disobedience*, that is, nonviolent protest against an unjust law or condition, as the best way to fight segregation.

The bus company finally agreed to integrate the buses and hire black drivers after the Supreme Court ruled that bus segregation violated the Constitution. Early on the morning of December 21, 1956, Reverend King signaled the end of the boycott by boarding one of Montgomery's newly integrated buses.

Protest against segregation grew as Eisenhower's term drew to a close. On February 1, 1960, a group of black college students were denied service at a department store lunch counter in Greensboro, North Carolina. The students refused to leave their seats at the lunch counter until closing time.

After several months of such "sit-ins," the lunch counter agreed to serve blacks and whites equally. Sit-ins spread to many southern communities. Within 18 months of the Greensboro protest, 70,000 people had participated in sit-ins throughout the South. Integrated eating facilities were won in a hundred communities. The sit-in movement drew national attention to the problem of segregation, as you will read in Chapter 38.

A Crisis in Education

In October 1957 the Soviet Union launched the first satellite into orbit around the earth. Americans had long believed that superior technology would keep the United States ahead of the Soviet Union. The successful *Sputnik I* flight undermined that confidence. National confidence was shaken further when the first American attempts to launch a satellite failed. In January 1958 the United States put a satellite, *Explorer I*, into orbit.

Concerned Americans charged that the nation had fallen behind in space technology because of weaknesses in education. Several months after the Sputnik launch, *Life*, a popular weekly magazine, featured a series of articles called "The Crisis in Education." The articles reported that American educational standards were "shockingly low." Many parents agreed that the schools had failed to challenge young people. Critics demanded a rigorous curriculum with heavy emphasis on science and mathematics. These subjects, it was argued, held the key to victory in the new "space race."

Congress responded to the criticism by passing the National Defense Education Act in 1958. The act provided federal aid to schools and colleges, especially for projects designed to improve instruction in science and math. Congress also increased the budget of the National Science Foundation, which provided research grants to scientists and funded curriculum projects.

New Forms in the Arts

During the 1930s and 1940s popular music had been dominated by the sentimental melodies of such "crooners" as Bing Crosby and Frank Sinatra and by the "big band" sound of such musicians as Glenn Miller and Duke Ellington. In the early 1950s a new type of popular music came into being. Rock 'n' roll, as the new music was called, was a uniquely American sound. It blended elements from country-and-western music with rhythm and blues. American teenagers liked the strong beat, repeated harmonies, and loud volume.

However, some people objected to the hair styles, clothing, and dance styles of rock stars like Elvis Presley, Chuck Berry, and Buddy Holly. Some complained about the volume of the music and the lyrics, which they could not understand. Others actually thought that rock music would contribute to teenage crime. A 1955 movie, *Blackboard Jungle* reinforced such concern. The film portrayed delinquent teenagers in a tough city high school and included the song "Rock Around the Clock," recorded by Bill Haley and the Comets.

Despite such objections, rock became the music of American youth. Rock stars became internationally famous, and rock 'n' roll

The new sound of the 1950s was rock 'n' roll. Like jazz, rock 'n' roll was an American music form that appealed to people around the world. One of its originators was Buddy Holly (shown with guitar). A plane crash in 1959 cut short his career.

By the 1950s a group of American painters called abstract expressionists had become a major force in world art. Because many of them worked or exhibited their art in New York City, they were also known as the New York School. Foremost among them was Jackson Pollock. In his finest paintings, such as this one, entitled Number 27, he applied swirling lines of color with the drip and splash technique that he originated.

still fills the air waves today. In the 1950s the driving beat of rock stood in sharp contrast to the quiet tone of much of the Eisenhower era.

After the war the visual arts underwent a minor revolution. American artists led an international movement away from realistic representation to a form known as abstract expressionism. Visitors to museums and galleries were often puzzled by what appeared to be little more than paint randomly splashed on canvasses. But the abstract expressionists were serious artists. Some, such as Jackson Pollock, used swirling colors to absorb the viewer in emotion. Other painters offered engaging repetitions of colors and lines.

While abstract expressionism led the viewer away from conventional representations of reality, "pop art" portrayed objects with cameralike precision. Pop art, which emerged during the late 1950s, made common items like soup cans and soda bottles the subject of art. Andy Warhol and Roy Lichtenstein emerged as leading figures of the pop art movement during the 1960s.

A Sense of Disillusionment

Although most people seemed content with American society during the 1950s, a few criticized the established order. One group, labeled "beatniks," refused to conform to accepted ways of dressing, thinking, and acting. Conformity, they insisted, stifled individualism. They ridiculed American attachment to material success and lived in voluntary poverty. The "beatniks" displayed their differences from American society by informal dress and colorful jargon.

Some social scientists wrote scholarly critiques of American society. William H. Whyte argued in his book *The Organization Man* (1956) that bureaucratic organizations tended to discourage creativity and individualism. In *The Lonely Crowd* (1950), David Riesman charged that many Americans cared too much about pleasing others. Riesman also lamented the power of advertising to mold public tastes.

Economist John Kenneth Galbraith argued that unplanned economic growth had resulted in great private fortunes but had left the public sector impoverished. In his book *The Affluent Society* (1958), Galbraith called for more resources to be invested in schools, theaters, and other public facilities.

In 1959 a scandal on a television quiz show convinced some critics that their concerns about American society were well founded. Charles Van Doren, a Columbia University instructor, revealed that the show's producers had given him the correct answers enabling him to win thousands of dollars.

Some Americans saw signs of national decline in the misconduct of Van Doren and the television executives. Novelist John Steinbeck claimed, "on all levels American society is rigged. . . . I am troubled by the cynical immorality of my country. It cannot survive on this basis." An article in the magazine *Look* lamented the emergence of "the freedom to chisel." Such feelings of disillusionment became a campaign issue in the presidential election of 1960.

The Election of 1960

In 1960 the Republicans nominated Vice-President Richard M. Nixon as their presidential candidate. Henry Cabot Lodge, Jr., of Massachusetts won the Republican nomination for Vice-President. The Democratic party nominated John F. Kennedy, a young senator from Massachusetts, for President and chose Senator Lyndon B. Johnson of Texas as his running mate.

Kennedy focused his campaign on the vague sense that the country was drifting under Eisenhower. The senator took advantage of his strong public image and promised to "get America moving again." In nationally publicized televised debates between Kennedy and Nixon, Kennedy seemed confident and vigorous while Nixon appeared nervous and unsure of himself.

During the campaign, Kennedy argued that the Republicans had allowed the Soviet Union to achieve nuclear superiority over the United States. He charged that there was a "missile gap," which he would close if elected President. Nixon campaigned on Eisenhower's record, stressing the peace and prosperity the United States had enjoyed under the Republicans. Although neither candidate made an issue of the fact that Kennedy was Catholic, his religion probably gained him votes in eastern cities and hurt his candidacy in rural areas and in the West.

The election was close. Kennedy received 34,227,096 popular votes to Nixon's

Televised debates between Richard Nixon (left) and John Kennedy (right) in 1960 marked a first in presidential elections. For the first time, millions of voters could watch and compare the candidates as they discussed the same points.

Major Events	
1944	GI Bill of Rights passed
1947	Taft-Hartley Act passed
1948	Truman orders end to segregation in armed forces; Truman reelected
1950	McCarthy charges there are communists in government
1952	Dwight D. Eisenhower elected President
1954	Army-McCarthy hearings; *Brown v. Board of Education of Topeka*
1955	Montgomery bus boycott
1957	Eisenhower orders troops to Little Rock; *Sputnik I* launched
1958	National Defense Education Act passed
1960	Sit-in movement begins; John F. Kennedy elected President

34,108,546, but in the electoral college Kennedy won by 303 to 219. At 43 years of age, Kennedy was the youngest person and first Catholic to be elected President of the United States.

SECTION REVIEW

1. Identify: Rosa Parks, Martin Luther King, Jr., *Sputnik I*, rock 'n' roll, beatniks, Richard M. Nixon, John F. Kennedy.
2. Define: civil disobedience.
3. (a) What did the Supreme Court rule in *Brown* v. *Board of Education of Topeka?* (b) What action did President Eisenhower take to enforce the Court ruling in Little Rock?
4. What two tactics did black Americans use against segregation during the 1950s?
5. How did Congress react to public outcry about the launch of *Sputnik I?*
6. Give two examples of new art forms that developed during the 1950s.
7. **Critical Thinking** How did writers and artists of the 1950s reflect concerns similar to those expressed in the 1920s?

Chapter 37 Review

In Perspective

The transition from war to peace was troubled by unemployment, inflation, and strikes. Discontent over these problems led many to believe that President Truman would be beaten easily in the election of 1948. However, Truman won and began to institute his Fair Deal program. He also used presidential authority to reduce discrimination against black Americans.

The Cold War contributed to anxieties about the potential threat of communism at home. The discovery of a few cases of disloyal activity fed such fears, and Senator Joseph McCarthy charged that many communists were active in high levels of government. McCarthy's investigations uncovered little evidence of such activity, and his popularity declined after the televised Army-McCarthy hearings.

Dwight D. Eisenhower, who easily won the election in 1952, pursued a moderate course. Although he resisted demands to use government action to end the recession of 1957–1958, he did not dismantle any New Deal programs. The Eisenhower years were generally viewed as a time of stability, but there were some significant social changes. The Supreme Court ruled that segregation in public schools was unconstitutional, and black citizens increased protest against segregation. The Soviet launching of *Sputnik I* shocked Americans into demanding a more rigorous educational system. In the 1960 presidential election, John F. Kennedy promised "to get America moving again."

Vocabulary

On a separate sheet of paper, write the word or words that best complete each of the following sentences.

1. The Servicemen's Readjustment Act was sometimes called the ___.
2. The ___ requires all workers to be union members.
3. ___ is segregation that existed in fact if not in law.
4. The term ___ referred to a technique of making sweeping accusations, frequently without evidence.
5. ___ is nonviolent protest against an unjust law or condition.

Chapter Checkup

1. (a) Why did the Republicans win a majority in both houses of Congress in 1946? (b) What impact did the Eightieth Congress have on Truman's legislative program? (c) What parts of Truman's Fair Deal did Congress pass after the 1948 election? (d) What parts of the Fair Deal failed to pass?
2. (a) How did segregation differ in the North and the South? (b) Describe how President Truman advanced the civil rights of black Americans.
3. (a) What type of charges did Senator Joseph McCarthy make? (b) What effect did he have? (c) Why did he eventually cease to be a political force?
4. (a) Describe general economic conditions during President Eisenhower's administration. (b) How did Eisenhower react to the recession of 1957–1958? Why?
5. (a) How did the Supreme Court decision in *Brown* v. *Board of Education of Topeka* differ from the 1896 Court decision on racial segragation? (b) What arguments did the NAACP lawyer make against "separate but equal" facilities?

Critical Thinking

1. **Recognizing Relationships** Review what you have learned about the attitude of the United States toward the Soviet Union after World War II. (See Chapter 36.) What relationship do you see between foreign policy and the domestic politics you studied in this chapter?
2. **Comparing** How did President Eisenhower's attitude toward government activity in the economy differ from President Truman's?

Developing Basic Skills

1. **Relating Past to Present** Observe how women are portrayed in television commercials today. (a) How does the view presented of women's roles in society differ from that presented in 1950s commercials? (b) How are the views similar?
2. **Collecting Evidence** Interview a friend or relative who lived during the 1950s. Ask the person what he or she remembers about the following topics: McCarthyism, television programs, the launching of Sputnik, the beginning of rock 'n' roll. Compare the person's recollections with what you have read in the text. (a) How are they similar? (b) How are they different? (c) What did you learn about life in the 1950s through your interview?

See page 833 for suggested readings.

Writer's Handbook

Informal Documentation

As you recall, there are times when you must cite a source used for a research paper. (See page 589.) The two common types of citations are informal citations and footnotes. Informal citations are placed immediately after the facts or quote you have taken from a source. To write informal citations, include in parentheses the author's name, the title of the source, and the page number where the information can be found. For example: (Thomas Bailey, *Diplomatic History of the United States*, 316–317). Of course, each of the sources you identify must also appear in your bibliography.

Practice: Using your textbook as your source, write an example of an informal citation.

38

A Turbulent Decade

(1960–1969)

The launching of a space flight

Chapter Outline

1 *Increased World Tension*

2 *The New Frontier*

3 *Building the Great Society*

4 *A Struggle for Equal Rights for Black Americans*

5 *A Continuing Struggle for Equality*

6 *Growing Involvement in World Affairs*

The 1960s dawned with much promise. The youthful confidence of John F. Kennedy reflected the hopes of many citizens for an era of economic, social, and technological progress. Yet the decade progressed differently from what most Americans could have guessed.

Blacks, Hispanics, Native Americans, and women pressed for an equal share of economic and social opportunities. On college campuses, students joined protest movements. By the end of the decade, over 500,000 Americans had been sent to fight in Vietnam. Genuine progress was made in many areas, but debate over how to achieve the goals shared by most Americans left the nation divided.

Johnson's Great Society

1960	1962	1964	1966	1968	1970

1961
Peace Corps created; Bay of Pigs invasion

1962
Cuban missile crisis

1963
President Kennedy assassinated

1964
Civil Rights Act passed; Johnson elected President

1965
Medicaid, Medicare, Voting Rights acts passed

1967
War between Israel and Egypt

1968
Martin Luther King, Jr., assassinated; Richard M. Nixon elected President

1 Increased World Tension

When John Kennedy took office in January 1961 the cold war still dominated relations between the Soviet Union and the United States. During President Kennedy's administration, a series of international crises threatened to erupt into actual warfare between the two nations.

The Kennedy Team

John Fitzgerald Kennedy brought to the White House a combination of youth, intelligence, and ideals, tempered by an eye for practical politics. He had used his charisma, family wealth, and organizational skills to achieve political success. However, Kennedy recognized that as President, his youth might be viewed as a liability. Consequently he chose his cabinet and advisers carefully. He appointed respected experts from the academic world and former military leaders, including a few Republicans.

The man who most symbolized the dynamism of the new administration was Secretary of Defense Robert McNamara. McNamara had been part of a young group of administrators known as the "whiz kids," who had helped save the Ford Motor Company from bankruptcy during the 1950s. McNamara was eventually appointed company president before coming to Washington to serve under President Kennedy.

A Shift in Foreign Relations

Despite President Eisenhower's military background, he had pursued a moderate defense policy. In the years following the Sputnik launching, for example, government expenditures on military weapons rose only 2 percent. When Eisenhower left office, he warned against the "unwarranted influence" that could come to be exerted by what he labeled "the military-industrial complex." However, during the 1960 campaign, John Kennedy spoke of a "missile gap." He claimed that the Soviet Union had a superior arsenal of military weapons, especially long-range missiles. Consequently he stepped up military spending once in office.

In the wake of the Cuban revolution, President Kennedy also wanted the armed forces to be prepared to combat possible Soviet-supported revolutions around the world. Premier Khrushchev had pledged Soviet support for such "wars of liberation."

To counter potential uprisings, the Kennedy administration began to develop *strategic forces*, that is, specially trained units that could be moved quickly to any part of the world. At Fort Bragg, North Carolina, and in the American-controlled Panama Canal Zone, the armed forces established jungle warfare schools to teach guerrilla fighting techniques.

Kennedy did not limit American response to the Soviet challenge to military measures. He also proposed a new type of foreign aid through the Peace Corps. The Peace Corps was to be composed of Americans volunteering to teach or to contribute technical advice in developing countries. Such foreign aid was designed to build

The youngest person ever elected President, John Kennedy, shown here, held a special appeal for young people. In his inaugural speech, he struck a responsive chord in young and old alike as he said, "Ask not what your country can do for you. Ask what you can do for your country."

friendship with countries in Africa, Asia, and South America. Further, President Kennedy hoped that such aid would persuade neutral nations that western-style democracy offered the best way to achieve peace, stability, and economic growth.

In 1961 the administration moved to improve relations with Latin American countries by organizing the Alliance for Progress. The United States pledged approximately $20 billion in aid to Latin American countries over a ten-year period. Latin American nations were to invest some $80 billion of their own funds in economic development.

Members of the alliance were required to reform unjust land or tax policies in order to develop more democratic economic systems and thereby reduce the chances of violent revolution. President Kennedy warned that, "those who make peaceful revolution impossible will make violent revolution inevitable." Although few governments were eager to comply with the reform provisions of the Alliance for Progress, its creation did improve the image of the United States among Latin American nations.

Trouble in the Bay of Pigs

Whatever goodwill the United States won through the Alliance for Progress was soon undermined when the Kennedy administration attempted to overthrow the government of Cuba. By the end of the Eisenhower administration the Central Intelligence Agency (CIA) had begun training anti-Castro Cuban exiles for such a task.

President Kennedy was briefed on the plan and told that with United States air support, success was likely. A secret invasion force trained in Guatemala was to land at the Bay of Pigs in Cuba. The assault group was to join up with anti-Castro forces in the mountains and march on Havana, the capital.

Convinced that Castro lacked support from the Cuban people, Kennedy allowed the invasion to begin on April 17, 1961. It was a disaster. The Cubans were well prepared. The "secret" training activities in Guatemala had been reported in the New York Times, and Cuban intelligence officials had apparently briefed the military about the invasion. The promised air strike, which was to destroy the six-plane Cuban air force, never took place. Furthermore, expected Cuban

support for the invaders did not materialize. Castro's forces cleared the beach at the Bay of Pigs in four days and captured some 1,200 attackers.

Initially President Kennedy denied United States involvement in the invasion, but eventually he assumed full responsibility. "All my life, I've known better than to depend on the experts," Kennedy remarked privately. "How could I have been so stupid, to let them go ahead?" The failure at the Bay of Pigs demonstrated the difficulties of using military tactics to achieve broad political goals.

Growing Tension in Europe

In June 1961 President Kennedy traveled to Vienna, Austria, to meet with Premier Nikita Khrushchev. The Soviet Union wanted NATO forces withdrawn from West Germany. The Soviet leader also voiced his concern over the increasing flow of East German youth, intellectuals, and technicians defecting to West Berlin.

Premier Khrushchev may have considered the President weak in light of the Bay of Pigs. Khrushchev threatened to sign a defense treaty with East Germany if NATO troops were not withdrawn by December. Kennedy refused to discuss a withdrawal.

On August 13 the East Germans suddenly erected a wall between East and West Berlin. The wall effectively cut off the flow of defectors, but it proved to be a valuable propaganda weapon for the western powers. It appeared to them that the communist governments of eastern Europe had to use force to keep their people from fleeing.

In 1963 the President visited West Berlin and was greeted by enormous crowds who heard him declare, *"Ich bin ein Berliner"* ("I am a Berliner"). With that statement he assured the residents of West Berlin that the United States would maintain its support of the city.

After the Berlin crisis, the Soviet Union and the United States increased efforts to strengthen their military capabilities. In September 1961 the Soviet Union broke the three-year moratorium on nuclear tests with a series of above-ground explosions. The United States began tests the following spring. President Kennedy also launched a program to build fallout shelters in case of a nuclear attack.

In 1961 East German authorities tried to stop East Berliners from fleeing into West Berlin by building a wall between the two sections of the city. To show American support for the free people of West Berlin, President Kennedy stood before the Berlin Wall in 1963 and declared in German, "Ich bin ein Berliner" ("I am a Berliner").

The Cuban Missile Crisis

In the midst of heightened tension, the President learned that Premier Khrushchev had placed offensive weapons in Cuba. Aerial photographs revealed missile launch pads under construction there. The insignia on the equipment were Soviet.

The President immediately convened a group of his advisers chaired by his brother Robert, the attorney general. For six days, while the advisers weighed alternatives, the President carried on public business as if nothing had happened. The President's advisers then proposed two options: a naval blockade of Cuba or an air strike against the missile sites.

On October 22, 1962, President Kennedy announced the presence of the Soviet missile launch pads to a shocked nation. Kennedy informed the public that a naval blockade would prevent further entry of offensive weapons to Cuba. As Soviet ships steamed toward Cuba, Kennedy placed the armed forces on full alert.

Tensions mounted as work continued on the Cuban bases and Soviet ships approached the blockade. Then the ships stopped. "We're eyeball to eyeball," reported Secretary of State Dean Rusk at the height of the crisis, "and I think the other fellow just blinked." Convinced of American determination, Premier Khrushchev ordered the ships to turn back and the bases to be dismantled.

The crisis was over, but the prospect of a nuclear war had been sobering indeed. American and Soviet leaders established a direct telephone link, known as the "hot line," between Washington and Moscow. The missile crisis also contributed to a new desire to limit the testing of nuclear weapons.

The Soviet Union was willing to limit nuclear tests because it wanted to devote more resources to improve its domestic economy. In addition, American public opinion strongly favored steps to reduce the radioactive fallout from nuclear tests. President Kennedy pronounced:

> If we cannot end now all our differences, at least we can help make the world safe for diversity. For . . . we all inhabit this small planet. We all breathe the same air. We all cherish our children's future. And we are all mortal.

In July 1963 the two powers concluded a treaty banning nuclear tests in the atmosphere, although underground tests were still permitted. In addition to the United States and the Soviet Union, Great Britain also ratified the treaty. The test-ban treaty proved to be a significant step in easing the international tensions that had played so great a part in the history of the previous two decades.

SECTION REVIEW

1. Identify: Robert McNamara, Peace Corps, Alliance for Progress.

2. Define: strategic forces.

3. (a) What was the purpose of the Peace Corps? (b) What was the purpose of the Alliance for Progress?

4. What event undermined the goodwill of the United States in Latin America?

5. What two responses did President Kennedy's advisers suggest to the building of missile bases in Cuba?

6. **Critical Thinking** What do you think were the benefits of having the Peace Corps made up of volunteers?

2 The New Frontier

During the Democratic nominating convention of 1960, John F. Kennedy had spoken of the frontiers Americans had conquered in the past. He had challenged the nation to turn to a "new frontier": those national goals that remained unfulfilled. As President, Kennedy tried to advance his New Frontier in the areas of economic development, civil rights, and the exploration of space.

The Frontier of Space

In the race to explore the new frontier of outer space, the Soviet Union had already proven its abilities with numerous satellite launches. It made further progress in April 1961, when Yuri Gagarin (YOO ree guh GAHR uhn) became the first person to orbit the earth. One month later United States Navy Commander Alan Shepard, Jr., rode a tiny Mercury capsule in a suborbital flight of 300 miles (about 500 kilometers). Shortly afterward President Kennedy pledged that the United States would put an American on the moon before 1970.

On February 20, 1962, Lieutenant Colonel John Glenn was launched into orbit from Cape Canaveral, Florida. Unlike the practice in the Soviet Union, the National Aeronautics and Space Administration (NASA) permitted live press coverage of the manned flights. Millions of Americans heard the slow countdown, watched the rocket's takeoff, and followed Glenn's conversations with ground control at Cape Canaveral. Glenn orbited the earth three times and returned home safely in what he called a "fireball of a ride."

Other manned and unmanned launches followed. Telstar, a commercial communications satellite, orbited the earth relaying live television broadcasts over long distances. The Mariner series of space probes came within 21,000 miles (about 34,000 kilometers) of the planet Venus and radioed back information.

Economic Policies

During the last years of President Eisenhower's administration, economic growth had slowed, yet the rate of inflation had steadily increased. President Kennedy hoped to stimulate economic growth while controlling inflation. An alliance of Republicans and conservative Democrats resisted the President's attempts to increase government spending, but Congress did raise the minimum wage. It also began debate on a tax cut. Many economists argued that a reduction in taxes would stimulate the economy by leaving the taxpayer more money to spend on consumer products.

President Kennedy urged Congress to pass several programs designed to reduce poverty, especially in urban slums and poor rural areas such as Appalachia, the hilly country stretching south from Pennsylvania through West Virginia, Kentucky, Tennessee, and Alabama. The programs were geared to involve local citizens in planning economic programs suited to local needs.

In an attempt to control inflation, the President established an informal standard of "wage-price guideposts" that he hoped business and labor would follow. He was particularly concerned about wages and prices in the steel industry. Steel was used in many industries, and a rise in steel costs would affect the entire economy.

In April 1962 the administration convinced steel workers to accept a contract with moderate wage increases. The union agreed with the understanding that the steel companies would not raise steel prices. But U.S. Steel and other major producers surprised the President by announcing a steep price increase. In a press conference Kennedy condemned the steel companies' actions. The Defense Department then announced it would purchase steel only from those companies that had not raised prices.

Inland Steel and many smaller companies kept their prices down, which forced the other producers to return to the old price levels. The President had won a major battle against inflation, but his attack on the steel companies damaged administration relations with big business.

Civil Rights

Because Kennedy had long advocated civil rights legislation, he received support from black Americans during the 1960 election. Once in office, Kennedy moved cautiously because he needed the backing of southern Democrats in Congress for his other programs. However, he did support a voting rights bill and the Twenty-fourth Amendment to the Constitution, prohibiting poll taxes. The Twenty-fourth Amendment was passed by Congress in August 1962 and ratified in 1964. (See page 834.) Kennedy also appointed blacks to key positions in government, including Robert Weaver as Home Finance administrator and Thurgood Marshall as a federal judge.

Attorney General Robert Kennedy dealt firmly with violations of civil rights. In 1961 he sent federal troops to Alabama to protect blacks trying to integrate buses and trains. Robert Kennedy personally supervised the case of James Meredith, a black Air Force veteran who attempted to enroll at the all-white University of Mississippi. When Meredith registered for classes in 1962, rioting erupted, and the President sent federal marshals to the campus to back the National Guard. Several hundred soldiers remained there until Meredith graduated.

In Alabama, Governor George Wallace gained national attention by temporarily halting federal marshals as they escorted black student Autherine Lucy to the formerly all-white University of Alabama. Lucy also continued her education with the protection of the National Guard.

In 1963 President Kennedy presented Congress with a comprehensive civil rights legislative package that would ban discrimination in employment and voting and in state programs receiving federal aid. The laws would also guarantee all Americans access to public accommodations. In a television message, the President asked:

> Are we to say to the world—and much more importantly, to each other—that this is the land of the free except for the Negroes; that we have no second-class citizens, except Negroes; that we have no class or caste system, no ghettos, no master race, except with respect to Negroes?

Tragedy in Dallas

On November 22, 1963, President Kennedy arrived in Dallas, Texas, on a political tour. As the presidential motorcade proceeded from the airport to the center of the city, the crowd was friendly and enthusiastic, and the President waved and smiled warmly in response.

Suddenly rifle shots rang out. The President lurched, then slumped in his seat. The limousine sped to Parkland Memorial Hospital, but the President was fatally wounded and could not be revived. That afternoon aboard an Air Force jet bound for Washington, Vice-President Lyndon Johnson was sworn in as the thirty-sixth President of the United States.

The nation and the world viewed the events of that November weekend with horror and grief. Lee Harvey Oswald was arrested and charged with the assassination. Millions watched television in disbelief as they saw Oswald, while being escorted by police, shot to death by Jack Ruby, a local nightclub operator.

From around the world the White House received expressions of grief and loss. Americans wept with the Kennedy family and a host of somber world leaders as television cameras followed the flag-draped casket carrying the President's body to Arlington National Cemetery. Although President Kennedy had not been in office long enough to test fully the measure of his leadership, his vigor and idealism had shaped the first years of the decade.

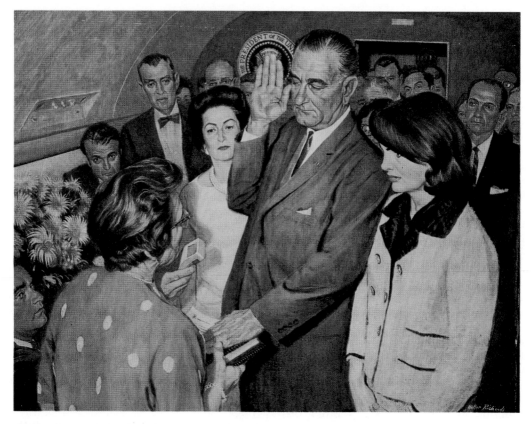

On the plane carrying the coffin of John Kennedy to Washington, Lyndon Johnson was sworn in as President. Shown here, from left, are federal Judge Sarah T. Hughes administering the oath, Lady Bird Johnson, the new President, and Jacqueline Kennedy.

SECTION REVIEW

1. Identify: Alan Shepard, John Glenn, Telstar, James Meredith, George Wallace.
2. (a) How did Kennedy try to control inflation? (b) What industry was he especially concerned about?
3. List two actions President Kennedy took in support of civil rights.
4. **Critical Thinking** What was the symbolism for Americans of the term the "new frontier"?

3 Building the Great Society

The outpouring of grief for the slain President brought with it an equal measure of support for his successor, Lyndon Johnson. In the first years of his administration, Johnson dedicated himself to fulfilling the Kennedy program, building what the new President called the Great Society. The Great Society, asserted Johnson, "asks not only how much, but how good; not only how to create wealth, but how to use it; not only how fast we are going, but where we are headed."

The Great Society Begins

When Lyndon Johnson arrived in Washington on November 22, 1963, he said simply, "I'll do my best. That's all I can do." Although he became President unexpectedly, few leaders in Washington had more experience for the job than Lyndon Johnson. He had first been elected to the House of Representatives from Texas in 1937. In 1948 he won a Senate post by 87 votes in a disputed election that earned him the nickname "Landslide Lyndon." By 1953 he was the Democratic minority leader in the Senate.

Johnson's success resulted from shrewd political sense and the ability to convince fellow senators to vote for legislation he favored. His vigorous persuasion became known as the "Johnson treatment." Senator George Smathers of Florida recalled the treatment as being like "a great overpowering thunderstorm that consumed you as it closed in around you." In 1958 when Johnson became majority leader of the Senate, he was perhaps the most influential politician on Capitol Hill.

As President, Johnson immediately urged Congress to pass the major bills of the Kennedy administration. He won over opponents to the tax cut proposal by promising a more efficient federal budget. Congress passed Kennedy's civil rights package as the Civil Rights Act of 1964. President Johnson also expanded government efforts to help the poor.

In 1964 approximately 30 million Americans (16 percent of the population) lived in families with incomes below the "poverty line," as defined by the government. The keystone to what Johnson called his War on Poverty was the Economic Opportunity Act of 1964. The act provided for job training programs for the poor, loans to encourage rural farm cooperatives and urban businesses, and aid to migrant laborers. It also created VISTA, Volunteers in Service to America, a domestic Peace Corps.

A Democratic Landslide

Johnson's active first year in office assured his nomination as the Democratic presidential candidate in 1964. As his running mate, he chose Hubert H. Humphrey, a well-known senator from Minnesota.

The Republicans were divided between New York Governor Nelson Rockefeller and Senator Barry Goldwater of Arizona. Rockefeller represented the moderate wing of the Republican party, with its strength in the Northeast. Goldwater represented the conservative wing of the party. He was a strong supporter of states' rights. Goldwater's rise to prominence also indicated the growing strength of the Southwest in United States politics.

Goldwater won the nomination and chose William Miller, a New York congress-

man, as his running mate. In accepting the nomination, Goldwater squarely faced the charge that his views were too extreme. "Extremism in the defense of liberty is no vice," he said. "Moderation in pursuit of justice is no virtue."

During the campaign Johnson and Humphrey portrayed themselves as moderate alternatives to Goldwater. Democratic political advertisements emphasized statements and positions that made Goldwater seem "dangerous" to many Americans. The tactic worked. Lyndon Johnson enjoyed the biggest victory since Franklin D. Roosevelt in 1936. Johnson received 61 percent of the popular vote compared to 39 percent for Goldwater.

Twenty-eight Democratic senators and 37 new representatives were also voted into office, giving the Democrats a large majority in both houses. President Johnson thus had the votes he needed to enact a long list of legislative bills.

A Flood of Legislation

During the election campaign, Lyndon Johnson summarized the goals he believed most Americans sought. "They want education for their children and an improving life for their families. They want to protect liberty and pursue peace. They expect justice for themselves and are willing to grant it to others." To meet these goals Johnson set before Congress an ambitious slate of social legislation, much of which was passed in 1965.

One of the most far-reaching pieces of legislation was the Medicare Act. It provided hospital coverage for citizens over 65 and allowed them to participate in a program that shared the cost of other medical expenses. In addition a Medicaid program provided funds for states to assist poor people of all ages who were not covered by Medicare. In passing Medicare, the federal government for the first time sought to guarantee a minimum level of health care for Americans.

President Johnson pressed for further civil rights legislation after the Reverend James J. Reeb, a black civil rights worker, was shot during a voter registration campaign in Selma, Alabama. The Voting Rights Act of 1965 authorized federal officials to register voters in states where state officials continued to discriminate on the basis of race. The enforcement of this law in Selma and throughout the country resulted in the

In 1965 black and white civil rights marchers from all over the nation joined the Reverend Martin Luther King, Jr., in a "freedom march." They walked the 65 miles from Selma, Alabama, to the state capital of Montgomery to demand voting rights.

registration of a million new black voters by the 1968 election.

The Immigration Act eliminated quotas that had limited immigration from certain parts of the world since the 1920s. (See page 547.) The Housing Act provided federal funds for constructing low- and middle-income housing. Congress created the Department of Housing and Urban Development (HUD), and President Johnson named Robert Weaver to head the department, making him the first black to serve in a presidential cabinet. Congress also expanded social security benefits, provided aid to higher education, began efforts to curb water pollution, and created the National Foundation for the Arts and Humanities.

In October 1965, after Congress had adjourned for the year, the President presented a display case of 50 pens to members of the White House press. The inscription read, "With these fifty pens President Lyndon B. Johnson signed into law the foundations of the Great Society, which was passed by the historical and fabulous first session of the Eighty-ninth Congress."

SECTION REVIEW

1. Identify: VISTA, Hubert H. Humphrey, Barry Goldwater.
2. Name two characteristics that contributed to Lyndon Johnson's political rise.
3. List two provisions of the Economic Opportunity Act of 1964.
4. What did the Medicare Act provide?
5. **Critical Thinking** Why do you think the Great Society programs have been called the "second Reconstruction"?

4 A Struggle for Equal Rights for Black Americans

In his appeal for the creation of the Great Society, President Johnson envisioned a nation in which economic and spiritual needs would be fully satisfied. Yet, as he himself recognized, not all citizens were able to share equally in that dream. The civil rights movement begun by black Americans in the 1950s would grow throughout the 1960s.

Tactics of Nonviolence

During the early 1960s advocates of greater civil rights generally used the nonviolent tactics followed by the Reverend Martin Luther King, Jr. His organization, the Southern Christian Leadership Conference, was joined by others, including the Congress of Racial

Equality (CORE) and the Student Non-violent Coordinating Committee (SNCC). The National Association for the Advancement of Colored People continued to work for equality through the courts, where it filed suits against acts of discrimination.

As you read in Chapter 37, a movement against the segregation of public facilities in the South began when a group of young blacks refused to leave an all-white lunch counter in 1960. Soon the tactic was adopted by black and white civil rights workers. "Freedom riders" quietly but firmly refused to be segregated on buses and trains or in depots, stations, or rest rooms. Groups marched in protest when voting rights were denied, or staged "sit-ins" at restaurant counters labeled "for whites only." Other protesters led campaigns to desegregate schools.

The response to such tactics was often violent. Angry mobs attacked buses of freedom riders. Police sometimes dispersed protesters with water hoses, police dogs, or electric cattle prods. Civil rights workers were frequently imprisoned and fined. Often

they sought arrest to bring national attention to their cause. In the North advocates of civil rights organized rent strikes to protest poor housing conditions and boycotted stores that refused to hire blacks.

In 1963 over 200,000 blacks and whites gathered in Washington, D.C., to demand racial equality. Civil rights leaders addressed the crowd, and Martin Luther King proclaimed in a ringing speech of hope: "I have a dream!" The protests had their effect as local communities began to repeal segregation laws. The federal government passed further civil rights legislation calling for an end to discrimination in public establishments and at polling places. Yet others were demanding more radical action.

A More Militant Movement

After 1963 a growing number of black leaders came to believe that King's philosophy of nonviolence was not bringing equality quickly enough. These radical leaders were especially concerned with the problems

---

★ Voices of Freedom ★

I Have a Dream

On August 28, 1963, over 200,000 people from all walks of life joined a public demonstration for racial equality at the Lincoln Memorial in Washington, D.C. Martin Luther King, Jr., was among ten speakers to address the crowd of black and white marchers. A portion of his stirring speech is printed below.

I say to you today, my friends, that in spite of the difficulties and frustrations of the moment I still have a dream. It is a dream deeply rooted in the American dream.

I have a dream that one day this nation will rise up and live out the true meaning of its creed: "We hold these truths to be self-evident; that all men are created equal." . . .

I have a dream that my four little children will one day live in a nation where they will not be judged by the color of their skin but by the content of their character. . . .

When we let freedom ring, when we let it ring from every village and every hamlet,

from every state and every city, we will be able to speed up that day when all of God's children, black men and white men, Jews and Gentiles, Protestants and Catholics, will be able to join hands and sing in the words of the old Negro spiritual, "Free at last! Free at last! Thank God Almighty, we are free at last!"

faced by northern blacks. Over the previous 50 years, blacks had moved in increasing numbers to northern cities.

Life in northern cities was hard and frustrating for most blacks. Although segregation laws did not exist in the North, widespread discrimination did. De facto segregation kept most blacks in rundown ghettos, where many lived in decayed buildings, often with inadequate plumbing and heating. Although the average income of black workers had risen since 1950, it remained much lower than the average income of whites. Unemployment was also higher among blacks than whites.

Radicals demanded immediate action to correct such conditions. One radical group was the Black Muslims, led by Elijah Muhammed. The Muslims believed that blacks would succeed only if they separated completely from white society. Founded in 1930, the movement received little national attention until its views were spread by Malcolm Little, an energetic Muslim minister who adopted the name Malcolm X.

By 1964 Malcolm X had rejected Elijah Muhammed's separatist ideas in favor of creating "a society in which there could exist honest white-black brotherhood." In February 1965 Malcolm X was shot and killed, presumably as the result of his dispute with the Black Muslims. His ideas, expressed in the *Autobiography of Malcolm X*, have remained influential.

Malcolm X and other blacks warned that frustration and despair in black ghettos might lead to violence. In 1964 and 1965 those warnings proved accurate. Harlem and Rochester, New York, were the sites of riots in the summer of 1964. In August 1965 even greater turmoil broke out in the Los Angeles ghetto known as Watts. For five days Watts was plagued by looting, rioting, and arson. The governor sent 14,000 National Guardsmen to restore order. By the time calm returned, 34 people were dead, 4,000 had been arrested, and $35 million worth of property had been destroyed or damaged.

In 1966 and 1967 riots erupted in other major cities, including Newark, Cincinnati, Atlanta, and Detroit. Although different incidents set off each riot, the violence and turmoil appeared to have spread because of the anger and frustration widely shared by blacks living in ghetto areas across the nation.

Black Power

During the late 1960s militant black leaders such as Stokely Carmichael and Floyd McKissick rejected cooperation with sympathetic whites and put forth a philosophy of "black power." Blacks, they argued, should take control of the economic and political aspects of their lives even if it required a violent revolution to do so. One radical group, the Black Panthers, urged blacks to arm themselves and fight for their rights when necessary.

Moderate black leaders stressed that black power should be expressed as self-reliance and pride, not as violence. Opinion polls revealed that most black Americans preferred the goals of integration and the more moderate interpretation of black power. However, the more violent rhetoric attracted widespread attention.

The mood of tension and violence increased in April 1968 when Dr. Martin Luther King, Jr., went to Memphis, Tennessee, to support a strike called by black sanitation workers. Having received many threats on his life, King told his followers, "I've seen the Promised Land. I may not get there with you. But I want you to know tonight that we as a people will get to the Promised Land." The next day, April 4, a sniper's bullets killed Dr. King, bringing sorrow and rage to the nation.

Riots broke out in over 170 cities across the nation. Amid the violence the body of Dr. King, the man who had won the Nobel Peace Prize "for the furtherance of brotherhood among men," was laid to rest at Morehouse College in Atlanta, Georgia. Inscribed on his gravestone are the words, "Free at last, free at last, thank God Almightly I'm free at last."

A Warning and Cautious Hope

The mixture of cautious hope and frustration that characterized most of the civil rights struggle was reflected in a report issued shortly before Martin Luther King's death. The Kerner Commission, appointed by President Johnson and headed by Illinois Governor Otto Kerner, spent six months studying the causes and consequences of the civil disorders that had swept the nation.

The commission report noted that black Americans had made significant progress in some areas. Freedom riders had largely succeeded in desegregating public places, and millions of blacks were voting. The Civil Rights Act of 1968 for the first time declared that no person could be denied housing on account of race. The only housing units not covered by the act were owner-occupied houses sold directly by the owners.

The Kerner report also stressed that more remained to be done. "Our nation is moving toward two societies," the commission warned, "one black, one white—separate but unequal." Despite the new laws, blacks still faced discrimination in housing, employment, and education. According to the report, only "a commitment to national action—compassionate, massive, and sustained" could bring equality for all.

SECTION REVIEW

1. Identify: Kerner Commission.
2. List three tactics black Americans used against segregation in the early 1960s.
3. What conditions led some black leaders to demand more radical action?
4. What goal did Malcolm X come to support before his death?
5. **Critical Thinking**   Why can nonviolent tactics be effective?

5 A Continuing Struggle for Equality

The struggle for equal rights among black Americans during the 1960s sparked other groups to demand their rights. The reform spirit of the decade especially affected Hispanics, Native Americans, and women.

Hispanic Americans

As the black civil rights movement grew, Hispanic groups also began to work more actively to overcome inequalities they faced. Such efforts were often more regional than national, however, because Hispanic groups with various heritages lived in different parts of the nation.

During the 1600s small groups of Spanish farmers had settled in what is now the southwestern United States. Many of their descendants, known as Hispanos, continued to live in the rural uplands and mountains of New Mexico and Colorado. The majority of the Hispanos raised sheep or tended small farms, as their ancestors had done.

A much larger Hispanic minority were the descendants of Mexicans who had lived in the Southwest when the United States annexed the territory in the Mexican War. Mexicans continued to migrate to the United States, especially after 1910. (See page 567.) By 1960 approximately 3.5 million Mexican Americans lived in the Southwest.

In the eastern United States most Hispanic immigrants came from Puerto Rico. The United States had annexed the island in 1898, and in 1917 Congress granted American citizenship to residents there. In 1952 the United States Congress and the citizens of Puerto Rico agreed to a commonwealth status for the island. Puerto Ricans drafted their own constitution and elected a governor and a legislature. At the same time, they retained the rights of United States citizens, were protected militarily by the United States, and came under the jurisdiction of federal agencies such as the post office and the customs service. Puerto Ricans could also immigrate to the United States and travel freely within its borders.

Before World War II, only about 70,000 Puerto Ricans had moved to the mainland, most of them settling in New York City. After the war, as the Puerto Rican population expanded rapidly, the number of emigrants increased. By 1960 some 600,000 had come to the mainland. Many continued to settle in New York, but some moved to other cities, including Chicago, San Francisco, and Bridgeport, Connecticut.

When Fidel Castro began setting up a communist state in Cuba in the early 1960s, thousands of Cubans sought to leave their country. Between 1961 and 1970 over 200,000 Cubans immigrated to the United States. Some fled the island in small boats. Most Cuban immigrants settled in southern Florida. Many resumed careers in medicine, law, and teaching. Miami, the city with the largest number of Cuban immigrants, acquired a new appearance. Shop windows displayed signs in Spanish. Cuban restaurants were built to cater to the new immigrants. Spanish-language radio stations began broadcasting. As their numbers grew, Cuban Americans became an increasingly powerful force in southern Florida.

The Problems of Discrimination

Hispanos, Mexican Americans, and Puerto Ricans faced many forms of discrimination. They lived in a land in which the dominant culture was English, while theirs was Spanish. Few schools had programs to teach English to students whose first language was Spanish. Consequently Hispanic students found themselves at a disadvantage. The lack of a good education in turn made it more difficult to obtain good jobs. But even well-educated Hispanics encountered discrimination among employers.

A government program started in the 1950s created special problems for Mexican American migrant workers. Under that program, Mexicans could obtain temporary permits to work in the United States. *Braceros*, as the Mexican workers were known, were willing to work for very low wages. Consequently migrant workers had to accept lower wages in order to compete with the braceros. The program was halted in 1965.

Hispanics who sought to correct the heritage of discrimination used a variety of tactics. In 1962 Cesar Chavez (SAY zahr CHAH vays) began a movement to unionize California grape pickers. The majority of grape pickers were Mexican Americans, or Chicanos, as younger activists were coming to call themselves. Chavez believed that a strong union would help migrant workers gain higher wages and better working conditions. Chavez adopted a nonviolent strategy similar to Martin Luther King's. He sought wide support by organizing sit-ins and protest demonstrations. During the late 1960s Chavez organized a nationwide boycott of table grapes that forced an increasing number of growers to accept the union by 1970.

In southwestern Texas, José Ángel Gutiérrez (hoh SAY AHN hehl goo TYEHR rehs) sought power for his people through political action. "Mexicanos need to be in control of their destiny," argued Gutiérrez. "We have been complacent for too long." His political party, La Raza Unida, called for bilingual education in public school systems, improved public services in Chicano neighborhoods, and an end to job discrimination.

In urban areas, more radical Chicano groups formed organizations such as the Brown Berets in Los Angeles and La Comunidad Latina in Chicago. Like the Black Panthers, such groups stressed militant self-defense and also sponsored health clinics and breakfast programs for schoolchildren.

By the end of the 1960s Hispanic groups had made definite gains. Cesar Chavez's efforts to unionize migrant workers spread to other fruit and vegetable industries, and a growing number of Americans of Spanish heritage gained access to better jobs. Some school districts had become more sensitive to their needs. Yet large numbers of Hispanics continued to face economic hardship and discrimination. Much remained to be done.

Native Americans

Toward the end of the 1960s Native Americans also adopted the techniques of protest. In addition to the problems of discrimination faced by other minorities, Native Americans were embittered by the government's long history of contradictory and changing policies.

As you read in Chapter 20, the Dawes Act of 1887 proposed a policy that sought to break up the old tribal system and divide reservation lands among individual Native Americans. In 1934 the government reversed that policy. The Indian Reorganization Act encouraged Native Americans to govern themselves through tribal arrangements.

The National Congress of American Indians was founded in 1940 in reaction to many years of discrimination and the confusion of government policy. The National Congress regularly petitioned Congress for greater recognition of Indian rights. During the 1950s government officials shifted policy again, recommending that the federal government turn the programs over to the states. Such inconsistency brought sharp protests from the National Congress and other Indian groups.

In the 1960s the federal government once again encouraged a return to a tribal system. But by then the Indian population was becoming increasingly urban. By 1969 an estimated 75 percent of all Native Americans lived in urban areas, most in the East. City life weakened traditional tribal ties and customs. In reaction many urban youth, especially, began to take a great pride in their heritage and make more radical demands for Indian rights. One group, led by Dennis Banks and Clyde Bellecourt, organized the militant American Indian Movement (AIM) in 1968.

A major confrontation between AIM members and federal authorities occurred at Wounded Knee, South Dakota, site of a massacre of Indians by the United States Army in 1890. (See page 383.) In March 1973 AIM members seized the trading post at Wounded Knee. The government responded by surrounding the area with federal law officers. The militants' position was weakened when other Native Americans did not support their demands, and they were forced to leave Wounded Knee.

Like the movements led by Hispanics and blacks, the Native American protests signaled a new attitude among minority groups. Native Americans demonstrated increasing pride in their heritage, confidence in their ability to contribute to the diversity of American society, and willingness to act to achieve their goals.

In 1973 members of the American Indian Movement seized a trading post at Wounded Knee, South Dakota. They demanded Senate hearings on United States treaties with Indian groups.

The Women's Rights Movement

Throughout the 1960s women had been active in urging social reform, as they had during the reform years of the 1830s and 1840s and during the progressive era of the early twentieth century. Although women in the 1960s had full political rights and many worked outside the home, some women argued that they continued to be victims of discrimination.

Betty Friedan presented that argument in her book *The Feminine Mystique*, published in 1963. Friedan argued that after World War II, society had forced women to retreat from the job market and from their careers back into the home. The business world continued to be dominated by men, she pointed out. Women's jobs were limited primarily to a few professions, such as nursing, teaching, and secretarial work. When women did perform the same jobs as men, women's salaries were consistently lower.

In 1966 Friedan founded the National Organization for Women (NOW) to press for legislation that would give women greater freedom and equality. The organization campaigned in favor of equal pay for equal work and the opening of opportunities for women at all levels of employment. It also worked to provide day care facilities for the children of mothers who worked outside the home.

Through the women's rights movement, women began to assume more diverse roles during the 1960s. The Equal Pay Act of 1963 guaranteed equal pay for equal work, and the Civil Rights Act of 1964 banned job discrimination on the basis of sex as well as race or ethnic origin. Although those acts were not always vigorously enforced, they provided a legal basis for greater equality. In the late 1960s and early 1970s women entered the work force in record numbers. Many companies made special efforts to promote women to management positions.

Despite such efforts much inequality remained. In 1970 only 2.8 percent of all lawyers and 9 percent of medical students were women. Only 7 percent of women working outside the home earned more than $10,000 a year, compared with 40 percent of working men. A California study in 1974 revealed that while more women were employed, their salaries were even farther behind men's in 1974 than they had been in 1960.

Median Income of Men and Women 1950–1970

—— Women   —— Men

$ Thousands

5
4
3
2
1
0

1950 1952 1954 1956 1958 1960 1962 1964 1966 1968 1970

Source: *Historical Statistics of the United States*

■ Incomes of women continued to lag far behind those of men. The chart shows the median incomes of men and women from 1950 to 1970. Although women's incomes rose, men's incomes rose even faster. ("Median income" means that half of all incomes are lower and half are higher than the figure named.)

A proposed constitutional amendment forbidding discrimination by sex was passed by Congress in 1972. The Equal Rights Amendment, as it became known, encountered strong opposition from men and women who believed that it would undermine certain traditional values. Opponents of the amendment also argued that women already had equal rights. The amendment was defeated when it was not ratified by June 1982. Like other groups, women were to continue their campaign for greater equality into the 1970s and 1980s.

SECTION REVIEW

1. Identify: Cesar Chavez, Dennis Banks, American Indian Movement, Betty Friedan, Equal Rights Amendment.

2. Define: bracero.

3. What status did Puerto Rico have after 1952?

4. List two tactics Cesar Chavez used to gain support for his union.

5. What two laws contributed to greater economic equality of men and women?

6. **Critical Thinking** How do you think the black civil rights movement affected other minorities?

The Equal Rights Amendment created great controversy. Opponents and proponents often demonstrated to convince state legislatures to vote their way.

6 Growing Involvement in World Affairs

President Johnson had begun his administration with the hope of building a Great Society. The struggle for equality by minorities and women reflected the aspirations of millions of Americans. Increasingly, however, national attention turned to a growing conflict in Southeast Asia. The war in Vietnam was to divide the nation. It also raised the question of what policy the United States should adopt toward nonindustrial, or developing, nations.

The Third World

By the 1960s the developing nations of Asia, Africa, and Latin America had become known as the Third World. (The other two "worlds" were the United States and its allies, and the Soviet Union and the communist bloc.) The Soviet Union and the United States frequently competed for the friendship of many of the nations that had become independent since World War II. Such competition contributed to a number of conflicts during the 1960s.

In 1960 the Belgian Congo became the independent Congo. (It is now Zaire.) Soon a civil war broke out between groups wanting to control the new government. President Kennedy decided to aid a pro-American faction. American assistance helped that faction win the civil war. Consequently many Africans resented American involvement, especially since white mercenaries from South Africa also took part.

For many years the governments of South Africa and Rhodesia (now Zimbabwe) practiced *apartheid* (ah PAHR tīd), a policy of racial separation by law. Although the majority of the population was black, the governments were controlled by the white descendants of European colonists.

For the United States, to oppose the white regimes was to risk the loss of valuable economic resources and strategic naval bases in South Africa. But to endorse the governments would violate principles of justice, as well as alienate newly independent black nations. For a while the United States compromised by publicly condemning apartheid while trading with South Africa and Rhodesia for important resources.

In Latin America civil war erupted in the Dominican Republic in the early 1960s. Juan Bosch, elected in 1962 as the country's first democratic leader, was ousted by the military seven months later. Reluctantly the United States recognized the new regime. In April 1965 Bosch and his followers attempted to overthrow the military leaders. They had nearly succeeded when President Johnson, fearing instability in the region, landed 23,000 marines in the Dominican Republic and called for a cease-fire. United States influence allowed the Dominican military to remain in power.

The United States had intervened, Johnson explained, to protect American civilians in the Dominican Republic and to prevent communists from taking over Bosch's revolution. Critics, however, claimed that the communist threat was more imagined than real. Bosch, an advocate of democratic reform, was bitter. "This was a democratic revolution smashed by the leading democracy in the world," he lamented.

In the Middle East the United States balanced massive Soviet aid to Egypt by sending military aid to Israel. In 1967 Israel drove Egyptian forces out of the Sinai Desert and across the Suez Canal during a six-day war. Israeli troops also routed Syrian forces from the Golan Heights and seized all of Jerusalem and lands on the West Bank of the Jordan River.

During the crisis American and Soviet leaders used the Moscow-Washington telephone hot line for the first time. They assured each other that they would not intervene in the conflict. However, continuing hostilities between Egypt and Israel insured that the Middle East would remain an area of concern for future administrations.

Growing Involvement in Vietnam

Southeast Asia represented another area of growing United States involvement. As you read in Chapter 36, when France withdrew from Vietnam in 1954, the country had been divided into two regions. North Vietnam was led by the communist government of Ho Chi Minh and South Vietnam by the government of President Ngo Dinh Diem. When Diem refused to hold the elections that had been proposed at the peace negotiations, the followers of Ho Chi Minh began a campaign to overthrow him.

The anti-Diem rebels were known as the National Liberation Front, or the Viet Cong. Using guerrilla warfare tactics, they killed village officials supporting Diem and tried to replace them with their own "shadow government." Viet Cong influence spread throughout South Vietnam, in part because of disciplined tactics and in part because Diem's government was unpopular. When Diem began widespread imprisonment of Buddhists who opposed his government, opposition to his regime grew.

In 1962 President Kennedy provided the South Vietnamese army of 150,000 men with United States military advisers and equip-

■ *The long war in Vietnam eventually affected most of Southeast Asia. The Ho Chi Minh Trail, shown on this map, was a main supply line from North Vietnam to Viet Cong guerrillas.*

Southeast Asia

ment. Still the South Vietnamese forces were unable to combat the estimated 15,000 Viet Cong. In 1963 the unpopular Diem was assassinated by military officers, but the situation did not improve. When President Johnson took office in 1963 approximately 16,000 United States troops were serving in Vietnam as advisers.

Escalation at the Gulf of Tonkin

During the early stages of the war, most Viet Cong guerrillas were South Vietnamese. North Vietnam had sent supplies and a few guerrilla fighters south. As American involvement grew, North Vietnam increased support to the Viet Cong. In 1964, 7,000 northern guerrillas traveled to the South.

Then, in August 1964, North Vietnamese torpedo boats attacked the United States destroyers *Maddox* and *Turner Joy* not far from the North Vietnamese coast. The destroyers were patrolling the Gulf of Tonkin while South Vietnamese ships attacked North Vietnamese islands in the gulf. North Vietnam claimed that it was rightfully chasing attackers from its territorial waters, but President Johnson argued that the attack was unprovoked. He ordered retaliatory air strikes against North Vietnam.

The President asked Congress for the authority to take "all necessary steps" to "prevent further aggression" by the North Vietnamese. The Gulf of Tonkin resolution, granting this far-reaching power, passed the House by a vote of 416 to 0 and the Senate by a vote of 88 to 2. Later in 1964 American involvement in Vietnam began to increase dramatically.

The United States initiated a bombing campaign called Rolling Thunder. The campaign was aimed at cutting the flow of supplies from North Vietnam to the Viet Cong. Beginning in February 1965, United States planes regularly flew missions over North Vietnam.

In April President Johnson ordered 20,000 American combat troops into Vietnam. By June General William Westmoreland, commander of United States forces in Vietnam, asked for an additional 200,000 troops. American forces grew to 385,000 by the end of 1966 and 536,000 by the end of 1968.

Escalation of the war was interrupted periodically as President Johnson sought

In 1965 President Johnson ordered United States combat troops into Vietnam. The Viet Cong frequently proved to be difficult to find because they seemed to melt away into jungles and villages. In this 1965 photograph American soldiers wade waist deep in water during a mission to "search and destroy" enemy forces.

peace through negotiation with North Vietnam. Neither side, however, could agree on conditions for peace. North Vietnam demanded a place for the National Liberation Front in any postwar government. The United States refused to negotiate on such terms. So the fighting continued.

Opposition at Home

Although President Johnson had received overwhelming support for the Gulf of Tonkin resolution in Congress, American opposition to the war increased as more American troops were sent to Vietnam. The costs of the war, both material and spiritual, were staggering. In 1967 the government spent $20 billion on the war. More important, by the end of 1968 over 25,000 Americans had been killed. The air war was destroying the Vietnamese countryside. Approximately 3.2 million tons (about 3 million metric tons) of explosive were dropped—50 percent more than all the explosives dropped on Europe and Asia during World War II.

In February 1968 American perception of the war began to change. During the Vietnamese holiday of Tet, the lunar new year, the Viet Cong launched attacks on major cities throughout South Vietnam. Although eventually repulsed by American and South Vietnamese forces and suffering major losses, the Viet Cong won a strategic victory by demonstrating that no part of Vietnam was safe, despite the massive American troop commitment.

In the United States thousands of college students protesting the war held "teach-ins" and marched on the Pentagon. The student protests against United States involvement in Vietnam were part of a spirit of political activism that characterized the decade. Young people were actively involved in the reform movements of the period, and college campuses were the scenes of numerous protest demonstrations. Student demands included greater participation in school administration and an end to military training and research. Increasingly, student protests centered on the war.

As the war escalated, so did protests against it. In 1967 some 35,000 antiwar protesters marched on the Pentagon. Met by the raised rifles of military police, one protester began silently placing carnations in their rifle barrels.

As casualties increased and the drafting of young men not in college continued, opposition to the war spread. The war became a major issue in the 1968 presidential election campaign. Democratic Senator Eugene McCarthy, an opponent of the war, ran a surprisingly strong race in the New Hampshire presidential primary. President Johnson won the primary by only a narrow margin. Growing antiwar sentiment put increasing pressure on the President.

In February 1968 General Westmoreland asked for an additional 200,000 troops. Even strong administration supporters of the war reluctantly concluded that the United States could not win using traditional military tactics. President Johnson refused Westmoreland's request. On March 31 the President announced that he was suspending the bombing of North Vietnam and that he would not run for reelection. North Vietnam responded by agreeing to enter negotiations, which were set in Paris.

The Election of 1968

When President Johnson withdrew from the race, Robert Kennedy and Vice-President Hubert Humphrey entered the presidential campaign. Humphrey cautiously supported administration policies in Vietnam. Although Kennedy had at first supported American intervention in Vietnam, by 1968 he was speaking out against the war. His energetic campaign produced an impressive string of victories over McCarthy and Humphrey. The greatest of those came in the important California primary of June 1968.

But on the evening of Kennedy's victory speech in Los Angeles, a young Palestinian named Sirhan Sirhan, angered by Kennedy's support of Israel, shot and killed him. The nation, still recovering from Martin Luther King's assassination, mourned another leader.

Robert Kennedy's death left Hubert Humphrey in the lead for the presidential nomination as the Democrats prepared for their convention in Chicago. Antiwar activists from around the country gathered in Chicago to protest the convention and Humphrey's support of the war. As Chicago police patrolled outside the convention hall, violence broke out.

Demonstrators assaulted the police with obscenities, bricks, bottles, and garbage. The police reacted with surprising force. Numerous police officers and demonstrators were injured. In addition, 49 reporters were arrested, beaten, or sprayed with mace, a caustic chemical designed for crowd control. Inside the hall the convention delegates nominated Humphrey, who chose Senator Edmund Muskie of Maine as his running mate.

Reacting to the antiwar movement and to urban riots, Alabama Governor George Wallace became a third-party candidate for President. He campaigned on the pledge to restore "law and order" to the nation.

In Miami the Republicans turned again to Richard Nixon as their candidate. His nomination was the result of a remarkable political comeback. Defeated as the Republican presidential candidate in 1960 and as a candidate for governor of California in 1962, Nixon had spent the following six years repairing his personal and political fortunes.

★ Arts in America ★

The Music of Protest and Change

Popular music reflected the diverse moods and movements of the 1960s. Folk singers with political messages found a large and receptive audience. With songs such as "Where Have All the Flowers Gone?" and "What Have They Done to the Rain?" folk singers protested war and radioactive fallout. Bob Dylan became the leader of folk protest. His musical poetry spoke out against war, bigotry, and injustice.

Dylan and other folk singers expressed the sentiments of a "counterculture." They rejected what they considered "dehumanizing" careers with large corporations and sought other paths to personal fulfillment. Some moved to the countryside, grew their own food, and tried to become self-sufficient. Others established rural communes where everyone shared the work.

Rock music underwent a type of revolution in the early 1960s when the Beatles and other British rock groups, such as the Rolling Stones and the Who, took the United States by storm. Thousands of screaming fans greeted the Beatles in February 1964 when they made their first national appearance on the *Ed Sullivan Show*. The Beatles were not simply another fad. Their 1967 album, *Sergeant Pepper's Lonely Hearts Club Band*, demonstrated their growing talent and opened the door to experimental rock music.

Dance crazes like the Twist, the Monkey, the Mashed Potato, and the Frug spawned musical styles of their own. The Beachboys kept alive the California "surf" sound they had introduced in the early 1960s. From Detroit came the "Motown" rhythms that introduced wide audiences to black stars. Such performers as the Temptations, the Four Tops, Martha and the Vandellas, Stevie Wonder, and the Supremes consistently topped the pop music charts.

A three-day outdoor rock festival in August 1969 brought the music of the 1960s to a climax. Over 300,000 people—most of them under age 30—gathered near Bethel, New York, for the Woodstock Music and Art Fair. Woodstock offered the nation a glimpse of the counterculture and became the symbol of the youth solidarity of the 1960s.

Bob Dylan.

Major Events

1961	Peace Corps and Alliance for Progress created; Bay of Pigs invasion
1962	Cuban missile crisis
1963	President Kennedy assassinated; Lyndon B. Johnson becomes President
1964	Civil Rights Act, Gulf of Tonkin resolution, and Economic Opportunity Act passed; Johnson elected President
1965	Regular bombing missions over North Vietnam begin; Medicare Act, Voting Rights Act, Housing Act, and Immigration Act passed
1967	Six-Day War between Israel and Egypt
1968	Tet offensive begins; Martin Luther King, Jr., assassinated; Robert Kennedy assassinated; Richard M. Nixon elected President

With his running mate, Spiro Agnew, governor of Maryland, Nixon narrowly won the election with 43.4 percent of the popular vote. Humphrey won 42.7 percent of the popular vote, Wallace 13.5 percent. The election results underscored the divisions in American society. Those divisions were to challenge Nixon's campaign promise to "bring us together."

SECTION REVIEW

1. Identify: Third World, Viet Cong, William Westmoreland, Eugene McCarthy.
2. Define: apartheid.
3. What was United States policy regarding the governments of South Africa and Rhodesia?
4. What was the main purpose of the Rolling Thunder campaign?
5. What two actions did President Johnson take in March of 1968 in reaction to growing opposition to the war in Vietnam?
6. **Critical Thinking** How did the Gulf of Tonkin resolution mark a turning point in the Vietnam conflict?

Chapter 38 Review

In Perspective

In contrast to the 1950s, the decade of the 1960s was a turbulent one. The Bay of Pigs invasion, construction of the Berlin Wall, and the Cuban missile crisis increased tensions between the United States and the Soviet Union. On the home front the decade began with high hopes. President John Kennedy urged Americans to turn to new frontiers, but his efforts were cut short by his assassination in November 1963. President Johnson continued Kennedy's programs and convinced Congress to pass legislation to create what he called the Great Society.

The movement among black Americans to gain equal rights grew dramatically during the 1960s. Many civil rights leaders adopted the nonviolent methods of Martin Luther King, Jr., but others demanded more radical action. Growing anger and frustration contributed to riots in many American cities in the mid-1960s. Hispanic Americans and Native Americans also began to organize to end discrimination. The women's rights movement of the 1960s contributed to a growing consciousness of the roles women could play in society.

By the end of the decade, the war in Vietnam overshadowed the struggle for equality. American involvement in the war grew after the Gulf of Tonkin incident. Opposition to the war grew also. In 1968 President Johnson withdrew from the presidential race and announced an end to the bombing of North Vietnam. The task of carrying out peace talks fell to the winner of the 1968 election, Richard Nixon.

Vocabulary

On a separate sheet of paper, write the word or words that best complete each of the following sentences.

1. ____ are specially trained military units that could be moved quickly to any part of the world.
2. The ____ is a group of volunteers who provide assistance to people in developing countries.
3. A (An) ____ was a Mexican who held a temporary permit to work in the United States.
4. ____ is a policy of separation of races enforced by law.
5. ____ is a term referring to developing nations.

Chapter Checkup

1. (a) What military actions did President Kennedy take in reaction to Khrushchev's pledge to support anti-American "wars of liberation"? (b) What actions did Kennedy take to try to win the friendship of Third World nations?
2. Describe John Kennedy's New Frontier goals in each of the following areas: (a) space exploration, (b) the economy, (c) civil rights. How did he begin to move toward those goals?
3. (a) What did President Johnson mean by the "Great Society"? (b) Describe the major pieces of legislation Congress passed as part of the Great Society.
4. (a) What tactics did black Americans use against segregation in the early 1960s? (b) Why did some black leaders demand more radical tactics? (c) What did black power mean to militant blacks? (d) What did it mean to moderate black leaders?
5. (a) What groups in addition to blacks struggled for equality in the 1960s? (b) What kinds of discrimination did each group face?
6. (a) What factors contributed to growing opposition to the war? (b) What impact did the opposition have on the 1968 presidential election?

Critical Thinking

1. **Supporting an Opinion** How did the Kerner Commission offer both warning and cautious hope? Explain.
2. **Comparing** (a) How did United States involvement in the Vietnam War differ from involvement in the Korean War? (b) How did it differ from involvement in World War II? (c) How do you think those differences affected public attitude?

Developing Basic Skills

1. **Placing Events in Time** Construct a time line of major developments from 1930 to 1968 in the struggle of black Americans for greater equality. (a) In which period were there the most developments? Why? (b) In which period was there the most government activity?
2. **Graph Reading** Study the graph on page 714. (a) How did the difference between the median income of men and that of women change? (b) What can you conclude?

See page 833 for suggested readings.

Writer's Handbook

Footnotes for Books

Footnotes are an important means of documentation. To write a footnote, place a small number to the right and slightly above the place where you have included borrowed information in your paper. Then identify the source at the bottom of the page or on a separate numbered list at the end of the paper. Study the examples.

[1] James Alonzo Bishop, *The Days of Martin Luther King, Jr.* (New York: Putnam, 1971), p. 387.

[2] Bishop, *The Days of Martin Luther King, Jr.*, pp. 411–412.

[3] Edwin S. Gaustad, ed., *A Documentary History of Religion in America Since 1865* (Grand Rapids, Michigan: William B. Eerdmans Publishing Co., 1983), p. 512.

Practice: Write two sample footnotes, using your textbook as the source.

Challenges at Home and Abroad

39

(1969–1976)

The 1976 bicentennial celebration in New York Harbor

In 1976 the United States was to celebrate its bicentennial, the two-hundredth anniversary of the Declaration of Independence. Yet as Richard Nixon took office in January 1969, an anniversary celebration was far from the minds of most Americans. The nation was seriously divided. Nixon had promised to bring Americans together, but that pledge proved difficult to fulfill.

For a time, there was evidence of increased stability. President Nixon tried to improve relations with the Soviet Union and the People's Republic of China. His appointments to the Supreme Court were to make the Court more conservative. A landing on the moon marked a high point of the space program. Yet Nixon's presidency ended early, with his resignation. To his successor, Gerald R. Ford, fell the task of healing the wounds dividing the nation.

"Vietnamization" of Vietnam War

1969	1970	1971	1972	1973	1974	1975	1976
1969 U.S. astronauts land on moon	**1970** Gulf of Tonkin resolution repealed		**1972** Nixon visits China, U.S.S.R.	**1973** Vietnam cease-fire signed; Watergate investigation begins	**1974** Nixon resigns; Gerald R. Ford becomes President	**1975** Saigon falls to North Vietnam; Helsinki Accords signed	**1976** Jimmy Carter elected President

1 A Balance of Power

Richard M. Nixon brought over two decades of political experience to the presidency. He had devoted much of his career to conservative Republican policies and strong anti-communism. As President, however, he surprised many of his supporters by pursuing a foreign policy that called for improved relations with the People's Republic of China and the Soviet Union. At the same time he worked to disengage the United States from Vietnam.

The New President

With his election as President in 1968, Richard Nixon capped a long political career. He had been elected to the House of Representatives from California in 1946, and in 1950 he went on to win a seat in the Senate. From 1953 to 1961, Nixon served as Vice-President under President Eisenhower.

In the first major defeat of his political career, Nixon narrowly lost the 1960 presidential election to John F. Kennedy. In 1962 he experienced a second bitter defeat when he ran for governor of California and lost. His political career seemed at an end. Throughout the 1960s, however, Nixon remained active in Republican party politics, and in 1968 the party chose him as its presidential candidate. (See page 719.) With Nixon's victory in that election, the nation had its first President from California.

Views on Foreign Affairs

Richard Nixon brought to the presidency a keen interest in foreign affairs. As Vice-President under Eisenhower, he had traveled to many nations and gained experience in the daily conduct of foreign affairs. As President, Nixon chose an expert in foreign affairs, Henry Kissinger, to be his national security adviser.

Kissinger was an analyst of diplomatic history. He had written extensively about international relations while a professor at Harvard University. Born in Germany, Kissinger and his family had fled to the United States in 1938 to escape the Nazis. He served in the United States Army during World War II. After the war, Kissinger took up his university studies and earned a doctorate degree.

Kissinger shared Nixon's view that the world had changed over the previous decade and that United States foreign policy had to change too. Nixon and Kissinger believed that the world could no longer be seen as two blocs, one communist and one noncommunist. Rather, there were many centers of world power—including Europe, Japan, the People's Republic of China, the Soviet Union, the Middle East, and the United States. Each of these centers of power had different interests and spheres of influence. Thus, in Kissinger's opinion, a foreign policy should seek a balance of world powers.

Within this framework, Nixon and Kissinger concluded that the United States had overextended itself militarily. The new administration moved to reduce obligations abroad, while maintaining a position of "strength and honor." According to Nixon:

> The United States will participate in the defense and development of allies and friends, but cannot—and will not—conceive *all* the plans, design *all* the programs, execute *all* the decisions and undertake *all* the defense of the free nations of the world. We will help where it will make a real difference and is considered in our interest.

The War in Vietnam

Over 540,000 American troops were in Vietnam when Richard Nixon took office. The President considered the Vietnam War a drain on vital American resources. Therefore, he wanted to reduce the commitment of troops and materials. Thus in 1969 he announced a policy of "Vietnamization." Under Vietnamization South Vietnam would take increased responsibility for fighting the war.

The new policy presented problems, however. Nixon ordered a resumption of the bombing of North Vietnam in order to give the South Vietnamese support while American troops withdrew. The bombing was unpopular among those Americans who wanted to see the war end immediately. In May 1970 the President ordered 32,000

United States troops to join the South Vietnamese in an invasion of Cambodia. Nixon said the move was necessary to stop the flow of supplies to the Vietcong. Critics charged that he was widening the war, and opposition to the war increased.

An incident at Kent State University in Kent, Ohio, four days after the invasion of Cambodia, symbolized the strong emotion generated by the war. A large number of Kent State students had gathered on campus to protest the war. They carried signs, sang protest songs, and chanted slogans. Troops from the Ohio National Guard were sent to maintain order. In the confusion, they fired their weapons into the crowd, killing four demonstrators and injuring nine. At Jackson State College in Mississippi, a similar incident left two students dead and twelve injured.

The deaths outraged many Americans. On May 5, 1970, the day after the killings at Kent State, the President announced that he would withdraw the troops from Cambodia within two months. But demonstrations against the war continued. Almost 100,000 protestors assembled in Washington, D.C., on May 9 to demonstrate opposition to the war. In December 1970 Congress voted to repeal the Gulf of Tonkin Resolution, which had provided the legal basis for the conduct of the war. However, Nixon argued that his position as commander in chief gave him the authority to keep troops in Vietnam.

Although the war continued, the policy of Vietnamization brought American troops home. By September 1972 only 60,000 remained in Vietnam. In the meantime, the President had increased the bombing of North Vietnam, hoping to force the North Vietnamese to make concessions at the Paris peace talks, which had stalled.

In October 1972, on the eve of the presidential election, Henry Kissinger announced that a tentative cease-fire had been agreed upon in Paris. "Peace is at hand," he promised, but negotiations faltered again. Finally, in January 1973, a cease-fire called an "Agreement on Ending the War and Restoring Peace in Vietnam" was signed. American troops were withdrawn over the next few months, and an uncertain calm settled over the two Vietnams.

This ended the direct involvement of United States troops in Vietnam. In the longest war in the nation's history, over 57,000 Americans lost their lives. More than 300,000 soldiers came home wounded. The economic costs of the war were enormous, amounting to about $150 billion. Furthermore, the war in Vietnam seriously divided the nation. For many years to come, Americans would debate the causes of the war and how such conflicts might be avoided in the future.

Members of Congress were especially troubled by the fact that a President had sent troops into battle without a formal declaration of war. A declaration of war would have required congressional approval. In November 1973 Congress passed the War Powers Act over President Nixon's veto. The act declared that a President could not send United States military forces into action for longer than 60 days unless authorized to do so by Congress.

Visits to the People's Republic of China and the Soviet Union

Few Americans expected Richard Nixon, long a strong opponent of communism, to improve American relations with the People's Republic of China and the Soviet Union. However, Kissinger and Nixon believed that the rift between China and the Soviet Union would allow the United States to make diplomatic gains.

In July 1971 Kissinger secretly traveled to China. He prepared the ground for President Nixon to visit China in February 1972. After 20 years the wall of suspicion that had separated China and the United States was coming down. The President was cordially received by Chinese leaders during his one-week visit. A large number of American television and newspaper reporters followed him as he toured the ancient Great Wall of China, attended banquets, and met with Mao Tse-tung.

Chinese and American leaders agreed to allow scientific, cultural, and journalistic exchanges between the two countries. They also announced an interest in increasing trade. A year after Nixon's visit, China and the United States established diplomatic offices in one another's capitals.

Soviet leaders also seemed willing to ease tensions. In May 1972 Richard Nixon became the first President to visit the Soviet Union since World War II. His trip marked the flowering of an era of *détente* (day TAHNT), a relaxation of tension between the United States and the Soviet Union.

Following the communist victory in China, there was no direct contact between the People's Republic of China and the United States for more than 20 years. When relations between the two countries thawed during the early 1970s, some of the first visitors to China were teenagers on the United States table tennis team. Part of the group is shown here with interpreters, visiting the Great Wall of China.

While in Moscow the President and Soviet leaders signed an arms control agreement. The Strategic Arms Limitation Talks (SALT) restricted the types and numbers of nuclear warheads and missiles that each country could deploy. Nixon also negotiated agreements that provided for increased trade and scientific cooperation.

President Nixon's visits to China and the Soviet Union opened new avenues of international cooperation. It was hoped that increased trade would benefit the American economy. Farmers in particular welcomed the higher grain prices that wheat sales to the Soviet Union brought. However, American consumers complained that such sales meant a rise in domestic food prices. Nevertheless, most Americans approved of détente. They were eager to diminish international tensions and the possibility of nuclear war.

SECTION REVIEW

1. Identify: Henry Kissinger, SALT.
2. Define: détente.
3. What centers of world power did Henry Kissinger identify?
4. How did United States military involvement in Vietnam end?
5. What agreement did President Nixon reach with Chinese leaders during his 1972 visit?
6. **Critical Thinking**   How did Nixon's reputation as an anticommunist help him to win acceptance of his foreign policy?

2 The Politics of Stability

During the presidential election campaign of 1968, Richard Nixon had won the support of those Americans who felt that the protest and reform movements of the 1960s had gone too far. His supporters, Nixon claimed, were the "silent majority" of Americans. He believed that the demonstrators were only a vocal minority. Once elected, Nixon promised, he would bring unity and stability to the nation.

A Lunar Triumph

One of the high points of the early years of the Nixon administration occurred when the United States made the first manned landing on the moon. In 1961 President Kennedy had vowed to send astronauts to the moon by 1970, and the American space program forged ahead. Tragedy struck in 1967 when a flash fire during launch practice killed three astronauts. But by 1968 a manned Apollo spacecraft had circled the moon, taken detailed pictures, and returned to earth.

In July 1969 Commander Neil Armstrong led the three-man mission that orbited the moon and then descended to its surface in a lunar module. Millions watched on television as Armstrong carefully stepped into a thin layer of lunar dust and said, "That's one small step for a man, one giant leap for mankind." Two other lunar landings followed in November 1969 and December 1972.

The space program brought many benefits beyond the excitement of exploration. Satellites improved communications, navigation, and weather forecasting on earth. The need for small computers aboard space capsules stimulated the new industry of microelectronics. Other space research led to the production of materials that insulated homes more efficiently, devices that generated solar energy, and freeze-dried foods for the supermarket.

Not everyone agreed that the achievements in space were worth the $24-billion cost. Critics of the space program thought the money could have been better spent to solve pressing problems such as poverty and disease. The dramatic moon landing temporarily overwhelmed critics. Further unmanned space probes such as the Viking missions to Mars in 1971 and 1976 radioed back valuable information at a much lower cost than the manned missions.

The Supreme Court and Crime

Nixon had stressed law enforcement throughout his campaign for the presidency. Once elected he supported a bill that granted federal funds to local police departments.

In 1969 United States astronauts Neil Armstrong and Edwin "Buzz" Aldrin landed on the moon and set up television cameras. Millions on earth watched on live television as the first humans hopped around in the moon's light gravity, collecting rock and soil samples.

The Apollo-Soyuz Mission: Détente in Space

In July 1975 millions in the United States and the Soviet Union watched on television as three Americans and two Russians lived, worked, and ate together in their joined spacecrafts. The successful Apollo-Soyuz mission represented the willingness of the two superpowers to cooperate. The agreement to conduct the joint mission was signed in May 1972, when détente was at its height.

For three years working groups for both countries met frequently to iron out technical and political difficulties. To solve the communication problem, each crew learned the other's language.

Finally, on July 15, 1975, the two spacecraft were launched—an Apollo from the United States and a Soyuz from the Soviet Union. Two days later the two craft successfully docked using equipment supplied by the United States. Four crew exchanges were made through the docking device.

In all, the Apollo crew conducted 17 experiments in space. Of these, 5 were conducted jointly with the Soyuz crew. One experiment allowed the Soyuz crew to photograph the outermost fringe of the sun. This view was made possible by the Apollo spacecraft's blocking out the sun's bright center as the two spacecraft moved apart. Later planned joint missions were scrapped as relations between the two nations cooled.

His most lasting influence on the legal system probably resulted from the four appointments he made to the Supreme Court.

During the 1960s, under Chief Justice Earl Warren, the Supreme Court had handed down several rulings protecting the rights of people accused of crimes. In *Gideon* v. *Wainwright* (1963), for example, the Warren Court held that the states had to provide free legal representation for defendants who could not afford to hire lawyers.

Other Warren Court decisions restricted the tactics police could use to gain evidence against suspected criminals. In *Mapp* v. *Ohio* (1961) the Supreme Court ruled that items illegally seized by police could not be used as evidence against the accused. In *Miranda* v. *Arizona* (1966) the Supreme Court held that, before questioning accused persons, police were required to inform them of their rights to remain silent and to be represented by a lawyer.

727

Reaction to the Warren Court

Many Americans believed that the Warren Court rulings unreasonably restricted the power of the police. Such rulings, critics argued, protected the rights of accused persons at the expense of victims and society as a whole. President Nixon agreed with this criticism.

In 1969 Chief Justice Warren resigned from the Court because of poor health. President Nixon then appointed Warren Burger, a respected judge from Minnesota, to replace him. The Senate confirmed Burger's appointment with little opposition. Burger shared the President's concern that the Supreme Court had been too liberal in protecting criminal suspects.

When Nixon had an opportunity to appoint a second justice, he nominated Judge Clement Haynsworth. But the Senate rejected Haynsworth because it discovered that as a judge he had ruled on cases involving corporations in which he owned stock. (Judges are required to disqualify themselves in cases in which they have a personal interest.)

The President then nominated Judge G. Harrold Carswell. Once again the Senate refused to approve the appointment because Carswell's record as a federal appeals judge had been unimpressive and because of his hostility to civil rights for blacks. Finally the President nominated Judge Harry Blackmun of Minnesota, whom the Senate quickly confirmed. President Nixon later filled two more vacancies on the Court, selecting Lewis F. Powell of Virginia and William H. Rehnquist of Arizona. Neither nominee encountered serious difficulty in his confirmation hearings.

Nixon's four appointments made the Supreme Court more conservative. The Burger Court did not reverse the landmark criminal procedure decisions handed down during the 1960s. But it did limit their scope. For example, the Supreme Court held that even if police violated the *Miranda* rule in obtaining a pretrial confession, that confession could still be used to discredit trial testimony of the defendant. The Burger Court also narrowed the scope of the *Mapp* decision by ruling that questions based on illegally seized evidence could be asked at a grand jury hearing, even if they could not be asked in a jury trial.

Domestic Policies

President Nixon's appointments to the Supreme Court were only one example of his concern with law-and-order issues in domestic policies. He supported strong anticrime measures that increased the power of law enforcement officials to deal with criminal suspects. Nixon's statements on law and order reflected the deep concern of many Americans about the rapid rise of crime, urban violence, and campus disorder.

Nixon opposed many of the programs established under Lyndon Johnson's Great Society. He closed the Office of Economic Opportunity, which had directed Johnson's War on Poverty, and he hoped to cut back other programs. But support for the Great Society remained strong in Congress. Nixon vetoed several major bills that provided funds for social programs, and Congress overrode some of the vetoes. In 1973 President Nixon began to *impound*, or refuse to spend, funds that had been appropriated by Congress.

Despite such actions, federal spending on social programs continued to rise during the Nixon years. For example, the federal contribution to Medicaid almost doubled between 1970 and 1974. However, aid to elementary and secondary education increased only slightly.

To many Americans, Nixon appeared to be far less interested in the rights of minorities than his predecessor was. His administration publicly opposed the extension of the Voting Rights Act of 1965. President Nixon also spoke out against court-ordered busing to achieve racial integration. And the White House loosened guidelines governing school desegregation in the North and South.

President Nixon's main goal for black Americans was to increase the number of jobs for skilled black workers and to develop programs to assist black-owned businesses. In these areas the administration had some success. During the Nixon years, for example, the number of small businesses owned by black Americans increased. The majority of blacks, however, considered the Nixon record disappointing.

The Problem of Stagflation

The war in Vietnam contributed to economic problems in the early 1970s. Huge military expenditures pushed the annual inflation rate to 5 percent in 1970. At the same time, recession slowed economic growth. Economists labeled the economic slump *stagflation*, a combination of stagnation and inflation. As more Vietnam veterans returned home and entered the job market, unemployment increased to over 6 percent.

As a conservative, President Nixon disliked government interference in the economy. Nevertheless, with inflation rising, Nixon ordered a 90-day freeze on wages, prices, and rents on August 15, 1971. The first part of the President's anti-inflation program was called Phase I.

In Phase II, which began on November 14, 1971, Nixon substituted broad price controls for the freeze. The Cost of Living Council was charged with monitoring prices and blocking unreasonable price hikes.

President Nixon urged Congress to cut taxes. He also lowered interest rates and increased government spending. Those measures encouraged consumer spending and lowered unemployment. By the end of 1972 stagflation seemed to be beaten. When the Phase II controls were lifted in early 1973, however, prices jumped at a record rate.

The Election of 1972

Nixon seemed assured of reelection in 1972. The economy appeared stable, and the President's trips to China and the Soviet Union were popular. Furthermore, Kissinger's first announcement of a breakthrough in the Paris peace talks came shortly before the election. (See page 724.)

The Democratic party, on the other hand, was badly split. A series of bitter primary elections had shown the party's deep divisions. Senator George McGovern of South Dakota won the nomination, but many Democrats felt he was too liberal. McGovern's problems mounted when reporters discovered that his running mate, Senator Thomas Eagleton of Missouri, had once suffered an emotional illness. With growing public concern about Eagleton's health, McGovern was forced to replace him with Sargent Shriver, former director of the Peace Corps and a brother-in-law of John and Robert Kennedy.

Meanwhile, President Nixon based a well-organized and well-financed campaign on his image as a statesman working in the White House. Nixon boasted about the strength of the economy and the progress in the Vietnam peace negotiations. He also promised stricter law enforcement. Not even the arrest of burglars who were publicly linked to the White House, at Democratic party headquarters in June 1972, detracted from the President's strength. He was widely seen as decisive and competent by the American people.

Nixon won the election in a landslide. He carried every state but Massachusetts and won almost 61 percent of the vote. In the electoral college, the margin was even more lopsided: 521 to 17 votes. Nixon began his second term with a strong national mandate. Few could have predicted that within two years his long political career would end in disgrace.

An Oil Embargo

Early in his second term President Nixon faced a new international crisis. In October 1973 Egyptian and Syrian troops launched a surprise attack on Israel on the Jewish holiday of Yom Kippur. Fighting raged for more than two weeks until a fragile peace was arranged by the United Nations.

In the tense days following the war, Henry Kissinger helped negotiate a cease-fire agreement between Egypt and Israel. (Kissinger had become secretary of state earlier in 1973.) In the spring of 1974 he shuttled back and forth between capitals in the Middle East, trying to work out a formal cease-fire between Israel and Syria. As a result of Kissinger's "shuttle diplomacy," the two countries signed a cease-fire agreement in May 1974.

The United States had been a strong supporter of Israel for many years. And it had provided military aid to Israel during the October War. Arab nations resented this American support of Israel. In reaction, on October 17 they ordered an embargo on oil shipments to the United States. Because Americans imported about 25 percent of the oil they used, the embargo soon disrupted life.

Americans found themselves waiting in long lines to buy gasoline—if they could get any at all. They wondered whether enough oil would be available to heat their homes during the coming winter. The oil embargo contributed to higher inflation. The price of

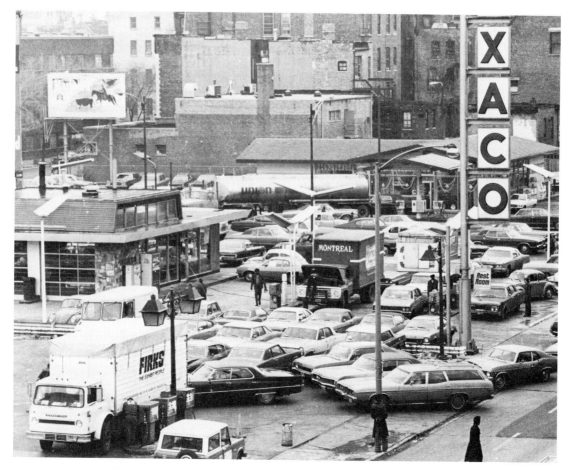

The oil embargo that began in October 1973 caused chaos at gas stations such as these in Chicago. By January 1974 many gas stations were closing early to conserve fuel. Other stations had closed down because they had run completely out of fuel.

fuel and thousands of other petroleum-based products, such as plastics, medicines, and fertilizers, soared. Consumer prices rose by 6 percent in 1973 and jumped by 11 percent the next year.

President Nixon reacted to the energy crisis by encouraging Americans to conserve energy. He asked the states to lower their highway speed limits to 55 miles per hour. In an effort to increase the production of domestic oil, he signed the Alaskan Pipeline Act. This act authorized construction of an oil pipeline across Alaska and Canada. Finally, in March 1974, the Arab nations lifted the oil embargo. The immediate energy crisis had passed, but the lesson was clear: Americans needed to take a closer look at the way they used energy.

SECTION REVIEW

1. Identify: Neil Armstrong, Earl Warren, Warren Burger, George McGovern.
2. Define: impound, stagflation.
3. List two benefits of the space program.
4. What did the Supreme Court rule in *Miranda* v. *Arizona?*
5. Describe two ways President Nixon tried to weaken Johnson's Great Society.
6. What role did Henry Kissinger play after the October War of 1973?
7. **Critical Thinking**   What advantages does a President in office have in an election campaign?

3 A Crisis in the Presidency

President Nixon and Vice-President Agnew had won a decisive victory in the 1972 election. Yet within two years, Agnew was to resign in disgrace, and Nixon was to become the first President to resign under the threat of impeachment and removal from office.

Behind the crisis in the executive branch lay a scandal that at first seemed to involve only a few minor officials of the President's reelection campaign. Further investigation revealed that higher officials and greater issues were involved.

A Puzzling Burglary

At 2:30 A.M. on June 17, 1972, Washington, D.C., police arrested five men who had broken into the headquarters of the Democratic National Committee, located in the Watergate apartment complex. The men were not ordinary burglars. They wore business suits and rubber surgical gloves. And they carried a walkie-talkie, 40 rolls of unexposed film, two cameras, lock picks, two pen-sized tear gas guns, and several bugging devices.

One of the Watergate burglars, James McCord, was a former CIA agent. McCord had been more recently employed as a security consultant to President Nixon's reelection committee. An address book carried by the burglars contained the name of another former CIA agent, E. Howard Hunt, a White House employee. Despite those links to the President, White House Press Secretary Ronald Ziegler called the break-in "a third-rate burglary attempt." He claimed that "certain elements may try to stretch this beyond what it is."

During the following months other disturbing facts came to light, many of them uncovered by Washington *Post* reporters Carl Bernstein and Bob Woodward. For example, one of the burglars had a checking account containing $89,000 from the Committee to Reelect the President (CREEP).

Reports pointed to the existence of a $350,000 cash "slush fund" controlled by CREEP to finance undercover projects designed to hinder Democratic party rivals. Former Nixon cabinet members Maurice Stans and John Mitchell knew of the fund, the reports suggested, and might have even approved the illegal activities.

Despite those reports, the Watergate break-in did not become a major issue in the 1972 presidential campaign. The President announced in August that White House counsel John Dean had conducted an investigation of the burglary and that "no one on the White House staff . . . was involved in this very bizarre situation."

After a lengthy inquiry by the Federal Bureau of Investigation (FBI), the five Watergate burglars, Howard Hunt, and G. Gordon Liddy, a lawyer for CREEP, were prosecuted. In January 1973 two defendants were found guilty, and five pleaded guilty. On March 23 the trial judge, John Sirica, sentenced all the defendants to prison terms.

On the day the sentences were imposed, Judge Sirica made public a letter he had received from James McCord. McCord charged that witnesses had committed perjury and that certain high officials had pressed the burglars to plead guilty so the trial would be concluded quickly. McCord's accusations heightened suspicions about the link between the burglars and the White House.

The Cover-up Unravels

McCord's revelations suggested that the White House was trying to hide the truth about the Watergate burglary. Further investigation linked high-level officials to the cover-up, including John Mitchell and Maurice Stans as well as President Nixon's two closest personal aides, H. R. Haldeman and John Ehrlichman. By April 1973 events forced President Nixon to accept the resignations of Haldeman and Ehrlichman.

Then in May a special committee set up by the Senate convened to hear testimony about Watergate. The Senate Select Committee on Presidential Campaign Activities was composed of seven senators and chaired by Senator Sam Ervin of North Carolina. Ervin was noted for his knowledge of constitutional law. He was determined to discover what the President knew about the Watergate burglary and cover-up. The committee hearings were televised for three

The televised Senate Watergate hearings showed the process of the American constitutional system in a time of crisis. The historic hearings were chaired by Senator Sam Ervin of North Carolina (left), shown questioning a witness. Sam Dash, chief counsel for the committee, is at the right.

months, giving the public a close look at the Watergate investigation.

Witnesses testified that Attorney General John Mitchell, the highest law enforcement officer in the country, had been present when Gordon Liddy outlined proposals for the Watergate burglary and other espionage activities.

The most astonishing testimony came from John Dean, who had been fired from his post as White House counsel in April. In a quiet voice Dean methodically confirmed much previous testimony and then went further. As recently as April, Haldeman, Ehrlichman, Mitchell—even President Nixon himself, Dean claimed—had continued to suppress information about the Watergate activities. Dean charged that the President had approved plans to pay the Watergate burglars "hush money" to remain silent.

Of all the witnesses, only Dean claimed that the President had tried to suppress information linking the Watergate burglary and the White House. Then, on July 16, 1973, Alexander Butterfield, an assistant to H. R. Haldeman, stunned committee members by

revealing that a secret White House tape recording system had been in existence for years. All conversations with the President had been routinely taped. Investigators immediately requested the tapes as a potential source of evidence.

Agnew's Undoing

While the Watergate affair was under investigation, another inquiry into unrelated matters was in progress. Officials charged that Vice-President Agnew, while governor of Maryland and even while Vice-President, had accepted bribes from construction companies doing business with the state.

Faced with a strong case against him and the prospect of going to prison, Agnew decided to resign as Vice-President on October 10, 1973. He also pleaded no contest, the equivalent of pleading guilty, to a single charge of federal income tax evasion. In exchange, the prosecutors dropped the other charges against him. The court fined him $10,000 and sentenced him to three years on probation.

According to the Twenty-fifth Amendment, the President must select a new Vice-President when that office becomes vacant. President Nixon chose Representative Gerald Ford of Michigan and submitted his name to Congress for confirmation. Congress confirmed Ford's appointment on October 12.

The Investigation Continues

In order to dispel charges that he was obstructing the Watergate investigation, President Nixon instructed his new attorney general, Elliot Richardson, to appoint a special Watergate prosecutor. Richardson chose Archibald Cox, a respected Harvard University law professor. When Butterfield disclosed the existence of the White House taping system, Cox moved to obtain the tapes.

On July 23 Cox requested a subpoena, a legally binding order, directing the President to turn over nine tapes to the special prosecutor's office. Judge Sirica granted the request. President Nixon appealed the decision. He claimed that "executive privilege" allowed him to retain the tapes for reasons of national security. But in October the United States Court of Appeals upheld Judge Sirica's ruling. In an attempt to prevent the release of the tapes, Nixon ordered Richardson to fire Cox.

Richardson refused and promptly resigned, as did his immediate subordinate, William Ruckelshaus. The solicitor general finally carried out the order, and on Saturday, October 20, Cox was removed. Reporters dubbed the resignations and firing the Saturday Night Massacre. Letters of protest poured into Congress. Sixteen separate bills calling for impeachment of the President were introduced. The House Judiciary Committee, under Chairman Peter Rodino of New Jersey, began deliberations.*

Under these pressures, President Nixon appointed a new special prosecutor, Leon Jaworski of Texas. The President also released the tapes to Judge Sirica. But embarrassed White House lawyers were forced to tell the court that some of the subpoenaed tapes were missing. Even worse, an apparently crucial 18½-minute segment had been erased from one tape. Experts testified that the erasures were most probably deliberate.

The crisis deepened in March 1974 when the grand jury investigating Watergate matters indicted Mitchell, Haldeman, Ehrlichman, and several other Nixon aides for perjury and obstruction of justice. The grand jury named the President as an unindicted co-conspirator.

In April, Special Prosecutor Jaworski and the House Judiciary Committee requested additional tapes. The President refused to submit them, but by the end of the month he agreed to supply edited transcripts. White House secretaries produced over 1,200 pages, which the President made public. The transcripts revealed the President discussing the Watergate cover-up.

Neither the Judiciary Committee nor Jaworski was satisfied with edited transcripts of the tapes. At the end of May, Jaworski obtained an order from Judge Sirica directing the President to turn over the Watergate tapes. Nixon appealed to the Supreme Court, but the Court upheld Sirica's order.

Late in July the Judiciary Committee passed three articles of impeachment against President Nixon. The articles claimed

that the President had obstructed justice, misused his presidential powers, and refused to comply with the committee's request for evidence.

At the insistence of his lawyers, the President then released transcripts of taped conversations recorded June 23, 1972, only a few days after the Watergate burglary. The transcripts demonstrated beyond all doubt that he had known of the burglars' connection to the White House and had acted to limit the FBI investigation. Even the President's staunchest supporters in Congress refused to defend him. Impeachment by the House seemed certain.

On August 8, 1974, President Richard M. Nixon appeared on national television and announced his resignation. He became the first President in the history of the republic to take such an action. Gerald Ford then became President.

On August 8, 1974, Richard Nixon became the first President in American history to resign from office. He resigned to avoid being impeached.

---

*The House of Representatives can impeach, or accuse, a President of high crimes and misdemeanors. The Senate then tries the case, and if it votes to convict, the President is removed from office.

The Imperial Presidency

Even before Watergate, some critics had charged that President Nixon was creating an "imperial presidency" by assuming too much power. During the Nixon years, the White House staff grew to 500 persons, more than double the size of any previous President's staff. Members of the White House staff did not have to be confirmed by the Senate, as cabinet members did. Thus, influential staff members, such as H. R. Haldeman and John Ehrlichman, were not responsible to anyone but the President.

Nixon's presidential style contributed to the uneasiness many Americans felt about the growing powers of the presidency. He would go for months without holding a press conference, and he often spent many hours during the day alone. This behavior created an image in many people's minds of a remote and secretive chief executive.

Furthermore, critics objected to policies they believed exceeded the President's authority. Nixon had defied the Democratic-controlled Congress by impounding funds Congress had appropriated. He also angered members of Congress when he claimed that he had the right as President to refuse to allow members of the executive branch to testify before congressional committees.

Richard Nixon had not created the powerful presidency. The executive branch of the federal government had been growing in size and authority since the 1930s. The events of Watergate, however, focused attention on the powers of the President and brought demands for reform.

Congress responded with several new laws. The Congressional Budget and Impoundment Act of 1974 revised congressional budget-making practices and forbade a President to impound funds appropriated by Congress. Congress strengthened the 1966 Freedom of Information Act, giving the public greater access to information on government decisions and activities.

In addition, the Federal Campaign Reform Act of 1974 provided tax funds to candidates for federal office who met certain qualifications. The act also placed limits on private campaign contributions. This was an effort to prevent the sort of misuse of funds that had occurred in the 1972 election. However, critics argued that even stronger laws were needed.

Watergate in Retrospect

The Watergate crisis was a traumatic experience for the United States. There had been other governmental scandals in American history, but a President had never resigned from office. The Watergate crisis shook the confidence of some Americans in their government. However, for many people, the crisis demonstrated the strength of the federal system of checks and balances. Congress and the Supreme Court had successfully checked the power of the President when he appeared to be abusing that power. The balance of powers as outlined in the Constitution had been maintained, and the transition from one administration to the next had been smooth.

With the presidency of the United States comes enormous power. The President is both the commander in chief of the armed forces and the principal designer of domestic and foreign policies. Watergate revealed the dangers of an imperial presidency, but it also demonstrated that no President is above the law. As Gerald Ford commented upon assuming the office of President, "Our great republic is a government of laws and not of men." That no President can ignore the laws of the United States seems to be one enduring lesson of the Watergate experience.

To some observers, the real end of the turbulent decade of the 1960s came with Nixon's resignation in August 1974. Strong feelings about the war in Vietnam and Watergate had sharply divided the nation. It was now up to Gerald Ford, the first President to assume the office without having been elected President or Vice-President, to try to heal the nation's wounds.

SECTION REVIEW

1. Identify: Sam Ervin, John Mitchell, John Dean, Archibald Cox, Leon Jaworski.

2. What did James McCord charge in the letter he wrote to Judge Sirica?

3. What was the Saturday Night Massacre?

4. What charges did the House Judiciary Committee make against Nixon?

5. **Critical Thinking** Why do you think there has been a willingness, if not a desire, in recent years to have a strong President?

4 A New Start

After taking the oath of office, President Gerald R. Ford proclaimed, "The Constitution works. . . . Our long national nightmare is over." Indeed, after the turmoil of Vietnam and Watergate, the public desperately wanted a return to stability.

The Unexpected President

Gerald Ford had served his congressional district in Michigan for 25 years, earning a reputation for hard work and dependability. From 1965 to 1973, he served as minority leader in the House of Representatives. His colleagues in the House liked him, and they had warmly supported his selection as Vice-President when Spiro Agnew resigned in October 1973.

After the disillusionment caused by the Watergate affair, Ford seemed an ideal person to hold the presidency. People saw him as outgoing and scrupulously honest. They responded to his simple lifestyle. Ford's pledge of "openness and candor" for his presidency drew wide praise. So too did his promise to hold regular news conferences and to make himself available to the nation.

Ford moved quickly to assure stability and to restore confidence in government. He selected Nelson Rockefeller, a former governor of New York, as his Vice-President. In foreign affairs, he announced that Henry Kissinger would be retained as secretary of state. Furthermore, he promised to follow the foreign policy guidelines established during the Nixon administration.

With a popular new President in the White House, the nation looked forward to a time of quiet healing. Early in the Ford presidency, however, new revelations ignited controversy.

New Controversies

Only a month after taking office, President Ford issued a blanket pardon to Richard Nixon that freed Nixon from prosecution for any crimes he might have committed while in office. Ford stated that he wanted to spare the country the agony of putting a former President on trial.

Some Americans supported the pardon because they agreed with President Ford that Richard Nixon had suffered enough. However, polls showed that the majority of Americans opposed the action. They questioned the justice of allowing Nixon to escape punishment while many of his subordinates had gone to jail.

The White House was flooded with phone calls and telegrams critical of the pardon. There were many charges that Ford's pardon was the result of a deal between Ford and Nixon. President Ford strongly denied that there had been any deal. Nevertheless, his popularity declined dramatically. He would never entirely regain the good will and support he had when he first took office.

Disclosures of misconduct in the CIA and FBI also startled the nation. In December 1974 the press revealed that the CIA had

Nixon's resignation brought Vice-President Gerald Ford to the White House. Ford had a reputation for being down-to-earth. The new President is shown here making breakfast in the family dining room.

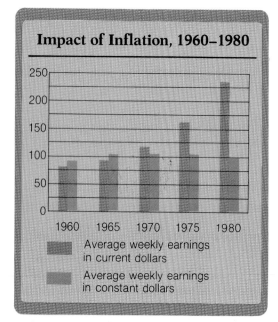

Impact of Inflation, 1960–1980

250
200
150
100
50
0

1960 1965 1970 1975 1980

Average weekly earnings in current dollars

Average weekly earnings in constant dollars

Source: *Statistical Abstract of the United States*

■ One of the most troubling problems of the modern economy has been persistent inflation. During an inflationary period it costs more dollars to buy the same goods and services. To make comparisons between years when the dollar had different values, economists use a concept called "constant dollars." That is, they choose a specific year, then use the amount of goods and services a dollar would buy in that year as a yardstick. On this graph, the "constant dollar" used is that of 1967. You can see that although wages increased dramatically, people's buying power did not.

kept files on American citizens, in direct violation of the agency's charter. It also came to light in February 1975 that J. Edgar Hoover, the longtime head of the FBI, had maintained secret files on prominent Americans.

President Ford appointed a high-level commission under the leadership of Vice-President Nelson Rockefeller to investigate the charges against the CIA. At the same time, Congress set up special committees to investigate the CIA and FBI and moved to restrict the undercover activities of the two agencies.

Ford sparked another heated controversy when he offered amnesty, or pardon, to those who had illegally avoided military service during the Vietnam War. The President said he wanted to heal the social divisions caused by the war. However, critics

charged that Ford's plan was too lenient on people who had refused to fight for their country. Few people took advantage of the offer of amnesty in any case. Some refused because they thought the requirement of alternative national service was an admission that resistance to military service had been wrong.

Troubled Economy

Serious economic challenges also faced the Ford administration. Soon after taking office, Ford targeted inflation as the nation's main economic problem. Following the 1973 oil embargo, steep increases in the price of oil had fueled a sharp jump in the rate of inflation. To counter rising prices, Ford began a voluntary program of controlling prices and wages called WIN (Whip Inflation Now), but he saw no success.

Instead of improving, the economy took a turn for the worse, moving into the worst recession since the 1930s. Factories closed down and consumer demand for goods dropped sharply. The rate of unemployment rose steadily, reaching about 9 percent by late 1975.

To stimulate the stagnant economy, Ford persuaded Congress to approve a tax cut. While the cut contributed to a modest economic recovery, it also stimulated a new round of inflation. The economy seemed to be stalled in a pattern, swinging between periods of recession and growing inflation. President Ford tried to curb inflation by cutting government spending. He vetoed a number of spending bills passed by the Democratic-controlled Congress. Despite such actions, inflation continued to plague the nation.

Continuity in Foreign Policy

In foreign affairs, President Ford continued the policies developed during the Nixon administration. With his secretary of state, Henry Kissinger, he promoted détente. Ford visited the Soviet Union in November 1974 and met with Soviet President Leonid Brezhnev to discuss a new treaty to limit nuclear arms.

The following year the President traveled to Helsinki, Finland, where he signed an agreement with the Soviet Union, Canada, and 32 nations in western and eastern Eu-

Henry Kissinger relished the art of diplomatic negotiations. Once he described himself as a "Lone Ranger"-style diplomat. He rode into town when there was trouble, solved the crisis, and rode out again in search of other crises. He is shown here visiting Israeli Prime Minister Golda Meir as part of his shuttle diplomacy following the 1973 October War.

rope. The agreement, known as the Helsinki Accords, fixed the national boundaries established after World War II. It also spelled out human rights standards that the signing nations pledged to observe.

Despite these examples of cooperation, by 1976 relations with the Soviet Union had begun to cool. Critics of détente charged that the Soviet Union had cheated on nuclear arms agreements and had steadily increased its arsenal of weapons. They believed that the Soviet Union had encouraged Egypt to attack Israel in 1973 and that it was arming other countries in the Third World. Some Americans cautioned that the Soviet Union should be viewed as an adversary rather than as a partner in détente.

In the Middle East, Ford and Kissinger could point to some success. Kissinger continued the shuttle diplomacy he had begun after the October War. As a result of his efforts, Israel agreed to withdraw from some of the territory it had occupied in the western Sinai Peninsula. The Middle East was just one area where Kissinger took an active role in foreign affairs. In all, he traveled about 650,000 miles as secretary of state.

The Fall of South Vietnam

The cease-fire signed in January 1973 brought about the withdrawal of American forces from Vietnam, but it did not bring peace to the region. The cease-fire soon broke down, and the war between South Vietnam and the Viet Cong and North Vietnam resumed. Without aid from the United States, the South Vietnamese army crumbled. In April 1975 it surrendered. On May 1 North Vietnamese forces entered Saigon. North and South Vietnam were reunited, and the former South Vietnamese capital was renamed Ho Chi Minh City.

At about the same time, the pro-American government in Cambodia collapsed and was replaced by a communist regime led by Pol Pot. Cambodia's new regime seized the American merchant ship *Mayaguez* after the ship had entered Cambodian waters. President Ford reacted forcefully. He sent a naval force and about 2,000 marines to free the crew of 39. Some Americans criticized the operation because it cost the United States 15 dead and 50 wounded, but most Americans supported President Ford.

Celebrating the Anniversary of the Nation's Birth

On July 4, 1976, in small towns and big cities all across the nation, millions of Americans celebrated the two-hundredth anniversary of the Declaration of Independence. Many towns sponsored firework displays and parades. In Seward, Nebraska, a time capsule containing such items as a 1976 car and letters from townspeople was sealed. Italian Americans in Rome, New York, planned one of the biggest spaghetti dinners ever held, preparing 600 pounds of pasta for a crowd of 3,000.

Special events in large cities drew enormous crowds. In Washington, D.C., the Declaration of Independence, the Constitution, and the Bill of Rights were on display for 76 consecutive hours to accommodate the thousands of tourists visiting the nation's capital. And in New York City hundreds of thousands of people were treated to a spectacular sight as a flotilla of 225 majestic sailing ships from 300 nations entered New York Harbor.

An occasion stirring national pride, the bicentennial reflected another celebration a century earlier. Philadelphia had been made the focal point of the 1876 centennial because of the city's important role in the founding of the nation. On July 4, 1876, a crowd of 200,000 gathered at Independence Hall in Philadelphia to hear a reading of the Declaration of Independence. Celebrations in all regions of the country marked the occasion. With the country still suffering the aftershocks of the Civil War, the South's participation in the centennial was considered an important step in reuniting the nation.

In 1976 the nation was again suffering from the memory of a recent and divisive war, the conflict in Vietnam. However, celebration of the nation's birthday was a time for drawing together and for renewing the spirit of independence and freedom created two centuries earlier.

At the Republican national convention President Ford was challenged by the conservative wing of the Republican party. The conservative Republicans backed Ronald Reagan, who had served as governor of California in the late 1960s and early 1970s. Despite spirited support from many convention delegates, Reagan's challenge was narrowly defeated.

Although the long years of fighting in Vietnam had finally ended, the effects of the war would be felt for years to come. More than 100,000 South Vietnamese left their country immediately after the communist takeover. Most of these people settled in the United States. Thousands later fled in small boats, some of which capsized in the open seas. When neighboring countries refused to accept the flood of South Vietnamese refugees, the problem became a serious international issue.

In Cambodia, the suffering brought about by a radical communist regime was devastating. The full extent of the tragedy may never be known, but more than 1 million people are believed to have starved or been executed under the Pol Pot regime.

The 1976 Election

The Ford administration had little time to forge its own policies, but the President's honesty and goodwill helped the nation recover from the atmosphere of Watergate. Most Americans welcomed the positive mood as they celebrated the nation's bicentennial anniversary on July 4, 1976.

Nonetheless, President Ford faced a strong challenge for the 1976 Republican presidential nomination. Ronald W. Reagan, former governor of California, had the support of the conservative wing of the Republican party. Ford won a narrow victory at the party convention, but the Watergate scandal damaged the Republicans' chances in the general election.

Former Georgia governor Jimmy Carter carried the Democratic banner. Carter had seemed an unlikely presidential candidate two years earlier, but his effective campaigning among the people won him the nomination. Carter's strong civil rights record as governor brought him overwhelming support from black voters. Labor also rallied behind him.

The primary issues during the election campaign were inflation, unemployment, and energy shortages, but neither candidate offered well-defined programs on those issues. Carter stressed humanitarian concerns in foreign policy and in all his dealings. "I

Major Events	
1969	American astronauts make first manned lunar landing; Vietnamization begins
1970	United States and South Vietnamese forces invade Cambodia; Congress repeals Gulf of Tonkin Resolution
1972	Nixon visits the People's Republic of China and Soviet Union; Nixon reelected
1973	Vietnam cease-fire signed; Watergate investigation begins; October War in Middle East; Ford appointed Vice-President; Arab oil embargo
1974	Nixon resigns; Gerald R. Ford becomes President
1975	Saigon falls to North Vietnam; *Mayaguez* seized by Cambodians; Helsinki Accords signed
1976	Bicentennial celebration; Jimmy Carter elected President

will never lie to you," he promised the American people. Jimmy Carter won a slim popular majority, with 40.8 million popular votes compared to 39.1 million for Ford. In the electoral college, Carter won 297 votes compared to 241 for Ford.

SECTION REVIEW

1. Identify: Nelson Rockefeller, WIN, Helsinki Accords, Jimmy Carter.
2. What revelations about the CIA and FBI startled the nation in 1974?
3. (a) How did President Ford try to stimulate the economy? (b) What effect did this measure have?
4. On what grounds did some Americans criticize the policy of détente during the mid-1960s?
5. (a) What happened to the cease-fire in Vietnam after the withdrawal of United States forces? (b) What was the result of this development?
6. What action did President Ford take when Cambodian forces seized the *Mayaguez?*
7. What were the main issues in the 1976 elections?
8. **Critical Thinking** How might a trial of Richard Nixon have benefited or harmed the nation?

 # Chapter 39 Review

In Perspective

Under President Nixon the United States began to disengage from the war in Vietnam. Nixon worked to improve relations with China and the Soviet Union, with the hope of contributing to a more stable world. He also sought to increase stability at home. The nation, however, continued to be troubled by inflation, which was aggravated by the rapid rise of oil prices after 1973.

In 1974 the Watergate crisis led to President Nixon's resignation. The nation was shaken by the events of Watergate, but the crisis also demonstrated that the system of checks and balances worked. Gerald Ford, a man known for his honesty, seemed to be the President the nation needed in 1974. However, President Ford was plagued by economic problems and by criticism of his pardon of Richard Nixon. In the 1976 presidential election, Ford lost to Democrat Jimmy Carter.

Vocabulary

On a separate sheet of paper, write the word or words that best complete each of the following sentences.

1. ___ was the relaxation of tension between the United States and the Soviet Union.
2. The United States and the Soviet Union participated in ___ to limit arms.
3. In 1973, Nixon ___, or refused to spend, funds appropriated by Congress.

4. ___ is a combination of stagnation and inflation.

5. Traveling back and forth between nations to negotiate has been called ___.

See page 833 for suggested readings.

Chapter Checkup

1. How did President Nixon reduce tensions with China and the Soviet Union in 1972?

2. (a) Why did Arab nations impose a boycott on oil shipments to the United States in 1973? (b) What impact did the boycott have on American life? Why?

3. (a) Why did the House Judiciary Committee begin hearings on the impeachment of President Nixon? (b) What did the committee decide? (c) What was Nixon's reaction?

4. (a) What economic problems faced the nation during the Nixon–Ford years? (b) What policies were implemented to deal with those problems? (c) To what extent were those policies successful?

Critical Thinking

1. Analyzing Why do you think it was probably easier for President Nixon to improve relations with China and the Soviet Union than it would have been for a person without a strong anti-communist background?

2. Relating Past to Present Review the system of checks and balances set up in the Constitution. (See pages 161–162.) (a) How did the system work during the Watergate crisis? Cite specific actions in your answer. (b) Does the presidency seem as powerful today as it was before the Watergate crisis? Explain.

Developing Basic Skills

1. Writing a Report Investigate one or more of the products you use that was developed through space technology. (You could begin with the products described on page 726, but there are many others.) Write a report in which you describe how the product was used in the space program and how it was adapted for everyday use.

2. Graph Reading Study the graph on page 736 and answer the following questions: (a) What were the average weekly earnings of American workers in current dollars in 1960? In 1980? (b) What were the average weekly earnings in constant dollars in 1960 and in 1980? (c) How did the relationship between current dollars and constant dollars change between 1960 and 1980? (d) How do you think the average American worker was affected by this development?

See page 833 for suggested readings.

Writer's Handbook

Footnotes for Signed and Unsigned Articles

Footnotes for different types of sources require different kinds of information. Study the following footnotes and notice the variations.

Signed and unsigned magazine articles:
  [1]D. M. Alpern, "Nixon in Prime Time," *Newsweek*, April 16, 1984, p. 34.
  [2]"What's Wrong with the Way We Pick Our Presidents," *U.S. News and World Report*, July 23, 1984, p. 29.

Signed and unsigned newspaper articles:
  [1]Philip Geyelin, "Sh! Says Richard Nixon," *Washington Post*, May 25, 1986, p. C7.
  [2]"10 Years Later," *Washington Post*, August 9, 1984, p. A22.

Signed and unsigned encyclopedia articles:
  [1]*Academic American Encyclopedia*, 1985 ed., "Gerald R. Ford," by Stanley W. Cloud.
  [2]*The New Columbia Encyclopedia*, 1975 ed., "Gerald R. Ford."

Practice: Rewrite the following footnotes correctly.

1. The New York Times, December 23, 1986: "OPEC Pact Sends Oil Prices Up," p. D1, by Lee A. Daniels.

2. Richard Corliss, Platoon, January 26, 1987, Newsweek, pp. 54–55.

3. Henry Kissinger, The New Columbia Encyclopedia, 1975 ed.

Beginning the Nation's Third Century

40

(1777–Present)

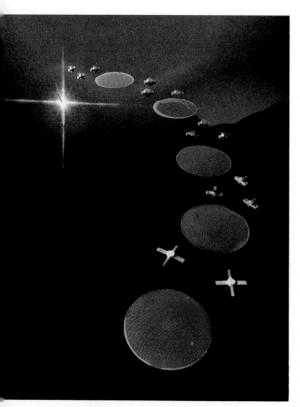

Silicon wafers used in computers

After the strains of the Vietnam War and Watergate, Americans were ready to seek new leadership. Both of the Presidents they chose at the beginning of the nation's third century were newcomers to Washington. Yet Jimmy Carter and Ronald Reagan had different styles of governing and sharply different views on political issues.

Both President Carter and President Reagan faced economic problems at home and the continued threat of nuclear conflict between the two superpowers. The voters decisively rejected President Carter's policies in the election of 1980. But President Reagan won popular approval for his programs when he was reelected in 1984. The Reagan administration broke new paths and steered the United States away from some of the policies it had followed since the election of Franklin D. Roosevelt in 1932.

Carter administration	Reagan administration

| 1976 | 1978 | 1980 | 1982 | 1984 | 1986 | PRESENT |

1978
Camp David Agreement signed

1979
U.S. recognizes China; Iranians seize American hostages

1981
Hostages released from Iran; Reaganomics begins

1984
Los Angeles Olympics; Reagan reelected

1986
Major tax reform and immigration laws passed

1 The Carter White House

During the presidential campaign of 1976, Jimmy Carter reminded voters that he had few ties to official Washington. His administration, he promised, would bring new faces and ideas to national government. However, as an "outsider" Carter had to convince the traditional leadership in Washington to enact his programs. This task was a difficult one in light of growing inflation and recession at home and mounting world tensions, particularly in the Middle East.

New Leadership in Washington

When James Earl Carter announced that he would seek the Democratic nomination for President, few people thought he could win. Carter had served as governor of Georgia, but he had little experience in national or international politics. No candidate from the deep South had won the presidency since before the Civil War. And Carter did not have much support from the leaders of the Democratic party. However, Carter proved to have wide appeal among rank-and-file Democrats.

He later described his political style as "a southern peanut farmer populist type." He promised honest government to a nation still struggling to forget the Watergate scandals. Many Americans welcomed his low-key, folksy manner and deep religious convictions. They thought that such a President would surely bring government in Washington back in touch with the people. Carter planned to appoint people to his administration who were new to Washington and national government.

Carter showed at his inauguration that he intended to transplant much of the simple, down-home style of his home town in Georgia to Washington. Rather than ride in the presidential limousine, he walked down Pennsylvania Avenue. He substituted a business suit for the formal attire Presidents usually wore for the ceremony. And when Carter was sworn in, the Chief Justice of the Supreme Court used his nickname, "Jimmy," rather than his given name, James Earl.

An Early Crisis

Even before Jimmy Carter assumed the presidency, an energy crisis loomed large. In 1960 the major oil exporting nations had formed the Organization of Petroleum Exporting Countries (OPEC). OPEC demanded a voice in setting prices and production quotas. It met with little success until the Arab oil embargo of 1973, when Arab nations cut oil shipments to the United States and other western countries who supported Israel. (See page 730.) Within a year oil prices

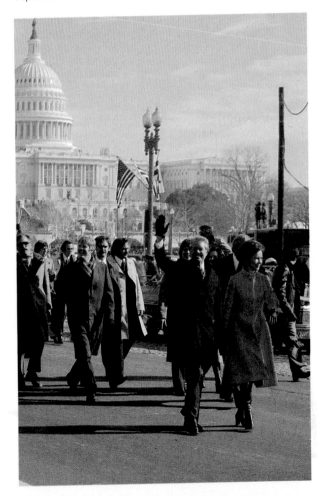

Jimmy Carter tried to bring the informality of his inaugural walk to his term in office. He discouraged the use of lavish ceremonies and often appeared in public in casual clothing. When he visited his home in Plains, Georgia, the President was often photographed playing softball with his staff and reporters.

soared from \$1.20 to \$10 per barrel. The sharp increase fueled inflation and threatened a worldwide recession.

The winter of 1976–1977 was an especially bitter one in parts of the United States. Shortages of natural gas and other fuels caused school and factory closings, business losses, and energy layoffs for many American workers. Thus energy policy became a major priority for the Carter administration.

A Stalemate With Congress

By itself, the energy crisis would have taxed any President, but Carter faced several difficult issues. After Vietnam and Watergate, Congress had tried to limit the authority of the executive branch to reduce the dangers of an "imperial presidency." Inflation, the energy crisis, and other domestic issues called for solutions that promised to be painful and unpopular. Efforts to improve relations with the People's Republic of China or the Soviet Union always provoked controversy. Furthermore, such issues as arms control seldom have broad popular appeal.

The new President's style sometimes made this difficult situation even worse. As an outsider, he did not have close ties with the Democratic leadership in the House and Senate. Many of his advisers were equally new to Washington. It took the administration a long time to master the intricacies of running the national government. Furthermore, Carter's critics charged that the President became so involved with details that he did not emphasize broad goals for his administration.

In his first year in office Carter presented Congress with almost a dozen major bills. The legislative program covered tax reform, social security, energy, and a host of other pressing matters. It immediately ran into strong opposition. As a result, no bill passed without major alterations. For example, the President asked Congress to pass a bill lowering income taxes for the poor and closing certain "loopholes" in current tax laws. Such loopholes allowed many people to avoid paying taxes no matter how much money they earned. The bill that Congress passed did lower some taxes. But it raised the social security tax, which increased the tax bill for most people.

In April 1977 Carter sent his National Energy Plan to Congress. The bill included high taxes on crude oil, which would increase the price of petroleum products. Carter hoped that higher prices would encourage conservation. The revenue raised would be used for mass public transportation. The energy bill passed the House with only minor changes. But by the time it passed the Senate, few of the President's ideas were left. Critics pointed to such failures as evidence that Carter had not displayed effective leadership.

Controversy in Foreign Policy

In his inauguration speech, Jimmy Carter made the idea of human rights* a central part of his foreign policy. "Our commitment to human rights must be absolute," he told the nation. "Because we are free we can never be indifferent to the face of freedom elsewhere."

In practice, Carter found a human rights policy easier to adopt than to enforce. He required the State Department to use the protection of human rights as a criterion for receiving aid from the United States. His administration suspended military aid to several nations guilty of severe violations of rights.

Yet, some of the United States' most loyal allies had the poorest records of political abuses. For example, the shah of Iran, Mohammed Reza Pahlavi, was an enthusiastic supporter of the United States in the Persian Gulf region. However, he ruled through a military dictatorship that became increasingly corrupt. President Carter might quietly urge the shah to improve his record on human rights, but he did not want to embarrass a loyal ally. As a result, critics charged that the policy was unfairly enforced. Nations less important to the United States were held to stricter standards.

The application of Carter's human rights policy did lead to a more active American role in Africa. Encouraged by UN Ambassador Andrew Young, the Carter administration condemned the apartheid policies of South Africa and Rhodesia. At times Young's

---

*"Human rights" refers to the opportunities of people to make political choices, to express their beliefs without the threat of persecution or violence, and to own personal property. Traditionally, governments in democratic countries such as Great Britain, Sweden, Japan, and the United States respect human rights more than do military dictatorships or governments in Soviet bloc nations.

candid remarks embarrassed the President. But Young was eager to forge new ties between the United States and black African nations. He participated in negotiations between representatives of the white minority and the black majority in Rhodesia. As a result of the negotiations, Rhodesia became Zimbabwe and majority rule was established.

Two other foreign policy issues sparked heated debate during the Carter administration—the Panama Canal treaties and diplomatic recognition of the People's Republic of China. In 1978 President Carter agreed to a series of treaties granting Panama control over the Canal Zone by the year 2000. Many critics did not recognize that the United States had never actually owned the Panama Canal. They charged that Carter was giving away American property.

President Carter saw the treaties as an important step toward improving the image of the United States in Latin America. Besides, he believed that the danger of sabotage would be reduced if the Panamanians gained control. The Senate voted its approval of the treaties in March 1978.

President Nixon had encouraged a thaw in United States relations with the People's Republic of China after his historic trip in February 1972. (See pages 724–725.) Trade and diplomatic talks had continued since then. In 1979 Jimmy Carter decided the time had come to renew the tradition of friendship between the two nations. He concluded a series of agreements that included formal diplomatic recognition and increased opportunities for trade.

Even though most Americans supported the President, diplomatic recognition led to considerable controversy. The Peking government had insisted that the United States withdraw its recognition of the nationalist government in Taiwan as the official government of China. Conservative Republicans accused Carter of abandoning a long-time ally of the United States.

The Camp David Summit

One of President Carter's successes in foreign affairs resulted from his efforts to settle the disputes between Israel and Egypt. In the years following the October War of 1973, Egyptian President Anwar el-Sadat began to develop closer ties with the United States. In

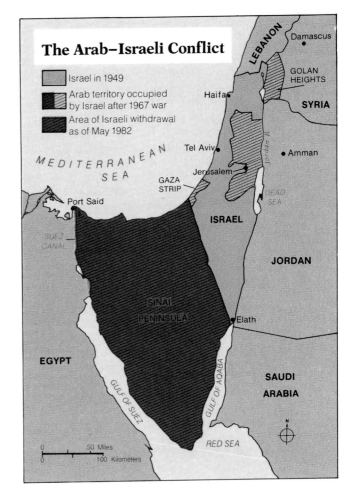

Israel gained territory in each of three wars fought in the Middle East—in 1948, 1967, and 1973. In a 1978 agreement reached at Camp David, Maryland, the leaders of Egypt and Israel agreed to initial steps toward resolving the long Middle East dispute. Israel agreed to withdraw from the Sinai Peninsula, the Gaza Strip, and part of Jordan over a five-year period. The withdrawal from the Sinai was completed in May 1982.

1975 Egypt canceled a treaty of friendship signed with the Soviet Union in 1971.

In November 1977 there was progress in the long-standing tension between Egypt and Israel. President Sadat visited Israel, becoming the first Arab head of state to do so. Shortly thereafter, Israeli Prime Minister Menachem Begin returned the visit. Sadat held cordial talks with Begin. Both sides agreed to work toward a peaceful settlement of their differences.

When negotiations faltered, President Carter invited Begin and Sadat to the United States to discuss their differences. For 12 days the three leaders met at the President's Camp David retreat in the mountains of Maryland to hammer out a settlement.

In September 1978 the tired but elated heads of state returned to Washington to sign the "Framework for Peace in the Middle East." The document proposed a five-year plan under which Israel, Jordan, and the Palestinians could work out a formula for Palestinian self-rule. It also laid the groundwork for a peace treaty between Egypt and Israel that would return the Sinai territory to Egypt.

Changing Relations With the Soviet Union

President Carter took office eager to conclude a new arms agreement with the Soviet Union. Negotiations for such an agreement had begun during the Ford administration. American and Soviet negotiators had met regularly in Vienna, Austria. They sought a formula to extend the limits on nuclear missiles agreed to in 1972 under SALT I. In June 1979 President Carter flew to Vienna to meet Soviet President Leonid Brezhnev. After a round of talks, the two men signed SALT II.

Carter found it easier to reach agreement with Brezhnev than with his opponents in the United States Senate. Critics of SALT II argued that the agreement would give the Soviets a dangerous advantage in warheads and missiles. For ten years, they pointed out, the Soviet Union had been outspending the United States on defense. Carter's supporters did not deny the risks, but they thought the treaty a necessary step toward reducing the danger of nuclear war.

Any chance of ratifying SALT II ended in December 1979 when the Soviet Union invaded Afghanistan to suppress a rebellion against the pro-Soviet government there. The international community generally condemned the Soviet action. President Carter spoke for many when he angrily declared, "The Soviet Union must pay a concrete price for its aggression."

Carter ordered a series of economic and political measures against the Soviet Union. He banned the sale of high-technology equipment and he severely limited grain sales to the Soviet Union. Carter also ordered United States athletes to boycott the summer Olympics scheduled for Moscow in 1980. Many people thought the President had been

In 1978 President Jimmy Carter brought together President Anwar el-Sadat of Egypt (left) and Prime Minister Menachem Begin of Israel (right) for private talks on the Middle East. At Camp David, Maryland, they agreed to the "Framework for Peace in the Middle East," a possible first step to peace in that region. For their efforts to bring peace to the Middle East, President Sadat and Prime Minister Begin were awarded the Nobel Peace Prize in 1978.

unfair in asking athletes and farmers to pay the price of showing American opposition to the invasion.

After the Soviet invasion of Afghanistan, President Carter warned that the United States would fight if the Soviets made any military move toward the Persian Gulf, the oil lifeline of the western powers. Carter also announced that he would increase the military budget over the next five years and that the United States would install new nuclear weapons in western Europe. The cold war threatened to heat up again.

Crisis in Iran

No sooner had Americans become concerned with events in Afghanistan than their attention was drawn to Iran. In 1979 right-wing Islamic fundamentalists, devoted to strict adherence to the Koran, overthrew the regime of the shah. Their religious leader, the Ayatollah Khomeini (i uh TOH luh hoh MEH nee), assumed the leadership of Iran when the shah fled the country.

In November 1979 the Carter administration allowed the exiled shah to enter the United States for medical treatment. When the United States refused to return the shah to Iran for trial, militant Iranians stormed the American embassy in Teheran, the capital of Iran. They took more than 50 American hostages and vowed to keep them until the United States returned the shah. Diplomatic efforts and economic sanctions aimed at the release of the hostages had little effect and a daring rescue mission failed because of mechanical difficulties.

The hostage crisis dominated newspaper headlines and weighed heavily on the minds of Americans throughout 1980. The situation grew increasingly tense as the United States built up its military presence in the Indian Ocean and Persian Gulf. When war broke out between Iran and Iraq, Iran blamed it on United States influence. Hostage negotiations remained stalemated.

Many thought the President had not shown sound judgment or strong leadership during the crisis. Yet there seemed little he could do without creating a grave threat to the hostages' lives. Until the last hours of his presidency Jimmy Carter devoted his energies to freeing the hostages.

The Soviet invasion of Afghanistan in December 1980 disrupted relations between the Soviet Union and the United States. This cartoon shows the action as another example of Soviet aggression toward neighboring countries.

A Developing Energy Policy

The revolution in Iran did more than weaken the strategic position of the United States in the Persian Gulf region. Iran's oil exports dropped to practically nothing. The resulting shortage helped drive the price of oil from about $13 per barrel in 1978 to over $31 in 1980. Only Saudi Arabia's willingness to make up Iran's lost oil supplies spared the United States from an even worse crisis.

Aware of the worldwide dangers of a deepening crisis, Congress moved to implement Carter's energy policy. Congress had already created a new Cabinet office, the Department of Energy. And Carter had won the tax credit provision of his energy program. Tax credits were offered to encourage conservation and the use of solar energy in homes and businesses. In 1979, $100 million was authorized for solar research. President Carter called for phasing out controls on the

This updated windmill was one of many alternative energy sources tried during the oil crisis in the 1970s.

price of domestic crude oil to allow domestic oil prices to rise to world levels.

In 1980 the United States paid $62 billion for imported oil, twice the 1976 figure. But the results of Carter's program had begun to show. Higher prices led to a boom in exploration and domestic drilling. They also produced a decline in oil consumption as both individuals and industries tried to conserve the more expensive fuel.

A Weakening Economy

The cost of oil contributed to a sharp increase in the rate of inflation. Inflation in 1979 soared to 11.3 percent, and in 1980 the prices consumers paid for goods rose by 13.5 percent.

At the same time interest rates on loans rose. Americans found it more difficult to borrow money for major purchases such as cars and homes. Auto sales went into a severe slump. New home sales, an important indicator of the state of the economy, dropped significantly. Businesses could not easily afford to borrow money for new investments in plants and equipment. Unemployment jumped from 5.8 percent in 1979 to 7.1 percent in 1980. Black Americans were particularly hard hit as their unemployment rate reached over 13 percent. As a result, Americans faced the 1980 election worried about the heatlh of the economy.

The 1980 Election

The combination of economic distress and the long, drawn-out hostage crisis undermined President Carter's popularity. In July 1980 just 21 percent of the people polled approved of Jimmy Carter's performance in office. Nonetheless, when the Democratic convention met, Carter easily won renomination.

The Republican party had been divided badly in the 1976 election. Moderate Republicans backing Gerald Ford resented the attacks of conservative supporters of Ronald Reagan. However, in 1980 the party rallied behind Reagan and his running mate, George Bush of Texas. Only the defection of John Anderson of Illinois, who ran for President as an independent, marred GOP unity.

Ronald Reagan made the economy and the hostage crisis major issues of his campaign. He asked voters to consider whether they were better off in 1980 than when Jimmy Carter had taken office in 1977. Double-digit inflation and high interest rates forced many Americans to agree with Reagan's charge that Carter did not have a sound economic program. In addition, Reagan stressed his determination to reduce the role of the federal government in the lives of Americans and to strengthen national defense.

Jimmy Carter did little active campaigning, although he agreed to television debates with Reagan. Reagan's skill as a public speaker helped persuade much of the television audience that he was the stronger candidate. While Carter stayed in Washington to work on the hostage crisis, other Democrats campaigned. They argued that Reagan's promise to lower the cost of government while greatly increasing defense spending did not make sense.

As election day drew near, public opinion polls and political commentators predicted a close election. The voters, however, proved them wrong. Ronald Reagan won 51 percent of the popular vote compared to 41 percent for President Carter and 7 percent for John Anderson. In the electoral college, Reagan won 489 electoral votes and Carter won 49.

Furthermore, for the first time in 26 years the Republicans gained a majority in the Senate, winning 53 seats compared to 41 in the 1978 mid-term election. In the House of Representatives they remained a minority, but they claimed 191 seats compared to 159 in 1978. Many traditional Democratic voters in labor unions, large cities, and the South had shifted to the Republicans.

749

SECTION REVIEW

1. Identify: OPEC, Mohammed Reza Pahlavi, Anwar el-Sadat, Menachem Begin.

2. How did President Carter try to make concern for human rights an important part of United States foreign policy?

3. What were the results of the Camp David summit?

4. (a) What agreement was reached with the Soviet Union in June 1979? (b) Why was this agreement not ratified by the Senate?

5. **Critical Thinking** How might dependence on foreign oil affect United States foreign policy?

2 A New Direction Under Reagan

Ronald Reagan's election in 1980 marked a new direction in American politics. Reagan wanted to limit government spending on social programs and lessen regulation by government agencies. In his first inaugural speech, Reagan stressed his basic political belief: "Government is not the solution to our problems. Government is the problem." Over the next four years he achieved many of his major goals. In 1984 he was reelected on his promise to complete the program his administration began in 1981.

The New President

For several reasons Ronald Reagan seemed an unusual choice as a Republican President. First, at the age of 69, he was the oldest person elected to the office. He was 73 when reelected to his second term. Second, until the 1970s, Reagan was better known as a movie and television personality than as a politician. Third, he had begun his political life as a liberal Democrat. Then in 1962 Reagan joined the Republican party. Four years later he was elected governor of California. By 1976 Reagan had emerged as the leader of the conservative wing of the Republican party.

The very first day of the Reagan administration was one of high drama and suspense. While the nation held its breath, intense negotiations in the final hours of the Carter administration produced agreement to free the American hostages in Iran. Just minutes after Ronald Reagan took the oath of office, word came of the hostages' release.

The 52 Americans held captive for 444 days in the United States Embassy in Teheran returned home to a joyous welcome.

Two months later an assassination attempt nearly ended the new President's life. Shots fired by a lone gunman outside a Washington, D.C., hotel wounded the President, his press secretary, and two security officials.

From the beginning, Reagan stamped the presidency with his own style. He left the details of government to his aides, while he devoted his energies to selling his program. Thus, he sometimes appeared uninformed about his own administration's activities. But few Presidents have had his talent for reaching the public. For a long time, even when controversy troubled his administration, the President seemed somehow apart from it.

Staying the Course

The poor state of the economy had been a major issue in the 1980 campaign. When Reagan took office he listed five economic problems: too much government spending, high taxes, inflation, high interest rates, and unemployment. His program for dealing with these problems called for major changes in the nation's economy. The program was called Reaganomics.

The two main parts of Reaganomics were a reduction in government spending and cuts in personal income taxes. Year after year the government spent more than it took in from taxes, creating large budget deficits that in turn fueled inflation. Reagan wanted to curb federal spending by cutting some social programs and reducing government regulation.

At the same time he wanted to cut taxes. If people had more money in their pockets, he argued, they would start new businesses, build more factories, and buy more products. Increased business activity would produce enough new revenue to make up for the money lost through the tax cuts. New businesses would also contribute to new economic growth.

Much of President Reagan's program was adopted in his first term. Shortly after taking office, Reagan signed an executive or-

■ *A high rate of inflation was a problem during much of the 1970s. The rate of inflation dropped in the early 1980s, but, as this graph shows, unemployment rose as the result of a deep recession. In 1983 and 1984 there was an economic recovery, but unemployment remained high.*

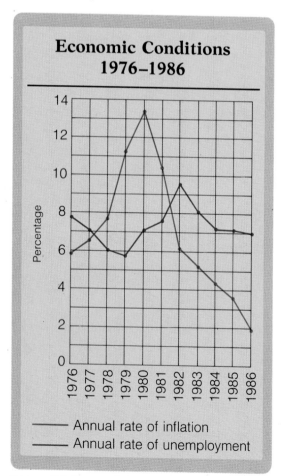

Economic Conditions 1976–1986

——— Annual rate of inflation
——— Annual rate of unemployment

Source: U.S. Bureau of Labor Statistics

der abolishing price controls on most domestic crude oil and its byproducts. In 1981 Congress approved a three-year cut in federal income taxes and a $35-billion cut in the budgets for several social programs, including food stamps, Medicaid, Medicare, and the school lunch program.

President Reagan also kept his promise to lessen government regulation of business. This process, known as *deregulation,* largely freed industries such as banking, trucking, and the airlines from government regulation. In some industries, the freedom to compete without government-set rules led to lower prices for consumers.

Deregulation, however, had some unexpected consequences. Critics claimed that increased competition could cause problems in the industries and that in some cases safety might be sacrificed as profit margins thinned. Indeed, price competition was a factor in the financial difficulties of several airlines in the 1980s.

Critics accused Reaganomics of indifference towards those who were the most vulnerable. Tax cuts, they argued, helped the rich far more than the poor. And cuts in government programs hurt the needy most of all. Voters showed their dissatisfaction in the 1982 congressional elections: they gave the Democrats 26 new seats in the House. The Republicans, however, maintained a majority of 54 to 46 in the Senate.

At first Reaganomics faltered, but the President did not heed his critics. He said he was going "to stay the course." By 1983 the economy had begun to turn around. The average family income, adjusted for inflation, rose for the first time in four years. The Gross National Product (GNP) increased at an annual rate of over 3 percent. Energy conservation programs begun in Carter's administration and a worldwide increase in oil production led to an oil glut. As oil prices dropped, so did the prices of many manufactured goods, lowering inflation and unemployment rates.

The Election of 1984

Ronald Reagan entered the 1984 election race confidently. Eight Democrats campaigned for their party's nomination. After a bitter struggle Walter Mondale, who had been Jimmy Carter's vice-president, emerged as the victor. His main competition had come from Senator Gary Hart of Colorado and the Reverend Jesse Jackson. Jackson's campaign created great excitement in the black community. He was the first black man to run as a presidential candidate of a major political party.

Walter Mondale made history by choosing Geraldine Ferraro as his running mate. Ferraro was the first woman to be the vice-presidential candidate of a major political party.

The outcome of the campaign seemed certain from the beginning. Polls showed Reagan with a commanding lead throughout. The results of the voting in November held few surprises. Reagan won with 59 percent of the popular vote.

President Reagan began his second term in office committed to tax simplification and a reduction of the deficit. In his inaugural speech he said:

> We are creating a nation once again vibrant, robust, and alive. But there are many mountains yet to climb. We will not rest until every American enjoys the fullness of freedom, dignity, and opportunity as our birthright. It is our birthright as citizens of this great republic.

Tax Reform

President Reagan made tax reform and tax simplification the highest priority of his second term. United States tax law was complex

OPEC Oil Prices, 1973–1987

Source: U.S. Department of Energy

■ *OPEC oil prices rose steadily between 1973 and 1981, as this graph shows. However, a world surplus of oil in the mid-1980s began to bring oil prices down.*

Ronald Reagan was overwhelmingly renominated at the 1984 Republican National Convention.

and over the years many deductions that had been written into the tax system benefited only those people who could afford to take advantage of them. However, there were strong pressure groups who were prepared to lobby against serious reform. Some argued that tax simplification might do away with deductions that were meant to encourage positive goals in the society, such as charitable contributions and lessening differences between the very rich and the very poor.

Nevertheless, politicians realized that most Americans believed that their tax system was unfair and that the code favored the wealthy. In 1986 Congress passed a major tax reform plan. The new rates took about 6 million of the poorest citizens off the tax rolls altogether and lowered the top tax rate for the highest incomes. Thus, many people in the middle class charged that the greatest benefits had gone to the poorest and the richest members of the society.

Most experts admitted that no one could accurately predict the long-range effects of the new tax code. Some critics felt that the new system would in fact bring in less money than before and cause greater deficits. Lawmakers hoped the elimination of many tax loopholes would produce greater revenue and increase the confidence of citizens in the fairness of the tax system.

The Federal Deficit

Although prosperity had returned to much of the nation by Ronald Reagan's second term in office, the nation was plagued with increasingly greater deficits in the federal budget. The annual deficit approached $200 billion for several years—far higher than it had ever been before. This meant that a greater percentage of the budget would be needed just to pay interest on the swelling national debt.

Many people worried about the deficit. President Reagan opposed any rise in taxes, arguing that Congress was not willing to cut social programs deeply enough. He called for a constitutional amendment that would bind his successors to maintain a balanced budget. In response Congress passed the Balanced Budget and Emergency Control Act of 1985, known as the Gramm-Rudman Act. This law called for automatic cuts to be made across the board in government spending if the deficit went beyond a target

point. Over time, the plan was intended to produce a balanced budget. This solution was popular because it forced cuts without making members of Congress responsible for approving specific cuts that might offend their *constituents*, the people whom they represented. However, the following year the Supreme Court struck down the provision of the act that automatically triggered across-the-board budget cuts, on the grounds that Congress could not give up its constitutional role of budget-maker.

Despite efforts to cut the budget without causing hardships for people, an increasing number of Americans were living below the poverty level in the later Reagan years. The "safety net" for the truly needy that the Reagan administration had promised did not save some of the most vulnerable members of the society from hardship. For the first time in American history, the greatest number of poor were found in the youngest part of the population.

The Supreme Court

Early in President Reagan's first administration, a vacancy on the Supreme Court allowed him to make a historic appointment. In July 1981 Reagan announced the nomination of Sandra Day O'Connor to fill the lifetime post of Associate Justice of the Supreme Court. O'Connor had been the first woman to serve as a majority leader of a state legislature. Since 1979 she had been a judge on the Arizona Court of Appeals. She developed a reputation as a scholarly jurist who delivered well-researched and well-written opinions. Her nomination was confirmed by the Senate by a vote of 99 to 0.

Reagan's next opportunity to change the Court came in 1986, when Chief Justice Warren Burger announced his intention to retire. The President named Associate Justice William Rehnquist to be Chief Justice and nominated Antonin Scalia to replace Rehnquist as Associate Justice. Both justices were known for their strong conservative views.

The effects of Reagan's appointments to the Supreme Court cannot be predicted. The Court still has members regarded as liberal, and the key to most decisions rests with those members whose positions do not fit neatly into liberal or conservative categories. The Court's position on social issues such as school prayer and the death penalty remained unchanged.

The Election of 1986

In November 1986 Americans went to the polls to elect the 100th Congress. President Reagan had campaigned for Republican senatorial candidates in the hopes of staving off a Democratic takeover of the Senate. However, Reagan's own personal appeal could not override some troubling issues. Huge foreign trade deficits were affecting the manufacturing segments of society and a faltering farm policy was endangering rural life.

As often happens in an off-year election, the political party out of office regains some of its losses. Several first-term senators who had been swept into office in the Reagan landslide in 1982 failed to keep their seats. The Republican loss of control of the Senate combined with Democratic control of the House posed a challenge to the Reagan administration. President Reagan would face opposition as issues became complicated by the politics of the 1988 presidential election.

On September 25, 1981, Sandra Day O'Connor was sworn in as an associate justice of the Supreme Court by Chief Justice Warren Burger. She took the oath of office on two family Bibles held by her husband, John J. O'Connor.

SECTION REVIEW

1. Identify: Reaganomics, Geraldine Ferraro, Sandra Day O'Connor, William Rehnquist.
2. Define: deregulation, constituent.
3. (a) What did Reagan see as the cause of the nation's economic problems? (b) What parts of his economic program did Congress enact in 1981?
4. What was the purpose of the Gramm-Rudman Act?
5. **Critical Thinking** Why is changing the tax system so difficult and risky?

3 Foreign Affairs During the Reagan Years

In foreign policy President Reagan was a vocal critic of the policy of détente, begun by Richard Nixon. (See page 724.) He called the policy "a one-way street the Soviet Union has used to pursue its own aims." In addition, Reagan tended to view conflicts throughout the world as part of the larger struggle between the superpowers. Reagan believed that a build-up of Soviet conventional and nuclear arms threatened the security of the United States. To counter the build-up he promised a large increase in American defense spending.

A Tough Stand

The President took a tough stand against Soviet actions. He said that the Soviet Union assumes the right "to commit any crime, to lie, to cheat to attain its ends." He spoke out against Soviet repression at home and the continuing occupation of Afghanistan. He also criticized Soviet actions in Poland.

In Poland an independent trade union known as Solidarity had organized strikes and demonstrations for economic reform and greater political freedom. In December 1981 the Polish government outlawed the union and imposed martial law. Charging that the Soviet Union had pressured Poland to take these actions, Reagan imposed trade and political sanctions. Many of the sanctions remained when the Polish government lifted martial law in 1983.

Soviet-American relations remained strained through the mid-1980s. In September 1983 a Soviet fighter plane shot down an unarmed South Korean airliner, killing all

269 passengers aboard, including a member of the United States Congress. The plane was flying over Soviet territory, and the Soviets claimed that they thought it was on a spy mission. Noting that the Soviets had not attempted to check the plane's identity, President Reagan denounced the act as unprovoked.

In 1984 the Soviet Union refused to send their athletes to the Olympic Games held in Los Angeles. Soviet officials said that they feared for the safety of the athletes. American observers generally felt that the Soviets were retaliating for the refusal of the United States to attend the 1980 Olympics in Moscow.

The growing tension between the United States and the Soviet Union increased pressure for arms control talks. But President Reagan could not easily meet with the Soviet leaders. Leonid Brezhnev went through a long illness before he died in November 1982. His successor, Yuri Andropov, had headed the Soviet secret police (KGB). He was better informed about the United States than any previous Soviet leader. But ill health troubled him, and after one year as premier he too died. His successor, Konstantin Chernenko (chair NYEHN koh), did not seem eager to improve relations with the United States. Like Reagan he adopted many of the slogans of the cold war. In late 1984, Chernenko died and was replaced by Mikhail Gorbachev (GOR buh chawf). Thus, there were continuing questions about Soviet leadership.

Reagan and Gorbachev

Mikhail Gorbachev, the new Soviet leader, was part of the new generation of Soviet leaders. He was a vigorous, relatively young man with a keen sense of public relations. In visits to western European nations, he professed a desire for peace and gave the impression that he was more reasonable than his predecessors. Yet his own associates recognized that his smile masked a strong will. Gorbachev became locked in a competition with President Reagan for international public opinion.

There were important differences between President Reagan's position on arms control and that of the Carter administration. Reagan sought an agreement with the Soviets to actually reduce the number of weapons, rather than simply agreeing on the numbers and kinds of weapons that would create a balance between the two sides. But Reagan's original proposal to the Soviets for arms reduction was not successful. It called for the deepest cuts to be made in land-based missiles, which were the key to Soviet defense strategy. In contrast, the United States had built its nuclear defense on a balance of land-based intercontinental missiles, bombers, and submarine-launched missiles.

In 1983 President Reagan announced that the United States would develop a weapons system that would provide an effective defense against incoming enemy missiles. This system was called the Strategic Defense Initiative (SDI), but it was popularly

The 1984 Olympic Games, held in Los Angeles, California, were an occasion of great national pride for Americans. Thousands of volunteers took turns carrying the Olympic torch from the east coast to Los Angeles. Gina Hemphill, granddaughter of Jesse Owens, star of the 1936 Olympics, carried the torch into the stadium.

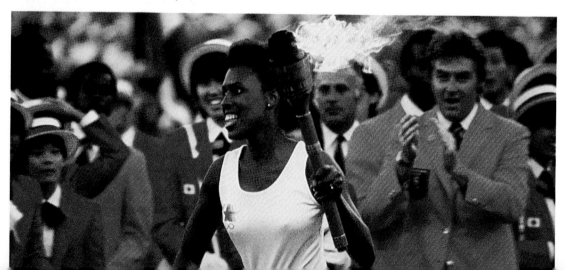

dubbed the "Star Wars defense." At Reagan's urging, Congress appropriated funds to develop the SDI system.

One of Premier Gorbachev's public aims was to stop the development of the SDI. He called for a moratorium on the testing of all nuclear weapons. He halted such testing by the Soviet Union in 1985. The Reagan administration continued underground testing, saying it was necessary to ensure the usability of weapons. In 1987, the Soviets resumed underground testing.

President Reagan and Gorbachev first met in 1985 to get acquainted and to explore grounds for agreement between the two countries. No arms control agreements were reached at the summit, but both leaders claimed to have a better sense of the other. In the same year Reagan announced that the United States would no longer be bound by the provisions of SALT II because of repeated Soviet violations.

President Reagan and Premier Gorbachev met briefly in Reykjavik, Iceland, in October 1986. Many people on both sides hoped the meeting would produce a general arms control agreement. But the Soviet leader pressed Reagan to abandon the 'SDI plans. Reagan refused, and the second summit meeting ended without an agreement. Despite this, arms control talks between the two sides continued in Geneva. New proposals kept hopes alive.

Problems in Latin America

United States policy toward Latin America changed under President Reagan. President Carter's policy had concentrated on reducing poverty and correcting human rights violations. Reagan tended to view problems in Latin America within the framework of the larger struggle with the Soviet Union. As a result, his administration has intervened actively in Latin American affairs, supporting strong governments that oppose communism. Sometimes these governments were military dictatorships.

In 1979 a popular revolution overthrew the dictator of Nicaragua, Anastasio Somoza. Somoza's family had ruled the country since the 1930s, when it took power with the help of the United States Marines. The new rulers of Nicaragua were members of a radical group called the Sandinistas, named after a Nicaraguan who had fought the American marines in Nicaragua in the 1930s. President

After arms reduction negotiations stalled, President Reagan and Mikhail Gorbachev met at Reykjavik, Iceland, to discuss a possible agreement.

Carter originally supported the Sandinista government with promises of aid, but relations between Nicaragua and the United States soured when the Sandinistas established close ties with Cuba.

President Reagan feared that Castro and the Soviet Union would establish a base in Nicaragua. Reagan authorized the CIA to support rebels known as contras who were fighting the Sandinistas. The contras were a mixed group—some had served under Somoza, others were former Sandinista rebels, others were from the democratic center.

The Reagan policy caused a great deal of controversy. Some Americans feared that the commitment to the contras would eventually lead to the involvement of United States troops. Others felt that it was illegal to support the overthrow of a government with which the United States maintained diplomatic relations. When it became known that the CIA had been involved in mining a Nicaraguan harbor, criticism mounted. But in the summer of 1986, Congress approved Reagan's request for funds to aid the contras.

Nicaragua's neighbor El Salvador also experienced a leftist rebellion against a military dictatorship. The Reagan administration claimed that the Nicaraguan Sandinistas were secretly aiding the Salvadoran rebellion. President Reagan backed the Salvadoran government. In 1983 El Salvador elected a civilian government led by moderate José Napoleón Duarte. Duarte opened talks with the rebels, but the differences between the two sides have not been settled, and violence continues to trouble the country.

In October 1983 President Reagan sent United States military forces to Grenada. The Reagan administration believed that Grenada's new radical government was building an airfield for Soviet and Cuban use. As a result of the invasion, a government more favorable to the United States was restored. Some Americans opposed the action fearing it was a dress rehearsal for military action in other areas.

Other changes in Latin America have been encouraging. During the 1980s in Argentina, Brazil, Uruguay, and Ecuador, military rulers stepped down, and democratically elected governments took their place. An elected government also replaced a dictator in Honduras. It remains to be seen, however, whether these new governments will be able to deal with the economic and social problems that beset much of Latin America.

The Philippines

The United States had given independence to the Philippines in 1946. Because of its former territorial status and the role of the United States in the Philippines in World War II, relations between the two countries were close. The United States maintained two of its most important strategic military bases there.

In the early years of independence, democracy flourished in the Philippines. In 1965, Ferdinand Marcos was elected president of the country. He became known as a staunch friend of the United States and a fervent anti-Communist. However, through the years his government became corrupt and repressive. In 1972, Marcos declared martial law and ruled as a dictator. The importance of the bases in the Philippines, however, kept the United States from taking action against him.

During the Marcos years the Philippine economy declined. Terrible poverty afflicted millions of Filipinos. In addition, the country faced two rebellions: one by the Moros, a Muslim group in the southern islands of the country, and the other by communist rebels in some remote areas.

One of the strongest Philippine opponents of Marcos was Benigno Aquino (beh NEE nyoh ah KEE noh), who lived in exile in the United States. In 1983 Marcos permitted Aquino to return to the Philippines, but Aquino was killed while leaving his plane in Manila. The assassination caused protests throughout the country. It soon became apparent that close associates of Marcos had not only been involved, but would go unpunished.

The Aquino assassination overshadowed the presidential elections Marcos held in 1986. Marcos's main opponent was Corazon Aquino, the widow of Benigno Aquino. She succeeded in uniting many of the forces opposing Marcos and, to the amazement of many, threatened Marcos's position.

Marcos, using all the resources of his regime, tried to steal the election. But the United States refused to support him. Finally, after military forces proved reluctant to support him further, Marcos fled to Hawaii. Aquino was sworn in as president.

Corazon Aquino faced many difficulties in solving the social and economic problems of the nation. She traveled to the United States in September 1986 to appeal for financial aid. She appeared before Congress and the public to plead her case. Many Americans felt that the United States should provide additional help to the Philippines in its struggle to make democracy work. In early

Corazon Aquino has sought help from the United States to rebuild the weakened Philippine economy. Aquino attended school in the United States and lived here in exile with her husband.

February 1987, less than a year after she took office, Corazon Aquino announced that a new, popularly-approved constitution would go into effect. She called upon the people of the Philippines to work together for democracy.

Turmoil in Lebanon

In the early 1980s a major war threatened to break out in Lebanon. Since the mid-1970s the Palestine Liberation Organization (PLO) had been using southern Lebanon as a base for raids on Israel. The PLO controlled many parts of Lebanon and was headquartered in Beirut. In addition, the Lebanese people were divided into several warring factions of Christians and Muslims, some of which were aided by neighboring countries.

In the summer of 1982 Israel invaded Lebanon to clear out PLO military bases and limit their striking capacity. Despite criticism from many countries, including the United States, Israeli troops swept northward until they were on the outskirts of Beirut. An agreement resulted in the PLO leaders leaving the country under the protection of an international peacekeeping force in return for a cease-fire.

In August 1982 a United Nations peacekeeping force returned to Beirut. It included troops from Italy, France, and Britain, as well as United States Marines. As fighting continued between the weak government of Lebanon and the country's many religious and political groups, the United States sought to support the government. An American battleship shelled inland villages controlled by opposition groups, and marines were assigned to protect an area around the airport. Then in October 1983 tragedy struck. Terrorists crashed a truck loaded with explosives into the marine barracks, killing 241 Americans. The deaths of these men raised grave questions about United States policy in Lebanon and caused President Reagan to withdraw United States forces in February 1984. Other countries kept their peacekeeping forces in place, but the civil war continued.

Other Issues in the Middle East

President Reagan's primary goal in the Middle East was to prevent Soviet gains in the area. Relations with Israel became closer because the United States regarded Israel as a strategic asset in that region. An agreement between the two countries provided for greater exchange of intelligence information, allowed United States troops the use of Israeli ports, and guaranteed Israel access to sophisticated American weaponry. With the oil glut, Saudi Arabia no longer played as important a role in United States strategic thinking as it had in the past.

Relations with Iran became an increasingly controversial issue in the late 1980s. The United States was officially neutral in the war between Iran and Iraq, but it regarded Iran under the Ayatollah Khomeini as an unfriendly nation. The United States also charged that Iran had encouraged terrorist acts against the United States, including the kidnapping of Americans in Lebanon. Therefore, the United States outlawed arms shipments to Iran and urged others to do likewise. For this reason, both the American people and United States allies were surprised when Iran revealed in 1986 that the United States had been shipping it arms. Although President Reagan protested that he was trying to make contacts with moderate elements within Iran, a commission appointed by the President reported that releases of hostages held by Islamic militants in Lebanon were related to the arms deals. Critics said that trading arms for hostages would encourage other hostage-taking and prolong the Iran-Iraq war. Later revelations linked the arms deals with secret and illegal payments to the Nicaraguan contras. The events surrounding the arms deal raised serious questions about the operations of some White House staff members. Several of the President's advisers, including his chief of staff and national security adviser, were replaced.

Terrorism

Conflicts in the Middle East have contributed to a worldwide increase in terrorism, with Americans often the targets. The taking of American hostages in Lebanon was just one of several incidents. In 1985 Lebanese Muslim terrorists hijacked a TWA plane and took it to Beirut. There, the passengers were kept hostage for two weeks under harrowing conditions, with the Lebanese government powerless to help. Later in 1985, Palestinian terrorists hijacked the Mediterranean cruise ship *Achille Lauro* at sea and killed one American passenger. This time, the United

States intercepted the hijackers and forced their escape plane to land in Italy, where they were put on trial.

The Reagan administration blamed Libyan dictator Muammar Qaddafi (kuh DAHF ee) for many of the terrorist activities. After a bomb killed an American serviceman in Berlin in April 1986, American planes bombed Libya's capital city, Tripoli. American strategists hoped that this action would lead to Qaddafi's overthrow, but he retained his hold on the country.

The source of terrorist activity was not always easy to pinpoint although there were strong suspicions that Syria and Iran were also involved. It was hard to identify the specific perpetrators and capture them without hurting innocent people. The United States allies in Europe feared a terrorist response in their countries if they cooperated fully with the United States.

A Policy Toward South Africa

Under President Carter, relations between South Africa and the United States were very cool, and the contacts between the two countries were limited. President Reagan believed that South Africa's strategic location and important mineral resources made it important in the global struggle against the Soviet Union. As a result, the Reagan administration has followed a policy known as "constructive engagement" to counter South Africa's apartheid policy. Reagan's policymakers used quiet diplomacy and kept public criticism of the South African government to a minimum. President Reagan disliked apartheid but argued that severe actions against South Africa would hurt the black majority of the population more than it would hurt the white government. The administration has also been suspicious of the main black opposition group, the African National Congress (ANC), because some of its members are communists.

In recent years the South African government of President P. W. Botha has made some changes. It has established parliaments for the country's other non-white groups, the Coloureds and the Indians. However, the black South Africans, more than 70 percent of the population, still cannot vote and have no representation in the government.

In the United States demonstrations and organized sit-ins at the South African consulate have dramatized the plight of the blacks in South Africa. Universities and some state governments, such as California's, have followed a strategy of *divestiture*, or refusal to hold stock in companies that have operations in South Africa. Many United States businesses have also withdrawn their sales outlets and factories from South Africa.

Members of Congress called for *economic sanctions*, or limits on trade and investment, to pressure the South African government into changing its policy. President Reagan tried to avoid sanctions by promising milder measures against the South African government. However, Congress passed a sanctions bill over the President's veto in October 1986. The sanctions include a ban on new investments in South Africa and the prohibition of imports of such South African products as steel, iron, uranium, coal, and farm implements. In addition, the bill suspended the rights of South African Airways to land in the United States. The overriding of his veto by both houses of Congress was a setback for the President.

East Asia

Asia has become more important to the United States because of its rapid economic development. The United States has sought closer economic ties with the People's Republic of China since full diplomatic relations were established in 1979. The new Chinese leadership under Deng Xiaoping (DUHNG syow PIHNG) has allowed private enterprise and trade. The United States, looking eagerly to a Chinese market of about one billion people, has helped to provide economic expertise.

The Reagan administration was also aware of the importance of China as a check to the Soviet Union. As a result, it has agreed to sell advanced weapons to the Chinese. President Reagan visited China in 1984, and the premier of China returned the visit. In spite of differences over Taiwan, the two nations maintain a strong relationship based on their mutual defense needs.

Japan, under Prime Minister Yasuhiro Nakasone (yah soo HEE roh nahk uh SOH nee), has enjoyed good relations with the United States. Nakasone has agreed to cooperate in the research for the Strategic Defense Initiative. But the Japanese resent pressure from the United States Congress to restrain their exports to the United States. Some American economic experts have claimed that Japanese companies sell under cost, or dump, their products abroad in order to establish markets. Nakasone has publically encouraged the Japanese to buy American products, but he has not lifted heavy restrictions against such American exports as farm products.

South Korea has taken a lesson from Japan's economic success. Since the 1970s, South Korea has enjoyed a booming economy. The Koreans have begun to sell electronic goods and automobiles in the United States. Korean products are considerably less expensive than American ones and also compete with Japanese-made goods.

759

SECTION REVIEW

1. Identify: Mikhail Gorbachev, contras, José Napoleón Duarte, Muammar Qaddafi, Yasuhiro Nakasone.
2. Define: divestiture, economic sanctions.
3. Why was Reagan's policy toward Nicaragua controversial?
4. Why were United States Marines sent to Lebanon in 1982?
5. What limitations has Congress placed on South African relations with the United States?
6. **Critical Thinking** Compare the foreign policy goals of President Carter and President Reagan. How did they differ?

4 Striving for Equality

One of the most important trends in United States history has been the struggle for equality among the nation's diverse groups. Discrimination has often stimulated groups to organize to combat disadvantages. In the 1970s and 1980s, the emphasis of the struggle for equality shifted as the federal government played a less significant role in supporting groups that had traditionally been the targets of discrimination.

■ Compare these two circle graphs showing the kinds of work done by men and women. In the 1960s and 1970s women entered the work force in unprecedente numbers, and many more women took professional or managerial jobs. Despite these changes, women still far outnumber men in service and clerical jobs.

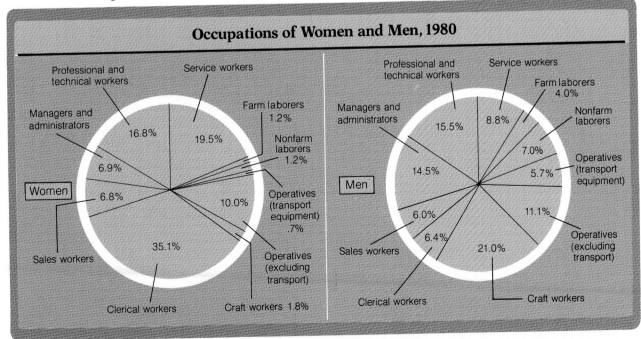

Occupations of Women and Men, 1980

Women:
Professional and technical workers 16.8%
Service workers 19.5%
Farm laborers 1.2%
Nonfarm laborers 1.2%
Managers and administrators 6.9%
Sales workers 6.8%
Operatives (transport equipment) .7%
Operatives (excluding transport) 10.0%
Clerical workers 35.1%
Craft workers 1.8%

Men:
Professional and technical workers 15.5%
Service workers 8.8%
Farm laborers 4.0%
Nonfarm laborers 7.0%
Managers and administrators 14.5%
Operatives (transport equipment) 5.7%
Sales workers 6.0%
6.4%
Clerical workers 21.0%
Operatives (excluding transport) 11.1%
Craft workers

Women in Sports

A widely publicized incident during the 1967 Boston Marathon involved an angry race official chasing Katherine Switzer in an attempt to remove her from the event. At that time, women were not allowed to run in the Boston Marathon. Only by registering as "K. Switzer" had Switzer been able to obtain an official number. After eluding the irate official, she became the first woman with an official number to finish the race.

Besides the inspiration of athletes like Switzer, the fitness boom of the 1970s and 1980s has contributed to women's increased interest in sports. Today there are an estimated 15 million women runners, many of whom participate in marathons, including the one in Boston. In 1984 a women's marathon was added to the Olympic games, a fitting symbol of the great strides taken by women athletes during the past decade.

Women have improved their performances in track-and-field events, swimming, and other sports. One reason for this is the growing number of women who participate in high school and college athletics. In 1970, women made up 7 percent of high school athletes and 2 percent of college athletes. By the early 1980s, the percentages were 35 and 30, respectively.

In addition, professional women athletes have seen a dramatic increase in prize money. For example, women golfers on the pro tour earned a total of $6.4 million in 1982, compared with $1.2 million in 1975. Women tennis pros, such as Chris Evert Lloyd, once earned purses far smaller than those of their male counterparts, but today they are paid at comparable levels.

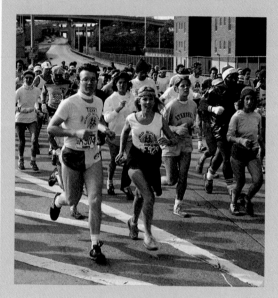

Gains for Women

The defeat of the Equal Rights Amendment in 1982 forced leaders of the women's movement to reconsider their tactics in promoting equality. Action then shifted to the courts. Groups and individuals brought suits against businesses and government agencies that were accused of discriminating against women.

Still, the 1980s have been a time of great achievement for American women. In record numbers women are entering careers that traditionally were dominated by men. The armed forces, police, and fire departments have seen an influx of women. In the 1980s, Sally Ride became the first American woman astronaut and Kathryn Sullivan was the first American woman to walk in space.

Women have also made significant inroads in other professions. For example, the percentage of women graduates of engineering schools rose from .8 percent in 1971 to 10.4 percent in 1981. Furthermore, the number of women managers doubled during the 1970s. In major corporations, women have been aiming for the highest executive positions and, in some cases, have achieved them.

Yet on the average, women workers still earn only about 65 percent of what men do. One reason for this phenomenon is that a majority of women continue to hold such traditional occupations as secretary, sales clerk, and registered nurse. These jobs tend to be low-paying, in spite of the fact that they require skills similar to those of higher-paying jobs traditionally held by men. For this reason, some women advocate a system called *comparable worth*. This system would pay comparable wages for jobs requiring comparable skills. Many women see this as the only way of ensuring equality of pay for women.

Black Americans

Black Americans were more seriously hurt by the recession of the early 1980s than many other Americans were. Unemployment was higher among black Americans, especially among black youth. In some cities, more than 40 percent of black teenagers were unemployed in 1982. In 1983, when the unemployment rate for the total population was 9.6 percent, it was 19.5 percent among blacks. Moreover, as economic recovery came to the rest of the population, the unemployment rate for black Americans remained high. To help young blacks into the job mainstream, some businesses are designing programs to provide training and jobs.

Government programs that had enabled blacks to make gains in the past have come under scrutiny in recent years. For example, critics sometimes described affirmative action as reverse discrimination. One interpretation of affirmative action was the decision of the Supreme Court in the case of *Regents of the University of California* v. *Bakke* in 1978. In this case, Allan Bakke sued to be admitted to the University of California on the grounds that he had been refused admission because the university set aside places for blacks. The Supreme Court ordered that Bakke be admitted to the university. The Court disallowed quotas but stated that race could be taken into account as a factor in admissions policy.

In 1987, however, a Supreme Court ruling once more adjusted the ground rules for affirmative action. To provide relief for the proven discrimination against black Alabama state troopers, a federal court ordered that one black trooper be promoted for each white trooper promoted to each rank. In a 5–4 decision in the case of *United States* v. *Paradise*, the Supreme Court upheld the strict promotion quota.

During President Reagan's administration, some members of the Civil Rights Commission have objected to the methods used to promote civil rights in the past. The President himself at first opposed extension of the Voting Rights Act, claiming that it was no longer needed. In 1982 Congress eliminated busing as a tool for integrating schools. On the other hand, Congress proclaimed the birthday of Martin Luther King, Jr., a na-

■ In the period from 1960 to 1980, the percentage of black Americans in white collar jobs almost tripled, growing to 39 percent in 1980. On the chart, these jobs are labeled Professional and technical workers, Managers and administrators, Sales workers, and Clerical workers. Yet incomes of blacks continue to trail those of whites.

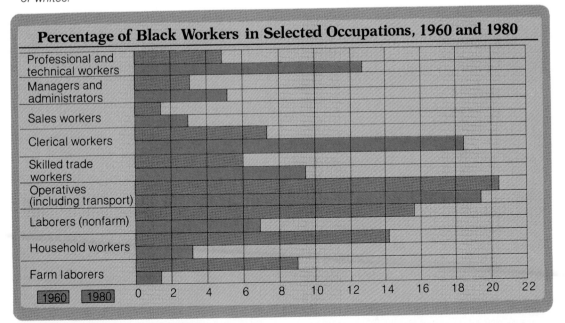

Percentage of Black Workers in Selected Occupations, 1960 and 1980

Source: *Statistical Abstract of the United States*

tional holiday in recognition of his contributions to the nation.

Many black Americans feel that some of the gains of the earlier civil rights movement have been lost. But there has been progress for some. Because more blacks were completing high school and attending college, more of them moved into the middle class and entered the professions than ever before. The percentage of blacks in professional and technical jobs almost tripled between 1960 and 1980, and the number of blacks in managerial positions doubled. Yet the median family income of black Americans remains between 50 and 60 percent of the median family income of whites.

Hispanic Americans

According to the 1980 census, there are 15 million people of Hispanic heritage in the United States. Hispanics thus make up the second largest minority group after black Americans. They form important percentages of the populations of such cities as Miami, New York, Los Angeles, and San An-

The states with the largest populations of Hispanic Americans are California, Texas, New York, and Florida.

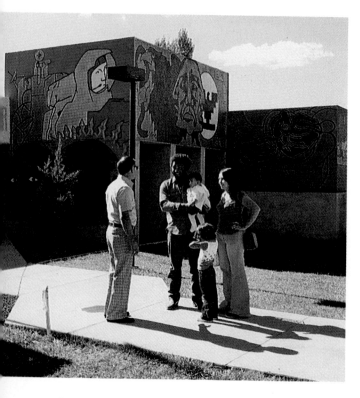

tonio. They have come from all parts of the Spanish-speaking world, but mainly from Mexico, Puerto Rico, and Cuba. Hispanic Americans have made great strides in recent years and have increased their participation in American life and in the prosperity of the country. Through gains in education, the numbers of Hispanic Americans in professions such as law and medicine has increased.

In the last 20 years, Miami has become an important center of Cuban American life. (See pages 711–712.) In 1980, more than 100,000 Cubans arrived in the exodus known as the Freedom Flotilla. Many of the new arrivals were friends and relatives of Cubans already living in the United States.

Most Mexican Americans, who make up the largest Hispanic group, live in the Southwest. All the major cities of this area have large Mexican American communities. In recent years, Mexican Americans have played an increasingly important role in the political and social life of that area.

The largest Puerto Rican community is in New York City, although smaller Puerto Rican communities are found in Chicago and Newark, New Jersey. Puerto Ricans make up about 10 percent of the population of New York City, around 700,000 people. Puerto Ricans are unique among Hispanic Americans because they are not an immigrant group. Though it has commonwealth status, Puerto Rico is politically part of the United States, and thus all its people are United States citizens at birth.

Native Americans

According to the 1980 census, there were 1,400,000 Native Americans living within the country. About 54 percent of them now live in urban areas, while others have chosen to retain their tribal identity and customs.

Under President Nixon, government policy was to promise Native Americans a degree of "self-determination." They were encouraged to develop tribal life on the reservations. The government pledged assistance in educational and economic development, housing, and vocational training. By 1973 Native Americans made up a majority of the members of the federal Bureau of Indian Affairs.

Recently there has been a small increase of Native Americans in the professions. Some Native Americans have become lawyers, doctors, and engineers. But many have remained at the bottom of the economic ladder. Mainly as a result of poor education, unemployment on the reservations in the early 1980s averaged around 50 percent.

Some groups of Native Americans have gone to the courts in an attempt to recover land taken from them earlier. The Taos Pueblo in New Mexico recovered land including the Blue Lake, which was sacred to their tribe and which formed part of a national park. In Maine, Indians sued for the recovery of more than one-third of the state. The courts awarded them $81 million with the provision that they be allowed to purchase 300,000 acres of land in Maine.

Because they are spread among more than 450 scattered groups, many speaking different languages, Native Americans have found it difficult to cooperate for national action. Ancient conflicts have also weakened their strength, as in the case of the Hopi and the Navajo, who have fought over rights to the same land in the Southwest.

Handicapped Americans

During the 1970s the handicapped started to move into the mainstream of American life. Inspired by gains made by other minorities, they organized to demand equal advantages that had been denied in the past. The Rehabilitation Act of 1973 forbade discrimination against the handicapped in jobs, education, and housing.

Federal and local governments have responded to lobbying by the handicapped by taking their special needs into account. Many public buildings and means of transportation now have facilities designed to meet the needs of handicapped Americans. For example, elevators often have Braille numbers to designate the floors. Ramps provide access to buildings for people in wheelchairs. Convenient parking spaces are designated for use by the handicapped.

In 1975 Congress passed the Education for All Handicapped Children Act. This required public schools to provide suitable education for children with physical or mental handicaps. Handicapped children were to attend classes with the nonhandicapped, rather than be placed in special facilities. Known as *mainstreaming*, in some areas this practice placed a burden on the resources of the school. Some criticize it on the grounds that handicapped children might need spe-

In recent years many people with physical handicaps have fought for their right to take advantage of the economic opportunities available to Americans. Special buses such as the one shown here enable people in wheelchairs to take public transportation to and from work.

cial attention that is not available in a regular classroom. Others argue that the benefit of being part of a normal school environment outweighs any drawbacks of this approach.

SECTION REVIEW

1. Identify: Sally Ride, Allan Bakke.
2. Define: comparable worth, mainstreaming.
3. In what areas have women recently made progress?
4. (a) What gains have blacks made in the 1970s and 1980s? (b) What setbacks have they faced?
5. Why have Hispanic Americans become a significant minority in the United States?
6. What gains have the handicapped made in recent years?
7. **Critical Thinking** Why do you think that comparable worth is such a controversial issue?

5 A Changing Population

American society has never remained the same. As the United States enters its third century, its society is being molded by new arrivals and a gradually aging population. Once more the nation must adjust to new conditions and face new challenges.

A Land of Immigrants

In 1965 Congress passed the Immigration and Nationality Act, which abolished the national origins quotas for immigrants. Since

■ *Since the 1960s immigrants to the United States have come increasingly from the nations of the Western Hemisphere and Asia. In the aftermath of the Vietnam War, many refugees from Vietnam and Cambodia settled in the United States. After Castro's revolution in 1959, and again in 1980, many Cuban refugees joined the ranks of immigrants.*

Sources of Immigration to the United States, 1820–1979

Millions of People

Years

— Europe
--- Americas
— Asia

Sources: *Statistical Abstract of the United States* and *Historical Statistics of the United States*

then, new groups of immigrants have arrived who are changing the face of the country.

In 1986 the United States celebrated the centennial of the Statue of Liberty. The statue represented the hopes of the millions of immigrants who entered New York harbor. Today, immigrants are more likely to arrive at airports in Florida, New York, and Los Angeles, or to cross the border from Mexico. The new Americans of today are most likely to come from Asia, Latin America, the Caribbean, or the Middle East, rather than from Europe.

Asians are the fastest-growing group of immigrants to the United States. In the 1960s, 13 percent of the people who immigrated to the United States came from Asia. The figure jumped to 34 percent in the 1970s. At the same time, immigration from Europe slowed—from 33 percent in the 1960s to 18 percent in the 1970s. In the 1980s these trends have continued.

Immigration from Asia has been increased by refugees from Vietnam and Cambodia fleeing turmoil in their homelands. The number of immigrants from China, Japan, and Korea, as well as from India and Pakistan, has also increased. The new Asian Americans have been highly successful in business and academic fields and are represented in the best universities and research laboratories of this country.

Immigration continues to increase from Latin America and the Caribbean as well. Of recent arrivals, the largest number, 1.3 million, have come from Latin America. About half of the newcomers came from Mexico, but Cubans and Haitians are heavily represented. By the end of the 1980s, some experts predict, Hispanics will pass blacks as the largest minority group in the United States.

Swelling the tide of immigration are the hundreds of thousands of people who enter the United States illegally each year. Some slip over the borders. Others overstay tourist visas. Estimates place the number of illegal immigrants at between 100,000 and 500,000 each year. Many Americans argue that illegal immigrants take jobs from Americans, a particular problem during times of high unemployment.

In 1986 Congress passed a law aimed at immigration control. It called for penalties for employers who hire people without proper documents and for amnesty for illegal aliens who lived in the United States before January 1, 1982. Tied to the bill was a large financial grant to states to help educate and provide social services for the immigrants given amnesty.

Cultural Diversity

For many years, historians wrote about the United States as a melting pot where different cultures merged into one. More recently, some observers have described the United States as a pluralistic society where many different cultures exist side by side. Whether a melting pot or a pluralistic society, the United States has always had a rich cultural heritage because of the diverse traditions immigrants brought from their homelands. These traditions can be seen in many aspects of American life: in the names of families, towns, and cities; in the variety of food and clothing; and in the diversity of religious worship and traditional festivals held across the country.

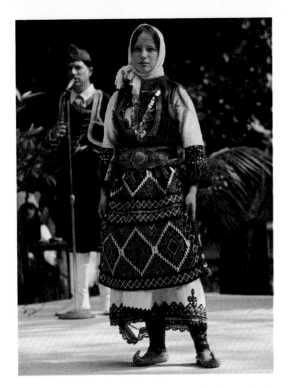

Americans cherish the traditions of the homelands of their ancestors. Across the country there are Puerto Rican parades, Chinese New Year feasts, Yugoslav and Italian festivals, and a dozen other salutes to the many heritages of Americans.

■ *One evidence of cultural diversity in the United States is the variety of religions. This graph shows the main religious groups in the United States. Most of the large categories contain dozens of smaller religious denominations.*

Major Religious Bodies in the United States

Eastern Churches of America	⛪
Jewish Congregations	🏠🏠
Roman Catholic	🏰🏰🏰🏰🏰🏰🏰🏰🏰🏰🏰
Protestant	⛪⛪⛪⛪⛪⛪⛪⛪⛪⛪⛪⛪⛪⛪
Other	🏠

One symbol represents 5 million members

The diversity of the nation's population has presented problems as well. New immigrants have often met with suspicion and hostility from some Americans. Many immigrants have faced a language barrier and unfamiliar customs that seemed to threaten their cherished traditions. Non-English speaking children of immigrants face many difficulties when they enter school.

Schools have tried to meet the needs of these children by introducing *bilingual education*. In bilingual education programs, students take some courses in English and some in their native languages. The 1980 census showed that 10 percent of schoolchildren came from homes where English was not the primary language.

Bilingual language programs have provoked much controversy. Critics say these programs do not encourage children to learn English and are too expensive. In addition, critics charge that the growing number of immigrant children in school, and the growing number of languages, have strained the capabilities of the schools. Supporters counter that teaching children in their native languages until they have the chance to learn English eases the transition to a new society.

■ *This graph is called a population pyramid. It shows the percentage of men and women in various age groups. At what age do males outnumber females? How will the shape of the pyramid change as the number of older people increases?*

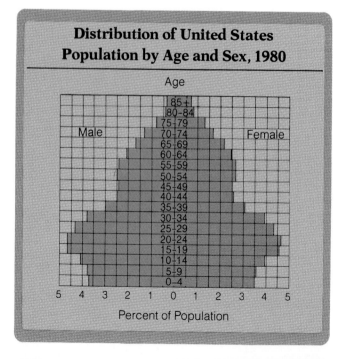

Distribution of United States Population by Age and Sex, 1980

Eventually, most new immigrants—old and young—learn English and adapt to American ways of life. The traditions they keep, however, have contributed to a unique American culture.

An Aging Population

If current trends continue, the nature of the country's population will be much different in the 1990s than it is today. One trend is slower population growth. Americans are marrying later and having fewer children. Throughout the 1970s the population increased by less than 1 percent a year. Some experts predict that by the year 2050 the United States will reach *zero population growth*. In other words, the population will stop increasing. The number of children born will equal the number of people who die in a given year.

In addition to growing more slowly, the population is becoming older. As fewer babies are born, the percentage of young people in the population drops. During the 1970s the number of children 14 years old and younger dropped by 11.5 percent. Experts predict that during the 1980s, teenagers will make up less than 30 percent of the population for the first time ever.

At the same time, the number of older people is growing as improved health care extends human life. In 1970 the median age of the population was about 28. That is, half of the population was older than 28 and half was younger. In 1983 the median age was 30.9. By 1990 it may be as high as 32 or 33. In addition, it is predicted that by 1990 one out of every eight Americans will be 65 years of age or older.

This aging population will have significant economic and social effects. If more people are in their thirties and forties, advertisers will aim their products at those age groups rather than at people in their teens or twenties. Eventually the proportion of people of working age will decline and the number of retired persons will increase more rapidly. This will put more pressure on the social security system, as fewer working people will be asked to support larger numbers of retired people.

Cities and Suburbs

By the end of the 1800s an increasing number of Americans were moving to the rapidly growing cities of the Northeast and Midwest.

That movement continued throughout the first half of the twentieth century. The United States, which had begun as a rural nation, became an urban one.

While some people were moving to cities, others began moving out of cities into suburbs. During the 1960s the population of suburbs increased by 27 percent while the population of the cities grew by only 6 percent. By 1970 more Americans lived in the suburbs than in cities and rural areas.

Suburbs grew in the 1970s, but the proportion of the population that lived in them dropped. In the 1990s suburbs will continue to grow but at an even slower rate than in the 1970s. Part of the suburban growth is due to an influx of black Americans. In 1970 less than 16 percent of Americans living in suburbs were black. By 1980 that figure had jumped to 23 percent.

The population of large cities—especially those in the Northeast and Midwest—declined in the 1970s and 1980s. For over 20 years, large cities have been plagued with rising unemployment as businesses and factories moved elsewhere. Poverty, decay, and crime have become characteristic of many urban areas that are losing middle-class residents. The 1980 census showed that cities had a higher poverty rate than rural areas.

Despite these problems, cities began to come back from decline. When the price of gasoline rose to new heights in the late 1970s and early 1980s, city living became more attractive than commuting. Moreover, many cities are undergoing massive facelifts as businesses and families seek an alternative to the suburbs.

During the 1984 election, political analysts discovered a voting group they termed young urban professionals. These "yuppies" were usually two-income families who found the joys of city life more attractive than suburban life. A new generation of younger Americans is repairing homes in once-blighted areas. "Urban homesteaders" are renovating factory lofts, waterfront warehouses, and old houses. Larimer Square in Denver, Georgetown in Washington, D.C., and the Upper West Side of Manhattan in New York City are only a few examples of city neighborhoods that residents are rebuilding. American cities may be on the threshold of a rebirth.

But small cities in economically depressed areas face continued hard times. In 1986 Congress ended the revenue-sharing

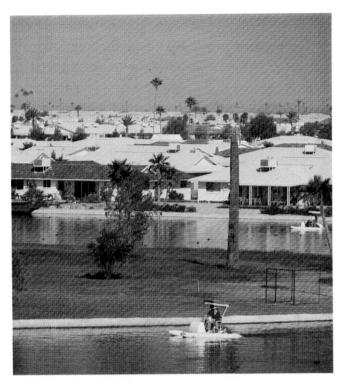

Sun City, Arizona, is a new kind of community designed for older people whose children are grown. Such communities, with golf courses and other recreational facilities, have become very popular.

program that in 14 years had poured $82 billion into communities throughout the country. Many cities used this money to pay for basic services such as police and fire departments. For cities without a growing tax base, the withdrawal of federal funds will hurt severely.

Rural America

During the 1970s a major shift in population movement occurred. For the first time since 1820, rural areas and small towns grew faster than metropolitan centers. Although some Americans returned to the cities, other Americans left to find jobs and a better quality of life. From 1970 to 1980 rural areas and small towns increased in population by 15.4 percent while the metropolitan areas increased by only 9.1 percent.

This increase came about despite the fact that there were fewer farmers. Improved transportation and communications made possible the relocation of business to small towns. High rents and taxes in cities have led many small businesses to relocate

Population Shifts Since 1950

Source: *Statistical Abstract of the United States*

■ *The desire to own a home led to an explosive growth of suburbs after World War II, but that growth has slowed in recent years. The percentage of people living in rural areas rose dramatically during the 1970s.*

Major Events

1977	Panama Canal treaties signed
1978	Camp David summit agreement signed
1979	United States recognizes People's Republic of China; SALT II signed; Iranians seize American hostages; Soviet Union invades Afghanistan
1980	Ronald Reagan elected president
1981	American hostages released from Iran; Reagan shot in assassination attempt; Sandra Day O'Connor appointed to Supreme Court
1982	Marines join international peacekeeping force in Lebanon
1983	United States invades Grenada
1985	Gramm-Rudman Act passed
1986	Reagan appoints William Rehnquist as Chief Justice of the Supreme Court and Antonin Scalia as an associate justice; tax reform bill passed

in less populated areas. Many advantages once found only in big cities were not available in towns.

In the 1980s, however, agricultural areas suffered from the crisis in farming. (See page 794.) Many businesses that depend on the agricultural sector of the economy have been adversely affected. The farm belt of the Midwest and South has seen bank failures and the bankruptcies of small businesses.

The Sunbelt and the Frostbelt

In the 1970s many people left northern and midwestern areas to move to the sunbelt, the name for the warm sunny states of the Southeast and Southwest. This westward movement of the population is a continuation of a historic trend.

The population of the western states has grown steadily since the Civil War. The population of the southern states generally decreased until the 1970s, when it began to grow dramatically. While the Northeast and

Midwest lost over 1 million people between 1970 and 1975, the South gained almost 2 million. During the 1970s the population of the West and South grew by 24 percent and 20 percent, respectively, almost twice the rate of growth of the country as a whole.

Forty percent of the population growth has occurred in three states: Texas, California, and Florida. (See the map on page 769.) Five sunbelt cities—Los Angeles, Dallas, San Diego, Houston, and San Antonio—now rank among the nation's ten largest cities. As a result of the move to the sunbelt, northeastern and midwestern states, sometimes called the frostbelt, lost 17 congressional seats in 1982 to states in the South and West.

However, changing economic conditions in the mid-1980s hurt some regions of the sunbelt. The drop in the price of imported oil cut the need for domestic oil. Many of the oil producers in such sunbelt states as Texas and Oklahoma laid off employees. The oil capital of the sunbelt, Houston, thrived during the 1970s and early 1980s when oil prices were high. By late 1986, however, about 70,000 of Houston workers in energy-related industries had lost their jobs, causing a local unemployment rate of over 10 percent. The textile industry, long a mainstay of manufacturing activity in parts of the South, suffered a similar decline in the face of cheap imported textiles from the Far East.

At the same time, many cities in the frostbelt have made a strong comeback in the 1980s. The many fine universities in the Boston area have enabled that city to attract new high-tech industries. New York, on the brink of bankruptcy in the 1970s, thrived in the 1980s. Its role as a world banking and financial center was strengthened by the rise in international trade.

SECTION REVIEW

1. Identify: sunbelt, frostbelt.
2. Define: bilingual education, zero population growth.
3. What groups of people have predominated in the immigration of the 1970s and 1980s?
4. How has the median age in the United States changed in the last twenty years?
5. How did changing economic conditions in the mid-1980s affect the sunbelt?
6. **Critical Thinking** Why do you think that immigration reform is such an emotional issue?

769

■ On this map you can see the distribution of population growth between 1970 and 1980. Which states lost population during this period? Explain why the map is titled "Move to the Sunbelt." Can you think of reasons why Alaska, which is outside the sunbelt, grew more than 30 percent in population during the period?

770

In Perspective

When Jimmy Carter became President in January 1977, he had high hopes that he could bring a fresh approach to the problems facing the nation. However, his position as an outsider made it difficult for him to work with Congress. Carter did play an important role in the successful conclusion of the Camp David agreement. Other parts of his foreign policy, however, created great controversy. The worsening economy and the hostage crisis in Iran contributed to Carter's defeat by Ronald Reagan in 1980.

During his first years in office, President Reagan introduced an economic program known as Reaganomics. Despite a deep recession, Reagan urged Congress and the American people to give his program time to work, and by the mid-1980s a recovery was underway. In his second term of office, Reagan focused on tax reform and reduction of the federal budget deficit. In foreign affairs Reagan took a firm stand in relations with the Soviet Union. With the election of a Congress dominated by Democrats in 1986, Reagan faced a challenge to some of his programs.

During the 1980s minority groups struggled to maintain gains made in the 1960s and 1970s and to develop new strategies. For many groups, the battles were being fought and progress was being made in the courts.

Immigrants from many lands have brought rich cultural traditions to American shores. Such traditions have helped make Americans a diverse people. In addition, the population has always seemed to be on the move, first from rural areas to cities and then to suburbs. Americans have migrated steadily westward, and more recently also to the South.

Vocabulary

Choose the answer that best completes each of the following sentences.

1. The people whom a representative represents are (a) colleagues; (b) constituents; (c) incumbents.

2. Equal payment for jobs requiring equally valuable but different skills is payment on the base of (a) comparable worth; (b) minimum wage; (c) fair labor standards.

3. The education of mentally or physically handicapped students with nonhandicapped students is called (a) individualized instruction; (b) group instruction; (c) mainstreaming.

4. The refusal to own stock in a company doing business in South Africa is called (a) apartheid; (b) deregulation; (c) divestiture.

5. The point at which the number of deaths in a society matches the number of births is (a) zero population growth; (b) population equalization; (c) gross national growth.

6. The education of students using their native language and English is (a) complementary education; (b) bilingual education; (c) secondary instruction.

Chapter Checkup

1. (a) Describe President Carter's relationship with Congress. (b) Why did this relationship develop? (c) What were the consequences of this relationship?

2. Describe the controversies surrounding each of the following aspects of Jimmy Carter's foreign policy: (a) human rights, (b) Panama Canal treaties, (c) recognition of the People's Republic of China, (d) ratification of SALT II.

3. How did the revolution in Iran affect the United States?

4. (a) What did President Reagan consider the major domestic problems of the nation when he first took office? (b) How did he deal with them?

5. Describe President Reagan's foreign policy toward (a) the Middle East, (b) Latin America, (c) South Africa.

6. What gains have women made in recent years?

7. (a) How did the case of the *Regents of the University of California* v. *Bakke* affect

the principle of affirmative action? (b) How did the case of the *United States* v. *Paradise* affect the principle of affirmative action?

8. How has the pattern of immigration to the United States changed since 1965?

9. What will some of the economic and social effects of a gradually aging population be?

10. (a) In what way is the movement to the sunbelt a continuation of a traditional movement? (b) What circumstances have led to the renewal of some older cities?

771

Critical Thinking

1. **Comparing**   Compare Ronald Reagan's response to the recession of the early 1980s with Franklin D. Roosevelt's response to the Great Depression of the early 1930s. (See Chapters 32 and 33.) (a) How did the basic approach of the two Presidents differ? (b) What developments of the past 50 years might help explain why their approaches were different?

2. **Analyzing**   How can policies of the federal government affect the direction in which society develops?

Developing Basic Skills

1. **Graph Reading**   Study the graph on page 750 and answer the following questions: (a) What was the unemployment rate in 1977? (b) In what year was the unemployment rate lowest? (c) In what year was the inflation rate highest? (d) During what period did the United States suffer from rising unemployment and rising inflation? (e) What generalization about the economy between 1980 and 1982 can you make from the information on the graph?

2. **Relating Past to Present**   Make a list of the foreign policy problems faced by the United States during the 1970s and 1980s. Compare these problems with the issues facing the United States after World War II. (See pages 667–682.) What are the similarities and differences between the two periods?

3. **Analyzing a Cartoon**   Study the cartoon on page 747. Then answer the following questions: (a) What event is portrayed in the cartoon? (b) What do the names on the tank represent? (c) What nations does the cartoonist indicate are in danger? (d) How would you describe the cartoonist's attitude toward Soviet foreign policy?

See page 833 for suggested readings.

Writer's Handbook

Creating a Graph

A chart or a graph can present a great deal of information clearly in a limited amount of space. You may find it useful to develop a graph to illustrate a research paper when you have statistical data that support your thesis. The most common types of graphs are circle graphs, line graphs, and bar graphs. Circle graphs show the relationship of a part to a whole. Bar graphs and line graphs are useful to show comparisons and change over a period of time. The choice of the type of graph you use depends on the information you want to display and the impact that you want to make.

Practice: Use the following table of federal debt from 1977 to 1986 to create a graph that shows trends in the federal debt. Figures are in millions of dollars (add 000,000).

Year	Millions of Dollars	Year	Millions of Dollars
1977	709,138	1982	1,146,987
1978	780,425	1983	1,381,886
1979	833,751	1984	1,576,748
1980	914,317	1985	1,841,853
1981	1,003,941	1986	2,073,864

Source: Office of Budget and Management

Speak American

What do the following words all have in common: *honcho, A-OK,* and *byte?*

The answer is that they are all relatively new words added to the English language by Americans. Honcho ("He's the head honcho on the day shift") was originally a Japanese term meaning squad leader. It was taken up by the Americans who occupied Japan after World War II. A-OK became popular in the 1960s, when astronauts assured launch commanders that their systems were "All okay." Byte, a product of the computer era, refers to a piece of data stored.

These are only three examples from the "recent history" of American English. Indeed, languages have histories every bit as rich as the histories of nations. Before the Normans invaded England in 1066 A.D., people in England spoke Anglo-Saxon, a Germanic tongue. After the conquest, English men and women adopted many French words. Most short English words, like *can, get,* and *hit,* come from Anglo-Saxon. Longer words, like *civilization* and *communication,* come from French. Century after century, the language grew. Today, some 80 percent of all English words can be traced to other languages.

In America, English developed even more quickly. For example, settlers adopted many Native American terms. *Raccoon, moose, squash,* and *pecan* are all Indian terms. So are *canoe, moccasin,* and *toboggan.* And the number of the place names taken from Indian languages is staggering. More than half of the 50 states have Native American names, from Massachusetts and Connecticut to the Dakotas and Hawaii.

American English did not develop simply by borrowing words. In sprawling, decentralized America, many local variations in language sprang up. The process began almost immediately in the colonies. In New York a youngster might get wet feet in a *kill* (Catskill), in New England, in a brook (Seabrook), in Virginia, in a *run* (Bull Run), and in a *creek* almost anywhere else.

By the 1800s the United States was known as the seedbed of hundreds of new words. Purists objected to the new terms. As one English magazine put it, "If the pure well of English is to remain undefiled, no Yankee should be allowed henceforth to throw mud into it." But Thomas Jefferson had recognized long before that the "new circumstances" in America called "for new words, new phrases, and the transfer of old words to new objects." Jefferson himself coined a word, *belittle,* which is still used today, although snobbish English critics of his day belittled the contribution!

Local regions have contributed their own phrases. When miners in the far West

---

As this menu board in a French cafe shows, English has absorbed words from other languages and other languages have adopted English words.

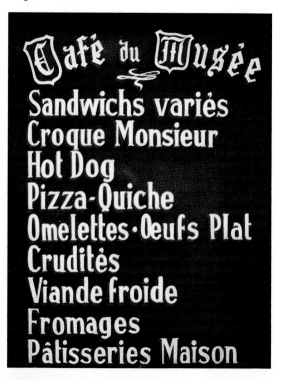

Café du Musée
Sandwichs variés
Croque Monsieur
Hot Dog
Pizza-Quiche
Omelettes·Oeufs Plat
Crudités
Viande froide
Fromages
Pâtisseries Maison

Many words such as skunk, tomahawk, *and* igloo *were adopted from Native American languages by early settlers.*

found a site that "panned out," they rushed to "stake a claim." Lumberjacks in the Pacific northwest used the term *backlog* for timber waiting to be shipped. Today *backlog* means unfinished work. In New England in the early twentieth century, Moxie was a popular soft drink. Soon, if a person had "moxie," it meant that he or she had the courage or pluck needed in difficult situations.

Contributions of Immigrants The mix of people in America also gave rise to new words. Immigrants brought with them many phrases that are now a part of our language. In fact, the word *immigrate* itself is American and was first used in 1789. Spanish-speaking people, who today make up the largest linguistic minority in the United States, have contributed more words to American English than has any other group. Spanish gave us the words we use when we take a stroll on the *plaza*, run for cover from a *tornado*, or witness a *stampede* of *mustangs*. The French language is the source of familiar words like *depot*, *dimes* and *cents*, *chowder*, and *gopher*.

Each group of immigrants added their own terms. Dutch Americans ate *coleslaw*, *cookies*, and *waffles*. They thought that

wild stories were *poppycock*, even if the story was told by their *boss*. German Americans asked for the *check* when they paid the bill at their local *delicatessen*, told *hoodlums* to *scram*, sent their children to *kindergarten*, and said *phooey!* Italian immigrants contributed words like *pizza*, *macaroni*, *ravioli*, *broccoli*, and *zucchini* to American cuisine as well as musical terms like *opera*, *virtuoso*, and *allegro*. Yiddish-speaking Jews from eastern Europe called a sentimental play or movie *schmaltzy* and said that shoddy merchandise was *schlock*.

Contributions of Blacks Black Americans have given many words to the language as well. *Okra* and *gumbo* are found on many menus. And most people know what it means to *bad-mouth* someone. But perhaps the most striking contribution is the terminology that is used for the different kinds of music black Americans pioneered. Black *spirituals* were first spoken of widely in the 1860s, *blues* in the 1870s, followed by *ragtime* in 1890s, *jazz* at the turn of the century, *boogie woogie* in the 1920s, *jitterbug* in the 1940s, *rhythm and blues* in the 1950s, and *soul music* in the 1960s. In the 1980s, *rap music* was originated by black groups.

The growth of American English shows no signs of slowing. Critics will no doubt try to keep it from running too far afield, as they have for hundreds of years. (Even in the 1660s, the English essayist Jonathan Swift complained of the "Enthusiastick Jargon" creeping into the language.) Some new words will be abandoned as passing fads; others will remain. But "speaking American" will always involve words drawn from all backgrounds and all walks of life. As the poet Walt Whitman observed, English is not "an abstract construction of dictionary makers," but a language that has "its basis broad and low, close to the ground." In that sense it has always been a democratic language, a language of the people.

1. What are some of the ways that new words are introduced into American English?
2. How does American English exempl[...] American society?

American Profiles

S.I. Hayakawa

Language has been important to S.I. Hayakawa as a student, teacher, and author. It has also been important to him as a citizen concerned with the quality and effectiveness of public communication.

Hayakawa, the son of Japanese immigrants, was born in Canada in 1906. After earning his undergraduate and graduate degrees in English Literature in Canada, he studied for his doctorate at the University of Wisconsin.

During the 1930s, Hayakawa recognized the role propaganda was playing in the rise of dictatorships in Europe. He analyzed how dictators were twisting words to mold public opinion. For example, Hitler's use of the innocent-sounding word "resettlement" masked the movement of Jews into concentration camps.

Hayakawa wanted Americans to be able to detect superstition, propaganda, and faulty reasoning in what they read and heard. He set out to make people aware of how words can be used and abused. Scholars had studied the meaning and use of words but Hayakawa brought the discussion from the lecture hall to the living room. In 1941, he published *Language in Action*—a book on language for the every-day reader. The book was an immediate success. Extensively revised in 1949 as *Language in Thought and Action*, Hayakawa's book has remained in print for over forty years.

Except for brief periods as a college president and United States senator, Hayakawa has devoted most of his adult life to teaching and writing about language. Even in his eighties, he has remained outspoken on the topic of public communication. In recent years this interest has embroiled him in the controversy over bilingualism.

Hayakawa is the honorary chairman of *U.S. English*, a group that seeks a constitutional amendment establishing English as the country's official language. He has stated, "We can speak any language we want at the dinner table, but English is the language of public discourses, of the marketplace, and of the voting booth." He argues that enabling people to avoid learning English denies them the full opportunities of American life.

Hayakawa's critics believe that a law making English the official language is unnecessary and is an insult to Americans whose home language is not English. Opponents of the law think it is unnecessary because non-English speakers are well aware that they must be able to speak English in order to better their economic situation. According to one Hispanic leader, "If you don't speak English, you're a dishwasher."

Former Senator S. I. Hayakawa (1906–) has devoted years to the study of semantics, or the meaning of words.

Although Hayakawa's ideas about bilingualism are controversial, they have contributed to the public debate on language. His writings on communication have increased our knowledge of the use and abuse of language for political ends.

1. What did Hayakawa hope to accomplish with *Language and Thought in Action*?
2. Do you agree or disagree with Hayakawa's views on establishing English as the country's official language? Explain your answer.

Voices of Freedom

Public and Private Language

Richard Rodriguez, a writer and lecturer, grew up in California, the son of Mexican immigrant parents. At home his family spoke in Spanish, but he recognized the need to learn English also. In the following excerpt from his autobiography, Rodriguez described his first days in an English-speaking school.

I remember to start with that day in Sacramento—a California now nearly thirty years past—when I first entered a classroom, able to understand some fifty stray English words.

The nun said in a friendly but oddly impersonal voice, "Boys and girls, this is Richard Rodriguez." (I heard her sound out: *Rich-heard Road-ree-guess.*) It was the first time I had heard anyone name me in English. "Richard," the nun repeated more slowly, writing my name down in her black leather book. . . .

Memory teaches me what I know of these matters; the boy reminds the adult. I was a bilingual child, . . . the son of working-class parents, both Mexican immigrants. . . . In public, my father and mother spoke a hesitant, accented, not always grammatical English. And they would have to strain—their bodies tense—to catch the sense of what was rapidly said by *los gringos*. At home they spoke Spanish. . . . The words would come quickly, with ease. Conveyed through those sounds was the pleasing, soothing, consoling reminder of being at home.

I learned my first words of English overhearing my parents speak to strangers.

At five years of age, I knew just enough English for my mother to trust me on errands to stores one block away. No more.

I was a listening child, careful to hear the different sounds of Spanish and English. . . . First, there were English (gringo) sounds. So many words were still unknown that when the butcher or the lady at the drugstore said something to me, exotic polysyllabic sounds would bloom in the midst of their sentences. Often, the speech of people in public seemed to be very loud, booming with confidence. The man behind the counter would literally ask, "What can I do for you?" But by being so firm and so clear, the sound of his voice said that he was a *gringo;* he belonged in public society.

But then there was Spanish. *Español:* my family's language. *Español:* the language that seemed to me a private language. I'd hear strangers on the radio and in the Mexican Catholic church across town speaking in Spanish, but I couldn't really believe that Spanish was a public language, like English. . . . Spanish seemed to be the language of home. . . . It became the language of joyful return.

From *Hunger of Memory* by Richard Rodriguez. Copyright © 1982 by Richard Rodriguez. Reprinted by permission of David R. Godine, Publisher.

1. Why does Rodriguez view Spanish as a private language?
2. What does he consider to be the essential importance of English in a bilingual family?

The United States: 41
Today and Tomorrow

A view of the earth from an Apollo flight

As the Apollo astronauts viewed the earth from their ship, they were awed by its beauty against the deep background of space. Photographs of that view inspired millions of Americans. The United States had crossed the threshold of outer space.

The American people have changed the face of the nation over hundreds of years. As the nation has expanded, its government and economy have grown.

Over the course of the nation's history, an increasing proportion of Americans have gained access to political rights and economic opportunities. The history of United States relations with other nations has been one of growing involvement. At home and abroad, economic, social, and political changes will continue to challenge American ingenuity.

Growing foreign economic competition

1950	1960	1970	1980	PRESENT
	1960s Peace Corps created to aid underdeveloped countries	**1970s** Oil crisis increases rate of inflation and trade deficit	**1971** 26th Amendment gives vote to 18-year-olds	**1980s** Use of computers expands; minorities make political gains

1 Advances in Science and Technology

Americans have long looked to science and technology to improve the quality of life. Advances in medical research, computer technology, and communications will continue to affect the way Americans live and work. The factories, offices, and homes of the future may be increasingly operated by machines. New video and computer devices will link Americans to vast networks of information, news, and entertainment as the home becomes a center for both work and recreation.

Toward a Healthier Life

Throughout the twentieth century improvements in nutrition, public sanitation, and medical care have extended life expectancy. Americans born in 1920 could expect to live about 54 years. Americans born in 1980 can reasonably hope to live about 74 years.

Medical researchers have contributed to this trend by finding ways to control or prevent many devastating diseases. Smallpox, once a great killer, has been virtually eliminated around the world. Vaccines have reduced the incidence of such childhood menaces as polio and measles. Antibiotics offer doctors additional weapons to combat many types of infections. However, overuse of some antibiotics has created superstrains of bacteria resistant to treatment.

Genetic engineering promises major advances for medicine and industry. Increasingly, scientists are able to alter the genetic codes of cells to eliminate diseases or produce new materials. For example, they have inserted human genes into bacteria to produce insulin, needed by millions of diabetics. Future genetic research may provide keys to eliminating diabetes and other diseases.

Advances in technology have also affected medical treatment. Microsurgery is now used successfully to reattach severed limbs. The development of nylon thread so fine that it can pierce a human hair is expected to speed the spread of microsurgery. Computer-assisted X-ray scanning can—with small risk—create pictures of areas inside the brain and other organs. The use of computers to help paraplegics gain muscle control is in the experimental stage.

Electronic devices have been developed to assist or replace the body's own organs. For example, pacemakers regulate the rhythm of irregular heartbeats. Dialysis machines cleanse the blood of patients whose kidneys have failed. In December 1982 surgeons implanted an artificial heart in Barney Clark who was dying from heart failure. With the artificial heart, Clark lived until March 1983.

Synthetic materials such as plastic and stainless steel are now widely used to repair damaged parts of the body. Doctors can replace knees, hips, and other joints crippled by arthritis.

The frontiers of medicine continued to expand. In the late-1980s, medical researchers were testing such devices as artificial skin grown in the laboratory, an artificial pancreas that would allow the body to produce its own supply of insulin, and an artificial

■ *Medical advances such as the development of vaccines have increased the number of years most Americans live. In 1900 the average person lived to age 47. Today average life expectancy is about 74 years of age. One result of this trend is a rising percentage of older people in the population.*

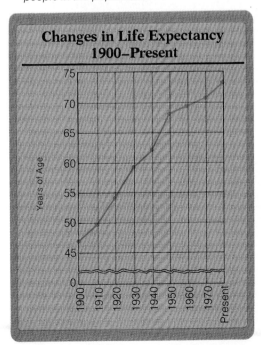

Changes in Life Expectancy 1900–Present

Source: *Statistical Abstract of the United States* and *Historical Statistics of the United States* eye that would be connected to the brain with electrodes.

The progress of medical technology has created problems as well. Medical advances have contributed to rising medical costs. In 1963 a hospital stay cost about $35 a day. By the early 1980s, that cost had soared to $250 a day.

In addition, some people felt that while medical technology might extend life, it did not improve the quality of life. The projected increase in the percentage of older citizens means that the need for nursing homes will probably increase greatly in the future. Such care is costly, and experts fear that government Medicare and Medicaid programs will be severely strained.

The Computer Age

In the past American families reminisced about the day they got their first telephone, first car, or first television. The generation of the 1980s will most likely ask, "Remember when we got our first computer?" As computers become smaller, less expensive, and more adaptable, they will become as common as televisions in American homes.

Computers are electronic machines that do calculations such as simple addition and computations involving complex numbers and logic. They are also used to assemble, store, process, and reproduce information. Computer programmers design programs that instruct the machines how to code or decode the information the user requests.

The computers of the 1950s were bulky and slow by today's standards. Such ma-

chines might fill several large rooms, require separate air conditioning systems, and cost millions of dollars. By using transistors and tiny silicon circuit chips instead of vacuum tubes, engineers made computers smaller, cheaper, and faster. Some personal computers that sold for under $3,000 in the late 1980s were more powerful than the million-dollar machines of 20 years earlier. Computers for home use dropped in price to under $1000. In 1984 alone, Americans bought nearly 15,000,000 computers for home use or business work stations.

A device called a modem can connect a computer through telephone lines to any similarly equipped computer. Home computers can link people to businesses, schools, and libraries. Consumers of the future may never have to leave home to go shopping. Letters and newspapers may be sent and received through computer networks. Some handicapped people are already using computers to take college courses.

In the 1980s a generations of computers for home and office was designed to be "user friendly." The machines could teach their operators how to make them work. This development would spark an even more explosive growth in the application of computers.

The uses of computer-based technology in factories and offices are extensive. By the mid-1980s factories were in operation in which computer-controlled robots did almost all the manufacturing. Computers ordered and shipped parts automatically. Computers also perform office tasks such as record keeping, inventory control, payroll accounting, and billing.

Banks are rapidly increasing their use of electronic funds transfer systems (EFTS). These replace the use of paper transfer documents, such as checks. Bankers predict that by the year 2000, we will have a "cashless society," in which people pay for all transactions with credit cards that immediately transfer funds from their bank accounts to pay for purchases. EFTS are less costly than paper-based systems, but they are vulnerable to abuse by persons who know how to use the system.

In areas where the work is repetitive or dangerous, computers have been a real benefit. This means, however, that machines do jobs that people once performed. Today's worker must adjust to a job market in which computers play an increasingly important role. One expert estimates that by 1990 com-

Computers have a wide variety of uses today. This student is using the computer to display a visual image of a football player.

puter skills will be necessary for up to 75 percent of all American jobs. Thus, workers will find it important to be "computer literate."

The Challenge of the Computer Age

Despite the many benefits of computers, some people view the computer age uneasily. Computer scientists are working on the development of "artificial intelligence"—programs that will allow computers to make deductions, draw inferences, and solve problems. Some people find the idea that a computer could "think" frightening. Experts point out, however, that it is humans who design and write the programs for computers. They say that the computer should be regarded as a powerful tool that will permit greater human progress.

Without advances in computer technology the United States could not have sent satellites or people into space. Yet those same advances have made modern weapons far more accurate and destructive than any before them. As new applications have been developed for computers, people have found that the benefits have not been without cost. Advertisers use computerized systems to bombard homes with huge quantities of unsolicited junk mail. Machines can automatically dial phone numbers and play prerecorded messages. Consumers have found that mistakes in computer-generated bills can be extremely frustrating to correct.

Are computers a threat to privacy? More and more information about people's personal lives is stored in computers. That information could be used to help or hurt people. In an emergency a doctor would have immediate access to a patient's medical history. But that same information in the wrong hands could be abused.

How safe are computer records? In the movie *War Games*, a teen-age computer expert begins by tapping into his school's computer to change his grades. Later, he gains entry into a Defense Department computer by using a modem and his personal computer, and accidentally nearly triggers a nuclear war. This was fiction, but in real life computer "hackers," or expert hobbyists, have entered business computers thought to be "protected" against invaders. Because computer technology is so new, there are few laws against such activity. The problem

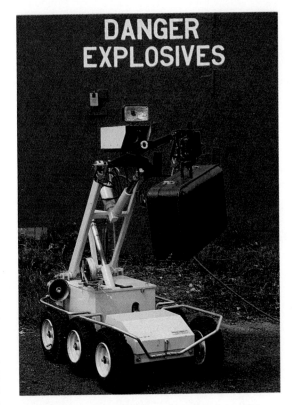

Law enforcement agencies use robots to assist their bomb squads. Robots can take risks that would be unacceptable for humans.

is likely to increase as more people have their own computers.

The computer age is just dawning. No one can say how far the computer revolution will go or what its long-term consequences may be. Sociologist Daniel Bell has argued that the new machines of the 1800s, such as the railroad and telephone, changed lives far more than the computer will. However, one of the pioneers of the computer revolution argues that computers, like many innovations, offer "unbounded possibilities for good and for evil."

Space Technology

The development of computer technology has made a crucial contribution to the success of the American space program. Computers helped design almost all the equipment and then allowed the engineers to make sure it worked properly. The millions of calculations that go into operating a space-bound rocket and determining its course could not be made without computer aid.

In most ways, the American space program has been a scientific triumph. Commu-

In 1984, for the first time, astronauts were able to move about outside the space shuttle without a tether. Bruce McCandless is shown here testing the jet-powered back pack a few yards from the shuttle. The earth is in the background.

nications satellites launched by *Columbia* transmit television signals around the globe. A space telescope launched in 1983 permits scientists to scan parts of the universe previously beyond human vision. Two unmanned Voyager spacecraft launched in 1977 are also providing a glimpse of the far reaches of the solar system by sending back pictures of the outer planets. *Voyager 1* came within 78,000 miles of Saturn in November 1980 and sent back clear pictures of the planet's rings. *Voyager 2* came even closer to the planet, passing within 63,000 miles in August 1981. The spacecraft took photographs and gathered information about Saturn, its moons, and its breathtaking series of rings. *Voyager 2* passed near Uranus in 1986 and will reach Neptune in 1989. After that, *Voyager 2*, which is carrying artifacts representing life on Earth, will leave the solar system to visit unknown parts of the universe.

For space experiments closer to Earth, NASA decided to concentrate its resources on a reusable space shuttle. Huge rockets took the shuttle into orbit. The small passenger-carrying shuttlecraft had enough power to carry it back to Earth and land much like an airplane. By the mid-1980s, the space shuttle was making regular trips into space.

The space shuttle program worked successfully for more than twenty missions after the first one went into space in April 1981. In 1985, United States Senator Jake Garn became the first civilian to fly on a shuttle mission. Then, on January 28, 1986, with millions of Americans watching on television, the space shuttle *Challenger* exploded just after leaving the launch pad. All seven passengers, including Christa McAuliffe, a New Hampshire social studies teacher, died in the accident. An investigation into the engineering of the space shuttle and the decision-making process at NASA led to important changes. The argument over the wisdom of concentrating United States space efforts on passenger flights resumed.

Laser Technology

In the 1930s and 1940s science fiction writers described such future weapons as ray guns. These weapons would shoot beams of light rather than bullets. Today, the laser has brought that vision close to reality. The term was coined in 1957 when scientist Gordon Gould created a device for Light Amplification by Stimulated Emission of Radiation (LASER). Lasers create intense light of a narrow range of wavelengths.

Lasers, like computers, have the potential for good and evil. Lasers used in medicine are so precise they can burn away diseased tissue without harming the healthy tissue around it. Their high heat seals off incisions with a minimum of bleeding. In the future, they may also be used for bone surgery. Lasers powerful enough to cut bone would make cleaner cuts, without the vibrations or tiny particles left by a saw.

Military planners are also examining the possible uses of lasers. Both the United States and the Soviet Union are experimenting with many military applications. The Strategic Defense Initiative involves the placement of laser guns on satellites orbiting the earth to destroy missiles. Experimental weapons using laser beams to destroy distant targets had been developed by the early 1980s.

Lasers are already part of everyday life. Most people are familiar with the black bar code on many packages. Lasers connected to computers read those codes to provide cashiers with the price and inventory number. In modern factories, gas torches have given way to cleaner and more powerful lasers that cut and weld metals.

The use of lasers promises to revolutionize entertainment. The newest stereo equipment uses lasers rather than a needle or stylus to play records. Video discs for television operate on a similar system. Lasers can be used to create stunning visual effects, as in many recent science fiction movies.

Lasers also have great potential use in the field of communications. Electronic messages can be sent by amplified light over flexible glass fiber wires called fiber-optic cables. These cables have many advantages over copper wires. They are far cheaper to make and install. Since they are much thinner, many more messages can be carried using the same amount of space.

In the future lasers will be tied in to computer-based communications systems. Fiber optics will make it practical to transmit the vast amounts of data stored by computer systems. Eventually, fiber optics may be used within computers themselves. The result would be machines that are even smaller, faster, and more powerful than those in use today.

The Information Age

Advances in computer technology and satellite communications have helped create a new age of information. By the late 1980s, many homes will be equipped to serve as information centers. The video cassette recorder (VCR) has made it possible for people to record programs and view them at their own convenience or rent or buy programs

★ Arts in America ★

The Making of *Star Wars*

The making of *Star Wars*, a fantasy film about a faraway galaxy, involved a blend of creativity and sophisticated computer technology. The result, for those who have seen *Star Wars* and its sequels, *The Empire Strikes Back* and *Return of the Jedi*, is a lifelike creation of a world inhabited by strange-looking creatures and technologically advanced machines. The sound, light, and action sequences represent significant achievements for the filmmakers and the standard against which future action films will be judged.

For the battle sequences in *Star Wars*, especially the final attack on the Death Star, the film crew created a special camera linked to a computer that recorded and memorized every shot. By consulting the camera's memory, new elements could be added to each scene.

To create the realistic look of many spacecraft swooping around each other, George Lucas, the director of *Star Wars*, spliced together footage of old war movies. After studying this film carefully, he used the special camera with computer memory to superimpose as many as twelve different pieces of film on one another to capture the right look.

With the money he earned from *Star Wars*, Lucas built one of the world's largest sound stages and a state-of-the-art special effects studio. His studio invented a $500,000 machine called a quad printer that contains four projectors each holding a separate piece of film. For *The Empire Strikes Back* the quad printer was used to film the voyage of the *Milennium Falcon* through an asteroid field. One of the projectors showed film of the *Falcon*, another showed the asteroids, another, the stars, and the fourth, shadows and laser beams. All four bits of film were projected through a prism that combined them into one seamless piece. A computer synchronized the four film sequences.

Techniques such as those used in science fiction films are revolutionizing filmmaking. Many of the techniques are used in other movies and even in television commercials.

and develop a home library of movies and features. Since the mid-1970s, cable television systems in many parts of the country have provided viewers with a greater variety of programs than ever before.

Some cable systems carry local government meetings and telephone talk shows that permit viewers to question their elected officials. Others contain special hookups that allow viewers to respond to questions posed over the air. Some have referred to this device as an electronic town meeting. In the future, cable systems will increasingly include means for two-way communication so that viewers can take part in television programs as well as watch them.

New technology has also revolutionized the way information is gathered. Many news organizations and business corporations are linked electronically to their offices around the world. News and information are spread almost instantaneously across the country and around the globe. Space satellites gather information about natural disasters or events such as the Chernobyl nuclear accident. The information is then broadcast within hours around the globe. The rapid increase in the amount of data available has created what has been called an information explosion. New scientific discoveries no longer take years to become generally known. Researchers and scientists have vastly more information to work with than ever before in history. The great difficulty in coping with the information explosion is in assembling all the available information to make practical use of it. Here, too, the computer has been a great aid.

SECTION REVIEW

1. Identify: EFTS, *Voyager 1*, *Voyager 2*, laser, VCR.
2. Describe three recent medical advances.
3. How are computers changing banking procedures?
4. How may lasers change the communications field?
5. **Critical Thinking** Do you agree with Daniel Bell that the new machines of the 1800s changed lives far more than the computer will? Explain.

2 Examining Social Issues

As the nation made material and scientific progress during the late 1970s and 1980s, questions about social issues increasingly became part of political debate. There was a general sense that the nation needed to return to more traditional values. Some Americans looked to their political leaders for help in guiding the nation in returning to these values.

Traditional American Values

In the 1960s there were great changes in the social structure of this country. Many advances were made in civil rights for groups that had long been the victims of discrimination. At the same time, there was a shift in what kind of behavior was considered acceptable by some people.

Dress and hairstyles reflected a growing interest in expressing one's individuality. People born in the "baby boom" of the post-World War II years were now becoming teen-agers. They created a youth culture with its own music, styles, and sense of proper behavior. From this era emerged the hippie who rejected society's rules. Protest against the Vietnam War added to a growing reluctance among many young people to follow the traditional leaders of society. Many of those who protested against the war rebelled against the standards of society as well. The Watergate scandal of the 1970s further eroded some people's confidence in their leaders.

As the 1970s progressed, however, many young people rejected the issues and youth culture of the sixties. They became preoccupied with individual material concerns. In the late 1970s, some observers created the term "the me generation" for the young people who abandoned political and social idealism in favor of a concern with self.

Some people felt that the search for inner values had given way to a new wave of materialism. The yuppie, the young urban professional who appeared less concerned with social or political action, seemed to

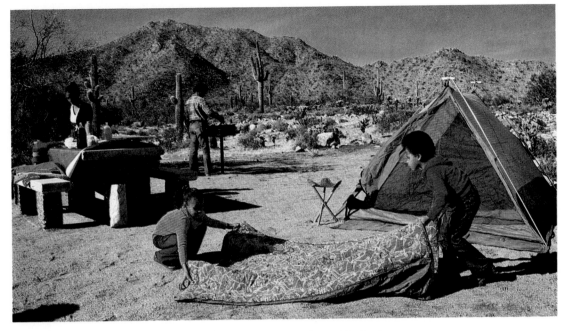

As society becomes more complex and more women work outside the home, families value vacation time spent together. Camping has become an increasingly popular family activity.

symbolize the era. Some people felt that the trend in the country was toward a life of material satisfaction. As a result, many people called for a renewed dedication to patriotism, loyalty, concern for others, and other traditional American values.

In the 1980s there was a general sense that the nation needed to return to those traditional American values. Reflecting the activities of religious groups in civil rights campaigns of the 1950s and 1960s, many churches today are becoming increasingly involved in the political process. Many religious groups now campaign for issues they believe are important and support candidates who favor their views.

One problem in dealing with such issues is that the United States is a pluralistic society with many different religious beliefs. Americans have long been proud of the Constitutional guarantee of freedom of religion. The federal government has usually steered away from religious matters. Members of some religious groups fear that their rights will suffer if values become a political issue. Many argue that values should remain a matter for the family and the churches. Others reply that many actions of government inevitably affect values.

In general, Americans agree that a sense of moral value is an important strength of society. A strong sense of values gives meaning and purpose to people's lives. There must be some common agreement on right and wrong behavior for a society to function effectively. On the other hand, conflicts over values cause tensions within the society. Conflict occurs when people feel that government action interferes with their personal values. Solving this conflict without limiting freedom of belief is a challenge that will face the nation in the years to come.

The Family

One institution that many Americans felt needed support was the family. Between 1960 and 1984, the divorce rate more than doubled. As a result single-parent families, usually headed by women, now make up over 10 percent of all households. They often face severe economic strain as a result of having only one wage earner. Another effect of the growing divorce rate is the so-called *blended family*. This family combines the children of more than one marriage into one household.

A recent development has been a large increase in the rate of illegitimacy. Teen-age pregnancy is a growing problem. It is predicted that one out of ten girls from 13 to 19 will become pregnant before she is married.

The illegitimacy rate in the United States is one of the highest among industrialized nations.

In addition, the increasing role of women in the workplace has had an effect on the family. The inflation of the 1970s, and the rise in single-parent families meant that more women returned to work. In some cases, this trend has been balanced by fathers playing a greater role in raising children than in the past.

The changing family has created a need for non-parental child care. Day care centers, where children are cared for from infancy through school age, have mushroomed throughout the country. Many question whether day-care centers or live-in baby sitters can provide for children's needs as effectively as parents can. Family life has always been the source of children's intellectual growth and sense of values. In addition, day care is expensive and some government programs that aided day-care centers have been cut.

Increased attention has focused on the quality of American education. In 1979 Congress created the cabinet-level Department of Education.

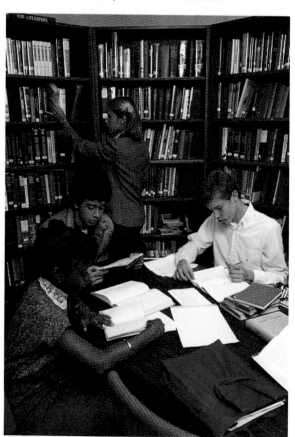

Many children are left on their own while parents work. Known as "latchkey children" because they are given the key to the home, they often have no supervision at all, even at a very young age. People are beginning to ask, "Who will raise our children?" No one really knows for sure what effects these changes in child care will have on society.

In recognition of these issues, President Carter called a White House Conference on the Family. Experts discussed the problems of the family and what could be done about them. They concluded that the population of families with the mother staying at home and taking care of the children would continue to decline. Many Americans oppose this trend feeling that the proper role of mothers is to raise their children. This view is opposed by many others who feel that society assigns childbearing and homemaking a status inferior to that of careers outside the home.

Some businesses have tried to accommodate women workers by granting maternity leaves or by establishing day-care centers within the workplace. But the pressures of career and parenthood have resulted in many disputes that have found their way into the courts.

The Education System

In the 1950s, after the Soviet Union launched *Sputnik I*, critics blamed the schools for the Soviet lead in the space race. Americans called for better education in science and mathematics. In the early 1980s concerns about the schools surfaced again. Some critics claimed that the nation's public schools had not done their job. Many claimed that this was a result of the lowering of standards in the 1960s when some nontraditional subjects were added to the curriculum. Today, the call for a return to traditional values in society is reflected in a demand that schools "return to basics."

In 1983 the U.S. Department of Education issued a report on the nation's educational system. Titled "A Nation at Risk," the report stated, "If an unfriendly power had attempted to impose on America the mediocre educational performance that exists today, we might well have viewed it as an act of war." The Department of Education recommended increasing the amount of time spent in school and increasing the number of required courses in such basic subjects as English, mathematics, science, and social studies. William J. Bennett, Secretary of Education, endorsed these proposals and called for more emphasis on moral training.

State legislatures and boards of education have responded to the criticism. In many states, the school year has been lengthened. In addition, the number of required courses has been increased. Many states have established competency exams as a requirement for graduation from high school. Many school districts refuse to allow students to participate in athletic programs unless they maintain satisfactory grades.

Overlooked in some of the criticism is the fact that more children are staying in school than ever before. About two-thirds of those who would have dropped out in the 1950s are now enrolled in school. The decline in student performance on standardized tests reflects this increase in the number of people being tested. When the top 9 percent of American students were compared with similar groups from other countries, the Americans held their own. Some reports have been particularly critical of the quality of science and mathematics education in the schools. Yet the scientific training in American colleges and universities draws students from all over the world.

The quality of the education system is crucial to the workings of a democratic society. The political system of the United States rests on the notion that a citizen is capable of making important decisions. The ideal of a democracy is the informed citizen. Without citizens who can understand the issues, the survival and strength of a democracy are threatened. As a result, the condition of the nation's education system will continue to be an important concern.

The Drug Crisis

Drugs have long been a problem in American society. Abuse of such substances as marijuana, heroin, and cocaine is not a new phenomenon. But their widespread use has created a major drug crisis.

Drug use is costly to society. In 1986, the government estimated that lost productivity from employee drug use amounted to $33 billion. Many feared that drug use might hamper the performance of such people as airline pilots and air traffic controllers. About one-third of the country's major cor-

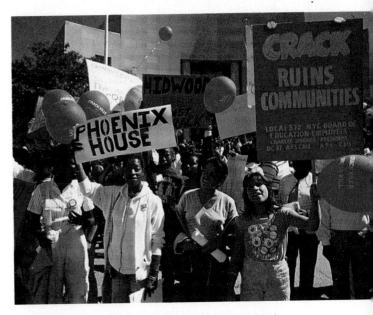

The rapid spread of the use of crack has galvanized communities into action. Concerned people have signalled their intolerance for drug abuse.

porations instituted some form of drug testing for their employees. The federal budget for drug enforcement nearly doubled from 1982 to 1986. However, money appropriated for drug treatment declined sharply in the same period.

By 1986, the drug crisis was attracting increased public attention. One reason for the greater concern with drugs was the appearance of a highly addictive form of cocaine known as *crack*. The use of this powerful drug was becoming widespread in such cities as Los Angeles, Houston, Miami, and New York.

President Reagan called for a "national crusade" against drugs. He and his wife, Nancy, made a televised appeal urging Americans to "Just Say No" to drugs.

Another serious concern is the spread of the disease known as Acquired Immune Deficiency Syndrome, or AIDS, which cripples the body's ability to fight off infection. AIDS is caused by a virus for which there is currently no cure nor means of immunization against its spread. Concerned parents, community leaders, and health care professionals are at work trying to educate young people and citizens at large who may be at risk. AIDS can be contracted through sexual contact with an infected partner or by using contaminated needles while taking drugs. As research continues into the control and prevention of AIDS, the disease is being treated as a serious public health problem.

SECTION REVIEW

1. Define: blended family, crack.

2. How has family life in the United States changed in the past 20 years?

3. What changes in education did "A Nation at Risk" recommend?

4. **Critical Thinking** Why is the dispute over values such a difficult one in a pluralistic society?

3 Governing a Growing Nation

The federal government has grown dramatically over the course of the nation's history. During the first years of the new nation, federal expenditures were just over $4,000 a year. In 1980 they were an estimated $690 billion, and in 1984 that figure increased to an estimated $997 billion. In other words, the federal government spends money at the rate of over $2.5 billion a day. The growth of expenditures reflects the growth of the role of the federal government. As the nation changed from an agricultural to an industrial nation, the role of the federal government expanded.

■ *Since World War II the total number of government jobs has increased dramatically. As the chart shows, the increase has been sharpest in local government employment.*

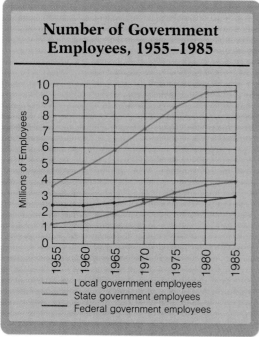

Number of Government Employees, 1955–1985

Millions of Employees

----- Local government employees
----- State government employees
—— Federal government employees

Source: U.S. Bureau of the Census

The Role of Government

Today hundreds of government agencies oversee and regulate aspects of the national economy. Government regulations affect nearly every aspect of American life, from the content of hot dogs to the air quality in textile mills. The regulations affect the food Americans eat, the clothes they wear, the cars they drive, and their work environment. Industry often passes on the costs of following regulations to consumers by raising prices.

During the late 1970s some of the regulatory agencies came under attack. Critics cited the existence of millions of regulations that required vast amounts of time, money, and paperwork to follow. While many people believe that some regulation is necessary to protect the public interest, they argue that the benefits of many regulations do not justify the expense of meeting their requirements. President Reagan shares this view.

During the past 50 years Americans have come to expect many services from their governments at the local, state, and national levels. For example, unemployment insurance protects people who lose their jobs. Social Security provides a guaranteed income for retired workers and their families. Governments build and maintain roads, mass transit systems, water purification plants, and airports.

Many such services were once provided only by private agencies and local governments. Until the 1930s few people believed the federal government should play a major role in providing social services. However, since then its role has grown tremendously. In 1929 the federal government spent $625 million on social programs. By 1939 that figure had grown to $3 billion, and in 1982

786

federal expenditures on social services amounted to $340 billion. From 1967 to 1982 the price tag of federal benefits programs increased from about 27 percent of the total federal budget to an estimated 49 percent. In addition to funding its own programs, the federal government has paid about one quarter of all expenditures by state and local governments. However, in 1986 Congress stopped the federal grants program for states and localities.

Many Americans have become increasingly concerned about the cost of government in the United States. Some groups have organized successful protests against rising state taxes. The most important of these efforts was Proposition 13 in California. Protesting taxpayers forced a cut in state taxes in the late 1970s. Similar actions have resulted in cuts in state budgets and services. Nationally, a proposed constitutional amendment requiring a balanced budget has gained some support. Such an amendment, its supporters say, would rein in congressional spending and taxation.

The election of President Reagan spurred the discussion of the role of the federal government in American life. Reagan believed that the federal government could not do some tasks as efficiently as private groups could. He called for greater investment by private concerns in some of the traditional welfare programs. He believed that by taking greater sums of money from individuals, the federal government hurt the private economy on which the wealth of the nation depends.

Special Interest Groups

The growth of government social programs created large groups of people who were interested in encouraging the government to continue these programs. For example, recipients of Social Security are directly affected by congressional decisions regarding the program. They, and people with similar interests, have banded together to make their positions known in Washington. These people, called *special interest groups*, often

■ These graphs show two ways of looking at federal spending. The circle graph at left shows how federal funds were allocated in 1983. The bar graph at right traces the increase in federal expenditures from 1930 to 1980. The Vietnam War and inflation were major reasons for the steep increase in the 1970s.

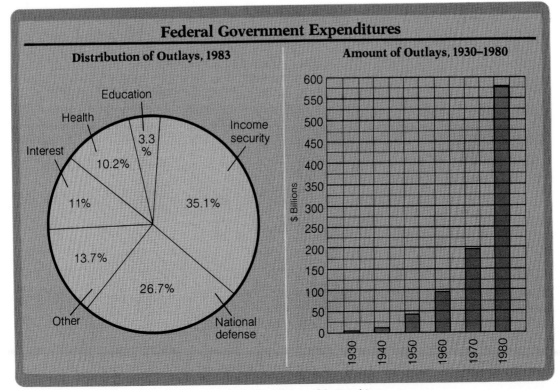

Federal Government Expenditures

Distribution of Outlays, 1983

Education, Health, Interest, Income security, National defense, Other — 3.3%, 10.2%, 11%, 35.1%, 13.7%, 26.7%

Amount of Outlays, 1930–1980

Source: *Historical Statistics of the United States* and *Statistical Abstract of the United States* work directly to influence the legislators or government officials who can affect their programs.

The growth of special interest groups is a political development that has caused concern among some people. Some critics feel that these groups are rarely interested in compromise or in more than one issue. Critics are concerned that the tactics of special interest groups, such as letter writing campaigns and demonstrations, may earn them more than their share of attention. Elected officials may feel that they cannot afford to ignore the demands of pressure groups.

But there is another side of the coin. Special interest groups serve a purpose in a democracy. They galvanize people into action and more often than not balance each other out. By bringing attention to an issue, they focus public interest and encourage debate. When special interest groups do not stir opposition, they probably reflect the national consensus on an issue.

Elections and the Media

Television has revolutionized the political process. Because campaign managers must develop strategies geared to television in order to be successful, television influences how candidates present the issues. A thoughtful, well-reasoned comment is less likely to be reported on television than a quick slogan or "photo opportunity" that will fit into the television news broadcast.

Candidates spend the bulk of their campaign budgets on television advertisements developed by media experts. Traditional campaigns, in which the candidate tried to appear in person before as many people as possible, are less efficient than television appearances and commercials. Recognizing the powerful influence of the media, many campaigners now engage in televised debates. In some large states, statewide political campaigns are conducted almost entirely on television.

Other technological developments have changed elections. Public opinion polls have become more accurate and sophisticated through the use of computers. A modern candidate polls prospective voters on all the major issues. Polling experts can use the computer to determine what different groups of voters feel about a given issue. Some candidates then fit their message to the audience they are addressing. The computer has enabled candidates to pinpoint accurately the interests and views of a given audience.

These developments have made the cost of campaigns much greater. Many modern candidates spend the bulk of their time doing nothing but raising funds. Restrictions have been placed on the amount of money that a presidential candidate can receive from a single individual. But for state and local elections there are fewer campaign spending limits. Some political observers feel that the trend toward expensive campaigns can influence the issues that are raised and keep qualified people out of politics because they do not have the economic resources to run a major campaign.

Political Parties Today

Television and other technology have weakened the traditional political parties. Since the Civil War, the Republican and Democratic parties have been the central factors in American politics. They survived by building coalitions of interest groups which cooperated to win elections. Many people identified with one or the other party and often voted for the party, rather than the individual. Today, television allows candidates to appeal to the voters over the head of the political parties. The long-time role of political parties as an intermediary between the candidates and the electorate is less important. As a result loyalty to political parties is weaker than it was in the past. Many candidates today proudly announce their independence from the positions of either party.

The victory of Ronald Reagan was a major boost for the Republican Party. The Democratic party coalition between labor, urban ethnic groups, minorities, and intellectuals, established by Franklin Roosevelt, has gradually weakened. Although more voters still identify themselves as Democrats, the Republican party is gaining. A 1986 Gallup poll showed that 32 percent of Americans supported the Republican party; 39 percent supported the Democratic party. As recently as 1979, Democrats had held a two-to-one advantage. Today in most elections, the independent voter holds the balance of power. Many candidates find it necessary to tailor their campaigns to appeal to independents who are interested in particular issues.

Blue-collar workers, usually union members, formerly voted overwhelmingly for the

Democratic party. In the 1984 election, many of these workers voted for Ronald Reagan, even though Walter Mondale had been a strong supporter of organized labor throughout his political career. Many workers liked the stronger defense stand taken by Reagan.

Third parties by and large have not been successful. There are none today that threaten to control a national election. Sometimes single-issue parties become important in local and state elections. So far none has drawn enough support to determine the results of a state-wide election.

Minorities in Government

As the minority population of the United States has increased—it is up 25 percent since 1960—more minority members have won positions in government, through election and appointment. Black Americans made dramatic gains in voting rights and have taken advantage of their new opportunities in politics. In Congress, the Black Caucus was formed in 1970 to strengthen the power of black Representatives. The caucus helped to mobilize support for the divestiture campaign against South Africa. Blacks are now commonly appointed as cabinet secretaries in all administrations. President Reagan appointed Samuel L. Pierce, Jr., to the post of Secretary of Housing and Urban Development.

In spite of the greater visibility of blacks at the national level, the most impressive gains have been at the state and local levels. In 1986 blacks held the position of mayor in some of the country's most important cities—Los Angeles, Chicago, Newark, Philadelphia, and Detroit. They have also demonstrated their political power by electing sheriffs and mayors of small towns in the South. Now that blacks hold a balance of power in the areas of the country where they are most numerous, they have much greater political influence.

Hispanic Americans, particularly those of Mexican and Cuban descent, made dramatic gains in the late 1970s and 1980s. The growing Cuban population of Miami elected a Cuban mayor in the 1980s, Xavier L. Suarez. Bob Martinez, whose grandparents came from Spain, was mayor of Tampa, Florida, and ran for governor of Florida in 1986. Mexican Americans have been politically successful throughout the Southwest. They have elected senators, and the mayor

Mayor Henry Cisneros (left) of San Antonio and Mayor Tom Bradley (right) of Los Angeles are among the growing number of elected minority officials.

of San Antonio, Texas, Henry Cisneros, won a national reputation for his administration of the city. Cisneros was one of the choices considered by Walter Mondale for his vice-presidential candidate.

Women have recently made great gains in political representation. The candidacy of Geraldine Ferraro for vice-president in 1984 reflected the growing strength of women in politics and government. In 1986, there were two women state governors, in Vermont and Kentucky. During the 1986 elections, six women ran for the United States Senate, and nine for governorships. Both major parties nominated women for governor of Nebraska. Women have also made great gains in city elections. Notable women mayors are Kathy Whitmire of Houston and Dianne Feinstein of San Francisco.

Increasing numbers of women have held posts in the federal government. Jeane Kirkpatrick, President Reagan's appointee as Ambassador to the United Nations, played a very visible role in foreign-policy making, an area traditionally dominated by men.

Extending Voting Rights

From 13 states on the east coast, the United States has grown to 50 states that span a continent and extend into the Pacific. The population of the country has expanded from about 4 million to over 200 million. The government of the nation has also grown. Today government employs more people, spends

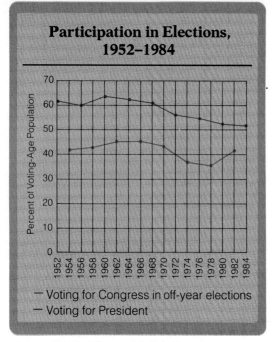

Participation in Elections, 1952–1984

Source: *Statistical Abstract of the United States*

- Voting for Congress in off-year elections
- Voting for President

■ *As you can see on this graph, more people vote in presidential elections than in elections when only members of Congress are being chosen.*

more money, and touches more lives than ever before. The people's role in government has also grown since the nation was founded.

In most of the colonies the right to vote was restricted to white male Protestant property owners. When the Constitution was ratified in 1789, the barriers of religion and property began to fall. By the 1830s most states had extended the vote to all adult white males.

The Fifteenth Amendment to the Constitution, ratified in 1870, stated that citizens could not be denied the right to vote on the basis of race. However, by the 1880s southern states were using devices to keep black citizens from voting. Voting rights legislation in the 1960s finally guaranteed the right to vote to all black Americans. The Twenty-fourth Amendment, ratified in 1964, outlawed the poll tax.

The long struggle for women's suffrage ended in 1920 when the states ratified the Nineteenth Amendment. The Twenty-sixth Amendment, ratified in 1971, guaranteed the right to vote to persons 18 years of age or older.

For the American political process, one of the most distressing developments since World War II has been the declining number of people who vote. Although a growing proportion of Americans has gained the right to vote, the percentage of eligible voters who take advantage of that right has declined significantly. For example, in the 1964 presidential election 62 percent of the electorate voted, while in 1980 only 53 percent went to the polls. Even fewer people participated in the congressional elections: 45 percent in 1966 compared to 35 percent in 1978. However, in the 1982 congressional elections this trend was reversed when the voter turnout reached 41 percent. Still, these figures are a cause for concern. In recent years, several attempts have been made to get more people to vote by simplifying the registration process. In some areas, citizens can register by mail. In others, volunteers set up registration tables on street corners or in shopping malls.

A More Direct Vote

As the right to vote has been extended, Americans have gained a more direct role in their government. The nation's founders limited the direct influence of the people. They believed that most people did not have the information or background needed to govern directly. Today books, radio, television, newspapers, and magazines provide a constant supply of information to American citizens.

In some states citizens can propose legislation in an initiative and vote on it directly in a referendum. In 1980 voters in 18 states and the District of Columbia placed a total of 42 issues on the ballot through initiative. In addition, voters in some states can remove officials from office by a recall election.

The initiative, referendum, and recall were introduced early in this century during the progressive era. That era also witnessed ratification of the Seventeenth Amendment to the Constitution, which called for the direct election of senators by the voters of each state. Today about half the states hold primary elections to select delegates to party nominating conventions, giving voters a more direct voice in selecting presidential candidates.

Although the direct influence of voters has increased during the past 100 years, Presidents continue to be chosen by the electoral college. Some people have proposed the direct election of the President, but opponents of the idea contend that such a method would give too much influence to densely populated areas of the nation. Continuation of the electoral college helps protect the interest of less populous areas.

SECTION REVIEW

1. Identify: Black Caucus.
2. Define: special interest groups.
3. Describe the political gains made by women in recent years.
4. What are two arguments in support of keeping the electoral college system?
5. **Critical Thinking** How are television and computer sources of benefit or harm in political campaigns?

4 A Land of Opportunity

The rich natural resources of North America and the industriousness of the American people have combined to create an economy of abundance unmatched in the rest of the world. Yet today, more Americans than ever are seeking a share of that abundance. Furthermore, other nations are competing vigorously for their own share of the world's business. These changing conditions are prompting new responses from the American people.

A Growing Economy

The United States with its rich supply of natural resources and long, navigable rivers has had an impressive history of economic growth. For decades manufacturing was the backbone of United States industrial strength. Although devastated by the Great Depression, the nation's economy emerged from World War II strong and vibrant, making the United States the world's leading economic power.

■ *The United States emerged from World War II with the world's strongest economy. One measure of economic strength is the gross national product (GNP). The GNP is the total dollar value of goods and services produced in a year. The growth of the GNP of the United States in the twentieth century is shown clearly on this graph.*

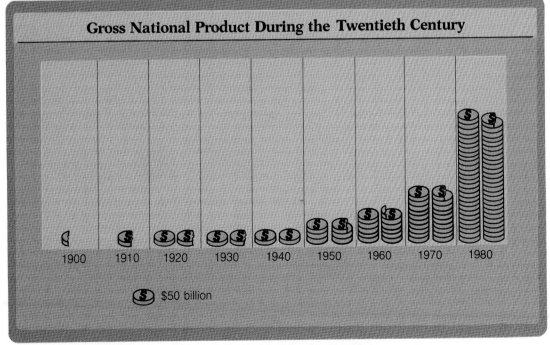

Gross National Product During the Twentieth Century

1900 1910 1920 1930 1940 1950 1960 1970 1980

$ $50 billion

Source: *Statistical Abstract of the United States* and *Historical Statistics of the United States*

The *gross national product* (GNP), the total dollar value of goods and services, has grown continually. From 1890 to 1970 the productivity of American workers more than quadrupled. In other words, a worker in 1970 produced four times as much dollar value per hour as did a worker in 1890.

As the variety and number of products available to Americans has increased, so has their income. From 1930 to 1980 the average real income of Americans tripled. From 1950 to 1980 the number of automobiles sold in the United States tripled. Today over 80 percent of American families own at least one car. Nearly all American families own a refrigerator and a television set, and the percentage who own VCRs, computers, and microwave ovens increases daily.

The basis of American economic strength has been changing in recent years. In the early twentieth century, the United States economy depended primarily on manufacturing. But in the last 50 years professions and service industries have increased in importance. During the 1960s, services overtook manufacturing as the major source of jobs. In the 1970s and 1980s American industry worked to maintain the clear-cut economic supremacy that it had enjoyed in the past. Although American manufacturing jobs were lost to overseas competition, millions of new jobs were being created at the same time in other areas of the economy. Government and industry have worked together to guarantee the economic health of the United States.

Industry Today

As the economy adapts to changing world conditions, American technology has once more met the demand for new products. These expanding industries have been dubbed the sunrise industries. They make up about 30 percent of current American manufacturing. Among these industries, high-technology manufacturing has had the greatest success despite competition from abroad.

High-technology industries, such as computers, have seen the rise of the entrepreneur as a major force in business. In contrast to the manager who is an employee of the corporation in which he or she works, the entrepreneur is self-employed and more likely to take risks. Many of the new products available on the market today have been pioneered as a result of the industry

and innovation of relatively small companies.

In contrast, basic smokestack industries such as automobiles and steel have declined. These industries have had greater difficulty dealing with stiff foreign competition. Cars made in Japan, West Germany, and other nations are a common sight on American streets. Even steel is now imported into the United States.

Maintaining Competitiveness

According to many economists, one key to strengthening the American economy is to increase *productivity*, that is, the output per hour of work. Although American productivity is increasing, the rate of increase has been slower than the rate of increase in Japan and some European countries. As a result, American products are more costly to produce and are less competitive on the world market.

Other factors have also contributed to the ability of foreign companies to sell their products for a lower price than American-made products. In some cases, foreign companies sell their products in the United States for less than it costs to produce them. This practice, known as dumping, is used to gain a foothold in certain industries. The United States government has tried to discourage dumping by monitoring the prices charged by foreign countries. In some countries, a foreign government subsidizes key industries, allowing companies to sell without making a profit.

A variety of approaches have been taken by American industry to reduce the impact of foreign competition. Some companies have tried to increase productivity by investing in new plants and equipment. They have also experimented with giving workers a larger role in solving on-the-job problems. Plant managers have found that as workers gain more responsibility they are less likely to be absent from their jobs. Businesses are also experimenting with more flexible working schedules, including job sharing, longer vacations, and a four-day workweek.

The United States government has also taken action. It has tried to reach agreements with foreign governments to restrict the quantity of foreign products that can be sold in the United States. For example, by an informal agreement with Japan, the number of Japanese cars exported to the United

States has been limited. Sterner measures have also been proposed. Some officials favor imposing tariffs on imported goods to raise their prices. Another proposal would require foreign cars sold in this country to have a specific percentage of American-made parts. The issue of what measures to take has sparked heated public debate.

A Changing Work Force

As the professional fields and service industries continue their rapid expansion, jobs are opening for people who do not produce goods. They are such workers as lawyers, teachers, doctors, nurses, computer programmers, and auto workers. Today about nine out of every ten jobs created are service or technical in nature. The need for people to service new sophisticated machinery has also created an important area of growth.

The service industries have created a demand for highly skilled people. Computers and other technological advances have transformed many jobs in the office and on the assembly line. The work force of the future will be more flexible than in the past. For those with skills, the job market will offer a greater variety of jobs throughout a worker's lifetime.

Labor and the Economy

A number of factors affect the rate of unemployment in the nation. One of these factors is that American workers compete with workers all over the world. Steelworkers compete for jobs with their counterparts in such countries as Japan. Even businesses based in the United States sometimes have their manufacturing work done abroad. Many products made with American parts are assembled by workers in Japan, South Korea, and Mexico. In recent years, this has led to calls for greater action by the federal government to protect the jobs of American workers. Congress has introduced legislation that would protect workers in key industries, but opposition has delayed enactment of these bills into law.

During the recession in 1982, national unemployment reached the level of 10 million persons. Much of this unemployment was the direct result of the recession. As the demand for products declined, many plants were closed and workers laid off. By the mid-1980s, however, economic conditions

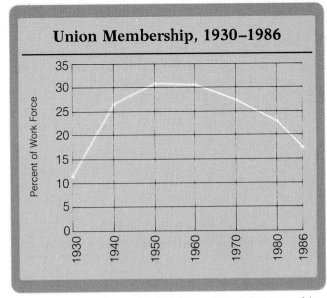

Source: *Statistical Abstract of the United States, Historical Statistics of the United States,* and U.S. Bureau of Labor Statistics

■ *Membership in labor unions has not grown as fast as the labor force. In fact, the percentage of the work force in unions has dropped in recent years, as this graph shows.*

had improved, and the unemployment rate had declined to about 7 percent. However, many available jobs remain unfilled because unemployed workers did not have the necessary skills. To put as many people to work as possible, government, industry, and educational institutions have been spending about $40 billion a year to retrain workers. One of the economic tasks of the future will be to devise new approaches to matching workers with available jobs.

Labor Unions Adjust to Change

Labor unions have had to face changes in industry in recent years. The strength of the labor movement has been in those industries that have been buffeted by competition from abroad. Auto and steel workers were strongly unionized, while white-collar workers were not. Many new job openings are for white-collar workers. Traditionally these people have been less attracted toward the union movement than have blue-collar industrial workers.

Membership in labor unions has declined since the 1950s. Then over 30 percent of the labor force was unionized. By 1985, labor union membership made up only 18 percent of the work force. This loss of numbers results in a loss of political and economic influence.

793

In recent years, some unions have not been able to get the kind of contract terms that they got in the past. Instead, particularly in heavy manufacturing industries, new contracts have sometimes included *givebacks*. These are previously won benefits that are now reduced or eliminated.

But unions are meeting these new conditions. Some unions have called for greater cooperation between management and labor. In an auto industry contract negotiation, the head of the auto workers' union was put on the board of directors of the automobile corporation. A push to organize workers in the expanding service industries is showing success. Greater emphasis is being placed on a new range of issues, such as working environment, flexible schedules, and maternity and child care leaves.

Agriculture in the United States

Until the late 1800s the United States was chiefly a farming nation. After the Civil War, manufacturing grew significantly and agriculture declined in economic importance. This trend continued into the twentieth century. By the 1980s less than 4 percent of the American work force was involved in agriculture. Yet farm production has increased significantly, partly as a result of the use of improved equipment, fertilizers, and pesticides.

The growth of productivity on the farm has not been accompanied by equal prosperity for farmers. On the contrary, many farmers have been forced off the farms because they cannot make a profit. Nearly 1 million jobs on farms and in rural businesses tied to agriculture have been lost since 1979.

The major reason for the farmer's dilemma has been that farmers are not able to match the supply of their product with the demand. When farmers have to make decisions on the amount of seed and fertilizer and the amount of acreage they will plant, they do not know what the price will be at harvest. If overall production is high, the price will be low and if production is low, then the price will be higher. In theory, if the farmers planted less, they would get a higher price for the amount that they grew. But from the point of view of the individual farmer, the risk of cutting back is greater than the potential benefits.

Government farm programs from the New Deal to the present have tried to deal with the problem of overproduction. In one type of program, the government promised support of a certain price level for particular crops. If the farmer's market price fell below that level, then the government would buy the crop at the higher price. In other programs, the government paid farmers of certain crops not to plant on some of their land. Through the years, this has not cut farm production enough, because developments in agriculture have brought greater yields per acre. The result has been a glut of farm products.

Agriculture in Crisis

In the 1970s, the Nixon administration agreed to sell a large amount of grain to the Soviet Union. This was a boon for the farm-

Farmers staged a protest in Washington, D.C. to focus attention on their plight. Increasing numbers of family farms have been lost due to debt.

ers, many of whom turned to the growing export trade. The 1970s were good years on most farms, as product prices rose along with the value of farmland. When petroleum prices rose, the federal government saw farm exports as vital to the economy. Government policy called for greater farm production, urging farmers to plant "fencerow to fencerow." Many farmers expanded their acreage and bought new equipment, often with borrowed money that they planned to repay out of future profits.

Then came the crunch. In 1980 the Carter administration placed an embargo on grain to the Soviet Union because of its invasion of Afghanistan. This occurred as interest rates were rising and the world economy was going into recession. Prices of farm products and land values fell, and the farmers were stuck with debt payments. Rising costs of farm equipment and fertilizer made the cost of producing grain higher than the price farmers received for grain. Many farmers were forced into bankruptcy because they could not pay their bills. At the same time exports to the less developed countries declined. These countries also had a debt problem (see page 798) and some had made efforts to develop their agriculture. Rural banks and businesses were also hard hit.

At first, the Reagan administration advocated phasing out price supports and subsidies. The goal of the Reagan administration was to make agriculture self-supporting. The administration urged farmers to pursue the export trade. When exports did not fill the needs of farmers for markets, the payment-in-kind program (PIK) was introduced in 1983. This program gave farmers grain from government storehouses in return for reduced plantings. This program was not successful since farmers worked the remaining land as intensively as possible. The federal government finally began subsidizing the farmers at the rate of $35 billion a year—far more than previous farm programs had cost.

Recent proposals have included plans that would place mandatory restrictions on farm production. One proposal calls for limits on both acreage and the number of bushels that could be sold. In return, the farmers would be guaranteed much higher prices. This proposal would raise the price of food at the supermarket by between 3 and 5 percent. Supporters compare this to the increased cost when the minimum wage of non-farm workers is raised. Others argue that the export trade for agriculture will improve and that such drastic controls will not be necessary. What there is agreement about is that agricultural policy must be adjusted to meet current needs.

A Healthy Living and Working Environment

One of the challenges facing Americans in the nation's third century is to maintain a balance between a healthy living environment and a healthy economy. The very abundance of American life has made that difficult.

Americans enjoy the freedom and convenience of owning and using their own automobiles. But the advantages are paid for with traffic jams and polluting exhaust. Growing communities are finding that their original plans for waste disposal cannot keep pace with expansion and development. They are searching for economical and environmentally sound ways to dispose of garbage and industrial waste, including radioactive wastes from nuclear power plants.

New scientific discoveries often benefit society, but some have had unexpected side effects. Some industrial chemicals, for example, have been linked to cancer and nerve disorders. Fumes, wastes, and chemicals can contaminate the air people breathe, the water they drink, and the food they eat. Chemical wastes containing powerful poisons have seeped into the water supply of communities, posing a grave health risk. In the cases of the contamination at Love Canal, New York, and Times Beach, Missouri, the towns had to be permanently evacuated. Emissions from oil- and coal-burning plants in the Ohio River Valley have fallen in the form of acid rain on New England and Canada, harming the forests, lakes, and wildlife of these areas.

Two events in other countries emphasized the dangers of ignoring environmental safeguards. In 1984, an accidental release of poison gas at a Union Carbide plant in Bhopal, India, killed thousands of people and blinded and wounded thousands more. The question after the tragedy was, "Could it happen here?"

In April 1986, a serious accident occurred in the Soviet Union. An explosion blew the roof off a nuclear reactor at a power plant in Chernobyl, near Kiev. Three seconds later a second blast shot a gigantic

Americans want to preserve the quality of their environment so that they can enjoy outdoor recreation. Bike riding saves gas and helps preserve air quality.

cloud of radioactive gas into the sky. The cloud drifted north across the Soviet Union and Europe. Winds spread lesser levels of the radioactivity around the world. Traces were detected as far away as the United States. The world's worst nuclear accident, Chernobyl contaminated hundreds of square miles of land and killed over thirty persons. Hundreds more were hospitalized indefinitely.

Federal Action

The search for a balance between the economic needs of a community and the need for a healthy environment has been a difficult one. The costs of a healthy environment are high, and difficult choices have to be made. How much risk is the country willing to run to produce needed chemicals? This has become an issue of intense debate in recent times. In the 1970s federal legislation set standards to ensure safe water and air. But some environmentalists have demanded that factories be required to follow even stricter antipollution requirements in order to protect the health of workers and local residents. Factory owners say that the measures already taken to protect the environment are sufficient. They contend that further regulations will not significantly improve environmental conditions, but will add to operating expenses. That, they argue, could increase the prices consumers pay for products and might even force plants to close. Consequently, some workers also oppose regulations they consider too strict.

Funding seems to have become the main stumbling block to environmental improvement. In 1980, Congress passed the Superfund Bill. This established a fund of over $1 billion to clean up extremely toxic wastes in targeted areas over a five-year period. The chemical companies that had done the polluting had to pay into this fund. When the fund expired, controversy over financing allowed the program to lapse. Then, in 1986, Congress passed a bill allotting another $9 billion to the Superfund. All corporations were to contribute to the fund. Though President Reagan opposed the proposal, he signed the bill after being assured that the corporation tax would not be used for other programs.

The continued growth of the American economy has depended on abundant natural resources. However, people are coming to realize that the supply of many resources is limited. The oil crises of the 1970s made this clear to many Americans. Practical limits require American industry and consumers to use resources efficiently and to find substitutes for those that are scarce.

SECTION REVIEW

1. Identify: sunrise industry, smokestack industry.

2. Define: gross national product, productivity, givebacks.

3. Which part of the work force has grown fastest over the last 50 years?

4. Explain why farmers were hard hit in the early 1980s.

5. What efforts have been made to make industries in the United States more competitive?

6. **Critical Thinking**   Why is it difficult to find a balance between a healthy living environment and a healthy economy?

5 The United States and the World

The world has become more interdependent. Political and economic developments in one area of the world affect other areas as nations compete in a changing world economy. Events thousands of miles away can affect the price Americans pay for sugar or oil, and events in the United States can affect the lives of people all over the world. This was not always the case, but the history of relations between the United States and the world has been one of growing involvement.

A Cautious New Nation

As part of the British Empire, the American colonies were closely tied to Europe. They could not avoid conflicts such as the French and Indian War. After 1783, however, the new nation hoped to stay out of European disputes. The early Presidents urged neutrality, but in 1812 the United States was drawn into a war with Great Britain. Following the war, the nation returned to its goal of avoiding involvement in European affairs.

The young republic was far from isolated, however. It expanded to the Pacific by treaties with France, Spain, and Britain and through a war with Mexico. Alaska was purchased from Russia. The United States also participated in world trade.

During the first half of the nineteenth century, the nation imported mostly manufactured goods and exported raw materials such as cotton and wood products. In 1830, for example, it exported $40 million worth of raw materials and only $5 million worth of manufactured products. That same year the United States imported $36 million worth of manufactured goods.

Toward World Leadership

Rapid industrialization after the Civil War contributed to a new world status for the United States. The country became a major producer of iron and steel, and it expanded its markets overseas. The value of United States exports rose from $845 million in 1890 to $2.3 billion in 1914. Almost one third of all exports in 1914 were manufactured goods.

American involvement in world politics also had increased by the end of the 1800s. President McKinley and his successors worked to protect American interests in Latin America, Asia, and Europe. The United States acquired an overseas empire, annexing Hawaii in 1898 and assuming control of several Spanish colonies after the Spanish-American War.

The United States reluctantly entered World War I in 1917 after attempts to remain neutral had failed. Following the war, Americans sought a return to peace, and for many that meant isolation from world events. However, aggression by Germany and Japan during the 1930s convinced national leaders to aid China and Britain. The United States entered World War II after the Japanese attack on Pearl Harbor in 1941 and emerged from the war as the most powerful nation—economically and militarily—in the world.

A Changing World Scene

As Japan and the nations of western Europe recovered from World War II, they entered a period of rapid economic growth. By the 1960s and 1970s they were competing successfully with the United States for world markets. Nevertheless, the United States remained unrivaled in the world for its output of goods and services. In 1980 the United States, with only 5.1 percent of the world's population, produced 21.3 percent of the world's goods.

■ *From the time of its emergence as a major industrial power, the United States has usually sold more goods to foreign countries than it has bought. On this chart you can trace imports and exports from 1900 to 1985. Note how the pattern shifted around 1970. As oil prices rose and the United States imported more petroleum, the cost of imports rose to record levels. At the same time, Japan and western Europe provided more competition for American companies selling products overseas.*

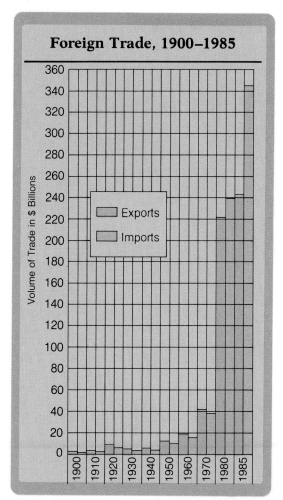

Foreign Trade, 1900–1985

Source: *Statistical Abstract of the United States, Historical Statistics of the United States,* and U.S. Department of Commerce

But a sharp rise in the cost of imported oil had a dramatic effect on the United States in the 1970s and 1980s. It not only showed Americans how dependent their country was on the world economy, but also affected the balance of trade. The *balance of trade* is the difference in value between imports and exports. In 1960 the United States had a trade surplus of $4.6 billion. By 1982 its trade deficit was about $44 billion.

Even after oil prices declined, the trade deficit keep increasing. Competition from foreign manufacturers contributed to this deficit.

United States officials met with representatives of Japan, Britain, France, and West Germany in 1985 to get help in bringing down the value of the dollar. The dollar had declined by 1987, but the trade deficit remained very high. Most experts believed it would remain so for the near future.

Problems of the Third World

Despite attempts to aid the poorer countries of the world, sometimes called the Third World, there has been an increasing gap between them and the more developed countries. The poverty of many Third World countries is tied to illiteracy and poor health conditions which hinder development. Events in these countries affect the economy of the United States and the lives of Americans. Third World nations are important markets for American products and are sources of raw materials important to the United States economy.

Many Third World countries were hard hit by higher oil prices in the 1970s. They borrowed large amounts of money from other governments and from banks in Europe and the United States. The world recession lowered demand for the minerals, metals, and farm products these nations export. Thus they found it difficult to pay their debts. If a nation *defaults*, or fails to pay its debts, the soundness of some major banks could be threatened. Economists worry that the failure of an important bank could trigger a worldwide financial panic.

To avoid this, international organizations have loaned money to developing countries at low interest rates. To get these loans, however, the recipient countries have had to agree to certain conditions. In some instances, financial institutions have insisted that government subsidies for such items as

Trends in American History: Forecasting Alternative Futures

In this chapter you have reviewed several trends in American history. But what lies ahead for the United States? Will the rate of technological change expand or will it slow down? Will the American people find a solution to the farm crisis? Will the United States maintain its economic position? These are just a few of the questions you might ask about the future.

While no one can predict exactly what will happen, you can forecast, or suggest, possible developments. Such forecasts can influence your decisions and actions in the present. For example, if you forecast that energy costs will continue to rise, you may decide to buy an energy-efficient automobile or a solar-heated house. Use the steps below to practice the skill of forecasting.

1. **Identify a trend.** Review this chapter and select one of the trends discussed. Write a paragraph in which you describe the trend in your own words.
2. **Project alternative future developments.** (a) What might happen if the trend continues? (b) What type of future events might change the trend? (c) How might each event affect the trend?
3. **Determine the likelihood of possible developments.** To complete this step use current news magazines, newspapers, and books. After researching the possible developments, decide which is most likely to occur and which is least likely to occur. Write a report explaining your conclusions about possible future developments.

food be dropped and prices be allowed to rise to their natural levels. Some American leaders have called for writing off, or forgiving, some of the debt and lowering interest rates.

Fashioning a Successful Foreign Policy

For many years after World War II, American foreign policy was primarily concerned with containing the growing power of the Soviet Union. The United States sent vast amounts of aid to western Europe and Japan to help rebuild their economies. It eventually extended aid to many Third World nations as well. Alliances such as NATO were aimed at checking Soviet expansion. By the 1980s, however, most Americans had come to realize that the world's economic and political balance was becoming increasingly complex.

Policy makers have found that classifying nations as pro-Soviet or pro-American is not as easy as it once was. Major powers such as China are pursuing independent courses, as are many smaller nations in Africa, Asia, and Latin America. Traditional American allies such as France and West Germany no longer automatically support American positions.

In addition, the system of alliances binds the United States to other countries. It must take into account the wishes and needs of its allies and friends when it makes decisions on foreign policy. For example, in arms talks with the Soviet Union, the United States has to consider the defense concerns of its European allies, who fear Soviet aggression. Keeping the alliance strong and united is one of the main foreign policy goals of the United States, and its leaders cannot normally make decisions that might weaken its relationship with Europe.

The relation of the United States and the United Nations is another concern. In its early years, the United States could command a majority in that organization to support its positions on different issues. With the addition of many new nations, this majority has disappeared. Because the United States often disagrees with the majority in the United Nations, there has been a loss of public support for the UN in the United States. In recent years, the United States cut back its annual financial contribution to the UN.

Peace Corps volunteers provide instruction in basic health practices in areas where there are few health care professionals. This volunteer is working in Senegal.

Finally, the United States government has to fashion a foreign policy that is domestically acceptable. This can be difficult. Conflicts often arise between Congress and the President over foreign policy. Since the Vietnam War, Congress has demanded a greater voice in foreign affairs. President Carter was unable to persuade the Senate to ratify SALT II, although it had been negotiated by both Republican and Democratic administrations. President Reagan has often faced congressional opposition to his policies in Central America.

A Tradition of Generosity

The United States has been generous in its aid to other countries. Recognizing the unique bounty of this nation, it has been part of the American tradition to give freely to less fortunate nations.

In the mid-1980s Americans became aware of the drought that was causing famine in sub-Saharan Africa. Hardest hit was the country of Ethiopia, ruled by a communist government. In spite of the government's hostility, Americans gave generously of money and food. Many citizens volunteered to help transport and distribute the aid. Moreover, the Reagan administration authorized the largest amount of aid by any single government.

Government agencies such as the Peace Corps, established during the administration of John F. Kennedy, have helped train Americans to go abroad to help in poorer countries. The Peace Corps has three major goals. It provides trained Americans to help people in developing countries. It tries to create a better impression of the United States throughout the world. Finally, by giving ordinary Americans a chance to work with those in other countries, it promotes a better understanding between peoples. Former members of the Peace Corps have recalled their experiences abroad as enriching ones. They have brought home a greater understanding of the world. Another program that began in the 1960s was Food for Peace. Through it, the United States has used its surplus food to help feed the hungry throughout the world.

A special financial agency that helps underdeveloped countries is the Agency for International Development (AID). This agency, part of the State Department, gives low-interest loans to projects that AID workers believe are particularly deserving of help. AID officials from the United States are found throughout the world.

This nation's tradition of generosity will continue through good times and bad. American generosity has had a positive impact on the lives of people throughout the world. One example of many is Nicholas Jacobs, who lives on the edge of the Kalahari Desert in Botswana. Unemployed in 1980, with only a seventh-grade education, Jacobs started a one-room shoe factory in 1983 with loans from the Botswana Development Bank. About half of the bank's funds had come from foreign aid from the United States. The aid has given Jacobs a chance for a more productive life. Multiplied many times, this use of American aid wins friends for the United States and creates a better world for all people to live in.

SECTION REVIEW

1. Define: balance of trade, default.
2. How did the United States balance of trade change between 1960 and 1982?
3. What was the primary concern of American foreign policy after World War II?
4. **Critical Thinking** Explain why it is so difficult today to fashion a successful foreign policy.

In Perspective

Advances in science and technology led to significant contributions in many fields, including medicine and communications. Computers have revolutionized both the work place and leisure time for many Americans. Satellites have helped locate deposits of scarce resources such as oil.

The 1980s witnessed a growing concern for traditional American values among people who were concerned with the apparent growth of materialism in society. The future of the traditional family was also examined. In the 1980s children were more likely to grow up in a single-parent household or in a blended family. Many children were being left on their own after school. The quality of education and the growth of drug use were other critical issues.

Over the years a growing proportion of the American population had gained the right to vote and acquired a more direct voice in government. The government itself had grown and become more involved in the economy and in the everyday lives of its citizens. The American economy of abundance had been challenged by foreign trade and by the need to balance economic growth and a healthy environment. Debts and changing market conditions strained American agriculture.

The United States role in world affairs had grown since the birth of the nation, despite strong sympathy for isolation during much of the nineteenth and part of the twentieth century. By the end of World War II the nation had become a major world power, and today it faces an increasingly complex world.

Vocabulary

On a separate piece of paper, write the word or words that best complete each of the following sentences.

1. Expert computer hobbyists are called ___.

2. A (An) ___ is a device for amplifying and concentrating light into a narrow beam.

3. ___ is a term used to identify a young city-dwelling professional.

4. A (An) ___ is a family in which there are children from more than one marriage.

5. ___ is a highly potent and highly addictive form of cocaine.

6. People with similar interests who band together to influence legislators are called a (an) ___.

7. ___ is the output of work per hour.

8. ___ are previously-won benefits that unions have had to give up in order to get new contracts.

9. The ___ is the difference in value between imports and exports.

10. A nation ___ when it fails to pay its debts.

Chapter Checkup

1. How have medical advances increased the life expectancy of Americans?

2. What is meant by the "computer age"?

3. Describe the two main components of the space program in the 1980s.

4. (a) What is one characteristic of a pluralistic society? (b) Why is it difficult to deal with issues relating to values in a pluralistic society?

5. (a) How have educators and the government responded to criticism that the schools were not preparing students for life? (b) What two issues were overlooked by critics?

6. How has President Reagan tried to change the role of the federal government?

7. (a) How has television affected how election campaigns are conducted? (b) How have computers affected election campaigns?

8. What factors have made it possible for foreign companies to compete with American industry?

9. (a) What are the problems facing farmers today? (b) What are some recent suggestions for programs to help the farmers?

10. How has the United States helped foreign nations to overcome economic and social problems?

Critical Thinking

1. **Analyzing** Few aspects of life today are unaffected by computers. How do you think computers will directly affect your life in the next ten years.

2. **Supporting an Opinion** (a) How does the federal government affect your daily life? (b) Do you think that government in the United States has grown too large? Why or why not?

Developing Basic Skills

1. **Ranking** List the challenges facing the United States during the 1980s and rank them from most to least important in your opinion. Then write an essay describing the possible consequences of not meeting the most important challenge.

2. **Reading Graphs** Study the circle graph on page 787. (a) What information is shown on the graph? (b) In what category does the government spend the most money? (c) What percentage of the budget does the government spend on defense? (d) If the national debt continues to rise, how will this graph change?

See page 833 for suggested readings.

Writer's Handbook

Typing the Final Draft

The appearance of a report is important because it reflects the care with which it was prepared. The following are general guidelines to follow when preparing a research paper. Of course, your teacher is the final authority.

Handwritten
Paper: Lined, white 8½" x 11"
           Ruled left margin
Text: Written or printed neatly
           in ink
           One side only
           Indent all paragraphs
           Single space
           Light corrections allowed

Typewritten
Paper: Unlined, white 8½" x 11"
Text: One side only
           Double space
           Margin settings—10 left
                          75 right
           5-space indent for paragraphs
           Single space and indent for
           longer quotations
               Margin settings—13 left
                              72 right
           Light corrections allowed

Wordprocessed:
Paper: Tractor guides removed
           Separated sheets
Text: Double-strike mode,
           if possible

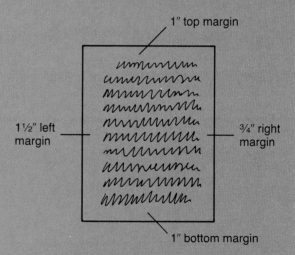

1" top margin

1½" left margin

¾" right margin

1" bottom margin

All pages should be numbered. Your last name should be written on each page. The sheets should be stapled, bound, or paper-clipped together.

Practice: Analyze a written or typed assignment that you have done. Note how it compares with the guidelines above. Write a brief paragraph explaining the reasons for these guidelines.

Reference Section

130°W   125°W   120°W   115°W   110°W   105°W   100°W

Pacific Time Zone

Mountain Time Zone

50°N

CANADA

Central Time Zone

45°N

Seattle • Spokane

★ Olympia

**WASHINGTON
1889**

Great Falls

Minot •

Grand Forks

**NORTH DAKOTA
1889**

• Portland

• Salem

• Eugene

Helena ★

**MONTANA
1889**

Billings •

Bismarck •

**OREGON
1859**

**IDAHO
1890**

★ Boise

Pocatello •

**WYOMING
1890**

Casper •

**SOUTH DAKOTA
1889**

Rapid City • ★ Pierre

Sioux Falls •

40°N

Ogden •

Great Salt Lake

★ Salt Lake City

Cheyenne ★

**NEBRASKA
1867**

• Reno

★ Carson City

**NEVADA
1864**

• Sacramento ★

San Francisco ★

• Oakland

• San Jose

**UTAH
1896**

Colorado Springs •

Denver ★

Lincoln ★

**COLORADO
1876**

**KANSAS
1861**

35°N

**CALIFORNIA
1850**

Las Vegas •

Wichita •

Long Beach •

Los Angeles •

San Diego •

PACIFIC OCEAN

**ARIZONA
1912**

★ Phoenix

★ Santa Fe

Albuquerque •

**NEW MEXICO
1912**

**OKLAHOMA
1907**

Oklahoma City •

30°N

Tucson •

Las Cruces •

El Paso •

Dallas •

Ft. Worth •

**TEXAS
1845**

Austin ★

120°W   115°W   110°W   105°W

San Antonio •

MEXICO

25°N

100°W

160°W   Hawaii–Aleutian Time Zone   155°W

Honolulu ★   **HAWAII
1959**

PACIFIC OCEAN

0   50   100 Miles

0   50 100 150 Kilometers

50°N   170°E

Hawaii–Aleutian Time Zone

PACIFIC OCEAN

180°   170°W   160°W   150°W

SOVIET UNION

Alaska Time Zone

70°N   140°W

Arctic Circle   130°W

Fairbanks •

**ALASKA
1959**

CANADA

Pacific Time Zone

60°N

BERING SEA

Anchorage •

Gulf of Alaska   Juneau ★

0   200   400 Miles

0   200   400   600 Kilometers

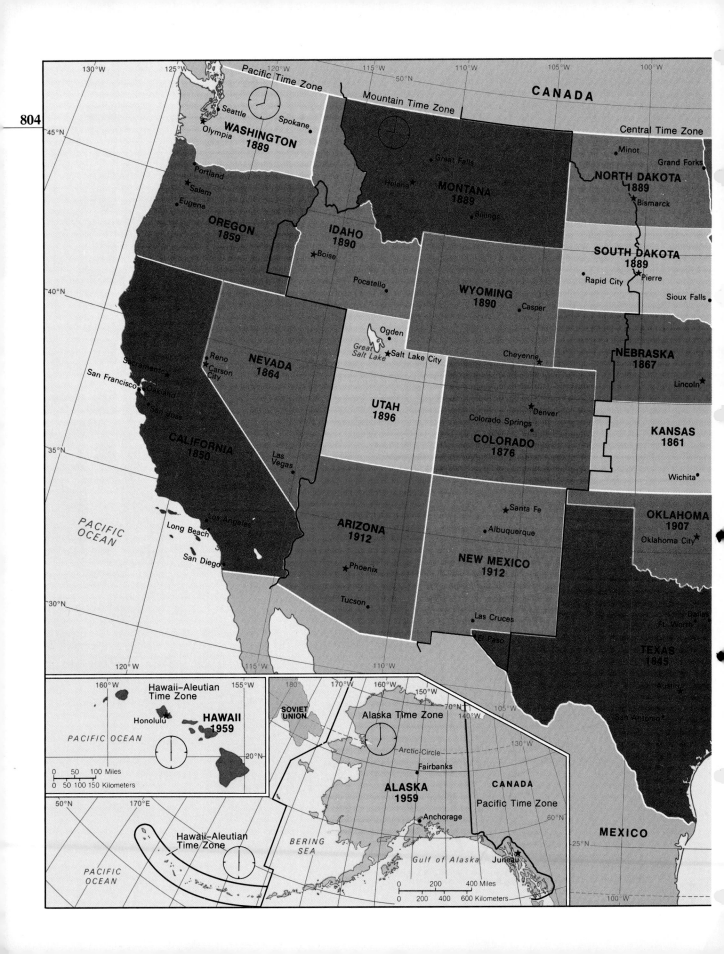

804

Pacific Time Zone

Mountain Time Zone

Central Time Zone

CANADA

WASHINGTON
1889

Seattle
Spokane
Olympia

OREGON
1859

Portland
Salem
Eugene

IDAHO
1890

Boise

Pocatello

MONTANA
1889

Great Falls
Helena
Billings

Great
Salt Lake

Ogden
Salt Lake City

WYOMING
1890

Casper

Cheyenne

NORTH DAKOTA
1889

Minot
Grand Forks
Bismarck

SOUTH DAKOTA
1889

Rapid City
Pierre
Sioux Falls

NEBRASKA
1867

Lincoln

NEVADA
1864

Reno
Carson
City

UTAH
1896

COLORADO
1876

Denver
Colorado Springs

KANSAS
1861

Wichita

Sacramento
San Francisco
Oakland
San Jose

CALIFORNIA
1850

Las
Vegas

Los Angeles
Long Beach
San Diego

PACIFIC
OCEAN

ARIZONA
1912

Phoenix

Tucson

NEW MEXICO
1912

Santa Fe
Albuquerque

Las Cruces
El Paso

OKLAHOMA
1907

Oklahoma City

TEXAS
1845

Dallas
Ft. Worth

Austin
San Antonio

MEXICO

Hawaii–Aleutian
Time Zone

HAWAII
1959

Honolulu

PACIFIC OCEAN

0   50   100 Miles
0 50 100 150 Kilometers

SOVIET
UNION

Alaska Time Zone

Arctic Circle

Fairbanks

ALASKA
1959

Anchorage

CANADA
Pacific Time Zone

BERING
SEA

Gulf of Alaska

Juneau

Hawaii–Aleutian
Time Zone

PACIFIC
OCEAN

0   200   400 Miles
0   200   400   600 Kilometers

Reference Section

807

The World

★ National capital

● Other city

| 0 | 500 | 1000 | 1500 | 2000 Miles |
| 0 | 1000 | 2000 | 3000 Kilometers |

OCEAN

ALASKA (U.S.)

Mackenzie

60°N

UNION OF SOVIET SOCIALIST REPUBLICS
(SOVIET UNION)

Lena

Ob

●Novosibirsk

Volga

ASIA

Ulan Bator★
MONGOLIA

Aleutian
Islands
(U.S.)

N. KOREA
Peking★ ●Pyongyang
Tientsin● ★Seoul
S. KOREA

JAPAN
★Tokyo

IRAN
AFGHANISTAN Kabul★ ●Islamabad
Tigris
Euphrates

New Delhi★
PAKISTAN

NEPAL BHUTAN
★ ★Thimphu
Kathmandu
BANGLADESH
Dacca★

CHINA

●Chungking
Huang

●Shanghai

★Taipei
TAIWAN

**NORTH
PACIFIC OCEAN**

Hawaii (U.S.)● 20°N

SAUDI
ARABIA

Calcutta●

INDIA
Bombay●

BURMA
Rangoon★

Mekong
★Hanoi
LAOS
●Vientiane
THAILAND VIETNAM
Bangkok★ KAMPUCHEA Manila●
(CAMBODIA) PHILIPPINES
★Phnom Penh
●Ho Chi Minh City

HONG
KONG
(U.K.)

SRI
LANKA
Colombo★
MALDIVES

BRUNEI

SOMALIA
★Mogadishu

KIRIBATI
NAURU

Equator 0°

SEYCHELLES

INDIAN OCEAN

Kuala Lumpur★ MALAYSIA
SINGAPORE

●Jakarta
INDONESIA

PAPUA
NEW GUINEA
★Port Moresby

SOLOMON
ISLANDS

TUVALU

COMORO
ISLANDS

MADAGASCAR
★Antananarivo

Reunion
(France) ●MAURITIUS

AUSTRALIA

VANUATU

New Caledonia
(France)

WESTERN
SAMOA

●FIJI

TONGA 20°S

SOUTH PACIFIC OCEAN

Adelaide● ●Canberra ●Sydney
★
●Melbourne

Wellington●
NEW
ZEALAND★

ANTARCTICA

MIDDLE EAST

| 0 | 500 | 1000 Miles |
| 0 | 500 | 1000 Kilometers |

ROMANIA
★Bucharest
BULGARIA
Tirane Sofia★ ●Istanbul
ALBANIA GREECE
★ TURKEY
Athens★ ★Ankara
TUNISIA
●Tunis
CYPRUS SYRIA
Beirut● ★Damascus
●Tripoli LEB. ★ ●Baghdad
Jerusalem IRAQ
★
Cairo★ ISRAEL JORDAN
★Amman

U.S.S.R.
(SOVIET UNION)

AFGHAN.

IRAN
●Tehran

LIBYA

EGYPT

RED SEA

KUWAIT
★
BAHRAIN
●Riyadh QATAR
SAUDI ARABIA ●Muscat
●Mecca U. ARAB
EMIR.

KWT.

OMAN

NIGER

CHAD
★Khartoum

●N'Djamena

SUDAN

P.D.R. OF
YEMEN
San'a
★
YEMEN
●Aden ●DJIBOUTI

ETHIOPIA
★Addis
Ababa

60°E 80°E 100°E 120°E 140°E 160°E 180° 160°W 140°W 120°W 100°W

Physical Features

CAPE COD

Long Island

Chesapeake Bay

CAPE HATTERAS

APPALACHIAN MOUNTAINS

ATLANTIC COASTAL PLAIN

Lake Ontario

Lake Erie

Lake Huron

Lake Michigan

Lake Superior

INTERIOR

PLAINS

OZARK
PLATEAU

OUACHITA MTS.

GULF
COASTAL
PLAIN

GREAT

PLAINS

BLACK
HILLS

Pikes Peak

Mt. Elbert

LLANO
ESTACADO

ROCKY

MOUNTAINS

CASCADE
RANGE

Mt. Rainier

GREAT
BASIN

Great Salt Lake

GRAND
CANYON

SIERRA NEVADA

Mt. Whitney

N
W — E
S

Elevations

Above 10,000 feet (3,000 meters)
7,000-10,000 feet (2,000-3,000 meters)
3,000-7,000 feet (1,000-2,000 meters)
700-3,000 feet (200-1,000 meters)
0-700 feet (0-200 meters)
Below sea level

0   250   500   750 Kilometers
0   250   500 Miles

BROOKS RANGE

Mt. McKinley

0   250   500   750 Kilometers
0   250   500 Miles

Kauai
Oahu
Molokai   Maui
Mauna
Kea
Hawaii

0   100   Miles
0   100 Kilometers

Natural Vegetation

Legend:
- Needleleaf forest
- Broadleaf forest
- Mixed forest
- Shrub and desert (tundra in Alaska)
- Western grassland
- Shrub and grassland
- Prairie grassland
- Central grassland and forest
- Barren

MAINE
VT.
N.H.
MASS.
CONN. R.I.
N.J.
DEL.
NEW YORK
PENNSYLVANIA
MD.
VIRGINIA
NORTH CAROLINA
SOUTH CAROLINA
W. VA.
OHIO
KENTUCKY
TENNESSEE
GEORGIA
FLORIDA
ALABAMA
MISSISSIPPI
MICHIGAN
INDIANA
ILLINOIS
WISCONSIN
MISSOURI
IOWA
ARKANSAS
LOUISIANA
MINNESOTA
NORTH DAKOTA
SOUTH DAKOTA
NEBRASKA
KANSAS
OKLAHOMA
TEXAS
COLORADO
WYOMING
NEW MEXICO
MONTANA
IDAHO
UTAH
ARIZONA
NEVADA
WASHINGTON
OREGON
CALIFORNIA

500 Miles
750 Kilometers

N
E
S
W

ALASKA
500 Miles
750 Kilometers

HAWAII
100 Miles
100 Kilometers

Patterns of Settlement

Extent of settlement in
1790
1810
1830
1850
1870
1890
Unsettled as of 1890

MAINE
VT. N.H. MASS. CONN. R.I.
NEW YORK
N.J. DEL.
PENNSYLVANIA
MD.
W. VA.
VIRGINIA
NORTH CAROLINA
SOUTH CAROLINA
GEORGIA
FLORIDA
OHIO
KENTUCKY
TENNESSEE
ALABAMA
MISSISSIPPI
MICHIGAN
INDIANA
ILLINOIS
MISSOURI
ARKANSAS
LOUISIANA
WISCONSIN
MINNESOTA
IOWA
NORTH DAKOTA
SOUTH DAKOTA
NEBRASKA
KANSAS
OKLAHOMA
TEXAS
MONTANA
WYOMING
COLORADO
NEW MEXICO
IDAHO
UTAH
ARIZONA
WASHINGTON
OREGON
NEVADA
CALIFORNIA

W E

ALASKA
500 Miles
750 Kilometers

HAWAII
100 Miles
100 Kilometers

500 Miles
750 Kilometers

Population Distribution

Persons per square mile	Persons per square kilometer
Over 500	Over 200
100-499	40-199
50-99	20-39
5-49	2-19
0-4	0-1

ALASKA

HAWAII

MAINE
VT.
N.H.
MASS.
CONN. R.I.
NEW YORK
PENNSYLVANIA
DEL.
MD.
OHIO
W. VA.
VIRGINIA
NORTH CAROLINA
SOUTH CAROLINA
GEORGIA
FLORIDA
MICHIGAN
INDIANA
KENTUCKY
TENNESSEE
ALABAMA
MISSISSIPPI
LOUISIANA
WISCONSIN
ILLINOIS
MISSOURI
ARKANSAS
MINNESOTA
IOWA
NORTH DAKOTA
SOUTH DAKOTA
NEBRASKA
KANSAS
OKLAHOMA
TEXAS
MONTANA
WYOMING
COLORADO
NEW MEXICO
IDAHO
UTAH
ARIZONA
WASHINGTON
OREGON
NEVADA
CALIFORNIA

Mineral Resources

MAINE
VT.
N.H.
MASS.
CONN. R.I.
N.Y.
NEW YORK
PENNSYLVANIA
N.J.
DEL.
MD.
OHIO
W. VA.
VIRGINIA
NORTH CAROLINA
SOUTH CAROLINA
KENTUCKY
TENNESSEE
GEORGIA
ALABAMA
FLORIDA
MISSISSIPPI
LOUISIANA
INDIANA
ILLINOIS
MICHIGAN
WISCONSIN
MINNESOTA
IOWA
MISSOURI
ARKANSAS
NORTH DAKOTA
SOUTH DAKOTA
NEBRASKA
KANSAS
OKLAHOMA
TEXAS
MONTANA
WYOMING
COLORADO
NEW MEXICO
IDAHO
UTAH
ARIZONA
WASHINGTON
OREGON
NEVADA
CALIFORNIA

ALASKA
HAWAII

N E S W

250 Miles
250 Kilometers
500 Miles
500 Kilometers
750 Kilometers

0 100 Miles
0 100 Kilometers

0 500 Miles
0 750 Kilometers

Aluminum	◄	Copper	●	Magnesium	✛	Natural gas	◄	Sulphur	○
Chromium	△	Gold	■	Manganese	●	Nickel	◆	Tin	■
Coal	🟫	Iron Ore	◄	Mercury	○	Oil	✛	Uranium	◆
Cobalt	◆	Lead	○	Molybdenum	△	Silver	●	Zinc	✚

Economic Activities

Agriculture

- Dairy cattle, hay
- Livestock, feed grains
- Wheat
- General farming
- Fruits and vegetables
- Grazing

Industry

- Iron and steel works
- Chemicals
- Petroleum and coal products
- Lumber
- Furniture
- Textiles

500 Miles

250   250   500

750 Kilometers

500 Miles

750 Kilometers

100 Miles

100 Kilometers

N
E
S
W

A Chronology of American History

This chronology includes some of the most important events and developments in American history. It can be used to trace developments in politics and government, exploration and innovation, society and economics, and culture and religion. The number following each entry refers to the chapter in which the event or development is discussed in the text.

	Politics and Government	Exploration and Innovation
Prehistory– 1499	Mayan Empire reaches its height 1 Crusades for Holy Land begin 1 Aztecs establish empire in Mexico 1 Strong monarchies develop in Europe 1 Incas establish empire in South America 1	Mayas predict eclipses of sun 1 Aztecs develop system of mathematics 1 Marco Polo travels to China 1 Columbus sails to America 2 Vasco da Gama reaches India 1
1500– 1599	Cortés defeats Aztecs 2 Pizarro captures Inca capital 2 Spanish enact Laws of the Indies 2 English colony established at Roanoke 2 English defeat Spanish Armada 2	Spanish explore North America 2 Magellan's expedition circles the globe 2 Cartier sails up St. Lawrence River 2 Drake sails around the world 2
1600– 1649	House of Burgesses set up in Virginia 3 Mayflower Compact signed 3 Massachusetts Bay colony founded 3 Maryland becomes first proprietary colony 3	English joint stock companies sponsor settlement in North America 3 Champlain founds Quebec 5 Spanish found Santa Fe 5 West Indian tobacco adapted to Virginia 3
1650– 1699	Town meetings held in New England 4 Restoration of Charles II in England 3 Royal colonies develop 3 France claims Louisiana 5 Glorious Revolution in England 3	Spanish explore Pacific coast 5 Joliet and Marquette explore Mississippi River 5 La Salle reaches Mississippi Delta 5
1700– 1749	Georgia founded 3 Molasses Act passed 4 English settlers move into Ohio Valley 5	Indigo developed as cash crop 4 Benjamin Franklin develops scientific approach to medicine 4
1750– 1799	French and Indian War 5 Intolerable Acts passed 6 Declaration of Independence signed 6 Revolutionary War 7 Articles of Confederation ratified 8 Constitution ratified 9	Watt patents steam engine 12 Fitch launches first steam-powered boat 12 Slater sets up textile mills in New England 12 Eli Whitney invents cotton gin 12

Society and Economics	Culture and Religion	
Agriculture develops in Americas 1 Rise of merchants and bankers in Europe 1 Trade between Europe and Asia expands 1 Incas develop diverse economy 1	Mayas develop system of writing 1 Aztecs build Tenochtitlan 1 Renaissance begins in Europe 1 Incas construct great cities 1	**Prehistory– 1499**
Native American population of Spanish America declines 2 Slave trade begins in Americas 2 French develop fishing and fur trading in North America 2	Spanish try to convert Native Americans to Christianity 2 Universities open in Spanish America 2 John White paints watercolors of life in North America 2	**1500– 1599**
John Smith organizes life in Jamestown 3 Slavery introduced in Virginia 3 Bible Commonwealth in Massachusetts 3	Persecution of Puritans in England 3 Harvard founded 4 Public school law passed in Massachusetts 3 Religious tolerance granted in Maryland 3	**1600– 1649**
New England becomes shipbuilding center 4 Navigation Acts passed 5 Royal African Company established 4 Bacon's Rebellion 4	Quakers seek religious freedom in Pennsylvania 3 Spanish missions in Southwest 5 Religious freedom granted in Massachusetts 4 College of William and Mary founded 4	**1650– 1699**
Triangular trade flourishes 5 Immigration to Middle Colonies grows 4 Plantations expand in Southern Colonies 4 Growth of port cities 4	Yale College founded 4 First regular newspaper in colonies founded 4 John Peter Zenger arrested for libel 4	**1700– 1749**
Proclamation of 1763 6 Parliament passes Sugar, Quartering, Stamp, Currency, and Townshend acts 6 Colonies boycott British goods 6 Northern states abolish slavery 8 Northwest Ordinance takes effect 8	American literature reflects nationalism 8 Southern states disestablish Episcopal Church 8 Noah Webster promotes an American language 8 National capital designed and built 10	**1750– 1799**

	Politics and Government	Exploration and Innovation
1800– 1824	Louisiana Purchase 11 War of 1812 11 Missouri Compromise passed 17 Monroe Doctrine 12	Lewis and Clark expedition 11 Steamboats improved 12 Steam-powered locomotives developed 15
1825– 1849	Jacksonian democracy 13 Indian Removal Act passed 13 Texas wins independence 14 Oregon divided along 49th parallel 14 Mexican War 14	Erie Canal opened 12 Mechanical reaper, steel plow, and telegraph developed 15 First commercial railroads in use 15 Gold discovered at Sutter's Mill 14
1850– 1874	Compromise of 1850 17 Kansas-Nebraska Act passed 17 Civil War 18 Reconstruction 19 Alaska purchased from Russia 24 Warfare on the Great Plains 20	Passenger elevator, sleeping car, and air brake invented 21 Bessemer process developed 21 Pony Express founded 20 Ironclad ships used in Civil War 17 Transcontinental railroad completed 20
1875– 1899	Battle of Little Big Horn 20 Populist movement 22 ICC created 22 Sherman Antitrust Act passed 22 Spanish-American War 24	Refrigeration in meatpacking developed 21 Telephone, phonograph, incandescent light bulb invented 21 First skyscraper built 23
1900– 1924	Progressive era 25, 26 Roosevelt Corollary 27 World War I 28 Fourteen Points 28 Treaty of Versailles rejected 28 Red Scare 29	Panama Canal built 27 Assembly line introduced 30 Scientific management introduced 30 Synthetic fibers developed 30 Electric appliances become widespread 30
1925– 1949	Bonus Army 31 New Deal 32, 33 World War II 34, 35 Truman Doctrine and Marshall Plan 36 NATO created 36	Transatlantic telephone service begins 30 First television pictures broadcast 30 Lindbergh flies across Atlantic 30 Iron lung developed 30 Atomic bomb developed 35
1950– 1974	Korean War 36 McCarthyism 37 Cuban missile crisis 38 Vietnam War 38, 39 Watergate crisis 39	*Explorer I* launched into orbit 37 Computers marketed commercially 40 American astronauts land on moon 39 Viking probe of Mars 39
1975– Present	Diplomatic recognition of China 40 Sandra Day O'Connor appointed to Supreme Court 40 Economic sanctions imposed on South Africa 40	Genetic engineering, computers, lasers, and artificial joints and organs advance medicine 41 Flights of *Columbia* 41 Voyager expeditions pass Saturn 41

Glossary

This glossary defines many important historical terms and phrases. Most of the entries appear in italics the first time they are used in the text. The page number following each definition refers to the page on which the term or phrase is first discussed in the text.

Pronunciation Key

When difficult terms or names first appear in the text, they are respelled to aid pronunciation. A syllable in LARGE CAPITAL LETTERS receives the most stress. Syllables with a secondary stress appear in SMALL CAPITAL LETTERS. The key below lists the letters used for respelling. It includes examples of words using each sound and shows how they would be respelled.

Symbol	Example	Respelling
a	hat	(hat)
ay	pay, late	(pay), (layt)
ah	star, hot	(stahr), (haht)
ai	air, dare	(air), (dair)
aw	law, all	(law), (awl)
eh	met	(meht)
ee	bee, eat	(bee), (eet)
er	learn, sir, fur	(lern), (ser), (fer)
ih	fit	(fiht)
i	mile	(mīl)
ir	ear	(ir)
oh	no	(noh)
oi	soil, boy	(soil), (boi)
oo	root, rule	(root), (rool)
or	born, door	(born), (dor)
ow	plow, out	(plow), (owt)

Symbol	Example	Respelling
u	put, book	(put), (buk)
uh	fun	(fuhn)
yoo	few, use	(fyoo), (yooz)
ch	chill, reach	(chihl), (reech)
g	go, dig	(goh), (dihg)
j	jet, gently, bridge	(jeht), (JEHNT-lee), (brihj)
k	kite, cup	(kīt), (kuhp)
ks	mix	(mihks)
kw	quick	(kwihk)
ng	bring	(brihng)
s	say, cent	(say), (sehnt)
sh	she, crash	(shee), (krash)
th	three	(three)
th	then, breathe	(thehn), (breeth)
y	yet, onion	(yeht), (UHN-yuhn)
z	zip, always	(zihp), (AWL-wayz)
zh	treasure	(TREH-zher)

abstinence   refraining from all alcohol (page 296)

adobe   sun-dried clay brick used by the Pueblo to construct buildings (page 7)

amendment   a revision or change; an addition to the Constitution, proposed by Congress or a national convention and ratified by the states (page 165)

amino acid racemization   a method that enables scientists to determine the age of archaeological remains up to a million years old and to test objects weighing less than an ounce (page 4)

anarchist   a person who opposes all organized government (page 408)

apartheid   a policy of racial separation by law as practiced in South Africa (page 715)

appeasement   a policy of giving in to the demands of a hostile power to prevent conflict; specifically, the policy followed by European leaders in the 1930s of granting Hitler's demands for more territory in order to avoid a second world war (page 631)

archaeologist   a scientist who studies the life and culture of ancient peoples (page 3)

arms race the competition between the United States and the Soviet Union since 1949 to develop the most powerful nuclear arsenal (page 678)

artifact an object made by an ancient people (page 3)

assembly line a grouping of machines and workers in which work passes from one worker to another, each performing one task in the production of an item (page 558)

assets the property and cash of a business or individual (page 395)

assimilate to merge into another culture by adopting its standards and values (page 276)

assumption the taking over of state debts by the federal government after the Revolutionary War (page 175)

astrolabe an invention of the Renaissance era that enabled a sailor to fix a ship's position by sighting the stars (page 14)

balance of trade the difference in value between a nation's imports and exports (page 798)

bank note paper money backed by a bank's reserves of gold or silver (page 215)

Bessemer process a method of producing strong steel quickly and cheaply by heating iron in a furnance and then introducing cold air to burn out the impurities (page 396)

bicameral legislature a legislature that has two chambers, or houses (page 142)

bilingual education the education of students in both their native language and English (page 766)

bill of attainder a legislative act that prescribes punishment for a person even though he or she has not been found guilty by a court (page 166)

blended family a family that includes children from more than one marriage (page 783)

Blitzkrieg in German, "lightning warfare"; a sudden, swift, large-scale offensive intended to win a quick victory; used by Germany during World War II (page 633)

bond a certificate issued to a person who lends money to a business or a unit of government; the certificate earns interest and is redeemed for cash on a given date (page 395)

bounty a sum paid to a recruit for signing up for military service; used by the Union during the Civil War (page 333)

bounty jumping a practice of signing up for military service more than once during the Civil War in order to receive payment for each enlistment (page 333)

bracero a Mexican worker who, under a government program started in the 1950s, obtained a temporary permit to work in the United States; program ended in 1965 (page 712)

brain trust a group of scholars and technical experts who advised President Franklin Roosevelt during the New Deal (page 593)

business inventory a list of unsold goods on hand (page 579)

capital money invested in a business (page 209)

caravel a sixteenth-century ship that had triangular sails and was able to sail into the wind (page 15)

carbon-14 test a method used by scientists to determine the age of plant and animal remains (page 4)

carpetbagger a northerner who settled in the South after the Civil War and supported Radical Reconstruction (page 360)

carrack a ship that looked like a squat wooden tub with square sails; was less efficient than the caravel which was developed later during the Renaissance (page 15)

cash crop a crop grown to be sold at a profit rather than to be consumed by the farmer (page 63)

caucus a meeting in which a few members of Congress decided on their party's presidential candidate; replaced in the mid-1800s by a nominating convention (page 237)

checks and balances a system established under the Constitution by which each branch of government can check or control the power of the other branches (page 161)

circumnavigate to sail around the globe; first accomplished by Magellan in 1522 (page 20)

city manager a professional administrator hired by an elected board of trustees of a city to manage the city government (page 481)

civil disobedience a form of nonviolent protest in which the protester violates the law but is willing to accept the penalties arising from his or her acts (page 694)

clipper ship a fast sailing vessel of the mid-1800s (page 271)

closed shop a business in which union membership is a requirement for employment (page 686)

collective bargaining the process by which a union represents a group of workers in negotiations with management (page 409)

company union an employee association sponsored by management (page 546)

comparable worth equivalent wages for jobs requiring comparable skills (page 761)

compass an invention of the Renaissance era that enabled a sailor to tell direction (page 14)

compulsory education the requirement that every child attend school until a certain age (page 297)

concurrent powers powers shared by the national and state governments (page 160)

confederation an alliance of independent states (page 143)

conquistador a professional Spanish soldier who explored and conquered lands in the New World (page 21)

consolidate to combine into a single unit, as to combine smaller companies into a larger one (page 394)

constituents those people whom an elected official represents (page 752)

containment foreign policy first outlined in 1947 stating that the United States would contain, or hold, Soviet influence within its existing limits (page 670)

contraband a fugitive slave behind Union lines during the Civil War whom the North refused to return to a southern master (page 340)

convoy a protective escort provided by navy warships for merchant vessels crossing the ocean during wartime (page 533)

copperhead a northerner who opposed the Civil War or supported the Confederacy (page 342)

corduroy road a road consisting of tree trunks laid side by side (page 218)

coureur de bois a French fur trader in New France (page 81)

crack a highly addictive form of cocaine (page 785)

craft union a union in which all members practice the same occupation (page 409)

dame school classes for girls and younger children that were held in colonial homes (page 69)

de facto segregation segregation that exists in fact, although not by law (page 686)

default to fail to pay a debt (page 798)

deficit spending a spending plan in which government spending exceeds tax revenues (page 611)

deflation an economic condition in which the price of goods and services declines (page 425)

delegated powers powers given by the Constitution exclusively to the national government and forbidden to the states (page 159)

depression an economic condition marked by a drastic decline in production and sales and a severe increase in unemployment (page 244)

deregulation a reduction of the amount of government regulation of an industry (page 750)

détente a relaxation of tensions between the United States and the Soviet Union beginning in the early 1970s (page 724)

devalue to reduce the value of the dollar in relation to other currencies (page 628)

disenfranchise to take away the right to vote (page 422)

divestiture a refusal to hold stock in companies that have operations in South Africa (page 758)

dividend a share of a company's profits issued to stockholders on a periodic basis (page 403)

dollar diplomacy a term describing President William Howard Taft's policy of encouraging financial investments in Asia as a means of increasing United States power there (page 519)

domino theory   the idea, prevalent during the Vietnam War, that if one Asian nation became communist, neighboring nations would follow (page 680)

due process   protection that guarantees individuals accused of crimes a fair, standardized, and open legal process (page 167)

durable good   a product designed to last several years before being replaced (page 579)

economic sanction   a refusal to trade with a nation until it changes its policies (page 758)

electoral college   an assembly elected by voters to formally elect the President and Vice-President of the United States (page 162)

embargo   a ban on trade with another nation (page 196)

empire   a system of territories governed by one nation (page 459)

encomiendas   the right granted to Spanish conquerors in the New World to demand a tax from Native Americans living on a given piece of land (page 26)

enumerated commodity   a colonial product that Parliament said could be shipped only to England (page 76)

established church   the official church of a colony that was supported by taxes on citizens regardless of their personal beliefs (page 69)

expatriate   a person who gives up his or her homeland to live in another country (page 568)

ex post facto law   a law that makes an act a crime after it has been committed (page 166)

faction   a group of people organized to pursue their own private advantages in eighteenth-century politics; known as political parties today (page 180)

factory system   a system for organizing labor in which all workers in the manufacturing process are brought together to work under one roof (page 209)

fall line   the area east of the Appalachian Mountains in which inland rivers begin dropping toward sea level (page 61)

federalism   a system of government in which authority is divided between national and state governments (page 159)

feeder line   a railroad route that carried freight to a river or a canal (page 270)

feudalism   the political and social system of Europe during the Middle Ages, characterized by self-sufficient manors, decentralized political control, and obligations of service and loyalty among classes (page 11)

fireside chat   an informal talk on nationwide radio by President Roosevelt (page 595)

freedman   a former slave freed as a result of the Civil War (page 353)

free enterprise   a system in which individuals make economic decisions, such as what products to make, how much to produce, and how to set prices (page 403)

free soiler   a person who opposed the expansion of slavery into United States territories during the 1850s; many joined the newly formed Republican party (page 320)

free state   a state in which slavery was not permitted before the Civil War (page 313)

funding   a process whereby a government raises or borrows money to pay off a debt (page 174)

gang system   a system of field work in which slaves worked together in gangs under an overseer (page 283)

general strike   a strike of the members of all unions in a particular location (page 546)

genocide   the systematic destruction of a race of people (page 655)

givebacks   previously-won benefits that workers have to give up in order to negotiate a new labor contract (page 794)

gold standard   a system in which a nation's currency is based on the value of gold (page 429)

graduated personal income tax   a system in which the tax rate is proportionate to a person's income (page 427)

grandfather clause   voting regulation adopted by a number of southern states after Reconstruction; allowed a man to satisfy voting requirements if his father or grandfather had been eligible to vote in 1867 (page 422)

Grange   an organization of farmers founded in 1867 for social reasons; later campaigned for state regulation of railroads and other reforms (page 426)

gross national product the total of all the goods and services produced in a country (page 792)

habeas corpus the right not to be imprisoned without a trial (page 331)

hogan Navajo home that consisted of an earthen dome with a log frame (page 7)

holding company a company that gains control of other companies by buying their stock (page 420)

horizontal integration a form of business organization in which a corporation acquires rival companies for the purpose of eliminating competition (page 402)

impeachment the process by which the House of Representatives makes an accusation of wrongdoing against the President or other high federal official (page 162)

impound to refuse to spend appropriated funds (page 728)

impressment the British practice of forcing American sailors to serve in the British navy during the early 1800s (page 196)

inalienable rights natural rights that governments cannot take away from citizens (page 142)

indentured servant a person from Europe or Africa who agreed to work for an employer in colonial America for a specified period of time in return for the cost of passage (page 65)

indigo a West Indian plant used to make dye; grown for profit in the Southern Colonies (page 63)

industrial union a union in which members work at various jobs in a single industry (page 612)

inflation an economic condition in which prices rise substantially over a significant period of time (page 123)

initiative a procedure that allows citizens to propose a bill by collecting a specific number of signatures from registered voters (page 481)

injunction a court order prohibiting a given action; used frequently against workers in nineteenth-century labor-management disputes (page 411)

interchangeable parts identical component parts that can be used in place of one another in the manufacturing process (page 210)

interlocking directorate a system under which the same people serve on the boards of directors of several firms within the same industry (page 503)

internationalism the belief, held by some Americans in the 1930s, that the United States should aid the victims of international aggression (page 627)

isolationism the belief, widely held during the 1920s and 1930s, that the United States should minimize its involvement in foreign affairs (page 625)

jingoism intense national pride particularly widespread in the United States before and during the Spanish-American War (page 463)

joint stock company a form of business organization devised around 1600 by European nations to finance business ventures and exploration; pooled the funds of many investors by selling shares in the company (page 37)

judicial review the power of the Supreme Court to determine the constitutionality of acts of the legislative and executive branches of the government (page 190)

kamikaze a World War II Japanese fighter pilot who sacrificed his life by deliberately crashing his plane into Allied ships (page 656)

kiva a room at the center of a Pueblo town where the men conducted religious ceremonies (page 7)

laissez-faire noninterference; has come to mean a policy by which the government minimizes its regulation of industry and the economy (page 190)

lame duck an elected official who has been defeated at the polls but whose term of office has not yet expired (page 325)

leapfrogging the technique used by the Allies in World War II of invading a few strategically placed Japanese-held islands and bypassing others in order to cut off Japanese supply lines to the other islands (page 651)

limited liability refers to a situation in which an investor's personal responsibility for the debts of a business does not exceed his or her initial investment (page 209)

limited war a war in which specific objectives are sought, rather than total victory over the enemy; became a major issue during the Korean War (page 676)

literacy rate the proportion of the population that can read and write (page 69)

localism the tendency of states or areas to act independently and not as part of a unified nation (page 121)

long drive a cattle drive during the mid-1800s in which a large herd was moved across hundreds or thousands of miles to a railhead, from which the cattle would be shipped to market (page 384)

loose construction an interpretation of the Constitution holding that the federal government has broad powers implied by its delegated powers (page 176)

Maine laws state laws of the 1850s that prohibited the sale of all alcoholic beverages (page 296)

mainstreaming placing handicapped students in classes with nonhandicapped students rather than in special facilities (page 763)

manifest destiny a commonly held belief in the first half of the nineteenth century that the United States had a mission to expand its borders to incorporate all land between the Atlantic and Pacific Oceans (page 259)

manor a large estate owned by a lord, during the Middle Ages, where peasants produced all the necessities (page 11)

manumission the freeing of slaves (page 139)

margin call a request by a stockbroker that an investor who has bought on margin put up more money to cover his or her loan on stocks that have decreased in value (page 578)

massive retaliation a military strategy proposed during the cold war of the 1950s in which the United States would retaliate directly against the Soviet Union or China, with nuclear weapons if necessary (page 678)

mercantilism an economic system prevalent in Europe after the Middle Ages in which each nation attempted to export more than it imported in order to strengthen its economy (page 75)

migrant worker an agricultural worker who travels from place to place doing seasonal work (page 567)

minuteman a member of a colonial Massachusetts militia ready to fight the British on a moment's notice (page 106)

monopoly complete control of a product or service in a particular market by a single company (page 403)

moral diplomacy a term describing President Woodrow Wilson's approach to foreign policy, which emphasized the use of negotiation and arbitration rather than force to settle international disputes (page 519)

mortality rate a death rate (page 250)

muckrakers early twentieth-century American journalists who tried to improve society by exposing political corruption, health hazards, and other social problems (page 477)

Mugwumps reformers within the Republican party who crusaded to end political corruption during the late 1800s (page 417)

nativist a person who wanted to limit immigration and preserve the virtues and way of life of native-born Americans (page 276)

naturalization the process by whch a citizen of one country becomes a citizen of another (page 196)

nomadic moving from place to place instead of living in permanent villages (page 8)

nonimportation agreement a promise made by colonial merchants and planters not to import certain goods taxed by the Townshend Acts (page 98)

normalcy President Warren G. Harding's term for the return to peace after World War I (page 549)

nullify to declare a law invalid and therefore unenforceable (page 185)

on margin refers to the practice of buying stock by which the buyer uses some of his or her own money and borrows the rest from a broker (page 576)

parity a system in which the government supports the price of certain farm products in order to maintain the purchasing power of farmers (page 554)

party platform a political party's declaration of its principles and programs (page 234)

patronage system the practice of giving out government jobs as favors to loyal party workers (page 417)

patroon a landowner in the Dutch colonies who received rent, taxes, and labor from tenant farmers (page 61)

pictogram a picture drawn on rock by the Anasazi that conveyed their ideas about life (page 7)

piedmont region a region of rolling hills; in the South, the piedmont lies between the Appalachian Mountains and the tidewater region (page 63)

planter a powerful plantation owner who planted cash crops and employed a large number of slaves (page 63)

pogrom a violent attack against a Jewish neighborhood in eastern Europe (page 440)

poll tax a fee that had to be paid in order to vote; instituted in the South after the Civil War to prevent blacks from voting; rendered unconstitutional by the Twenty-fourth Amendment (page 422)

pooling an agreement among railroad administrators to divide the total volume of freight among their lines (page 395)

popular sovereignty the method suggested by Stephen Douglas in the 1850s by which the voters of a territory would decide whether to allow slavery within the territory (page 314)

potlatch a feast held by an early Native American family of the northwest Pacific coast to demonstrate its prosperity (page 6)

prehistoric period the time before recorded history (page 3)

presidio A Spanish settlement in the New World constructed for military activities (page 25)

primary election an election held before the general election to choose candidates for office (page 481)

primer an illustrated textbook that taught Puritan children reading, spelling, and the tenets of the Puritan faith (page 69)

productivity the output per hour of work (page 792)

prohibition the ban on the sale and manufacture of alcoholic beverages resulting from ratification of the Eighteenth Amendment in 1919 (page 505)

proprietor an individual who received colonial land in America from the king of England and who was expected to administer that land in accordance with the laws of England (page 45)

protective tariff a tax on imports designed to discourage their sale and to favor the development of domestic industry (page 176)

public domain land that belongs to the nation rather than to individuals or corporations (page 378)

pueblo a Spanish settlement in the New World that included farming, trade, and town life; villa (page 25)

quadrant an invention of the Renaissance era that enabled a sailor to take bearings from the sun or the stars in order to plot a ship's position on a map (page 14)

ranchero a Mexican ranch owner (page 250)

ratification the process of officially approving a proposal (page 144)

rebate a discount; in the nineteenth century some railroads offered rebates on shipping charges to attract business (page 395)

recall election a special election that allows voters to remove an elected official before the completion of his or her term (page 481)

recession an economic condition characterized by a mild increase in unemployment and a moderate decline in production and sales (page 408)

reconcentration a policy of General Weyler of Spain in 1896 whereby people in Cuban towns and villages were marched into detention camps and guarded by Spanish soldiers (page 463)

referendum   the process by which people can vote directly on a bill (page 481)

reparations   payments made by nations defeated in war as compensation for the damage they caused (page 535)

reservation   an area of land specifically set aside by the federal government for Native Americans (page 381)

reserved powers   powers retained by the states because they are not expressly given to the federal government nor denied to the states (page 159)

revival   a meeting held to revive a religious spirit in people (page 295)

royal colony   an American colony in which the governor and counsil were appointed by the king (page 49)

sachem   one of 50 specially chosen leaders who, along with the chiefs of each tribe, governed the Iroquois League during the 1500s (page 8)

scalawag   a white southerner who supported Radical Reconstruction (page 360)

scientific management   the systematic study of the performance of workers and machines for the purpose of increasing efficiency (page 557)

sea dogs   English sailors who pirated Spanish ships carrying precious minerals from the New World back to Spain (page 30)

secede   to withdraw from a large political body (page 191)

segregation   the practice of separating people on a racial basis (page 138)

self-determination   the freedom of a country to determine its own future and form of government (page 535)

self-sufficient   having the resources to get along without help, as a farm family in the New England Colonies (page 57)

separation of powers   a system in which the branches of government exercise distinct powers (page 160)

serf   a peasant of the Middle Ages who was bound by custom to a lord's land (page 11)

sharecropper   an agricultural worker who works part of another person's land, receives supplies and equipment from the landowner, and in return gives the landowner part of the harvest (page 360)

sitdown strike   a strike in which workers sit down on the job and refuse to leave the work place until their demands are met (page 613)

slave codes   laws regulating the conduct of slaves before the Civil War (page 66)

slave state   a state in which slavery was permitted before the Civil War (page 313)

sovereignty   the source of a government's power or authority (page 159)

special interest group   a group of people with a common interest organized for political action (page 787)

sphere of influence   an area in China during the late 1800s where trade was controlled by a foreign power (page 470)

spoils system   the practice of dismissing government job holders affiliated with a defeated party and replacing them with supporters of the victorious party (page 241)

squatter   a person who settles on land without a legal right to do so (page 146)

stagflation   an economic condition characterized by both inflation and recession (page 729)

stock certificate   a document stating that the holder owns a share of a corporation (page 395)

strategic forces   specially trained armed forces units that can be moved quickly to any part of the world (page 701)

strict construction   a literal interpretation of the Constitution, holding that the federal government has only those powers explicitly delegated to it in the Constitution (page 176)

strike   an organized work stoppage by employees, conducted for the purpose of improving pay or working conditions (page 273)

subsistence farming   a level of farming at which farmers produce just enough to feed their families (page 57)

sunbelt   a term referring to southeastern and southwestern states known for their mild climates and expanding economies (page 768)

synthetic   a chemically produced fiber (page 559)

task system a system by which individual slaves were assigned specific jobs each day (page 283)

telephoto a process for sending pictures by wire (page 559)

temperance movement a campaign against the consumption of alcohol (page 296)

tenant farmer an agricultural worker who rents land from another person and pays the rent either in cash or by giving the landowner a portion of the crop; tenants provide their own seed and supplies (page 360)

territorial integrity condition in which a nation's borders are guaranteed against disturbance by other nations (page 535)

tidewater region a flat coastal plain where the land is so low that rivers crossing it flow backwards with incoming tides (page 63)

totalitarian state a country in which the government is supreme and individuals have few rights (page 627)

town meeting a meeting in which residents of a town in the New England Colonies discussed matters of importance and elected representatives to the colonial assembly (page 57)

trade deficit a situation in which the value of a nation's imports exceeds the value of its exports (page 798)

trade surplus a situation in which the value of a nation's exports exceeds the value of its imports (page 798)

triangular trade the pattern of trade during the colonial era in which merchant ships traveled a triangular route, stopping in New England, Africa, and the West Indies (page 77)

trunk line a heavily traveled railroad route that links major cities (page 270)

trust a form of business organization, widespread during the late 1800s, in which investors in rival corporations exchanged their stock certificates and voice in management for trust certificates issued by a giant firm (page 403)

unconstitutional refers to a legislative act or executive action that violates the Constitution (page 162)

underground railroad the network of people who helped slaves escape to the northern states or to Canada (page 304)

union an association of workers formed to improve wages and working conditions (page 273)

utility company a company that distributes gas and electricity (page 605)

utopian founded on the idea of achieving perfection, or the ideal (page 299)

vassal a lord who received land from a king, an emperor, or a higher lord during the Middle Ages in return for loyalty (page 11)

vertical integration a form of business organization in which a manufacturing corporation acquires firms that contribute to the completion of a finished product (page 402)

veto an action by which a chief executive rejects a bill submitted to him or her by the legislature (page 142)

vigilante a self-appointed enforcer of the law (page 377)

villa a Spanish settlement in the New World that included farming, trade, and town life; pueblo (page 25)

watered stock shares of ownership in a company that are not actually backed by the company's property and cash (page 395)

white manhood suffrage voting by all white males (page 236)

workingmen's party an organization of workers of the early 1800s that sought universal white manhood suffrage, free public education, and abolition of debtor imprisonment laws (page 274)

writ of assistance a document issued by British authorities during the colonial period that allowed officials to conduct unrestricted searches (page 98)

writ of habeas corpus a court order directing authorities to bring a prisoner to court to explain the basis for his or her detention (page 166)

yellow journalism a style of newspaper writing in the late 1890s that featured sensational headlines and stories (page 463)

zero population growth a point at which the number of births equals the numbers of death in a population (page 766)

Suggested Readings

General Works

Commager, Henry Steele, ed. *Documents of American History*. Appleton-Century-Crofts. A large selection of government documents.

Ferrell, Robert H. *American Diplomacy*. Norton. A general history of American diplomacy.

Franklin, John Hope. *From Slavery to Freedom: A History of American Negroes*. Knopf. A standard history of black people in America.

Handlin, Oscar and Mary F. *The Wealth of the American People*. McGraw-Hill. A history of the growth of the American economy since colonial times.

Josephy, Alvin. *The Indian Heritage of America*. Knopf. One of the most complete and accurate treatments of Native Americans in North, Central, and South America from prehistoric times to the present.

Malone, Dumas, ed. *Dictionary of American Biography*. Scribner. A multivolume work useful to the student who wants to compare the backgrounds of people who participated in an historical event.

Moquin, Wayne, and Van Doren, Charles, eds. *A Documentary History of the Mexican Americans*. Praeger. A collection of documents that trace the history of Mexican Americans from the 1500s to the late 1960s.

Morris, Richard B. *Encyclopedia of American History*. Harper & Row. A well-organized guide to American history.

O'Neill, William L. *Everyone Was Brave: A History of Feminism in America*. Quadrangle. A history of the women's rights movement from its mid-nineteenth-century origins to the late 1960s.

Unit One The Americas

Chapter 1

Cheyney, E.P. *The European Background of American History, 1300–1600*. Scholarly Press. A discussion of the social, political, and economic developments in Europe that led to the discovery of the New World.

Davies, Nigel. *The Aztecs*. Putnam. A political history of the Aztec civilization; contains illustrations of Aztec art and architecture.

Hyams, Edward, and Ordish, George. *The Last of the Incas*. Simon & Schuster. A comprehensive, illustrated account of Inca rulers and accomplishments.

Terrell, John Upton. *Pueblos, Gods and Spaniards*. Dial. A history of the Pueblo after the arrival of the Spanish; good general reading.

Thompson, J. Eric. *The Rise and Fall of Maya Civilization*. University of Oklahoma. A classic account of Maya cultural, political, and social patterns.

Chapter 2

Builders of America. Funk & Wagnalls. Biographies of early American explorers and colonial leaders.

Cumming, W.P.; Skelton, R.A., and Quinn, D.B. *The Discovery of North America*. McGraw-Hill. A fascinating collection of original paintings, engraved maps, and primary source narratives of French, Spanish, and English exploration of the New World.

Horgan, Paul. *Conquistadores in North American History*. Farrar, Straus. A fast-reading book about Spanish exploration in North America, focusing on individual conquistadores.

Marshall, James V. *The Wind at Morning*. Morrow. An historical novel based on Magellan's journey around the world.

Morison, Samuel Eliot. *The European Discovery of America*. Oxford University. An illustrated history of European explorations in North and South America.

Chapter 3

Covey, Cyclone. *The Gentle Radical: A Biography of Roger Williams*. Macmillan. Williams's life provides the focus for historical events and life in seventeenth-century New England.

Morgan, Edmund S. *The Puritan Dilemma: The Story of John Winthrop*. Little, Brown. A clear but sophisticated analysis of Puritan thought.

Peare, Catherine Owens. *William Penn*. Holt. A comprehensive account of the life of William Penn and his devotion to the founding of Pennsylvania.

Vaughan, Alden. *American Genesis: Captain John Smith and the Founding of Virginia*. Little, Brown. A biography of Smith that explores the problems of organizing a distant overseas colony.

Chapter 4

Hofstadter, Richard. *America at 1750: A Social Portrait*. Knopf. A descriptive portrait of American culture, economics, and society in the mid-1700s.

Land, Aubrey C., ed. *Letters From America*. Harvard University. Letters of William Eddis to a friend in England; provide valuable insight into the life of the planter class in the Southern Colonies.

Nash, Gary B. *Red, White, and Black: The Peoples of Early America.* Prentice-Hall. An account of the interaction of European, African, and Native American cultures before the Revolutionary War.

Sandburg, Carl. *Remembrance Rock.* Harcourt. A novel about life in New England from Puritan days to the dawn of the Revolutionary War.

Williams, Selma R. *Demeter's Daughters: The Women Who Founded America, 1587–1792.* Atheneum. A discussion of the roles, rights, and responsibilities of colonial women; includes biographical sketches of prominent women.

Wright, L.B., ed. *The American Heritage History of the Thirteen Colonies.* American Heritage. An illustrated history of colonial life.

Chapter 5

Chidsey, Donald Barr. *The French and Indian Wars: An Informal History.* Crown. A history of the rivalry between England and France in the New World; includes information about the roles of Native Americans and English colonists.

Cooper, James Fenimore. *The Last of the Mohicans.* Scribner. A classic novel about events in upper New York during the French and Indian War, despite the inaccurate description of Native Americans.

Lawson, Don. *The Colonial Wars.* Abelard. A fast-reading account of the Spanish, French, and British struggle for supremacy in North America.

Segal, Charles M., and Stineback, David. *Puritans, Indians, and Manifest Destiny.* Putnam. An examination of relations between Puritans and Native Americans in the 1600s; set around the theme of conflict between different cultures.

Unit Two Creating a Republic

Chapter 6

Acheson, Patricia C. *America's Colonial Heritage.* Dodd, Mead. A discussion of the ideas and events contributing to the movement toward independence.

Allen, Harvey. *The City in the Dawn.* Rinehart. A novel about the life of a Native American before, during, and after the American Revolutionary War, set in Ohio and Pennsylvania.

Chidsey, Donald Barr. *The World of Samuel Adams.* Thomas Nelson. An account of Adams's activities as a politician and patriot.

Freeman, Douglas Southall. *George Washington,* vol. 3, *Planter and Patriot.* Scribner. An enjoyable account of George Washington's transformation from farmer to leader of the American revolution.

Gipson, Lawrence Henry. *The Coming of the Revolution, 1763–1775.* Harper & Row. An in-depth examination of the causes of the American Revolution.

Chapter 7

Booth, Sally Smith. *Women of '76.* Hastings House. Information about colonial, Native American, and European women of the revolutionary period.

Canfield, Cass. *Samuel Adams's Revolution, 1765–1776.* Harper & Row. A description of the causes, events, and heroes of the American Revolution; enjoyable reading.

Catton, Bruce, ed. *The American Heritage Book of the Revolution.* Simon & Schuster. An illustrated History of the Revolutionary War.

Cooper, James Fenimore. *The Pilot.* Dodd, Mead. A classic novel inspired by the adventures of John Paul Jones.

Smith, Page. *A New Age Now Begins: A People's History of the American Revolution.* McGraw-Hill. A history of the Revolutionary War that makes good use of anecdotes.

Vaughan, Alden T., ed. *Chronicles of the American Revolution.* Grosset & Dunlap. A collection of articles, speeches, sketches, journals, and illustrations from the Revolutionary War period.

Whitney, Janet. *Abigail Adams.* Little, Brown. A fast-reading biography of Abigail Adams during the American revolution. One of the few biographies about a woman of the revolutionary period.

Chapter 8

Jensen, Merrill. *The New Nation: A History of the United States During the Confederation, 1781–1789.* Random House. A classic account of political developments during the 1780s.

Morgan, Edmund S. *The Birth of the Republic, 1763–1789.* University of Chicago. An historical account that emphasizes the development of a common heritage in the colonies and the new republic.

Nye, Russell B. *The Cultural Life of the New Nation, 1776–1830.* Harper & Row. Interesting material on education, literature, and religion in the newly established nation.

Chapter 9

Chidsey, Donald Barr. *The Birth of the Constitution.* Crown. An informal history of the issues and individuals that created the Constitution.

Hamilton, Alexander; Jay, John; and Madison, James. *The Federalist.* Random House. A collection of essays written in support of ratification of the Constitution.

Kenyon, Cecelia, ed. *The Antifederalists.* Bobbs-Merrill. A collection of letters, pamphlets, and documents written by opponents of ratification of the Constitution.

Rossiter, Clinton. *1787: The Grand Convention*. Macmillan. A detailed and thorough description of the people, setting, and consequences of the Constitutional Convention.

Unit Three **An Emerging Nation**

Chapter 10

Cunliffe, Marcus. *The Nation Takes Shape, 1789–1837*. University of Chicago. An interesting analysis of conflicting forces in the early years of the nation.

Hendrickson, Robert. *Hamilton*, vol. 2, *1789–1804*. Mason/Charter. An absorbing biography of Washington's secretary of the treasury.

Hofstadter, Richard. *The Idea of a Party System*. University of California. An account of how early political leaders came to accept a party system.

Smith, Page. *John Adams*, vol. 1, *1735–1784*. Greenwood. A scholarly description of Adams's public and private life.

Chapter 11

Brodie, Fawn M. *Thomas Jefferson: An Intimate History*. Norton. A biography revealing Jefferson's personal and public life.

Chidsey, Donald Barr. *Lewis and Clark: The Great Adventure*. Crown. A popular history that uses entries from the explorers' original diaries to highlight adventurous episodes.

Gerson, Noel B. *Mr. Madison's War: 1812, the Second War for Independence*. Julian Messner. A vivid examination of the issues and personalities involved in the bitter struggle between the United States and Great Britain.

Smith, Page. *Jefferson: A Revealing Biography*. McGraw-Hill. An illustrated biography of Thomas Jefferson; interesting reading.

Vidal, Gore. *Burr: A Novel*. Random House. A biographical novel based on the life of Aaron Burr.

Chapter 12

Ammon, Harry. *James Monroe: The Quest for National Identity*. McGraw-Hill. A biography of Monroe; reveals the political and private life of the fifth President.

Billington, Ray A. *Westward Expansion: A History of the American Frontier*. Macmillan. A comprehensive treatment of westward growth in the United States.

Dangerfield, George. *The Awakening of American Nationalism, 1815–1828*. Harper & Row. An exploration of economic and political nationalism in the early nineteenth century.

Garraty, John A., ed. *Quarrels That Have Shaped the Constitution*. Harper & Row. An account of landmark Supreme Court cases, including

an absorbing account of the Court under John Marshall.

Unit Four **An Era of Expansion**

Chapter 13

Bartlett, Irving H. *Daniel Webster*. Norton. A recent biography of this charismatic symbol of American nationalism.

Jahoda, Gloria. *The Trail of Tears*. Holt. A moving account of the removals of American Indians from 1813 to 1855.

Schlesinger, Arthur M., Jr. *The Age of Jackson*. Little, Brown. A wide-ranging, favorable account of Jackson's presidency.

Taylor, George Rogers, ed. *Jackson vs. Biddle's Bank*. D.C. Heath. A history of the dispute over the second Bank of the United States.

Chapter 14

Chidsey, Donald Barr. *The War With Mexico*. Crown. A clear description of the causes, events, heroes, and villains of the Mexican War.

Egan, Ferol. *Frémont*. Doubleday. An exciting biography of John Frémont, who epitomizes the era of expansion.

Parkman, Francis. *The Oregon Trail*. New American Library. A record of Parkman's adventurous journey west in the 1840s.

Webb, Todd. *The Gold Rush Trail and the Road to Oregon*. Doubleday. A photographic record of the way west; includes excerpts from letters and diaries.

Chapter 15

Eaton, Clement. *The Growth of Southern Civilization, 1790–1860*. Harper & Row. A widely respected history of the pre–Civil War South.

Groner, Alex. *The American Heritage History of American Business and Industry*. American Heritage. An illustrated history of business and industry in the United States.

Litwack, Leon. *North of Slavery*. University of Chicago. An analysis of the position of free blacks in the North before the Civil War.

Rayback, Joseph G. *A History of American Labor*. Macmillan. A comprehensive overview that includes a discussion of early trade unions and labor parties.

Stampp, Kenneth M. *The Peculiar Institution: Slavery in the Ante-Bellum South*. Knopf. A searching and critical examination of American slavery; valuable for its portrayal of daily life on the plantation.

Chapter 16

The Beauty of America in Great American Art. Morrow. Full-color reproductions of American paintings accompanied by selections from poets and authors.

Mabee, Carleton. *Black Freedom*. Macmillan. An historical account that focuses on the abolitionist movement from 1830 through the Civil War.

Miller, Douglas. *Then Was the Future*. Knopf. A social history of the North from 1815 to 1850 as portrayed in letters, diaries, songs, speeches, and art.

Thomas, John R. *The Liberator: William Lloyd Garrison*. Little, Brown. A biography of Garrison portraying him as a controversial and moralistic individualist.

Unit Five A Nation Torn Apart

Chapter 17

Catton, Bruce. *The Coming Fury*. Doubleday. An historical account that traces the split between the North and South from the election of 1860 through the first battle of Bull Run.

Nevins, Allan. *The Emergence of Lincoln*, vol. 2. Scribner. A political history of people and events from 1857 to 1861.

Nevins, Allan. *Ordeal of the Union*, vol. 2, *A House Dividing, 1852–1857*. Scribner. Classic work on the conflicts that divided North and South from 1852 to 1857.

Truman, Nelson. *The Old Man: John Brown at Harpers Ferry*. Holt. A biography of John Brown, focusing on his later years.

Chapter 18

Crane, Stephen. *The Red Badge of Courage*. Norton. A classic Civil War novel about the feelings of a Union soldier in the face of enemy fire; originally published in 1895.

Eaton, Clement. *Jefferson Davis*. Free Press. A biography of the President of the Confederacy.

Ketchum, Richard, ed. *The American Heritage Picture History of the Civil War*. American Heritage. A large collection of photographs, sketches, paintings, drawings, and maps of the Civil War; both North and South are covered.

Luthin, Reinhard H. *The Real Abraham Lincoln*. Prentice-Hall. A scholarly biography of Lincoln's adult years.

Nevins, Allan. *The War for the Union*. Scribner. An account of the Civil War that emphasizes the problems of a war-torn nation rather than a series of military engagements.

Quarles, Benjamin. *The Negro in the Civil War*. Little, Brown. An absorbing account of the role of black Americans in the Civil War.

Wheeler, Richard. *Voices of the Civil War*. Crowell. A collection of eyewitness accounts of the Civil War by foot soldiers, generals, and civilians.

Young, Agatha. *The Women and the Crisis*. McDowell, Obolensky. A history of women in the North during the Civil War.

Chapter 19

Carter, Hodding. *The Angry Scar: The Story of Reconstruction*. Greenwood. An account of southerners' reactions to Reconstruction.

Fast, Howard. *Freedom Road*. Crown. A novel about a black congressman during Reconstruction.

Franklin, John Hope. *Reconstruction After the Civil War*. University of Chicago. A sympathetic treatment of congressional efforts to reconstruct the old Confederacy.

Stampp, Kenneth M. *Era of Reconstruction: 1865–1877*. Random House. A scholarly reexamination of Reconstruction.

Unit Six Transforming a Nation

Chapter 20

Beebe, Lucius, and Clegg, Charles. *The American West: The Pictorial Epic of a Continent*. Dutton. The Old West in pictures including introductions to people and events.

Brown, Dee. *The Gentle Tamers*. Bantam. Easily read, entertaining social history of women in the West.

Cather, Willa. *O Pioneers!* Houghton Mifflin. A major American author's fast-reading novel about immigrants to the Midwest and their struggles against adversity.

Haines, Francis. *The Plains Indians*. Crowell. A recent study of the Plains Indians, including their confrontation with white society.

Katz, William Loren. *The Black West*. Doubleday. A collection of rare documents and photographs of black Americans on the frontier.

Chapter 21

Allen, Frederick Lewis. *The Lords of Creation*. Quadrangle. A history of the corporations and industrialists prominent in American economic expansion during the late 1800s and early 1900s.

Maddow, Ben. *A Sunday Between Wars*. Norton. An illustrated history of the building of American industry and the human costs of that progress; good general reading.

Norris, Frank. *The Octopus*. Airmont. Readable novel about California farmers and their struggle with railroad injustices.

Weisberger, Bernard, and Nevins, Allan. *Captains of Industry*. American Heritage. A fast-moving description of industrial leaders including contemporary illustrations.

Chapter 22

Boardman, Fon W., Jr. *America and the Gilded Age, 1876–1900*. Henry Z. Walck. A brief portrait of a period of rapid changes.

Hicks, John D. *The Populist Revolt: A History of the Farmer's Alliance and the People's Party*. University of Nebraska. A comprehensive treatment of the origins of the populist movement.

Twain, Mark. *The Gilded Age.* Bobbs-Merrill. A readable novel portraying the materialism and corruption of the post–Civil War period.

Washington, Booker T.; Johnson, James Weldon; and DuBois, William E.B. *Three Negro Classics.* Avon. Includes DuBois's *Souls of Black Folk* and Washington's *Up From Slavery;* particularly interesting for DuBois's appraisal of Washington.

Woodward, C. Vann. *The Strange Career of Jim Crow.* Oxford University. Discussion of race relations in the South after the Civil War.

Chapter 23

Beard, Annie E. *Our Foreign Born Citizens.* Crowell. A compilation of short biographies of 23 distinguished immigrants.

Davis, Allen F. *American Heroine: The Life and Legend of Jane Addams.* Oxford University. A detailed biography of Jane Addams; explores her motivations and accomplishments.

McKelvey, Blake. *The Urbanization of America, 1860–1915.* Rutgers University. A detailed book about the growth of American cities in the late 1800s and early 1900s.

Riis, Jacob August. *How the Other Half Lives.* Peter Smith. An illustrated study of tenements in New York City at the turn of the century by a contemporary reporter.

Chapter 24

Azoy, Colonel A.C.M. *Charge!* Longman. Entertaining description of the battle of San Juan Hill.

Chidsey, Donald Barr. *The Spanish-American War.* Crown. Popularized behind-the-scenes account of the Spanish-American War.

Pratt, Julius W. *America's Colonial Experiment.* Peter Smith. An account of how the United States gained and governed a widespread colonial empire.

Weems, John Edward. *The Fate of the* Maine. Holt. An enjoyable description of the ship and the crew, based on original documents and interviews with survivors.

Unit Seven Entering a Modern Age

Chapter 25

Goldman, Eric. *Rendezvous With Destiny.* Knopf. Contains interesting descriptions of the politics and personalities of the progressive era.

Morris, Edmond. *The Rise of Theodore Roosevelt.* Coward, McCann & Geoghegan. Recent biography of Roosevelt focusing on the many facets of his life and career.

Pinchot, Gifford. *Breaking New Ground.* University of Washington. The story of American forestry and conservation.

Reiger, C.C. *The Era of the Muckrakers.* Peter Smith. Discussion of the role of muckraking journalism during the first decade of the twentieth century.

Sinclair, Upton. *The Jungle.* New American Library. A classic contemporary attack on unsanitary practices and conditions in the meatpacking industry.

Chapter 26

Anthony, Susan B.; Stanton, Elizabeth Cady; et al., eds. *History of Woman Suffrage.* Arno. A collection of documents from the leaders of the women's rights movement in the late 1800s and early 1900s.

Faulkner, Harold V. *The Decline of Laissez-Faire, 1897–1917.* M. E. Sharpe. Account of the growth of federal regulatory power during the progressive era.

Link, Arthur. *Woodrow Wilson and the Progressive Era, 1910–1917.* Harper & Row. A scholarly account of the politics of progressivism by Wilson's leading biographer.

Scott, Anne Firor, and Scott, Andrew M. *One Half the People: The Fight for Women's Suffrage.* Lippincott. A brisk, lively analysis of the suffrage movement in the United States; includes documents.

Stein, Leon. *The Triangle Fire.* Lippincott. An interesting recreation of the Triangle Shirt Waist Company fire, based on original documents and interviews with survivors.

Chapter 27

Beale, Howard K. *Theodore Roosevelt and the Rise of America to World Power.* Johns Hopkins University. A detailed, scholarly account of American expansion under Roosevelt.

Kennan, George F. *American Diplomacy, 1900–1950.* New American Library. The early chapters present a concise history of early twentieth-century foreign policy.

Mason, Herbert Molloy, Jr. *The Great Pursuit.* Random House. An illustrated account of Pershing's expedition into Mexico in search of Pancho Villa.

McCullough, David. *The Path Between the Seas.* Simon & Schuster. The exciting account of the people. nations, and money behind the construction of the Panama Canal.

Chapter 28

Barbeau, Arthur E., and Henri, Florette. *The Unknown Soldiers.* Temple University. A history of black American troops in World War I.

Hemingway, Ernest. *A Farewell to Arms.* Scribner. A classic American novel about fighting on the Italian front.

Hoehling, A.A. *The Great War at Sea.* Crowell. Fast-reading discussion of American naval action between 1914 and 1918.

Leckie, Robert. *The Story of World War I.*

Random House. A lavishly illustrated history of the first world war.

Sinclair, Upton. *World's End*. Viking. A novel about the role of munitions makers during the war.

Unit Eight **The Roaring Twenties**

Chapter 29

Hicks, John D. *Republican Ascendancy, 1921–1933*. Harper & Row. A thorough political history of the era.

Lathem, Edward Connery, ed. *Meet Calvin Coolidge*. Stephen Greene. An enjoyable description of how Coolidge was seen by family, friends, neighbors, and colleagues.

Murray, R.K. *Red Scare: A Study in National Hysteria*. University of Minnesota. The roots, major events, and effects of the Red Scare.

Sinclair, Andrew. *The Available Man*. Quadrangle. A description of Warren G. Harding's political and personal life.

Chapter 30

Allen, Frederick Lewis. *Only Yesterday*. Harper & Row. Popular, lively social history of the 1920s.

Dodds, John W. *Everyday Life in Twentieth Century America*. Putnam. A social history of the 1920s.

Fitzgerald, F. Scott. *The Great Gatsby*. Scribner. A classic American novel about jazz-age society on Long Island in the 1920s.

Huggins, Nathan Irvin. *Harlem Renaissance*. Oxford University. An account of the flowering of black culture during the 1920s.

Morrden, Ethan. *That Jazz*. Putnam. Entertaining look at jazz as the symbol of the times.

This Fabulous Century, vol. 3, *The Twenties*. Time-Life. Fascinating collection of photographs of the people, places, and events of the 1920s.

Chapter 31

Bernstein, Irving. *The Lean Years. A History of the American Worker, 1920–1933*. Houghton Mifflin. A discussion of the growth of the labor movement during the prosperous twenties and the early years of the Great Depression.

Emery, Anne. *American Friend: Herbert Hoover*. Rand McNally. The last chapters of this sympathetic biography tell the story of the early years of the Great Depression.

Galbraith, John. *The Great Crash, Nineteen Twenty-Nine*. Houghton Mifflin. Easy-to-understand economic history of the causes and effects of the stock market crash.

Schlesinger, Arthur M., and Fox, Dixon R., eds. *The Age of the Great Depression, 1929–1941*. Franklin Watts. Discussion of popular reactions and moods during the depression.

Unit Nine **A Time of Trial**

Chapter 32

Deal, Bordon. *Dunbar's Cove*. Scribner. Novel based on a family's fight with the Tennessee Valley Authority over the condemnation of their land for a dam.

Graff, Robert D.; Ginna, Emmett; and Butterfield, Roger. *FDR*. Harper & Row. A pictorial account of Roosevelt's life and politics integrated with interesting text.

Gunther, John. *Roosevelt in Retrospect*. Harper & Row. Fast-reading anecdotal biography of Franklin Roosevelt.

Hurd, Charles. *When the New Deal Was Young and Gay*. Hawthorn. A nostalgic look at Roosevelt's first four years in office.

Chapter 33

Allen, Frederick Lewis. *Since Yesterday*. Harper & Row. Popularized social history of the 1930s, including an account of the Great Depression.

Bourke-White, Margaret, and Caldwell, Erskine, eds. *You Have Seen Their Faces*. Arno. Day-to-day existence of black and white rural poor in the South during the 1930s portrayed in poignant photographs with sensitive text.

Einaudi, Mario. *The Roosevelt Revolution*. Greenwood. Analysis of the permanent changes in American life and thought brought on by the New Deal.

Ellison, Ralph. *Invisible Man*. Random House. Discussion of relations between blacks and whites during the depression years.

Flynn, John T. *Country Squire in the White House*. Da Capo. A highly critical view of Roosevelt and the New Deal.

Steinbeck, John. *Grapes of Wrath*. Penguin. Classic American novel about Oklahoma Dust Bowl families who become migrant fruit pickers to survive.

Chapter 34

Ferrell, Robert H. *American Diplomacy in the Great Depression: Hoover-Stimson Foreign Policy, 1929–1933*. Norton. Detailed, scholarly study of President Hoover's foreign policy.

Rauch, Basil. *Roosevelt: From Munich to Pearl Harbor*. Da Capo. Detailed but readable political study of the era.

Sinclair, Upton. *Presidential Agent*. Curtis. Novel about an American secret agent during the late 1930s.

Williams, Ben Ames. *Time of Peace*. Houghton Mifflin. Exploration of the changing reactions of Americans to the threat of war.

Chapter 35

Beach, Edward. *Run Silent, Run Deep*. Holt. A novel about submarine warfare in the Pacific.

Buchanan, A. Russell. *The United States and World War II*. Harper & Row. Excellent survey of the military history of World War II, including discussion of diplomacy and the home front.

Conrat, Maisie and Richard. *Executive Order 9066*. Massachusetts Institute of Technology. Sensitive photographic study of Japanese internment in the United States during World War II.

Hoehling, A.A. *Homefront U.S.A.* Crowell. Illustrated story of the public and private citizens who fought the war at home.

Motley, Mary Penick, ed. *The Invisible Soldier*. Wayne State University. Anthology of 55 oral histories of the experiences of black American soldiers in World War II.

Unit Ten The United States in a Changing World

Chapter 36

Agar, Herbert. *The Price of Power: America Since 1945*. University of Chicago. Fast-moving history of the decade after World War II.

Jones, Joseph M. *The Fifteen Weeks*. Harcourt. Detailed account of people and events from the inception of the Truman Doctrine to the launching of the Marshall Plan.

Michener, James A. *The Bridges at Toko-ri*. Random House. Novel about a United States naval task force assigned to bomb enemy supply lines during the Korean War.

Chapter 37

Archer, Jules. *Battlefield President: Dwight D. Eisenhower*. Julian Messner. Readable biography of President Eisenhower stressing the military and political aspects of his career.

Handlin, Oscar. *Fire-Bell in the Night: Crisis in Civil Rights*. Little, Brown. A study of the racial crises of the 1950s.

Hayman, Leroy. *Harry S. Truman: A Biography*. Crowell. Easy-to-read account of Truman's personal and political life.

Keylin, Arleen, ed. *The Fabulous Fifties as Reported by the New York* Times. Arno. Excellent coverage of the era, with photographs of television shows, movies, musicians, and other aspects of social life juxtaposed with front pages of the *Times*.

Chapter 38

Browne, Malcolm. *The New Face of War*. Bobbs-Merrill. Inside look at the Vietnam War by a newspaper reporter.

Burns, James MacGregor. *John Kennedy: A Political Profile*. Harcourt. Comprehensive biography of Kennedy based on the author's access to Kennedy's files, family records, and letters.

Deloria, Vine, Jr. *Custer Died for Your Sins: An Indian Manifesto*. Macmillan. Biting, witty indictment of white actions toward Native

Americans and description of the situation in the 1960s by a member of the Sioux tribe.

Friedan, Betty. *The Feminine Mystique*. Dell. A critique of post–World War II inequities and discrimination against women.

Harwood, Richard, and Johnson, Haynes. *Lyndon*. Praeger. Somewhat sentimental portrait of Lyndon Johnson illustrated with over 100 photographs.

King, Martin Luther, Jr. *Stride Toward Freedom: The Montgomery Story*. Harper & Row. Account of the struggle of black citizens against segregation in Montgomery, Alabama.

O'Neill, William C. *Coming Apart: An Informal History of America in the 1960s*. Quadrangle. A lively treatment of politics and protest during the 1960s.

Chapter 39

Ford, Gerald. *A Time to Heal*. Harper & Row. The former President's autobiography, with special emphasis on his White House years.

Kalb, Bernard and Kalb, Marvin. *Kissinger*. Little, Brown. A richly detailed biography of the former secretary of state.

White, Theodore. *Breach of Faith: Fall of Richard Nixon*. Atheneum. The Watergate story, by one of America's most distinguished journalists.

Chapter 40

Evans, Rowland and Novak, Robert. *The Reagan Revolution*. Dutton. A sympathetic account of Ronald Reagan's political and economic ideas.

Friedman, S. David. *Energy: The New Era*. Random House. A scholarly discussion of America's energy policies and prospects.

Lasky, Victor. *Jimmy Carter: The Man and the Myth*. Richard Marek. An analysis of Carter's rise to the presidency, the problems he confronted, and the questions raised during his administration.

Olson, James Stuart. *The Ethnic Dimension in American History*. St. Martin's. Discusses the role of ethnic identity in American history.

Sale, Kirkpatrick. *Power Shift: The Rise of the Southern Rim and Its Challenge to the Eastern Establishment*. Random House. Discussion of the causes of the rise of the sun belt and its political consequences.

Chapter 41

Drucker, Peter F. *The Age of Discontinuity: Guidelines to Our Changing Society*. Harper & Row. A critic of government regulation of the economy presents an optimistic view of America's ability to meet coming economic challenges.

Evans, Christopher. *The Making of the Micro: A History of the Computer*. Van Nostrand Reinhold. A brief history of electronic computing.

The Fifty States

State	Capital	Date of Entry to Union (Order of Entry)	Area in Square Miles	Population (1985)	Number of Representatives in House
Alabama	Montgomery	1819 (22)	51,705	4,004,435	7
Alaska	Juneau	1959 (49)	591,004	514,819	1
Arizona	Phoenix	1912 (48)	114,000	3,086,827	5
Arkansas	Little Rock	1836 (25)	53,187	2,345,431	4
California	Sacramento	1850 (31)	158,706	25,816,590	45
Colorado	Denver	1876 (38)	104,091	3,253,425	6
Connecticut	Hartford	1788 (5)	5,018	3,160,280	6
Delaware	Dover	1787 (1)	2,044	605,711	1
Florida	Tallahassee	1845 (27)	58,664	11,071,358	19
Georgia	Atlanta	1788 (4)	58,910	5,878,225	10
Hawaii	Honolulu	1959 (50)	6,471	1,050,270	2
Idaho	Boise	1890 (43)	83,564	1,004,071	2
Illinois	Springfield	1818 (21)	56,345	11,502,433	22
Indiana	Indianapolis	1816 (19)	36,185	5,489,287	10
Iowa	Des Moines	1846 (29)	56,275	2,894,273	6
Kansas	Topeka	1861 (34)	82,277	2,453,581	5
Kentucky	Frankfort	1792 (15)	40,409	3,747,769	7
Louisiana	Baton Rouge	1812 (18)	47,751	4,553,903	8
Maine	Augusta	1820 (23)	33,265	1,158,539	2
Maryland	Annapolis	1788 (7)	10,460	4,342,562	8
Massachusetts	Boston	1788 (6)	8,284	5,764,125	11
Michigan	Lansing	1837 (26)	58,527	8,992,766	18
Minnesota	St. Paul	1858 (32)	84,402	4,199,749	8
Mississippi	Jackson	1817 (20)	47,689	2,623,069	5
Missouri	Jefferson City	1821 (24)	69,697	5,004,162	9
Montana	Helena	1889 (41)	147,046	826,933	2
Nebraska	Lincoln	1867 (37)	77,355	1,606,779	3
Nevada	Carson City	1864 (36)	110,561	933,451	2
New Hampshire	Concord	1788 (9)	9,279	980,841	2
New Jersey	Trenton	1787 (3)	7,787	7,509,625	14
New Mexico	Santa Fe	1912 (47)	121,593	1,446,347	3
New York	Albany	1788 (11)	49,108	17,676,828	34
North Carolina	Raleigh	1789 (12)	52,669	6,178,329	11
North Dakota	Bismarck	1889 (39)	70,703	692,027	1
Ohio	Columbus	1803 (17)	41,330	10,763,309	21
Oklahoma	Oklahoma City	1907 (46)	69,956	3,427,371	6
Oregon	Salem	1859 (33)	97,073	2,680,087	5
Pennsylvania	Harrisburg	1787 (2)	45,308	11,895,301	23
Rhode Island	Providence	1790 (13)	1,212	958,151	2
South Carolina	Columbia	1788 (8)	31,113	3,321.520	6
South Dakota	Pierre	1889 (40)	77,116	705,027	1
Tennessee	Nashville	1796 (16)	42,144	4,723,332	9
Texas	Austin	1845 (28)	266,807	16,384,800	27
Utah	Salt Lake City	1896 (45)	84,899	1,684,942	3
Vermont	Montpelier	1791 (14)	8,614	529,396	1
Virginia	Richmond	1788 (10)	40,767	5,642,183	10
Washington	Olympia	1889 (42)	68,138	4,366,248	8
West Virginia	Charleston	1863 (35)	24,231	1,968,989	4
Wisconsin	Madison	1848 (30)	56,153	4,792,115	9
Wyoming	Cheyenne	1890 (44)	97,809	534,744	1
District of Columbia			69	621,251	1 (nonvoting)

Presidents and Vice-Presidents of the United States

President	Term(s) Served	Political Party	Vice-President	Term(s) Served
1. **George Washington** (b. 1732, d. 1799)	1789–1797	None	John Adams	1789–1797
2. **John Adams** (b. 1735, d. 1826)	1797–1801	Federalist	Thomas Jefferson	1797–1801
3. **Thomas Jefferson** (b. 1743, d. 1826)	1801–1809	Dem.-Rep.	Aaron Burr	1801–1805
			George Clinton	1805–1809
4. **James Madison** (b. 1751, d. 1836)	1809–1817	Dem.-Rep.	George Clinton	1809–1812
			Elbridge Gerry	1813–1814
5. **James Monroe** (b. 1758, d. 1831)	1817–1825	Dem.-Rep.	Daniel D. Tompkins	1817–1825
6. **John Quincy Adams** (b. 1767, d. 1848)	1825–1829	Dem.-Rep.	John C. Calhoun	1825–1829
7. **Andrew Jackson** (b. 1767, d. 1845)	1829–1837	Democrat	John C. Calhoun	1829–1832
			Martin Van Buren	1833–1837
8. **Martin Van Buren** (b. 1782, d. 1862)	1837–1841	Democrat	Richard M. Johnson	1837–1841
9. **William H. Harrison** (b. 1773, d. 1841)	1841	Whig	John Tyler	1841
10. **John Tyler** (b. 1790, d. 1862)	1841–1845	Whig	*	
11. **James K. Polk** (b. 1795, d. 1849)	1845–1849	Democrat	George M. Dallas	1845–1849
12. **Zachary Taylor** (b. 1784, d. 1850)	1849–1850	Whig	Millard Fillmore	1849–1850
13. **Millard Fillmore** (b. 1800, d. 1874)	1850–1853	Whig	*	
14. **Franklin Pierce** (b. 1804, d. 1869)	1853–1857	Democrat	William R. King	1853
15. **James Buchanan** (b. 1791, d. 1868)	1857–1861	Democrat	John C. Breckinridge	1857–1861
16. **Abraham Lincoln** (b. 1809, d. 1865)	1861–1865	Republican	Hannibal Hamlin	1861–1865
			Andrew Johnson	1865
17. **Andrew Johnson** (b. 1808, d. 1875)	1865–1869	Republican	*	
18. **Ulysses S. Grant** (b. 1822, d. 1885)	1869–1877	Republican	Schuyler Colfax	1869–1873
			Henry Wilson	1873–1875
19. **Rutherford B. Hayes** (b. 1822, d. 1893)	1877–1881	Republican	William A. Wheeler	1877–1881
20. **James A. Garfield** (b. 1831, d. 1881)	1881	Republican	Chester A. Arthur	1881
21. **Chester A. Arthur** (b. 1829, d. 1886)	1881–1885	Republican	*	
22. **Grover Cleveland** (b. 1837, d. 1908)	1885–1889	Democrat	Thomas A. Hendricks	1885
23. **Benjamin Harrison** (b. 1833, d. 1901)	1889–1893	Republican	Levi P. Morton	1889–1893
24. **Grover Cleveland** (b. 1837, d. 1908)	1893–1897	Democrat	Adlai E. Stevenson	1893–1897
25. **William McKinley** (b. 1843, d. 1901)	1897–1901	Republican	Garret A. Hobart	1897–1899
			Theodore Roosevelt	1901
26. **Theodore Roosevelt** (b. 1858, d. 1919)	1901–1909	Republican	Charles W. Fairbanks	1905–1909
27. **William H. Taft** (b. 1857, d. 1930)	1909–1913	Republican	James S. Sherman	1909–1912
28. **Woodrow Wilson** (b. 1856, d. 1924)	1913–1921	Democrat	Thomas R. Marshall	1913–1921
29. **Warren G. Harding** (b. 1865, d. 1923)	1921–1923	Republican	Calvin Coolidge	1921–1923
30. **Calvin Coolidge** (b. 1872, d. 1933)	1923–1929	Republican	Charles G. Dawes	1925–1929
31. **Herbert C. Hoover** (b. 1874, d. 1964)	1929–1933	Republican	Charles Curtis	1929–1933
32. **Franklin D. Roosevelt** (b. 1882, d. 1945)	1933–1945	Democrat	John N. Garner	1933–1941
			Henry A. Wallace	1941–1945
			Harry S. Truman	1945
33. **Harry S. Truman** (b. 1884, d. 1972)	1945–1953	Democrat	Alben W. Barkley	1949–1953
34. **Dwight D. Eisenhower** (b. 1890, d. 1969)	1953–1961	Republican	Richard M. Nixon	1953–1961
35. **John F. Kennedy** (b. 1917, d. 1963)	1961–1963	Democrat	Lyndon B. Johnson	1961–1963
36. **Lyndon B. Johnson** (b. 1908, d. 1973)	1963–1969	Democrat	Hubert H. Humphrey	1965–1969
37. **Richard M. Nixon** (b. 1913)	1969–1974	Republican	Spiro T. Agnew	1969–1973
			Gerald R. Ford	1973–1974
38. **Gerald R. Ford** [†] (b. 1913)	1974–1977	Republican	Nelson A. Rockefeller	1974–1977
39. **Jimmy Carter** (b. 1924)	1977–1981	Democrat	Walter F. Mondale	1977–1981
40. **Ronald Reagan** (b. 1911)	1981–	Republican	George Bush	1981–

* Prior to ratification of the Twenty-fifth Amendment in 1967, there was no constitutional provision for replacing a Vice-President if that office became vacant.

† Inaugurated August 9, 1974, to replace Nixon, who resigned the same day.

The Declaration of Independence

When in the course of human events it becomes necessary for one people to dissolve the political bands which have connected them with another and to assume, among the powers of the earth, the separate and equal station to which the laws of nature and of nature's God entitle them, a decent respect to the opinions of mankind requires that they should declare the causes which impel them to the separation.

We hold these truths to be self-evident, that all men are created equal; that they are endowed by their Creator with certain unalienable rights; that among these are life, liberty, and the pursuit of happiness. That, to secure these rights, governments are instituted among men, deriving their just powers from the consent of the governed; that, whenever any form of government becomes destructive of these ends, it is the right of the people to alter or to abolish it, and to institute a new government, laying its foundation on such principles, and organizing its powers in such form, as to them shall seem most likely to effect their safety and happiness. Prudence, indeed, will dictate that governments long established should not be changed for light and transient causes; and, accordingly, all experience hath shown that mankind are more disposed to suffer, while evils are sufferable, than to right themselves by abolishing the forms to which they are accustomed. But when a long train of abuses and usurpations, pursuing invariably the same object, evinces a design to reduce them under absolute despotism, it is their right, it is their duty, to throw off such government and to provide new guards for their future security. Such has been the patient sufferance of these colonies, and such is now the necessity which constrains them to alter their former systems of government. The history of the present King of Great Britain is a history of repeated injuries and usurpations, all having, in direct object, the establishment of an absolute tyranny over these States. To prove this, let facts be submitted to a candid world:

He has refused his assent to laws the most wholesome and necessary for the public good.

He has forbidden his governors to pass laws of immediate and pressing importance, unless suspended in their operation till his assent should be obtained; and, when so suspended, he has utterly neglected to attend to them.

He has refused to pass other laws for the accommodation of the large districts of people, unless those people would relinquish the right of representation in the legislature: a right inestimable to them and formidable to tyrants only.

He has called together legislative bodies at places unusual, uncomfortable, and distant from the depository of their public records, for the sole purpose of fatiguing them into compliance with his measures.

He has dissolved representative houses, repeatedly for opposing, with manly firmness, his invasions on the rights of the people.

He has refused, for a long time after such dissolutions, to cause others to be elected: whereby the legislative powers, incapable of annihilation, have returned to the people at large for their exercise; the state remaining, in the meantime, exposed to all the danger of invasion from without and convulsions within.

He has endeavored to prevent the population of these States; for that purpose, obstructing the laws for naturalization of foreigners, refusing to pass others to encourage their migration hither, and raising the conditions of new appropriations of lands.

He has obstructed the administration of justice by refusing his assent to laws for establishing judiciary powers.

He has made judges dependent on his will alone for the tenure of their offices and the amount and payment of their salaries.

He has erected a multitude of new offices and sent hither swarms of officers to harass our people and eat out their substance.

He has kept among us, in time of peace, standing armies, without the consent of our legislatures.

He has affected to render the military independent of, and superior to, the civil power.

He has combined with others to subject us to a jurisdiction foreign to our Constitution and unacknowledged by our laws, giving his assent to their acts of pretended legislation—

For quartering large bodies of armed troops among us;

For protecting them by a mock trial from punishment for any murders which they should commit on the inhabitants of these States;

For cutting off our trade with all parts of the world;

For imposing taxes on us without our consent;

For depriving us, in many cases, of the benefit of trial by jury;

For transporting us beyond seas to be tried for pretended offences;

For abolishing the free system of English laws in a neighboring province, establishing therein an arbitrary government, and enlarging its boundaries, so as to render it at once an example and fit instrument for introducing the same absolute rule into these colonies;

For taking away our charters, abolishing our most valuable laws, and altering, fundamentally, the powers of our governments;

For suspending our own legislatures and declaring themselves invested with power to legislate for us in all cases whatsoever.

He has abdicated government here by declaring us out of his protection and waging war against us.

He has plundered our seas, ravaged our coasts, burnt our towns, and destroyed the lives of our people.

He is, at this time, transporting large armies of foreign mercenaries to complete the works of death, desolation, and tyranny already begun with circumstances of cruelty and perfidy scarcely paralleled in the most barbarous ages, and totally unworthy, the head of a civilized nation.

He has constrained our fellow citizens, taken captive on the high seas, to bear arms against their country, to become the executioners of their friends and brethren, or to fall themselves by their hands.

He has excited domestic insurrections amongst us and has endeavored to bring on the inhabitants of our frontiers, the merciless Indian savages, whose known rule of warfare is an undistinguished destruction of all ages, sexes, and conditions.

In every stage of these oppressions, we have petitioned for redress in the most humble terms; our repeated petitions have been answered only by repeated injury. A prince whose character is thus marked by every act which may define a tyrant is unfit to be the ruler of a free people.

Nor have we been wanting in attention to our British brethren. We have warned them, from time to time, of attempts made by their legislature to extend an unwarrantable jurisdiction over us. We have reminded them of the circumstances of our emigration and settlement here. We have appealed to their native justice and magnanimity, and we have conjured them, by the ties of our common kindred, to disavow these usurpations, which would inevitably interrupt our connections and correspondence. They, too, have been deaf to the voice of justice and consanguinity. We must, therefore, acquiesce in the necessity which denounces our separation, and hold them, as we hold the rest of mankind, enemies in war, in peace, friends.

We, therefore, the representatives of the United States of America, in general Congress assembled, appealing to the Supreme Judge of the world for the rectitude of our intentions, do, in the name and by the authority of the good people of these colonies, solemnly publish and declare, that these united colonies are, and of right ought to be, free and independent states: that they are absolved from all allegiance to the British Crown, and that all political connection between them and the state of Great Britain is, and ought to be, totally dissolved; and that, as free and independent states, they have full power to levy war, conclude peace, contract alliances, establish commerce, and to do all other acts and things which independent states may of right do. And, for the support of this declaration, with a firm reliance on the protection of Divine Providence, we mutually pledge to each other our lives, our fortunes, and our sacred honor.

The Constitution of the United States of America

The text of the Constitution is printed in black. Annotations are printed in blue. The titles of articles, sections, and clauses have been added for clarity. They are not part of the original document. The portions of the Constitution in brackets have been changed by amendments or no longer apply. Page numbers in the annotations refer to relevant material in your textbook. Difficult terms in the Constitution are italicized and defined in the annotations.

Preamble

We, the people of the United States, in order to form a more perfect Union, establish justice, insure domestic tranquillity, provide for the common defense, promote the general welfare, and secure the blessings of liberty to ourselves and our posterity, do ordain and establish this Constitution for the United States of America.

The Preamble introduces the purposes of the government established by the Constitution. It does not have the force of law. Therefore, parties to lawsuits cannot base claims on the provisions contained in the Preamble.

Article 1. The Legislative Branch

Legislative powers refers to the power to make law. The Senate and the House of Representatives make up the federal government's legislative branch.

Section 1. A Two-House Legislature

All legislative powers herein granted shall be vested in a Congress of the United States, which shall consist of a Senate and House of Representatives.

Through custom other branches of the federal government also possess law-making power. When judges interpret the Constitution, they are, in effect, making law (page 208). Furthermore, such regulatory agencies as the Federal Trade Commission can make rules that have the effect of law. The powers of the federal regulatory agencies, however, are subject to the control of Congress.

Section 2. House of Representatives

1. Election of Members The House of Representatives shall be composed of members chosen every second year by the people of the several states, and the electors in each state shall have the qualifications requisite for electors of the most numerous branch of the state legislature.

Clause 1 *Electors* refers to voters. Members of the House run for election every two years. The original Constitution does not specify voting qualifications. It provides that people qualified to vote in elections for the largest house of the state legislature must be allowed to vote in elections for the House of Representatives. Four amendments to the Constitution—the Fifteenth, Nineteenth, Twenty-fourth, and Twenty-sixth—have restricted state power to limit the right to vote.

2. Qualifications No person shall be a Representative who shall not have attained to the age of twenty-five years, and been seven years a citizen of the United States, and who shall not, when elected, be an inhabitant of that state in which he shall be chosen.

Clause 2 A member of the House must live in the state he or she represents, but members need not be legal residents of the district they represent. Tradition, however, dictates that candidates run for election in the districts in which they legally reside.

3. Determining Representation Representatives [and direct taxes] shall be apportioned among the several states which may be

Clause 3 *Persons bound to service* refers to indentured servants, while *all other persons* refers to the slave population. The *enumeration* that will be made every ten years refers to a census.

included within this Union, according to their respective numbers [which shall be determined by adding to the whole number of free persons, including those bound to service for a term of years, and excluding Indians not taxed, three-fifths of all other persons]. The actual enumeration shall be made within three years after the first meeting of the Congress of the United States, and within every subsequent term of ten years, in such manner as they shall by law direct. The number of Representatives shall not exceed one for every 30,000, but each state shall have at least one Representative; [and until such enumeration shall be made, the state of New Hampshire shall be entitled to choose three; Massachusetts, eight; Rhode Island and Providence Plantations, one; Connecticut, five; New York, six; New Jersey, four; Pennsylvania, eight; Delaware, one; Maryland, six; Virginia, ten; North Carolina, five; South Carolina, five; and Georgia, three.]

A state's representation in the House is based on its population. According to the original clause, the state's entire free population is counted for the purpose of representation, but only three fifths of the slaves were to be counted. This arrangement resulted from a compromise at the Constitutional Convention (page 157). The so-called three-fifths clause became meaningless when the Thirteenth Amendment, which freed the slaves, was added to the Constitution. An act of Congress has fixed the number of members in the House at 435.

4. Filling Vacancies When vacancies happen in the representation from any state, the executive authority thereof shall issue writs of election to fill such vacancies.

Clause 4 *Executive authority* refers to the governor of a state. A *writ of election* is an order to hold an election. When a member of the House leaves office prior to the end of his or her term, the governor must fill that vacancy by calling a special election.

5. Selection of Officers; Power of Impeachment The House of Representatives shall choose their Speaker and other officers; and shall have the sole power of impeachment.

Clause 5 The *speaker of the House* is a member who acts as its presiding officer. By modern practice, the speaker is chosen by the party that has a majority in the House. The speaker applies House rules and determines when members will be allowed to address the House. *Impeachment* is an accusation of misconduct that can be made against the President and Vice-President, federal judges, and other high federal officials. Impeachment and removal from office are discussed in Section 3.

Section 3. The Senate

1. Selection of Members The Senate of the United States shall be composed of two Senators from each state [chosen by the legislature thereof], for six years, and each Senator shall have one vote.

Clause 1 According to the original clause, the legislature of each state was to elect two senators. This clause was nullified by the Seventeenth Amendment, ratified in 1913.

2. Alternating Terms; Filling Vacancies Immediately after they shall be assembled in consequence of the first election, they shall be divided as equally as may be into three classes. [The seats of the Senators of the first class shall be vacated at the expiration of the second year, of the second class at the expiration of the fourth year, and of the third class at the expiration of the sixth year,] so that one-third may be chosen every second year; [and if vacancies happen by resignation, or otherwise, during the recess of the legislature

Clause 2 Unlike the House, in which the terms of all members expire at the same time, the terms of only one third of the senators expire in any congressional election year. Thus every two years one third of the Senate stands for reelection. Normally only one of a state's senators would run in any election year. The election of the Senate by thirds insures that the body will not be totally transformed in any one election.

This clause allows the governor, the *executive*, to fill vacancies that occur between elections by making temporary appointments if the state legislature is not in session. Under this clause, when the legislature reconvenes it has the power to fill any existing vacancies. The method for filling vacancies was changed by the Seventeenth Amendment.

of any state, the executive thereof may make temporary appointments until the next meeting of the legislature, which shall then fill such vacancies.]

3. Qualifications No person shall be a Senator who shall not have attained to the age of thirty years, and been nine years a citizen of the United States, and who shall not, when elected, be an inhabitant of that state for which he shall be chosen.

Clause 3 The qualifications for membership in the Senate are more restrictive than qualifications for membership in the House. The age qualifications must be met at the time the oath of office is taken.

4. President of the Senate The Vice-President of the United States shall be president of the Senate, but shall have no vote, unless they be equally divided.

Clause 4 The Vice-President of the United States is the president of the Senate. As presiding officer, he or she applies the rules of the Senate. The president of the Senate may vote only to break a tie. The first Vice-President, John Adams, cast 20 votes during his term in office. Besides filling a vacancy created by the President's death or resignation, these are the only powers the Constitution assigns to the Vice-President.

5. Election of Senate Officers The Senate shall choose their other officers, and also a president *pro tempore*, in the absence of the Vice-President, or when he shall exercise the office of the President of the United States.

Clause 5 *Pro tempore* means temporary. The president pro tempore must be a member of the Senate. He or she presides over the Senate in the absence of the Vice-President. Under the Presidential Succession Act of 1947, the president pro tempore of the Senate follows the Vice-President and the speaker of the House in the line of succession if the office of President becomes vacant.

6. Impeachment Trials The Senate shall have the sole power to try all impeachments. When sitting for that purpose, they shall be on oath or affirmation. When the President of the United States is tried, the Chief Justice shall preside; and no person shall be convicted without the concurrence of two-thirds of the members present.

Clause 6 The *Chief Justice* refers to the Chief Justice of the Supreme Court. By a majority vote the House may impeach the President and Vice-President, federal judges, and cabinet officers for "treason, bribery, or other high crimes and misdemeanors." (See Article 2, Section 4).

The Senate acts as a jury in impeachment cases. A two-thirds vote against the accused results in conviction. Although several federal judges have been convicted by the Senate, no President has ever been convicted. The House impeached President Andrew Johnson in 1868, but the Senate acquitted him of the charges (page 359). President Richard Nixon faced the possibility of impeachment and conviction, but his resignation ended the impeachment proceedings in progress (page 733).

7. Penalties Upon Conviction Judgment in cases of impeachment shall not extend further than to removal from office, and disqualification to hold and enjoy any office of honor, trust, or profit under the United States; but the party convicted shall nevertheless be liable and subject to indictment, trial, judgment, and punishment, according to law.

Clause 7 *Judgment* in this clause means conviction by the Senate. Government officials convicted in impeachment proceedings are removed from office and barred from holding office in the future. The Senate does not have the power to impose any other penalty on convicted officials. However, they may be tried subsequently in criminal courts.

Section 4. Times of Elections and Meetings

1. Election of Congress The times, places, and manner of holding elections for Senators and Representatives shall be prescribed in

Clause 1 Under this clause the state legislatures are free to determine the time and manner of congressional elections unless Congress acts. Prior to 1842 Congress allowed the states to regulate congressional elections. In each state by the legislature thereof; but the Congress may at any time by law make or alter such regulations, except as to the places of choosing Senators.

some states members of the House were chosen on a state-wide basis. In 1842 Congress required the states to create congressional districts. One representative was to be elected from each district. In 1872 Congress provided that congressional elections be held in every state on the same date in even-numbered years.

2. Annual Sessions The Congress shall assemble at least once in every year, [and such meeting shall be on the first Monday in December, unless they shall by law appoint a different day.]

Clause 2 The Twentieth Amendment changed the date for the beginning of each congressional session to January 3 unless Congress resolves to meet on another day.

Section 5. Rules for the Conduct of Business

1. Organization Each house shall be the judge of the elections, returns, and qualifications of its own members, and a majority of each shall constitute a quorum to do business; but a smaller number may adjourn from day to day, and may be authorized to compel the attendance of absent members, in such manner, and under such penalties, as each house may provide.

Clause 1 A *quorum* is the minimum number of members required to be present for the conduct of business. Each house of Congress has the right to decide the qualifications of its members. Until 1969 it was generally held that Congress could impose qualifications not specified in the Constitution. Thus some members have been barred from Congress because they were found to have engaged in misconduct.

For example, in 1967 the House of Representatives refused to seat Adam Clayton Powell of New York because of "gross misconduct." When Powell's suit challenging his exclusion reached the Supreme Court, the Court held that the Constitution does not permit Congress to exclude legally elected members who have met all the requirements specified in Article 1, Section 2.

2. Procedures Each house may determine the rules of its proceedings, punish its members for disorderly behavior, and with the concurrence of two-thirds, expel a member.

Clause 2 This clause gives both houses of Congress wide power to conduct their business. The Senate, for example, has established rules for debate that allow *filibustering*, the practice of giving lengthy speeches for the purpose of obstructing pending legislation. In 1917 the Senate passed a *cloture* rule, a rule allowing the Senate to vote to stop a filibuster. The right to filibuster does not exist in the House.

3. A Written Record Each house shall keep a journal of its proceedings, and from time to time publish the same, excepting such parts as may in their judgment require secrecy; and the yeas and nays of the members of either house on any question shall, at the desire of one-fifth of those present, be entered on the journal.

Clause 3 The *Congressional Record*, published daily, prints all speeches made on the floor of the House and the Senate. It also records the votes cast.

4. Rules for Adjournment Neither house, during the session of Congress, shall, without the consent of the other, adjourn for more than three days, nor to any other place than that in which the two houses shall be sitting.

Clause 4 Neither the House nor the Senate can adjourn for more than three days without the approval of the other body. This clause requires the two houses of Congress to meet in the same place. For example, the House cannot adjourn its session in Washington, D.C., and reconvene in another place.

Article 2, Section 3 gives the President the power to adjourn both houses of Congress if they cannot agree on a time to adjourn. To date the President has never exercised this power.

Section 6. Privileges and Restrictions

1. Salaries and Immunities The Senators and Representatives shall receive a compensation for their services, to be ascertained by law and paid out of the Treasury of the United States. They shall in all cases, except treason, felony, and breach of the peace, be privileged from arrest during their attendance at the session of their respective houses, and in going to and returning from the same; and for any speech or debate in either house, they shall not be questioned in any other place.

Clause 1 The salary for members of Congress is set by an act of Congress. Members with special responsibilities, such as the speaker of the House, receive larger salaries.

This clause provides that when Congress is in session its members shall enjoy an immunity from arrest in civil cases. Thus the clause protects members of Congress from imprisonment for debt. The clause does not provide immunity from arrest in state or federal criminal cases.

A member of Congress is protected from libel and slander suits for things he or she says in Congress while it is in session. This provision also protects members of Congress from lawsuits concerning their written words. Immunity under the speech and debate provision does not extend to words spoken outside Congress.

2. Restrictions on Other Employment No Senator or Representative shall, during the time for which he was elected, be appointed to any civil office under the authority of the United States, which shall have been created, or the emoluments whereof shall have been increased, during such time; and no person holding any office under the United States shall be a member of either house during his continuance in office.

Clause 2 *Emolument* means salary. The first part of this clause bars a member of Congress from holding a federal office that was created or the salary of which was increased during his or her term in Congress. The second part of the clause prevents officeholders in the executive and judicial branches from serving in Congress. This provision strengthens the separation of powers.

Section 7. Law-Making Process

1. Tax Bills All bills for raising revenue shall originate in the House of Representatives; but the Senate may propose or concur with amendments as on other bills.

Clause 1 *Revenue* is income raised by a unit of government through taxation. Under this clause, federal revenue bills must originate in the House. This was a democratic measure because when the Constitution was written, the House was the only branch of government elected directly by the people. The Senate can amend revenue legislation. By custom, bills authorizing the expenditure of federal money also originate in the House.

2. How a Bill Becomes a Law Every bill which shall have passed the House of Representatives and the Senate shall, before it become a law, be presented to the President of the United States; if he approve, he shall sign it, but if not, he shall return it, with his objections, to that house in which it shall have originated, who shall enter the objections at large on their journal, and proceed to reconsider it. If after such reconsideration two-thirds of that house shall agree to pass the bill, it shall be sent, together with the objections, to the other house, by which it shall likewise be reconsidered, and, if approved by two-thirds of that house, it shall become a law. But in all such cases the votes of both houses shall be determined by yeas and nays, and the names of the persons voting for and against the bill shall be entered on the journal of each house

Clause 2 A *bill* is a proposal for a law. Bills passed by a majority of the House and Senate are presented to the President. If the President signs the bill it becomes law. A bill can also become law without the President's signature. The President can refuse to act on a bill. If Congress is in session at the time, the bill becomes law ten days after the President receives it.

The President can *veto*, or reject, a bill in two ways. He or she can veto it by sending it back to the house where it originated or by refusing to take any action on it. If the President withholds action and Congress adjourns within ten days of the President's receipt of the bill, the bill is dead. This method of killing a bill without taking action is known as the *pocket veto*.

A bill vetoed by the President can still become law if it is passed again by a two-thirds vote in each house of Congress. This clause is an important part of the system of checks and balances established by the Constitution (pages 161–162).

respectively. If any bill shall not be returned by the President within ten days (Sundays excepted) after it shall have been presented to him, the same bill shall be a law, in like manner as if he had signed it, unless the Congress by their adjournment prevent its return, in which case it shall not be a law.

3. Resolutions Passed by Congress Every order, resolution, or vote to which the concurrence of the Senate and House of Representatives may be necessary (except on a question of adjournment) shall be presented to the President of the United States; and before the same shall take effect, shall be approved by him, or being disapproved by him, shall be repassed by two-thirds of the Senate and House of Representatives, according to the rules and limitations prescribed in the case of a bill.

Clause 3 This clause was inserted to prevent Congress from bypassing the President by calling pieces of legislation resolutions rather than bills. *Joint resolutions* go through the same process as bills and have the force of law. Such resolutions are passed when there is no need for prolonged examination of a measure before Congress. For example, proposals to renew an existing piece of legislation sometimes take the form of a joint resolution.

Concurrent resolutions are the expression of the will of Congress. They are not submitted to the President and do not have the force of law. Changes in rules of legislative procedure typically take the form of concurrent resolutions. Congressional resolutions proposing constitutional amendments are not presented to the President.

Section 8. Powers Delegated to Congress
The Congress shall have power

1. To lay and collect taxes, duties, imposts, and excises, to pay the debts and provide for the common defense and general welfare of the United States; but all duties, imposts, and excises shall be uniform throughout the United States;

Clause 1 *Duties* are tariffs, and *excises* are taxes on the production or sale of particular goods. *Imposts* refers to taxes generally. This clause gives Congress the power to tax and to spend tax revenues.

The clause does not give Congress unlimited taxation power. For example, Congress may not tax exports (see Section 9, Clause 5) or the activities of state governments. Until the ratification of the Sixteenth Amendment in 1913, Congress could not impose an income tax unless the tax was apportioned among the states according to population. Taxes under this clause must be imposed uniformly.

2. To borrow money on the credit of the United States;

Clause 2 Congress may authorize the sale of bonds to the public to raise money for the operation of the government. The government thus borrows money from the bond holders. People and banks invest in bonds on the assumption that the government will meet its obligations to creditors. The Constitution sets no limit on the total indebtedness of the federal government.

3. To regulate commerce with foreign nations, and among the several states, and with the Indian tribes;

Clause 3 This clause gives the federal government exclusive power to regulate foreign and interstate trade. For example, only the federal government may impose tariffs on foreign goods or regulate the freight rates of railroads crossing state lines. The so-called commerce clause provided the constitutional basis for the Interstate Commerce Act (page 419), the Sherman Antitrust Act (page 420), as well as other federal regulatory legislation.

4. To establish a uniform rule of naturalization, and uniform laws on the subject of bankruptcies throughout the United States;

Clause 4 *Naturalization* is the process by which a citizen of one country becomes a citizen of another country. This clause requires that the naturalization process be the same throughout the United States. A business or individual is *bankrupt* when it is unable to pay its debts. The clause empowers Congress to pass laws to supervise the collection of debts from bankrupt businesses or individuals.

5. To coin money, regulate the value thereof, and of foreign coin, and fix the standard of weights and measures;

Clause 5 Under this clause Congress is authorized to coin metallic currency. The clause also provides the legal basis for the printing of paper currency by the government. The government determines the metallic content of coins and the amount of gold and silver that backs printed currency. It also has the power to adjust the value of the dollar in relation to foreign currencies.

6. To provide for the punishment of counterfeiting the securities and current coin of the United States;

Clause 6 *Counterfeiting* is the act of making an unauthorized copy of United States currency for the purpose of using it as legal tender. Law enforcement agents from the Treasury Department investigate this crime.

7. To establish post offices and post roads;

Clause 7 By virtue of this clause Congress has the power to establish a government monopoly over delivery of mail.

8. To promote the progress of science and useful arts by securing for limited times to authors and inventors the exclusive right to their respective writings and discoveries;

Clause 8 Under this clause Congress may pass *copyright* laws that enable a person to register his or her work in the United States Copyright Office. Once copyrighted, a work may not be used or copied without the author's permission. A copyright registered prior to January 1978 lasts for 28 years and may be renewed for an additional 28 years. A copyright registered after January 1978 lasts for the author's lifetime plus 50 years.

The clause also allows Congress to enact legislation to protect the work of inventors. The government issues *patents* to people who invent new goods or manufacturing processes. An invention registered with the Patent Office may not be manufactured and sold without the permission of the patent holder. Patents for inventions last for 17 years.

9. To constitute tribunals inferior to the Supreme Court;

Clause 9 Article 3, Section 1, establishes the Supreme Court. This clause gives Congress the power to create *inferior*, or lower, federal courts.

10. To define and punish piracies and felonies committed on the high seas and offenses against the law of nations;

Clause 10 *Piracy* is robbery of ships on the high seas. Under this clause United States courts have jurisdiction over piracy cases even though the crime may have been committed outside national territorial limits.

11. To declare war, [grant letters of marque and reprisal,] and make rules concerning captures on land and water;

Clause 11 *Letters of marque and reprisal* are documents issued by the government authorizing an armed merchant vessel to attack ships of an enemy nation.

Congress has the exclusive power to declare war. Declarations of war are granted upon request of the President. This procedure was followed in the War of 1812, the Spanish-American War, and the two world wars. But the United States has engaged in armed conflict without a congressional declaration of war, as in Korea and Vietnam (page 724). The legal basis of a war fought without congressional declaration is the President's authority as commander-in-chief (Article 2, Section 2, Clause 1) to order American forces into action. During the late 1960s and early 1970s the Supreme Court refused to review claims that challenged the constitutionality of the Vietnam War. The War Powers Act of 1973 placed restrictions on the President's power to engage American forces without an official declaration of war (page 724).

12. To raise and support armies, but no appropriation of money to that use shall be for a longer term than two years;

13. To provide and maintain a navy;

14. To make rules for the government and regulation of the land and naval forces;

Clauses 12, 13, 14 These clauses subordinate the military to the control of Congress. Congress determines the level of funding for the army and navy, and it has the power to fix the size of the armed forces. Although these clauses do not mention a military draft, the power "to raise and support armies" suggests the authority to establish a draft. Clause 14 empowers Congress to write a code governing military discipline.

15. To provide for calling forth the militia to execute the laws of the Union, suppress insurrections, and repel invasions;

16. To provide for organizing, arming, and disciplining the militia, and for governing such part of them as may be employed in the service of the United States, reserving to the states, respectively, the appointment of the officers, and the authority of training the militia according to the discipline prescribed by Congress;

Clauses 15, 16 *Militia* refers to the various state militias. The militia exists to protect the United States from insurrection and foreign invasion. Although the militia, now called the National Guard, is organized along state lines and is under the command of the governor of each state, it can be placed under the command of the President. President Eisenhower placed the Arkansas National Guard under federal control during the Little Rock school integration crisis (page 694).

17. To exercise exclusive legislation in all cases whatsoever, over such district (not exceeding ten miles square) as may, by cession of particular states, and the acceptance of Congress, become the seat of government of the United States, and to exercise like authority over all places purchased by the consent of the legislature of the state in which the same shall be, for the erection of forts, magazines, arsenals, dock-yards, and other needful buildings;—and

Clause 17 This clause provides that the site of the nation's capital be outside the jurisdiction of any state. It calls upon the federal government to exercise full control over the district in which the capital is located. In 1790, after much discussion, Congress made Washington, D.C., the nation's capital (page 174). Congress has the power to legislate for Washington, D.C., but in 1973 it gave the district's residents the right to elect local officials.

18. To make all laws which shall be necessary and proper for carrying into execution the foregoing powers, and all other powers vested by this Constitution in the government of the United States, or in any department or officer thereof.

Clause 18 The first 17 clauses in this section list the powers that the Constitution specifically delegates to Congress (page 159). The framers of the Constitution realized that Congress could not deal with the changing needs of the nation if it was limited to only those powers explicitly listed. They therefore added this clause. Under the clause Congress may pass legislation that is "necessary and proper" for implementing its delegated powers. It is sometimes called the elastic clause because it allows Congress to stretch the meaning of its delegated powers.

Section 9. Powers Denied to the Federal Government

1. The Slave Trade [The migration or importation of such persons as any of the states now existing shall think proper to admit shall not be prohibited by the Congress prior to the year 1808; but a tax or duty may be imposed on such importation, not exceeding $10 for each person.]

Clause 1 This clause, which deals with the importation of slaves, was the result of a compromise between supporters and defenders of the slave trade (page 157). To satisfy slave owners, the Constitution barred Congress from immediately prohibiting the importation of slaves. But the Constitution did provide that Congress could prohibit the slave trade after 1808. The $10 import tax was never imposed. This clause is now obsolete.

2. Writ of Habeas Corpus The privilege of the writ of *habeas corpus* shall not be suspended, unless when in cases of rebellion or invasion the public safety may require it.

Clause 2 A *writ* is a court order directing an action. A *writ of habeas corpus* is a court order directing government officials to bring a prisoner to court and explain why he or she is being held. The writ of habeas corpus is an important safeguard against unlawful imprisonment. A judge can order the release of a prisoner if he or she finds that there are insufficient grounds for the prisoner's detention.

The clause allows for the suspension of the writ of habeas corpus in times of rebellion or invasion. But it does not state which branch of government has the power to suspend the writ. In 1861, in the case of *ex parte Merryman*, Chief Justice of the Supreme Court Roger B. Taney ruled that Congress, not the President, has the power to suspend the writ of habeas corpus. Congress subsequently passed legislation authorizing the President to suspend the writ. President Abraham Lincoln suspended the writ of habeas corpus during the Civil War.

3. Bills of Attainder and Ex Post Facto Laws No bill of attainder or *ex post facto* law shall be passed.

Clause 3 A *bill of attainder* is a legislative act declaring that a person is guilty of a particular crime. *Ex post facto* laws impose penalties on acts that were committed when the conduct was not forbidden by law.

Bills of attainder punish the accused without giving him or her the benefit of a trial by jury. For example, during World War II Congress prohibited the payment of salaries to three government officials accused of being unpatriotic. In 1946 the Supreme Court nullified the act, holding that the legislation constituted a bill of attainder. Legislation requiring communists to register with the government, however, has been held not to constitute a bill of attainder.

There have been many court decisions explaining what constitutes an ex post facto law. For example, in 1972 a United States district court held that a law barring the payment of government pensions to persons previously found guilty of *perjury,* or lying under oath, in national security matters constituted an ex post facto law and thus could not be enforced. In this case the people claiming the pensions had not been federal employees at the time the pension law was passed.

4. Apportionment of Direct Taxes [No capitation or other direct tax shall be laid, unless in proportion to the census or enumeration herein before directed to be taken.]

Clause 4 A *capitation tax* is a tax levied directly on each person. Direct taxes, according to this clause, can be imposed only if they are divided among the states according to population. The Sixteenth Amendment gives Congress the right to establish an income tax without regard to the population of the states.

5. Taxes on Exports No tax or duty shall be laid on articles exported from any state.

Clause 5 Congress is explicitly barred from taxing exports. The clause was inserted at the insistence of southern states, since their economies depended on exporting agricultural products (page 157).

6. Special Preference for Trade No preference shall be given any regulation of commerce or revenue to the ports of one state over those of another; nor shall vessels bound to, or from, one state, be obliged to enter, clear, or pay duties in another.

Clause 6 To *enter* means to report to the customs house. A vessel is *cleared* when it obtains the proper documents at the customs house. The clause bars Congress from passing legislation that would promote the commerce of one state to the disadvantage of others. It also prohibits states from imposing tariffs on interstate commerce.

7. Spending No money shall be drawn from the Treasury, but in consequence of appropriations made by law; and a regular statement and account of the receipts and expenditures of all public money shall be published from time to time.

Clause 7 The federal government may not spend any money unless Congress has authorized its expenditure. Thus the President is prohibited from drawing money from the treasury for programs that have not been approved by Congress. This power provides Congress with an important check on the President.

Whether the President must spend money authorized by Congress is unclear. For example, President Lyndon Johnson refused to release federal aid for highway funds to the states, and President Richard Nixon refused to spend food stamp money appropriated by Congress. The refusal of the President to spend money authorized by Congress is called *impoundment.*

8. Creation of Titles of Nobility No title of nobility shall be granted by the United States; and no person holding any office of profit or trust under them, shall, without the consent of the Congress, accept of any present, emolument, office, or title, of any kind whatever, from any king, prince, or foreign state.

Clause 8 Meeting at a time when feeling against monarchy ran high, the framers inserted a clause prohibiting the government from awarding titles of nobility. American citizens are not allowed to accept titles of nobility from foreign governments without the consent of Congress. Consistent with the provisions of this clause, Congress has passed legislation permitting government officials to receive small gifts from foreign officials. But gifts that exceed "minimal value" must be accepted in behalf of the United States and become the property of the nation.

Section 10. Powers Denied to the States

1. Unconditional Prohibitions No state shall enter into any treaty, alliance, or confederation; grant letters of marque and reprisal; coin money; emit bills of credit; make anything but gold and silver coin a tender in payment of debts; pass any bill of attainder, *ex post facto* law, or law impairing the obligation of contracts, or grant any title of nobility.

Clause 1 See Article 1, Section 8, Clause 11, for letters of marque and reprisal. Some of the powers denied to the states are similarly denied to the federal government. The prohibition against bills of attainder, ex post facto laws, and the creation of titles of nobility fall into this category.

Other prohibitions apply only to the states. For example, the states are barred from making treaties and coining money. The framers of the Constitution feared the prospect of a nation divided by conflicting diplomatic obligations and separate currencies. The obligations of contracts provision bars a state from nullifying valid contracts, that is, from declaring them void.

The prohibitions listed in this clause are unconditional. Congress cannot pass a law granting these powers to the states.

2. Powers Conditionally Denied No state shall, without the consent of the Congress, lay any imposts or duties on imports or exports, except what may be absolutely necessary for executing its inspection laws; and the net produce of all duties and imposts, laid by any state on imports or exports, shall be for the use of the Treasury of the United States; and all such laws shall be subject to the revision and control of the Congress.

Clauses 2, 3 Powers listed in Clauses 2 and 3 are denied to the states, but Congress can lift the prohibitions by passing appropriate legislation.

Clause 2 bars the states from taxing imports and exports unless permitted by Congress. The clause allows the states to charge inspection fees on goods entering the states if approved by Congress. Fees collected by the states must be turned over to the United States Treasury.

Tonnage refers to the carrying capacity of a ship. A duty on tonnage would be based on a ship's cargo capacity. States may not impose tonnage taxes unless authorized by Congress.

Clause 3 forbids the states to maintain an army and navy without the consent of Congress. The states are similarly barred from entering into agreements with foreign nations or engaging in war unless the threat of invasion is imminent.

3. Other Denied Powers No state shall, without the consent of Congress, lay any duty of tonnage, keep troops, or ships of war in time of peace, enter into any agreement or compact with another state, or with a foreign power, or engage in war, unless actually invaded, or in such imminent danger as will not admit of delay.

Article 2. The Executive Branch

Section 1. President and Vice-President

1. Chief Executive The executive power shall be vested in a President of the United States of America. He shall hold his office during the term of four years, and together with the Vice-President, chosen for the same term, be elected as follows:

Clause 1 As chief executive the President is responsible for enforcing laws passed by Congress. Whether the President has additional power as chief executive has been a matter of dispute. President Theodore Roosevelt believed that the President could do "anything that the needs of the nation demanded unless such action was forbidden by the Constitution and the law." Others have argued that the authority of the chief executive should be limited to enforcing the law. See Article 2, Section 3, for a further discussion of the powers of the President.

2. Selection of Electors Each state shall appoint, in such manner as the legislature thereof may direct, a number of electors, equal to the whole number of Senators and Representatives to which the state may be entitled in the Congress; but no Senator or Representative, or person holding an office or trust or profit under the United States, shall be appointed an elector.

Clauses 2, 3 Some of the framers of the Constitution feared allowing the people to elect the President directly (page 162). Consequently, the Constitutional Convention established the electoral college. According to Clause 2 each state's electoral vote is to equal its combined number of senators and representatives. The states may decide the procedure for selecting electors. Members of Congress and federal officeholders are barred from serving as electors. This much of the original electoral college system is still in effect.

3. Electoral College Procedures [The electors shall meet in their respective states, and vote by ballot for two persons, of whom one at least shall not be an inhabitant of the same state with themselves. And they shall make a list of all the persons voted for, and of the number of votes for each; which list they shall sign and certify, and transmit sealed to the seat of the government of the United States, directed to the president of the Senate. The president of the Senate shall, in the presence of the Senate and House of Representatives, open all the certificates, and the votes shall then be counted. The person having the greatest number of votes shall be the President, if such number be a majority of the whole number of electors appointed; and if there be more than one who have such majority, and have an equal number of votes, then the House of Representatives shall immediately choose by ballot one of them for President; and if no person have a majority, then from the five highest on the list the said House shall in like manner choose the President. But in choosing the President the votes shall be taken by states, the representation from each state having one vote. A quorum for this purpose shall consist of a member or members from two-thirds of the states, and a majority of all the states shall be necessary to a choice. In every case, after the choice of the President, the person having the greatest number of votes of the electors shall be the Vice-President. But if there should remain two

Clause 3 called upon each elector to vote for two candidates without designating one for President and one for Vice-President. The candidate who received the most electoral votes (provided it was a majority) would become President. In cases in which no candidate won a majority of the electoral vote, the House would choose the President, and the Senate would choose the Vice-President.

The election of 1800 revealed a defect in the original electoral college system (page 186). Thomas Jefferson was the presidential candidate of the Republican party, and Aaron Burr was the vice-presidential candidate. But since the vote ended in a tie, either could have become President. The House finally elected Jefferson. The Twelfth Amendment altered electoral college procedures.

or more who have equal votes, the Senate shall choose from them by ballot the Vice-President.]

4. Time of Elections The Congress may determine the time of choosing the electors, and the day on which they shall give their votes; which day shall be the same throughout the United States.

5. Qualifications for President No person except a natural-born citizen [or a citizen of the United States, at the time of the adoption of this Constitution], shall be eligible to the office of the President; neither shall any person be eligible to that office who shall not have attained to the age of thirty-five years, and been fourteen years a resident within the United States.

6. Presidential Succession In case of the removal of the President from office, or of his death, resignation, or inability to discharge the powers and duties of the said office, the same shall devolve on the Vice-President, and the Congress may by law provide for the case of removal, death, resignation, or inability, both of the President and Vice-President, declaring what officer shall then act as President, and such officer shall act accordingly, until the disability be removed, or a President shall be elected.

7. Salary The President shall, at stated times, receive for his services, a compensation, which shall neither be increased nor diminished during the period for which he shall have been elected, and he shall not receive within that period any other emolument from the United States, or any of them.

8. The Oath of Office Before he enter on the execution of his office, he shall take the following oath or affirmation:—"I do solemnly swear (or affirm) that I will faithfully execute

Clause 4 According to legislation passed in 1792 electors are chosen on the Tuesday following the first Monday of November every four years. Congress has required that the electors of each state meet to cast their ballots on the first Monday after the second Wednesday in December, following the election in November. The votes of the electoral college are counted in the House of Representatives on January 6.

Today voters in each state cast ballots for slates of electors pledged to presidential candidates. The candidate receiving most of a state's popular vote wins that state's electoral vote. Neither the Constitution nor federal law requires electors to vote for the candidate to whom they are pledged. However, according to custom, electors nearly always do so. Thus the general election in November settles the issue of who will be the next President, and the balloting in December attracts little interest.

Clause 5 The first seven Presidents of the United States could not claim to be natural-born citizens of the United States, because they were born subjects of the British crown. But they qualified for the presidency because they were citizens "of the United States at the time of the adoption of this Constitution."

Although the issue has never been resolved by the courts, scholarly opinion suggests that the children of American citizens born abroad meet the citizenship requirements of this clause. Note that natural-born and native-born are not identical terms. A child of American parents who is born abroad is a natural- but not a native-born citizen of the United States.

Clause 6 This clause states that the powers of the President shall pass to the Vice-President if the President leaves office or is unable to discharge the duties of the office. The language of this clause caused confusion the first time a President died in office. When President William Henry Harrison died, it was uncertain whether Vice-President John Tyler should remain Vice-President and simply act as President or actually be sworn in as President. Tyler persuaded a federal judge to swear him in, and the precedent was created that the Vice-President assumes the office of President when that office becomes vacant. The Twenty-fifth Amendment superseded this clause.

Clause 7 In 1983 the President received a salary of $200,000. The Constitution prohibits the salary from being increased or decreased during a President's term. This clause bars the President from accepting any other federal or state position during his or her term in office.

Clause 8 By custom the presidential oath is administered by the Chief Justice of the Supreme Court. But this has not always been the case. After President John Kennedy's assassination, Vice-President Lyndon Johnson was sworn in by a federal district judge.

the office of President of the United States, and will to the best of my ability, preserve, protect, and defend the Constitution of the United States."

Section 2. Powers of the President

1. Commander in Chief of the Armed Forces The President shall be Commander in Chief of the Army and Navy of the United States, and of the militia of the several states, when called into the actual service of the United States; he may require the option, in writing, of the principal officer in each of the executive departments, upon any subject relating to the duties of their respective offices, and he shall have power to grant reprieves and pardons for offenses against the United States, except in cases of impeachment.

Clause 1 This clause, combined with the provisions outlining congressional control over the military (see Article 1, Section 8, Clauses 11-15), established the principle of civilian control of the armed forces. Although the President may not serve in the armed forces while in office, he or she occupies the highest position in the military chain of command. President Harry Truman exercised the principle of civilian control of the military during the Korean War. He relieved General Douglas MacArthur of his command after MacArthur criticized Truman's handling of the war (page 676).

Since President Lincoln's administration, the definition of the commander-in-chief's powers has expanded beyond narrowly military actions. For example, Lincoln based his issuance of the Emancipation Proclamation on this power (page 340). During World War II President Franklin Roosevelt supervised labor relations, claiming that his power as commander-in-chief enabled him to impose sanctions on employers and employees who threatened industrial peace.

A *reprieve* suspends punishment prescribed by law. A *pardon* issued before trial bars prosecution. If a pardon is issued after conviction, it wipes out the judgment of the court. The President may not issue pardons in impeachment cases. President Gerald Ford's pardon of Richard Nixon barred the government from prosecuting the former President for possible criminal offenses (page 732). Because Nixon had already resigned from office, impeachment was no longer an issue.

2. Making Treaties and Nominations He shall have power, by and with the advice and consent of the Senate, to make treaties, provided two-thirds of the Senators present concur; and he shall nominate, and by and with the advice and consent of the Senate, shall appoint ambassadors, other public ministers and consuls, judges of the Supreme Court, and all other officers of the United States, whose appointments are not herein otherwise provided for, and which shall be established by law; but the Congress may by law vest the appointment of such inferior officers, as they think proper, in the President alone, in the courts of law, or in the heads of departments.

Clause 2 As part of the system of checks and balances, this clause requires that treaties negotiated by the President be approved by two thirds of the Senate. The Senate defeat of the Versailles Treaty in 1919 illustrates the President's dependence on the consent of the Senate (page 540).

Executive agreements made with foreign heads of state are not subject to Senate approval. For example, President Franklin Roosevelt bypassed the Senate in the 1940 bases-for-destroyers deal with Britain. Roosevelt declared that his power as commander-in-chief enabled him to execute that agreement. The Supreme Court has sanctioned executive agreements as a valid exercise of presidential power.

This clause also requires that the President's appointments to high public office be confirmed by the Senate. Most presidential appointments are routinely confirmed, but the Senate refused to confirm two of President Nixon's nominations to the Supreme Court (page 728).

3. Temporary Appointments The President shall have power to fill up all vacancies that may happen during the recess of the Senate, by granting commissions which shall expire at the end of their next session.

Clause 3 If the Senate is recessed, the President may fill high government posts with temporary appointments.

Section 3. Duties

He shall from time to time give to the Congress information of the state of the Union, and recommend to their consideration such measures as he shall judge necessary and expedient; he may, on extraordinary occasions, convene both houses, or either of them, and in case of disagreement between them, with respect to the time of adjournment, he may adjourn them to such time as he shall think proper; he shall receive ambassadors and other public ministers; he shall take care that the laws be faithfully executed, and shall commission all the officers of the United States.

This section has helped make the President a legislative leader. The President has the power to recommend the enactment of legislation. Section 3 requires the President to give a state of the union address to Congress. This address is given in January, and since 1913 it has been delivered in person by the President.

The provision empowering the President to receive ambassadors and other public ministers, together with the powers to command the armed forces and negotiate treaties, gives him or her a predominant role in shaping foreign policy.

This section also requires that the President "take care that the laws be faithfully executed." President Dwight Eisenhower's dispatch of troops to Little Rock, Arkansas, during the 1957 school integration crisis was an application of this principle (page 694). Administration of programs created by Congress are primary examples of the President's execution of the law.

Section 4. Impeachment and Removal From Office

The President, Vice-President, and all civil officers of the United States, shall be removed from office on impeachment for, and conviction of, treason, bribery, or other high crimes and misdemeanors.

Civil officers include federal judges and members of the cabinet. The role of Congress in the impeachment and removal process is discussed in Article 1, Section 2, Clauses 6 and 7.

The term *high crimes and misdemeanors* is ambiguous. When applied to the impeachment of judges, the phrase has included violations of particular laws as well as general noncriminal misconduct. Because only one President—Andrew Johnson—has been impeached, the courts have not had occasion to decide whether "high crimes and misdemeanors" must include violations of law when applied to impeachment of a President. During the Watergate affair President Nixon's lawyers insisted that impeachable offenses must be violations of law. But some members of the House argued that noncriminal misconduct could provide the basis for impeachment.

Article 3. The Judicial Branch

Section 1. Federal Courts

The judicial power of the United States shall be vested in one Supreme Court, and in such inferior courts as the Congress may from time to time ordain and establish. The judges, both of the Supreme and inferior courts, shall hold their offices during good behavior, and shall, at stated times, receive for their services a compensation, which shall not be diminished during their continuance in office.

Judicial refers to the courts. The Constitution created the Supreme Court, but it does not specify the size of the Court, nor does it establish additional federal courts. The framers left these tasks to Congress. This section does provide, however, that all federal judges shall serve for life, dependent upon good behavior.

According to the Judiciary Act of 1789 the membership of the Supreme Court was fixed at six (nine justices now sit on the Court), and a system of lower courts was established (page 173). Congress created 13 district courts and three courts of appeals. Today there are 94 district courts and 13 courts of appeals.

District courts conduct trials of criminal and civil cases. Courts of appeals hear claims that a district court committed errors in the conduct of a trial or pretrial proceedings. While the Congress may abolish the district courts or courts of appeals, it may not abolish the Supreme Court.

Section 2. Jurisdiction of Federal Courts

1. Scope of Judicial Power The judicial power shall extend to all cases, in law and equity, arising under this Constitution, the laws of the United States, and treaties made or

Clause 1 *Jurisdiction* refers to the right of a court to hear a case. The distinction between courts of law and courts of equity is now largely obsolete. Federal courts can decide only cases brought by parties to a lawsuit. Federal courts cannot make rules of law when no lawsuit exists.

852

which shall be made, under their authority; to all cases affecting ambassadors, other public ministers and consuls; to all cases of admiralty and maritime jurisdiction; to controversies to which the United States shall be a party; to controversies between two or more states; [between a state and citizens of another state;] between citizens of the same state claiming lands under grants of different states, and between a state or the citizens thereof, and foreign states, citizens, or subjects.

Federal courts are empowered to hear cases *under this Constitution.* This means that the federal judiciary can determine the constitutionality of acts of Congress and state legislatures as well as of actions of the President and other government officials.

The right of a court to rule on the constitutionality of laws and official acts is known as *judicial review.* Already exercised by the state courts, the doctrine was reaffirmed in *Marbury* v. *Madison* (page 190), when the Supreme Court held that "a legislative act, contrary to the Constitution, is not law." Federal courts also have jurisdiction in cases involving ambassadors and cases in which the United States is a party. The provision allowing federal jurisdiction in cases "between a State and citizens of another State" has been modified by the Eleventh Amendment.

2. The Supreme Court In all cases affecting ambassadors, other public ministers and consuls, and those in which a state shall be a party, the Supreme Court shall have original jurisdiction. In all the other cases before mentioned, the Supreme Court shall have appellate jurisdiction, both as to law and fact, with such exceptions, and under such regulations as the Congress shall make.

Clause 2 *Original jurisdiction* refers to the power of a court to hear a case when it originates. Typically courts of original jurisdiction find the facts of a case and determine the issue of guilt or liability. Courts of *appellate jurisdiction* do not decide the question of guilt or liability. They review claims that a lower court judge made legal errors in conducting the trial or pretrial proceedings.

Under this clause the Supreme Court exercises original jurisdiction over a narrow range of cases: disputes in which a state is involved and cases involving ambassadors or public ministers. In recent times the Supreme Court has exercised its original jurisdiction infrequently. Instead it functions almost exclusively as an appellate court.

3. Trial by Jury The trial of all crimes, except in cases of impeachment, shall be by jury; and such trial shall be held in the state where the said crimes shall have been committed; but when not committed within any state, the trial shall be at such place or places as the Congress may by law have directed.

Clause 3 This clause does not guarantee trial by jury in *civil cases,* legal disputes that do not involve allegations of criminal wrongdoing. Nor does it require the states to provide jury trials. The clause applies to federal criminal prosecutions. See the Sixth Amendment for a more extended discussion of the right to trial by jury.

Section 3. Treason
1. Definition Treason against the United States shall consist only in levying war against them, or in adhering to their enemies, giving them aid and comfort. No person shall be convicted of treason unless on the testimony of two witnesses to the same overt act, or on confession in open court.

Clause 1 An *overt act* refers to a concrete action, not merely a state of mind.

2. Punishment The Congress shall have power to declare the punishment of treason, but no attainder of treason shall work corruption of blood or forfeiture except during the life of the person attainted.

Clause 2 This clause allows Congress to punish traitors, but it forbids punishment of the traitor's children for the crime of the parent. *Attainder* refers to the loss of rights that accompanies conviction for a serious crime. Under English law attainder of treason was transmitted to the children of traitors. In England *corruption of blood* meant that the children of criminals could not inherit or retain property owned by the parents. Such a punishment is prohibited by this clause, and it has been abolished in England.

Article 4. Relations Among the States and Between States and Federal Government

Section 1. Official Records and Acts

Full faith and credit shall be given in each state to the public acts, records, and judicial proceedings of every other state. And the Congress may by general laws prescribe the manner in which such acts, records, and proceedings shall be proved, and the effect thereof.

The purpose of this section is to guarantee that the official records and acts of one state are recognized by the other states. For example, the section requires a state to recognize valid marriage certificates issued by another state.

Section 2. Privileges and Rights of Citizens

1. Privileges The citizens of each state shall be entitled to all privileges and immunities of citizens in the several states.

Clause 1 Despite this clause, the Constitution, as interpreted by the courts, does not forbid state residence requirements for lower tuition rates, hunting, fishing, and professional licenses.

2. Extradition A person charged in any state with treason, felony, or other crime, who shall flee from justice, and be found in another state, shall on demand of the executive authority of the state from which he fled, be delivered up, to be removed to the state having jurisdiction of the crime.

Clause 2 *Extradition* is the process of returning an alleged criminal or fugitive found in one state to the state in which he or she is sought. The Supreme Court has ruled that federal courts are powerless to order a governor to extradite a fugitive from justice. The Court interpreted this clause to mean that governors may deliver an escaped criminal to the authorities of another state but are not required to do so.

3. Return of Fugitive Slaves [No person held to service or labor in one state, under the laws thereof, escaping into another, shall in consequence of any law or regulation therein, be discharged from such service or labor, but shall be delivered up on claim of the party to whom such service or labor may be due.]

Clause 3 *Persons held to service or labor* refers to slaves and indentured servants. This clause required states to return runaway slaves to their owners. See pages 316–318 for a discussion of the fugitive slave controversy. The Thirteenth Amendment nullified this clause.

Section 3. Admission of States and Governing Territories

1. New States New states may be admitted by the Congress into this Union; but no new state shall be formed or erected within the jurisdiction of any other state; nor any state be formed by the junction of two or more states, or parts of states, without the consent of the legislatures of the states concerned as well as of the Congress.

Clause 1 This clause gives Congress the power to admit new states. However, Congress does not have unrestricted authority to set conditions for admission. For example, when Oklahoma applied for admission to the Union, Congress made the location of the state capital a condition for admission. In *Coyle* v. *Smith* (1911) the Supreme Court held that Congress may not set admission requirements in areas exclusively under state control.

2. Federal Lands The Congress shall have power to dispose of and make all needful rules and regulations respecting the territory or other property belonging to the United States; and nothing in this Constitution shall be so construed as to prejudice any claims of the United States, or of any particular state.

Clause 2 Congress can make rules for the administration of land owned by the United States. This includes territories not organized into states and federal land located within a state. See page 146 for a description of how Congress administered the Northwest Territory. The Supreme Court has prohibited states from taxing federal property.

Section 4. Guarantees to the States

The United States shall guarantee to every state in this Union a republican form of government, and shall protect each of them against invasion; and on application of the legislature, or of the executive (when the legislature cannot be convened) against domestic violence.

A *republic* is a form of government in which the voters have supreme authority and power is exercised by elected representatives. According to this section the United States government must protect the existence of a republican form of government in every state. The federal government must also protect the states from foreign invasion and supply armed forces to suppress disorder when asked to do so by a state. The President may also, on his or her own initiative, send troops to a state to enforce the laws and preserve order. See Article 2, Section 2, Clause 1.

Article 5. Amendment of the Constitution

The Congress, whenever two-thirds of both houses shall deem it necessary, shall propose amendments to this Constitution, or, on the application of the legislatures of two-thirds of the several states, shall call a convention for proposing amendments, which, in either case, shall be valid to all intents and purposes, as part of this Constitution, when ratified by the legislatures of three-fourths of the several states, or by conventions in three-fourths thereof, as the one or the other mode of ratification may be proposed by the Congress; provided that [no amendments which may be made prior to the year 1808 shall in any manner affect the first and fourth clauses in the Ninth Section of the First Article; and that] no state, without its consent, shall be deprived of its equal suffrage in the Senate.

This article provides that amendments to the Constitution can be proposed by a two-thirds vote of both houses of Congress or by a national convention called by Congress at the request of two thirds of the state legislatures. No amendment has ever been proposed by the latter method. Proposed constitutional amendments can be ratified either by the legislatures of three fourths of the states or by three fourths of special state conventions. The latter method has been used only once. Congress determines by which method a proposed amendment will be ratified.

The Constitution does not specify the period of time in which a proposed amendment must be ratified. However, Congress may establish a time limit for ratification. Since the passage of the Twentieth Amendment, Congress has provided that proposed amendments will be void unless ratified within seven years. Such a limitation has been upheld by the Supreme Court.

In October 1978 Congress extended the ratification deadline for the proposed Equal Rights Amendment. The constitutionality of that resolution is the subject of debate. The question of whether a state may rescind, or withdraw, its ratification of an amendment is also disputed. Several state legislatures rescinded their approval of the proposed Equal Rights Amendment, but the legality of that action has not yet been determined by the Supreme Court.

Article 6. Other Provisions

Section 1. Prior Public Debts

All debts contracted and engagements entered into, before the adoption of this Constitution, shall be as valid against the United States under this Constitution, as under the Confederation.

According to this clause the United States government agreed to pay debts incurred prior to the adoption of the Constitution.

Section 2. Supreme Law of the Land

This Constitution, and the laws of the United States which shall be made in pursuance thereof, and all treaties made, or which shall be made, under the authority of the United States, shall be the supreme law of the land; and the judges in every state shall be bound thereby, anything in the constitution or

This section makes the Constitution, acts of Congress, and treaties ratified by the Senate the "supreme law of the land." The Supreme Court has held that a state may not regulate the operation of any federal activity. For example, a state may not examine the qualifications of federal mail truck drivers, nor may it impose dietary standards in federal institutions.

The section requires state judges to strike down state laws that conflict with the Constitution or an act of laws of any state to the contrary notwithstanding.

Congress. State courts are bound by the decisions of the United States Supreme Court, although the extent to which they must follow the rulings of lower federal courts is less clear.

855

Section 3. Oaths to Support the Constitution

The Senators and Representatives before mentioned, and the members of the several state legislatures, and all executive and judicial officers, both of the United States and of the several states, shall be bound by oath or affirmation, to support this Constitution; but no religious test shall ever be required as a qualification to any office or public trust under the United States.

State and federal officeholders must take an oath to support the Constitution. Persons whose conscience does not permit the swearing of oaths may affirm their support of the Constitution.

During the colonial period England and all the colonies except Rhode Island imposed a religious test for the holding of public office. Typically the religious test required an officeholder to profess belief in the faith of one of the Protestant denominations. Intent on barring this practice in the United States, the framers of the Constitution provided that religious affiliation may not be a qualification for office holding.

Article 7. Ratification

The ratification of the convention of nine states shall be sufficient for the establishment of the Constitution between the states so ratifying the same.

During 1787 and 1788 the states held conventions to ratify the Constitution. By October 1788 the required nine states had ratified the Constitution. The Constitution went into effect on the first Wednesday of March 1789.

Done in Convention, by the unanimous consent of the states present, the seventeenth day of September, in the year of our Lord one thousand seven hundred and eighty-seven, and of the independence of the United States of America the twelfth. *In Witness* whereof, we have hereunto subscribed our names.

Attest:

William Jackson,
Secretary

George Washington,
President and Deputy from Virginia

New Hampshire
John Langdon
Nicholas Gilman

Massachusetts
Nathaniel Gorham
Rufus King

Connecticut
William Samuel Johnson
Roger Sherman

New York
Alexander Hamilton

New Jersey
William Livingston
David Brearley
William Paterson
Jonathan Dayton

Pennsylvania
Benjamin Franklin
Thomas Mifflin
Robert Morris
George Clymer
Thomas Fitzsimons
Jared Ingersoll
James Wilson
Gouverneur Morris

Delaware
George Read
Gunning Bedford, Jr.
John Dickinson
Richard Bassett
Jacob Broom

Maryland
James McHenry
Dan of St. Thomas Jennifer
Daniel Carroll

Virginia
John Blair
James Madison, Jr.

North Carolina
William Blount
Richard Dobbs Spaight
Hugh Williamson

South Carolina
John Rutledge
Charles Cotesworth Pinckney
Charles Pinckney
Pierce Butler

Georgia
William Few
Abraham Baldwin

Amendments to the Constitution

The first ten amendments, which were added to the Constitution in 1791, are called the Bill of Rights. Originally the Bill of Rights applied only to actions of the federal government. However, the Supreme Court has used the due process clause of the Fourteenth Amendment to extend many of the rights to protect individuals against action by the states.

Amendment 1. Freedoms of Religion, Speech, Press, Assembly, and Petition

Congress shall make no law respecting an establishment of religion, or prohibiting the free exercise thereof; or abridging the freedom of speech, or of the press; or the right of the people peaceably to assemble, and to petition the government for a redress of grievances.

5 of 10

The First Amendment prohibits the government from *abridging*, or limiting, freedom of expression. Freedom of the press protects all forms of the press from government control or censorship. Freedom of assembly is the right to peaceably gather to express a point of view. *Petition* refers to the expression of complaints directly to government officials. *Redress* means to set right, or correct. Americans have the right to present grievances to the government and ask that the source of the grievances be eliminated.

An *established religion* is one that is officially recognized by a government and has privileges denied other denominations. During the colonial period, established churches were common (page 69). The authors of the First Amendment wanted to separate government and religion. Defining the government's proper relationship to religion, however, has presented problems for the courts. The Supreme Court has upheld state aid for the transportation of students to parochial schools, but it has invalidated devotional Bible reading in public schools. The First Amendment also bars government restriction on the *free exercise of religion.* This means, in part, that the state cannot penalize an individual for the exercise of his or her religious beliefs.

Determining the range of conduct protected by the free speech clause has been an important task of the courts. In *Schenk* v. *United States* (1919) the Court upheld Schenk's conviction for distributing antidraft pamphlets during World War I. It ruled that Schenk's actions presented a "clear and present danger" to the United States. In the absence of "clear and present danger" the courts have generally not upheld restrictions on freedom of speech.

Amendment 2. Right to Bear Arms

A well-regulated militia, being necessary to the security of a free state, the right of the people to keep and bear arms shall not be infringed.

This amendment guarantees the right of a state militia to keep weapons. Courts have generally ruled that government can regulate the ownership of weapons by private citizens.

Amendment 3. Lodging Troops in Private Homes

No soldier shall, in time of peace, be quartered in any house, without the consent of the owner; nor in time of war, but in a manner to be prescribed by law.

During the colonial period the British lodged soldiers in private homes without the consent of the owners (page 103). This amendment restricts the government's right to use private residences as military barracks.

Amendment 4. Search and Seizure

The right of the people to be secure in their persons, houses, papers, and effects, against unreasonable searches and seizures, shall not be violated; and no warrants shall issue but upon probable cause, supported by oath or affirmation, and particularly describing the place to be searched, and the persons or things to be seized.

This amendment protects Americans from unreasonable searches and seizures. A reasonable search is defined as one authorized by a judge who issues a search warrant. A warrant is issued only if there is *probable cause.* This means that it is likely the search will produce evidence that a particular crime has been committed. A warrant must specify the exact place to be searched and the things to be seized.

Courts have ruled that in some cases searches are permissible without a warrant. For example, courts have held that police may search a person who is under arrest. The Supreme Court has also upheld the right of police to stop and search a person if the officer reasonably concludes that the suspect may be armed. Furthermore, a warrant is not needed if a person freely consents to a search.

The Supreme Court has ruled that items discovered in the course of an unlawful search may not be used as evidence against the accused during trial for a criminal offense. This ban is called the *exclusionary rule.*

Amendment 5. Rights of the Accused

No person shall be held to answer for a capital, or otherwise infamous, crime, unless on a presentment or indictment of a grand jury, except in cases arising in the land or naval forces, or in the militia, when in actual service in time of war or public danger; nor shall any person be subject for the same offense to be twice put in jeopardy of life and limb; nor shall be compelled, in any criminal case, to be a witness against himself; nor be deprived of life, liberty, or property, without due process of law; nor shall private property be taken for public use, without just compensation.

A *capital* crime is one for which the penalty may be death. An *infamous* crime is one punishable by imprisonment or loss of political privileges. According to the Fifth Amendment prosecutions of both types of crimes in federal court must be based on the accusation of a grand jury. The *grand jury,* a panel of between 12 and 23 citizens, may issue an *indictment,* or accusation, at the request of the public prosecutor. *Presentments,* now rarely used, are grand jury accusations not sought by the public prosecutor.

Double jeopardy is forbidden by the Fifth Amendment. This means that an accused person may not be tried twice for the same crime. The double jeopardy rule does not bar prosecution when the original conviction was set aside by an appellate court.

This amendment also prohibits the government from forcing accused persons to testify against themselves. Thus an accused person may not be required to testify in his or her own defense during trial. Nor can the prosecutor suggest to the jury that failure to testify is a sign of guilt.

Due process refers to fair procedure. In the context of criminal procedure, due process includes the right of the accused to be heard, to be represented by a lawyer, and to confront prosecution witnesses. In noncriminal matters, due process requires authorities to provide a forum in which the affected individual can be heard. The last provision of the amendment bars the government from seizing private property without compensating the owner.

Amendment 6. Right to Speedy Trial by Jury

In all criminal prosecutions, the accused shall enjoy the right to a speedy and public trial, by an impartial jury of the state and district wherein the crime shall have been committed, which district shall have been pre-

The Sixth Amendment does not require a trial by jury in cases in which the maximum punishment is six months in prison or less, or in cases in military courts. Although juries traditionally have 12 members, convictions by six-person juries have been upheld by the courts. The amendment does not require unanimous verdicts.

viously ascertained by law, and to be informed of the nature and cause of the accusation; to be confronted with the witnesses against him; to have compulsory process for obtaining witnesses in his favor, and to have the assistance of counsel for his defense.

Defendants have the right to a speedy trial, although this does not mean that courts are bound to try defendants within a specified period of time. However, delays that are purposeful and that prejudice the defendant's right to a fair trial may result in a dismissal of the charge. The requirement that trials be public does not prohibit trial judges from excluding television camera crews and newspaper photographers from the courtroom. The requirement that a jury be *impartial* means the jury members must lay aside their opinions and render a verdict based solely on the evidence presented in court. The *compulsory process* provision refers to a defendant's right to force witnesses to testify by issuing *subpoenas,* legal orders requiring a person to appear in court.

Since 1942 the federal government has been obligated to provide free legal counsel to defendants in criminal trials if the defendants cannot afford to hire a lawyer. In 1963 the Supreme Court imposed the same requirement on the states (page 727).

Amendment 7. Jury Trial in Civil Cases

In suits at common law, where the value in controversy shall exceed $20, the right of trial by jury shall be preserved, and no fact tried by a jury shall be otherwise re-examined in any court of the United States than according to the rules of the common law.

Common law refers to rules of law established by judges in past cases. This amendment establishes the right to a jury trial in civil cases in which the amount of money disputed meets a specified dollar limit.

The second part of the amendment limits the power of federal appellate courts to reexamine facts tried by juries in civil cases. This means that an appellate court may not overturn a verdict solely because it disagrees with the jury's interpretation of the evidence. An appellate court may set aside a verdict only on the grounds that the trial court committed errors in law that deprived the defendant of his or her right to a fair trial.

Amendment 8. Bail and Punishment

Excessive bail shall not be required, nor excessive fines imposed, nor cruel and unusual punishments inflicted.

Bail is money a defendant gives to the court as a pledge that he or she will appear for trial. The amendment prohibits unreasonable denial of bail. The decision to deny bail depends on such factors as the defendant's family and community ties, the seriousness of the charge, and the weight of the evidence.

Courts have held that bail is excessive if it is set at a figure higher than necessary to secure the appearance of the accused at trial. A defendant's inability to pay bail is not in itself proof that excessive bail has been imposed.

Cruel and unusual punishments are barred by the amendment. These include various forms of physical and mental abuse.

Amendment 9. Powers Reserved to the People

The enumeration in the Constitution, of certain rights, shall not be construed to deny or disparage others retained by the people.

This amendment asserts that the people have rights not listed in the Constitution. It assumes that there are rights so basic that they exist even though not specifically mentioned. This amendment was added to satisfy critics of the original Constitution who feared that a Bill of Rights would be used to limit rights to only those listed (page 166).

Amendment 10. Powers Reserved to the States

The powers not delegated to the United States by the Constitution, nor prohibited by it to the states, are reserved to the states respectively, or to the people.

This amendment limits federal power by providing that the states shall exercise those powers that are neither denied to them nor specifically delegated to the federal government. The powers reserved to the states are not listed in the Constitution.

Amendment 11. Suits Against States

Passed by Congress on March 4, 1794. Ratified on January 23, 1795.

The judicial power of the United States shall not be construed to extend to any suit in law or equity, commenced or prosecuted against one of the United States, by citizens of another state, or by citizens or subjects of any foreign state.

See the note for Article 3, Section 2, Clause 1.

Amendment 12. Election of President and Vice-President

Passed by Congress on December 9, 1803. Ratified on June 15, 1804.

The electors shall meet in their respective states, and vote by ballot for President and Vice-President, one of whom, at least, shall not be an inhabitant of the same state with themselves; they shall name in their ballots the person voted for as President, and in distinct ballots the person voted for as Vice-President, and they shall make distinct lists of all persons voted for as President, and of all persons voted for as Vice-President, and of the number of votes for each, which lists they shall sign and certify, and transmit, sealed, to the seat of government of the United States, directed to the President of the Senate; the President of the Senate shall, in the presence of the Senate and House of Representatives, open all the certificates and the votes shall then be counted; the person having the greatest number of votes for President shall be the President, if such number be a majority of the whole number of electors appointed; and if no person have such majority, then from the persons having the highest numbers not exceeding three on the list of those voted for as President, the House of Representatives shall choose immediately, by ballot, the President. But in choosing the President, the votes shall be taken by states, the representation from each state having one vote; a quorum for this purpose shall consist of a member or members from two-thirds of the states, and a majority of all the states shall be necessary to a choice. And if the House of Representatives

Before the adoption of this amendment the candidates for President and Vice-President were not specified. The candidate who received the most electoral votes became President, and the runner-up became Vice-President. See the note for Article 2, Section 1, Clause 3. The Twelfth Amendment sought to prevent a repetition of the deadlocked election of 1800. It provides that there be separate ballots for President and Vice-President.

According to this amendment, the House of Representatives elects the President if no candidate receives a majority in the electoral college (page 233).

shall not choose a President whenever the right of choice shall devolve upon them, [before the fourth day of March next following,] then the Vice-President shall act as President, as in the case of the death or other constitutional disability of the President. The person having the greatest number of votes as Vice-President, shall be the Vice-President, if such number be a majority of the whole number of electors appointed, and if no person have a majority, then, from the two highest numbers on the list, the Senate shall choose the Vice-President; a quorum for the purpose shall consist of two-thirds of the whole number of Senators, and a majority of the whole number shall be necessary to a choice. But no person constitutionally ineligible to the office of President shall be eligible to that of Vice-President of the United States.

Amendment 13. Abolition of Slavery

Passed by Congress on January 31, 1865. Ratified on December 6, 1865.

Section 1. Neither slavery nor involuntary servitude, except as a punishment for crime whereof the party shall have been duly convicted, shall exist within the United States, or any place subject to their jurisdiction.

Section 2. Congress shall have power to enforce this article by appropriate legislation.

The Emancipation Proclamation, issued by President Lincoln in 1863, freed only those slaves residing in states controlled by the Confederacy (page 340). This amendment completed the emancipation process.

In addition to abolishing slavery, the amendment prohibits *involuntary servitude*, or labor done against one's will. This does not apply to persons convicted of a crime. Courts have held that forced labor in payment of a debt violates the ban on involuntary servitude.

Amendment 14. Rights of Citizens

Passed by Congress on June 13, 1866. Ratified on July 9, 1868.

Section 1. Citizenship All persons born or naturalized in the United States and subject to the jurisdiction thereof, are citizens of the United States and of the state wherein they reside. No state shall make or enforce any law which shall abridge the privileges or immunities of citizens of the United States; nor shall any state deprive any person of life, liberty, or property, without due process of law; nor deny to any person within its jurisdiction the equal protection of the laws.

This section defines citizenship for the first time in the Constitution, and it extends citizenship to blacks. It also prohibits states from denying the rights and privileges of citizenship to any citizen. The guarantee of due process contained in the Fifth Amendment applies to the federal government, while this section forbids states to deny due process of law.

During the late nineteenth and early twentieth centuries, the due process clause was used to strike down state laws that regulated business practices and labor conditions. The courts held that state regulatory legislation deprived corporations of the right to manage their property as they saw fit. Since the 1930s, however, courts have generally held that the due process clause does not necessarily invalidate regulatory legislation. Courts have ruled that legislation protecting the health and safety of citizens is not prohibited by the due process clause.

Section 1 also guarantees all citizens "equal protection under the law." The authors of the amendment included this clause to prevent states from discriminating against black citizens. In 1896, however, in *Plessy* v. *Ferguson*, the Supreme Court ruled that separate facilities for blacks and whites did not violate this clause as long as the facilities were equal (page 422). This view was upheld until the 1954 ruling in *Brown* v. *Board of Education* that separate facilities were inherently unequal (page 693).

Section 2. Apportionment of Representatives

Representatives shall be apportioned among the several states according to their respective numbers, counting the whole number of persons in each state, excluding Indians not taxed. But when the right to vote at any election for the choice of electors for President and Vice-President of the United States, Representatives in Congress, the executive and judicial officers of a state, or the members of the legislature thereof, is denied to any of the male inhabitants of such state, being twenty-one years of age and citizens of the United States, or in any way abridged, except for participation in rebellion, or other crime, the basis of representation therein shall be reduced in the proportion which the number of such male citizens shall bear to the whole number of male citizens twenty-one years of age in such state.

This section provides that states would have their representation in the House of Representatives reduced if they infringed on the right of citizens to vote. This specific provision has never been enforced. However, federal voting legislation passed during the 1960s largely ended voting discrimination.

Section 3. Former Confederate Officials

No person shall be a Senator or Representative in Congress, or elector of President and Vice-President, or hold any office, civil or military, under the United States, or under any state, who, having previously taken an oath, as a member of Congress, or as an officer of the United States, or as a member of any state legislature, or as an executive or judicial officer of any state, to support the Constitution of the United States, shall have engaged in insurrection or rebellion against the same, or given aid or comfort to the enemies thereof. But Congress may, by vote of two-thirds of each house, remove such disability.

This section prohibited persons who had been federal or state government officials before the Civil War and who had participated in the Confederate cause from serving again as government officials. In 1872 Congress restored the political rights of former Confederate officials.

Section 4. Government Debt

The validity of the public debt of the United States, authorized by law, including debts incurred for payment of pensions and bounties for services in suppressing insurrection or rebellion, shall not be questioned. But neither the United States nor any state shall assume or pay any debt or obligation incurred in aid of insurrection or rebellion against the United States or any claim for the loss or emancipation of any slave; but all such debts, obligations, and claims shall be held illegal and void.

The validity of debts owed to the United States was recognized by this section, but it barred the repayment of debts owed to the Confederacy. Thus the Confederacy's creditors were punished for aiding the rebellion. The states of the former Confederacy were also barred from compensating slave owners for the loss of slaves.

Section 5. Enforcing the Amendment The Congress shall have power to enforce, by appropriate legislation, the provisions of this article.

Congress passed a Civil Rights Act in 1875 that barred segregation in hotels, public transportation, theaters, and other public places. But in 1883 the Supreme Court struck down the act, holding that the Fourteenth Amendment applied only to discriminatory actions by the states, not by individuals. The Court has held that the amendment does apply to businesses if they rent their premises from the state.

Amendment 15. Right of Suffrage

Passed by Congress on February 26, 1869. Ratified on February 2, 1870.

Section 1. Extending the Right to Vote The right of citizens of the United States to vote shall not be denied or abridged by the United States or any state on account of race, color, or previous condition of servitude.

This section bars voting discrimination on the grounds of race or "previous condition of servitude." It thus extended suffrage to former slaves and to blacks who had been free before the Civil War. Despite the Fifteenth Amendment, during the late nineteenth century the southern states began to deny the right to vote to blacks through the use of grandfather clauses, literacy tests, and poll taxes (page 422).

Section 2. Enforcement The Congress shall have power to enforce this article by appropriate legislation.

The Twenty-fourth Amendment prohibited the use of poll taxes in national elections. The Voting Rights Act of 1965 suspended literacy tests and authorized federal supervision of voter registration in places where a pattern of discrimination had been found (page 707).

Amendment 16. The Income Tax

Passed by Congress on July 12, 1909. Ratified on February 3, 1913.

The Congress shall have power to lay and collect taxes on incomes, from whatever source derived, without apportionment among the several states, and without regard to any census or enumeration.

In 1894 the Supreme Court invalidated an income tax law by ruling that the Constitution prohibited a "direct tax" unless it was collected in proportion to each state's population. Congress had not provided for this method of collection in the 1894 tax legislation. This amendment provides that income taxes can be collected without regard to a state's population (page 505). It thereby nullifies Article 1, Section 9, Clause 4.

Amendment 17. The Election of Senators

Passed by Congress on May 13, 1912. Ratified on April 8, 1913.

Section 1. Method of election The Senate of the United States shall be composed of two Senators from each state, elected by the people thereof, for six years; and each Senator shall have one vote. The electors in each state shall have the qualifications requisite for electors of the most numerous branch of the state legislatures.

This amendment replaces Article 1, Section 2, Clause 1. According to the amendment senators are directly elected by the people of each state. The amendment reflected the efforts of progressives to make the election process more democratic (page 505).

Section 2. Vacancies When vacancies happen in the representation of any state in the Senate, the executive authority of such state shall issue writs of election to fill such vacancies: *Provided* that the legislature of any state may empower the executive thereof to

When a Senate seat becomes vacant, the governor of the state must order an election to fill the vacancy. The state legislature may empower the governor to make a temporary appointment until an election is held.

make temporary appointments until the people fill the vacancies by election as the legislature may direct.

[Section 3. Those Elected Under Previous Procedure This amendment shall not be so construed as to affect the election or term of any Senator chosen before it becomes valid as part of the Constitution.]

The terms of senators who had already been elected by state legislatures were not affected by the Seventeenth Amendment.

Amendment 18. Prohibition of Alcoholic Beverages

Passed by Congress on December 18, 1917. Ratified on January 16, 1919.

[Section 1. Ban on Alcohol After one year from the ratification of this article the manufacture, sale, or transportation of intoxicating liquors within, the importation thereof into, or the exportation thereof from, the United States and all territory subject to the jurisdiction thereof for beverage purposes is hereby prohibited.

This amendment banned the manufacture, sale, and transportation of alcoholic beverages (pages 505–506). It was repealed by the Twenty-first Amendment.

Section 2. Enforcement The Congress and the several states shall have concurrent power to enforce this article by appropriate legislation.

Both the states and the federal government had the power to pass legislation to enforce the amendment.

Section 3. Method of Ratification This article shall be inoperative unless it shall have been ratified as an amendment to the Constitution by the legislatures of the several states, as provided in the Constitution, within seven years from the date of the submission hereof to the states by the Congress.]

The Eighteenth Amendment was the first to include a specific time limit for ratification by the required number of states.

Amendment 19. Women's Suffrage

Passed by Congress on June 4, 1919. Ratified on August 18, 1920.

Section 1. The Right to Vote The right of citizens of the United States to vote shall not be denied or abridged by the United States or by any state on account of sex.

According to this amendment neither the federal nor the state governments can deny the right to vote on account of sex. Prior to the enactment of the amendment many individual states had extended suffrage to women (page 507–508).

Section 2. Enforcement Congress shall have power to enforce this article by appropriate legislation.

Amendment 20. Presidential Terms; Sessions of Congress

Passed by Congress on March 2, 1932. Ratified on January 23, 1933.

Section 1. Beginning of Term The terms of the President and Vice-President shall end at noon on the 20th day of January, and the terms of Senators and Representatives at noon on the 3rd day of January, of the years

This section changes the date of the beginning of presidential terms from March 4 to January 20. This shortened the waiting period between the November election and the inauguration of the President. It also changed the date for the beginning of congressional terms from March 4 to January 3.

in which such terms would have ended if this article had not been ratified; and the terms of their successors shall then begin.

Section 2. Congressional Sessions The Congress shall assemble at least once in every year, and such meeting shall begin at noon on the 3d day of January, unless they shall by law appoint a different day.

According to this section annual sessions of Congress are to begin on January 3 rather than in December. Prior to the amendment members of Congress who were defeated in November served in a new session of Congress from December until March. Such members were known as *lame ducks.* Thus the amendment is often called the lame duck amendment. By establishing the same date for the beginning of a member's term and the beginning of a new session, the overlap was eliminated.

Section 3. Presidential Succession If at the time fixed for the beginning of the term of the President, the President-elect shall have died, the Vice-President-elect shall become President. If a President shall not have been chosen before the time fixed for the beginning of his term, or if the President-elect shall have failed to qualify, then the Vice-President-elect shall act as President until a President shall have qualified; and the Congress may by law provide for the case wherein neither a President-elect nor a Vice-President-elect shall have qualified, declaring who shall then act as President, or the manner in which one who is to act shall be selected, and such person shall act accordingly until a President or Vice-President shall have qualified.

If the President-elect dies, the Vice-President-elect will become President.

Section 4. Elections Decided by Congress The Congress may by law provide for the case of the death of any of the persons from whom the House of Representatives may choose a President whenever the right of choice shall have devolved upon them, and for the case of the death of any of the persons from whom the Senate may choose a Vice-President whenever the right of choice shall have devolved upon them.

Congress is empowered to pass legislation to deal with a situation in which a presidential candidate dies while an election is being decided by the House. Similar authorization is given to Congress in cases in which the Senate elects the Vice-President.

[Section 5. Date of Implementation Sections 1 and 2 shall take effect on the 15th day of October following the ratification of this article.

Section 6. Ratification Period This article shall be inoperative unless it shall have been ratified as an amendment to the Constitution by the legislatures of three-fourths of the several states within seven years from the date of its submission.]

Amendment 21. Repeal of Prohibition

Passed by Congress on February 20, 1933. Ratified on December 5, 1933.

Section 1. Repeal of National Prohibition The eighteenth article of amendment to the Constitution of the United States is hereby repealed.

Congress directed that special state conventions be called to ratify the amendment. Prohibition ended on December 5, 1933. This is the only time an amendment was ratified by state conventions rather than by state legislatures.

Section 2. State Laws The transportation or importation into any state, territory, or possession of the United States for delivery or use therein of intoxicating liquors, in violation of the laws thereof, is hereby prohibited.

Each state remained free to ban the sale or manufacture of alcoholic beverages within its borders. This section makes the importation of liquor into a so-called dry state a federal offense.

[**Section 3. Ratification Period** This article shall be inoperative unless it shall have been ratified as an amendment to the Constitution by conventions in the several states, as provided in the Constitution, within seven years from the date of the submission hereof to the states by the Congress.]

Amendment 22. Limit on Number of President's Terms

Passed by Congress on March 12, 1947. Ratified on March 1, 1951.

Section 1. Two-Term Limit No person shall be elected to the office of the President more than twice, and no person who has held the office of President, or acted as President, for more than two years of a term to which some other person was elected President shall be elected to the office of the President more than once. [But this Article shall not apply to any person holding the office of President when this Article was proposed by the Congress, and shall not prevent any person who may be holding the office of President, or acting as President, during the term within which this Article becomes operative from holding the office of President or acting as President during the remainder of such term.]

Before Franklin D. Roosevelt no President served for more than two terms (pages 634 and 653). Roosevelt's four-term presidency convinced many Americans that the two-term tradition should be reinforced by a constitutional amendment.

[**Section 2. Ratification Period** This Article shall be inoperative unless it shall have been ratified as an amendment to the Constitution by the legislatures of three-fourths of the several states within seven years from the date of its submission to the states by the Congress.]

Amendment 23. Presidential Electors for District of Columbia

Passed by Congress on June 16, 1960. Ratified on April 3, 1961.

Section 1. Determining the Number of Electors The District constituting the seat of Government of the United States shall appoint in such manner as the Congress may direct:

A number of electors of President and Vice-President equal to the whole number of Senators and Representatives in Congress to which the District would be entitled if it were a State, but in no event more than the least populous State; they shall be in addition to those appointed by the States, but they shall be considered, for the purposes of the election of President and Vice-President, to be electors appointed by a State; and they shall meet in the District and perform such duties as provided by the twelfth article of amendment.

Section 2. Enforcement The Congress shall have power to enforce this article by appropriate legislation.

This amendment gives residents of Washington, D.C., the right to vote in presidential elections. Washington, D.C., has three electoral votes.

Amendment 24. Abolition of Poll Tax in National Elections

Passed by Congress on August 27, 1962. Ratified on January 23, 1964.

Section 1. Poll Tax Banned The right of citizens of the United States to vote in any primary or other election for President or Vice-President, for electors for President or Vice-President, or for Senator or Representative in Congress, shall not be denied or abridged by the United States or any state by reason of failure to pay any poll tax or other tax.

Section 2. Enforcement The Congress shall have the power to enforce this article by appropriate legislation.

No state can impose the payment of a poll tax as a requirement for voting in national elections. Some states had used poll taxes to deprive blacks of the right to vote. The amendment bars poll taxes only in presidential and congressional elections. A Supreme Court decision in 1966 nullified poll taxes in state elections on the grounds that such taxes constitute a denial of equal protection of the laws under the Fourteenth Amendment.

Amendment 25. Presidential Succession and Disability

Passed by Congress on July 6, 1965. Ratified on February 11, 1967.

Section 1. President's Death or Resignation In case of the removal of the President from office or his death or resignation, the Vice-President shall become President.

Section 2. Vacancies in Vice-Presidency Whenever there is a vacancy in the office of the Vice-President, the President shall nomi-

This section clarifies Article 2, Section 1, which ambiguously provides that in case of the President's death his powers "shall devolve on the Vice-President." Amendment 25 states simply that "the Vice-President shall become President" in the event of the President's death or resignation from office.

When Vice-President Lyndon Johnson became President after the death of President John Kennedy, the vice-presidency remained vacant for the balance of Johnson's nate a Vice-President who shall take the office upon confirmation by a majority vote of both houses of Congress.

Section 3. Disability of the President

Whenever the President transmits to the President pro tempore of the Senate and the Speaker of the House of Representatives his written declaration that he is unable to discharge the powers and duties of his office, and until he transmits to them a written declaration to the contrary, such powers and duties shall be discharged by the Vice-President as Acting President.

Section 4.

Whenever the Vice-President and a majority of either the principal officers of the executive departments or of such other body as Congress may by law provide, transmit to the President pro tempore of the Senate and the Speaker of the House of Representatives their written declaration that the President is unable to discharge the powers and duties of his office, the Vice-President shall immediately assume the powers and duties of the office as Acting President.

Thereafter, when the President transmits to the President pro tempore of the Senate and the Speaker of the House of Representatives his written declaration that no inability exists, he shall resume the powers and duties of his office unless the Vice-President and a majority of either the principal officers of the executive department or of such other body as Congress may by law provide, transmit within four days to the President pro tempore of the Senate and the Speaker of the House of Representatives their written declaration that the President is unable to discharge the powers and duties of his office. Thereupon Congress shall decide the issue, assembling within 48 hours for that purpose if not in session. If the Congress, within 21 days after receipt of the latter written declaration, or, if Congress is not in session, within 21 days after Congress is required to assemble, determines by two-thirds vote of both houses that the President is unable to discharge the powers and duties of his office, the Vice-President shall continue to discharge the same as Acting President; otherwise, the President shall assume the powers and duties of his office.

first term in office. The problem of a vacant vice-presidency was remedied by the Twenty-fifth Amendment, which provides that the President shall fill vacancies in the vice-presidency. Acting under this amendment President Richard Nixon appointed Gerald Ford Vice-President after Spiro Agnew resigned (page 732). The amendment was used a second time, after Nixon resigned as President. Gerald Ford, who succeeded Nixon, appointed Nelson Rockefeller Vice-President.

During the twentieth century there have been times when poor health prevented a President from exercising the powers of office. Presidents Woodrow Wilson and Dwight Eisenhower both fell gravely ill while in office. The Constitution, as it then stood, did not prescribe who should exercise presidential powers if a President became disabled. This section states that the Vice-President will serve as Acting President if the President declares in writing that he or she is unable to execute the powers of office.

This section provides that the Vice-President and the cabinet may declare that the President is unable to execute the powers of office, whereupon the Vice-President becomes Acting President. In turn, the President may declare that no disability exists and resume office. However, the Vice-President and cabinet may challenge the President's assertion of no disability. At that point the Congress would determine whether the President was in fact disabled.

Amendment 26. Suffrage for Persons 18 Years or Older

Passed by Congress on March 23, 1971. Ratified on July 1, 1971.

Section 1. Lowering of Voting Age The right of citizens of the United States, who are 18 years of age or older, to vote shall not be denied or abridged by the United States or any state on account of age.

Section 2. Enforcement The Congress shall have the power to enforce this article by appropriate legislation.

Prior to ratification of the amendment most states disqualified persons under age 21 from voting. Legislation passed by Congress in 1970 lowered the minimum voting age to 18 for state and federal elections, but the Supreme Court ruled the same year that Congress could not set minimum age qualifications for state elections. As a result, this amendment was proposed and ratified.

Index

Italicized page numbers refer to illustrations. The *m, c,* or *p* preceding the number refers to a map *(m),* chart *(c),* or picture *(p)* on that page. An *n* following a page number refers to a footnote.

881

883

Illustration Credits *(continued from page iv)*

Cover: The Art Source **Page v** *t* Collection of Laurie Platt Winfrey, *b* Mr. & Mrs. Paul Mellon, Upperville, N.Y.; **vi** *t* MFA, *b* Patrick Henry Memorial Foundation; **vii** *t* Lee Boltin, *b* NG, gift of William and Bernice Chrysler Garbisch; **viii** *t* NYHS, *b* The Boatmen's National Bank; **ix** St. Louis Art Museum (detail); **x** *t* Collection of Laurie Platt Winfrey, *b* Taft Museum, Cincinnati, Ohio; **xi** *t* MCNY, *b* Fine Arts Museum of San Francisco; **xii** NYHS; **xiii** White House Historical Association; **xiv** *t* Courtesy of the Franklin Delano Roosevelt Library, *b* Civic Center Department, City of Detroit; **xv** WW; **xvi** Dan Budnik/Woodfin Camp; **xxi** Corcoran Gallery of Art; **xxii** James West Davidson; **xxiii** Gretchen Lytle.

UNIT ONE Page xxvi, *tl* Collection of Laurie Platt Winfrey, *tr* NYPL, *bl* The Granger Collection, *br* The British Museum; **1** *tl* Mr. & Mrs. Paul Mellon, Upperville, N.Y., *tr* NYHS, *bl* Collection of Laurie Platt Winfrey, *br* NYHS; **2** British Museum; **3** Arizona State Museum, University of Arizona, silk-screen print by Robert Spray for Margaret Schevill Link; **6** AMNH; **10** AMNH; **12** Bibliothèque Nationale; **13** Bibliothèque Nationale; **14** British Museum; **18** MMA; **22** AMNH; **24** AMNH; **26** Courtesy of Santa Barbara Mission; **27** Hispanic Society of America; **29** British Museum; **30** National Portrait Gallery, London; **31** LC; **33** Public Archives of Canada, Map Division; **36** Pilgrim Society; **39** National Portrait Gallery, Washington, D.C.; **43** Mansell Collection; **46** Enoch Pratt Free Library, Baltimore, Md.; **52** Architect of the Capitol; **54** Bettmann Archive; **56** MFA; **64** Colonial Williamsburg Foundation; **67** *t* National Maritime Museum, Greenwich, England, *b* NYPL; **68** Historical Society of Pennsylvania; **69** LC; **70** Colonial Williamsburg Foundation; **74** Anne S.K. Brown Military Collection, Brown University Library; **75** NYHS; **80** NYPL; **81** The National Gallery of Canada, Ottawa, Gift of the estate of the Hon. W.C. Edwards, Ottawa, 1928; **82** National Gallery of Canada, Ottawa; **83** Public Archives of Canada; **84** State Historical Society of Wisconsin; **86** Royal Ontario Museum, Canadiana Gallery.

UNIT TWO Page 90 *tl* Collection of Historical Paintings, Williams Center, LaFayette College, Eaton, Pa., *tr* Chicago Historical Society, *b* The Granger Collection (both); **91** *tl* NYSHA, *tr* The Granger Collection, *bl* The Corning Glass Museum, *br* Lee Boltin; **92** Patrick Henry Memorial Foundation; **96** Brown University Library; **98** LC; **99** LC; **101** The Granger Collection; **102** MFA; **103** LC; **104** MFA; **105** MFA; **107** Connecticut Historical Society; **112** Yale (detail); **118** WW; **119** LC; **120** Fraunces Tavern Museum; **122** *l* Chicago Historical Society, *r* Anne S.K. Brown Military Collection, Brown University Library; **125** NYPL; **133** Bettmann Archive; **134** Courtesy of Fort Ticonderoga Museum, N.Y.; **136** Peale Museum; **138** Bettmann Archive; **139** Museum of Art, Rhode Island School of Design, gift of Miss Lucy T. Aldrich; **145** NYHS; **147** *t* Scala/Art Resources; *b* Peabody Museum, Salem, Mass.; **149** Filson Club; **154** Mystic Seaport Museum, Mystic, Conn.; **156** Independence National Historic Park; **164** NYHS; **166** Boatmen's National Bank.

UNIT THREE Page 170 *tl* Lee Boltin, *tr* Massachusetts Historical Society, *bl* The Granger Collection, *br* AMNH Photo—P. Hollembeak; **171** *tl* U.S. Naval Academy, *tr* Collection of Laurie Platt Winfrey, *bl* Old Dartmouth Historical Society Whaling Museum, *br* The Granger Collection; **172** NG, gift of Edgar William and Bernice Chrysler Garbisch; **174** LC; **175** NYHS; **177** MMA, gift of Edgar William and Bernice Chrysler Garbisch; **183** NYSHA; **184** The Granger Collection; **188** NYHS; **195** NYPL, Rare Book Division; **196** British Museum; **200** Field Museum of Natural History, Chicago; **203** New Orleans Museum of Art; **206** MMA (detail); **208** Library of the Boston Athenaeum; **210** SI; **211** MFA, M. and M. Karolik Collection; **214** Henry Clay Memorial Foundation; **218** MFA; **220** NYHS; **226** National Gallery of Art; **227** MFA, M. and M. Karolik Collection; **228** The Granger Collection.

UNIT FOUR Page 230 *tl* The Boatmen's National Bank, *tr* The Granger Collection, *bl* SEF/Art Resource, *br* © Yale; **231** *tl* Bettmann Archive, *tr* Thomas Gilcrease Institute, Tulsa, Okla., *bl* The Granger Collection, *br* Collection of Laurie Platt Winfrey; **232** NG; **236** NYPL, Prints Division; **237** Museum of Art, Rhode Island School of Design, Gift of Edith Jackson Green and Ellis Jackson;

238 The Granger Collection; **240** Michal Heron, courtesy of Cherokee Museum; **243** Boston Public Library; **245** NYHS; **248** C.R. Smith Collection, University Art Museum, University of Texas at Austin; **250** Thomas Gilcrease Institute of American History and Art, Tulsa, Okla.; **252** Oregon Historical Society; **256** The Granger Collection; **258** Institute of Texan Cultures; **264** California Historical Society, San Francisco; **268** Kennedy Galleries, Inc., New York; **271** SI; **273** Newark Museum, gift of William F. LaPort, 1925; **280** Musee de Pau; **282** Louisiana State Museum; **284** Missouri Historical Society; **285** LC; **290** The Granger Collection; **291** The Granger Collection; **292** National Portrait Gallery, SI; **294** St. Louis Art Museum (detail); **299** by permission of Houghton Library, Harvard University; **300** NYHS; **301** LC; **302** Vassar College Library; **305** LC; **307** MMA, gift of Russell Sage, 1908.

UNIT FIVE Page 310 *tl* NYHS, *tr* Collection of Laurie Platt Winfrey, *bl* Charlestown Museum, *br* Brooklyn Museum; **311** *tl* Bettmann Archive, *tr* Collection of Laurie Platt Winfrey, *bl* National Portrait Gallery, *br* The Granger Collection; **312** Cincinnati Art Museum (detail) purchased from the Webber estate by a popular subscription fund, NYHS; **317** NYPL; **322** LC (both); **324** Pennsylvania Academy of Fine Arts; **330** LC; **335** LC; **338** *l* LC, *r* NA; **341** State of North Carolina, Division of Archives and History; **345** NYPL; **350** West Point Museum; **352** LC; **354** Bettmann Archive; **359** LC; **360** LC; **361** Chicago Historical Society; **362** NYPL; **364** Alabama Department of Archives and History; **368** The Granger Collection; **369** The Granger Collection; **370** The Granger Collection (both).

UNIT SIX Page 372 *tl* City Library, DeSmet, S. Dak., *tr* MCNY, *bl* Taft Museum, Cincinnati, Ohio, *br* Collection of Laurie Platt Winfrey; **373** *tl* MMA, Gift of Hugh J. Grant, 1974, *tr* LC, *bl* Fine Arts Museum of San Francisco, Calif., *br* LC; **374** City Library, DeSmet, S. Dak. (detail); **375** SI; **378** Thomas Gilcrease Institute of American History and Art, Tulsa, Okla.; **379** Thomas Gilcrease Institute of American History and Art, Tulsa, Okla.; **381** LC; **383** SI; **385** *l* Wichita Art Museum, *r* The Granger Collection; **389** Western History Collections, University of Oklahoma Library; **392** MCNY, J. Clarence Davies Collection; **394** Newberry Library; **395** Coverdale and Colpitts; **397** Bethlehem Steel Corporation; **402** American Petroleum Institute; **405** Abby Aldrich Rockefeller Folk Art Center, Colonial Williamsburg Foundation; **407** Metropolitan Life Insurance Co.; **409** The Granger Collection; **410** NYPL; **414** Chicago Historical Society, Solomon D. Butcher Collection; **415** Newberry Library; **419** NYPL; **423** Nebraska State Historical Society; **424** LC; **426** U.S. Department of Agriculture; **428** Kansas State Historical Society; **429** LC; **430** LC; **434** Indianapolis Museum of Art, gift of a Couple of Old Hoosiers (detail); **439** LC; **441** George Hall/Woodfin Camp; **442** MCNY; **443** MCNY; **444** F.W. Woolworth Co.; **445** The Granger Collection; **446** Philadelphia Museum of Art; **447** MCNY, photograph by Jacob A. Riis, Jacob A. Riis Collection; **448** International Museum of Photography at George Eastman House; **449** LC; **450** Wyoming State Archives, Museums and Historical Department; **454** New York Historical Society, Bella Landauer Collection; **455** Bettmann Archive; **456** © Rosetta Records; **458** LC; **459** LC; **461** LC; **462** LC; **463** LC; **467** The Granger Collection; **468** LC; **471** LC.

UNIT SEVEN Page 474 *t* The Granger Collection (both), *bl* Los Angeles County Museum of Art, *br* Scala/Art Resource; **475** *tl* NYHS, *tr* The Granger Collection, *bl* LC, *br* Imperial War Museum; **476** University of Hartford, J. Doyle De Witt Collection; **478** *t* LC, *b* NAACP; **480** UPI; **482** Phillips Collection, Whitney Museum of American Art; **483** LC; **485** LC; **486** National Archives; **488** Blaine Harrington III/Stock Market; **489** The Granger Collection; **492** Bettmann Archive; **493** International Sports and Games Research Collection, University of Notre Dame; **494** The Boy Scouts of America; **496** National Portrait Gallery, Washington, D.C.; **498** Theodore Roosevelt Collection, Harvard Library; **500** LC; **503** LC; **504** AMNH; **506** UPI; **510** U.S. Military Academy at West Point; **512** LC; **515** LC; **517** LC; **521** NA; **524** SI; **527** *t* WW, *b* NA; **529** NA; **531** NA; **532** New Jersey Historical Society; **535** NA; **537** NA.

UNIT EIGHT Page 542 *tl* Scala/Art Resource, *tr* Norton Gallery & School of Art, *bl* Collection of Laurie Platt Winfrey, *br* LC; **543** *tl* Memorial Art Gallery of the University of Rochester, Marion Stratton Gould Fund, *tr* California State Library, *b* LC (both); **544**

White House Historical Association; **547** LC; **549** LC; **550** LC; **551** LC; **556** LC; **557** LC; **558** Culver Pictures, Inc.; **561** Bettmann Archive; **562** Westinghouse Electrical Corporation; **563** Culver Pictures, Inc.; **564** LC; **566** Joslyn Art Museum; **570** International Sports and Games Research Collection, University of Notre Dame; **571** Bettmann Archive; **572** National Baseball Hall of Fame; **574** LC; **576** LC; **577** Miami Dade Public Library, Romer Collection (both); **579** WW; **580** Collection of the Whitney Museum of American Art; **585** NA; **586** LC.

UNIT NINE **Page 590** *tl* NYHS, *tr* San Francisco Art Museum, *bl* Giraudon/Art Resource, *br* University of Hartford, J. Doyle DeWitt Collection; **591** *tl* The Granger Collection, *tr* LC, *bl* © Turner Entertainments, *br* Courtesy of the Franklin Delano Roosevelt Library; **592** Courtesy of the Franklin Delano Roosevelt Library; **594** LC; **596** NA; **598** *t* LC, Farm Security Administration, *b* UPI; **599** LC; **601** U.S. Department of Agriculture; **602** LC; **604** Bettmann Archive; **606** LC; **608** LC; **610** LC; **613** LC; **616** LC, Farm Security Administration (all); **617** King's Highway Elementary School, Westport, Conn.; **619** National Collection of Fine Art, SI; **620** LC; **624** Bettmann Archive; **628** The Pentagon; **629** LC; **631** LC; **632** LC; **635** Thomson Organization; **638** NA; **640** Civic Center Department, City of Detroit; **643** U.S. Army photograph; **645** LC; **646** LC; **647** LC; **650** *l* LC, *r* U.S. Army photograph; **652** NA; **655** LC; **656** Navy Combat Art Collection; **657** U.S. Army photograph; **660** WW; **661** LC; **662** Bettmann Archive.

UNIT TEN **Page 664** *tl* Saturday Evening Post cover, 1946, The Curtis Publishing Co., *tr* UPI/Bettmann Newsphotos, *bl* UPI/Bettmann Newsphotos, *br* WW; **665** *tl* Wally McNamee/Woodfin Camp, *tr* J.P. Laffont/Sygma, *bl* Wally McNamee/Woodfin Camp, *br* Chuck O'Rear/Woodfin Camp; **666** LC; **672** Fenno Jacobs/Black Star; **673** LC; **675** U.S. Department of Defense photograph, U.S. Marine Corps; **677** UPI; **680** NA; **684** Hallmark Cards, Inc.; **687** UPI; **689** UPI; **691** UPI; **692** *t* UPI, *b* WW; **694** UPI (both); **695** Michael Ochs Archives; **696** Collection of the Whitney Museum of American Art; **697** American Broadcasting Company; **700** National Aeronautics and Space Administration; **701** NA; **703** LC; **706** LC; **708** James H. Karales/Design Photographers International; **709** UPI/Bettmann Newsphotos; **713** Michael Abramson/Black Star; **714** *l* Frank Johnston/Black Star, *r* Owen Franken/Stock Boston; **717** LC; **718** Paul Conklin for Time, Inc.; **719** John Launois/Black Star; **722** Dan Budnik/Woodfin Camp; **725** Frank Fishbeck for *Life* Magazine, © 1971 Time, Inc.; **726** NASA; **727** NASA; **730** UPI; **732** UPI; **733** UPI/Bettmann Newsphotos; **735** WW; **737** David Rubinger/Black Star; **738** *l* Don Holway/Contact Press Images, *rt* Tiziou/Sygma, *rb* Sygma; **739** Franken/Liaison Agency; **742** David Madison/Bruce Coleman, Inc.; **743** Naythons/Gamma-Liaison; **746** Wally McNamee/Woodfin Camp; **748** Energy Research and Development Administration; **751** Sygma; **753** Breese/Gamma-Liaison; **754** UPI; **756** John Ficara/Woodfin Camp; **760** Globe Photos, Inc.; **762** Michal Heron/Woodfin Camp; **763** Glen Donahue/Globe Photos; **765** Nick Sapicha/Stock Boston; **767** John Running/Stock Boston; **772** Mark Antman/The Image Works; **773** Newberry Library; **774** WW; **776** NASA; **778** David Madison/Bruce Coleman, Inc.; **779** Diego Goldberg/Sygma; **780** NASA; **781** Movie Still Archives; **783** Michal Heron; **784** Ken Karp/Omni-Photo Communications; **785** A. Tannenbaum/Sygma; **789** Bill Nation/Sygma; **794** Lee Lockwood/Black Star; **800** Olivier Rebbot/Woodfin Camp.

REFERENCE SECTION **Page 814** *l* Independence National Historical Park, *r* Peale Museum; **815** Colonial Williamsburg Foundation (both); **816** *l* Chicago Historical Society, Solomon D. Butcher Collection, *r* Thomas Gilcrease Institute of American History and Art, Tulsa, Okla.; **817** *l* Bethlehem Steel Corporation, *r* Joslyn Art Museum.

890